# THE HANDBOOK OF ROAD SAFETY MEASURES SECOND EDITION

## RELATED BOOKS

HIMANEN, LEE-GOSSELIN & PERRELS – *Building Blocks for Sustainable Transport: Obstacles, Trends, Solutions*

DAVID SHINAR – *Traffic Safety and Human Behaviour*

STOPHER & STECHER – *Travel Survey Methods Quality and Future Directions*

HENSHER & BUTTON (eds.) – *Handbooks in Transport*

FULLER & SANTOS – *Human Factors for Highway Engineers*

GAUDRY & LASSARE (eds.) – *Structural Road Accident Models*

DAGANZO – *Fundamentals of Transportation and Traffic Operations*

# THE HANDBOOK OF ROAD SAFETY MEASURES

# SECOND EDITION

BY

Rune Elvik
*Institute of Transport Economics, Oslo, Norway*

Alena Høye
*Institute of Transport Economics, Oslo, Norway*

Truls Vaa
*Institute of Transport Economics, Oslo, Norway*

Michael Sørensen
*Institute of Transport Economics, Oslo, Norway*

Emerald

United Kingdom – North America – Japan
India – Malaysia – China

Emerald Group Publishing Limited
Howard House, Wagon Lane, Bingley BD16 1WA, UK

First edition 2004

Second edition 2009



**Reprints and permission service**
Contact: booksandseries@emeraldinsight.com



**British Library Cataloguing in Publication Data**
A catalogue record for this book is available from the British Library

ISBN: 978-1-84855-250-0

Awarded in recognition of Emerald's production department's adherence to quality systems and processes when preparing scholarly journals for print

INVESTOR IN PEOPLE

# Table of Contents

# PREFACE

The second, revised edition of *The Handbook of Road Safety Measures*, first published by Elsevier Science in 2004, gives a systematic overview of current knowledge regarding the effects of road safety measures. The book gives state-of-the-art summaries of current knowledge regarding the effects of 128 road safety measures. Since 2004, the introduction part and 65 chapters have been revised and 5 chapters have been added.

Easily accessible knowledge on how to prevent traffic injury is in increasing demand, as the number of people killed or injured in road accidents continues to grow on a global basis. It is hoped that this book may serve as a reference manual for road safety professionals in every country. The 2004 edition of the book was published in Spanish in 2006.

The book is based on the Norwegian edition of the book, first published in 1982 and continuously updated and expanded since 2001. Work on this book started as far back as 1980. During the whole period from 1980 until now, the endeavour to develop and update the book has been funded by the Norwegian Ministry of Transport and Communications and the Norwegian Public Roads Administration. In recent years, the Swedish Road Administration has been an important contributor as well. The Institute of Transport Economics (TØI) would like to thank these institutions for their financial support and their long-term commitment to this research effort. Without the original Norwegian edition, the current English version could never have been produced.

The present edition is the result of the coordinated effort of Chief Research Officer Rune Elvik and researchers Alena Høye, Truls Vaa and Michael Sørensen – all belonging to the Institute of Transport Economics. The final preparation of the manuscript for publication was made by Unni Wettergreen. The points of view expressed in the book are those of the authors and do not necessarily reflect the positions of the funding agencies. Errors and omissions, if any, are the sole responsibility of the authors.

Oslo, May 2009
Institute of Transport Economics

Lasse Fridstrøm
Managing Director

# PART I

## Introduction

# 1.

# Background and Guide to Readers

## 1.1 Purpose of the *Handbook of Road Safety Measures*

As the title of this book is *Handbook of Road Safety Measures*, most readers will perhaps expect a handbook to give instructions or advice concerning its main topic, but not all readers will expect the same kind of instructions or advice. It is therefore appropriate to start the book by describing its background and purpose.

Although this book is called a 'handbook', it does not provide any instructions or advice of a general nature with respect to how best to design or implement road safety measures. The term 'handbook' rather denotes a reference manual, a catalogue or an encyclopaedia of road safety measures.

Why is this book written and what is its main purpose? The book is written in order to summarise and present in an easily accessible form what is currently known about the effects of road safety measures. A road safety measure is any technical device or programme that has improving road safety as the only objective or at least one of its stated objectives. Road safety measures may be directed at any element of the road system: patterns of land use, the road itself, road furniture, traffic control devices, motor vehicles, police enforcement and road users and their behaviour.

This book takes a broad view of what constitutes a road safety measure. It is not limited to a particular class of safety programmes, but tries to cover everything that is intended to improve road safety. A total of 128 road safety measures are included. Improving road safety is, unfortunately, not a concept that has a standard scientific definition. In this book, it refers to a reduction in the expected number of accidents, a

**The Handbook of Road Safety Measures**

**ISBN: 978-1-84855-250-0**

reduction in accident or injury severity or a reduction in the rate of accidents or injuries per kilometre of travel.

The main purpose of the book is to describe, as objectively as possible, the effects of road safety measures on road safety. Some road safety measures influence not only road safety but also the ease of travel and the quality of the environment. Ease of travel is a broad concept that includes aspects such as accessibility (the availability of a certain destination for travel), out-of-pocket expenses (like motor vehicle operating costs) and travel time. In this book, the term mobility is used to denote the ease of travel in terms of accessibility, cost and travel time. Environmental impacts of road safety measures refer primarily to impacts on traffic noise and air pollution, but in some cases, other impacts are briefly mentioned, for example, impacts on the working conditions of professional drivers.

Some of the terms that have been used to describe the contents of this book, such as 'current knowledge' and 'objective description', require a more extensive discussion. This will be undertaken in later chapters of Part I (in particular, Chapters 4 and 5). Before describing the main questions, the book tries to answer, its structure and the role of research in promoting road safety, what this book is not intended to be needs to be explained.

This book is not a technical design handbook. It does not tell readers how to design a junction or how to build a car. This book does not offer a prescription for road safety policy. It does not tell readers which road safety measures ought to be taken, nor does it instruct policymakers in how to set priorities for the provision of road safety. Section 1.4 outlines how the line separating road safety research from road safety policymaking is understood in the book.

This book does not tell you how to do road safety research; however, it tries to assess systematically the quality of current knowledge about the effects of road safety measures. In doing so, this book of course invokes widely accepted standards of technical rigour and quality in applied research. However, assessing the quality of what is known is not the same thing as instructing researchers about how to improve knowledge.

This book does not tell readers how to set up an accident recording system or how to investigate accidents, but discusses the concept of accident causation and briefly summarises what is known about factors that contribute to road accidents. Although this presentation may perhaps give readers some ideas about what they should be looking for when trying to find out why road accidents happen, it is highly deficient in acting a guide as to how best to investigate and record road accidents.

Some readers may take exception to the consistent use of the word ‘accident’ in the book, preferring perhaps other words like crash or unintentional injury event (Langley 1988). Hopefully, these readers will not be deterred from using the book. Some of the arguments for not using the word ‘accident’ are, we believe, based on misunderstanding. For example, it has been argued that the word ‘accident’ has traditionally been used to represent events that occur at random, and which are therefore unpreventable.

This point of view is both correct and incorrect. It is correct in that there is an element of randomness in accident occurrence. However, the occurrence of accidents is never entirely random. Young male drivers are systematically over-involved in road accidents. The gender and age of drivers involved in road accidents are, therefore, not entirely a matter of chance. On the contrary, the occurrence of a specific road accident is random in the absolute sense that if it could have been accurately predicted, it would not have happened (assuming that accidents are not deliberate; that nobody wants to become involved in an accident).

Part of the nature of random events is that the precise time and place of their occurrence, as well as the precise nature of their impacts, are unpredictable. But unpredictability in this sense does not necessarily imply un-preventability. To illustrate this, imagine a 100-km-long road, chopped up into 100 consecutive 1-km sections. The number of accidents recorded on each 1-km section is counted, and the distribution of accident counts among the 100 sections is found to closely follow the Poisson probability law, which means that accident occurrence in these 100 road sections is random in the sense that it is not statistically possible to identify one road section that has a higher expected number of accidents than any other road section. Yet it hardly follows from this observation that the accidents occurring along the 100-km road cannot be prevented. Suppose, for example, that all drivers using the road slowed down by 10 km per hour. It is very likely that there would then be fewer accidents. Or, suppose road lighting is installed along the road. Again, it is likely that there would be a reduction in the number of accidents.

‘Accident’ is the right word for a road crash, precisely because it connotes randomness. It is a matter of fact that there is a large, but not always dominant, element of randomness in accident occurrence. It is, however, a serious misunderstanding to suggest that randomness as such implies that accidents cannot be prevented.

## 1.2 Which questions does the book answer?

This book provides answers to the following questions:

- Which measures can be used to reduce the number of traffic accidents or the severity of injury in such accidents?

- Which accident problems and types of injury are affected by the different measures?
- What effects on accidents and injuries do the various road safety measures have according to international research?
- What effects do the measures have on mobility and the environment?
- What are the costs of road safety measures?
- Is it possible to make cost–benefit evaluations of the measures?
- Which measures give the greatest benefits for traffic safety seen in relation to the cost of the measures?

Not all these questions are equally easy to answer, and it is not always possible to give a precise or conclusive answer. For example, the effect of a measure on accidents may vary from place to place, depending on the design of the measure, the number of accidents at the spot, any other measures that have been implemented, etc. As a result, different studies of the same measure may provide different conclusions. An attempt has been made to identify sources of variation in study findings and to try to form as homogeneous groups as possible when presenting estimates of the effects of measures on road safety. This will be discussed more detail in Chapter 2.

## 1.3 Structure of the book

The book consists of three parts, each of which can be read independently. The chapters in each part are also designed to be read independently.

**Part I** describes the purpose of the book and its structure, the method used in surveying and analysing the literature the book is based on, factors contributing to road accidents, basic concepts of road safety research, the quality of road safety evaluation research and scientific approaches to planning and policymaking.

**Part II** describes road safety measures in 10 different areas. Within each area, a number of different types of measures are described in individual sections. The 10 areas are

1. Road design and road equipment (20 measures)
2. Road maintenance (9 measures)
3. Traffic control (21 measures)
4. Vehicle design and protective devices (29 measures)
5. Vehicle and garage inspection (4 measures)
6. Driver training and regulation of professional drivers (12 measures)
7. Public education and information (4 measures)
8. Police enforcement and sanctions (13 measures)

9. Post-accident care (3 measures)
10. General purpose policy instruments (14 measures).

**Part III** contains a glossary of words, symbols and abbreviations, which are used in the book and a subject index.

In **Part II**, each chapter and each of the sections within each chapter has been written following the same structure. The first section in each chapter gives an overview of the amount of research available and summaries of the effects on accidents, environment and mobility, as well as an overview of costs and cost–benefit analyses. The sections that described specific types of road safety measures all consist of the same subsections, a short description of which is given in the following.

***Problem and objective.*** This section describes the road safety problem, which the measure is designed to solve or reduce. A road safety problem can be described in terms of a high number of accidents, a high accident rate or a high proportion of serious injuries. For example, it is widely seen as a problem that pedestrians and cyclists are more often involved in injury accidents per kilometre travelled in traffic than car occupants, and that they tend to be more seriously injured than car occupants when involved in an accident. As far as possible, the size of the road safety problem which each measure is intended to affect is shown by means of accident figures or estimates of risk. However, not all road safety problems can be described exhaustively in numerical terms only. This applies, for example, to the feeling of insecurity that some road users experience.

Many road safety measures are intended to tackle local problems, having a fairly clearly limited scope in time and space. However, this does not apply to all measures. Some measures are directed towards more general problems, which may affect all road users and all places. In such cases, it is difficult to state precisely the number and nature of accidents which these measures are designed to affect. For some road safety measures, the concept of 'target accidents' is thus somewhat ill defined (Hauer 1997).

***Description of the measure.*** This section gives information concerning the design of a road safety measure and its intended function. Detailed technical descriptions are not given. Illustrations showing the measure are given in some cases.

***Effect on accidents.*** This section deals with the effects on accidents, or on the severity of injury in accidents, which have been found in research. Whenever possible, effects are stated in terms of the percentage change of the number of accidents or injuries attributable to a certain measure. All estimates of effect presented in this book are uncertain. The most important sources of such uncertainty are identified for each measure. Statistical uncertainty is stated in terms of a 95% confidence interval for the estimate of effect. For measures where no studies have been found that quantify effects on road safety, the effect is described in other ways.

***Effect on mobility***. In addition to the effect on accidents and injuries, many road safety measures also have effects on mobility. These impacts are briefly described, but not in as great detail as safety effects.

***Effects on the environment***. Effects on the environment are briefly described. Such effects include traffic noise and air pollution in a wide sense. Major incursions into the landscape and changes in land use should also be regarded as important environmental effects.

***Costs***. For the majority of measures, information is given regarding the cost of the measure. The information is taken partly from official budgets and accounts, partly from research reports and partly from producers or dealers in safety equipment. Good estimates of cost have not always been found. The cost figures presented are usually an estimate of the average cost for a 'unit' of a measure, for example, 1 km of track for walking and cycling, one roundabout, one signalised junction, one seat belt, one set of ABS brakes, etc. In addition, total costs are presented for measures whose extent of usage is sufficiently well known.

***Cost–benefit analysis***. Examples are given of cost–benefit analysis of most measures. It is important to bear in mind that the results of cost–benefit analyses depend strongly on the context to which they refer. Monetary valuations of impacts, which are a key element of cost–benefit analysis, vary substantially between countries. As a rule, one would therefore not expect the results of cost–benefit analyses made in one country to apply directly to another country. The context to which most of the analyses presented refer is the current situation in Norway. However, where cost–benefit analyses have been reported in other countries, they are quoted. The applicability of cost–benefit analyses to road safety measures is discussed in detail in Chapter 6 of Part I.

## 1.4 Science and politics in road safety

Road safety research, in particular road safety evaluation research, is highly applied. This type of research is carried out mostly to help reduce the number of road accidents and the injuries resulting from them. Can science and politics be kept apart in such a highly applied field of research? Where is the dividing line between science and politics in road safety?

A distinction can be made between three types of issues that arise in policymaking. The three types of issues can be stated in the following terms:

- Normative: A is a good thing (or the right thing to do).
- Empirical: If action B is performed, A will be produced.
- Prescriptive: Therefore, we ought to take action B.

Normative issues are about deciding what we think is good or right and are ultimately matters of moral judgement. Most people would probably agree that reducing traffic injury is a good outcome. Hence, most people would probably also endorse a policy objective stating that traffic injuries should be reduced.

Formulating the ideals and objectives that policy should strive to realise clearly lies within the realm of politics rather than science. Policy objectives represent human value systems and seek to articulate these in an attractive way. Does this mean that science has nothing to say about normative issues? No. A scientific evaluation of the solutions proposed to normative issues can be made by relying on principles of logical consistency. For example, a policy objective stating that every road user has the right to safer travel than the average risk faced by road users can be rejected as logically inconsistent, since it is impossible for everyone to be safer than average.

A broader scientific analysis of human value systems belongs to ethics and moral philosophy, and is outside the scope of this book. The main topic of road safety evaluation research is to determine whether road safety measures are effective in improving road safety. This is entirely an empirical issue.

It was stated in Section 1.1 that this book describes, as objectively as possible, what is known about the effects of road safety measures, in particular their effects on road safety. What does this statement mean? How can any description of knowledge claim to be objective? Objectivity is not something that can be meaningfully measured in numerical terms. It is, however, an ideal of science to which this book strives by

- seeking to present objective knowledge about the effects of road safety measures,
- assessing knowledge according to standards of validity that are independent of the content of that knowledge, and depend solely on how it was produced, and
- refraining from advocacy.

Let us elaborate on each of these points.

***Objective knowledge***. In discussing what we mean by scientific knowledge, epistemology has traditionally relied on a subjective conception of knowledge, in which knowledge is defined as justified true belief. Within this framework, knowledge cannot exist without a knowing subject. In short, a justified and true statement does not constitute knowledge unless someone is aware of the statement and believes it.

This conception of knowledge lies close to everyday usage of the term. Hauer, for example, in discussing the state of knowledge with respect to the effects of road safety measures, states (1988, 3): 'My own critical views about the amount of factual knowledge that is available in the field of road safety delivery rest on years of study. As I moved from one inquiry to another and began to notice how shallow are the foundations of what passes for knowledge, I gradually realized that ignorance about the safety repercussions of the many common measures is not the exception.' Three years later, he remarked (Hauer 1991, 135): 'How little we know about the safety consequences of our road design decisions and about the repercussions of our traffic control actions is simple to demonstrate. One needs only to ask the engineer: "Approximately how many accidents per year do you expect to occur with design X?" While the engineer might venture an opinion, in truth, the arsenal of knowledge at the disposal of the North American engineer just does not suffice to give an answer.'

While conforming both to everyday usage and the traditions of epistemology, the subjective concept of knowledge creates a number of difficulties. Although it makes sense to say that person A knows more about a subject than person B, if person A can pass a more difficult examination about the subject than person B, it hardly makes sense to say that the amount of knowledge that is available to the general public concerning a subject is determined primarily by how much person A can remember when undergoing an examination in the subject.

Karl Popper introduced the concept of objective knowledge (Popper 1979), which he defines (1979, 73) as 'the logical content of our theories, conjectures, guesses'. He adds that 'Examples of objective knowledge are theories published in journals and books and stored in libraries; discussions of such theories; difficulties or problems pointed out in connection with such theories, and so on.' Knowledge in the objective sense, according to Popper (1979, 109), is knowledge without a knower; it is knowledge without a knowing subject.

In short, the concept of objective knowledge can be defined as all results of research, theoretical or empirical, that are available to the general public by virtue of being written or otherwise stored in a medium that is accessible to anyone who wants to learn its contents. Knowledge in this sense exists, as pointed out by Popper, in the shelves of libraries and archives. This kind of knowledge is objective in the sense that it exists irrespective of whether anyone keeps it inside his or her head. It is, however, not necessarily objective in the sense that everyone who reads a certain paper in a journal will find the results reported in the paper convincing and therefore believe them, as required according to the subjective conception of knowledge.

This book seeks to develop objective knowledge about the effects of road safety measures by relying on an extensive and systematic search of the literature, described in detail in Chapter 2, and by summarising this literature by means of formal techniques of meta-analysis that minimise the contribution of subjective factors that are endemic in traditional, narrative literature surveys.

***Assessing the validity of knowledge***. Can the results of road safety evaluation studies be trusted? Do these studies always show the true effects on road safety of the measures that have been evaluated? Regrettably, the answer to these questions is no. Hauer (2002, 3) laments: 'By publishing many biased accounts on a variety of treatment, all giving inflated estimates of safety effect, one creates an entirely incorrect lore about what is achievable. ... The publication of incorrect results is like the release of toxin into a pristine body of water. It does not take much to make an entire lake unfit for drinking. ... The remedy to knowledge pollution is not reader education. While it is useful to educate potential readers to assess critically the results of safety studies, it is too much to hope that reader education can undo the damage done by publishing poorly done research.' In this book, a systematic framework has been used to assess the validity of the studies that are quoted. This framework applies to published or at least written studies, and not to oral communications, personal beliefs, tacit knowledge or other forms of subjective knowledge.

***Checking studies according to a set of criteria of validity*** may be regarded as an overly restrictive and simplistic way of assessing the validity of knowledge. Three points can be made in defence of this approach. First, the set of criteria for assessing the validity of evaluation studies are intended as *normative* criteria, not as descriptive criteria. All too often, controversies about research revolve around the contents of the results, rather than the methodological rigour of the research, and are heavily influenced by vested interests, rather than a disinterested search for the truth (see Crossen 1994, for some striking examples of these tendencies).

Second, it is conceded that a set of normative criteria is bound to be incomplete, in the sense that it does not exhaust the considerations that are regarded as relevant in assessing the validity of studies. Some considerations about study quality may apply just to one particular study and are thus not easily stated in general terms.

Third, while an informal and subjective assessment of the validity of research can reflect considerations that are difficult to formalise, it is nevertheless likely to be subject to more or less unknown biases. No matter how hard we try to be objective, there is always a risk that we go by the rule that 'bad studies are ... those whose results we do not like' (Rosenthal 1991, 130). By assessing validity in terms of formally stated, normative criteria, the role of personal prejudices in the assessment can be minimised.

***Refraining from advocacy***. Suppose an effective remedy for road accidents is found. Surely that is good news. Let us apply the remedy at once. Advocacy in research reports refers to statements recommending or calling for the use of specific road safety measures. To offer policy recommendations is to engage in advocacy. While advocacy may be tempting to many researchers ('Hey look, I've found a wonderful solution to an important social problem! Please give me some applause'), it is a temptation that should be resisted. Let us explain why.

In the first place, advocacy will, at least in the long term, undermine the confidence in research. Many road safety measures are controversial. The fact that a certain road safety measure is effective does not always mean that people like it. A researcher who has repeatedly advocated lower speed limits to improve road safety will find his credibility greatly reduced next time he publishes a study that, once again, concludes that lowering speed limits is an effective way of improving road safety.

In the second place, there is nearly always more than one way of improving road safety. Treatment A may be effective for a particular accident problem, but so are treatments B, C, D, E and F. To choose between these treatments, policymakers need to know more than simply the fact that they are all likely to reduce the number of accidents. Perhaps costs differ greatly. Perhaps the impacts on mobility and the environment are different. Perhaps public opposition is strong to three of the measures, but not to the other three. And so on. In short, making road safety policy involves complex trade-offs that tend to be overlooked by those who advocate a particular road safety measure.

In the third place, to advocate something one should really be sure that it works. If knowledge is not firmly established, one can get nasty surprises when introducing a treatment that was erroneously believed to be effective. Unfortunately, knowledge about the effects of road safety measures is not always very firmly established.

Some readers may object to these arguments by saying that this book offers covert policy recommendations by presenting cost–benefit analyses of the road safety measures it covers. However, a cost–benefit analysis is not a policy recommendation. It is simply a way of showing, in terms of a common scale, the relative importance of various impacts of a programme. Trying to identify the practical implications of a cost–benefit analysis is not as straightforward as some people think. It is not the case that an action should always be adopted if the benefits of that action are greater than its costs, and should never be adopted if the costs are greater than benefits. This point is made in virtually every textbook on cost–benefit analysis. Moreover, it is not obvious that road safety policy can or ought to be based slavishly on the results of cost–benefit analyses. To determine the weight that cost–benefit analysis should carry in road safety policy requires judgements that must be made outside the framework of cost–benefit analysis, and are not part of the analysis as such.

# 2.

# Literature Survey and Meta-Analysis

## 2.1 Systematic literature search

A comprehensive survey of studies evaluating the effects of road safety measures has been made. These studies have been identified by means of a systematic literature search. This section describes how the literature search was done.

The literature search consists of a 'fixed' part and a 'variable' part. The fixed part is a comprehensive search for studies in a sample of sources. The variable part is based on the results of the fixed part of the search. This approach is sometimes referred to as the ancestry approach. The fixed part of the literature search is a systematic survey of the following main groups of sources:

- Previous Norwegian editions of *Handbook of Road Safety Measures*
- Scientific journals
- Reports issued by selected research institutes
- Conference proceedings from a sample of regular conferences
- The library of the Institute of Transport Economics
- Bibliographical databases.

The variable part of the literature search comprises references found in studies that were retrieved from these sources.

***Previous Norwegian editions of Handbook of Road Safety Measures***. Previous editions of this book have been published in Norwegian and in English. The previous editions

**The Handbook of Road Safety Measures**

**ISBN: 978-1-84855-250-0**

of the book (Pedersen, Elvik and Berard-Andersen 1982, Elvik, Vaa and Østvik 1989, Elvik, Mysen and Vaa 1997, Elvik and Vaa 2004) have been examined, and we have tried to obtain studies to which references were made. No studies that have been referred to in the earlier editions of the book have been omitted. Even though the first edition of the book refers to many studies that by now are relatively old (over 30 years), none of these studies have been omitted. There are two main reasons for this. First, by keeping old studies, one has the opportunity of finding whether new and old studies reach the same conclusions. Second, the research is cumulative. This means that new studies are based on and add to the results of older studies, but attempt to refine, confirm, falsify, or develop these results by replicating studies or by applying better research methods.

***Scientific journals***. A number of scientific journals has been hand-searched and relevant papers have been identified. Table 2.1 shows the journals that have been searched and the volumes included for each journal.

The journals that were judged to be the most important have been examined from around 1970 or from the first published volume. Less important journals have been searched from 1980. *Highway Research Record* ceased publication in 1974 and was replaced by *Transportation Research Record*.

***Reports issued by research institutes***. Reports issued by a number of research institutions and public agencies in different countries have been searched. Table 2.2 shows the institutions whose publications have been systematically surveyed in the literature search.

Volumes included for the different series of reports issued by these institutions largely cover the period for which the report series in question has been in existence. For report series that were regarded as less important, only volumes from after 1980 have been studied.

***Conference proceedings***. Every year, or at other fixed intervals, a number of international conferences or seminars are held that deal with the questions of road safety. Normally, conference proceedings, which contain the contributions to these conferences, are published. For conferences that are held regularly, the proceedings from conferences in recent years have been searched systematically. Table 2.3 shows the conferences concerned.

In addition to these regular conferences, a number of other conferences are held. Proceedings of these conferences have been obtained if there was reason to believe they might contain relevant papers.

*Table 2.1: Scientific journals surveyed as part of the literature search*

| Journal | Volumes included |
|---|---|
| Accident Analysis and Prevention | 1969– |
| Australian Road Research (ceased publication in 1991) | 1970–91 |
| Dansk Vejtidsskrift (Danish Road Journal) | 1980– |
| Ergonomics | 1980– |
| Highway Research Record (ceased publication in 1974) | 1960–74 |
| Human Factors | 1980– |
| IATSS Research | 1980– |
| ITE-Journal (formerly Traffic Engineering) | 1970– |
| Journal of Risk and Uncertainty | 1988– |
| Journal of Safety Research | 1969– |
| Journal of Traffic Medicine | 1974– |
| Journal of Transport Economics and Policy | 1970– |
| Journal of Transportation Engineering | 1970– |
| Nordic Road and Transport Research | 1989– |
| NTR-nytt (News from Nordic Research) | 1992– |
| Policy Sciences | 1980– |
| Public Roads | 1980– |
| Recherche-Transports-Sécurité (RTS – INRETS Research Review) | 1984– |
| Risk Analysis | 1981– |
| Samferdsel | 1970– |
| Safety Science (formerly Journal of Occupational Accidents) | 1980– |
| Strassenverkehrstechnik | 1980– |
| Traffic Engineering and Control | 1970– |
| Transportation Research Part F | 1998– |
| Trafikken og Vi | 1970– |
| Transportation Research (series A and B) | 1980– |
| Transportation Research (series C) | 1993– |
| Traffic Injury Prevention | 1999– |
| Transportation Research Record (replaced Highway Research Record) | 1974– |
| Zeitschrift für Verkehrssicherheit | 1970– |

***Literature search in the library of the Institute of Transport Economics.*** Literature searches have been made in the library of the Institute of Transport Economics using subject words. These searches were done on a supplementary basis, designed to identify studies that were not found in the other sources that were searched systematically.

***Bibliographical databases.*** Literature searches have been carried out using several international bibliographical databases. These are ROADLINE at VTI (Swedish Road

*Table 2.2: Institutions (listed alphabetically) whose publications have been searched in literature survey*

| Institution | Period covered |
|---|---|
| Australian Road Research Board (ARRB, Australia) | 1970– |
| Beratungsstelle für Unfallverhüting (BFU, Switzerland) | 1980– |
| Bundesanstalt für Strassenwesen (BASt, Germany) | 1974– |
| Danmarks Transportforskning (DTF) | 2001– |
| Kommunikationsforskningsberedningen (KFB, TFB, TFD, Sweden) | 1977– |
| Lunds Tekniske Høgskole (Lund Institute of Technology, Sweden) | 1977– |
| Nordisk Ministerråd (Nordic Council of Ministers, Nordic countries) | 1973– |
| Nordisk Vegteknisk Forbund (NVF, Nordic Road Federation, Nordic countries) | 1970– |
| Organization of Economic Cooperation and Development (OECD) | 1970– |
| Rådet for Trafiksikkerhedsforskning (Danish Council for Road Safety Research, Denmark) | 1969–2001 |
| SINTEF Samferdselsteknikk/NTH Samferdselsteknikk (Norwegian Institute of Technology, Norway) | 1975– |
| Society of Automotive Engineers (SAE, USA) | 1980– |
| Statens vegvesen (Public Roads Administration, Norway) | 1980– |
| Statens Väg- och Trafikinstitut (VTI, Swedish Road and Transport Research Institute, Sweden) | 1975– |
| SWOV (Institute for Road Safety Research, The Netherlands) | 1970– |
| TØI (Institute of Transport Economics, Norway) | 1963– |
| Transport Research Laboratory (TRL, TRRL, RRL, Great Britain) | 1965– |
| US Department of Transportation (USA) | 1980– |
| US Transportation Research Board (TRB, USA) | 1960– |
| Vejdirektoratet (Public Roads Administration, Denmark) | 1980– |
| Vägverket (National Roads Administration, Sweden | 1980– |

*Table 2.3: Conference proceedings which have been studied as part of the literature search*

| Conference (frequency) | Year |
|---|---|
| Alcohol, Drugs and Traffic Safety (every 3 years) | 1971– |
| Australian Road Research Board Conference (every second year) | 1980– |
| PTRC Summer Annual Conference (now: European Transport Forum, annual) | 1985– |
| Road Safety in Europe (VTI et al.) (every second year) | 1985– |
| Road Safety on Four Continents (VTI and TRB) (every second year) | 1985– |
| TRB Annual Meeting (annual) | 1985– |
| VTI/TFBs Research Days (annual) | 1989– |

and Transport Research Institute), OECD's database IRRD, the database TRANSPORT (Silverplatter), Sciencedirect (the online database from Elsevier), PubMed (of the US National Library of Medicine) and the Cochrane Library.

A large number of road safety evaluation studies have been found in the sources listed above. Many of these studies refer to other studies, which were obtained if the references appeared to be relevant. Relevance was judged according to study titles and abstracts (if available). This approach to searching the literature does not guarantee 100% coverage. We do believe, however, that we have retrieved a large proportion of the best road safety evaluation research that has been published.

## 2.2 Criteria for study inclusion

The main objective of the literature search was to find studies that have quantified, or at least have tried to quantify, the effect of one or more road safety measures on the number of accidents, accident rate and the number of injuries or risk of injuries. Studies that have evaluated the effects of road safety measures by relying on proxy measures for safety, such as conflicts between road users or changes in road user behaviour, rather than accidents or injuries, are less relevant. One reason for this is the fact that for many forms of behaviour, the relationship to accident occurrence is unknown. Another reason is that the ultimate objective of all road safety measures is to reduce the expected number of accidents or injury severity.

This does not mean that measurements of road user behaviour, for example, are not of interest. On the contrary, they can make a study more valuable by supplementing accident records. For example, the validity of a study is greater if it describes changes in both speed and accidents – and shows that these changes are closely related to each other – than if an otherwise similar study provides information only on speed or accidents by itself.

## 2.3 Study classification

Studies have been classified according to the road safety measure whose effects they have evaluated. Some studies have evaluated several measures and are therefore included for each of the measures evaluated. However, the majority of studies evaluate the effects of just one road safety measure.

It has traditionally been regarded as a strength if a study tried to evaluate the effects of a particular road safety measure. However, as far as road safety policy is concerned, several measures are usually combined in one programme. In that case, it is important to know not just the effects of each measure that goes into the programme but the combined effects of all measures put together. It is not obvious that the effects of a road safety programme will be equal to the sum of the effects of the individual measures that make up the programme. The effect of a measure will not necessarily be the same when it is implemented in combination with other measures, as when it is implemented on its own.

Another general limitation of road safety evaluation research is that it often requires that the measures are implemented fairly extensively to provide enough data to evaluate effects. This means that evaluation research does not always provide a good basis for predicting the effects of new measures. Those who develop new measures would like to be able to predict the effects of the measures before they are introduced. Such prediction is not always possible. In Chapter 5, the possibility of giving a theoretical account for the findings of road safety evaluation research will be discussed.

## 2.4 The use of meta-analysis to summarise study results

The results of studies that have evaluated the effects on accidents and injuries of different measures are summarised by means of meta-analysis, provided it is applicable. Meta-analysis is a quantified synthesis of results of several studies that have evaluated the same road safety measure stated in the form of a weighted mean estimate of effect (Elvik 1999). As a part of the meta-analysis, moderating factors are investigated that influence the size of the effect of a road safety measure on accidents or injuries.

There are a number of textbooks on meta-analysis (Cooper and Hedges 1994, Petitti 2000, Lipsey and Wilson 2001) that describe various techniques in detail. Here, only the main elements are described to help readers understand the results that are presented in the individual chapters.

***Main elements of meta-analysis***. The study unit in a meta-analysis is a result, or an estimate of effect. An estimate of effect has to be stated as a precise point estimate in order to be included in a meta-analysis. If a result is stated simply as: 'No statistically significant changes in the number of accidents were found', it cannot be included in a meta-analysis. Moreover, the standard error of an estimate of effect has to be known, at least if results are to be weighted according to their statistical precision. A single study can contain more than one result. In such cases, all results, or the most important results from studies with a very large number of results, have been included in the meta-analyses. Multiple results from the same study have been treated as statistically independent, although this assumption may not always be correct.

Study results can be summarised by means of meta-analysis if the studies

- provide at least one numerical estimate of the effect of a road safety measure, or provide information that can be used to derive such an estimate and
- state the number of accidents on which the estimate of effect is based or provide other information that allows the calculation of the statistical uncertainty of the effect estimate, such as the confidence interval.

***Basics of the log odds method of meta-analysis***. The log odds method of meta-analysis has been applied throughout (Fleiss 1981, Shadish and Haddock 1994). According to this method, a weighted mean estimate of effect is calculated on the basis of the estimates of effect found in the studies that have been retrieved. This method of meta-analysis was chosen because the odds ratio (OR) is the most commonly found estimate of effect in road safety evaluation studies. An example of how an OR is calculated is as follows: If a study finds that there were 75 accidents on road X before a measure was implemented, and 23 accidents afterwards, whereas on a comparison road, there were 67 before the implementation of the measure on road X and 25 afterwards (no measure was implemented on the comparison road), the OR is $(23/75)/(25/67) = 0.307/0.373 = 0.822$. This corresponds to an accident reduction of 17.8% $(-1 + 0.822)$. In studies that employ multivariate techniques of analysis, effects are normally stated in terms of an OR that has been adjusted for confounding.

When applying the log odds method of meta-analysis, a summary effect is calculated as the weighted mean of the logarithms of the individual estimates of effect (ORs). Combining logarithms of ORs yields an unbiased estimate of the weighted mean effect of a set of studies. The steps in a log odds meta-analysis are

- calculation of estimates of effect,
- calculation of statistical weights and choice of the model of meta-analysis: Fixed effects when there is no systematic variation in the estimates of effect or random effects when there is systematic variation in the estimates of effect,
- calculation of summary estimates of effect, and
- confidence intervals: for each summary effect, a 95% confidence interval is calculated.

***Calculation of estimates of effect***. Estimates of effect are calculated as ORs. Some of the estimators of effect commonly found in road safety evaluation studies are listed in Table 2.4. The list is not exhaustive. Estimates of effect based on coefficients produced by multivariate analyses, which have the statistical properties of ORs, are not as common, but have increasingly been used in recent studies. The different estimators of effect should not be mixed up. Producing summary estimates of effect in meta-analysis

*Table 2.4: Commonly used estimators of effect in road safety evaluation studies*

| Name of dependent variable | Formal definition |
|---|---|
| Odds | Uat/Ubt |
| Odds ratio (simple or adjusted) | (Uat/Ubt)/(Uac/Ubc) |
| Ratio of odds ratios | [(Uati/Ubti)/(Uaci/Ubci)]/[(Uatj/Ubtj)/(Uacj/Ubcj)] |
| Ratio of relative risk | [Uati/(Uati+Ubti)]{[Uatj/(Uatj+Ubtj)] |
| Accident rate ratio | (Ua/Ta)/(Ub/Tb) |

U = number of accidents, T = traffic volume, exposure to risk, a = after, or with, some measure whose effect is evaluated, b = before, or without, some measure whose effect is evaluated, t = test group, c = comparison group, i = category I, j = category j.

based on studies that employ different estimators of effect can be misleading because both the statistical properties and the substantive interpretations of the various estimators differ. When other estimates of effect other than ORs are reported, ORs are calculated as far as possible based on the available information.

***Calculation of statistical weights and choice of model.*** There are two methods of combining estimates of effect in meta-analysis, the fixed effects model and the random effects model. The fixed effects model of analysis is based on the assumption that there is no systematic variation in effects in the set of studies considered, that is, all estimates of effect are samples of the same 'true' effect. When there is systematic variation, or heterogeneity, in the estimates of effect, the estimates cannot be regarded as representing the same 'true' effect. In this case, a random effects model is more adequate. In a random effects model, an account is taken of heterogeneity in the results and an underestimation of the uncertainty of the summary effect is avoided.

The differences between the fixed effects and the random effects models can be summarised as follows: The fixed effects model is adequate only if there is no heterogeneity in the results. Otherwise it will assign too much weight to results with large statistical weights and the confidence interval of the summary effect will be underestimated. The random effects model can be applied whether or not there is heterogeneity in the results. When there is significant heterogeneity, it assigns relatively less weight to results with large fixed effects weights, and confidence intervals of summary effects are larger than that in the fixed effects model. The less heterogeneity there is in the estimates of effect, the more similar will be the results from the two models.

When applying fixed effects and random effects models in meta-analysis, they differ with respect to how the statistical weights are calculated. In the fixed effects model, the statistical weight of the natural logarithm of each effect estimate is the inverse of its variance:

$$w_i = \frac{1}{v_i}$$

The variance of the logarithm of the OR is

$$v_i = \frac{1}{A} + \frac{1}{B} + \frac{1}{C} + \frac{1}{D}$$

where *A*, *B*, *C* and *D* are the four numbers that enter the calculation of the estimate of effect. In studies that do not use comparison groups, the terms $1/C$ and $1/D$ drop out. The same applies to studies that state the effects of a road safety measures in terms of an accident rate ratio. Statistical weights are estimated on the basis of the recorded number of accidents. In case of zero accidents, 0.5 is added to all four (or two) numbers used in estimating the statistical weight of a result.

In a random effects model, the statistical weights are calculated as a function of the fixed effects weights and a measure of the heterogeneity in the estimates of effect. The more heterogeneity there is in the results, the more similar will the statistical weights of the estimates of effect become, that is estimates based on large fixed effects weights will have their weights adjusted more than estimates based on small fixed effects weights.

In order to test the amount of heterogeneity in the estimates of effect, the following test statistic, *Q*, is estimated:

$$Q = \sum_{i=1}^{g} w_i y_i^2 - \frac{\left(\sum_{i=1}^{g} w_i y_i\right)^2}{\sum_{i=1}^{g} w_i}$$

where $y_i$ is the estimate of effect *i* and $w_i$ the fixed effects weight of estimate *i*. This test statistic has a $\chi^2$ distribution with $g-1$ degrees of freedom, where *g* is the number of estimates of effect that have been combined. If this test statistic is statistically significant, a random effects model is more adequate than a fixed effects model. In a random effects model, the statistical weights are modified to include a component reflecting the systematic variation of estimated effects between cases. This component is estimated as follows (Shadish and Haddock 1994):

$$\tau^2 = \frac{Q - (g - 1)}{C}$$

$Q$ is the test statistic described earlier, $g$ the number of estimates and $c$ the following estimator:

$$c = \sum_{i=1}^{g} w_i - \left[ \frac{\sum_{i=1}^{g} w_i^2}{\sum_{i=1}^{g} w_i} \right]$$

The variance of each result now becomes

$$v_i^* = \tau^2 + v_i$$

The corresponding statistical weight becomes the inverse of the variance.

***Random or fixed effects?*** Most meta-analyses that are presented in the book have been calculated based on a random effects model. Fixed effects models have been applied only when too few estimates of effect are available for calculating a random effects model. In meta-analyses that have not been updated after 1997, the fixed effects model is the most commonly used model.

***Summary effects***. The weighted summary effect based on a set of $g$ estimates is calculated as follows:

$$\bar{y} = \exp\left( \frac{\sum_{i=1}^{g} w_i y_i}{\sum_{i=1}^{g} w_i} \right)$$

where 'exp' is the exponential function (i.e., 2.71828 raised to the power of the expression in parenthesis), $y_i$ the logarithm of each estimate of effect and $w_i$ the statistical weight of each estimate of effect.

***Confidence intervals***. A 95% confidence interval for the weighted mean estimate of effect is obtained according to the following expression:

$$95\% \text{ confidence interval (upper/lower limit)} = \exp\left[ \left( \frac{\sum_{i=1}^{g} w_i y_i}{\sum_{i=1}^{g} w_i} \right) \pm \frac{1.96 \cdot 1}{\sqrt{\sum_{i=1}^{g} w_i}} \right]$$

The weights in this expression are either the fixed effects weights or the random effects weights, depending on the model of analysis adopted.

## 2.5 Does a weighted mean estimate of effect make sense?

A concern that many people have about meta-analysis is the so-called apples and oranges problem. This refers to the fact that studies that may differ greatly among themselves are combined into an overall estimate of the average effect of a road safety measure. It is argued that this does not make sense if studies are very heterogeneous, for example, with respect to different versions of the measure, countries or methods used in the studies.

Fortunately, the relevance of this argument can to some extent be tested in a meta-analysis. By doing so, one gains an impression of how meaningful it is to generalise a set of findings of evaluation studies in terms of a weighted average result. A way of checking whether a weighted mean estimate of effect makes sense is to prepare a funnel graph plot. An example of such a graph is shown in Figure 2.1.

The graph shows 94 results of studies that have evaluated the effects of road lighting on the number of accidents. The horizontal axis shows the natural logarithms of the estimates of effect. Values below 0 mean that the number of accidents is reduced, the

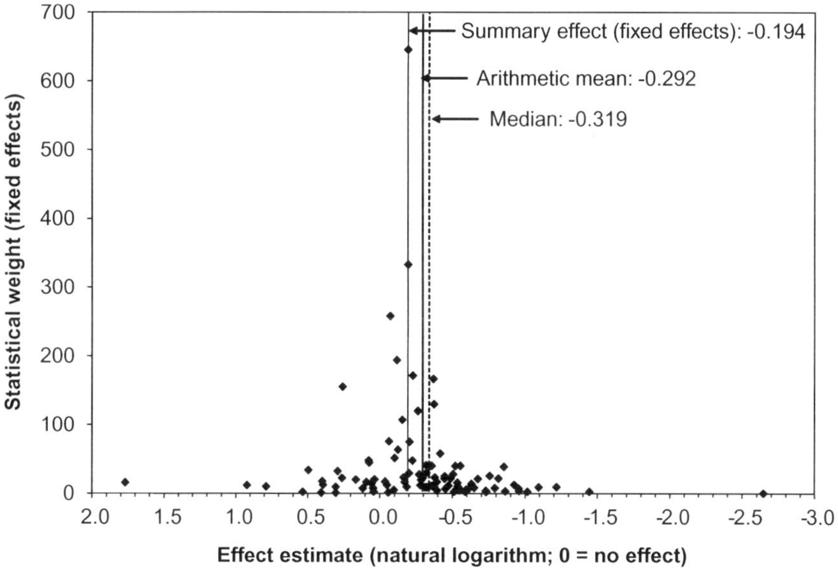


*Figure 2.1: Funnel graph of studies that have evaluated the effects of road lighting on the number of accidents (unspecified severity).*

value 0 means that the number of accidents is unchanged and values above 0 mean that the number of accidents increases. The vertical axis shows the statistical weight (fixed effects) of the results. The greater the statistical weight, the more the accidents which form the basis of a result. The dots indicate the individual results. Furthermore, three measures of the main tendency of the results are shown: the median, the arithmetic (unweighted) mean and the summary effect that has been calculated with the fixed effects model.

By studying such funnel graphs, an informed opinion can be formed of how reasonable a weighted mean result is. Properties of the distribution of estimates of effect that are investigated based on the funnel graph are the modality and dispersion of the results, the skewness and the sensitivity to outliers.

***Modality and dispersion of the results*** refers to the shape of the distribution of estimates of effect and how many humps or peaks it has. Figure 2.1 shows a unimodal distribution, that is, a distribution where the data points gather round a single peak. In this type of distribution, the weighted summary effect lies close to the highest peak of the distribution and thus is representative of the centre of gravity of the distribution. A bimodal distribution is one that has two peaks. In this type of distribution, the average will often lie between the two peaks and thus will not really be very informative. If possible, bimodal distributions should be divided into two, and an average should be calculated for each mode.

There may also be distributions with no clear pattern at all, randomly scattered distributions. In these types of distributions, the results are highly dispersed, with no clear tendency in any direction. An average may then be arbitrary and any differences concealed as a result of arbitrary assignment would be important to highlight. Ideally, the distribution of the results should not only be unimodal but also exhibit a systematic pattern where the results that have the largest statistical weights are closest to the mean and results that are further away from the mean have smaller statistical weights. It is not always easy to see if the results follow an ideal distribution or not. There are statistical methods for investigating the distribution of the results and for treating results that are not ideal.

First, heterogeneity can be tested statistically as has been described earlier, and a random effects model can be applied that takes into account heterogeneity. A random effects model takes into account that there is heterogeneity, but does not explain it.

Second, there are possibilities for explaining heterogeneity. The simplest way is to divide results into sub-groups and to calculate new summary effects for each of the sub-groups of results. Results may be grouped, for example, according to injury severity or variants of the measure. When summary effects differ between sub-groups, and when heterogeneity is reduced within the sub-groups, the sorting variable is likely to have contributed to the heterogeneity. It is then called a moderator variable.

Heterogeneity can also be explained by using meta-regression. In meta-regression analysis, regression models are developed on study level with the estimates of effect as dependent variable and characteristics of the studies as predictors. Characteristics of the studies may be the same variables as the sorting variables in the sub-group analysis (e.g., type of measure investigated, type of roads, methodological aspects, and so on). Thereby, it is possible to investigate which characteristics of the studies affect the outcome of the studies, while controlling for several factors at the same time. One restriction of meta-regression is that it requires quite large numbers of estimates of effect. As a rule of thumb, there should be at least 10 estimates of effect for each predictor included in the model. When there are few estimates of effect, the results may be arbitrary and highly sensitive to, for example, adding or omitting predictors or individual estimates of effect from the analysis.

A third possibility that should be considered in some cases is to refrain from calculating a summary effect. When the distribution of estimates of effect is highly heterogeneous without showing any signs of unimodality, a summary effect would not be meaningful. Indications for such a distribution are results that are highly different between the fixed effects and the random effects model and extremely large confidence intervals in the random effects model. This is illustrated by a numerical example in which six estimates of effect have been generated that have a highly heterogeneous and non-unimodal distribution. In this example, the result from the fixed effects model is a summary effect of −57% (95% confidence interval [−58; −55]), and that from the random effects model is a summary effect of +6% (95% confidence interval [−62; +195]).

***Skewness*** in a distribution refers to how the data points are distributed around the average, that is, how the individual results distribute themselves around a weighted average result. Ideally, the distribution should be symmetrical around (the natural logarithm of) the summary effect. If a distribution is very skew, the mean will give a misleading impression of where the majority of the results lies. An indication of skewness is a large difference between the median and the arithmetic mean of the distribution. An unskewed distribution will have very similar median and arithmetic mean.

***Publication bias*** is one possible source of skewness. Publication bias means that studies are more likely to be published when the results are in accordance with the expectation. In most accident studies, the expectation is that one will find accident reductions following the implementation of a safety measure. Publication bias leads to a skewed distribution of the estimates of effect because there will be fewer results on its 'undesired' side. Moreover, results (also in the desired direction) are more likely to be significant when based on large numbers of accidents. Results from small studies that find large effects in the expected direction will therefore be over-represented, and results from small studies that are unexpected will be under-represented. In the absence of publication bias (and other biases), the distribution will be symmetrical.

When there is publication bias, the summary effect is likely to show larger accident reductions than would be the case if all studies had been published, and none had been omitted because of insignificant or unexpected results.

A statistical possibility for controlling for publication bias is the trim and fill method. This method simulates studies that are assumed to have been suppressed by a tendency to publish (large) effects in the expected direction (Christensen 2003). The distribution of all original estimates of effect and the simulated estimates of effect that are generated in a trim and fill analysis is symmetrical around the peak of the original distribution. The simulated estimates of effect are mostly effects from small studies in the unexpected direction. A summary effect is then calculated based on all, original and simulated, estimates of effect. This summary effect is usually less favourable for the measure that has been evaluated than the summary effect that is based on the published estimates only. The trim and fill method can be applied both to a fixed effects and a random effects model of meta-analysis. An example is shown in Figure 2.2.

Figure 2.2 shows the results of the same studies as in Figure 2.1. The 'funnel'-shaped dotted lines (which are drawn by hand, not fitted to the data) indicate roughly the outer limits of the distribution of the estimates of effect. All original estimates of effect are located inside these lines and seem to be almost symmetrically distributed. All the same, 15 new data points have been generated in the trim and fill analysis. All of them show increases in accident numbers on roads with road lighting and have relatively small weights. The summary effect that is based on all, original and simulated, results is consequently somewhat less favourable (−15% accidents on lit roads compared with unlit roads) than the summary effect that is based on the original estimates of effect only (−18% accidents on lit roads compared with unlit roads). The difference is, however, not large.

***Other biases*** can produce results that resemble those expected when there is publication bias. The most frequent such bias occurs when results that refer to different accident severities are combined in one analysis. Many road safety measures have larger effects on more severe accidents. One such measure is road lighting; other measures are guardrails, roundabouts, electronic stability control, seat belts and numerous others. Evaluation studies of such measures are likely to find larger effects on fatal accidents

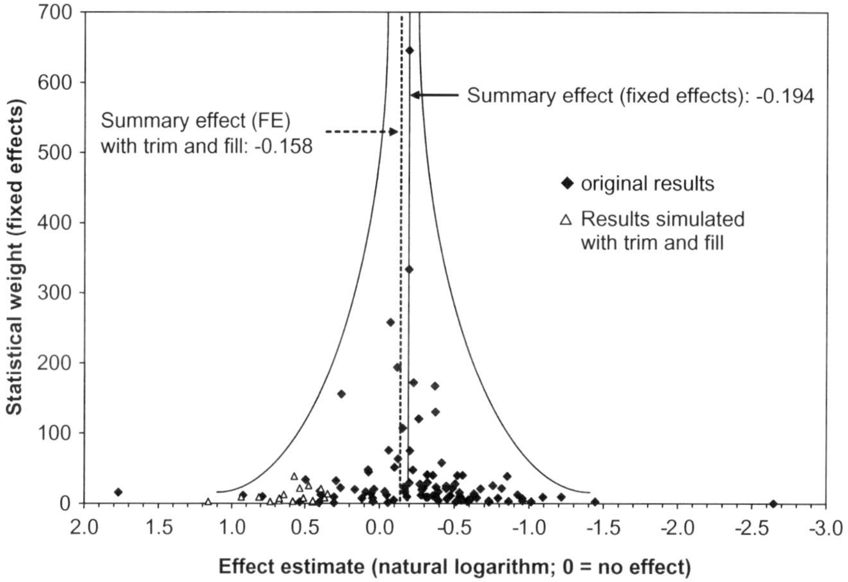


*Figure 2.2: Funnel graph of studies that have evaluated the effects of road lighting on the number of accidents (unspecified severity), results from trim and fill analysis.*

than on injury accidents. Since there are usually far more injury accidents than fatal accidents, the (large) estimates of effect that refer to fatal accidents will have smaller statistical weights than the (smaller) estimates of effect that refer to injury accidents. A distribution of estimates of effect that refer to a mixture of fatal and injury accidents may therefore tempt one to conclude that there is publication bias. This is illustrated in Figure 2.3, which consists of the same data points as Figure 2.1. The results that refer to fatal accidents (black) have small statistical weights and on the average are more on the right side of the distribution, that is, show larger accident reductions than the results that refer to non-fatal accidents (white).

The trim and fill analysis that has been applied to the data in Figure 2.2 should therefore not have been applied to these data. The skewness of the distribution is more likely to be due to the mixing of accident severities, and not due to the publication bias. In this case, there is an apples and oranges problem and a summary effect should not be calculated based on all results.

***Sensitivity to outliers*** denotes how strongly the mean in a distribution is affected by one single atypical result (outlier). If a single, outlying result decisively influences the weighted mean, this will hardly be representative of the majority of the results.

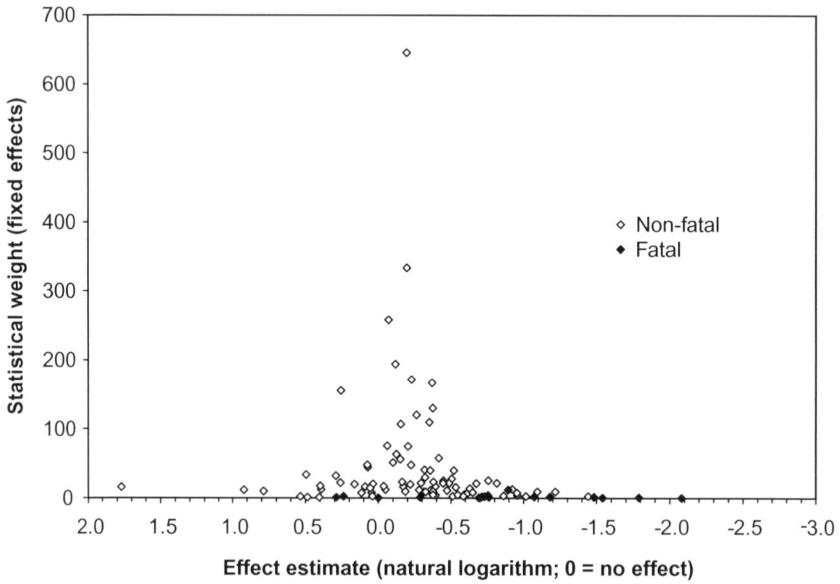


*Figure 2.3: Funnel graph of studies that have evaluated the effects of road lighting on the number of accidents (unspecified severity), results for fatal and non-fatal accidents.*

Sensitivity to outliers can be tested by calculating the $g-1$ average, where one result after another is excluded and comparing these averages with the average of all $g$ results. If no differences are found, then the weighted mean result is robust against outliers. When outliers are found, it may be investigated if there are characteristics of the respective study that can explain the result. However, there are no (objective) criteria for what results can be regarded as outliers. Whether a result is regarded as an outlier and the explanations that may be found are to a large degree subjective and may be arbitrary. Moreover, whether the result is affected by individual estimates of effect is highly dependent on the number of available estimates of effect. When there are only few, almost any effect estimate may be regarded as an outlier, whereas almost no estimates of effect will seem to be outliers when there are a large number of estimates of effect. Therefore, outliers are normally not omitted from the analysis.

## 2.6 Developing accident modification functions

It is increasingly recognised that the effects of road safety measures cannot always be adequately described in terms of a single point estimate, such as a given percentage change in the expected number of accidents. The effects of many road safety measures are likely to vary, depending on characteristics of the measure and of the context into which it is introduced. To describe systematic variation in the effects of road safety measures, accident modification functions need to be developed (Elvik 2009).

Figure 2.4 gives an example of an effect modification function (Elvik 2009). It is based on studies in Norway, Sweden and Denmark that evaluated the effects on road safety of constructing bypass roads, which lead to long-distance traffic outside towns. In Figure 2.4, the percentage change in the number of injury accidents is given as a function of the number of inhabitants in the bypassed town.

The function in Figure 2.4 has been fitted to 10 data points. Each data point is shown by a dot, surrounded by the 95% confidence interval for the data point. As can be seen from the function fitted to the data points, the effects of bypass roads are largest in small towns and decline as the size of the town increases. An accident modification factor of 0.80 corresponds to an accident reduction of 20%. An accident modification factor of 1.00 suggests that the number of accidents did not change.

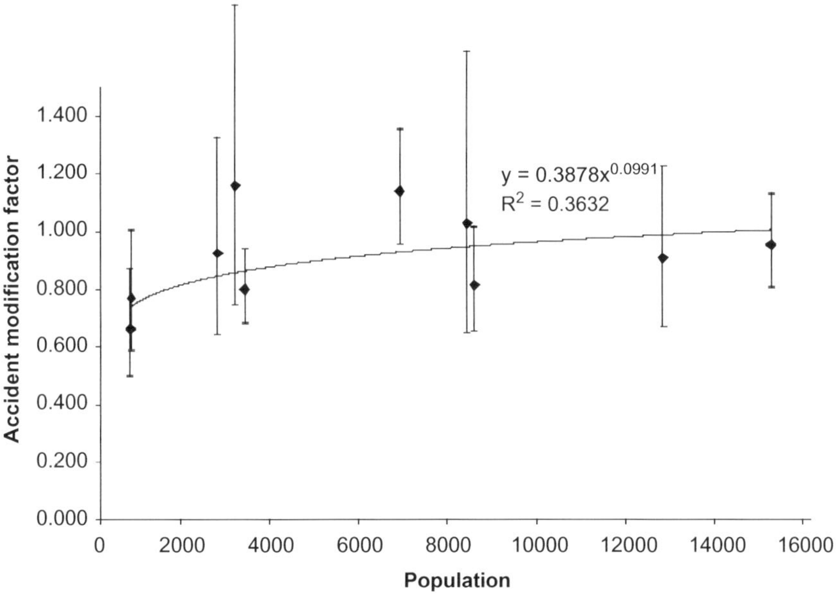


*Figure 2.4: Accident modification function for bypasses. Effect on accidents as a function of the size of the population in the bypassed town.*

## 2.7 Specification of accident or injury severity

Results that refer to accidents at different levels of severity have for the most part been kept apart. On a few occasions, it has been impossible to avoid mixing results that refer to different levels of severity because the studies we refer to have combined accidents and injuries with different levels of severity. For measures that primarily affect the number of accidents, a distinction is made between the following levels of accident severity:

- Fatal accidents, which normally refer to accidents where at least one person is killed immediately or dies within 30 days of the accident
- Injury accidents; in the majority of cases, these also include fatal accidents
- Property damage only accidents
- Accidents of unspecified severity, which in a majority of cases will include a mixture of fatal, injury and property damage only accidents, in unknown proportions.

For measures that primarily affect injury severity, a distinction is often made between the following levels of severity:

- Fatal injury
- Serious injury (mostly injuries that require hospitalisation)
- Slight injury (mostly injuries that require medical treatment, but not hospitalization)
- No injury.

No standard definition of injury severity is used in road safety evaluation studies. The above definitions represent those that are found most often in evaluation studies.

Injury severity is often classified by means of the Abbreviated Injury Scale (AIS scale), the Maximum Abbreviated Injury Scale (MAIS) or the Injury Severity Score (ISS). AIS has six values: AIS 6 is killed, AIS 3, 4 and 5 are seriously injured, AIS 2 is moderately injured and AIS 1 is slightly injured. Each of six regions of the body is assigned one value that refers to the most serious injury to the respective body region. MAIS is based on the AIS. The MAIS value of an injured person is the highest AIS value that person has on any body region. ISS is also based on the AIS. The human body is divided into six regions, and each of these regions is assigned an AIS score. ISS is calculated as the sum of the squared values of the three body regions with the highest AIS scores.

## 2.8 Updated estimates of effect: Revision of the book

The Norwegian edition of this book was finished in late 1997. By 2009, Part I and over half of all chapters in Part II have been revised. The dates when each of the chapters in Part II has been last revised are stated in the introductory sections of the chapters. Readers may wonder why we publish a book in which part of the material is by now up to 10 years old. The answer is that this is a choice we had to make in view of the amount of resources we have available for this work. Revising the whole book is a major research project, which would have taken a number of years and further delayed publication of the English edition. Therefore, the chapters that were chosen for revision since 1997 are those where most recent accident studies were available. As research is going on, the revision of this handbook will never be finished.

# 3.

# Factors Contributing to Road Accidents

## 3.1 A simple conceptual framework

The number of people killed or injured in road accidents depends basically on the three factors: exposure, accident rate and injury severity (Nilsson 2002).

***Exposure*** denotes the amount of activity in which accidents may occur. Any human activity is exposed to the risk of accident, but as far as road traffic is concerned, the amount of activity usually refers to the amount of travel, that is the number of person kilometres of travel performed. Despite the apparent simplicity of this definition (the amount of travel), measuring exposure in a theoretically satisfactory way is difficult. Some of these difficulties are discussed in Section 3.4.

There are various ways in which one can travel by road: as a pedestrian, by cycling, by driving a car, by taking the bus, etc. Not all of these ways involve the same level of accident risk. The type of exposure chosen is therefore an aspect of exposure that influences the number of people killed or injured in road accidents. Furthermore, the risk to which one is exposed as a road user is probably not independent of the combination of various means of transport in traffic. The risk of accident to each pedestrian, for example, is usually lower, the higher the proportion of pedestrians in traffic. Hence, the relative proportions of the various means of transport in a traffic stream may influence the overall level of risk represented by that traffic stream.

***Accident rate*** is the risk of accident per unit of exposure and is an indicator of the probability of accident occurrence. Although an accident rate is not identical to an estimate of probability, it is a useful indicator as the probability of accident occurrence,

**The Handbook of Road Safety Measures**

**ISBN: 978-1-84855-250-0**

in the theoretical sense, can be assumed to be proportional to the accident rate. The higher the accident rate, the higher the probability of an accident on a given trip of a given length. Sometimes the terms risk of accident, level of risk, or accident risk will be used synonymously with accident rate. Although the accident rate is defined per unit of exposure, it is not independent of exposure. Ideally, an exposure measure ought to be defined in a way that accident rate and exposure are independent. Such an exposure measure is, however, not available to date.

The probability of accident occurrence is affected by a very large number of risk factors related to the elements of the traffic system: infrastructure and traffic control devices, vehicles and road users. A risk factor for accidents is any factor that increases the probability of accident occurrence. Risk factors are, in other words, statistically related to the probability of accidents, but not all risk factors can be regarded as causes of accidents in a stricter sense of the term.

***Injury severity*** refers to the outcome of accidents in terms of injuries to people or damage to property. The severity of the consequences of an accident is, in theory, a continuous variable ranging from the smallest fender bender to disasters with multiple fatalities. In practice, simple scales that take on just a few discrete values are often constructed to indicate accident or injury severity. As an example, official road accident statistics in most countries classify accidents by severity according to the following simple scale: fatal accident, accident resulting in serious injury, accident resulting in slight injury and property damage accidents. These crude categories are not comparable even between countries.

The outcome of an accident in terms of injury to people or damage to property is also affected by a very large number of factors, related to the same elements of the traffic system as the risk factors for accidents. In this book, no attempt will be made to survey everything that is known about risk factors contributing to road accidents. An exhaustive review of this huge topic would easily fill the pages of a large book. The review is therefore limited to some of the factors that have been identified as important.

A simple taxonomy of the main factors that influence road safety is presented in Figure 3.1.

In principle, there are four ways of reducing the number of persons killed or injured in road accidents:

- By reducing exposure to the risk of accident, that is, by reducing the amount of travel
- By shifting travel to means of transport that have a lower level of risk

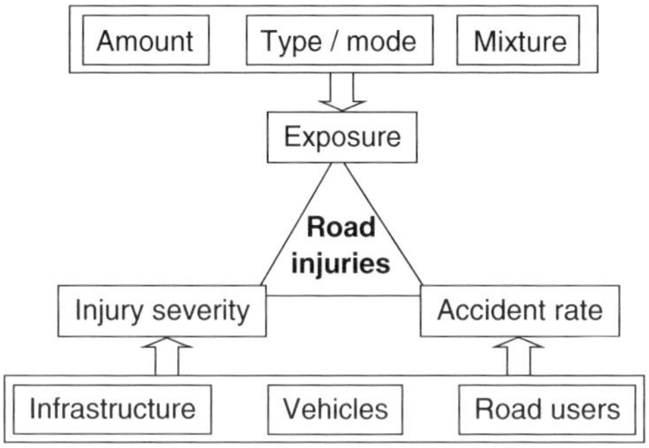


*Figure 3.1: A taxonomy of factors affecting road safety.*

- By reducing the accident rate for a given amount of travel
- By reducing accident severity, that is, by protecting people better from injury

This chapter gives a brief overview of the scope of the road accident problem worldwide, as well as of the most important factors that contribute to road accidents. First, a survey of the number of road accident fatalities worldwide is presented.

## 3.2 The scope of the road accident problem worldwide

There is no statistics showing the total number of people killed or injured in road accidents in the world. According to the World Health Organization (2008), nearly 1.2 million people are killed in road accidents annually, but no reliable estimate of the number of people injured worldwide in road accidents can be given. Rules for the reporting of road accidents and actual levels in reporting are incomparable and incomplete. As shown in Section 3.3, reporting in official statistics of road accidents leading to injury is very incomplete even in the most highly developed countries of the world with a significant number of motorised vehicles.

In many highly motorised countries belonging to the Organization for Economic Co-operation and Development (OECD), the number of road accident fatalities has been reduced after a peak was reached in about 1970. The current number of road accident fatalities in some of the OECD countries is less than 50% of its peak value. Against this background, some people might think that road accidents are gradually becoming a less serious problem in the world as a whole. This impression is not correct. The number of road accident fatalities in the world as a whole continues to grow every year. In the Global Burden of Disease study performed by the World Health Organization (Murray and Lopez 1996), it was concluded that, worldwide, traffic fatalities are becoming more important as a cause of death. This study predicted that road accidents would become the sixth largest cause of death in the world in 2020, whereas it was the ninth largest cause of death in 1990. The number of disability-adjusted life years caused by road accidents was predicted to increase from ninth largest in 1990 to third largest in 2020. A disability-adjusted life year is a measure of how the quality of life is affected by disease or injury, on a scale ranging from 0 (no disability) to 1 (dead).

Probably the best international database on road accidents is the International Road and Traffic Database (IRTAD) that operates within the framework of the Joint OECD/ECMT Transport Research Centre, and gathers data on road accidents from 37 countries, 28 of which are the members of the OECD (no data are available from Turkey and Mexico, which also are OECD members). Key figures from this database can be accessed from the homepage of the http://internationaltransportforum.org/irtad/index.html. An advantage of the IRTAD database is that it applies the 30-day definition of a traffic fatality for all member countries. This definition states that a person is counted as a traffic accident fatality if he or she dies within 30 days after the accident. Table 3.1 presents the most recent figures concerning traffic fatalities in the countries that are members of IRTAD. Table 3.1 also shows two measures of road accident fatality risk that are labelled 'health risk' and 'traffic risk'.

***Health risk*** is the number of road accident fatalities per year per 100,000 inhabitants. Health risk attributable to road accidents can be compared with the health risk represented by other causes of death, as was done in the Global Burden of Disease Study. The size of the health risk posed by road accidents in a country depends on three main factors: (1) the amount of travel per year per inhabitant in a country, (2) the level of traffic risk and (3) the resources available to protect road users from fatal injury or provide rapid medical treatment for serious injuries, to prevent them from becoming fatal.

***Traffic risk*** is the number of road accident fatalities per year per 1 billion motor vehicle kilometres of travel. The level of traffic risk indicates how safe road travel is in a country.

Table 3.1 shows that there are fairly large variations in both health risk and traffic risk between the IRTAD countries. All these countries are highly motorised, having at least 0.14 motor vehicles per inhabitant in 2000.

As far as road accident fatalities in other countries of the world are concerned, the available statistics are less comprehensive. The most inclusive statistics are the World Road Statistics, collected by the International Road Federation. These statistics can be accessed via the website of the International Road Federation (http://www.irfnet.org).

*Table 3.1: Road accident fatalities, health risk and traffic risk in IRTAD member countries (IRTAD)*

| | Motor vehicles per inhabitant | Road accident fatalities | | Health risk[1] | Traffic risk[2] |
|---|---|---|---|---|---|
| | 2006 | 1980 | 2006 | 2006 | 2006 |
| Australia | 0.68 | 3,272 | 1,598 | 8.0 | |
| Austria | 0.64 | 2,003 | 730 | 8.8 | 8.9 |
| Belgium | 0.59 | 2,396 | 1,069 | 10.2 | 11.1 |
| Bulgaria | | | 1,043 | 13.5 | |
| Canada | 0.62 | 5,461 | 2,925 | 9.1 | 9.2 |
| Cyprus | | | 86 | 11.2 | |
| Czech Republic | 0.48 | 1,261 | 1,063 | 10.4 | 20.5 |
| Denmark | 0.45 | 690 | 306 | 5.6 | |
| Estonia | | | 204 | 15.2 | |
| Finland | 0.57 | 551 | 336 | 6.4 | 6.4 |
| France | 0.61 | 13,499 | 4,709 | 7.5 | 8.5 |
| Germany | 0.67 | 15,050 | 5,091 | 6.2 | 7.4 |
| Greece | 0.63 | 1,446 | 1,657 | 14.9 | |
| Hungary | 0.34 | 1,630 | 1,305 | 13.0 | |
| Iceland | 0.79 | 25 | 31 | 10.3 | 10.9 |
| Ireland | 0.50 | 564 | 368 | 8.7 | 10.9 |
| Israel | 0.31 | 434 | 414 | 5.9 | 9.6 |
| Italy | 0.75 | 9,220 | 669 | 9.6 | |
| Japan | 0.65 | 11,388 | 7,272 | 4.7 | |
| Latvia | | | 407 | 17.7 | |
| Lithuania | | | 759 | 22.3 | |
| Luxembourg | 0.82 | 98 | 36 | 7.7 | |
| Malta | | | 10 | 2.5 | |
| The Netherlands | 0.53 | 1,996 | 730 | 4.5 | 7.7 |
| New Zealand | 0.75 | 597 | 391 | 9.3 | 10.1 |
| Norway | 0.66 | 362 | 242 | 5.2 | 6.5 |
| Poland | 0.47 | 6,002 | 5,243 | 13.7 | |
| Portugal | 0.52 | 2,579 | 969 | 9.2 | |
| Romania | | | 2,478 | 11.5 | |
| Slowakia | | | 579 | 10.7 | |
| Slovenia | 0.58 | 558 | 262 | 13.1 | 16.5 |
| South Korea | 0.38 | 6,449 | 6,376 | 13.0 | 19.3 |
| Spain | 0.65 | 6,522 | 4,104 | 9.4 | |
| Sweden | 0.58 | | 445 | 4.9 | 5.9 |

*Table 3.1: (Continued)*

| | Motor vehicles per inhabitant | Road accident fatalities | | Health risk[1] | Traffic risk[2] |
|---|---|---|---|---|---|
| | 2006 | 1980 | 2006 | 2006 | 2006 |
| Switzerland | 0.68 | 848 | 370 | 5.0 | 5.9 |
| UK | 0.57 | 6,182 | 3,297 | 5.5 | |
| USA | 0.83 | 51,091 | 43,443 | 14.7 | 9.0 |
| Total IRTAD | 0.67 | 152,174 | 101,017 | 10.1 | 9.3 |
| Total IRTAD (1980 available): | | 95,006 | | | |

[1]Killed per 100,000 inhabitants.
[2]Killed per 1 billion vehicle km.

It includes more than 185 countries. Key figures from these countries, including the IRTAD member countries, are presented in Table 3.2a (all countries) and Table 3.2b (summarised for continents/regions). These statistics are by no means complete. They are limited to those countries that had reported traffic fatalities, the number of motor vehicles and the size of the population to the International Road Federation for the years 2001–06. One should also keep in mind that different countries may apply different definitions of a traffic fatality – not all countries use the 30-day definition – and that the reporting of road accident fatalities is not complete in all countries. Moreover, it is not known to what degree the numbers of registered motor vehicles correspond to the numbers of motor vehicles actually in use.

As a whole, Australia/New Zealand and Europe have the most favourable road safety records, with traffic risk being lower than in other parts of the world and health risk among the lowest. North, Central and South America and the former East Bloc countries have somewhat higher traffic risk.

In South and Central America, the low health risk is related to the fact that the motorisation rate is quite low. However, the standard deviations of both health and traffic risk are high compared with the average risks. The countries of the former East Bloc, more than half of which are members of the IRTAD, are performing better than the former USSR countries on both safety indicators. Other parts of the world have poorer road safety records, especially Africa that has the highest traffic risk. In Asia and Africa, the health risk is about the same as that in Europe, while traffic risk is about 10 times as high or higher. The large standard deviations in the traffic risk are mainly due to some countries with extremely high health risk (over 1,000 fatalities per 100,000 motor vehicles). These countries are Ethiopia, Uganda, Bangladesh and

*Table 3.2a: Road accident fatalities, health risk and traffic risk for selected countries (International Road Federation, World Road Statistics, 2008)*

| Country | Year | Number of road accident fatalities | Health risk (fatalities per 100,000 inhabitants) | Traffic risk (fatalities per 100,000 motor vehicles) |
|---|---|---|---|---|
| ***Africa*** | | | | |
| Algeria | 2005/2003 | 4,000 | 12.6 | 134.5 |
| Angola | 2002/2001 | 942 | 6.6 | |
| Botswana | 2005/2004 | 532 | 30.1 | 267.2 |
| Brunei Darussalam | 2000/2006 | 32 | 8.4 | 24.7 |
| Congo, Rep. | 2002/2004 | 126 | 3.2 | |
| Ethiopia | 2003/2002 | 1,628 | 2.4 | 1,132.8 |
| Gabon | 2000 | 293 | 23.0 | |
| Ghana | 2006/2001 | 1,242 | 6.1 | 302.0 |
| Kenya | 2004 | 2,264 | 6.8 | 372.9 |
| Lesotho | 2000 | 290 | 16.4 | |
| Malawi | 2005 | 903 | 7.0 | |
| Mauritania | 2006 | 186 | 6.1 | |
| Mauritius | 2006 | 134 | 10.7 | 74.8 |
| Morocco | 2003/2006 | 3,754 | 12.3 | 220.7 |
| Namibia | 2002 | 340 | 17.4 | 203.6 |
| Niger | 2005/2006 | 371 | 2.7 | 487.8 |
| Nigeria | 2004 | 5,351 | 4.2 | |
| Senegal | 2000 | 646 | 6.4 | 473.4 |
| Sierra Leone | 2002/2003 | 70 | 1.3 | 365.9 |
| South Africa | 2006 | 15,419 | 32.5 | 215.3 |
| Swaziland | 2003/2001 | 255 | 23.9 | 273.9 |
| Tunisia | 2004 | 1,533 | 15.4 | 162.2 |
| Uganda | 2000 | 1,527 | 6.5 | 1,272.0 |
| Zimbabwe | 2002/2000 | 1,433 | 11.4 | |
| ***Asia*** | | | | |
| Bangladesh | 2006/2003 | 4,000 | 2.9 | 1,250.8 |
| Cambodia | 2000/2003 | 824 | 6.1 | 180.2 |
| China | 2006/2005 | 98,738 | 7.6 | 268.4 |
| China, Hong Kong | 2006/2005 | 151 | 2.2 | 31.1 |
| China, Macao | 2004 | 16 | 3.5 | 23.8 |
| Chinese Taipei | 2006 | 3,140 | 13.7 | 45.9 |
| India | 2003/2005 | 94,968 | 8.7 | 740.0 |
| Indonesia | 2002/2005 | 11,451 | 5.2 | 49.8 |

*Table 3.2a: (Continued)*

| | Country | Year | Number of road accident fatalities | Health risk (fatalities per 100,000 inhabitants) | Traffic risk (fatalities per 100,000 motor vehicles) |
|---|---|---|---|---|---|
| IRTAD | Japan | 2004 | 8,492 | 6.7 | 11.3 |
| | Korea, Republic of | 2006/2005 | 6,376 | 13.2 | 40.1 |
| | Lao PDR | 2002/2006 | 608 | 10.5 | 193.0 |
| | Malaysia | 2003 | 6,282 | 25.7 | 94.4 |
| | Maldives | 2004 | – | | – |
| | Mongolia | 2003/2002 | 415 | 17.0 | 390.5 |
| | Myanmar (Burma) | 2006/2003 | 1,308 | 2.6 | 466.7 |
| | Pakistan | 2004/2006 | 4,428 | 2.8 | 214.2 |
| | Singapore | 2006 | 190 | 4.2 | 30.0 |
| | Sri Lanka | 2006/2002 | 2,029 | 10.7 | 186.6 |
| | St Vincent & Grenadines | 2003/2002 | 10 | 8.5 | 61.5 |
| | Thailand | 2003 | 14,446 | 22.9 | |
| | Vietnam | 2002/2003 | 11,319 | 13.9 | 1,788.6 |
| | ***Australia/New Zealand*** | | | | |
| IRTAD | Australia | 2005 | 1,627 | 8.1 | 12.1 |
| IRTAD | New Zealand | 2006 | 393 | 9.4 | 13.0 |
| | ***Europe*** | | | | |
| IRTAD | Austria | 2006 | 730 | 8.8 | 15.9 |
| IRTAD | Belgium | 2006 | 1,069 | 10.2 | 19.0 |
| IRTAD | Cyprus | 2005 | 102 | 13.5 | 18.1 |
| IRTAD | Denmark | 2005/2006 | 306 | 5.6 | 12.9 |
| IRTAD | Finland | 2006 | 336 | 6.3 | 11.7 |
| IRTAD | France | 2006 | 4,708 | 7.7 | 12.8 |
| IRTAD | Germany | 2006 | 5,091 | 6.2 | 10.3 |
| IRTAD | Greece | 2005/2006 | 1,657 | 14.9 | 30.0 |
| IRTAD | Iceland | 2005/2006 | 31 | 10.3 | 14.4 |
| IRTAD | Ireland | 2003/2004 | 379 | 9.3 | 21.2 |
| IRTAD | Italy | 2005/2006 | 5,669 | 9.6 | 14.5 |
| IRTAD | Luxembourg | 2004 | 50 | 11.0 | 15.1 |
| IRTAD | Malta | 2004 | 13 | 3.2 | 5.1 |
| IRTAD | The Netherlands | 2002/2006 | 730 | 4.5 | 9.3 |
| IRTAD | Norway | 2005/2004 | 259 | 5.6 | 10.3 |
| IRTAD | Poland | 2005/2006 | 5,243 | 13.8 | 35.6 |
| IRTAD | Portugal | 2003/2006 | 969 | 9.2 | 18.3 |
| IRTAD | Spain | 2003/2004 | 4,741 | 11.1 | 20.5 |

*Table 3.2a: (Continued)*

| | Country | Year | Number of road accident fatalities | Health risk (fatalities per 100,000 inhabitants) | Traffic risk (fatalities per 100,000 motor vehicles) |
|---|---|---|---|---|---|
| IRTAD | Sweden | 2006 | 445 | 4.9 | 9.5 |
| IRTAD | Switzerland | 2006 | 370 | 4.9 | 8.7 |
| | Turkey | 2005/2006 | 4,633 | 6.4 | 55.0 |
| IRTAD | United Kingdom | 2005/2006 | 3,172 | 5.2 | 10.2 |
| | ***Former East Bloc*** | | | | |
| | Albania | 2006 | 277 | 8.7 | 89.7 |
| | Bosnia and Herzegovina | 2004 | 251 | 6.4 | |
| IRTAD | Bulgaria | 2004/2006 | 1,043 | 13.6 | 37.4 |
| | Croatia | 2006 | 614 | 14.0 | 38.1 |
| IRTAD | Czech Republic | 2002/2006 | 1,063 | 10.3 | 26.5 |
| IRTAD | Hungary | 2003/2006 | 1,303 | 12.9 | 40.7 |
| | Macedonia, FYR | 2002/2004 | 155 | 7.6 | 46.9 |
| | Moldova | 2005/2006 | 382 | 10.1 | 96.8 |
| IRTAD | Romania | 2005/2006 | 2,478 | 11.5 | 63.6 |
| | Serbia | 2006 | 900 | 12.2 | 49.9 |
| IRTAD | Slovakia | 2006 | 608 | 11.3 | 39.2 |
| IRTAD | Slovenia | 2006 | 262 | 13.1 | 24.7 |
| | ***Former USSR*** | | | | |
| | Armenia | 2006 | 332 | 11.1 | |
| | Azerbaijan | 2005/2006 | 1,027 | 12.1 | 199.4 |
| | Belarus | 2006 | 1,726 | 17.8 | |
| IRTAD | Estonia | 2005/2006 | 204 | 15.2 | 31.8 |
| | Georgia | 2003/2006 | 675 | 15.3 | 208.5 |
| | Kazakhstan | 2006 | 4,271 | 27.9 | 200.3 |
| | Kyrgyzstan | 2005 | 893 | 17.4 | |
| IRTAD | Latvia | 2006 | 407 | 17.7 | 42.7 |
| IRTAD | Lithuania | 2006 | 759 | 22.3 | 43.5 |
| | Russian Federation | 2006 | 32,700 | 23.0 | 100.5 |
| | Tajikistan | 2000/2004 | 415 | 6.5 | |
| | Turkmenistan | 2002 | 519 | 11.2 | |
| | Ukraine | 2005/2006 | 7,592 | 16.2 | 125.9 |
| | ***Middle East*** | | | | |
| | Bahrain | 2003/2002 | 81 | 11.6 | 30.0 |
| | Egypt | 2005/2006 | 6,000 | 8.1 | |
| | Iran | 2002/2006 | 8,257 | 11.8 | |

*Table 3.2a: (Continued)*

| | Country | Year | Number of road accident fatalities | Health risk (fatalities per 100,000 inhabitants) | Traffic risk (fatalities per 100,000 motor vehicles) |
|---|---|---|---|---|---|
| IRTAD | Israel | 2005/2006 | 414 | 5.9 | 20.4 |
| | Jordan | 2006 | 899 | 16.3 | 128.6 |
| | Kuwait | 2004 | 400 | 16.3 | 38.5 |
| | Lebanon | 2000/2006 | 375 | 9.3 | |
| | Oman | 2002/2003 | 578 | 23.0 | |
| | Palestine | 2005 | 159 | 4.4 | 120.5 |
| | Qatar | 2002/2006 | 270 | 32.9 | 77.4 |
| | Saudi Arabia | 2005 | 5,982 | 25.3 | 134.5 |
| | Syria | 2006 | 2,197 | 11.3 | 245.1 |
| | United Arab Emirates | 2001/2003 | 873 | 21.6 | |
| | ***North America*** | | | | |
| IRTAD | Canada | 2003/2004 | 2,730 | 8.5 | 14.8 |
| IRTAD | United States | 2005 | 43,443 | 14.7 | 21.7 |
| | ***South/Central America*** | | | | |
| | Anguilla | 2004 | 1 | | 15.0 |
| | Bahamas | 2002/2005 | 68 | 21.1 | |
| | Barbados | 2004/2002 | 24 | 9.0 | 23.8 |
| | Bolivia | 2004/2001 | 823 | 9.7 | 187.2 |
| | Brazil | 2004 | 6,119 | 3.3 | 19.6 |
| | Chile | 2006/2001 | 1,562 | 10.0 | 60.5 |
| | Colombia | 2005/2006 | 5,486 | 12.0 | 204.2 |
| | Costa Rica | 2004/2006 | 329 | 7.5 | 39.1 |
| | Ecuador | 2006 | 1,801 | 13.6 | 205.5 |
| | Jamaica | 2006/2005 | 326 | 12.3 | 64.2 |
| | Mexico | 2006 | 4,908 | 4.7 | 21.2 |
| | Nicaragua | 2004/2002 | 473 | 9.2 | 190.9 |
| | Panama | 2002 | 401 | 13.1 | 127.3 |
| | Paraguay | 2000 | 160 | 3.0 | 35.4 |
| | Peru | 2004/2006 | 3,481 | 12.6 | 270.4 |
| | Philippines | 2005/2006 | 961 | 1.1 | 34.4 |
| | Puerto Rico | 2001 | 496 | 12.9 | |
| | Suriname | 2004 | 69 | 15.5 | 64.8 |
| | Uruguay | 2005 | 150 | 4.3 | 24.7 |

*Table 3.2b: Road accident fatalities, health risk and traffic risk summarised for several continents/regions (International Road Federation, World Road Statistics, 2008)*

| | Number of countries | Number of motor vehicles per 100 population | Number of road accident fatalities | Health risk (SD) | Traffic risk (SD) |
|---|---|---|---|---|---|
| Australia/New Zealand | 2 | 68 | 2,020 | 8.3 (0.9) | 12.2 (0.6) |
| Europe | 22 | 49 | 40,703 | 8.0 (3.3) | 16.2 (11) |
| North America | 2 | 67 | 46,173 | 14.1 (4.3) | 21.1 (4.9) |
| South/Central America | 18 | 13 | 27,638 | 5.4 (5.1) | 39.7 (84.6) |
| Former East Bloc | 12 | 27 | 9,336 | 11.4 (2.4) | 43.3 (23.8) |
| Middle East | 13 | 16 | 26,485 | 12.2 (8.4) | 105.5 (74.7) |
| Former USSR | 13 | 20 | 51,520 | 20.3 (5.7) | 106.1 (76.2) |
| Asia | 20 | 6 | 269,191 | 8.0 (6.7) | 138.9 (463.7) |
| Africa | 24 | 5 | 43,271 | 9.0 (8.6) | 224.0 (348.6) |

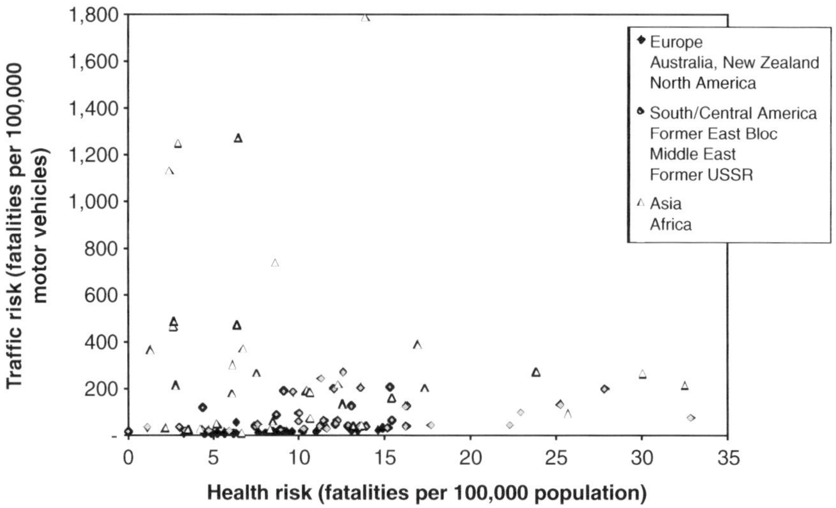


*Figure 3.2: Relationship between health risk and traffic risk in different countries (International Road Federation, World Road Statistics, 2008).*

Vietnam; India has 750 fatalities per 100,000 motor vehicles. It is not known to what degree the high risk can be explained with unregistered motor vehicles.

Figure 3.2 shows the relationship between health risk and traffic risk in all countries listed in Tables 3.1, 3.2a and 3.2b. It appears that there is a negative relationship between health risk and traffic risk in Asia and Africa, that is a high health risk is related to a low traffic risk and vice versa. In other countries, there is no such relationship. In the North American European and North American countries, Australia and New Zealand, there is a slight tendency for higher health risk to be associated with higher traffic risk.

Many years ago, Smeed (1949) postulated a law-like relationship between health risk and motorisation rate, stating essentially that as the motorisation rate goes up, the number of road accident fatalities per inhabitant goes down. The data presented in Tables 3.1, 3.2a and 3.2b do not lend support to the idea of such a relationship. The relationship between motorisation (motor vehicles per 100 inhabitants) and health risk is shown in Figure 3.3 for countries that are included in Table 3.1, 3.2a and 3.2b.

Figure 3.4 shows the relationship between motorisation (vehicles per 100 inhabitants) and traffic risk (fatalities per 100,000 vehicles). There are only five countries with more than 500 fatalities per 100,000 vehicles, which are not shown in Figure 3.3. The motorisation rate in these countries is very low (between 0.2 and 1.2 motor vehicles per 100 inhabitants). The data suggest that traffic risk decreases as motorisation increases. For the countries with a low motorisation rate, the spread of the data points seems to be particularly great.

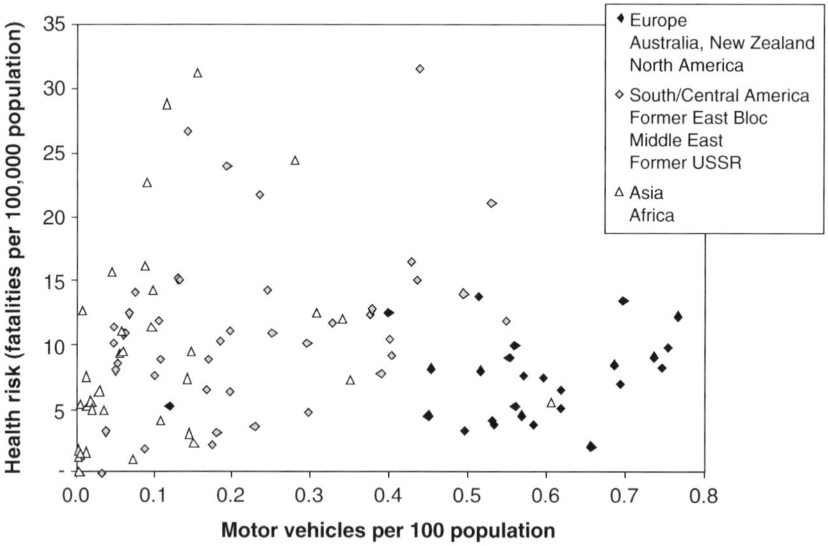


*Figure 3.3: Relationship between motorisation and health risk.*

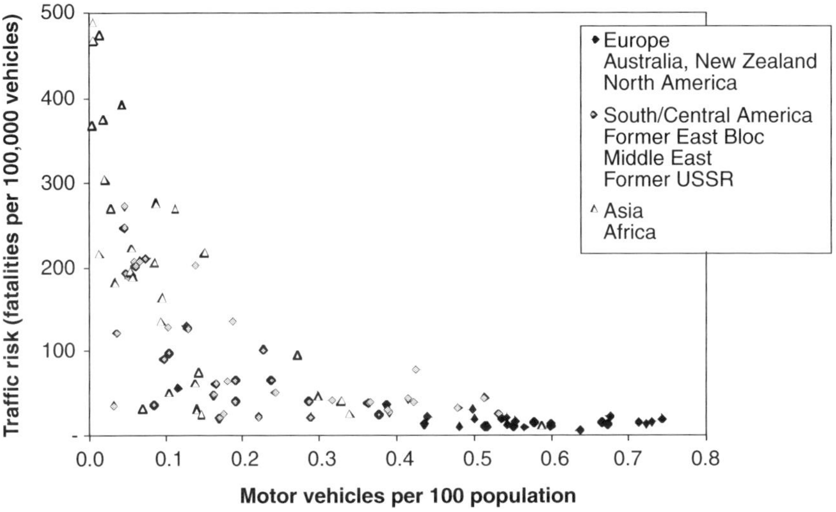


*Figure 3.4: Relationship between motorisation and traffic risk.*

## 3.3 Incomplete reporting in official road accident statistics

It is well known that the reporting of road accidents in official statistics is incomplete and biased. Incomplete road accident reporting is part of a larger problem concerning the availability of accurate information about road accidents. Figure 3.5 traces the sources of error and loss of data in official accident records. Starting with all accidents that actually occur on public roads, the first loss of information occurs because some of these accidents are not defined as reportable to the police. In Norway, for example, accidents that are not reportable include all accidents involving pedestrians only and all accidents in which inconsequential personal injuries are sustained.

It is known from a large number of studies, summarised by Elvik and Mysen (1999), that the reporting of reportable injury accidents in official statistics is very incomplete. A large number of potentially important data elements, related to human factors in particular (Elvik and Vaa 1990), are not recorded. Finally, there are errors or missing information in some of the recorded data elements. In Norway, for example, information about the use of seat belts is missing for about 55% of car drivers who are killed.

Virtually all studies of the effects of road safety measures are based exclusively on official accident statistics. However, very few studies seem to have probed the implications of these, more or less inevitable, errors. Hauer and Hakkert (1988) have

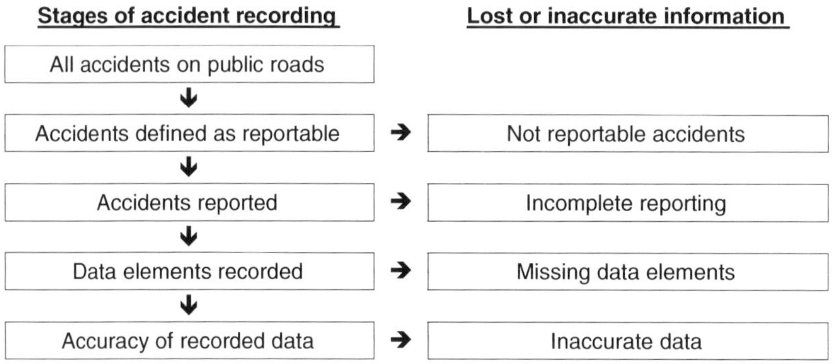


*Figure 3.5: Sources of error and data loss in official accident records.*

examined some of the implications of incomplete accident reporting. One of the most important implications is that incomplete accident reporting increases the uncertainty of the estimated effects of road safety measures. Elvik and Mysen (1999) have conducted a meta-analysis of studies of accident reporting in official statistics reported in 13 countries. The study was based on earlier reviews made by Borger (1995), Hauer and Hakkert (1988), Hvoslef (1994) and James (1991), but included more studies than any of those reviews.

***The definition of the level of accident reporting***. Most studies of the level of accident reporting in official statistics involve comparing accidents and injuries recorded at hospitals with those recorded by the police in the area serviced by the hospital or hospitals. There are two reasons why such a comparison is unlikely to show the true reporting level for injury accidents in official road accident statistics. First, at least three definitions of reporting level can be derived from a comparison of police records and hospital records (Figure 3.6).

$$\text{Definition } 1 = \frac{B}{B+C}$$

$$\text{Definition } 2 = \frac{A+B}{B+C}$$

$$\text{Definition } 3 = \frac{A+B}{A+B+C}$$

The simplest definition, and the one most commonly used in studies that rely on hospital records, is the proportion of cases recorded by the hospital for which a police report is found. Another common definition of the reporting level is simply to count the total number of cases recorded by the police as a proportion of the total number of cases recorded by the hospital. The theoretically most correct definition counts police

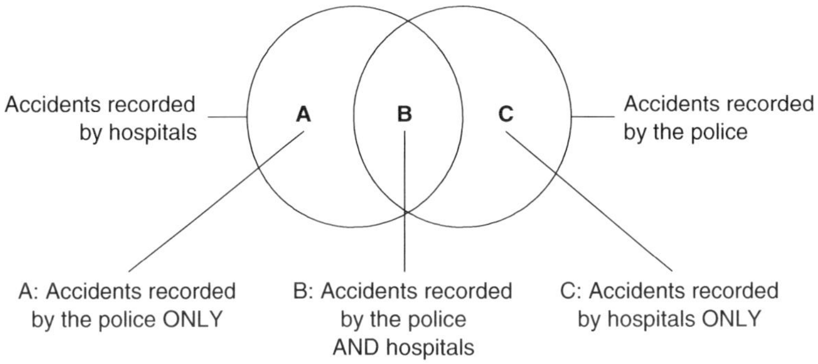


*Figure 3.6: Illustration of three definitions of the level of accident reporting.*

reported cases as a proportion of cases recorded by *A* – the police alone, *B* – both the hospital and the police and *C* – the hospitals alone.

The choice of definition can make a big difference for the estimated level of reporting. In Figure 3.6, if *A* is 100, *B* is 200 and *C* is 400, definition 1 gives a reporting level of 33% (200/600), definition 2 a reporting level of 50% (300/600) and definition 3 a reporting level of 43% (300/700). Unfortunately, not all studies state precisely how reporting level was defined. The use of definition 3 requires a study of individual records to find the number of cases that belong to each of the categories *A*, *B* and *C*. In studies that simply compare the total number of cases recorded by the police and the hospital, the reporting level is defined according to either definition 1 or definition 2 in Figure 3.6. Neither of these definitions is theoretically correct.

The second reason why a definition of reporting level based on a comparison of police and hospital records is unlikely to show the true reporting level for injury accidents is that hospital records are unlikely to be complete. There are a number of sources of road accident data, including police records, hospital records, insurance records, other company records and self-reported accidents. It is widely agreed that none of these sources is likely to be complete. In order to get the most complete coverage of accidents, ideally data from all these sources should be combined and their degree of overlap should be determined exactly; however, this has never been done. Virtually all studies of road accident reporting compare just two sources of data, the most common comparison being between police records and hospital records.

It follows that no exact determination of the level of reporting for road accidents is possible. The true number of accidents is unknown and is not recorded anywhere. Any estimate based on available sources is likely to show the lower bound for the true number of road accidents.

***Meta-analysis of studies of accident reporting***. Elvik and Mysen (1999) made a meta-analysis of 49 studies that have evaluated the reporting level for road accidents involving personal injury. The studies included are listed in the paper by Elvik and Mysen (1999). Reporting level was defined as the number of police reported cases divided by the number of cases in the main source of data. No distinction was made between the various definitions of reporting level discussed above because not all studies state exactly how the reporting level was defined.

***Reporting levels by injury severity***. The reporting level for injury accidents in official road accident statistics depends on injury severity. Injury severity is, however, a variable that is likely to be defined in different ways in different countries. In the meta-analysis of accident reporting, a crude distinction has been made between the following levels of injury severity:

- Fatal injuries: death within 30 days after the accident
- Serious injuries: injuries that result in admission to hospital as an in-patient
- Slight injuries: injuries treated at hospitals, but not resulting in admission as an in-patient
- Very slight injuries: injuries treated medically outside hospitals
- Property damage only, accidents in which nobody was injured. In many countries, property damage only accidents do not have to be reported.

Figure 3.7 shows the mean reporting level for injury accidents according to these levels. The mean reporting level given for each level of injury severity is a weighted average based on studies reported in several countries. The vertical bars indicate the range of reporting levels found in the studies.

***Reporting levels by groups of road users.*** Table 3.3 shows the mean reporting level for injury accidents in various countries for various groups of road users and types of accident.

Table 3.3 shows a remarkably consistent pattern in accident reporting in various countries. In general, the reporting level is highest for car occupants. It is generally slightly lower for pedestrians, still lower for motorcycle riders and lowest for cyclists. With the exception of Great Britain, the reporting of cyclist injuries is roughly between 10% and 25%. For single vehicle accidents among cyclists, reporting is very low, below 10% in all the countries that have evaluated the reporting level for single vehicle bicycle accidents.

Despite this consistency, the overall level of accident reporting differs greatly between countries. To compare the level of road safety between countries, one must therefore

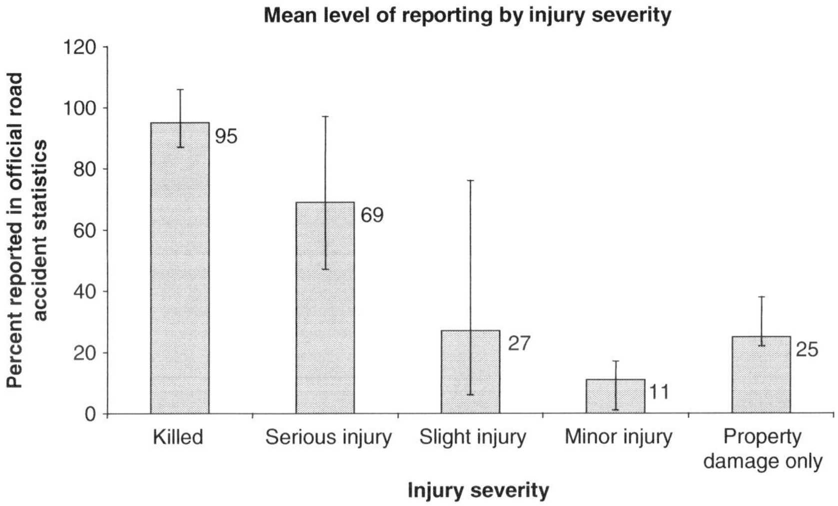


*Figure 3.7: Mean level of accident reporting by injury severity (Elvik and Mysen 1999).*

*Table 3.3: Percentage of injury accidents reported by road user group and type of accident*

| | Car occupants | | | Motor cycle riders | | | Cyclists | | | Pedestrians |
|---|---|---|---|---|---|---|---|---|---|---|
| Country | All | Drivers | Passengers | All | Collisions | Single | All | Collisions | Single | All |
| Australia | 73 | 79 | 66 | 53 | | | 7 | | | 69 |
| Denmark | 48 | | | 31 | 53 | 16 | 10 | 31 | 3 | 39 |
| France | 63 | | | 45 | | | 11 | | | 83 |
| Germany | 52 | | | 44 | | | 22 | | | 45 |
| Great Britain | 68 | 67 | 67 | 44 | | | 66 | 85 | 3 | 81 |
| The Netherlands | 63 | | | 56 | | | 24 | | | 49 |
| Norway | 56 | 52 | 45 | 37 | | | 16 | 46 | 2 | 45 |
| Reunion | 45 | | | 35 | | | 16 | | | 46 |
| Sri Lanka | 78 | | | 81 | | | 26 | | | 75 |
| Sweden | 77 | 80 | 76 | 55 | 67 | 25 | 29 | 59 | 8 | 70 |
| Switzerland | 44 | | | 22 | | | 8 | | | 38 |
| USA | 65 | 82 | 40 | (not available) | | | 26 | 51 | 0 | 56 |

*Table 3.4: Reporting of road accident fatalities and injuries in different countries (Hutchinson 1984)*

| | Fatalities | Injuries |
|---|---|---|
| The Netherlands | 106 | 43 |
| Germany | 104 | 39 |
| Denmark | 97 | 21 |
| Finland | 96 | |
| Canada | 95 | 88 |
| USA | 95 | 49 |
| Belgium | 93 | |
| Sweden | 93 | 55 |
| Australia | 92 | 64 |
| UK | 90 | 57 |
| Norway | 87 | 37 |
| France | | 54 |
| Switzerland | | 25 |

rely on fatalities only. The officially recorded numbers of injured road users are too greatly affected by varying levels of reporting to be directly comparable.

***The reporting of road accident fatalities and injuries in different countries***. Hutchinson (1984) compared the number of fatalities and injuries reported in official road accident statistics with the number reported in official mortality statistics (Table 3.4). The results that refer to fatalities are based on death certificates for a large number of countries. In all cases, the 30-day definition of a road accident fatality is applied. The results that refer to injuries are estimated as weighted mean of the results from several studies.

In most countries, the reporting of fatalities in official road accident statistics is incomplete. In two countries, there is apparently a reporting of more than 100% of traffic accident fatalities. Hutchinson remarks that the reasons for this are unknown. Possible explanations for the apparent over-reporting are that persons who committed suicide, who died immediately before the accident of an acute illness or who are foreigners are assigned a different cause of death in the official death records, but retained as traffic fatalities in the road accident statistics.

On average, the reporting level for traffic accident fatalities for the 11 countries included in Table 3.4 is about 95%. The reporting level for fatalities differs significantly between countries ($\chi^2 = 69.554$, $df = 10$, $p < 0.001$). For injuries, the reporting level ranges from 88% to 21%. The (weighted) mean reporting level is 39%. The differences in reporting level between the countries are very highly significant ($X^2_{hom} = 43,117.324$, $df = 12$, $p < 0.001$).

A closer look at some of the studies shows that few differences between countries in reporting level are probably attributable to differences with respect to the severity of the injuries that are included. The studies in Canada were based on data dominated by serious injuries, that is, by injuries that resulted in admission to hospital as an in-patient. This clearly illustrates how difficult it is to obtain comparable accident data for different countries.

## 3.4 Exposure: Traffic volume

Ideally speaking, a study of the relationship between traffic volume and accidents ought to control for the effects of all other factors that affect accident occurrence. 'To control for' means to remove, so that the effects of the amount of travel are not mixed up with the effects of other factors. Such other factors are, for example, road category (lower accident rate on better roads) and time of the year or day (higher accident rates in darkness).

Studies of the relationship between exposure and accidents usually refer to traffic volume, not the amount of travel, that is normally defined as the number of motor vehicles using a road per unit of time. Pedestrians and cyclists tend not to be included, usually because there are no reliable counts of their numbers. The volume of travel includes passengers in addition to drivers.

The relationship between exposure and accidents is reviewed in Chapter 10.5; here only a summary is given. The effects of the amount of travel on the number of accidents can be expressed in many ways. Two of the most informative are to

- describe, by means of a mathematical function, the shape of the relationship between traffic volume and accidents, and
- indicate the contribution that traffic volume makes to explaining systematic variation of the number of accidents.

***The relationship between traffic volume and accidents***. Increasing traffic volumes are usually related to increasing numbers of accidents. However, the number of accidents is not linearly related to traffic volume. Usually, the percentage increase of the number of accidents is less than the percentage increase of traffic volume. Increasing traffic volumes are often related to better road standards, and drivers may pay more attention at high volumes than at low volumes.

On the basis of a large number of studies, the estimated relationship between traffic volume and accidents is shown in Figure 3.8. Traffic volume is expressed as the annual average daily traffic (AADT), which is the most commonly used, although not necessarily the best, measure of traffic volume. The mathematical function used to describe the relationship

$$N = \text{AADT}^{\beta}$$

As volume increases by 10%, the estimated increase of the number of accidents is 8.8% with a 95% confidence interval from 7.7% to 9.9%. The uncertainty in the estimated change of the number of accidents is due to a number of factors. First, the form of the mathematical function may not be optimal. The percentage change of the number of

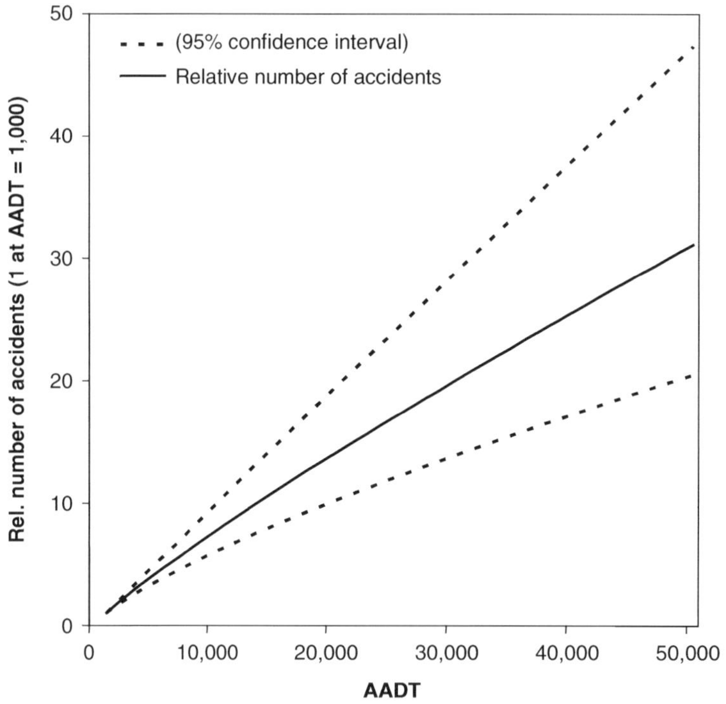


*Figure 3.8: Relationship between traffic volume (AADT) and the number of accidents, estimated by means of meta-analysis based on 28 studies.*

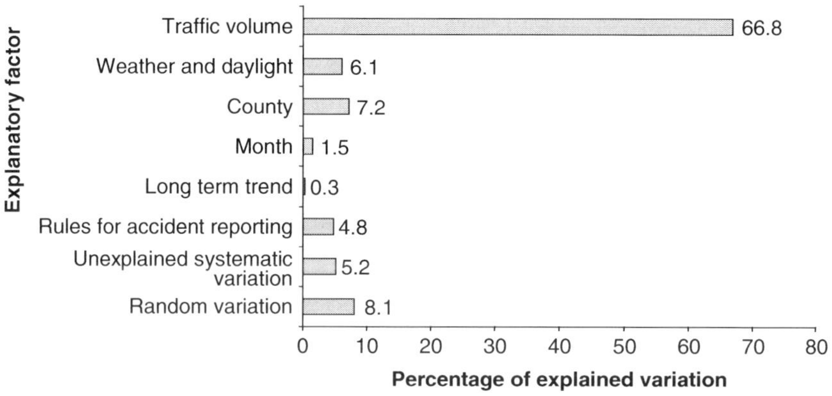


*Figure 3.9: Contribution of various factors to explaining the variation in injury accidents by county and month in Norway (Fridtstrøm et al., 1993, 1995).*

accidents may be different at different volumes. Second, the relationship between volume and accidents is likely to be different under different conditions, for example, depending on the type and capacity of the road, the type of accidents and variations of volume over time.

***The contribution of traffic volume to explaining systematic variation of the number of accidents.*** Figure 3.9 shows the results of a multivariate analysis of some factors that influence the number of injury accidents per county per month in Norway (Fridstrøm et al. 1993, 1995). The effects of traffic volume alone is about twice as great as the effects of all other factors combined.

Some readers may raise the following objections: What about the effects of road safety measures? What about road user behaviour? Why do these factors not show up in the diagram to explain at least part of the variation of the number of accidents? The simple answer is that these factors were not included in the analysis. Even if road safety measures and road user behaviour had been included, these factors would not necessarily have explained very much of the variation in the number of accidents. To have explanatory power, these variables would have to exhibit sufficient variation in the data set. It is doubtful whether that would be the case for road safety measures. Such measures tend to be introduced gradually in small doses, so that significant variations would not be expected between counties in Norway.

Despite these reservations, there is hardly any doubt that traffic volume is the single most important factor that influences the number of road accidents. This is likely to be the case all over the world, although of course the precise shape of the relationship between traffic volume and the number of accidents will vary from place to place.

## 3.5 Accident rates for different types of exposure

When travelling by road, the main means of transport available are walking, cycling, riding a moped or motorcycle, driving a car, being a passenger in a car and going by bus. In a number of countries, injury rates have been compared for these means of transport:

Sweden: Nilsson (2002)
Denmark: Brems and Munch (2008)
Great Britain: UK Department for Transport (2008)
The Netherlands: SWOV (2008)
Norway: Bjørnskau (2008)

The absolute injury rates are not comparable, due to differences in accident reporting discussed earlier. Figure 3.10 presents relative injury rates, in which the injury rate of a car driver has been set 1.0. A simple mean for the five countries has been estimated.

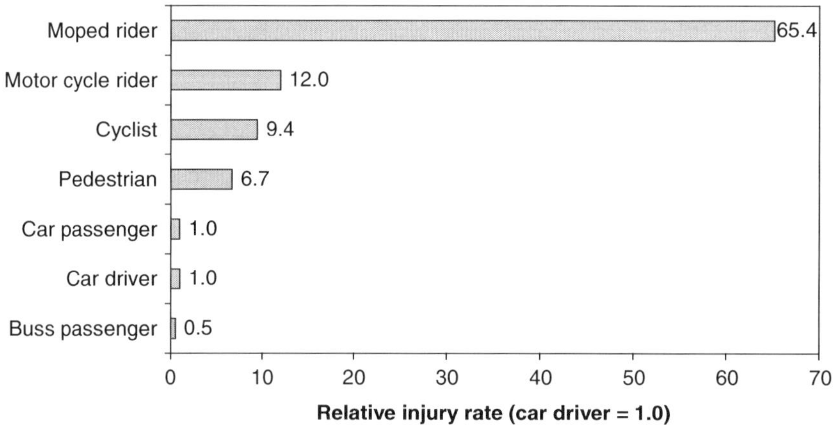


*Figure 3.10: Relative injury rates for different means of transport – mean for five countries.*

A very similar pattern was found for all five countries. Travelling by moped or motorcycle involves a risk of injury, which is over 10 times higher than that of a car driver. Pedestrians and cyclists also run a high risk of being injured per kilometre of travel. Car passengers have the same risk of injury as car drivers. Travelling by bus is the safest. These estimates of relative injury rates are all based on accidents reported in official accident statistics. The differences in injury rates would probably have been even greater if these rates had been estimated on the basis of injuries recorded in hospitals.

Why are pedestrians, cyclists and riders of mopeds and motorcycles at such a high risk of getting injured in road traffic? There are many reasons, and we will not go into them in detail. Referring to the conceptual model in Section 3.1, there are two classes of reasons for the high injury rate of pedestrians, cyclists and riders of mopeds and motorcycles:

- factors affecting accident involvement rate and
- factors affecting the probability of injury, given that a road user is involved in an accident (vulnerability).

Pedestrians and cyclists tend to do most of their travel in urban areas, where the overall risk of accidents is higher than in rural areas. Moped riders are often young and inexperienced. Motorcycle riders may be more experienced; on the contrary, a motorcycle is capable of going at a higher speed than a moped. Much of the difference in injury rate between pedestrians, cyclists and rider of mopeds and motorcycles on the one hand, and car occupants on the other, is attributable to differences in the protection from injury offered in an accident. The accident involvement rates of car drivers is not very different from that of pedestrians and cyclists, but a far higher proportion of car accidents result in property damage only.

## 3.6 The mixture of road users

Most of the road system carries mixed traffic, that is, all or most categories of road users use the same area for travel. Urban roads may have separate facilities for pedestrians and/or cyclists, but at junctions, pedestrians and cyclists normally mix with car traffic. Do the relative proportions of different road users in traffic affect the number of accidents?

There is reason to believe that this is the case. Few studies have estimated the relationship between composite measures of exposure and the number of accidents or injured road users. By way of illustration, a study by Brüde and Larsson (1993) estimated the relationship between accidents involving pedestrians or cyclists and motor vehicles by means of the following composite measure of exposure:

Number of accidents involving groups 1 and 2 $= \alpha Q_1^b Q_2^c$

In this formula, $Q_1$ is the number of road users of type 1, $Q_2$ is the number of road users of type 2, $b$ and $c$ are coefficients to be estimated and $\alpha$ is a scaling constant.

Brüde and Larsson (1993) estimated the following functions:

Number of pedestrian accidents $= 0.0000734 \times \text{MV}^{0.50} \times \text{PED}^{0.72}$

Number of bicycle accidents $= 0.0000180 \times \text{MV}^{0.52} \times \text{CYC}^{0.65}$

where MV is the number of motor vehicles (AADT = annual average daily traffic), PED is pedestrian volume and CYC is cyclist volume.

On the basis of these functions, the number of accidents can be estimated for any combination of values for the number of motor vehicles and the numbers of pedestrians or cyclists.

These functions suggest a highly non-linear relationship between exposure and the number of accidents. If, as an example, the number of pedestrians increases from 500 to 1,000, and the number of motor vehicles increases from 5,000 to 10,000, the number of pedestrian accidents (i.e., accidents in which pedestrians are struck by cars) increases by a factor of nearly 2.33. In other words, the number of accidents is more than double when total traffic volume is doubled (from 5,500 to 11,000 in total). Despite this, the risk run by each pedestrian, at a given amount of motor traffic, declines strongly as the number of pedestrians increases. If the number of pedestrians increases from 100 to 1,000, the risk of getting injured, stated as the number of pedestrian accidents per pedestrian exposed, drops by about 50%. A further increase in the number of pedestrians from 1,000 to 2,000 is associated with a further reduction in the injury rate per pedestrian of some 17%.

Likewise, the risk of a motor vehicle striking a pedestrian declines as a function of the number of motor vehicles interacting with pedestrians. Thus, for a given amount of pedestrian traffic, the risk of each motor vehicle hitting a pedestrian drops by more than 50% if the number of motor vehicles increases from 2,000 to 10,000.

For both pedestrians and motor vehicles, a high traffic volume alone confers some protection from injury accidents. There is safety in numbers: each pedestrian is safer if more pedestrians there are. The precise behavioural mechanisms leading to this relationship are not very well known. More dense traffic is likely to have at least two effects that are beneficial to safety: First, in dense traffic, there are more things to pay attention to. Assuming that nobody wants to be involved in an accident, drivers may strive to pay at least sufficient attention to the traffic to be reasonably sure of avoiding accidents. Moreover, driving in dense traffic is less monotonous than driving in very sparse traffic. Second, in very dense traffic, speed goes down. As speed goes down, accidents become both less likely and less severe. Pedestrians are better able to enforce their right of way when crossing the road if there are many of them than if there is just one pedestrian waiting to cross the road.

Similar comments apply to accidents involving cyclists and motor vehicles. The situation almost resembles a paradox: While each road user, in each of the groups that interact, is safer in heavy traffic than in light traffic, the total number of accidents involving the interacting categories of road users increases more than in proportion to the total interacting volumes.

As noted, few studies have examined the relationship between exposure and accident occurrence using composite measures of exposure. Virtually, the only applications that can be found in the literature refer to accidents at junctions, modelled as a function of intersecting traffic volumes, and studies of accidents involving pedestrians or cyclists and motor vehicles. This means that the precise nature of the relationship between exposure to risk and the number of accidents remains largely unknown at its most basic level. In most studies, only aggregate measures of exposure have been used, in most cases including motor vehicles only. Important aspects of the relationship between exposure and accidents remain hidden as long as exposure is not broken down into categories of road users that differ greatly with respect to their accident involvement rate.

## 3.7 A SURVEY OF SOME RISK FACTORS FOR ACCIDENT INVOLVEMENT

A large number of risk factors have been found to be statistically associated with accident rates, that is, with the number of accidents per unit of exposure. In this brief survey, only a few of these factors will be mentioned.

***Type of road or traffic environment***. The rate of road accidents, given as accidents per million vehicle kilometres of travel, varies greatly between different types of road and different types of traffic environment. An international comparison is given in Table 3.5 which is taken from the chapter dealing with urban and regional planning. Sources are as follows:

*Table 3.5: Relative risk on different types of roads in different countries: injury accidents (risk on motorways = 1.00)*

| | Relative risk of injury accidents in different countries | | | | | | | |
|---|---|---|---|---|---|---|---|---|
| Type of road | Denmark | Finland | Germany | UK | Norway | The Netherlands | Sweden | USA |
| | | | | ***Rural areas*** | | | | |
| Motorway | 1.00 | 1.00 | 1.00 | 1.00 | 1.00 | 1.00 | 1.00 | 1.00 |
| Main road | 3.97 | 2.91 | 3.00 | 2.82 | 2.28 | 1.33 | 1.29 | 2.72 |
| Collector road | 4.67 | 3.27 | | | 3.46 | 3.67 | 2.34 | 4.56 |
| Access road | 5.67 | 6.11 | | 5.11 | 5.53 | 7.17 | 1.34 | 8.66 |
| | | | | ***Urban areas*** | | | | |
| Main road | 11.00 | 7.86 | | 7.17 | 5.22 | | 2.15 | 5.68 |
| Collector | 9.11 | 6.82 | | | 6.46 | 18.33 | 3.96 | 5.61 |
| Access road | 9.98 | 7.35 | | 7.06 | 12.13 | 9.50 | 3.09 | 8.81 |
| All | 4.61 | 3.75 | 5.33 | 4.42 | 4.04 | | 2.22 | 4.64 |

*Source:* See the text.

Denmark: Greibe and Hemdorff (2001)
Finland: Tielaitos (1997)
Germany: BASt (2008)
UK: UK Department for Transport (2008)
Norway: Erke and Elvik (2006)
The Netherlands: SWOV (2008)
Sweden: Thulin (1991)
USA: US Department of Transportation (1991)

Relative accident rates are used because absolute rates are not comparable between different countries due to differences in accident reporting and in the estimated amounts of travel. The classification of road types in this table is rough and approximate and is only intended to demonstrate main patterns. It has not been possible to obtain accident rates for all types of roads in all countries included in the table. Thus, some cells do not show any accident rate.

Table 3.5 shows that motorways have the lowest risk of injury accidents of all roads. On average, the rate of injury accidents per million vehicle kilometres of travel on motorways is about 25% of the average for all the public roads. Main roads in rural areas also have a lower accident rate than the average for all public roads.

All roads in urban areas have a higher rate of injury accidents than the average for public roads. The relative accident rate on access roads in urban areas is on average around 7, when the rate on motorways is set equal to 1.00. The variations in accident rate are very consistent across countries. Despite the fact that only seven countries are included in the table, the main tendencies observed are likely to apply to most highly motorised countries.

***Elements of the design of roads.*** The design of roads can be described in terms of number of lanes, lane width, horizontal and vertical alignment, design of junctions and numerous other elements. A detailed description of how each element of road design affects the number of accidents is given in Part II, Chapter 1. In this introductory chapter, only a few items will be mentioned.

The effect of road width on accident rates depends on whether the road is located in an urban or a rural area. In rural areas, accident rate declines as road width increases, whereas in urban areas, accident rate increases as road width increases. Differences in speed and the mix of traffic using the road may account for this difference in the effect of road width. In rural areas, speed is higher than in urban areas, and a wider road may provide an added margin of safety, which is not as essential in urban areas. In urban areas, more traffic will cross the road than in rural areas. The time it takes to cross a road increases, the wider the road becomes.

The number of junctions and access points has a major impact on accident rate. At junctions, the accident rate increases if a junction has more legs and if a higher proportion of traffic enters the junction from the minor road (which by definition would always have less than 50% of the vehicles entering a junction).

Both horizontal and vertical alignment affect accident rate. As an example, Figure 3.11 shows the injury accident rate for horizontal curves in Norway depending on the radius of the curve. It is seen that accident rate increases as curves get sharper. In addition to the sharpness of a curve, the number of curves per kilometre of road is related to the accident rate. Surprising curves have higher accident rates than curves that are anticipated by the drivers. The expectations of drivers are affected by the number of curves per kilometre of road. A curve of a given radius has a smaller effect on accident rate on a road with many curves than on a road with few curves.

***Environmental risk factors.*** Darkness, precipitation and difficult road surface conditions contribute to increasing the risk of accidents. This has been shown in a number of studies (Hvoslef 1976, Satterthwaite 1976, Sherretz and Farhar 1978, Ivey et al. 1981, Brodsky and Hakkert 1988, Ragnøy 1989, Fridstrøm and Ingebrigtsen 1991, Fridstrøm et al. 1995, Sakshaug and Vaa 1995, Vaa 1995, Johansson 2008,

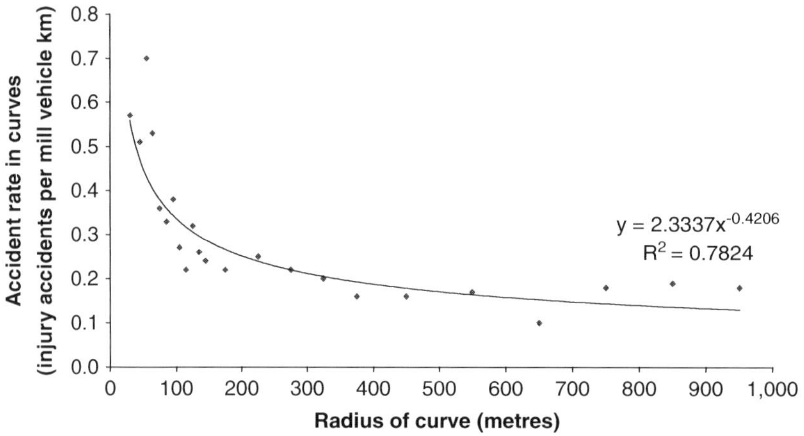


*Figure 3.11: Effect of radius of curve on accident rate, based on Norwegian data.*

*Table 3.6: Relative risk of injury accidents in different environmental conditions: estimate for Norway*

| Factor | Value of factor | Relative accident rate | Confidence interval |
|---|---|---|---|
| Light conditions | Daylight | 1.0 | |
| | Darkness – vehicle accidents | 1.0 | (0.9; 1.1) |
| | Darkness – pedestrian accidents | 2.1 | (1.7; 2.5) |
| | Darkness – bicycle accidents | 1.6 | (1.2; 2.0) |
| Road surface conditions | Dry bare road | 1.0 | |
| | Wet bare road | 1.3 | (1.1–1.8) |
| | Wet snow | 1.5 | (1.1–2.0) |
| | Snow or ice covered road | 2.5 | (1.5–4.0) |

Wanvik 2009). On the basis of these studies, the relative accident rates in Table 3.6 have been estimated. They are intended to give a best estimate of the relative risk of injury associated with different light conditions and road surface conditions. The risk of accidents increases in the dark, on the wet roads and when the roads are covered with snow or ice.

***Age and gender of road user***. The relationship between the age and gender of road users and their accident rate has been studied extensively. One of the reasons for this is that information about age and gender is usually easily available from accident records, whereas many other human factors are not recorded in official accident records. The

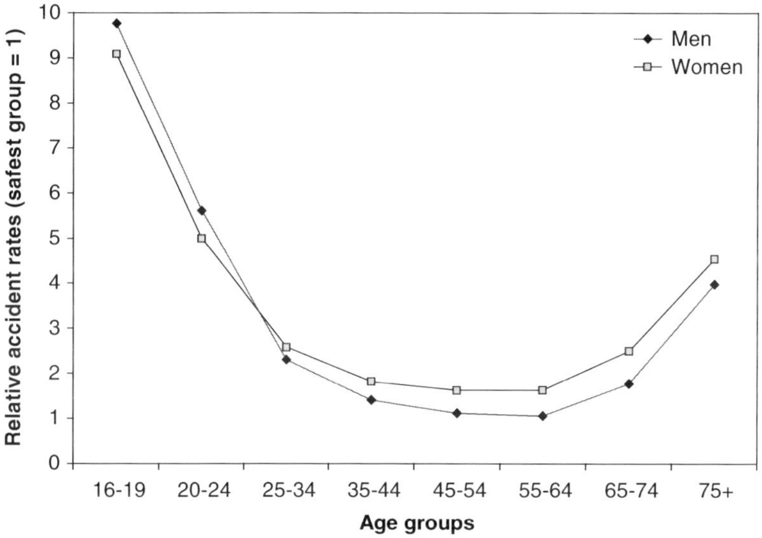


*Figure 3.12: Relative rates of involvement in injury accidents by driver age and gender. Source: see text.*

most detailed studies refer to the age and gender of car drivers. Figure 3.12 presents the relationships derived from the following studies:

The Netherlands: SWOV (2008)
Denmark: Brems and Munch (2008)
Norway: Bjørnskau (2008)
Sweden: Nilsson (2002)
USA: Massie, Green and Campbell (1997)
Victoria, Australia: Diamantopoulou, Skalova, Dyte and Cameron (1996)

All these studies have investigated the relationship between the age and gender of car drivers and their involvement in injury accidents per miles or kilometres of exposure. In each study, the lowest involvement rate found in any group was set at 1.0. Involvement rates for other groups were then expressed relative to this value. Figure 3.12 presents the average relative accident involvement rate of men and women based on these nine studies.

The results are remarkably consistent. Accident involvement rate is a U-shaped function of driver age, both for men and for women. The group with the lowest accident rate is in all studies men at the age of 45–55 or 55–64 years. In young drivers, men tend to have a higher average accident rate than women. From about the age of 30, the mean accident rate is higher for women than for men. The mean accident involvement rate, all ages taken together, is higher for women than for men.

This finding will probably strike many readers as surprising. Women are generally considered to be more careful drivers than men and are charged for traffic offences much less often than men. Despite this, there may be a number of reasons why the mean injury accident rate tends to be higher among women than among men. First, women drive less than men. Accident involvement rate per kilometre of driving is not independent of the distance driven, but decreases as driving distances increase. In recent years, an increase in the number of women involved in fatal accidents has been observed. This increase is likely to be due to an increase in exposure, although young women also were found to be increasingly involved in risk-taking behaviour (Romano, Kelley-Baker and Voas 2008). Second, women tend to drive smaller cars than men. Small cars do not give as good protection against injury in an accident as large cars. Third, women tend to drive more in towns and cities, where the risk of accidents is higher than in rural areas. Men, especially young men, were found to be involved in more loss of control accidents and the primary actor in head-on collisions than women (Richardson, Kim, Li and Nitz 1996, Tavris, Kuhn and Layde 2001). These accidents are on average more severe than most other types of accidents.

The variation of injury risk by age tends to be U-shaped for pedestrians, cyclists and riders of mopeds and motorcycles as well. As far as bus passengers are concerned, less is known about the variation of injury rate according to passenger age and gender. However, children, teenagers and older women tend to travel by bus more often than other groups in the population, and would therefore be more exposed to risk.

***Medical condition of road user***. Another area where a large amount of research has been reported concerns the effects of different illnesses and health problems on drivers' risk of accidents. Almost all these studies apply to drivers, and the methodological quality of many studies is rather weak. The results should be interpreted as indications of statistical associations between different health problems and the risk of accidents, not as well-established causal relationships.

Table 3.7 is taken from the chapter on health requirements for drivers and shows the association between different illnesses and health problems and the risk of accidents. In the table, the risk faced by healthy drivers is set equal to 1.00, and the risk associated with different illness and health problems is stated relative to this value.

*Table 3.7: Association between health problems and drivers' accident rate: relative accident rates for drivers with certain illnesses (relative accident rate for healthy drivers = 1)*

| Groups of diseases | Best estimate | 95% Confidence interval |
|---|---|---|
| Renal diseases | 0.87 | (0.54; 1.34) |
| Visual impairments | 1.09 | (1.04; 1.15) |
| Arthritis | 1.17 | (1.004; 1.36) |
| Hearing impairments | 1.19 | (1.02; 1.40) |
| Coronary diseases | 1.23 | (1.09; 1.38) |
| Diabetes mellitus | 1.56 | (1.31; 1.86) |
| Medication/psychoactive substances | 1.58 | (1.45; 1.73) |
| Psychiatric diseases | 1.72 | (1.48; 1.99) |
| Neurological diseases | 1.75 | (1.61; 1.89) |
| Alcoholism | 2.00 | (1.89; 2.12) |

It can be seen from Table 3.7 that a number of illnesses and health problems contribute to increasing the accident rate, but often not by very much. A relative accident rate of less than two indicates a rather weak association, much weaker than the association between driver age and accident involvement rate (Figure 3.12). Drivers probably try their best to compensate for ill health by driving more carefully and perhaps refraining from driving at all in dense traffic at night or when circumstances are otherwise difficult.

***Impairment through the use of alcohol.*** Drinking and driving has been recognised as an important road safety problem for a long time. Many studies have reported how alcohol reduces performance. A number of studies, based on roadside surveys, have evaluated the relationship between impairment by alcohol and involvement in road accidents. Results from a sample of these studies are reported in Figure 3.13 based on the following studies:

Norway: Glad (1985)
Sweden: Nilsson (1986)
Norway: Assum and Ingebrigtsen (1990)
USA: Zador, Krawchuk and Voas (2000)
New Zealand: Keall, Frith and Patterson (2004)
Norway: Assum (2005)
The Netherlands: Mathijssen (2005)

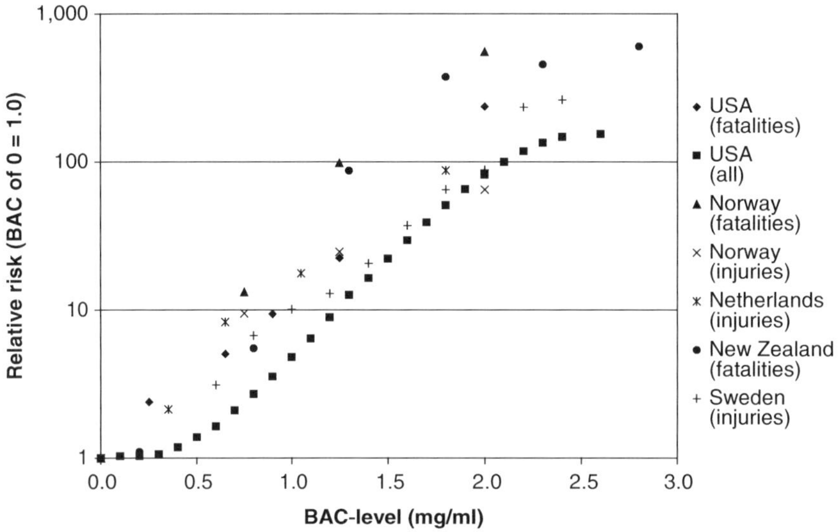


*Figure 3.13: Association between blood alcohol level and relative accident involvement rate. Source: see text.*

Although there is considerable variation in the risk estimates, especially at high BAC levels, it is beyond dispute that accident rate increases dramatically as blood alcohol level increases. Note the use of a logarithmic scale for relative accident involvement rate in Figure 3.13. There are few, if any, other risk factors that have been found to increase accident rate by a factor of more than 100. The increase of accident rate has been found to be steeper for injury accidents and fatal accidents than for property-damage-only accidents.

***Speed of travel.*** Speed is an important risk factor. A large number of studies have evaluated the effects of changes in traffic speed on the number and severity of accidents. Considerably, fewer studies have evaluated how the choice of speed made by each driver affects the accident rate of that driver. Studies that are often quoted include those of Solomon (1964), Munden (1967), Cirillo (1968), West and Dunn (1971), Harkey, Robertson and Davis (1990) and Kloeden, Ponte and McLean (1997, 2001). With the exception of the two studies by Kloeden et al., all these studies suggested that drivers who drive more slowly than the mean speed of traffic and drivers who driver faster than the mean speed of traffic have a higher rate of accident involvement than drivers whose speed is close to the mean speed of traffic.

It has been shown (White and Nelson 1970) that errors in speed measurements can generate an artificial U-shaped curve for the relationship between deviation from mean speed and relative rate of accident involvement. Another potential source of error is the precise definition of the accident involvement variable. If this variable is defined in terms of the number of cars involved in accidents, all accidents that involve two cars will be counted twice. Finally, if estimates of the pre-crash speeds of vehicles involved in accidents are less precise than estimates of the speeds of vehicles not involved in accidents, this could generate an artificial U-shaped relationship between speed and accident involvement.

On the whole, there is therefore a significant chance that the findings of the studies indicating a U-shaped relationship between speed and accident involvement are to a large extent attributable to methodological weaknesses of the studies.

## 3.8 A SURVEY OF RISK FACTORS FOR INJURY SEVERITY

***Type of motor vehicle – vehicle mass.*** The significance of the mass of the vehicle and whether one is protected by the body of the vehicle or not are described in Section 4.19 of Part II. It is well known that the greater the mass, the more protection people have against being injured in accidents. According to official Norwegian accidents statistics, the importance of mass and a surrounding car body can be shown by studying how the probability of being injured, given that a driver, pedestrian or cyclist is involved in an injury accident reported to the police, varies between different groups of road users and types of vehicle. This is possible because uninjured drivers who are involved in injury accidents (including uninjured pedestrians and cyclists) are recorded in official accident statistics. Figure 3.14 shows how the probability of being injured as a driver when one is involved in an injury accident reported to the police varies between road user groups and types of vehicle.

The figure is based on official Norwegian accident statistics. Among pedestrians and cyclists, more than 95% of those who are involved in injury accidents reported to the police are injured. Among people riding mopeds and motorcycles, the proportion injured is around 90%. About 45% of car drivers involved in injury accidents reported to police are injured. Among drivers of trucks or buses, the proportion injured is between 10% and 20%. These differences would be even more distinct if property damage only accidents were included. The statistics that are available for property damage accidents, however, do not allow such a detailed description of vehicle types as the injury accident statistics.

The differences in the mass of passenger cars do not matter very much for the overall number of injured car occupants. Occupants are better protected in large cars than in small cars. However, the protection a large car offers is at the expense of those who use

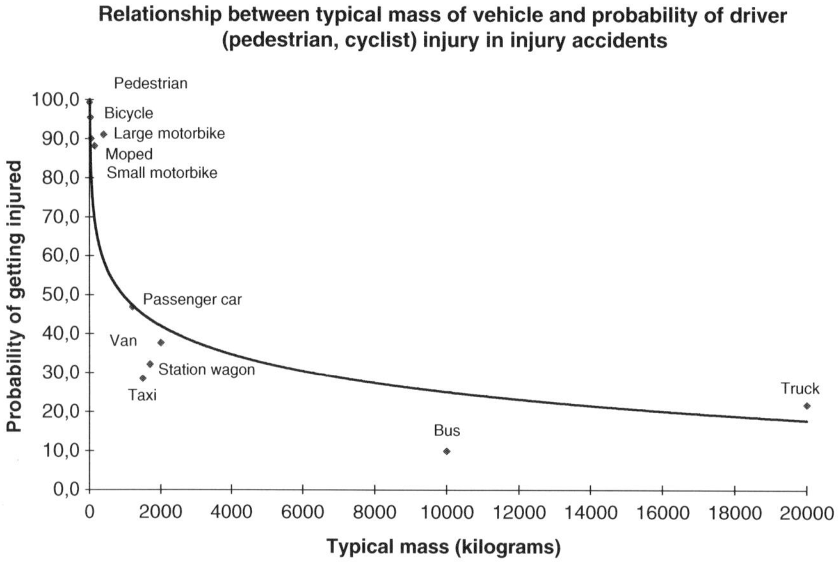


*Figure 3.14: Relationship between mass of vehicle (or road user) and probability of getting injured when involved in an injury accident. Based on Norwegian accident statistics.*

smaller cars. The risk of a driver being injured is reduced by almost 50% if the mass of the car increases from less than 850 kg to more than 1,500 kg. At the same time, a car of more than 1,500 kg poses a 75% higher risk of injuring other cars than a car of less than 850 kg.

***Impact speed.*** Figure 3.15 shows how the probability of serious injury to drivers of private cars in a traffic accident depends on impact speed ($\Delta V$ or the change in speed that occurs on impact). The figure is taken from Evans (1996) and shows how the probability of being seriously injured varies by changes in speed for drivers with and without seat belts. Figure 3.15 shows that up to an impact speed of around 70 km/h, it is more likely that a serious injury will be avoided than not. When impact speed is above 100 km/h, it is impossible to avoid serious injury, whether or not seat belts are worn. Serious injuries are roughly defined here as injuries that require hospitalisation.

The relationship between impact speed and the probability of being injured has the same form for pedestrians and cyclists as for car drivers, but shifts towards a lower speed. For pedestrians, there is a considerable increase in the chances of being killed when impact speed is more than 30 km/h (Pasanen 1996).

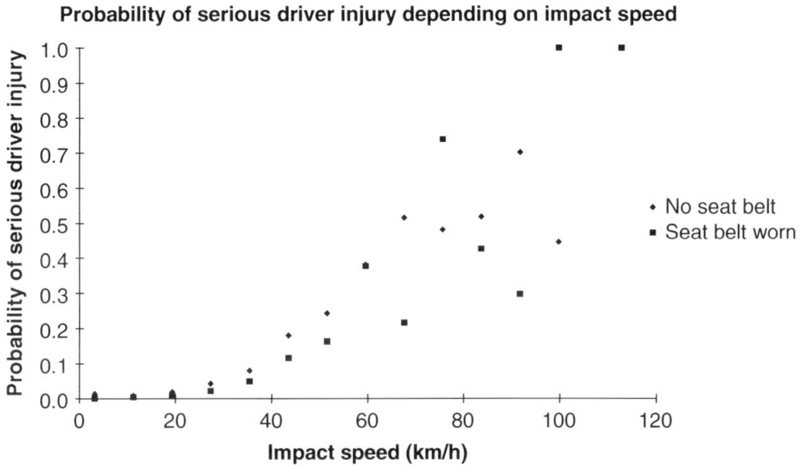


*Figure 3.15: Relationship between impact speed and probability of serious driver injury (Evans 1996).*

***Wearing personal protective equipment.*** Use of personal safety equipment is of considerable importance for the probability of being injured in a traffic accident, especially for otherwise unprotected road users, that is, pedestrians, cyclists or riders of mopeds or motorcycles.

A moped or motorcycle rider reduces the probability of being injured by around 25% by wearing a helmet. If protective leather clothing is also worn, the probability of being injured is reduced by a further 30%. Together, such protective equipment gives reduction in the probability of being injured of approximately 50% [1–(0.75 × 0.70)]. A pedestrian who uses a reflector reduces the probability of being hit in the dark by 70–90%. A car occupant wearing a seat belt has a 20–30% lower probability of being injured than a car occupant not wearing a seat belt, and a 40–50% lower probability of being killed.

## 3.9 Assessing the relative importance of risk factors

Describing factors contributing to road accidents and injuries by listing factors that have been found to be statistically associated with the frequency of accident occurrence and the severity of injuries sustained in accidents represents only the rudiments of a scientific explanation. Can the importance of factors contributing to road accidents be assessed more formally? Is it possible to give a more coherent scientific account of various aspects of road safety problems?

It has sometimes been claimed that there is no rational way of defining road safety problems and assessing how easily these problems can be solved. Thus, for example, Pedersen, Elvik and Berard-Andersen (1982, page 29) state:

> *"What do we mean by a road safety problem? There are many answers to this question that all make sense. The risk that children run on their trip to school is a road safety problem. Drinking and driving is a road safety problem, driving in the dark is a road safety problem, and young driver risk is a road safety problem. By making such lists of problems, it is possible to cover all areas of road safety. The snag is that the various problems on such a list tend to overlap. Children are at risk when travelling to school partly because young drivers have a high risk of accident involvement, partly because of drinking and driving, and partly because driving in the dark increases the risk of accident. Drinking and driving is a major problem partly because it takes place in the dark and on roads where there are pedestrians and cyclists. These examples show how difficult it is to define road safety problems in an orderly and logical way. This difficulty is particularly relevant when we want to give an exhaustive definition of road safety problems."*

It is obviously correct that the risk factors that contribute to accidents and injuries interact in complex ways that are not fully known. It is equally true that there does not exist any scientifically 'correct' way of defining road safety problems, at least not in a strict sense of the term. But it is wrong to conclude that any list of factors contributing to road accidents is completely arbitrary and therefore of no use either as a scientific explanation or for the purpose of developing an effective road safety programme. A rational approach to assessing the importance of risk factors in contributing to accidents and injuries can be developed by relying on concepts taken from epidemiology.

***Describing the importance of risk factors in terms of attributable risks***. One of the basic notions of epidemiology is that of attributable risk, also known as etiologic fraction (Kleinbaum, Kupper and Morgenstern 1982). Attributable risk is the fraction of accidents or injuries that is attributable to a certain risk factor, that is, the size of the reduction in the number of accidents or injuries that could be achieved by removing the risk factor.

Attributable risk is generally expressed as a fraction and assumes values in the range from 0 to 1. To illustrate the concept, consider the case of unprotected road users. Unprotected road users are all road users who are not enclosed by a deformable

*Table 3.8: Number of fatalities, police reported injuries, amount of travel and relative risks of fatality and injury for unprotected and protected road users in Sweden (Thulin and Nilsson, 1994)*

| Injuries, travel and risk | Unprotected road users | Protected road users | All road users |
|---|---|---|---|
| Killed road users | 259 | 466 | 725 |
| Injured road users | 6,454 | 14,633 | 21,087 |
| Mill person km of travel | 6,661 | 114,861 | 121,522 |
| Relative fatality rate | 9.58 | 1.00 | 1.47 |
| Relative injury rate | 7.61 | 1.00 | 1.36 |
| Attributable fatality risk | 0.896 | Reference | 0.320 |
| Attributable injury risk | 0.869 | Reference | 0.266 |

structure absorbing energy in case of an accident. They include pedestrians, cyclists and riders of mopeds and motorcycles. Protected road users are drivers and passengers using cars and buses.

Table 3.8 shows the number of fatalities, the number of injuries recorded by the police, the annual amount of travel and the relative fatality and injury rate of unprotected and protected road users in Sweden according to the 1992 National Household Travel Survey (Thulin and Nilsson 1994).

This table can be used to illustrate the meaning of the concept of attributable risk. It is seen that unprotected road users run a risk of being killed that is nearly 10 times higher than the risk run by protected road users. To bring down the fatality risk to unprotected road users to the same level as that of protected road users, a reduction of nearly 90% would be needed. This is the attributable risk of a fatal injury for unprotected road users as shown in the table (0.896), which is estimated simply as the ratio (9.58–1)/9.58. This measure of attributable risk will be referred to as *the target attributable risk*, that is, the reduction in risk that must be achieved within the target group (in this case unprotected road users) in order get the same risk level as the reference group (in this case protected road users).

*The overall* or *population attributable risk* (PAR) for unprotected road users is the contribution that their enhanced risk level makes to the total number of people killed or injured. The overall attributable risk has been estimated at 0.320 for fatality risk and 0.266 for injury risk, as shown in Table 3.8.

To explain how PAR is estimated, denote the proportion of exposure to the risk factor of interest by PE. In Table 3.8, this proportion is $6{,}661/121{,}522 = 0.055$, that is the proportion of all travel done by unprotected road users. Denote by RR the relative risk run when exposed to the risk factor of interest. In Table 3.6, this is 9.58 for fatality risk. In computing relative risk, the safest category of any risk factor is always used as reference. PAR is then defined as:

$$PAR = \frac{PE(RR - 1)}{[PE(RR - 1)] + 1}$$

For fatality risk in Table 3.8, the numerator comes to $0.055 \times 8.58 = 0.47$. The denominator is $0.47+1 = 1.47$. Attributable risk is $0.47/1.47 = 0.32$.

By estimating the risks attributable to various risk factors, it is possible to obtain a quantified notion of their importance in contributing to accidents and injuries. This makes it possible, in principle, to rank various risk factors in order of their importance as contributing factors to accidents and injuries. In a report written for the Swedish National Roads Administration (Elvik and Amundsen 2000), an attempt was made to quantify the importance of various road safety problems in Sweden by estimating the risks attributable to them.

Several notes of caution with respect to the use of attributable risks as a measure of the importance of various road safety problems are pertinent:

- There are many important risk factors for which no meaningful estimate of attributable risk is possible. Inattention on the part of road users is a case in point. There is little doubt that inattention causes many accidents. However, trying to quantify the contribution of this risk factor to accidents is very difficult because exposure to it is virtually impossible to measure. (What is the proportion of kilometres driven by inattentive drivers?)
- Risk factors tend to be correlated, but these correlations are not very well known. In most cases, it is probably not correct to add the risks attributable to two risk factors to find their joint contributions to accidents or injuries.
- Some road safety problems are not adequately described in terms of enhanced risk. Children, for example, do not have an excessive risk of injury in traffic compared with adults. However, there is a strong desire to provide a higher level of safety for children than for other groups of road users. As long as it remains possible to reduce the risk of injury to children, accidents will be regarded as a problem, despite the fact that estimates of attributable risk will not identify children as a group exposed to a particularly high risk.
- Accidents and injuries are not fully reported in official accident statistics. If the level of reporting is associated with a risk factor, an estimate of the risk attributable to that factor will be biased. This may apply to the risk attributable to being an unprotected road user, at least as far as injuries is concerned. Injuries to

unprotected road users, especially cyclists, are known to be less fully reported in official statistics than injuries to car occupants. An estimate of attributable risk based on official accident statistics will then be an underestimate of the true risk attributable to being an unprotected road user.

Despite these limitations, the concept of attributable risk is fruitful when trying to assess the importance of various road safety problems. The contribution of a number of risk factors to the current number of road accident fatalities and injuries in Sweden was therefore estimated by putting together information from a large number of sources.

***Correlations among risk factors.*** When the contributions of various risk factors to current road safety problems are to be assessed, it is important to try to account for the correlations between risk factors. Otherwise, the contributions of a set of risk factors to injuries may be counted twice, and thereby the potential for injury reduction by removing or controlling the risk factors may be overestimated. This can be illustrated by means of a numerical example.

Consider the data given in Table 3.9. These data are fictitious and are used only to illustrate how the existence of correlations between risk factors may bias estimates of the risks attributable to them. In this table, the risks attributable to two risk factors are considered. It is assumed that each risk factor increases risk by 50%, which gives a relative risk of RR = 1.50 for those who are exposed to the risk factor. Relative risk when exposed to both risk factors is $1.5 \times 1.5 = 2.25$. Moreover, it is assumed that 20% of all road users are exposed to each factor.

If exposure to one of the risk factors is independent of exposure to the other, it can easily be calculated that 64% of all road users will not be exposed to any of the two factors ($0.8 \times 0.8 = 0.64$). Thirty-two per cent will be exposed to one factor only [$2 \times (0.8 \times 0.2 = 0.16)$], and 4% will be exposed to both factors ($0.2 \times 0.2 = 0.04$). This distribution of exposure is shown in the first row of Table 3.9, for the case, in which there is no correlation in exposure to the two risk factors. In this case the risk, attributable to both risk factors is 0.174. The crude estimate of the risk attributable to each risk factor is 0.115. The sum of the crude attributable risks is 0.230, which is more than the total risk attributable to both risk factors. The source of the problem is the fact that crude estimates counts the cell in which both risk factors are present twice. This double counting gets worse as the correlation between the risk factors gets stronger. Attributable risks are shown in bold italics in Table 3.9.

As shown in Table 3.9, estimates of the risk attributable to each risk factor grow to 0.138 for a moderate correlation in exposure to the two risk factors, to 0.160 when

*Table 3.9: Illustration of how the existence of correlations between risk factors may bias estimates of risks attributable to them (fictitious data)*

| Correlation in exposure | Exposure and risk | Risk factors present in exposure and injuries | | | | |
|---|---|---|---|---|---|---|
| | | None | Factor 1 | Factor 2 | Both | Total |
| None (0.00–0.15) | Exposure | 640 | 160 | 160 | 40 | 1000 |
| | Injuries | 640 | 240 | 240 | 90 | 1210 |
| | True relative risk | 1.00 | 1.50 | 1.50 | 2.25 | |
| | Crude risk attributed to factor 1 | 1.00 | 1.65 | | | ***0.115*** |
| | Crude risk attributed to factor 2 | 1.00 | | 1.65 | | ***0.115*** |
| | Total attributable risk | | | | 1.58 | ***0.174*** |
| Moderate (0.15–0.50) | Exposure | 680 | 120 | 120 | 80 | 1000 |
| | Injuries | 680 | 180 | 180 | 180 | 1220 |
| | True relative risk | 1.00 | 1.50 | 1.50 | 2.25 | |
| | Crude risk attributed to factor 1 | 1.00 | 1.80 | | | ***0.138*** |
| | Crude risk attributed to factor 2 | 1.00 | | 1.80 | | ***0.138*** |
| | Total attributable risk | 1.00 | | | 1.69 | ***0.180*** |
| Strong (0.50–0.85) | Exposure | 720 | 80 | 80 | 120 | 1000 |
| | Injuries | 720 | 120 | 120 | 270 | 1230 |
| | True relative risk | 1.00 | 1.50 | 1.50 | 2.25 | |
| | Crude risk attributed to factor 1 | 1.00 | 1.95 | | | ***0.160*** |
| | Crude risk attributed to factor 2 | 1.00 | | 1.95 | | ***0.160*** |
| | Total attributable risk | 1.00 | | | 1.82 | ***0.187*** |
| Perfect (0.85–1.00) | Exposure | 760 | 40 | 40 | 160 | 1000 |
| | Injuries | 760 | 60 | 60 | 360 | 1240 |
| | True relative risk | 1.00 | 1.50 | 1.50 | 2.25 | |
| | Crude risk attributed to factor 1 | 1.00 | 2.00 | | | ***0.167*** |
| | Crude risk attributed to factor 2 | 1.00 | | 2.00 | | ***0.167*** |
| | Total attributable risk | 1.00 | | | 2.00 | ***0.194*** |

exposure is strongly correlated and to 0.167 when exposure is very strongly correlated. Thus, crude estimates of both relative risk and attributable risk become more and more biased when the correlation between risk factors is stronger. One would accordingly expect that estimates of risk that are adjusted for correlations with other risk factors are lower than crude estimates.

Ideally speaking, estimates of the risks attributable to specific risk factors ought to be derived from multivariate analyses, in which the partial effects of each risk factor have been estimated while controlling for as many other risk factors as possible. Very few multivariate analyses of this nature, based on Swedish data, are available (Fridstrøm et al. 1993, Tegnér and Loncar-Lucassi 1996). Besides, the results of those few studies have not been presented in a format that easily allows attributable risks to be estimated. It must be therefore concluded that studies allowing well-controlled estimates of the contributions of various risk factors to injuries in road accidents do not exist. Any estimate based on available data is likely to be incomplete and possibly misleading. Nevertheless, it has been concluded that it is better to try to make the best use of current data, rather than not attempting to quantify the contributions of various risk factors to current road problems.

***Quantification of the importance of risk factors – a case illustration.*** The contribution of various factors to current road safety problems in Sweden was estimated in stages. Details of the estimation are given in the full report in Elvik and Amundsen (2000). The following points are important to note with respect to the interpretation of the estimates that are presented:

- The attributable risks refer to the risks of sustaining a fatal injury or an injury reported to the police. No account has been taken of incomplete accident reporting.
- The assessment is limited to a total of 20 risk factors for which data of acceptable quality could be found.
- The estimates of attributable risk represent the contributions of the various factors as of the early or mid nineteen nineties. The contribution of a specific risk factor to fatalities and injuries may change over time.

***Simple first-order attributable risks.*** The first stage of analysis was to estimate the *first-order attributable risks* of the risk factors included in the study. These estimates did *not* account for *overlaps* between types of accidents affected by various risk factors or *correlations in exposure* to the various risk factors. The results of this first stage of estimation are given in Figure 3.16. To keep the figure simple, confidence intervals are not shown. Risk factors have been assigned to five main groups:

- Bad system design, which includes risk factors related to the design of roads and the traffic environment
- Environmental risks, which includes the effects on accidents of daylight and weather
- Vulnerability of road users, which includes the enhanced risk run by pedestrians, cyclists and inexperienced drivers
- Unsafe road user behaviour, which comprises violations of road traffic legislation
- Provision of medical services, which refers to the limited availability of rapid rescue services in remote and sparsely populated areas of Sweden.

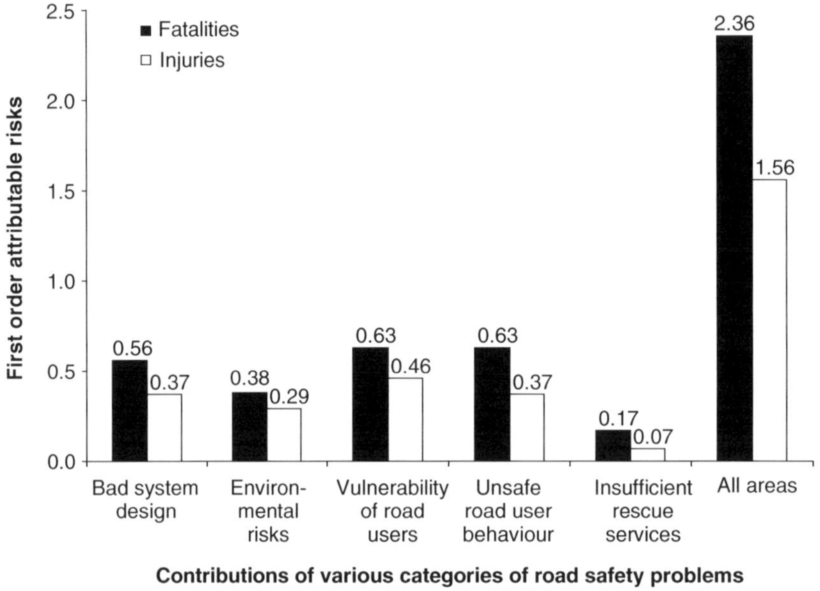


*Figure 3.16: First-order attributable risks of major road safety problems in Sweden.*

Bad system design, vulnerability of road users and road user behaviour are the three most important main categories of roads safety problems as evidenced in the first-order risks attributable to these problems. Each of these problems accounts for about 60% of fatalities and about 40% of all injuries. If violations of road traffic law did not occur, the number of fatalities could be reduced by 63% and the total number of injuries could be reduced by 37% (Figure 3.16).

The sum of all first-order attributable risks is 2.36 for fatalities and 1.56 for injuries. This simply demonstrates the widely known fact that more than one risk factor may contribute to each accident. This fact is known from in-depth studies of accidents, which usually list several factors that may have contributed to each accident. Hence, if the contributions of a set of risk factors to accidents are simply added, the answer will nearly always come to more than 100%. In fact, if more factors had been included in the analysis, the sum of the first-order contributions would have been greater than the numbers given in Figure 3.16.

The single most important contributing factor out of the 20 factors that were included in the analysis is violation of speed limits. Speeding represents an attributable risk of 0.38 for fatalities and 0.21 for injuries.

***Adjusting for overlapping problem definitions and correlations among risk factors***. The second stage of the analysis was to adjust the simple first-order attributable risks for overlapping types of accidents affected and the presence of correlations in exposure to the various risk factors. The following categories of road safety problems partly overlap:

- *High risk in urban areas and high risk for unprotected road users:* Since most unprotected road users are injured in urban areas, the higher risk in urban areas compared with the countryside is partly attributable to the presence of more unprotected road users in urban areas. The overlap between these problems was removed by subtracting from the risk attributed to urban areas the proportion due to accidents involving unprotected road users.
- *High risk in urban areas and high risk in some junctions:* Most accidents in junctions occur in urban areas and thereby contribute to the high risk in those areas. The overlap was removed by subtracting from the risk attributed to junctions the proportion of junction accidents that occur in urban areas.
- *Roads standards are low and some roads are poor with respect to crashworthiness:* These problems partly overlap. The overlap was removed by subtracting from the risk attributed to roadside objects the part that refers to narrow roads with poor alignment.
- *High risk for unprotected road users and safety problems of children:* These problems overlap to the extent that children are injured as unprotected road users. Risks attributable to children as unprotected road users were subtracted from the overall risk attributed to children to remove the overlap between the problems.
- *High risk for unprotected road users and for older road users:* These problems overlap to the extent that older road users are injured as pedestrians and cyclists. Removing the overlap involved subtracting from the overall risk attributed to being an older road user the part that was due to being unprotected as well.

It was assumed that exposure to darkness and to winter road conditions are correlated. This assumption is reasonable because there is less daylight in winter than in summer. A correlation of 0.5 was assumed, and the first-order attributable risks from darkness and winter conditions were, somewhat conservatively, reduced by 30% each.

Violations of road traffic law, except for speeding, were assumed to be correlated. A three-way (multiple) correlation of 0.3 between drinking and driving, not wearing seat belts and other violations was assumed. The risk attributable to each of these violations was reduced by 10%.

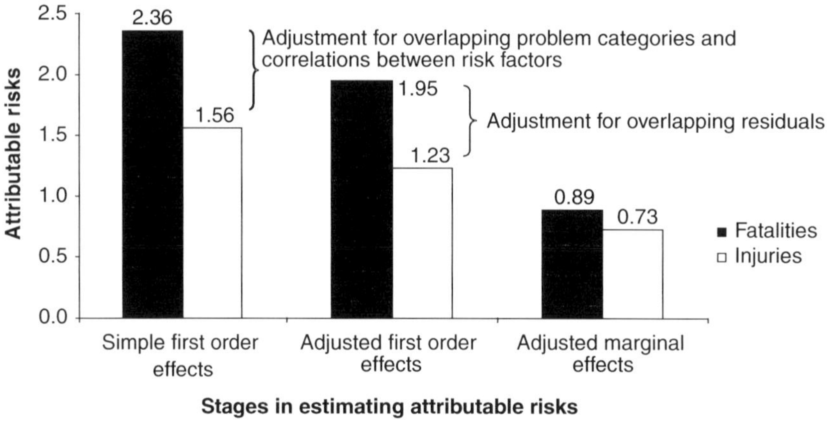


*Figure 3.17: Adjustments in first-order attributable risks.*

Once these adjustments had been made, the marginal effect of each risk factor was estimated by applying the method of joint residuals. Figure 3.17 shows the results of the estimation.

Adjusting for overlaps and correlations reduces the sum of the attributable risks from 2.36 to 1.95 for fatalities and from 1.56 to 1.23 for injuries. The sum of the marginal effects of the risk factors is 0.89 for fatalities and 0.73 for injuries. By definition, the sum of marginal effects cannot exceed 1, since it is logically impossible to reduce the number of injuries by more than 100% (which equals a proportion of 1). Figure 3.17 shows that by removing all risk factors included in this analysis, it is theoretically possible to reduce the number of fatalities by 89% and the total number of injuries by 73%. In practice, of course, the potentials for reduction are smaller. It is almost never possible to entirely remove a risk factor.

***Marginal contributions of various risk factors.*** Table 3.10 presents estimates of the marginal contributions of various risk factors to current road safety problems in Sweden. The marginal contribution of a risk factor to fatalities and injuries denotes the partial contribution it represents in a set of risk factors whose combined effects have been estimated according to the method of joint residuals.

If the problems are ranked according to the size of their contributions to fatalities and injuries, the following five problems are at the top of the list:

- Speed limit violations (0.172 for fatalities; 0.125 for injuries)
- Poor vehicle crashworthiness (0.156 for fatalities; 0.039 for injuries)

*Table 3.10: Adjusted marginal attributable risks for various risk factors in Sweden (Elvik and Amundsen 2000)*

| | | Marginal attributable risk | |
|---|---|---|---|
| Exposed group | Comparison group | Fatalities | Injuries |
| 1. Roads in urban areas | All roads in rural areas | −0.060 | 0.127 |
| 2. Poor road standard | Motorway road standard | 0.016 | 0.006 |
| 3. Roadside obstacles | Clear side zones | 0.070 | 0.021 |
| 4. Poor vehicle crashworthiness | Best performing cars | 0.156 | 0.039 |
| 5. Erroneous highway signs | Correct highway signs | 0.005 | 0.009 |
| 6. Heavy vehicles | Light vehicles | 0.049 | 0.003 |
| 7. High risk junctions | Low risk junctions | 0.010 | 0.004 |
| ***A. Bad system design (total)*** | ***Good system design*** | ***0.245*** | ***0.210*** |
| 8. Risk at night | Risk during daytime | 0.053 | 0.045 |
| 9. Risk in winter | Risk in summer | 0.063 | 0.061 |
| 10. Risk of animal crashes | Zero risk of animal crashes | 0.007 | 0.023 |
| ***B. Environmental risks (total)*** | ***Less hazardous environment*** | ***0.123*** | ***0.128*** |
| 11. Children's traffic risks | Safest age group (any mode) | 0.005 | 0.005 |
| 12. Unprotected road users | Protected road users | 0.081 | 0.052 |
| 13. Young drivers' traffic risks | Safest age group of drivers | 0.039 | 0.060 |
| 14. Older road users' traffic risks | Safest age group (any mode) | 0.044 | 0.025 |
| ***C. Vulnerable road users (total)*** | ***Safest groups of road users*** | ***0.169*** | ***0.142*** |
| 15. Speed limit violations | Legal speed | 0.172 | 0.125 |
| 16. Drinking and driving | Sober driving | 0.030 | 0.026 |
| 17. Not wearing seat belts | Wearing seat belts | 0.035 | 0.017 |
| 18. Other violations of traffic law | Behaviour complying with the law | 0.038 | 0.033 |
| 19. Excessive driving in towns | Removal of 3% of urban driving | 0.002 | 0.009 |
| ***D. Unsafe behaviour (total)*** | ***Safe road user behaviour*** | ***0.277*** | ***0.209*** |
| 20. Standard of medical services | Ambulance helicopters | 0.076 | 0.042 |
| ***E. Current rescue services (total)*** | ***Best available service level*** | ***0.076*** | ***0.042*** |
| ***All problem areas*** | ***Best currently available safety*** | ***0.890*** | ***0.730*** |

- High risks of unprotected road users (0.081 for fatalities; 0.052 for injuries)
- Insufficient medical and rescue services for accident victims (0.076 for fatalities; 0.042 for injuries)
- Roadside obstacles (0.070 for fatalities; 0.021 for injuries).

The problems have been ranked according to their contributions to fatal injuries. High risk in urban areas makes a major contribution to injuries in general, but is actually a safety factor for fatalities. This means that the risk of injury is higher in urban areas than outside, but that the risk of fatal injury is lower in urban areas than outside.

This example indicates that, despite the great limitations in available data, it is possible to gain an impression of the relative importance of various risk factors in contributing to road accident fatalities and injuries. To make use of available data, several adjustments had to be made, but these were to some extent based on official accident data.

The next step of an analysis in which the importance of risk factors has been assessed would be to try to sort risk factors into categories with respect to how easily the factors can be modified or influenced by means of road safety measures.

# 4.

# Basic Concepts of Road Safety Research

## 4.1 Random and systematic variation in accident counts

Road safety is usually defined and evaluated in terms of the recorded number of accidents or the number of killed or injured road users. The number of accidents or injured road users recorded during a certain period is the result of a complex process. There are two problems associated with the use of the recorded number of accidents to estimate safety: under-reporting of accidents (see Chapter 3) and random variation in the recorded accident numbers.

When looking for explanations of accidents and for ways of preventing them, it is important not to mix up random and systematic variation in the number of accidents. Systematic variation is the 'true' variation in the accident counts, i.e. variation of the expected number of accidents. Random variation is variation of the observed accident counts around the expected number of accidents. These concepts are described in more detail below. When evaluating safety measures, it is often better to use estimates of the expected, rather than the recorded, number of accidents by using the Empirical Bayes (EB) method, which also is described below.

***Expected number of accidents***. The expected number of accidents is the number of accidents (e.g. on a specific road or in a specific junction) that one can expect per time unit, based on known properties of the road or junction. It is the average number of accidents that will occur per unit of time in the long run, given that exposure and all risk factors remain constant.

**The Handbook of Road Safety Measures**

**ISBN: 978-1-84855-250-0**

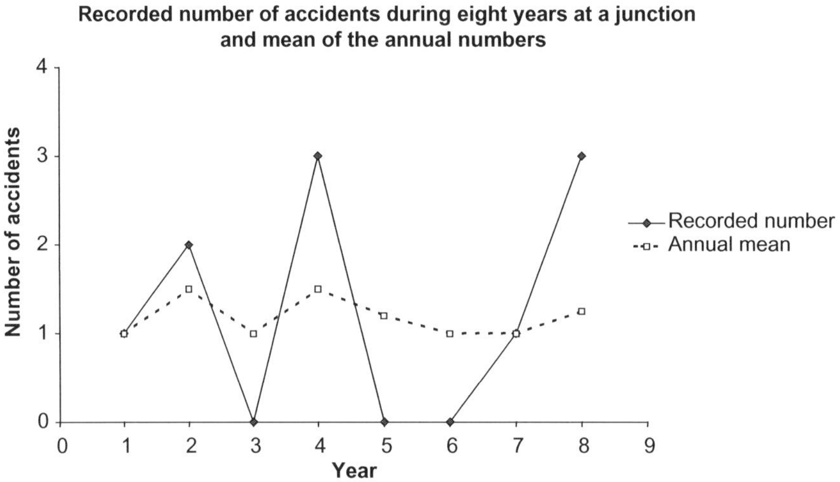


*Figure 4.1: Illustration of the concept of the expected number of accidents.*

The meaning of the expected number of accidents can be clarified by means of an example. Figure 4.1 shows hypothetical numbers of accidents recorded in a junction during a period of eight years. The black dots represent the recorded number of accidents per year and the white dots show the moving average of the annual counts of accidents. In the first year, this is the same as the count of accidents for that year. In the second year, it is the average of the two first years; in the third year, it is the average of first three years, etc.

It can be seen that the recorded number of accidents in a given year is not necessarily representative of the mean annual number of accidents at the junction in the period we are studying. We also see that as accident counts are accumulated for more years, the annual average number becomes more stable and less affected by the recorded number in a single year. If one were to collect accident data for the same junction over a very long period, e.g. 50 or 100 years, the annual average number of accidents for this period would eventually hardly be affected at all by the recorded number of accidents for a given year. In the limit, the annual average would be insensitive to the recorded number of accidents in a specific year. It would then be an estimate of the long-term *expected number of accidents*. This is the average number of accidents per unit time, which would be expected to occur in the long run at a constant exposure (amount of traffic) and at a constant accident rate per unit of exposure.

However, during such a long period, it cannot be assumed that the junction has an unchanged amount of traffic or otherwise remains unchanged. Thus the expected number of accidents would not remain constant during such a long period. In practice, the expected number of accidents is seldom estimated by observing the accident history for a single junction, a single road section, or a single driver for a period of 50 or 100 years.

The true value of the expected number of accidents for a given unit of observation, such as a junction or a driver, cannot be observed directly but has to be estimated. The most common method of estimating the expected number of accidents is to study a large number of units (junctions, road sections, drivers, vehicles, etc.), which vary with respect to characteristics that are believed to influence the expected number of accidents. By means of statistical analysis, we then try to determine the amount of systematic variation in accident counts and identify factors that produce it.

***Random and systematic variation in accident counts.*** There is *systematic variation* in the number of accidents when some units (junctions, drivers, vehicles, roads) have a higher or lower long-term expected number of accidents than other units of the same type. *Random variation* in the number of accidents is variation in the recorded number of accidents around a given expected number of accidents. Two sets of factors generate systematic variation in the number of accidents:

- The amount of traffic (exposure)
- Risk factors (factors that affect the probability of accidents at a given exposure).

On top of these come vehicle occupancy and other factors that influence the number of injury victims per accident.

The fact that road accidents are subject to random variation means that not all changes in the recorded number of accidents imply changes in the expected number of accidents. For example, a decrease from 280 fatalities per year to 250 is not more than random variation. A decrease from 10,000 injured to 9,500 people injured is large enough for it not to be exclusively attributable to chance.

The problem of not mixing up random fluctuations of the number of accidents with changes in the long-term expected number of accidents is most severe when the mean expected number of accidents per study unit is small. To illustrate the problem, consider the hypothetical case of 100 junctions that have a mean expected number of accidents of 1.5 per junction per year. Assume further that the recorded number of accidents in any junction is the result of pure random variation, i.e. all junctions have the same expected number of accidents. Suppose a road safety measure reduces the mean expected number of accidents per junction per year to 1.0, still assume a random distribution of accidents in the set of junctions.

A simple before-and-after study will then most likely observe a reduction of the recorded number of accidents in 50 junctions, an increase in 24 junctions, and an unchanged number of accidents in 26 junctions. Apparently, the safety measure will be most effective in those junctions that had the highest recorded number of accidents in the year before. In the 20 junctions that had three or more accidents in the before-period, and a total of 69 accidents, one would find a reduction to 17 accidents (a 75% reduction). This appears to be a far greater reduction than the mean reduction of 33% (from a total of 150 to 100 accidents). Such an impression is, however, misleading. Under the assumptions made in this example, the true effect is identical in all junctions – any observed variation in effect is random only. Identifying junctions where the safety measure was particularly effective, based on the recorded number of accidents in the before-period, would be capitalising on chance.

***Statistical modelling of systematic and random variation in accident numbers.*** Pure random variation in accidents is usually modelled by the Poisson probability law. According to the Poisson probability law, the variance of the count of accidents equals the mean. The smaller the size of the standard deviation, calculated as a percentage of the number of accidents, the greater the number is. For example, the standard deviation in 10 accidents is equal to about three accidents, i.e. 30%. The standard deviation in 100 accidents is equal to 10 accidents, i.e. to say 10%. A 95% confidence interval for random variation in the number of accidents can be obtained by multiplying the square root of the number of accidents by 1.96. For example, the 95% confidence interval for an expected number of accidents of 10 is

$$10 \pm 1.96 \times \sqrt{10} = 10 \pm 1.96 \times 3.16 = 10 \pm 6.2$$

The lower limit of the confidence interval is 3.8 and the upper limit is 16.2.

Multivariate statistical models, often Poisson regression models or negative binomial regression models, are increasingly used to analyse factors that explain systematic variation of the number of accidents. The most common specification of these models is

$$\text{Expected number of accidents} = \alpha Q^{\beta} \exp^{\sum \kappa x}$$

where $Q$ measures exposure, i.e. some variable describing traffic volume. Exp is the exponential function, i.e. the base of natural logarithms (e = 2.71828) raised to the sum of parameter estimates multiplied by the relevant values of the explanatory variables, representing risk factors ($\Sigma \kappa x$). For an in-depth presentation of multivariate accident modelling, the reader is referred to Gaudry and Lassarre (2000).

***Modelling the expected number of accidents in before-and-after studies with the Empirical Bayes method.*** Results from before-and-after studies may be misleading when evaluation studies are based on the recorded number of accidents, especially when the recorded number is small, and when the study units selected had higher than normal recorded numbers of accidents in the before period. When a measure is implemented only for units with high numbers of accidents in the before-period, the number of accidents will most likely be smaller in the after period, even if the measure has no effect at all. This is referred to as the regression to the mean effect. Regression to the mean may be controlled by using the expected, instead of the recorded, number of accidents in the before-period. Since the expected number is never known exactly, it has to be estimated. By means of the EB method, the expected number of accidents (e.g. on a road section or at a junction) can be estimated as follows:

- It is estimated how many accidents would normally be expected in a unit with comparable properties (risk factors and exposure), based on a multivariate model of accident occurrence in a (preferably large) number of the same type of units, with varying properties. In addition to the normal expected number of accidents, the uncertainty of this estimate is calculated.
- It is estimated how many accidents would be expected for the actual unit, by combining the normal expected number of accidents (step 1) and the recorded number of accidents. The observed number of accidents is included in order to take into account specific unobserved risk factors (that are not included in the accident model in step 1). The expected number of accidents is assigned a statistical weight that corresponds to the uncertainty of this estimate and that can assume values between 0 and 1. The expected number of accidents for the specific unit is calculated as follows:

$$\begin{aligned}&\text{Expected number of accidents for the specific unit}\\&\quad = \text{Expected number of accidents} \times \text{Statistical weight}\\&\qquad + \text{Observed number of accidents} \times (1 - \text{Statistical weight})\end{aligned}$$

- The observed number of accidents in the after period is compared to the expected number of accidents that has been estimated for the specific unit in the before period.

A more detailed description of the EB method, the statistical background and applications are given in Hauer (1997).

## 4.2 The use of accident rates to measure safety

It has traditionally been assumed that the effects of traffic volume on the number of accidents can be removed – controlled for – by estimating an accident rate:

$$\text{Accident rate} = \frac{\text{Number of accidents}}{\text{Traffic volume}}$$

This assumption is not correct (Hauer 1995). Most accident rates, which are defined per vehicle kilometre or per person kilometre, have a significant non-linearity, i.e. the assumption that the number of accidents is independent of the distance driven or the amount of travel does not hold. Figure 4.2 shows a very striking example of this, taken from a British study (Forsyth, Maycock and Sexton 1995).

Accident rate declines sharply as annual driving distance increases. The mean accident rate for men is 0.345 and for women is 0.389. Women have a higher mean accident rate than men, despite the fact that their accident rate for any given annual mileage is lower than the accident rate for men. If this fact were not known, one might erroneously conclude that women are poorer drivers than men.

The finding presented in Figure 4.2 is a case of Simpson's paradox, which may occur when data exhibiting strong non-linearity, or a strong interaction between two or more

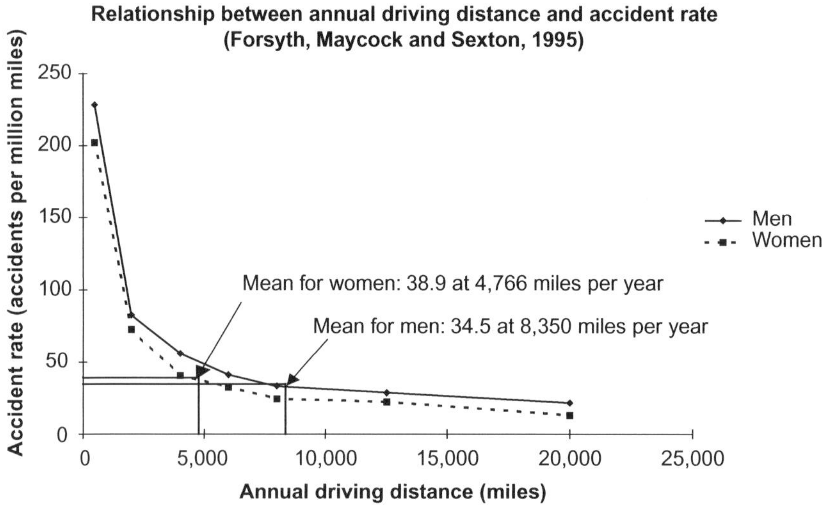


*Figure 4.2: Relationship between annual driving distance and accident rate (Forsyth Maycock and Sexton 1995).*

factors, are aggregated across categories of the non-linear function or the variables that interact. This can result in a fallacy of aggregation: in this case to an erroneous conclusion that the accident rate for women is higher than it is for men.

Non-linear relationships between traffic volume and accidents have also been found in most studies that have developed accident models for roads or junctions. In most studies, the percentage increase of the number of accidents is smaller than would be expected if there were a linear relationship, i.e. the number of accidents increases at a lower rate than traffic volume (see also Section 3.4).

Consequently, the effects of exposure on accidents are not adequately controlled by estimating accident rates and accident rates may have limited value as a measure of road safety. Road safety evaluation studies that use accident rate ratios as the dependent variable are of dubious validity unless the accident rate ratio applies to study units that have an identical amount of exposure and are otherwise identical with respect to at least major risk factors affecting the number of accidents.

## 4.3 Explaining road accidents – the concept of cause

Do accidents have causes? If they do, how can we make sense of the term 'cause of accident'? Until around 1960, it was widely believed that it was not possible to reduce road accidents effectively without knowing the 'real causes of traffic accidents'. This opinion was expressed in the first parliamentary report on traffic safety in Norway (Ministry of Justice, Parliamentary report 83, 1961–62, *On measures for promoting traffic safety*), stating:

> *"A thorough planning of measures to prevent traffic accidents is of great significance if good results are to be achieved. If planning is to be effective, it is necessary to know and analyse the problems in traffic at which the measures can be directed. It is not possible at present to implement road safety planning in a totally satisfactory way. Sufficient knowledge of the real causes of accidents is not available and as a result, the best remedies are not known either. It is usually a complex set of causes that result in traffic accidents; this makes it difficult to evaluate the importance of the individual causal elements."*

Others have rejected the use of the concept of cause in explaining accidents (Haight 1980). Accidents are the outcome of a vastly complex random process, whose general characteristics can be modelled statistically. Some of the factors that influence the stochastic process leading to accidents are known; others will never be known.

The logic of the argument that you need to know the causes of a problem in order to solve it seems irresistible. Yet, there is not necessarily a very close connection between the causes of the problem and its solution. To see why this is not the case, it may be instructive to consider in detail some of the approaches that have been taken to explaining road accidents and discuss their implications.

***Theories of accident causation – a brief chronology***. The scientific study of accidents started about 100 years ago. At least since that time, theories have been proposed to answer the question: Why do accidents happen?

While easily asked, this is indeed a very difficult question to answer. Useful discussions can be found in a number of books. In particular, books by the following authors are recommended:

Cresswell and Froggatt (1963)
Shaw and Sichel (1971)
Evans (1991)
Wilde (1994).

Five different theories trying to explain accidents will be briefly discussed. Figure 4.3 lists the theories in chronological order and indicates the heyday periods of the various theories.

***Accidents as random events***. Accident research started 100 years ago when Bortkiewicz published his book entitled *The Law of Small Numbers* (Leipzig 1898). Bortkiewicz studied the frequency of deaths from horse kicks in the Prussian army. He found that the distribution of the number of deaths per army corps per year was almost perfectly random. To describe the random process leading to accidents, he used the Poisson model. This model fitted the actual distribution of accidents very closely. Bortkiewicz's results led to acceptance of the idea that accidents were purely random events over which humans had no control.

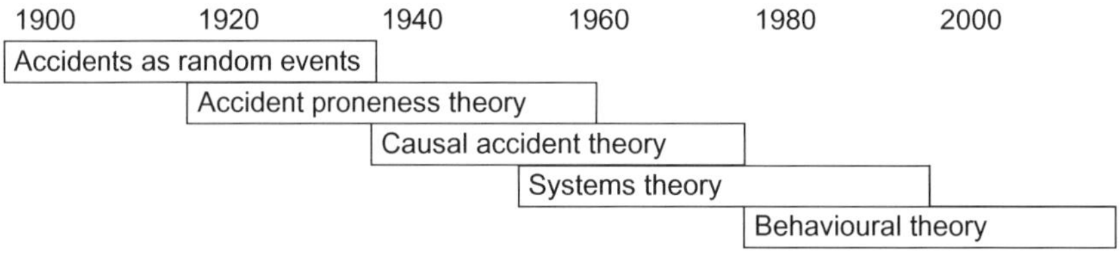


*Figure 4.3: The heyday periods of various accident theories.*

***Accident proneness theory.*** The view that accidents were purely random events was shaken during the First World War, when Greenwood and Yule (1920) discovered an abnormal concentration of accidents involving a few workers in munitions factories. These workers had far more accidents than randomness alone could explain. Greenwood and Yule proposed different statistical models to explain the observed distribution of accidents. The simplest of these models that adequately described the observed distribution of accidents was the negative binomial model.

This model was based on an assumption of different initial accident liabilities. Some people were, in other words, more prone to have accidents than others. This reorientation of accident theory coincided with a surge of innovations in psychology. Psychoanalysis became widely known through the writings of Sigmund Freud. The first intelligence tests and personality tests were developed. The belief soon took hold that it was possible by means of psychological tests to identify people who were particularly prone to accidents and deny them access to the activities where they were causing accidents. This point of view was predominant in accident research from about 1920 until about 1950.

The pendulum had moved from one extreme to the other. From maintaining that accidents were entirely random, the conventional wisdom now held that accidents were the fault of a few people with some sort of personality disorder. An important finding undermining accident proneness theory was made as early as 1939 by Thomas Forbes (1939). He found that most car accidents were caused by ordinary drivers. Although only 1% of the drivers were involved in 23% of all accidents during the 1931–33 period, the same 1% of drivers were only involved in 4% of all accidents during the 1934–36 period. Most accidents during the latter period involved drivers who did not have any accidents during the first period. Forbes had actually demonstrated the effects of regression to the mean, although he did not himself use that term to describe his finding.

Growth of mass automobilism in the 1940s and 1950s in the United States, and the attendant growth in the number of accidents, made it clear that road accidents can happen to everybody, not just a few particularly clumsy people. It was felt that the theory of accident proneness could no longer fully explain road accidents.

***Causal accident theory*** argued that it was only by finding the real causes of accidents that successful prevention was possible, and that the real causes of accidents can only be found by studying in detail each accident, the circumstances surrounding it and the events leading to it. This approach is perhaps modelled on microbiology and its search for the causes of disease by identifying microorganisms transmitting infections or other mechanisms triggering disease. Proponents of the theory took the fact that the number of accidents kept rising as conclusive evidence that the established approaches to the study of accident causation had not been able to find the real causes.

The in-depth case study approach ended up by concluding that accidents typically have more than one cause. It is almost never possible to identify any one of the potentially contributing causes as more decisive than the others. Human factors were found to contribute to most accidents. In particular, many in-depth studies attributed accidents to errors made by road users.

The strong focus of causal accident theory on human errors led, in the 1950s, to a misplaced emphasis on trying to modify human behaviour as the only effective measure to prevent accidents. It soon became apparent that these efforts were only modestly successful. It was also soon realised that merely finding that man is fallible was not enough to prevent accidents. It was necessary to find out why human errors were made. This realisation led to transition to a new kind of accident theory.

***Systems theory (and epidemiological theory)*** emerged in the 1950s and was popular in the 1960s and 1970s. The basic proposition of systems theory is that accidents are the result of maladjustments in the interaction between the components of complex systems. According to this theory, it is not possible to pick out any part of the road transport system as more crucial than others for its successful operation. Humans, for example, err, but why do they make errors? The answer proposed by systems theory was that errors are made because the system is not adequately designed and matched to human capabilities.

Systems theory sought to find the solution to accidents by modifying the technical components of the road transport system. Highway and vehicle safety engineering became important factors in this work. As a theory of accident prevention, systems theory has been more successful than any other accident theory. The improvements that have been made to the road system, traffic control and motor vehicle design have dramatically reduced the accident rate per kilometre of travel in Western motorised countries.

During the last 15–20 years, it has become apparent, however, that not even systems theory can provide a fully satisfactory solution to the road accident problem.

***Behavioural theory***. Perhaps accidents are an insoluble problem? That is suggested in Gerald Wilde's risk homeostasis theory, which figures prominently among the various behavioural accident theories that have been proposed after 1980. This theory will be discussed more in depth in the next section. The basic idea of all the behavioural theories is that human risk assessment and human risk acceptance is a very important determinant of the actual number of accidents in an activity. More specifically, Wilde proposes that every society has the number of accidents it wants to have and that the only way of permanently lowering this number is by changing the target level of risk (the desired level of safety).

***What can be concluded from this brief survey of accident theories?*** Firstly, it is probably fair to say that all accident theories that have been proposed contain an element of truth. It is true that accidents are, to some extent, random events. It is also true that some people are more likely to become involved in accidents than others. It is true, indeed trivially true, that man is fallible, that errors will be made and that some of these errors will result in accidents. It is true that the more we try to adapt technical systems to human limitations, the fewer errors will be made and the fewer accidents will occur. However, no system is ever entirely foolproof and the human desire to test limits and experience the thrill of hazards cannot be suppressed.

Secondly, none of the theories provide a complete scientific explanation for accidents. Each theory represents a partial perspective that offers a partial explanation. The relationship between the theories is somewhat complex, as some theories seek to explain single vehicle accidents, while other theories look for explanations of variation in the number of accidents, and yet other theories attempt to explain the overall level of safety of a system. The factors that are relevant at one of these levels of analysis may not be relevant at another level.

Thirdly, almost all the theories about accident causation have been proposed as means of reducing accidents, rather than out of intellectual curiosity. The desire to have a theory, which not just explains, but also tells you how to prevent the phenomenon you are seeking to explain, has been unfortunate in many ways. Some theories have obviously had a too narrow focus. Other theories are really only frameworks of concepts, not coherent deductive systems of hypotheses and empirical propositions. The accident theories that have been proposed so far have therefore not resulted in a general theory of accident causation, which can be stated in terms of law-like propositions that form a closed deductive system. By the same token, as will be discussed in Chapter 5, it is difficult to give a coherent theoretical account of the results of road safety evaluation studies.

***Nature of accident causes – a statistical concept of causation.*** Historically speaking, the concept of cause has been applied in a deterministic sense. The cause always produces the effect, and the same cause always has the same effect. If you heat an iron rod, it will always expand, and always – to within a small measurement error – expand by the same amount if a given amount of heat is applied.

The association between the factors that contribute to accidents and accident occurrence is irreducibly statistical. By studying accidents without having any idea of how frequently various hazards occur in traffic, no conclusions whatsoever can be drawn concerning the relative importance of factors contributing to accidents. At best, some educated guesses regarding potentially contributing factors can be done.

The association between various risk factors and accidents can only be detected if we know the frequency and distribution of road user exposure to the risk factors. This is no less true in the case of human factors than it is the case of road-related risk factors or vehicle-related factors.

The chief merit of in-depth accident studies is that they provide more detailed accident data than ordinary accident records do. Clearly, ordinary accident records are not sufficiently detailed for studying the role of human factors in road accidents. Besides, in-depth studies are often conducted by scientific teams or trained experts. This means that the recording of information will often be more complete and more accurate than it is in the case of ordinary accident reporting by the police.

***Criteria of causality for statistical associations***. If it is accepted that it makes sense to use the notion of causality to refer to statistical associations between variables, the next question is how to separate those statistical associations that are causal in nature from those that are not. It is obviously not true that any statistical relationship found in a data set is causal. Much work has been put into developing criteria for assessing causality in non-experimental data. The following brief discussion is based on Elvik (2001a, 2008b). In order to claim that A causally influences B, the following conditions should ideally be present:

- There should be a strong statistical relationship between the presumed cause (A) and the presumed effect (B), which is consistent in subsets of the data. If the cause can reasonably be assumed to be effective only within a certain subset of the data, effects should be found only in that subset and not outside it.
- The direction of causality should be clear, that is it should be clear which variable is the cause and which is the effect. The cause should precede the effect in time.
- If the cause manifests itself at different doses, there should be a dose–response pattern between cause and effect. As an example, the higher the blood alcohol level, the greater the increase in accident rate one would expect.
- The statistical relationship between cause and effect should not disappear when confounding factors are controlled. Confounding factors are all factors that could have similar effects to those of the causal factor of interest. They are, as it were, competing explanations to the relationships observed.

- The findings of the study should be supported by theory. The causal mechanism through which effects are transmitted, i.e. the process through which a cause produces its effects, should be known.

A more detailed discussion of these conditions for causal interpretations of statistical relationships can be found in Section 5.2. By critically assessing statistical relationships according to these criteria, an informed opinion about the likelihood of these relationships being causal can be formed. In this sense, the concept of causality makes sense not just for deterministic laws of nature, but also for stochastic process like those leading to road accidents.

## 4.4 Road accidents as a self-regulatory problem

***Theory of risk homeostasis – a general explanatory model for accidents?*** During the last 15–20 years, there has been a lively discussion in road safety research about different models, which are intended to explain why accidents occur and the possibilities of formulating a general theory to explain accidents. The researcher, who has gone furthest in the direction of proposing a general theory for explaining accidents, is the Canadian researcher Gerald Wilde. He has put forward the theory of risk homeostasis, which briefly stated claims that the only factor that can lead to lasting changes in the number of accidents per unit of time in the long term is changes in the strength of the desire for safety in the population.

Wilde's model has provoked an extensive international discussion (Slovic and Fischhoff 1982, Graham 1982, Lund and Zador 1984, Evans 1985, 1991, Haight 1986, McKenna 1985, 1988, Summala 1988, Howarth 1988, OECD 1990, Elvik 1991, Evans and Graham 1991, Hoyes and Glendon 1993, Underwood, Jiang and Howarth 1993, Bjørnskau 1994, Bjørnskau and Fosser 1996, Fosser, Sagberg and Sætermo 1996, Sagberg, Fosser and Sætermo 1997). A detailed discussion of this research is not undertaken here for want of space. The main points of view, on which the majority of researchers agree with Wilde's theory of risk homeostasis, can be summarised as follows:

- It is not possible to refute Wilde's theory of risk homeostasis. If it is found that a measure does not reduce the number of accidents, this confirms the theory, showing that people adapt their behaviour to a lower level of risk so that the number of accidents remains unchanged. If the opposite is found – that the number of accidents reduces – this can be explained by stating that the target level of risk has been reduced. Thus no result would lead to rejection of the theory. The theory can be invoked to explain any finding and thus has no explanatory value.

- One may interpret Wilde's theory as an assertion that no measure is effective. According to such an interpretation, the theory is wrong. There are many examples of road safety measures that have reduced the number of accidents and/or injury severity.
- Wilde does not state how the 'target level of risk' can best be measured and how it can be influenced. This then becomes a 'black box' into which anything that cannot be measured can be put.

Nonetheless, many researchers would probably agree that Wilde has identified important mechanisms in his theory and that not all road safety measures have the intended effects. There is no doubt that the strength of demand for road safety is of major importance for the success of an accident prevention programme. The stronger the desire to prevent accidents, the stronger the measures it would be acceptable to take in order to prevent accidents.

***Theory of behavioural adaptation and factors affecting such adaptations***. Wilde's attempt to formulate a general theory to explain accidents has not been successful. A more limited theory is the theory of behavioural adaptation or risk compensation. This theory states that road users adapt their behaviour to risk factors and road safety measures to a greater or lesser extent, but not necessarily in such a way as to fully compensate for the risk factors or measures, which trigger the behavioural adaptation, as Wilde maintains. The logic in this theory is shown in Figure 4.4.

It is assumed that every road safety measure is intended to affect accidents by affecting one or more of the risk factors, which contribute to accidents or injury severity (risk factors that the measure is meant to affect). In addition to these factors, a road safety measure may have unintentional effects on one or more other risk factors, which affect accidents or injury severity. If these risk factors are adversely affected, this can partly or fully outweigh the favourable effects on the risk factors, which the measure is designed to affect. It is these compensatory changes in other risk factors, rather than those that the measure is primarily designed to affect, which are referred to as risk

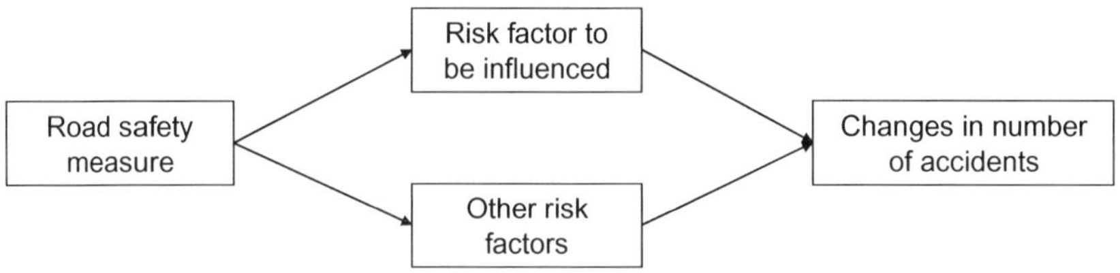


*Figure 4.4: The logic of the theory of behavioural adaptation (risk compensation).*

compensation. The conceptual scheme, which is used as a basis for Figure 4.4, has been developed by Evans (1985, 1991).

Let us illustrate this model by means of an example. Road lighting is intended to affect accidents by making it easier to see other road users and objects in the dark. The *detection distance in the dark* is the risk factor that road lighting is meant to influence. The effect road lighting has on accidents if the detection distance alone is increased, and road users do not change their behaviour, is referred to as the *engineering effect* of the measure. The engineering effect is shown by the uppermost arrows in Figure 4.4. Suppose that road lighting also leads to road users driving faster and reducing their alertness. Such behavioural changes are not intended by the road authorities and can lead to road lighting having a smaller effect on accidents than it would otherwise have had. The behavioural changes can be labelled the *behavioural effect* of the measure and go through the lowest row of arrows in Figure 4.4. The *net effect* of a measure is determined by the engineering effect and the behavioural effect, and the direction and strength of these effects.

Much of the research into behavioural adaptation in traffic has tried to find out why behavioural adaptation occurs in some cases and not in others, and to describe better the forms that behavioural adaptation can take. One form of behavioural adaptation, which is probably important, but which is very difficult to study, is the change in alertness among road users. Lower alertness is not necessarily easily observable. For example, reduced alertness does not necessarily lead to a change in speed.

Some of the factors that influence the likelihood of behavioural adaptations include (Bjørnskau 1994, Elvik 2004):

- *Noticeability of the measure*: Measures that lead to noticeable improvements, which road users believe reduce the risk of accidents are more liable to risk compensation (behavioural adaptation) than measures that do not lead to noticeable improvements. Example: Road markings are assumed to be more liable to behavioural adaptation than collapsible steering columns.
- *Whether the measure reduces accidents or injuries*: Measures that reduce the risk of accidents are more liable to risk compensation than measures that reduce the severity of injuries in accidents. Example: Airbag system (ABS) is assumed to be more liable to behavioural adaptation than airbags.
- *Whether road users have already compensated for the risk factors that the measure is meant to influence or not*: If road users have already adapted their behaviour to the risk factor that the measure is meant to affect, the measure is more liable to risk compensation than if such an adaptation has not taken place. Example: Periodic inspections of private cars must be assumed to be more liable to behavioural

adaptation than road lighting, because road users try to compensate for technical defects so that the accident rate does not increase, but they do not adapt their behaviour in the dark in such a way that the increase in risk in the dark disappears.

- *The size of the engineering effect*: The greater the engineering effect, the greater the probability that there will be behavioural adaptation. Example: It is more likely that improving a car's headlights will lead to behavioural adaptation when driving in the dark than when driving in daylight.
- *The benefits of changing behaviour*: A measure can only lead to behavioural adaptation if road users experience some benefit in changing behaviour. Example: It is difficult to think of a behavioural adaptation to gates at level crossings between roads and railroads, which would increase the benefit to road users. Driving in a zigzag pattern between gates that are lowered is extremely dangerous and may also lead to damage to the vehicle if one hits the barriers. The vast majority would hardly perceive this as either beneficial or comfortable. Reducing alertness, so that one reacts later confers no benefit either, because it only means that one would have to brake harder in order to stop in front of the gate.

Can behavioural adaptation explain why some road safety measures do not seem to reduce accidents? Among the road safety measures that are included in this book are both measures that, according to the studies available, reduce the number of accidents, and measures that do not do so. The latter group includes tracks for walking and cycling, resurfacing of roads, bright road surfaces, and basic driver training. Can behavioural adaptation among road users explain why these measures, and others, do not lead to fewer accidents?

The answer to this question is yes in the majority of cases, but with a number of reservations. Obviously, it can always be claimed that behavioural adaptation explains the lack of effect on accidents of a measure. However, very often, such behavioural adaptation is not fully documented. Unfortunately, convincing evidence of changed behaviour is only rarely found. For example, no one has shown that the ineffectiveness of edge lines in reducing accidents is due to behavioural adaptation among road users. We cannot rule it out, but we do not know if behavioural adaptation is the reason why no reduction in accidents has been found.

Behavioural adaptation does not necessarily fully eliminate the effect of a measure on accidents. For example, road lighting reduces the number of injury accidents in darkness by around 30%. This is a major effect. Few would believe that this measure leads to behavioural adaptation. Figure 4.5 shows the results of a study of drivers' speed adaptation on a road section where road lighting was installed.

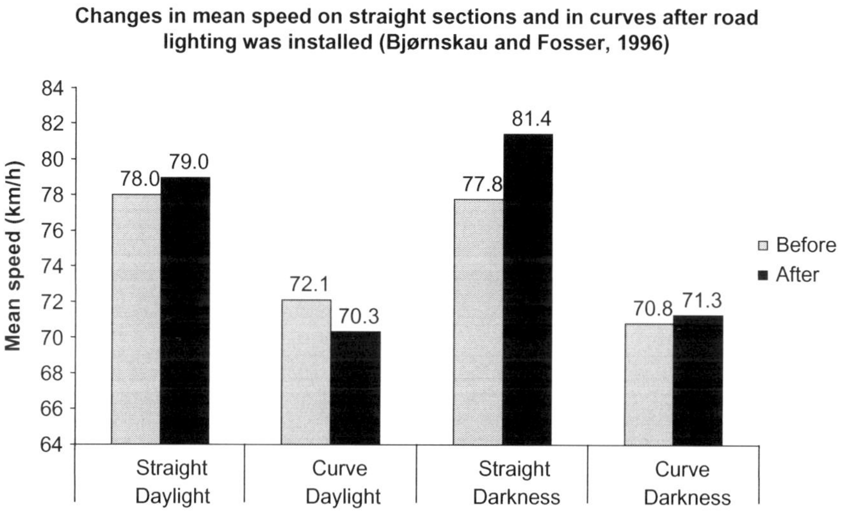


*Figure 4.5: Changes in mean speed following the introduction of road lighting (Bjørnskau and Fosser 1996).*

4.5 shows the average speed in kilometres on straight roads and in curves, in daylight and the dark, before and after road lighting was introduced. Speed increased in the dark, especially on straight roads. If the changes in speed from the before to the after periods in daylight is used as a comparison group, the net increase in speed in the dark can be estimated to 3%, both on straight roads and in curves. The study also found that drivers were less attentive on lit roads than on unlit roads.

The increase in the detection distance to given objects in the dark, measured under controlled conditions, can be used as a measure of the engineering effect of road lighting. According to Ketvirtis (1977), the detection distance increases from a maximum of 50 to 75 m with correctly installed vehicle lights as the only source of light, to around 250 m when the road has road lighting of the standard required for national highways in Norway (light intensity of 1–2 cd/sqm). At a driving speed of 78 km/h, with a 1 s reaction time and a friction coefficient of 0.8, the stopping distance is about 52 m. Road lighting thus provided an increase in the safety margin from $75 - 52 = 23$ m before it was installed to $250 - 52 = 198$ m after it was installed. The engineering effect of road lighting, in other words, corresponds to a potential decrease in accidents in the dark of at least 80%. The actual decrease in accidents is around 30%. This indicates that road lighting leads to significant behavioural adaptation, which contributes to reducing, but not eliminating, the effect on accidents.

Nonetheless, it is rarely possible to estimate how behavioural adaptation modifies the effects of a measure on accidents in this way. Firstly, the engineering effect of many measures is not known or is impossible to calculate. Secondly, the incidence of behavioural adaptation is rarely known. Thirdly, it is not known, even with regard to road lighting, which form of behavioural adaptation has the greater effect. Is it increased speed or reduced alertness? The only effect that one can expect to quantify is, at best, the total effect of all forms of behavioural adaptation, and not the partial contributions of the many forms such adaptation may take.

# 5.

# Assessing the Quality of Evaluation Studies

## 5.1 The concept of study quality

Study quality is used synonymously with study validity. *Validity* denotes the degree to which research approximates the truth. This definition is taken from Cook and Campbell (1979). The words 'approximates the truth' in the definition are used deliberately, since researchers can never claim to know the truth for sure. The best that can be accomplished in empirical social research is to conduct studies in ways that are not known to lead to systematic errors and to argue on that basis that the results are not (positively) known to deviate from the truth. This, however, is not the same as to claim that the truth has been found.

Study quality is affected by a large number of characteristics of study design and conduct. The various aspects of study quality will be referred to as types of validity and are discussed in greater detail below.

## 5.2 Assessing study quality

Study quality is assessed by making a systematic evaluation of the validity of a study or a set of studies in terms of specific criteria of study validity. Ideally speaking, an assessment of study quality ought be standardised and expressed in numerical terms by means of a scale for study quality. So far, however, no formal scoring system for assessing the quality of road safety evaluation studies has been developed. The

**The Handbook of Road Safety Measures**

**ISBN: 978-1-84855-250-0**

assessment of study quality that has been done in this book is systematic, in the sense that it relies on explicitly stated criteria of study quality that are applied consistently to all studies. It is, however, not numerical, that is, the results of the assessment are not summarised quantitatively. Research is ongoing with the aim of developing a quantified study quality score. The task has turned out to be more difficult than originally believed.

Study quality comes in degrees. It is not the case that studies are either perfect or worthless. Most often, if a study is checked systematically according to a list of criteria for study quality, it will be found that the study satisfies some of these criteria, but not all of them. The question then arises: Can we trust the findings of a study that is known to have some shortcomings? Are some shortcomings more important than others?

It is not always simple to answer these questions. The answers given in this book are based on what past experience has taught us about the shortcomings that most strongly affect the results of road safety evaluation studies. A certain weakness found in a study is important if it is known that it may strongly influence the results of a study. It is, on the other hand, rather less important if it is known not to have an impact on study findings.

***Criteria of study quality***. The criteria of study quality that have been applied to assess the road safety evaluation studies referred to in this book, are to a great extent based on the validity framework of Cook and Campbell (1979). According to this framework, the quality of a study can be assessed in terms of four types of validity:

- *Statistical conclusion validity*: Sampling techniques, statistical analyses
- *Theoretical validity*: Operational definition of theoretical concepts and propositions
- *External validity*: Generalisability of the results of a study
- *Internal validity*: Basis for inferring a causal relationship between treatment and effect.

***Statistical conclusion validity*** refers to the accurateness and the representativeness of the data and the results of statistical analyses in a study. Study results are statistically valid if they cannot be attributed to randomness or bias of the measurements and if they are representative of a known population of units. The statistical conclusion validity is assessed in terms of the following criteria,

*Sampling technique*: The best way of sampling study units is by means of random sampling from a known sampling frame. Random sampling ensures that there is no systematic bias in the sample. However, a sampling frame from which random sampling of study units can be made does not always exist. In that case, other sampling techniques are employed. In road safety evaluation studies, samples defined according to warrants or criteria for the use of a road safety measure and convenience samples (or self-selected samples) are common.

*Sample size*: Sample size refers to the number of study units included in a study. Larger sample sizes are associated with smaller statistical uncertainty of the results. In most road safety evaluation studies, sample size refers to the number of accidents. However, in some studies, data refer to aggregates of elementary study units, for example, to numbers of accidents per state per month or per year. This involves the risk of an error of aggregation, and the statistical validity of such studies may be reduced. An example of this was given in Section 4.2, in the discussion of accident rates for men and women.

*Reporting of statistical uncertainty in results*: In order to assess the statistical uncertainty of the results from a study, the sample size, or alternatively, the standard error (or information sufficient to derive the standard error) has to be reported. Studies that fail to report this information cannot be included in meta-analysis.

*Measurement errors:* Measurement errors may contribute to systematic bias, which may lead to a systematic over- or underestimation of the effects of a measure. An example of measurement errors in road safety studies is under-reporting of accidents.

*Specification of accident or injury severity*: Studies that specify the severity of the accidents or injuries to which results apply are rated as better than studies that do not specify accident or injury severity. Firstly, the effects of many road safety measures have been found to vary, depending on accident severity. Secondly, fatalities and severe injuries are regarded as a more serious problem than minor injuries or accidents that result in property damage only.

***Theoretical validity***, or construct validity, refers to the theoretical foundation and the operational definition of theoretical concepts and propositions. Criteria for theoretical validity are as follows.

*Identification of relevant concepts and variables:* Relevant concepts and variables and how they can best be measured are specified. Relevant variables may be independent, dependent, confounding, mediating and moderator variables (Figure 5.1). Mediator variables are variables that are affected by the independent variable and that have an effect on the dependent variable. Moderator variables are variables that affect the relationship between independent and dependent variable, that is, the relationship differs between different groups or levels of the moderator variable. Confounding variables are variables that are related to both independent and dependent variable, and whose relationship to the dependent variable may be mistaken for an effect of the

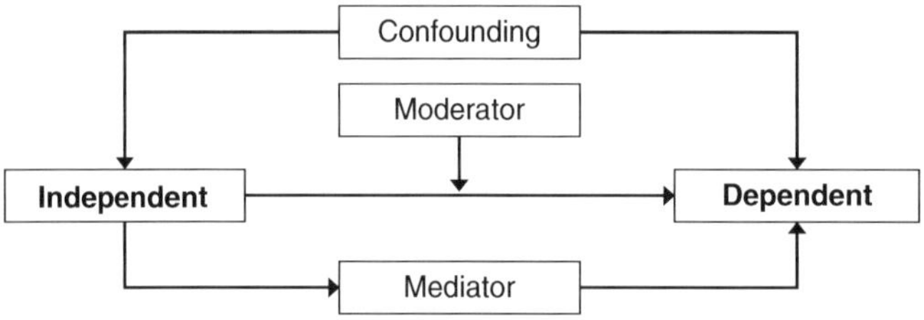


*Figure 5.1: Relationships between relevant study variables.*

independent variable. Confounding variables may also be uncontrolled moderator variables.

*Hypotheses describing the relationships between variables:* Hypotheses are formulated on the relationships between those variables that are assumed to be relevant, based on an explicitly stated theoretical background. The hypotheses contain assumptions about the direction and strength of the relationships between the variables. Additionally, the most important alternative hypotheses are identified, which may explain study findings if the proposed theory is contradicted.

*Knowledge of causal mechanism*: If a study can identify the causal mechanism through which a road safety measure influences accidents or injuries, the theoretical validity is strengthened, provided observations of the causal mechanism make sense. It would, for example, make sense if a study found that a reduced speed limit was associated with lower speeds and less serious accidents. If, on the other hand, speed was reduced but accidents became more serious, it would be more difficult to accept this finding as showing the true effect of reduced speed on accident severity.

Unfortunately, most of the road safety evaluation research does not rely on an explicitly stated theoretical foundation. Some studies test explicitly stated hypotheses, but the hypotheses are rarely based on a well-established theory. This is one of the major problems of this research, because it means that few results can be ruled out as nonsensical on theoretical grounds. If you heat an iron rod, and it does not expand, you can rule out the possibility that you have made an important new discovery in physics. It is far more likely that there is something wrong with your experiment or measurements. If road lighting were installed, could we rule out the possibility that the number of accidents in the dark would increase? Not really. While common sense and general knowledge about visibility at night lead us to expect that safety will be improved, the possibility of an opposite result cannot be ruled out. If road users take advantage of road lighting by driving faster, by driving more at night, or by driving when they are more tired or less attentive, there may be no benefits for road safety.

***External validity*** refers to the generalisability of study results. A study has high external validity if its findings are valid for different settings than those in which the study was made. It is difficult to assess the external validity of a single study. External validity is best assessed by comparing the findings of studies that have been made in different settings. If the findings are similar, the external validity of the set of studies is high. If findings differ greatly, external validity is more doubtful. However, context-specific effects of safety measures are not necessarily a methodological weakness, but rather a property of reality. Nevertheless, the generalisiability of context-specific effects is reduced.

To some extent, high external validity can make up for the absence of a strong theoretical foundation for road safety evaluation studies. Results that have been replicated a large number of times, in many studies made in many countries, are more likely to show true effects than results reported by just a few studies in just a few countries.

***Internal validity*** refers to the inference of a causal relationship between treatment and effect. This aspect of study validity is very important. The objective of a road safety evaluation study is to determine the *effects* on safety of a road safety measure. To measure the effects of something is the same as describing the causal relationship between the action taken and the associated changes in road safety. Criteria for causality were discussed in Section 4.3, but are worth repeating here. The following criteria indicate that there is a causal relationship between a safety measure A and a safety indicator B (Elvik 2008a):

*Statistical association between treatment and effect*: There is a (strong) statistical relationship between A and B, which is consistent between different data sets or subgroups, and which is found only within the target group for measure A. The strength of the relationship is assessed both in terms of the size of the effect and in terms of statistical significance or confidence intervals. When different effects are found within different subgroups, these should be predicted from hypotheses proposed before the study. If a statistical relationship is inconsistent, and no moderator variable can be found to account for this, it weakens a causal inference.

*Clear direction of causality*: The direction of the relationship can be explained in both theoretical and empirical terms. Causal direction can be determined if there is a clear temporal relationship between the variables (the cause comes before the effect), and there should be a known mechanism that explains the effect of A on B. It should be ruled out that A is caused by B.

*Dose–response pattern*: If a treatment comes in different doses, one should expect to find a dose–response pattern. The larger the dose, the greater the effect. If this is found, it strengthens a causal inference.

*Specificity of effect*: It is sometimes possible to identify a certain group of road users, a certain type of accident, or some other category in which one would expect a treatment to be effective. If the treatment is found to be effective in the 'target group', but not in other groups, then internal validity is strengthened. A limitation of this criterion is that it is sometimes difficult to define the target group for a measure very precisely (Hauer 1997).

*Control of confounding factors*: The relationship between A and B does not disappear when potential confounding variables are controlled for. Confounding variables are all variables that are related to both A and B, when the relationship of these variables with B can be mistaken for an effect of A on B. Examples of confounding variables are other safety measures that are implemented at the same time as A, or general trends in accident numbers. When confounding variables are not controlled for, the effects of measure A are often systematically over- or underestimated. When effects of other safety measures or accident trends are not controlled for, the effects of measure A will most likely be overestimated.

Adequate control of confounding variables is perhaps the single most important aspect of study quality for road safety evaluation studies. Lack of control for confounding variables can profoundly influence the results of an evaluation study, as will be shown by some examples in the next section.

Studies may control for confounding variables in two ways. Firstly, the study design contributes to the degree to which confounding variables are controlled for. The best way of controlling for confounding variables by study design is randomisation, that is, each unit of the whole population has the same probability of being selected for the treatment group (in which a measure is applied) or for the control group (in which no measure is applied). When possible confounding variables are known, matching may be an alternative to randomization, that is, study units with and without the application of a measure are compared pairwise, each pair being equal with respect to confounding variables. A study may also be restricted to study units, which are identical with respect to confounding variables. In this case, the generalisability of the results may be limited.

Secondly, control for confounding variables may be achieved by statistical techniques. In multivariate analysis, potential confounding variables can be included as predictor variables whereby the effects of those confounding variables that are included in the analysis are statistically controlled for. However, multivariate analyses are no guarantee for internal validity.

In the following, the most common factors that reduce the internal validity of studies are summarised.

- *Regression to the mean:* It means that accident numbers that have been exceptionally high or low at one time are most likely to be closer to the mean at a later time. Regression to the mean is often a problem in before-and-after studies in which measures are applied only in cases (e.g. on roads) where the number of accidents has been exceptionally high. Without control for regression to the mean, the number of accidents will decrease in the after-period even if the measure has no effect at all. How regression to the mean can be treated statistically has been described in Section 4.1.
- *Self-selection bias:* There are often systematic differences between persons (or other study units) who choose to apply a measure on a voluntary basis and those who do not. If self-selection bias is not controlled for, the effects of a measure will almost always be overestimated.
- *Accident migration:* Safety measures may reduce accidents in those places or at those times where/when the measures are implemented. In other places or at other times, accidents may increase.
- *Study effects:* The fact that a study is conducted or that measurements are made may have an influence on those aspects that are measured in a study (e.g. if speed measurement devices are not hidden for drivers, drivers may reduce speed because of the measurement equipment).

In multivariate analyses, there are a number of further possible sources of error that may reduce the internal validity of the study results (Elvik 2008a):

- *Endogeneity*: When a measure is used only where there have been many accidents, the number of accidents may remain higher than elsewhere after the measure has been applied, even if the number of accidents actually has been reduced over time.
- *Incorrect functional form of the independent variable:* When a functional form of the independent variable is used in a multivariate model that does not correspond to the relationship of this variable to the dependent variable, the relationship that is found between the independent and dependent variable will be weaker than when a more adequate functional form is chosen (e.g. if a linear function is applied when a U-shaped relationship exists).
- *Collinearity and omitted variables:* Results from multivariate analysis may be biased if too many predictor variables are included in the model, and if relevant predictor variables are not included in the model. It is a problem that one never knows for sure that all relevant variables, but not more, are included in a model.

## 5.3 The importance of study quality: Some illustrations

This section will give some examples of how various aspects of study quality can influence study findings.

***Case 1: Errors in data and their correction.*** Road safety evaluation studies are sometimes based on data that may contain systematic errors. A case in point is studies that evaluate the effects of seat belts on injury severity.

The results of studies that evaluate the effect of seatbelts can be strongly influenced by how reliable the information is regarding the use of seat belts and injury severity. People who are uninjured or slightly injured will often have left the vehicle before the police arrive at the accident scene. When the police ask whether belts were used or not, a number of those who were not using a seatbelt will say that they were using a seat belt, in order to avoid problems. In this way, the use of seatbelts may be systematically over-reported among uninjured and slightly injured people involved in traffic accidents.

A study that took this source of error into account was carried out by Dean, Reading and Nechodom (1995). Table 5.1 shows the results of the study, with and without adjustment for possible over-reporting of seat belt use in accidents. Dean, Reading and Nechodom estimated the actual use of seat belts in accidents on the basis of information on seat belt use in traffic and an assumption that seat belt use was correctly stated for fatal injuries. The way correct seat belt use was estimated is of course subject to debate. The main point here is to show that errors in data can have a major impact on the estimates of effect reported in an evaluation study.

***Case 2: Misleading statistical analysis of data.*** Lyles, Lighthizer, Drakopoulos and Woods (1986) report a before-and-after study of jurisdiction-wide upgrading of traffic control devices in cities in Michigan. They conclude that: "Results of assessing the

*Table 5.1: Estimated effect of seat belts on the probability of different injuries in accidents, depending on adjustment for over-reporting of seat belt use in accidents (Dean et al. 1995)*

| | Percentage change in number of injuries attributed to seat belts | |
|---|---|---|
| Injury severity | Stated seat belt use | Adjusted seat belt use |
| Killed | −85 | −54 |
| Seriously injured | −80 | −49 |
| Slightly injured | −52 | −25 |
| All injured | −55 | −28 |

overall effectiveness of traffic control device upgrading on a jurisdiction-wide basis were mixed at best." Tables 1 and 2 of the paper report changes in the distribution of accidents by type in all cities that were included, except for Pontiac, which was by far the largest of the cities where traffic control devices were upgraded. Based on the analyses of the data in these two tables, the authors conclude that: "The overall results are not particularly enlightening in terms of the effects of the Traffic Control Device upgrading." Table 3 of the paper presents the total number of accidents before and after upgrading for treated and untreated roads in seven cities. The authors, however, concentrate more on changes in the distribution of accidents by type and conclude that: "The results are inconsistent in general." Table 5.2 reproduces the data presented in Table 3 of the original paper.

Table 5.2 shows that the effects of upgrading traffic control devices do indeed seem to be inconsistent, as stated by the authors. The estimate of effect in each city ranges from about 21% accident reduction to about 15% increase in the number of accidents. However, five of the seven estimates indicate a reduction in the number of accidents.

If the seven estimates of effect are combined by means of a fixed-effects log odds meta-analysis, the summary estimate of effect is a 9% reduction in the number of accidents, with a 95% confidence interval ranging from 14% to 3% accident reduction.

A test of the homogeneity of the seven estimates of effect shows that these estimates do not differ significantly. Combining them by means of a fixed-effects model is therefore correct. If, however, Pontiac is omitted, the summary estimate of effect becomes a 4% accident reduction, with a 95% confidence interval and 14% reduction to 7% increase.

*Table 5.2: Changes in the number of accidents associated with upgrading of traffic control devices (Lyles et al. 1986, Table 3)*

| | Treated roads | | Comparison roads | | |
|---|---|---|---|---|---|
| City | Before | After | Before | After | Estimate of effect (odds ratio) |
| Albion | 304 | 161 | 256 | 171 | 0.793 |
| Dundee | 44 | 41 | 109 | 88 | 1.154 |
| East Tawas | 115 | 83 | 79 | 58 | 0.983 |
| Hudsonville | 122 | 108 | 74 | 67 | 0.978 |
| Mackinaw City | 69 | 44 | 44 | 27 | 1.039 |
| Mt Pleasant | 727 | 747 | 876 | 913 | 0.986 |
| Pontiac | 4483 | 4019 | 3106 | 3104 | 0.897 |

In short, the conclusions drawn by the authors of this study are misleading, because

- the authors focussed on changes in the distribution of accidents by type, rather than the total number of accidents;
- the authors incorrectly state that there was no overall effect on safety; and
- the authors incorrectly claim that the effects were inconsistent, suggesting that there was more than random variation in effects between cities.

***Case 3: How approaches taken to the analysis of data can influence results?*** Little (1971) has published a paper aptly titled "Uncertainties in evaluating periodic motor vehicle inspection by death rates." In the paper, Little tries to determine the effect of periodic motor vehicle inspection on population death rates from road accidents in American states. Excerpts of the data used for this purpose are shown in Table 5.3.

Based on these data, several estimates of the effect of periodic motor vehicle inspection can be generated (Table 5.4). If one simply compares the fatality rate before and after periodic motor vehicle inspection was introduced in the treated states, a 10% increase is observed. If these states are compared with comparison group 1, a 5% increase of fatality rate can be estimated. The following estimates of the effects of periodic motor vehicle inspection on population fatality rate can be derived from the information given in Table 5.3.

Estimates ranging from a 25% reduction of fatality rate to a 10% increase of fatality rate can be generated merely by varying the cells of the data table, which are included in an analysis. Which of these estimates is the best one? An estimate that utilises as much of the available data as possible would often be regarded as the best one. In this case, that would be the before-and-after estimate, using comparison group 3. This estimate utilises data from all the states, rather than just a particular group of states.

*Table 5.3: Data for evaluating the effects of periodic motor vehicle inspection on population death rates*

| | Road accident fatalities per 100,000 inhabitants per year | |
|---|---|---|
| Group of states | Before | After |
| Treated group: States that introduced periodic inspection | 25.88 | 28.52 |
| Comparison group 1: States that had periodic inspection all the time | 17.89 | 18.74 |
| Comparison group 2: States that did not have periodic inspection | 22.28 | 23.29 |
| Comparison group 3: All other U.S. states | 22.63 | 23.06 |

*Source:* Adapted from Little (1971).

*Table 5.4: Estimates of effects of periodic motor vehicle inspection on population death rates, based on the results in Table 5.3*

| Way of analysing data | Effect attributed to periodic motor vehicle inspection (%) |
|---|---|
| Simple before-and-after in treated group | +10 |
| Before-and-after using comparison group 1 | +5 |
| Before-and-after using comparison group 2 | +5 |
| Before-and-after using comparison group 3 | +8 |
| Comparison of states with and without inspection–before (comparison group 1 compared to comparison group 2) | −20 |
| Comparison of states with and without inspection–after (comparison group 1 compared to comparison group 2) | −20 |
| Comparison of states with and without inspection–before (comparison group 1 compared to treated group+comparison group 2) | −25 |
| Comparison of states with and without inspection–after (comparison group 1 compared to treated group+comparison group 2) | −2 |

***Case 4: Inadequate control of confounding factors – black spot treatment.*** It has repeatedly been found that the effects attributed to a measure or programme in evaluation studies depend on the quality of those studies. In fact, this has been found so often that Rossi and Freeman, as early as 1985, launched 'the Iron Law of Evaluation Studies', which states

> *"The better an evaluation study is technically, the less likely it is to show positive program effects." (p. 391)*

In a paper published in Accident Analysis and Prevention in 1997 (Elvik 1997, reprinted in Elvik 1999), an attempt was made to test the Iron Law of Evaluation Studies by using studies that have evaluated the effects on accidents of black spot treatment as a case. Studies were classified according to whether or not they controlled for regression to the mean, changes in traffic volume, long-term trends in numbers of accidents and accident migration. The classification of studies was generous: studies that claimed to have controlled for any of the confounding factors were treated as having done so, although some studies did not explain in sufficient detail how they had controlled for the confounding factors. Figure 5.2 gives a sample of the results of the study. It shows the percentage change in the number of injury accidents attributed to black spot treatment, depending on which confounding factors studies controlled for.

In simple before-and-after studies that did not control for any of the four confounding factors, an impressive accident reduction of 55% was attributed to black spot treatment. In studies that controlled for regression to the mean, long-term trends and

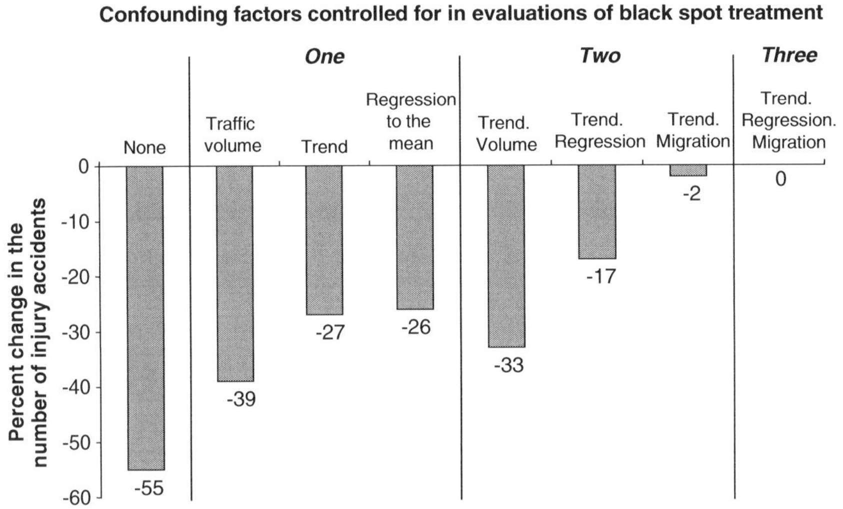


*Figure 5.2: The importance of confounding factors in before-and-after studies of black spot treatment (Elvik 1997).*

accident migration, the effect attributed to black spot treatment was zero. There is clear tendency in support of the Iron Law of Evaluation Studies: The more the confounding factors a study controlled for, the smaller the effects attributed to black spot treatment.

Now, some people might wonder how we can know that a potentially confounding factor, say long-term trends, actually did confound a study. The answer is simple. If the effect attributed to the road safety measure differs depending on whether or not the potentially confounding factor is controlled for, then it does in fact confound study results. Potentially confounding factors do not, of course, always actually confound the results of a study. If there are no long-term trends in accidents, then this factor cannot confound. The point is that we cannot know whether or not a potentially confounding factor actually confounds a study unless we control for it. The fact that a certain factor is potentially confounding is, in other words, a sufficient condition for trying to control for it.

Only an experimental study design in which units are assigned randomly to a treated and untreated group makes sure all potentially confounding factors are controlled for. In non-experimental studies, the best we can do is to control for the confounding factors that are known at any time, and for which relevant data can be obtained.

Let us return for a moment to Figure 5.2. It has been claimed that: "considerable safety benefits may accrue from application of appropriate road engineering or traffic management measures at hazardous road locations. Results from such applications at 'black spots' demonstrating high returns from relatively low cost measures have been reported worldwide." (quoted from Elvik 1997). Is this claim justified? The pattern shown in Figure 5.2 would seem to support a rather harsh verdict: The claim that black spot treatment is an effective way of preventing road accidents is totally unsubstantiated. It is based on an uncritical acceptance of studies that must be rejected because they did not control for important, and well-known, confounding factors.

***Case 5: Confounding factors are important for study findings.*** Another illustration of the importance of confounding factors in before-and-after studies is based on a number of evaluations of road safety measures in Norway. Figure 5.3 presents the key findings of this study (Elvik 2002). Seven different road safety measures were evaluated, all by means of before-and-after studies. For some of the measures, more than one evaluation study has been reported. Each study controlled for regression to the mean and general trends in a larger area in which study sites were located. Controls for these confounding factors were introduced in such a way that it was easy to remove them, thus producing the results a simple before-and-after study would have yielded.

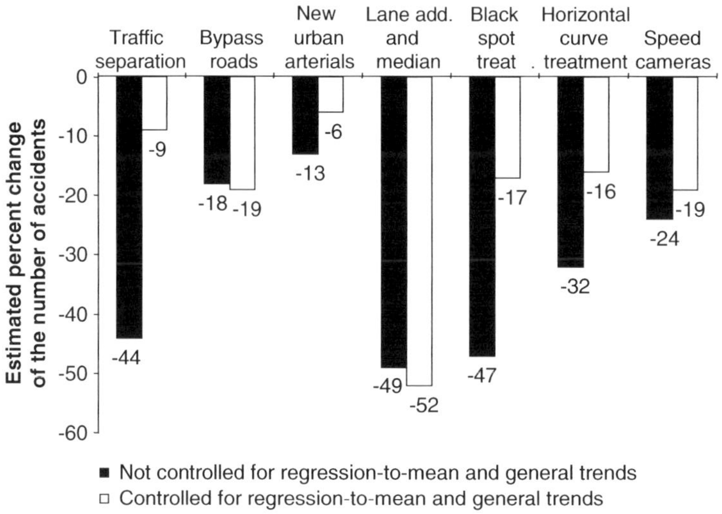


*Figure 5.3: Comparison of controlled and uncontrolled estimates of the effects of seven road safety measures evaluated in Norway (Elvik 2002).*

As can be seen from Figure 5.3, the effects attributed to the seven road safety measures were almost always greater, in some cases substantially greater, when no confounding factors were controlled for, than when the effects of the confounding factors were removed. On the average, a 32% accident reduction was found in the uncontrolled studies. The studies that controlled for regression to the mean and general trends found a 16% accident reduction.

Once more, there was support for the Iron Law of Evaluation Studies. Countless such examples could be given. There are so many examples of poor studies that the really good ones are to be highly valued.

***Case 6: Ambiguous direction of causality***. It is common to evaluate the effects of safety measures by comparing accident rate between groups (or roads, drivers or vehicles) where the measure is applied or not. The results of such comparisons will be absurd if the implementation of measures depends on the accident rate. An example is the relationship between speed and accidents (Elvik 2008a). Figure 5.4 shows accident rates on roads with different average speed. At first sight, higher speed seems to be related to reduced accident rates – only that speed limits are lower on roads with higher accident rates. When only roads with the same speed limit are taken into consideration (the four groups of data points, each of which are roads with an identical speed limit), it can be seen that accident rate increases with increasing speed.

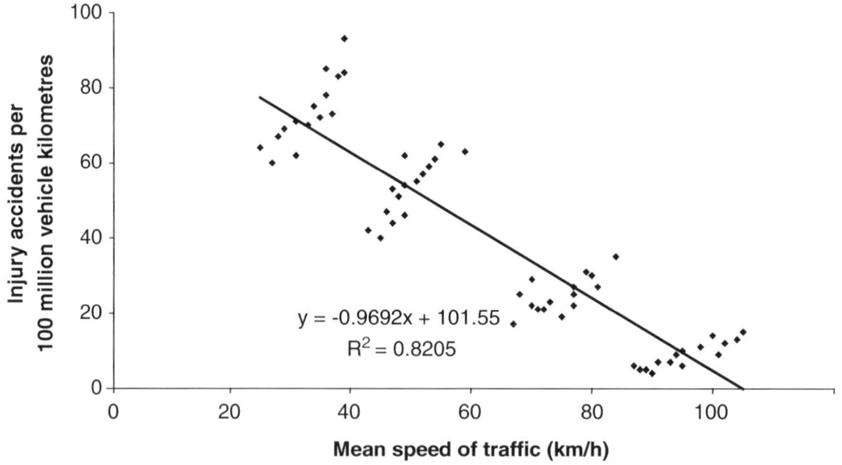


*Figure 5.4: Simple bivariate relationship between the mean speed of traffic and injury accident rate (Elvik 2008a).*

## 5.4 The treatment of study quality in meta-analysis

How has study quality been treated in the meta-analyses reported in this book? Briefly stated, study quality has been assessed in terms of the criteria stated in Section 5.2, the influence of study quality on the outcome of studies has been investigated, and as far as possible the results from the best studies are presented.

The main criterion for assessing study quality was how well a study controlled for confounding factors. In order to assess the influence of study quality on the outcomes, the available studies have been grouped according to study quality. Then differences between – otherwise comparable – results from studies of varying quality are identified, or the effect of study quality is investigated with meta-regression analysis. When significant differences are found, that is, if results from studies are affected by study quality, the findings of the best studies only are presented.

In some cases, all available studies are rather weak. In such cases, comments are given to alert the reader to the possibility that the study findings quoted could be misleading. It cannot be concluded that such study findings are positively wrong or misleading, only that the studies quoted did not control very well for confounding factors, and that a causal inference is therefore not possible. The amount and quality of evaluation studies vary substantially from one road safety measure to another.

## 5.5 Can the findings of road safety evaluation studies be accounted for in theoretical terms?

As already noted, one of the major problems of road safety evaluation research is the fact that most of this research does not have a strong theoretical basis, which guides the design of studies and the interpretation of study findings. The lack of a strong theoretical basis for research means that few results of road safety evaluation studies can be ruled out on theoretical grounds. Results of road safety evaluation studies that initially strike us as counter-intuitive can usually be given some ad hoc and post hoc explanation, but could almost never have been predicted in advance based on law like relationships or other precise theoretical notions.

In general, there are two ways to interpret the findings of empirical studies:

- Substantive interpretations, which, ideally speaking, offer a validated explanation of study findings in theoretical terms, for example, by referring to causal relationships.

- Methodological interpretations, which usually amount to rejecting the findings of a study or set of studies because the studies relied on poor data or employed flawed research methods.

Ideally speaking, researchers want to do research in ways that rule out methodological explanations of study findings. Regrettably, road safety evaluation research does not have a strong theoretical foundation, or a strong tradition for using experimental study designs. Most of this research does not refer explicitly to any theoretical framework at all, and often relies on relatively weak, non-experimental study designs that make it impossible to rule out methodological interpretations of the findings. The prospects of giving a coherent theoretical account of the findings of such studies would therefore seem to be bleak.

Although the findings of road safety evaluation studies do not conform closely to a set of law-like statements, some quite general concepts could be imagined that could be used in trying to discern patterns in the finding of these studies that would lend some credibility to them. Such concepts include:

- *Complexity*: The amount of new information a road user has to process per unit of time. When complexity is high, road users have to pay attention to rapidly changing traffic situations, in addition to performing the usual perceptual-motor tasks of walking, cycling or driving a motor vehicle.
- *Compatibility*: The differences between categories of road users in terms of the kinetic energy produced by their movements. The smaller these differences, the more compatible are road users.
- *Energy*: Kinetic energy that is converted to others forms, such as deformation, in case of accident. Kinetic energy is a function of speed and mass.
- *Predictability*: The reliability with which the behaviour of a road user can be predicted in a given situation. Lane-keeping is an example of very predictable behaviour.
- *Visibility*: The possibility of seeing something at a distance. The greater the distance at which an object can be seen and identified, the greater the visibility.
- *Individual rationality*: Choice of the best means to realise given ends. It might be assumed that road users do not want to become involved in an accident. Hence, an accident can always be treated as a breakdown of rationality.

On the basis of these concepts, the following hypotheses could be developed regarding the effects of road safety measures. Road safety will normally be improved when

- complexity is reduced,
- incompatible road users are separated,

- the amount of energy released in accidents is reduced,
- road user behaviour is more predictable,
- visibility is enhanced, and
- incentives road users get for safe behaviour are strengthened.

To the extent that the findings of road safety evaluation studies conform to predictions based on these hypotheses, it could be said that the overall pattern of these results makes sense. Let us consider a few examples of findings in evaluation studies that can be interpreted on the basis of the six hypotheses listed above.

Motorways (freeways) are, in many ways a very simple road system from which at least some of the complexities found in other types of traffic environment have been removed (Hypothesis 1). There are no access points to adjacent properties. There are no at-grade junctions. Pedestrians, cyclists and slow-moving motor vehicles are not allowed to use motorways. The road surface is generally kept in a good state. There are no sharp and surprising curves along the road. Oncoming traffic is separated by means of the median, which often has guardrails. In view of these design features of motorways, one would expect the accident rate to be lower than it is in more complex traffic environments – as is indeed the case.

Road lighting and daytime running lights both enhance visibility and reduce accidents (Hypothesis 5). Seat belts and crash helmets reduce injury severity (Hypothesis 3). Rewarding safe driving has been found to reduce accident rates (Hypothesis 6).

Many more examples could be given of findings that are explicable in terms of the hypotheses listed above. Yet, this does not amount to much by way of giving a theoretical account of the findings of road safety evaluation studies. The six hypotheses proposed do not represent a well-established body of theory: six different hypotheses could easily have been proposed in order to account for the findings of road safety evaluation studies. Besides, giving examples of study findings that are supported by the hypotheses does not rule out the possibility of alternative, methodological interpretations of the same study findings. Undertaking a rigorous test of whether what we know from road safety evaluation research makes sense from a theoretical point of view is a major research project that is beyond the scope of this book.

# 6.

# The Contribution of Research to Road Safety Policy-Making

## 6.1 An idealised model of the policy-making process

An analytical model of the policy-making process is presented in Figure 6.1 as a starting point for discussing the nature of the contribution research can make to road safety policy-making. This model is used as a heuristic device only. It is not meant to be a literally correct description of how road safety policy-making actually proceeds. The stages identified are listed in logical order, but in actual policy-making, this does not necessarily correspond to chronological order.

As noted in Chapter 3, research can make a contribution to the description of road safety problems by means of epidemiological studies of the contributions that various risk factors make to the current number of road accident fatalities and injuries (Stage 1 in Figure 6.1). Setting targets for improving road safety (Stage 2) is a profoundly political activity. Still, research can make a contribution by showing examples of targets that have been found to be more or less effective in the past. Research can also help prevent a self-contradictory formulation of a set of targets.

Potentially effective road safety measures (Stage 3 in Figure 6.1) are described in this book. Making a survey of potentially effective road safety measure is therefore an activity that, to a large extent, has to be based on research. Stage 4 of the model sketched in Figure 6.1 again involves a more prominent political element. A framework for analysis of alternative policy options consists, among other things, of decisions

**The Handbook of Road Safety Measures**

**ISBN: 978-1-84855-250-0**

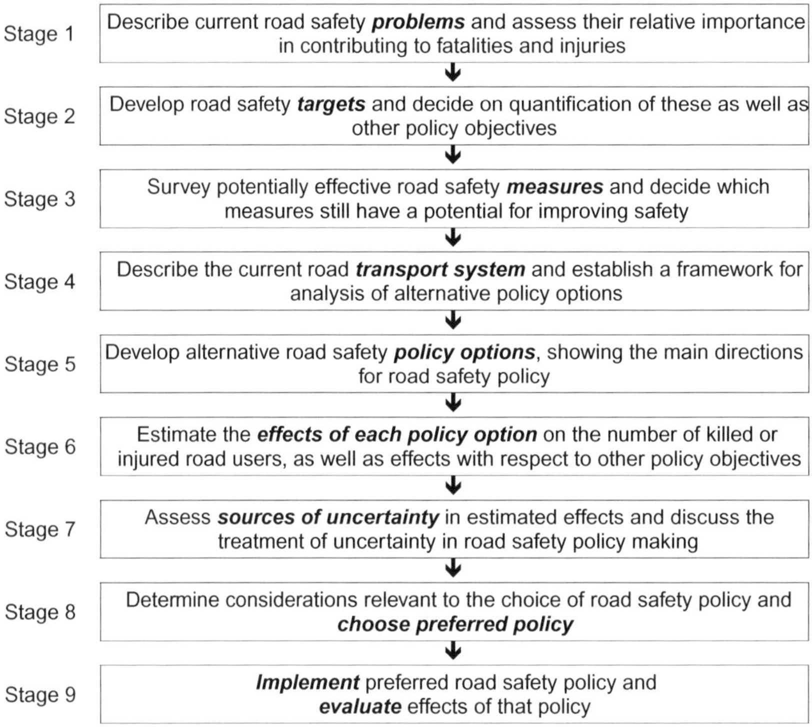


*Figure 6.1: An analytical model of road safety policy-making.*

made with respect to the constraints of road safety policy-making. For example, it is not uncommon to accept the following as constraints on road safety policy:

- Current traffic volume and traffic growth is allowed to continue.
- No interventions are made with respect to the right of road users to choose mode of travel.
- Current budgets and their allocation between major items is continued.

Whether or not these constraints should be accepted as binding is, of course, entirely a political issue. Normative models of priority setting for public policy, such as cost–benefit analysis are intended to help policy-makers choose between alternative policy options. However, these models do not show how best to develop these options. Developing alternative policy options (Stage 5) is a political activity that involves judgements regarding both practical and political feasibility.

Estimating the effects of each policy option on road safety is an activity to which research can make a major contribution (Stage 6). The same applies to estimating uncertainty in the expected effects of a road safety policy option (Stage 7). The choice of a preferred policy is a political act (Stage 8). Research can inform this choice by analysing costs and benefits of alternative policy options. It is, however, a misunderstanding to think that the results of a cost–benefit analysis amount to a policy recommendation. A cost–benefit analysis sheds light on the efficiency in economic terms of alternative policy options. However, considerations other than efficiency in the strict sense of that term within the framework of cost–benefit analysis will nearly always be relevant for policy choice. It would therefore rarely, if ever, be the case that a cost–benefit analysis was the only basis for making a policy choice.

Once road safety policy has been chosen, it is important to monitor and evaluate it (Stage 9). Unfortunately, this is not always done in a systematic way.

## 6.2 The applicability of cost–benefit analysis

The use of cost–benefit analysis to inform the basis for making road safety policy is controversial. It is therefore perhaps instructive to discuss in more detail the applicability of cost–benefit analysis to road safety policy-making. To a large extent, the discussion is based on a paper by Elvik (2001b).

Cost–benefit analysis has been applied for many years to set priorities for road safety measures. Its application goes at least 25 years back (Trilling 1978), but has remained controversial (Hauer 1994). In an early appraisal of the applicability of cost–benefit analysis to road safety measures, Joksch (1975) concluded that there were so many problems in estimating both costs and benefits and that one should not rely on cost–benefit analysis to decide whether road safety measures ought to be introduced. His objections did not, however, question the basic principles of cost–benefit analysis. Critics like Hauer (1991, 1994) and Haukeland (1994) have been more fundamental and reject the basic principles of cost–benefit analysis as put forward in the field of welfare economics to be applicable in the field of road safety. They state that the very idea of putting a monetary value on human life does not make sense and is ethically unacceptable.

The implications for the applicability of cost–benefit analysis of various types of criticism against its use depend on the nature of the arguments made. If the basic principles of cost–benefit analysis are rejected, then the technique cannot be applied at all. If, on the other hand, the economic valuation of a certain non-marketed good is considered to be too uncertain, then more research is called for to obtain a more precise valuation.

Most textbooks on cost–benefit analysis and applied economic welfare theory (Boadway and Bruce 1984, Dasgupta and Pearce 1972, Gramlich 1990, Hanley and Spash 1993, Johansson 1991, Layard and Glaister 1994, Mishan 1988, Sassone and Schaffer 1978, Sugden and Williams 1978, Williams and Giardina 1993) contain examples of such analyses, intended to show their basic logic. In general, the examples used to illustrate cost–benefit analysis in textbooks share the following characteristics:

- *They involve public expenditures*, often investments. Projects are sometimes financed by direct user payment, but more often by general taxation.
- *There are multiple policy objectives*, often partly conflicting and requiring trade-offs to be made. It is assumed that policy-makers want solutions that realise all policy objectives to the maximum extent possible.
- One or more policy objectives concern the provision of a non-market public good, like less crime, a cleaner environment or safer roads.
- *It is assumed that an efficient use of public funds is desirable*, since such funds are scarce and alternative uses for them are numerous.

These are the main characteristics of problems that economists regard as well suited for cost–benefit analysis.

***The main principles of cost–benefit analysis***. Applied welfare economics supplies the basic principles of cost–benefit analysis. There are four main principles:

- *Consumer sovereignty:* The principle of consumer sovereignty, briefly stated, means that welfare is defined in terms of how consumers choose to spend their income between commodity bundles. The right of consumers to choose how to spend their income is respected.
- *Valuation of goods according to willingness to pay:* The strength of consumer preferences for the provision of public goods is measured by the amount of money that consumers are willing to pay for these goods. Various techniques have been developed to assess willingness to pay for non-marketed goods. It is beyond the scope of this book to discuss these techniques in detail.
- *Welfare maximisation:* The objective of cost–benefit analysis is welfare maximisation.
- *Neutrality with respect to distribution of outcomes:* Results from cost–benefit analyses are neutral with respect to the distribution of outcomes in the sense that they only show for which measures the benefits (in total) exceed the total costs. Cost–benefit analyses do not take into account possible differences between

different persons or groups and the costs may exceed benefits for some persons or groups.

***The applicability of cost–benefit analysis to road safety policy.*** The applicability of cost–benefit analysis to an area of public policy can be assessed by going through five stages. The stages are as follows:

- Assess the basic principles of cost–benefit analysis
- Determine the type of issue to be decided
- Evaluate the suitability of policy objectives for cost–benefit analysis
- Determine if suitable policy programmes can be developed
- Evaluate the consequences of policy programmes, especially with respect to the possibility of monetary valuation.

***Assess the basic principles of cost–benefit analysis.*** The first stage is to assess the basic principles of cost–benefit analysis. Those who reject these principles, rule out the use of cost–benefit analysis. A commonly held argument for rejecting the principle of consumer sovereignty is that road users are poorly informed about accident risks and have no idea of what it is like to be severely injured. Hence, it is argued that road users are not in a position to form well-informed preferences with respect to the need for improving road safety. Hauer (1994, 112) argues that trying to put a monetary value on human life is impossible, because it is 'impossible to have preferences for an option involving the death of the deciding organism and it is meaningless to speak about them'.

Against this, it can be argued that very many activities and choices that people are allowed to make influence their survival prospects. This is true of choice of occupation, where to live, how much and by what means to travel and lifestyle habits with respect to, for example, eating, exercising, sexual activity, smoking and alcohol consumption. All these choices can reasonably be modelled as lotteries involving death as one of their possible outcomes. It is far-fetched indeed to claim that people cannot intelligently make these choices, because there is a certain probability that death will be the outcome. There is always a certain probability that death may occur – in every human activity. There is nothing special about road traffic in this respect.

Another common objection to using cost–benefit analysis to assess road safety measures is that the major policy objective ought to be to reduce the differences in accident rate between different groups of road users. Objections to cost–benefit analysis referring to how benefits and costs are distributed are based on the perception of the nature of the policy issue to be decided. Cost–benefit analysis is not equally well suited for all types of policy issues.

***Determine the type of issue to be decided.*** The second stage in an assessment of the applicability of cost–benefit analysis is, therefore, to determine the nature of the policy issue to be decided. Proponents of cost–benefit analysis recognise the fact that it is not appropriate to use the technique as an aid to help decide every type of issue. Some issues concern universal human rights, whose existence is not subject to a calculation of costs and benefits. Issues that concern the existence, exercise or protection of these rights are widely held to lie outside the scope of economic reasoning in terms of calculating costs and benefits. Issues that mainly concern justice and fairness are also widely held to lie outside the scope of cost–benefit analysis. It is important to note that the perception of a public policy issue is, at least to some extent, subjective. Whereas some people regard the provision of road safety mainly as a technical and economic issue, others regard it as a matter of bringing justice to those who are disproportionately at risk in the present road system. The former group may accept the use of cost–benefit analysis of road safety measures, whereas the latter group is likely to reject it.

***Evaluate the suitability of policy objectives for cost–benefit analysis.*** In order to allow for a cost–benefit analysis of policy options, policy objectives have to satisfy certain formal requirements. The first requirement is that policy objectives must be sufficiently clearly stated to make it possible to value their attainment in monetary terms. This does not necessarily require policy objectives to be quantified. On the contrary, quantified policy objectives may, depending on how they are formulated, be inconsistent with the principles of cost–benefit analysis. A policy objective must, however, be sufficiently clearly stated so that economists can design a study intended to assign monetary values to various levels of goal attainment.

The second assumption made in cost–benefit analysis is that trade-offs between multiple policy objectives are legitimate. This means that a policy objective, which is lexicographically prior to all other objectives, is ruled out. An example of a target formulation fitting this description is Vision Zero for road accident fatalities. It states that there should not be any deaths or injuries resulting in permanent impairment in road traffic and explicitly rules out any trade-off of this objective against other policy objectives (Vägverket 1997).

The third assumption, not explicitly stated in most textbooks, but recognised as important in practice by Eriksen, Killi and Minken (1994), is that policy objectives should not be highly controversial. Political controversies cannot be resolved by resorting to calculations of how much various policy objectives are 'worth' in monetary terms. If people disagree about the political objectives worth pursuing, this disagreement must be resolved either by majority vote or by negotiations that bring the different opinions closer together.

***Determine if suitable policy programmes can be developed.*** The theory of cost–benefit analysis tells decision-makers to choose those policy programmes that give the greatest benefits in relation to costs. However, it does not tell decision-makers how best to develop alternative policy programmes to choose from. The policy options are simply taken as given, very little is said about how to obtain them. A policy programme will be judged acceptable according to a cost–benefit analysis only if its benefits are greater than costs. Purely symbolic programmes, designed merely to give an impression that something is being done to solve a problem, are not sanctioned by cost–benefit analysis.

Cost–benefit analysis rests on an assumption that it is possible to separate means from ends. What this means can perhaps be clarified by means of an example. Suppose that an acceptably reliable estimate of the willingness to pay of the population for safer roads is available. A road safety programme is developed and a cost–benefit analysis is performed. Suppose it turns out that cost-effective road safety measures (measures for which benefits are greater than costs) can reduce the number of road accident fatalities by 25%. Assume further that a quantified target has been set for reducing the number of road accident fatalities by 50%. It is then against the rules of cost–benefit analysis to tamper with the willingness-to-pay estimate in order to design a programme, which reduces the number of fatalities by 50% cost-effective. A more appropriate conclusion is that the target is inconsistent with the willingness to pay for improved road safety.

This example illustrates both what the principle of consumer sovereignty implies and how a quantified policy target can be inconsistent with the application of cost–benefit analysis. It also touches on a point that some safety advocates find particularly offensive, which is that one should limit the provision of road safety to what the population demands, as shown by willingness to pay.

***Evaluate the consequences of policy programmes, especially with respect to the possibility of monetary valuation***. Cost–benefit analysis rests on the assumption that all economically relevant impacts of a project are valued in monetary terms according to the principles of welfare economics (Hanley and Spash 1993). An economically relevant impact is one that affects the utility of an individual. Roughly speaking, this means that all impacts that are subject to individual preferences are relevant.

It is of course difficult to know when all economically relevant impacts have been included in a cost–benefit analysis. In recent years, the list of impacts that are included in a cost–benefit analysis has grown, as more and more items are valued in monetary terms. Despite this, there are still impacts that are not included in cost–benefit analyses. Road user security (feeling of safety) is a case in point.

## 6.3 Monetary valuation of road safety in different countries

A survey of official monetary valuations of road safety used in cost–benefit analyses in more than 20 motorised countries has been made at the Institute of Transport Economics (Elvik 2008b). The survey included valuations of traffic fatalities only. Figure 6.2 presents official valuations of the benefit to society of preventing a road accident fatality in 23 motorised countries. Figures are given in EUR at 2002 prices, adjusted to purchasing power parity. It is seen that the valuation of a traffic fatality varies enormously. Those factors that have been found to have the greatest influence on the valuation are real income per capita and the use of a willingness-to-pay method in order to obtain a monetary valuation of the benefits to society arising out of preventing traffic fatalities. Both these factors were associated with an increased valuation of road safety.

The large differences found in the monetary valuation assigned to traffic fatalities clearly shows that one should be very careful about applying the results of cost–benefit analyses of road safety measures made in one country to another. Although the costs of many road safety measures are likely to be somewhat lower in those countries that assign a low value to the prevention of a traffic fatality than in countries that assign a high value, it is unlikely that differences in cost fully compensate for the differences in the value given to the benefits of preventing road accident fatalities.

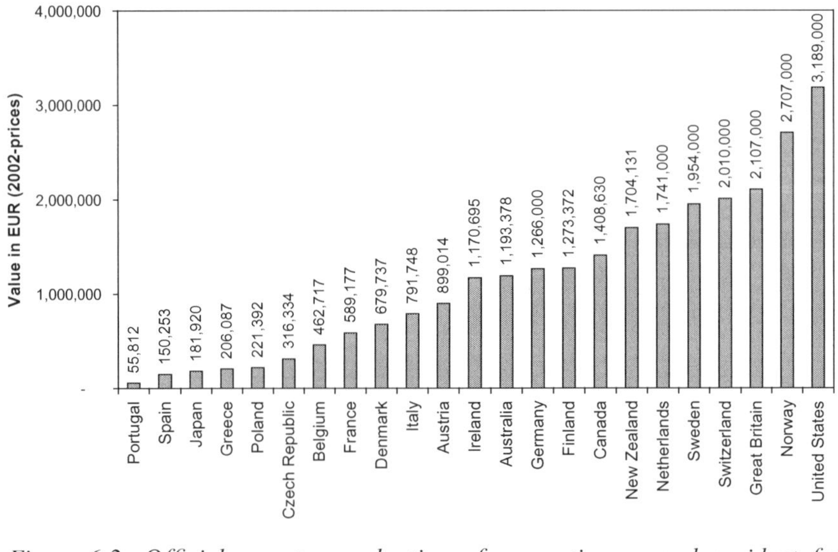


*Figure 6.2: Official monetary valuation of preventing a road accident fatality in 23 motorised countries – EUR 2002 prices at purchasing power parity.*

Examples of cost–benefit analyses are given in many chapters of this book. These examples should be treated as numerical examples only, intended to illustrate the logic of cost–benefit analysis of the various road safety measures, and not as fully developed analyses whose results apply to other countries.

## 6.4 Current monetary valuations of impacts of road safety measures in Norway

In several chapters in this book, examples are given of cost–benefit analyses that refer to Norwegian conditions. As an aid to understanding these examples, the monetary valuations of impacts of road safety measures that have been applied in the examples are presented below.

***Accident costs.*** The accident costs that are currently used in cost–benefit analyses were estimated in 1993 (Elvik 1993) and adjusted to 2005 prices in 2005 (Samstad, Killi and Hagman 2005). The accident costs are the sum of five main items:

- Medical costs
- Loss of production capacity
- Costs of property damage
- Administrative costs
- Economic valuation of lost quality of life.

Given in 2005 prices, the unit costs per case of injury are stated in Table 6.1.

The cost figures in Table 6.1 apply to each reported injured person and per injury accident reported to the police. In calculating the costs, account was taken of under-reporting of accidents and injuries in official accident statistics. The cost figures therefore also include the costs of the unreported injuries.

***Vehicle operating costs, cost of travel time and environmental costs.*** Cost–benefit analyses include not only accident costs but also an economic evaluation of vehicle operating costs, cost of travel time and environmental costs. These costs will not be surveyed in detail in this book. Estimates for Norway stated in 2005 prices are presented in Table 6.2.

These figures are social opportunity costs. This means that special taxes on petrol, for example, are not included in the operating costs for vehicles. Costs of travel time are stated per vehicle hour. This means that these costs cover both drivers and passengers

*Table 6.1: Costs of traffic accidents per injured person and per accident in Norway (NOK 2005 prices)*

| Valuation unit | Total costs | Proportion loss of welfare (%) |
|---|---|---|
| ***Injured person*** | | |
| Fatal injury | 26,344,313 | 79 |
| Very seriously injured | 18,044,268 | 51 |
| Seriously injured | 5,998,886 | 50 |
| Slightly injured | 793,503 | 58 |
| Property damage only | 49,374 | 0 |
| Average injuries | 2,269,420 | 58 |
| ***Accident*** | | |
| Fatal accident | 29,835,728 | 79 |
| Injury accident | 3,174,014 | 54 |
| Property damage only accidents | 86,405 | 0 |

*Table 6.2: Vehicle operating costs and costs of travel time (NOK 2005 prices)*

| Type of vehicle | Operating costs, NOK per kilometre driven | Costs of travel time, NOK per vehicle hour | Costs of travel time, NOK per person hour |
|---|---|---|---|
| Light vehicles | 1.30 | 135 | 83.6 |
| Business travel | 1.30 | 287 | 205.0 |
| Trips to/from work | 1.30 | 77 | 63.0 |
| Private | 1.30 | 115 | 57.0 |
| Heavy vehicles | 3.73 | 468 | |
| Bus | 3.73 | 318 | |
| Bus (including person hours for passengers) | 3.73 | 998 | |

in vehicles. A valuation of travel time for bus passengers is included in travel time costs for buses.

Environmental costs for road traffic have been estimated by Sælensminde and Hammer (1994). The costs include a monetary valuation of local air pollution, traffic noise and dust and dirt. Valuation is stated per person affected and varies depending on the size of the change in the environmental impacts. Calculated in 1995 NOK, the value of changes in environmental problems is given in Table 6.3.

*Table 6.3: Valuation of the change in environmental problems stated per affected person (NOK 1995 prices, rounded to the nearest 50)*

| Percentage change | Local air pollution | Traffic noise | Dust and dirt |
|---|---|---|---|
| +20 | 5,150 | 2,550 | 1,750 |
| +10 | 2,550 | 1,300 | 900 |
| −10 | 1,650 | 550 | 500 |
| −20 | 3,300 | 1,150 | 1,050 |
| −30 | 5,050 | 1,700 | 1,550 |
| −40 | 6,100 | 2,050 | 1,850 |
| −50 | 7,150 | 2,350 | 2,200 |
| −60 | 8,200 | 2,650 | 2,500 |
| −70 | 9,300 | 2,950 | 2,800 |
| −80 | 10,400 | 3,250 | 3,100 |
| −90 | 11,450 | 3,600 | 3,450 |

In the cost–benefit analyses presented in this book, we have found it convenient to state environmental costs per kilometre driven, based on work done by Eriksen and Hovi (1995). Eriksen and Hovi have calculated environmental costs per kilometre driven for different types of vehicles. They also included the emission of carbon dioxide, in addition to the three environmental factors, which Sælensminde and Hammer have evaluated. Table 6.4 shows estimates of the environmental costs per kilometre driven for different types of vehicles, in 2005 prices, based on Samstad, Killi and Hagman (2005).

***The time horizon of cost–benefit analyses.*** In cost–benefit analyses, benefits and costs are estimated for the whole technical and economic lifetime of the measure. Future impacts are converted to present values using a discount rate. Table 6.5 shows the service life that is assumed for different main groups of road safety measures. The discount rate that has been used is 4.5% per year.

## 6.5 The preventability of road accident fatalities and injuries

Which risk factors can easily be controlled and how great a role do they play in the number of accidents? Fridstrøm (1999) has suggested that the factors that affect the number of accidents can be divided into the following groups with respect to how easily they can be influenced.

*Table 6.4: Environmental costs calculated in NOK per kilometre driven for different types of vehicle according to density of population (NOK 2005 prices, Samstad, Killi and Hagman 2005)*

| | Local emissions | | | Noise | | |
|---|---|---|---|---|---|---|
| Vehicles | Cities | Other densely built-up areas | Rural areas | Cities | Other densely built-up areas | Rural areas |
| Car (petrol) | 0.064 | 0.041 | 0.016 | 0.311 | 0.310 | 0.000 |
| Car (diesel) | 0.600 | 0.191 | 0.009 | 0.309 | 0.309 | 0.000 |
| Bus | 4.575 | 2.038 | 0.178 | 2.906 | 2.925 | 0.000 |
| Moped/mc | 0.049 | 0.037 | 0.031 | 1.101 | 1.102 | 0.000 |
| Passenger transport road | 0.247 | 0.105 | 0.020 | 0.382 | 0.382 | 0.000 |
| Truck (petrol) 3.5t + | 0.619 | 0.619 | 0.151 | 1.856 | 2.010 | 0.000 |
| Truck (diesel) 3.5–7.5t | 1.745 | 0.799 | 0.075 | 1.967 | 1.942 | 0.000 |
| Truck (diesel) 7.5–16t | 2.563 | 1.146 | 0.097 | 3.181 | 3.253 | 0.000 |
| Truck (diesel) 16–23t | 4.065 | 1.742 | 0.126 | 3.252 | 3.206 | 0.000 |
| Truck (diesel) 23t+ | 4.003 | 1.747 | 0.167 | 3.226 | 3.214 | 0.000 |
| Trucks | 3.136 | 1.397 | 0.123 | 2.818 | 2.832 | 0.000 |

*Table 6.5: Service life for different groups of road safety measures*

| Group of measures | Service life |
|---|---|
| Road investment measures | 25 years |
| Traffic signs, minor improvements to roads | 10 years |
| Road markings | 1–10 years (depending on amount of traffic) |
| Re-asphalting, new road surfaces | 1–10 years (depending on amount of traffic) |
| Winter maintenance measures | 1 year (1 winter) |
| Vehicle safety features for new vehicles | 18 years |
| Vehicle safety features – retrofitted on the entire vehicle fleet | 7.5 years |
| Vehicle inspections | 1 year |
| Driver training measures | 1–3 years |
| Traffic education for children | 1–3 years |
| Information campaigns | 1 year |
| Police enforcement | 1 year |
| Sanctions (fines, imprisonment) | 1 year |
| Withdrawal of driving licence | Period of withdrawal |

First, accident numbers depend on a number of truly *autonomous factors, determined outside the (national) social system*, which can hardly be influenced by any (single) government, no matter how strong the political commitment is. Examples are weather, natural resources, the state of technology, the international price of oil, the size and structure of the population, etc.

Second, they depend on a number of *general socio-economic conditions*, some of which are subject to political intervention. However, changes in such conditions are seldom an intended part of transport policy and they are rarely made with the primary purpose of promoting road safety. Examples are industrial development, unemployment, disposable income, consumption, taxation, inflation, public education, etc.

At the third level, the size and structure of the *transport sector*, and the policy directed towards it have an influence on accident counts, although they usually are not intended as elements of road safety policy. Most importantly, many of these factors are strongly associated with *exposure*, that is, with the total volume of activities exposing the members of society to road accident risk. Examples are transport infrastructure, public transport, overall travel demand, modal choice, fuel and vehicle tax rates, size and structure of vehicle fleet, driving licence penetration rates, etc.

Fourth, the accident statistics depend, of course, on the system of *data collection*. Accident under-reporting is the rule rather than the exception. Changes in the reporting routines are liable to produce fictitious changes in the accident counts.

Fifth, accident counts, much like the throws of a die, are strongly influenced by sheer *randomness*, producing literally unexplainable variation. This source of variation is particularly prominent in small accident counts. For larger accident counts, the law of large numbers prevails, producing a relatively high degree of long-run stability.

Finally, accident counts are susceptible to influence – and, indeed, influenced – by *accident counter-measures*.

Although generally at the centre of attention among policy-makers and practitioners in the field of accident prevention, this last source of influence is far from being the only one, and may not even be the most important. To effectively reduce road casualties at the societal level, it appears necessary to broaden the perspective on accident prevention, so as to incorporate *exposure* as an important intermediate variable for policy analysis and intervention at the very least.

It was suggested in Chapter 1 that some safety activists caution against using the word accident, arguing that the random nature of accidents implies that they are not preventable. This point of view was dismissed as nonsense. To what extent are road accidents preventable? What do ordinary people and governments think about this?

According to a survey reported by Girasek (2001), a sample of the US population believe that 62% of road accident fatalities can be prevented. Recent analyses of road safety policy in Norway and Sweden (Elvik 2001c) found that by applying all effective road safety measures extensively during the next 10 years, the number of road accident fatalities could be reduced by 81% in Norway and 77% in Sweden. These very large reductions would, however, be very expensive to achieve. If only those road safety measures whose benefits are greater than the costs are used, it is possible to reduce the number of road accident fatalities by 60% in Norway and 53% in Sweden.

## 6.6 Vision Zero

In Sweden, a long-term vision for road safety, Vision Zero, has been adopted as the basis for road safety policy. Vision Zero states (Kommunikationsdepartementet 1996; Vägverket 1996): 'No one shall be killed or seriously injured in traffic accidents.'

Serious injuries are taken to mean injuries leading to permanent impairment. The basis for Vision Zero is the idea that zero fatalities and serious injuries are regarded as the only ethically defensible objective for road safety policy. There is no specific number of fatalities or serious injuries that can be defended as ethically correct or defensible. Consequently, proponents of Vision Zero argue that vehicles and traffic systems must be designed in such a way that no one is killed or seriously injured when they travel in the system in accordance with the rules, which apply to travel in such systems.

The responsibility for accidents is often attributed to individual road users. It is almost always possible to find something that a road user might have done differently, thereby avoiding the accident. In contrast to this, Vision Zero states that the responsibility for accidents is shared by the system designers and the road user (Ministry of Transport and Communications 1997):

- The designers of the system are always ultimately responsible for the design, operation and use of the road transport system and thereby responsible for the level of safety within the entire system.

- Road users are responsible for following the rules for using the road transport system set by the system designers.
- If road users fail to obey these rules due to lack of knowledge, acceptance or ability, or if injuries occur, the system designers are required to take necessary further steps to counteract people being killed or seriously injured.

It is neither assumed in Vision Zero that road accidents can be fully prevented nor is it considered an ethical problem, or a problem that can be solved fully, but some accidents lead to minor injuries, which will heal. Attention is directed towards the prevention of serious injuries and fatalities. Vision Zero is presented as a long-term, ideal objective for a traffic system where the amount of biomechanical energy to which people can be exposed without sustaining serious injury is the basic design parameter. Once this has been established, it is possible to deduce the level of speed that can be permitted and how vehicles should be designed in order not to cause more injuries in accidents that exceed the threshold for permanent injuries.

It is easy to object that Vision Zero is unrealistic or that it will be far too expensive to implement. A critical analysis of Vision Zero is outside the scope of this book.

## References

Assum, T. (2005). *The prevalence and relative risk of drink and drug driving in Norway.* TØI Report 805/2005. Oslo: Institute of Transport Economics.

Assum, T. & Ingebrigtsen, S. (1990). *Trafikkulykker med alkoholpåvirkede førere 1987 (Road accidents and drivers under the influence of alcohol)*. TØI notat 915. Oslo, Institute of Transport Economics.

BASt (2008). *Strassenverkehrsunfaelle in Deutschland.*

Bjørnskau, T. (1994). *Hypoteser om atferdstilpasning (risikokompensasjon)*. Arbeidsdokument TST/0512/94. Oslo: Institute of Transport Economics.

Bjørnskau, T. (2008). *Risiko i vegtrafikken 2005-2007 (Road traffic risk in Norway 2005-2007)*. TØI-rapport 986/2008. Oslo: Institute of Transport economics.

Bjørnskau, T. & S. Fosser (1996). *Bilisters atferdstilpasning til innføring av vegbelysning. Resultater fra en før- og etterundersøkelse på E-18 i Aust-Agder*. TØI Report 332. Oslo: Institute of Transport Economics.

Boadway, R.W. & N. Bruce. (1984). *Welfare economics*. Blackwell, Oxford.

Borger A. (1995). *Underrapportering av trafikkulykker. Metaanalyse av rapporteringsgrad.* Arbeidsdokument TST/0690/95. Oslo: Institute of Transport Economics.

Bortkiewicz, L. von. (1898). *Das Gesetz der kleinen Zahlen (The law of small numbers)*. B. G. Teubner, Leipzig.

Brems, C. & Munch, K. (2008). *Risiko i trafiken 2000–2007*. Rapport 2:2008. Lyngby: DTU Transport.

Brodsky, H. & A. S. Hakkert (1988). Risk of a road accident in rainy weather. *Accident Analysis and Prevention,* **20,** 161–176.

Brüde, U. & J. Larsson. (1993). Models for predicting accidents at junctions where pedestrians and cyclists are involved. How well do they fit? *Accident Analysis and Prevention*, **25**, 499–509.

Christensen, P. (2003). *Topics in meta-analysis*. Report 692/2003. Oslo: Institute of Transport Economics.

Cirillo, J. A. (1968). Interstate System Accident Research Study II, Interim Report II. Public Roads, 35, 71–75.

Cook, T. D. & D. T. Campbell (1979). *Quasi-Experimentation. Design and Analysis Issues for Field Settings*. RandMcNally, Chicago.

Cooper, H. & L. V. Hedges (Eds) (1994). *The Handbook of Research Synthesis*. Russell Sage Foundation, New York, NY.

Cresswell, W. L. & P. Froggatt. (1963). *The causation of bus driver accidents. En epidemiological study*. Oxford University Press, London.

Crossen, C. (1994). *Tainted Truth. The Manipulation of Fact in America*. Simon and Schuster, New York, NY.

Dasgupta, A. K. & D. W. Pearce. (1972). *Cost-benefit analysis: Theory and practice*. Macmillan, London.

Dean, J. M., J. C. Reading & P. J. Nechodom (1995). Overreporting and Measured Effectiveness of Seat Belts in Motor Vehicle Crashes in Utah. *Transportation Research Record,* **1485**, 186–191.

Diamantopoulou, K., Skalova, M., Dyte, D. & Cameron, M. (1996). *Crash risks of road user groups in Victoria*. Report 88. Monash University Accident Research Centre, Melbourne.

Elvik, R. (1991).*Ulykkesteori. Historisk utvikling og status i dag*. Metode-teori rapport 6. Oslo: Institute of Transport Economics.

Elvik, R. (1993). *Økonomisk verdsetting av velferdstap ved trafikkulykker*. TØI-Report 203. Oslo: Institute of Transport Economics.

Elvik, R. (1997). Evaluations of road accident blackspot treatment: A Case of the Iron Law of evaluation studies? *Accident Analysis and Prevention*, **29**, 191–199.

Elvik, R. (1999). *Assessing the validity of evaluation research by means of meta-analysis.* Report 430. Institute of Transport Economics, Oslo.

Elvik, R. (2001a). *Quantified road safety targets. An assessment of evaluation methodology.* Report 539. Institute of Transport Economics, Oslo.

Elvik, R. (2001b). Cost-benefit analysis of road safety measures: applicability and controversies. *Accident Analysis and Prevention*, **33**, 9–17.

Elvik, R. (2001c). Improving road safety in Norway and Sweden: analysing the efficiency of policy priorities. *Traffic Engineering and Control*, **42**, 9–16.

Elvik, R. (2002). The importance of confounding in observational before-and-after studies of road safety measures. *Accident Analysis and Prevention*, **34**, 631–635.

Elvik, R. (2004). To what extent can theory account for the findings of road safety evaluation studies? *Accident Analysis & Prevention*, **36**, 841–849.

Elvik, R. (2008a). Criteria for causal inference: lessons from epidemiology applied to safety evaluation. *Paper prepared for Workshop on Future Directions in Highway Crash Data Modeling, Washington D. C.* November 20–21, 2008.

Elvik, R. (2008b). *Cost-benefit analysis.* Text prepared for ERSO website (ERSO = European Road Safety Observatory). Available at www.erso.eu.

Elvik, R. (2009). Developing accident modification functions. Paper 09-0299. Transportation Research Board, Annual Meeting, January 2009, Washington, DC. Available on TRB Annual Meeting CD Rom.

Elvik, R. & Amundsen, A. H. (2000). *Improving road safety in Sweden. Main report.* Report 490. Institute of Transport Economics, Oslo.

Elvik, R. & A. B. Mysen. (1999). Incomplete accident reporting. Meta-analysis of studies made in 13 countries. *Transportation Research Record*, **1665**, 133–140.

Elvik, R., Mysen, A.B. & Vaa, T. (1997). *Trafikksikkerhetshåndboken (Handbook of road safety measures).* Oslo: Institute of Transport Economics.

Elvik, R. & T. Vaa (1990). *Human factors, road accident data and information technology.* Report 67. Institute of Transport Economics, Oslo.

Elvik, R. & Vaa, T. (2004). *Handbook of road safety measures.* Amsterdam: Elsevier.

Elvik, R., T. Vaa & E. Østvik (1989). *Trafikksikkerhetshåndbok. Revidert utgave.* Oslo: Institute of Transport Economics.

Erke, A. & Elvik, R. (2006). *Effektkatalog for trafikksikkerhetstiltak (Road safety measures: A catalogue of estimated effects).* TØI-Report 851/2006. Oslo: Institute of Transport Economics.

Eriksen, K. S. & I. B. Hovi (1995). *Transportmidlenes marginale kostnadsansvar.* TØI notat 1019. Oslo: Institute of Transport Economics.

Eriksen, K. S., M. Killi and H. Minken. (1994). *Samfunnsøkonomiske analyser*. TØI-Report 242. Oslo: Institute of Transport Economics.

Evans, L. (1985). Human Behavior Feedback and Traffic Safety. *Human Factors*, **27**, 555–576.

Evans, L. (1991). *Traffic Safety and the Driver*, VanNostrand Reinhold, New York, NY.

Evans, L. (1996). Safety-belt effectiveness: the influence of crash severity and selective recruitment. *Accident Analysis and Prevention*, **28**, 423–433.

Evans, W. L. & J. D. Graham (1991). Risk Reduction or Risk Compensation? The Case of Mandatory Safety-Belt Use Laws. *Journal of Risk and Uncertainty*, **5**, 61–73.

Fleiss, J. L. (1981). *Statistical Methods for Rates and Proportions. Second Edition*. John Wiley and Sons, New York, NY.

Forbes, T. W. (1939). The normal automobile driver as a traffic problem. *Journal of General Psychology*, **20**, 471–474.

Forsyth, E., G. Maycock & B. Sexton (1995). *Cohort study of learner and novice drivers: Part 3, accidents, offences and driving experience in the first three years of driving*. Project Report 111. Transport Research Laboratory, Crowthorne, Berkshire.

Fosser, S., F. Sagberg & I.-A. Sætermo (1996). *Atferdstilpasning til kollisjonsputer og blokkeringsfrie bremser*. TØI Report 335. Oslo: Institute of Transport Economics.

Fridstrøm, L. (1999). *Econometric models of road use, accidents, and road investment decisions. Volume II*. TØI report 457. Institute of Transport Economics, Oslo.

Fridstrøm, L. , Ifver, J., Ingebrigtsen, S., Kulmala & Thomsen, L.K. (1993). *Explaining the variation in road accident counts*. Report Nord 1993:35. Nordic Council of Ministers, Copenhagen.

Fridstrøm, L. , Ifver, J., Ingebrigtsen, S., Kulmala & Thomsen, L.K. (1995). Measuring the contribution of randomness, exposure, weather, and daylight to the variation in road accident counts. *Accident Analysis and Prevention*, **27**, 1–20.

Fridstrøm, L. & S. Ingebrigtsen (1991). An aggregate accident model based on pooled, regional time-series data. *Accident Analysis and Prevention*, **23**, 363–378.

Gaudry, M. & S. Lassarre, S. (Eds) (2000): *Structural road accident models. The international DRAG family*. Pergamon Press, Oxford.

Girasek, D. C. (2001). Public beliefs about the preventability of unintentional injury deaths. *Accident Analysis and Prevention*, **33**, 455–465.

Glad, A. (1985). *Omfanget av og variasjonen i promillekjøringen. Reviderte resultater fra en landsomfattende promilleundersøkelse i 1981–82 (Amount and variation of drink driving. Updated rseults from a national study of drink driving in 1981–82).* TØI notat 740. Oslo, Institute of Transport Economics.

Graham, J. D. (1982). On Wilde's theory of risk homeostasis. *Risk Analysis*, **2**, 235–237.

Gramlich, E. M. (1990). *A guide to benefit-cost analysis. Second edition.* Prentice Hall, Englewood Cliffs, NJ.

Greenwood, M & G. U. Yule (1920). An inquiery into the nature of frequency distributilns representative of multiple happenings, with particular reference to the occurrence of multiple attacks of decease or repeated accidents. *Journal of the Royal Statistical Society*, **83**, 255–279.

Greibe, P. & Hemdorff, S. (2001). *Håndbog i trafiksikkerhedsberegninger.* Rapport 220. København: Vejdirektoratet.

Haight, F. A. (1980). What causes accidents? – a semantic analysis. In Evans, L. (Ed): *Accident Causation*, 51–54. Report SP-461. Society of Automotive Engineers. Warrendale, PA.

Haight, F. A. (1986). Risk, especially risk of traffic accident. *Accident Analysis and Prevention*, **18**, 359–366.

Hanley, N. & C. L. Spash. (1993). *Cost-benefit analysis and the environment.* Edward Elgar, Aldershot.

Harkey, D. L., Robertson, H. D. & Davis, S. E. (1990). Assessment of current speed zoning criteria. *Transportation Research Record*, **1281**, 40–51.

Hauer, E. (1988). A Case for Science-Based Road Safety Design and Management. Paper presented at the conference "*Highway Safety: At the Crossroads*", San Antonio, Texas, March 1988. Proceedings published by American Society of Civil Engineers.

Hauer, E. (1991). The behaviour of public bodies and the delivery of road safety. In Koornstra, M. J.; Christensen, J. (Eds): *Enforcement and Rewarding. Strategies and Effects, Proceedings of the International Road Safety Symposium in Copenhagen*, Denmark, September 19–21, 1990, 134–138. SWOV Institute for Road Safety Research, Leidschendam.

Hauer, E. (1994). Can one estimate the value of life or is it better to be dead than stuck in traffic? *Transportation Research*, series A, **28**, 109–118.

Hauer, E. (1995). On exposure and accident rate. *Traffic Engineering and Control*, **36**, 134–138.

Hauer, E. (1997). *Observational Before-After Studies in Road Safety.* Pergamon, Oxford.

Hauer, E. (2002). *Fishing for safety information in the murky waters of research reports.* Paper prepared for session 539, critically assessing the results of safety studies, Annual Meeting of Transportation Research Board, January 13–17, Washington DC.

Hauer, E. & A. S. Hakkert. (1988). Extent and Some Implications of Incomplete Accident Reporting. *Transportation Research Record*, **1185**, 1–10.

Haukeland, J.V. (1994). Om å sette pris på livet. *Samferdsel*, Mai 1994, 28–29.

Howarth, C. I. (1988). The relationship between objective risk, subjective risk and behaviour. *Ergonomics*, **31**, 527–535.

Hoyes, T. W. & A. I. Glendon (1993). Risk homeostasis: issues for future research. *Safety Science*, **16**, 19–33

Hutchinson, T. P. (1984). Medical statistics on road accident injury in several countries. In Yagar, S. (Ed): *Transport Risk Assessment*, 43–76. University of Waterloo Press, Waterloo, Ontario.

Hvoslef, H. (1976). *Sommertid gir færre trafikkulykker*. Manuskript 1976. Oslo: Institute of Transport Economics.

Hvoslef, H. (1994). *Under-reporting of road traffic accidents recorded by the police, at the international level.* Paper prepared for IRTAD. OECD, Paris.

International Road Federation (IRF) (2008). *World Road Statistics 2008. Data 2001–2006*. Geneva, International Road Federation.

Ivey, D., Griffin, L., Newton, T., Lytten, R. & Hankins, K. (1981). Predicting wet weather accidents. *Accident Analysis and Prevention*, **13**, 83–99.

James, H. F. (1991). Under-reporting of road traffic accidents. *Traffic Engineering and Control*, **32**, 574–583.

Johansson, P-O. (1991). *An introduction to modern welfare economics*. Cambridge University Press, Cambridge.

Johansson, Ö. (2008). *A new method for assessing the risk of accidents associated with darkness*. Unpublished manuscript. Swedish National Roads Administration, Borlänge.

Joksch, H. C. (1975). A critical appraisal of the applicability of cost-benefit analysis to highway traffic safety. *Accident Analysis and Prevention*, **7**, 133–153.

Keall, M. D., Frith, W. J., Patterson, T. L. (2004). The influence of alcohol, age and number of passengers on the night-time risk of driver fatal injury in New Zealand. *Accident Analysis and Prevention*, **36**, 49–61.

Ketvirtis, A. (1977). *Road Illumination and Traffic Safety*. Prepared for Road and Motor Vehicle Traffic Safety Branch, Transport Canada. Ottawa, Transport Canada,

Kleinbaum, D. G., L. L. Kupper, & H. Morgenstern, (1982). *Epidemiologic Research. Principles and Quantitative Methods*. Van Nostrand Reinhold, New York, NY.

Kloeden, C. N., McLean, A. J., Moore, V. M. & Ponte, G. (1997). Travelling speed and the risk of crash involvement. University of Adelaide, Road Accident Research Unit, Adelaide.

Kloeden, C. N., Ponte, G. & McLean, A. J. (2001). *Traveling speed and the risk of crash involvement on rural roads.* Report CR 204. Road Accident Research Unit, Adelaide University.

Kommunikationsdepartementet. (1996). *Nollvisionen. En rapport från två trafiksäkerhetsdagar nittonhundranittiosex.* Stockholm.

Langley, J. (1988). The need to discontinue the use of the term "accident" when referring to unintentional injury events. *Accident Analysis and Prevention*, **20**, 1–8.

Layard, R. & S. Glaister (Eds). (1994). *Cost-Benefit Analysis. Second edition.* Cambridge University Press, Cambridge.

Lipsey, M. W. & D. B. Wilson (2001). *Practical meta-analysis.* Applied social research methods series, volume 49. Sage Publications, Thousand Oaks, CA.

Little, J. W. (1971). Uncertainties in evaluating periodic motor vehicle inspection by death rates. *Accident Analysis and Prevention*, **3**, 301–313.

Lund, A. K. & P. L. Zador. (1984). Mandatory belt use and driver risk taking. *Risk Analysis*, **4**, 41–53.

Lyles, R.W., Lighthizer, D.R., Drakopoulus, A. & Woods, S. (1986). Efficacy of Jurisdiction-Wide Traffic Control Device Upgrading. *Transportation Research Record*, **1068**, 34–41.

Massie, D. L., Green, P.E. & Campbell, K.L. (1997). Crash involvement rates by driver gender and the role of average annual mileage. *Accident Analysis and Prevention*, **29**, 675–685.

Mathijssen, M. P. M. (2005). Drink driving policy and road safety in the Netherlands: a retrospective analysis. *Transportation Research Part E*, **41**, 395–408.

McKenna, F. P. (1985). Do safety measures really work? An examination of risk homeostasis theory. *Ergonomics*, **28**, 489–498.

McKenna, F. P. (1988). What role should the concept of risk play in theories of accident involvement? *Ergonomics*, **31**, 449–464.

Ministry of Justice, Norway. (1962). Parliamentary report 83, 1961–62. *On measures to promote road safety.* (in Norwegian). Oslo.

Ministry of Transport and Communications (1997). *En route to a society with safe road traffic.* Selected extract from Memorandum prepared by the Swedish Ministry of Transport and Communications. Memorandum, DS 1997:13.

Mishan, E. J. (1988). *Cost-benefit analysis. An informal introduction. Fourth edition.* Unwin Hyman, London.

Munden, J. M. (1967). *The relation between a driver's speed and his accident rate*. RRL Report LR 88. Crowthorne, Berkshire, Road Research Laboratory.

Murray, C. J. L. & A. D. Lopez. (1996). *The Global burden of disease: a comprehensive assessment of mortality and disability from diseases, injuries, and risk factors in 1990 and projected to 2020*. Harvard University Press, Baltimore, MD.

Nilsson, E. (1986). Olycksrisk och promillehalt (Accident risk and blood alcohol concentration). TFB Report 1986:14. Stockholm: Transportforskningsberedningen.

Nilsson, G. (2002). *The three dimensions of exposure, risk and consequence*. Unpublished manuscript. Swedish national road and transport research institute, Linköping.

OECD Scientific Expert Group. (1990). Behavioural adaptations to changes in the road transport system. OECD, Paris.

Pasanen, E. (1996). Bicycle/car-accidents at crossings. *Proceedings of the Conference Road Safety in Europe*, Birmingham, United Kingdom, September 9–11, 1996, **Vol 7A**, **Part 1**, 133–143. Swedish National Road and Transport Research Institute, Linköping.

Pedersen, T. O., R. Elvik & K. Berard-Andersen. (1982). *Trafikksikkerhetshåndbok*. Oslo: Institute of Transport Economics.

Petitti, D. B. (2000). *Meta-analysis, decision analysis, and cost-effectiveness analysis*. Second edition. Oxford University Press, New York, NY.

Popper, K. R. (1979). *Objective Knowledge. An Evolutionary Approach. Revised Edition*. Oxford University Press, Oxford.

Ragnøy, A. (1989). *Trafikksikkerhet og drensasfalt*. Arbeidsdokument TST/0143/89. Oslo: Institute of Transport Economics.

Richardson, J., Kim, K., Li, L. & Nitz, L. (1996). Patterns of motor vehicle crash involvement by driver age and sex in Hawaii. *Journal of Safety Research*, **27**, 117–125.

Romano, E., Kelley-Baker, T. & Voas, R.B. (2008). Female involvement in fatal crashes: increasingly riskier or increasingly exposed? *Accident Analysis and Prevention*, **40**, 1781–1788.

Rosenthal, R. (1991). *Meta-Analytic Procedures for Social Research*. Applied Social Research Methods Series Volume 6. Sage Publications, Newbury Park, CA.

Rossi, P. H. & H. E. Freeman. (1985). *Evaluation. A Systematic Approach*. Third Edition. Sage Publications, Beverly Hills, Ca.

Sagberg, F., S. Fosser, & I.-A. Sætermo. (1997). An investigation of behavioural adaptation to airbags and antilock brakes among taxi drivers. *Accident Analysis and Prevention*, **29**, 293–302.

Sakshaug, K. & T. Vaa. (1995). *Salting og trafikksikkerhet. Saltingens effekt på ulykker og kjørefart*. Report. SINTEF Samferdselsteknikk, Trondheim.

Samstad, H., Killi, M. & Hagman, R. (2005). *Transport cost-benefit analysis: Parameters, unit costs and indices*. TØI Report 797/2005. Oslo: Institute of Transport Economics.

Sassone, P. G. & W. A. Schaffer. (1978). *Cost-benefit analysis. A handbook*. Academic Press, New York, NY.

Satterthwaite, S. P. (1976). An assessment of seasonal and weather effects on the frequency of road accidents in California. *Accident Analysis and Prevention*, **8**, 87–96.

Shadish, W. R. & C. K. Haddock. (1994). Combining estimates of effect size. In Cooper, H.; Hedges, L. V. (Eds): *The Handbook of Research Synthesis*, Chapter 18, 261–281. Russell Sage Foundation, New York, NY.

Shaw, L. & H. S. Sichel. (1971). *Accident proneness. Research in the occurrence, causation and prevention of road accidents*. Pergamon Press, Oxford.

Sherretz, L. A. & B. C. Farhar. (1978). An Analysis of the Relationship Between Rainfall and the Occurrence of Traffic Accidents. *Journal of Applied Meteorology*, **17**, 711–715.

Slovic, P. & B. Fischhoff. (1982). Targeting risks. *Risk Analysis*, **2**, 227–234.

Smeed, R. J. (1949). Some statistical aspects of road safety research. *Journal of the Royal Statistical Society*, Series A, **1**, 1–34.

Solomon, D. R. (1964). *Accidents on Main Rural highways related to Speed, Driver and Vehicle*. US Department of Commerce, Federal Bureau of Highways, Washington DC.

Sugden, R. & A. Williams. (1978). *The principles of practical cost-benefit analysis*. Oxford University Press, Oxford.

Summala, H. (1988). Risk control is not risk adjustment: the zero-risk theory of driver behaviour and its implications. *Ergonomics*, **31**, 491–506.

SWOV (2008). *Slachtoffers/reizigerskilometers (mld)*. http://www.swov.nl/cognos/cgi-bin/ppdscgi.exe?DC = Q&E = /Nederlands/Risico/Slachtoffers%20per%20miljard %20reizigerskilometers (last accessed 03. March 2009).

Sælensminde, K. & F. Hammer. (1994). *Verdsetting av miljøgoder ved bruk av samvalganalyse. Hovedundersøkelse*. TØI Report 251. Oslo: Institute of Transport Economics.

Tavris, D.R., Kuhn, E.M. & Layde, P.M. (2001). Age and gender patterns in motor vehicle crash injuries. importance of type of crash and occupant role. *Accident Analysis and Prevention*, **33**, 167–172.

Tegnér, G.; Loncar-Lucassi, V. M. (1996). *Tidsseriemodeller över trafik- och olycksutveklingen. Mätning och analys av Dennispaketets verkliga effekter*. Transek AB, Stockholm.

Thulin, H. (1991). *Trafikantgruppers skadetal, risker och hälsoförluster i olika trafikmiljöer-en tabellsammanställning*. Bilaga 2 till Samhällsekonomisk prioritering av trafiksäkerhetsåtgärder. TFB & VTI forskning/research Report 7:2 1991. Transportforskningsberedningen og Statens väg- och trafikinstitut, Stockholm og Linköping.

Thulin, H. & G. Nilsson. (1994). *Vägtrafik. Exponering, skaderisker och skadekonsekvenser för olika färdsätt och åldersgrupper*. VTI-Report 390. Väg- og transportforskningsinstitutet, Linköping.

Tielaitos-Finnish National Road Administration. (1997). *Public Roads in Finland 1.1.1997*. Finnra Statistical Reports 1/1997. Finnish National Road Administration, Helsinki.

Trilling, D. R. (1978). A Cost-Effectiveness Evaluation of Highway Safety Countermeasures. *Traffic Quarterly*, **32**, (January 1978), 41–67.

UK Department for Transport (2008). Transport Statistics Great Britain: 2008 edition.

Underwood, G., C. Jiang & C. I. Howarth. (1993). Modelling of safety measure effects and risk compensation. *Accident Analysis and Prevention*, **25**, 277–288.

US Department of Transportation. (1991). *Fatal and Injury Accident Rates on Public Roads in the United States*. Washington DC, US Department of Transportation, Federal Highway Administration.

Vägverket. (1996). *Nollvisionen. En idé om trafiksäkerhet*. Statens Vägverk, Borlänge.

Vägverket. (1997). *Nollvisionen, fördjupning*. Vägverket, Borlänge. Text located at http://www.vv.se/ts/nollvisn.htm.

Vaa, T. (1995). *Effekt av salting av veger i Sør-Trøndelag*. Report STF63 A95021. SINTEF Samferdselsteknikk, Trondheim.

Wanvik, P. O. (2009). Effects of road lighting. An analysis based on Dutch accident statistics 1987–2006. *Accident Analysis and Prevention*, **41**, 123–128.

West, L. B. & Dunn, J. W. (1971). Accidents, Speed Deviation and Speed Limits. Traffic Engineering, 41, 52–55.

Wilde, G. J. S. (1994). *Target Risk. Dealing with the danger of death, disease and damage in everyday decisions*. PDE Publications, Toronto.

Williams, A. & E. Giardina (Eds). (1993). *Efficiency in the public sector. The theory and practice of cost-benefit analysis*. Edward Elgar, Aldershot.

White, S. B. & A. C. Nelson. (1970). Some effects of measurement errors in estimating involvement rate as a function of deviation from mean traffic speed. *Journal of Safety Research*, **2**, 67–72.

World Health Organization (2008). *Global status report on road safety*. http://www.who.int/violence_injury_prevention/road_traffic/global_status_report/en/print.html.

Zador, P.L., Krawchuk, S.A., & Voas, R.B. (2000). Alcohol-related relative risk of driver fatalities and driver involvement in fatal crashes in relation to driver age and gender: An update using 1996 data. *Journal of Studies on Alcohol*, **61**, 387–395.

# PART II

# Road Safety Measures

# 1.

# Road Design and Road Equipment

## 1.0 Introduction and overview of 20 measures

This chapter describes the effects of 20 measures based on road design and road equipment. These 20 measures are as follows:

1.1 Cycle lanes and tracks
1.2 Motorways
1.3 Bypasses
1.4 Urban arterial roads
1.5 Channelisation of junctions
1.6 Roundabouts
1.7 Redesigning junctions
1.8 Staggered junctions (reconfiguring crossroads to two T-junctions)
1.9 Grade-separated junctions
1.10 Black spot treatment
1.11 Cross-section improvements
1.12 Roadside safety treatment
1.13 Improving road alignment and sight distance
1.14 Reconstruction and rehabilitation of roads
1.15 Guardrails and crash cushions
1.16 Game accident measures
1.17 Horizontal curve treatments
1.18 Road lighting
1.19 Improving tunnel safety
1.20 Roadside rest and service areas

The Handbook of Road Safety Measures

ISBN: 978-1-84855-250-0

The main features of current knowledge of the effects of these measures on accidents, mobility and the environment are described in this introductory chapter. Emphasis is placed on describing the effects on accidents. The effects on mobility and environmental conditions are described more briefly. Costs and salient points of cost–benefit analyses are described as well.

## Amount and quality of research

Table 1.0.1 shows the number of studies, the number of results and the sum of the statistical weights of the studies retrieved on the effects of road design and road

*Table 1.0.1: The amount of research evaluating the effects on accidents of road design and road equipment*

| Measure | Number of studies | Number of results | Sum of statistical weights | Results last updated |
|---|---|---|---|---|
| 1.1 Cycle lanes and tracks | 46 | 257 | 18,536 | 2009 |
| 1.2 Motorways | 13 | 55 | 15,463 | 1997 |
| 1.3 Bypasses | 8 | 73 | 2,271 | 2001 |
| 1.4 Urban arterial roads | 12 | 86 | 7,844 | 2001 |
| 1.5 Channelisation of junctions | 39 | 210 | 7,531 | 2007 |
| 1.6 Roundabouts | 39 | 141 | 7,692 | 2009 |
| 1.7 Redesigning junctions | 11 | 56 | 2,618 | 2008 |
| 1.8 Staggered junctions | 9 | 79 | 1,929 | 1997 |
| 1.9 Grade-separated junctions | 20 | 150 | 24,751 | 2006 |
| 1.10 Black spot treatment | 53 | 341 | 55,757 | 2009 |
| 1.11 Cross-section improvements | 66[1] | 908 | 168,093 | 2007 |
| 1.12 Roadside safety treatment | 6 | 61 | 19,643 | 1997 |
| 1.13 Improving road alignment and sight distance | 27[2] | 790 | 30,0024 | 2007 |
| 1.14 Reconstruction and rehabilitation of roads | 11 | 93 | 6,484 | 2008 |
| 1.15 Guard rails and crash cushions | 38 | 250 | 27,668 | 2001 |
| 1.16 Game accident measures | 25 | 59 | 838 | 2008 |
| 1.17 Horizontal curve treatments | 12 | 41 | 1,037 | 2007 |
| 1.18 Road lighting | 70 | 503 | 163,306 | 2007 |
| 1.19 Improving tunnel safety | 9 | 36 | 1,684 | 2009 |
| 1.20 Roadside rest and service areas | 0 | 0 | – | 1997 |

[1]An additional 17 accident studies could not be summarised in the log odds metaanalysis.
[2]An additional 28 accident studies could not be summarised in the log odds metaanalysis.

equipment on the number of traffic accidents and injuries. The statistical weights are based on the size of the accident sample used in the evaluation studies. The largest numbers of studies are available for road lighting and cross-section improvements. For roadside rest and service areas, no studies have been found that quantify the effect on the number of accidents.

The size of the sample (number of sites and accidents) in studies on the effects of road layout and road equipment on accidents shows significant variations. Small samples, i.e. few sites and few accidents, pose a problem in many studies. This is particularly true regarding studies of the redesign of junctions, measures against accidents involving wild animals and horizontal curve treatments. Thus the statistical uncertainty in the results is particularly large in these measures.

The quality of research evaluating the effects of road layout and road equipment can be judged according to a number of criteria. The majority of studies on the effects of road layout and road equipment on accidents tend not to be based on a random sample of sites drawn from a known population or sampling frame. Strictly speaking, this means that the results of many studies cannot be generalised to places and conditions other than precisely those for which they were carried out. Only when a result is reproduced a number of times can it be assumed to have general validity. For road lighting and guardrails, the studies have, to a large extent, reached the same conclusion, although different study designs have been used. For black spot treatments, the opposite case holds. Here, the results diverge significantly, depending on the extent to which confounding factors were controlled for. The same is true to some extent of cycle tracks and lanes and channelisation of junctions.

Random and systematic measurement errors cannot be excluded in some studies. Incomplete accident reporting is a general problem. Only a handful of studies have used more than one source of data for accidents, for example, accidents reported to the police and accidents registered at hospitals in order to test whether accident reporting affects the results.

In order to claim that a particular measure is a cause of changes in the accident figures, one must rule out that these changes are due to other events or factors, or to regression to the mean. Strictly speaking, such a requirement can only be fulfilled in experiments. Only some of the measures against game accidents have been studied experimentally. For all other measures affecting road layout and road equipment, the results presented come from more or less well-controlled non-experimental studies.

Many studies have not studied accidents on sites before and after a measure was implemented. Instead they compare accidents on road sections or at junctions with different properties. The results of such studies do not necessarily say anything about how accident numbers can be expected to change after the implementation of a measure. This concerns mainly evaluations of channelisation of junctions, grade-separated junctions, cross-section improvements, and improving alignment and sight conditions. Differences in accident numbers may be due to other factors, e.g. a very narrow road may have more sharp curves than a wider road.

For some of the measures described in this chapter, studies are available that have estimated the effects of measures with regression models. That means these studies compare accident rates at sites with and without measure, or with different amounts of a measure, while at the same time controlling for a number of other factors. These studies are for the most part better in terms of control for confounding factors than ordinary case–control or before–after studies. The results could, however, not be included in the regular log odds meta-analysis and are therefore summarised only qualitatively.

For some measures, including cross-section improvement, improving alignment and sight distances and road lighting, there is a clear so-called dose–response relationship. This means that the greater the dose of the measure that is implemented, the greater the change in the number of accidents. For example, a major improvement in road lighting reduces the number of accidents in darkness more than a minor improvement.

Some of the results are probably surprising for most people. It is important to find explanations for such surprising results. Nonetheless, in the majority of cases, it is difficult to point to any clear explanation of the results. Tracks for walking and cycling can serve as an example. No statistically significant changes in the number of accidents can be attributed to this measure. This may be due partly to the fact that more walking and cycling is induced by the tracks, partly that not all pedestrians or cyclists use the tracks for walking and cycling and partly that motor vehicles increase their speed. Evidence of these and other possible changes in road user behaviour is, to a large extent, missing. As a result, these explanations, although reasonable, are no more than hypotheses of possible, but unsubstantiated explanations.

### Main points of the effects of the measures on accidents

Measures that have been found to reduce the number of accidents include motorways, bypasses, grade-separated junctions, channelisation of junctions, roundabouts, road-side safety treatments, guardrails and crash cushions, some of the game accident measures and road lighting. Guardrails and crash cushions are effective in injury control, reducing the number of injury accidents but not always the number of property-damage-only accidents. Many cross-section improvements and improvements of the alignment of roads reduce accidents as well.

For a number of measures, the effect varies substantially, depending on the design of the measure and site conditions. Certain forms of channelisation of junctions reduce the number of accidents but not all forms of channelisation do this. Roundabouts reduce the number of injury accidents, but appear to lead to more property damage only accidents. Improving the cross-section and alignment of roads may reduce the number of accidents, the effects are however complex and dependent, among other things, on the road standard, the consistency of geometric properties and on the effects on speed. It is therefore for the most part difficult to establish simple relationships between isolated geometric properties of roads and accidents. Combinations of geometric properties are mostly more important for accidents. Some game accident measures have also been found to reduce accidents when biological and ecological factors are taken into account in the design of the measures.

Certain road construction measures, including the construction of tracks for walking and cycling and new arterial roads in towns and cities do not appear to reduce the number of injury accidents. A possible explanation for this may be that the measures result in more traffic. These measures reduce the accident rate, but in certain cases, the reduction is totally or partially offset by an increase in the number of vehicle kilometres.

In some cases, there are indications that measures that have reduced the number of accidents at places where they have been implemented have led to an increased number of accidents elsewhere. This type of accident displacement from treated spots to other nearby locations is called accident migration. Tendencies towards accident migration have been found for game accident measures that lead to a reduction of game crossing at some road sections but to increased game crossings at other road sections (e.g. at the ends of fenced road sections). Tendencies towards accident migration have also been found for black spot treatment. Explanations are not very well known. In addition, there are so few studies that have found this type of tendency that it cannot be ascertained how widespread accident migration is in general.

**Main points of the effects of the measures on mobility**

Mobility is here taken to mean the quality of traffic flow in terms of the average speed over a given stretch of road, as well as the capacity of roads. Inducing new traffic can also be regarded as an increase of mobility. Table 1.0.2 shows the main points in current knowledge of the effect of the measures on mobility. New roads can lead to

*Table 1.0.2: Effects of road design and road equipment on mobility*

| | Aspect of mobility | |
|---|---|---|
| Measure | Amount of traffic | Speed level |
| 1.1 Cycle lanes and tracks | Increase | Unknown |
| 1.2 Motorways | Increase | Increase |
| 1.3 Bypasses | Increase | Increase |
| 1.4 Urban arterial roads | Increase | Increase |
| 1.5 Channelisation of junctions | None | Increase |
| 1.6 Roundabouts | None | Increase |
| 1.7 Redesigning junctions | None | Unknown |
| 1.8 Staggered junctions | Unknown | Unknown |
| 1.9 Grade-separated junctions | Unknown | Increase |
| 1.10 Black spot treatment | Unknown | Unknown |
| 1.11 Cross-section improvements | Unknown/increase | Increase |
| 1.12 Roadside safety treatment | Unknown | Unknown |
| 1.13 Improving road alignment and sight distance | Unknown | Increase |
| 1.14 Reconstruction and rehabilitation of roads | Unknown | Increase |
| 1.15 Guard rails and crash cushions | None | None |
| 1.16 Game accident measures | None | None/decrease |
| 1.17 Horizontal curve treatments | None | Increase |
| 1.18 Road lighting | None | Increase |
| 1.19 Improving tunnel safety | None | Unknown |
| 1.20 Roadside rest and service areas | Unknown | Unknown |

induced traffic. For cycle lanes and tracks and tracks for walking and cycling, this means more walking and cycling, and for other new roads, more car traffic. However, the effects can vary substantially and are often modest, for example, for bypasses around smaller towns. Many measures have probably little or no effect on traffic volume. For a number of measures, the effect is unknown.

Most measures lead to increased speed, while only one measure leads to a reduction in speed, namely roundabouts. Nevertheless, the total passing time at a roundabout is, in many cases, less than, for example, at a signalised junction, since the waiting time is shorter and fewer vehicles have to come to a complete halt. Some game accident measures aim at reducing speed. Not all measures are however successful in reducing speed.

For some measures, the effect on the speed level is unknown. A number of such measures must, in many cases, be assumed to increase speed. Examples of these are cycle tracks and lanes and roadside safety treatments.

Taken together, it can be concluded that the majority of measures in this area either increase or have a neutral effect on mobility. This is not surprising, since the main aim of extending and improving the road system is to increase mobility and reduce transport costs.

### Main points on the effects of the measures on environmental conditions

Information about the effect of the measures on environmental conditions is relatively poor. For the majority of measures, either no studies are available or the available studies deal only with a few environmental aspects. Nonetheless, it is possible to indicate the likely effects of a number of measures based on general knowledge about the relationships between the amount of traffic and speed levels on the one hand and, for example, noise, exhaust emission and the spread of dust and dirt on the other hand. Table 1.0.3 summarises the main points in current knowledge about the effects of the

*Table 1.0.3: Main elements of the information available about effects on environmental conditions of road design and road equipment*

| Measure | Changes in noise levels and pollution |
|---|---|
| 1.1 Cycle lanes and tracks | Unknown |
| 1.2 Motorways | Unknown |
| 1.3 Bypasses | Decrease |
| 1.4 Urban arterial roads | Decrease |
| 1.5 Channelisation of junctions | Unknown |
| 1.6 Roundabouts | Decrease |
| 1.7 Redesigning junctions | Unknown |
| 1.8 Staggered junctions | Unknown |
| 1.9 Grade-separated junctions | Decrease |
| 1.10 Black spot treatment | Unknown |
| 1.11 Cross-section improvements | Unknown |
| 1.12 Roadside safety treatment | Unknown |
| 1.13 Improving road alignment and sight distance | Unknown |
| 1.14 Reconstruction and rehabilitation of roads | Unknown |
| 1.15 Guard rails and crash cushions | None |
| 1.16 Game accident measures | None |
| 1.17 Horizontal curve treatments | None |
| 1.18 Road lighting | Increase |
| 1.19 Improving tunnel safety | Unknown |
| 1.20 Roadside rest and service areas | Unknown |

measures on environmental conditions. The table refers to local environmental conditions, rather than regional or global conditions. Table 1.0.3 shows that the effects on noise and pollution are unknown for the majority of measures. Constructing new roads can reduce noise and pollution near the old road, since the old road is relieved of traffic. New roads are normally built further away from dwellings than existing roads.

All measures that affect mobility also are likely to affect noise and pollution. Increased traffic volumes will, all else being equal, increase noise and pollution. Increased speed may increase noise and pollution. However, when speed variations are reduced, noise and pollution may decrease. An example are roundabouts where fewer vehicles have to stop, or curve improvements that reduce the amount of braking and accelerating between curves or between curves and straight sections.

Some of the game accident measures have environmental impacts other than noise and pollution. Measures that aim at preventing game from crossing roads impair seasonal movements of game. Other measures affect both forestry and wood ecology.

### Main elements in the costs of the measures

Table 1.0.4 summarises the main points in the unit costs of the measures. Unit costs refer to the costs per kilometre of road where a measure is implemented, per junction or per curve. The cost figures in Table 1.0.4 are average costs. The costs at individual sites can deviate significantly from the average. The unit costs of the measures vary considerably. Table 1.0.4 shows only the investment costs for the measures described. Some measures also entail operating and maintenance costs, for example guard rails and road lighting.

It is emphasised that the cost figures are uncertain for a number of measures. This is particularly true with regard to grade-separated junctions, roadside safety treatment and building roads through tunnels. No cost estimates are available for cross-section improvements and improvements of road alignment and sight conditions. These types of improvements can be achieved by numerous different measures and the depend, among other things, on the specific measure, the road type and standard and traffic volume.

### Main points in the cost–benefit analyses

Cost–benefit analyses of the measures have been carried out to varying degrees. Where cost–benefit analyses are lacking, numerical examples have been worked out to indicate

*Table 1.0.4: Main elements in the cost figures for road design and road equipment*

| Measure | Unit | Average cost (million NOK) | Costs from year |
|---|---|---|---|
| 1.1 Cycle lanes and tracks | Kilometre road | 3–7.8 | 2005[1,2] |
| 1.2 Motorway – class A | Kilometre road | 75.0 | 1995 |
| 1.2 Motorways – class B | Kilometre road | 22.5 | 1995 |
| 1.3 Bypasses | Kilometre road | 20.0 | 1995 |
| 1.4 Arterial roads in and around cities | Kilometre road | 60.0 | 1995 |
| 1.5 Channelisation of junctions – left turn lane main road | Junction | 0.5–0.8 | 2005[2] |
| 1.5 Channelisation of junctions-side road channelisation | Junction | 0.2–0.4 | 2005[2] |
| 1.5 Channelisation of junction-full channelisation | Junction | 1.2–1.8 | 2005[2] |
| 1.6 Roundabouts (T-junction) | Junction | 2–4.8 | 2005[1,2] |
| 1.6 Roundabouts (X-junction) | Junction | 4.0–6.0 | 2005[1,2] |
| 1.7 Redesigning junction geometrics | Junction | 6.0 | 1995 |
| 1.8 Staggered junctions | Junction | 6.0 | 1995 |
| 1.9 Grade-separated junctions | Junction | 40.0 | 1995 |
| 1.10 Black spot treatment (average) | Location | 0.2 | 2009 |
| 1.11 Cross-section improvements | Kilometre road | – | – |
| 1.12 Roadside safety treatment | Kilometre road | 0.36 | 2005[1] |
| 1.13 Improving road alignment and sight conditions | Kilometre road | – | – |
| 1.14 General rehabilitation and reconstruction of road | Kilometre road | 4.0 | 1995 |
| 1.15 New safety guard rails (AADT 1,500–50,000) | Kilometre road | 0.6–0.8 | 2005[1] |
| 1.16 Game accident measures – at-grade crossing | Location | 0.1 | 2008 |
| 1.16 Game accident measures – wood clearance (first-time) | Kilometre road | 0.04 | 1995 |
| 1.16 Game accident measures – wood clearance (annually) | Kilometre road | 0.004 | 1995 |
| 1.17 Marking signs in horizontal curves | Curve | 0.035 | 2005[2] |
| 1.18 New road lighting (AADT 3,000–50,000) | Kilometre road | 0.4–1.3 | 2005[1,2] |
| 1.18 Improving road lighting | Kilometre road | 0.3 | 2007 |
| 1.19 Building road tunnels (four lanes, two tubes) | Kilometre road | 130–190 | 1995 |
| 1.20 Roadside rest and service areas | Location | 0.5 | 1995 |

[1]Erke and Elvik (2006).
[2]Statens vegvesen, Handbook 015 (2005; utkast 11 aug.).

the typical benefit–cost ratio if available data are good enough. Table 1.0.5 sums up the results of the cost–benefit evaluations of the measures. The benefit–cost ratios vary substantially between the measures.

Measures that have been found to be cost-effective are bypasses, urban arterial roads, channelisation of junctions, roundabouts, grade-separated junctions, guardrails, curve improvements (background and directional marking), road lighting and building new

*Table 1.0.5: Cost–benefit evaluations of measures affecting road layout and road equipment*

| Measure | Benefit–cost ratio |
|---|---|
| 1.1 Cycle lanes | 10 |
| 1.2 New motorway – class A (sparsely populated area) | 0.15 |
| 1.2 New motorway – class B (sparsely populated area) | 0.35 |
| 1.3 Bypasses (densely populated areas) | 1.1 |
| 1.4 New urban arterial road | 1.3 |
| 1.4 Expansion of main road in city from two to four lanes | 2.3 |
| 1.5 Left turn lane at crossroads | 3.4 |
| 1.5 Full channelisation of crossroads | 3.4 |
| 1.5 Left turn lane at T-junction | 1.6 |
| 1.6 Roundabouts at crossroads | 2.2 |
| 1.6 Roundabouts at T-junctions | 1.8 |
| 1.7 Redesigning junction geometric | – |
| 1.8 Staggered junctions | 0.2–2.1 |
| 1.9 Grade-separated junctions | 2.2 |
| 1.10 Black spot treatment | 1.1–5.7 |
| 1.11 Cross section improvement | – |
| 1.13 Improvements of the alignment and sight distance | – |
| 1.14 General rehabilitation and reconstruction of roads | 0.5 |
| 1.15 New guard rails | 2.00 |
| 1.15 Repairing old guard rails | 2.00 |
| 1.16 Game accident measures | >1.00 |
| 1.16 Game accident measures – woodlance clearance annually | 5.60 |
| 1.17 Background and directional markings on curves | >1.00 |
| 1.18 New road lighting on motorways | 0.21 |
| 1.18 New road lighting on rural roads (AADT < 12,500) | 0.27–0.95 |
| 1.18 New road lighting on rural roads (AADT > 12,500) | 1.36–4.01 |
| 1.18 New road lighting in towns | <1 |
| 1.19 Urban arterial road in tunnel | 1.10 |
| 1.19 Rural road in tunnel | 0.20 |
| 1.20 Roadside rest and service areas | – |

arterial roads in tunnels. The cost–benefit ratios of these measures are for the most part dependent on the traffic volumes and number and severity of accidents. The cost for the measures also vary and are different, e.g. between different road types and terrains. Cost–benefit ratios are therefore not always directly comparable between two alternative measures. For example, a roundabout requires more space than channelisation of a junction, but is usually associated with larger benefits to a junction's capacity and may have more favourable effects on severe accidents.

For some measures, the benefit–cost ratio is unknown. For all measures in this chapter, both costs and benefits depend highly on traffic volume and the type or design of the measure. Overall cost–benefit ratios must therefore be treated with some caution.

## 1.1 Cycle lanes and tracks

**Problem and objective**

Cyclists run a greater risk of being injured in traffic than car occupants. An estimate based on official accident statistics and the national household travel survey in Norway (Bjørnskau 2008) shows that the accident rate for cyclists is five to six times higher per kilometre travelled than for drivers and passengers in cars. The real accident rate for cyclists is most likely higher. A Norwegian study (Bjørnskau 2005) showed that there are approximately seven to eight bicycle accidents for each bicycle accident that is reported in official accident statistics. When underreporting of bicycle accidents in official accident statistics is taken into account, the accident rate for cyclists is ca. 20 times that of car occupants (car accidents are also underreported, but to a lesser degree than bicycle accidents).

About 80% of all bicycle accidents occur in urban areas. More than 80% of all bicycle accidents that are reported in official accident statistics are collisions with cars, most of them at junctions. Single-vehicle bicycle accidents have a particularly low level of reporting in official accident statistics. The majority of all traffic accidents (over 70%) involving cyclists are single-vehicle accidents where other road users or vehicles are not involved (Bjørnskau 2008).

Many cyclists do not feel safe in traffic, especially when they are travelling in mixed traffic on roads with heavy car traffic (Schioldborg 1979, Hvoslef 1980). According to Bjørnskau (2004), 28% of all cyclists feel unsafe. Only among motorcyclists there is a larger proportion feeling unsafe.

Cycle tracks and lanes are intended to reduce bicycle accident risk. Another objective is to give cyclists increased mobility and feeling of security when travelling in public traffic areas.

## Description of the measure

A distinction is made between the following cycling facilities which represent varying degrees of separation from motor traffic:

- Cycle lanes are a protected space on the carriageway, separated from motor traffic by means of road markings, and often additionally announced by road signs;
- Cycle tracks (or cycle paths) are space that is physically separated from the carriageway, e.g. by kerbstones, lawn or a ditch;
- Tracks for walking and cycling are roads for pedestrians and cycles travelling in both traffic directions, which are physically separated from the carriageway, tracks for walking and cycling are usually constructed on one side of the road only.

At junctions, cycle lanes and cycle tracks can be designed in numerous ways (Sørensen 2009, Statens vegvesen 2003). Some of the most common designs have been investigated empirically and are described in the section 'Effect on Accidents'.

## Effect on accidents

***Cycle lanes.*** The following studies have evaluated the effects on accidents of cycle lanes (Table 1.1.1):

Lott and Lott (1976) (USA)
Welleman and Dijkstra (1985) (Netherlands)
Smith and Walsh (1988) (USA)
Agustsson and Lei (1994) (Denmark)
Jensen (1996) (Denmark)
Nielsen, Andersen and Lei (1996) (Denmark)
Coates (1999) (UK)
Nilsson (2003) (Sweden)
Jensen (2006a) (Denmark)

On roads with cycle lanes there are fewer accidents than on roads without cycle lanes. However, at junctions the total number of accidents is greater on roads with cycle lanes. For bicycle accidents, the reduction of the total number of accidents is smaller than for other road users. Possible explanations are increased numbers of cyclists and increased speed among cyclists. Most of the studies have not controlled for the number of cyclists, i.e. the results refer to changes in the total numbers of accidents after cycle lanes were installed, compared to before the installation.

*Table 1.1.1: Effect on accidents of cycle lanes*

| | | Percentage change in the number of accidents | |
|---|---|---|---|
| Accident severity | Type of accident affected | Best estimate | 95% confidence interval |
| Injury accidents | All accidents | −21 | (−25; −16) |
| Injury accidents | All accidents along the road | −13 | (−19; −6) |
| Injury accidents | All accidents at junctions | +20 | (+6; +35) |
| Injury accidents | All accidents at signalised junctions | +14 | (−7; +38) |
| Injury accidents | Cycle accidents | −9 | (−17; 0) |
| Injury accidents | Cycle accidents along the road | −19 | (−36; +3) |
| Injury accidents | Cycle accidents at junctions | −25 | (−35; −13) |
| Injury accidents | Cycle accidents at signalised junctions | −9 | (−29; +16) |
| Injury accidents | Pedestrian accidents | −30 | (−42; −16) |
| Injury accidents | Motor vehicle accidents | −37 | (−42; −31) |
| Injury accidents | Motor vehicle accidents along the road | −24 | (−31; −15) |
| Injury accidents | Motor vehicle accidents at junctions | −51 | (−57; −44) |

*Table 1.1.2: Effect on accidents of cycle tracks*

| | | Percentage change in the number of accidents | |
|---|---|---|---|
| Accident severity | Type of accident affected | Best estimate | 95% confidence interval |
| Injury accidents | All accidents | −2 | (−5; +1) |
| Injury accidents | All accidents along the road | −8 | (−13; −3) |
| Injury accidents | All accidents at junctions | +4 | (−2; +10) |
| Injury accidents | Cycle accidents | +7 | (−3; +18) |
| Injury accidents | Cycle accidents along the road | −11 | (−18; −3) |
| Injury accidents | Cycle accidents at junctions | +24 | (+11; +38) |
| Injury accidents | Pedestrian accidents | −3 | (−11; +4) |
| Injury accidents | Motor vehicle accidents | −7 | (−12; −1) |

***Cycle tracks.*** The following studies have evaluated the effects on accidents of cycle tracks (Table 1.1.2):

Jørgensen and Rabani (1969) (Denmark)
Jørgensen and Herrstedt (1979) (Denmark)
Knoche (1981) (Germany)
Bach, Rosbach and Jørgensen (1985) (Denmark)

Welleman and Dijkstra (1985) (Netherlands)
Nettelblad (1987) (Sweden)
COWI-consult and Vejdirektoratet (1990) (Denmark)
Harland and Gercans (1993) (UK)
Agustsson and Lei (1994) (Denmark)
Rystam (1995) (Sweden)
Leden et al. (1997) (Sweden)
Jensen (2006a) (Denmark)
Agerholm, Caspersen, Madsen and Lahrmann (2008) (Denmark)

Cycle tracks only lead to small changes in the total number of accidents. However, most of the studies have not controlled for the number of cyclists, i.e. the results refer to changes in the total numbers of accidents after cycle tracks were installed, compared to before the installation.

Along stretches of road, a significant decrease of accident numbers was found, while accidents at junctions increase. Cycle tracks aim at making cycling safer and more attractive. However, cycle tracks do not seem to improve safety for cyclists. For the total number of cycle accidents, a non-significant increase was found and the number of cycle accidents at junctions increases significantly. It seems thus that cycle accidents are transferred from along the road to junctions.

A possible explanation for the accident increase at junctions is that the physical separation of cyclist and motor traffic makes cyclists and drivers pay less attention to each other. At the same time, cyclists may be tempted to overestimate their own safety. Lack of attention is a problem at junctions where cyclists and drivers have to interact (Statens vegvesen 2003, Jensen 2006a, Agerholm, Caspersen, Madsen and Lahrmann 2008).

***Tracks for walking and cycling***. The following studies have evaluated the effects on accidents of cycle tracks (Table 1.1.3):

Quenault (1981) (UK)
Ørnes (1981) (Norway)
Kallberg and Salusjärvi (1982) (Nordic countries)
Claesson and Sjölinder (1985) (Sweden)
Wheeler and Morgan (1987) (UK)
Frøysadal (1988) (Norway)
Stølan (1988) (Norway)
Blakstad and Giæver (1989) (Norway)

*Table 1.1.3: Effect on accidents of tracks for walking and cycling*

| | | Percentage change in the number of accidents | |
|---|---|---|---|
| Accident severity | Type of accident affected | Best estimate | 95% confidence interval |
| Injury accidents | All accidents | 0 | (−10; +11) |
| Injury accidents | Cycle accidents | +1 | (−29; +45) |
| Injury accidents | Cycle accidents along the road | +2 | (−42; +78) |
| Injury accidents | Cycle accidents at junctions | +1 | (−37; +62) |
| Injury accidents | Pedestrian accidents | −10 | (−32; +21) |
| Injury accidents | Pedestrian accidents along the road | −35 | (−67; +29) |
| Injury accidents | Pedestrian accidents at junctions | +1 | (−32; +52) |
| Injury accidents | Motor vehicle accidents | +1 | (−10; +14) |

Leden (1989) (Nordic countries)
Elvik (1990) (Norway)
Dietrichs (1991) (Norway)
Thingwall (1991) (Norway)
Borger and Frøysadal (1993) (Norway)
Downing, Sayer and Zaheer-Ul-Islam (1993) (Papua New Guinea)
Borger and Frøysadal (1994) (Norway)
Jensen (2006b) (Denmark)

The total number of accidents, as well as the number of cycle accidents, seems to be unaffected. For pedestrian accidents, a non-significant reduction was found along the road. The studies have not controlled for the number of cyclists, i.e. the results refer to changes in the total numbers of accidents after tracks for walking and cycling were installed compared with those before the installation.

A number of studies found that building tracks for walking and cycling increases pedestrian and cyclist traffic (Nettelblad 1987, Wheeler and Morgan 1987, Gabestad 1989). This will also increase the numbers of pedestrians and cyclists at junctions and crossing facilities. Moreover, not all pedestrians and cyclists use the tracks for walking and cycling (Strugstad 1985, Thingwall 1991). Those who continue walking/cycling on the road may have increased accident risk. In some cases the speed limit was increased (e.g. from 60 to 70 km/h) at the same time as tracks for walking and cycling were built, which is likely to increase speed and thereby accident rates for motor vehicles.

When tracks for walking and cycling increase the number of pedestrians and cyclists, the accident rates for these user groups is most likely to decrease, even if the number of accidents increases, i.e. more pedestrians and cyclists make walking/cycling safer for each pedestrian or cyclist.

***Design at junctions.*** The following studies have investigated the effects on accidents of different designs of cycle facilities at junctions (Table 1.1.4):

Nielsen (1993) (Denmark): Advanced stop line
Wheeler, Leicester and Underwood (1993) (UK): Advanced stop line
Nielsen (1994) (Denmark): Advanced stop line
Gårder, Leden and Pulkkinen (1998) (Sweden): Continuing cycle path
Coates (1999) (UK): Coloured cycle lane
Jensen and Nielsen (1999) (Denmark): Advanced stop line, interrupted cycle path, harlequin pattern
Pfeifer (1999) (Denmark): Interrupted cycle path
Jensen (2002) (Denmark): Advanced stop line
Jensen (2006c) (Denmark): Coloured cycle lane in junctions, continuing cycle path
König (2006) (Sweden): Coloured cycle lane in junctions

*Table 1.1.4: Effects on accidents of the design of cycle lanes and paths at junctions*

| | Percentage change in the number of injury accidents | | |
|---|---|---|---|
| Measure | Type of accident affected | Best estimate | 95% confidence interval |
| Interrupted cycle path | Cycle accidents | −31 | (−45; −12) |
| Continuing cycle path | Cycle accidents | −13 | (−36; +16) |
| | Pedestrian accidents | −54 | (−77; −6) |
| | Motor vehicle accidents | 11 | (−14; +43) |
| Advanced stop line at signalised junctions | All accidents | −16 | (−39; +16) |
| | Cycle accidents | −19 | (−47; +23) |
| | Motor vehicle accidents | −11 | (−46; +49) |
| Coloured cycle lane | All accidents | −2 | (−15; +22) |
| | Cycle accidents | −22 | (−33; −8) |
| | Pedestrian accidents | +23 | (−14; +77) |
| | Motor vehicle accidents | +14 | (0; +30) |
| Coloured cycle lane in one arm of the junction | All accidents (all severities) | −10 | (−20; +1) |
| Coloured cycle lane in two arms of the junction | All accidents (all severities) | +23 | (0; +51) |
| Coloured cycle lane in four arms of the junction | All accidents (all severities) | +60 | (+15; +122) |
| Other road markings for cyclists in yield junctions | Cycle accidents | −6 | (−31; +29) |
| Harlequin pattern | Cycle accidents | −16 | (−61; +80) |
| Cycle symbol | Cycle accidents | −5 | (−33; +34) |

Berggrein and Bach (2007) (Denmark): Harlequin pattern and cycle symbols
Jensen (2008) (Denmark): Coloured cycle lane in junctions

***Interrupted cycle path.*** The cycle path ends immediately before the junction. In the junction, there is either a marked cycle lane or no separate cycle facility. This measure was found to significantly reduce the number of cycle accidents. A likely explanation is that cyclists and drivers pay more attention to each other in mixed traffic, and that cyclists are feeling more unsafe (Pfeifer 1999, Agerholm, Caspersen, Madsen and Lahrmann 2008). Interrupted cycle paths are a recommended measure in many countries (Denmark, Sweden, Netherlands, Belgium, Germany, UK, USA, Canada, and Australia; Sørensen 2009).

***Continuing cycle path.*** The cycle path continues in yield junctions. A non-significant reduction of cycle accidents was found for this measure. Pedestrian accidents were found to be reduced as well, probably because the pavement usually continues in junctions. According to a Danish study, the accident rate for cyclists is 26% lower at junctions with a continuing cycle paths than at junctions with an interrupted cycle path, and the number of killed or seriously injured cyclists is higher at junction with a continuing cycle path.

***Advanced stop line at signalised junctions.*** Advanced stop line arrangements comprise a stop line for motor vehicles, an additional stop line for cyclists nearer the signal heads and a leading lane that allows cyclists to pass the first stop line. In front of the stop line for motor vehicles, there is in some cases a reservoir for waiting cyclists to occupy. The results in Table 1.1.4 refer to advanced stop lines without such a reservoir. The aim is to make cyclists more visible to drivers and to prevent vehicles turning right from colliding with cyclists cycling straight ahead. Advanced stop lines were found to reduce accident numbers, although the effects are not significant. A study conducted by Hunter (2000a) showed that cyclists who used the advanced stop line correctly were not involved in conflicts with motor vehicles. However, only 22% of all cyclists used the advanced stop line, for the most part because cars stopped at the cyclist stop line, not at the stop line intended for motor vehicles. About 50% of all cars did so. A Danish study found similar results (Andersson and Lund 2009). A possible explanation is that drivers do not want to have cyclists in front of them (Newman 2002). Advanced stop lines (with or without reservoir) are recommended in a number of countries (Norway, Denmark, Germany, Sweden, UK, Australia, Netherlands, Belgium, Germany, Canada, USA; Sørensen 2009).

***Coloured cycle lane.*** In the junction a cycle lane is marked, which is painted for the whole width of the cycle lane (e.g. in blue, green or red), and additionally marked with cycle symbols. A significant reduction of cycle accidents was found at junctions with coloured cycle lanes. Coloured cycle lanes are recommended in many countries, especially in complex junctions (Sørensen 2009). However, results from a Danish study (Jensen 2008) indicate that coloured cycle lanes are most favourable in non-complex junctions and may have detrimental effects in complex junctions.

***Other types of road markings for cyclists in yield junctions***. Other types of road markings were found to reduce the number of cycle accidents. The results are however not significant.

***Bent-out cycle track crossing.*** On a bent-out crossing, the cycle track approaches are deflected away from the main carriageway to create a gap of one or two car lengths between the main road and the crossing. The aim of this measure is to give drivers turning into the side road extra time to notice crossing cyclists, and to allow vehicles waiting to exit the side road to do so without blocking the crossing point. Only one evaluation study was found (Andersen, Nielsen and Olesen 2004). This study is based on too few accidents to draw any conclusions about the safety effects of this measure.

***Bent-in cycle track crossing.*** In contrast to a bent-out cycle track crossing, the cycle track approaches are deflected towards the main carriageway. The aim is to make cyclists more visible to drivers. No evaluations of the effects on accidents have been found.

***Exclusive cycle lanes to the left of exclusive right turn lanes.*** This measure is recommended i a number of countries (e.g. Denmark, Netherlands, Germany, UK, USA, Australia; Sørensen 2009) and has been used over many years, e.g. in Denmark. But the safety effects have only been evaluated indirectly and in small studies (Sørensen 2008). None of the studies has reached clear conclusions as to whether or not accidents or conflicts between cyclists and motor vehicles are reduced (Nielsen 1995, Ryley 1996, Hunter 2000b, City of Portland 1999, Hunter, Harkey, Stewart and Birk 2000).

## Effect on mobility

The average driving speeds for cars may be reduced when cycle lanes and cycle paths reduce the width of the driving lanes (Sakshaug 1986, Gabestad 1989). Bolling (2000) found 2–4 km/h lower speed on roads with cycle paths than on other roads. Fowler (2005) found speed reductions on roads with cycle lanes of between 1.5 km/h outside rush hour and 0.9 km/h in rush hour. According to Wittink (2001), average speed is normally reduced by ca. 5% on roads with cycle lanes. In Norway, the speed limit was increased from 60 to 70 km/h on a number of stretches of road after tracks for walking and cycling were constructed (Elvik 1990). This may increase speed. A Swedish study found no speed reductions on roads where cycle lanes were installed, and not difference in the speed at which vehicles passed cyclists (Nilsson 2001).

Cycle lanes and tracks may improve mobility for cyclists. As mentioned above, it was found that the amount of walking and cycling increases. This represents an improvement in mobility for pedestrians and cyclists. Cycle tracks may also improve mobility for cyclists when they are built so as to minimise the travel distance for cyclists. Cycle paths were found to increase average speed among cyclists (Nilsson 2000).

At junctions, advanced stop lines were found to improve mobility for cyclists (Sørensen 2009). Motor vehicles however may be slowed down by cyclists, and many drivers do therefore not stop at their stop line, but drive partly or wholly into the area that is reserved for cyclists (Hunter 2000a, Andersson and Lund 2009, Newman 2002). Cycle paths that are interrupted, bent-in or bent-out are most likely to reduce speed for cyclists (Sørensen 2009). Interrupted cycle paths may lead to vehicles blocking the way for cyclists. This problem may be reduced by a marked cycle lane in the junction. Bent-in cycle paths force cyclists to slow down and eventually to stop.

Exclusive cycle lanes to the left of exclusive right turn lanes have most likely only limited effects for cyclists' mobility (Sørensen 2009).

**Effect on the environment**

Cycle lanes and tracks, together with other measures, may in the long run increase the number of cyclists. Jensen (2006a) found that cycle tracks increase cycle traffic by around 18–20%, while cycle lanes increase cycle traffic by around 5–7%. Motorized traffic decreased by 9–10% after the installation of cycle tracks and remained unchanged after the installation of cycle lanes. An increase of cycle traffic, at the cost of reduced motorized traffic, has favourable effects on the environment (energy consumption, climate, noise, emissions, health).

The construction of cycle paths increases the space needed for road construction.

The subjective feeling of safety usually increases among cyclists when cycle traffic is physically separated from motorized traffic. Cycle lanes also increase the subjective feeling of safety but to a lesser degree than cycle tracks (Backer-Grøndahl, Amundsen, Fyhri and Ulleberg 2007, Jensen 2006b, 2006d, Nilsson 2003, Statens vegvesen 2003, Vejdirektoratet 2000). In junctions, measures that separate cycle and motorised traffic also are likely to increase the subjective feeling of safety, i.e. coloured cycle lane and bent-out cycle path. Measures that contribute to an increased mix of cycle and motorized traffic on the other hand are likely to make cyclists feel more unsafe, i.e. interrupted cycle track, bent-in cycle path and exclusive cycle lanes to the left of exclusive right turn lanes. Advanced stop line for cyclists may increase the feeling of safety for cyclists because they become more visible. On the other hand, cyclists may also feel pressured from vehicles waiting behind them (Sørensen 2009).

### Costs

Typical costs of cycle lanes and tracks in Norway are ca. NOK 1 million per kilometre for cycle lanes, and ca. NOK 8 million for cycle tracks and for tracks for walking and cycling (2009 prices; Statens vegvesen 2007a, 2007b, Sælensminde 2002, Vejdirektoratet 2000). The costs for establishing a separate network for cyclists will depend on the size and the standard of the network, and on the degree to which existing road infrastructure can be used.

In addition, an annual maintenance cost of around NOK 38,000 per kilometre road for cycle tracks and tracks for walking and cycling should be included. The maintenance costs for cycle lanes are lower. The costs vary depending on local conditions and the maintenance standard (Amundsen and Kolbenstvedt 2009).

### Cost–benefit analysis

According to a Norwegian study, the socioeconomic benefit of establishing a coherent network of routes for pedestrians and cyclists is at least four to five times the costs (Sælensminde 2002). This analysis includes investment and maintenance costs, and benefits in the form of health effects, reduced accidents, travel times and feeling unsafe. Additionally, reduced external costs of motorised traffic are included in the analysis.

The cost–benefit ratio of marking cycle lanes on existing roads has been estimated to be around 10, and the benefit–cost ratio of advanced stop lines for cyclists has been estimated to be around 13 (Elvik 1999).

## 1.2 Motorways

### Problem and objective

Many older main roads were built to carry far less traffic than the traffic carried by them at the present time. This leads to a mixture of local traffic and long-distance traffic, poor traffic flow and numerous accidents. Demands for shorter journey times, lower transport costs and fewer accidents generates a demand for roads that can carry large amounts of traffic at high speed without traffic safety becoming any worse than on roads with lower speed levels.

Motorways are designed to carry heavy traffic at high speed with the lowest possible number of accidents. Motorways are designed to collect long-distance traffic from other roads, so that conflicts between long-distance traffic and local traffic are avoided.

## Description of the measure

There are different definitions of motorways in different countries, but for the most part, motorways are roads for automobile traffic only, which have a median barrier and no at-grade junctions. Most motorways have more than one lane per direction. The speed limit is often 90, 100 or 110 km/h, and sometimes (e.g. in Germany) there is no speed limit. The road standard is generally high, motorways have wide lanes, wide shoulders, are often equipped with road lighting and have a high maintenance standard.

## Effect on accidents

***Accident rate on motorways compared with other types of road.*** Motorways have much lower accident rates than other roads. Accident rate is expressed in terms of the number of injury accidents reported to the police per million vehicle kilometre. Table 1.2.1 shows accident rates for national highways in Norway for different time periods (Muskaug 1981, 1985, Elvik 1991, Erke and Elvik 2006). Motorway A are motorways

*Table 1.2.1: Accident rates on national highways in Norway*

| | Injury accidents reported to the police per million vehicle kilometres | | | | |
|---|---|---|---|---|---|
| Road type | 1971–75* | 1977–80* | 1986–89 | 1991–94 | 2005 |
| Motorway A | 0.06 | 0.08 | 0.08 | 0.07 | 0.07 |
| Motorway B | 0.09 | 0.11 | 0.15 | 0.10 | 0.11 |
| Roads in rural areas | 0.33 | 0.30 | 0.25 | 0.17 | 0.14 |
| Roads in urban areas | 0.59 | 0.57 | 0.36 | 0.38 | 0.37 |

*Between 1971 and 1975, accident reporting in Norway was lower than for the period after 1977 (Fridstrøm and Bjørnskau 1989). The accident rates for these two periods are, therefore, not entirely comparable.

as described above, while motorway B are two-lane roads without median barrier with a speed limit of 90 km/h on most roads.

Type A motorways have an accident rate that is 70–90% lower than the accident rate for standard country roads and roads in cities and towns. Type B motorways have an accident rate that is 40–80% lower than on other roads. Recent figures from Sweden (Thulin 1991), Denmark (Vejdatalaboratoriet 1991), Finland (Leden 1993), Great Britain (UK Department of Transport 1991), Germany (Marburger, Klöckner and Stöckner 1989), The Netherlands (Koornstra 1993) and USA (US Department of Transportation 1992) show a corresponding pattern for all these countries. Motorways are the safest roads, especially when compared to roads in towns and cities.

***Before-and-after studies of new motorways.*** When a new motorway is constructed, the reduction in the number of accidents is not normally as large as the difference in accident rates between motorways and other roads might lead one to expect. First, not all traffic transfers from existing roads to the motorway. And second, motorways often generates new traffic, especially where there are capacity problems on existing roads.

Before-and-after studies of motorways built in Norway (Holt 1993) Sweden (Statens Vägverk 1983a), Denmark (Jørgensen 1991a) Great Britain (Newby and Johnson 1964, Leeming 1969) and USA (Olsson 1970, Cirillo 1992) have found an average decrease in the number of injury accidents of around 7% (95% CI [−4; −9]). The same studies did not find any statistically significant changes in the number of property-damage-only accidents.

The size of the effect on accidents of building motorways depends to some extent on how existing traffic is distributed between the motorway and the old road network, and on how large the induced traffic is. The average increase in vehicle km of travel on the affected road network for the motorways for which information is available in Norway (Holt 1993), Sweden (Statens Vägverk 1983a), Denmark (Jørgensen 1991a) and USA (Cirillo 1992) was around 35%. The increases varied from 2% to 95%. Decreases were not found in any of these cases. The 'affected road network' includes the old road or roads which the motorway has relieved of traffic, and the motorway, taken together.

***Effect of equipment and traffic control on motorways.*** The effect on road safety of the layout and equipment on motorways has been evaluated in the following studies, which are summarised in Table 1.2.2:

Coleman and Sacks (1967) (USA): anti-dazzle screens in central reservations
Walker and Chapman (1980) (Great Britain): anti-dazzle screens in central reservations
Cooper, Sawyer and Rutley (1992) (Great Britain): automatic queue warnings

*Table 1.2.2: Effect on accidents of a number of measures on motorways*

| | | Percentage change in the number of accidents | |
|---|---|---|---|
| Accident severity | Type of accident affected | Best estimate | 95% confidence interval |
| ***Increasing from two to three traffic lanes on class B motorways*** | | | |
| Injury accidents | All accidents | +3 | (−22; +35) |
| ***Automatic queue warnings with variable signs*** | | | |
| Injury accidents | All accidents | −14 | (−22; −8) |
| Property damage only accidents | All accidents | +16 | (+1; +34) |
| Injury accidents | Accidents involving rear-end collisions | −22 | (−29;−13) |
| Property damage only accidents | Accident involving rear-end collisions | +65 | (+28;+112) |
| ***Anti-dazzle screens in central reservations on motorways*** | | | |
| Injury accidents | Accidents in darkness | −11 | (−45; +45) |
| Property damage only accidents | Accidents in darkness | +6 | (−25; +51) |

Vaa et al. (1994) (Norway): three lanes on class B motorways
Persaud, Mucsi and Ugge (1996) (Canada): automatic queue warnings

Class B motorways with three traffic lanes have, in practice, the same accident rates as otherwise identical class B motorways with two lanes. Automatic queue warnings appear to reduce the number of injury accidents, but are associated with an increase in the number of property-damage-only accidents (see also Section 3.29).

Anti-dazzle screens in central reservations of motorways make it possible to drive with full beam headlights without causing glare for oncoming traffic. There is a tendency for anti-dazzle screens to reduce the number of injury accidents in darkness.

### Effects on mobility

Motorways improve mobility for motor vehicles. Speed is higher and motorways have a higher capacity than other roads.

### Effect on the environment

Motorways often entail a major intrusion into the landscape. High geometric design standards mean that motorways, to a greater extent than other roads, must be built on embankments, in cuttings or using tunnels and bridges. Heavy traffic and a high speed on motorways lead to noise. Noise barriers for buildings near motorways are often necessary at a greater distance from the road than is the case for other roads. Motorways are a barrier for local traffic, especially for pedestrians and cyclists, who do not have access to motorways. They also hinder the movements of wildlife. High speed levels on motorways lead to increased fuel consumption and increased pollution.

**Costs**

The cost of building motorways varies from place to place. On the basis of recent Norwegian experiences (Elvik 1996), the average cost of building a class A motorway can be estimated to around NOK 75 million per kilometre ($\pm$20 million kroner). The average cost of building a class B motorway is estimated to around NOK 22.5 million per kilometre ($\pm$1.5 million kroner). Annual maintenance costs are estimated at around NOK 350,000 per kilometre road per year for Class A motorways and NOK 175,000 per kilometre road per year for Class B motorways.

**Cost–benefit analysis**

Cost–benefit analyses of new motorways are carried out by the Norwegian Public Roads Administration as part of the planning process for new motorways. Costs and benefits vary from case to case. An example is given to show the significance of different factors in a cost–benefit evaluation.

For class A motorways, it is assumed that the old road had an annual average daily traffic of either 20,000 or 15,000, 0.17 injury accidents per million vehicle kilometres and a speed level of 70 km/h. It is assumed that a motorway takes 75% of the traffic from the old road and that the speed level on the motorway is 90 km/h. Vehicle operating costs are assumed to increase by NOK 0.10 per kilometre. The environmental costs are assumed to increase by NOK 0.02 per kilometre as a result of increased $CO_2$ emission due to increases in speed. Corresponding assumptions are made for class B motorways, except that the annual average daily traffic on the old road is assumed to be either 15,000 or 7,500.

Under these conditions, the benefit–cost ratio of building a motorway of class A is calculated to be 0.17 with an annual average daily traffic of 20,000 and 0.13 with an annual average daily traffic of 15,000. The benefit–cost ratio of building a class B motorway is calculated to be 0.43 with an annual average daily traffic of 15,000 and 0.22 with an annual average daily traffic of 7,500. The biggest contributor to the benefit is travel time savings. The increase in vehicle operating costs and environmental costs reduces the benefit. However, even if it is assumed that an increase in these costs can be avoided, the benefits of motorways remain smaller than the costs.

## 1.3 Bypasses

### Problem and objective

The accident rate in towns and cities is usually higher than in rural areas. In the central business district of towns, pedestrians, cyclists and motor vehicles are often mixed on the same street. There are many junctions and other points where pedestrians cross the road. A high traffic volume inside towns causes environmental problems in addition to increasing the risk of accidents. Roads in urban areas have an accident rate which is 2–10 times higher than roads in rural areas (Elvik and Muskaug 1994). The accident rate is particularly high on arterial roads and access roads.

Bypasses are designed to carry long-distance traffic outside towns and cities, so that conflicts between local traffic and long-distance traffic are avoided. The construction of bypasses makes it easier to introduce traffic-calming measures on the main road through a town than when this road serves through traffic.

### Description of the measure

Bypass roads are normally built without access roads and designed for a speed limit of least 80 km/h. Connections to existing roads are made using junctions or interchanges of a high standard. Where bypasses border on existing built up areas, roundabouts are sometimes used to establish links to the local road network.

### Effect on accidents

The following studies have evaluated the effects of bypasses on the number of accidents:

Newland and Newby (1962) (Great Britain)
Stølen (1969) (Norway)
Brandsæter (1973) (Norway)
Haakenaasen (1980) (Norway)
Statens Vägverk (1983a) (Sweden)
Weissbrodt (1984) (Germany)

Furuseth (1987) (Norway)
Nilsson (1994) (Sweden)
Amundsen and Hofset (2000) (Norway)
Andersson, La Cour Lund and Greibe (2001) (Denmark)

The results of these studies have been summarised in a meta-analysis reported by Elvik, Amundsen and Hofset (2001). Table 1.3.1 present estimates of the effect of bypasses on accidents, based on this meta-analysis.

On average, a decrease in the number of injury accidents of around 25% has been found following the construction of bypasses. The number of property-damage-only accidents is reduced by 27%. These figures include accidents both on the old road network and on the bypass. The effect of bypasses on the number of accidents varies from place to place, depending on the following factors:

- The higher the accident rate on the road through the town where the bypass is built, the greater the decrease in the number of accidents usually is.
- The more traffic shifted to the bypass road, the greater the decrease in the number of accidents usually is.
- The more induced traffic, the smaller the reduction in number of accidents.
- If the accident rate is reduced on the old road through the town, for example using speed-reducing measures, greater decrease in the number of accidents can be attained.
- The design of junctions built between the old road and the bypass also influences the accident rate.

A Norwegian study (Amundsen and Hofset 2000) found a 19% reduction of the number of injury accidents. The mean accident rate on the old main road increased from 0.42 injury accidents per million vehicle kilometres before the bypass was built to 0.48 injury accidents per million vehicle kilometres after the bypass was built. The mean accident rate on the bypass roads was 0.17 injury accidents per million vehicle

*Table 1.3.1: Effects of bypasses on accidents*

| | Percentage change in number of accidents | | |
|---|---|---|---|
| Accident severity | Types of accident affected | Best estimate | 95% confidence interval |
| Injury accidents | All accidents | −25 | (−33, −16) |
| Property-damage-only accidents | All accidents | −27 | (−38, −13) |
| Accident severity not stated | All accidents | −21 | (−38, +1) |

kilometres of driving. A possible explanation of an increased accident rate on the old main road is that speeds may increase, since traffic volume no longer hinders the choice of speed to the same extent as before.

The construction of a bypass road does not appear to affect accident severity. According to recent Norwegian (Amundsen and Hofset 2000) and Danish (Andersson, La Cour Lund and Greibe 2001) studies, the severity of accidents remains the same after a bypass roads has been opened to traffic as it was on the old main road.

### Effect on mobility

Bypass roads increase mobility for both long-distance traffic and local traffic. A British study (Mackie and Griffin 1978) found that the average speed in a sample of towns before bypasses were built was between 38 and 44 km/h. The average speed on the bypass was between 78 and 95 km/h. Bypasses can make it easier for pedestrians and cyclists to cross roads in towns, since less traffic reduces waiting times. On the other hand, an increase in speed may make it more difficult to cross the road. A bypass road can be a barrier to local travel.

### Effect on the environment

A distinction should be made between local and regional impacts on the environment (Nielsen 2000). Local impacts on the environment include reduced traffic volume on the old main road, which may in turn reduce traffic noise, vibrations, local air pollution and barriers to local travel. Opportunities for introducing environmental measures in a town may be improved, since the needs of long-distance travel no longer need to be taken into account. Finally, there will be less congestion, which in turn reduces vehicle emissions.

On the other hand, any new road involves intruding the landscape and increasing the area used for transport facilities. In the long run, the provision of increased road capacity may lead to urban sprawl and to a pattern of development inducing more transport.

### Costs

A compilation of recent Norwegian experiences (Elvik 1996) shows that the average cost of building a bypass is around NOK 20 million per kilometre road ($\pm$4 million NOK).

**Cost–benefit analysis**

A numerical example has been worked out, based on data from the most recent Norwegian study of the effects of bypasses (Amundsen and Hofset 2000). Mean AADT for the old road before the bypass was built was 4,525. This reduced to a mean AADT of 1,785 after the bypass road was opened to traffic. Mean AADT on the bypass roads was 4,105. The number of injury accidents was reduced by 19% on the average. Mean length of the bypass roads was 4.3 km. The effects of a bypass road on travel time were estimated by assuming a mean speed, before as well as after, of 50 km/h in the town (the old main road) and 80 km/h on the bypass road. Valuation of travel time, vehicle operating costs and environmental impacts were taken from an analysis of optimal speed limits (Elvik 2002). Total benefits of a typical bypass road in Norway were estimated to NOK 113 million (present value). Costs were estimated to be NOK 110 million. The benefits are marginally greater than the costs, indicating that bypass roads built in Norway in recent years may have conferred a small net benefit to the society.

## 1.4 Urban arterial roads

**Problem and objective**

In many large town and cities, the main road network was designed for less traffic than it carries today. This leads to congestion and dense traffic. If the capacity of the main road network is too small, some of the traffic will be diverted to collector roads and access roads, which are not designed for through traffic. Heavy traffic in residential areas spoils residential environments, making it unsafe and unpleasant to be outside, especially for children and the elderly.

An American study (Zhou and Sisiopiku 1997) investigated the relationship between the degree of capacity utilisation on a road and accident rate. The degree of capacity utilisation is the ratio between the actual hourly traffic and the road's capacity (the volume/capacity ratio). Figure 1.4.1 shows the results of the study.

A distinction is made between injury accidents and property damage only accidents. For both types of accidents, the accident rate drops when volume capacity ratio increases from around 0.10 to around 0.50. When there is little traffic on a road, accident rate can be high for several reasons. Firstly, speeds are often higher when there is little traffic than when there is a lot of traffic. Secondly, traffic is lowest at night, when accident rate is high because of darkness. When the volume capacity ratio increases from around 0.50 to 0.90, the accident rate increases again, especially for

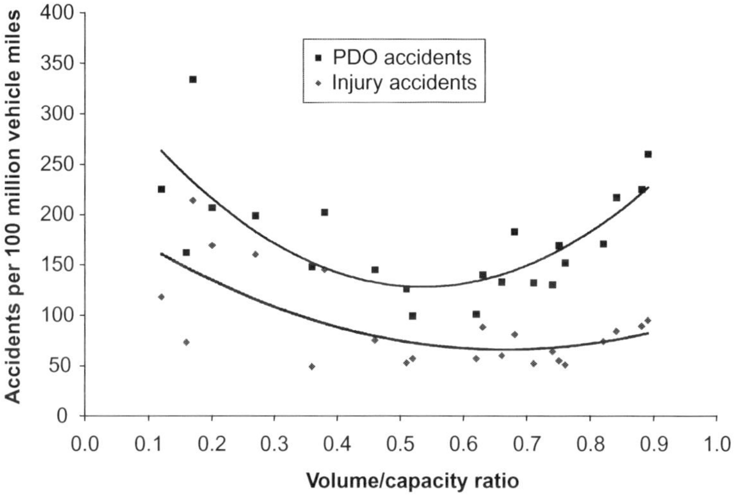


*Figure 1.4.1: Variations in the accident rate as a function in the capacity utilisation on a road (Zhou and Sisiopiku 1997).*

property damage only accidents. In other words, there is a high level of risk in dense traffic.

A number of studies have evaluated the relationship between traffic congestion and the accident rate (Hall and Pendleton 1990, Sullivan 1990, Hall and Polanco de Hurtado 1992, Persaud and Dzbik 1993, Sandhu and Al-Kazily 1996). The results are inconsistent. In rural areas, most roads carry too little traffic for capacity problems to arise (Hall and Pendleton 1990). In the San Francisco area, it was found that the accident rate in rush-hour traffic increased by around 90% for injury accidents (relative rate of 1.9 when other traffic has a rate of 1.0) and around 160% for property-damage-only accidents (relative rate 2.6) (Sullivan 1990). A study of the relationship between capacity utilisation and accident rate at intersections in the town of Albuquerque in New Mexico in the USA found no clear pattern (Hall and Polanco de Hurtado 1992). However, a study in Toronto, Ontario (Persaud and Dzbik 1993), found an increased accident rate in rush-hour traffic, for both injury accidents and property-damage-only accidents. The accident rate in rush-hour traffic was about twice as high as during the rest of the day. A study in California (Sandhu and Al-Kazily 1996) also found that the accident rate in rush-hour traffic was about twice as high as outside the rush-hour.

In summary, the studies discussed above indicate that congestion and rush-hour traffic increase the accident rate. Building new arterial roads in towns and cities and expanding the capacity of existing main roads is intended, *as a traffic safety measure*, to direct long-distance traffic on to main roads with adequate capacity and high levels of safety and to make it possible to screen residential areas from through traffic. Other important goals in building urban arterial roads are increasing mobility, reducing time spent in traffic, reducing vehicle operating costs and improving the environment through a reduction in noise and pollution.

### Description of the measure

Arterial roads inside towns and cities are designed to carry traffic to and from the centre and through the town or city. In this chapter, the following measures related to the provision of urban arterial roads are treated:

- Building new arterial roads
- Increasing the capacity of existing arterial roads
- Minor improvements of existing arterial roads

### Effect on accidents

***Building new arterial roads.*** The following studies have evaluated the effects of new urban arterial roads on road safety:

Jadaan and Nicholson (1988) (Christchurch, New Zealand)
Jørgensen (1991a) (Odense, Denmark)
Holt (1993) (Trondheim, Norway)
Sæverås (1998) (Bergen, Norway)
Amundsen and Elvik (2004) (Oslo, Norway)

These studies have been summarised by Amundsen and Elvik (2004). On the average, a new urban arterial road, added to the existing road system, does not affect the number of accidents. The best estimate of the mean effect, based on the studies above is 1% accident reduction (−9%, +8%). New arterial roads induce traffic. On the average, traffic grew by 16% for the arterial roads included. Accident rate was reduced by 17%. These two effects almost cancel, leaving the number of accidents unchanged.

***Increasing the capacity of existing arterial roads.*** The capacity of an arterial road can be increased, for example, by adding lanes, by banning parking and by altering traffic control at junctions. Lane addition projects have been included in this chapter. Studies of the effects of increasing the number of traffic lanes on arterial roads include:

Foley (1967) (USA)
Thorson and Mouritsen (1971) (Denmark)
Hvoslef (1974) (Norway)
Andersen (1977) (Denmark)
Vejdirektoratet (1980) (Denmark)
Krenk (1985) (Denmark)
Harwood (1986) (USA)
Köhler and Schwamb (1993) (Germany)
Langeland (1999) (Norway)
Amundsen and Elvik (2004) (Norway)

These studies have been summarised by Amundsen and Elvik (2004). Table 1.4.1 shows the changes in the number of accidents associated with an increase in the number of traffic lanes according to these studies.

The studies indicate that four-lane arterial roads have a lower injury accident rate than two-lane arterial roads. For property-damage-only accidents, results indicate a higher

*Table 1.4.1: Effects on accidents of increasing the number of lanes on main roads in cities*

| | Percentage change in the number of accidents | | |
|---|---|---|---|
| Accident severity | Types of accident affected | Best estimate | 95% confidence interval |
| ***Comparison of roads with 2 or 3 lanes without a median*** | | | |
| Injury accidents | All accidents | −12 | (−15; −8) |
| Property damage only accidents | All accidents | +32 | (+24; +40) |
| ***Comparison of roads with 2 or 4 lanes without a median*** | | | |
| Injury accidents | All accidents | −11 | (−13; −8) |
| Property damage only accidents | All accidents | +13 | (+8; +18) |
| ***Comparison of roads with 2 or 4 lanes with a median*** | | | |
| Injury accidents | All accidents | −4 | (−9; +2) |
| Property damage only accidents | All accidents | +15 | (+8; +22) |
| ***Increasing the number of lanes from 2 or 4 to 4 or 6 with a median (Norwegian results only)*** | | | |
| Injury accidents | All accidents | −51 | (−65; −33) |

accident rate on four-lane roads than on two-lane roads. It should be noted that all results, except those reported in the last row of the table, are based on comparative studies of the accident rate on different types of road, not on before-and-after studies. In comparative studies of accident rates, it is always difficult to adequately control for all factors that influence accident rate in addition to the design elements of primary interest. The Norwegian before-and-after studies, controlling for trends and regression to the mean, found that increasing the number of lanes from 2 to 4, or from 4 to 6, and adding a median reduced the number of injury accidents by 51%.

***Minor improvement of existing urban arterial roads.*** Only one study of minor improvements of existing urban arterial roads has been retrieved (Flagstad 1990). The study evaluated minor improvements of arterial roads in Bergen, Norway. The study did not find any statistically significant changes in the number of accidents associated with any of the improvements. The number of injury accidents increased by 15% (−20%; +65%).

## Effect on mobility

During the rush hour, the average speed of traffic on a road with capacity problems is often between 10 and 20 km/h, depending on how large the capacity problems are. The length of the rush hour in Norway varies from half-an-hour to between 3 and 4 h per day on weekdays (except Saturdays) (Nielsen and Larsen 1988). On an arterial road with sufficient capacity, the driving speed in normal traffic is around 50–80 km/h, depending on the width, alignment, the number of junctions and the form of traffic control at junctions.

## Effect on the environment

A necessary condition for improving the environment by building new urban arterial roads is that the gains along the old road system are large enough to offset the disadvantages of a new road. In Norway, many of the recently built arterial roads have been built-in tunnels. Traffic volume on the old arterial roads has been reduced. The net effect has been to improve the environment. Residents of the eastern part of Oslo, where a new arterial road has been built in a tunnel, are less exposed to and report being less annoyed by noise and air pollution after the new arterial road was built than before (Klæboe et al. 2000, Clench-Aas et al. 2000). On the other hand, expanding road capacity to meet urban travel demand tends to induce new traffic, which in the long run may lead to more congestion.

### Costs

A compilation of recent Norwegian cost figures (Elvik 1996) shows that the cost of building new urban arterial roads is on average around NOK 60 million per kilometre (NOK $\pm$20 million). Improving existing urban arterial roads cost on average around NOK 20 million per kilometre ($\pm$1 million NOK). Expanding the bypass in Trondheim, Norway from two to four lanes cost around NOK 30 million per kilometre for the affected road network. The mean construction cost per kilometre of recently constructed new urban arterial roads in Norway was NOK 288 million.

### Cost–benefit analysis

The long-term effects of new urban arterial roads are complex and difficult to include in cost–benefit analyses. These long-term effects include urban sprawl, changes in the modal split of travel and changes in car ownership rates. Short-term impacts on the flow of traffic can, however, be analysed within the conventional framework for cost–benefit analyses of road investment projects. Numerical examples based on recent Norwegian experiences have been worked out.

One example refers to the construction of a new arterial road. It has been assumed that the old arterial road had an AADT of 42,000. It has further been assumed that 20% of traffic is rush-hour traffic, flowing at a mean speed of 15 km/h. The rest of traffic is assumed to flow at 50 km/h. On the new arterial road, it has been assumed that 80% of traffic flows at 70 km/h and 20% of traffic flows at 50 km/h. It has been assumed that 80% of the initial traffic is transferred to the new arterial road, 20% remains on the old road. Induced traffic is set to 15%. Induced traffic is assumed to use the new arterial road. No effect on accidents of the new arterial road has been assumed. Applying official Norwegian monetary valuations of travel time, vehicle operating cost and environmental impacts time gives benefits (present value) of about NOK 1,486 million for a typical urban arterial road project. Costs were estimated to be NOK 1,114 million. Benefits are greater than costs, but this numerical example does not consider the possibility that congestion may worsen again in the long run.

Another numerical example has been worked out for adding lanes and a median to an urban arterial road. It was again assumed that traffic congestion would be greatly reduced. Both the number and severity of accidents were assumed to reduce, resulting in a reduction of 75% in the total cost of accidents. For typical Norwegian conditions, benefits were estimated to be NOK 1,169 million and costs to be NOK 549 million. Again, benefits are greater than costs.

## 1.5 Channelisation of junctions

### Problem and objective

Around 40% of all police reported injury accidents in Norway occur at junctions. The proportion of injury accidents at junctions is higher in urban areas (ca. 50%) than in rural areas (ca. 35%). Road junctions are dangerous and difficult areas for all road users. The vast majority of accident black spots identified on national highways are road junctions (Christensen 1988, Statens vegvesen 2007c, 2007d).

Accidents at junctions are, however, less severe than other accidents, both in urban and in rural areas. This is probably due to lower speed in junctions compared to straight sections. The most common types of accidents at junctions are side impact, turning accidents, and collisions with pedestrians or cyclists. About 20–30% of all accidents at junctions are collisions between a left turning vehicle with oncoming traffic. According to a Norwegian study in 1986 (Vodahl and Giæver 1986), accident rates at four-legged junctions are greater than accident rates at three-legged junctions. Accident costs, which depend on both number of accidents and accident severity, are according to Norwegian accident analyses (Sakshaug and Johannessen 2005).

- Higher at junctions with priority to traffic entering from the right hand side than in signalised junctions
- Higher at signalised junctions than at junctions where traffic on the minor approaches must give way,
- Higher at four-legged junctions than at three-legged junctions
- Higher at higher speed limits in all junctions
- Higher at higher proportions of minor road volumes

Channelisation of junctions aims at improving safety in junctions by separating traffic flows, improving sight and making driving patterns and right-of-way rules transparent.

### Description of the measure

Channelisation of junctions is a physical measure to segregate different streams of traffic at junctions. Channelisation can be carried out using traffic islands (physical channelisation) or road markings (painted channelisation). Distinctions can be made between different forms of channelisation:

- Side road channelisation with traffic islands or road markings on side roads at junctions.

- Left turn lanes, which separate vehicles turning left off the main road at a junction from those going straight ahead.
- Right turn lanes, which separate traffic turning right from the main road at a junction from straight-through traffic.
- Passing lanes, which are wider areas of the traffic lane for traffic which is going straight ahead at an intersection, so that this traffic can pass vehicles which are waiting to turn left. Passing lanes are an alternative to left turn lanes.
- Full channelisation includes both side road channelisation and left turn lanes, possibly also right turn lanes.

**Effect on accidents**

The effect on accidents of different forms of channelisation at junctions has been evaluated in a number of studies:

Exnicios (1967) (USA): left turn lanes, full channelisation
Wilson (1967) (USA): left turn lanes
Hammer (1969) (USA): left turn lanes
Lyager and Løschenkohl (1972) (Denmark): full channelisation
Bennett (1973) (Great Britain): left turn lanes
Johannessen and Heir (1974) (Norway): side road channelisation, full channelisation
Faulkner and Eaton (1977) (Great Britain): side road channelisation
Vodahl and Johannessen (1977) (Norway): side road channelisation, full channelisation
Vaa and Johannessen (1978) (Norway): side road channelisation, full channelisation
Jørgensen (1979) (Denmark): various forms of channelisation
Brüde and Larsson (1981) (Sweden): side road channelisation, full channelisation
Statens Vägverk (1981) (Sweden): side road channelisation, left turn lanes
Schiøtz (1982) (Nordic countries): side road channelisation
Engel and Krogsgård Thomsen (1983) (Denmark): left turn lanes
Brüde and Larsson (1985) (Sweden): side road channelisation, left turn lanes
Craus and Mahalel (1986) (Israel): left turn lanes
Jørgensen (1986) (Denmark): right turn lanes
Vodahl and Giæver (1986) (Norway): side road channelisation, full channelisation
Brüde and Larsson (1987a) (Sweden): side road channelisation, left turn lanes
McCoy and Malone (1989) (USA): left turn lanes
Kølster Pedersen et al (1992) (Denmark): side road channelisation, right turn lanes
Kulmala (1992) (Finland): several types of channelisation
Giæver and Holt (1994) (Norway): passing lanes

Jørgensen (1994) (Denmark): side road channelisation
Seim (1994) (Norway): full channelisation
Vogt and Bared (1998) (USA): right turn lanes
Vogt (1999) (USA): left turn lanes
Preston and Schoenecker (2000) (USA): left turn lanes
Newstead and Corben (2001) (Australia): right turn lanes, left turn lanes
Strathman, Duecker, Zhang and Williams (2001) (USA): right turn lanes, left turn lanes
Thomas and Smith (2001) (USA): right turn lanes, left turn lanes
Chin and Quddus (2003) (Singapore): left turn lanes
Kumara and Chin (2003) (Singapore): right turn lanes, left turn lanes
Rimiller, Ivan and Garrick (2003) (USA): left turn lanes
Khattak Naik and Kannan (2004) (USA): left turn lanes
Naik (2005) (USA): left turn lanes
Hochstein (2006) (USA): right turn lanes
Kim, Washington and Oh (2006) (USA): left turn lanes

The results from these studies vary somewhat, depending among other things, on which method was used in the study. Here only the results of the methodologically best studies are shown. Furthermore, results are only shown when more than one study has evaluated a specific form of channelisation. Tables 1.5.1–1.5.3 show the estimated effects on accidents of different forms of channelisation at junctions.

Most results in Tables 1.5.1–1.5.3 are non-significant. This reflects the problem of many studies, which is that only few junctions have been studied. If the results are interpreted as showing true effects, the results can be summarised as follows:

- Left turn lanes reduce injury accidents. The effects of physical channelisation are greater than of marked channelisation, and the effects are greater at T-junctions than at X-junctions.
- Right turn lanes reduce injury accidents at X-junctions, but not at T-junctions. No effect has been found on property-damage-only accidents.
- Full channelisation reduces injury accidents at X-junctions, but not at T-junctions. The effects of physical channelisation are greater than that of marked channelisation. The effects of full channelisation are slightly larger than the effects of left turn lanes or right turn lanes only.
- Side road channelisation increases injury accidents at T-junctions and reduces injury accidents at X-junctions.
- Passing lanes reduce injury accidents at X-junctions and increase accidents at T-junctions.

*Table 1.5.1: Effects of left turn lanes on the number of accidents at junctions*

| | Percentage change in the number of accidents | | |
|---|---|---|---|
| Accident severity | Types of accidents affected | Best estimate | 95% confidence interval |
| ***Left turn lane at T-junctions: Physical/marked*** | | | |
| Injury accidents | All accidents | −17 | (−36; +7) |
| Property damage only accidents | All accidents | +1 | (−18; +25) |
| Unspecified | All accidents | −18 | (−29; −6) |
| ***Left turn lane at T-junctions: Physical*** | | | |
| Injury accidents | All accidents | −27 | (−52; +10) |
| ***Left turn lane at T-junctions: Marked*** | | | |
| Injury accidents | All accidents | −19 | (−63; +79) |
| ***Left turn lane at X-junctions: Physical/marked*** | | | |
| Injury accidents | All accidents | −24 | (−43; +1) |
| Property damage only accidents | All accidents | −77 | (−97; +76) |
| Unspecified | All accidents | −31 | (−45; −13) |
| ***Left turn lane at X-junctions: Physical*** | | | |
| Injury accidents | All accidents | −4 | (−25; +22) |
| ***Left turn lane at X-junctions: Marked*** | | | |
| Injury accidents | All accidents | +14 | (−52; +170) |

*Table 1.5.2: Effects of right turn lanes on the number of accidents at junctions*

| | Percentage change in the number of accidents | | |
|---|---|---|---|
| Accident severity | Types of accidents affected | Best estimate | 95% confidence interval |
| ***Right turn lane at T- or X-junction: Physical or marked*** | | | |
| Injury accidents | All accidents | −7 | (−22; +11) |
| Property damage only accidents | All accidents | +1 | (−39; +67) |
| Unspecified | All accidents | +3 | (−7; +15) |
| ***Right turn lane at T- junction: Physical or marked*** | | | |
| Injury accidents | All accidents | +12 | (−15; +48) |
| ***Right turn lane at X-junction: Physical or marked*** | | | |
| Injury accidents | All accidents | −19 | (−25; −12) |

*Table 1.5.3: Effects of other types of channelisation on the number of accidents at junctions*

| | Percentage change in the number of accidents | | |
|---|---|---|---|
| Accident severity | Types of accidents affected | Best estimate | 95% confidence interval |
| ***Full channelisation at T- junction: Physical*** | | | |
| Injury accidents | All accidents | +24 | (−2; +58) |
| ***Full channelisation at X- junction: Physical*** | | | |
| Injury accidents | All accidents | −32 | (−52; −5) |
| ***Full channelisation at X- junction: Marked*** | | | |
| Injury accidents | All accidents | −57 | (−70; −41) |
| ***Side road channelisation at T-junctions: Physical*** | | | |
| Injury accidents | All accidents | +18 | (+1; +38) |
| ***Side road channelisation at X-junctions: Physical*** | | | |
| Injury accidents | All accidents | −20 | (−31; −7) |
| Property damage only accidents | All accidents | −35 | (−71; +47) |
| ***Passing lane at T-junction: Physical*** | | | |
| Injury accidents | All accidents | +26 | (−16; +89) |
| ***Passing lane at X-junction: Physical*** | | | |
| Injury accidents | All accidents | −11 | (−68; +145) |

Most types of channelisation seem to be more favourable at X-junctions than at T-junctions. The only exception are left turn lanes, which are more favourable at T-junctions. There is no clear difference between physical and marked channelisation.

The explanation of these results is not known. A traffic island is in itself a fixed obstacle and in the event of collision can lead to vehicle damage, or in the worst case that the vehicle overturns and personal injuries result. On the other hand, physical channelisation is more clearly visible and marked channelisation may cause confusion in bad weather conditions or when the markings are worn off. Some forms of channelisation make the intersection wider, so that the area of conflict is enlarged. Right hand turn lanes may create blind spots, where a vehicle turning right can obscure approaching through traffic for road users who are coming from the right on a side road. Comprehensive channelisation measures can make an intersection large and complicated. This can increase the chance of mistaking traffic lanes or other errors among road users.

In most studies of channelisation of junctions, it is not specified whether junctions are signalised. Harwood et al. (2002) found greater effects of left-turn lanes at signalised junctions than at non-signalised junctions. The effects of right turn lanes on the contrary were greater at non-signalised junctions than at signalised junctions.

### Effect on mobility

Left turn lanes, right turn lanes, passing lanes and full channelisation are all intended to improve traffic flow, largely by preventing turning vehicles (left or right), from hindering or delaying traffic, which is going straight ahead at the junction (Craus and Mahalel 1986). Left turn lanes increase the capacity at junctions on the average by about 25% (S/K Transportation Consultants, Inc. 2000). The effect of right turn lanes on capacity is usually smaller. Capacity increases become more marked on roads with larger volumes of through traffic, and with larger volumes of left turning traffic (left turn lanes) or right turning traffic (right turn lanes; Craus and Mahalel 1986).

Side road channelisation is normally introduced on roads where the traffic is required to give way. At such intersections, it is the amount of traffic on the main road, not the channelisation, which determines the length of the waiting time for side road traffic.

### Effect on the environment

No studies have been found that indicate anything about the effect on environmental conditions of channelisation of intersections. Some forms of channelisation increase the area of the intersection. Positive effects may be achieved because fewer vehicles have to stop and accelerate.

### Costs

Table 1.5.4 shows estimated average costs of channelisation of junctions. Local variations in costs of at least 50% must be expected around these mean values.

### Cost–benefit analysis

Numerical examples have been calculated for channelisation of junctions. It is assumed that the traffic volume is 10,000 vehicles per day at crossroads and 5,000 vehicles per day at T-junctions. The number of injury accidents per million vehicles is assumed to

*Table 1.5.4: Suggested costs for channelisation at intersections: costs per intersection (2005 prices) (Statens vegvesen, Hb155, draft, 2005)*

| Form of channelisation | Costs (NOK) |
|---|---|
| Left turn lane at crossroads | 800,000 |
| Side road channelisation at crossroads | 400,000 |
| Full channelisation at crossroads | 1,650,000 |
| Left turn lane at T-junctions | 500,000 |
| Side road channelisation at T-junctions | 200,000 |
| Full channelisation at T-junctions | 1,200,000 |

*Table 1.5.5: Cost–benefit analyses of channelisation at junctions*

| | | Cost–benefit ratio | |
|---|---|---|---|
| Form of channelisation | Effect on injury accidents (%) | Benefit: accident reduction | Benefit: accident reduction and time savings |
| ***Channelisation at crossroads (AADT 10,000; injury rate 0.178)*** | | | |
| Left turn lane | −10 | 1.8 | 3.4 |
| Side road channelisation | −20 | 7.3 | 7.3 |
| Full channelisation | −30 | 2.7 | 3.4 |
| ***Channelisation at T-junctions (AADT 10,000; injury rate 0.067)*** | | | |
| Left turn lane | −20 | 1.1 | 1.6 |
| Side road channelisation | +18 | – | – |
| Full channelisation | +24 | – | – |

be 0.178 at crossroads and 0.067 at T-junctions. These figures correspond to the average accident rates at give-way controlled junctions where the speed limit is 80 km/h and where the proportion of traffic from the side road or side roads is approximately 30%. The costs are assumed to be as described in the preceding section. The assumed effects on injury accidents are as shown in Table 1.5.5, which shows cost–benefit ratios under the assumption that only safety is affected and when time savings are assumed in addition to the effects on safety. Time savings are only assumed for left-turn lanes and full channelisation, but not for side-road channelisation.

The numerical examples show that the benefits of all types of channelisation at crossroads and of left turn lanes at T-junctions exceed the costs even if no time savings are taken into account. For side-road and full channelisation at T-junctions, no cost–benefit ratios are shown in Table 1.5.5 because no accident reductions have been found.

The cost–benefit ratios are dependent, among other things, on the traffic volumes at the junctions. Under the assumptions described above, the benefits of left turn lanes at crossroads exceed the costs when the traffic volume is at least 5,600 vehicles per day when no time savings are taken into account. Time savings will be greater at larger traffic volumes.

## 1.6 Roundabouts

### Problem and objectives

At road junctions with heavy traffic, waiting times for traffic required to give way may be long. This may tempt road users to enter the junction with small safety margins. Frequent crossing and turning manoeuvres can create dangerous situations and make the traffic situation complex. Around 40% of all injury accidents reported to the police occur at intersections.

Converting intersections to roundabouts can improve safety and traffic flow in several ways. The number of potential conflict points between the traffic streams passing through an intersection is reduced from 32 to 20 at crossroads and from 9 to 8 at T-junctions. Road users entering a roundabout are required to give way to road users already in the roundabout, no matter which road they are coming from, and thus are forced to observe traffic at the roundabout more carefully. All traffic comes from one direction. Road users therefore do not have to observe traffic from several directions at the same time in order to find a gap to enter the roundabout. Roundabouts with offside priority eliminate left turns in front of oncoming traffic. Roundabouts are built so that road users cannot drive a straight path through the junction but must drive round a traffic island located in the middle of the junction. This reduces speed.

### Description of the measure

A roundabout is a road intersection with circulatory traffic. The traffic passing through the intersection is regulated in one direction anti-clockwise (in countries driving on the right) around a circular traffic island placed in the centre. The traffic approaching a roundabout is usually required to give way to the traffic already in the roundabout (offside priority). All the results presented here refer to this type of roundabout.

*Table 1.6.1: Effects on accidents of converting intersections to roundabouts*

| | Percentage change in the number of accidents | | |
|---|---|---|---|
| | Accident severity | Best estimate | 95% confidence interval |
| All roundabouts | All severities | −36 | (−43; −29) |
| All roundabouts | Fatal accidents | −66 | (−85; −24) |
| All roundabouts | Injury accidents | −46 | (−51; −40) |
| All roundabouts | Property damage only accidents | +10 | (−10; +35) |
| Previous yield junctions | All severities | −40 | (−47; −31) |
| Privious signalised junctions | All severities | −14 | (−27; +1) |
| X-junctions | All severities | −34 | (−42; −25) |
| T-junctions | All severities | −8 | (−28; +18) |
| Roundabouts in rural areas | All severities | −69 | (−79; −54) |
| Roundabouts in urban areas | All severities | −25 | (−34; −15) |

## Effect on accidents

A number of studies have evaluated the effects of roundabouts on the number of accidents. The summary estimates of the effect on accidents given below (Table 1.6.1) are based on the following studies:

Lalani (1975) (UK)
Green (1977) (UK)
Lahrmann (1981) (Denmark)
Cedersund (1983a, 1983b) (Sweden)
Senneset (1983) (Norway)
Brüde and Larsson (1985) (Sweden)
Johannessen (1985) (Norway)
Hall and McDonald (1988) (UK)
Nygaard (1988) (Norway)
Corben, Ambrose and Wai (1990) (Australia)
Giæver (1990) (Norway)
Tudge (1990) (Australia)
Van Minnen (1990) (Netherlands)
Jørgensen (1991b) (Denmark)
Brüde and Larsson (1992) (Sweden)
Dagersten (1992) (Switzerland)

Holzwarth (1992) (Germany)
Hydén, Odelid and Várhelyi (1992) (Sweden)
Jørgensen and Jørgensen (1992) (Denmark)
Kristiansen (1992) (Norway)
Schnüll, Haller and Von Lübke (1992) (Germany)
Værø (1992a, 1992b, 1992c, 199d) (Denmark)
Brilon, Stuwe and Drews (1993) (Germany)
Huber and Bühlmann (1994) (Switzerland)
Jørgensen and Jørgensen (1994) (Denmark)
Schoon and Van Minnen (1993) (Netherlands)
Seim (1994) (Norway)
Voss (1994) (Germany)
BTCE (1995) and Motha, Musidlak and Williams (1995) (Australia)
Oslo Veivesen (1995) (Norway)
Flannery and Datta (1996) (USA)
Giæver (1997) (Norway)
Flannery, Elefteriadou, Koza and McFadden (1998) (USA)
Mountain, Maher and Fawaz (1998) (GB)
Persaud, Retting, Gårder and Lord (2001) (USA)
Newstead and Corben (2001) (AUS)
Brabander and Vereeck (2005) (Belgium)
Traffic Engineering Branch (2005, 2007) (Australia)
Meuleners, Hendrie, Legge and Cercarelli (2005), Meuleners, Hendrie, Lee and Legge (2008) (Australia)

The results show that the total number of accidents is significantly reduced in roundabouts. The greatest effect was found for fatal accidents. Property damage accidents increase, but their effect is however not significant. These results refer to all types of roundabouts.

The results indicate further that the conversion of previous yield junctions and of X-junctions has greater effects than the conversion of other types of junctions. Greater effects were also found in rural areas compared to urban areas. This may be related to the finding that effects of roundabouts are greater at higher speed limits (Brabander and Vereeck 2005).

More detailed analyses show that there are no significant differences in the effects of roundabouts between different countries (Elvik 2003). The results do not seem to be affected to a large degree by publication bias. Results from a meta-regression analysis show that all the factors that are repesented in Table 1.6.1 are significant predictors for the effectiveness of roundabouts. However, there is large heterogeneity in the results, which indicates that the effectiveness of roundabouts is likely to be affected by further factors, which could not be investigated in the present analysis.

The relationship between the size of the central island in roundabouts and the accident rate was studied by Cedersund (1983a) and Maycock and Hall (1984). Both studies have controlled for a number of other factors. None of them found a relationship between the size of the central island and the accident rate. Studies from Norway (Tran 1999) and Sweden (Brüde and Larsson 1999) indicate that injury accident rates are higher in large roundabouts than in small roundabouts. However, this result is uncertain and it is not controlled for other factors that may affect accident rates in roundabouts. According to Jørgensen and Jørgensen (2002), accident rates are greater in roundabouts, which require larger speed reductions on roads with 80 km/h speed limit. On roads with lower speed limits, no relationship was found between required speed reductions and accident rates.

Some studies (Lalani 1975, Van Minnen 1990, Jørgensen 1991b, Schoon and Van Minnen 1993) have evaluated the effects of roundabouts on accidents for different groups of road users. The studies indicate that pedestrian accidents are reduced to the same extent as other types of accidents when roundabouts are built. The reduction in number of accidents involving cyclists is somewhat smaller – around 10–20% (compared to 30–40% for the total number of injury accidents). The results of various studies are highly conflicting and uncertain. The figures are based on Nordic studies.

**Effect on mobility**

Roundabouts have a greater capacity than normal give-way regulated intersections and signalised junctions. The increase in capacity is due to the fact that both crossing and turning manoeuvres, which often lead to waiting times and can delay other traffic, are removed. Road users appear to accept smaller gaps at roundabouts than at other intersections. In spite of the fact that roundabouts lead to lower speeds (Senneset 1983), the total passing time at a roundabout can be reduced compared with other intersections.

The size of the time gain depends on the amount of traffic at the particular intersection, variations in traffic over the 24-h period and the distribution of entering vehicles between the approaches to the junction. It is therefore difficult to give general figures. A German study (Brilon and Stuwe 1991) indicates that the waiting time per car at a roundabout is about 15 s less than at an intersection with traffic lights with an hourly traffic flow of between 500 and 2,000 vehicles. A study of 20 intersections with give-way regulations, which were converted to roundabouts in Växjö in Sweden (Várhelyi 1993), found that cars coming from the main road on average lost 2.3 s per intersection per car when these were converted to roundabouts. Cars coming from minor roads achieved a time gain of 4.4 s per intersection per car. The intersections had on average 9,700 entering cars from the main road per 24-h period and 3,130 entering cars per 24-h period from side roads. The same study (Várhelyi 1993) found that conversion of a signalised junction with 23,500 incoming vehicles per day to a roundabout gave an average time gain of 10.1 s per car.

### Effect on the environment

A Danish study (Bendtsen 1992) found that emission of hydrocarbons (HC), carbon monoxide (CO) and nitrogen oxide (NOx), calculated in grams per kilometre driven per car are around 5–10% lower at roundabouts than signalised junctions. A Swedish study (Várhelyi 1993) found a reduction of 29% in the emission of carbon monoxide and a reduction of 21% in the emission of nitrogen oxide after a signalised junction was converted to a roundabout. At intersections, which were previously give-way regulated, less favourable results were achieved. Emissions of carbon monoxide increased by 6% and emissions of nitrogen oxide increased by 4% following conversions to roundabouts (Várhelyi 1993).

### Costs

The costs of building a roundabout can vary from several hundred thousand kroner to NOK 5–10 million. According to information collected by Elvik and Rydningen (2002), the mean cost of converting a three-leg junction in Norway to a roundabout is about NOK 4.8 million. For four leg junctions, the mean cost of conversion was about NOK 3.5 million.

### Cost–benefit analysis

The costs and benefits of converting junctions to roundabouts will vary substantially from place to place. Data collected by Elvik and Rydningen (2002) provide a basis for assessing the costs and benefits of recently constructed roundabouts in Norway. For three-leg junctions, mean AADT was 9,094 and the mean accident rate was 0.23 injury accidents per million entering vehicles. The latter value is substantially higher than the normal accident rate for three-leg junctions in Norway. The benefits of converting a typical three-leg junction to a roundabout were estimated to be NOK 9.15 million

(25 years, 5% discount rate). Costs were estimated to be NOK 5.15 million. For four-leg junctions, mean AADT was 10,432 and the mean accident rate was 0.15 injury accidents per million entering vehicles. The accident rate is rather close to the normal value for a four-leg junction. The benefits of converting a typical four-leg junction to a roundabout were estimated to NOK 9.20 million, costs were estimated to be NOK 4.16 million. Benefits are greater than costs in both these cases, suggesting that the conversion of junctions to roundabouts is cost-effective, at least at the traffic volumes observed in this sample.

## 1.7 Redesigning junctions

### Problem and objectives

Older junctions, or junctions which were built in difficult terrain may have a substandard geometric lay-out. The angle between roads can reduce the overview and make simple turning manoeuvres difficult. Steep gradients when approaching an intersection can also reduce visibility and make it difficult to stop or to start again after having stopped. A common cause of traffic accidents is that the road users cannot see each other in time or do not see each other at all. Junctions have been found to have higher accident rates when requirements concerning sight conditions are not fulfilled, compared to junctions where these requirements are fulfilled (Vodahl and Giæver 1986). This does not apply to roundabouts, where sight obstructions have been found to reduce accident rates (Giæver 2000).

Redesigning of junctions is intended to improve sight conditions at intersections, simplify turns and make the intersection more visible to road users who are approaching it.

### Description of the measure

Redesigning junctions includes

- changes to the angle between roads,
- changes to the gradients of roads approaching the intersection,
- measures to improve sight conditions at intersections and
- changes to the roads cross profile (lane width, median, shoulder) and curvature.

These measures are often implemented in conjunction with channelisation of intersections (see Section 1.5) or other measures.

**Effect on accidents**

Estimated effects on accidents of geometrical changes to junctions are for the most part based on studies of the relationship between geometric properties of junctions and accidents. Only improvements of visibility conditions have been evaluated in before-and-after studies.

Three studies have investigated the relationships between several geometrical properties of junctions and accidents (Bauer and Harwood 1998, Lyon et al. 2003, Vogt and Bared 1998). The strongest and most consistent relationship was found between volumes and accidents. No consistent relationships have been found between any of the geometrical properties of junctions and accidents.

***Angles between roads at junctions*** have been investigated in the following studies:

Hanna, Flynn and Tyler (1976) (USA)
Vaa and Johannessen (1978) (Norge)
Brüde and Larsson (1985) (Sverige)
McCoy, Tripi and Bonneson (1994) (USA)
Kumara and Chin (2003) (Singapore)

Based on these studies, how accident numbers differ between skewed junctions (junctions where the angle between the roads is different from 90°), compared to junctions with 90° angles is summarised in Table 1.7.1. According to the available studies, skewed junctions seem to be related to more accidents than junctions with 90° angles between the roads. According to the study by Fildes et al. (2000), skewed junctions are most problematic for older drivers. However, Maze and Burchett (2006) found that accidents at junctions with 90o angles are less serious than at skewed junctions.

*Table 1.7.1: Effects on the number of accidents at junctions of changes to angles between roads at intersections: Angles different from 90 degrees, compared to 90 degree angles*

| | Percentage change in number of accidents | | |
|---|---|---|---|
| Accident severity | Types of accident affected | Best estimate | 95% confidence interval |
| Unspecified | All accidents at T-junctions | +34 | (+2; +76) |
| Unspecified | All accidents at X-junctions | +6 | (−2; +15) |

***Gradients on approaches to junctions.*** The significance of gradients on approaches to junctions have been studied by

Johannessen and Heir (1974) (Norway)
Hanna, Flynn and Tyler (1976) (USA)
Vodahl and Giæver (1986) (Norway)
Vogt and Bared (1998) (USA)
Harwood et al. (2000) (USA)
Savolainen and Tarko (2004) (USA)
Kumara and Chin (2003) (Singapore)

On the basis of these studies, the relationship between gradients on one or more arms of a junction and the number of accidents has been estimated as shown in Table 1.7.2. The results refer to both uphill and downhill gradients. The results indicate that there are more accidents at junctions with (steep) gradients than at junctions with no or small gradients. However, the results are not significant. Small gradients are mostly defined as 2 or 3 m height difference per kilometre. The results for steep instead of small gradients refer to gradients of above versus below 2, 3 or 5 m/km. Two studies have used multivariate models that control for a number of other factors than gradients (Lyon et al. 2003, Oh, Washington and Choi 2004). No relationships between gradients and accidents were found in these studies either.

***Improved sight conditions at junctions.*** The effect on accidents of improving sight conditions at junctions has been studied by

Johannessen and Heir (1974) (Norge)
Hanna, Flynn and Tyler (1976) (USA)
Vaa and Johannessen (1978) (Norge)
Brüde and Larsson (1985) (Norge)

*Table 1.7.2: Effects on number of accidents of changing gradients on roads leading to an intersection*

| | Percentage change in number of accidents | | |
|---|---|---|---|
| Accident severity | Types of accident affected | Best estimate | 95% confidence interval |
| ***Small instead of no gradient*** | | | |
| Unspecified | All accidents at junctions | +11 | (−9; +35) |
| ***Steep instead of small gradient*** | | | |
| Unspecified | All accidents at junctions | −17 | (−23; +69) |

*Table 1.7.3: Effects on accidents of improved sight conditions at intersections*

| | | Percentage change in number of accidents | |
|---|---|---|---|
| Accident severity | Types of accident affected | Best estimate | 95% confidence interval |
| Unspecified | All accidents at junctions | −12 | (−19; −4) |
| Injury accidents | All accidents at junctions | −3 | (−18; +14) |
| Property damage only | All accidents at junctions | −16 | (−24; −7) |

Vodahl and Giæver (1986) (Norge)
Kulmala (1992) (Finland)
Kumara and Chin (2003) (Singapore)

For the most part, these studies have investigated increased sight distances from approaches to the junction into crossing roads. Based on these studies, the effect on accidents of improving sight conditions can be estimated as follows (Table 1.7.3):

Sight improvements at junctions give a weak, but not statistically significant reduction in the number of injury accidents and a decrease of around 16% in the number of property-damage-only accidents. A possible explanation of why sight improvements at intersections do not lead to a greater decrease in the number of accidents is that road users adapt their behaviour to the sight conditions at intersections and are particularly careful when visibility is poor.

***Cross-section design and curvature at junctions.*** Relationships between the road cross-section design (lane width, median, shoulder) and curvature and accidents have been investigated in a number of relatively well-controlled studies. Consistent relationships are found only in a very few instances. The relationship between geometrical properties of junctions and accidents is likely to depend, among other things, on the type of junction and the traffic environment. The results from studies of the relationships between geometrical characteristics of road sections and accidents (see Sections 1.11 and 1.13) can therefore not easily be transferred to junctions.

***Lane width.*** Bauer and Harwood (1998) found that there are fewer accidents at junctions with wider lanes in urban areas. Wong, Sze and Li (2007) found that there are fewer fatal and serious injury accidents at junctions with wider lanes. An 0.5 m increase of lane width has been found to be related to a reduction of the number of fatal and serious injury accidents by ca. 45%. No relationships between lane width and junction safety were found in rural areas (Harwood et al. 2000) and for minor injury accidents (Wong, Sze and Li 2007).

***Shoulder width***. Bauer and Harwood (1998) found no relationship between shoulder width and accidents, except at T-junctions in rural areas, where wider shoulders were associated with fewer accidents. Kim, Lee, Washington and Choi (2007) found that junctions with road shoulders had fewer sideswipe accidents and more rear-end collisions than junctions with no road shoulders.

***Median***. Bauer and Harwood (1998) did not find significant differences in accident number between junctions with and without a median. Only in T-junctions with stop-regulation in urban areas, it was found that a median is related to fewer accidents. Kumara and Chin (2003) found 19% fewer accidents at junctions with a median on the main road than at junctions without a median on the main road. The result is however not significant.

***Curvature***. Savolainen and Tarko (2004) have investigated the relationship between curvature and accidents at junctions on two- and four-lane roads. On two-lane roads, fewer accidents were found at junctions with a small degree of curvature than at junctions with a high degree of curvature. On four-lane roads, the result is reverse, and accident numbers have been found to increase with increasing curvature. Hower, none of the results are significant. Kumara and Chin (2003) and Wong, Sze and Li (2007) found significantly more accidents at junctions with a curve on at least one of the approaches than at junctions with no curves on any of the approaches.

### Effect on mobility

No studies have been found that indicate the effect on mobility of altering the geometric lay-out at intersections. To the extent that such changes improve sight conditions and make it easier to turn at intersection, it is reasonable to assume that mobility is improved.

### Effect on the environment

The effect on the environment of altering the geometric lay-out intersections has not been documented.

### Costs

The costs of redesigning junctions vary considerably, depending on the scope of the measures and the terrain conditions. A compilation of cost data from conversions of intersections in Norway (Elvik 1996) suggests that the cost of a complete rebuilding of an intersection may be in the order of magnitude of NOK 6 million (1995 prices) per intersection.

### Cost–benefit analysis

A numerical example has been made for a T-junction with 5,000 vehicles per day and an accident rate of 0.10 injury accidents per million entering vehicles. If the number of injury accidents is reduced by 5%, the saved accident costs (present value) will be NOK 0.42 million. If the measure costs more than this, it will not be cost-effective from an economic point of view.

## 1.8 Staggered junctions (reconfiguring crossroads to two T-junctions)

### Problem and objective

Junctions with four approaches (crossroads) make higher demands on road user alertness and behaviour than junctions with three approaches (T-junctions). A four-leg junction has 32 conflict points between the streams of traffic passing though the junction. A three-leg junction has 9 conflict points between the streams of traffic. Norwegian studies of accident rates at junctions (Giæver 1990, Sakshaug and Johannessen 2005) show that four-leg junctions have double the accident rate of three-leg junctions. According to the studies, the number of injury accidents reported to the police per million entering vehicles at different types of road junctions are as shown in Table 1.8.1.

It should be noted that crossroads with a high proportion of minor road traffic have higher accident rates than T-junctions.

Staggered junctions reduce the number of conflict points at junctions and thus make the task of crossing the junction simpler for road users.

### Description of the measure

Staggered junctions can be constructed in two ways: left–right staggering and right–left staggering. Figure 1.8.1 shows these two forms of staggering.

*Table 1.8.1: Injury accidents per million entering vehicles at different types of road junctions*

| Type of control | Type of junction | Speed limit (km/hr) | Percentage of minor road traffic | | |
|---|---|---|---|---|---|
| | | | 0–14.9 | 15.0–29.9 | 30.0– |
| Right hand rule | T-junctions | 50 | 0.07 | 0.07 | 0.13 |
| | Crossroads | 50 | 0.10 | 0.19 | 0.18 |
| Give way (yield) | T-junctions | 80 or 90 | 0.06 | 0.12 | 0.26 |
| | Crossroads | 80 or 90 | 0.07 | 0.27 | 0.58 |
| | T-junctions | 60 or 70 | 0.07 | 0.11 | 0.14 |
| | Crossroads | 60 or 70 | 0.12 | 0.19 | 0.28 |
| | T-junctions | 50 | 0.08 | 0.11 | 0.11 |
| | Crossroads | 50 | — | 0.10 | 0.31 |
| Traffic signals | T-junctions | 50 | 0.04 | 0.06 | 0.05 |
| | Crossroads | 50 | 0.12 | 0.09 | 0.10 |
| Roundabouts | T-junctions | All | All types of side road traffic: 0.03 | | |
| | Crossroads | All | All types of side road traffic: 0.05 | | |

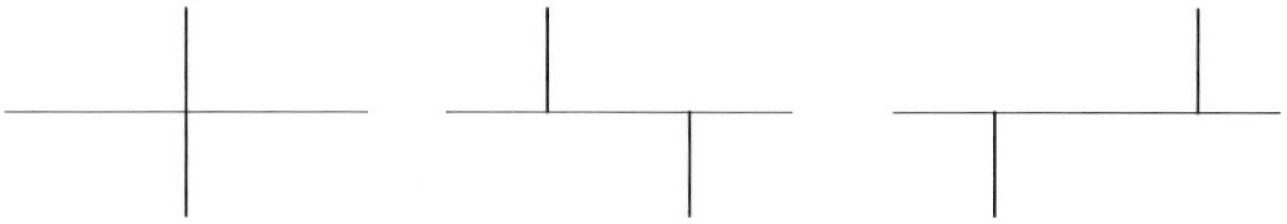


*Figure 1.8.1: Different ways of dividing one crossroad into one staggered junction.*

## Effect on accidents

A number of studies of accident rates at crossroads and T-junctions with different amounts of minor road traffic can be applied in order to estimate how staggering the crossroads will affect accidents. The results given below are taken from the following studies:

Lyager and Løschenkohl (1972) (Denmark)
Johannessen and Heir (1974) (Norway)
Hanna, Flynn and Tyler (1976) (USA)
Vaa and Johannessen (1978) (Norway)
Brüde and Larsson (1981) (Sweden)
Cedersund (1983b) (Sweden)

*Table 1.8.2: Effects of staggering crossroads on the number of accidents at junctions*

| | | Percentage change in the number of accidents | |
|---|---|---|---|
| Accident severity | Type of junctions affected | Best estimate | 95% confidence interval |
| Injury accidents | Junctions with little minor road traffic (< 15%) | +35 | (+10; +70) |
| | Junctions with some minor road traffic (15–30%) | −25 | (−33; −15) |
| | Junctions with heavy minor road traffic (> 30%) | −33 | (−43; −21) |
| | All Junctions | −20 | (−25; −10) |
| Property damage only | Junctions with little minor road traffic (< 15%) | +15 | (+5; +30) |
| | Junctions with average minor road traffic (15–30%) | 0 | (−10; +10) |
| | Junctions with heavy minor road traffic (> 30%) | −10 | (−20; 0) |
| | All Junctions | +3 | (−3; +9) |

Vodahl and Giæver (1986) (Norway)
Brüde and Larsson (1987b) (Sweden)
Montgomery and Carstens (1987) (United States)

On the basis of these studies, the effect on accidents of staggering a four-leg junction (using either pattern shown in Figure 1.8.1) is estimated as follows (Table 1.8.2):

The effect of staggered junctions depends on the proportion of minor road traffic at the crossroads before staggering. When minor road traffic is small, no safety gains are obtained by dividing the crossroads into a staggered junction. Where minor road traffic is heavy, the number of injury accidents is reduced by around 33%. The number of property-damage-only accidents is reduced by around 10%. The effect on property damage only accidents is smaller than the effect on the number of injury accidents.

Only one study (Brüde and Larsson 1987b) has compared the two methods of staggering at crossroads. The study indicates that the left–right stagger has a more favourable effect on traffic safety than the right–left stagger. The left–right pattern reduced the number of accidents by 4%, while the right–left pattern increased it by 7%. The difference in effect is, however, not statistically significant.

**Effect on mobility**

Mahalel, Craus and Polus (1986) have studied traffic flow at crossroads compared with staggered junctions created either by left–right stagger or right–left stagger. The average waiting time for crossing the main road for traffic from a minor road is shortest with the right–left stagger and longest with the left–right stagger. Crossroads occupy a position in-between. The explanation for this is that with the right–left stagger, the traffic from the minor road has to give way to only one stream of traffic when it turns (to the right) onto the main road. With an hourly traffic rate of 1,000 vehicles (both directions taken together), the difference in waiting time between right–left staggering and left–right staggering is around 15 s per car.

According to Mahalel, Craus and Polus (1986) right–left staggering creates greater disturbances for traffic on the main road than left–right staggering. Traffic disturbance on a main road occurs when a vehicle on a minor road turning on to a main road forces a vehicle on the main road to reduce speed, in order to maintain a reasonable distance between the vehicles. The reason why such disturbances are greater with right–left staggering than left–right staggering is that drivers coming from a minor road are assumed to accept shorter gaps when they are turning right onto the road than when they are turning left.

**Effect on the environment**

No studies have been found which show how staggering of crossroads affects the environment.

**Costs**

No figures are available that show the costs of staggering a crossroads. At least one new junction must be constructed when staggering a four-leg junction. The costs of this and any alterations to the road may be of the order of magnitude of NOK 1–10 million.

**Cost–benefit analysis**

No cost–benefit analyses of staggering cross roads have been found. Therefore a numerical example has been made to show the typical costs and benefits of this measure. It is assumed that the measure is implemented at a yield-controlled crossroads in a rural area, where the minor road traffic is more than 30%. The junction is assumed to have an annual average daily traffic of 5,000 incoming vehicles, of which 2,000 come from the minor roads (1,000 from each minor road). The accident rate is 0.50 injury accidents per million entering vehicles. It is assumed that 10 property-damage-only accidents occur per injury accident. Staggering the crossroads is assumed to reduce the number of injury accidents by 30% and the number of property-damage-only accidents by 10%.

The present value of saved accident costs have been estimated to around NOK 4.8 million. In addition, there may be a gain in mobility. However, with the assumed amount of traffic, this will be small. If the measure costs less than the gain of NOK 4.8 million, it will provide benefits that are greater than costs in monetary terms.

## 1.9 Grade-separated junctions

### Problem and objective

At very large traffic volumes, at-grade junctions cannot serve traffic satisfactorily, no matter what form of traffic control is used. Queues may form, as well as dense traffic, with numerous turning manoeuvres, which often create unstable and dangerous situations. This increases the number of accidents, especially the number of accidents involving property damage only.

In order to improve traffic flow and reduce the chances of conflict between different traffic streams, grade-separated junctions (interchanges) can be built. In full grade-separated junctions, all movements, which require crossing other streams of traffic, are removed and are reduced to changing traffic lanes for traffic in the same direction.

### Description of the measure

A grade-separated junction (interchange) is a junction where the primary traffic streams are segregated from each other by being placed on separate levels. Various forms of interchanges have been developed, such as diamond interchanges, trumpet interchanges, and full or partial cloverleaf interchanges. These interchanges differ with respect to the types of ramps that are built for turning traffic.

### Effect on accidents

***Grade-separated junctions instead of at-grade junctions.*** Effects of replacing at-grade junctions by grade-separated junctions have been estimated based on studies from several European countries:

Hvoslef (1974) (Norway)
Statens vägverk (1983b) (Sweden)
Tie- ja vesirakennushallitus (1983) (Finland)
Johansen (1985) (Norway)

Pajunen (1999) (Finland)
Tielaitos (2000) (Finland)
Meewes (2002) (Germany)

Based on these studies, the effects on the numbers of accidents of replacing at-grade junctions by grade-separated junctions are estimated as shown in Table 1.9.1. The studies have not evaluated the conversion of junctions from one type of junction to another but compared accident rates between different types of junctions.

According to the results shown in Table 1.9.1 the accident rate is lower at-grade-separated junctions than at at-grade junctions. The largest differences have been found in X-junctions. At X-junctions, the reduction of the number of injury accidents is larger than the reduction of the number of property-damage-only accidents.

*Table 1.9.1: Effects of grade-separated junctions on accidents in the area of the junctions*

| | Percentage change in the number of accidents | | |
|---|---|---|---|
| Accident severity | Types of accidents affected | Best estimate | 95% confidence interval |
| ***T-junction: grade-separated instead of at-grade*** | | | |
| Unspecified | All accidents | −16 | (−33; +4) |
| Injury accidents | All accidents | −24 | (−57; +33) |
| ***X-junction: grade-separated instead of at-grade*** | | | |
| Unspecified | All accidents | −42 | (−52; −30) |
| Injury accidents | All accidents | −57 | (−62; −51) |
| Property damage only accidents | All accidents | −36 | (−50; −19) |
| ***Signalised junctions: grade-separated instead of at-grade*** | | | |
| Unspecified | All accidents | −27 | (−36; −18) |
| Injury accidents | All accidents | −28 | (−40; −15) |
| ***Grade-separated instead of partly at-grade junctions*** | | | |
| Unspecified | All accidents | −15 | (−24; −5) |
| ***Partly grade-separated junctions instead of at-grade X-junction*** | | | |
| Unspecified | All accidents | −26 | (−38; −13) |
| ***Partly grade-separated junctions instead of at-grade X-junction with speed camera*** | | | |
| Unspecified | All accidents | +115 | (+52; +205) |
| ***Partly grade-separated instead of signalised junctions*** | | | |
| Unspecified | All accidents | −22 | (−41; +3) |

The accidents in the area of the junctions include accidents on ramps for grade-separated junctions, but not accidents on comparable stretches of road immediately before and after at-grade junctions. If these accidents were included in the calculation of the effects on accidents, still larger reductions of the number of accidents on grade-separated junctions would probably have been found. However, ramps are a new road element when grade-separated junctions are constructed, and their effects on safety should be included in the effects of grade-separated junctions.

Partly grade-separated junctions are junctions where there is no at-grade connection between two main roads, but where the connections between ramps and main roads are at-grade (instead of acceleration/deceleration lanes). These types of junctions have been investigated in Germany by Meewes (2002). Partly grade-separated junctions have been found to be less safe than grade-separated junctions, but safer than at-grade X-junctions. When at-grade X-junctions are equipped with speed cameras, these are safer than partly grade-separated junctions without speed cameras. No significant difference has been found between partly grade-separated and signalised junctions.

***Effects of the design of grade-separated junctions.*** Effects of the design of grade-separated junctions have been investigated in the following studies:

Lundy (1967) (USA)
Cirillo (1968, 1970) (USA)
Yates (1970) (USA)
Wold (1995) (Norway)
Bauer and Harwood (1998) (USA)
Janson et al. (1998) (USA)
Khorashadi (1998) (USA)
Bared, Giering and Warren (1999) (USA)
Pajunen (1999) (Finland)
Tielaitos (2000) (Finland)
Lee, Bonneson, Kidd and Larwin (2002) (USA)
Golob, Recker and Alvarez (2004) (USA)
McCartt, Shabanova Northrup and Retting (2004) (USA)

The results of these studies are summarised in Table 1.9.2 for diamond interchanges compared to other types of interchanges. The effects of different design elements of grade-separated junctions are summarised in Table 1.9.3. Design elements for which results from accident studies are available are layout of the junction, ramp types, curve radius of ramps, acceleration/ deceleration-, and merging-lanes and the number of

*Table 1.9.2: Effects on accidents in the area of intersections of diamond interchanges compared to other types of interchanges*

| | Percent change in the number of accidents | | |
|---|---|---|---|
| Accident severity | Types of accidents affected | Best estimate | 95% confidence interval |
| ***Diamond instead of trumpet*** | | | |
| Unspecified | All accidents | −38 | (−59; −7) |
| ***Diamond instead of junction with direct access ramps*** | | | |
| Unspecified | All accidents | −25 | (−59; +40) |
| ***Diamond instead of clover-leaf*** | | | |
| Unspecified | All accidents | −2 | (−19; +18) |
| ***Diamond instead of loop*** | | | |
| Unspecified | All accidents | −9 | (−25; +10) |
| ***Diamond instead of other*** | | | |
| Unspecified | All accidents | −7 | (−17; +4) |
| ***Diamond instead of other*** | | | |
| Unspecified | Truck accidents, *not* on ramps | −11 | (−23; +3) |
| ***Diamond instead of other except loop*** | | | |
| Unspecified | Truck accidents on ramps | +43 | (+33; +54) |
| ***Diamond instead of loop*** | | | |
| Unspecified | Truck accidents on ramps | −10 | (−20; +2) |
| ***TUDI instead of SPUI (see text for explanation)*** | | | |
| Unspecified | All accidents | +2 | (−11; +17) |

lanes. All results refer to comparisons of accident rate between different types of intersections or between different variants of the design elements of interchanges. None of the studies evaluated the effects of converting interchanges into a different type of interchange.

According to the results in Table 1.9.1, diamond interchanges have lower accident rates than most other types of interchanges. Most differences are only small and not significant. Diamond interchanges are most favourable in comparison with trumpet interchanges and junctions with direct access ramps. There are several factors that make diamond interchanges relatively safe. The layout is relatively simple and thereby reduces confusion or errors among drivers. Ramps in diamond interchanges are straight, and accident rates are smaller on straight ramps than on curved ramps (see below).

*Table 1.9.3: Effects on accidents in the area of intersections of design elements of grade-separated junctions*

| | Percent change in the number of accidents | | |
|---|---|---|---|
| Accident severity | Types of accidents affected | Best estimate | 95% confidence interval |
| ***Ramp types*** | | | |
| Unspecified | Straight ramp instead of clover-leaf | −45 | (−60; −25) |
| Unspecified | Clover-leaf instead of long ramp | −23 | (−39; −3) |
| Unspecified | Long instead of short ramp | −38 | (−49; −24) |
| Unspecified | Short ramp instead of loop | −30 | (−45; −10) |
| ***Straightening of curves on ramps (larger curve radius)*** | | | |
| Unspecified | Accidents on ramps | −13 | (−36; +17) |
| ***Crossroad above instead of below main road*** | | | |
| Unspecified | All accidents | −4 | (−17; +10) |
| ***Extension of acceleration lane by 30 m*** | | | |
| Unspecified | Accidents in acceleration lane | −11 | (−17; −5) |
| ***Extension of deceleration lane by 30 m*** | | | |
| Unspecified | Accidents in deceleration lane | −7 | (−13; +0) |
| ***Extension of acceleration and deceleration lane by ca 30 metres*** | | | |
| Unspecified | Accidents in acceleration/deceleration lane | −5 | (−11; +2) |
| ***Merging lanes requiring less than 2 lane changes instead of merging lanes requiring 2 lane changes for driving on/off ramp*** | | | |
| Unspecified | Accidents in merging lane | −32 | (−36; −27) |
| ***4-lane road instead of 2-lane road*** | | | |
| Unspecified | All accidents | +30 | (+5; +61) |
| ***Off-ramp instead of on-ramp*** | | | |
| Unspecified | Accidents on ramps | +73 | (+70; +75) |

Truck accidents in different types of grade-separated junctions have been investigated by Janson et al. (1998). Diamond interchanges are safer for trucks than other types of grade-separated intersections, when accidents on ramps are not taken into account. Truck accident rates on ramps in diamond interchanges are lower than on loop ramps, but higher than on other types of ramps (ramps on which direction changes are below 180°). The rate of truck accidents on grade-separated junctions is lower when traffic volumes are high than when traffic volumes are low.

No difference has been found between accident rates in TUDI (tight urban diamond interchange) and SPUI (single-point urban interchange). These results are based on the study by Lee, Bonneson, Kidd and Larwin (2002). Both types of interchange are designed so as to be as little space-consuming as possible.

Accident rates on different types of ramps have been studied by McCartt, Shabanova Northrup and Retting (2004) and Janson et al. (1998). Accident rates on ramps increase in the following order: straight ramp (lowest accident rates), clover ramp, long ramp, short ramp, loop (highest accident rates). These results are in accordance with the results from the comparisons between different layouts of grade-separated junctions. The lowest accident rates have been found in diamond interchanges, which are built with straight ramps only. The results are also in accordance with the result that shows lower accident rates on straighter ramps.

Accident rates seem to be lower in grade-separated junctions where the side road crosses over (instead of under) the main road, possibly because of better sight conditions for merging traffic from the side road. A relationship between the length of acceleration and deceleration lanes and accident rate has been found on lanes with a length of up to 200 m. Longer acceleration or deceleration lanes have not been found to be associated with a lower accident rate. The most common type of accident on ramps are road departure and rollover accidents (Janson et al. 1998, McCartt, Shabanova Northrup and Retting 2004).

Merging lanes have been investigated by Golob, Recker and Alvarez (2004). The accident rate increases with an increasing number of lane changes that are required for driving on or off a ramp. Most accidents in merging lanes do however not involve personal injury (Hoffmann, Kölle and Mennicken 2000).

Accident rates in grade-separated junctions are higher on four-lane roads than on two-lane roads. This is contrary to accident rates on sections, which usually are higher on two-lane roads than on four-lane roads.

Accident rates have been found to be larger on off- than on on-ramps. Road departure accidents are three times as frequent on off-ramps compared to on-ramps. Rear-end collisions occur equally often on on- and off-ramps. Side impacts (sidswipe) are twice as frequent on on-ramps compared to off-ramps (McCartt, Shabanova Northrup and Retting 2004).

Ramp metering is a measure that increases the capacity of grade-separated junctions by preventing vehicles from entering the main road in platoons. Ramp metering reduces stop-and-go traffic and thereby fuel consumption and it may reduce collisions (Cambridge Systematics 2001, Lee, Hellinga and Ozbay 2006).

### Effect on mobility

Grade-separated junctions are primarily constructed where traffic volume is too great to flow satisfactorily through an intersection, particularly on roads where high-speed levels imply that an intersection represents a particularly great hazard. It is therefore reasonable to assume that mobility in the majority of cases will increase.

Model calculations on the basis of general relationships between traffic levels, capacity and waiting times at intersections indicate that the average time gain per car at interchanges may be between 5 and 15 s (Elvik 1993). In a Finnish study (Tuovinen, Kosonen and Enberg 2002) a somewhat larger effect was estimated, depending on the traffic volume. The average time gain is estimated at 7–9 s per vehicle when the traffic volume is 500 vehicles per hour on the main road and 100–250 vehicles on the ramp. When the traffic volumes are twice as large, the estimated time savings are between 14 and 160 s per vehicle.

Acceleration lanes have additionally positive effects on driving speeds, which are higher and thereby also allow for acceptance of smaller gaps, than when there are no acceleration lanes.

### Effect on the environment

No studies have been found that indicate an effect of grade-separated junctions on environmental conditions. A grade-separated interchange requires more space than an intersection. Artificially elevated ramps and bridges can appear dominant in the landscape and spoil the view for people living along the road. Fuel consumption may be reduced because of reduced braking and accelerating.

### Costs

On the basis of figures for a small number of interchanges built in Norway, the average cost of constructing an interchange is estimated at NOK 40 million (Elvik 1996). This figure is very uncertain. The costs depend among other things on the type of interchange and required space.

### Cost–benefit analysis

A numerical example has been calculated for converting an X-junction into a grade-separated junction. The junction is assumed to have an annual average daily traffic of

20,000 vehicles and an accident rate of 0.25 injury accidents per million entering vehicles. The number of injury accidents is assumed to be reduced by 50%. Each vehicle is assumed to save 10 s when passing through the intersection. Under these assumptions, the benefit in the form of saved accident costs is calculated at NOK 41.5 million. The saved costs of travel time comprise NOK 46.6 million. The total benefit is NOK 88.2 million. This is more than twice as much as the estimated average costs, this cost estimate is however uncertain and not based on recent projects.

## 1.10 Black spot treatment

### Problem and objective

In towns and cities, but also in rural areas, traffic accidents often cluster at specific places. These are often junctions, but may also be private access roads, curves, railway-highway level crossings, hilltops, narrow road stretches or bridges. A concentration of accidents at a specific spot may partly be due to incorrect, inappropriate or inadequate road design or traffic control at that place. In such cases, the clustering of accidents may be avoided or reduced by improving road design or traffic control.

Black spot treatment aims at identifying, analysing and improving roads at places with a concentration of accidents by improving road design or traffic regulation at such spots in order to reduce the expected number of accidents.

### Description of the measure

There is no international standard definition of accident black spots or hazardous road sections. From a theoretical point of view, an accident black spot should be defined as follows (Elvik 2007, Sørensen and Elvik 2007):

> *The expected number of accidents is higher than at other similar locations as a result of local risk factors.*

The definition of accident black spots should be based on the local expected number of accidents instead of the recorded number of accidents. The recorded number is always influenced by both random and systematic variation. However, only the systematic variation is of interest for road safety improvements. Comparisons should be made with the expected number of accidents at other similar locations in order to identify locations with inadequate design. Finally, local risk factors should be identified, which may explain the higher expected number of accidents and which may be removed or amended by means of road design improvements (Elvik 2007, Sørensen and Elvik 2007).

The identification of hazardous locations should rely on the empirical Bayes method, which controls for regression to the mean effects (Elvik 2007). The results of black spot treatment evaluations are especially prone to regression to the mean, since black spots are per definition locations with exceptionally high accident numbers. If the necessary resources or data are not available, a simpler accident model or category-based method should be used (Sørensen 2007).

Accident black spot identification and improvement may be supplemented by a network safety management, which focuses on longer hazardous stretches of road, and which is increasingly used e.g. in Denmark, Sweden, Finland, the Netherlands and the UK (EU 2003, Sørensen 2006, SWOV 2007). Many accident black spots have been improved, while at the same time new roads are increasingly built based on improved knowledge of road safety, and road safety audits are conducted before new roads are built.

In Norway, there are two definitions of hazardous road locations (Statens vegvesen 2007c), accident black spots with at least four police reported injury accidents during five years over a stretch of road of maximum of 100 m, and hazardous road sections with at least 10 police reported injury accidents during five years on a stretch of road of maximum 1 km. Additionally, hazardous road locations are identified based on the injury severity density, or accident costs. In this approach a distinction is made between accidents of varying severity and accident costs are calculated by weighting the numbers of fatal, critical, serious and slight injuries according to economic valuations of the respective injuries (e.g. NOK 26.5 million per fatality; Ragnøy Christensen and Elvik 2002). Hazardous road locations are identified by comparing the actual accident costs with the accident costs that would be expected on a road with similar geometric and traffic characteristics. The 10% of the road network with the highest accident costs and where there were registered fatally or critically injured are classified as 'hazardous'. Accident analyses are recommended for adjoining road stretches with high accident costs Ragnøy and Elvik (2003).

**Effect on accidents**

The measures taken to treat accident black spots vary from place to place. Black spot treatment can be seen as a *general approach* to improving road safety, where the accident record and other information are used to identify those locations where it is most worthwhile to improve safety. It is therefore of some interest to summarise general experiences with black spot treatment. A number of studies cover these:

Exnicios (1967) (USA)
Malo (1967) (USA)
Wilson (1967) (USA)
Tamburri, Hammer, Glennon and Lew (1968) (USA)
Hammer (1969) (USA)
Dearinger and Hutchinson (1970) (UK and USA)
Duff (1971) (UK)
Hatherly and Lamb (1971) (UK)
Karr (1972) (USA)
Hvoslef (1974) (Norway)
OECD (1976) (France)
Hatherly and Young (1977) (UK)
Vodahl and Johannessen (1977) (Norway)
Jørgensen (1979) (Denmark)
Statens vegvesen (1983) (Norway)
Boyle and Wright (1984) (UK)
Elvik (1985) (Norway)
Lovell and Hauer (1986) (USA)
Persaud (1987) (Canada)
Christensen (1988) (Norway)
Mountain and Fawaz (1989) (UK)
Corben, Ambrose and Wai (1990) (Australia)
Flagstad (1990) (Norway)
Wong (1990) (USA)
Lalani (1991) (USA)
Retting (1991) (USA)
Sørensen (1991) (Denmark)
Kølster Pedersen et al. (1992) (Nordic countries)
Mountain and Fawaz (1992) (UK)
Mountain, Fawaz and Sineng (1992) (UK)
Værø (1992a, 1992b, 1992c, 199d) (Denmark)
Holmskov and Lahrmann (1993) (Denmark)
Tziotis (1993) (Australia)
Gregory and Jarrett (1994) (UK)
Mountain et al. (1994) (UK)
BTCE (1995) and Motha, Musidlak and Williams (1995) (Australia)

Mountain, Jarrett and Fawaz (1995) (UK)
Legassick (1996) (UK)
Proctor (1996) (UK)
Weinert (1996) (Germany)
Corben and Hamish (1998) (Australia)
Mountain, Maher and Fawaz (1998) (UK)
Giæver (1999) (Norway)
Corben, Newstead, Diamantopoulou and Cameron (1996) and Newstead and Corben (2001) (Australia)
Bureau of Transport Economics (2001) (Australia)
Københavns Amt (2001) (Denmark)
Larsen (2002) (Denmark)
Sørensen and Jensen (2004) (Denmark)
Statens vegvesen (2005) (Norway)
Traffic Engineering Branch (2005, 2007) (Australia)
Meuleners, Hendrie, Legge and Cercarelli (2005), Meuleners, Hendrie, Lee and Legge (2008) (Australia)
Scully, Newstead, Corben and Candappa (2006) and Corben, Scully, Newstead and Candappa (2008) (Australia).

It was found that the results of studies of the effects of black spot treatment depend very much on the confounding factors the studies have controlled for (Elvik 1997). Whether or not the studies have controlled for regression to the mean in the number of accidents is particularly significant. Table 1.10.1 summarises the results from studies that have controlled for time trends and for regression to the mean.

The results in Table 1.10.1 indicate that both accident black spot and black section treatment reduce accidents significantly. The percentage change in the number of injury accidents is somewhat greater for accident black spot treatment than for accident black section treatment, and greater in rural than in urban areas. Effects on injury accidents are greater than the effects on property-damage-only accidents. According to the study by Corben, Scully, Newstead and Candappa (2008) effects are greater on local roads (−56%) than on main roads (−24%).

The effects on accidents vary between different measures. Most of the results in Table 1.10.1 refer to treatments where a number of measures has been implemented simultaneously. The effects vary also between countries. The greatest effects were found in countries with no long tradition for accident black spot/section treatment (Sørensen and Elvik 2007). The estimated reduction of injury accidents by 26% is

*Table 1.10.1: Effects on accidents black spot treatment*

| | | Percentage change in number of accidents | |
|---|---|---|---|
| Accident severity | Types of accident affected | Best estimate | 95% confidence interval |
| ***Black spot and black section treatment*** | | | |
| Injury accidents | All accidents at the spot/on the section | −26 | (−25; −27) |
| Property damage only accidents | All accidents at the spot/on the section | −19 | (−31; −6) |
| Injury accidents | All accidents at the spot/on the section in urban areas | −30 | (−31, −28) |
| Injury accidents | All accidents at the spot/on the section in rural areas | −43 | (−47, −39) |
| ***Black spot section treatment*** | | | |
| Injury accidents | All accidents at the spot | −33 | (−36; −30) |
| Property damage only accidents | All accidents at the spot | +0 | (−27; +38) |
| ***Black section treatment*** | | | |
| Injury accidents | All accidents on the section | −28 | (−31; −28) |
| Property damage only accidents | All accidents on the section | −16 | (−39; +15) |

strongly affected by a number of large Australian studies. When only European studies are included in the analysis, the effect estimate is a reduction by 22%.

Studies that have not controlled for regression to the mean found for the most part greater accident reductions than those presented above. However, these results are not methodologically tenable and are therefore not presented here.

Some studies have investigated possible accident migration effects of accident black spot treatment. Accident migration means an increase of the number of accidents at nearby locations where no improvements have been made. Accident migration may be controlled for by investigating changes in the total number of accidents at both improved and non-improved locations. The results do not indicate that the number of injury accidents changes significantly when accident migration is controlled for. For accident black spot treatment, a reduction of the number of injury accidents by 5% was found (95% CI [−21; +14]) and for accident black section treatment an increase by 2% was found (95% CI [−6; +11]). These results should be considered with a certain amount of scepticism (Elvik 1997). Only a handful of studies have considered possible accident migration as a result of black spot treatment. These studies have not, as yet, given any good explanation for the phenomenon. As a result, it is not known how widespread a tendency towards accident migration may be, and what causes it.

**Effect on mobility**

The effect on mobility of black spot treatment depends on the measures used. Measures that may improve mobility, especially when traffic is heavy, include channelisation of junctions, roundabouts, traffic signal control of junctions, upgrading traffic signals and improving the friction of the road surface. Measures that reduce mobility are reduced speed limits and other speed-reducing measures. Measures, which have small effects on mobility, are background and directional markings in curves, minor sight improvement measures and various road marking treatments.

**Effect on the environment**

The environmental effects of road traffic depend, among other things, on traffic volume, variation in speed, composition of the traffic, the road alignment and the road surroundings. A significant change in environmental effects can be achieved by changing these conditions.

Measures that reduce speed or that improve the quality of traffic flow, i.e. reduce congestion and lead to less dispersion with respect to speed, normally reduce the environmental problems along a road. The same is true of measures that reduce traffic volume. Reducing traffic volume is however not normally an aim of black spot treatment.

**Costs**

The costs of black spot treatment depend on the measures used and may vary from a few thousand NOK (e.g. for road signs) to several million NOK (e.g. conversion of a junction into a roundabout). Black spot improvements in the Norwegian county Østfold (300 sites) cost between NOK 10,000 and 1.6 million per site, the average cost was NOK 0.2 million per site, not including maintenance costs (Statens vegvesen 2005). The average costs of impovements of hazardous road sections following road safety inspections are NOK 0.6 million per kilometre road for the implementation of short-term measures (not including maintenance costs and costs for conducting the audits) (Statens vegvesen 2005).

**Cost–benefit analysis**

The main aim of black spot treatment is the identification of sites where local risk factors contribute to high accident rates. These risk factors are often related to details, not to more general aspects of road design. Improvements are therefore often relatively cheap. The benefit–cost ratio of cheap black spot treatments can be very high. A report proposing black spot treatments at Hamar, Norway (Stigre 1993a) shows that the majority of measures have a benefit–cost ratio between 30 and 60. More comprehensive measures normally have a lower benefit–cost ratio.

A numerical example has been made for the improvement of an accident black spot with four injury accidents over a period of five years (which corresponds to the official Norwegian definition of an accident black spot). The measure is assumed to reduce the number of injury accidents by 25%. No change is assumed for the number of property-damage-only accidents. The time period for the example is 25 years. The annual maintenance costs of the measure are assumed to be 2.5% of the investment costs. Under these assumptions, a measure that costs NOK 10 million will have a benefit–cost ratio of one. Measures that cost less will have a greater benefit–cost ratio. When the same calculation is made for a hazardous road section with 10 injury accidents over a period of five years, measures with a cost of NOK 25 million or less will have a benefit–cost ratio of 1 or greater.

In Norway, cost–benefit ratios for short-term measures following road safety inspections on 345 km roads is estimated to be ca. 2.5. Benefit–cost ratios vary between 1.1 on roads with a traffic volume of AADT 5,000 and a cost–benefit ratio of 5.7 on roads with a traffic volume of AADT 30,000. The analyses show that road safety inspections have greater benefits than costs on roads with a traffic volume of AADT 5,000 or more (Erke and Elvik 2007).

## 1.11 Cross-section improvements

### Problem and objective

Dangerous situations can easily arise on narrow roads when the amount of traffic increases. A narrow road allows drivers less room to manoeuvre their vehicles and as a result, there is less margin for errors than on a wide road, especially at high speeds. When braking, encountering other vehicles, turning onto or off a road, and overtaking, the amount of available road area influences normal driving and the chances of avoiding an accident. Pedestrians and cyclists may also have less room on narrow roads than on wider roads, especially when motor vehicle traffic is heavy.

Improving the cross-section of the road is intended to give all roads users increased safety margins by making the road wider, by constructing hard shoulders along the road and by increasing the number of traffic lanes and by constructing central reservations between the carriageways. Another important objective is to increase mobility by increasing the capacity of the road.

**Description of the measure**

The cross-section of a road is the design elements it consists of when a cut is made across it. Elements in the cross-section are shown in Figure 1.11.1

Road width consists of the traffic lanes and the hard shoulders. The shoulder is a driveable area between the edge of the lanes and the edge of the road. The carriageway consists of one or more traffic lanes, which are normally next to each other and are divided by lane lines (centre lines on two-lane roads). Central reservations (medians) may take the form of earth or grass mounds with a V-shaped profile, or barriers.

Cross-section improvements include the following measures:

- Increasing the number of traffic lanes
- Increasing the width of the road
- Constructing passing lanes (on one or both sides)
- Constructing hard shoulders
- Increasing the width of the hard shoulder
- Simultaneously altering the width of the traffic lanes and of the hard shoulder
- Installing central reservations (medians)
- Increasing median width
- Increasing the width of bridges
- Emergency lanes for trucks

Combinations of these measures (and other possible measures) are dealt with in Section 1.14, dealing with reconstruction and rehabilitation of roads.

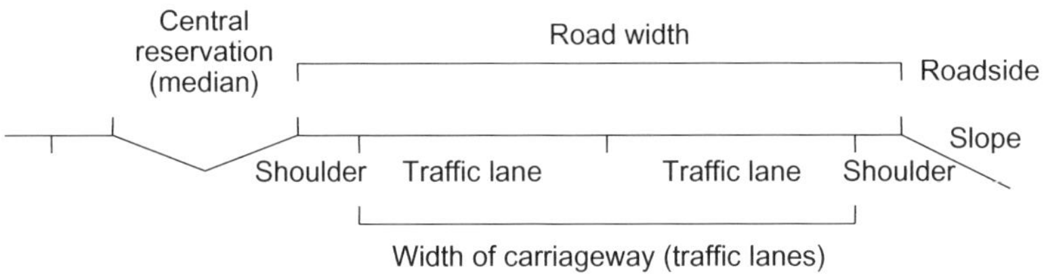


*Figure 1.11.1: Elements in the cross-section (traffic lanes in one direction only).*

**Effect on accidents**

***Number of traffic lanes.*** The relationships between the number of driving lanes and accident rates have been investigated in the following studies:

Kihlberg and Tharp (1968) (USA)
Thorson and Mouritsen (1971) (Denmark)
Andersen (1977) (Denmark)
Nordtyp-projektgruppen (1980) (Nordic countries)
Vejdirektoratet (1980) (Denmark)
Muskaug (1981) (Norway)
Rogness, Fambro and Turner (1982) (USA)
Krenk (1985) (Denmark)
Harwood (1986) (USA)
Levine, Golob and Recker (1988) (USA)
Blakstad and Giæver (1989) (Norway)
Goble (1994) (New Zealand)
Bauer and Harwood (2000) (USA)
Buss (2000) (Germany)
Agent and Pigman (2001) (USA)

Most of these studies have compared accident rates between roads with different numbers of lanes, and not evaluated remarking or reconstruction projects. Based on these studies, it is estimated how increasing the number of lanes affects accidents.

When the number of lanes is increased from 2 to 4, a non-significant decrease of accident rates has been found. The overall effect of increasing the number of lanes is zero, i.e. no effect. The results are very heterogeneous and inconsistent. However, the results are highly heterogeneous, indicating that moderator variables are likely to affect the size and direction of the effects. The results are likely to be affected by other differences between roads with different numbers of lanes, e.g. traffic volumes, road standard, median barrier, curvature, mean speed, traffic volumes etc., which are related to accident rates and which are not controlled for.

A number of other studies (not included in the results in Table 1.11.1) have estimated the relationship between the number of lanes and accidents in regression models, which control for a number of other factors. These studies are

Poch and Mannering (1996) (USA)
Milton and Mannering (1996) (USA)

*Table 1.11.1: Effects on accidents of number of driving lanes*

| | Percentage change in the number of accidents | | |
|---|---|---|---|
| Specification of measure | Accident severity | Best estimate | 95% confidence interval |
| *Increased number of lanes* | Unspecified | 0 | (−7; +7) |
| *4 instead of 2 lanes* | Injury accidents | −11 | (−25; +5) |
| | Property damage only accidents | −7 | (−31; +25) |
| | Unspecified | −12 | (−23; +2) |

Forckenbrock and Foster (1997) (USA)
Shankar, Milton and Mannering (1997) (USA)
Milton and Mannering (1998) (USA)
Sawalha and Sayed (2001) (Canada)
Noland and Oh (2004) (USA)

Most of these studies have found higher accident rates on roads with a larger number of lanes. According to Bauer and Harwood (2000) roads with 4 or more lanes are safer than roads with fewer lanes in rural areas. In urban areas, they found the reverse, roads with 3 or fewer lanes were safer than roads with more lanes.

Even if the number of accidents is greater on 4 lane roads, injury severity seems to be lower. In the study by Forckenbrock and Foster (1997) the proportion of fatal accidents is 44% lower on four-lane roads compared to two-lane roads. An investigation of data on accident numbers and accident costs in Norway also indicates lower injury severity on four-lane roads than on two-lane roads. In Figure 1.11.2, accident numbers and accident costs are compared between two- and four-lane roads with speed limit 50 or 80 km/h. At both speed limits, accident numbers are higher on four-lane roads than on two-lane roads. Accident costs on the contrary are lower on four-lane roads than on two-lane roads. These estimates are based on regression models in which the effect of traffic volume is controlled for.

Based on the present analyses, no straightforward conclusions can be drawn about the relationship between number of lanes and accidents. There are many potential moderator variables. On the whole, the number of accidents may increase, but accident severity seems to decrease.

***Road width.*** A number of studies have been made to determine the effects of road width on the number of accidents. The results, which are given here, are taken from the following studies:

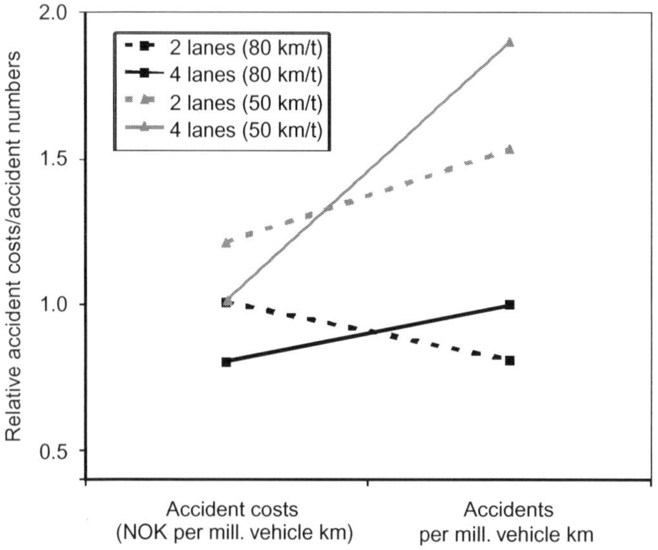


*Figure 1.11.2: Accident costs and accident numbers on roads with different numbers of driving lanes (AADT 10,000).*

Brüde and Nilsson (1976) (Sweden)
Brüde and Larsson (1977) (Sweden)
Brüde, Larsson and Thulin (1980) (Sweden)
Nordtyp-projektgruppen (1980) (Nordic countries)
Vejdirektoratet (1980) (Denmark)
Muskaug (1981) (Norway)
Björketun (1984) (Sweden)
Krenk (1985) (Denmark)
Muskaug (1985) (Norway)
Statens Vägverk (1985a) (Sweden)
Zegeer and Deacon (1987) (USA)
English (1988) (Australia)
Björketun (1991) (Sweden)
Elvik (1991) (Norway)
Corben, Newstead, Diamantopoulou and Cameron (1996) (USA)

Based on these studies, the effect on the number of accidents of increasing the width of the road is estimated as shown in Table 1.11.2.

*Table 1.11.2: Effects on accidents of road width*

| | Percentage change in the number of accidents | | |
|---|---|---|---|
| Accident severity | Types of accidents affected | Best estimate | 95% confidence interval |
| ***Increase of road width from narrower than design standard to road width conforming to design standards*** | | | |
| Injury accidents | Accidents in rural areas | −5 | (−7; −3) |
| Property damage only accidents | Accidents in rural areas | −13 | (−22; −3) |
| Injury accidents | Accidents in urban areas | +11 | (+7; +15) |
| Property damage only accidents | Accidents in urban areas | −21 | (−38; +0) |
| ***Increase of road width within design standards*** | | | |
| Injury accidents | Accidents in rural areas | −8 | (−10; −6) |
| Property damage only accidents | Accidents in rural areas | −10 | (−14; −6) |
| Injury accidents | Accidents in urban areas | +4 | (+0; +8) |
| Property damage only accidents | Accidents in urban areas | +10 | (+3; +18) |

Increasing the width of the road has been found to reduce the number of accidents on roads in rural areas, but may lead to a small increase in the number of accidents in urban areas. The increases in road widths, which form the basis for the figures given above, are mostly between 1 and 3 m. A possible explanation as to why increased road width does not appear to reduce the number of accidents in urban areas is that wider roads in towns and cities make crossings wider, so that pedestrians need more time to cross the road. In rural areas, increased road width may have greater importance as a safety margin, because speed is higher than in towns. Additionally, there may be differences between roads of different widths as regards lane width, shoulder width, median barrier etc. When controlling for traffic volumes and speed, Garber and Erhard (2000) did not find any relationship between road width and accidents.

***Lane width***. Relationships between lane width and accidents have been estimated in the following studies:

Thorson and Mouritsen (1971) (Denmark)
Zegeer, Deen and Mayes (1981) (USA)
Rosbach (1984) (Denmark)
Tsyganov, Machemehl and Warrenchuk (2005) (USA)

The differences of lane width that have been investigated are between 0.3 and 0.5 m. Based on these studies, the effects of increasing lane width have been estimated as shown in Table 1.11.3.

*Table 1.11.3: Effects on accidents of lane width*

| | | Percentage change in the number of accidents | |
|---|---|---|---|
| Accident severity | Accident type affected | Best estimate | 95% confidence interval |
| ***Increase by ca. 0.3–0.5 m*** | | | |
| Unspecified | All accidents | −4 | (−12; +4) |
| Unspecified | Accidents on sections | +19 | (+3; +37) |
| Unspecified | Accidents in curves | −8 | (−32; +26) |
| ***Increase of lane width from narrower than design standard to lane width conforming to design standards*** | | | |
| Injury accidents | Accidents in rural areas | +9 | (+4; +14) |
| Unspecified | Accidents in rural areas | −5 | (−8; −1) |
| Injury accidents | Accidents in urban areas | +14 | (+7; +20) |
| ***Increase of lane width within design standards*** | | | |
| Injury accidents | Accidents in urban areas | −8 | (−14; −1) |
| Unspecified | Accidents in urban areas | −19 | (−24; −15) |

The results are contradictory. They do not show any clear pattern of effects in urban versus in rural areas or on accidents of different severity (most results of unspecified severity include both injury and property damage only accidents). Increasing lane width within the range permitted by design standards seems to reduce the number of accidents in urban areas. The results for accidents on sections and accidents in curves are based on the study by Tsyganov, Machemehl and Warrenchuk (2005). These results indicate that increased lane width is favourable in curves, but not on sections.

The relationships between lane width and accident rates have also been investigated in the following studies by means of regression models that control for a number of other factors:

Milton and Mannering (1996) (USA)
Milton and Mannering (1998) (USA)
Vogt and Bared (1998) (USA)
Abdel-Aty and Radwan (2000) (USA)
Strathman, Duecker, Zhang and Williams (2001) (USA)
Harnen, Umar, Wong and Hashim (2003) (Malaysia)
Noland and Oh (2004) (USA)

The results from these studies are as inconsistent as those shown in Table 1.11.3. Half of the studies found increasing accident rates when lane width increases, and the other half of the studies found decreasing accident rates when lane width increases.

There are numerous potential moderator variables that may affect the relationship between lane width and accident rate.

- A decrease of lane width in combination with an increase of the number of lanes increases accident rates, especially at junctions (Harwood 2003, Abdel-Aty and Radwan 2000). However, roads with narrow lanes have often lower speed limits, and lower speed is mostly associated with a lower accident rate.
- When shoulder width is increased in addition to increasing lane width, Hanley, Gibby and Ferrara (2000) found reduced accident rates. When wider lanes imply narrower shoulder, this may be an explanation of findings of higher accident rates on roads with wider lanes.
- Effects of lane widening may differ between curves and straight sections. Lane widenings were found to reduce accident rates in curves, but to increase accident rates on straight sections (Tsyganov, Machemehl and Warrenchuk 2005). A simultaneous increase of lane and shoulder width in curves has been found to increase accident rates (Hanley, Gibby and Ferrara 2000).
- Studies in Bavaria and Canada (Frost and Keller 1990, Frost and Morrall 1998) found that extra-wide driving lanes reduced both accident numbers and accident severity, although speed increased. The lanes were wide enough to allow overtaking while there was oncoming traffic.
- Effects of lane width may be different between urban and rural areas, the results are however not consistent (see above).

In summary, lane width seems to be related to accidents, but the relationship depends on many other factors and may be positive or negative. No clear relationship between design speed (which is related to lane width amongst other things) and accidents has been found either (Harwood 2003).

***Passing lanes.*** On roads with large differences in speed, e.g. gradients, roads with heavy traffic or scenic roads, queues and irritation can occur which may encourage dangerous overtaking. By providing an extra traffic lane, a passing lane, such problems can be reduced. The effects of passing lanes on the number of accidents have been investigated in the following studies, the results of which are summarised in Table 1.11.4.

Sinclair, Knight and Partners (1973) (USA)
Statens Vägverk (1979) (Sweden)
Harwood and St John (1985) (USA)
Frost and Morrall (1998) (USA)
Tiehallinto (1998) (Finland)
Mutabazi Russell and Stokes (1999) (USA)
Potts and Harwood (2004) (USA)

*Table 1.11.4: Effects on accidents of passing lanes*

| Accident severity | Accident type affected | Percentage change in the number of accidents: Best estimate | 95% confidence interval |
|---|---|---|---|
| ***Passing lane in one direction only*** | | | |
| Injury accidents | All accidents | −13 | (−27; +4) |
| Property damage only accidents | All accidents | −18 | (−27; −7) |
| Unspecified | All accidents | −15 | (−23; −7) |
| Unspecified | Accidents in passing lane | −30 | (−37; −22) |
| Unspecified | Accidents on road section before and after passing lane | −20 | (−35; 0) |
| ***Passing lanes in both directions*** | | | |
| Injury accidents | All accidents | −40 | (−55; −25) |
| Property damage only accidents | All accidents | −6 | (−37; +42) |

Passing lanes in one direction have been found to reduce the number of injury accidents by about 13%. The results refer to accidents on road sections with a passing lane, as well as the stretches of road upstream and downstream of the passing lane.

The results from the studies of Statens Vägverk (1979) and Tiehallinto (1998), which have investigated effects on accidents on the road stretches with passing lanes and effects on accidents upstream and downstream of the passing lanes separately, indicate that accidents are reduced also upstream and downstream of the passing lanes, possibly because of a reduction of overtaking manoeuvres on road stretches without passing lanes. Accident rates related to passing lanes can be further reduced by marking a flush median where the passing lane and the regular driving lane are merging at the end of the passing lane (Tuovinen and Enberg 2003). Double-sided passing lanes reduce the number of injury accidents by about 40%. The effectiveness of passing lanes increases with increasing traffic volumes (Potts and Harwood 2004).

On the whole, passing lanes seem to reduce accidents, especially severe accidents and mostly on roads with large traffic volumes.

***Hard shoulders.*** The significance of hard shoulders has been studied in Denmark and USA:

Zegeer, Deen and Mayes (1981) (USA)
Rogness, Fambro and Turner (1982) (USA)

*Table 1.11.5: Effects on accidents of hard shoulders*

| | Percentage change in the number of accidents | | |
|---|---|---|---|
| Accident severity | Accident type affected | Best estimate | 95% confidence interval |
| ***Constructing hard shoulders*** | | | |
| Injury accidents | All accidents | −17 | (−30; −2) |
| Property damage only accidents | All accidents | −49 | (−60; −43) |
| Unspecified | All accidents | −26 | (−40; −11) |
| ***Extra-wide shoulders*** | | | |
| Injury accidents | All accidents | −19 | (−29; −7) |

Rosbach (1984) (Denmark)
Wang, Hughes and Steward (1998) (USA)
Brown and Tarko (1999) (USA)

The effects of extra-wide shoulders on motorways have been studies in Germany by Heidemann, Bäumer, Hamacher and Hautzinger (1998). Based on these studies, the effects of constructing hard shoulders on accidents are summarised in Table 1.11.5.

On roads with hard shoulder (mostly 0.3–1 m shoulder width) there are on average 17% fewer injury accidents than on roads without hard shoulder. The results refer to accidents in rural areas. The effect on property damage only accidents is larger than the effect on injury accidents. However, the result for property damage only accidents is based on only one study. When the relationship between hard shoulders and accidents is investigated in regression models, which control for several road characteristics and traffic volume, the result is similar; there are fewer accidents on roads with than without hard shoulders (Brown and Tarko 1999).

The effect of extra-wide shoulders has been investigated in Germany on motorways with 4 to 6 lanes with median guardrail and different traffic volumes (AADT between 40,000 and 60,000). Injury accidents were reduced significantly by between ca. 10% and 30%. Extra-wide shoulders have been found to reduce road departure accidents and they provide space for broke down cars and can be used as additional driving lanes.

In summary, the results are consistent in that they show lower accident rates on roads with hard shoulders than on roads without hard shoulders.

***Shoulder width and paving shoulders.*** The relationship between shoulder width and accidents has been investigated by

Zegeer, Deen and Mayes (1981) (USA)
Barbaresso and Bair (1983) (USA)
Rosbach (1984) (Denmark)
Navin and Appeadu (1995) (USA)
Wang, Hughes and Steward (1998) (USA)

The effects of paving shoulders on accidents have been investigated by

Corben, Deery, Mullan and Dyte (1996) (USA)
Ogden (1997) (Australia)
Wang, Hughes and Steward (1998) (USA)

Based on these studies the effects of increasing shoulder width and of paving shoulders are estimated as shown in Table 1.11.6.

Increasing shoulder width has been found to reduce the number of accidents, mostly injury accidents. The effect is larger on motorways than on other rural roads. These results are overall results from comparisons of roads with shoulders of different widths. The results for shoulder width include both roads with paved and unpaved shoulders. Paving shoulders is associated with a large and significant reduction of all types of accidents.

A number of studies have estimated the relationship between shoulder width and accidents with regression models, which control for several other road characteristics and traffic volumes:

Knuiman, Council and Reinfurt (1993)
Miaou (1994)
Milton and Mannering (1996)

*Table 1.11.6: Effects on accidents of increasing shoulder width and of paving shoulders*

| | Percentage change in the number of accidents | | |
|---|---|---|---|
| Accident severity | Accident type affected | Best estimate | 95% confidence interval |
| ***Increasing shoulder width on rural roads*** | | | |
| Injury accidents | All accidents | −18 | (−27; −7) |
| Unspecified | All accidents | −12 | (−23; 0) |
| ***Increasing shoulder width on motorways*** | | | |
| Unspecified | All accidents | −27 | (−43; −8) |
| ***Paving shoulders*** | | | |
| Unspecified | All accidents | −37 | (−48; −24) |

Forckenbrock and Foster (1997)
Shankar, Milton and Mannering (1997)
Milton and Mannering (1998)
Vogt and Bared (1998)
Wang, Hughes and Steward (1998)
Council and Steward (1999)
Hanley, Gibby and Ferrara (2000)
Ivan, Wang and Bernardo (2000)
Strathman, Duecker, Zhang and Williams (2001)
Noland and Oh (2004)

The majority of studies have found significantly fewer accidents on roads with wider shoulders. When roads are divided into roads with wide and narrow shoulders, 1.5 m shoulder width is often used as the limit. Unfavourable effects of wider shoulders have been found only in few studies and under special circumstances. Ivan, Wang and Bernardo found more single-vehicle accidents on roads with wider shoulders. This result is however based on only very few accidents. Strathman, Duecker, Zhang and Williams (2001) found more accidents on motorways with wider shoulders than on motorways with narrow shoulders. Such an effect was not found on other roads than motorways. Wide shoulder may increase accident rates when the shoulders are used as driving lanes and when there are rock or other walls beside the road or when the shoulders are not continuous but interrupted by rock walls (Milton and Mannering 1996, Shankar, Milton and Mannering 1997).

Based on these results, it can be concluded that wider shoulders almost always result in fewer accidents.

***Lane and shoulder width***. Several studies from Denmark, Sweden and USA have investigated the combined effects of lane and shoulder width on accidents:

Brüde and Larsson (1996): increasing lane width from 3.75 to 5.5 m and reduction of shoulder width from 3.25 to 1 m.
DeLuca (1986): reduction of lane width by 0.3 m and increasing shoulder width by 1.2 m.
Carlsson and Lundkvist (1992): increasing lane width from 3.75 to 5.5 m reduction of shoulder width from 2.75 to 1.00 m.
Rosbach (1984): reduction of lane width by 0.25 m and increasing shoulder width by 0.25 m.

The results are inconsistent. The number of injury accidents appears to decrease both when the traffic lanes are made narrower and the shoulders wider (–7%; 95%

CI [−10; −2]) and when the opposite is done, i.e. when the traffic lanes are made wider and the hard shoulder narrower (−5%; 95% CI [−16; +7]). However, it is not unlikely that the results are due to regression to the mean.

***Median***. The effect of medians on accidents have been investigated by:

Kihlberg and Tharp (1968) (USA)
Leong (1970) (Australia)
Thorson and Mouritsen (1971) (Denmark)
Garner and Deen (1973) (USA)
Andersen (1977) (Denmark)
Muskaug (1985) (Norway)
Harwood (1986) (USA)
Scriven (1986) (Australia)
Blakstad and Giæver (1989) (Norway)
Squires and Parsonson (1989) (USA)
Dijkstra (1990) (Netherlands)
Köhler and Schwamb (1993) (Germany)
Bowman and Vecellio (1994) (USA)
Bretherton (1994) (USA)
Claessen and Jones (1994) (Australia)
Oregon Department of Transportation (1996) (USA)
Bonneson and McCoy (1997) (USA)
Beca Carter Hollings & Ferner Ltd. (1998) (New Zealand)
Harwood, Pietrucha, Fitzpatrick and Woolridge (1998) (USA)
Wang, Hughes and Steward (1998) (USA)
Brown and Tarko (1999) (USA)
Bauer and Harwood (2000) (USA)
Eisele, Frawley and Toycen (2004) (USA)
Saito, Cox and Jin (2005) (USA)

Most of these studies have compared accident rates on roads with and without median. Medians in most studies are either curbed medians or other medians without guardrail. Whether or not guardrails are present is however not specified in all studies. The results are summarised in Table 1.11.7.

Medians have been found to reduce accidents in most situations. The largest accidents reductions have been found in urban areas. No effects have been found on property-damage-only accidents. In curves, accidents have been found to increase. However, most of the accident reductions that have been found according to Table 1.11.7 are

*Table 1.11.7: Effects on accidents of medians*

| | Percentage change in the number of accidents | | |
|---|---|---|---|
| Accident severity | Accident type affected | Best estimate | 95% confidence interval |
| ***Median (vs. no median)*** | | | |
| Injury accidents | All accidents | −15 | (−27; −1) |
| Property damage only accidents | All accidents | −2 | (−19; +19) |
| Unspecified | All accidents | −8 | (−15; 0) |
| Unspecified | Accidents in rural areas (no estimate, see text) | | |
| Unspecified | Accidents in semi-urban areas | −9 | (−26; +13) |
| Unspecified | Accidents in urban areas | −19 | (−33; −3) |
| Unspecified | Accidents on straight sections | −11 | (−33; +18) |
| Unspecified | Accidents in curves | +51 | (0; +128) |
| ***Median instead of two-way left turn lane*** | | | |
| Unspecified | All accidents | −29 | (−37; −18) |
| ***Median instead of no median and wider lanes*** | | | |
| Unspecified | All accidents | +15 | (−49; +163) |

likely to be overestimated. A more detailed analysis indicates that the results are either affected by publication bias or by confounding variables, which are not controlled for. When publication bias is controlled for, the overall effect on injury accidents is approximately zero. Table 1.11.7 shows the uncorrected results. For accidents in rural areas, no effect estimate is shown because the results are so inconsistent that an overall effect would not be meaningful.

Medians may have both favourable and unfavourable effects on factors that may be relevant to safety. They increase the distance between opposing traffic flows, reduce the numbers of turning vehicles and may make pedestrian crossings safer. Medians without a barrier may however also increase the number of pedestrian crossings and thereby increase the total number of pedestrian accidents (Zegeer, Stewart, Huang and Lagerwey 2002). Medians seem to change the distribution of accidents by type. Gabler, Gabauer and Bowen (2005) found reduced numbers of head-on collisions, but increased number of less severe accidents. Another study found reduced numbers of side impacts and increased numbers of rear-end collisions (Saito, Cox and Jin 2005). They reduce also passing opportunities.

Unfavourable effects of medians have been found in curves and when medians imply narrower lanes. In both cases, significant increases of accident numbers have been found. Curbed medians and medians with guardrails may cause accidents which otherwise would not have occurred, i.e. vehicles may crash into them (Zegeer and Council 1995).

The main conclusion about the effect of medians on accidents is that accidents may be reduced. The results are, however, uncertain and most likely affected by confounding factors.

***Median type and width.*** The effects of median type and median width on accidents have been investigated in the following studies, the results of which are summarised in Table 1.11.8:

Garner and Deen (1973)
Scriven (1986)
Knuiman, Council and Reinfurt (1993)
Wang, Hughes and Steward (1998)
Claessen and Jones (1994)
Harwood, Pietrucha, Fitzpatrick and Woolridge (1998)

The results indicate that wide curbed medians are safer than narrow medians or flush medians. These results are based on studies in mostly urban areas. A flush median only has no effect on accidents (see Section 3.13 on Road markings). A V-shaped median (ditch) seems to be safer than a curbed median, and there is no significant difference

*Table 1.11.8: Effects on accidents of median width and type of median*

| | Percentage change in the number of accidents | | |
|---|---|---|---|
| Accident severity | Accident type affected | Best estimate | 95% confidence interval |
| ***Wide instead of narrow curbed median*** | | | |
| Unspecified | All accidents | −42 | (−46; −38) |
| ***Curbed instead of flush median*** | | | |
| Unspecified | All accidents | −56 | (−58; −54) |
| ***Median barrier instead of V-shaped median (ditch)*** | | | |
| Unspecified | All accidents | −14 | (−72; +168) |
| ***V-shaped median (ditch) instead of curbed median*** | | | |
| Unspecified | All accidents | −68 | (−71; −65) |
| ***Increasing median width*** | | | |
| Unspecified | All accidents | −5 | (−6; −4) |
| Unspecified | Accidents in rural areas | −54 | (−58; −51) |
| Unspecified | Accidents in urban areas | +86 | (+78; +95) |

between a V-shaped median and a median barrier. These results are based on only one study of motorway accidents.

Increasing median width seems to reduce accidents only in rural areas. A significant increase of accidents on roads with wider medians has been found in urban areas. This result may be due to increased intersection accidents. These results are based on several studies, which have compared different categories of median widths. Since all studies have used different width categories, it is not possible to estimate the relationship between median width and accidents.

Relationships between median width and accidents has also been investigated in a number of studies that have estimated regression models.

1. Knuiman, Council and Reinfurt (1993) (USA; motorways)
2. Wang, Hughes and Steward (1998) (USA; four lane roads in rural areas)
3. Abdel-Aty and Radwan (2000) (USA; principal arterials, urban and rural areas)

All of these studies have found reduced numbers of accidents on roads with wider medians up to 20 m width. When median width gets as large as 20 m or more, no further reductions of accidents have been found.

The main conclusion from these results is that wider medians are safer than narrower medians in rural areas, but not in urban areas.

***Bridge width.*** Two studies have been found of the effects of bridge width on accidents: Mak (1987) and Corben, Newstead, Diamantopoulou and Cameron (1996). The summary effect of increased bridge width from these studies is a significant reduction of accidents by 35% (−51%; −14%). Zegeer and Council (1995) found that the difference between bridge and road width is related to accident numbers. Accident numbers increase as bridge width decreases as long as the bridge is wider than the road. Navin and Appeadu (1995), on the contrary, found no relationship between bridge width (measured as the width of the bridge, in relation to the width of the road immediately before the bridge) and accidents.

No effect on accidents has been found of paving shoulders on bridges (Corben, Newstead, Diamantopoulou and Cameron 1996). No studies have been found that have compared accident rates between bridges and roads with a similar cross profile. The results from Mak and Corben et al. indicate that bridge width affects accidents to a larger degree than road width.

***Escape ramps for trucks.*** Escape ramps for trucks may reduce truck accidents, which are caused by brake failures, especially in long downhill slopes (Abdelwahab and Morral 1997). However, no numerical estimates of the effect on accidents are available.

## Effect on mobility

The cross profile of roads affects strongly the capacity of roads. It also affects speed and the perception of speed by drivers. Increased road capacity and improved road standard often increases traffic volumes.

***Number of lanes.*** Road capacity and speed increase with increasing numbers of lanes. Buss (2000) showed that increased number of lanes with unchanged road width led to an increase of speed by 21%, and congestions were reduced by over 50%.

***Road width.*** A narrow road reinforces the feeling of driving fast, and lane keeping becomes more demanding. Speed has been found to increase with increasing road width (Nilsson, Rigefalk and Koronna-Vilhelmsson 1992a, 1992b). A Norwegian study (Sakshaug 1986) of the factors that influence the mean speed of traffic at a given speed limit found that speed increases by 1.4 km/h per metre of increased road width at a speed limit of 50 km/h and by 0.6 km/h per metre of increased road width at a speed limit of 80 km/h.

***Lane width.*** On wider lanes, speed is higher and there are more passing opportunities. Large effects on speed have been found of extra-wide lanes in Canada and Bavaria (Frost and Keller 1990) without impairing safety. Harwood (1990) has compared the capacity on roads with different lane width. Compared to 12 ft. lanes, the capacity on roads with 11 ft. lane width was reduced by 3%, the capacity on roads with 10 ft. lane width was reduced by 7% and the capacity on roads with 10 ft. lane width was reduced by 10%.

***Passing lanes.*** Passing lanes increase mobility. An American study (Harwood and St John 1985) found that the average speed increased by 3.5 km/h on stretches with passing lanes (speed limit 85 km/h). The percentage of cars queuing was reduced from 35% directly upstream of the lane to 21% in the lane and 29% immediately downstream of the passing lane. The roads, which were studied, had an hourly traffic (in daytime) carrying between 35 and 560 cars.

***Hard shoulders.*** Hard shoulders may reduce congestion because they provide space for broke down vehicles (Heidemann, Bäumer, Hamacher and Hautzinger 1998). Wide hard shoulders may also be used as additional driving lanes, and thereby reduce congestion at high traffic volumes.

### Effect on the environment

No studies have been found that indicate the effects on environmental conditions of cross-section improvements. Increasing the number of traffic lanes and the road width increases the area that is used for the road. A wide road may represent a greater barrier to pedestrians crossing the road than a narrow road. Increased speed and increased traffic volumes increase energy consumption and traffic noise.

### Costs

The costs of cross-section improvements vary greatly, depending on the type of measure, terrain conditions at the site and the density of buildings. Cross-section improvements, which require a widening of the road, are more expensive and more technically complicated in towns and cities than in sparsely populated areas. The measures are also more expensive in rocky terrain than in soil (Gabestad 1981).

A study of traffic safety measures carried out on national highways in Norway in 1986 (Elvik 1987) has found that reconstruction and rehabilitation of roads on average NOK 4 million per kilometre road. Reconstruction and rehabilitation often entail both the cross-section and the alignment being improved at the same time as well as road surface renewal.

### Cost–benefit analysis

A numerical example has been calculated for general cross-section improvements on a road with 80 km/h speed limit and traffic volumes between 1,000 and 20,000 vehicles (AADT). The example is based on data on Norwegian accidents and accident costs. Accident costs are assumed to be reduced by 20%. Speed is assumed to increase from 80 to 90 km/h. The valuation of travel time from a societal perspective is currently NOK 155 per hour (Killi 1999). Table 1.11.9 shows the estimated reductions of accident and time costs.

The example shows that cost savings increase with increasing traffic volumes. Reductions of the costs of travel time increase more than reductions of accident costs because of the logarithmic relationship between volume and accident numbers. The

*Table 1.11.9: Estimated reductions of accident and time costs per kilometre road*

| | ADT | | | |
|---|---|---|---|---|
| Costs per kilometre per year | 1,000 | 5,000 | 10,000 | 20,000 |
| Accident costs (NOK) | 294,637 | 1,163,649 | 2,110,733 | 3,838,005 |
| Reduction of accident costs (NOK) | 58,927 | 232,730 | 422,147 | 767,601 |
| Reduction of costs of travel time (NOK) | 78,576 | 392,882 | 785,764 | 1,571,528 |
| **Sum of reduced costs** | **117,226** | **524,223** | **1,005,133** | **1,933,573** |

total reductions of accident and time costs indicate how much road improvements may cost per year, without being socio-economically unprofitable.

A cost–benefit analysis of installing a median has been conducted by Glad, Albin, McIntosh and Olson (2002). The analysis is based on accidents on 677 km state highway with traffic volumes above 5,000 vehicles. The benefits have been found to be greater than the costs for medians below 15 m width. The cost–benefit ratios are dependent on traffic volume.

## 1.12 Roadside safety treatment

### Problem and objective

The terrain along the roadside may affect for both the number of accidents and the severity of injuries. Steep slopes increase the probability of a vehicle rolling over in the event of running off the road. Rollover increases the probability of the driver or passenger being ejected from the vehicle or the body of the car being crushed. In both cases, the danger of being killed or severely injured increases significantly (Evans 1991). The probability of personal injury or death occurring when leaving the roadway has been found to increase the steeper and higher the slope is (Glennon and Tamburri 1967, Pettersson 1977).

Permanent obstacles close to the road can increase the number of accidents and leave a smaller margin for regaining vehicle control when it has been lost. The distance between the roadside and the obstacle influences the probability of colliding with the obstacle, and if the obstacle is located on an outer bend or on a traffic island, the probability of collision increases even more. It is neither possible nor desirable to protect all fixed obstacles along the roadside using guardrails. The guardrail is in itself a fixed obstacle and in some cases it may reduce visibility.

Roadside safety treatment aims to remove particularly dangerous and sight-reducing obstacles from the roadside and give drivers greater opportunities to regain control of vehicles in the event of running off the road, particularly by levelling out slopes so that the probability of rolling over is reduced.

## Description of the measure

In this chapter, three types of roadside safety treatment are described. These are flattening side slopes, increasing the distance between the edge of the road and fixed obstacles and the removal of such obstacles.

## Effect on accidents

***Flattening side slopes.*** American studies (Dotson 1974, Missouri Dept of Transportation 1980, Graham and Harwood 1982) show that flattening side slopes reduces both the number and severity of accidents. On the basis of these studies, the effect on the number of accidents of flattening side slopes can be estimated as shown in Table 1.12.1.

Flattening a side slope from 1:3 to a slope of 1:4 reduces the number of injury accidents by around 40% and the number of property-damage-only accidents by around 30%. Flattening from 1:4 to 1:6 reduced the number of accidents by a further 20%. A possible explanation of this may be that flatter slopes make it easier to regain control over a vehicle, so that when a vehicle leaves the road, it does not necessarily lead to an accident. Flatter slopes may also have fewer fixed obstacles than steeper slopes and can also improve sight distances.

*Table 1.12.1: Effects of flattening side slopes on the number of accidents*

| | Percentage change in the number of accidents | | |
|---|---|---|---|
| Accident severity | Types of accident affected | Best estimate | 95% confidence interval |
| ***Flattening slope from 1:3 to 1:4*** | | | |
| Injury accidents | All accidents | −42 | (−46; −38) |
| Property damage only | All accidents | −29 | (−33; −25) |
| ***Flattening slope from 1:4 to 1:6*** | | | |
| Injury accidents | All accidents | −22 | (−26; −18) |
| Property damage only | All accidents | −24 | (−26; −21) |

***Increasing the distance to fixed obstacles.*** Increasing the distance to fixed obstacles along the roadside has been studied by Cirillo (1967) and Zegeer et al. (1988). In summary, increasing the distance from around 1 metre to around 5 metres has been found to reduce accidents (unspecified severity) significantly by 22% (95% CI [−24; −20]). Increasing the distance from around 5 metres to around 9 meters has been found to reduce accidents (unspecified severity) significantly by 44% (95% CI [−46; −43]). It is emphasised that these results are based only on two studies. It is unknown whether the results show the effect of increased distances to roadside obstacles alone, or if they also include the effects of other improvements such as improved sight conditions along the road, and to what degree the results may be affected by regression to the mean.

***Removal and marking of roadside obstacles.*** An Australian study (Corben, Deery, Mullan and Dyte 1996) studied the effects on accidents of removing roadside obstacles and of marking them to make them more visible. Following the removal of roadside obstacles, the number of injury accidents decreased by 2% (−20%; +20%). Marking the roadside obstacles led to a 23% reduction in the number of injury accidents (−65%; +69%). The changes in the number of accidents were not statistically significant.

### Effect on mobility

No studies have been found, which indicate how roadside safety treatment affects mobility. To the extent that such improvements improve visibility, speed may increase.

### Effect on the environment

No studies have been found that show how roadside safety treatment affects the environment. Deeper cuttings and higher embankments are major landscape incursions and can spoil the landscape. Planting along embankments can reduce this negative effect.

### Costs

The costs of flattening side slopes and removing roadside obstacles vary with the terrain conditions. Relevant cost figures are not available.

### Cost–benefit analysis

A numerical example has been calculated for a national highway with an annual average daily traffic of 1,500 vehicles and an accident rate of 0.20 injury accidents per million vehicle km. The number of injury accidents is assumed to decrease by 20% and the number of property-damage-only accidents by 5%. It is further assumed that the average speed increases from 60 to 70 km/h. Vehicle operating costs are assumed to decrease by NOK 0.05 per kilometre driven. The benefit of improving 1 km of road is calculated at NOK 0.7 million in saved accident costs, NOK 1.5 million in saved costs of travel time and NOK 0.3 million in reduced vehicle operating costs, comprising NOK 2.5 million in total. The cost of the measure is calculated at NOK 4.8 million. The benefit in this case is smaller than the costs.

## 1.13 Improving road alignment and sight distance

### Problem and objective

Road alignment affects speed, speed variation, friction demand, drivers' expectations about the road ahead, the tolerance for errors and visibility conditions. Surprising changes in road alignment can be demanding and lead to driver errors. Sharp curves and steep gradients also increase the demands on vehicle suspension systems and brakes. They require speed reductions, especially for heavy vehicles. Sight can be reduced in curves and on crests.

About one-third of all injury accidents in Norway, and more than half of all head-on collisions and road departure accidents occur in curves on rural roads (Elvik and Muskaug 1994). According to Milton and Mannering (1996), accident rates in curves are between 1.5 and 4 times as high as on straight sections. Geometric properties of curves that affect accident rates are curve radius, deflection angle, superelevation, cross profile, vertical curves and distance to other curves (tangent length). Based on Norwegian accident statistics, it has been found that accident rates increase only slightly when curve radius decreases from 1,000 to ca. 400 m. From a radius of 200 m and below, a steep increase of accident rates has been found. Accident types, which are overrepresented in curves, are single-vehicle accidents, turn-over, head-on collisions, accidents in darkness and accidents involving illegal BAC levels.

Improvements of road alignment and visibility conditions aim at reducing the demands on driver attention and driving skills, improving the consistency and predictability of roads. Another objective is to increase mobility by improving curves and gradients, which lead to significant reductions in speed.

**Description of the measure**

The alignment of a road is defined as the road's path in a horizontal and vertical plane. It is described by horizontal and vertical curvature. Horizontal curves (bends) are normally described by curve radius, deflection angle and the shape of the transition curve. Curves with different radius and deflection angle are shown in Figure 1.13.1. Transition curves means changes of the radius between the tangent section and the curve.

Longer stretches of road can be described in terms of different indicators of geometric consistency, e.g. the number of curves per kilometre, the sum of all deflection angles per kilometre, or the length of tangents, i.e. straight sections between curves. Vertical curves are transitions from one gradient to another, e.g. from a flat section to an uphill gradient. There are two types of vertical curves, crest and sag. A crest is a hilltop, while sag is the bottom of a downhill stretch. Gradients are normally described according to how steep they are, given as a percentage. The increase in percentage shows how the height of the road varies, in metres, per kilometre of road. The concept of gradient is used for all changes in the height of the road, no matter what the direction of the traffic. Depending on the direction of the traffic, a distinction can be made between fall (downhill) and rise (uphill). The degree of gradient denotes the sum of the changes in

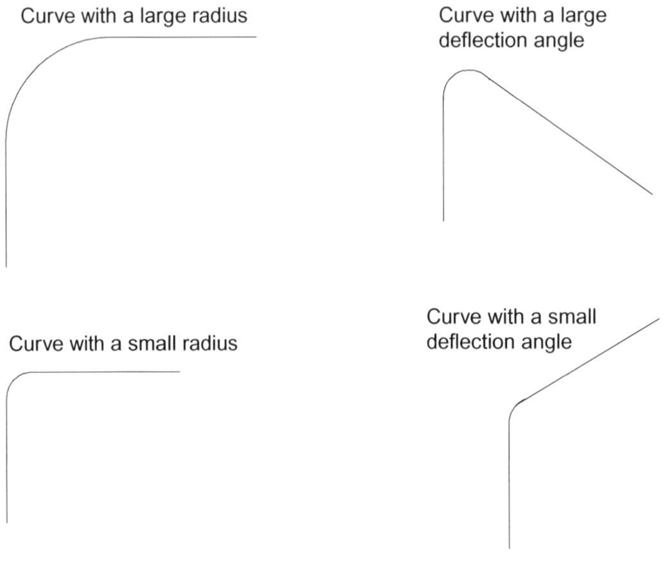


*Figure 1.13.1: Curves with different radius and deflection angle.*

the height of the road calculated per unit of length, e.g. per kilometre. Sight distances along a road depend partially on the alignment, partially on the roadside surroundings, partially on weather, road surface and conditions and partially on traffic conditions.

In this chapter, how the following characteristics of road alignment and sight conditions are related to accidents is described:

- Radius, deflection angle and length of horizontal curves
- Superelevation and side friction demands
- Transition curves (clothoides)
- Geometric consistency
- Gradients and the proportion of road which lies in sharp crest or sag curves
- Sight distance

**Effect on accidents**

Most studies, which have investigated effects of alignment or sight distance on accidents, have compared accident rates on different roads, and only few have evaluated the effects of changing the road geometry. In interpreting results from accident studies, several factors should be taken into account. The results from older studies cannot necessarily be generalised to the present. Relationships between road geometry and accidents are complex and may depend, among other things, on road standard, vehicles, traffic volumes and speed, and may therefore also change over time. Most geometric characteristics of roads are additionally highly related (confounded) and effects of different aspects of road geometry can be difficult or impossible to separate. For example, curves with a larger radius are longer and associated with shorter tangent lengths than curves with a smaller radius when the deflection angle is identical. Curves with a larger radius are additionally often associated with longer sight distances than curves with a smaller radius, but with a shorter sight distance than a straight road over a longer distance, and consequently less passing opportunities. Sharp horizontal or vertical curves are often near other sharp vertical or horizontal curves and are located in different types of terrain than roads, which are mostly straight. On roads with many horizontal or vertical curves, the roadside is often more dangerous, visibility conditions are worse and the terrain may make it more difficult to build wider roads or wide paved shoulders.

The effects of radius and deflection angle have been studies in different types of studies. Some studies have compared accident numbers or accident rates in curves with different geometric properties. Other studies have estimated regression models for the prediction of accident numbers in curves, with a number of different road and traffic characteristics as predictor variables. Results from the latter type of study are for the most part better controlled for potential confounding variables than results from the first type of studies. The results from these two types of studies are not combined to overall results, but reported separately.

***Curve radius.*** Several studies have investigated the effect of curve radius on accidents:

Brüde and Nilsson (1976) (Sweden)
Brüde, Larsson and Thulin (1980) (Sweden)
Nordtyp-projektgruppen (1980) (Denmark)
McBean (1982) (Great Britain)
Matthews and Barnes (1988) (New Zealand)
Stewart and Chudworth (1990) (Great Britain)
Zegeer et al. (1991) (USA)
Rasmussen, Herrstedt and Hemdorff (1992) (Denmark)
Fink and Krammes (1995) (USA)

Based on these studies, the effects of increasing curve radius have been estimated as shown in Table 1.13.1. The studies have compared accident rates in curves with different radii.

The studies have found that there are more accidents in curves with a smaller radius than in curves with a larger radius. The strongest relationship between curve radius and accidents has been found in sharp curves. Increasing the radius in curves with radii greater than 2,000 m has no effect on accidents. Straightening slack curves (radius more than ca. 1,000 m) to straight roads has been found to significantly increase the number of accidents. The best design for traffic safety appears to be a road with gentle curves

*Table 1.13.1: Effects on accidents in curves of curve radius*

| | Percentage change in the number of accidents | | |
|---|---|---|---|
| Increase of curve radius | Injury severity | Best estimate | 95% confidence interval |
| From <200 m to 200–400 m | Unspecified | −50 | (−55; −45) |
| From 200–400 m to 400–600 m | Unspecified | −33 | (−36; −29) |
| From 400–600 m to 600–1000 m | Unspecified | −23 | (−27; −19) |
| From 600–1000 m to 1000–2000 m | Unspecified | −18 | (−22; −14) |
| From 1,000–2,000 m to >2,000 m | Unspecified | −12 | (−16; −8) |
| From >2,000 to greater but finite | Unspecified | 0 | (−5; +5) |
| From >1,000 m to straight road | Unspecified | +10 | (+4; +16) |

but with sight conditions sufficient for overtaking. No differences have been found between results that refer to injury accidents and results that refer to accidents of unspecified severity (injury and property-damage-only accidents). The results have therefore been combined.

One potential source of error in the studies that are summarised in Table 1.13.1 is that most studies have not controlled for other curve and road characteristics, such as deflection angle, road and shoulder width or terrain. If for example curves with a smaller radius also have larger deflection angles than curves with a larger radius, the small radius is not necessarily the only factor that contributes to higher accident rates.

Several studies have estimated the effects of curve characteristics by computing regression models or by estimating other models of curve accidents. Studies that have investigated effects of curve radius are:

Choueiri and Lamm (1987) (USA)
Fink and Krammes (1995) (USA)
Milton and Mannering (1996) (USA)
Voigt (1996) (USA)
Shankar, Milton and Mannering (1997) (USA)
Milton and Mannering (1998) (USA)
Hauer (1999) (USA)
Hanley, Gibby and Ferrara (2000) (USA)
Cairney and McGann (2000) (Australia)

The results are summarised as follows.

- Curves with a smaller radius have higher accident rates than curves with a larger radius. The results are inconsistent as to whether or not the relationship between radius and accident rate is linear.
- The results are also inconsistent as to whether or not the relationship between radius and accident rate depends on the deflection angle.
- Stronger relationships between curve radius and accidents have been found in curves on narrow roads (under 8.1 m), compared to wider roads.
- Curve radius has a greater effect on accidents in curves with long tangents.
- On straight roads, accident rates have been found to be higher than would be expected based on geometric characteristics such as curve radius (infinite) or deflection angle (zero) (Shankar, Milton and Mannering 1997).

***Deflection angle.*** The relationship between deflection angle and accidents in curves has been investigated in several studies that have estimated regression models of curve accidents:

Knuiman, Council and Reinfurt (1993) (USA)
Miaou (1994) (USA)
Milton and Mannering (1996) (USA)
Forckenbrock and Foster (1997) (USA)
Shankar, Milton and Mannering (1997) (USA)
Milton and Mannering (1998) (USA)
Vogt and Bared (1998) (USA)
Abdel-Aty and Radwan (2000) (USA)
Strathman, Duecker, Zhang and Williams (2001) (USA)
Noland and Oh (2004) (USA)

Some of the studies have found greater, some have found unchanged and some have found smaller accident numbers in curves with smaller deflection angles. This may be due to interaction effects between deflection angle, curve radius and other curve characteristics. Milton and Mannering (1996, 1998) found decreasing accident numbers in sharp curves (small radius and large deflection angle), and decreasing accident numbers with increasing radius. An explanation of these seemingly contradictory results may be that curves with small radius and large deflection angle often are near other sharp curves, and that these curves are less unexpected and that speed is lower in such curves. Miaou (1994) found a significant interaction between deflection angle and curve length. There were more accidents in curves that are both sharp (large deflection angle) and long than would be expected based on the effects of curve length and deflection angle alone.

***Curve length.*** Effects of curve length were studied by Milton and Mannering (1996), Miaou (1994) and Strathman, Duecker, Zhang and Williams (2001). When controlling for other curve characteristics, increasing curve length is related to more accidents in all three studies, but not all effects are significant. This indicates that curves are a continuous risk, not a point risk (Hauer 1999).

***Superelevation.*** Superelevation in curves is usually constructed so that the outside of the curve is somewhat higher than the inside. Superelevation affects the side friction in a curve, which affects the risk of accidents. Side friction in curves depends not only on superelevation, but also on curve radius, deflection angle, length of the curve and vehicle speed among other things. Speed on the other hand has been found to be affected by curve radius and side friction (Voigt and Krammes 1998). Superelevation improves also the drainage of water from the road. Studies that have investigated the effects of superelevation on accidents are the following:

Zador, Stein, Hall and Wright (1985) (USA)
Zegeer et al. (1991) (USA)
Corben, Newstead, Diamantopoulou and Cameron (1996) (Australia)
Sakshaug (1998) (Norway)
Hanley, Gibby and Ferrara (2000) (USA)
Christensen and Ragnøy (2006) (Norway)

Most of these studies have investigated improvements of superelevation according to design standards or curve speed models, and not the effect of increased or reduced superelevation. Reduced accident rates in curves with improved superelevation were found by Corben, Newstead, Diamantopoulou and Cameron (1996), Zador, Stein, Hall and Wright (1985) and Zegeer et al. (1991). In the Norwegian studies, increased accident rate was found when superelevation increased. However, these studies included accidents in curves and on straight sections and no effects have been estimated for curves only.

***Transition curves (clothoids).*** Transition curves are defined as the transition between a tangent (straight road section) and a circular curve, i.e. the point where the radius of curvature reaches its minimum. In a transition curve, the road will curve gradually more and more. Transition curves are often designed as clothoids. A clothoid is a curve where the radius of curvature decreases linearly as a function of the arc length. The effects on accidents of clothoids have been investigated by Zegeer et al. (1991) and Tom (1995). The results are summarised in Table 1.13.2.

*Table 1.13.2: Effects on accidents in curves of transition curves (clothoids)*

| | Percentage change in the number of accidents | | |
|---|---|---|---|
| Roads/curves | Injury severity | Best estimate | 95% confidence interval |
| All | Unspecified | −11 | (−19; −1) |
| Curve radius under 165 m | Unspecified | +112 | (+17; +282) |
| Curve radius between 165 and 345 m | Unspecified | +4 | (−55; +138) |
| Curve radius over 165 m | Unspecified | −80 | (−99; +390) |
| Road width under 9 m | Unspecified | −3 | (−17; +14) |
| Road width between 9 and 11 m | Unspecified | −11 | (−22; +1) |
| Road width over 11 m | Unspecified | −19 | (−32; −3) |

According to these results, the overall effect of transition curves is a reduction of accidents. The results that refer to different curve radius are based on the study by Tom (1995). In sharp curves, increasing accident numbers have been found. The results are based on all accidents in curves, including transition curves.

Council (1998) has investigated effects of transition curves on accidents and found different results depending on the horizontal and vertical curvature of the roads. Reduced accident rates have been found in sharp curves (deflection angle under 3°) in flat terrain. In rolling terrain, increased accident rates have been found in curves with transition curves, compared to curves without transition curves, except on roads with wide lanes and wide shoulders. In rolling terrain, the sight distances are shorter than in flat terrain. Drivers may therefore underestimate the sharpness of curves when they only see the beginning of the curve, which is less sharp when the curve is constructed with a transition curve. Sharp curves with clothoids may therefore be more often unexpected in rolling terrain than in flat terrain. In flat terrain, where there are longer sight distances, sharp curves may be less unexpected, which make it easier to adjust speed. Passetti and Fambro (1999) have compared speed in different types of curves. In sharp curves (radius under 145 m), they found higher speed when the curves have a transition curve than when the curves did not have a transition curve.

An explanation of favourable effects of transition curves in flat terrain (Council 1998) is that steering wheel movements are smoother than in curves without transition curve. Superelevation is also often more favourable and changes less abruptly in curves with transition curves, thereby side friction may be improved. As indicated by the results by Council, the sight distance may be decisive for whether transition curves have positive effects on steering wheel movements and friction, or negative effects in terms of predictability and speed.

***Geometric consistency.*** The results that have been presented above indicate that curve geometry affects accidents. However, no straightforward conclusions can be drawn about the effects of isolated curve characteristics. Accident rates seem to be largest in curves with unfavourable combinations of different geometric properties, e.g. a small radius, a large deflection angle and a long straight section before the curve. The geometric consistency of road stretches can be described in terms of numerous indicators. By investigating relationships between geometric consistency and accidents account is taken of the fact that characteristics of longer road stretches can affect accident rates, not only characteristics of individual curves or straight sections. The characteristics of longer road stretches affect drivers' expectations and may thereby affect speed and the degree to which curves are expected. In the following, some results for different indicators of geometric consistency are summarised.

***Geometric consistency: Alignment classes.*** In studies from Sweden (Brüde and Nilsson 1976, Brüde and Larsson 1977) and Denmark (Nordtyp-projektgruppen 1980), roads have been divided into three groups, according to the proportion of road that lies in sharp curves and steep gradients. Fewer accidents have been found on roads with fewer sharp curves and steep gradients. Accident rates were reduced by an average 12% (95% confidence interval [−15; −9]) on roads in group 1 or 2 (fewer sharp curves and steep gradients), compared to roads in group 2 or 3 (more sharp curves and steep gradients), respectively. The study by Corben, Newstead, Diamantopoulou and Cameron (1996), however, did not find any significant effect of general improvements of horizontal curvature. The average effect was an accident reduction by 7% (95% confidence interval [−44; +55]).

***Geometric consistency: Tangent length.*** Tangent length is assumed to affect accident rates in curves because on longer tangents speed is higher and curves may be more unexpected than after short tangents. Decreasing accident rates in curves with shorter tangents have been found in the studies by Eick and Vikane (1992), Eriksen (1993) and Stigre (1993b). Based on the study by Matthews and Barnes (1988), the effects on accidents of increasing tangent length have been estimated as shown in Table 1.13.3. Shorter tangents seem to be more favourable, all results are however non-significant.

Milton and Mannering (1996, 1998) have found a significant interaction between tangent length and deflection angle. Accident rates have been found to increase when tangent length increases and when the deflection angle increases at the same time, more than would be expected based on the effects of tangent length and deflection angle alone.

***Geometric consistency: Speed changes and design speed.*** A number of studies found higher accident rates in curves where there are larger differences of speed between tangent and curve (Anderson, Bauer, Harwood and Fitzpatrick 1999, Anderson and Krammes 2000, Brenac 1996, Hauer 1999, Krammes 1997). Voigt (1996) found a larger

*Table 1.13.3: Effects on accidents in curves of different tangent length*

| | Percentage change in the number of accidents | | |
|---|---|---|---|
| Increase of tangent length | Injury severity | Best estimate | 95% confidence interval |
| from 0 to 200 m | Injury accidents | −9 | (−31; +19) |
| from 200 to 400 m | Injury accidents | −5 | (−18; +10) |
| from 400 to 600 m | Injury accidents | +3 | (−41; +77) |
| from 600 m to longer tangent | Injury accidents | +9 | (−32; +76) |

effect on accidents of speed reductions in curves than of individual geometric characteristics of curves. In the study by Fink and Krammes (1995), increased accident rates were not only found in curves following long tangents, but also in curves following very short tangents. Lamm et al. (1998) have divided curves according to the reduction of the 85 percentile of speed (V85) into three groups (reduction of V85 by 10 km/h, between 10 and 20 km/h, and over 20 km/h). The results of three of the mentioned studies are summarised in Figure 1.13.2.

Relationships have also been found between design speed and accidents. Design speed is the highest speed that can be driven along a stretch of road, and it determines minimum requirements to e.g. curvature and sight distance (Brenac 1996). Krammes (1997) found more accidents on roads with low design speed. In this study, design speed referred to longer road sections with several curves and the results are explained in terms of larger variations of speed when design speed is low. Shankar, Mannering and Barfield (1995) have investigated the effects of the design speed of individual curves. They found fewer and less serious accidents on roads with lower design speed. Low design speed of curves is not necessarily tantamount to larger speed variations.

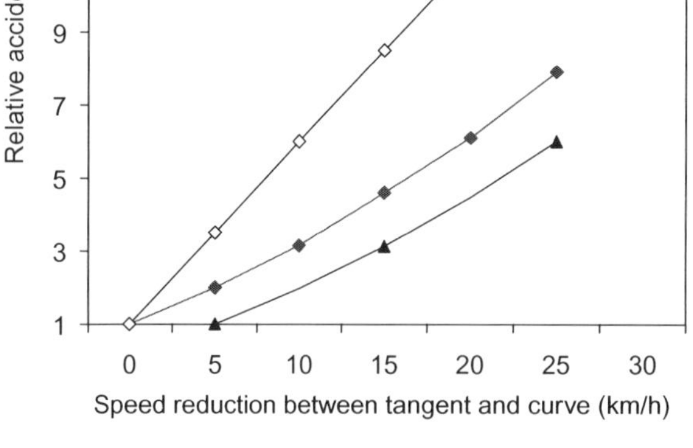


*Figure 1.13.2: Relationship between accident rate and speed reduction between tangent and curve.*

***Geometric consistency: Curvature.*** The curvature of a road can be expressed e.g. in terms of the number of curves per kilometre or the sum of all deflection angles on a stretch of road. Curvature is assumed to affect accidents in two ways. Firstly, sharp bends are usually associated with higher accident rates (than less sharp bends or straight sections), and roads with many sharp bends may therefore be expected to have more accidents than comparable roads with fewer sharp bends. Secondly, the more sharp bends there are on a road, the less unexpected will each bend be, which may reduce accident rates compared to sharp bends that are not in the vicinity of other sharp bends, and the accident rates per curve may therefore be smaller than would be expected based on the effects of the curves alone.

Two studies have found more accidents on roads with a larger proportion of the road in sharp bends (Björketun 1991, Lamm, Zumkeller and Beck 2000). These studies have not controlled for the effects of the curves on accidents and the results do therefore not say anything about the risk per curve on roads with many or few curves per kilometre.

A number of studies have investigated the effects of road curvature on accidents. Brenac (1996) and Matthews and Barnes (1988) have found that accident rates in curves with a small radius are greater when the road otherwise only has curves with large radius than when the road otherwise has more curves with a small radius. When there only are few curves on a stretch of road, rollover accidents are the accident type that increases most compared to roads with many curves (Shankar, Mannering and Barfield 1995). A number of studies that have estimated regression models for curves have also investigated the effects on accidents of road curvature:

Milton and Mannering (1996) (USA)
Milton and Mannering (1998) (USA)
Garber and Wu (2001) (USA)
Strathman, Duecker, Zhang and Williams (2001) (USA)
Noland and Oh (2004) (USA)

Most of these studies have found significantly fewer accidents on roads with many curves, larger changes of direction (sum of deflection angles over a longer stretch of road) and with shorter tangents than would be expected based on the effects of the curves alone. A possible explanation for reduced accident rates in curves on roads with many curves, compared to roads with few curves, is a better speed adaptation and more adequate drivers' expectations. The results also show that isolated curve characteristics may not be sufficient as predictors of accidents without taking into account the rest of the road.

*Table 1.13.4: Effects on accidents of reducing gradients*

| | Percentage change in the number of accidents | | |
|---|---|---|---|
| Reduction of gradient | Injury severity | Best estimate | 95% confidence interval |
| From over 70 to 50–70 per thousand | Unspecified | −20 | (−38; +1) |
| From 50–70 to 30–50 per thousand | Unspecified | −10 | (−20; 0) |
| From 30–50 to 20–30 per thousand | Unspecified | −10 | (−15; −5) |
| From 20–30 to 10–20 per thousand | Unspecified | −7 | (−12; −1) |
| From 10–20 to less than 10 per thousand | Unspecified | −2 | (−8; +6) |

***Gradients.*** The effects of reducing gradients have been estimated (Table 1.13.4) based on the following studies of the relationship between gradients and accidents:

Brüde and Nilsson (1976) (Sweden)
Brüde, Larsson and Thulin (1980) (Sweden)
English (1988) (Australia)
Matthews and Barnes (1988) (New Zealand)
McBean (1982) (Great Britain)
Statens Vägverk (1979) (Sweden)

The studies indicate that reducing gradients reduces the number of accidents. The effect is greater for the steepest gradients. Reducing gradients to below 10 per 1,000 has no statistically significant effect on the number of accidents. In accordance with these results, several studies, which have estimated regression models for accident numbers, have found more accidents on steeper gradients (Milton and Mannering 1998, Noland and Oh 2004, Miaou 1994, Strathman, Duecker, Zhang and Williams 2001, Shankar, Mannering and Barfield 1995, Shankar, Milton and Mannering 1997, Vogt and Bared 1998).

Uphill grades have been found to be safer than downhill grades (Matthews and Barnes 1988, Björketun 1991). On uphill stretches, the accident rate is around 7% lower than for similar downhill stretches (lower 95% limit 13%, upper 95% limit 0%). Brinkman and Perchonk (1979) found that the rate of fatal accidents is not different between an uphill gradient and a flat road, and about 13% greater in a downhill gradient than on a flat road.

The proportion of a road that lies in sharp crest or sag curves may be expected to affect accidents in a similar way as horizontal curves. Sharp crest or sag curves in themselves may be risk factors, because of short sight distances in crest curves and long braking distances in sag curves. The study by Bjørketun (1991) could not confirm the expectation of more accidents in sharp crest or sag curves. Brinkman and Perchonk (1979), on the contrary, found 23% lower rate of fatal accidents in uphill and downhill gradients, which had sharp crest or sag curves than in uphill and downhill gradients without sharp crest or sag curves. The number of sharp crest or sag curves has been found to affect accidents in the study by Noland and Oh (2004). On roads with more sharp crest or sag curves, there were fewer accidents. A possible explanation is that vertical curves are less unexpected when there are many of them. A relationship between the number of gradients on a road and accidents has however not been found in the study by Shankar, Mannering and Barfield (1995).

***Sight distance.*** The sight distance affects the time it takes a driver to brake and stop the vehicle. Results from accident studies are inconsistent. Two studies have found that increasing sight distances leads to an increased number of accidents (Nordtyp-projektgruppen 1980, McBean 1982). The two studies indicate that increasing the sight length from less than 200 to more than 200 metres (but below 1 km) leads to 23% higher accident rate (lower 95% limit 6% increase, upper 95% limit 43%). Above 1 km, the sight distance no relationship between sight distance and accidents was found. A possible explanation is that the majority of drivers regard sight obstructions as a hazard and reduce speed when sight is reduced. Other studies have not found any relationship between sight distance and accidents on road sections without junctions (Glennon 1987, Urbanik, Hinshaw and Fambro 1989, Fitzpatrick, Fambro and Stoddard 2000). Two studies have been found in which increasing sight distance is associated with a reduced number of accidents. Fambro, Fitzpatrick and Koppa (1997) found that accident rates increase when sight distances become shorter than required by design standards. A study from Italy (Caliendo 2001) found that accident numbers decreased when the sight distance on motorways increased.

Removing visual obstacles on road sections (without junctions) seems mostly not to lead to reductions of accidents. In an Australian study (Corben, Deery, Mullan and Dyte 1996), removing sight obstacles had no effect on accidents. Marking of sight obstacles on the other hand reduced accidents by 23%, but this effect was not significant. Vaa (1991) did not find any effect of removing visual obstacle either. Statens Vägverk (1987) has studied the effect or removing sight obstacles along roads in order to reduce came accidents by making it easier for drivers to notice game coming out of the woods. A reduction of accidents by about 20% was found (95% confidence interval [−38; +6]).

Shorter sight distances in junctions are associated with higher accident numbers according to the study results from Mayer and Bruce (1988), Fambro et al. (1989) and Urbanik, Hinshaw and Fambro (1989). These results refer to at-grade junctions, which are not roundabouts. Poch and Mannering (1996) found significantly more accidents in junctions with sight obstacles than in junctions without sight obstacles, when controlling for a number of other factors, e.g. geometric characteristics of the junctions. A possible explanation of increased accident rates in junctions with short sight distance or with sight obstacles is that drivers do not sufficiently adjust speed in order to compensate for increased braking distance. This explanation is confirmed by the results from Fambro et al. (1989), who found that speed was not different depending on the sight distance in junctions.

In roundabouts, a Norwegian study found the contrary effect of sight distance. Giæver (2000) found better visibility conditions in roundabouts where there had been many accidents than in roundabouts where no accidents had occurred. Schurr and Abos-Sanchez (2005) found reduced speed in roundabouts after sight obstacles (vegetation) were planted in the central island.

Possible explanations for the seemingly inconsistent effects on accidents of sight distance and sight obstacles are drivers expectations and behaviour. Long sight distances may increase speed and encourage passing manoeuvres, which may increase accidents. Braking distances on the other hand are also longer at longer sight distances, which may reduce accident rates. When short sight distances are recognized by drivers as a potential danger, they may lead to reduced speed and accident rates, as has been found in roundabouts. However, when something requires braking, e.g. a junction, accidents may increase all the same.

**Effect on mobility**

Road alignment affects the mean speed of traffic and the speed profile of vehicles over a given distance. The effect on speed is greater for heavy vehicles than for light vehicles (Skarra and Gabestad 1983). On two-lane roads without passing lanes, reduced speed of heavy vehicles will also lead to reduced speed for light vehicles, especially when sight distances are not sufficient for passing, which is often the case on roads with many sharp curves or gradients. Curves with larger radius may provide better passing possibilities than curves with a smaller radius, but they are associated with short tangents, all else being equal, which may reduce passing possibilities (Brenac 1996).

An analysis of factors influencing mean speed at a given speed limit (Vaa 1991) found that speed was strongly related to road alignment. On uphill stretches of 40 per 1,000, the average speed was around 7–8 km/h lower than on flat roads (around 70–72 km/h as opposed to around 78–79 km/h). On downhill stretches of 40 per 1,000, the average speed was around 1–4 km/h higher than on flat roads (76–77 km/h vs. 73–76 km/h). The radius of horizontal curves also affects the speed level. The sharper the curve, the lower the speed level.

### Effect on the environment

No studies have been found, which show the effect on the environment of altering road alignment and sight conditions. Measures affecting speed can affect both noise and pollution emissions. Increased speed can lead to both increased noise levels and increased emissions of certain types of exhaust gases. On the other hand, improving the alignment reduces variations in speed and thus fuel consumption.

Roads with rigid alignments have to be built on embankments or in cuttings to a greater extent than other roads and thus may entail uglier incursions into the natural landscape than roads where the alignment can be better adapted to the local terrain formation.

### Costs

The costs of improving road alignment vary strongly depending on the type of improvement, how comprehensive the improvement is, terrain conditions at the site and density of buildings. Technically it is more difficult and more expensive to alter road alignments in towns and cities than in sparsely populated areas. Roads built on rock are more expensive than otherwise identical roads in earth terrain.

General improvements of national highways in Norway in the period 1990–92 cost, on average, between NOK 2.2 and 5.0 million per kilometre road (Hagen 1991, 1993, 1994). The corresponding cost for general improvements of county highways in the same years were, on average, between NOK 0.25 and 1.8 million per kilometre road. It is not known how large a proportion of these costs can be attributed to improving the road alignment and sight conditions. The average cost of general improvements of existing roads were NOK 4.7 million per kilometre road (Elvik and Rydningen 2002).

### Cost–benefit analysis

A numerical example has been calculated for general geometric improvements of a rural road with a 80 km/h speed limit. It is assumed that the improvements will reduce accidents and travel times. The costs are highly dependent on the type of road, the terrain and the changes to be made. Therefore, monetary values of safety and travel

*Table 1.13.5: Estimated reduction of accident costs (million NOK, 2005 prices) per km road per year*

| | | ÅDT | | | |
|---|---|---|---|---|---|
| | | 1,000 | 5,000 | 10,000 | 20,000 |
| Effect on accidents | −5% | 0.01 | 0.06 | 0.11 | 0.19 |
| | −10% | 0.03 | 0.12 | 0.21 | 0.38 |
| | −20% | 0.06 | 0.23 | 0.42 | 0.77 |
| | −30% | 0.09 | 0.35 | 0.63 | 1.15 |
| Increase of speed | 65–70 km/h | 0.04 | 0.18 | 0.36 | 0.72 |
| | 50–70 km/h | 0.13 | 0.67 | 1.35 | 2.69 |
| Maximum costs per km per year at which improvements are beneficial | | 0.1–0.2 | 0.2–1.0 | 0.5–2.0 | 0.9–3.8 |
| Maximum investment costs per km per year at which improvements are beneficial | | 0.8–3.3 | 3.5–15.2 | 6.9–29.4 | 13.6–57.0 |

time benefits have been calculated in order to show at what cost improvements can be expected to be profitable from a societal point of view. Expected reductions of accident costs are estimated for different effects on accidents and for different traffic volumes. Expected reductions of costs of travel time are estimated for speed increases from 67 to 70 km/h and from 60 to 70 km/h. The valuation of travel time is NOK 155 per hour per vehicle (Killi 1999). Improved geometric consistency is likely to reduce vehicle operation costs as well because braking and accelerating is reduced. However, no cost estimates are available. Table 1.13.5 summarizes the results of the numerical example and show at which ranges of annual costs per kilometre road (in million NOK) geometric improvements may be expected to be profitable. The maximum investment costs per kilometre at which the benefits of realignment are greater than the costs have been calculated with a 4.5% discount rate and 25 years life time. The ranges of the maximum costs refer to the smallest estimates of both effects on accidents and speed increase (lower value) and to the largest estimates of both effects on accidents and speed increase (upper value).

## 1.14 Reconstruction and rehabilitation of roads

### Problem and objective

Narrow roads with curves make driving more demanding and leave drivers with smaller safety margins in critical situations than wider, straighter roads.

Reconstruction, rehabilitation and resurfacing of existing roads is intended to give roads a design and traffic control which corresponds to the current design standards. This will contribute to removing hazardous locations attributable to the layout of the road and increase mobility on the road.

**Description of the measure**

Reconstruction, rehabilitation and resurfacing of roads consists of altering the existing road to bring it up to current design standards and other improvements, which include *both* the road cross-section *and* the road alignment. When general improvements are made to a road, it is usually the case that the road surface and road equipment, such as guardrails and traffic signs, are also replaced. In some cases, traffic control, e.g. the speed limit, may also be changed.

**Effect on accidents**

The effect on accidents of reconstruction, rehabilitation and resurfacing of roads has been studied in Sweden (Brüde and Nilsson 1976, Nilsson 1978, Statens vägverk 1983a, Björketun 1991, Slätis 1994), Denmark (Nordtyp-projektgruppen 1980), Great Britain (Walker and Lines 1991) and USA (Nemeth and Migletz 1978, Larsen 1986, Goldstine 1991, Benekohal and Hashmi 1992). On the basis of these studies, the effect on accidents of reconstruction, rehabilitation and resurfacing of roads can be estimated to the figures given in Table 1.14.1.

The effect of reconstruction, rehabilitation and resurfacing of roads has most extensively been studied for rural areas. In rural areas, such improvements reduce the number of injury accidents by around 20%. The number of property-damage-only

*Table 1.14.1: Effects of reconstruction, rehabilitation and resurfacing of roads on the number of accidents*

| | Percentage change in number of accidents | | |
|---|---|---|---|
| Accident severity | Types of accident affected | Best estimate | 95% confidence interval |
| Injury accidents | Accidents in rural areas | −20 | (−25; −15) |
| Property damage only | Accidents in rural areas | −5 | (−12; +3) |
| Injury accidents | Accidents in urban areas | −7 | (−12; −1) |
| Property damage only | Accidents in urban areas | −5 | (−12; +3) |

accidents is reduced by around 5%. The effect on property-damage-only accidents is more uncertain than for injury accidents. In urban areas, the effect of general improvements is smaller. Here, the number of accidents is reduced by some 5–10%.

**Effect on mobility**

Reconstruction, rehabilitation and resurfacing of existing roads increase mobility, especially in sparsely populated areas, where cross-section and alignment affect the speed levels to a greater extent than in densely populated areas. A clear relationship between cross-section and speed level has been found (Nilsson, Rigefalk and Koronna-Vilhelmsson 1992a, 1992b) as well as between alignment and speed level (Vaa 1991). The difference in the mean speed of traffic between a narrow road with poor alignment and a wide road with good alignment can be more than 20 km/h (from less than 60 km/h to more than 80 km/h).

**Effect on the environment**

No studies have been found that indicate the effect on the environment of reconstruction, rehabilitation and resurfacing of existing roads. Increases in speed can lead to increased environmental problems such as the level of noise and the emission of air pollution. On the other hand, a more even flow of traffic, especially reductions in differences in speed between light and heavy vehicles, can reduce fuel consumption and thus the emission of pollution, which depend on fuel consumption.

**Costs**

The costs of reconstruction, rehabilitation and resurfacing of roads can vary hugely, depending on the extent of the measures, terrain conditions at the site and the density of buildings. The measures are more expensive, and technically more complicated, in towns and cities than in sparsely populated areas. The measures are also more expensive in rocky terrain than in terrain comprising earth or scree (Gabestad 1981). A Norwegian study of traffic safety measures carried out on national highways in 1986 (Elvik 1987) showed that reconstruction, rehabilitation and resurfacing of roads cost on average NOK 4 million per kilometre road.

**Cost–benefit analysis**

A cost–benefit analysis of general improvements of national highways, based on data from measures implemented in 1986, found that the benefit–cost ratio of this measure was around 0.5 (Elvik 1993). The roads included in the study had an annual average daily traffic of 1,500 vehicles and an accident rate of 0.43 injury accidents per million vehicle kilometres. A compilation of information from the Norwegian Public Roads Administration project database for investment projects on national highways in the road plan period 1990–93 (Elvik 1992) shows that the Norwegian Public Roads Administration evaluated the average benefit–cost ratio of general improvements of roads in this road planning period at around 1.0.

A numerical example has been worked out which covers reconstruction, rehabilitation and resurfacing of a national highway with an annual average daily traffic of 1,500 vehicles and an accident rate of 0.20 injury accidents per million vehicle kilometres. The number of injury accidents is assumed to go down by 20%, the number of property damage only accidents by 5%. It is further assumed that the average speed increases from 60 to 70 km/h. Vehicle operating costs are assumed to go down by NOK 0.05 per kilometre driven. The benefit of improving 1 km of road is calculated to be NOK 0.7 million in saved accident costs, NOK 1.5 million in saved travel time costs and NOK 0.3 million in reduced vehicle operating costs, making a total of NOK 2.5 million. The cost is calculated to be NOK 4.8 million. The benefit in this case is smaller than the costs.

## 1.15 Guardrails and crash cushions

**Problem and objective**

Along public roads in Norway there are many steep slopes, rocks, water, trees and other fixed obstacles that may cause injuries when accidents occur. Driving off the road accidents represents about 25% of the police reported persons injured per accident (Statistisk sentralbyrå 2000). 35% of all road accident fatalities in 2002 were killed in single vehicle off the roads accidents. When leaving the road in steep terrain, where there may be trees and large rocks the chances of severe injury are high. The probability of being killed or injured increases the steeper and higher the slope (Glennon and Tamburri 1967, Pettersson 1977). On motorways without a median barrier (class B motorways in Norway), head-on collisions represents 36% of all police-reported personal injuries, compared to only 14% for all public roads (Ranes 1998). On motorways, accidents involving crossing the median and accidents involving collisions with construction elements on access ramps or on bridges are particular hazards. Such accidents often occur at high speed and end by stopping abruptly at an obstacle that does not yield. The probability of death or serious personal injury is therefore high.

In Norway, the type of obstacle that is hit in is a rock/mountain in 28% of all off-the road accidents, a guardrail in 18%, a lighting pole in 20%, a tree in 13% and a wall or building in 4% (Elvik 2001). These figures refer to off-the road accidents in which an obstacle is hit and in which it is known what type of obstacle is hit (4,766 accidents, of a total of 7,255 off-the-road accidents). The distance to the struck obstacles is over 10 m in 57% of all cases. Below 10 m, the distances are quite evenly distributed between zero and 10 m, with most obstacles between 1 and 3 m.

Guardrails and crash cushions are designed to reduce the extent of damage and injury in the event of an accident. Guardrails in medians on divided roads are intended to prevent accidents involving crossing the median. Guardrails and crash cushions should ideally stop a vehicle and direct it to a controlled halt, without throwing it back onto the carriageway. In addition, guardrails and crash cushions must be installed in such a way that they do not obstruct visibility or give a misleading impression of the road alignment.

**Description of the measure**

Warrants for the use of guardrails have been developed in Norway and many other countries. These warrants usually refer to the height and steepness of side slopes or to the presence of certain fixed obstacles close to the road. A distinction is sometimes made between more or less yielding guardrails. Listed from the least yielding to the softest form of guardrail, the following types are found: bridge rail, concrete guardrail, steel guardrail and wire guardrail. In Norway, guardrails and crash cushions are only erected where it would be more dangerous to drive off the road or into the obstacle from which the road users are protected, than it would be to drive into guardrails or crash cushions (Statens vegvesen 2000). Guardrail end terminals can also be designed in many different ways. Currently, the recommended design in Norway is to flare out the guardrail and attach it on the backslope.

The effects on accident shave been investigated of

- guardrails along the roadside,
- median guardrails on divided highways, and
- crash cushions.

## Effect on accidents

Guardrails and crash cushions are not primarily intended to prevent accidents from occurring, but to reduce the extent of the damage when an accident has occurred. Nonetheless, it is possible that both guardrails and crash cushions affect the number of accidents. Guardrails are fixed obstacles that drivers will try to avoid. The driver's wish to avoid driving into the guardrail can in itself reduce the number of accidents. Guardrails can also lead to improved optical guidance. On the other hand, a guardrail may lead to drivers being less careful, especially on roads in dangerous terrain, where the driver, if a guardrail is missing, will try to concentrate on not driving off the road. Guardrails in medians on divided roads can reduce available space for emergency manoeuvres and thus lead to accidents. When evaluating the net effect of guardrails and crash cushions on accidents is therefore important to take into account both changes in the probability of accidents in the severity of the accidents.

***Guardrails along the roadside.*** The effect on road accidents of setting up guardrails along the roadside has been investigated in the following studies, the results of which are summarised in Table 1.15.1.

Glennon and Tamburri (1967) (United States)
Tamburri, Hammer, Glennon and Lew (1968) (United States)
Williston (1969) (United States)
Good and Joubert (1971) (Australia)
Woods, Bohuslav and Keese (1976) (United States)
Pettersson (1977) (Sweden)
Ricker et al. (1977) (United States)
Perchonok et al. (1978) (United States)

*Table 1.15.1: Effects on accidents of guardrails along the roadside*

| | | Percentage change in the number of accidents | |
|---|---|---|---|
| Accident severity | Types of accident affected | Best estimate | 95% confidence interval |
| ***New guardrail along embankment*** | | | |
| Fatal accidents | Running-off-the-road | −44 | (−54, −32) |
| Injury accidents | Running-off-the-road | −47 | (−52, −41) |
| Unspecified | Running-off-the-road | −7 | (−35, +33) |
| ***Changing to softer guardrails*** | | | |
| Fatal accidents | Running-off-the-road | −41 | (−66, +2) |
| Injury accidents | Running-off-the-road | −32 | (−42, −20) |

Schandersson (1979) (Sweden)
Hall (1982) (United States)
Boyle and Wright (1984) (Great Britain)
Bryden and Fortuniewicz (1986) (United States)
Domhan (1985) (Germany)
Schultz (1986) (United States)
Ray, Troxel and Carney (1991) (United States)
Hunter, Stewart and Council (1993) (United States)
Gattis, Alguire and Narla (1996)
Corben, Deery, Mullan and Dyte (1996) (Australia)
Short and Robertson (1998) (United States)
Ljungblad (2000) (Sweden)

Guardrails along embankments strongly reduce the number of fatal and injury off-the-road accidents. The effect on the total number of accidents, including property-damage-only accidents, is smaller and more uncertain. Changing to more pliant guardrails also has a damage-reducing effect as well, but this is smaller than the effect of setting up guardrails in places where previously there were none.

Guardrails do not have an equally great effect on all types of obstacles. Guardrails lead to a significant reduction in the severity of injuries sustained in collisions with trees, rock faces and driving off the road in steep slopes. The reduction in the severity of injuries is, however, smaller with regard to hitting signposts or ditches.

***Median guardrails on divided highways.*** The effect on accidents of median guardrails on divided highways has been evaluated in a number of studies. The results given below (Table 1.15.2) are based on the following studies:

Billion (1956) (USA)
Moskowitz and Schaefer (1960) (USA)
Beaton, Field and Moskowitz (1962) (USA)
Billion and Parsons (1962) (USA)
Billion, Taragin and Cross (1962) (USA)
Sacks (1965) (USA)
Johnson (1966) (USA)
Moore and Jehu (1968) (Great Britain)
Williston (1969) (USA)
Galati (1970) (USA)
Good and Joubert (1971) (Great Britain)
Tye (1975) (USA)

*Table 1.15.2: Effects on accidents of guardrails in central reservations on multi-lane highways*

| | Percentage change in number of accidents | | |
|---|---|---|---|
| Accident severity | Types of accident affected | Best estimate | 95% confidence interval |
| ***Median guardrail on multi lane divided highways*** | | | |
| Fatal accidents | All accidents | −43 | (−53, −31) |
| Injury accidents | All accidents | −30 | (−36, −23) |
| Unspecified | All accidents | +24 | (+21, +27) |
| ***Type of guardrail in median*** | | | |
| Injury accidents | Concrete | +15 | (−18, +61) |
| Injury accidents | Steel | −35 | (−43, −26) |
| Injury accidents | Wire | −29 | (−40, −15) |

Andersen (1977) (Denmark)
Ricker et al. (1977) (USA)
Johnson (1980) (Great Britain)
Statens vägverk (1980) (Sweden)
Hunter, Stewart and Council (1993) (USA)
Martin et al. (1998) (France)
Sposito and Johnston (1999) (USA)
Hancock and Ray (2000) (USA)
Nilsson and Ljungblad (1999) (Sweden)
Hunter et al. (2001) (USA)

Significant reductions have been found of fatal and injury accidents. Larger reductions have been found for more yielding types of guardrails (steel, wire). For property-damage-only accidents, a significant increase by 24% has been found.

The figures given in Table 1.15.2 refer to all accidents. Martin and Quincy (2001) have investigated accidents on French motorways in which a median barrier was struck. Only in 0.6% of all accidents in which a median was struck, a car crossed the median. For buses and trucks the respective figure is 6.4%. Accident in which the median is not crossed are far less severe than accidents in which the median is crossed. For cars, the proportion of fatal accidents is 94% lower when the median is not crossed, compared to when the median is crossed. For serious and slight injuries, the respective reductions are 83% and 30%. The proportion of property damage only accident increased by 66% when the median is not crossed. The proportion of median crossings was smallest for concrete barriers. However the number of injuries and fatalities was 1.7 higher than with other types of median guardrails.

***Median guardrails on undivided highways.*** Trials have been made in Norway and Sweden using wire guardrails placed between the lanes of undivided highways in order to prevent or reduce the severity of head-on collisions. These trials have been evaluated in Sweden. The most recently published evaluation (Carlsson, Brüde and Bergh 2001) produced the estimates presented in Table 1.15.3. The total number of accidents has increased. There has, however, been a very marked reduction of accident severity, as evidenced by the large reductions of the number of fatally or seriously injured road users.

***Crash cushions.*** Crash cushions are energy-absorbing structures put up in front of tunnel portals, fixed obstacles where the road divides into exit ramps or in front of bridge pillars. The effect on road accidents of crash cushions has been investigated in the following studies, the results of which are summarised in Table 1.15.4.

Viner and Tamanini (1973) (United States)
Griffin (1984) (United States)

*Table 1.15.3: Guardrails to prevent head-on collisions on undivided highways in Sweden (Carlsson, Brüde and Bergh 2001)*

| Number of accidents or injured persons | Expected without guardrail | Actual number with guardrail |
|---|---|---|
| All accidents (including property-damage-only) | 106 | 142 |
| Slightly injured persons | 47.3 | 39 |
| Seriously injurted persons | 15.0 | 7 |
| Fatally injured persons | 5.2 | 0 |

*Table 1.15.4: Costs of guardrails. Norwegian data (Elvik 2001)*

| | Unit cost (1 km or 1 crash cushion) | |
|---|---|---|
| Type of guardrail | Investment | Annual maintenance |
| Steel, 4 m between poles, no blocking | 250,000 | 7,500–15,000 |
| Steel, 4 m between poles, blocking | 280,000 | 8,000–16,000 |
| Steel, 2 m between poles, no blocking | 350,000 | 10,000–20,000 |
| Steel, 2 m between poles, blocking | 400,000 | 12,000–24,000 |
| Concrete | 750,000 | 25,000–50,000 |
| Wire | 300,000 | 20,000–40,000 |
| Crash cushion | 150,000 | 5,000–10,000 |

Kurucz (1984) (United States)
Schoon (1990) (The Netherlands)
Proctor (1994) (Great Britain)

Large reductions have been found in fatal accidents (−69%; 95% CI [−83; −46]), injury accidents (−69%; 95% CI [−75; −62]) and of property damage only accidents (−46%; 95% CI [−63; −23]). However, the results for the different studies are quite heterogeneous and may be affected by regression to the mean.

### Effect on mobility

The effects of guardrails and crash cushions on mobility have hardly been evaluated. The few studies available are old and mostly refer to guardrails in medians of divided highways. Billion (1956) found no significant changes in speed after concrete guardrails were erected in the median of the Long Island Parkway in New York. Billion, Taragin and Cross (1962), in a similar study, found increased speed on straight road sections and reduced speed in curves. Sacks (1965) found that speed increased by 3–5 km/h after median guardrails were set up. Guardrails on undivided highways in Sweden have been associated with an increase in mean speed of about 2 km/h (Carlsson, Brüde and Bergh 2001).

### Effect on the environment

No studies have been found that indicate the effect of guardrails on the environment. Guardrails probably have no effect on noise or air pollution. A guardrail can increase the barrier effect of a road for game, pedestrians, cyclists and emergency vehicles.

### Costs

In a recent cost–benefit analysis (Elvik 2001), the following cost estimates were applied (Table 1.15.4):

### Cost–benefit analysis

A cost–benefit analysis made for Norway (Elvik 2001) indicates that guardrails along embankments provide benefits that are greater than the costs for roads that have an AADT of more than about 3,000. If traffic volume is less than this, the expected number of accidents per kilometre of road will usually be too small to offset the costs of putting up guardrails. On the other hand, it can be argued that driving off the road is equally dangerous no matter what the traffic volume on the road is. Current requirements for the use of guardrails in Norway therefore disregard traffic volume to some extent and are based on descriptions of the terrain along a road. Guardrails to prevent head-on collisions on undivided highways may provide benefits that are greater than costs if traffic volume exceeds an AADT of about 5,000 (Elvik 2001).

## 1.16 Game accident measures

### Problem and objective

Every year about 5,000 deers are being killed on Norwegian roads. Of these, 1,300 are moose. Most game accidents do not cause personal injuries. The most severe game accidents are vehicle–moose collisions. Studies from Norway (Messelt 1994) and Sweden (Almkvist et al. 1980) have shown that the risk of being injured in a moose collision is about 12 times as high as in a collision with other deer (85% of which are roe-deer and 15% red-deer). A study from Maine, USA (Center for Disease Control and Prevention 2006) has shown that the risk of being injured is about six times as high in a moose–collision compared to a collision with red-deer and that the risk of being killed is about 26 as high.

According to a number of studies, game accidents are mainly concentrated at the following times and places:

- Most vehicle–moose collisions occur in forests and near watercourses (Bruinderink and Hazebroek 1996, Finder, Roseberry and Woolf 1999). Moose are most often hit by vehicles in (young) pine woods (Ball and Dahlgren 2002).
- Most vehicle–moose collisions occur during migration between winter and summer habitats (Gibby and Clewell 2006, Rogers 2004) and in the winter habitats during the winter (Lavsund and Sandegren 1991, Høye 2005). Moose migration follows mostly the same routes every year (Putman 1997, Gibby and Clewell 2006). Winter habitats are mostly woodlands in lower areas with little snow in winter, and they are often near roads and railways. In Hedmark, the part of Norway with most forest and moose, 81% of all vehicle–moose collisions occur during the months November–March (Storaas, Nicolaysen, Gundersen and Zimmermann 2005).
- The risk of vehicle–moose collisions is greatest during the first 2–3 h after sunset and after sunrise (Haikonen and Summala 2001). During these hours, moose is most active and not well visible for drivers.

- Increasing moose-populations are related to increasing numbers of vehicle–moose collisions. The rate of increase in the number of collisions has been found to be increasing with increasing moose populations (Beilinson 2001, Bruinderink and Hazebroek 1996, SSB). Local movements of moose within an area are also related to increased collisions (Storaas, Nicolaysen, Gundersen and Zimmermann 2005, Nysted 2005).

Game accident measures aim at reducing the number of game accidents and the severity of such accidents.

**Description of the measure**

Game accident measures include measures that aim at changing driver behaviour, animal behaviour or the population of animals. Measures include infrastructure measures (road signs and similar measures, game fences and crossing facilities, speed limits and road lighting) vehicle measures (seat-belts) and measures involving forestry and wildlife administration.

**Effect on accidents**

The effects of a number of measures that have been found on accidents, speed and deer are summarised in Table 1.16.1. The results show that the 'classical measures' (warning signs, game mirrors, scent signals, game fence) do not reduce accidents. Temporary warnings signs and variable message signs may reduce accidents, at least on the short term.

The most effective measure seems to be fencing in combination with safe crossing facilities. The effects are, however, dependent on the design of the crossing facilities and the degree to which these are accepted by deer. Clearance of woodlands along roads and feeding moose in winter habitats during the winter has been found to reduce accidents as well. A reduction of moose density in winter habitats is likely to reduce the number of vehicle–moose collisions.

***Warning signs.*** Effects on accidents of warning signs is not documented (Blamey and Blamey 1990, Meyer 2006, Putman 1997, Voß 2007). A possible explanation is that drivers are becoming used to the signs and that they virtually never observe game at the signs (Putman 1997). Effects on driver behaviour or attention have not been found either (Gibby and Clewell 2006, Transportforskningsdelegationen 1980).

*Table 1.16.1: Effects of game accident measures on accidents, speed and deer/game*

| | Effect on accidents | Effect on speed | Effect on deer/game |
|---|---|---|---|
| Warning signs | (0) No effect | (0) No effect | |
| Temporary warning signs | (+) Possible reduction, mostly short term effects | (0) No effect | |
| Variable road signs | | (+) Reduction | |
| Game mirrors | (0) No effect | (–) Possible increase | (0) No effect |
| Scent signals | (0) No effect | | (0) Possible short term effect, no long-term effects |
| Game fences | (0) No effect | | (–) Hinders natural movements/migration |
| Game fence with grade-separated crossings | (+) Reduction (–80%) | | (+) Reduces negative effects of fencing alone |
| Game fence with at-grade crossings | (+) Reduction (–40%) | | (+) Reduces negative effects of fencing alone |
| Reduced speed limit | (+) Reduction | (+) Reduction | |
| Road lighting | (+) Reduction | (–) Possible increase | (0) No effect |
| Seat belt use | (+) Reduced accident severity | (0) No effect | |
| Clearance of vegetation alongside roads | (+) Reduction | | (+) Roadsides less attractive |
| Feeding of moose in winter | (+) Reduction | | (+/–) Attracted away from road sides |
| Reduction of moose density in winter habitats | (+) Likely reduction | | (+) Reduced moose density in winter habitats |

Summary of results: (+) indicates favourable result, (–) indicates unfavourable result.

***Temporary warning signs.*** The effects on accidents of temporary warning signs, which are put up only during times when there is an especially high risk of game accidents, have been investigated in two studies. Sullivan et al. (2004) have investigated the effects of well visible warning signs with red flags and flashing beacons in an experimental study. The number of vehicle–red-deer collisions was reduced by 51% (95% CI [–3; –75]). Speed reductions were also found, but only during the first year in which the signs were used, not in the second year. The latter result indicates that drivers become used to the signs and that the effect is likely to diminish over time. Rogers (2004) have studied the effects of game warning signs with the additional sign 'high crash area', which were set up in winter. Accidents were reduced by 18% (95% CI [–39; +10]). The effect is not significant and no effect was found on speed.

***Variable road signs*** that are activated only when animals are actually approaching a road have been investigated in Switzerland (Kistler 1998, Romer and Mosler-Berger

2003). In these studies, the variable signs consisted of a warning sign and a reduced speed limit (40 km/h). Game accidents were reduced by 81% on roads were such signs were installed. Speed was also reduced.

A number of other studies have investigated the effects of different types of variable message signs on speed, with varying results. Speed has been found to be either reduced, unchanged or increased (Huijser et al. 2007). Not all of these signs were combined with reduced speed limits as in Switzerland. Reduced speed was found in two studies of the effects of variable warning signs with flashing beacons that were activated when game was approaching openings in game fences along motorways (Beilinson 2001).

***Education and campaigns.*** No empirical studies have been found of the effects of education or campaigns. In a Swedish study, it was found that moose hunters had more knowledge about moose, but had not fewer moose accidents than non-hunters (Transportforskningsdelegationen 1980).

***Game mirrors and reflectors.*** Game mirrors are coloured prism glass, mounted on wooden posts, which reflect light from car headlights. In nordic countries, game mirrors are no longer used. In the USA, they are still in use (Schafer, Penland and Carr 1985). Deer have only a limited colour vision, they do not see red colours (Sielecki 2001). Acoustic signals that are often used in combination with game mirrors are often outside the range of deer's acoustic abilities (D'Angelo, Warren, Miller and Gallagher 2004, Knapp et al. 2004).

Effects on accidents of game mirrors have been investigated in a number of methodologically strong studies from different countries. None of those studies found large or significant accident reductions (Almkvist et al. 1980, Armstrong 1992, Bruinderink and Hazebroek 1996, Cottrell 2003, Ford and Villa 1993, Gilbert 1982, Gulen et al., 2006, Lehtimäki 1979, Reeve and Anderson 1993, Waring, Griffis and Vaugh 1991, Woodard, Reed and Pojar 1973). A summary effect has been calculated based on the following well controlled studies:

Lehtimäki (1979) (Finland)
Almkvist et al. (1980) (Sweden)
Voß (2007) (Germany)
Rogers (2004) (USA)
Armstrong (1992) (USA)

In summary, an increase of the number of game accidents by 7% has been found, which is not statistically significant (95% CI [−11; +28]). Only immediately after the game mirrors were set up, accidents may be reduced. A significant increase in game accidents has been found by Reeve and Anderson (1993). A significant increase of the number of night-time accidents was found by Rogers (2004). A possible explanation for increased night-time accidents is increased speed. Increased speed on roads with game mirrors were found by Lehtimäki (1981).

According to a number of observational studies, not all deer are affected by game mirrors and most animals get quickly used to them (Almkvist et al. 1980, Armstrong 1992, Rogers 2004, Lien Aune 2004, Putman 1997, Storaas, Nicolaysen, Gundersen and Zimmermann 2005, Waring, Griffis and Vaugh 1991).

***Scent signals*** are sometimes used to deter game from crossing roads. Substances are applied to poles beside the road that are assumed to be aversive to game. No accident reductions have been found in the study by Lutz (1994) and an increase of the number of accidents was found by Voß (2007). Observational studies of moose behaviour found that only some animals react to scent marks and that the effects are not long-lasting (Lutz 1994, Storaas, Nicolaysen, Gundersen, and Zimmermann 2005).

***Game fences*** are often installed along roads with high traffic volumes and where game is frequently crossing. The height of the fences varies depending on the type of game (e.g. at least 1.5 m for roe deer and 2.7 m for white-tail deer). Fences are a hinder for migration and deer go therefore often around the fence and cross the roads where the fence ends (Gordon and Anderson 2003, Clevenger, Chruszcz and Gunson 2001, Väre 1995). Consequently, game accidents have often been found to increase at the ends of fences and in junctions (Clevenger, Chruszcz and Gunson 2001, Lehtimäki 1984, Ludwig and Bremicker 1983, Statens vägverk 1985b, Ward 1982). Deer has also been found to regularly cross fences either by jumping or through holes or weak points (Väre 1995).

Some studies have evaluated the effects of game fences on road stretches that include both the fenced part and both ends of the fences. These studies have been conducted in Finland (Lehtimäki 1981, Väre 1995), Sweden (Statens vägverk 1979) and the USA (Ludwig and Bremicker 1983, Ward 1982). The results are highly heterogeneous. The estimated effects on accidents range from a 92% reduction (Statens vägverk 1979) to increases by 22% (Ward 1982) and 120% (Väre 1995). The fences in these studies hat no crossing facilities. A reduction of game accidents was found by Ward (1982) after the fences were extended and tunnels were built in order to allow safe crossing. In Sweden, game fences have been found to reduce vehicle–moose collisions by 12% when controlling for a number of factors such as speed, traffic volume and moose density (Seiler 2005). When game crosses a fence and gets caught between fence and road, the survival chances are small and exit ramps have not been found to be effective (Lehnert and Bissonette 1997, Olsson 2007).

Even if fences do not prevent all game from crossing roads, natural movements, access to resources and gene flow are negatively affected (D'Angelo, Warren, Miller and Gallagher 2004). Measures that hinder migration will therefore have a negative impact on deer populations and other wildlife species (Gibby and Clewell 2006, Olsson, Widén and Larkin 2008). Moreover, fences may during migration lead to gatherings of large number of deer on one side of the fence, with forest damage as a consequence.

Most drawbacks of game fences can be avoided by installing sufficiently long and impenetrable fences with safe crossing facilities for game and other animals.

***Safe crossing facilities: Bridges and tunnels.*** Fenced roads may be crossed safely by game when bridges or tunnels are built. Several studies have found reductions of game accidents by 80% or more along fenced roads with safe crossing facilities (Clevenger, Chruszcz and Gunson 2001, Ward 1982). Bridges or tunnels along unfenced roads have not been found to affect accident numbers (Dodd, Gagnon and Schweingsburg 2003). Not all bridges and tunnes are equally popular among deer. A number of studies have investigated factors that contribute to the degree bridges and tunnels actually are used by game (Bruinderink and Hazebroek 1996, Clevenger and Waltho 2005, Dodd, Gagnon and Schweingsburg 2003, Gordon and Anderson 2003, Kruger and Wolfel 1991, Ng et al. 2004, Olbrich 1984, Reed, Woodard and Pojar 1975). These studies found that crossing facilities are used most when the road is fenced, when they are lying on existing migration routes, when tunnels are large, when bridges are wide, when entrances to bridges and tunnels are constructed in a funnel shape and planted with bushes and trees when the road is not heavily trafficked. It has been found that it may take some time before game starts using the crossing facilities.

***Safe crossing facilities: Level crossings.*** Effects of level crossings that were installed on fenced roads have been studied by Lehnert and Bissonette (1997). The number of vehicle–deer collisions has been found to be reduced by 40% (95% CI [−58; −15]). The crossings were marked on the roads and announced by road signs.

***Reduced speed limits.*** Reduced speed may increase the chances of drivers to detect animal that is crossing a road, and collisions are likely to have less severe consequences. In a Swedish study (Seiler 2005), the relationship between speed and game accidents has been investigated, while controlling for a number of other factors such as traffic volume, game fences and moose density. It has been estimated that a speed reduction by 2 km/h would lead to a reduction of game accidents by 15% and that a speed reduction with 10 km/h would reduce game accidents by 56%.

Two studies have investigated the relationship between speed limit and game accidents. Gunther, Biel and Robinson (1998) found a reduction of the number of game accidents by 50% (95% CI [−58; −40]) on road stretches where the speed limit was 70 km/h or below than on other road stretches. However, this study has not controlled for other factors that speed limit. Bertwistle (1999) found that the number of vehicle–moose collisions decreased on a stretch of road where the speed limit was reduced from 90 to 70 km/h.

***Road lighting***. A number of older studies have not found any relationship between road lighting and game accidents (Bruinderink and Hazebroek 1996). A Finnish study (Mäkelä and Kärki 2004) found that game accidents were reduced by 6% on roads where road lighting was installed. The result is statistically significant, but the effect of road lighting on game accidents has been found to be smaller than on other types of accidents. A possible explanation is that moose density has increased by ca. 36% during the study period.

Reed, Woodard and Beck (1977, 1981) have investigated the effects of road lighting on vehicle–deer collisions by switching on and off road lighting for periods of one week over 5 years. For each 1-week period, it was estimated how many deer had crossed the road and the number of vehicle–deer collisions was registered. The results show that there were 18% fewer collisions in the periods with the light switched on. The effect is, however, not significant (95% CI [−40; +13]). Observations did not indicate that deer behaviour was affected by whether or not the lights were switched on. Effects on vehicle speed were not found either.

***Seat-belts and motorcycle helmets.*** Williams and Wells (2005) studied 147 game accidents that were fatal to a vehicle occupant. Most of these involved only one vehicle. Forty percent of all killed drivers were motor cycle riders (only 2.4% of all registered vehicles were motorcycles). Sixty percent of all killed drivers had not used the seat belt. Among the killed motorcyclists, 57% had not used a helmet. According to Williams and Wells, seat belts and helmets would have reduced the severity of the injuries in most cases. Farrell et al. (1996) found that the most severe injuries to car occupants were head injuries (70% of all severe injuries) or neck injuries (25% of all severe injuries). Injuries were less severe among drivers who had used the seat belt than among drivers who had not. Even if these studies indicate that seat-belts may reduce injury severity in vehicle–deer collisions, results from simulator tests indicate that the effects may not be great because the speed reductions often are only small Gens (2001).

***Vehicle crashworthiness***. No studies have been found of the vehicles crashworthiness on the severity of game accidents.

***Clearance of woodland.*** Trees and bushes along the road can be sight hindrances for drivers and make it difficult to detect animals. Moreover, young vegetation attracts deer because it is popular food. In experimental studies in Norway, it was found that removing food (young trees and bushes) alongside railway tracks, in combination with increasing food availability further away from the railway tracks (feeding), reduced the number of mooses hit by trains by about 50% (Andreassen, Gundersen and Storaas 2005, Storaas, Nicolaysen, Gundersen and Zimmermann 2005) and that removing vegetation on a 20–30 m wide stripe alongside railway tracks also reduced accidents.

A number of studies has shown that sight clearance of woodland along roads may reduce vehicle–deer collisions (Putman 1997, Seiler 2005, Statens vägverk 1987). In an experimental study in Sweden, trees were pruned up to three metres above ground level at a distance of up to 20 m from the edge of the road (Statens vägverk 1987). Vehicle–deer collisions were reduced by 20%.

***Feeding of moose in winter.*** High moose density in winter moose habitats is associated with increasing vehicle–moose collisions on roads in the winter habitats. Norwegian studies have found that feeding moose in such areas attracts moose away from the roads and reduces vehicle–moose collisions by about 50% (Storaas, Nicolaysen, Gundersen and Zimmermann 2005). The total number of moose did not increase (Nysted 2005). However, there were considerable damages to young pinewood within ca. 1 km of the feeding stations (Gundersen, Andreassen and Storaas 2004). An experimental study of feeding mule deer (Wood and Wolfe 1988) found that mule deer–vehicle collisions in winter were reduced by 37% (95% CI [−48; −22]). Observations of mule deer confirmed that animals were attracted away from the roads and toward the feeding stations.

***Reducing moose density in winter habitats.*** In Norway, moose–vehicle collisions are highly concentrated in winter habitats during the winter. A reduction of the number of moose is likely to reduce the number of moose–vehicle collisions. Today, moose density is regulated in autumn and does not take into account changes of moose density during the year.

### Effect on mobility

Most game accident measures do not affect mobility for motor vehicles. A Finnish study (Lehtimäki 1979) found that the average speed on roads with game mirrors was 2–5 km/h higher than on roads without game mirrors. Reduced speed limits will reduce speed to the degree that drivers comply with the speed limits. Game fences limit animals' freedom of movement and can hinder access to woodland (see next section).

**Effect on the environment**

A number of game accident measures reduce natural movements of game. This refers especially to game fences without safe crossing facilities. Consequences are reduced food availability, gene flow and the deer populations (D'Angelo, Warren, Miller and Gallagher 2004). When highly trafficked roads are unfenced, they may also hinder crossings. Roads with volumes above AADT 4,000 can be regarded as a hinder, while on roads with an AADT above 10,000 practically no deer manage to stay alive while crossing (Olsson 2007).

Clearance of woodland may change the landscape and affect forestry. Hunting and feeding moose affect forestry as well, especially when moose density is high. Forest damages, especially to young pines and broad-leaved trees, will be reduced when deer density is reduced, and they may increase when deer concentrates around feeding stations.

**Costs**

Average costs for several game accident measures that are used as standard costs by the Norwegian Public Roads Administration are summarised in Table 1.16.2 (Statens vegvesen (2005, håndbok 115).

The costs for installing at-grade game crossings have been estimated at between US 15,000 and 28,000 (1997 prices) by Lehnert and Bissonette (1997). Costs for constructing a tunnel under an existing road have been estimated at between US 92,000 and 173,000 (1997 prices).

*Table 1.16.2: Average costs of game accident measures*

| Measures | Cost per unit (NOK, 2005 prices) |
|---|---|
| Erecting warning signs, per sign | 2,000–5,000 |
| Erecting game fence, per fence meter (annual maintenance costs unknown) | 250–300 |
| At-grade crossing with four light poles | 100,000 |
| Wood clearance (first-time), per road kilometer | 40,000 |
| Wood clearance (annual maintenenance, per road km) | 4,000 |
| Wood clearance, per junction | 10,000 |

**Cost–benefit analysis**

No cost–benefit analyses have been calculated for game accident measures because both costs and effects are highly dependent on local conditions and the design of the measures. Instead, it has been estimated how much money can be spent on game accident measures, without the costs being greater than the benefits. The average societal costs of personal injuries in game accidents have been estimated based on Norwegian accident statistics and the results from several international studies (Almkvist et al. 1980, Center for Disease Control and Prevention 2006, Messelt 1994) as follows:

- NOK 2 million per game accident in which at least one person injured
- NOK 156,121 per vehicle–moose collision in which the moose is killed (independent of whether or not a person actually is injured)
- NOK 12,896 per deer–vehicle collision (deer other than moose) in which the deer is killed (independent of whether or not a person actually is injured)

In addition to personal injuries, deer–vehicle collisions usually cause damage to the vehicles, even if no person is injured. These costs are not taken into account in the above mentioned average costs. The value of the killed deer (loss of income from hunting and meat sales) and administrative costs of game accidents (e.g. search for hit deer, removing cadavers) are not included either.

Based on these figures, the average annual accident costs on a road with 0.29 vehicle–moose collisions per kilometre per year is about NOK 45,000 per kilometre. The annual average on a Norwegian road is 0.29 vehicle–moose collisions per road kilometre, which is within a winter habitat for moose, with an AADT of ca. 2,000 and a moose density in winter, which is between 5 and 10 times as large as in summer and autumn (most moose–vehicle collisions occur in winter). On such a road, measures that reduce moose–vehicle collisions by 50% may cost NOK 22,500 per kilometre per year without being unprofitable from a societal point of view. E.g. annual clearance of woodlands would have a cost–benefit ratio of 5.6. Measures may cost even more if also costs not directly related to personal injuries are taken into account.

In a cost–benefit analysis from the USA, Lehnert and Bissonette (1997) have estimated that game fences with at-grade crossings have greater benefits than costs when at least the first 6 years after construction are regarded. This result is based on an estimated accident cost of NOK 12,000 per deer–vehicle collision. These accident costs include only the losses associated with killed deer and vehicle damage. Personal injuries are not taken into account.

## 1.17 Horizontal curve treatments

### Problem and objective

While driving on country roads, drivers form expectations of the trajectory of the road on the basis of the road alignment. When the road is mainly straight, drivers do not always expect sudden sharp curves to occur. When the road has numerous curves, on the other hand, drivers are more likely to expect further curves on the road ahead. Accordingly, higher accident rates have been found in sharp curves on roads with only few curves, compared to sharp curves on roads with many (sharp) curves (Elvik and Muskaug 1994). Accident rates in unexpected curves have been found to be around three times as high when there are fewer than 0.5 such curves per kilometre road as when there are more than 0.75 curves per kilometre road. This corresponds to the results on geometric consistency and tangent length, which are described in Section 1.13. Almost all accidents in curves are driving off the road accidents or head-on collisions between vehicles (Elvik and Muskaug 1994).

It is not always possible to improve sharp curves by rebuilding the road. Measures in horizontal curves are designed to reduce the accident rate in curves by giving good prior warning of these curves, indicating the path of the curve as clearly as possible and possibly providing road users with information about safe speeds in the curve.

### Description of the measure

Measures in horizontal curves include warning measures and optical lines of sight, which prepare road users for a curve and indicate the path of curve more exactly. These include

- Warning signs before curves
- Background or directional marking and painted guardrails in curves
- Recommended speeds
- Reduced speed limits

### Effect on accidents

***Curve improvements.*** The effects on accidents of curve improvements are estimated based on the following studies, the results of which are summarised in Table 1.17.1.

McCamment (1959) (USA): Danger warning signs and recommended speed

*Table 1.17.1: Effects on accidents of horizontal curve treatments*

| | Percentage change in number of accidents | | |
|---|---|---|---|
| Accident severity | Types of accident affected | Best estimate | 95% confidence interval |
| ***Curve warning signs*** | | | |
| Injury accidents | Accidents in curves | −30 | (−73; +84) |
| Property damage only accidents | Accidents in curves | −8 | (−60; +108) |
| ***Accident black spot warning signs*** | | | |
| Injury accidents | Accidents in curves | −33 | * |
| ***Background or directional marking in curves*** | | | |
| Injury accidents | Accidents in curves | −21 | (−52; +8) |
| Injury accidents | Accidents on road sections with curves | +8 | (−3; +20) |
| Property damage only accidents | Accidents in curves | −18 | (−44; +21) |
| ***Painted guardrails in curves*** | | | |
| Injury accidents | Accidents in curves | −38 | (−61; −2) |
| Injury accidents | Whole affected section | +42 | (+18; +72) |
| ***Recommended speed in curves*** | | | |
| Injury accidents | Accidents in curves | −13 | (−22; −2) |
| Property damage only accidents | Accidents in curves | −29 | (−50; −0) |

*Statistically significant ($p<0.1$).

Tamburri, Hammer, Glennon and Lew (1968) (USA): Background marking (directional marking)
Hammer (1969) (USA): Danger warning signs, recommended speed
Rutley (1972) (Great Britain): Danger warning signs, recommended speed
Schandersson (1982) (Sweden): Background and directional marking, widening road, profile adjustment
Statens vegvesen (1983) (Norway): Background and directional marking
Eick and Vikane (1992) (Norway): Background and directional marking
Kølster Pedersen et al. (1992) (Denmark): Background and directional marking
Eriksen (1993) (Norway): Painted guardrails, background and directional marking
Stigre (1993b) (Norway): Background and directional marking
Tom (1995) (USA): Transition curves
Giæver (1999) (Norway): Accident black spot warning signs

***Warning signs.*** Advance warning of curves using warning signs appears to reduce the number of accidents. However, the results are not significant. In the study by Giæver

(1999), warning signs were combined with accident black spot warnings. A reduction of accidents by 33% was found when controlling for trend, traffic volume and regression to the mean.

***Background marking/directional marking and painted guardrails in curves.*** The results for background and directional markings and painted guardrails in curves indicate that injury accidents in curves are reduced, although not significantly. Norwegian studies showed that accidents may increase in untreated curves, when only some curves are treated with background or directional marking (Eick and Vikane 1992, Eriksen 1993, Stigre 1993b). However, more rigorous studies are needed before this can be concluded with certainty. According to a literature review by Lyles and Taylor (2006), background and directional marking leads to increased speed, moves the lateral placement of the vehicles further away from the edge line and reduces accidents. The effects are greatest at night, in sharp curves, and when edge lines are marked additionally.

***Recommended speed.*** Signs showing the recommended speed have been found to reduce the number of accidents by about 15–30%. These results are based on three studies from 1972 or earlier. The effects that have been found on speed are inconsistent between different studies (Lyles and Taylor 2006). For example Rutley (1972) found no speed changes. A study from New Zealand (Koorey, Wanty and Cenek 1998) found that driving speeds were on the average 5 km/h above the recommended speed when the recommended speed was 50 km/h, and about 20 km/h above the recommended speed when 70 km/h was recommended. Badeau, Baass and Barber (1998) explain these results with inconsistencies in the recommended speeds, and with the drivers experiences that it is safe to drive (much faster than the recommended speed. On the whole, recommended speed in curves does not seem to lead to lower speed, but to fewer accidents. A possible explanation is that drivers, based on their experience, do not take the recommendations seriously as maximum safe speeds, but interpret the signs rather as general warnings and drive more carefully in curves with recommended speed.

***Reduced speed limits.*** Studies of the effects on speed have found larger and more consistent effects of speed limit changes than of recommended speed. Speed reductions are usually smaller than the reduction of the speed limit. Based on a review of studies reported in many countries, it has been estimated that the change of mean driving speed in kilometres per hour is on average:

$$(\text{Change of speed limit}) * 0.2525 - 1.2204.$$

According to the power model of speed and accidents, changes of the average speed are related to changes of accident numbers as described in the following formula:

$$\frac{\text{Accidents after}}{\text{Accidents before}} = \left(\frac{\text{Speed after}}{\text{speed before}}\right)^{\text{Exponent}}$$

The exponent is 3.6 for fatal accidents, and 2.0 for injury accidents (Elvik, Christensen and Amundsen 2004). If the average speed in a curve where the speed limit is 80 km/h was 70 km/h, and if the speed limit is reduced to 60 km/h, it would be expected that speed is reduced by 6.3 km/h, that fatal accidents are reduced by 29% and that injury accidents are reduced by 17%. The assumptions regarding effects of speed limit changes on speed and the effects of speed on accidents refer to all types of roads. No results are available that refer specifically to curves. The relationships between speed limit, speed and accident may be different in curves compared to straight roads. The speed is for example more likely to be lower than the speed limit in curves than on straight sections of road, and there may be other differences.

**Effect on mobility**

Background and directional markings have led to increased speed in some studies (see above, effects on accidents). Studies of effects of recommended speed in curves have found small or no effects on speed (see above, Effects on accidents).

**Effect on the environment**

No studies have been found, which document the effect on the environment of the measures described in this chapter.

**Costs**

On average, the costs of signs warning of curves, showing recommended speed in curves and background and directional marking are on average NOK 35,000 per curve, depending on the number of signs which are put up.

**Cost–benefit analysis**

A numerical example has been calculated for background and directional markings in curves, combined with recommended speed. It is assumed that the number of fatalities is reduced by 29%, that the number of severely injured is reduced by 23% and that the number of slightly injured is reduced by 16%. Speed is assumed to be reduced from 55 to 50 km/h. The investment costs are assumed to be NOK 35,000 per kilometre. The cost–benefit ratios are greater than one when the traffic volume is 500 vehicles per day or more. Cost–benefit ratios increase with a decreasing slope as traffic volume increases.

## 1.18 Road lighting

### Problem and objective

For motor vehicles, the risk of having an accident in darkness is about 1.5–2 times higher than in daylight (Bjørnskau 1993, Mäkelä and Kärki 2004, OECD 1979, Vaaje 1982). Around 35% of all police reported injury accidents in Norway occur in the twilight or in the dark. The percentage is the same both within and outside densely populated areas. Only some 20–25% of traffic travels during the hours of darkness. The risk in the dark increases more for more serious accidents. According to a study from the USA, about 25% of all traffic travels in darkness while 50% of all fatal accidents occur in darkness (Griffith 1994). In the dark, the risk increases more for younger drivers than for older age groups (Massie, Campbell and Williams 1995), more for pedestrians than for people travelling by motor vehicle, and more for accidents where a vehicle runs off the road (Elvik and Muskaug 1994).

Most of the information drivers utilise in traffic is visual. Visual conditions can therefore be very significant for safe travel. In the dark, the eye picks up contrast, detail and movement to a far lesser extent than in daylight. This is one of the reasons why the risk of an accident is higher during darkness than during daylight for all road users. Other factors that may contribute to increased accident rates in the dark are more drivers with illegal BAC levels, drowsiness, higher speed and lower proportions of seat belt use.

The objective of road lighting is to reduce the accident rate in the dark by making it easier to see the road, other drivers and the immediate surroundings of the road. Road lighting may also make it less unpleasant to travel in the dark and may prevent crime.

### Description of the measure

Road lighting is defined as all artificial lighting of roads, streets, crossroads and crosswalks. Lighting in tunnels is dealt with in Section 1.19, safety in tunnels. In towns and cities, the street network is usually well lit to a greater or lesser extent. Outside towns and cities, few stretches of road are lit.

### Effect on accidents

***Lighting of previously unlit roads.*** A number of studies have evaluated the effect on accidents of road lighting along previously unlit roads. The results presented here are based on the following studies, the results of which are summarised in Table 1.18.1.

Seburn (1948) (USA)
Tanner and Christie (1955) (Great Britain)
Borel (1958) (Switzerland)
Tanner (1958) (Great Britain)
Taragin and Rudy (1960) (USA)
Billion and Parsons (1962) (USA)
Christie (1962) (Great Britain)
Ives (1962) (USA)
Transportforskningskommissionen (1965) (Sweden)
Christie (1966) (Great Britain)
Institute of Traffic Engineers (1966) (USA)
Tamburri, Hammer, Glennon and Lew (1968) (USA)
Cleveland (1969) (USA)
Tennessee Valley Authority (1969) (USA)
Walthert, Mäder and Hehlen (1970) (Switzerland)
Fisher (1971) (Australia)
Jørgensen and Rabani (1971) (Denmark)
Box (1972a) (USA)
Cornwell and Mackay (1972) (Great Britain)
Pegrum (1972) (Australia)
Sabey and Johnson (1973) (Great Britain)
Austin (1976) (Great Britain)
Lipinski and Wortman (1976) (USA)
Walker and Roberts (1976) (USA)
Andersen (1977) (Denmark)
Fisher (1977) (Australia)
Ketvirtis (1977) (Japan, USA)
National Board of Public Roads and Waterways (1978) (Finland)
Polus and Katz (1978) (Israel)

*Table 1.18.1: Effects on accidents of lighting of previously unlit roads*

| | Percentage change in the number of accidents | | |
|---|---|---|---|
| Accident severity | Types of accidents affected | Best estimate | 95% confidence interval |
| ***Accidents in darkness on all types of roads*** | | | |
| Fatal accidents | All accidents | −60 | (−62; −57) |
| Injury accidents | All accidents | | |
| *Controlled for publication bias* | | −14 | (−23; −4) |
| *Not controlled for publication bias* | | −23 | (−34; −11) |
| Property damage only accidents | All accidents | −16 | (−23; −10) |
| Unspecified | Head-on collisions | −52 | (−57; −46) |
| Unspecified* | Head-on collisions | −20 | (−54; +44) |
| Unspecified | Rear-end collisions | −54 | (−68; −33) |
| Unspecified* | Rear-end collisions | −41 | (−71; +21) |
| Unspecified | Single vehicle accidents | −39 | (−64; +3) |
| Unspecified* | Single vehicle accidents | −5 | (−50; +79) |
| ***Accidents in darkness in rural areas*** | | | |
| Fatal accidents | All accidents | −87 | (−98; −34) |
| Injury accidents | All accidents | | |
| *Controlled for publication bias* | | −14 | (−57; +71) |
| *Not controlled for publication bias* | | −26 | (−51; +10) |
| Property damage only accidents | All accidents | −27 | (−62; +40) |
| Injury accidents | Accidents at junctions | −22 | (−28; −15) |
| Property damage only accidents | Accidents at junctions | −30 | (−39; −20) |
| ***Accidents in darkness in urban areas*** | | | |
| Fatal accidents | All accidents | −43 | (−61; −15) |
| Injury accidents | All accidents | −29 | (−34; −23) |
| Property damage only accidents | All accidents | −14 | (−20; −8) |
| Fatal accidents | Pedestrian accidents | −78 | (−88; −62) |
| Injury accidents | Pedestrian accidents | −50 | (−57; −43) |
| Injury accidents | Accidents at junctions | −40 | (−51; −27) |
| Property damage only accidents | Accidents at junctions | −32 | (−47; −13) |
| ***Accidents in darkness on motorways*** | | | |
| Injury accidents | All accidents | | |
| *Controlled for publication bias* | | −4 | (−32; +35) |
| *Not controlled for publication bias* | | −13 | (−31; +8) |
| Unspecified | Rear-end collisions | −20 | (−36; +0) |
| Unspecified | Single vehicle accidents | +44 | (−2; +110) |
| Unspecified | Accidents at junctions | −41 | (−64; −5) |

*Results from Wanvik (2007b) omitted. This study is based on a large number of accidents and has therefore a large effect on the summary effects, however, the study has several methodological weaknesses, which may have contributed to an overestimation of the effects.

Jørgensen (1980) (Denmark)
Brüde and Larsson (1981) (Sweden)
Schwab, Walton, Mounce and Rosenbaum (1982) (several countries)
Brüde and Larsson (1985) (Sweden)
Lamm, Klöckner and Choueiri (1985) (Germany)
Brüde and Larsson (1986) (Sweden)
Cobb (1987) (Great Britain)
Box (1989) (USA)
Griffith (1994) (USA)
Jacoby and Pollard (1995) (GBR)
Hogema and Van der Horst (1998) (NL)
Painter (1998) (Great Britain)
Preston and Schoenecker (1999) (USA)
Bauer and Harwood (2000) (USA)
Isebrands et al. (2004) (USA)
Mäkelä and Kärki (2004) (Finland)
Wanvik (2007a) (Norway)
Wanvik (2007b) (Netherlands)
Wanvik (2007c) (Sweden)
Helai, Chor and Haque (2008) (Singapore)

According to the results in Table 1.18.1, road lighting reduces fatal accidents by 60% and injury and property damage only accidents by around 15%. These effects are statistically significant. However, most studies have methodological weaknesses, and other factors than road lighting may have contributed to the differences in accident rates between lit and unlit roads. All results that are based on a sufficient number of effect estimates have been tested for publication bias. When the results indicate that there is publication bias, summary effects with and without control for publication bias are shown in Table 1.18.1. When no results are presented with control for publication bias, this indicates for the most part that not enough effect estimates are available, not that the results are not affected by publication bias.

The results indicate that the effects of road lighting are greater for more serious accidents. The effects are also greater for pedestrian accidents and for accidents at junctions than for other accidents. The effect on injury accidents is greater in urban than in rural areas. This may be partly due to larger proportions of pedestrian accidents and accidents at junctions in urban areas, compared to rural areas. The effect on fatal accidents, however, seems to be greater in rural areas. No significant effects of road lighting have been found on motorways, except at junctions.

When different accident types are regarded, the results are not consistent with the finding that more severe accidents are more strongly affected by road lighting. Rear-end collisions, for which large reductions have been found, are for the most part less severe than head-on collisions or single vehicle accidents. An interpretation of the effects on different accident types is further complicated by the fact that the summary effects that are based on all studies are strongly affected by the results from one individual study (Wanvik 2007b), and change when the results from this study are omitted. Some studies have reported results for the effects of road lighting under different road and weather conditions. The results are, however, highly inconsistent and no summary effects have therefore been computed.

***Improving existing lighting.*** A number of studies have evaluated the effect on accidents of improving existing lighting. The results shown here are based on the following studies:

Seburn (1948) (USA)
Tanner and Christie (1955) (Great Britain)
Wyatt and Lozano (1957) (USA)
Tanner (1958) (Great Britain)
Turner (1962) (Australia)
Christie (1966) (Great Britain)
Sielski (1967) (USA)
Huber and Tracy (1968) (USA)
Tamburri, Hammer, Glennon and Lew (1968) (USA)
Box (1972a) (USA)
Box (1972b) (USA)
Box (1976) (USA)
Friis, Jørgensen and Schiøtz (1976) (Denmark)
Andersen (1977) (Denmark)
Fisher (1977) (Australia)
Richards (1981) (USA)
Lamm, Klöckner and Choueiri (1985) (Germany)
Ludvigsen and Sørensen (1985) (Denmark)
Foyster and Thompson (1986) (Great Britain)
Pfundt (1986) (Germany)
Danielsson (1987) (Sweden)
Janoff (1988) (USA)
Schreuder (1989) (Netherlands)
Schreuder (1993) (Netherlands)
Uschkamp, Hecker, Thäsler and Breuer (1993) (Germany)

*Table 1.18.2: Effects of improved road lighting on the number of accidents*

| | | Percentage change in number of accidents | |
|---|---|---|---|
| Accident sevrerity | Accident types affected | Best estimate | 95% confidence interval |
| ***Increasing the level of lighting by up to double the previous level of lighting*** | | | |
| Injury accidents | Accidents in darkness | −8 | (−20; +6) |
| Property-damage-only | Accidents in darkness | −1 | (−4; +3) |
| ***Increasing the level of lighting by up to 2–5 times the previous level of lighting*** | | | |
| Injury accidents | Accidents in darkness | −13 | (−17; −9) |
| Property-damage-only | Accidents in darkness | −9 | (−14; −4) |
| ***Increasing the level of lighting by 5 times the previous level of lighting or more*** | | | |
| Fatal accidents | Accidents in darkness | −50 | (−79; +15) |
| Injury accidents | Accidents in darkness | −32 | (−39; −25) |
| Property-damage-only | Accidents in darkness | −47 | (−62; −25) |

Studies of the effect on accidents of reducing the level of lighting in order to save energy have also been included here. By switching the before and after periods, these studies can also show the possible effects of improving lighting levels. The results of the studies about the effects of reducing the level of lighting are discussed in greater detail in the next section. On the basis of the reports listed above, the effect of improving existing lighting on accidents is presented in Table 1.18.2.

Increasing the level of lighting by up to double the previous level has a limited effect on the number of accidents. The best estimate is a reduction in the order of magnitude of 5% but this reduction is not statistically significant according to the studies quoted. When the level of lighting is increased to between two and five times the original level, the number of accidents occurring in the dark is reduced by about 10%. When the level of lighting is increased to more than five times the original level, the effect on accidents is as great as when a previously unlit road is lit, that is to say a reduction in the number of accidents involving personal injury in the dark of around 30%. The results clearly show that the size of the effect of improved lighting on accidents depends on the size of the improvement.

***Reduction of existing lighting.*** In some countries, road and street lighting is reduced during certain periods in order to save energy. The effect of reducing lighting on the number of accidents has been studied by

Huber and Tracy (1968) (USA)
Box (1976) (USA)

Friis, Jørgensen and Schiøtz (1976) (Denmark)
Richards (1981) (USA)
Lamm, Klöckner and Choueiri (1985) (Germany)
Ludvigsen and Sørensen (1985) (Denmark)
Pfundt (1986) (Germany)
Danielsson (1987) (Sweden)
Yin (2005) (USA)

The usual way of reducing lighting is to turn off every other lamp. The reports can therefore broadly represent the effects of halving the level of lighting. On the basis of these studies, the estimated effect on injury accidents in darkness is a significant increase by 17% (95% CI [+9; +25]), and the estimated effect on property-damage-only accidents in darkness is a significant increase by 27% (95% CI [+9; +50]).

***Deformable light poles.*** Road lighting may increase the seriousness of road accidents where collisions with lampposts are involved. In Norway, there have been about 300 accidents per year which involve personal injury and where collisions occur with lamp posts or similar structures (e.g. telegraph poles etc.) in the years 2001–05. The severity of accidents involving lampposts can be reduced by using deformable lampposts. Two main types of posts are available (Statens vegvesen, Handbook 017, 2007e). These are poles of a frangible design, which are mounted in such a way that they break loose from their foundations in the event of a collision, and posts of a breakaway design, which have elements that deform in the event of a collision.

The effect on injury severity in the event of a collision of installing deformable lampposts has been studied in Great Britain (Walker 1974) and the USA (Ricker et al. 1977, Kurucz 1984). On the basis of these studies, non-rigid lampposts are estimated to reduce the probability of personal injury in the event of a collision by about 50% (95% CI [−72; −25]).

Two studies have evaluated the effects of non-rigid lampposts on the number of accidents (Corben, Deery, Mullan and Dyte 1996, Ricker et al. 1977). These studies found a reduction of 29% in the number of accidents (unspecified severity) (95% CI [−40; −14]). However, this result is likely to be totally or partially due to regression to the mean.

## Effect on mobility

A Norwegian survey (Bjørnskau and Fosser 1996) showed that how road lighting increased mean speed increased in the dark, particularly along straight roads. The net speed increase in the dark can be calculated to roughly 3%, both on straight roads and in curves. Other studies have not found changed speed on roads where road lighting had been installed (Cornwell 1972, Huber and Tracy 1968, Mäkelä and Kärki 2004). Nor is there anything to indicate that road lighting affects the distribution of traffic over a 24-h period to any significant extent (Elvik 1995). Studies in the Netherlands found increased capacity of roads where lighting was installed (Folles, Ijsselstijn, Hogema and van der Horst 1999).

**Effect on the environment**

No studies have been found on the effects of road lighting on noise or pollution. One possible effect of road lighting is that it becomes more pleasurable to drive in the dark. Road lighting consumes electricity. Environmental effects of power consumption will depend on how the energy is produced. Road lighting usually aims at improving visibility conditions for drivers, and not to make it more pleasurable to travel in the dark, e.g. for pedestrians or cyclists (Gardner 1998). It is all the same likely that road lighting makes it more pleasurable and reduces feelings of insecurity.

A survey of the inhabitants in a suburb in Västerås in Sweden, where one-third of the lighting was turned off at night showed that around 40% of those questioned had not noticed that this had been done (Dahlstedt 1981). Some 80% of those questioned thought it was a good idea that the municipality tried to save money by reducing the road lighting.

To studies have found reduced crime after road lighting was installed. A Dutch study found that fewer crimes were reported during the evening and at night in streets with high levels of lighting than in streets where the level of lighting was low (Schreuder 1993). An evaluation of street lighting in Great Britain also found significant reductions of crime by about 20% after street lighting was installed (Painter 1998). At the same time, activity in the streets increased.

**Costs**

The average costs for installing road lighting in Norway are about NOK 0.72–1.25 million per kilometre road. The annual maintenance costs are up to 10% of the investment costs depending on the type of lighting. (Erke and Elvik 2006).

## Cost–benefit analysis

Cost–benefit ratios of road lighting are dependent on the traffic volume and on the accident rate. Numerical examples are calculated for road lighting on roads with different traffic volumes. The calculations are based on the following assumptions:

- Investment costs per kilometre road are NOK 1 million.
- Annual maintenance costs are between about NOK 0.11 million.
- On motorways the number of fatalities and serious injuries in darkness is reduced by 5% and the number of slightly injured in darkness is reduced by 5%.
- On other roads in rural areas the number of fatalities and serious injuries in darkness is reduced by 60% and the number of slightly injured in darkness is reduced by 14%.
- The proportion of accidents that occur in darkness is 35%.

The accident rates on roads with different traffic volumes are estimated based on accidents on Norwegian motorways and other roads in rural areas where the speed limit is 80 km/h. The cost–benefit ratios of road lighting are as shown in Table 1.18.3. The numerical examples show that road lighting is beneficial on roads with a traffic volume above 15,000 vehicles per day, except for motorways. On roads with lower traffic volumes and on motorways road lighting is not beneficial. These results do not take into account different effects of road lighting at junctions and on sections.

A numerical example is also calculated for improving existing lighting in urban areas. The calculation is based on the same assumptions as above. It is assumed that improved lighting reduces injury accidents in darkness by 15%. The investment costs are assumed to be NOK 300,000 per kilometre road and the annual maintenance costs

*Table 1.18.3: Cost–benefit ratios of road lighting in Norway*

| | Traffic volume (AADT) | Injury accidents per mill. vehicle km | Cost–benefit ratio |
|---|---|---|---|
| Motorway | 30,000 | 0.072 | 0.21 |
| 80 km/h speed limit | 2,500 | 0.164 | 0.27 |
| 80 km/h speed limit | 3,000 | 0.161 | 0.32 |
| 80 km/h speed limit | 5,000 | 0.152 | 0.51 |
| 80 km/h speed limit | 10,000 | 0.142 | 0.95 |
| 80 km/h speed limit | 15,000 | 0.136 | 1.36 |
| 80 km/h speed limit | 20,000 | 0.132 | 1.76 |
| 80 km/h speed limit | 30,000 | 0.126 | 2.53 |
| 80 km/h speed limit | 50,000 | 0.120 | 4.01 |

are assumed to increase by NOK 15,000 per year. Under these assumptions, improving road lighting is not beneficial, independent of the traffic volume.

A British study of the effects of road lighting on crime (Painter 1998) has estimated a cost–benefit ratio of between 1.4 and 3. Only reduced crime is taken into account in these ratios.

## 1.19 Improving tunnel safety

### Problem and objective

Steep mountainsides, narrow valleys and poor ground conditions make road construction difficult and expensive. In order to keep construction costs down, many roads (in particular older roads and road with less traffic), which lie in difficult terrain, are narrow, full of curves and with dangerous side terrain. This contributes to increasing the accident rate. In such terrain, building roads in tunnels is often chosen in order to achieve better mobility and increased traffic safety. Compared with above-ground roads, a road in a tunnel has a number of characteristics, which can both increase and reduce safety (Siemens 1989). Factors, which make roads in tunnels safer than roads above-ground, are

- roads in tunnels do not normally have intersections or access roads,
- there is usually little or no pedestrian and cycle traffic in tunnels,
- roads in tunnels often have a more gentle alignment then roads above-ground (fewer sharp curves and steep gradients),
- roads in tunnels are not exposed to avalanches or landslides,
- roads in tunnels are not exposed to rain or typical winter driving conditions and snow ploughing problems.

Factors, which can make roads and tunnels less safe than roads above-ground, include

- traffic space is limited, opportunities for evasive manoeuvres are small;
- there is no daylight, and light conditions often change dramatically when driving in and out of a tunnel;
- access to fresh air is reduced and steam, mist or exhaust gases can reduce visibility;
- in the event of accidents or fires, the escape route may be blocked and rescue work may be more difficult than on roads above ground.

A number of studies have been carried out in Norway to determine accident rates in tunnels and factors influencing them. These studies are

Mo (1980) (accident rate in tunnels and on roads above ground)
Hovd (1981) (accident rate in tunnels and on roads above ground)
Thoma (1989) (accident rate in tunnels and on roads above ground)
Hvoslef (1991) (factors which affect accident rate in tunnels)
Stabell (1992) (factors which affect accident rate in tunnels)
Amundsen and Gabestad (1991) (Oslo tunnel: first year of operation)
Amundsen (1993) (frequency of different events in tunnels)
Amundsen (1996) (frequency of different events in tunnels)
Amundsen and Ranes (1997) (accident rate in tunnels and factors influencing it)
Mysen (1997) (accident rate in two-lane tunnels with a single tube and heavy traffic)
Salvisberg et al. (2004) (accident rates in single and dual tube tunnels)
Robatsch and Nussbaumer (2005) (accident rates in single and dual tube tunnels)
Amundsen and Engebretsen (2008) (several risk factors)

On the basis of the most recent estimates of the accident rate in tunnels, Figure 1.19.1 shows the number of injury accidents per million vehicle kilometres for different zones in tunnels.

The injury accident rate in tunnels is highest in the transition zones between the tunnel and the road above ground. The above ground zone nearest the tunnel has the highest rate. One reason for this could be that the road often lies in the shade, and thus may be more exposed to slippery driving conditions than roads more exposed to sunlight. The relatively high risk in the first part the tunnel may be attributable to the fact that the eye has not yet adapted to the level of lighting in the tunnel. Lighting in the tunnel is, however, strongest near the portals and reduces in the central zone.

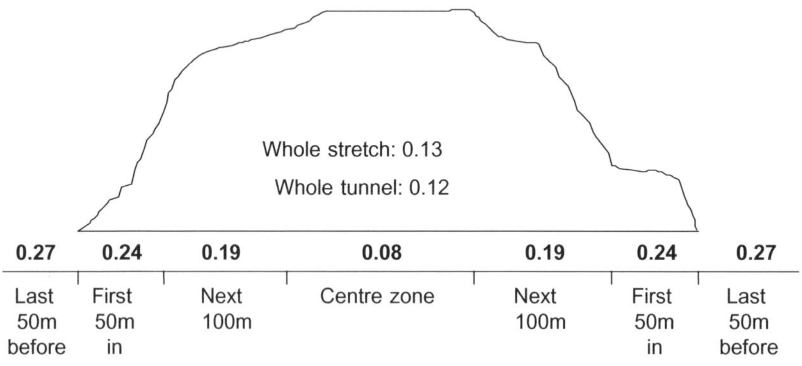


*Figure 1.19.1: Number of injury accidents per million vehicle kilometres in different zones in tunnels (Amundsen and Engebretsen 2008).*

For the tunnel as a whole, the accident rate is relatively low. Many roads above-ground in rural areas, and the great majority of roads in towns and cities, have a higher rate of injury accidents than tunnels. Studies of the frequency of different events in tunnels (Amundsen 1993, 1996) indicate that the relative frequency of events, when the number of injury accidents is set equal to 1, is approximately:

| Type of event | Relative frequency |
|---|---|
| Injury accidents | 1 |
| Property damage only accidents | 2 |
| Fires in vehicles | 0.1–0.2 |
| Other events (engine cut-out etc.) | 40–80 |

Safety measures in tunnels are intended to ensure that the accident rate is no higher than on roads above ground, and ideally lower, since rescue work in the event of accidents in tunnels is more difficult than for accidents on roads above-ground.

**Description of the measure**

In rural areas, tunnels are usually built to shorten the road and to keep it open in winter. In densely populated areas, tunnels are also built to avoid conflict with existing buildings and to improve the environment. In this chapter, tunnel safety comprises the following measures:

- Choice between building a road in a tunnel or above ground
- Choice of tunnel length
- Choice of tunnel width
- Choice of gradient in tunnels
- Choice of radius of horizontal curves in tunnels
- Tunnel lighting
- Choice between a single tube (traffic in both directions) and dual tubes (one-way traffic in each tube)
- Sub-sea tunnels compared to tunnels on land
- Lighting of tunnels

Factors, which may affect safety in tunnels, but which are not discussed in this chapter, include ventilation system, emergency bays, emergency telephones and continuous traffic monitoring using cameras. The reason why these measures are not included is that studies of their effect on accidents have not been identified.

## Effect on accidents

Based on the studies listed above, the effects on accidents of different measures in tunnels are given in Table 1.19.1.

Roads in tunnels are safer than roads above-ground in towns and cities. In sparsely populated areas, and on motorways, there appears to be no significant difference in accident rate between tunnels and roads in the day. Lighting in tunnels, increasing the width of tunnels and reducing gradients in tunnels all contribute to increasing safety. The same is true for longer tunnels, but this is due to the fact that the transition zones contribute less to the accident rate in a long tunnel than in a short one.

Doubling the radius of horizontal curves reduces accident rate in tunnels. The changes represented in Table 1.19.1 are from 112 to 225 m, 225 to 450 m and 450 to 900 m. Dual tube tunnels appear to be slightly safer than single-tube tunnels, but the differences are not statistically significant. Norwegian data (Amundsen and Engebretsen 2008) indicate that dual tunnels are safer than single tunnels in rural areas

*Table 1.19.1: Effects on accidents of different measures in tunnels*

| | Percentage change in the number of accidents | | |
|---|---|---|---|
| Accident severity | Types of accident affected | Best estimate | 95% confidence interval |
| ***Road in tunnel vs. road above-ground*** | | | |
| Injury accidents | All accidents: motorways | −2 | (−15; +12) |
| Injury accidents | All accidents: rural | −4 | (−17; +11) |
| Injury accidents | All accidents: urban | −61 | (−77; −35) |
| ***Lighting in tunnels*** | | | |
| Injury accidents | Accidents in tunnels | −35 | (−51; −14) |
| ***Increasing the width of the tunnel from less than 6 m to more than 6 m*** | | | |
| Injury accidents | Accidents in tunnels | −40 | (−49; −30) |
| ***Tunnels with a gradient of more than about 5% compared to flat tunnels*** | | | |
| Injury accidents | Accidents in tunnels | +13 | (−4; +32) |
| ***Doubling the radius of horizontal curves*** | | | |
| Injury accidents | Accidents in tunnels | −35 | (−45; −24) |
| ***Dual tube tunnels compared to single tube tunnels*** | | | |
| Injury accidents | Accidents in tunnels | −5 | (−15; +6) |
| ***Sub-sea tunnels compared to tunnels on land*** | | | |
| Injury accidents | Accidents in tunnels | +16 | (−15; +38) |

but not in urban areas. Sub-sea tunnels appears to have a slightly higher accident rate than tunnels on land, but this could be because sub-sea tunnels tend to have steeper gradients than tunnels on land.

**Effect on mobility**

The effect of tunnels on mobility depends to a large extent on the type of traffic environment in which the tunnels are built. On motorways, the speed level in tunnels is about the same as on motorways above-ground. Tunnels on roads in sparsely populated areas can shorten journey times compared to roads above-ground, since tunnels tend to be shorter and curves are avoided. Tunnels on roads in densely populated areas can also result in a gain in journey time for motor vehicles, because the number of stops due to intersections and access roads is reduced, while, at the same time, there is little pedestrian and cycle traffic in tunnels.

Speed measurements in a tunnel in Ålesund, Norway (length 3,481 m, steepest gradient 8.5%, speed limit 80 km/h) shows that light vehicles maintain a speed of between 80 and 90 km/h, scarcely affected by the gradient. For heavy vehicles, the gradients have a significant effect on speed. Speeds drop to 30–40 km/h (Stabell 1992). In tunnels with steep gradients, major differences in speed between light and heavy vehicles can obviously occur. The difference in speed is greatest on downhill sections.

**Effect on the environment**

In tunnels with heavy traffic, good ventilation is necessary for maintaining acceptable air quality in the tunnel. Tunnels in urban areas, which remove traffic from residential areas, can improve the environment for those living along the road. A study of the short-term effects of the Vålereng-tunnel, Norway (Kolbenstvedt et al. 1990), found that the number of dwellings exposed to an outdoor noise level of 65 decibels or more was reduced. In living rooms, the reduction was around 8%, while for bedrooms it was around 28%. Pollution, measured as concentrations of carbon monoxide (CO) and nitrogen dioxide ($NO_2$) per cubic metre of air were also reduced.

Some people may feel unsafe when travelling through tunnels, because it is dark and because it is an enclosed space (Rein 1986). It is estimated that 6.3 out of every 1,000 persons suffer mild degrees of claustrophobia. Also, 2.2 out of every 1,000 persons suffer from serious claustrophobia disabling.

## Costs

Cost figures for a number of large tunnels, which were opened to traffic between 1988 and 1993, have been taken from the annual reports of the Norwegian Public Roads Administration. These data show very large variations in costs. The average construction cost for the tunnels represented was NOK 55.2 million per kilometre of tunnel built. The tunnels can be divided into three main groups with respect to construction costs:

- Tunnels of at least four lanes (2+2) and separate tubes for each traffic direction in larger towns and cities: construction cost NOK 130–190 million per kilometre road.
- Underwater tunnels with at least two traffic lanes: construction costs NOK 25–50 million per kilometre road.
- Ordinary mountain tunnels with two traffic lanes: construction costs NOK 10–30 million per kilometre road.

The annual maintenance costs for tunnels are higher than for roads aboveground. Maintenance costs of NOK 0.5–1.0 million per kilometre road per year are not unusual.

## Cost–benefit analysis

The costs and benefits of building a tunnel depend very much on local conditions. It is therefore difficult to give general figures. In order to indicate possible effects, two numerical examples have been developed.

One example concerns building a main road in a tunnel in a city. It is assumed that the old road had an annual average daily traffic of 30,000 and an accident rate of 0.50 injury accidents per million vehicle kilometres. These figures are roughly representative of major tunnels that have been built in cities in Norway in recent years. It is assumed that there is a 40% reduction in the number of accidents. It is further assumed that the tunnel takes over 60% of the traffic from the old road. An average speed of 35 km/h is assumed for the old road; 70 km/h is assumed for the tunnel. Vehicle operating costs are assumed to be reduced by NOK 0.10 per kilometre driven. It is further assumed that there is an environmental gain corresponding to NOK 0.30 in saved environmental costs per kilometre driven. Building the tunnel is assumed to cost NOK 150 million per kilometre of road. The annual maintenance costs for the tunnel are set at around NOK 1.5 million per kilometre of road. Given these assumptions, the benefit is estimated at NOK 57.7 million in saved accident costs, NOK 109.4 million in saved travel time costs, NOK 7.7 million in saved vehicle operating costs and NOK 38.3 million in saved environmental costs, making a total of NOK 213 million. The costs are estimated to be NOK 201 million. The example indicates that it may be cost-effective to move the biggest main roads in cities into tunnels, assuming that a high percentage of the traffic transfers to the tunnel.

A numerical example has also been developed for a road in a rural area. It is assumed that there is an annual average daily traffic of 3,000 vehicles and an accident rate of 0.20 injury accidents per million vehicle kilometres on the old road. The number of accidents is assumed to reduce by 25%. It is assumed that all traffic transfers to the tunnel. Speed is assumed to increase from 65 to 75 km/h. Vehicle operating costs are assumed to reduce by NOK 0.05 per kilometre driven. The benefit of building a 1 km long tunnel given these assumptions is estimated to be NOK 1.7 million in saved accident costs, NOK 0.6 million in saved costs of travel time and NOK 0.6 million in saved vehicle operating costs, making it a total of NOK 5 million. The costs of building and maintaining the tunnel are estimated as NOK 21.5 million. This is more than the benefit of the tunnel. Clearly, it is not normally cost-effective to build roads in tunnels in sparsely populated areas.

## 1.20 Rest stops and service areas

### Problem and objective

Driving for long periods without a break reduces driver performance and may lead to an increase in the accident rate, as has been shown in a Norwegian study (Fosser 1988). After several hours' driving, the majority of drivers will need food, rest, toilet facilities or other breaks from driving. Rest stops and service areas along the road are intended to meet such needs. It is very difficult to know how many accidents are due to long periods of driving without a break or to a lack of services along the road. Accidents have normally more than one cause, and the length of the journey is seldom known.

Studies of the relationship between driving time without breaks and accident rate amongst professional drivers show that the accident rate starts to increase after 6 h driving without a break. For continuous driving periods of up to 10 h, the risk increases by 10–80%. For continuous driving periods over 10 h, the risk increases by 100–250% (Fosser 1988). Corresponding studies of private car drivers have not been carried out. In American studies, it has been assumed that lack of service provision along a road leads to parking on the road shoulder. In the USA, accidents where cars parked on the hard shoulder have been hit are estimated to comprise 1–5% of all accidents on motorways in sparsely populated areas.

Rest stops and other service facilities along the road are intended to prevent drivers from stopping for breaks on the hard shoulder or in the traffic lane, and give drivers on long journeys services en route, so that long periods of driving without breaks can be avoided.

## Description of the measure

Rest stops and service areas on Norwegian roads include the following facilities (Ragnøy 1978): unserviced lay-byes and parking areas without equipment, rest stops (equipped with tables and chairs, rubbish bins and toilets), emergency telephones, kiosks, petrol stations/service stations, cafés, and overnight facilities. In Norway, the recommendation is that major rest stops be constructed every 45 km on national highways and minor rest stops every 15 km. Major rest stops should be equipped with tables, chairs, rubbish bins and toilets. On motorways, it is recommended that rest shops should serve one traffic direction only.

## Effect on accidents

Only one study has been found that has tried to quantify the effect of rest stops on the number of accidents (King 1989). The study is based on the assumption that the lack of rest stops leads the driver to stop on the hard shoulder instead. It is assumed that rest stops contribute to the prevention of accidents where vehicles parked on the hard shoulder are hit. On the motorway network in the United States in 1981, it was estimated that the number of accidents where vehicles parked on the hard shoulder were hit would have been 50% higher without rest stops than with the actual number of rest stops available that year. The average distance between rest stops on motorways in the United States in 1981 was around 70 km. This is a purely hypothetical estimate of effect. The report emphasises that there are major problems of research method involved in estimating the effect on accidents of rest stops, because it is difficult know with certainty which types of accidents rest stops prevent (King 1989).

## Effect on mobility

No studies have been found that show the effects of rest stops and other service facilities along the road on mobility. The measures are not primarily intended to increase mobility but to meet the other needs.

### Effect on the environment

No studies have been found that show the effects of rest stops and other service facilities on roads on physical environmental factors. Such facilities can, however, contribute to making long journeys more pleasant. A Norwegian survey of motorists using rest stops in the summer of 1978 found that meal breaks and rest breaks were given as the most important reasons for using the rest stop. The average rest period was 15–30 min (Ragnøy 1978). The proportion who stopped en route had a clear relationship to the length of the journey. For journeys under 50 km, 11% stopped en route. This increased to 35% for journeys of 51–100 km, 61% for journeys of 101–200 km and over 85% for journeys of more than 200 km per day.

### Costs

Few cost figures are available for construction and maintenance of rest stops and other service facilities along the road. Construction costs depend on the size of the rest stop and ground conditions at the site. In Norway the construction cost of a rest stop was between NOK 150,000 and 300,000, and the cost of toilet facilities was about NOK 200,000 per rest stop in 1982 (Statens vegvesen 1985). Annual running and maintenance costs were between NOK 5,000 (small lay-bys) and NOK 42,000 (main rest stop with toilets) depending on the type of facility.

### Cost–benefit analysis

An American cost–benefit analysis concluded that rest stops along motorways in the USA had a benefit–cost ratio of around 3.2 (King 1989). Prevention of accidents comprised 30% of the benefit, the reduction of unnecessary driving (looking for a suitable place to stop) 26% and driver satisfaction (user comfort and convenience) 44%. However, this analysis is based on a purely hypothetical estimate of the effects on safety.

## References

Abdel-Aty, M. & Radwan, A.E. (2000). Modeling traffic accident occurrence and involvement. Accident Analysis and Prevention, 32, 633–642.

Abdelwahab, W. & Morral, J.F. (1997). Determining the need for and location of truck escape ramps. Journal of Transportation Engineering, 123, 350–356.

Agent, K.R. & Pigman, J.G. (2001). Safety impacts of rural road construction. Report KTC-01-01/SPR219-00-1I. Lexington, Kentucky: Kentucky Transportation Center, College of Engineering, University of Kentucky.

Agerholm, N.; Caspersen, S.; Madsen, J. C. O.; Lahrmann, L. (2008). Traffic safety on bicycle paths – results from a new large scale Danish study, 6th ICTCT Extra Workshop, Intersections: Points of communication and points of risk, Innovative intersection design for safety and mobility, Melbourne, april.

Agustsson, L. & K. M. Lei. (1994). Trafiksikkerhedseffekten af cykelbaner på strækninger mellem kryds i byområder. Notat 12. Vejdirektoratet, København.

Almkvist, B.et al. (1980). Viltolyckor med vägtrafik (VIOL) (Game accidents in road traffic). Slutrapport. 1980-02-21. Report TU 143. Statens vägverk, Utvecklingssektionen, Borlänge.

Amundsen, A. H. & R. Elvik. (2004). Effects on road safety of new urban arterial roads. *Accident Analysis and Prevention*, **36**, 115–123.

Amundsen, A. & Kolbenstvedt, M. (2009). Miljøhåndboken, http://miljo.toi.no/, Transportøkonomisk institutt, Oslo.

Amundsen, F. H. (1993). Hendelser and havarier i norske vegtunneler. Registreringer 1992. Rapport 7029. Vegdirektoratet, Plan- og anleggsavdelingen, Oslo.

Amundsen, F. H. (1996). Bilbranner og andre hendelser i norske vegtunneler 1990–95. Rapport TTS 11 1996. Vegdirektoratet, Transport- og trafikksikkerhetsavdelingen, Transportanalysekontoret, Oslo.

Amundsen, F.H. & Engebretsen, A. (2008). Traffic accidents in road tunnels. An analysis of traffic accidents in tunnels on national roads for the period 2001–2006. TS Report 7-2008. Oslo: Public Roads Administration.

Amundsen, F. H. & K. O. Gabestad. (1991). Oslotunnelen. Erfaringer fra planleggingen og det første driftsåret. Rapport 14, 1991. Vegdirektoratet, Plan- og anleggsavdelingen, Oslo.

Amundsen, F. H. & F. Hofset (2000). Omkjøringsveger – en analyse av trafikkulykker og trafikkutvikling. Rapport TTS 8 2000. Vegdirektoratet, Kontor for trafikkanalyse, Oslo

Amundsen, F. H. & G. Ranes. (1997). Vegtrafikkulykker i vegtunneler. Rapport TTS 9 1997. Vegdirektoratet, Transport- og trafikksikkerhetsavdelingen, Transportanalysekontoret, Oslo.

Andersen, K. B. (1977). Uheldsmønsteret på almindelige 4-sporede veje. RfT-rapport 20. Rådet for Trafiksikkerhedsforskning (RfT), København.

Andersen, T., Nielsen, M. A. and Olesen, S. (2004). Cyklister i kryds, Dansk Vejtidsskrift, 11, 18–19.

Anderson, I.B., Bauer, K.M., Harwood, D.W. & Fitzpatrick, K. (1999). Relationship to safety of geometrical design consistency measures for rural two-lane highways. Transportation Research Record, 1658, 43–51.

Anderson, I.B. & Krammes, R.A. (2000). Speed reduction as a surrogate for accident experience at horizontal curves on rural two-lane highways. Transportation Research Record, 1701, 86–94.

Andersson, P. K.; B. La Cour Lund & P. Greibe (2001). Omfartsveje. Den sikkerhedsmessige effekt. Rapport 4, 2001. Danmarks Transport Forskning, Lyngby.

Andersson, P. K. & Lund, B. L. C. (2009). Adfærd ved stopstreg – Fire Københavnske bykryss, Trafitec for Københavns Kommune.

Andreassen, H.P., Gundersen, H. & Storaas, T. (2005). The effect of scent-marking, forest cleaning and supplemental feeding on moose-train collisions. Journal of Wildlife Management, 69, 1125–1132.

Armstrong, J. J. (1992). An evaluation of the effectiveness of Swareflex deer reflectors. Ontario Ministry of Transportation Research and Development Branch Report No. MAT-91-12.

Austin, B. R. (1976). Public lighting the deadly reckoning. Traffic Engineering and Control, 17, 262–263.

Bach, O., O. Rosbach & E. Jørgensen. (1985). Cykelstier i byer. Den sikkerhedsmæssige effekt. Vejdirektoratet, Sekretariatet for Sikkerhedsfremmende Vejforanstaltninger, Vejdatalaboratoriet, Næstved.

Backer-Grøndahl, A., Amundsen, A. H., Fyhri, A., & Ulleberg, P. (2007). Trygt eller truende? Opplevelse av risiko på reisen, TØI-rapport 913, Transportøkonomisk institutt, Oslo.

Badeau, N., Baass, K. & Barber, P. (1998). Method proposed to determinde the safe and advisory speeds in curves. Conference of the Transportation Association of Canada, September 20–23, Regina, Saskatchewan.

Ball, J.P. & Dahlgren, J. (2002). Browsing damage on pine (Pinus sylvestris and Pinus contorta) by a migrating moose (Alces alces) population in winter: relation to habitat compositions and road barriers. Scandinavian Journal of Forest Research, 17, 427–435.

Barbaresso, J. C. & B. O. Bair. (1983). Accident Implications of Shoulder Width on Two-Lane Roadways. Transportation Resarch Record, 923, 90–97.

Bared, J., Giering, G.L. & Warren, D.L. (1999). Safety evaluation of acceleration and deceleration lane length. ITE Journal, 69, 50–54.

Bauer, K.M. & Harwood, D.W. (1998). Statistical models of accidents on interchange ramps and speed change lanes. Report FHWA-RD-97-106.

Bauer, K.M. & Harwood, D.W. (2000). Statistical models of at-grade intersection accidents – addendum. Report FHWA-RD-99-094.

Beaton, J. L., R. N. Field & K. Moskowitz. (1962). Median Barriers: One Year's Experience and Further Controlled Full-Scale Tests. Highway Research Board Proceedings, 41, 433–468.

Beca, Carter Hollings & Ferner Ltd. (1998). Safety benefits of median barriers on New Zealand motorways. Transfund New Zealand Research Report No. 107.

Beilinson, L. (2001). Using transport telematics in preventing animal accidents. Proceedings of the conference road safety on three continents in Pretoria, South Africa.

Bendtsen, H. (1992). Rundkørsler reducerer luftforureningen. Dansk Vejtidsskrift, 10, 34.

Benekohal, R. F. & A. M. Hashmi. (1992). Procedures for Estimating Accident Reductions on Two-Lane Highways. Journal of Transportation Engineering, 118, 111–129.

Bennett, G. T. (1973). Carriageway markings for rural junctions. Traffic Engineering and Control, 15, 137–139.

Berggrein, B. & Bach, U. (2007). Uheldsevaluering af cykelsymboler og harlakinmønster, Dansk Vejtidsskrift, 4, 40–41.

Bertwistle, J. (1999). The Effects of Reduced Speed Zones on Reducing Bighorn Sheep and Elk Collisions with Vehicles on the Yellowhead Highway in Jasper National Park. In the Proceedings of the International Conference on Wildlife Ecology and Transportation. Held in Missoula, MT, September 13 to 16, 1999, pp. 727–735.

Billion, C. E. (1956). Effect of Median Barriers on Driver Behavior. Highway Research Board Bulletin, 137, 1–17.

Billion, C. E. & N. C. Parsons. (1962). Median Accident Study – Long Island, New York. Highway Research Board Bulletin, 308, 64–79.

Billion, C. E., A. Taragin & E. C. Cross. (1962). Effect of Parkway Medians on Driver Behavior - Westchester County Parkways. Highway Research Board Bulletin, 308, 36–63.

Björketun, U. (1984). Samband mellan vägbeläggningar och trafikolyckor vid olika väderlek. VTI-meddelande 393. Statens väg- och trafikinstitut (VTI), Linköping.

Björketun, U. (1991). Linjeföring samt prediktion av olyckor utifrån linjeföringsdata för vägar projekterade/byggda under 1950-, 1960- respektive 1970-talet. VTI-meddelande 641. Statens väg- och trafikinstitut (VTI), Linköping.

Bjørnskau, T. (1993). Risiko i vegtrafikken 1991–92. TØI-rapport 216. Transportøkonomisk institutt, Oslo.

Bjørnskau, T. (2004). Trygghet i transport. Oppfatninger av trygghet ved bruk av ulike transportmidler, TØI-rapport 702, Transportøkonomisk institutt, Oslo.

Bjørnskau, T. (2005). Sykkelulykker – ulykkestyper, skadekonsekvenser og risikofaktorer, TØI-rapport 793, Transportøkonomisk institutt, Oslo.

Bjørnskau, T. (2008). Risiko i trafikken 2005–2007, TØI-rapport 986, Transportøkonomisk institutt, Oslo.

Bjørnskau, T. & S. Fosser. (1996). Bilisters atferdstilpasning til innføring av vegbelysning. Resultater fra en før- og etterundersøkelse på E-18 i Aust-Agder. TØI-rapport 332. Transportøkonomisk institutt, Oslo.

Blakstad, F. & T. Giæver. (1989). Ulykkesfrekvenser på vegstrekninger i tett og middels tett bebyggelse. Rapport STF63 A89005. SINTEF Samferdselsteknikk, Trondheim.

Blamey, G. & Blamey, G. (1990). The results of a deer survey carried out on an area between Hatfield forest and Dunnow, Essex. Ove Arup and Parterns, London.

Bolling, A. (2000). Demonstrationsstråk for cykel – för och eftermätningar avseende trafikantgruppers beteende – Flöde – Hastighet – Köremönster – Samspell, VTI meddelande 905, Väg- och transportforskningsinstitutet, Linköping.

Bonneson, J. A. & P. T. McCoy. (1997). Effect of median treatment on urban arterial safety: an accident prediction model. Paper 970101. Transportation Research Board, 76th Annual Meeting, January 12–16, 1997, Washington DC.

Borel, P. (1958). Accident prevention and public lighting. Bulletin des Schweitzerisches Elektrotechnisches Verbands, 49, 1, 8–11, 1958 (Sitert etter Ketvirtis 1977).

Borger, A. & E. Frøysadal. (1993). Sykkelundersøkelsen 1992. TØI-rapport 217. Transportøkonomisk institutt, Oslo.

Borger, A. & E. Frøysadal. (1994). Sykkelbyprosjektet. Intervjuundersøkelser i sykkelbyene Sandnes og Tønsberg/Nøtterøy i 1992. TØI-rapport 234. Transportøkonomisk institutt, Oslo.

Bowman, B. L. & R. L. Vecellio. (1994). Effect of urban and suburban median types on both vehicular and pedestrian safety. Transportation Research Record, 1445, 169–179.

Box, P. C. (1972a). Freeway Accidents and Illumination. Highway Research Record, 416, 10–20.

Box, P. C. (1972b). Comparison of Accidents and Illumination. Highway Research Record, 416, 1–9.

Box, P. C. (1976). Effect of Lighting Reduction On an Urban Major Route. Traffic Engineering, October 1976, 26–27.

Box. P. C. (1989). Major Road Accident Reduction by Illumination. Transportation Research Record, 1247, 32–38.

Boyle, A. J.; Wright, C. C. (1984). Accident 'migration' after remedial treatment at accident blackspots. Traffic Engineering and Control, 25, 260–267,

Brabander, B.D. & Lode Vereeck, E.N. (2005). Road safety effects of roundabouts in Flanders. Journal of Safety Research, 36, 289–296.

Brandsæter, P. B. (1973). Virkninger av omkjøringsvegene ved seks tettsteder på Østlandet. Biri, Eina, Gran, Stange, Nesbyen, Ål. TØI-rapport. Transportøkonomisk institutt, Oslo.

Brenac, T. (1996). Safety at curves and road geometric standards in some European countries. Transportation Research Record, 1523, 99–106.

Bretherton, W. M. (1994) Are Raised Medians Safer Than Two-Way Left-Turn Lanes? ITE-Journal, December 1994, 20–25.

Brilon, W. & B. Stuwe. (1991). Kreisverkehrsplätze - Leistungsfähigkeit, Sicherheit und verkehrstechnische Gestaltung. Strassenverkehrstechnik, 35, 296–304.

Brilon, W., B. Stuwe & O. Drews. (1993). Sicherheit und Leistungsfähigkeit von Kreisverkehrsplätzen. FE Nr 77359/91. Lehrstuhl für Verkehrswesen, Ruhr-Universität Bochum.

Brinkman, C. & Perchonk, K. (1979). Hazardous effects of highway features and roadside objects – Highlights. Public Roads, Federal Highway Administration, Washington D.C., pp.8–14.

Brown, H. & Tarko, A. (1999). Effects of access control on safety of urban arterial streets. Transportation Research Record 1665, 68–74.

Brüde, U. & G. Nilsson. (1976). Prediktionsmodell för trafikloyckor för kvalitetsbestämning av vägars trafiksäkerhet. VTI-rapport 77. Statens väg- och trafikinstitut (VTI), Linköping.

Brüde, U. & J. Larsson. (1977). En olycksanalys av tvåfältiga huvudvägar med hastighetsbegränsning 90 km/h. VTI-meddelande 55. Statens väg- och trafikinstitut (VTI), Linköping.

Brüde, U. & J. Larsson. (1981). Vägkorsningar på landsbygd inom huvudvägnätet. Olycksanalys. VTI-rapport 233. Statens väg- och trafikinstitut (VTI), Linköping.

Brüde, U. & J. Larsson. (1985). Korsningsåtgärder vidtagna inom vägförvaltningarnas trafiksäkerhetsarbete. Regressions- och åtgärdseffekter. VTI-rapport 292. Statens väg- och trafikinstitut (VTI), Linköping.

Brüde, U. & J. Larsson. (1986). Trafiksäkerhetseffekter av korsningsåtgärder. VTI-rapport 310. Statens väg- och trafikinstitut (VTI), Linköping.

Brüde, U. & Larsson, J. (1987a). Före-efter studier avseende olyckor i landsbygdskorsningar ingående i "Korsningsinventering 1983". VTI-meddelande 545. Statens väg- och trafikinstitut (VTI), Linköping.

Brüde, U. & Larsson, J. (1987b). Förskjutna 3-vägskorsningar på landsbygd. Effekt på trafiksäkerhet. VTI-meddelande 544. Statens väg- och trafikinstitut (VTI), Linköping.

Brüde, U. & J. Larsson. (1992). Trafiksäkerhet i tätortskorsningar. VTI-meddelande 685. Statens väg- och trafikinstitut (VTI), Linköping.

Brüde, U. & J. Larsson. (1996). Breda körfält - effekt på trafiksäkerhet. VTI-meddelande 807. Väg- och transportforskningsinstitutet, Linköping.

Brüde, U. & J. Larsson. (1999). Trafiksäkerhet i cirkulationsplatser avseende motorfordon. VTI meddelande 865. Väg- och Transportforskningsinstitutet, Linköping.

Brüde, U., J. Larsson & H. Thulin. (1980). Trafikolyckors samband med linjeföring - för olika belagd bredd, hastighetsgräns, årstid, ljusförhållanden och region. VTI-meddelande 235. Statens väg- och trafikinstitut (VTI), Linköping.

Bruinderink, G. & Hazebroek, E. (1996). Ungulate traffic collisions in Europe. Conservation Biology, 10, 1059–1067.

Bryden, J. E. & J. S. Fortuniewicz. (1986). Performance of highway traffic barriers. In: Effectiveness of Highway Safety Improvements, 242–252 (Carney, J. F. III ed). American Society of Civil Engineers, New York, NY.

BTCE (1995). Evaluation of the black spot program, report 90, Bureau of Transport and Communication Economics (BTCE), Canberra.

Bureau of Transport Economics (2001). The black spot program 1996–2002 – An evaluation of the first three years, Report 104, Bureau of Transport Economics (BTE), Canberra.

Buss, E. (2000). Using hard shoulders on autobahns as additional traffic lanes. Conference Traffic Safety on two Continents, Malmö, september, 20–22 (VTI konferens).

Cairney, P. & McGann, A. (2000). Relationships between crash risk and geometric characterisitcs of rural highways. Austroads Report Nr. 0-85588-555-6.

Caliendo, C. (2001). Relationships between accidents and geometric characteristics for four lanes median separated roads. Conference Traffic safety on three continents, Moscow, 19–21 September 2001.

Cambridge Systematics (2001). Twin cities metro area ramp meter study. Minnesota Department of Transportation.

Carlsson, A.; Brüde, U. & T. Bergh. (2001).Utvärdering av alternativ 13 m väg. Halvårsrapport 2001:1. VTI notat 69-2001. Väg- och Transportforskningsinstitutet, Linköping.

Carlsson, A. & Lundkvist, S.O. (1992). Breda körfält på motortrafikled. Trafikanteffekter vid alternativ vägbanemålning på motortrafikled. VTI-meddelande 687. Statens väg- och trafikinstitut (VTI), Linköping.

Cedersund, H-Å. (1983a). Cirkulationsplatser. VTI-meddelande 361. Statens väg- och trafikinstitut (VTI), Linköping.

Cedersund, H-Å. (1983b). Olyckor i tätortskorsningar. VTI-meddelande 362. Statens väg- och trafikinstitut (VTI), Linköping.

Centers for Disease Control and Prevention (CDC) (2006). Injuries from motor-vehicle collisions with moose – Maine, 2000–2004. Morbidity and Mortality Weekly Report, 55, 1272–1274.

Chin, H.C. & Quddus, M.A. (2003). Applying the random effect negative binomial model to examine traffic accident occurrence at signalized intersections. Accident Analysis and Prevention, 35, 253–259.

Choueiri, E. M. & Lamm, R. (1987). Rural Roads Speed Inconsistencies Design Methods: Part I, Operating Speeds and Accident Rates on Two-Lane Rural

Highway Curved Sections. Department of Civil and Environmental Engineering, Clarkson University, NY.
Christensen, P. (1988). Utbedringer av ulykkespunkter på riksveger og kommunale veger i perioden 1976–1983. Erfaringsrapport. TØI-rapport 0009. Transportøkonomisk institutt, Oslo.
Christensen, P. & Ragnøy, A. (2006). Vegdekkets tilstand og trafikksikkerhet. Rapport 840/2006. Oslo: Transportøkonomisk institutt.
Christie, A. W. (1962). Some investigations concerning the lighting of traffic routes. Public Lighting, 27, 189–204.
Christie, A. W. (1966). Street Lighting and Road Safety. Traffic Engineering and Control, 7, 229–231.
Cirillo, J. A. (1967). Interstate System Accident Research - Study II. Highway Research Record, 188, 1–7.
Cirillo, J. A. (1968). Interstate System Accident Research Study II, Interim Report II. Public Roads, 35, 71–75.
Cirillo, J. A. (1970). The Relationship of Accidents to Length of Speed-Change Lanes and Weaving Areas on Interstate Highways. Highway Research Record, 312, 17–32.
Cirillo, J. A. (1992). Safety Effectiveness of Highway Design Features. Volume 1. Access Control. Report FHWA-RD-91-044. US Department of Transportation, Federal Highway Administration, Washington DC.
City of Portland (1999). Portland's Blue Bike Lanes – Improved Safety Through Enhanced Visibility, City of Portland, Office of Transportation, Portland.
Claessen, J. G. & D. R. Jones. (1994). The road safety effectiveness of wide raised medians. Proceedings 17th ARRB Conference, Part 5, 269–284. South, Australian Road Research Board, Vermont.
Claesson, B. & Sjölinder, K. (1985). Kriterier för separering av cykeltrafik. ARGUS.
Clench-Aas, J. et al. (2000). Oslo traffic study – part 2: quantifying effects of traffic measures using individual exposure modelling. Atmospheric Environment, 34 (27), 4737–4744.
Cleveland, D. E. (1969). Illumination. Chapter 3 of Traffic Control and Roadway Elements - Their Relationship to Highway Safety, Revised. Automotive Safety Foundation, Washington DC.
Clevenger, A.P., Chruszcz, B. & Gunson, K.E. (2001). Highway mitigation fencing reduces wildlife-vehicle collisions. Wildlife Society Bulletin, 29, 646–653.
Clevenger, A.P. & Waltho, N. (2005). Performance indices to identify attributes of highway crossing structures facilitating movement of large mammals. Biological Conservation, 121, 453–464.
Coates, N. (1999). The safety benefits of cycle lanes, Velo-city '99, Graz-Maribor.
Cobb, J. (1987). Light on Motorway Accident Rates. The Journal of The Institution of Highways and Transportation, October 1987, 29–33.

Coleman, R. R. & W. L. Sacks. (1967). An Investigation of the Use of Expanded Metal Mesh as an Anti-Glare Screen. Highway Research Record, 179, 68–73.

Cooper, B. R., H. E. Sawyer & K. S. Rutley. (1992). Analysis of accidents before and after implementation of improved motorway signalling. Research Report 342. Transport and Road Research Laboratory, Crowthorne, Berkshire.

Corben, B. & Hamish, A. D. (1998). Road Engineering countermeasures: An evaluation of their effectiveness and in-depth investigations of the unsuccessful treatments, Road Engineering Association of Asia and Australian (REEAAA), 9th conference, Wellington, New Zealand, 1, 197–2002.

Corben, B., Newstead, S., Diamantopoulou, K. & Cameron, M. (1996). Result of an evaluation of TAC funded accident black spot treatment, 18th ARRB Transport Research Conference, Christchurch.

Corben, B., Scully, J., Newstead, S. & Candappa, N. (2008). An evaluation of the effectiveness of a large scale accident black spot program, 23rd PIARC Road World Conference, Paris.

Corben, B., C. Ambrose & F. C. Wai. (1990). Evaluation of accident black spot treatments. Report 11. Monash University (Melbourne, Australia), Accident Research Centre, Melbourne, Australia.

Corben, B.F., Deery, H.A., Mullan, N.G. & Dyte, D.S. (1996). The general effectiveness of countermeasures for crashes into fixed roadside objects. Monash University, Report 1996/111.

Cornwell, P. R. (1972). Lighting and road traffic. Part 2. Highway capacity, vehicle speeds and public lighting. Traffic Engineering and Control, 13, 297–298.

Cornwell, P. R. & G. M. Mackay. (1972). Lighting and road traffic. Part 1. Public lighting and road accidents. Traffic Engineering and Control, 13, 142–144.

Cottrell, B.H. (2003). Evaluation of deer warning reflectors in Virginia. Technical Assistance Report VTRC 03-TAR6. Charlottesville, Virginia: Virginia Transportation Research Council.

Council, F. & Steward, J. (1999). Safety effects of the conversion of rural two-lane to four-lane roadways based on cross-sectional models. Transportation Research Record 1665, 35–43.

Council, F.M. (1998). Safety benefits of spiral transitions on horizontal curves on two-lane rural roads. Transportation Research Record, 1635, 10–17.

COWI-consult; Vejdirektoratet. (1990). Cykelruter i 4 byer. Sikkerhedsmæssig effekt. COWI-consult and Vejdirektoratet, København.

Craus, J. & D. Mahalel. (1986). Analysis of Operation and Safety Characteristics of Left-Turn Lanes. ITE-Journal, July, 34–39.

D'Angelo, G.J., Warren, R.J., Miller, K.V. & Gallagher, G.R. (2004). Evaluation of strategies designed to reduce deer-vehicle collisions. Report. Georgia Department of Transport.

Dagersten, A. (1992). Roundabouts in Switzerland and Sweden. Thesis 72. University of Lund, Lund Institute of Technology, Department of Traffic Planning and Engineering, Lund, Sweden.

Dahlstedt, S. (1981). Allmänhetens upplevelse av en reducerad offentlig belysning inom en stadsdel i Västerås. VTI-meddelande 278. Statens väg- och trafikinstitut (VTI), Linköping.

Danielsson, S. (1987). Trafiksäkerhetseffekter vid en dämpning av gatubelysningen. VTI-rapport 315. Statens väg- och trafikinstitut (VTI), Linköping.

Dearinger, J. A. & J. W. Hutchinson. (1970). Cross Section and Pavement Surface. Chapter 7 of Traffic Control and Roadway Elements - Their Relationship to Highway Safety. Revised Edition. Highway Users Federation for Safety and Mobility, Washington DC.

DeLuca, F. J. (1986). Effect of Lane Width Reduction on Safety and Flow. In: Effectiveness of Highway Safety Improvements. Proceedings of the Conference, 218–230 (Carney, J. F. ed). American Society of Civil Engineers, New York, NY.

Dietrichs, B. (1991). Gang- og sykkelveger i Buskerud. Trafikksikkerhet. Sykkel som transportmiddel. TS-konsult, Drammen.

Dijkstra, A. (1990). Problemsituaties op verkeersaders in de bebouwde kom: Tweede fase: Selectie van problemsituaties. SWOV Rapport R-90-13. Stichting Wetenschappelijk Onderzoek Verkeersveiligheid SWOV, Leidschendam.

Dodd, N.L., Gagnon, J.W. & Schweingsburg, R.E. (2003). Evaluation of Measures to minimize wildlife-vehicle collisions and maintain wildlife permeability across highways in Arizona, USA. ICOET 2003 Proceedings, 353–354.

Domhan, M. (1985). Die Bewährung von Schutzplanken in der Praxis. Strassenverkehrstechnik, Heft 6, 201–206.

Dotson, V. E. (1974). An Evaluation of the Thirty-Foot Clear Zone. Master of Science Thesis, University of Illinois, Urbana, Ill, 1974 (quoted by Graham & Harwood, 1982). Illinois.

Downing, A., I. Sayer & M. Zaheer-Ul-Islam. (1993). Pedestrian Safety in the Developing World. Proceedings of Conference on Asian Road Safety 1993 (CARS '93), Chapter 7, 10–25. Published by OECD and others, Kuala Lumpur.

Duff, J. T. (1971). The effect of small road improvements on accidents. Traffic Engineering and Control, 12, 244–245.

Eick, H. & G. Vikane. (1992). Verknaden av URF-tiltak i Hordaland. Rapport. Statens vegvesen Hordaland, Trafikkseksjonen, juli 1992. Bergen.

Eisele, W.L., Frawley, W.E. & Toycen, C.M. (2004). Estimating the impact of access management techniques: Final results. Report FHWA/TX-04/0-4221-2.

Elvik, R. (1985). Regresjonseffekt i ulykkespunkter. En empirisk undersøkelse på riksveger i Vest-Agder. Arbeidsdokument av 9.9.1985 (prosjekt O-1146). Transportøkonomisk institutt, Oslo.

Elvik, R. (1987). Trafikksikkerhetstiltak gjennomført på riksveger i 1986. Beskrivelse av omfang, nytte og kostnader. TØI-notat 0844. Transportøkonomisk institutt, Oslo.

Elvik, R. (1990). Gang- og sykkelvegers virkning på trafikkulykker. En før og etterundersøkelse i Østfold og Aust-Agder. TØI-rapport 63. Transportøkonomisk institutt, Oslo.

Elvik, R. (1991). Ulykkesrisiko på riksveger 1986–89. TØI-rapport 81. Transportøkonomisk institutt, Oslo.

Elvik, R. (1992). Nytte-kostnadsanalysers rolle som grunnlag for riksveginvesteringer. Arbeidsdokument TST/0321/92 konfidensielt. Transportøkonomisk institutt, Oslo.

Elvik, R. (1993). Hvor rasjonell er trafikksikkerhetspolitikken? En analyse av investeringsprogrammet på Norsk veg- og vegtrafikkplan. TØI-rapport 0175. Transportøkonomisk institutt, Oslo.

Elvik R. (1995). A meta-analysis of evaluations of public lighting as accident countermeasure. Transportation Research Record, 485, 112–23.

Elvik, R. (1996). Enhetskostnader for veg- og trafikktekniske tiltak. Arbeidsdokument TST/0722/96. Transportøkonomisk instiutt, Oslo.

Elvik, R. (1997). Evaluations of road accident blackspot treatment: a case of the Iron Law of evaluation studies? Accident Analysis and Prevention, 29, 191–199,

Elvik, R. (1999). Cost-benefit analysis of safety measures for vulnerable and inexperienced road users, TØI-rapport 435, Transportøkonomisk institutt, Oslo.

Elvik, R. (2001). Nytte-kostnadsanalyse av ny rekkverksnormal. TØI rapport 547. Transportøkonomisk institutt, Oslo.

Elvik, R. (2002). Optimal Speed Limits. The limits of optimality models. Transportation Research Record, 1818, 32–38.

Elvik, R. (2003). Road safety effects of converting intersections to roundabouts. Paper 03-2106. Transportation Research Board, Annual Meeting, 2003, Washington DC.

Elvik, R. (2007). State-of-the-art approaches to road accident black spot management and safety analysis of road networks, TØI-rapport 883, Transportøkonomisk institutt, Oslo.

Elvik, R.; F. H. Amundsen, & F. Hofset. (2001). Road safety effects of bypasses. TRB paper 01-0525. Transportation Research Board, Washington DC.

Elvik, R., Christensen, P. & Amundsen, A.H. (2004). Speed and road accidents. An evaluation of the power modell. TØI-report 740/2004. Oslo: Institute of Transport Economics.

Elvik, R. & R. Muskaug. (1994). Konsekvensanalyser og trafikksikkerhet. Metode for beregning av konsekvenser for trafikksikkerheten av tiltak på vegnettet. TØI-rapport 0281. Transportøkonomisk institutt, Oslo.

Elvik, R. & U. Rydningen. (2002). Effektkatalog for trafikksikkerhetstiltak. TØI rapport 572. Transportøkonomisk institutt, Oslo.

Engel, U. & L. Krogsgård Thomsen. (1983). Trafiksanering på Østerbro. Del 1-ulykkesanalyse. RfT-notat 1/1983. Rådet for Trafiksikkerhedsforskning (RfT), København.

English, N. (1988). An analysis of the relationship between road improvements and road safety. CR 75 July 1988. Transport and Communications, Federal Office of Road Safety, Canberra, Australia.

Eriksen, T. (1993). Analyse av Running-off-the-road i Akershus fylke 1987–92. Hovedoppgave i samferdselsteknikk. Norges Tekniske Høgskole, Institutt for Samferdselsteknikk, Trondheim.

Erke, A. & Elvik, R. (2006). Effektkatalog for trafikksikkerhet. TØI-report 851/2006. Oslo: Institute of Transport Economics.

Erke, A. & Elvik, R. (2007). Nyttekostnadsanalyse av skadeforebyggende tiltak, TØI-rapport 933, Transportøkonomisk institutt, Oslo.

EU (2003). Road infrastructure safety management, European Commission, DG Energy and Transport, High Level Group Road safety.

Evans, L. (1991). Traffic Safety and the Driver. Van Nostrand Reinhold, New York, NY.

Exnicios, J. F. (1967). Accident Reduction Through Channelization of Complex Intersections. In: Improved Street Utilization Through Traffic Engineering, 160–165. Highway Research Board, Special Report 93. Highway Research Board, Washington DC.

Fambro, D.B., Urbanik, T. I., Hinshaw, W. M. et al. (1989). Stopping sight distance considerations at crest vertical curves on rural two-lane highways in Texas. Texas Transportation Institute, Texas State Department of Highway & Public Transportation, Transportation Planning Division: Report TX-90/1125-1F.

Fambro, D.B., Fitzpatrick, K. & Koppa, R. (1997). Determination of stopping sight distance. NCHRP Report 400. Transportation Research Board, National Research Council, Washington DC.

Farrell, T.M., Sutton, J.E., Clark, D.E., Horner, W.R., Morris, K.I., Finison, K.S., Menchen, G.E. & Cohn, K.H. (1996). Moose-motor vehicle collisions. An increasing hazard in northern New England. Archives of Surgery, 131, 377–381.

Faulkner, C. R. & J. E. Eaton. (1977). Accident investigation and prevention by applying the location sampling technique to rural crossroads. TRRL Laboratory Report 780. Transport and Road Research Laboratory, Crowthorne, Berkshire.

Fildes, B., Corben, B., Morris, A. et al. (2000). Road safety environment and design for older drivers. Report AP-R169. Sydney, Australia: Austroads.

Finder, R.A., Roseberry, J.L. & Woolf, A. (1999). Site and landscape conditions at white-tailed deer/vehicle collision locations in Illinois. Landscape and Urban Planning, 44, 77–85.

Fink, K. L. & R. A. Krammes. (1995). Tangent length and sight distance effects on accident rates at horizontal curves on rural, two-lane highways. Paper No 950616, 74th Annual Meeting of the Transportation Research Board, January 22–28, Washington, DC.

Fisher, A. J. (1971). A review of street lighting in relation to road safety. Report Nr 18. Australian Department of Transport, Australian Government Publishing Service, Canberra.

Fisher, A. J. (1977). Road lighting as an accident countermeasure. Australian Road Research, 7, 4, 3–15.

Fitzpatrick, K., Fambro, D.B. & Stoddard, A.M. (2000). Safety effects of limited stopping sight distance on crest vertical curves. Transportation Research Record, 1701, 17–24.

Flagstad, K. (1990). Før-etter analyse av trafikksikkerhetstiltak i Bergen. Hovedoppgave i samferdselsteknikk. Norges Tekniske Høgskole, Institutt for samferdselsteknikk, Trondheim.

Flannery, A. & T. K. Datta (1996). Modern Roundabouts and Traffic Crash Experience in the United States. Paper 960658. Transportation Research Board 75th Annual Meeting January 7–11, 1996 Washington DC.

Flannery, A., Elefteriadou, L., Koza, P. & McFadden, J. (1998). Safety, delay, and capacity of single-lane roundabouts in the United States. Transportation Research Record, 1646, 63–70.

Foley, J. L. (1967). Major Route Improvements. In: Improved Street Utilization Through Traffic Engineering, 166–171. Highway Research Board Special Report 93. National Research Council, Highway Research Board, Washington DC.

Folles, E., Ijsselstijn, J., Hogema, J.H. & van der Horst, A.R.A (1999). Dynamic public lighting. Ministry of Transport, Public Works and Water Management: Cover report.

Forckenbrock, D.J. & Foster, N.S.J. (1997). Accident cost savings and highway attributes. Transportation, 24, 97–100.

Ford, S.G. & Villa, S.L. (1993). Reflector use and the effect they have on the number of mule deer killed on California highways. Report FHWA/CA/PD94/01. Sacramento, CA, Department of Transport.

Fosser, S. (1988). Kjøre- og hviletidsbestemmelsenes betydning for trafikksikkerheten. TØI-rapport 8. Transportøkonomisk institutt, Oslo.

Fowler, M. (2005). The effects of the pages Road Cycle lane on Cyclist Safety and Traffic Flow Operations, ENCI 495 project Report, Bachelor prosjekt, University of Canterbury, Christchurch, New Zealand.

Foyster, M. J. & M. Thompson. (1986). The effect of road lighting improvements in Westminster on road accidents. Proceedings of Seminar P held at the PTRC Summer Annual Meeting, University of Sussex, England, 14–17 July 1985, 161–172. PTRC, Sussex, England.

Fridstrøm, L. & T. Bjørnskau. (1989). Trafikkulykkenes drivkrefter. En analyse av ulykkestallenes variasjon i tid og rom. TØI-rapport 39. Transportøkonomisk institutt, Oslo.

Friis, A., N. O. Jørgensen & I. Schiøtz. (1976). Færdselsuheld og vejbelysning under oliekrisen. En undersøgelse af om den neddæmpede vejbelysning under oliekrisen i vinteren 1973/74 havde nogen virkning på færdselsuheldstallet. RfT-notat 129. Rådet for Trafiksikkerhedsforskning (RfT), København.

Frost, U. & Keller, H. (1990). Empirical studies on extra-wide highways in Bavaria. European Transport and Planning 18th Summer Annual Meeting, Sussex.

Frost, U. & Morrall, J. (1998). A comparison and evaluation of the geometric design practices with passing lanes, wide-paved shoulders and extra-wide two-lane highways in Canada and in Germany. International Symposium on Highway Geometric Design Practices. Boston, Massachusetts.

Frøysadal, E. (1988). Syklistenes transportarbeid og risiko. TØI-notat 883. Transportøkonomisk institutt, Oslo.

Furuseth, E. (1987). Mange roper på tunge tiltak. Foredrag under kurset "Samordnet trafikksikkerhetsarbeid", arrangert av Norske Sivilingeniørers Forening, Gol, mars 1987. Norske Sivilingeniørers Forening, Oslo.

Gabestad, K. O. (1981). En trafikkøkonomisk analyse av lønnsomheten av en reduksjon i kravet til vegers linjeføringsstandard. TØI-notat 599. Transportøkonomisk institutt, Oslo.

Gabestad, K. O. (1989). Gang/sykkelveg gjennom Åsen i Nord-Trøndelag. Før/etterundersøkelse. TØI-notat 903. Transportøkonomisk institutt, Oslo.

Gabler, H.C., Gabauer, D.J. & Bowen, D. (2005). Evaluation of cross median crashes. Report FHWA-NJ-2005-04.

Galati, J. V. (1970). Study of Box-Beam Median Barrier Accidents. Highway Research Board Special Report 107, Highway Safety, 133–139.

Garber, N. & Erhard, A. (2000). Effect of speed, flow, and geometric characteristics on crash frequency for two-lane highways. Transportation Research Record, 1717, 76–83.

Garber, N.J. & Wu, L. (2001). Stochastic models relating crash probabilities with geometric and corresponding traffic characteristics. Center for Transportation Studies at the University of Virginia: Research Report No. UVACTS-5-15-74.

Gardner, C. (1998). Re-thinking urban lighting. Lighting Journal, 63, 18–19.

Garner, G. R. & R. C. Deen. (1973). Elements of Median Design in Relation to Accident Occurrence. Highway Research Record, 432, 1–11.

Gattis, J. L., M. S. Alguire & S. R. K. Narla (1996). Guardrail End-Types, Vehicle Weights, and Accident Severities. Journal of Transportation Engineering, 12, 210–214.

Gens, M. (2001). Moose crash test dummy. VTI särtryck 342.

Gibby, A.R. & Clewell, R. (2006). Evaluation of wildlife warning systems and other countermeasures. Report NV-RTD-06-010. Nevada Department of Transportation.

Gilbert, J.R. (1982). Evaluation of deer mirrors for reducing deer-vehicle collisions. Report FHWA/RD/82/061. Washington DC.

Giæver, T. (1990). Ulykkesfrekvenser i rund kjøringer og signalregulerte kryss. STF63 A90002. SINTEF Samferdselsteknikk, Trondheim.

Giæver, T. (1997). Rundkjøringer i Hordaland – ulykkesanalyser, utforming og trafikantatferd. Rapport STF22 A97601. SINTEF Bygg og miljøteknikk, samferdsel, Trondheim.

Giæver, T. (1999). Før-/etterundersøkelse av ulykkespunkter og strekninger med spesiell skilting. SINTEF rapport STF22 A99554.

Giæver, T. (2000). Rundkjøringer – sammenheng mellom geometrisk utforming og ulykker. SINTEF rapport STF22 A00558.

Giæver, T. & A. G. Holt (1994). Ukanaliserte kryss med passeringslomme - utbredelsen av denne type kryss, og sikkerhet i disse. Rapport STF63 A93003. SINTEF Samferdselsteknikk, Trondheim.

Glad, R.W., Albin, R.B., McIntosh, D.M. & Olson, D.K. (2002). Median treatment study of Washington state highways. Washington State Department of Transportation: Report WA-RD-516.1.

Glennon, J. (1987). Effects of sight distance on highway safety. Relationship between safety and key highway features: State of the art report 6. Transportation Research Board, Washington DC.

Glennon, J. C. & T. N. Tamburri. (1967). Objective Criteria for Guardrail Installation. Highway Research Record, 174, 184–206.

Goble, C. (1994). Improving road safety – reducing four lane arterials to two: the effects. 17th ARRB Conference, Queensland, Vol 17(5), 303–321.

Goldstine, R. (1991). Influence of Road Width on Accident Rates by Traffic Volume. Transportation Research Record, 1318, 64–69.

Golob, T.F., Recker, W.W. & Alvarez, V.M. (2004). Safety aspects of freeway weaving sections. Transportation Research Part A, 38, 35–51.

Good, M. C. and P. N. Joubert. (1971) A review of roadside objects in relation to road safety. University of Melbourne, Department of Mechanical Engineering, 1971 (Published by Australian Government Publishing Service, 1973, as Report no NR/12 by Expert Group on Road Safety), Australia.

Gordon, K. & Anderson, S. (2003). Evaluation of an underpass installed in US Highway 30 at Nugget Canyon, Wyoming, for migrating mule deer. Report FHWA-WY-03/01F.

Graham, J. L. & D. W. Harwood. (1982). Effectiveness of Clear Recovery Zones. National Cooperative Highway Research Program Report 247. Transportation Research Board, Washington DC.

Green, H. (1977). Accidents at off-side priority roundabouts with mini or small islands. TRRL Laboratory Report 774. Transport and Road Research Laboratory, Crowthorne, Berkshire.

Gregory, M. & D. F. Jarrett. (1994). The long-term analysis of accident remedial measures at high-risk sites in Essex. Traffic Engineering and Control, 35, 8–11.

Griffin, L. I. (1984). How Effective are Crash Cushions in Reducing Deaths and Injuries? Public Roads, March 1984, 132–134.

Griffith, M. S. (1994). Comparison of the Safety of Lighting Options on Urban Freeways. Public Roads, Autumn 1994, 8–15.

Gulen, S., McCabe, G., Anderson, V.L., Rosenthal, I. & Wolfe, S.E. (2006). Evaluation of wildlife reflectors in reducing vehicle-deer collisions on Indiana interstate I-80/90. Indiana Department of Transport, TRB Annual Meeting 2006.

Gundersen, H., Andreassen, H. P. & Storaas, T. (2004) Supplemental feeding of migratory moose Alces alces: Forest damage at two spatial scales. Wildlife Biology, 10, 213–223.

Gunther, K.A., Biel, M.J. & Robinson, H.L. (1998). Factors Influencing the Frequency of Road-killed Wildlife in Yellowstone National Park. In the Proceedings of the International Conference on Wildlife Ecology and Transportation. Held in Fort Myers, FL, February 9–12,1998, pp. 395–405.

Gårder, P.; Leden, L.; Pulkkinen, U. (1998). Measuring the Safety Effect of Raised Bicycle Crossings Using a New Research Methodology, Transportation Research Record, 1636, 64–70.

Haakenaasen B. (1980). Virkninger av trafikkløsninger. Korttidsvirkninger av omkjøringsvegen på Gol. Rapport. Transportøkonomisk institutt, Oslo.

Hagen, K-E. (1991). Veg- og trafikktekniske tiltak i det samfunnsmessige regnskapssystemet for trafikkulykker (SRT). Arbeidsdokument TST/0307/91. Transportøkonomisk institutt, Oslo.

Hagen, K-E. (1993). Samfunnsøkonomisk regnskapssystem for trafikkulykker og trafikksikkerhetstiltak. TØI-rapport 0182. Transportøkonomisk institutt, Oslo.

Hagen, K-E. (1994). Rullering av samfunnsøkonomisk regnskapssystem for trafikkulykker og trafikksikkerhetstiltak (SRT) for 1992. Arbeidsdokument TST/0570/94. Transportøkonomisk institutt, Oslo.

Haikonen, H. & Summala, H. (2001). Deer-vehicle crashes – Extensive peak at 1 hour after sunset. American Journal of Preventive Medicine, 21, 209–213.

Hall, J. W. (1982). Guardrail Installation and Improvement Priorities. Transportation Research Record, 868, 47–53.

Hall, J. W. & O. J. Pendleton. (1990). Rural Accident Rate Variations with Traffic Volume. Transportation Research Record, 1281, 62–70.

Hall, J. W. & M. Polanco de Hurtado. (1992). Effect of Intersection Congestion on Accident Rates. Transportation Research Record, 1376, 71–77.

Hall, R. D. & M. McDonald. (1988). Junction design for safety. Paper presented at Roads and Traffic 2000, International Road and Traffic Conference, Berlin, 6–9 September 1988. Proceedings, Vol 4–2, 147–151.

Hammer, C. G. (1969). Evaluation of Minor Improvements. Highway Research Record, 286, 33–45.

Hancock, K. L. & M. H. Ray. (2000). Assessment of collision rates for longitudinal barriers. Paper (not numbered). Transportation Research Board Annual Meeting, Washington, DC (available on CD-rom).

Hanley, K.A., Gibby, A. & Ferrara, T. (2000). Analysis of accident reduction factors on California state highways. Transportation Research Record, 1717, 37–45.

Hanna, J. T., T. E. Flynn & W. E. Tyler. (1976). Characteristics of Intersection Accidents in Rural Municipalities. Transportation Research Record, 601, 79–82.

Harland, G. & R. Gercans. (1993). Cycle Routes. Project Report 42. Crowthorne, Berkshire, Transport Research Laboratory,

Harnen, S., Umar, R.S.R., Wong, S.V. & Hashim, W.I.W. (2003). Motorcycle crash prediction model for non-signalized intersections in Malaysia. IATSS Research – Transportation, 27(2), 58–65.

Harwood, D. W. (1986). Multilane Design Alternatives for Improving Suburban Highways. National Cooperative Highway research Program Report 282. National Research Council, Transportation Research Board, Washington, DC.

Harwood, D.W. (1990). Effective Utilization of Street Width on Urban Arterials. NCHRP Report 330, Transportation Research Board.

Harwood, D.W. (2003). Relationship between lane width and speed: review of the literature. Prepared for the Columbia Pike Street Space Planning Task Force by the Parsons Transportation Group, September 2003.

Harwood, D.W., Bauer, K.M., Potts, I.B. et al. (2002). Safety effectiveness of intersection left- and right-turn lanes. Report FHWA-RD-02-089.

Harwood, D.W., Council, F.M., Hauer, E. et al. (2000). Prediction of the expected safety performance of rural two-lane highways. Report FHWA-RD-99-207. Kansas City, Missouri. Midwestern Research Institute.

Harwood, D.W., Pietrucha, M.T., Fitzpatrick, K. & Woolridge, M.D. (1998). Design of intersections on divided highways. International Symposium on Highway Geometric Design Practices. Boston, Massachusetts.

Harwood, D. W. & A. D. St John. (1985). Passing lanes and other operational improvements on two-lane highways. Report FHWA/RD-85/028. US Department of

Transportation, Federal Highway Administration, Office of Research, Development and Technology, Turner-Fairbank Highway Research Center, Washington DC.
Hatherly, L. W. & D. R. Lamb. (1971). Accident prevention in London by road surface improvements. Traffic Engineering and Control, 12, 524–529.
Hatherly, L. W. & A. E. Young. (1977). The Location and Treatment of Urban Skidding Hazard Sites. Transportation Research Record, 623, 21–28.
Hauer, E. (1999). Safety and the choice of degree of curve. Transportation Research Record, 1665, 22–27.
Heidemann, D., Bäumer, M., Hamacher, R. & Hautzinger, H. (1998). Standstreifen und Verkehrssicherheit auf BAB. Bonn: Berichte der Bundesanstalt für Straßenwesen, Verkehrstechnik, Heft V55.
Helai, H., Chor, C.H. & Haque, M.M. (2008). Severity of driver injury and vehicle damage in traffic crashes at intersections: A Bayesian hierarchical analysis. Accident Analysis and Prevention, 40, 45–54.
Hochstein, J.L. (2006). Safety effects of offset right-turn lanes at rural expressway intersections. Iowa State University, Midwest Transportation Consortium Fall 2006 Student Paper Competition.
Hoffmann, S., Kölle, M. & Mennicken, C. (2000). Kapazität von Verflechtungsstrecken an planfreien Knotenpunkten. Straßenverkehrstechnik, 11, 573–580.
Hogema, J.H., & Van der Horst, A.R.A. (1998). Dynamische Openbare Verlichting (DYNO). Fase 4: Synthese [Dynamic Public Lighting. Phase 4: Synthesis](Report TM 98 C065). Soesterberg, The Netherlands: TNO Human Factors Research Institute.
Holmskov, O. & H. Lahrmann (1993). Er sortpletbekæmpelse vejen frem? Dansk Vejtidsskrift, 2, 3–9.
Holt, A. G. (1993). Trafikksikkerhetsvurdering E6 Øst. Notat 794/93. SINTEF Samferdselsteknikk, Trondheim.
Holzwarth, J. (1992). Ausserorts-Kreisverkehrsplätze zur Unfallstellenbeseitigung. Ergebnisse zweier Modellvorhaben in Baden-Württemberg. Strassensverkehrstechnik, 36, 142–146.
Hovd, A. (1981). Trafikkulykker i vegtunneller. Rapport STF61 A81012. SINTEF Vegteknikk, Trondheim.
Huber, C. A. & F. Bühlmann (1994). Sicherheit von Kreiselanlagen. Erfahrungen und vorläufige Empfehlungen. Pilotstudie. Schweitzerische Beratungsstelle für Unfallverhütung, Bern,.
Huber, M. J. & J. L. Tracy. (1968). Effects of Illumination on Operating Characteristics of Freeways. National Cooperative Highway Research Program Report 60. Highway Research Board, Washington DC.
Huijser, M.P., P. McGowen, J. Fuller, A. Hardy, A. Kociolek, A.P. Clevenger, D. Smith & R. Ament. (2007). Wildlife-vehicle collision reduction study. Report to

congress. U.S. Department of Transportation, Federal Highway Administration, Washington DC, USA.
Hunter, W. W. (2000a). Evaluation of innovative bike-box application in Eugene, Oregon, Trasportation Research Record, 1705, 99–106.
Hunter, W. W. (2000b). Evaluation of a combined bicycle lane/Right turn lane in Eugene, Oregon, rapport FHWA-RD-OO-151, federal Highway Administration, U.S. Department of Transportation.
Hunter, W.W.et al. (2001). Three-strand cable median barrier in North Carolina. In-service evaluation. Transportation Research Record, 1743, 97–103.
Hunter, W. W., Harkey, D. L., Stewart, R. J. & Birk, m. L. (2000). Evaluation of blue bike-lane treatment in Portland, Oregon, Transportation Research Record, 1705, 107–115.
Hunter, W. W., J. R. Stewart & F. M. Council. (1993). Comparative Performance Study of Barrier and End Treatments Types Using the Longitudinal Barrier Special Study File. Transportation Research Record, 1419, 63–77.
Hvoslef, H. (1974). Trafikksikkerhet i Oslo. Problemstilling, analyse og løsninger. Oslo veivesen, Oslo.
Hvoslef, H. (1980). Trafikanters skaderisiko i bytrafikk. En anlyse av ulykker og reiseaktivitet i Haugesund. TØI-rapport. Transportøkonomisk institutt, Oslo.
Hvoslef, H. (1991). Trafikksikkerhet i vegtunneler. Informasjon fra Trafikksikkerhetskontoret, 6, 1991. Statens vegvesen, Vegdirektoratet, Miljø- og trafikksikkerhetsavdelingen, Trafikksikkerhetskontoret, Oslo.
Hydén, C., K. Odelid & A. Várhelyi. (1992). Effekten av generell hastighetsdämpning i tätort. Resultat av et storskaligt försök i Växjö. I. Huvudrapport. Lunds Tekniske Høgskola, Institutionen för trafikteknik, Lund.
Høye, J.K. (2005). Elgforvaltning i ubalanse. Glommen, 2, 4–5.
Institute of Traffic Engineers and Illuminating Engineering Society. (1966). Joint Committee of Public Lighting. Public Lighting Needs. Special Report to US Senate, 1966 (Sitert etter Ketvirtis 1977).
Isebrands, H., Hallmark, S., Hans, Z, McDonald, T., Preston, H. & Storm, R. (2004). Safety impacts of street lighting at isolated rural intersections – Part II, year 1. Iowa State University: Report.
Ivan, J.N., Wang, C. & Bernardo, N.R. (2000). Explaining two-lane highway crash rates using land use and hourly exposure. Accident Analysis and Prevention, 32, 787–795.
Ives, H. S. (1962). Does Highway Illumination Affect Accident Occurrence? Traffic Quarterly, 16, 229–241.
Jacoby, R.G. & Pollard, N.E. (1995). The lighting of rural roundabouts. Lighting Journal, 149–159.

Jadaan, K. S. & Nicholson, A.J. (1988). Effect of a New Urban Arterial on Road Safety. Australian Road Research, 18, 213–223.

Janoff, M. S. (1988). Effect of Bridge Lighting on Nighttime Traffic Safety. Transportation Research Record, 1172, 88–92.

Janson, B.N., Award, W., Robles, J., Kononov, J. & Pinkerton, B. (1998). Truck accidents at freeway ramps: Data analysis and high-risk site identification. Journal of Transportation and Statistics, 1, 75–92.

Jensen, S. U. (1996). Cykelfelter. Sikkerhedsmæssig effekt i signalregulerede kryds. I: Trafikdage på Aalborg Universitet 1996. Konferencerapport, Bind 2, 743.753 (Lahrmann, H. & L.H. Pedersen ed). Aalborg Universitet, Transportrådet og Trafikforskningsgruppen, Aalborg.

Jensen, S. U. (2002). Mer sikker på cykel i Randers – Før-og-efter uheldsevaluering, notat 5, Danmarks Transportforskning.

Jensen, S. U. (2006a). Effekter af sykelstier og cykelbaner – før-og-efter evaluering af trafiksikkerhed og trafikmængde ved anlæg af ensrettede sykelstier og cykelbaner i Københavns Kommune, Trafitec.

Jensen, S. U. (2006b). Svendborg Sikker Cykelby – Evaluering af trafiksikkerhed, tryghed og cykeltrafik, Trafitec.

Jensen, S. U. (2006c). Effekter af overkørsler og blå cykelfelter – før-og-efter evaluering af trafiksikkerhed ved anlæg af overkørsler u vigepligtsregulerede kryds og blå cykelfelter i signalregulerede kryds i Københavns Kommune, Trafitec.

Jensen, S. U. (2006d). Cyklisters oplevede tryghed og tilfredshed – forskelle i tryghed og tilfredshed afhængig af strækningers og kryds' udformning, Trafitec.

Jensen, S. U. (2008). Safety effects of blue cycle Crossings: A before–after study, Accident Analysis and Prevention, 40, 742–750.

Jensen, S. U.; Nielsen, M. A. (1999). Sikkerhedseffekter af nye vejudformninger for cyklister, notat nr. 63, Vejdirektoratet.

Johannessen, S. (1985). Rundkjøringer. Forslag til retningslinjer basert på data om 35 rundkjøringer. STF63 A85008. SINTEF Samferdselsteknikk, Trondheim.

Johannessen, S. & J. Heir. (1974). Trafikksikkerhet i vegkryss. En analyse av ulykkesforholdene i 187 vegkryss i perioden 1968–72. Oppdragsrapport 4. Norges Tekniske Høgskole, Forskningsgruppen, Institutt for samferdselsteknikk, Trondheim.

Johansen, T. M. (1985). Trafikksikkerhet i planskilte kryss. Hovedoppgave ved Institutt for samferdselsteknikk, Norges Tekniske Høgskole, høsten 1985. Norges Tekniske Høgskole, Trondheim.

Johnson, H. D. (1980). Cross-over accidents on all-purpose dual carriageways. TRRL Supplementary Report 617. Transport and Road Research Laboratory, Crowthorne, Berkshire.

Johnson, R. T. (1966). Effectiveness of Median Barriers. Highway Research Record, 105, 99–109.

Jørgensen, E. (1979). Sikkerhedsmæssig effekt af mindre anlægsarbejder. Effektstudie. Vejdirektoratet, Sekretariatet for Sikkerhedsfremmende Vejforanstaltninger (SSV), Næstved.

Jørgensen, E. (1980). Eksempler på effektstudier fra SSV. Vejdirektoratet, Sekretariatet for Sikkerhedsfremmende Vejforanstaltninger (SSV), Næstved.

Jørgensen, E. (1986). Er højresvingsspor sikkerhedsfremmende? Dansk Vejtidsskrift, 9, 229–231.

Jørgensen, E. & N. O. Jørgensen. (1992). Er der mere nyt om rundkørsler? Dansk Vejtidsskrift, 12, 29–31.

Jørgensen, E. & N. O. Jørgensen. (1994). Sikkerhed i nyere danske rundkørsler. Paper presentert ved Trafikdage ved Aalborg Universitets Center (AUC), 28–30 August 1994. Proceedings, 191–198. Aalborg.

Jørgensen, E. & Jørgensen, N.O. (2002). Trafiksikkerhed i rundkørsler i Danmark. Rapport 235 2002. København, Vejdirektoratet.

Jørgensen, N. O. (1991a). The Safety Effects of a Major Infrastructure Project. Paper presented at Euro Traffic '91. In: Conference Proceedings. Aalborg, Denmark.

Jørgensen, N. O. (1991b). Rundkørslers kapacitet og sikkerhed. Dokumentasjonsrapport. Danmarks Tekniske Højskole, Institut for veje, trafik og byplan, København.

Jørgensen, N. O. & L. Herrstedt. (1979). Sikkerhed for cyklister og knallertkørere i Københavnsområdet. RfT-rapport 24. Rådet for Trafiksikkerhedsforskning, København.

Jørgensen, N. O. & Z. Rabani. (1969). Cykelstiers betydning for færdselssikkerheden. RfT-rapport 1. Rådet for Trafiksikkerhedsforskning, København.

Jørgensen, N. O. & Z. Rabani. (1971). Fodgængeres sikkerhed i og ved fodgængerovergange. RfT-rapport 7. Rådet for Trafiksikkerhedsforskning (RfT), København.

Jørgensen, P. (1994). "Klumpheller" - en god trafiksikkerhedsløsning. Dansk Vejtidsskrift, 4, 23–24.

Kallberg, V-P. & M. Salusjärvi. (1982). Trafiksäkerhetseffekter av gång- och cykelvägar. EMMA-rapport 5. Forskningsrapport 58. Statens Tekniska Forskningscentral, Väg- och Trafiklaboratoriet, Esbo.

Karr, J. I. (1972). Evaluation of minor improvements - part 8, grooved pavements. Final Report. Report CA-HY-TR-2151-4-71-00. Division of Highways, Sacramento, CA, California.

Ketvirtis, A. (1977). Road Illumination and Traffic Safety. Prepared for Road and Motor Vehicle Traffic Safety Branch, Transport Canada. Transport Canada, Ottawa.

Khattak, A.J., Naik, B. & Kannan, V. (2004). Safety evaluation of left-turn lane width at intersections with opposing left-turn lanes. Report SPR-P1(03) P554. Lincoln, Nebraska: University of Nebraska, Mid-America Transportation Center.

Khorashadi, A. (1998). Effect of ramp type and geometry on accidents. Report FHWA/CA/TE-98/13.

Kihlberg, J.K. & K. J. Tharp. (1968). Accident rates as related to design elements of rural highways. National Cooperative Highway Research Program Report 47. Highway Research Board, Washington DC.

Killi, M. (1999). Anbefalte tidsverdier i persontransport (Recommended time values for passenger transport). TØI Report 459/1999. Oslo. Transportøkonomisk institutt.

Kim, D.-G., Lee, Y., Washington, S. & Choi, K. (2007). Modeling crash outcome probabilities at rural intersections: Application of hierarchical binomial logistic models. Accident Analysis and Prevention, 39, 125–134.

Kim, D.-G., Washington, S. & Oh, J. (2006). Modeling Crash Types: New Insights into the Effects of Covariates on Crashes at Rural Intersections. Journal of Transportation Engineering, 132, 282–292.

King, G. F. (1989). Evaluation of safety roadside rest areas. National Cooperative Highway Research Program. Report 324. Transportation Research Board, Washington, DC.

Kistler, R. (1998). Wissenschaftliche Begleitung der Wildwarnanlagen CALSTROM WWA-12-S. Zürich: Infodienst Wildbiologie & Oekologie.

Klæboe, R. et al. (2000). Oslo traffic study – part 1: an integrated approach to assess the combined effects of noise and air pollution om annoyance. Atmospheric Environment, 34 (27), 4727–4736.

Knapp, K.K., Yi, X., Oakasa, T., Thimm, W., Hudson, E. & Rathmann, C. (2004). Deer-vehicle crash countermeasure toolbox: A decision and choice resource. Final Report. University of Wisconsin-Madison, Midwest Regional University Transportation Center.

Knoche, G. (1981). Einfluss von Radwegen auf die Verkehrssicherheit. Band 2. Radfahrerunfälle auf Stadtstrassen. Forschungsberichte der Bundesanstalt für Strassenwesen, Bereich Unfallforschung, 62. Bundesanstalt für Strassenwesen, Bergisch-Gladbach.

Knuiman, M., Council, F. & Reinfurt, D. (1993). The effects of median width on highway accident rates. Transportation Research Record, 1401, 70–80.

Köhler, U. & R. Schwamb. (1993). Erweiterung und Verifizierung des Modells zur Abschätzung des Unfallgeschehens und der Unfallkosten auf Innerörtlichen Netzelementen. Schlussbericht. Forschungsbericht FE-Nr 70186/88. Ingenieursozietät BGS. Frankfurt am Main.

König, S. (2006). Evaluation of the effect of rebuilt bicycle paths at intersections on arterial streets in Lund – a case study, Thesis 146, Lund University, Department of Technology an Society, Lund.

Kolbenstvedt, M. et al. (1990). Korttidsvirkninger av Vålerenga-tunnelen i noen gatestrekninger i Vålerenga/Gamlebyen. Før/etterundersøkelse av trafikale virkninger og støy- og forurensningsbelastning. TØI-notat 0907 (revidert 20.7.1990). Transportøkonomisk institutt, Oslo.

Koorey, G., Wanty, D. & Cenek, P. (1998). Applications of road geometry data for highway safety in New Zealand. Road Safety - Research, Policing, Education Conference, Wellington.

Koornstra, M. J. (1993). Future developments of motorized traffic and fatalities in Asia. Proceedings of Conference on Asian Road Safety 1993 (CARS '93), Chapter 10, 1–15.Published by OECD and others, Kuala Lumpur.

Krammes, R. (1997). Interactive highway safety design module: design consistency module. FHWA (http://www.tfhrc.gov/pubrds/pr97-10/p47.htm; 22.11.2006).

Krenk, F. (1985). Metoder og resultater i den koordinerede uheldsstatistik 1978–82. Rapport 27. Vejdatalaboratoriet, Herlev.

Kristiansen, P. (1992). Erfaringer med rundkjøringer i Akershus. Statens vegvesen Akershus, Oslo.

Kruger, H.-H. & Wolfel, H. (1991). Behavioral response of fallow deer to various types of simulated underpasses. Proceedings of the XXth Congress of the International Union of Game Biologists, 591.

Kulmala, R. (1992). Pääteiden tasoliittymissä tehtyjen toimenpiteiden vaikutukset onnettomukksiin. Tielatoksen tutkimuksia 2/1992. Tielaitos, Tiehallitus, Helsinki.

Kumara, S.S.P. & Chin, H.C. (2003). Modelling accident occurrence at signalized tee intersections with special emphasis on excess zero. Traffic Injury Prevention, 4, 53–57.

Kurucz, C. N. (1984). An analysis of the injury reduction capabilities of breakaway light standards and various guardrails. Accident Analysis and Prevention, 16, 105–114.

Københavns Amt (2001). Ombygning af 24 vejkryds – vurdering af den sikkerhedsmæssige effekt, Københavns Amt, Vejafdelingen, København.

Kølster Pedersen, S. et al. (1992). Trafiksäkerhetsåtgärder i Väg- och Gatumiljö. Exempel hämtade från de nordiska länderna under 1980-talet. Nordiske Seminar- och Arbejdsrapporter 1992:607. Nordisk Ministerråd, København.

Lahrmann, H. (1981). Rundkørsler: trafiksikkerhed, geometrisk udformning, kapacitet. Vejdirektoratet, Sekretariatet for Sikkerhedsfremmende Vejforanstaltninger (SVV), Næstved.

Lalani, N. (1975). The impact on accidents of the introduction of mini, small and large roundabouts at major/minor priority junctions. Traffic Engineering and Control, 16, 560–561.

Lalani, N. (1991). Comprehensive Safety Program Produces Dramatic Results. ITE-Journal, October, 31–34.
Lamm, R., J. H. Klöckner & E. M. Choueiri. (1985). Freeway Lighting and Traffic safety - A Long Term Investigation. Transportation Research Record, 1027, 57–63.
Lamm, R., Psarianos, B., Choueiri, E.M. & Soilemezoglou, G. (1998). A practical safety approach to highway geometric design international case studies: Germany, Greece, Lebanon and the United States. International Symposium on Highway Geometric Design Practices. Boston, Massachusetts.
Lamm, R., Zumkeller, K. Beck, A. (2000). Traffic safety – The relative effectiveness if a variety of road markings and traffic control devices. International Conference, Road Safety on Three Continents, 20.–22. September 2000, Pretoria, South Africa, Conference Proceedings, Session 3, pp.1–14.
Langeland, P. A. (1999). Virkninger av ombygging av E6 Okstadbakken – Tunga N. Notat av 4. november 1999. Statens vegvesen, Sør-Trøndelag vegkontor, Trondheim.
Larsen, G. E. (1986). Non-freeway programwide 3R accident analysis New York. In: Effectiveness of Highway Safety Improvements, 22–30. (Carney, J. F. III ed) American Society of Civil Engineers, New York, NY.
Larsen, U. (2002). Udbedring af sorte pletter i Storstrøms Amt – en god forretning, Vejdtidskrift, 12, 50–52.
Lavsund, S. & Sandegren, F. (1991). Moose vehicle relations in Sweden: a review. Alces, 27, 118–126.
Leden, L. (1989). The safety of cycling children. Effect of the street environment. Publications 55. The Technical Research Centre of Finland, Espoo.
Leden, L. (1993). Methods to estimate traffic safety. Unpublished manuscript dated 21 September 1993. Technical Research Centre of Finland, Road Traffic and Geotechnical Laboratory, Espoo.
Leden, L. et al. (1997). Metodik för före-/efterstudier. Tillämpat på cyklisters trafiksäkerhet. KFB Rapport 1997:15. Kommunikationsforskningsberedningen, Stockholm.
Lee, J.C., Bonneson, J.A., Kidd, B.D. & Larwin, T.F. (2002). Evaluation of operational efficiencies, cost, and accident experience of four phase single point urban interchanges. FHWA-AZ01-501.
Lee, C., Hellinga, B. & Ozbay, K. (2006). Quanitfying effects of ramp metering on freeway safety. Accident Analysis and Prevention, 38, 279–288.
Leeming, J. J. (1969). Road accidents. Prevent or punish? Cassell, London.
Legassick, R. (1996). The case for route studies in road traffic accident analysis investigations. In: Proceedings of the Conference Road Safety in Europe and Strategic Highway Research Program (SHRP), Prague, the Czech Republic,

September 20–22, 1995, Vol 4A, Part 1, 37–53. Swedish National Road and Transport Research Institute, Linköping.

Lehnert, M.E. & Bissonette, J.A. (1997). Effectiveness of Highway Crosswalk Structures at Reducing Deer-Vehicle Collisions. Wildlife Society Bulletin, 25, 809–818.

Lehtimäki, R. (1979). Elk Mirrors and Traffic. Report from Liikenneturva 27/1979. The Central Organization for Traffic Safety (Liikenneturva), Helsinki.

Lehtimäki, R. (1981). Fences for protection of traffic and deer. Summary. Duplicates of Research Section of Liikenneturva 37/1981. The Central Organization for Traffic Safety (Liikenneturva), Helsinki.

Lehtimäki, R. (1984). Elk and white tail deer as traffic hazards. Liikenneturva, Reseach Department, Helsinki.

Leong, H. J. W. (1970). Effect of kerbed raised median strips on accident rates of urban roads. ARRB Proceedings, 1970, Vol 5, 338–364.

Levine, D. W., T. F. Golob & W. W. Recker. (1988). Accident migration associated with lane-addition projects on urban freeways. Traffic Engineering and Control, 29, 624–629,

Lien Aune, L. (2004). Viltreflektorers virkning på elgens kryssing av vei. Bachelor-oppgave, Høgskolen i Hedmark.

Lipinski, M. E. & R. H. Wortman. (1976). Effect of Illumination on Rural At-Grade Intersection Accidents. Transportation Research Record, 611, 25–27.

Ljungblad, L. (2000).Vägens sidoområden och sidoräcken. VTI rapport 453. Väg- och transportforskningsinstitutet, Linköping.

Lott, D.F. & Lott, D.Y. (1976). Differential Effect of Bicycle Lanes on Ten Classes of Bicycle-Automobile Accidents. Transportation Research Record, 605, 20–24.

Lovell, J. & E. Hauer. (1986). The Safety Effect of Conversion To All-Way Stop Control. Transportation Research Record, 1068, 103–107.

Ludvigsen, H. S. & K. Sørensen. (1985). Natreduktion af vejbelysning - den sikkerhedsmæssige effekt. Vejregelforberedende rapport 1. Vejdirektoratet, Sekretariatet for Sikkerhedsfremmende Vejforanstaltninger (SVV), København.

Ludwig, J., & T. Bremicker. 1983. Evaluation of 2.4-m fences and one-way gates for reducing deer-vehicle collisions in Minnesota. Transportation Research Record, 913, 19–22.

Lundy, R. A. (1967). The Effect of Ramp Type and Geometry On Accidents. Highway Research Record, 163, 80–119.

Lutz, W. (1994). Ergebnisse der Anwendung eines sogenannten Duftzaunes zur Vermeidung von Wildverslusten durch den Strasseverkehr nach Gehege- und Freilandorientierungen. Zeitschrift fuer Jagdwissenschaft, 40, 91–108.

Lyager, P. & C. Løschenkohl. (1972). Uheldsmønstre i kanaliserede landevejskryds. Sammenfatning. RfT-rapport 14. Rådet for Trafiksikkerhedsforskning (RfT), København.

Lyles, R.W. & Taylor, W.C. (2006). Communicating changes in horizontal alignment. NCHRP Report 559.

Lyon, C., Oh., J., Persaud, B., Washington, S. & Bared, J. (2003). Empirical investigation of Interactive highway safety design model accident Prediction algorithm. Transportation Research Record, 1840, 78–86.

Mackie, A. M. & L. J. Griffin. (1978). Environmental effects of by-passing small towns. TRRL Supplementary Report 349. Transport and road Research Laboratory, Crowthorne, Berkshire.

Mahalel, D., J. Craus & A. Polus. (1986). Evaluation of Staggered and Cross Intersections. Journal of Transportation Engineering, 112, 495–506.

Mak, K. K. (1987). Effect of Bridge Width on Highway Safety. In: State of the Art Report 6. Relationship Between Safety and Key Highway Features. A Synthesis of Previous Research, 22–35. Transportation Research Board, Washington DC.

Malo, A. F. (1967). Signal Modernization. In: Improved Street Utilization Through Traffic Engineering, 96–113. Highway Research Board, Special Report 93. Highway Research Board, Washington DC.

Marburger, E. A., J. H. Klöckner & U. Stöckner. (1989). Assessment of the potential accident reduction by selected Prometheus functions. Preliminary Report of PROGENERAL. Bundesanstalt für Strassenwesen, Bergisch-Gladbach.

Martin, J. L. & R. Quincy. (2001). Crossover crashes at median strips equipped with barriers on a French motorway network. Transportation Research Record, 1758, 6–12. National Research Council, Washington DC.

Martin, J. L.et al. (1998). The severity of primary impact with metal or concrete central median barriers on French motorways. In: VTI-konferens 9A, part 2, 109–123. Proceedings of the conference Traffic Safety on Two Continents in Lisbon, Portugal, September 22–24, 1997. Swedish National Road and Transport Research Institute, Linköping.

Massie, D. L., K. L. Campbell & A. F. Williams. (1995). Traffic accident involvement rates by driver age and gender. Accident Analysis and Prevention, 27, 73–87.

Matthews, L. R. & J. W. Barnes. (1988). Relation between road environment and curve accidents. Proceedings of 14th ARRB Conference, Part 4, 105–120. Australian Road Research Board, Vermont South, Victoria, Australia.

Maycock, G. & Hall, R.D. (1984). Accidents at 4-arm roundabouts. Transport and road Research Laboratory, Report LR 1120.Crowthorne.

Mayer, W. & Bruce, S. (1988). Departures from visibility standards – the implications for safety. Proceedings of the PTRC Transport and Planning Annual Meeting, University of Bath, England, Vol P307, 57–68.

Maze, T.H. & Burchett, G.D. (2006). Rural expressway intersection characteristics: Factor in reducing safety performance. Washington: Transportation Research Board 85th Annual Meeting.

McBean, P. A. (1982). The influence of road geometry at a sample of accident sites. TRRL Laboratory Report 1053. Transport and Road Research Laboratory, Crowthorne, Berkshire.

McCamment C. W. (1959) New Kansas Curve Signs Reduce Deaths. Traffic Engineering, February 1959, 14–15.

McCartt, A.T., Shabanova Northrup, V. & Retting, R.A. (2004). Types and characteristics of ramp-related motor vehicle crashes on urban interstate roadways in Northern Virginia. Journal of Safety Research, 35, 107–114.

McCoy, P. T. & M. S. Malone. (1989). Safety Effects of Left-Turn Lanes on Urban Four-Lane Roadways. Transportation Research Record, 1239, 17–22.

McCoy, P.T., Tripi, E.J. & Bonneson, J.A. (1994). Guidelines for realignment of skewed intersections. Lincoln, Nebraska: Department of Vicil Engineering College of Engineering and Technology.

Meewes, V. (2002). Knotenpunktformen außerorts – Sicherheitsvergleich als Entscheidungshilfe (Vegkryss i spredtbygd strøk – sammenligning av sikkerheten som beslutningsgrunnlag). Köln: Institut für Straßenverkehrstechnik.

Messelt, H. (1994). Vilt på tvers av veien. Seminar om viltpåkjørsler 22 juni 1994 i Drammen. Koppang vegstasjon, Koppang.

Meuleners, L., Hendrie, D., Lee, A. H. & Legge, M. (2008). Effectiveness of the Black Spot Programs in Western Australia, Accident Analysis and Prevention, 40, 1211–1216.

Meuleners, L., Hendrie, D., Legge, M. & Cercarelli, L. R. (2005). An Evaluation of the Effectiveness of the Black Sport Programs in Western Australia 2000–2002, Rapport RR 155, Injury Research Centre, The University of Western Australia, Crawley.

Meyer, E. (2006). Assessing the effectiveness of deer warning signs. Report No. K-TRAN: KU-03-6. University of Michigan.

Miaou, S.-P. (1994). The relationship between truck accidents and geometric design of road sections: Poisson versus negative binomial regressions. Accident Analysis and Prevention, 26, 471–482.

Milton, J. & Mannering, F. (1996). The relationship between highway geometrics, traffic related elements, and motor vehicle accidents. Report WA-RD 403.1. Washington State Department of Transportation.

Milton, J. & Mannering, F. (1998). The relationship among highway geometries, traffic-related elements and motor-vehicle accident frequencies. Transportation, 25, 395–413.

Missouri Dept of Transportation. (1980) Comparison of Accident Rates Related to 4:1 and 6:1 Inslopes on 2-Lane Rural Trunk Highways. Unpublished Report, June 1980 (sitert etter Graham & Harwood, 1982). Missouri.

Mo, M. (1980). Trafikkulykker i tilknytning til vegtunneler. Hovedoppgave ved Institutt for veg- og jernbanebygging. Norges Tekniske Høgskole, Trondheim.

Montgomery, R. E. & R. L. Carstens. (1987). Uncontrolled T Intersections: Who Should Yield? Journal of Transportation Engineering, 113, 299–314.

Moore, R. L. & V. J. Jehu. (1968). OTA Study Week Theme II. Recent developments in barrier design. Traffic Engineering and Control, 10, 421–429.

Moskowitz, K. & W. E. Schaefer. (1960). California Median Study 1958. Highway Research Board Bulletin, 266, 34–62.

Motha, J., Musidlak B. & Williams, C. (1995). An economic evaluation of the australian federal black spot road safety program, Prodeedings of the 7th World Conference on Transport Research, volume 3, Transport Policy, 137–149, Sydney.

Mountain, L. & B. Fawaz. (1989). The area-wide effects of engineering measures on road accident occurrence. Traffic Engineering and Control, 30, 355–360.

Mountain, L. & B. Fawaz. (1992). The effects of engineering measures on safety at adjacent sites. Traffic Engineering and Control, 33, 15–22.

Mountain, L., B. Fawaz, B. & L. Sineng. (1992). The assessment of changes in accident frequencies on link segments: a comparison of four methods. Traffic Engineering and Control, 33, 429–431.

Mountain, L. et al. (1994) Highway improvements and maintenance: their effects on road accidents. Paper presented at the 22nd PTRC Summar Annual Meeting, 12–16 September, 1994. Proceedings of Seminar J, 151–161.

Mountain, L., D. Jarrett & B. Fawaz. (1995). The safety effects of highway engineering schemes. Proceedings of the Institution of Civil Engineers Transport, 111, 298–309.

Mountain L., Maher, M. & Fawaz, B. (1998). Improved estimates of the safety effects of accident remedial schemes, Traffik Engineering and Control, 10, 554–554.

Muskaug, R. (1981). Riksvegnettets ulykkesrisiko. En analyse av risikoen for personskadeulykker på det norske riks- og europavegnettet utenfor Oslo avhengig av vegbredde, fartsgrense og trafikkmengde. TØI-notat 579. Transportøkonomisk institutt, Oslo.

Muskaug, R. (1985). Risiko på norske riksveger. En analyse av risikoen for trafikkulykker med personskade på riks- og europaveger utenfor Oslo. avhengig av vegbredde, fartsgrense, trafikkmengde og avkjørselstettet. TØI-rapport. Transportøkonomisk institutt, Oslo.

Mutabazi, M., Russell, E.R. & Stokes, R.W. (1999). Review of the effectiveness, location, design, and safety of passing lanes in Kansas. Kansas: University of Kansas, Report No. K-TRAN: KSU-97-1.

Mysen, A. B. (1997). Beregning av ulykkesfrekvens i tunneler med ett rør og ett kjørefelt i hver retning. Arbeidsdokument TST/0832/97. Transportøkonomisk institutt, Oslo.

Mäkelä, O. & Kärki, J.-L. (2004). Tievalaistuksen vaikutus liikenneturvallisuuteen ja ajonopeuksiin (Impact of road lighting on road safety and driving speeds). Helsinki: Tiehallinnon selvityksiä 18/2004.

Naik, B. (2005). Offsetting opposing left-turn lanes at signalized intersections: A safety assessment case study in Lincoln, Nebraska. Midwest Transportation Consortium Student Conference, Fall 2005.

National Board of Public Roads and Waterways. (1978). Traffic Safety Effects of Road Lights. Väg- och Vattenbyggnadsstyrelsen, Helsinki.

Navin, F. & Appeadu, C. (1995). Estimating vehicle accidents on British Columbia roads. Transportation Planning and Technology, 19, 45–62.

Nemeth, Z. A. & D. J. Migletz, D. J. (1978). Accident Characteristics Before, During, and After Safety Upgrading Projects on Ohio's Rural Interstate System. Transportation Research Record, 672, 19–24.

Nettelblad, P. (1987). Olycksrisken ökar med dubbelriktade cykelbanor. En undersökning av 11 cykelbanor i Malmö. Gatukontoret, Trafikdivisionen, Malmö.

Newby, R. F. & H. D. Johnson. (1964). Changes in the numbers of accidents and casualties on main roads near the London-Birmingham motorway. Proceedings of Australian Road Research Board, Vol 2, Part 1, 558–564.

Newland, V. J. & R. F. Newby. (1962). Changes in Accident Frequency after the Provision of By-Passes. Traffic Engineering and Control, 3, 614–616.

Newman, A. (2002). The marking of avanced cycle lanes and advanced stop boxes at signalised intersections, Christchurch City Council, Christchurch.

Newstead, S., & Corben, B. (2001). Evaluation of the 1992–1996 Transport Accident Commission funded accident black spot treatment program in Victoria. Report No. 182. Melbourne, Australia: Monash University Accident Research Centre.

Ng, S.J., Dole, J.W., Sauvajot, R.M., Riley, S.P.D. & Valone, T.J. (2004). Use of highway undercrossings by wildlife in southern California. Biological Conservation, 115, 499–507.

Nielsen, E. D., K. V. Andersen & K. M. Lei. (1996). Trafiksikkerhedseffekten af cykelbaner i byområder. Rapport 50. Vejdirektoratet, København.

Nielsen, G. (2000). Omkjøringsveger. I: Kolbenstvedt, M.; Solheim, T.; Amundsen, A. H. Miljøhåndboken. Trafikk og miljøtiltak i byer og tettsteder, 237–242. Transportøkonomisk institutt, Oslo.

Nielsen, G. & O. I. Larsen. (1988). Vegtrafikk i by. Problemer og perspektiver. Arbeidsdokument TP/0057/88. Transportøkonomisk institutt, Oslo.

Nielsen, M.A. (1993). Cyklisternes sikkerhed forbedret. Dansk Vejtidsskrift, 1, 9–10.

Nielsen, M.A. (1994). Safety of Cyclists in Urban Areas. Proceedings of Seminar J, Traffic Management and Road Safety, held at PTRC Summer Annual Meeting, 1994, 113–123. PTRC Education and Research Services Ltd, publication P381.

Nielsen, M.A. (1995). Cykelbane på venstreside af højresvingsbane, Dansk Vejtidskrift, 4, 26–28.

Nilsson, A. (2000). Kunskapsöversikt om cykelfält - om cykelfälts användning, utformning och betydelse för cyklisters säkerhet och cykelns konkurrenskraft, Lunds Universitet, Lund Tekniska Högskola, Institutionen för Teknik och samhälle, Lund.

Nilsson, A. (2001). Re-allocating road space for motor vehicles to bicycles: effects on cyclist's opinion and motor vehicle speed, The AET European Transport Conference, Cambrigde.

Nilsson, A. (2003). Utvärdering av cykelfälts effekter på cyklisters säkerhet och cykelns konkurrenskraft mot bil, Doktoraavhandling, Bulletin 217, Lunds Universitet, Lund Tekniska Högskola, Institutionen för Teknik och samhälle, Lund.

Nilsson, G. (1978). Behov av trafiksäkerhetsmått för vägplanering. VTI-meddelande 97. Statens väg- och trafikinstitut (VTI), Linköping.

Nilsson, G. (1994). Förbifarter del 1. Inventering av förbifarter och trafikeffekter av förbifartslösningar. VTI-rapport 396. Väg- och transportforskningsinstitutet, Linköping.

Nilsson, G. & Ljungblad, L. (1999). Stållineräcken i mittremsan på motorvägar. VTI rapport 442. Väg- och transportforskningsinstitutet, Linköping.

Nilsson, G. K., Rigefalk, S. & Koronna-Vilhelmsson, I. (1992a). Follow up study of speeds on rural roads. VTI-meddelande 675.

Nilsson, G. K., Rigefalk, S. & Koronna-Vilhelmsson, I. (1992b). Hastighetsuppföljning på landsväg. Mätresultat 1991. VTI-meddelande 690. Statens väg- och trafikinstitut (VTI), Linköping.

Noland, R.B. & Oh, L. (2004). The effect of infrastructure and demographic change on traffic-related fatalities and crashes. a case study of Illinois county-level data. Accident Analysis and Prevention, 36, 525–532.

Nordtyp-projektgruppen. (1980). Trafikulykker på vejstrækninger. En sammenstilling af ulykkesfrekvenser for nordiske typesektioner. Utarbeidet for vegmyndighetene i Danmark, Norge og Sverige. Vejdirektoratet, København.

Nygaard, H. C. (1988). Erfaringer med rundkjøringer i Akershus. Statens vegvesen Akershus, Oslo.

Nysted, E. (2005). Feeding stations as a measure to re-distribute moose in their winter habitat. Examensarbete (2005:11) i ämnet skoglig zooekologi. Umeå, Sverige: Sveriges Landbruksuniversitet.

OECD Road Research Group. (1976). Hazardous Road Locations. Identification and Countermeasures. OECD, Paris.

OECD Road Research Group. (1979). Road Safety at Night. OECD, Paris.

Oh, J., Washington, S. & Choi, K. (2004). Development of accident prediction models for rural highway intersections, Transportation Research Record, 1897, 18–27.

Ogden, K.W. (1997). The effects of paved shoulders on accidents on rural highways. Accident Analysis and Prevention, 29, 353–362.

Olbrich, P. (1984). Untersuchung der Wirksamkeit von Wildwarnreflektoren und der Eignung von Wilddurchlassen. Zeitschrift für Jagdwissenschaft, 30, 101–116.

Olsson, L. (1970). Trafikolyckornas samband med trafikmiljön. Trafiksäkerhet hos motorvägar. Meddelande 30. Chalmers Tekniska Högskola, Institutionen för stadsbyggnad, Forskargruppen Scaft, Gøteborg.

Olsson, M.P.O. (2007). The use of highway crossings to maintain landscape connectivity for moose and roe deer. Dissertation, Karlstad University Studies.

Olsson, M.P.O., Widén, P. & Larkin, J.L. (2008). Effectiveness of a highway overpass to promote landscape connectivity and movement of moose and roe deer in Sweden. Landscape and Urban Planning, 85, 133–139.

Oregon Department of Transportation (1996). Medians. Salem, Oregon: Discussion Paper No. 4.

Oslo Veivesen (1995). Ulykkesanalyse. Rundkjøringer i Oslo. Statens Vegvesen, Oslo.

Painter, K. (1998). Value for money: Street lighting and crime reduktion. Lighting Journal, 63, 24–27.

Pajunen, K. (1999). Perusverkon eritasoliittymien turvallisuus (trafikksikkerhet i planskilte kryss i stamvegnettet). Helsinki: Tielaitoksen selvityksiä, 21.

Passetti, K.A. & Fambro, D.B. (1999). Operating speeds on curves with and without spiral transitions. Transportation Research Record, 1658, 9–16.

Pegrum, B. V. (1972). The application of certain traffic management techniques and their effect on road safety. National Road Safety Symposium. Canberra, Australian Department of Transport, 1972 (Sitert etter OECD 1979). Canberra.

Perchonok, K.et al. (1978). Hazardous Effects of Highway Features and Roadside Objects. Volume 2: Findings. Report FHWA-RD-78-202. US Department of Transportation, Federal Highway Administration, Washington.

Persaud, B. N. (1987). 'Migration' of accident risk after remedial blackspot treatment. Traffic Engineering and Control, 28, 23–26.

Persaud, B. N. & L. Dzbik. (1993). Accident Prediction Models for Freeways. Transportation Research Record, 1401, 55–60.

Persaud, B., K. Mucsi & A. Ugge, A. (1996). Development and application of microscopic accident potential models to evaluate the safety impact of freeway traffic management systems. In: Proceedings of the Conference Road Safety in Europe and Strategic Highway Research Program (SHRP), Prague, the Czech Republic, September 20–22, 1995, Vol 4A, Part 1, 227–240. Swedish National Road and Transport Research Institute, Linköping.

Persaud, B.N., Retting, R.A., Gårder, P.E. & Lord, D. (2001). Observational before-after study of the safety effect of US roundabout conversions using the Empirical Bayes method. TRB paper 01-0562. Washington DC, Transportation Research Board.

Pettersson, R. (1977). Avkörningsolyckor och vägens sidoutrymme. Etapp 2. Olycksrisk samt samband mellan skadeföljd och utformingen av vägens sidoutrymme. VTI-rapport 127. Statens väg- och trafikinstitut (VTI), Linköping.

Pfeifer, J. P. C. (1999). Sikkerhed for cyklister i kryds, Aalborg Universitet.
Pfundt, K. (1986), Strassenbeleuchtung und Verkehrssicherheit. Strassenverkehrstechnik, Heft 1, 1–9.
Poch, M. & Mannering, F. (1996). Negative binomial analysis of intersection accident frequencies. Journal of Transportation Engineering, 122, 105–113.
Polus, A. & A. Katz. (1978). An analysis of nighttime pedestrian accidents at specially illuminated crosswalks. Accident Analysis and Prevention, 10, 223–228.
Potts, I.B. & Harwood, D.W. (2004). Benefits and design/location criteria for passing lanes. Kansas: Midwest Research Institute, report No. RDT 04-008.
Preston, H. & Schoenecker, T. (1999). Safety Impact of Street Lighting at Isolated Rural Intersections. Final Report MN/RC-1999-17. Minnesota Department of Transportation, April.
Preston, H. & Schoenecker, T. (2000). Bypass lane safety, operations, and design study. Report MN/RC – 2000–22. Minneapolis: BRW, Inc.
Proctor, S. (1994). Improvements to Impact Protection Standards in Great Britain. Paper presented at Road Safety in Europe and Strategic Highway Research Program, Lille, France, 26–28 September, 1994. Preprint of papers for 27 September.
Proctor, S. (1996). An independent review of 3M «Road Safety» products. In: Proceedings of the Conference Road Safety in Europe and Strategic Highway Research Program (SHRP), Prague, the Czech Republic, September 20–22, 1995, Vol 4A, Part 5, 179–192. Swedish National Road and Transport Research Institute, Linköping.
Putman, R.J. (1997). Deer and road traffic accidents: Options for management. Journal of Environmental Management, 51, 43–57.
Quenault, S. W. (1981). Peterborough experimental cycle route. TRRL Laboratory Report 975. Transport and Road Research Laboratory, Crowthorne, Berkshire.
Ragnøy, A. (1978). Serviceanlegg langs riksveger. Hovedoppgave i samferdselsteknikk. Norges Tekniske Høgskole, Institutt for Samferdselsteknikk, Trondheim.
Ragnøy, A., Christensen, P. & Elvik, R. (2002). Skadegradstetthet – SGT Et nytt mål på hvor farlig en vegstrekning er, TØI-rapport 618, Transportøkonomisk institutt, Oslo.
Ragnøy, A. & Elvik, R. (2003). Trafiksikkerhetsanalyse av stamvegnettet i Norge, TØI-rapport 649, Transportøkonomisk institutt, Oslo.
Ranes, G. (1998). Analyse av personskadeulykker på motorveg. Notat datert 22 april 1998. Vegdirektoratet, Oslo.
Rasmussen, S., L. Herrstedt & S. Hemdorff. (1992). Trafiksikkerhed på motortrafikveje. Notat 8. Vejdatalaboratoriet, Herlev.
Ray, M. H., L. A. Troxel & J. F. Carney. (1991). III. Characteristics of Fixed-Roadside-Object Side-Impact Accidents. Journal of Transportation Engineering, 117, 281–297.

Reed, D. F. & Woodard, T.N. (1981). Effectiveness of Highway Lighting in Reducing Deer–Vehicle Accidents. Journal of Wildlife Management, 45, 721 to 726.

Reed, D. F., Woodard, T.N. & Beck, T.D.I. (1977). Highway Lighting to Prevent Deer-Auto Accidents. Final Report. Report CDOH-P&R-R-77-5. Colorado Division of Highways, 1977.

Reed, D.F. ,Woodard, T.N. & Pojar, T.M. (1975). Behavioral response of mule deer to a highway underpass. Journal of Wildlife Management, 39, 361–367.

Reeve, A.F. & Anderson, S.H. (1993). Ineffectiveness of Swareflex reflectors at reducing deer-vehicle collisions. Wildlife Society Bulletin, 21, 127–132.

Rein, J. G. (1986). Agorafobi, tunneler og tiltak. Arbeidsdokument av 1.9.1986 (prosjekt O-1286). Transportøkonomisk institutt, Oslo.

Retting, R. A. (1991). Improving Urban Traffic Safety: A Multidisciplinary Approach. Experiences From New York City 1983–1989. Prepared in conjunction with the Volvo Traffic Safety Award 1991. Thompson Printing, Belleville, NJ.

Richards, S. H. (1981). Effects of Turning Off Selected Roadway Lighting as an Energy Conservation Measure. Transportation Research Record, 811, 23–25.

Ricker, E. R. et al. (1977). Evaluation of Highway Safety Program Standards Within the Purview of the Federal Highway Administration - Final Report. Report DOT-FH-11-9129. US Department of Transportation, Federal Highway Administration, Washington.

Rimiller, J., Ivan, J. & Garrick, N. (2003). Estimating benefits from specific highway safety improvements. Phase III safety benefits from left turn treatment. Report JHR 02-290. University of Connecticut, Connecticut Transportation Institute.

Robatsch, K. & Nussbaumer, C. (2005). Sicherhetsvergleich von Tunnels. Verkehrssicherheitsvergleich von Tunnels mit Gegenverkehr und Tunnels mit Richtungsverkehr mit anderen Strassen arten. Kuratorium für Verkehrssicherheit, Wien.

Rogers, E. (2004). An ecological landscape study of deer vehicle collisions in Kent County, Michigan. Report by White Water Associates Inc. Prepared for Kent County Road Commission, Grand Rapids, Michigan.

Rogness, R. O., D. B. Fambro & D. S. Turner. (1982). Before-After Analysis for Two Shoulder Upgrading Alternatives. Transportation Research Record, 855, 41–47.

Romer, J. & Mosler-Berger, C. (2003). Preventing wildlife-vehicle accidents. The animal detection system CALSTROM: 3 Proceedings of Infra Eco Network Europe (IENE) Conference. Habitat fragmentation due to Transport Infrastructure and Presentation of the COST 341 action, 13–15 November 2003, Brussels, Belgium.

Rosbach, O. (1984). Kantlinier forbedrer både bilisters og cyklisters sikkerhed. Dansk Vejtidsskrift, 11, 1984. Særtryk utgivet af Vejdirektoratet, Sekretariatet for Sikkerhedsfremmende Vejforanstaltninger (SSV).

Rutley, K. S. (1972). Advisory speed limits for bends. TRRL Report LR 461. Transport and Road Research Laboratory, Crowthorne, Berkshire.

Ryley, T. J. (1996). Advanced stop lines for cyclists: The role of central cycle lane approaches and signal timings, TRL report 181, Transport Research Laboratory, Berkshire.

Rystam, Å. (1995). Demonstrationscykelstråk i Göteborg. Bulletin 127. Tekniska Högskolan i i Lund, Institutionen för trafikteknik, Lund.

S/K Transportation Consultants, Inc. (2000), National Highway Institute Course Number 133078: Access Management, Location, and Design, April.

Sabey, B. E. & H. D. Johnson. (1973). Road lighting and accidents: before and after studies on trunk road sites. TRRL Report LR 586. Transport and Road Research Laboratory, Crowthorne, Berkshire.

Sacks, W. L. (1965). Effect of Guardrail in a Narrow Median Upon Pennsylvania Drivers. Highway Research Record, 83, 114–131.

Saito, M., Cox, D.D. & Jin, T.G. (2005). Evaluation of four recent traffic and safety initiatives, Vol II: Developing a procedure for evaluating the need for raised medians. Utah Department of Transportation Research and Development Division: Final Report.

Sakshaug, K. (1986). Fartsgrenseundersøkelsen -85. Detaljerte resultater fra fartsdelen og ulykkesdelen. Notat 535/86 og 536/86. SINTEF Samferdselsteknikk, Trondheim.

Sakshaug, K. (1998). Effekt av overhøyde i kurver. SINTEF rapport.

Sakshaug, K. & Johannessen, S. (2005). Revisjon av håndbok 115 "Analyse av ulykkessteder": Verdier for normal ulykkesfrekvens og skadekostnad ved normal og god standard. SINTEF notat datert 2005-05-03. Trondheim, SINTEF teknologi og samfunn, transportsikkerhet og – informatikk.

Salvisberg, U., Allenbach, R., Cavegn, M. et al. (2004). Verkehrssicherheit in Autobahn- und Autostrassentunneln des Nationalstrassennetzes. Bfu-report 51. Beratungsstelle für Unfallverhütung, Bern.

Sandhu, B., and J. Al-Kazily. (1996). Safety impacts of freeway traffic congestion. Paper 960702. Transportation Research Board, 75th Annual Meeting, January 7–11, 1996, Washington DC.

Savolainen, P. & Tarko, A. (2004). Safety of Intersections on High-Speed Road Segments with Superelevation. Report FHWA/IN/JTRP-2004/25. West lafayette, IN: Purdue University.

Sawalha, Z. & Sayed, T. (2001). Evaluating safety of urban arterial roadways. Journal of Transportation Engineering, 127, 151–158.

Schafer, J. A., S. Penland & W. P. Carr. (1985). Effectiveness of Wildlife Warning Reflectors in Reducing Deer-Vehicle Accidents in Washington State. Transportation Research Record, 1010, 85–88.

Schandersson, R. (1979). Avkörningsolyckor och vägens sidoutrymme. Etapp 3. Olyckskostnader samt beräkning av olycksrisker och olyckskostnader för objekt i sidoutrymmet. VTI-rapport 185. Statens väg- och trafikinstitut (VTI), Linköping.

Schandersson, R. (1982). Effekten på trafikolyckor av några åtgärder i horisontalkurvor. VTI-meddelande 298. Statens väg- och trafikinstitut (VTI), Linköping.

Schioldborg, P. (1979). Fotgjenger og bilfører - to forskjellige verdener? Psykologisk institutt, Universitetet i Oslo.

Schiøtz, I. (1982). Sidevejsheller. Sikkerhedsmæssig effekt. EMMA-rapport 2. Vejdirektoratet, Sekretariatet for Sikkerhedsfremmende Vejforanstaltninger (SSV), Næstved.

Schnüll, R., W. Haller & H. Von Lübke. (1992). Sicherheitsanliegen bei der Umgestaltung von Knotenpunkten in Städten. Forschungsberichte der Bundesanstalt für Strassenwesen (BASt) 253. Bundesanstalt für Strassenwesen, Bergisch-Gladbach.

Schoon, C. C. (1990). After seven years RIMOB in practice. An evaluation of the Dutch impact attenuator RIMOB. SWOV Report R-90-49. SWOV Institute for Road Safety Research, Leidschendam.

Schoon, C. C. & J. Van Minnen. (1993). Ongevallen op rotondes II. Tweede onderzoek naar de onveiligheid van rotondes vooral voor fietsers en bromfietsers. R-93-16. Stichting Wetenschappelijk Onderzoek Verkeersveiligheid, SWOV, Leidschendam.

Schreuder, D. A. (1989). The relationship between the level of street lighting and the traffic safety. R-89-55. SWOV Institute for Road Safety Research, Leidschendam.

Schreuder, D. A. (1993) Relation between lighting, accidents and crime in urban streets. The VIIth European Lighting Conference, 4–7 April 1993, Heriot-Watt University, Edinburgh, Scotland. Proceedings, Volume 1, 117–123.

Schultz, L. C. (1986). Pennsylvania's Guide Rail Standards: A Cost-Effective Change. Transportation Research Record, 1065, 12–18.

Schurr, K.S. & Abos-Sanchez, J. (2005). Effects of central island landscape treatments at single-lane roundabouts. DOT-Report SPR-P1(03)P550.

Schwab, R. N. et al. (1982). Roadway Lighting. Chapter 12 of Synthesis of Safety Research Related to Traffic Control and Roadway Elements, Volume 2. Report FHWA-TS-82-233. US Department of Transportation, Federal Highway Administration, Washington DC.

Scriven, R. W. (1986). Raised Median Strips - A Highly Effective Road Safety Measure. ARRB Proceedings, 1986, Vol 13, Part 5, 46–53.

Scully, J., Newstead, S., Corben, B. & Candappa, N. (2006). Evaluation of the effectiveness of the $240 M Statewide blackspot program – accident blackspot component, Monash University Accident Research Centre, Melbourne.

Seburn, T. C. (1948) Relighting A City. Proceedings of the Institute of Traffic Engineers Nineteenth Annual Meeting, 58–72, 1948 (Sitert etter Ketvirtis 1977).

Seiler, A. (2005). Predicting locations of moose vehicle collisions in Sweden. Journal of Applied Ecology, 42, 371–382.

Seim, R. (1994). Analyse av kryssulykker i Akershus fylke 1990–93. Hovedoppgave i samferdselsteknikk høsten 1994. Norges Tekniske Høgskole, Institutt for samferdselsteknikk, Trondheim.

Senneset, G. (1983). Rundkjøringer. Del II Hovedrapport. Erfaringer fra utvalgte rundkjøringer i Norge. STF63 A83001 II. SINTEF Samferdselsteknikk, Trondheim.

Shankar, V., Mannering, F. & Barfield, W. (1995). Effect of roadway geometrics and environmental factors on rural freeway accident frequencies. Accident Analysis and Prevention, 27, 371–389.

Shankar, V., Milton, J. & Mannering, F. (1997). Modelling accident frequencies as zero-altered probability processes: An empirical inquiry. Accident Analysis and Prevention, 29, 829–837.

Short, D. & L. S. Robertson. (1998). Motor vehicle death reductions from guardrail installation. Journal of Transportation Engineering, 124, 501–502.

Sielecki, L. E. 2001. Evaluating the effectiveness of wildlife accident mitigation installations with the Wildlife Accident Reporting System (WARS) in British Columbia. Pages 473–489 in Proceedings of the International Conference on Ecology and Transportation. Center for Transportation and the Environment, North Carolina State University.

Sielski, M. C. (1967). Relationship of Roadway Lighting and Traffic Accidents. In: Highway Research Board Special Report 93, Improved Street Utilization through Traffic Engineering, 172–177. Highway Research Board, Washington DC.

Siemens A/S. (1989). Sikkerhet i veitunneler. Siemens Norge A/S, Oslo.

Sinclair, Knight & Partners Ltd. (1973). A Review of Road Design in Relation to Road Safety. October 1971. Report NR/11. Expert Group on Road Safety, Australian Government Publishing Service, Canberra, Australia.

Skarra, N. & K. O. Gabestad. (1983). Kjørekostnadshåndboken. Transportøkonomisk institutt og Vegdirektoratet, Oslo.

Slätis, A. (1994). Så här har trafikolyckorna på Sveavägen halverats. Paper presentert ved VTIs och KFBs forskardagar, Linköping, 12 och 13 januar 1994. KFB och VTI forskning/research, 12, del 3, 188–198. Kommunikationsforskningsberedningen, Stockholm.

Smith, R.L. & Walsh, T. (1988). Safety Impacts of Bicycle Lanes. Transportation Research Record, 1168, 49–56.

Sposito, B. & S. Johnston. (1999). Three cable median barrier performance and costs in Oregon. Paper 99-0370. Transportation Research Board Annual Meeting, Washington DC (available on CD-rom).

Squires, C. A. & P. S. Parsonson. (1989). Accident Comparison of Raised Median and Two-Way Left-Turn Lane Median Treatments. Transportation Research Record, 1239, 30–40.

Stabell, P. (1992). Trafikkavvikling i tunneler. Paper presentert ved Nordisk Vegteknisk Forbunds XVI Kongress, Tammerfors, Finland, 9–11 juni, 1992. I Via Nordica, Dokument, 468–478. Helsinki, Nordiska Vägtekniska Förbundet.
Statens vegvesen (1983). Veiledning. Håndbok 115. Analyse av ulykkessteder. Statens vegvesen, Oslo.
Statens vegvesen (1985). Veiledning. Planlegging av serviceanlegg. Rutevis, overordnet planlegging av serviceanlegg langs vegnettet. Håndbok 124. Statens vegvesen, Oslo.
Statens vegvesen (2000). Rekkverksnormal. Foreløpig. 6 November 2000. Vegdirektoratet, Oslo.
Statens vegvesen (2003). Sykkelhåndboka – Utforming av sykkelanlegg, Veiledning, Håndbok 233, Statens vegvesen, Oslo.
Statens vegvesen (2005). Effektberegninger – Østfold – ulykkespunkter og ulykkesstrekninger, Statens vegvesen, Trafikksikkerhetsseksjonen.
Statens vegvesen (2007a). Nasjonal transportplan 2010–2019 – Nasjonal sykkelstrategi – attraktivt å sykle for alle – Grunnlagsdokument for NTP 2010–2019 Vegdirektoratet, Staten vegvesen, Oslo.
Statens vegvesen (2007b). Statusrapport for Statens vegvesens oppfølging av Nasjonal sykkelstrategi, rapport 2007/09, Utbyggingsavdelingen, Oslo.
Statens vegvesen (2007c). Analyse av ulykkessteder, Veiledning, Håndbok 115, Statens vegvesen, Oslo.
Statens vegvesen (2007d). Analyse av ulykkessteder – vedleggsdel for manuelle beregninger, Veiledning, Håndbok 115, Statens vegvesen, Oslo.
Statens vegvesen (2007e). Håndbok 017 Veg- og gateutforming. Oslo: Statens vegvesen.
Statens vägverk. (1979). Trafiksäkerhet vid stigningsfält. En olycksanalys från 1972–77. Meddelande TU 1979:5. Statens vägverk, Tekniska avdelningen, Utvecklingssektionen, Borlänge.
Statens vägverk. (1980). Trafiksäkerhet på vägar med midträcke. Rapport TU 143. Statens vägverk, Utvecklingssektionen, Borlänge.
Statens Vägverk. (1981). Olycksreducerande åtgärder i tätort. En føre/efter studie. PP-meddelande 19. Statens vägverk, Sektionen för planeringsunderlag, Borlänge.
Statens vägverk. (1983a). Trafiksäkerhetseffekt av väginvesteringar. 20 exempel på uppföljda objekt. PP-Meddelande nr 27. Borlänge, Statens vägverk, Sektionen för planeringsunderlag,
Statens vägverk. (1983b). Trafiksäkerheten i trafikplatser på 2-fältig väg. Rapport TU 153. Statens vägverk, Utvecklingssektionen, Borlänge.
Statens vägverk. (1985a). Trafiksäkerhet på vägar projekterade/byggda under 1950-, 1960- och 1970-talet. Meddelande TU 1985:5. Statens vägverk, Tekniska avdelningen, Utvecklingssektionen, Borlänge.
Statens vägverk. (1985b). Viltstängsel. Olika typers effekt och kostnad. Meddelande TU 1985:2. Statens vägverk, Utvecklingssektionen, Borlänge.

Statens vägverk. (1987). Sikträjning som viltolycksminskande åtgärd. Rapport VV 1987:14. Statens vägverk, Serviceavdelning Planering och Projektering, Trafiksäkerhetssektionen, Borlänge.

Statistisk sentralbyrå (2000). Vegtrafikkulykker. Årlig utgave. 1996–2000 (årgangene 1995–1999). Oslo- Kongsvinger.

Stewart, D. & C. J. Chudworth. (1990). A remedy for accidents at bends. Traffic Engineering and Control, 31, 88–93.

Stigre, S. A. (1993a). Trafikksikring i Hamar. Ulykkesanalyse og forslag til trafikksikkerhetstiltak. Del 1 og 2. Statens vegvesen Hedmark og Hamar kommune, Hamar.

Stigre, S. A. (1993b). Tiltak mot utforkjøringsulykker i Vestfold. Effektundersøkelse. Oppdragsrapport til Statens vegvesen Vestfold. Svein A. Stigre, Rykkinn.

Storaas, T., Nicolaysen, K.B., Gundersen, H., Zimmermann, B. (2005). Prosjekt elgtrafikk i Stor-Elvdal 2000–2004 – hvordan unngå elgpåkjørsler på veg og jernbane. Oppdragsrapport nr. 1. Høgskolen i Hedmark.

Strathman, J.G., Duecker, K.J., Zhang, J. & Williams, T. (2001). Analysis of design attributes and crashes on the Oregon highway system. Oregon: Center for Urban Studies, Portland State University, Report SPER 312.

Strugstad, R. (1985). Bruk av gang- og sykkelveganlegg. Utformingens og vedlikeholdets betydning. Rapport STF63 A85006. SINTEF Samferdselsteknikk, Trondheim.

Stølan, A. (1988). Erfaringer med trafikksaneringer og sammenhengende gang- og sykkelveger. Asplan Samferdsel. Utgitt av Samferdselsdepartementet, Miljøverndepartementet, Kommunal- og arbeidsdepartementet og Vegdirektoratet. Oslo.

Stølen, J. A. (1969). Virkninger av omkjøringsvegene ved Lillesand og Sande. Oslo. Norsk institutt for by- og regionforskning, (Magisteravhandling i geografi ved Universitetet i Oslo), Oslo,

Sullivan, E. C. (1990). Estimating Accident Benefits of Reduced Freeway Congestion. Journal of Transportation Engineering, 116, 167–180.

Sullivan, T.L., Williams, A.F., Messmer, T.A., Hellinga, L.A. & Kyrychenko, S.Y. (2004). Effectiveness of temporary warning signs in reducing deer-vehicle collisions during mule deer migrations. Wildlife Society Bulletin, 32, 907–915.

SWOV (2007). SWOV fact sheet - The high risk location approach, Intitute for road safety research, Leidschendam.

Sælensminde, K. (2002). Gang- og sykkelvegnet i norske byer – Nyttekostnadsanalyser inkludert helseeffekter og eksterne kostnader av motorisert vegtrafikk, TØI-rapport 567, Transportøkonomisk institutt, Oslo.

Sæverås, O. J. (1998). Vestre innfartsåre. Sammenligning av ulykkessituasjonen før og etter åpning av ny innfartsåre fra vest (ytre del). Statens vegvesen, Trafikksikkerhetsseksjonen, Bergen.

Sørensen, M. (1991). Forsøg med særlig afmærkning af uheldskryds. Dansk Vejtidsskrift, 5, 17–19.
Sørensen, M. (2006). Grå strækninger i det åbne land – udvikling, anvendelse og vurdering af uheldsbaseret metode til udpegning, analyse og udbedring af grå strækninger, ph.d.-afhandling, Aalborg Universitet, Institut for Samfundsudvikling og Planlægning, Aalborg.
Sørensen, M. (2007). Best practice guidelines on black spot management and safet analysis of road network, TØI-rapport 898, Transportøkonomisk institutt, Oslo.
Sørensen, M. (2008). Midtstilte sykkelfelt i Oslo - Litteraturstudie av utenlandske anbefalinger og erfaringer, TØI-arbeidsdokument SM/2002/2008, Transportøkonomisk institutt, Oslo.
Sørensen, M. (2009). Kryssløsninger i by – Internasjonale anbefalinger for å sikre miljøvennlig bytransport, TØI-rapport 1004, Transportøkonomisk institutt, Oslo.
Sørensen, M. & Elvik, E. (2007). Black spot management and safety analysis of road networks – best practice guidelines and implementation steps, TØI-rapport 919, Transportøkonomisk institutt, Oslo.
Sørensen, M. & Jensen, H. (2004). Evaluering af sortpletbekæmpelse i Århus Amt, Dansk Vejdtidskrift, 1, 11–13.
Tamburri, T. N., Hammer, C.J., Glennon, J. C. & Lew, A. (1968). Evaluation of Minor Improvements. Highway Research Record, 257, 34–79.
Tanner, J. C. (1958). Reduction of Accidents by Improved Street Lighting. Light and Lighting, 51, 353–355.
Tanner, J. C. & A. W. Christie. (1955). Street lighting and accidents – a study of some new installations in the London area. Light and Lighting, 48, 395–397.
Taragin, A. & B. M. Rudy. (1960). Traffic Operations as Related to Highway Illumination and Delineation. Highway Research Board Bulletin, 255, 1–22,
Tennessee Valley Authority. (1969). A Study of the Benefits of Suburban Highway Lighting. Illuminating Engineering, April, 359–363.
Thingwall, L. (1991). Trafikksikkerhetsmessig effekt av gang og sykkelveganlegg i Akershus. Hovedoppgave ved Institutt for Samferdselsteknikk. Norges Tekniske Høgskole, Institutt for Samferdselsteknikk, Trondheim.
Thoma, J. (1989). Verkehrssicherheit in Autobahntunnels. Unfallkennzahlenvergleich Freie Strecke/Tunnel. BFU Report R8927. Schweitzerische Beratungsstelle für Unfallverhütung, Bern.
Thomas, G.B. & Smith, D.J. (2001). Effectiveness of roadway safety improvements. Final Report. Ames, IA: Iowa State University Research Park.
Thorson, O. & I. Mouritsen. (1971). Den koordinerede uheldsstatistik 1962–1966. En analyse af 38.000 uheld på de danske hovedlandeveje og landeveje. RfT-rapport 6. Rådet for Trafiksikkerhedsforskning (RfT), København.

Thulin, H. (1991). Trafikantgruppers skadetal, risker och hälsoförluster i olika trafikmiljöer - en tabellsammanställning. Bilaga 2 till Samhällsekonomisk prioritering av trafiksäkerhetsåtgärder. TFB & VTI forskning/research rapport 7:2 1991. Transportforskningsberedningen och Statens väg- och trafikinstitut, Stockholm och Linköping.

Tie- ja vesirakennushallitus (1983). Perusverkon eritasoliittymien liikenneturvallisuus. Helsinki, Tie- ja vesirakennushallitus, Liikennetoimisto, Insinööritoimisto Y-Suunnittelu.

Tiehallinto (1998). Ohituskaistojen turvallisuus (The safety of passing lanes). Tiehallinnon Selvityksiä. Helsinki: Tiehallinto.

Tielaitos, Tie- ja liikennetekniikka (2000). Perusverkon eritasoliittymien turvallisuus turvallisuus (The safety of grade-separated junctions). Tietoa tiensuunnittelun, 47.

Tom, G. K. J. (1995). Accidents on Spiral Transition Curves. ITE-Journal, September 1995, 49–53.

Traffic Engineering Branch (2005). An Evaluation of the National Black Spot Programme in Tasmania. Traffic Engineering Branch, Department of Energy and Resources, Tasmania, Australia.

Traffic Engineering Branch (2007). State Black Spot Program. Notes on Administration. Traffic Engineering Branch, Department of Energy and Resources, Tasmania, Australia.

Tran, T. (1999). Vegtrafikkulykker i rundkjøringer – 1999. TTS rapport 2, 1999. Vegdirektoratet, Transport- and trafikksikkerhetsavdelingen, Oslo.

Transportforskningsdelegationen. (1980). Viltolyckor. Trafikanters beteende och möjligheter att påverka detta. Rapport 1980:3. Transportforskningsdelegationen, Stockholm.

Transportforskningskommissionen. (1965). Väg- och gatubelysningens inverkan på trafiksäkerheten. Meddelande nr 60. Transportforskningskommissionen, Stockholm.

Tsyganov, A.R., Machemehl, R.B. & Warrenchuk, N.M. (2005). Safety impact of edge lines on rural two lane highways. Report FHWA/TX-05/0-5090-1. Austin, TX: Center for Transportation Research, The University of Texas at Austin.

Tudge, R. T. (1990). Accidents at roundabouts in New South Wales. Proceedings of the 15th ARRB Conference, Part 5, 331–349. Australian Road Research Board, Vermont South, Australia.

Tuovinen, P. & Enberg, A. (2003). Tiemerkinnat ohituskaistakohdissa – Sulkuviivojen vaikutus ajokäyttäytymiseen (Marking of passing lanes, effects on driver behaviour). Helsinki: Tiehallinnon Selvityksiä, 50/2003.

Tuovinen, P., Kosonen, T. & Enberg, Å. (2002). Kiihdytyskaistat perusverkon erityisliittymissä. Helsinki: Tiehallinnon Selvityksiä, 47/2002.

Turner, H. J. (1962). Influence of road lighting on traffic safety and service. Proceedings of the Australian Road Research Board, Volume 1, Part 1, 596–611.

Tye, E. J. (1975) Median Barriers in California. Traffic Engineering, 25, 28–29.

Tziotis, M. (1993). Evaluation of mid-block accident black spot treatment, report 48, Monash University Accident Research Centre, Melbourne.

UK Department of Transport. (1991). Transport Statistics Great Britain 1991. Her Majesty's Stationary Office, London.

Urbanik, T.I., Hinshaw, W. & Fambro, D.B. (1989). Safety effects of limited sight distance on crest vertical curves. Transportation Research Record, 1208, 23,35.

US Department of Transportation. (1992). Fatal and Injury Accident Rates on Public Roads in the United States 1991. US Department of Transportation, Federal Highway Administration, Washington DC.

Uschkamp, G., et al. (1993). Zusammenhang zwischen Beleuchtungsgüte und Strassenverkehrsunfällen. FE 70300/89. Schlussbericht 31.8.1993. ISV Ingenieurgruppe Stadt+Verkehr.

Vaa, T. (1991) Effekt av siktforbedrende tiltak på strekninger. Rapport STF63 A91014. SINTEF Samferdselsteknikk, (utgitt av Vegdirektoratet, Driftsavdelingen). Trondheim,

Vaa, T. & S. Johannessen, S. (1978). Ulykkesfrekvenser i kryss. En landsomfattende undersøkelse av ulykkesforholdene i 803 kryss i perioden januar 1970 - juni 1976. Oppdragsrapport 22. Norges Tekniske Høgskole, Forskningsgruppen, Institutt for samferdselsteknikk, Trondheim.

Vaa, T. et al. (1994). Utredning av tofargesystemet. Rapport STF63 A94003. SINTEF Samferdselsteknikk, Trondheim.

Vaaje, T. (1982). Risiko i vegtrafikken - med sammenligning av risiko ved andre transportmåter og aktiviteter for øvrig. Temahefte 11 i temaserien Samferdsel. Transportøkonomisk institutt, Oslo.

Van Minnen, J. (1990). Ongevallen op rotondes. Vergelijkende studie van de onveiligheid op een aantal locaties waar een kruispunt werd vervangen door een "nieuwe" rotonde. R-90-47. Stichting Wetenschappelijk Onderzoek Verkeersveiligheid, SWOV, Leidschendam.

Várhelyi, A. (1993). Minirondeller. Energi- ofch miljöeffekter. TFB-rapport 1993:6. Transportforskningsberedningen, Stockholm.

Vejdatalaboratoriet - Vejdirektoratet. (1991). Trafikuheld i 1990 på kommuneveje, landeveje og hovedlandeveje. Rapport 97. Vejdatalaboratoriet, Næstved.

Vejdirektoratet. (1980). Farlige og sikre veje. Den koordinerede uheldsstatistik 1976–78. Rapport 26. Vejdatalaboratoriet, Økonomisk-statistisk afdeling, København.

Vejdirektoratet (2000). Idékatalog for cykeltrafik, Vejdirektoratet, København.

Viner, J. G. & F. J. Tamanini. (1973). Effective Highway Barriers. Accident Analysis and Prevention, 5, 203–214.

Vodahl, S. B. & S. Johannessen. (1977). Ulykkesfrekvenser i kryss. Arbeidsnotat nr 7. Resultater av før/etterundersøkelsen. Oppdragsrapport 178. Norges Tekniske Høgskole, Forskningsgruppen, Institutt for samferdselsteknikk, Trondheim.

Vodahl, S. B. & T. Giæver. (1986). Risiko i vegkryss. Dokumentasjonsrapport. Rapport STF63 A86011. SINTEF Samferdselsteknikk, Trondheim.

Vogt, A. (1999). Crash models for rural intersections: Four-lane by two-lane stop-controlled and two-lane by two-lane signalized. Report FHWA-RD-99-128.

Vogt, A. & Bared, J.G. (1998). Accident models for two lane rural roads: segments and intersections. Report FHWA-RD-98-133.

Voigt, A.P. (1996) An evaluation of alternative horizontal curve design approaches on rural two-lane highways. Report TTI-04690-3, Texas Transportation Institute.

Voigt, A.P. & Krammes, R.A. (1998). An operational and safety evaluation of alternative horizontal curve design approaches on rural two-lane highways. International Symposium on Highway Geometric Design Practices. Boston, Massachusetts.

Voss, H. (1994). Zur Verkehrssicherheit innenörtlicher Knotenpunkte. Zeitschrift für Verkehrssicherheit, 40, 68–72.

Voß, H. (2007). Unfallhäufungen mit Wildunfällen. Modellversuch im oberbergischen Kreis. Unfallforschung der Versicherer. Berlin: Gesamtverband der Deutschen Versicherer.

Väre, S. (1995). Riista-aitakokeilu valtatiellä 6. Tielaitoksen Selvityksiä 63/1995. Helsinki: Tiehallinto, Keskushallinto.

Værø, H. (1992a). Effekt af sortpletbekæmpelse i Hillerød. Vejdirektoratet, Trafiksikkerhedsafdelingen, København.

Værø, H. (1992b). Effekt af sortpletbekæmpelse i Nyborg. Vejdirektoratet, Trafiksikkerhedsafdelingen, København.

Værø, H. (1992c). Effekt af sortpletbekæmpelse i Silkeborg. Vejdirektoratet, Trafiksikkerhedsafdelingen, København.

Værø, H. (1992d). Effekt af sortpletbekæmpelse i Skælskør. Vejdirektoratet, Trafiksikkerhedsafdelingen, København.

Walker, A. E. (1974). Field experience of breakaway lighting columns. TRRL Laboratory Report 660. Transport and Road Research Laboratory, Crowthorne, Berkshire.

Walker, A. E. & R. G. Chapman. (1980). Assessment of anti-dazzle screen on M6. TRRL Laboratory Report 955. Transport and Road Research Laboratory, Crowthorne, Berkshire.

Walker, C. D. & C. J. Lines. (1991). Accident reductions from trunk road improvements. Research Report 321. Transport and Road Research Laboratory, Crowthorne, Berkshire.

Walker, F. W. & S. E. Roberts. (1976). Influence of lighting on accident frequency at highway intersections. Transportation Research Record, 562, 73–78.

Walthert, R., F. Mäder & P. Hehlen. (1970) Données Statistiques sur la Proportion des Accidents le Jour et la Nuit, leurs Causes et Conséquences. La Conduite de Nuit, Automobil Club de Suisse, 1970 (Sitert etter Ketvirtis 1977).

Wang, J., Hughes, W.E. & Steward, R. (1998). Safety effects of cross-section design on rural multi-lane highways. International Symposium on Highway Geometric Design Practices. Boston, Massachusetts.

Wanvik, P.O. (2007a). The effect of road lighting on accidents. A Norwegian before-and-after study. Paper No. 2 PhD project.

Wanvik, P.O. (2007b). Injury risk on Dutch roads related to light conditions. Paper No. 3 PhD project.

Wanvik, P.O. (2007c). The accident reducing effect of road lighting in various situations. Paper No. 4 PhD project.

Ward, A.L. (1982). Mule deer behaviour in relation to fencing and underpasses on Interstate 80 in Wyoming. Transportation Research Record, 859, 8–13.

Waring, G.H., Griffis, J.L. & Vaugh, M.E. (1991). White-tailed deer roadside behaviour, wildlife warning reflectors and highway mortality. Applied Animal Behavior Science, 29, 215–223.

Weinert, R. (1996). Effects of accident remedial measures on urban roads. Proceedings of Seminar H held at the PTRC European Transport Forum, Brunel University, England, 2–6 September 1996, Vol P 407. Published by PTRC Education and Research Services Ltd.

Weissbrodt, G. (1984). Auswirkungen von Ortsumgehungen auf die Verkehrssicherheit. Heft 48, Unfall- und Sicherheitsforschung Strassenverkehr. Bundesanstalt für Strassenwesen, Bergisch-Gladbach.

Welleman, A. G. & A. Dijkstra, A. (1985). Fietsvoorzieningen op weggedeelten binnen de bebouwde kom II. Inventarisatie en voorbereiding analyses. Rapport R-85-46. Stichting Wetenschappelijk Onderzoek Verkeersveiligheid, SWOV, Leidschendam.

Wheeler, A.H., Leicester, M.A. & Underwood, G. (1993). Advanced stop-lines for cyclists. Traffic Engineering & Control, 34, 54–60.

Wheeler, A. H. & J. M. Morgan. (1987). The Albert Gate and Albion Gate cycle schemes in London. Traffic Engineering and Control, 28, 628–635.

Williams, A.F. & Wells, J.K. (2005). Characteristics of vehicle-animal crashes in which vehicle occupants are killed. Traffic Injury Prevention, 6, 56–59.

Williston, R. M. (1969) Motor vehicle traffic accidents: limited access expressway system. Connecticut State Highway Department, Bureau of Traffic, Technical Report 10, 1969 (quoted from Good & Joubert, 1971), Connecticut.

Wilson, J. E. (1967). Simple Types of Intersection Improvements. In: Improved Street Utilization Through Traffic Engineering, 144–159. Highway Research Board Special Report 93. National Research Council, Highway Research Board, Washington DC.

Wittink, R. (2001). Promoting of mobility and safety of vullnerable road users, D-2001-3, Institute for Road Safety Research (SWOV), Leidschendam, Nederland.

Wold, H. (1995) Trafikkulykker i planskilte kryss. Hovedoppgave i samferdselsteknikk høsten 1995. Norges Tekniske Høgskole, Institutt for samferdselsteknikk,) Trondheim.

Wong, S-Y. (1990) Effectiveness of Pavement Grooving in Accident Reduction. ITE Journal, July 1990, 34–37.

Wong, S.C., Sze, N.N. & Li, Y.C. (2007). Contributory factors to traffic crashes at signalized intersections in Hong Kong. Accident Analysis and Prevention, 39, 1107–1113.

Wood, P. & Wolfe, M.L. (1988). Intercept feeding as a means of reducing deer-vehicle collisions. Wildlife Society Bulletin, 16, 376–380.

Woodard, T.N., Reed, D.F. & Pojar, T.M. (1973). Effectiveness of Swarflex wildlife warning reflectors in reducing deer-vehicle accidents. Internal Report, Colorado Division of Wildlife, Fort Collins, Colorado.

Woods, D.L., B. Bohuslav & C. J. Keese. (1976). Remedial Safety Treatment Of Narrow Bridges. Traffic Engineering, March 1976, 11–16.

Wyatt, F.D. & E. Lozano. (1957). Effect of Street Lighting on Night Traffic Accident Rate. Highway Research Board Bulletin, 146, 51–55.

Yates, J.G. (1970). Relationship Between Curvature and Accident Experience on Loop and Outer Connection Ramps. Highway Research Record, 312, 64–75.

Yin, T. (2005). Effects of highway illumination reduction on highway safety performance. Portland State University.

Zador, P., Stein, H., Hall, J. & Wright, P. (1985). Superelevation and roadway geometry. Deficiency at crash sites and on grades (Abridgement). Insurance Institute for Highway Safety, Washington, D.C.

Zegeer, C.V. & J. A. Deacon. (1987). Effect of Lane Width, Shoulder Width, and Shoulder Type on Highway Safety. In: State of the Art Report 6. Relationship between Safety and Key Highway Features. A Synthesis of Prior Research. Transportation Research Board, Wahington DC.

Zegeer, C.V., R. C. Deen & J. G. Mayes. (1981). Effect of Lane and Shoulder Widhts on Accident Reduction on Rural, Two-Lane Roads. Transportation Research Record, 806, 33–43.

Zegeer, C.V. et al. (1988). Accident Effects of Sideslope and Other Roadside Features on Two-Lane Roads. Transportation Research Record, 1195, 33–47.

Zegeer, C.V., Stewart, J.R., Reinfurt, D.W. et al. (1991). Cost-Effective Geometric Improvements for Safety Upgrading of Horizontal Curves. Report FHWA-RD-90-021. US Department of Transportation, Federal Highway Administration, Turner-Fairbank Highway Research Center, McLean, VA.

Zegeer, C.V. & Council, F.M. (1995). safety relationships associated with cross sectional roadway elements. Transportation Research Record, 1512, 29–36.

Zegeer, C.V., Stewart, J.R., Huang, H.H. & Lagerwey, P.A. (2002). Safety effects of marked vs. unmarked crosswalks at uncontrolled locations: Executive summary and recommended guidelines. FHWA-RD-01-075.

Zhou, M. & Sisiopiku, V. (1997). On the relationship between volume to capacity ratios and accident rates. Transportation Research Record, 1581, 47–52.

Ørnes, A. L. (1981). Trafikksikkerhetseffekten av gang- og sykkelveger. Oppdragsrapport 56. Norges Tekniske Høgskole, Forskningsgruppen, Institutt for samferdselsteknikk, Trondheim.

# 2.

# Road Maintenance

## 2.0 Introduction and overview of nine measures

This chapter covers nine measures involving road maintenance. These measures are as follows:

2.1 Resurfacing of roads
2.2 Treatment of unevenness and rut depth of the road surface
2.3 Improving road surface friction
2.4 Bright road surfaces
2.5 Landslide protection measures
2.6 Winter maintenance of roads
2.7 Winter maintenance of pavements, foot and cycle paths and other public areas
2.8 Correcting erroneous traffic signs
2.9 Traffic control at roadwork sites

These measures are carried out on existing roads and do not normally involve any long-term changes of the road. This introductory section describes the main points in the current knowledge of the effects of these measures on accidents, mobility and environmental conditions. The main features of the costs of the measures and their cost–benefit value are also described.

**The Handbook of Road Safety Measures**

**ISBN: 978-1-84855-250-0**

## Amount and quality of research

The amount of research evaluating the effect of maintenance measures on accidents is highly variable. For example, many studies have evaluated the road safety effects of resurfacing and of improving the friction of road surfaces and winter maintenance of roads. Relatively, few studies have evaluated the other measures. The effect on accidents of protecting roads against landslides has not been quantified. The effects of the other measures on accidents can be quantified on the basis of the available evaluation studies. Table 2.0.1 shows the amount of research into the effects of road maintenance measures on accidents. It also shows the number of studies, the number of results and the total of statistical weights for the studies to which reference is made regarding the effect of the measures on accidents. Meta-analysis has been used to synthesise results for all measures with the exception of landslide protection.

The quality of research is also variable. Experiments have been done on winter maintenance of roads, in particular, salting roads. Only non-experimental studies are available for the other measures. A common problem for the majority of measures in this area is that either just one or only a few studies have been carried out to evaluate their effects on accidents.

## Main features of the effects on accidents

***Resurfacing*** of roads, which normally involves re-asphalting, appears to lead only to small accident reductions. Some studies indicate that accidents may increase in the first

*Table 2.0.1: The amount of research evaluating the effects on accidents of road maintenance measures*

| Measure | Number of studies | Number of results | Sum of statistical weights | Results last updated |
|---|---|---|---|---|
| 2.1 Resurfacing of roads | 12 | 174 | 9,654 | 2008 |
| 2.2 Treatment of unevenness and rut depth of the road surface | 3[1] | 13 | 6,564 | 2008 |
| 2.3 Improving road surface friction | 21[2] | 131 | 24,943 | 2008 |
| 2.4 Bright road surfaces | 1 | 1 | 229 | 1997 |
| 2.5 Landslide protection | 2 | 2 | – | 1997 |
| 2.6 Winter maintenance of roads | 22 | 185 | 59,862 | 1997 |
| 2.7 Winter maintenance of footpaths etc. | 2 | 24 | 602 | 1997 |
| 2.8 Correcting erroneous traffic signs | 1 | 13 | 1,217 | 1997 |
| 2.9 Traffic control at roadworks sites | 4 | 21 | 2,034 | 2009 |

[1]In addition seven studies that are not included in the meta-analysis.
[2]In addition four studies that are not included in the meta-analysis.

period immediately after re-asphalting, probably due to increasing speed. More favourable effects have been found in the long term. The relationship between unevenness and accidents is somewhat unclear, multi-vehicle accidents may increase on more uneven roads. Increasing rut depth is related to increased accident rates. The combined effect of increasing unevenness and increasing rut depth over the years is an increase in the number of accidents. Improving unevenness and rut depth without resurfacing does not improve friction and is therefore not necessarily associated with a decrease of accidents.

***Improving road surface friction*** reduces the number of accidents. The effects are greatest on wet roads, in sharp bends and when friction initially is low. Friction seems to be more important for accident rates than unevenness. No significant effects on accidents have been found of porous asphalt.

***Bright road surfaces*** have not been found to reduce the number of accidents, but only one study has been found. These surfaces appear to lead to higher driving speeds.

***Landslide protection*** must be assumed to reduce the number of landslides and their consequences; however, the effects of this measure on the number of accidents have not been quantified.

***Winter maintenance of roads*** improves safety. This is true both for salting roads and for raising the standard of snow clearance. At the same time, a number of winter maintenance measures contribute to maintaining mobility during the winter period. Winter maintenance of pavements, footpaths and cycle paths and other public areas does not always appear to reduce the number of accidents. Instead, clearing snow from pathways may in certain cases make these more slippery than they were before and thus contribute to more falls among pedestrians. Heated surfaces, which remain bare throughout the winter, contribute to reducing the number of pedestrian falls.

***Correcting erroneous traffic signs***, i.e. road signs not conforming to the norms for traffic signs, reduces the number of accidents. Safeguarding roadworks can reduce the number of accidents in areas where roadworks are taking place.

### Main features of the effects on mobility

Many of the measures in this area lead to higher driving speeds. These include resurfacing, improvements to the evenness of road surfaces, bright road surfaces and winter maintenance of roads. An important goal in road maintenance is to improve or maintain mobility. Several of these measures appear to promote this goal.

## Main features of effects on the environment

Asphalting work leads to noise and smells. Improving the friction of road surfaces by using so-called porous asphalt reduces the level of noise from traffic. Salting roads leads to damage to plants along the roadside, pollution of ground water, an increase in the amount of slush thrown up by cars, rust on cars and disintegration of concrete structures. The remaining measures in this area have no documented effects on the environment.

## Main features of costs

Table 2.0.2 summarises the main points in the unit costs of road maintenance measures. The costs of most types of maintenance depend on the type of road, road width, traffic volume among other things. The costs in Table 2.0.2 are average costs for maintenance in Norway and refer to all roads where the respective types of maintenance have been carried out in the respective years. The costs for resurfacing, for example, refer to the average costs of resurfacing main roads, irrespective of road width and load carrying capacity demands, in the whole country in 2007. No cost

*Table 2.0.2: Main elements in the cost of road maintenance measures*

| Measure | Unit | Average cost (million NOK) | Costs from year |
|---|---|---|---|
| 2.1 Surfacing of, e.g., road shoulders | Square metre road surface | 0.0002 | 2005[1] |
| 2.1 Resurfacing of roads, all main roads | Kilometre road | 0.50 | 2007[2] |
| 2.2 Treatment of unevenness and rut depth of the road surface | Kilometre road | – | |
| 2.3 Improving road surface friction | Kilometre road | – | |
| 2.4 Bright road surfaces | Kilometre road | 0.55 | 2007[2,3] |
| 2.5 Landslide protection | Kilometre road | – | |
| 2.6 Winter maintenance of roads – snow clearance (roads with AADT 2,000–25,000) | Kilometre road | 0.0042–0.0183 | 1995 |
| 2.6 Winter maintenance of roads – salting (roads with AADT 7,000–25,000) | Kilometre road | 0.0142–0.0153 | 1995 |
| 2.7 Winter maintenance of footpaths etc. (annual cost) | Kilometre road | 0.010 | 1995 |
| 2.8 Correcting erroneous traffic signs | Sign | 0.002–0.005 | 2005[1] |
| 2.9 Traffic control at roadwork sites | Kilometre road | – | |

[1]Statens vegvesen, Handbook 015 (2005; utkast 11. aug.).
[2]Statens vegvesen, projects in 2007.
[3]Amundsen (1983).

estimates for the treatment of unevenness and rut depth of road surfaces and improving road surface friction are shown. These measures can be assumed to cost less than re-asphalting, but the actual costs will depend on the type and severity of damages to the road surface and the specific type and amount of measures. Landslide protection and traffic control at roadwork may be of varying extent, from setting up signs to extensive geological works and realignment of roads.

### Main features of cost–benefit analyses

The standard of road maintenance depends on the amount of traffic on the roads. Roads with heavy traffic have higher standards of maintenance than those with light traffic. Since both costs and benefits of road maintenance vary greatly depending on the amount of traffic, it is difficult to state generally whether benefits are greater than costs for these measures.

Resurfacing, improvements to the unevenness and rut depth of road surfaces and improving friction have been found to improve both safety and mobility. The numerical examples developed show that the benefits from these measures can, in certain cases, be large enough to offset the costs. One numerical example indicates that using porous asphalt can give benefits that exceed costs in places where many accidents occur on wet roads. Better winter maintenance is also cost-effective on many roads. The effect on accidents of landslide protection is not sufficiently known for cost–benefit analysis to be meaningful.

## 2.1 Resurfacing of roads

### Problem and objective

Traffic, weather conditions and ground conditions expose the road surfaces to wear and tear. Ruts, cracks and unevenness in the road surface reduce driving comfort and can be a traffic hazard. Water collecting in ruts in the road surface increases the danger of aquaplaning. Ruts and cracks in the road surface may make it more difficult to keep a motor vehicle on a steady course. Large holes in the road surface can damage vehicles and lead to the driver losing control of the vehicle. It is not known how many traffic accidents are due in whole or in part to the standard of the road surface.

Resurfacing is intended to prevent dangerous unevenness and damage due to wear and tear on the road surface, to increase driver comfort, maintain the road's loading capacity (permitted axle loads) and to reduce wear and tear on vehicles.

## Description of the measure

Ordinary resurfacing denotes the normal replacement of existing road surfaces with new road surfaces, for example, in the form of re-asphalting. Asphalting of gravel roads is also included here as one type of renewal of road surfaces. Bright road surfaces, high-friction road surfaces and porous (drainage) asphalt are dealt with in Sections 2.2–2.4.

## Effect on accidents

***Asphalting gravel roads.*** A Swedish study (Carlsson and Öberg 1977) shows that roads with sealed surfaces have a lower accident rate than gravel roads. Compared with gravel roads, the risk of injury accidents is around 20% lower on roads with oil-gravel surfaces and around 40% lower for roads with asphalt (bituminous) surfaces. The risk of accidents involving property damage only is some 15% lower for roads with oil-gravel surfaces than for gravel surfaces, and around 35% lower for roads with asphalt surfaces than for gravel roads. It is emphasised in this report that the differences in accident rate between gravel roads and other roads are not only attributable to the road surface but also to other differences in road standards, such as width of roads, alignment and sight conditions (Carlsson and Öberg 1977).

***Concrete instead of asphalt.*** On asphalt surface, drainage of water is improved compared with a concrete surface. This may lead to increased accident rates on concrete surfaces. The relationship between the type of surface (concrete vs. asphalt) and accidents has been studied by Strathman, Duecker, Zhang and Williams (2001). Regression models have been estimated in which it is controlled for a number of other factors such as the cross section and alignment of the roads. On freeways, accident rates were found to be significantly higher when the surface is concrete than when the surface is asphalt. On other types of roads, no significant differences have been found.

***Re-asphalting***. The effects of re-asphalting and of the quality of the asphalted surface on road safety have been evaluated in a number of studies:

Miller and Johnson (1973) (Great Britain, re-asphalting)
Schandersson (1981) (Sweden, index for road surface standard)
Schandersson (1989) (Nordic countries, index for road surface standard)
Leden and Salusjärvi (1989) (Nordic countries, age of the rod surface)
Hauer, Terry and Griffith (1994) (USA, re-asphalting)
Leden and Hämäläinen (1994) (Finland, re-asphalting)

Leden, Hämäläinen and Manninen (1998) (Finland, re-asphalting)
Geedipally (2005) (Sweden, re-asphalting)

The studies that have investigated the effects of road surface standard have used an index for the state of the road surface, based among other things on the depth of ruts, evenness and cracks. The results of these different studies are very similar. Best estimates of the effects on accidents of re-asphalting roads are shown in Table 2.1.1.

Re-asphalting roads does not appear to lead to statistically significant changes in the number of accidents. There do not seem to be differences between different levels of injury severity or between wet and dry roads. Two studies that are not included in the results in Table 2.1.1 found increased accident rates immediately after re-asphalting, but reduced accident rates in the longer term (Hauer, Terry and Griffith 1994, Harwood et al. 2003). The age of the road surface and an index for road surface standard do not seem to affect accident rates either.

## Effect on mobility

Asphalting gravel roads leads to higher driving speeds (Arnberg 1976, Carlsson and Öberg 1977, Carlsson 1978, Kolsrud and Nilsson 1983). Available studies have shown

*Table 2.1.1: Effects on accidents of re-asphalting*

| | | Percentage change in the number of accidents | |
|---|---|---|---|
| Accident severity | Types of accidents affected | Best estimate | 95% Confidence interval |
| ***Re-asphalting*** | | | |
| Unspecified | All accidents | +1 | (−4; +6) |
| Injury accidents | All accidents | −4 | (−13; +6) |
| Unspecified | Accidents on dry roads | −2 | (−13; +10) |
| Unspecified | Accidents on wet roads | +10 | (−6; +28) |
| Injury accidents | All accidents during the first year after re-asphalting | −5 | (−31; +31) |
| Unspecified | All accidents during the second year after re-asphalting | −3 | (−14; +9) |
| ***Age of the road surface (asphalt): New vs. old surface*** | | | |
| Unspecified | All accidents | 0 | (−2; +2) |
| ***Index for road surface standard: Good vs. poor surface standard*** | | | |
| Injury accidents | All accidents | −4 | (−13; +7) |
| Property damage only | All accidents | +6 | (−2; +14) |

somewhat different results, varying from 1.5–3.5 km/h increase in average speed (median speed) to 1.6–5.2 km/h increase. However, asphalting gravel roads also leads to a net reduction in calculated stopping distances of up to 25%.

Re-asphalting also affects driving speed, especially where the evenness of the road surface is improved (Anund 1992, Cooper, Jordan and Young 1980, Cleveland 1987, Karan, Haas and Kher 1976). Increases of up to 10 km/h have been found, but more typical values are in the region of 2–5 km/h. Harwood et al. (2003) found varying results on different roads. Speed changes were between minus 6.4 km/h (−4 mph) and plus 9.7 km/h (+6 mph). On the average, speed increased with 1.6 km/h (1 mph). A Finnish study found a small increase of speed by 0.6 km/h on dry roads (Leden, Hämäläinen and Manninen 1998).

### Effect on the environment

Dust from dry gravel roads can cause problems for road users and people living close to the road. This problem disappears when the road is sealed. No studies have been found of the effects of re-asphalting roads on the environment.

### Costs

The costs for re-asphalting depend, among other things, on the size and type of the re-asphalting projects. Average costs for re-asphalting projects in Norway (www.vegvesen.no) are ca. NOK 0.5 million per kilometre of road. This is an average cost for different types of roads and no information is available on which or how many of the layers of the road surface are renewed. On a road with 12.5 m surface width, the corresponding cost per square metre would be NOK 40. The costs for re-asphalting of road shoulders are NOK 200 per square metre (Statens vegvesen, Håndbok 115, utkast aug. 2005).

### Cost–benefit analysis

Numerical examples have been calculated for re-asphalting of different types of roads. The first numerical example is calculated under the assumption that re-asphalting is the alternative to no re-asphalting at all during the lifetime of the new asphalt layer. In this scenario, investment costs for re-asphalting occur, but no maintenance costs are assumed. Investment costs are assumed to be 100 NOK per square metre; surface width is assumed to be in accordance with Norwegian road standards. A road that, according to road standards, needs re-asphalting can be assumed to have higher maintenance costs if not re-asphalted, and the maintenance costs will increase with proceeding decay of the existing asphalt layer. The assumption of no maintenance costs is therefore conservative. Maintenance costs are most likely to decrease when a road is re-asphalted, but no estimates of the difference are available. Injury accidents are assumed to be reduced by 4% and travel times are assumed to be reduced with 2 s per vehicle per kilometre. This corresponds to an increase of speed, e.g. from 58 to 60 km/h, from 77 to 80 km/h or from 95 to 100 km/h. Accident cost and time savings are assumed over the whole lifetime of the new asphalt layer. If accident and time costs increase at the same rate without re-asphalting as on a re-asphalted road, this assumption is realistic. If accident and time costs would increase at a higher rate without re-asphalting, the accident and time cost savings of re-asphalting would be underestimated. Vehicle operation costs are assumed to be reduced by 0.06 NOK per vehicle per kilometre, which corresponds to a reduction by about 2%.

The results in Table 2.1.2 show that the benefits of re-asphalting are greater than the benefits on roads with traffic volumes above 2,000 under the current assumptions. The cost–benefit ratios are most likely to be underestimated. If roads are not re-asphalted, it is most likely that accident, travel time and vehicle operation costs would increase at a higher rate than when roads are re-asphalted. Moreover, maintenance costs are likely to be reduced after re-asphalting, which is not taken into account in the calculation.

A second numerical example is calculated for re-asphalting a road with a traffic volume of 25,000 in the actual year (year 0) instead of delaying re-asphalting by one ore more years. The example refers to a road surface that has reached the end of its lifetime according to road standards. The assumptions as regards investment costs and accident, travel time and vehicle operation cost savings are identical to the numerical example presented in Table 2.1.2. It is taken into account that accident, travel time and

*Table 2.1.2: Cost–benefit analysis of re-asphalting instead of no re-asphalting*

| Traffic volume (AADT) | Life time (years) | Investment costs per kilometre road (million NOK) | Cost savings during whole life time (million NOK) | | | |
|---|---|---|---|---|---|---|
| | | | Accident cost savings | Time cost savings | Vehicle operation cost savings | Cost–benefit ratio |
| 500 | 11.3 | 0.65 | 0.13 | 0.13 | 0.09 | 0.56 |
| 2,000 | 9.3 | 0.85 | 0.04 | 0.46 | 0.32 | 0.96 |
| 7,000 | 8.4 | 1.25 | 0.10 | 1.45 | 1.01 | 2.05 |
| 12,000 | 5.5 | 1.60 | 0.12 | 1.95 | 1.36 | 2.14 |
| 25,000 | 4.7 | 2.20 | 0.19 | 3.45 | 2.40 | 2.87 |
| 40,000 | 3.3 | 2.20 | 0.17 | 3.46 | 2.41 | 2.74 |

vehicle operation costs are increasing during the lifetime of an asphalt layer. From the year, in which asphalt is renewed in the comparison scenario, these costs are therefore assumed to be lower than when asphalt is renewed in the actual year. The cost–benefit ratios of re-asphalting in year 0 instead of year $x$ are as follows:

| Re-asphalting in year 0 instead of | Cost–benefit ratio |
|---|---|
| Year 1 | 0.70 |
| Year 2 | 0.80 |
| Year 3 | 1.67 |
| Year 4 | 2.08 |
| Year 5 | 2.87 |

Delaying re-asphalting may be beneficial up to 2 years. The total lifetime is 5 years, and the benefit–cost ratio of delaying re-asphalting by 5 years is therefore identical to the benefit–cost ratio of re-asphalting instead of no re-asphalting at all. These calculations do not take into account changes of maintenance costs. Maintenance costs are likely to be higher on older roads, and delaying resurfacing may therefore be less beneficial than suggested by the present analysis.

## 2.2 Treatment of unevenness and rut depth of the road surface

### Problem and objective

Potholes and other irregularities in the road surface are potential dangers that may cause the driver to lose control of the vehicle. Major unevenness in the road surface increases wear and tear on vehicles and can also damage vehicles. The significance of unevenness in the road surface as a risk factor for traffic accidents in Norway is not known. In 1988, the factor 'hole in the road' was listed for 10 traffic accidents involving personal injury, of a total of 8,167 injury accidents reported that year (Statistics Norway 1989). This comprises 0.1% of all accidents. However, an uneven road surface may contribute to traffic accidents, even though the factor seen in isolation does not cause the accident by itself.

Improving the evenness of road surfaces is intended to remove dangerous irregularities in the road surface, so that the danger of losing control of a vehicle is reduced. Other objectives are to reduce wear and tear on vehicles and to increase driver comfort.

**Description of the measure**

The unevenness of the road surface refers to the megatexture, i.e. surface variations of between 50 and 500 mm (Cairney and Styles 2005). Megatexture affects water drainage. Low megatexture reduces the wear of vehicles tyres and suspension systems. Holes and cracks may reduce the directional stability and increase breaking distances. The most common index for megatexture is international roughness index (IRI).

Macrotexture refers to minor variations in the road surface of between 0.5 and 50 mm, whereas microtexture refers to variations of under 0.5 mm. Both macro- and microtexture affect friction. The effects are described in Section 2.3.

Asphalt wear in longitudinal direction leads to rutting. In ruts, water can accumulate and ruts can negatively affect a vehicle's directional stability and manoeuvrability.

Improving the evenness of road surfaces involves filling potholes in the road surface, sealing large cracks, repairing damage following frost heave and other measures in areas where the road surface is abnormally uneven. Such measures reduce the megatexture of a road surface, but they do not improve friction. General renewal of road surfaces, which often leads to the road surface becoming smoother, is dealt with in Section 2.1. This chapter deals with the effects of megatexture and rut depth and of measures on short sections of road where particular unevenness in the road surface has occurred.

**Effect on accidents**

The relationships between the unevenness (megatexture) of the road surface, rut depth and accidents have been investigated in a number of studies. Only few studies have directly investigated the effects on accidents of treating unevenness and rut depth.

***Unevenness (megatexture).*** The relationship between unevenness and accidents has been reviewed in several studies from different countries, in which different indices of unevenness have been used. An overall relationship cannot be calculated. Table 2.2.1 gives an overview of the results of the studies.

The results are highly inconsistent. Increasing unevenness has been found to be related to increased, decreased and unchanged accident numbers. There do not appear to be systematic differences between the results depending on whether or not confounding variables have been controlled for.

One consistent result is that all studies that have investigated effects on head-on collisions or on multi-vehicle accidents found that increasing unevenness is related to

*Table 2.2.1: Studies of the relationship between unevenness of the road surface and accidents*

| Study | Type of accidents affected | Effect on accidents | Comment |
|---|---|---|---|
| Al-Masaeid (1997) (Jordan; IRI) | Single-vehicle accidents | Decrease | Controlled for some other factors |
| | Multi-vehicle accidents | Increase | Generally low standard |
| Christensen and Ragnøy (2006) (Norway; IRI) | All accidents | Decrease | Controlled for several other factors |
| DeSilva (2001) (Australia) | Accident costs | No change | Controlled for several other factors |
| Gothie (2001) (France; IRI) | Accident costs | No change | Not controlled for other factors |
| Ihs, Velin and Wicklund (2002) (Sweden) | All accidents | Increase | Partly controlled for other factors |
| | Single-vehicle accidents, head-on collisions | Increase | Generally good standard (IRI < 5,1 mm on 95% of road length) |
| | Other accidents | Unclear | |
| Nelson English, Loxton & Andrews Pty Ltd (1988) (Australia; Australian index of unevenness) | All accidents | Decrease | Not controlled for other factors |
| Souleyrette et al. (2001) (USA; IRI) | Head-on collisions | Increase | Controlled for several other factors |

increasing accident numbers. Holes, cracks and other damages to the road surface lead to larger variations in the lateral placement of vehicles and may cause abrupt breakings (Al-Masaeid 1997). On the other hand, speed may decrease on uneven roads, and thereby contribute to reduced accident rates (Al-Masaeid 1997, Christensen and Ragnøy 2006, Oxley et al. 2004).

The results from Norway and Sweden are contradictory. In Norway (Christensen and Ragnøy 2006), it was found that reduced unevenness increases the number of accidents. A reduction of IRI from 4 to 2 was associated with an accident increase of 7% and from 8 to 2 was associated with an accident increase of 23%. The Swedish study (Ihs, Velin and Wicklund 2002) found increased accident numbers on more uneven roads. A possible explanation for the contradictory results according to Christensen and Ragnøy (2006) is a generally better road standard in Sweden and a better control for confounding factors (e.g. speed limit and traffic volumes) in the Norwegian study.

***Rut depth***. The relationship between rut depth and accidents has been investigated in three studies. An overall relationship cannot be calculated. Table 2.2.2 gives an overview of the results of the studies.

In the studies from Norway and United States, increasing rut depth was found to be associated with an increasing number of accidents. According to these studies, the

*Table 2.2.2: Studies of the relationship between rut depth and accidents*

| Study | Rut depths studied (groups) | Effect on accidents | Comments |
|---|---|---|---|
| Start, Kim and Berg (1996) (USA) | Between 1, 3 and 10 mm vs. above 10 mm | Increase: ca. 16% more accidents per increase of rut depth by 2.5 mm | Not controlled for other factors |
| Christensen and Ragnøy (2006) (Norway) | Between 0 and 25 mm vs. above 25 mm | Increase: ca. 5% more accidents per increase of rut depth by 5–10 mm | Controlled for several other factors |
| Ihs, Velin and Wicklund (2002) (Sweden) | Between 0 and 18 mm vs. above 18 mm | Increase in winter, decrease in summer | Partly controlled for other factors |

number of accidents is not linearly related to rut depth, but increases most at rut depths above a certain limit (ca. 10 to 30 mm). The largest increase of accidents in the US study was found on roads with a rut depth above 7.6 mm. In the Norwegian study, accidents decreased by 5% when rut depth was reduced from 10 to 0 mm, and by 15% when it decreased from 30 to 0 mm. In the Swedish study, no clear relationship between rut depth and accidents was found, but the sign of the relationship differed between summer and winter (see Table 2.2.2). The results of the Norwegian study indicate that the effects of rut depth on accidents depend on a number of other factors, such as the unevenness of the road surface.

***Combined effects of unevenness and rut depth***. Christensen and Ragnøy (2006) have investigated the effects of increasing unevenness and rut depth over time. It is estimated that increasing unevenness and rut depth lead to an increase in accidents by 2.3% after 10 years and by 4.8% after 20 years. A reduction of IRI and rut depth to the original level (i.e. of a newly asphalted road) is consequently expected to reduce the number of accidents by 2.2% on a 10-year old-road surface and by 4.6% on a 20-year-old road surface. Re-asphalting will, however, also improve friction, and when estimating the effects of re-asphalting, friction improvements have to be taken into account as well.

Effects of improving both unevenness and rut depth have been investigated by Al-Masaeid, Sinha and Kuczek (1993). A non-significant increase in accident numbers by 8% has been found. A possible explanation for an increase in accident numbers according to Al-Masaeid et al. is increasing speed and that patching holes and ruts do not improve friction.

### Effect on mobility

It has been documented that an uneven road surface leads to reductions in speed (Anund 1992, Karan, Haas and Kher 1976). The size of the change in speed depends among other things on the traffic volume and how large the irregularities in the road surface are, but can be up to 10 km/h.

### Effect on the environment

No studies have been found that show how improving evenness in the road surface affects the environment. Holes in the road and rut formation lead to pools of water, which can increase vehicle spray. This can be a problem for both drivers and pedestrians and cyclists. Unevennesses can also increase noise from vehicles driving over holes or braking abruptly in order to avoid holes.

### Costs

The costs of treating a roads unevenness and rut depth depend among other things on the degree of deterioration of the road surface and on the type of treatment applied. A simple assumption is made that the costs per kilometre road are ca. 20% of the costs for re-asphalting per kilometre road at a cost of NOK 100 per square metre (Section 2.1).

### Cost–benefit analysis

No cost–benefit analysis has been found of treatment of unevenness and rut depth. A numerical example has therefore been calculated. The assumptions are made as in the numerical example for re-asphalting (Section 2.1.7), with two exceptions. First, no effect on the number of accidents is assumed. Second, the investment cost is assumed to be as described in the section above. The treatments are assumed to last for 2 years. The results are summarised in Table 2.2.3. The benefits are larger than the costs on roads with a traffic volume of at least 2,000 vehicles per day. If the treatments last only for 1 year, the benefits exceed the costs from a traffic volume of 7,000 vehicles per day or more. These results show that maintaining a high standard of road surfaces can be beneficial even if there is no effect on road safety.

## 2.3 Improving road surface friction

### Problem and objective

Good friction is an essential condition for safe vehicle traffic. Friction affects both steering and braking distances. It denotes the resistance against sliding between two

*Table 2.2.3: Cost–benefit analysis of improving a roads unevenness and rut depth*

| Traffic volume (AADT) | Investment costs per kilometre road (million NOK) | Cost savings during whole life time (million NOK) | | | |
|---|---|---|---|---|---|
| | | Accident costs | Time costs | Vehicle operation cost | Cost–benefit ratio |
| 500 | 0,13 | 0,00 | 0,03 | 0,02 | 0,40 |
| 2,000 | 0,17 | 0,00 | 0,12 | 0,09 | 1,23 |
| 7,000 | 0,25 | 0,00 | 0,43 | 0,30 | 2,92 |
| 12,000 | 0,32 | 0,00 | 0,74 | 0,51 | 3,91 |
| 25,000 | 0,44 | 0,00 | 1,54 | 1,07 | 5,93 |
| 40,000 | 0,44 | 0,00 | 2,46 | 1,71 | 9,49 |

surfaces that are in contact with each other. It is affected by the macro- and microtexture of a road surface. Microtexture refers to variations in the surface below 0.5 mm, and affects the adhesion between the road surface and vehicle tyres, and thereby the braking distance at low speed. Macrotexture refers to surface variations between 0.5 and 50 mm, and It affects the deformation of vehicle tyres, the contact between tyres and the road surface when water is on the road, and water drainage. Low micro- and macrotexture reduce friction and increase the braking distance. Reduced macrotexture also reduce noise and tyre wear. Micro- and macrotexture are usually not related to each other, i.e. a road surface with a low microtexture does not necessarily also have a low macrotexture.

Surface variations above 50 mm are denoted as megatexture (unevenness). Unevenness and its effects on accidents are described in Section 2.1.

Friction is measured using a coefficient, the friction coefficient, which varies between 0 and 1. If the friction coefficient is reduced from say 0.5 to 0.3, the stopping distance for a car driving at 80 km/h increases from 73 to 106 m (Ragnøy 1986). This applies assuming that the driver's reaction time is one second. Typical values for the friction of the road surface are 0.7–0.9 on dry bare asphalt, 0.4–0.7 on wet bare asphalt and 0.1–0.4 on snow or ice-covered roads. Improving friction (e.g. by re-asphalting) leads to reduced braking distance. An increase of friction from 0.4 to 0.6 has the same effect on braking distance as a reduction of speed from 40 to 33 km/h or from 60 to 49 km/h (Cairney and Styles 2005). Friction coefficients can be measured with different types of measuring equipment and at different speeds. Friction measurements from different countries are not always comparable. Acceptable values for friction vary as well, e.g. between 0.3 and 0.4 at 80 km/h and 0.6 at higher speed (Noyce, Bahia, Yambo and Kim 2005).

On dry bare roads, friction is unrelated to driving speed (Brudal 1961, Hegmon 1987, Ivey, Keese, Neill and Brenner 1971, Thurmann-Moe 1976). On wet bare roads,

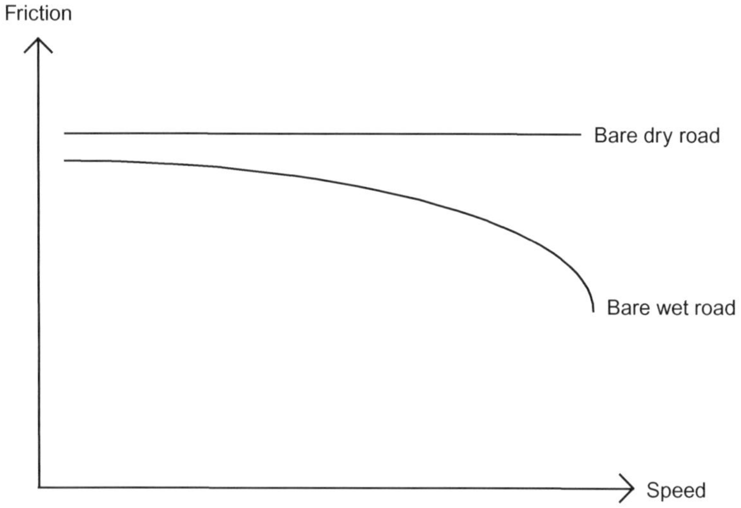


*Figure 2.3.1: The relationship between speed and friction. Schematic diagram.*

however, friction is reduced with increased speeds. The relationship between speed and friction is shown in Figure 2.3.1.

Surveys show that drivers of motor vehicles do not sufficiently adapt their speed to compensate for the difference in friction between dry and wet roads (Cleveland 1987, Wallman and Åström 2001, Noyce, Bahia, Yambo and Kim 2005). According to Swedish and Finnish studies, drivers adjust their speed to the visual impression of the road surface. These impressions are not always related to objective friction and the relationship between speed and (objective) friction is therefore weak (Wallman and Åström 2001).

The accident rate is therefore higher on wet roads than on dry roads (Brodsky and Hakkert, 1988, Ivey, Griffin, Newton and Lytton 1981, Ragnøy 1989, Satterthwaite 1976). If the rate of injury accidents on dry bare roads is set to 1.0, the corresponding rate on wet bare roads is about 1.2 during daytime and around 1.4 at nighttime (Ragnøy 1989). The increase in risk on wet roads is proportional to the amount of precipitation, particularly on worn-out road surfaces (Schandersson 1989).

On dry roads, friction is normally better in winter than in the summer. This is due to the differences in temperature. At high temperatures, the binding agent in asphalt is more viscous and mixes more easily with the stone material. This reduces friction. After long dry periods in the summer in particular, the road surface can become slippery when it starts to rain. This is due to the fact that dust, oil spills and other elements, which lie on the road surface in dry weather, polish the stones in the road surface.

Improving the friction of the road surface is intended to ensure a sufficient road grip for manoeuvring and braking during all weather and road surface conditions and for normal traffic conditions.

## Description of the measure

Improving the friction of the road surface can be achieved in several ways. The most common method is to lay a new road surface with extra good friction, or which is suitable to drain water, on top of the old surface. Such road surfaces are known as high-friction surfaces. One such type of road surface is porous (drainage) asphalt. Porous asphalt is mostly used on motorways in order to reduce noise and to increase capacity in rainy weather.

Porous asphalt has a different stone composition from normal asphalt. Porous asphalt consists only of relatively large stones. Air pockets are formed between these that drain water and contribute to reducing noise (Kielland 1988). Porous asphalt has an inverted texture with a relatively smooth surface and small indentations. New porous asphalt has a pore volume of about 20%. In order to maintain the water drainage properties of the surface, a clogging of the pores has to be prevented by regular cleaning. Another disadvantage of porous asphalt is its low resistance to studded tyres. During the last years, techniques have been developed to make porous asphalt more durable, but porous asphalt is still less durable than other asphalt types. Porous asphalt can also be problematic in winter because it freezes more quickly (Bonnot 1997). Preventing freezing by salting requires far more salt than on ordinary asphalt.

Another method is to sink grooves in the road surface. Grooving is used on dense asphalt in order to improve water drainage and to reduce spray. Grooving has only a limited lifetime and increases noise.

## Effect on accidents

***Friction.*** A number of studies have investigated the relationship between friction and accidents:

Hankins, Morgan, Ashkar and Tutt (1971) (USA)
Hatherly and Lamb (1971) (Great Britain)

Mahone and Runkle (1972) (USA)
Rizenbergs, Burchett and Napier (1973) (USA)
Adam and Shah (1974) (USA)
Rizenbergs, Burchett and Warren (1976) (USA)
Hatherly and Young (1977) (Great Britain)
Schulze, Gerbaldi and Chavet (1977) (France)

Improving friction has been found to reduce accidents on wet roads. Larger effects have been found for initially lower friction and for larger increases of friction. On dry roads, the effects are smaller and for the most part, not significant.

The relationships between friction and accidents have also been investigated by several more recent studies, the results of which could not be integrated in Table 2.3.1.

*Table 2.3.1: Effects on accidents of improving friction*

| | Percentage change in the number of accidents | | |
|---|---|---|---|
| Accident severity | Types of accidents affected | Best estimate | 95% Confidence interval |
| ***Increase of friction by ca. 0.05; initial friction below 0.50*** | | | |
| Unspecified | All accidents | −10 | (−25, +7) |
| Unspecified | Accidents on wet roads | −35 | (−52, −12) |
| Unspecified | Accidents on dry roads | −1 | (−18, +20) |
| ***Increase of friction by ca. 0.10; initial friction below 0.50*** | | | |
| Unspecified | All accidents | −17 | (−31, +1) |
| Unspecified | Accidents on wet roads | −42 | (−61, −14) |
| Unspecified | Accidents on dry roads | −10 | (−22, +5) |
| ***Increase of friction by ca. 0.25; initial friction below 0.50*** | | | |
| Unspecified | All accidents | −32 | (−40, −22) |
| Unspecified | Accidents on wet roads | −56 | (−71, −35) |
| Unspecified | Accidents on dry roads | −12 | (−25, +4) |
| ***Increase of friction by ca. 0.10; initial friction between 0.50–0.60*** | | | |
| Unspecified | All accidents | −11 | (−21, −1) |
| Unspecified | Accidents on wet roads | −40 | (−51, −26) |
| Unspecified | Accidents on dry roads | −4 | (−13, +5) |
| ***Increase of friction by ca. 0.10; initial friction between 0.50–0.60*** | | | |
| Unspecified | All accidents | −26 | (−45, +1) |
| Unspecified | Accidents on wet roads | −32 | (−53, +1) |
| Unspecified | Accidents on dry roads | −26 | (−44, −1) |

Cairney and Styles (2005) (Australia)
Caliendo, Guida and Parisi (2007) (Italy)
Davies, Cenek and Henderson (2005) (New Zealand)
DeSilva (2001) (Australia)
Parry and Viner (2005) (Great Britain)
Viner, Sinhal and Parry (2005) (Great Britain)

The results from these studies are consistent and most of these studies have controlled for a number of potential confounding variables. In summary, these studies have found that

- friction has larger effects on accidents than macrotexture or unevenness (megatexture, IRI),
- the effects of friction are greater on roads with a low macrotexture,
- friction has a greater effect on accidents in curves with a small radius than in curves with a large radius or on straight road sections.

***Macrotexture*** is one of the factors affecting accident rates. The following studies have investigated the relationship between macrotexture and accidents (Table 2.3.2):

Cairney and Styles (2005) (Australia)
Davies, Cenek and Henderson (2005) (New Zealand)
Cairney (2006) (Australia)

Accident rates have been found to be lower on roads with high macrotexture than on roads with low macrotexture. However, not all results are significant. The largest effects have been found on accidents at junctions and on straight sections in rural areas.

These results are consistent with a number of other accident studies, the results of which could not be included in the results shown in Table 2.3.2. Increased accident rates on roads with low friction were found in the studies by Gothie (2001), Roe, Webster and West (1991) and Tredrea (2001). Increased accident rates at junctions on roads with low macrotexture have also been found by Cairney (2006) and Roe, Webster and West (1991). Increased accident rates on rural roads with low macrotexture, but not on urban roads, have been found by Tredrea (2001). Cairney (2006) has not found any relationship between macrotexture and accidents on wet roads. Roe, Webster and West (1991), on the contrary, found no difference between the effects on dry versus wet roads or between different types of accidents. Cairney (2006) found no effect of macrotexture on fatal or serious injury accidents but only on accidents involving heavy vehicles or young drivers.

*Table 2.3.2: Effects on accidents of increasing macrotexture*

| | | Percentage change in the number of accidents | |
|---|---|---|---|
| Accident severity | Types of accidents affected | Best estimate | 95% Confidence interval |
| ***Rural areas, macrotexture above 0.4 instead of below 0.4*** | | | |
| Unspecified | Accidents on straight sections | −28 | (−37; −18) |
| Unspecified | Accidents on straight sections on wet roads | −16 | (−40; +17) |
| Injury accidents | Accidents on straight sections | +2 | (−24; +37) |
| Unspecified | Accidents at junctions | −65 | (−75; −50) |
| Unspecified | Accidents in curves | +8 | (−22; +51) |
| ***Urban areas, macrotexture above 0.3 instead of below 0.3*** | | | |
| Unspecified | Accidents on straight sections | −22 | (−45; +11) |
| Unspecified | Accidents on straight sections on wet roads | +15 | (−23; +73) |

All of these studies indicate that accident rates increase only when macrotexture is below a certain value, but that accident rates are relatively independent of macrotexture above that value. The values that may be regarded as a threshold for increasing accident rates are different between different studies, probably due to differences between the roads or between measurement methods and calibration of measuring equipment.

***Pavement grooving***. The effects on accidents of pavement grooving have been investigated in the following studies:

Dearinger and Hutchinson (1970) (Great Britain, USA)
Karr (1972) (USA)
Hatcher (1974) (USA)
Zipkes (1977) (Switzerland)
Burns (1981) (USA)
Gallaway et al. (1982) (Canada and USA)
Wong (1990) (USA)
Hanley, Gibby and Ferrara (2000) (USA)

The results are summarised in Table 2.3.3.

The results indicate that grooving has more favourable effects on wet roads than on dry roads, and more favourable effects on property damage only accidents than on injury accidents. The results are, however, strongly related to the study methods. Many studies are of weak methodological quality. Most studies are simple before-after studies of accident black spot treatments, which have not controlled for regression to

*Table 2.3.3: Effects on accidents of pavement grooving*

| | Percentage change in the number of accidents | | |
|---|---|---|---|
| Accident severity | Types of accidents affected | Best estimate | 95% Confidence interval |
| Injury accidents | All accidents | +8 | (−25; +57) |
| | Accidents on wet roads | −39 | (−73; +36) |
| | Accidents on dry roads | +39 | (−27; +163) |
| Property damage only accidents | All accidents | −13 | (−20; −6) |
| | Accidents on wet roads | −67 | (−74; −58) |
| | Accidents on dry roads | −1 | (−9; +8) |
| Unspecified | Accidents on wet roads | −29 | (−55; +14) |

the mean. The effects are therefore most likely over-estimated. The only study that has controlled for regression to the mean is the study by Hanley, Gibby and Ferrara (2000). The result in Table 2.3.3 that refers to unspecified accident severity is based on this study.

Two studies have compared longitudinal and transverse grooves in the pavement (Burgè, Travis and Rado 2001, Drakopolous and Kuemmel 2007). Both studies found increased friction and reduced noise on roads with longitudinal grooves compared with roads with transverse grooves. Differences in accident rates were not found (Drakopolous and Kuemmel 2007).

***Porous asphalt***. The effects on accidents of porous asphalt have been investigated by

Tromp (1993) (The Netherlands)
Herbst and Holzhammer (1995) (Austria)
Bonnot (1997) (France)
Brailly (1998) (France)
Commandeur, Bijleveld, Braimaister and Janssen (2002) (the Netherlands)
Sliwa (2003) (Germany, unpublished data)

No significant effects on accidents have been found of porous asphalt (Table 2.3.4). The studies are not of good methodological quality, but the results do not seem to be affected by methodological aspects (Elvik and Greibe 2005). Porous asphalt affects a number of risk factors. These effects are summarised in Table 2.3.5 according to Elvik and Greibe (2005). Some risk factors are positively affected, some negatively affected and rest not affected at all. This may be an explanation for the inconsistent and small effects that have been found on accidents.

*Table 2.3.4: Effects on accidents of porous asphalt*

| | Percentage change in the number of accidents | | |
|---|---|---|---|
| Accident severity | Types of accidents affected | Best estimate | 95% Confidence interval |
| Unspecified | All accidents | −13 | (−26, +3) |
| Unspecified | Accidents on wet roads | −3 | (−33, +40) |
| Unspecified | Accidents on dry roads | 1 | (−31, +48) |

*Table 2.3.5: Effects of porous asphalt on accident risk factors (Elvik and Greibe 2005)*

| Risk factor | Effect of porous asphalt |
|---|---|
| Noise in the car | No effect |
| Friction, braking distance | No effect |
| Spray, visibility conditions | Favourable effect |
| Water drainage | Favourable effect |
| Glare | Favourable effect |
| Rutting | Favourable effect |
| Winter driving conditions | Unfavourable effect (porous asphalt freezes more easily) |
| Speed | Unfavourable effect (increased speed, smaller speed reductions on wet roads) |
| Wear, maintenance requirements | Unfavourable effect (porous asphalt requires re-asphalting twice as much as dense asphalt) |

According to Elvik and Greibe (2005), other types of asphalt than porous asphalt have favourable effects on both noise and friction. Examples are Italgrip (Spinoglio 2003) and chipseal asphalt (e.g. calcined bauxite), which has a positive texture and improves friction especially in unfavourable driving conditions. Calcined bauxite is more durable than porous asphalt and friction is reduced less over time (Hudson and Mumm 2003).

### Effect on mobility

Improving road surface friction can affect driving speeds, especially where the evenness of the road surface is also improved (Anund 1992, Cleveland 1987, Cooper, Jordan and Young 1980, Karan, Haas and Kher 1976). Increases of up to 10 km/h have been found, but more typical values lie in the region of 2–5 km/h. Porous asphalt increases mobility on wet roads by improving water drainage and reducing spray.

### Effect on the environment

When using normal thickness of the layer of porous asphalt, a reduction of traffic noise of 3–5 dBA outdoors close to roads is achieved (Storeheier 2000). The highest value is achieved when an old worn-out asphalt surface is replaced with a new drainage asphalt surface with suitably high porosity and stone sizes not exceeding 16 mm. This applies to roads with a speed limit of 50 km/h and above, with reasonably even traffic flow. In addition to reducing noise, porous asphalt can reduce water spray from vehicles. This improves visibility in rainy weather and can lead to reduced use of windscreen washing fluid in cars.

The effects on noise levels stated above refer to the time shortly after the measure is implemented. Without special maintenance measures, most of the noise reduction for porous asphalt will have disappeared after the first winter season. Where traffic is light and the speed of traffic is high, the effect of the measure can last somewhat longer. In countries where studded tyres are not used, the noise reduction effect of porous asphalt has been found to last 3–5 years (Storeheier 1996).

The lifetime of porous asphalt is about half as long as that of dense asphalt. Porous asphalt requires therefore twice as much re-asphalting. Porous asphalt also requires more maintenance. In winter, more salting is needed to avoid freezing. Salting has negative environmental impacts. Pavement grooving increases noise.

### Costs

Porous asphalt has higher costs than other types of asphalt. Investment costs are higher and porous asphalt requires more maintenance and cleaning and salting. Sælensminde (2002) has compared the costs of porous asphalt with the costs and benefits of other types of asphalt on a road with a traffic volume of 25,000 vehicles per day and four lanes. The total costs (investment and maintenance costs) that are assumed in the analysis are ca. NOK 3.4 million for porous asphalt and NOK 1.3 million for usual asphalt. The lifetime of porous asphalt is 3 years for the top layer and 7 years for the basic layer. The lifetime of usual asphalt is 7 years for all layers.

### Cost–benefit analysis

Sælensminde (2002) has compared the costs and benefits of porous and usual asphalt in a cost–benefit analysis. This analysis refers to a four-lane road with a traffic volume of 25,000 vehicles per day. The speed limit is assumed to be either 60 or 80 km/h. It is assumed that porous asphalt reduces noise with 3.5 dB(A) for a period of 3 years when the speed limit is 60 km/h. When the speed limit is 80 km/h, it is assumed that the noise is reduced with 4.5 dB(A) for a period of 3 years. It is further assumed that porous asphalt has no effect on the number of accidents, speed or vehicles operating costs. Possible costs and environmental effects of increased salting are not included in the analysis. At a speed limit of 80 km/h, the benefits of porous asphalt are estimated at NOK 16.3 million (present value). The benefits exceed the costs.

Cost–benefit analyses for measures that aim at improving friction are not calculated. There are numerous different types of measures and both effects and costs are highly dependent on the type of measure, road category, traffic volumes, among other things.

## 2.4 Bright road surfaces

### Problem and objective

The reflective properties of the road surface influence visual conditions when travelling on roads, especially in the dark. A normal, dark road surface absorbs most of the light reaching the road surface. By using brighter-coloured types of stone in road surfaces, the amount of reflection can be increased. Research carried out in Norway at the Road Laboratory (Thurmann-Moe and Dørum 1980) shows that it is possible to increase sight distance in the dark by 10–20% by replacing dark road surfaces with brighter road surfaces. Sight distance affects the distance at which other road users and permanent obstacles can be detected and thus the chance of avoiding accidents. On the contrary, road markings are more visible on dark road surfaces (Amundsen 1983).

Bright road surfaces are intended to improve sight conditions while driving, especially when driving in the dark on unlit roads, so that other road users and permanent obstacles can be noticed more quickly.

### Description of the measure

The brightness of a road surface is determined by the type of stone used in the road surface and the age of the surface itself. Newly laid asphalt of the normal type is very dark. By using brighter stone, the road surface can be made brighter.

### Effect on accidents

Only one study has been found that has evaluated effect on accidents of bright road surfaces (Amundsen 1983). This Norwegian study showed that bright road surfaces do not reduce the number of injury accidents. An increase of 1% in the number of injury accidents was found, which was not statistically significant (lower 95% limit 11% decrease in number of accidents, upper 95% limit 15% increase in number of accidents). Bright road surfaces were not associated with any changes in the number of accidents either in the dark or in daylight.

### Effect on mobility

The Norwegian study of how bright road surfaces affect traffic safety (Amundsen 1983) found that bright roads surfaces were associated with an increase in the average speed of 1.4 km/h. The increase in speed was greatest in the dark and on wet roads (around 3–4 km/h).

### Effect on the environment

No studies have been found that show the effect on the environment of bright road surfaces. Bright road services may make it more comfortable to travel, especially during the dark. No studies have been found that have quantified any such effect.

### Costs

Cost figures for bright road surfaces are not available. According to Amundsen (1983), bright road surfaces cost around 10% more than normal road surfaces in Norway. This amounts to NOK 20,000–25,000 per kilometre of road where new road surfaces are laid. Bright road surfaces can also be more quickly worn down than normal road surfaces and for this reason need to be renewed more often.

### Cost–benefit analysis

No cost–benefit analyses of bright road surfaces are available. A numerical example has been worked out to indicate possible effects. It is assumed that the road has an annual average daily traffic of 2,000, that the number of traffic accidents is not affected, but driving speed increases by 1.5 km/h from 73.5 to 75 km/h, that the additional cost of a bright road surface is NOK 25,000 per kilometre of road and that the lifetime of the surface is 5 years. During this period, the increase in speed disappears gradually.

The present value of saved costs of travel time calculated over 5 years is estimated at around NOK 43,000 per kilometre of road. The cost of the measure is calculated at around NOK 30,000 per kilometre of road. The numerical example suggests that the travel time gain associated with bright road surfaces may be large enough to justify the additional cost of such road surfaces compared with normal road surfaces.

## 2.5 Landslide protection measures

### Problem and objective

Road users have no chance on their own of preventing landslides and few chances of avoiding being hit by a landslide if they happens to find themselves at a place where a landslide is occurring. As a result, landslides are often regarded as a hazard from which people should be totally protected when travelling on public roads. Avalanches or the danger of avalanche comprises some 55% of all registered road closures in Norway. Avalanches are therefore an important cause of poor accessibility on the road network. The total closure time for national and county highways can be roughly estimated to be 1,500–2,000 h/year (Statens vegvesen håndbok 056 1994a, 1994b).

Parts of the road network in Norway run through areas where it is very difficult to achieve full protection against landslides. In such areas, controlled release of landslides or periodic closure of roads may be used as protective measures. The objective of landslide protection is to reduce the probability of the road of being exposed to landslide and reduce the damaging effects of landslides by protecting road users from being caught by landslides, which cannot be prevented.

### Description of the measure

Landslide protection measures include (Tøndel 1977, Samferdselsdepartementet, st.meld. 32, 1998–89) re-routing of roads, landslide superstructures, walls, embankments or landslide screens, bolting rocks, covering rock faces with nets or similar material, the controlled release of landslides and warnings of landslide hazard and closing exposed roads in periods of particularly high risk.

### Effect on accidents

***Re-routing roads through tunnels or across terrain safe from landslide danger.*** The accident rate in tunnels in sparsely populated areas is almost the same as for roads in daylight. The accident rate in tunnels in densely populated areas is lower than for roads in the day (see Section 1.19, *safety of road tunnels*).

***Landslide superstructures, walls, embankments and landslide screens.*** No studies have been found that evaluate the effect on accidents of landslide superstructures, walls, embankments and landslide screens. An American study of snow screens on a high mountain pass, erected to prevent snow drifts and the formation of snow drifts on the road, found that the number of accidents during strong winds and snow drifts was reduced by around 10% when the length of the road covered by snow screens increased from 0% to 50% (Tabler and Furnish 1982) (see Section 2.6, *winter maintenance of roads*).

***Bolting and safety nets.*** On roads that are exposed to rock falls, loose rocks can be secured using bolts or by cladding the rock face with a safety net. Studies of the effects on accidents of these measures have not been found.

***Controlled release of landslides.*** Norwegian studies (Tøndel 1977) have shown that it is possible to dynamite away snowdrifts, which are likely to slide. Whenever controlled release of landslides is made, it is assumed that the road is closed in advance. Use of controlled landslide release as a preventive measure is best suited for avalanches and requires systematic monitoring of the risk of avalanches in the areas affected. The effect on accidents is not known.

***Avalanche warnings.*** The risk of avalanches depends among other things on the amount of snow, the formation of the terrain, wind conditions and temperature conditions (Tøndel 1977). By means of exploiting knowledge about the relationship between the number of avalanches and risk factors for them, it is possible to warn of avalanche danger. Roads known to be particularly exposed to avalanches can be closed in periods when a high risk of avalanches is forecast. Meteorological institutes routinely forecast avalanche danger. The effect on accidents of warning of avalanches has not been documented.

## Effect on mobility

Avalanches leading to road closures in Norway can lead to long delays for road users. On the basis of records made in 1970 in two Norwegian counties, Tøndel (1977) produced the following figures for delays resulting from avalanches:

| Road section | No. of avalanches | Total time of road closure (h) | Variation in length of road closure (h) | Total waiting time for road users (h) |
|---|---|---|---|---|
| Veblungsnes-Innfjorden | 5 | 24.5 | 0.5–17.5 | 5,555 |
| Volda-Hunnes | 5 | 21.5 | 1.0–11.5 | 1,057 |
| Kvænangsfjellet | 2 | 19.0 | 2.0–17.0 | 657 |
| Laksvatn-Fagernes | 5 | 17.0 | 2.0–10.0 | 3,140 |

There is a great variation with respect to how long the road is closed following an avalanche. On average, for the avalanches given above, the road was closed for around 5 h after each avalanche. The delays that occur in this period depend on the amount of traffic on the road. Road users who reach the place directly after an avalanche will suffer the maximum delay. Road users who arrive just after the road is re-opened will not be delayed. If the arrivals of road users are evenly distributed over the period when the road is closed, the total delay on a road with an annual average daily traffic above 2,000, which is closed for 5 h after an avalanche, can be estimated to 1,000 vehicle hours (of 2,000 vehicles, some 420 will arrive during the period when the road is closed; average delay per vehicle is 2.5 h).

**Effect on the environment**

No studies have been found that show the effects on the environment of landslide protection. Those who travel on roads that are particularly exposed to landslides may feel safer when a road is protected against landslides.

**Costs**

Relatively few cost figures are available for measures designed to protect against landslides in Norway. Constructing roads in tunnels in sparsely populated areas costs between NOK 10 and 30 million per kilometre of road (see Section 1.19, *safety of tunnels*). Tøndel (1977) gives the costs of building snow screens in areas with a high amount of loose snow to NOK 850,000–1 million per hectare (1975 prices). The costs of fully protecting all the roads exposed to landslides are estimated at around NOK 3.1 thousand million for national highways and NOK 2.2 thousand million for county highways (Samferdselsdepartementet, st. meld. 32, 1988–1989).

**Cost–benefit analysis**

The effects on accidents and mobility of landslide protection are not sufficiently known for cost–benefit analyses to be meaningful. A total annual cost of around NOK 100 million for landslide protections (as in the period 1990–93) seems extremely high when set against the number of accidents that are due to landslides. For example, the costs of fatal accidents due to landslides are around NOK 35 million per year. Landslide safety measures can, however, improve mobility as well as traffic safety. For example, preventing a road closure, which would otherwise have led to 1,000 vehicle hours delay, is equivalent to NOK 100,000 in saved travel time costs.

## 2.6 Winter maintenance of roads

### Problem and objective

During winter, friction and visual conditions are often poorer than in summer. Snow and ice on the road reduce friction (Hvoslef 1976, Ruud 1981, Öberg 1981, Gabestad 1988). This increases the stopping distance and creates a danger of losing control of the vehicle. On a road completely covered with snow and slush, the friction coefficient (which varies between 0 and 1) can be reduced to less than 0.1. Normal values for roads that are wholly or partially covered by snow or ice are 0.1–0.4. On wet bare roads, the friction coefficient is as a rule around 0.4–0.7. On dry bare roads, it lies as a rule in the region of 0.7–0.9. Banks of snow reduce vision and may reduce the width of the road.

A number of studies (Väg- och vattenbyggnadsstyrelsen 1972, Ruud 1981, Öberg 1981, Öberg et al. 1985) have shown that drivers of motor vehicles do not reduce their speed enough in slippery driving conditions to maintain the same braking distance as on dry bare roads. This is one of the reasons why the accident rate is higher on snow and ice-covered roads than on dry bare roads. On the basis of a study of the risk on salted and unsalted roads in Norway (Vaa 1995), Vaa (1996) has estimated the relative accident rate for different road surface conditions as follows:

| Road surface conditions | Relative risk |
|---|---|
| Dry bare roads | 1.0 |
| Wet bare roads | 1.3 |
| Slush | 1.5 |
| Hard snow | 2.5 |
| Loose snow and ice-covered roads | 4.4 |

On average for the period 1990–93, 16% of injury accidents reported to the police occurred on snow or ice-covered roads, 5% on roads partially covered with snow or ice and 1% on roads that were slippery for other reasons. Winter maintenance of roads is intended to reduce the number of accidents during winter by removing snow and ice from the road and thus improving friction.

### Description of the measure

The most important winter maintenance measures are snow clearance, sanding and salting.

National highways in Norway are divided into maintenance classes on the basis of traffic volume. The standards for winter maintenance are most stringent on the roads with the heaviest traffic. Salting of roads in Norway is done as preventative salting that stops falling snow from sticking to the road surface, prevents freezing rain from freezing to the road surface, prevents the formation of frost and dissolves thin layers of ice. Salting is carried out when weather conditions indicate that these problems may occur. In order to salt a road, the air and road surface temperature should normally be above −6 °C. In 1994, around 8,000 km of national highway were salted, of which 5,000 km were salted during the whole of the winter and 3,000 km were salted only during spring and autumn. The length of salted roads has been expanded in recent years.

Winter maintenance of pavements, foot and cycle paths is discussed in Section 2.7.

**Effect on accidents**

Winter maintenance measures are implemented either after it has started to snow (snow clearance, sanding) or when weather conditions are forecast which that reduced friction (preventive salting). If these measures are not implemented, reduced friction normally leads to an increased accident rate. Swedish and German studies have found a pattern of risk over the 24-h period on roads where the effects of winter maintenance measures have been studied (Schandersson 1986, Sävenhed 1994) as shown in Figure 2.6.1.

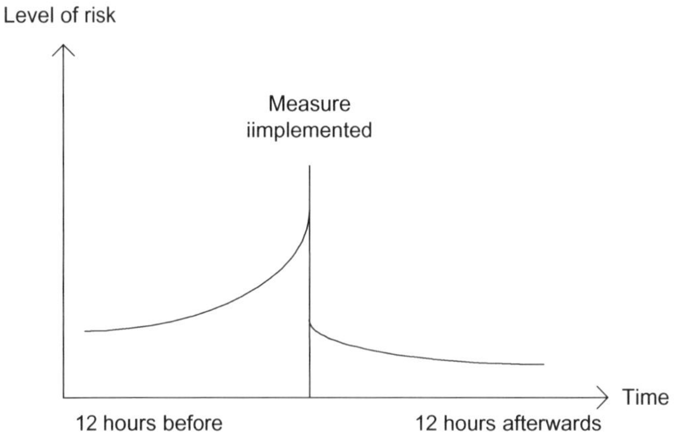


*Figure 2.6.1: Risk pattern before and after implementation of winter maintenance measures.*

In the period before a measure is implemented, the accident rate increases gradually more as the result of increasingly poor driving conditions. Directly after the measure is implemented, the rate drops significantly. Thereafter the accident rate drops slowly, down towards approximately the same level as before poor driving conditions set in.

It follows from this that the size of the effect of a winter maintenance measure depends very much on the length of the period being considered. The effect is greatest immediately after a measure is implemented, but it will be 'watered down' if a longer period is considered. The effect throughout a whole winter season depends how often precipitation or weather conditions that require maintenance measures occur, and how quickly the measure is implemented. On roads with high winter maintenance standards, it is assumed that the measures will be implemented more quickly than on roads with low winter maintenance standards. The following studies have evaluated the effects of different winter maintenance measures on accidents:

Väg- och Vattenbyggnadsstyrelsen (1972) (Finland): cessation of salting
Andersson (1978) (Sweden): introduction of salting
Brüde and Larsson (1980) (Sweden): introduction of salting
Lie (1981) (Norway): introduction of salting
Tabler and Furnish (1982) (USA): snow screens on high mountain passes
Björketun (1983) (Sweden): more rapid deployment of maintenance
Ragnøy (1985a) (Norway): general winter maintenance standards
Öberg et al. (1985) (Sweden): cessation of salting
Schandersson (1986) (Sweden): sanding, salting, snow clearance and other measures
Bertilsson (1987) (Sweden): general winter maintenance standard
Schandersson (1988) (Sweden): general winter maintenance standard
Möller (1988) (Sweden): introduction of salting
Nilsson and Vaa (1991) (Norway): introduction of salting
Öberg, Gustafson and Axelson (1991) (Sweden): cessation of salting
Kallberg (1993) (Finland): cessation of salting
Eriksen and Vaa (1994) (Norway): increased winter maintenance standard
Sävenhed (1994) (Sweden): general winter maintenance standard
Öberg (1994) (Sweden): point salting
Sakshaug and Vaa (1995) (Norway): introduction of salting
Kallberg (1996) (Finland): cessation of salting
Vaa (1996) (Norway): increased general winter maintenance standard.

Table 2.6.1 shows the results of these studies regarding their effects on accidents.

*Table 2.6.1: Effects on accidents of winter maintenance measures*

| | Percentage change in the number of accidents | | |
|---|---|---|---|
| Accident severity | Type of accident affected | Best estimate | 95% Confidence interval |
| ***Increasing standard of maintenance by one class throughout the whole winter season*** | | | |
| Injury accidents | All accidents | −12 | (−14; −10) |
| Property damage only accidents | All accidents | −30 | (−32;−29) |
| ***Introduction of salting throughout the whole winter season*** | | | |
| Injury accidents | All accidents | −15 | (−22; −7) |
| Property damage only accidents | All accidents | −19 | (−39; +6) |
| ***Cessation of salting throughout the whole winter season*** | | | |
| Injury accidents | All accidents | +12 | (−4; +30) |
| Property damage only accidents | All accidents | +1 | (−15; +21) |
| ***Increased maintenance preparedness (more rapid deployment) throughout the winter*** | | | |
| Unspecified | All accidents | −8 | (−14; −1) |
| ***Salting-effect first 24 h after measure*** | | | |
| Unspecified | All accidents | −24 | (−42; 0) |
| Unspecified | All accidents | −35 | (−59; +3) |
| ***Sanding-effect first 24 h after measure*** | | | |
| Unspecified | All accidents | −62 | (−85; −5) |
| ***Increasing length of road protected by snow screens from 0% to 50%*** | | | |
| Unspecified | Accidents in mountains | −11 | (−24; +6) |

In all Nordic countries, public roads are divided into ***maintenance classes*** based on traffic volume and the importance of the road in the transport system. A distinction is made between three or four maintenance classes. In the highest maintenance classes, the standards for winter maintenance are stricter than for the lower maintenance classes. Increasing maintenance standards by one class was found to reduce the number of injury accidents by around 10% and the number of property damage only accidents by around 30%. The fact that there is a greater reduction in the number of property damage only accidents than in the number of injury accidents is due to the fact that winter driving appears to increase the risk of property damage only accidents more than the risk for personal injury accidents (Hvoslef 1976).

***Introducing salting*** reduces the number of accidents. If salting is stopped, the number of accidents increases. The earliest studies of salting (Väg- och Vattenbyggnadsstyrelsen 1972, Andersson 1978, Vejdirektoratet 1979) did not find any effect of this measure on accidents. Later studies (Öberg et al. 1985, Öberg, Gustafson and Axelson 1991,

Nilsson and Vaa 1991, Kallberg 1993, Sakshaug and Vaa 1995) have shown that salting reduces the number of accidents. At least two explanations for this development can be imagined. First, salting methods have improved over time. In a Norwegian before-and-after study (Sakshaug and Vaa 1995), no decrease in the number of accidents on roads where salting began before 1988 could be found. On roads where salting began after 1988, however, the number of accidents went down. Second, the very first studies evaluating salting, in particular the Finnish study in 1972 (Väg- och Vattenbyggnadsstyrelsen 1972), were carried out on roads with no speed limits. Speed limits must be assumed to inhibit the tendency of drivers to increase speed when friction is improved.

In a Swedish study (Björketun 1983), the effects on accidents of ***increased maintenance preparedness*** were studied. Two forms of increased preparedness were implemented on selected roads during the night between 0300 and 0700 h. One method was to allow a salting vehicle to patrol the road during this time period. The other was a surveillance system where surveillance personnel monitored weather and road surface forecasts particularly closely. Both methods reduced the number of accidents. Seen as a whole, increased preparedness reduces the number of accidents (injury and property damage only accidents), calculated over a 24-h period, by 8%. The surveillance method was associated with a 30% reduction in accidents in the period monitored (0300–0700 h), whereas the patrol car was associated with a 23% reduction in accidents on the patrolled roads during the patrol period. During the rest of the day, these measures had little or no effect on the number of accidents.

***Salting, snow clearance and sanding*** appear to have a significant effect on the number of accidents during the first 24 h after the measures are implemented. However, the results are very uncertain. There is reason to believe that the effect of sanding decreases strongly over time since the sand is blown away by passing cars. A Swedish study (Öberg 1978) found that sanding produced an increase in the friction coefficient of around 0.1 from a baseline level of around 0.2–0.3 Speed increased on average by 2.4 km/h. Nonetheless, a net reduction in the calculated stopping distance of around 8 m (corresponding to about 10% reduction) was achieved. After some 300 cars had passed, most of the sand had blown away from the carriageway. The effect on friction and stopping distances thus disappeared. This shows that sanding must be repeated frequently in order to maintain the effect on roads with heavy traffic.

An American study (Tabler and Furnish 1982) of a high mountain pass, where the road was exposed to snowdrifts, shows that the number of accidents (injury and property damage only accidents) during strong winds and snow drift was reduced by around 10% when 50% of the road was protected by snow screens. The estimate of the effect on accidents is very uncertain. The road studied was particularly exposed to snowdrifts.

Any effects of regression to the mean in the number of accidents were not controlled for. It is therefore uncertain how valid the results of this study are.

**Effect on mobility**

Winter maintenance of roads has a major effect on mobility (Table 2.6.2.). Good mobility is the main objective of the majority of winter maintenance measures. A number of studies have evaluated how different winter maintenance measures affect speed. An overview of the results of these studies is given below:

These studies indicate that winter maintenance measures increase the average speed of traffic by up to 7 km/h. The increase in speed depends on how large improvements in friction are as a result of the measures. During snowy weather, speed is reduced greatly, by 10–15 km/h (Ruud 1981, Möller, Wallman and Gregersen 1991, Sakshaug and Vaa 1995). The distances between cars are also greater in snowy weather (Ruud 1981, Möller, Wallman and Gregersen 1991).

During poor weather and with poor road surface conditions, road users may choose to cancel or delay a journey they otherwise would have made. Different studies have come to somewhat conflicting results with regard to the extent of such behaviour. A Swedish study concluded that traffic volume was 1–5% lower when a road was covered with snow than when the same road was bare. Another Swedish study (Möller, Wallman and Gregersen 1991) where variations in the amount of traffic over a 24-h period were studied found no indication that the number of motor vehicles was reduced during snowy weather. However, the number of cyclists was extremely sensitive to weather conditions. Norwegian studies have found that between 6% and 9% of all drivers stated that they had cancelled or postponed one or more journeys by car during the winter because of snow or ice (Gabestad, Amundsen and Skarra 1988).

*Table 2.6.2: Effects of winter maintenance on speed*

| Study | Measure studied | Speed limit (km/h) | Changes of average speed (km/h) |
|---|---|---|---|
| Öberg (1978) | Sanding | Not stated | +2.4 |
| Ruud (1981) | Salting | 80 | +5.1 |
| Öberg (1981) | Snow clearance | 90 | +2.0–7.0 |
| Öberg et al. (1985) | Salting | Not stated | +0.0–2.0 |
| Öberg, Gustafson and Axelsson (1991) | Salting | 90 | +2.3–5.9 |
| Sakshaug and Vaa (1995) | Salting | 80 | +4.0 |

*Table 2.6.3: Effects on environmental factors of salting*

| Study | Measure | Environmental factor | Effect found |
|---|---|---|---|
| Bäckman (1980) | Salting | Groundwater | Increased salt content |
| | | Soil | Salt content increased by a factor of 4–10 |
| | | Vegetation | Damage to spruce trees |
| Öberg et al. (1985) | Salting | Wear and tear on roads | Increase of 70% |
| | | Spray | Increase of 60–120% |
| | | Corrosion | Rust formation 3–5 times higher |
| Öberg, Gustafson and Axelsson (1991) | Salting | Groundwater | Salt content 2–8 times higher |
| | | Soil | Salt content 2–5 times higher |
| | | Vegetation | Dead trees increased by 750% |
| | | | Healthy trees reduced by 50% |
| | | Corrosion | Rust corrosion increased by circa 100% |

## Effect on the environment

Winter maintenance measures, especially salting, can have a number of effects on the environment. The overview given below (Table 2.6.3) summarises the effects on environmental factors of salting, which have been found.

Salting roads greatly increases the salt content in groundwater and in soil near the road. Damage to vegetation, in particular spruce trees, on streets has been found due to increased salt content in soil and water, combined with salt-containing spray on trees close to the road. Salting roads increases the wear and tear on roads, largely due to traffic driving on wet bare roads. Wear and tear from studded tyres on wet dry roads is approximately twice as large as on dry bare roads. Salt corrodes concrete structures, which can particularly affect bridges (Öberg et al. 1985). On salted roads, increased costs for bridge maintenance are to be expected. Salt also contributes to increased rust on cars. The effect is difficult to isolate since many factors affect rust formation on cars. Studies of untreated steel plates, which have been exposed to salt water spray in the course for a winter season, found that rust formation is three to five times as great. On cars treated for rust, the effect is smaller, approximately a doubling of rust formation.

Many road users are critical of salting roads. In a Norwegian roadside survey carried out in the winter of 1992–93 (Holt 1993), 65% of road users stated that they were totally or partially against a statement that 'salting is desirable', 35% were completely or partially in agreement with the statement, 19% considered increased salting to be very important or somewhat important and 64% felt that it was unnecessary or less important.

*Table 2.6.4: Costs of winter maintenance per kilometre of road for different types of road in Norway*

| | NOK per kilometre road for different road types in Norway 1995 prices | | |
|---|---|---|---|
| Maintenance task | Rural road AADT 2,000 | Urban road AADT 7,000 | Motorway AADT 25,000 |
| Snow clearance | 4,200 | 9,200 | 18,300 |
| Salting* | | 14,200 | 15,300 |
| Other winter maintenance | 9,500 | 14,500 | 2,900 |
| Sum maintenance | 13,700 | 37,900 | 36,500 |

*Roads with an AADT less than 2,000 are normally not salted.

### Costs

In 1995, a total of NOK 673 million was used for winter maintenance of national highways in Norway. The cost per kilometre of various winter maintenance operations calculated on the basis of a cost model developed by the Norwegian Public Roads Administration (Statens vegvesen handbook 140, part IIB 1995, Elvik 1996) is shown in Table 2.6.4.

The cost of winter maintenance of roads varies depending on the amount of traffic on the road, the degree of urbanisation, maintenance standards and whether the road is salted or not.

### Cost–benefit analysis

A Norwegian analysis (Gabestad and Ragnøy 1982) examined 10 different strategies in winter maintenance of roads, as well as different regulations of the use of studded tyres. The strategies were evaluated on the basis of their effect on costs to road users and to the road authorities. Road user costs included were costs of accidents, travel time, fuel, corrosion, studded tyres and loss of benefit from cancelled journeys. The costs to the road authorities included were costs of re-asphalting, road markings, washing signs, increased bridge maintenance and sanding and salting. One strategy was a ban on studded tyres combined with increased salting. The strategy was calculated to give an annual net saving of between NOK 74 and 111 million, depending on which roads are being salted. The strategy gave a net reduction in costs for the road authorities, since the reduction in costs of re-asphalting clearly exceeded the increased costs of sanding and salting. For road users, the strategy only gave a net saving if all roads with an annual average daily traffic of over 1,000 vehicles were salted (where the climate made this possible). A similar strategy where a ban on studded tyres was combined with increased sanding gave a calculated annual net saving of between NOK 169 and 190 million. This strategy was estimated to give net savings both for road users and for road authorities. For road users, the greatest difference in relation to the salting strategy is that increased corrosion costs were avoided. On the contrary, sanding was assumed to have less effect on accidents than salting, so that the accident costs in the sanding strategy were higher than with the salting strategy. A strategy where a ban on use of studded tyres was combined with improved snow and ice clearance standards was calculated to give an annual net saving of NOK 147 million. The strategy produced savings both for road users and road authorities. A strategy where salting and sanding were assumed to cease, while current use of studded tyres continued, gave a calculated annual saving of NOK 164 million. The saving was largely due to reduced corrosion costs.

In Sweden, costs and benefits involved in stopping salting were calculated on the basis of the results of a study where salting of specific roads was stopped as an experiment (Öberg et al. 1985). The benefits of stopping road salting included reductions of corrosion, car washing, wear and tear on roads and costs for bridge maintenance. The disadvantages of stopping salting roads consisted of an increased number of accidents, increased journey time and increased costs of other winter maintenance. The benefits of stopping salting were calculated at NOK 5,932 million. The reduced corrosion costs comprised 97% of this figure. The cost of stopping salting was calculated at NOK 4,349 million. Of this, increased accident costs comprise 93%. The benefit of stopping salting was somewhat greater than the costs. Both of the items that contributed the most to the results of the analysis were, however, highly uncertain. The decrease in corrosion was estimated at between SEK 2.7 and 7.94 million SEK with 5.75 million SEK as the best estimate. Changes in accident costs varied from 1,635 million in savings to SEK 6,625 million increases with SEK 4,065 million increase as best estimate. This shows the uncertainty of knowledge about the effects of salting.

In a Norwegian study, winter maintenance on the outer ring road in Trondheim was stepped up (Eriksen and Vaa 1994). The effect on accidents was studied and it was estimated that the saved accident costs exceeded the costs of the measure by a factor of 70. Any gain for mobility was not included in this report. Increased salting was an important part of the increased maintenance strategy. Possible increased corrosion costs due to salting were not included in the analysis. In a later report on the increased winter maintenance on the outer ring road in Trondheim, Norway (Vaa 1996), the benefit of the measure during the course of one winter was estimated to be NOK 5,327,000 in saved accident costs. The cost of the measure was estimated to be NOK 117,000. Effects on mobility and environmental conditions were not included in this analysis.

It is difficult to draw general conclusions on the basis of the cost–benefit analyses discussed above. None of the studies described above take into account the effects of salting on the environment.

In order to give an impression of the costs and benefits of current winter maintenance in Norway, a numerical example has been prepared for national highways. The national highway network is divided into four winter maintenance classes. Roads of the highest class (class 1) are salted throughout the winter and cleared to the highest snow clearance standard. Roads of the lowest class (class 4) are only cleared to the lowest standard. Table 2.6.5 shows the assumptions made in the cost–benefit analysis.

On the basis of these assumptions, annual costs and benefits of current maintenance standards in different maintenance classes are given in Table 2.6.6. The numerical example indicates that the benefits of current winter maintenance standards are greater than the costs for the majority of national highways. It is emphasised that the environmental costs of salting roads are not included in the calculation. The environmental costs include damage to trees and plants near the road and pollution of ground water. When these costs are included, the benefit of the maintenance standard in class 1 and class 2 will be reduced.

*Table 2.6.5: Assumptions for calculating costs and benefits of current winter maintenance in different maintenance classes in Norway*

| Factor | Class 1 | Class 2 | Class 3 | Class 4 |
|---|---|---|---|---|
| Road length (km) | 5,000 | 3,000 | 12,000 | 6,000 |
| Annual average daily traffic (typical value) | 7,000 | 3,500 | 1,500 | 600 |
| Injury accidents per million vehicle kilometres | 0.16 | 0.19 | 0.22 | 0.25 |
| Property damage only accidents per injury accident | 20 | 18 | 16 | 14 |
| Maintenance standards effect on injury accidents | −15% | −12% | −10% | −5% |
| Maintenance standards effect on property damage only | −35% | −30% | −20% | −15% |
| Average vehicle speed kilometre per hour | 64 | 63 | 62 | 61 |
| Maintenance standards effect on speed level | +4 | +3 | +2 | +1 |
| Maintenance standards effect on vehicle operating costs | −0.04 | −0.03 | −0.025 | −0.02 |
| Corrosion costs per car per kilometre driven (salting)[1] | 0.10 | 0.03 | 0.00 | 0.00 |
| Increased road maintenance costs million NOK per kilometre road per year (sign washing, road surface renewal, bridge maintenance [2] | 10,000 | 3,000 | | |
| Costs of winter maintenance per kilometre road per year | 35,000 | 29,000 | 22,000 | 14,000 |

[1]Corrosion costs per kilometre driven based on Ragnøy (1996).
[2]Calculated on the basis of Elvik 1996.

*Table 2.6.6: Costs and benefits of current winter maintenance standards for national highways in Norway*

| Factor | Annual amount in million NOK | | | |
|---|---|---|---|---|
| | Class 1 | Class 2 | Class 3 | Class 4 |
| Saved accident costs (+) | 470 | 132 | 192 | 24 |
| Saved costs of travel time (+) | 1,175 | 276 | 336 | 36 |
| Saved vehicle operating costs (+) | 510 | 114 | 168 | 24 |
| Increased corrosion costs (−) | 1,280 | 114 | 0 | 0 |
| Increased road maintenance costs (−) | 50 | 10 | | |
| Total benefits | 825 | 398 | 696 | 84 |
| Budget costs for implementing the measure | 175 | 87 | 264 | 84 |
| Opportunity cost of public funds | 35 | 17 | 53 | 16 |
| Total costs | 210 | 104 | 317 | 100 |

## 2.7 Winter maintenance of pavements, footpaths, cycle paths and other public areas

### Problem and objective

Official Norwegian road accident statistics are limited to accidents where at least one vehicle is involved. Injury recording systems at Norwegian hospitals and accident and emergency departments (Ragnøy 1985b, Lund 1989, Hagen 1990, Borger 1991, Guldvog, Thorgersen and Ueland 1992) show that a larger number of injury accidents involve pedestrian falls. Estimates of the number of falls among pedestrians range from 17,750 in 1990 (Borger 1991) to 37,370 in the same year (Elvik 1991) and 32,000 in 1991 (Guldvog, Thorgersen and Ueland 1992). The difference between these figures is probably due to different definitions of the accidents included, as well as different methods of estimating the national figure based on data from the National Institute for Public Health (SIFF). Nonetheless, it is clear that the number of falls involving personal injury, no matter what the definition, is higher than the official number of injuries that occur in all traffic accidents that are reported to the police (around 11,00–12,000 per year).

Around 75% of falls occur during the months of November, December, January and February. Many falls incurred by pedestrians are due to slippery conditions. Snow and ice was stated as the cause for 35% of falls recorded in the SIFF register of injuries in 1985–86, looking at the year as a whole (Lund 1989). A record of falls at the Oslo Accident and Emergency Clinic, Norway for the winter of 1983–84 showed that 83% of accidents occurred on snow or ice-covered ground (Ragnøy 1985b). A corresponding study in Drammen in Norway in 1988 (Hagen 1990) indicates that the percentage was the same. Winter maintenance of streets, pavements, footpaths and cycle paths and other pedestrian areas thus may potentially affect the number of falls during the winter significantly.

Many cycle accidents may also be related to the standard of winter maintenance of public roads and streets in Norway (Hvoslef 1994). Nonetheless, slippery conditions are stated less frequently as the cause of cycle accidents than for pedestrian falls since cycling has a different distribution over the year than walking.

Inadequate winter maintenance of footpaths and cycle paths can indirectly lead to an increase in the number of traffic accidents where pedestrians or cyclists are hit by motor vehicles, since pedestrians and cyclists choose to use areas designed for cars when they feel it is less slippery to travel there than in areas specifically designated for walking and cycling. The number of accidents occurring in this way is not known.

Winter maintenance of pavements, footpaths and cycle paths and other pedestrian areas is intended to make these traffic areas just as attractive to use in winter as areas for car traffic, by ensuring that pedestrians and cyclists have the best possible friction in all weather conditions.

### Description of the measure

Winter maintenance of pavements, footpaths, cycle paths and other pedestrian areas (bus stops, crossings, etc.) includes snow clearance and snow removal, sanding or salting and heating pavements to prevent snow from freezing and sticking to the pavement.

### Effect on accidents

Only one study has been found that has evaluated the effects of improved winter maintenance measures on accidents involving falls (Möller, Wallman and Gregersen 1991). The study involved a residential area of the town of Skellefteå in Sweden, where winter maintenance was intensified by means of increased snow clearance and sanding. The study found that the number of accidents involving falls *increased* by 57% after the winter maintenance was stepped up (95% CI [+1; +145]). This shows that the increased winter maintenance was not sufficient to improve conditions in pedestrian areas. The percentage of snow and ice-covered areas was not reduced. It cannot be ruled out that the pedestrian areas became even *more slippery* after snow clearance increased. This can be blamed on the fact that the underside of the snowplough may have glazed the surface, which was cleared (Möller, Wallman and Gregersen

1991). The researchers recommend snow clearance of pedestrian areas with a 'ridged' plough, not one that is smooth on the underside.

Other studies can indirectly indicate the *potential* effects on the number of falls of reducing the amount of snow and ice-covered pedestrian areas. A Swedish study (Möller, Wallman and Gregersen 1991) shows that the risk to pedestrians of falling is significantly higher in snow and icy conditions than on bare areas. The risk to pedestrians of falling in snowy and icy conditions when compared with bare pedestrian areas was studied during three winters in Gothenburg and Skellefteå (Möller, Wallman and Gregersen 1991). In Gothenburg, pedestrians ran five times the risk of falling on snow or ice compared with bare ground. The percentage of pedestrian traffic on snow or ice during the three winters varied between 14% and 34%. In Skellefteå, the risk to pedestrian's risk of falling on snow or ice was 7–10 times higher than on bare ground. The percentage of pedestrian traffic on snow or ice-covered ground during the three winters varied between 88% and 95%.

On the basis of figures from Oslo, Gothenburg and Skellefteå, it is estimated that a reduction of pedestrian traffic in snow and ice by 10% may lead to a reduction in falls by 15% (95% CI [−22; −7]). A total removal of snow and ice may reduce pedestrian falls in winter by 52% (95% CI [−62; −39]). The study in Skellefteå ((Möller, Wallman and Gregersen 1991) indicates that it is difficult to remove snow and ice for pedestrian areas simply through snow clearance and sanding. The most effective measure for complete removal of snow and ice from pedestrian areas is probably through heating such areas (Hagen 1990).

**Effect on mobility**

Snow and ice in pedestrian areas reduce accessibility for pedestrians. Many choose to remain indoors instead of going out when it is snowy or icy. In a survey of some 500 inhabitants above the age of 67 in Oslo in the winter of 1983–84 (Ragnøy 1985b), 72% said that they went out less often in the winter than in the summer. Slippery pavements were the reason given most often for this. Around 45% of those questioned would like to go out more often in winter than they in fact do. About one-third stated that they had to have help to do errands out of doors during the winter.

**Effect on the environment**

No studies have been found that show the effect on the environment of better winter maintenance of pedestrian areas. Sand must be swept away in the spring. This may cause temporary local dust problems. Salt brought into the house must be washed out.

### Costs

If it is assumed that a pavement is cleared of snow on average 10 times during the winter and is sanded about 5 times, the total costs of winter maintenance of pavements in Norway can be estimated at NOK 580 million per year (Hagen 1995). This corresponds to a cost of around NOK 10,000 per kilometre of pavement per year.

### Cost–benefit analysis

The costs of 1,210 falls among pedestrians in Oslo during the winter of 1983–84 were calculated to be NOK 2.3 million (Ragnøy 1985b). Corresponding costs of 240 falls in Drammen, Norway in 1988 were calculated at between NOK 14 and 16 million (Hagen 1990). None of the calculations include a monetary valuation of the loss of welfare in the event of traffic accidents. On the basis of the calculations for Drammen, the total costs in Norway for falls in winter conditions are estimated to be in the order of magnitude of NOK 800–900 million (Hagen 1990).

In a more recent Norwegian calculation, Hagen (1995) has estimated the costs of falls where pedestrians slip or stumble to be around NOK 880 million or more. If a rough estimate of the loss of welfare as a result of these accidents is included, the costs are in the region of NOK 1.670 million per year.

Normal snow clearance does not appear to reduce the number of pedestrian falls. Heating the pavement can, however, be a good alternative. In winters, when there is plenty of snow and frequent snow clearance and sanding are required, it is no more expensive to have heated pavements than to clear snow and to sand. A reallocation of resources from snow clearance and sanding to heating can have a favourable effect on the number of injuries. However, as yet we do not know the optimal mix of heating pavements and other forms of winter maintenance. The variation in the amount of pedestrian traffic is important in such discussions.

## 2.8 Correcting erroneous traffic signs

### Problem and objective

In order for traffic signs to function appropriately, a number of conditions must be fulfilled: The signs must be located so that they are easy to see and readable both in daylight and in the dark, understandable and taken seriously by the road users, and must be enforced in order to prevent violations. In order to ensure that traffic signs are used in accordance with these conditions, the Norwegian government has issued guidelines for the design, location and use of traffic signs. Standards for maintenance of traffic signs have also been established (Statens vegvesen, Handbook 111, 1994a, 1994b). However, studies suggest that these guidelines are not always implemented in practice. A survey of the condition and maintenance of traffic signs (Amundsen 1986) found that 32% of 6,484 signs surveyed were damaged. There was also damage to 19% of signposts. The survey also found that many older road signs had poor reflective properties, i.e. they were difficult to read in the dark.

A study of 731 road signs on eight sections of road in Norway (Ragnøy, Vaa and Nilsen 1990) found that there were faults on 60% of the signs. A distinction was made between the following types of error (percentage of errors in brackets):

1. Location: sign is placed at a position so that it is not easily visible, at the wrong height or too close to other road signs (30%).
2. Design: sign was of the wrong size, wrong text or the wrong colour (27%).
3. Repetition: sign was wrongly placed in relation to crossroads or other signs that must be repeated (4%).
4. Lack of correspondence with road markings (2%).
5. Wrong use of sign or a poor combination of signs (9%).
6. Too many signs, a sign is not necessary, or is repeated too many times (19%).
7. Lack of road sign (9%).

Corresponding studies in the other Nordic countries (Vaa et al. 1990, Muskaug 1995) showed that there were faults in 45% of traffic signs in Finland, 15% of all traffic signs in Denmark and 14% of the traffic signs in Sweden.

Erroneous traffic signs and deficient maintenance of signs can lead to signs being missed or misunderstood. Depending on the type of sign concerned, this may lead to dangerous behaviour such as speeding, ignoring yield rules, driving against the permitted direction of traffic or illegal parking. Correcting erroneous traffic signs is intended to ensure that road signs and maintenance of signs corresponds with the guidelines laid down by the authorities so that the signs function as intended.

**Description of the measure**

The Norwegian regulations concerning the use of traffic signs (Statens vegvesen, Handbook 050, 1987) give guidelines for the design, location and use of individual traffic signs. For a number of signs, for example, stop signs at cross roads, detailed guidelines are given for the use of the sign in order to ensure that the sign is used so restrictively that road users take it seriously. The regulations also indicate who has the authority to set up traffic signs. The meaning of the signs is explained in the Road Traffic Act, and related legislation. Standards for maintenance of signs are given in maintenance standards for the Norwegian Public Roads Administration (Statens vegvesen handbook 111, 1994a, 1994b). Each year, thousands of traffic signs are replaced along public roads in Norway as part of the maintenance procedure. The signs are washed several times a year, at least along the roads where traffic is heaviest.

**Effects on accidents**

Only one study has been found on the effect on accidents of improving incorrect road signs. This is an American study (Lyles, Lighthizer, Drakopoulus and Woods 1986) of upgrading the highway signs in towns so that they correspond to the American *Manual on Uniform Traffic Control Devices* (MUTCD). The study found that improvements to make traffic signs conform to the MUTCD led to a 15% decrease in the number of injury accidents (lower 95% limit 25% decrease, upper 95% limit 3% decrease). Property damage only accidents were reduced by 7% (lower 95% limit 14% decrease, upper 95% limit 0.3% decrease). The authors of the study incorrectly conclude that upgrading substandard signs do not reduce the number of accidents, on the basis of an inadequate statistical analysis of the data.

Since only one study has been carried out, the result should be interpreted with caution, since it is not known how representative it is. The study does not report which different types of errors in traffic signs were corrected and how serious these errors were.

**Effect on mobility**

No studies have been found about the effects on mobility of correcting erroneous traffic signs.

**Effect on the environment**

No studies have been found that show the effects on the environment of correcting defective traffic signs.

## Costs

It is estimated that the capital value of the 1.1 million signs erected along public roads in Norway is around NOK 2 thousand million (Amundsen 1986). In 1993, the costs of erecting and maintaining traffic signs and road markings were as follows:

| | Costs in million NOK (1993) | |
|---|---|---|
| Type of work | National highways | County highways |
| Erecting traffic signs | 42.2 | 2.5 |
| Erecting delineator posts | 1.9 | 0.0 |
| Road markings | 150.0 | 18.6 |
| Replacing and maintaining signs | 60.3 | 13.2 |
| Replacing delineator posts | 8.1 | 0.1 |
| Washing signs etc | 2.6 | 0.3 |
| Sum all measures | 265.1 | 34.7 |

The average cost of replacing a traffic sign in Norway is around NOK 1,500–3,000. The costs per kilometre for washing signs depends on traffic volume and whether the road is salted or nor. The costs are highest on roads with heavy traffic and that are salted.

## Cost–benefit analysis

No cost–benefit analyses of correcting erroneous traffic signs have been found. On the basis of the information given above, a numerical example can be made that indicates possible effects of the measure. It is assumed that correcting erroneous traffic signs can be carried out at a cost of NOK 10,000 per kilometre of road. It is assumed that the measure is implemented on a national highway in a town with an annual average daily traffic of 6,000 and 0.40 injury accidents per million vehicle kilometre. The number of injury accidents is assumed to go down by 15% and the number of property damage only accidents by 7%. The effect of the measure is assumed to last for 5 years. The benefit will be around NOK 1.24 million per kilometre of road, which is more than 100 times the cost of the measure. Correcting erroneous traffic signs is, in other words, very cost-effective, even if the effect on accidents were to be considerably smaller, or the costs considerably higher than assumed in this example.

## 2.9 Traffic control at roadwork sites

### Problem and objective

Increasing traffic and the resultant wear and tear on roads increase the need for maintenance and improvement work on public roads if a reduction in the road standard is to be avoided. The majority of roadworks have to be carried out while the road is open to traffic. This leads to disadvantages for road users and can increase the accident rate. Roadworks personnel who have to work in direct proximity to the traffic are particularly exposed.

A number of studies have evaluated how roadworks affect the accident rate (Graham, Paulsen and Glennon 1978, Nemeth and Migltez 1978, MacLean 1979, Kemper, Lum and Tignor 1984, Summersgill 1985, Marlow and Coombe 1989, Garber and Hugh Woo 1991). Most studies found that accident rates are higher in work zones. However, the results vary substantially, and not all studies found large of significant increases in accident rates (Jin et al. 2008, Khattak, Khattak and Council 2002). As regards injury severity, results are inconsistent. Although some studies found more severe accidents in work zones, other studies found less severe accidents and others found no difference in accidents between roads with and without work zones (Garber and Zhao 2002).

There are likely to be differences depending on the type and location of the work zones. For example, Daniel, Dixon and Jared (2000) found more severe accidents in construction work zones, rather than maintenance work zones. More severe accidents were also found when work zones are idle compared with accidents occurring in work zones in progress (Daniel, Dixon and Jared 2000), and at night compared with during daytime (Arditi, Lee and Polat 2007, Garber and Zhao 2002). Study results are quite inconsistent as to where in a work zone most accidents occur, but most studies found the greatest proportions of accidents in the activity area (Garber and Zhao 2002).

The types of accidents that are most over-represented at work zones are rear-end collisions (Garber and Zhao 2002). Increases were also found for head-on collisions, sideswipe and collisions with fixed objects, whereas side impacts and road departure accidents were found to be reduced in work zones; in general, the proportion of multi-vehicle accidents is greater at work zones than on other roads (Graham, Paulsen and Glennon 1978, Khattak, Khattak and Council 2002). Common factors are congestion (rear-end collisions), restricted lane width, construction equipment and uneven road surface (Tsyganov, Machemehl and Harrison 2003)

A consistent system for traffic control at roadwork sites can increase the safety for roadworkers and reduce the accident rate for road users. Traffic control at roadworks is intended to safeguard and protect roadworkers and road users, direct traffic past the roadworks with the minimum amount of delay and inconvenience and to allow an effective progression of the roadworks.

## Description of the measure

Traffic control at roadwork sites encompasses all measures for warning of and protecting roadworks on existing roads. Normally, a number of measures are used in combination that depend on the road standard, level of speed, traffic volume and the nature of the work.

***Temporary traffic control*** may use several different options such as temporary speed limits, traffic signals at areas where only one driving lane can be used at a time, temporary road markings, cones or reflective blocks to direct traffic into new temporary lanes, manual traffic direction when the road area is too narrow for traffic in both directions, flagging to warn of roadworks, cordoning off the work area with barriers or work at night in order to reduce the problems for traffic.

***Road closure***. Closing a road makes it possible to carry out roadworks without interruptions from passing traffic. This gives the best possible safety conditions for roadworkers, since all risk from passing traffic is removed. At the same time, road closure can make it possible to carry out roadworks more effectively. Road closure where no diversion routes are available can only be used for short-term work.

***Diversions.*** In cases of both road closure and roadworks that greatly reduce road capacity, it is necessary to direct traffic to temporary diversions in order to avoid major delays.

***Marking of machinery.*** Yellow flashing warning lights can only be used when ordinary rules of the road cannot apply and only when they are necessary to prevent an unacceptable hazard. This means during work with snow clearance, sanding and salting, as well as when lorries or machinery used in roadworks must stop or be parked on the road, if they are parked in such a way that they represent a particular hazard to other traffic or where the vehicle or machinery is wider than 2.5 m.

***Personal safety equipment***. Roadworkers must use orange work clothes with reflectors sewn onto them. During poor weather and light conditions, a protective vest must also be used. The protective vests must be fluorescent orange with good retro-reflection. The use of protective clothing makes the workers more visible.

**Effect on accidents**

***Traffic control***. In an American study (Garber, Hugh Woo 1991), the accident rate during roadworks was compared for different types of warning and safety measures that comprise cordoning off the roadworks, reduced speed limits, arrows and flagging. According to the study, more stringent traffic control at roadworks appears to reduce accidents on two-lane roads by 40% (95% CI [−65; −5]). On multi-lane roads, a significant increase of the number of injury accidents by 70% (95% CI [+55; +90]) was found. The study does not offer any explanation for these results. Driving patterns on multi-lane roads past roadworks may be more complicated than on two-lane roads.

***Temporary road markings***. Temporary road markings can lead to speed reductions. In the United States, the use of cones combined with warnings about roadworks led to an average reduction in speed of 7% (Richards, Wunderlich and Dudek 1985). Such a reduction implies a reduction in the expected number of injury accidents of around 15% (see Section 3.9, *speed limits*).

***Flagging***. A study has shown that the average speed when flagging takes place was reduced by 19% (Richards, Wunderlich and Dudek 1985). Such a reduction implies a reduction in the expected number of injury accidents of around 40% (see Section 3.9, *speed limits*).

***Closing traffic lanes***. Three studies have been reported in which the number of accidents is compared when traffic on class A motorways is redirected to full contra flow (i.e. right over to the opposite carriageway, which is narrowed down and used by traffic in both directions) in relation to partial contra flow (i.e. where only part of the opposite carriageway is taken into use) (Summersgill 1985, Marlow and Coombe 1989, Burns, Dudek and Pendleton 1989). Best estimates of the effect on accidents of full contra flow in relation to partial contra flow on the basis of these studies are given in Table 2.9.1.

Driving in full contra flow when compared with partial contra flow reduces the number of accidents at roadworks by about 20%. Possible explanations for this may be that full contra flow forces drivers to reduce speed more than partial contra flow, increases alertness and creates less chance of confusing traffic lanes than partial contra flow. Table 2.9.1 also shows the result of a study into how separate traffic lane changes in connection with contra flow work in relation to mixed lane changes (Summersgill 1985). Separate lane change means that traffic on each lane of the class A motorway is re-directed towards the opposite carriageway without it being possible to change lanes in the transition area. With mixed lane changing, it is possible to change lanes even in

*Table 2.9.1: Effects on accidents of traffic control at roadworks on motorways*

| | Percentage change in the number of accidents | | |
|---|---|---|---|
| Accident severity | Type of accident affected | Best estimate | 95% Confidence interval |
| ***Transition from partial to full contra flow*** | | | |
| Injury accidents | Accidents at roadworks | −23 | (−28; −17) |
| Property damage only accidents | Accidents at roadworks | −23 | (−28; −18) |
| ***Segregated vs. mixed lane changes on motorways*** | | | |
| Injury accidents | Accidents at roadworks | +35 | (+5, +75) |

the transition area towards the opposite carriageway. According to the study, segregated lane changes result in poorer road safety than mixed lane changing. The study does not give any explanation for this result.

A Swedish study (Nygaard and Pettersson 1982) found that a reduction in speed past roadworks on a motorway was 20 km greater when traffic was first directed into the right lane and thereafter through a speed-reducing curve before the roadworks, compared with conventional narrowing.

***Work at night***. Two studies found that accident rates at work zones increased more at night than during daytime (Summersgill 1985, Ullman, Ullman and Finley 2006), and several studies found that accidents at work zones are more severe at night than during daytime (Arditi, Lee and Polat 2007, Garber and Zhao 2002). However, there may be differences between work zones at night and during daytime, e.g. nighttime work periods usually involve more lane closures than daytime work periods. Even if accident rates increase at night, the total number of accidents will depend on the amount of traffic at night and during the day.

***Personal protective equipment***. Retro-reflective personal safety garments were found to increase conspicuity and detection distances for pedestrians in work zones, although the effects became smaller in complex surroundings (Sayer and Mefford 2004, Sayer and Buonarosa 2008).

No studies were found of the effects on accidents of traffic signals, manual traffic control, cordoning off roadworks and marking of machinery. The effects on accidents of temporary diversion routes depends on whether the diversion routes can carry traffic at a lower accident rate than the accident rate along the road where the roadworks are taking place.

### Effect on mobility

Scandinavian studies found that speed limits of under 50 km/h have little effect on the level of speed past roadworks. Physical measures such as rumble strips or narrower traffic lanes were found to be important for the speed level (Pettersson 1978, Eikanger 1983).

In the United States, it has been shown that flagging has a major effect on speed levels. The average speed was reduced by 19% (Richards, Wunderlich and Dudek 1985). Using cones reduces the average speed by 7%.

### Effect on the environment

The effect on noise, pollution and subjective safety of the measures described in this chapter are not known. At very low driving speeds, the emission of poisonous gases from cars can increase. This may be a problem for roadworkers who are working close to the source of the emissions.

### Costs

The cost of traffic control at roadwork sites depends on which measure is implemented and which equipment is used. In Norway, a traffic sign costs around NOK 1,000–2,000, but can normally be used again. A vehicle-activated, mobile traffic signal system using radars as detectors costs about NOK 84,000 (old estimate), whereas a normal mobile system costs around NOK 44,000 (old estimate).

### Cost–benefit analysis

It is not known how many accidents occur in connection with roadworks and how serious these are. It is therefore impossible to know how great the benefits of traffic control at roadwork sites are. Measures reducing the speed of passing vehicles can lead to fewer and less serious accidents. On the contrary, reduced speeds delay traffic. A numerical example can indicate possible effects of roadwork warnings.

It is assumed that the road has an annual average daily traffic of 2,300 vehicles (about average for national highways) and an accident rate of 0.25 injury accidents per million vehicle kilometre. Roadworks warnings are assumed to reduce this risk by 40%. The speed is assumed to go down from 66 to 61 km/h. The roadworks are assumed to last for 1 month. Warning measures are assumed to cost NOK 10,000.

The saved accident costs are calculated to be NOK 19,000 and increased travel time costs to be NOK 9,000. Thus, the net benefit is NOK 10,000, which is the same as the cost of the measure. On roads with more traffic than assumed in this example, it may be cost-effective to implement more comprehensive warning of roadworks than assumed in the example.

## References


Adam, V. & S. C. Shah. (1974). Evaluation of Open-Graded Plant-Mix Seal Surfaces for Correction of Slippery Pavements. *Transportation Research Record*, **523**, 88–96.

Al-Masaeid, H. R. (1997). Impact of pavement condition on rural road accidents. *Canadian Journal of Civil Engineering*, **24**, 523–531.

Al-Masaeid, H. R., Sinha, K. C. & Kuczek, T. (1993). Evaluation of safety impact of highway projects. *Transportation Research Record*, **1401**, 9–16.

Amundsen, F. H. (1983). *Trafikkulykker og kjøreatferd på mørke og lyse vegdekker*. TØI-notat 654. Transportøkonomisk institutt, Oslo.

Amundsen, F. H. (1986) *Trafikkskiltenes tilstand og vedlikehold. En gjennomgang av trafikkskiltenes betydning og vedlikeholdsmessige standard*. Rapport. Transportøkonomisk institutt, Oslo.

Andersson, K. (1978). *Kemisk halkbekämpning. Effekt på trafikolyckor*. VTI-rapport 145. Statens väg- och trafikinstitut (VTI), Linköping.

Anund, A. (1992). *Vägytans inverkan på fordonshastigheter*. VTI-meddelande 680. Väg- och TrafikInstitutet (VTI), Linköping.

Arditi, D., Lee, D. E. & Polat, G. (2007). Fatal accidents in nighttime vs. daytime highway construction work zones. *Journal of Safety Research*, **38**, 399–405

Arnberg, P. W. (1976). *Fordons hastigheter och sidaccelerationer före och efter ytandbehandling av grusvägar*. VTI-rapport 112. Statens väg- och trafikandinstitut (VTI), Linköping.

Bertilsson, S. (1987). *Trafiksäkerhetseffekter av Vägverkets vinterhållningsåtgärder 1972–1985*. Publikasjon 1987:55. Statens Vägverk, Borlänge.

Björketun, U. (1983). *Försök med förbättrad vinterberedskap. Analys av inträffade trafikolyckor*. VTI-rapport 248. Statens väg- och trafikinstitut (VTI), Linköping.

Bonnot, J. (1997). French experience of porous asphalt. *Proceedings of second European conference on porous asphalt*, Madrid, March 12–14, 1997.

Borger, A. (1991). *Underrapportering av trafikkulykker*. TØI-notat 975. Transportøkonomisk institutt, Oslo.

Brailly, M. C. Porous macadam and road safety. In *VTI-konferens 10A, Part 7, 9th International Conference Road Safety in Europe*, Bergisch-Gladbach, September 21–23, 1998.

Brodsky, H. & A. S. Hakkert (1988). Risk of a road accident in rainy weather. *Accident Analysis and Prevention*, **20**, 161–176.

Brudal, H. (1961). *Vegdekkers ruhet. Fortsatt forskning*. Rapporter og diskusjon i forandbindelse med Nordisk Vegteknisk Forbunds utvalg for bituminøse bindemidler og belegningers møte i Norge 18–20 oktober 1960. Meddelelse 13. Statens vegvesen, Veglaboratoriet, Oslo.

Brüde, U. & J. Larsson. (1980). *Samband vintertid mellan väderlek-väglag-trafikolyckor. Statistisk bearbetning och analys*. VTI-rapport 210. Statens väg- och trafikinstitut (VTI), Linköping.

Burgè, P. L., Travis, K. & Rado, Z. (2001). *A comparison of transverse tined and longitudinal diamond ground pavement texturing for newly constructed concrete pavement*. Transportation research Board.

Burns, E. N., C. J. Dudek & O. J. Pendleton. (1989) *Construction Costs and Safety Impacts of Work Zone Traffic Control Strategies, Volume II: Informational Guide*. FHWA-RD-89-210. Federal Highway Administration, Georgetown Pike.

Burns, J. C. (1981). Roughness and Roadway Safety. *Transportation Research Record*, **836**, 8–14.

Bäckman, L. (1980). *Vintervägsaltets miljöpåverkan*. VTI-rapport 197. Statens väg- och trafikinstitut (VTI), Linköping.

Cairney, P. (2006). *Road Surfacing Revisited* – a new look at an old countermeasure. ARRB.

Cairney, P. & Styles, E. (2005). *A pilot study of the relationship between macrotexture and crash occurence*. Road Safety Research Report CR223. ARRB Transport Research Victoria, Australia.

Caliendo, C., Guida, M. & Parisi, A. (2007). A crash-prediction model for multilane roads. *Accident Analysis & Prevention*, **39**, 657–670.

Carlsson, G. (1978). *Ytbehandling av grusvägar. Uppföljning av friktion, hastigheter och sidoläge efter ett år*. VTI-meddelande 98. Statens väg- och trafikandinstitut (VTI), Linköping.

Carlsson, G. & G. Öberg. (1977). *Ytbehandling av grusvägar. Trafik- och friktionsstudier*. VTI-rapport 119. Statens väg- och trafikinstitut (VTI), Linköping.

Cleveland, D. E. (1987). Effects of Resurfacing on Highway Safety. In: *Relationship Between Safety and Key Highway Features, A Synthesis of Prior Research*, 78–95. State of the Art Report 6, Transportation Research Board, Washington DC.

Commandeur, J.J.F.; Bijleveld, F.D.; Braimaister, L.G.; Janssen, S.T.M.C. (2002). *De analyse van ongeval-, weg-, en verkeerskenmerken van de Nederlandse rijkswegen.* Report R-2002-19. Leidschendam, SWOV Institute for Road Safety Research.

Cooper, D. R. C., P. G. Jordan & J. C. Young. (1980). *The effect on traffic speeds of resurfacing a road.* TRRL Supplementary Report 571. Transport and Road Research Laboratory, Crowthorne, Berkshire.

Christensen, P. & Ragnøy, A. (2006). *Vegdekkets tilstand og trafikksikkerhet (The condition of the road surface and safety).* TØI Report 840/2006. Oslo: Transportøkonomisk institutt.

Daniel, J., Dixon, K. & Jared, D. (2000). Analysis of fatal crashes in Georgia work zones. *Transportation Research Record*, **1270**. Washington: TRB, National Research Council.

Davies, R. B., Cenek, P. D. & Henderson, R. J. (2005). The effect of skid resistance and texture on crash risk. *International Surface Friction Conferencem Christchurch*, New Zealand. http://www.surfacefriction.org.nz/.

Dearinger, J. A. & J. W. Hutchinson. (1970). *Cross Section and Pavement Surface. Chapter 7 of Traffic Control and Roadway Elements - Their Relationship to Highway Safety.* Revised Edition. Highway Users Federation for Safety and Mobility, Washington DC.

DeSilva, H. (2001). *Road safety benefits of improved skid resistance: a valuation procedure.* ARRB Transport Research Conference. Melbourne, Victoria.

Drakopolous, A. & Kuemmel, D. A. (2007). *Wet pavements crash study of longitudinal and transverse tined pavement.* Report WHRP 07-04. Madison: University of Wisconsin.

Eikanger, M. (1983). *Hastighetsmålinger ved asfalteringsarbeid.* Arbeidsdokument av 22.7.1983 (prosjekt O-1005, revisjon arbeidsvarsling). Transportandøkonomisk institutt, Oslo.

Elvik, R. (1991). *Hva koster ulykkene samfunnet?* Rapport 100. Transportandøkonomisk institutt og Skadeforebyggende Forum, Oslo.

Elvik, R. (1996). *Enhetskostnader for veg- og trafikktekniske tiltak.* Arbeidsdokument TST/0722/96. Transportøkonomisk institutt, Oslo.

Elvik, R. & Greibe, P. (2005). Road safety effects of porous asphalt: a systematic review of evaluation studies. *Accident Analysis and Prevention,* **37**, 515–522.

Eriksen, T. & T. Vaa. (1994). *Bedre vintervedlikehold gir færre ulykker. Resultater fra prøveprosjekt på Ytre Ringveg.* Rapport STF63 A94009. SINTEF Samferdselsteknikk, Trondheim.

Gabestad, K. O. (1988). *Føreforholdsbeskrivelse. Føreforholdsbegreper i Norden.* TØI-notat 839. Transportøkonomisk institutt, Oslo.

Gabestad, K. O., F. H. Amundsen & N. Skarra. (1988). *Trafikantatferd på vinterføre. En undersøkelse av biltrafikantenes tilpasning av reiseomfang og reisetidspunkt.* Rapport 10. Transportøkonomisk institutt, Oslo.

Gabestad, K. O. & A. Ragnøy. (1982). *Samfunnsøkonomiske konsekvenser i vinterandvedlikeholdet.* Sammendrag. Rapport. Transportøkonomisk institutt og Vegdirektoratet, Oslo.

Gallaway, B. M., Benson, F. C., Mounce, J. M., Bissell, H. H. & Rosenbaum, M. J. (1982). *Pavement Surface. Chapter 2 of Synthesis of Safety Research Related to Traffic Control and Roadway Elements.* Volume 1. Report FHWA-TS-82-232. US Department of Transportation, Federal Highway Administration, Offices of Research, Development, and Technology, Washington DC.

Garber, N. J. & T.-S. Hugh Woo. (1991). Effectiveness of Traffic Control Devices in Reducing Accident Rates at Urban Work Zones. *Transportation Quarterly*, **45** (2), 259–270.

Garber, N. J. & Zhao, M. (2002). *Crash characteristics at work zones.* Report VTRC 02-R12. Virginia Transportation Research Council.

Geedipally, S. R. (2005). *Analysis of traffic accidents before and after resurfacing -a statistical approach.* Examensarbete Linköpings universitet, Tekniska högskolan.

Gothie, M. (2001). Could adherence and road geometry be used to identify the areas of risk? *International Conference Traffic safety on Three Continents*, Moskva.

Graham, J. L., R. J. Paulsen & J. C. Glennon. (1978). Accident Analyses of Highway Construction Zones. *Transportation Research Record*, **693**, 25–32.

Guldvog, B., A. Thorgersen & Ø. Ueland. (1992). *Ulykker, vold og selvpåført skade. Personskaderapport.* Rapport nr 1/92. Seksjon for forebyggende og helseandfremmende arbeid. Statens Institutt for Folkehelse, Oslo.

Hagen, K-E. (1990). *Økonomisk vurdering av fotgjengerfall på vinterføre i Drammen.* Rapport 64. Transportøkonomisk institutt, Oslo.

Hagen, K-E. (1995). Gateulykker - et forsømt område for ulykkesforebygging i Norge? I: *Kostnader til skadeforebygging.* Innlegg presentert på seminar på Vettre Hotell, Asker, 28. og 29. august 1995, 15–22. (Elvik, R.; Lund, J. eds). TØI-notat 1012. Transportøkonomisk institutt, Oslo.

Hankins, K.D., Morgan, R.B., Ashkar, B., Tutt, P.R. (1971). Influence of Vehicle and Pavement Factors on Wet-Pavement Accidents. *Highway Research Record*, **376**, 66–84.

Hanley, K.E., Gibby, A.R. & Ferrara, T.C. (2000). Analysis of accident reduction factors on California state highways. *Transportation Research Record*, **1717**, 37–45.

Harwood, D. W., Rabbani, E. R. K., Richard, R., McGee, H. W. & Gittings, G. L. (2003). *Systemwide impact of safety and traffic operations design decisions for 3R projects*. NCHRP Report 486.

Hatcher, C. W. (1974). Grooving streets and highways can help stop skid crashes. *Traffic Engineering*, **April**, 14–15.

Hatherly, L. W. & D. R. Lamb. (1971). Accident prevention in London by road surface improvements. *Traffic Engineering and Control*, **12**, 524–529.

Hatherly, L. W. & A. E. Young. (1977). The Location and Treatment of Urban Skidding Hazard Sites. *Transportation Research Record*, **623**, 21–28.

Hauer, E., D. Terry & M. S. Griffith. (1994). Effect of Resurfacing on Safety of Two-Lane Rural Roads in New York state. *Transportation Research Record*, **1467**, 30–37.

Herbst, G. H. & Holzhammer, C. (1995). Performance of porous asphalts on Austrian motorways. *Proceedings of XXth world road congress*, Montreal.

Hegmon, R. R. (1987). Tire-Pavement Interaction. *Public Roads*, **51**, 1, 5–11.

Holt, A. G. (1993) *Undersøkelse av vegvedlikehold og kjøreforhold-vinteren 1992/93*. Rapport STF63 A93008. SINTEF Samferdselsteknikk (Utgitt av Vegdirektoratet, Driftsavdelingen). Trondheim.

Hudson, K. C. & Mumm, P. (2003). Six years of calcined bauxite. *ARRB Transport Research Conference*. Cairns, Queensland.

Hvoslef, H. (1976). *Vegsalting og trafikksikkerhet*. TØI-notat 238, revidert utgave mars 1976. Transportøkonomisk institutt, Oslo.

Hvoslef, H. (1994). *Syklistulykker i Norge. Hva er problemet?* Notat 30.94.853. Revidert 23.3.1994. Statens vegvesen, Vegdirektoratet, Trafikksikkerhetsandkontoret, Oslo.

Ihs, A., Velin, H. & Wicklund, M. (2002). *Vägytans inverkan på trafiksäkerheten. Data från 1992–1998*. VTI meddelande 909.

Ivey, D. L., Keese, C.J.; Neill, A.H.; Brenner, C. (1971). Interaction of Vehicle and Road Surface. *Highway Research Record*, **376**, 40–53.

Ivey, D.L. Griffin, L.I.; Newton, T. M.; Lytton, R.L. (1981). Predicting wet weather accidents. *Accident Analysis and Prevention*, **13**, 83–99.

Jin, T.G., Saito, M. & Eggett, D.L. (2008). Statistical comparisons of the crash characteristics on highways between construction time and non-construction time. Accident Analysis and Prevention, 40, 2015–2023.

Kallberg, V-P. (1993). *Teiden suolauksen vähentämiskokeilu Kuopion tiepiirissä. Vaikuandtukset talvella 1992–1993*. Tielaitoksen selvityksIä 86/1993. Tielaitos, Liikenteen palvelukeskus, Helsinki.

Kallberg, V-P. (1996). Experiment with reduced Salting of Rural Main Roads in Finland. *Transportation Research Record*, **1533**, 32–37.

Karan, M. A., R. Haas & R. Kher. (1976). Effects of Pavement Roughness on Vehicle Speeds. *Transportation Research Record*, **602**, 122–127.

Karr, J. I. (1972). *Evaluation of minor improvements-part 8, grooved pavements. Final Report.* Report CA-HY-TR-2151-4-71-00. Diviandsion of Highways, Sacramento, CA, California.

Kemper, W. J., H. S. Lum & S. C. Tignor (1984). The Safety of Narrow Lanes for Traffic Control at a Construction Site. *Public Roads*, **47 (4)**, 119–124.

Khattak, A.J., Khattak, A.J. & Council, F.M. (2002). Effects of work zone presence on injury and non-injury crashes. *Accident Analysis and Prevention*, **34**, 19–29.

Kielland, J. B. (1988). *Kostnad og nytte av drensasfalt. En eksempelstudie for hovedvegnettet i Sarpsborg/Fredrikstad-området.* Statens Forurensningsandtilsyn, Oslo.

Kolsrud, B. & G. K. Nilsson. (1983). *Belägging av grusvägar med Y1G.* VTI-meddelande 282. Statens väg- och trafikinstitut (VTI), Linköping.

Leden, L. & O. Hämäläinen. (1994). The effect of resurfacing on friction, speeds and safety on main roads in Finland. Paper submitted to *Accident Analysis and Prevention*, draft 11.11.

Leden, L., Hämäläinen, O. & Manninen, E. (1998). The effect of resurfacing on friction, speeds and safety on main roads in Finland. *Accident Analysis and Prevention,* **30**, 75–85.

Leden, L. & M. Salusjärvi. (1989). *Trafiksäkerhet och vägytans egenskaper (TOVE). Samband mellan beläggningens ålder och trafiksäkerheten.* VTT meddelanden 1076. Statens Tekniska Forskningscentral (VTT), Esbo.

Lie, D. A. (1981). *Salting og ulykker. En undersøkelse av saltingens betydning for ulykandkestallet. For perioden 1974–1980.* Statens vegvesen, Vegdirektoratet, Oslo.

Lund, J. (1989). *Nasjonal ulykkes- og skadestatistikk. Oversikt over ulykkes- og skadeandmønsteret i Norge basert på ett års skadedata ved sykehusene/legeandvaktene i Harstad, Trondheim og Stavanger 1/7 1985–30/6 1986.* Rapport fra Skadeandregisteret nr 4–1989. Statens Institutt for Folkehelse, Oslo.

Lyles, R.W.; Lighthizer, D.R.; Drakopoulus, A.; Woods, S. (1986). Efficacy of Jurisdiction-Wide Traffic Control Device Upgrading. *Transportation Research Record*, **1068**, 34–41.

Maclean, A. D. (1979). *M6 reconstruction 1976: two-way traffic using narrow lanes.* TRRL Supplementary Report 474. Transport and Road Research Laboratory, Crowthorne, Berkshire.

Mahone, D. C. & S. N. Runkle. (1972). Pavement Friction Needs. *Highway Research Record*, **396**, 1–11.

Marlow, M. & R. D. Coombe (1989). *A study of the safety of major motorway roadworks in 1987.* Research Report 223. Transport and Road Research Laboratory, Crowthorne, Berkshire.

Miller, M. M. & Johnson, H. D. (1973). *Effects of resistance to skidding on accidents: surface dressing on an elevated section of the M4 motorway*. Transport and Road Research Laboratory Report LR 542.

Möller, S. (1988). *Beräkning av olyckskvot vid olika väglag med hjälp av schabloner*. VTI-meddelande 584. Statens väg- och trafikinstitut (VTI), Linköping.

Möller, S., C-G. Wallman & N. P. Gregersen. (1991). *Vinterväghållning i tätort-trafikandsäkerhet och framkomlighet*. TFB og VTI forskning/research 2, 1991. Transportforskningsberedningen, Stockandholm.

Muskaug, R. (1995). Trafikkskilting i Norden. Situasjonsbeskrivelse og grunnlag for framtidig forenkling og harmonisering. *TemaNord* 1995, 547. Nordisk Ministerråd, København.

Nelson English, Loxton & Andrews Pty Ltd. (1988). *An analysis of the relationship between road improvements and road safety*. Report CR 75.

Nemeth, Z. A. & D. J. Migletz (1978). Accident Characteristics Before, During and After Safety Upgrading Projects on Ohio's Rural Interstate System. *Transportation Research Record*, **672**, 19–24.

Nilsson, B. & T. Vaa. (1991). *Salting og trafikksikkerhet. Forprosjekt*. Rapport STF63 A91013. SINTEF Samferdselsteknikk, Trondheim.

Noyce, D. A., Bahia, H. U., Yambo, J. M. & Kim, G. (2005). *Incorporating road safety into pavement management. maximizing asphalt pavement surface friction for road safety improvements*. Midwest Regional University Transportation Center Traffic Operations and Safety TOPS Laboratory.

Nygaard, B. & H.-E. Pettersson (1982). *Effektmätning av ny metod för körfältsreduktion vid vägarbete på motorvägar*. VTI-meddelande 275. Statens väg- och trafikinstitut, Linköping.

Oxley, J., Corben, B., Koppel, S., Fildes, B., Jacques, N., Symmons, M. & Johnston, I. (2004). *Cost-effective infrastructure measures on rural roads*. MUARC Report 217.

Parry, A.R. & Viner, H.E. (2005). *Accidents and the skidding resistance standard for strategic roads in England*. Report TRL 622. Berkshire, UK: Transport Research Laboratory.

Pettersson, H-E. (1978). *Utvärdering av en hastighetsreducerande anordning i vägbanan i samband med vägarbete på Essingeleden*. VTI-meddelande 146. Statens väg- och trafikinstitut, Linköping.

Ragnøy, A. (1985a). *Vintervedlikeholdsprosjektet. Vegtrafikkulykker om vinteren*. Rapport. Transportøkonomisk institutt og Vegdirektoratet, Oslo.

Ragnøy, A. (1985b). *Gangtrafikk på vinterføre i Oslo. Kan vintervedlikeholdet hjelpe?* Rapport. Transportøkonomisk institutt, Oslo.

Ragnøy, A. (1986). *Bremsing og ulykker*. TØI-notat 806. Transportøkonomisk institutt, Oslo.

Ragnøy, A. (1989). *Trafikksikkerhet og drensasfalt.* Arbeidsdokument TST/0143/89. Transportøkonomisk institutt, Oslo.

Ragnøy, A. (1996). *Bilkorrosjon, omfang og kostnader. Litteraturstudie.* Arbeidsand-dokument TST/0769/96. Transportøkonomisk institutt, Oslo.

Ragnøy, A., T. Vaa & R. H. Nilsen (1990). *Skilting i Norge. Resultater fra registrering og evaluering av 8 vegstrekninger i Østlandsområdet.* TØI-notat 945. Transandpor-tøkonomisk institutt, Oslo.

Richards, S. H., R. C. Wunderlich & C. L. Dudek (1985). Field Evaluation of Work Zone Speed Control Techniques. *Transportation Research Board,* **1035**, 66–77.

Rizenbergs, R. L., J. L. Burchett & Napier, C. T. (1973). *Accidents on rural interstate and parkway roads and their relation to pavement friction.* Report 377. Division of Research, Kentucky Bureau of Highways, Lexington, KY.

Rizenbergs, R. L., J. L. Burchett & L. A. Warren (1976). *Accidents on rural, two-lane roads and their relation to pavement friction.* Report 443. Division of Research, Kentucky Department of Highways, Lexington, KY.

Roe, P., Webster, D. & West, G. (1991). *The relation between the surface texture of roads and accidents.* Transport Road Research Laboratory. Research Report 296

Ruud, H. H. (1981). *Kjørefart på saltede og usaltede veger. Målinger i Akershus og Vestfold 1980 og 1981.* Rapport. Transportøkonomisk institutt, Oslo.

Sakshaug, K. & T. Vaa. (1995). *Salting og trafikksikkerhet. Del 1: Før-etterundersøkels av saltingens effekt på personskadeulykker.* Rapport STF63 A95003. SINTEF Samferdselsteknikk, Trondheim.

Samferdselsdepartementet. (1989). *Stortingsmelding 32, 1988–89.* Norsk veg- og vegtrafikkplan 1990–93. Oslo.

Satterthwaite, S. P. (1976). An assessment of seasonal and weather effects on the frequency of road accidents in California. *Accident Analysis and Prevention,* **8**, 87–96.

Sayer, J. R. & Buonarosa, M. L. (2008). The roles of garment design and scene complexity in the daytime conspicuity of high-visibility safety apparel. *Journal of Safety Research,* **39**, 281–286.

Sayer, J. R. & Mefford, M. L. (2004). High visibility safety apparel and nighttime conspicuity of pedestrians in work zones. *Journal of Safety Research,* **35**, 537–546.

Schandersson, R. (1981). *Samband mellan vägbeläggningar och trafikolyckor 1977.* VTI-meddelande 242. Statens väg- och trafikinstitut (VTI), Linköping.

Schandersson, R. (1986). *Samband mellan trafikolyckor, väglag och vinterväghållning-sandåtgärder. En pilotstudie av olycksriskens nivå timmerna före och efter åtgärd.* VTI-meddelande 483. Statens väg- och trafikinstitut (VTI), Linköping.

Schandersson, R. (1988). *Samband mellan trafikolyckor, väglag och vinterväghållningsandåtgärder. Olycksrisker vid olika mängd snönederbörd.* VTI-meddelande 514. Statens väg- och trafikinstitut (VTI), Linköping.

Schandersson, R. (1989). *Trafiksäkerhet och vägytans egenskaper (TOVE). En underandsökning av belaga vägar med olika yttilstånd baserad på data från fyra nordiska länder 1982–1986.* VTI-meddelande 594. Statens väg- och trafikinstitut (VTI), Linköping.

Schulze, K-H., A. Gerbaldi & J. Chavet. (1977). Skidding accidents, friction numbers and the legal aspects involved. Report of the PIARC Technical Committee on slipperiness and evenness. *Transportation Research Record*, **623**, 1–10.

Sliwa, N. (2003). *BASt safety study of porous asphalt.* Unpublished data forwarded to the Institute of Transport Economics.

Souleyrette, R., Kamyab, A., Knapp, K.K., Khattak, A., Basavaraju, R. & Storm, B. (2001). *Systematic identification of high crash locations.* Final Report. Iowa State University, Center for Transportation Research and Education.

Spinoglio, S. (2003). *Performance of Italgrip sections.* Unpublished data forwarded to the Institute of Transport Economics.

Start, M. R., J. Kim, & W. D. Berg. (1996). Development of safety-based guidelines for treatment of pavement rutting. In: *Proceedings of the Conference Road Safety in Europe and Strategic Highway Research Program (SHRP)*, Prague, the Czech Republic, September 20–22, 1995, **No 4A**, **Part 5**, 79–98. Swedish National Road and Transport Research Institute, Linköping.

Statens vegvesen. (1987). *Normaler. Skiltnormaler. Tekniske bestemmelser og retningslinjer for offentlige trafikkskilt, vegoppmerking og trafikklysandsignaler.* Håndbok 050. Statens vegvesen, Oslo.

Statens vegvesen. (1994a). *Retningslinjer. Vedlikeholdsstandard. Minimum prosesskode for riksveger.* Håndbok 111. Statens vegvesen, Oslo.

Statens vegvesen. (1994b). *Vegdata. Driftsregnskap. Driftsstatistikk 1993.* Håndbok 056. Statens vegvesen, Oslo.

Statens vegvesen. (1995). *Håndbok 140. Konsekvensanalyser. Del IIB. Metodikk for beregning av prissatte konsekvenser.* Brukerveiledning for EFFEKT 5. Vegdirektoratet, Oslo.

Statens vegvesen (2005). Handbook 115 Analyse av ulykkessteder. Oslo. Statens vegvesen.

Storeheier, S. Å. (1996). Vegdekke. I: *Miljøhåndboken*, 276–278. (Kolbenstvedt, M., H. Silborn & T. Solheim eds): Transportøkonomisk institutt, Oslo.

Storeheier, S. Å. (2000). Vegdekke. I: Kolbenstvedt, M.; Silborn, H.; Solheim, T.: *Miljøhåndboken*, 276–278. Oslo, Transportøkonomisk institutt.

Strathman, J.G., Duecker, K.J., Zhang, J., Williams, T. (2001). *Analysis of design attributes and crashes on the Oregon highway system.* Report FHWA-OR-RD-02-01.

Summersgill, I. (1985). *Safety performance of traffic management at major roadworks on motorways in 1982.* TRRL Research Report 42. Transport and Road Research Laboratory, Crowthorne, Berkshire.

Sælensminde, K. (2002) Støysvake vegdekker bør prøves ut også i Norge. *Samferdsel*, **10**, 24–25.

Sävenhed, H. (1994). Relation between Winter Road Maintenance and Road Safety. VTI-särtryck 214. Reprint from *Technical Report IXth PIARC International Road Congress*, March 21–25, 1994, Seefeld, Austria. Väg- och transportandforskningsinstitutet (VTI), Linköping.

Tabler, R. D. & R. P. Furnish. (1982). Benefits and Costs of Snow Fences on Wyoming Interstate 80. *Transportation Research Record*, **860**, 13–20.

Thurmann-Moe, T. (1976). *Vegdekkers friksjonsforhold på sommerføre. En utredning fra Veglaboratoriet.* Internrapport 692. Statens vegvesen, Veglaboratoriet, Oslo.

Thurmann-Moe, T. & S. Dørum. (1980). *Lyse vegdekker.* Meddelelse 22. Statens vegvesen, Veglaboratoriet, Oslo.

Tredrea, P. (2001). *Relationships between surface texture & accidents for selected rural and urban roads.* ARRB Transport Research Ltd Contract Report.

Tromp, J. P. M. (1993). *Verkeersveiligheid en drainerend asfaltbeton (ZOAB) (Road safety and drain asphalt (ZOAB)).* Report R-93-35. Leidschendam, SWOV institute for road safety research.

Tsyganov, A., Machemehl, R. & Harrison, R. (2003). *Complex work zone safety.* Report FHWA/TX-03/4021-3.

Tøndel, I. (1977). *Sikring av veger mot snøskred.* Avhandling til lic techn graden. Meddelelse nr 17 fra Institutt for veg- og jernbanebygging. Norges Tekniske Høgskole, Trondheim.

Ullman, G.L., Ullman, B.R. & Finley, M.D. (2006). *Analysis of Crashes at Active Night Work Zones in Texas.* Transportation Research Board 2006 Annual Meeting CDROM. National Research Council, Washington, DC.

Vaa, T. (1995). *Salting og trafikksikkerhet. Del 2: sammenligning av ulykkesfrekvens på saltet og usaltet vegnett. Saltingens effekt på kjørefart.* Rapport STF63 A95004. SINTEF Samferdselsteknikk, Trondheim.

Vaa, T. (1996). *Bedre vintervedlikehold gir færre ulykker. Resultater fra prøveprosjekt på Ytre Ringveg sesongene 1993/94, 1994/95 og 1995/96.* Rapport STF22 A96613. SINTEF Bygg- og miljøteknikk, Samferdsel, Trondheim.

Vaa, T., Beilinson, L., Helmers, G. et al. (1990). *Registrering av faktisk skiltbruk i Norden. Resultater fra registrering og evaluering av 32 vegstrekninger i Danmark, Finland, Norge og Sverige.* Rapport 69. Transportøkonomisk institutt, Oslo.

Vejdirektoratet (1979). *Samfundsøkonomisk analyse af anvendelsen af vejsalt i vinterandvedligeholdelsen*. Rapport fra projektgruppe M. Vejdirektoratet, Vejregelsekretariatet, København.

Viner, H., Sinhal, R. & Parry, T. (2005). Review of United Kingdom skid resistance policy. *Roads*, **326**, 66–77.

Väg- och Vattenbyggnadsstyrelsen. (1972). *Försöket osaltad väg. Slutrapport*. Väg- och Vattenbyggnadsstyrelsen, Helsinki.

Wallman, C.-G. & Åström, H. (2001). *Friction measurement methods and the correlation between road friction and traffic safety*. VTI meddelande 911A.

Wong, S-Y. (1990). Effectiveness of Pavement Grooving in Accident Reduction. *ITE Journal*, **July**, 34–37.

Zipkes, E. (1977). The Influence of Grooving of Road Pavements on Accident Frequency. *Transportation Research Record*, **623**, 70–75.

Öberg, G. (1978). *Effekter av sandning. Trafik- och friktionsstudier*. VTI-rapport 164. Statens väg- och trafikinstitut (VTI), Linköping.

Öberg, G. (1981). *Friktion och reshastighet på vägar med olika vinterväghållning*. VTI-rapport 218. Statens väg- och trafikinstitut (VTI), Linköping.

Öberg, G. (1994). Effekter av saltning och punktsaltning på gator. *TemaNord* 1994, 511. Nordisk Ministerråd, København.

Öberg, G., K. Gustafson & L. Axelson. (1991). *Effektivare halkbekämpning med mindre salt. MINSALT-projektets huvudrapport*. VTI-rapport 369. Statens väg- och trafikinstitut (VTI), Linköping.

Öberg, G., Arnberg, R.W., Carlson, G., Helmers, G., Jutengren, K. & Land, P-G. (1985). *Experiments with unsalted roads. Final report*. VTI-rapport 282A. Swedish Road and Traffic Research Institute (VTI), Linköping.

# 3.

# Traffic Control

## 3.0 Introduction and overview of 22 measures

This chapter covers the effects of 22 traffic control measures on accidents, mobility and the environment. The 22 measures are

3.1 Area-wide traffic calming
3.2 Environmental streets
3.3 Pedestrian streets
3.4 Urban play streets
3.5 Access control
3.6 Priority control
3.7 Yield signs at junctions
3.8 Stop signs at junctions
3.9 Traffic signal control at junctions
3.10 Signalised pedestrian crossings
3.11 Speed limits
3.12 Speed-reducing devices
3.13 Road markings
3.14 Traffic control for pedestrians
3.15 Stopping and parking control
3.16 One-way streets
3.17 Reversible traffic lanes
3.18 Bus lanes and bus stop design
3.19 Dynamic route guidance

**The Handbook of Road Safety Measures**

**ISBN: 978-1-84855-250-0**

3.20 Variable message signs
3.21 Protecting railway-highway level crossings
3.22 Environmental zones

This introductory section describes the essential elements in current knowledge of the effects of these measures on accidents, mobility and the environment. The emphasis is on describing effects on accidents. The main elements in current knowledge of costs and cost–benefit analyses are also described.

**Amount and quality of research**

The amount of the research evaluating the effects of traffic control measures on accidents is indicated by the number of studies of the individual measures, the number of results of the studies and the sum of the statistical weights in meta-analyses of studies of the effects on accidents. Table 3.0.1 shows the indices of the amount of research that has evaluated the effects of traffic control measures on accidents.

Table 3.0.1 shows that traffic signal control at intersections and speed limits are the traffic control measures for which there are most studies evaluating effects on accidents. Other measures that have been studied extensively include area-wide traffic calming, speed-reducing devices, road markings and traffic control for pedestrians and cyclists. These measures have been evaluated based on relatively large numbers of accidents. Measures where the basis is less comprehensive are reversible traffic lanes, environmental streets, urban play streets, pedestrian streets, dynamic route guidance and variable message signs (VMS). In summarising knowledge of the effects of the measures on accidents, meta-analyses have been used for all measures except dynamic route guidance.

The quality of the studies that have evaluated the effects of traffic control measures on accidents varies. For the majority of measures, the method by which study locations were sampled is not described in detail. This probably means that most studies rely on convenience samples, i.e. locations for which data happened to be available, and which were of interest for the study. This sampling technique does not ensure that the results are statistically representative of a known population or the road system in general. Speed limits are an exception to this pattern. In many cases, the effects of speed limits have been studied for an entire country, which ensures that results are representative for the road network under consideration.

The great majority of studies are based on official accident records. This means that incomplete accident reporting may have influenced the results. However, no examples

*Table 3.0.1: The amount of research evaluating the effects of traffic regulating measures on accidents*

| Measure | Number of studies | Number of results | Sum of statistical weights | Results last updated |
|---|---|---|---|---|
| 3.1 Area-wide traffic calming | 33 | 76 | 8,728 | 1997 |
| 3.2 Environmental streets | 11 | 62 | 457 | 2004 |
| 3.3 Pedestrian streets | 6 | 6 | 87 | 1997 |
| 3.4 Urban play streets | 4 | 9 | 145 | 1997 |
| 3.5 Access control | 7 | 39 | 7,424 | 1997 |
| 3.6 Priority control | 6 | 18 | 2,559 | 1997 |
| 3.7 Yield signs at junctions | 14 | 46 | 2,109 | 1997 |
| 3.8 Stop signs at junctions | 15 | 63 | 1,757 | 1997 |
| 3.9 Traffic signal control at junctions | 60 | 225 | 53,687 | 1997 |
| 3.10 Signalised pedestrian crossings | 21 | 69 | 1,511 | 2009 |
| 3.11 Speed limits | 51 | 245 | 167,431 | 2004 |
| 3.12 Speed-reducing devices | 32 | 202 | 4,912 | 2004 |
| 3.13 Road markings | 57 | 175 | 52,310 | 2006 |
| 3.14 Traffic control for pedestrians | 38 | 119 | 2,677 | 2009 |
| 3.15 Stopping and parking control | 13 | 71 | 7,060 | 1997 |
| 3.16 One-way streets | 5 | 147 | 7,863 | 1997 |
| 3.17 Reversible traffic lanes | 5 | 16 | 1,567 | 2008 |
| 3.18 Bus lanes and bus stop design | 13 | 79 | 6,116 | 1997 |
| 3.19 Dynamic route guidance | 2 | – | – | 2009 |
| 3.20 Variable message signs | 13 | 38 | 1,026 | 2009 |
| 3.21 Protecting railway-highway level crossings | 20 | 40 | 7,584 | 2009 |
| 3.22 Environmental zones | 0 | 0 | – | 2004 |

of studies have been found that show if and how incomplete accident reporting has affected the results.

Experimental study designs ensure that all confounding factors are controlled. Experimental studies have been made to evaluate the effects of speed limits and road markings on accidents. Good quasi-experimental studies have been made of area-wide traffic calming and signal-controlled pedestrian crossings. Apart from this, most studies do not control very well for confounding factors. Results may also be affected by regression to the mean.

A characteristic of most forms of traffic control is that they are local, that is, they apply to a given crossroads, a city quarter or another clearly defined part of the road network. It has been suggested that traffic control measures do not solve problems, but merely move them elsewhere. Only a very few studies of the effects of traffic control measures on accidents have probed for this possible effect. In the majority of cases, the effects have only been studied at the locations where a specific type of traffic control has been introduced.

Traffic control measures are intended to change road user behaviour. The greater the change in behaviour, the greater the expected changes in the number of accidents. Such dose–response relationships have been studied for a number of traffic control measures including environment streets, speed limits and speed-reducing measures. Relatively clear dose–response patterns have been found for all these measures. The more the speed reduction, the greater is the reduction in the number of accidents. The more the speed increases, the greater is the increase in the number of accidents, especially the number of serious accidents.

The extent to which study results can be explained varies greatly. More detailed information on road user behaviour will, in many cases, lead to a better explanation of the study results. For example, the available results indicate that marking a pedestrian crossing, without any other measures, leads to more pedestrian accidents. It is not unlikely that the explanation for this can be found in behavioural changes among road users. Pedestrians may become less careful when crossing the road and the car drivers may not become correspondingly more considerate. More detailed information on pedestrian and driver behaviour is needed in order to explain why this measure does not appear to have the intended effect on accidents.

**Main elements in effects on accidents**

Traffic control measures have varying effects on the number of accidents. Measures that have been found to reduce the number of accidents are area-wide traffic calming, environmental streets, pedestrian streets, urban play streets, access control, stop signs at junctions, traffic signal control at junctions, signalised pedestrian crossings, reduced speed limits, speed-reducing devices, parking regulations, bus stop bays, some VMS, variable feedback signs and protecting railway-highway level crossings. However, some of the results may be affected by regression to the mean.

Measures that do not have statistically significant effects on the number of accidents include priority control, yield signs at intersections, most forms of road markings, some traffic control measures for pedestrians and cyclists, one-way streets and reversible lanes.

Measures that appear to lead to an increased number of accidents are flashing yellow traffic signals and permission to turn right on a red signal, increased speed limits, marking pedestrian crossings without using other measures and bus lanes.

It may seem that traffic control measures primarily intended to increase mobility or improve traffic flow do not necessarily reduce the number of accidents. Such measures include increased speed limits, right turn on red and reversible traffic lanes. On the other hand, traffic control measures that reduce speed or otherwise simplify the road users' tasks (e.g. lower speed limits, traffic signals) often appear to lead to fewer accidents.

**Main elements in effects on mobility**

The choice of traffic control measures is always a compromise between mobility and traffic safety. Other considerations, such as accessibility, environmental conditions and costs also influence choices.

Traffic control measures that improve mobility are priority control of roads (for road users on priority roads, which normally have the heaviest traffic), traffic signal control at junctions with heavy traffic, increased speed limits, stopping and parking control (for road users who do not need to stop or park), one-way streets, reversible traffic lanes, bus lanes (for public transport services) and, probably, dynamic route guidance.

Measures reducing mobility include lower speed limits, speed-reducing devices, variable feedback signs for speed and protecting railway-highway level crossings (for road users). A number of measures increase mobility for some road users but may reduce it for others. These include, for example, area-wide traffic calming, yield signs at junctions, traffic signal control at pedestrian mid-block crossings and a number of control measures for pedestrians and cyclists. Other measures have little or no effect on mobility.

**Main elements in the effects of the measures on the environment**

The effects of traffic control measures on the environment have been studied to a lesser extent than the effects on traffic safety and mobility. Measures reducing traffic volume will, under otherwise identical conditions, reduce the environmental problems caused by traffic. Measures that lead to lower and less variable speeds will normally lead to less noise and lower air pollution emissions, except where speed is very low (less than around 30–40 km/h). Measures that will often improve the environment are area-wide traffic calming, environmental streets, pedestrian streets, urban play streets, lower speed limits and parking regulations.

## Main elements in costs

Table 3.0.2 summarises the main points in the unit costs of several traffic control measures. For many measures, no cost estimates are available. Many traffic control measures are introduced by means of traffic signs alone and thus entail very small direct costs. These include priority control, yield signs at junctions, stop signs at intersections, speed limits, stopping and parking control and one-way streets.

A number of measures consist of combinations of traffic signs and other traffic control measures. These include protection of railway grade crossings. Area-wide traffic calming, environmental streets, pedestrian streets, urban play streets and speed-reducing devices are often introduced in a city quarter or other large areas as a part of a reclassification of the street network. The total costs of such measures will therefore vary depending on the size of the area and the number of measures implemented.

*Table 3.0.2: Main elements in the cost figures for traffic control*

| Measure | Average unit cost (million NOK) | Costs from year |
|---|---|---|
| 3.2 Environmental streets | 3.2–16.5 | 1995 |
| 3.6, 3.7, 3.8, 3.11, 3.15, 3.16 Traffic signs, per sign | 0.002–0.005 | 2005[2] |
| 3.9 Traffic signal control at junctions, per junction | 1.3–1.9 | 2006[1] |
| 3.10 Signalised pedestrian crossing, per crossing | 0.5–1.0 | 2005[1] |
| 3.12 Speed-reducing devices: Speed hump | 0.01–0.03 | 2003 |
| 3.12 Speed-reducing devices: Marking rumble strips, per km marking | 0.004 | 2003 |
| 3.13 Road markings: Marking of line, per line km | 0.011–0.035 | 2005[2] |
| 3.17 Reversible traffic lanes, per km road | 3–5 | 2007 |
| 3.20 Variable message sign | 0.18–0.30 | 2007[1, 3] |
| 3.21 Variable feedback signs (installation) | 0.18 | 2005 |
| 3.21 Variable feedback signs (annual maintenance) | 0.015 | |

[1]Erke and Elvik (2006).
[2]Statens vegvesen, Handbook 115 (2005; utkast 11. aug.).
[3]US Department of Transportation, www.itscosts.its.dot.gov.

### Main elements in cost–benefit analyses

In addition to referring to cost–benefit analyses reported earlier, numerical examples have been worked out for the majority of measures to indicate possible costs and benefits.

Among measures where the benefit is greater than the costs, at least in Norway today, are area-wide traffic calming, pedestrian streets, priority control, introducing yield or stop signs at intersections, traffic signal control at crossroads and upgrading traffic signals, edge lines marked as rumble strips, improving pedestrian crossings by constructing refuges, raised pedestrian crossings, pedestrian guard rails, one-way streets and creating bus lanes.

Cost–benefit analyses of speed limits on national highways carried out by the Norwegian Public Roads Administration show that there are virtually no savings to be made from increasing speed limits on class A motorways from 90 to 100 or 110 km/h. Reducing speed limits from 90 to 80 km or from 80 to 70 km/h on rural roads may however be beneficial. Introducing a winter speed limit from 15 November to 15 March, which is 10 km/h below the speed limit for the rest of the year, has also be found to be cost-effective.

Measures where the benefits are smaller than their costs according to current cost–benefit analyses include urban play streets, speed-reducing devices in residential areas and marked pedestrian crossings. For marked pedestrian crossings, the reason why benefits are smaller than costs is the fact that the number of accidents increases. This can be counteracted by a number of measures, including refuges, raised pedestrian crossings, traffic signals, lighting and pedestrian guardrails. For the speed-reducing measures (urban play streets and speed-reducing devices), the increase in the cost of travel time outweighs the decrease in accident costs. On the other hand, it is doubtful whether current cost–benefit analyses fully reflect the environmental qualities, which are the reason why many people in residential areas often want speed-reducing measures to be introduced.

## 3.1 Area-wide traffic calming

### Problem and objective

The road network in older parts of towns and cities was often constructed for less traffic than it carries today. Older areas were not planned according to the principles for separation and differentiation of the road network (Forskargruppen Scaft 1972), which are now used as a basis for planning roads and streets in Norway (Statens vegvesen, Handbook 017 1993). Through traffic in residential areas increases the accident rate and reduces security, which, among other things, reduces children's opportunities for play and outdoor activities.

Traditionally, black spot treatment (see Section 1.10) has been an important road safety measure in towns and cities (Hvoslef 1974, Christensen 1988). This type of strategy cannot always solve traffic safety problems in areas with an undifferentiated road network. In typical residential areas, accidents are, as a rule, more randomly spread across the road network than on main roads (OECD 1979, Kraay, Mathijssen and Wegman 1984). It is difficult to find clusters of accidents. At the same time, the accident rate, that is, accidents per million vehicle kilometre can be high. In order to improve safety, either traffic volume must be reduced or the accident rate must be reduced using measures affecting the whole road network.

Area-wide traffic calming is a systematic use of the principles of separation and differentiation of the road network in developed areas. By means of traffic control measures, area-wide traffic calming is intended to remove through traffic from residential districts and direct it onto a main road network upgraded to carry increased traffic without an increase in the accident rate. Another objective is to create a more pleasant residential environment and to make outdoor play less dangerous.

**Description of the measure**

Area-wide traffic calming is the co-ordinated use of traffic control measures in a large, defined area in order to improve traffic safety and environmental conditions. Measures that may be a part of area-wide traffic calming are

- a ban on through traffic in residential streets using traffic signs, or physical closure,
- speed-reducing devices in residential streets, either in the form of reduced signposted speed limits (speed limit zones of 30 km/h are common) or by using physical measures (speed humps, chicanes) combined with road signs,
- one-way traffic in residential streets to reduce through traffic,
- improving main roads, e.g. in the form of parking bans, improving stops for buses and trams, traffic signal control at intersections and signalised pedestrian crossings and
- changing parking regulations in residential streets and access roads, e.g. in the form of reserved parking for residents.

Other measures that may be included in area-wide traffic calming are bus lanes, pedestrian streets and urban play streets. These measures are described in other chapters.

## Effect on accidents

A number of studies have evaluated the effects of area-wide traffic calming on accidents, implemented in the form of a street reclassification plan for a defined area, based on the measures listed above. The results presented in this chapter originate from these studies, the results of which are summarised in Table 3.1.1.

Boëthius et al. (1971) (Sweden)
Muskaug (1976a) (Norway)
Muskaug (1976b) (Norway)
Vreugdenhil (1976) (Australia)
Oslo Byplankontor (1978) (Norway)
Dalby (1979) (Great Britain)
Brownfield (1980) (Great Britain)
Bærum Reguleringsvesen (1980) (Norway)
Drammen Byplankontor (1980) (Norway)
Fahlman, Norberg and Bylund (1980) (Sweden)
Hvoslef (1980) (Sweden)
Rauhala (1980) (Finland)
Dalby and Ward (1981) (Great Britain)
Haakenaasen (1981) (Norway)
Haakenaasen (1982) (Norway)

*Table 3.1.1: Effects of area-wide traffic calming on the number of accidents*

| | Percentage change in the number of accidents | | |
|---|---|---|---|
| Accident severity | Type of accident affected | Best estimate | 95% confidence interval |
| ***The whole area where area-wide traffic calming has been introduced (main streets and local streets)*** | | | |
| Injury accidents | All accidents | −15 | (−17; −12) |
| Property-damage-only accidents | All accidents | −15 | (−19; −12) |
| ***Local roads in the area where area-wide traffic calming has been introduced (residential streets)*** | | | |
| Injury accidents | All accidents | −24 | (−29; −18) |
| Property-damage-only accidents | All accidents | −29 | (−35; −22) |
| ***Main roads in the area where area-wide traffic calming has been introduced (main streets)*** | | | |
| Injury accidents | All accidents | −8 | (−12; −5) |
| Property-damage-only accidents | All accidents | −11 | (−16; −6) |

Hart (1982) (The Netherlands)
Engel and Krogsgård Thomsen (1983) (Denmark)
Muskaug (1983a) (Norway)
Brilon et al. (1985) (Germany)
Stølan (1988) (Norway)
Fisher, Van Den Dool and Ho (1989) (Australia)
Janssen and Verhoef (1989) (The Netherlands)
Walker, Gardner and McFetridge (1989) (Great Britain)
Walker and McFetridge (1989) (Great Britain)
Ward, Norrie, Allsop and Sang (1989a) (Great Britain)
Ward, Norrie, Allsop and Sang (1989b) (Great Britain)
Ward, Norrie, Allsop and Sang (1989c) (Great Britain)
Brilon and Blanke (1990) (Germany)
Fairlie and Taylor (1990) (Australia)
Chua and Fisher (1991) (Australia)
Brilon and Blanke (1992) (Germany)
Baier et al. (1992) (Germany)
Gunnarsson and Hagson (1992) (Sweden)
Chick (1994) (Great Britain)

Area-wide traffic calming reduces the number of accidents by around 15%, when all roads in the area subject to area-wide traffic calming are included in the analysis. On local roads within the area subject to area-wide traffic calming, greater accident reductions have been found than on the main roads forming the boundaries for the area. Most of the reduction in the number of accidents in residential streets is due to reduced traffic. The reduction in the number of accidents on main streets is largely due to a reduced accident rate. Traffic increased slightly (1–5%) on main streets.

**Effect on mobility**

The effect of area-wide traffic calming on mobility has been studied in a number of areas where area-wide traffic calming has been introduced in Norway (Muskaug 1976a, 1976b, 1983b, Haakenaasen 1981, 1982). The studies show that travel times increase on different routes within the traffic calming areas as well as on selected routes in and out of the traffic calming area. This may be due, among other things, to one-way streets, reduced speed limits and other speed-reducing devices and fewer access points in an area subject to area-wide traffic calming.

An English study (Dalby and Ward 1981) shows that area-wide traffic calming affects journey times on main streets only to a small extent. In areas with speed-reducing devices, the average speed is reduced to 15–25 km/h. This is a reduction of 5–10 km/h compared to mean speed before the speed-reducing devices were implemented.

**Effect on the environment**

Area-wide traffic calming can significantly reduce the number of dwellings exposed to noise when traffic volumes in residential streets are reduced and traffic is directed to streets with fewer inhabitants (Øvstedal 1996). The recommended limit in Norway for outdoor noise is 55 dBA, measured 2 m from the facade. Measurements show that a reduction of traffic to less than 500 vehicles per 24-h period is necessary to obtain satisfactory conditions. However, studies in Norway have shown that on streets with average traffic (2,000–8,000), significant improvements can be achieved, even with relatively small reductions in the number of vehicles.

**Costs**

On the basis of a survey of several sources, Elvik (1996) estimates the average cost of area-wide traffic calming of an area to be around NOK 2 million per area. Annual maintenance costs for the area can be expected to increase by around NOK 0.1 million. There are considerable variations in costs from one area to another. For areas subject to area-wide traffic calming in Norway, costs have varied between NOK 0.16 and NOK 5.90 million per area. The costs of the individual measures that are often included in area-wide traffic calming are (Elvik 1996) around NOK 1.2 million (±NOK 0.15 million ) for traffic signal control at an intersection, around NOK 0.27 million (±NOK 0.02 million) for a mid-block signalised pedestrian crossing, around NOK 150,000 (±NOK 10,000) for constructing a bus bay, around NOK 100,000 (±NOK 50,000) for widening the pavement at an intersection, around NOK 15,000 (±NOK 5,000) for physical closure of a street using a barrier or similar, around NOK 15,000 (±NOK 5,000) for constructing a speed hump, around NOK 5,000 (±NOK 3,000) for marking an ordinary pedestrian crossing and around NOK 2,000 (±NOK 1,000) for putting up a road sign.

**Cost–benefit analysis**

In order to indicate possible effects of area-wide traffic calming, a numerical example has been worked out. It is assumed that the area is limited by a main street with an annual average daily traffic (AADT) of 6,000 and an accident rate of 0.50 injury accidents per million vehicle kilometres. The average traffic volume on local streets within the area is assumed to be 800 and the accident rate 1.10 injury accidents per million vehicle kilometres. Traffic volume on local streets is assumed to reduce by 25% (200 vehicles). It is assumed that this traffic is transferred to the adjoining main street. The number of accidents will be reduced by 10% on the main street and 25% on the local streets. The mean speed of the remaining traffic on the local streets is assumed to reduce from 35 to 30 km/h. It is assumed that traffic transferred from local streets to the main streets saves NOK 0.15 per vehicle kilometre in operating costs. For remaining traffic on local streets, it is assumed that vehicle operating costs increase by NOK 0.10 per vehicle kilometre. On local streets, it is assumed that the environmental costs are reduced by NOK 0.25 per vehicle kilometre. The construction costs for area-wide traffic calming (budget costs) are assumed to be NOK 2 million per year. Annual maintenance costs for the area subject to area-wide traffic calming are assumed to increase by NOK 0.1 million. Under these assumptions, the present value of reduced accident costs are estimated to NOK to 5.1 million, increased costs of travel time to NOK 1.2 million, increased vehicle operating costs to NOK 0.1 million and reduced environmental costs to NOK 0.6 million. The total benefit is estimated to NOK 4.4 million. The social opportunity cost of the measure is estimated to be NOK 3.8 million. The benefit is therefore greater than the costs (4.4/3.8 = 1.15).

## 3.2 Environmental streets

### Problem and objective

For inhabitants and others who use roads with heavy traffic, traffic is often experienced as a problem, especially when speeds are high. Heavy traffic and high speeds lead to high accident rates and create noise, pollution and a feeling of insecurity. The road becomes a barrier and opportunities for social contact are reduced. In order to reduce the conflict between a road's transport function and the need for safety and a liveable environment in towns, the road can be redesigned to reduce speed, and at the same time, the traffic environment can be made more pleasant. Converting a main road to an environmental street is intended to improve the environment in towns by reducing accidents, the feeling of insecurity and environmental problems caused by traffic. Measures designed to achieve this are speed-reducing devices and environmental measures such as planting, decorative use of kerbstones and other aesthetic measures.

### Description of the measure

An environmental street is a road where through traffic is permitted, but where the road is built in such a way that it leads to low speed and a high degree of alertness and consideration with regard to local traffic. Elements that may be included in the construction are

- Tracks for walking and cycling
- Speed humps and/or raised pedestrian crossings
- Widening the pavement at intersections
- Alternate narrowing of the carriageways (zigzag pattern = chicanes)
- Continuous kerbstones across side roads at intersections to emphasise the obligation to give way
- Bus bays/Bus stops delineated by kerbstones
- Marked parking places, combined with parking bans outside designated places
- Refuges on pedestrian crossings
- Planting and furnishing of pavements and traffic islands
- Lighting.

In order to create an aesthetically pleasing impression, materials of good quality and varied designs are often used, such as different types of flagstones and paving stones, which are used, for example, on pavements and on raised pedestrian crossings.

**Effect on accidents**

A number of studies have evaluated the effects of environmental streets on accidents:

Borges, Hansen and Meulengracht-Madsen (1985) (Denmark)
Stølan (1988) (Norway)
Angenendt (1991) (Germany)
Freiholtz (1991) (Sweden)
Baier et al. (1992) (Germany)
Schnüll and Lange (1992) (Germany)
Nielsen and Herrstedt (1993) (Denmark)
Herrstedt, Kjemtrup, Borges and Andersen (1993) (Denmark, France)
Engel and Andersen (1994) (Denmark)
Wheeler and Taylor (1995) (Great Britain)
Statens vegvesen (2003) (Norway)

Based on these studies, it is estimated that the number of injury accidents is reduced by 35% (95% CI [−43; −26]), and that the number of property-damage-only accidents is reduced by 27% (95% CI [−36; −18]). However, none of the studies controlled for regression to the mean in the number of accidents and the results may therefore be overestimated.

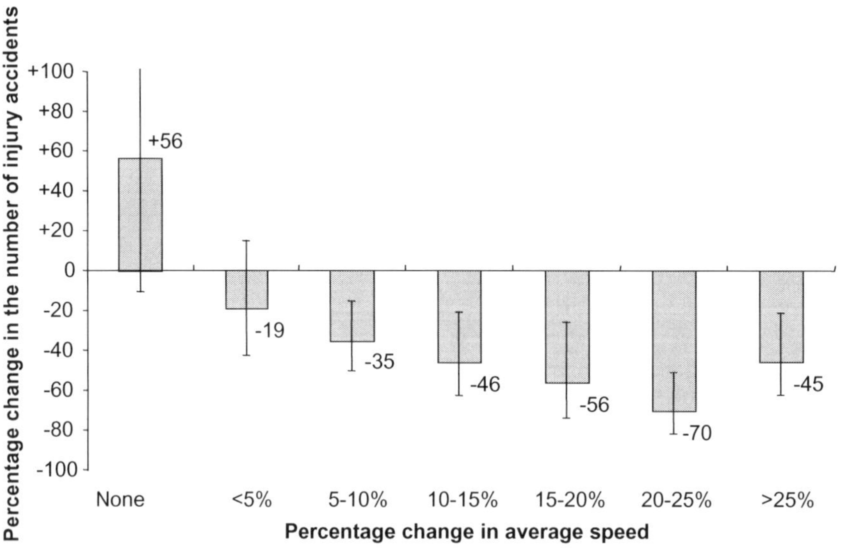


*Figure 3.2.1: Relationship between changes in mean speed (percentage) and changes in the number of injury accidents (percentage) after construction of environment streets.*

The effect on accidents is related to the size of the reduction in speed associated with the introduction of environmental streets. On average, speed reduced from 54.9 to 46.0 km/h and the amount of traffic reduced by around 3.5%. Figure 3.2.1 shows the relationship between changes in mean speed and changes in the number of injury accidents. The vertical lines indicate the uncertainty in changes in the number of accidents. No effects on accidents have been found when speed was unchanged, and larger reductions of speed are related to greater accident reductions.

**Effect on mobility**

Environment streets reduce speeds for through traffic in a town. If, for example, speed is reduced from 50 to 45 km/h for a length of 500 m, this corresponds to 4 s additional driving time. A couple of studies (Solberg 1986a, Nielsen and Herrstedt 1993) indicate that speed increases on roads outside a town where environment streets have been built. It was further found that the waiting time for minor road traffic at intersections can be slightly reduced where environment streets are built, since lower speeds on the main road mean that it is easier to finds a suitable gap to turn onto the main road.

## Effect on the environment

In five test areas selected by Norwegian Public Roads Administration (Batnfjordsøra, Os, Stryn, Hokksund and Rakkestad), the changes in noise and vibrations were measured (Lie and Bettum 1996). No clear changes in the noise level were found. In two areas, an increase in vibration was registered. However, the vibrations in both places are below the recommended maximum values (Lie and Bettum 1996).

A summary of experiences from environment streets in 24 towns and cities (Haddeland and Nielsen 1991) shows that the noise level is reduced by up to 6 dB in towns where environment streets have been built. In the majority of cases, the noise reduction is around 1–3 dB. In certain places, increased noise levels have been found in connection with rumble strips and areas with cobblestones, raised intersections and pedestrian crossings.

The effects of environment streets on pollution have only been studied in a few places. The results are contradictory. A reduction in emissions has been found in some places but not in others (Haddeland and Nielsen 1991). The results are, as yet, too uncertain to be quantified. Environmental streets are assumed to increase well-being and a feeling of security (Statens vegvesen 2003).

## Costs

The cost figures available for environment streets vary substantially. On the basis of 23 km of roads, which have been converted to environment streets, Elvik (1996) has calculated the average cost at around NOK 3.2 million (1995 prices) per kilometre of road. The average cost of 16 environmental streets in Norway has been estimated at NOK 19 million (Statens vegvesen 2003). There were, however, large differences between individual projects. A compilation of cost figures for 23 cities in Denmark, Germany and France (Herrstedt, Kjemtrup, Borges and Andersen 1993) found an average cost of DKK 9 million (at 1990 prices) per kilometre of road. Lie and Bettum (1996) gives the average cost of building environment streets in the five towns selected by the Norwegian Public Roads Administration as around NOK 16.5 million per kilometre of road. A compilation of information from 13 Danish cities (Vejdirektoratet 1996) found an average cost of DKK 5.2 million per kilometre of road (at approximately 1995 prices).

## Cost–benefit analysis

No cost–benefit analyses of environmental streets based on the most recent experiences with such streets have been found. A numerical example has been worked out. It is assumed that a main street with an AADT of 6,000 and an accident rate of 0.50 injury accidents per million vehicle kilometres is converted to an environmental street. This is assumed to cost NOK 5 million for converting the street and an annual additional cost for road maintenance of NOK 500,000 per kilometre of road. The number of injury accidents is assumed to be reduced by 40% and the number of property-damage-only accidents by 25%. Average speed is assumed to reduce from 54 to 46 km/h. In addition to increased travel time costs, it is assumed that this reduction in speed leads to an increase in vehicle operating costs of NOK 0.03 km per vehicle kilometre. It is assumed that environmental costs are reduced by NOK 0.10 per vehicle kilometre, as a result of reduced noise and a more pleasant environment.

Under these assumptions, the reduction of accident costs for an environmental street of 1 km is estimated to be NOK 10.3 million. Increased cost of travel time is estimated to be NOK 8.2 million. Increased vehicle operating costs are estimated to be NOK 0.8 million and saved environmental costs to be NOK 2.6 million. The total benefit is estimated to be NOK 3.8 million. The social opportunity costs of the measure are estimated to be NOK 6.7 million. The benefit in this numerical example is smaller than the costs.

## 3.3 Pedestrian streets

### Problem and objective

Commercial streets in the centre of towns tend to have a high number of pedestrian accidents. There are several reasons for this. Parking and delivering goods create many visual obstructions. Heavy pedestrian traffic and a large amount of traffic crossing roads create conflicts between vehicles and pedestrians. Commercial streets often have a high density of intersections and access roads.

By converting commercial streets to pedestrian streets, conflicts between motor traffic and pedestrians can be reduced. At the same time, it is easier to introduce environmental measures, such as planting and possibly outdoor trading in summer.

### Description of the measure

A pedestrian street is a street where motor vehicles are not permitted, apart from delivering goods at given times of the day. Pedestrian streets are normally signposted at both ends. Normally, pedestrian streets are rebuilt by removing the kerbstone so that

*Table 3.3.1: Effects of pedestrian streets on the number of accidents*

| | | Percentage change in the number of accidents | |
|---|---|---|---|
| Accident severity | Types of accident affected | Best estimate | 95% confidence interval |
| ***Accidents in pedestrian streets*** | | | |
| Injury accidents | All accidents | −60 | (−80; −20) |
| ***Accidents in streets adjoining pedestrian streets*** | | | |
| Injury accidents | All accidents | +5 | (−15; +30) |
| ***Accidents both in pedestrian streets and adjoining streets around the pedestrian street*** | | | |
| Injury accidents | All accidents | −25 | (−40; −10) |

the division between the road and the pavement disappears. Pedestrian streets often have a surface of paving stones.

## Effect on accidents

The effect of pedestrian streets on accidents has been studied in Norway (Frøysadal et al. 1979), Sweden (Lillienberg 1971, Lillienberg, Birgersson and Husberg 1971), Denmark (Værø 1992), Finland (Kølster Pedersen et al. 1992) and Great Britain (Dalby 1979). On the basis of the studies, the best estimate of the effect of building pedestrian streets on accidents is shown in Table 3.3.1.

Pedestrian streets are associated with a large reduction in the number of accidents in the pedestrian streets. In surrounding streets, a non-significant increase in the number of accidents has been found. Taking pedestrian streets and the surrounding streets together, the number of accidents is reduced. The studies of pedestrian streets have, to some extent, been carried out in areas where there were previously a high number of pedestrian accidents. The effects may therefore be smaller at places where there are fewer pedestrian accidents.

## Effect on mobility

No studies have been found that show the effects on mobility of creating pedestrian streets. In pedestrian streets, pedestrians and cyclists have better mobility, since conflicts with motorists either disappear or are greatly reduced. Conditions for delivering goods can be improved, since those delivering goods no longer have to compete for parking places with customers of nearby shops. Access to shops in the streets is reduced for customers who want access by car, right to the shop door. If pedestrian streets lead to increased car traffic in neighbouring streets, movement of traffic in these streets may become worse.

## Effect on the environment

Creating pedestrian streets reduces noise and air pollution in streets that are pedestrianised. In Prästgatan in Östersund, Sweden the noise level reduced by 6–9 dB (Lillienberg 1971). In Odda, Norway, noise reductions of 4–8 dB were registered in the area of the pedestrian street (Frøysadal et al. 1979). In the surrounding streets, noise levels increased by around 3 dB. In Prästgatan in Östersund, the concentration of carbon monoxide (CO) per cubic metre of air in the area of the pedestrian street was reduced by 75% after the conversion (Lillienberg 1971). The concentrations of a number of other gases were also reduced. In Odda, far fewer residents and business people stated that they were annoyed by traffic noise after the pedestrian street was created than before (Frøysadal et al. 1979). Business owners in pedestrian streets felt that access conditions for customers in cars and for delivery of goods had become worse after the pedestrian street was created. Profits did not go down.

## Costs

The costs of converting a street to a pedestrian street vary, depending on local conditions. Pedestrian street construction in Odda, Norway, cost NOK 750,000 (at the end of the 1970s) (Frøysadal et al. 1979). The main cost involved in creating pedestrian streets is renewing the street surface. The overview given in Table 3.3.2 shows unit costs for replacing street surfaces and putting up traffic signs. The figures are based on information from Trondheim municipality, Norway, for the summer of 1990 (Øvstedal 1996).

*Table 3.3.2: Cost involved in creating pedestrian streets*

| Task | Costs (1990) |
|---|---|
| Removing asphalt | Around NOK 30 $m^{-2}$ |
| Laying paving stones, including removal of earth | NOK 200–400 $m^{-2}$ (concrete) |
| | NOK 700–900 $m^{-2}$ (paving stones) |
| Laying kerbstones | NOK 350–500 $lm^{-1}$ |
| Putting up traffic signs | NOK 2,200 per sign |

The unit costs vary depending on the quantity, type and quality of the material used. The figures above do not include all work involved in creating pedestrian streets. Planting, for example, has not been included. If a street that is 8 m wide and 200 m long is to be converted to a pedestrian street, with kerbstones at each end and six traffic signs, the total cost can be estimated to around NOK 800,000 on the basis of the unit costs given in Table 3.3.2. Planning and planting costs should be added to this.

### Cost–benefit analysis

No cost–benefit analyses of pedestrian streets have been found. In order to indicate the possible effects of the measure, a numerical example has been prepared. It is assumed that a commercial street with an AADT of 5,000 and 1.1 injury accidents per million vehicle kilometres is converted to a pedestrian street. It is assumed that 40% of the traffic transfers to an adjoining street with an AADT (before transfer) of 3,000 and an accident rate of 0.6 injury accidents per million vehicle kilometres. Forty percent of the traffic is assumed to disappear. Thus, the total reduction in traffic in the pedestrian street will be 80%. The number of accidents is assumed to reduce by 60% in pedestrian streets and to increase by 50% in the adjoining streets where traffic volume increases. The environmental costs in both the pedestrian street and the adjoining street are assumed to change in proportion to traffic volume. Creating pedestrian streets is assumed to cost NOK 4 million of public money.

Under these assumptions, the reduction of accident costs is estimated to be NOK 23.1 million. The loss of benefit for displaced traffic is estimated to NOK 14.3 million. Saved environmental costs are estimated at NOK 6.1 million. The total benefit is estimated to NOK 14.9 million. The social opportunity cost of the measure is estimated to NOK 4.8 million. In this case, the benefit is significantly greater than the cost.

## 3.4 Urban play streets

### Problem and objective

City streets in residential areas have traditionally served a social function. Increasing traffic and the associated parking in the streets can reduce this (Appleyard and Lintell 1972, Rasmussen 1990). Residential streets with no speed-reducing devices have a higher risk of injury accidents than any other type of road. A Norwegian study (Blakstad and Giæver 1989) found that access roads in areas with detached family houses have an accident rate of 1.10 injury accidents per million vehicle kilometres. Access roads in urban areas have an accident rate of 2.17 injury accidents per million vehicle kilometres. By way of comparison, main roads in detached family house areas and in urban areas have an accident rate of respectively 0.48 and 0.87 injury accidents per million vehicle kilometres.

Converting streets to urban play streets is designed to give the residents a safe and attractive outdoor environment, without too great a reduction in access to buildings. The streets are modified so that they become more attractive for walking or living in. Traffic volume can be reduced in streets that have through traffic. Increased safety is achieved by greatly reducing car speeds.

## Description of the measure

Urban play streets are, above all, intended to encourage recreation and outdoor play in areas where vehicle traffic is limited. Urban play areas permit mixed traffic at walking speed and may be one of a number of measures used in area-wide traffic calming for a specific area. Urban play streets are planted with trees and shrubs, sandpits, play equipment, tables and benches. The road itself is not rectilinear and is not delineated using kerbstones or anything else that creates differences in levels between the road and other areas. Parking places must be clearly marked. Urban play streets must not carry through traffic. Driving in and out of urban play streets will be over kerbstones.

Urban play streets are primarily an environmental measure, even though they can also improve traffic safety. The concept of urban play streets comes from the Netherlands, where it was launched as an alternative to the Stadsbyggnad, Chalmers, Arbetsgruppen För Trafiksäkerhet (SCAFT) principles for separation and differentiation of the road network (Kraay, Mathijssen and Wegman 1984).

In Norway, urban play streets can only be established if the area does not have through traffic, no building within the urban play street is more than 300 m driving distance along the most appropriate road out of the zone, the division between road and pavement is removed, speed-reducing devices are introduced (all vehicles that are permitted to drive within the area must be able to negotiate the speed-reducing devices), parking places for cars are specially marked and if kerbstones are used to mark vehicle entrances and exits to the area.

## Effect on accidents

The effect of urban play streets on accidents has been studied in Norway (Muskaug 1983a, 1983b), Germany (Kahrmann 1988), The Netherlands (Janssen and Verhoef

1989) and Denmark (Engel and Krogsgård Thomsen 1990). In the majority of studies, the development of urban play streets was included in more comprehensive area-wide traffic calming. The effects given below, however, only refer to the streets that have been developed as urban play streets, and not the whole area subjected to area-wide traffic calming. In summary, urban play streets have been found to reduce injury accidents by 25% (95% CI [−45; −5]) and property-damage-only accidents by 20% (95% CI [−40; +5]). The reduction in accidents is probably due to a combination of less car traffic and lower speeds.

**Effect on mobility**

Urban play streets can reduce mobility for car drivers, but increase mobility for pedestrians and cyclists. The amount of car traffic reduced significantly in two urban play streets in Sandefjord, Norway. Speed was reduced to 15–25 km/h (Muskaug 1983a, 1983b). The percentage of pedestrians who relax outdoors, as opposed to walking, in the streets, increased in urban play streets. The average time spent outdoors increased by 10–30%. In comparable streets without urban play streets, a reduction of 10–30% in recreation time was found (Muskaug 1983a, 1983b). Urban play streets can create delays and reduce access for emergency vehicles and maintenance vehicles.

**Effect on the environment**

No studies have been found that show how urban play streets affect noise, dust and air pollution. As a rule, urban play streets will lead to a reduction in speed and a reduction in the proportion of heavy traffic. This can lead to less noise (Haakenaasen 1982).

Urban play streets create common outdoor areas, which encourage recreation and social activities. People often feel it is easier and more pleasant to be a pedestrian or a cyclist on these streets and often let their children play outside (Muskaug 1983a). There may be more parked cars in urban play streets. In Sofienberg, Oslo, Norway, parking times increased. Up to twice as many cars were parked in urban play streets than there were in marked parking places (Muskaug 1983b).

**Costs**

The costs of creating urban play streets vary greatly, depending on the length of the streets and the standard of the measures adopted, among other things. The main cost in creating urban play streets is the replacement of the street surface. The overview given below (Table 3.4.1) gives unit costs for replacing the street surface and putting up

*Table 3.4.1: Costs involved in creating urban play streets*

| Task | Costs (1990) |
|---|---|
| Removing asphalt | Around NOK 30 $m^{-2}$ |
| Laying paving stones, including removal of earth | NOK 200–400 $m^{-2}$ (concrete); NOK 700–900 $m^{-2}$ (paving stones) |
| Laying kerbstones | NOK 350–500 $lm^{-1}$ |
| Putting up traffic signs | NOK 2,200 per sign |

traffic signs. The figures are based on information from Trondheim municipality, Norway, for the summer of 1990 (Øvstedal 1996).

The unit costs vary depending on the quantity, type and quality of the material used. The figures above do not include all work involved in creating urban play streets. Planting, for example, has not been included. If a street that is 8 m wide and 200 m long is to be converted to an urban play street, with kerbstones at each end and six traffic signs, the total cost can be estimated at around NOK 800,000 on the basis of the unit costs given above. Planning and planting costs should be added.

Winter maintenance of urban play streets can be more expensive than winter maintenance of city streets, since it is more difficult to use snow clearance equipment (Amundsen 1984). A study of winter maintenance costs in urban play streets (Amundsen 1984) found that the total costs of winter maintenance, excluding removal of snow, were around NOK 0.14–6.87 $m^{-2}$. If snow removal is included, the costs were more than double the highest of these figures (over NOK 16 $m^{-2}$). Major cost savings can be achieved by designing urban play streets in such a way that it is not necessary to remove snow or such that this needs to be done less often (Amundsen 1984).

### Cost–benefit analysis

In order to obtain an impression of the factors that influence the costs and benefits of urban play streets, a numerical example has been worked out. It is assumed that an access street with an AADT of 500 and 1.1 injury accidents per million vehicle kilometres is converted to an urban play street. The number of injury accidents is assumed to reduce by 25% and the number of property-damage-only accidents by 20%. It is assumed that speed is reduced from 30 to 20 km/h. At such low speeds, vehicle operating costs and pollution emissions both increase. Nonetheless, it is assumed that an environmental benefit corresponding to NOK 0.09 per vehicle kilometre is achieved (Grue, Langeland and Larsen 1997). This benefit corresponds to the increase in value of houses associated with the removal of one vehicle kilometre of driving in the immediate vicinity of a house. Increase in property values are assumed to reflect social benefits such as increased feeling of security, greater opportunities for children to play outside unsupervised and lower noise levels. Under these assumptions, the benefit for traffic safety of an urban play street of 1 km is estimated to be NOK 1.25 million in reduced accident costs. Travel time costs increase by around NOK 3.55 million and vehicle operating costs by around NOK 0.64 million. The environmental costs are reduced by around NOK 0.19 million. The total benefit, however, is negative, at minus NOK −2.75 million, which is primarily due to the increased costs of travel time. The social opportunity costs of the measure are estimated to NOK 4.8 million per kilometre of road.

## 3.5 Access control

### Problem and objective

A private access road (driveway in US parlance) is any road connecting a private property to a public road. In addition to the actual point of connection, part of the private road is also regarded as part of the access point. The accident rate increases strongly with increasing numbers of private access roads per kilometre of road. A study of accident rates on Norwegian national highways in the period 1977–80 (Muskaug 1985) has investigated the relationship between the number of private access roads per kilometre of road and the accident rate (Table 3.5.1). A similar study of a sample of road sections in Norway found the same relationship (Blakstad and Giæver 1989).

*Table 3.5.1: Relationship between accident rate on national highways and the number of private access roads per km road in Norway*

| Number of access points per kilometre road | Accidents per million vehicle kilometres |
|---|---|
| None – motorway class A | 0.08 |
| None – motorway class B | 0.11 |
| 0–5 | 0.21 |
| 6–10 | 0.27 |
| 11–15 | 0.29 |
| 16–30 | 0.38 |
| Over 30 | 0.47 |
| City centre areas (over 50) | 0.80 |

Access control is intended to reduce the number of private access roads along public roads, to make each access point as safe as possible and to distribute traffic between private access roads in such a way that the total accident rate is minimised.

**Description of the measure**

The following measures are described in this chapter:

- constructing roads without access to private properties along the road,
- removing access points on existing roads,
- merging access points on existing roads, and
- improving the design of each access point.

**Effect on accidents**

***Constructing roads without access points.*** When new roads are built in Norway, the number of accesses is determined according to the choice of road standard class (Statens vegvesen, Handbook 017 1993). Motorways have no private access roads and there are different types of main roads, both with and without access points. New main roads are often built without private access roads. According to the studies presented in Section 1.2, motorways have lower accident rates than most other roads.

***Removing private access roads.*** Removing private access roads is normally only possible when the need for them disappears, for example, because a business has closed or moved. The effect of removing private access roads on accidents can be estimated on the basis of a number of Norwegian studies of the relationship between the density of private access roads and accident rate. The results presented here are based on the studies by Jensen (1968), Grimsgaard (1976), Hvoslef (1977), Amundsen (1979), Grimsgaard (1979), Hovd (1979) and Muskaug (1985). The results are summarised in Table 3.5.2. In summary, reducing the number of private access roads and the traffic using them by about 50% reduces the number of injury accident by around 25–30%.

***Merging private access roads.*** Normally, it is not possible to remove private access roads to the extent discussed above. As long as a business needs access to the road, the issue is whether the access should be designed in the form of a separate access point to each property or a communal access road, possibly a public intersection, which serves traffic to several properties. When traffic from a number of small access roads is merged, the result is fewer private access roads, each with more traffic. It is not obvious that this will reduce the number of accidents. Studies (Hovd 1981, Vodahl and Giæver

*Table 3.5.2: Effects of reductions of the number of private access roads on accidents*

| | | Percentage change in the number of accidents | |
|---|---|---|---|
| Accidents severity | Types of accident affected | Best estimate | 95% confidence interval |
| ***From over 30 to 16–30 access roads per km*** | | | |
| Injury accidents | All accidents | −29 | (−33; −25) |
| ***From 16–30 to 6–15 access roads per km*** | | | |
| Injury accidents | All accidents | −31 | (−34; −29) |
| ***Form 6–15 to under 6 access roads per km*** | | | |
| Injury accidents | All accidents | −25 | (−28; −22) |

*Table 3.5.3: Level of risk associated with different densities of private access roads, depending on the amount of traffic on private access roadss*

| | Injury accidents per million vehicle kilometres | | | | | |
|---|---|---|---|---|---|---|
| | Amount of traffic per 0.5 km road | | | | | |
| Number of private access roads per 0.5 km road | 0–59 | 60–129 | 130–299 | 300–499 | Over 500 | Total |
| 0–5 | 0.23 | 0.32 | 0.46 | 0.45 | 0.57 | 0.26 |
| 6–10 | 0.22 | 0.28 | 0.32 | 0.46 | 0.60 | 0.30 |
| 11–15 | 0.17 | 0.25 | 0.42 | 0.43 | 0.60 | 0.39 |
| Over 15 | | | 0.30 | 0.68 | 0.81 | 0.65 |
| Total | 0.22 | 0.29 | 0.37 | 0.49 | 0.70 | 0.31 |

1986a, 1986b) show that the accident rate at intersections and private access roads increases with an increasing proportion of minor road traffic. Only one study has been found evaluating how the accident rate on public roads varies depending on the amount of traffic on the private access road (Hovd 1981). The study showed the following accident rates (injury accidents reported to the police per million vehicle kilometres) associated with different levels of activity (amount of traffic) (Table 3.5.3).

The figures show that the accident rate for a given number of private access roads per kilometre of road increases with increasing amounts of traffic. This is shown by the figures in each line of the table. When private access roads are merged, each access road carries heavier traffic. On the basis of Table 3.5.3, it has been estimated that mergers, which represent a halving of the number of private access roads, do not affect the number of accidents (−8%; +8%). The explanation for this may be that by merging private access roads, several minor intersections with little minor road traffic are replaced by one large intersection with a high proportion of minor road traffic. Other studies (Vodahl and Giæver 1986a, 1986b) show that intersections with a high proportion of minor road traffic have higher accident rates than intersections with a small proportion of side road traffic.

***Improving access point design.*** The effects of the design of each access point on the accident rate for the private access road has been studied in Norway (Hovd 1979). The study investigated increasing sight distances on private access roads and the curve radius on the main road in private access roads. The study found that increasing the sight distance along the main road did not reduce the number of accidents at private access roads. An increase roughly corresponding to a doubling of the sight distance is associated with a non-significant increase of around 10% in the number of accidents related to private access roads (95% CI [−5; +30]). Increasing the curve radius on the main road did not lead to fewer accidents either. An increase in the curve radius by a factor of around 3–5 led to around 30% more accidents (95% CI [+8; +59]). The study concludes that the results 'may indicate that road users regard the most poorly designed private access roads as hazardous and thus drive such a way that, overall, fewer and less serious accidents occurred' (Hovd 1979, 187).

## Effect on mobility

Removing or merging private access roads can lead to more difficult access conditions for properties along the road. In some places, access roads are combined with tracks for walking and cycling, where the track for walking and cycling can be used as an access road to the properties. This is only done in places where relatively few properties use the track as an access road. Increased density of private access roads reduces the mean speed of traffic (Sakshaug 1986). A Norwegian study found that increasing the number of private access roads by 10 per 500 m reduced the average traffic speed by 1 km/h at a speed limit of 50 km/h and by 8.8 km/h at a speed limit of 80 km/h.

## Effect on the environment

No studies have been found that show how the measures discussed in this chapter affect the environment. The effects probably depend on which measure is used. Constructing roads without private access roads can remove through traffic from built-up areas and thus can improve the local environment. Removing private access roads can lead to increased safety, but may sometimes lead to detours for local traffic.

*Table 3.5.4: Costs of access control measures: 1995 prices, Norway (Elvik 1996)*

| Measure | Cost per km of road in NOK million |
|---|---|
| Constructing roads without private access roads (motorway B) | 22.50 (± 1.50) |
| Constructing tracks for walking and cycling | 3.80 (± 0.50) |
| Access control along existing roads | 0.75 (± 0.30) |
| Closing private access roads with barriers or similar | 0.015 (± 0.005) |

### Costs

The costs depend on which measure is used. The approximate cost figures are given on the basis of available studies (Elvik 1996) in Table 3.5.4. In some cases, tracks for walking and cycling can function as access roads to a small number of properties and thus make it possible to remove private access roads along existing roads.

### Cost–benefit analysis

No cost–benefit analyses of all the measures discussed in this chapter are available. Cost–benefit analyses of constructing roads without private access roads are described in Section 1.2, motorways.

The number of private access roads along a road is one of the criteria for reducing the speed limit along the road. By merging private access roads, the speed limit could, in principle, be raised, for example, from 60 to 70 km/h. Assume that by building new access roads costing, for example, NOK 4 million per kilometre of road, it is possible to reduce the number of private access roads to the extent that the speed limit can be raised from 60 to 70 km/h. The number of accidents is assumed not to change. If the mean speed of traffic increases, for example, from 62 to 67 km/h on roads with an AADT of 4,000 vehicles, the present value of costs of travel time calculated over 25 years will be NOK 2 million. This is less than the cost of the measure, indicating that it does not give good value for money.

## 3.6 Priority control

### Problem and objective

Heavy through traffic in towns and cities with many intersections can lead to confusion about priority rules and poor traffic flow, if all intersections are governed by the rule of giving way to traffic from the right (the right hand priority rule). At intersections between a road with heavy traffic and a road with light traffic, the right hand priority rule functions poorly, according to a Norwegian study (Johannessen 1984). Almost half of traffic drives as through traffic from the road with least traffic is required to yield at such intersections. Consistent application of the right hand priority rule at intersections along main roads in towns and cities leads to delays for through traffic. By signposting main roads in towns and cities as priority roads and requiring minor road traffic to yield, the interaction between road users is simplified and the capacity of main roads is increased. Priority control of roads is intended to create unambiguous right-of-way conditions and to improve traffic flow and safety on roads designated as main roads (priority roads).

**Description of the measure**

All roads can be made priority roads, apart from access roads. Roads that make a 90° turn through intersections cannot normally be made priority roads until the intersection has been reconstructed so that the road runs straight ahead at the intersection.

**Effect on accidents**

The effects of priority roads on accidents have been investigated in the following studies:

Pegrum, Lloyd and Willett (1972) (Australia)
Amundsen (1973a) (Norway)
Amundsen (1973b) (Norway)
Daltrey, Howie and Randall (1978) (Australia)
Dimmen and Giæver (1990) (Norway)
Stigre (1991) (Norway)
Stigre (1993) (Norway)
Buran, Heieraas and Hovin (1995) (Norway)

In summary, non-significant increases of the number of injury accidents (+5%; 95% CI [−2; +12]) and of the number of property-damage-only accidents (+3%; 95% CI [−3; +7]) have been found. This may be somewhat surprising, since priority control has been found to lead to more predictable behaviour at intersections and better compliance with prevailing right-of-way regulations (more people adhere to yield signs than to the right hand priority rule). On the other hand, it has been found that an increase in speed results from priority control of roads. Possible changes in road user alertness and expectations of the behaviour of other road users have not been studied.

### Effect on mobility

The effect of priority control of roads on the mean speed of traffic has been the subject of a number of studies (Amundsen 1973a, Hallion and Michael 1978, Johannessen 1984, 1985, Stigre 1991, 1993). Recent Norwegian studies are summarised in Table 3.6.1. Speed measurements on control sections are not available for all studies. However, where such measurements are available, the net change in mean speed on the test section of road has been adjusted for changes observed on the control sections.

All results indicate that speed increases when priority control is introduced, especially at intersections. A possible explanation for this is that drivers, who are approaching an intersection on a priority-controlled road, increase their speed when they see yield signs. When intersections are governed by the rule of giving way to traffic from the right, drivers have to observe traffic from the side road more carefully and be ready to stop.

Changes in yield behaviour at intersections and pedestrian crossings are shown in Table 3.6.2. In the before-period, the right hand priority rule controlled traffic at intersections, while in the after-period, the yield rule is applied.

### Effect on the environment

No studies have been found that show how priority control of roads affects environment. Increased speeds may lead to increased emissions of certain types of exhaust gas from motor vehicles. Priority control of roads leads to longer waiting times

*Table 3.6.1: Changes in speed following priority control of roads (average speed in km/h)*

| | | Test (km/h) | | Control (km/h) | | |
|---|---|---|---|---|---|---|
| Study | Site | Before | After | Before | After | Percentage change |
| Stigre (1991) | Intersection | 37.8 | 41.1 | 41.1 | 39.5 | +13.1 |
| | Road | 45.6 | 47.5 | 48.4 | 48.9 | +3.1 |
| Stigre (1993) | Intersection | 47.4 | 48.7 | | | +2.7 |
| | Road | 51.4 | 52.2 | | | +1.6 |
| Buran, Heieraas and Hovin (1995) | Pedestrian crossing | 43.1 | 43.0 | 47.9 | 45.7 | +4.6 |
| | Road | 40.2 | 41.5 | | | +3.2 |

*Table 3.6.2: Changes in observance of yield rules at intersections and at pedestrian crossings on priority-controlled of road. Percentage observing yield rule*

| | | Percentage who observe yield rule | | | Number of vehicles recorded | |
|---|---|---|---|---|---|---|
| Study | Site | Before | After | % Change | Before | After |
| Stigre (1991) | Intersection | 87 | 95 | 9 | 1,557 | 1,410 |
| | Pedestrian crossing | 57 | 65 | 14 | 97 | 74 |
| Stigre (1993) | Intersection | 56 | 93 | 66 | 1,854 | 1,479 |
| | Pedestrian crossing | 42 | 66 | 57 | 219 | 125 |
| Buran, Heieraas and Hovin (1995) | Intersection | 80 | 91 | 14 | 198 | 105 |
| | Pedestrian crossing | 43 | 76 | 77 | 114 | 133 |

for traffic required to yield (Amundsen 1973a). This can lead to increased emission of exhaust gases. The actual effects on pollution emissions have not been documented.

## Costs

The direct costs of priority control of roads include installing road signs and yield markings on the carriageway. Data for 35 km of road in sparsely populated areas in Norway (Ragnøy, Vaa and Nilsen 1990) indicated an average road sign density of around 4.3 signs per kilometre of road, of which around 6–7% were yield and priority signs (corresponding to around 0.25–0.30 signs per kilometre of road). Corresponding data for some 22 km of road in towns and cities indicated an average sign density of around 20 signs per kilometre of road of which around 7% were yield and priority signs (corresponding to around 1.3–1.4 signs per kilometre of road.) It is not known how many of the roads studied were priority controlled. In towns and cities, a small part of the road network is priority controlled. If it is assumed that priority control in towns and cities requires 5–10 signs (priority roads and minor roads together) per kilometre of priority road, the costs of the measure will be around NOK 10,000–25,000 per kilometre of road. Planning costs should be added.

## Cost–benefit analysis

A numerical example has been prepared to indicate possible effects of the measure. It is assumed that the measure is implemented in a town with an average density of houses. It is assumed that the road that is priority controlled is a main road with an AADT of 4,000 vehicles and an accident rate of 0.35 injury accidents per million vehicle kilometres. The number of accidents is assumed to remain unchanged. The average speed on the road that is priority controlled is assumed to increase from 45 to 48 km/h. It is assumed that the road has three intersections per kilometre, with a total of 2,000 incoming vehicles from the minor roads (in total). Vehicles coming from the minor roads are assumed to sustain a delay of 3 s per car.

The estimates indicate that saved costs of travel time (present values calculated for 10 years) for traffic on the priority-controlled road (1 km) are around NOK 1.4 million. Increased costs of travel time for minor road traffic are around NOK 0.7 million. The total benefit will then be NOK 0.7 million. The social opportunity costs of the measure are estimated at NOK 30,000 per kilometre of road. The benefit is substantially greater than the costs.

## 3.7 Yield signs at junctions

### Problem and objective

At road junctions where no other type of traffic control has been introduced, the rule of giving way to traffic from the right applies. The right hand priority rule applies at most junctions in towns and cities in Norway (Elvestad et al. 1991). The right hand priority rule does not always function as intended (Helmers and Åberg 1978, Johannessen 1984). At junctions where one road is wider than the other or has significantly more traffic than the other road, compliance with the right hand priority rule is poor. Only about 50–60% of road users comply with the right hand priority rule at such junctions. Lack of clarity regarding rules of the right-of-way can lead to dangerous behaviour and accidents.

Increasing traffic may lead to so-called compound yield situations at right hand priority-controlled junctions. These are situations where a number of road users are required to yield to each other. In such situations, many road users are in doubt as to how they are to proceed (Bjørnskau 1994). Traffic flow becomes unstable and sluggish. Main road traffic through a town or city, in particular, can be delayed where there are numerous junctions. The purpose of introducing yield signs is to simplify road user decision-making, improve the flow of traffic and increase safety.

### Description of the measure

Yield rules at junctions are introduced by putting up yield signs on the approach or approaches where traffic is required to give way. The signs are supplemented with road markings and yield lines marked on the road surface. Along the main road, another sign, priority junction, can be erected (this is not compulsory).

### Effect on accidents

Several studies have evaluated the effect of introducing yield control at junctions on accidents. The results presented in this chapter are based on the following studies:

Pegrum, Lloyd and Willett (1972) (Australia)
Amundsen (1973a, 1973b) (Norway)
Johannessen and Heir (1974) (Norway)
Vodahl and Johannessen (1977) (Norway)
Daltrey, Howie and Randall (1978) (Australia)
Vaa and Johannessen (1978) (Norway)
Statens Vägverk (1981) (Sweden)
Cedersund (1983) (Sweden)
Rosenbaum (1983) (USA)
Polus (1985) (Israel)
Rutherford, McLaughlin and VonBorstel (1985) (USA)
Frith and Harte (1986) (New Zealand)
Vodahl and Giæver (1986a, 1986b) (Norway)

On the basis of these studies, it is estimated that injury accidents are reduced by 3% (95% CI [−9; +3]) and that property-damage-only accidents are reduced by 3% (95% CI [−12; +7]). These results do not indicate that yield signs at junctions have any statistically significant effect on the number of accidents. Some studies (Vaa and Johannessen 1978, Vodahl and Giæver 1986a, 1986b) have found larger increases of accident numbers at junctions with little minor road traffic. The explanation why yield signs at junctions do not reduce the number of accidents may be that speed increases. Yielding behaviour, on the other hand, becomes more consistent as evidenced by the fact that more people observe the yield rule than the right hand priority rule.

### Effect on mobility

A number of studies (Amundsen 1973a, Johannessen 1984, 1985, Stigre 1991, 1993) have found that yield signs at junctions leads to increased speeds on the main road and reduced speed on the approaches subject to the yield rule. The increase in speed on the main road is, as a rule, between 1 and 4 km/h (average speed of around 45 km/h). The reduction in speed on the minor road is normally around 2–3 km/h.

## Effect on the environment

No studies have been found that report on the effect of yield signs at junctions on the environment. Increased speed may lead to an increase in noise and increased emission of certain types of exhaust gases from motor vehicles. Increased waiting times for minor road traffic can also lead to increased exhaust emissions. The actual effects are not known.

## Costs

This measure is implemented in Norway using traffic signs and is usually quite inexpensive. The costs of signposting and road markings are around NOK 2,000–5,000 per junction. The costs of accident analyses, inspections and other activities related to planning must be added to this. These costs are not known.

## Cost–benefit analysis

A numerical example has been worked out, which may indicate possible effects of the measure. It is assumed that the junction where yield signs are introduced is a T-junction with an AADT of 5,000 vehicles, 20% minor road traffic and 0.10 injury accidents per million entering vehicles. It is assumed that the number of accidents does not change. It is assumed that traffic on the main road (4,000 vehicles) saves 1 s per car, while traffic on the minor road (1,000 vehicles) loses 3 s per car.

The estimation shows that saved costs of travel time for main road traffic (present value 10 years) are NOK 285,000 and the increased costs of travel time for minor road traffic are NOK 215,000. The net savings in costs of travel time are NOK 70,000. The cost of the measure is estimated to NOK 12,000 per junction. In other words, yield signs at junctions give a net saving in time when minor road traffic is relatively light, if, at the same time, the traffic on the main road is not so heavy that the minor road traffic has problems in finding gaps in reasonable time. At junctions with more traffic, it is probably more cost-effective to control traffic using signals or in the form of a roundabout.

Both the effect on accidents and the effect on travel time are, at any rate, very small and for this reason uncertain. The results of a cost–benefit analysis will therefore be extremely sensitive to small changes in the assumptions made about these effects.

## 3.8 Stop signs at junctions

### Problem and objective

One of the most common factors associated with road accidents is the failure of road users involved to see each other in time, or at all (Englund 1978). The design of a junction, visibility, traffic volume and road user behaviour are some of the factors that influence the probability that road users will see each other in time to avoid an accident. Doubts as to who should give way at a junction may also lead to accidents.

Highway agencies can influence some of the factors that influence the probability that road users will see each other at junctions. By putting up stop signs, road users are obliged to come to a complete halt before passing the junction. This ought to give better time to observe traffic. Stop signs at junctions are intended to reduce accidents by giving road users more time to observe traffic before entering the junction.

### Description of the measure

The use of stop signs in junctions comes in two versions: two-way stop and all-way stop. Two-way stop means that stop signs are put up on the minor road only. All-way stop means that stop signs are put up on all roads entering a junction. If a junction is controlled by all-way stop, whoever arrives first, goes first. If there is two-way stop, vehicles from the minor road have to wait until there is a sufficient gap in traffic on the major road to enter it.

The use of all-way stop, sometimes referred to as four-way stop, is very widespread in North America. Outside North America, this type of traffic control is less common. In Norway, the use of stop signs is very restrictive. In many countries, formal warrants for the use of stop signs have been developed, intended to ensure that stop signs are only used in junctions that have a bad accident record associated with inadequate road user observation.

### Effect on accidents

A number of studies have evaluated the effects of stop signs in junctions on accidents. The results presented below are based on the following studies:

Pegrum, Lloyd and Willett (1972) (Australia)
Andersson (1982) (Nordic countries)

Cedersund (1983) (Sweden)
Rosenbaum (1983) (United Stares)
Polus (1985) (Israel)
Frith and Harte (1986) (New Zealand)
Lovell and Hauer (1986) (USA and Canada)
Frith and Derby (1987) (New Zealand)
Trafiksäkerhetsverket (1988) (Sweden)
McGee and Blankenship (1989) (USA)
Brüde and Larsson (1990) (Sweden)
Brüde and Larsson (1992a) (Sweden)
Kulmala (1995) (Finland)
Helberg et al. (1996) (Denmark)
Persaud et al. (1997) (USA)

The results of these evaluation studies vary substantially. The estimates presented below (Table 3.8.1) are based on studies that have controlled for regression to the mean and long-term trends in the number of accidents.

Putting up stop signs reduces the number of injury accidents by about 20% in three-leg junctions and by about 35% in four-leg junctions. The effects on property-damage-only accidents are very uncertain; none of the estimates are statistically significant at the 5% level. When stop signs are removed and replaced by yield signs, the number of injury accidents increases by about 40% and the number of property-damage-only accidents by about 15%. Four-way stop reduces the number of accidents (severity not stated) by about 45%.

**Effect on mobility**

Stop signs will usually impose a slight delay on motorists. According to a Swedish study (Henriksson 1992), the mean delay per car entering a stop-controlled junction from the minor road was about 7 s. In junctions with all-way stop, the mean delay per car was estimated to 11 s. If a junction with the same traffic volume had traffic signals, rather than stop signs, mean delay per car would be about 12 s.

**Effect on the environment**

A Swedish study (Henriksson 1992) estimated the effects of stop signs on the emission of hydrocarbons (HC), CO, carbon dioxide ($CO_2$) and nitrogen oxide (NOx). For these pollutants, emissions were estimated to be about 10–20% if a junction has four-way

*Table 3.8.1: Effects of stop signs in junctions on accidents*

| | | Percentage change of the number of accidents | |
|---|---|---|---|
| Accident severity | Types of accident affected | Best estimate | 95% confidence interval |
| ***One-way stop in three-leg junctions*** | | | |
| Injury accidents | Accidents in junctions | −19 | (−38; +7) |
| Property-damage-only | Accidents in junctions | −60 | (−95; +224) |
| ***Two-way stop in four-leg junctions*** | | | |
| Injury accidents | Accidents in junctions | −35 | (−44; -25) |
| Property-damage-only | Accidents in junctions | −16 | (−34; +8) |
| ***Replacing stop signs by yield signs (all types of junction)*** | | | |
| Injury accidents | Accidents in junctions | +39 | (+19; +62) |
| Property-damage-only | Accidents in junctions | +14 | (+2; +26) |
| ***Four-way stop*** | | | |
| Unspecified severity | Accidents in junctions | −45 | (−49; −40) |

stop than if it has two-way stop only. Emissions in stop-controlled junctions were not compared to other types of traffic control. It is nevertheless reasonable to assume that the emission of air pollution will increase, since stopping and starting is associated with higher emissions than driving at a constant speed.

## Costs

Stop control is introduced by putting up stop signs at a junction. The cost of doing this is about NOK 2,000 to NOK 5,000 per junction. In addition to these costs, the costs of identifying junctions that would benefit from having stop signs and of analysing accidents for those junctions are also included. These costs are less known.

## Cost–benefit analysis

A couple of numerical examples have been worked out in order to indicate the potential costs and benefits associated with the use of stop signs in junctions. These examples refer to (1) stop signs on the minor road of a three-leg junction in a rural area and (2) four-way stop in a four-leg junction in an urban area.

For the first of these cases, it has been assumed that the junction has an AADT of 5,000 entering vehicles, of which 20% enter from the minor road. The accident rate is assumed to be 0.10 injury accidents per million entering vehicles. The number of injury accidents is assumed to reduce by 20% when stop signs are introduced. Vehicles entering from the minor road are delayed by 5 s, on the average. Additional emission of air pollution is assumed to represent a cost of NOK 0.05 per vehicle entering from the minor road.

Given these assumptions, the present value of the reduction in accident costs comes to NOK 690,000. Additional costs of travel time amount to NOK 356,000 and additional costs of air pollution amount to NOK 128,000. Total benefits are NOK 205,000. A cost of NOK 30,000 per junction is a reasonable estimate. Benefits are substantially greater than costs.

As for the four-leg junction, an AADT for 7,500 was assumed, 40% entering from the minor roads, and an injury accident rate of 0.20. When four-way stop is introduced, all vehicles are delayed by 9 s. It is assumed that the number of injury accidents is reduced by 45% and the number of property-damage-only accidents reduced by 30%. Air pollution emissions are assumed to increase at a rate representing a societal cost of NOK 0.09 per vehicle.

The present value of the reduction of accident costs is NOK 4.9 million. The increase in the costs of travel time amounts to NOK 4.8 million. The increase in environmental cost is estimated to NOK 1.7 million. Overall benefits in this case are negative, at NOK −1.6 million. Costs can be estimated to about NOK 60,000 per junction.

These examples show that stop control can give a net benefit to society if applied to minor roads in rural junctions. Four-way stop in urban junctions does not appear to be a cost-effective measure.

## 3.9 Traffic signal control at junctions

### Problem and objective

The majority of traffic accidents in towns and cities occur at junctions. This is true for all groups of road users (Elvik and Muskaug 1994). As traffic volume increases, the probability of conflict between road users at junctions increases, and traffic flow worsens. Traffic signal control at junctions separates different streams of traffic from each other, and can improve the flow of traffic at junctions. According to the Norwegian guidelines for traffic control devices, traffic signal control at junctions aims at improving traffic safety, reducing delays, making school roads safer and prioritising public transport. The emphasis placed on each objective will vary depending on the conditions at the individual junction.

### Description of the measure

Traffic signal control is introduced using traffic signals, which can either be time-controlled (phases change after a given time, irrespective of the amount of traffic) or vehicle-actuated (the length of the phases is adapted to the amount of vehicles up to a given maximum phase length). Traffic signals can be designed with separate phases for each traffic stream at a junction (conflict-free control) or with shared phases for some of the traffic streams. In Norway, it is normal for drivers who are turning right to share the same phase as pedestrians crossing the road, and for drivers who are turning left to share the same phase as oncoming traffic.

In this chapter, the introduction of traffic signal controls at junctions, which were previously controlled in other ways, and a number of improvements to existing traffic signals are described. Measures to prevent red-light running are described in Section 8.5.

### Effect on accidents

***New traffic signals.*** A number of studies have evaluated the effect of traffic signal control at junctions on accidents. The results presented in Table 3.9.1 are based on the following studies:

Young (1967) (USA)
Andreassen (1970) (Australia)
Cribbins and Walton (1970) (USA)
Gunnarsson and Olsson (1974a, 1974b) (Sweden)
Johannessen and Heir (1974) (Norway)
King and Goldblatt (1975) (USA)

*Table 3.9.1: Effects on accidents at junctions of traffic signal control at junctions*

| | Percentage change in the number of accidents | | |
|---|---|---|---|
| Accident severity | Type of accident which is affected | Best estimate | 95% confidence interval |
| ***Traffic signal control at three-leg junctions*** | | | |
| Injury accidents | Accidents at junctions | −15 | (−25; −5) |
| Property-damage-only accidents | Accidents at junctions | −15 | (−40; +15) |
| ***Traffic signal control at four-leg junctions*** | | | |
| Injury accidents | Accidents at junctions | −30 | (−35; −25) |
| Property-damage-only accidents | Accidents at junctions | −35 | (−45; −25) |

Amundsen et al. (1976) (Norway)
Grønnerød (1976) (Finland)
Hoff and Overgaard (1976) (Denmark)
Vodahl and Johannessen (1977) (Norway)
Hakkert and Mahalel (1978) (Israel)
Vaa and Johannessen (1978) (Norway)
Dahlen and Toftenes (1979) (Norway)
Hvoslef (1979) (Norway)
Short, Woelfl and Chang (1982) (USA)
Cedersund (1983) (Sweden)
Dahlen and Toftenes (1984) (Norway)
Brüde and Larsson (1985) (Sweden)
Craven (1986) (USA)
Frith and Harte (1986) (New Zealand)
Vodahl and Giæver (1986a, 1986b) (Norway)
Brüde and Larsson (1988) (Sweden)
Dagestad (1989) (Norway)
Datta and Dutta (1990) (USA)
Lalani (1991) (USA)
Brüde and Larsson (1992b) (Sweden)
Seim (1994) (Norway)
Kulmala (1995) (Finland)

Traffic signal control reduces the number of accidents by around 15% at T-junctions and around 30% at crossroads. The effect is the same for property-damage-only accidents as it is for injury accidents. More detailed studies show that traffic signal control has different effects on different types of accidents. Accidents involving vehicles crossing the junction are greatly reduced, while rear-end collisions increase.

***Upgrading traffic signals.*** Many studies have evaluated the effect of different types of upgrading of traffic signals on accidents. The results presented in this chapter are based on the following studies:

Malo (1967) (USA)
Andreassen (1970) (Australia)
Crook (1970) (Great Britain)
Grønnerød (1976) (Finland)
McGee and Warren (1976) (USA)
McGee (1977) (USA)
Hakkert and Mahalel (1978) (Israel)

Bastable (1980) (Australia)
Baier and Schlabbach (1981) (Germany)
DeWerd (1982) (The Netherlands)
Preusser et al. (1982) (USA)
Senneset and Skjetne (1982) (Norway)
Zador, Moshman and Marcus (1982) (USA)
Zegeer, Opiela and Cynecki (1982) (USA)
Wu, Lee, Machemehl and Williams (1982) (USA)
Perfater (1983) (USA)
Mahalel and Zaidel (1985) (Israel)
Schlabbach, Scharffetter, Lauer and Guttenberger (1984) (Germany)
Bach and Jørgensen (1986) (Denmark)
Craven (1986) (USA)
Greiwe (1986) (USA)
Hodge, Daley and Nguyen (1986) (Australia)
Barbaresso (1987) (USA)
Zaidel and Hocherman (1987) (Israel)
Bhesania (1991) (USA)
Hauer (1991) (USA)
Lalani (1991) (USA)
Kølster Pedersen et al. (1992) (Denmark)
Shebeeb (1995) (USA)
Hanbali and Fornal (1997) (USA)
Stamatiadis and Agent (1997) (USA)

On the basis of the studies, best estimates of the effect of different improvements to traffic signals on accidents are given in Table 3.9.2.

Most improvements appear to reduce the number of accidents at traffic signal-controlled junctions. Improvements that do not appear to reduce the number of accidents include:

- installing pedestrian signals with mixed phases with motor vehicles,
- flashing green lights to warn of phase changes,
- yellow flashing lights at low traffic, and
- permission to turn right on red light.

Many of the results given are very uncertain and should be treated with scepticism. Many of the available studies have been carried out at junctions that were accident black spots. None of these studies controlled for regression to the mean. Many studies

*Table 3.9.2: Effects of upgrading traffic signals on the number of accidents at junctions*

| | Percentage change in the number of accidents | | |
|---|---|---|---|
| Accident severity | Type of accident affected | Best estimate | 95% confidence interval |
| ***Installing secondary signal*** | | | |
| Unspecified severity | Accidents at traffic signal-controlled junctions | −25 | (−50; +5) |
| ***Installing pedestrian crossing signal – mixed phase with motor vehicles*** | | | |
| Injury accidents | Pedestrian accidents | +8 | (−1; +17) |
| Injury accidents | Vehicle accidents | −12 | (−21; −3) |
| ***Installing pedestrian crossing signals – separate phase*** | | | |
| Injury accidents | Pedestrian accidents | −30 | (−40; −15) |
| Injury accidents | Vehicle accidents | −18 | (−27; −9) |
| ***Extended all-red period*** | | | |
| Unspecified severity | Accidents at traffic signal-controlled junctions | −55 | (−65; −40) |
| ***Establishing left turn phase*** | | | |
| Unspecified severity | Accidents on left turns | −10 | (−15; −5) |
| ***Separate left turn phase*** | | | |
| Unspecified severity | Accidents at left turns | −58 | (−64; −50) |
| ***Conflict-free phase changes*** | | | |
| Injury accidents | Accidents at traffic signal-controlled junctions | −75 | (−90; −35) |
| Property-damage-only accidents | Accidents at traffic signal-controlled junction | −25 | (−65; +60) |
| ***Changed phase development (order, length)*** | | | |
| Injury accidents | Accidents at traffic signal-controlled junctions | −55 | (−75; −15) |
| Property-damage-only accidents | Accidents at traffic signal-controlled junctions | +15 | (−25; +70) |
| ***Improving sight conditions, signal heads and signal posts*** | | | |
| Unspecified severity | Accidents at traffic signal-controlled junctions | −40 | (−45; −35) |
| ***Improvements to road markings and channelisation*** | | | |
| Unspecified severity | Accidents at traffic signal-controlled junctions | −15 | (−35; +10) |
| ***Vehicle-actuated phase changes*** | | | |
| Unspecified severity | Accidents at traffic signal-controlled junctions | −25 | (−33; −15) |
| ***Co-ordinating signals («green wave»)*** | | | |
| Injury accidents | Accidents in co-ordinated areas | −19 | (−22; −15) |
| Property-damage-only accidents | Accidents in co-ordinated areas | −23 | (−26; −20) |
| ***Green flashing signal warning of phase changes*** | | | |
| Injury accidents | Accidents at traffic signal-controlled junctions | +42 | (+30; +56) |

*Table 3.9.2: (Continued)*

| | Percentage change in the number of accidents | | |
|---|---|---|---|
| Accident severity | Type of accident affected | Best estimate | 95% confidence interval |
| ***Yellow flashing light in low traffic*** | | | |
| Injury accidents | Accidents during yellow flashing lights | +55 | (−7; +165) |
| Property-damage-only accidents | Accidents during yellow flashing lights | +40 | (+30; +55) |
| ***Permission to turn right on a red light (with yield requirement)*** | | | |
| Injury accidents | Right turn accidents | +60 | (+50; +70) |
| Property-damage-only accidents | Right turn accidents | +10 | (+9; +11) |

have not specified accident severity, but are based on a mixture of injury accidents and property-damage-only accidents. Care should be taken in generalising the results to all signalised junctions. It is possible that upgrading is effective only in junctions that have particular problems.

### Effect on mobility

At junctions with heavy traffic (more than 600 cars during the peak hour), traffic signal control will, as a rule, reduce waiting times for all traffic movements taken together (Blakstad 1988). Traffic streams that would otherwise be required to yield can gain time, while those with priority can be delayed. Pedestrians often gain time when there is traffic signal control.

Co-ordinating traffic signals can reduce waiting times and considerably increase the average speed in city streets with traffic flow problems. A German study (Schlabbach, Scharffetter, Lauer and Guttenberger 1984) found increases to around 40–45 km/h, irrespective of the previous level of speed. Norwegian studies (Senneset and Skjetne 1982) show minor effects on mobility of co-ordinating traffic signals.

### Effect on the environment

No studies have been found that show how traffic signal control at junctions affects the emission of exhaust gases and noise levels in traffic. A German study (Schlabbach, Scharffetter, Lauer and Guttenberger 1984) found that co-ordinating traffic signals can lead to lower fuel consumption and lower emission of exhaust gases. How large this effect is, depends on the extent to which co-ordination of traffic signals improves the traffic flow.

### Costs

A compilation of cost figures from a number of sources (Elvik 1996) shows that the average cost of traffic signal control at a junction on a national highway can be estimated to be NOK 1.1 million (±NOK 0.15 million) at 1995 prices. Annual maintenance costs can be estimated at NOK 50,000 per junction. Corresponding figures for county roads are around NOK 430,000 (±NOK 42,000) for constructing a traffic signal-controlled junction and NOK 30,000 per year for operation and maintenance. Cost figures for upgrading traffic signals have not been found.

### Cost–benefit analysis

The benefit–cost ratio of a traffic signal-controlled junction depends on how the measure affects accidents and mobility. Three numerical examples have been prepared.

It is assumed that a three-leg junction with an AADT of 12,000 vehicles, 25% minor road traffic and 0.10 injury accidents per million incoming vehicles is traffic signal-controlled. It is assumed that the number of accidents is reduced by 15%. Entering vehicles are assumed to be delayed by an average of 1 s. Increased exhaust emissions are assumed to increase the environmental costs by NOK 0.03 per car. The cost of a traffic signal-controlled junction is assumed to be ca. NOK 0.9 million in construction costs. The saved accident costs are estimated to be NOK 2.3 million. The increased costs of travel time are estimated to be NOK 1.4 million and the increased environmental costs to be NOK 1.5 million. The total benefit is negative, around NOK –0.6 million. In other words, the measure is not cost-effective.

For a four-leg junction, the corresponding AADT is assumed to be 20,000 vehicles, 40% minor road traffic and 0.20 injury accidents per million entering vehicles. The number of injury accidents is assumed to reduce by 30% and the number of property-damage-only accidents by 35%. Incoming vehicles are assumed to save, on average, 3 s. Increased exhaust emissions are assumed to increase the environmental costs by NOK 0.07 per vehicle. The cost of a traffic signal-controlled junction is assumed to be NOK 1.44 million in construction costs. The reduction of accident costs are estimated to NOK 15.6 million. Saved costs of travel time are estimated to be NOK 7.1 million, and the increased environmental costs NOK 6.0 million. The total benefit is estimated to be NOK 16.8 million. The costs of the measure are estimated at around NOK 2.1 million (including present value of operating and maintenance costs). The benefit is greater than the costs.

An example has also been drawn up concerning upgrading signal-controlled crossroads with an AADT of 15,000 and an accident rate of 0.25 injury accidents per million incoming vehicles. The number of accidents is assumed to reduce by 20%. Time consumption and pollution emissions are assumed not to change. Costs are set at NOK 0.72 million. The benefit is greater than the costs. Saved accident costs are estimated to be NOK 9.5 million and the cost of the measure is estimated at around NOK 1.1 million.

## 3.10 Signalised pedestrian crossings

### Problem and objective

Crossing roads can be difficult. Children and the elderly in particular have problems in crossing public roads. Official Norwegian accident statistics show that around 70% of pedestrian accidents occur while crossing a road. Marking a pedestrian crossing does not always provide good enough safety for pedestrians crossing the road. Drivers do not always observe the duty to yield for pedestrians crossing the road on marked pedestrian crossings (Amundsen et al. 1976, Muskaug et al. 1979, Varhelyi 1998). In order to improve pedestrian crossings, the crossing point can be signalised.

### Description of the measure

Pedestrian crossings can be signal-controlled by means of traffic signals that change automatically or that only change when a pedestrian presses a button to obtain a green light. A type of signalised pedestrian crossing used in Great Britain and a number of other countries is a pelican crossing (pelican = pedestrian light-controlled). This is a push-button-activated signalling system, where flashing yellow lights for vehicles appear at the end of the crossing phase. When the flashing yellow light shows, vehicles may cross the pedestrian crossing provided there are no pedestrians on it. The purpose of the yellow blinking light phase is to shorten waiting times for motor vehicles. Experience shows that push buttons are little used (Dahlen and Toftenes 1979, Huang and Zegeer 2001).

## Effect on accidents

The effects of signalised pedestrian crossings on accidents are summarised in Table 3.10.1. The results are based on the following studies:

Mackie and Older (1965) (Great Britain)
Jacobs and Wilson (1967) (Great Britain)
Jørgensen and Rabani (1971) (Denmark)
Rayner (1975) (Great Britain)
Schmutz (1977) (Switzerland)
Willett (1977) (Australia)
Arndt (1978) (Australia)
Inwood and Grayson (1979) (Great Britain)
Kildebogaard and Wass (1982) (Denmark)
Dahlen and Toftenes (1984) (Norway)
Bagley (1985) (Great Britain)
Harper (1985) (Great Britain)
Vodahl and Giæver (1986b) (Norway)
Giæver (1987) (N)

*Table 3.10.1: Effect of signalised pedestrian crossings on accidents*

| | Percentage change in the number of accidents | | |
|---|---|---|---|
| Accident severity | Types of accidents affected | Best estimate | 95% confidence interval |
| ***Signalised pedestrian crossing vs. no crosswalk*** | | | |
| Injury accidents | Pedestrian accidents mid-block | −49 | (−81; +35) |
| Injury accidents | Pedestrian accidents at junctions | −2 | (−48; +84) |
| ***Signalised pedestrian crossing vs. marked crosswalk*** | | | |
| Injury accidents | Pedestrian accidents | −27 | (−59; +29) |
| Injury accidents | Vehicle accidents | +53 | (−45; +309) |
| Injury accidents | All accidents | −23 | (−56; +32) |
| ***Pelican crossing vs. no crosswalk*** | | | |
| Injury accidents | Pedestrian accidents | −20 | (−34; −2) |
| Injury accidents | Vehicle accidents | +3 | (−22; +36) |
| Injury accidents | All accidents | −9 | (−21; +5) |
| ***Pelican crossing vs. marked crosswalk*** | | | |
| Injury accidents | Pedestrian accidents | +3 | (−25; +42) |
| Injury accidents | Vehicle accidents | −23 | (−35; −10) |
| Injury accidents | All accidents | −16 | (−30; +1) |

Lindenmann, Riedel and Thoma (1987) (Switzerland)
Ekman (1988) (Sweden)
Hunt and Griffiths (1989) (Great Britain)
Daly, McGrath and vanEmst (1991) (Great Britain)
Ward et al. (1994) (Great Britain)
Summersgill and Layfield (1996) (Great Britain)
Gårder (2004) (USA)

Ordinary ***signalised pedestrian crossings*** at locations where there previously was no crosswalk were not found to affect accidents significantly. A large but non-significant reduction of pedestrian accidents was found at midblock crossings. However, the results are highly heterogeneous and most studies have not applied a comparison group.

***Signalised pedestrian crossings*** at locations where there previously was a marked crosswalk were found to reduce pedestrian accidents and to increase vehicle accidents. The result for vehicle accident is based on only two studies with a very weak study design (e.g. exposure is not controlled for and no comparison group was applied). Most of the studies that have investigated effects on pedestrian accidents have not applied a comparison group either, many have not controlled for exposure, and none has controlled for both pedestrian and vehicle exposure. As indicated by the large confidence intervals, the results are highly uncertain and likely to be affected by factors, such as methodological weaknesses and differences between the pedestrian crossings and crossing locations (e.g. volumes, numbers of lanes, junction vs. mid-block).

***Pelican crossings*** at locations where there previously was no crosswalk were found to significantly reduce pedestrian accidents, while no effects were found on vehicle accidents. At locations where there previously were ordinary marked crosswalks, no effect was found on pedestrian accidents, but vehicle accidents were found to decrease.

### Effect on mobility

Signalised pedestrian crossings affect waiting times at crossing points for both pedestrians and motor vehicles. A British study (Hunt 1990) compared average waiting times for pedestrians and drivers at different types of crossing points. Based on this study Figure 3.10.1 shows the results for pedestrian waiting times and Figure 3.10.2 shows the results for motor vehicle waiting times.

Figure 3.10.1 shows that an ordinary, marked pedestrian crossing gives the shortest waiting time for pedestrians, at all levels of vehicle traffic. If all drivers observe the duty to give way to pedestrians at pedestrian crossings, there will only be a minimal waiting

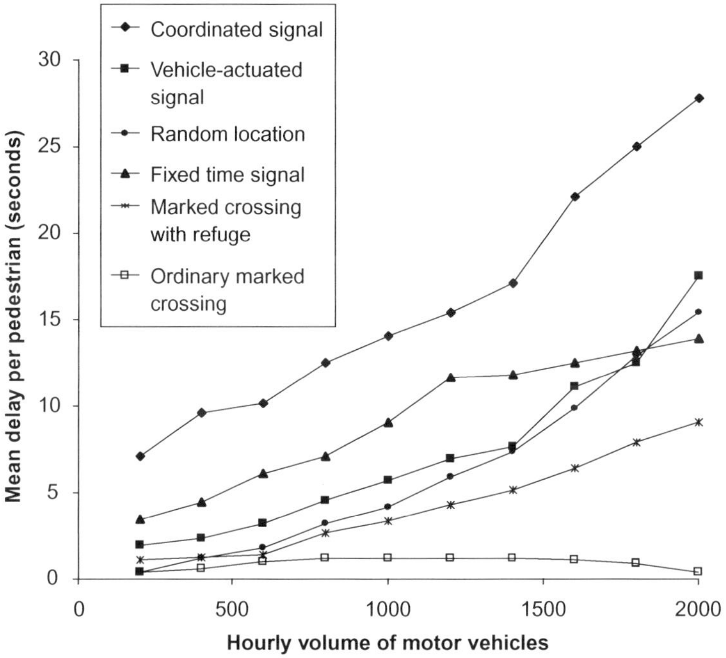


*Figure 3.10.1: Average delay per pedestrian in seconds per road crossing at different types of crossing facilities (Hunt 1990).*

time for pedestrians on pedestrian crossings. On pedestrian crossings with refuges, the waiting time is somewhat longer than on ordinary pedestrian crossings. All forms of signalised pedestrian crossings result in longer waiting times for pedestrians. On average, pedestrians must wait for around half the circuit time for the signal.

Figure 3.10.2 shows that fixed time signals forming part of a co-ordinated system give the shortest waiting times for motorised traffic. Ordinary pedestrian crossings can lead to long waiting times if both pedestrian traffic and road traffic is high. Figures 3.10.1 and 3.10.2 show that there are conflicting interests between pedestrians and motorists with respect to the type of crossing facilities that give the shortest waiting time.

**Effect on the environment**

Pedestrians feel safer crossing the road at a signalised pedestrian crossing than at other crossing points (Schioldborg 1979). No studies have been found that show the effects on noise and pollution emissions of signalised pedestrian crossings.

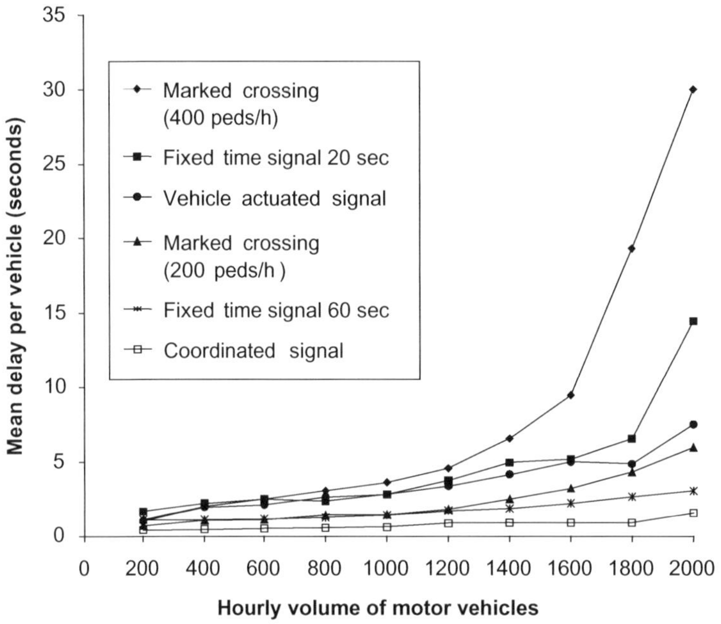


*Figure 3.10.2: Average waiting time per vehicle calculated in seconds at different types of crossings (Hunt 1990). Relationship between changes in the number of accidents and changes in speed.*

### Costs

A compilation of cost figures from the Norwegian Public Roads Administration (Elvik and Rydningen 2002) shows that introducing traffic signal control of pedestrian crossings cost, on average, around NOK 340,000 (±NOK 25,000) (2000 prices). Annual operating and maintenance costs can be estimated at around NOK 25,000 per traffic signal–regulated pedestrian crossing per year.

### Cost–benefit analysis

A numerical example has been worked out to indicate costs and benefits of signalised pedestrian crossings. It is assumed that the crossing has an AADT of 15,000 vehicles and 5,000 pedestrians. During the daytime (8 h), it is assumed that the hourly vehicle traffic is 1,000 and the hourly pedestrian traffic is 400. The site is assumed to have 0.05 pedestrian accident per 1 million incoming vehicles and 0.05 vehicle accidents per million incoming vehicles. The number of pedestrian accidents is assumed to be reduced by 12%, and the number of vehicle accidents by 2%. The expected delay is calculated on the basis of Figures 3.10.1 and 3.10.2 to an average for the whole 24-h period of less than 3 s per pedestrian and per vehicle. Saving in accident costs are estimated to around NOK 0.9 million. Increased costs of travel time are estimated to around NOK 7.1 million. The total benefit is therefore negative, NOK –6.2 million. This calculation does not include an economic valuation of the increased feeling of safety among pedestrians.

It may be argued that delays of 3 s are not significant. However, this length of delay is only an average. The delays are not evenly distributed. For example, some delays may be of 1 min while in other cases there may be no delay at all. The fact that around 25% of pedestrians cross the road at a red light (Askildsen, Leite and Muskaug 1996), may indicate that some pedestrians regard the saving of a few seconds as a benefit, which more than offsets the increased risk of accident.

## 3.11 Speed limits

### Problem and objectives

A driver usually wants to get from A to B using as little time as possible and with a reasonable feeling of comfort and safety while travelling. The majority of drivers trade off travel time against safety for themselves and for other road users. In this evaluation, factors such as road geometry, driving and light conditions, the amount of traffic, the characteristics of the car, one's own skills and motives, accident rates and the possibility of police enforcement are all included (Samferdselsdepartementet, st. meld. 72 1977–78, Glad, Rein and Fosser 1990). Many drivers have an expectation of being able to control their car at much higher speeds than the posted speed limits. This is particularly true of young and inexperienced drivers, who have a tendency to overestimate their own ability and to underestimate traffic hazards (Johansson 1982, Spolander 1983, Rumar 1985). If car drivers could choose their own speed, many would probably have chosen a much higher speed than they do today.

In practice, there are major differences in the speed at which different drivers drive given the same external conditions. High speeds and great variations in speed increase the probability of accidents and serious personal injuries, because the demands on the road user's observation and reactions increase, and because braking distance increases proportionally with the square of the speed. Furthermore, the risk of fatal injuries increases by the fourth power of the change in speed to which the body is exposed in an accident. High speeds increase energy consumption and the emission of polluting gases. The noise level from traffic also increases with increasing driving speeds.

General and signposted speed limits state the highest permitted driving speed on a road. Ideally, speed limits are set as a compromise between the need for mobility for drivers and of the need for safety and the environmental protection both for drivers and others who use the road.

**Description of the measure**

In the majority of European countries, unrestricted speeds on the entire or part of the road network existed from the 1930s. It was only after around 1970–75 that permanent speed limits became common on the main road network. Norway has had general speed limits on the whole road network since 1912. The limits were gradually adjusted upwards up until 1965 (Samferdselsdepartementet, st. meld. 72 1977–78). Residential roads often have a speed limit reduced from 50 to 40 or 30 km/h (Amundsen 1983). In 2001, the speed limit was reduced from 90 to 80 km/h or from 80 to 70 km/h on many roads with exceptionally high injury severity density (Ragnøy 2004).

**Effect on accidents**

There are a great number of studies of the effects of speed limits on accidents. Only studies that have investigated effects of speed limits on both speed and accidents or injuries have been included in the present analysis. These studies are

Hall, Hearne and O'Flynn (1970) (Ireland): 97 km/h
Jönrup and Svensson (1971) (Sweden and other countries): 113, 110, 105, 100, 90, 80 km/h
Wahlgren (1972) (Finland): 110, 90 km/h
Andersson and Nilsson (1974) (Sweden): 110 km/h
Brodersen, Jørgensen and Lund (1975) (Denmark): 110, 90, 60 km/h
Brodin and Ringhagen (1975) (Sweden): 30 km/h
Nilsson (1976) (Sweden): 110, 70 km/h
Burritt, Moghrabi and Matthias (1976) (USA): 88 km/h
Scott and Barton (1976) (Great Britain): 97, 80 km/h
Kemper and Byington (1977) (USA): 88 km/h
Daltrey and Healy (1980) (Australia): 100 km/h
Nilsson (1980) (Sweden): 90 km/h
Amundsen (1981) (Norway): 70, 60 km/h
Christensen (1981) (Denmark): 110, 90 km/h
Koshi and Kashima (1981) (Japan): 50 km/h

Salusjärvi (1981) (Finland): 120, 100, 80, 60 km/h
Frith and Toomath (1982) (New Zealand): 80 km/h
Salusjärvi (1982) (Norway): 60 km/h
Amundsen (1983) (Norway): 60 km/h
Jørgensen et al. (1985) (Nordic countries): 110, 100, 90 km/h
Sakshaug (1986) (Norway): 90, 60, 50 km/h
Engel and Krogsgård Thomsen (1987) (Denmark): 50 km/h
Ullman and Dudek (1987) (USA): 72 km/h
Dietrich, Lindenmann, Hehlen and Thoma (1988) (Switzerland): 120, 80 km/h
Engel and Krogsgård Thomsen (1988) (Denmark): 50 km/h
Upchurch (1989) (USA): 105 km/h
US Department of Transportation (1989) (USA): 105 km/h
Gallaher et al. (1989) (USA): 105 km/h
Rijkswaterstaat (1989) (Netherlands): 120 km/h
Brown, Maghsoodloo and McArdle (1990) (USA): 105 km/h
Nilsson (1990) (Sweden): 90 km/h
Smith (1990) (USA): 105 km/h
Roszbach (1990) (Netherlands): 120 km/h
Sidhu (1990) (USA): 105 km/h
Jernigan and Lynn (1991) (USA): 105 km/h
Sliogeris (1992) (Australia): 110 km/h
Godwin (1992) (USA): 105, 88 km/h
Sammer (1994) (Austria): 30 km/h
Rock (1995) (USA): 105 km/h
Parker (1997) (USA): 105, 88, 72, 64, 56 km/h
Antov and Roivas (1999) (Estonia): 110 km/h
Farmer, Retting and Lund (1999) (USA): 113 km/h
Peltola (2000) (Finland): 80 km/h
Andersson (2000) (Sweden): 90, 70 km/h
Wretling (2000) (Sweden): 90 km/h
Burns, Johnstone and Macdonald (2001) (Great Britain): 32 km/h
Abel and Matthes (2001) (Germany): 30 km/h
Amundsen, Roald and Engebretsen (2004) (Norway): 100 km/h
Richter et al. (2004) (Israel): 100 km/h
Ragnøy (2004) (Norway): 80, 70 km/h
Vernon, Cook, Peterson and Dean (2004) (USA): 113 km/h

Results from countries using miles (per hour) as a unit are converted to kilometres per hour (1 mile = 1,609 m). On the whole, the summarised results are based on 248 effect estimates from 51 studies. The results from these studies have been summarised by Elvik, Christensen and Amundsen (2004). The effects on accidents, injuries and fatalities of changing speed limits depend on the effect of the speed limit changes on speed. Elvik, Christensen and Amundsen (2004) have summarised the relationship between speed limit changes and speed as shown in Figure 3.11.1 based on the studies shown above. As a rule of thumb, when the speed limit is changed by 10 km/h, speed changes by about 2.5 km/h.

The changes in the numbers of fatalities, injuries and accidents can be estimated based on changes of speed. According to the power model of speed (Elvik, Christensen and Amundsen 2004), the relationship between speed changes and changes in numbers of accidents and injuries can be described as power functions according to the following formula:

$$\frac{\text{Accidents after}}{\text{Accidents before}} = \left(\frac{\text{Average speed after}}{\text{Average speed before}}\right)^{\text{Exponent}}$$

The effects of speed changes on injuries and fatalities are estimated accordingly. The exponents for the best estimates of the effects and the confidence intervals are as shown in Table 3.11.1. The relationship between speed changes and changes in numbers of accidents and injuries is illustrated in Figure 3.11.2.

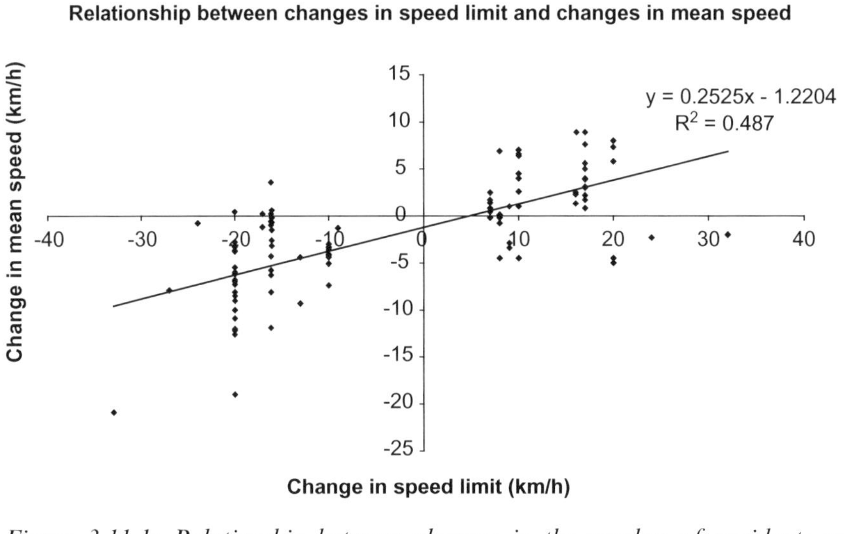


*Figure 3.11.1: Relationship between changes in the number of accidents and changes in speed.*

*Table 3.11.1: Exponents for the best estimates and the confidence intervals of the effects of speed changes on accidents, injuries and fatalities*

| Accident/injury severity | Best estimate | 95% confidence interval |
|---|---|---|
| Fatalities | 4.5 | (4.1–4.9) |
| Serious injuries | 3.0 | (2.2–3.8) |
| Slight injuries | 1.5 | (1.0–2.0) |
| All injuries | 2.7 | (0.9–4.5) |
| Fatal accidents | 3.6 | (2.4–4.8) |
| Accidents with serious injuries | 2.4 | (1.1–3.7) |
| Accidents with slight injuries | 1.2 | (0.1–2.3) |
| All injury accidents | 2.0 | (1.3–2.7) |
| Property-damage-only accidents | 1.0 | (0.2–1.8) |

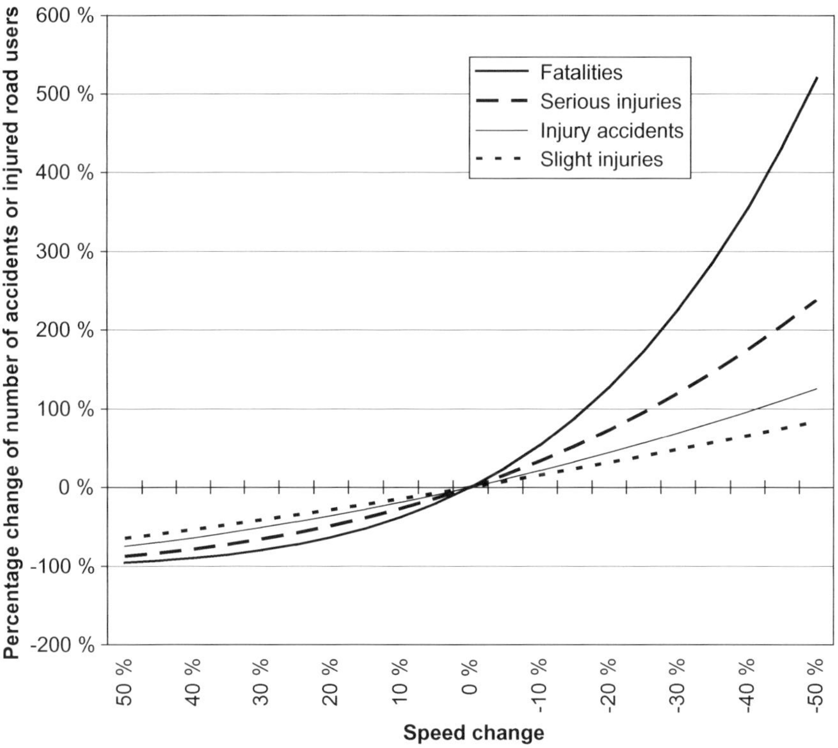


*Figure 3.11.2: Effect on numbers of accidents, injuries and fatalities of reducing speed as estimated with the power model.*

*Table 3.11.2: Relationship between speed and travel time*

| Speed (km/h) | Travel time (minutes) (distance 60 km) |
|---|---|
| 100 | 36 |
| 90 | 40 |
| 80 | 45 |
| 70 | 51 |
| 60 | 60 |
| 50 | 72 |
| 40 | 90 |
| 30 | 120 |

### Effect on mobility

Lower speed reduces mobility by increasing the time taken to travel and transport goods (Table 3.11.2).

By reducing speed from, for example, 80 to 70 km/h over a 60 km length of road, travel time increases from 45 min to around 51 min. More equal distribution of speed between vehicles in a traffic stream may increase the capacity of the road. This can give better mobility in cases where traffic volume is nearly the capacity of the road. A reduction of speed by, for example, 10 km/h increases travel times more at lower speeds (e.g. from 50 to 40 km/h) than at higher speeds (e.g. from 100 to 90 km/h).

### Effect on the environment

The effect of speed limits on the environment is, to a large extent, influenced by how fuel consumption, exhaust emissions and noise vary with speed. For light cars, fuel consumption per kilometre driven is greatest at low speeds (Ragnøy 1994). It decreases with increasing speed levels up to around 60–70 km/h. At higher speeds, fuel consumption increases, but not up to the level of low speeds. For heavy vehicles, fuel consumption also decreases with increasing speed up to around 50 km/h. At high speeds, fuel consumption increases. The increase is greater than for light vehicles. Heavy vehicles consume almost as much fuel at high speeds (90 km/h or more) as at very low speeds (10 km/h). Emissions of $CO_2$ are linearly related to fuel consumption. Fuel consumption for a given vehicle is influenced by whether the driving speed is constant or varies on a given section of road. The more variable the driving speed, the higher the fuel consumption.

Pollution emission is – as a rule of thumb – proportional to fuel consumption. Reducing speed limits has nearly always led to lower average speeds. It can therefore be assumed that reducing the speed level to 50–70 km/h – whatever the previous speed limit –

normally reduces exhaust emission from vehicles. The effects on air pollution of further reductions in speed depend on how much the variation in speed is reduced. Very low driving speeds (below 30 km/h) lead to increased emission, but this effect can be countered by reducing the variation in speed (Public Roads Administration, Norwegian Pollution Control Authority and Directorate for Nature Management, 1992).

Noise caused by motor vehicles increases with increasing speeds (Public Roads Administration, Norwegian Pollution Control Authority and Directorate for Nature Management, 1992). Reducing speed will therefore, under otherwise identical conditions, reduce the noise problems caused by road traffic.

### Costs

In Norway, speed limits are introduced by putting up speed limit signs. The cost of purchasing and installing a traffic sign is around NOK 2,000–5,000 per sign.

### Cost–benefit analysis

Speed limits can be set according to different principles (Nilsson and Roosmark 1976, Jørgensen et al. 1985, Vägverket 1997). One of these principles is to define optimal speed limits, so that the total costs to society are minimised. The total costs include accident costs, the costs of travel time, vehicle operating costs, environmental costs and road maintenance costs. Other principles for setting speed limits are

- adapting the speed limit to actual speed levels, measured, for example, in terms of 85% percentile (the speed below which 85% of vehicles drive) or the average speed.
- varying the speed limit according to the standard of the road (e.g. road geometry, number of access roads).
- adapting the speed limit to human biomechanical tolerances (vision zero speed limit), i.e. not higher than 30 km/h on roads where there are pedestrians, not higher than 50 km/h where motor vehicles are crossing and not above 70 km/h where head-on collisions may occur.

In practice, a mixture of the different principles for setting speed limits is almost always used. Optimal speed limits have been calculated and compared to the actual speed limits and speed (Table 3.11.3). Most actual speed limits are quite near the optimal speed limits.

Optimal speed limits have several limitations. It is questionable if all relevant effects of speed are taken into account. Which effects are taken into account is dependent on the availability of economic valuations, and several effects, for example, the security of

*Table 3.11.3: Optimal speed limits and actual speed limits and speed in Norway and Sweden*

| Road category | Average speed (km/h) | Actual speed limit (km/h) | Optimal speed limit (km/h) |
|---|---|---|---|
| ***Norway*** | | | |
| Motorway A | 95 | 90 or 100 | 100 |
| Motorway B | 86 | 90 or 80 | 80 |
| Rural road | 77 | 80 | 70 |
| Urban arterial | 50 | 50 | 50 |
| Access road | 40 | 30 | 40 |
| ***Sweden*** | | | |
| Motorway A | 109 | 110 | 110 |
| Motorway B | 108 | 110 | 90 |
| Motorway B | 96 | 90 | 80 |
| Rural road | 95 | 90 | 80 |
| Urban arterial | 50 | 50 | 60 |
| Access road | 39 | 30 | 60 |

pedestrians and cyclists, are therefore currently not included in the calculation of optimal speed limits. Valuation is not an exact science, and valuations of the same things may be different in different countries. Optimal speed limits are, for example, based on different values of the effects of speed in Norway and in Sweden (Elvik 2002). On motorways, the optimal speed limit is somewhere between 70 and 110 km/h. The cost curve is almost flat in this interval and the optimal speed limit can therefore not be determined more exactly. The effects on road safety however are widely different between 70 and 110 km/h.

When determining optimal speed limits, the need for enforcement should be taken into account. Enforcement costs can be very different between two different speed limits, even if the societal costs of these two speed limits are approximately equal. The costs of enforcement can therefore be decisive in determining the optimal speed limits.

## 3.12 Speed-reducing devices

### Problem and objective

High speeds in residential streets, access roads and other places where children play result in a high accident rate and strong feelings of insecurity. Access roads in urban and semi-urban areas in Norway have higher accident rates than most other types of road (Blakstad and Giæver 1989). Accident rates on access roads without speed-reducing devices in urban and semi-urban areas are between 1.4 and 3.0 injury accidents per million vehicle kilometres. On other roads in urban areas, there are between 0.3 and 1.0 injury accidents per million vehicle kilometres.

Reduced speeds in residential areas in Norway lead to a lower risk (Blakstad and Giæver 1989), but road signs stating particularly low speed levels (20, 30 or 40 km/h) do not always have the desired effect on speed in residential areas. On wide, straight roads in particular, speeds are high (Amundsen and Christensen 1986). In order to get speeds down to the desired level, speed-reducing devices, that make fast driving uncomfortable or impossible, may be necessary.

### Description of the measure

Speed-reducing devices are intended to force vehicles to keep to low speeds, so that the risk of accidents is reduced and feelings of safety increase. Speed-reducing devices include speed humps, raised pedestrian crossings, raised junctions (plateau junctions), rumble strips, narrowing road width and speed zones.

***Speed humps*** are artificial elevations on the carriageway. A hump is often designed as part of a circle (circle segment), part of a trapeze or as a sinusoidal curve. Speed dumps (artificial depressions in the carriageway) are no longer used. Circle-shaped speed humps, which were recommended in 1973 (Watts 1973), give increasing discomfort when driven over at increasing speeds. This can be avoided by designing the hump as a sinusoidal curve, which has no breaking point with the longitudinal profile of the road (Lahrmann and Mathiasen 1992). Speed humps may be designed so that they can be used as raised pedestrian crossings.

***Raised junctions (plateau junctions)*** mean that the junction area is raised to the same level as the surrounding pavement. Ramps are constructed on the access to the raised junction area. Raised junctions can be combined with pavement widening, as well as bollards on the edge of the pavement to separate pedestrians and vehicles.

***Rumble strips*** are changes in the road surface that lead to knocks, vibration and /or noise within the car. Rumble strips can be constructed using coarse road surfaces or strips of plastic, which are placed across the road on top of the road surface.

***Speed zones*** refers to co-ordinating several speed-reducing devices within one area, e.g. 30 km/h zones, speed humps, raised junctions, road narrowing, bollards to prevent cars from driving on pavements, chicanes (narrowing alternate sides of the road), rumble strips (mini), roundabouts, portals etc. This measure is known as the '30 km/h zone' or 'quiet roads'. The zone can include major residential areas and villa areas (Behrendt et al. 1989, Engel and Krogsgård Thomsen 1989, Forschungsgesellschaft 1989, Mackie, Hodge and Webster 1993, Mackie and Webster 1995).

**Effect on accidents**

The effects of speed-reducing devices have been evaluated in a number of studies. The results presented here were taken from the following studies:

Kermit and Hein (1962) (USA): rumble strips
Owens (1967) (USA): rumble strips
Kermit (1968) (USA): rumble strips
Hoyt (1968) (USA): rumble strips
Bellis (1969) (USA): rumble strips
Illinois Division of Highways (1970) (USA): rumble strips
Sumner and Shippey (1977) (UK): rumble strips
Helliar-Symons (1981) (UK): rumble strips
Baguley (1982) (UK): speed humps
Mailand, Obst and Strack (1987) (Germany): speed zones
Moore (1987) (USA): rumble strips
Behrendt et al. (1989) (Germany): speed zones
Blakstad and Giæver (1989) (Norway): speed humps
Engel and Krogsgård Thomsen (1989) (Denmark): speed zones
Engel and Krogsgård Thomsen (1990) (Denmark): speed zones
Forschungsgesellschaft für Strassen- und Verkehrswesen (1989) (Germany): speed zones
Giæver and Meland (1990) (Norway): speed humps
Virginia Department of Highways and Transportation (1991) (USA): rumble strips
Baier (1992) (Germany): speed zones
Faure and de Neuville (1992) (France): speed zones
Schnüll, Haller and Von Lübke (1992) (Germany): raised junctions
Harwood (1993) (USA): rumble strips
Mackie, Hodge and Webster (1993) (UK): speed zones
Webster (1993) (UK): speed humps
Webster and Layfield (1993) (UK): rumble strips
Mackie and Webster (1995) (UK): speed zones
European Transport Safety Council (1996) (Denmark): speed humps
Webster and Mackie (1996) (UK): speed humps

Al-Masaeid (1997) (Jordan): speed humps
Eriksson and Agustsson (1999) (Denmark): speed humps
Ewing (1999) (USA): speed humps
Agustsson (2001) (Denmark): speed humps

Table 3.12.1 shows the effects of speed-reducing devices on the number of accidents estimated on the basis of these studies.

***Speed humps*** have been found to reduce injury accidents by about 41%. This result is based on methodologically weak studies and may be influenced by regression to the mean. The studies by Baguley (1982), Webster (1993) and Webster and Mackie (1996) have found reduced traffic volumes in roads where speed humps have been constructed. The accident rate on roads in the area around the road with speed humps does not increase. On average, for all studies where information is available about speed, mean speed was reduced from 47.7 to 36.6 km/h in streets where speed humps were installed. This corresponds to a 24% reduction in speed. Based on knowledge about the relationship between speed and accidents, this corresponds to an expected reduction of injury accidents by 42%.

*Table 3.12.1: Effects of speed-reducing devices on accidents*

| | Percentage change in the number of accidents | | |
|---|---|---|---|
| Accident severity | Types of accidents affected | Best estimate | 95% confidence interval |
| ***Speed humps*** | | | |
| Injury accidents | All accidents on roads with speed humps | −41 | (−57; −34) |
| Injury accidents | All accidents on roads nearby roads with speed humps | −7 | (−14; −0) |
| ***Raised junctions*** | | | |
| Injury accidents | Accidents at junctions | +5 | (−34; +68) |
| Property-damage-only accidents | Accidents at junctions | +13 | (−55; +183) |
| ***Rumble strips in front of junctions*** | | | |
| Injury accidents | Accidents at junctions | −33 | (−40; −25) |
| Property-damage-only accidents | Accidents at junctions | −25 | (−45; −5) |
| Unspecified | Accidents at junctions | −20 | (−25; −5) |
| ***Speed zones*** | | | |
| Injury accidents | All accidents | −27 | (−30; −24) |
| Property-damage-only accidents | All accidents | −16 | (−19; −12) |

***Raised junctions*** have been found to increase the number of accidents, although the results are not significant. The studies have not used any comparison group and the authors advice against generalizing the results.

***Rumble strips*** have been particularly used on approaches to junctions. Rumble strips reduce the number of injury accidents at junctions by around 33% and the number of property-damage-only accidents by around 25%. The results do not seem to be affected by methodological aspects of the studies.

***Speed zones (30 km/h zones in residential areas with speed humps).*** Speed-zones appear to reduce the number of injury accidents by around 27%. For property-damage-only accidents, the decrease appears to be somewhat smaller, around 16%. It must be emphasised that the majority of results are based on simple before-and-after studies. Regression to the mean was not controlled for.

### Effect on mobility

All speed-reducing devices reduce mobility in that speed is reduced. The measures may also deter traffic. Speed-reducing devices can deter heavy vehicles in particular (Amundsen 1986). On a typical access road with a length of up to 0.5 km, a reduction in speed from 35 to 25 km/h will lead to a delay of a maximum of 20 s per car. In a questionnaire, 35% of the bus companies asked said that they were against speed humps. The most common arguments against speed humps in streets with bus traffic concern back injuries to the drivers, injuries to passengers and wear and tear on materials (Amundsen 1986). It is not known whether speed humps create problems for winter maintenance of roads.

### Effect on the environment

Measurements carried out at three sites in England where speed humps have been installed show a reduction in noise (Sumner and Baguley 1979a, 1979b). Rumble strips can increase the noise level by 2–6 dB (Statens vegvesen 1985). In a Danish study, the noise from five different types of rumble strips was measured (Høj 1990). The increase in noise levels varied between 1.6 and 3.7 dB. It was lowest for paving stones and highest for grooves in the road surface. An increase of 2 dB is almost the limit of being audible.

The emission of pollutants from vehicles can increase, particularly at low speeds. Table 3.12.2 shows the estimated emission of NOx, CO and HC in grams while driving along

*Table 3.12.2: Exhaust emissions at different speeds. Grams per 250 m driven*

| | Discharge in grams while driving 250 m | | |
|---|---|---|---|
| | NOx | CO | HC |
| 20 km/h | 0.27 | 4.90 | 0.68 |
| 30 km/h | 0.42 | 3.78 | 0.66 |
| 50 km/h | 0.81 | 4.72 | 0.96 |

a 250 m of road with one stop at top speeds of respectively 20, 30 and 50 km/h (Public Roads Administration, Norwegian Pollution Control Authority and Directorate for Nature Management, 1992). Table 3.12.2 is based on German results. The possible health-related effects of these variations in exhaust emissions are unknown.

### Costs

Constructing a speed hump on a road in Norway of normal width (4–8 m) costs around NOK 10,000–30,000. Signs warning of the measure cost around NOK 2,000–5,000 per sign. Making rumble strips using plastic costs NOK 15–40 $m^{-1}$.

### Cost–benefit analysis

A numerical example has been worked out to indicate possible effects in a residential road. It is assumed that the road carries 200 vehicles per day and has an accident rate of 1.0 injury accidents per million vehicle kilometres. The example concerns a road of 1 km, but the majority of access roads are shorter than this. Speed humps are assumed to reduce speed from 35 to 25 km/h. The number of accidents is assumed to reduce by 50%. The environmental costs, related to with exhaust emissions, are assumed to increase by NOK 0.10 per vehicle kilometre. It is assumed that there are 10 speed humps, constructed at total cost of NOK 150,000. Under these assumptions, the savings in accident costs are estimated at NOK 960,000. The increase in the costs of travel time is estimated at NOK 970,000 and the increase in vehicle operating costs is estimated to be NOK 210,000. The increase in environmental costs is estimated at NOK 85,000. The increase in these costs is more than large enough to offset the decrease in accident costs, resulting in an overall benefit of NOK –305,000. However, this analysis does not include increased feelings of safety or improvements to other qualities of the residential environment, for example, increased opportunities for outdoor play. Speed-reducing devices are in demand in many residential areas, which indicates that those living in these areas consider the benefits of the measure as greater than the costs.

A numerical example has also been prepared concerning laying rumble strips in front of a junction. It is assumed that the junction is located in a rural area. The junction is assumed to have an AADT of 5,000 and an accident rate of 0.10 injury accidents per million entering vehicles. It is assumed that rumble strips are laid on the approach where the traffic is required to yield, at a cost of NOK 5,000. This corresponds to around 15 rumble strips across an 8 m-wide road. The number of injury accidents is assumed to reduce by 33% and property-damage-only accidents by 25%. The effect is assumed to last for 3 years. The rumble strips must then be renewed. The rumble strips are assumed to have an effect for the last 100 m ahead of the junction. The speed on this stretch is assumed to reduce from 35 to 25 km/h, which corresponds to a delay of around 4 s per vehicle. The reduction of accident costs is estimated at NOK 350,000 and increased costs of travel time at NOK 530,000. In this case, the increase in the costs of travel time is greater than the reduction in accident costs, so that the total benefit is negative.

## 3.13 Road markings

### Problem and objective

In order to drive safely and comfortably, drivers depend on reference points in the proximity of the vehicle and further ahead in the direction they are driving. In the dark, in particular, but also in other poor visibility conditions (for example in fog), such reference points are essential when it is hard to identify the road from its surroundings. At complicated junctions, it is important for road users to be able to find the right place on the carriageway using reference points. Road markings are intended, among other things, to give drivers such reference points.

In Norway, in 2001–05, about 16% of all injury accidents were head-on collisions, and about 28% of all injury accidents were run-off-the-road accidents and about 2% of all injury accidents were passing accidents. Taken together, this is somewhat more (44%) than in 1995, where 37% of all injury accidents were head-on collisions or run-off-the-road accidents. An analysis of contributing factors to fatal head-on collisions in Finland in the years 1991–98 (Summala, Karola, Radun and Couyoumdjian 2003) found that perception errors or drowsiness had contributed to 31%, driver errors had contributed to 36% and wrong driving lane had contributed to 15% of all fatal head-on collisions.

Road markings are intended to direct traffic by indicating the path of the carriageway and marking the road in relation to the surroundings. They may also warn road users about specific conditions related to the road alignment.

## Description of the measure

Road markings include several measures. Longitudinal lines on the road surface include centre lines, lane lines and edge lines. The centre line separates opposite traffic streams. It can either be a prohibitory line (solid line), which it is not allowed to cross, a warning line or a traffic lane line. Lane marking lines separate traffic lanes for traffic in the same direction. Edge lines mark the outer edge of the carriageway. Other types of road markings and related measures, which are described in this chapter are rumble strips, flush medians, chevron markings and combined measures.

Marking prohibited areas at intersections, reversible lanes and bus lanes are described in other chapters.

## Effect on accidents

Effects of road markings on accidents have been investigated by

Thomas (1958) (USA): edge lines
Musick (1960) (USA): edge lines
Williston (1960) (USA): edge lines
Basile (1962) (USA): edge lines
Sawhill and Neuzil (1963) (USA): two-way left turn lanes
Taylor and Foody (1966) (USA): delineator posts
Tamburri, Hammer, Glennon and Lew (1968) (USA): centre lines and edge lines
Roth (1970) (USA): edge lines and delineator posts
Hoffman (1974) (USA): two-way left turn lane
Johns and Matthias (1977) (USA): transition from white to yellow centre lines
Daas (1978) (Norway): delineator posts
Charnock and Chessell (1978) (Great Britain): edge lines
Bali et al. (1978) (USA): various types of road marking
Åkerlund and Johansson (1980a) (Sweden): delineator posts
Åkerlund and Johansson (1980b) (Sweden): delineator posts
McBean (1982) (Great Britain): edge lines
Engel and Krogsgård Thomsen (1983) (Denmark): centre lines and lane lines

Rosbach (1984) (Denmark): edge lines
Thakkar (1984) (USA): two-way left turn lane
Willis, Scott and Barnes (1984) (Great Britain): edge lines
Glennon (1986) (USA): centre lines
Harwood and St John (1985) (USA): two-way left turn lane
Ligon, Carter, Joost and Wolman (1985) (USA): shoulder rumble strips
Emerson and West (1986) (USA): shoulder rumble strips
Johansson (1986) (Sweden): delineator posts
Yee and Bell (1986) (Great Britain): lane lines
Hall (1987) (USA): wide edge lines
Cottrell (1988) (USA): wide edge lines
Creasey, Ullman and Dudek (1989) (USA): raised pavement markers
Griffin (1990) (USA): raised pavement markers
Lum and Hughes (1990) (USA): wide edge lines
Haynes, Copley, Farmer and Helliar-Symons (1993) (USA): chevron markings
Kallberg (1993) (Finland): delineator posts
Bowman and Vecellio (1994) (USA): two-way left turn lane
Fitzpatrick and Balke (1995) (USA): two-way left turn lane
Helliar-Symons, Webster and Skinner (1995) (USA): chevron markings
Bonneson and McCoy (1997) (USA): two-way left turn lane
Corben et al. (1997) (Australia): various types of road markings
Hickey (1997) (USA): shoulder rumble strips
Perrillo (1998) (USA): shoulder rumble strips
Brown and Tarko (1999) (USA): two-way left turn lane
Giæver, Sakshaug, Jenssen and Berge (1999) (Norway): shoulder and centre rumble strips
Welch (1999) (USA): two-way left turn lane
Cheng, Gonzalez and Christensen (2000) (USA): shoulder rumble strips
Griffith (2000) (USA): shoulder rumble strips
Outcalt (2001) (USA): centre rumble strips
Annino (2003) (USA): shoulder rumble strips
Drakopoulos and Vergou (2003) (USA): chevron markings
Ford and Calvert (2003) (USA): road inspections
Jurisich, Segedin, Dunn and Smith (2003) (USA): flush median
Marvin and Clark (2003) (USA): shoulder rumble strips
McFadden and Chandhok (2003) (USA): shoulder rumble strips
Noyce and Elango (2004) (USA): centre rumble strips
Persaud, Bahar, Mollett and Lyon (2004) (USA): raised pavement markers
Persaud, Retting and Lyon (2004) (USA): centre rumble strips

The results of these studies are summarised below. When measures have been evaluated by means of methodologically sound and methodologically weak studies, only the results from the methodologically sound studies are presented. The main impression is that many types of road markings only have small effects on accidents. Exceptions are rumble strips, two-way left turn lanes, and combined measures, which have been found to reduce accidents.

***Edge and centre lines.*** The results for edge and centre lines are summarised in Table 3.13.1. No effects on accidents have been found after the installation of different types of marked edge or centre lines. A meta-analysis of the effects of centre and edge lines on roads that previously had no centre or edge lines found higher speed and smaller distance to the road shoulder (Davidse, van Driel and Goldenbeld 2004).

***Rumble strips*** are installed along centre or edge lines. They may be milled into the road surface, or the lane markings may contain transverse elevated elements. Rumble strips produce vibrations and noise when a vehicle drives over them. Effects on accidents are summarised in Table 3.13.2. Rumble strips have been found to reduce accidents, mostly the types of accidents that the shoulder and centre rumble strips aim to prevent, i.e. road departure accidents and head-on collisions respectively. The effects of shoulder rumble strips on road departure accidents are somewhat larger than the effects of centre rumble strips on head-on collisions. Most studies have not provided

*Table 3.13.1: Effects of edge and centre lines on accidents*

| | Percentage change in the number of accidents | | |
|---|---|---|---|
| Accident severity | Types of accidents affected | Best estimate | 95% confidence interval |
| ***Normal edge line*** | | | |
| Injury accidents | All accidents | −3 | (−7; +1) |
| Property-damage-only accidents | All accidents | −3 | (−14; +10) |
| ***Wide edge line (20 cm instead of 10 cm)*** | | | |
| Injury accidents | All accidents | +5 | (−4; +14) |
| Property-damage-only accidents | All accidents | −1 | (−16; +17) |
| ***Centre lines (division between traffic in opposite directions)*** | | | |
| Injury accidents | All accidents | −1 | (−8; +6) |
| Property-damage-only accidents | All accidents | +1 | (−5; +6) |
| ***Changing from white to yellow centre lines*** | | | |
| Injury accidents | All accidents | −6 | (−31; +29) |
| ***Traffic lane line (between traffic lanes for traffic in the same direction)*** | | | |
| Injury accidents | All accidents | −18 | (−51; +36) |

*Table 3.13.2: Effects of shoulder and centre rumble strips on accidents*

| | Percentage change in the number of accidents | | |
|---|---|---|---|
| Accident severity | Types of accidents affected | Best estimate | 95% confidence interval |
| ***Shoulder rumble strips*** | | | |
| Unspecified | All accidents | −10 | (−21; +4) |
| Unspecified | Single vehicle accidents | −25 | (−41; −5) |
| Unspecified | Road departure accidents | | |
| | *Controlled for publication bias:* | −16 | (−41; +20) |
| | *Not controlled for publication bias:* | −44 | (−59; −24) |
| Injury accidents | Road departure accidents | −52 | (−80; +14) |
| ***Centre rumble strips*** | | | |
| Unspecified | All accidents | −4 | (−19; +13) |
| Unspecified | Head-on collisions | −24 | (−33; −13) |
| Unspecified | Accidents in daylight | −8 | (−16; +0) |
| Unspecified | Accidents at night | −15 | (−23; −7) |

enough information about the type of rumble strips to allow a comparison between different techniques for installing rumble strips. No negative side effects have been found of rumble strips, such as panicking or accident migration, in the study by Griffith (2000). A Finnish study found that both speed and the variation of the lateral position of vehicles on the road were reduced on roads with rumble strips.

***Flush medians*** are marked medians of varying width with diagonal lines, which are not allowed to be crossed. The results for flush medians are summarised in Table 3.13.3. A non-significant accident reduction has been found of flush medians, which are not more than 2 m in width. According to Jurisich, Segedin, Dunn and Smith (2003), the reduction of accidents is greatest at night for accidents that involve pedestrians, loss of control accidents and turning accidents.

***Two-way left turn lanes*** are lanes in the middle of the road designed for left turning traffic in both directions. These are used to some extent in the USA on multi-lane roads with many intersections and access roads and a large amount of left turning traffic. The results for two-way left turn lanes are summarised in Table 3.13.4. Installing two-way left turn lanes on roads than previously had four driving lanes has been found to reduce injury accidents and no significant effect has been found on property-damage-only accidents. After the installation of the two-way left turn lanes, only one driving lane remained per direction, in addition to the two-way left turn lanes in the middle of the road. A trim-and-fill analysis indicates that the results for injury accidents and for unspecified severity may be affected by publication bias. Results are therefore shown

*Table 3.13.3: Effects of flush medians on accidents*

| | Percentage change in the number of accidents | | |
|---|---|---|---|
| Accident severity | Types of accidents affected | Best estimate | 95% confidence interval |
| ***Flush median (all)*** | | | |
| Unspecified | All accidents | −1 | (−8; +6) |
| ***Flush median, width under 2 m*** | | | |
| Unspecified | All accidents | -11 | (−30; +13) |
| ***Flush median, width over 2 m*** | | | |
| Unspecified | All accidents | +2 | (−4; +9) |

*Table 3.13.4: Effects of two-way left turn lanes on accidents*

| | Percentage change in the number of accidents | | |
|---|---|---|---|
| Accident severity | Types of accidents affected | Best estimate | 95% confidence interval |
| Unspecified | All accidents | | |
| | *Controlled for publication bias* | −13 | (−24; 0) |
| | *Not controlled for publication bias* | −24 | (−33; −12) |
| Injury accidents | All accidents | | |
| | *Controlled for publication bias* | −15 | (−30; +2) |
| | *Not controlled for publication bias* | −23 | (−36; −6) |
| Property-damage-only accidents | All accidents | −19 | (−38; +7) |

both with and without control for publication bias. The corrected result for injury accident is significant but the result for unspecified severity fails significance.

***Raised pavement markers*** are coloured glass prisms that are partially sunk into the asphalt and reflect light from car headlights. They are often used on roads where visual guidance is of special importance. ***Delineator posts*** are plastic posts about 1 m high, equipped with a reflector on the top. They are mounted on both sides of the road at distances of 50 m from each other on straight sections and 25 m in curves. Delineator posts mark the edge of the road.

The results for raised pavement markers and delineator posts are summarised in Table 3.13.5. No significant effects have been found of raised pavement markers, when these are the only measure (see below, combined road marking measures). Pavement markers lose some of their reflecting properties already during the first year after installation, and they cannot be expected to affect accidents when there is snow or ice on the roads

*Table 3.13.5: Effects of raised pavement markers and delineator posts on accidents*

| | Percentage change in the number of accidents | | |
|---|---|---|---|
| Accident severity | Types of accidents affected | Best estimate | 95% confidence interval |
| ***Raised pavement markers*** | | | |
| Unspecified | All accidents | −1 | (−3; +1) |
| Injury accidents | All accidents | −3 | (−7; +1) |
| Unspecified | Accidents in darkness | −2 | (−7; +4) |
| Injury accidents | Accidents in darkness | −1 | (−25; +29) |
| Unspecified | Daylight accidents | +1 | (−4; +6) |
| Unspecified | Head-on collisions | −1 | (−33; +46) |
| Unspecified | Loss of control accidents | −3 | (−12; +7) |
| ***Delineator posts*** | | | |
| Unspecified | All accidents | −4 | (−17; +10) |
| Injury accidents | All accidents | −7 | (−22; +12) |
| Property-damage-only accidents | All accidents | −3 | (−27; +28) |

(Krammes and Tyer 1991). Delineator posts have been found to reduce accidents, the results are however not significant. Studies of driver behaviour have found that delineator posts increase speed, and the lateral placement of vehicles moves away from the road shoulder (Schumann 2003, Lyles and Taylor 2006). The possibly opposite effects these two changes might have on accidents may explain the small effects that have been found of delineator posts on accidents.

***Chevron markings*** on motorways are angle symbols marked on the carriageway. They aim at helping drivers maintain an adequate distance to the vehicles in front. In the approaches to junctions or roundabouts, chevrons aim at reducing speed. Chevron markings have been found to reduce accidents by 32% (95% CI [−59; +13]). On British motorways, chevrons have been found to increase headways, and both collisions and single vehicle accidents have been reduced (Helliar-Symons, Webster and Skinner 1995).

***Combined measures*** are combinations of the above road marking measures, such as edge lines and delineator posts, centre lines and edge lines or centre lines, edge lines and delineator posts. The results are summarised in Table 3.13.6. Combined measures seem to have larger effects on accidents than each of the measures separately. This concerns especially raised pavement markers and delineator posts, for which only small or no effects were found when these were the only measures implemented. For systematic improvements of road markings after road inspections in order to improve compliance with design standards, a large accident reduction has been found. The result is based on

*Table 3.13.6: Effects of combined measures and systematic improvements of road markings after road inspections on accidents*

| | Percentage change in the number of accidents | | |
|---|---|---|---|
| Accident severity | Types of accidents affected | Best estimate | 95% confidence interval |
| ***Edge lines and pavement markers*** | | | |
| Unspecified | All accidents | −47 | (−66; −18) |
| ***Edge lines and directional markings in curves*** | | | |
| Injury accidents | All accidents | −19 | (−46; +23) |
| ***Pavement markers and directional markings in curves*** | | | |
| Injury accidents | All accidents | −45 | (−58; −28) |
| ***Edge line and centre line*** | | | |
| Injury accidents | All accidents | −24 | (−35; −11) |
| ***Edge line, centre line and delineator posts*** | | | |
| Injury accidents | All accidents | −45 | (−56; −32) |
| ***Improvement of road markings after road inspection*** | | | |
| Injury accidents | All accidents | −36 | (−45; −25) |

the study by Ford and Calvert (2003), in which improved road markings in combination with improved signposting were investigated. This study did not control for regression to the mean and the result is therefore likely to be overestimated.

## Effect on mobility

British and American studies (Mullowney 1982, Stimpson, McGee and Kittelson 1977, Thomas 1958, Williston 1960, Willis and Scott Barnes 1984) show that road markings have little effect on driving speeds. As a rule, speeds increase a little immediately after the road is marked, but this increase gradually disappears. An American study (Cottrell 1988) found that increasing the width of the edge line from 10 to 20 cm did not lead to changes in vehicles' average speed. A Finnish study (Kallberg 1993) concluded that delineator posts contributed to increased speed. Increases of up to 5–10 km/h were found. No effect on speed was found of rumble strips (Giæver, Sakshaug, Jenssen and Berge 1999). However, rumble strips can be a hindrance to cyclists (Perrillo 1998) and ambulances (Russel and Rys 2005).

A Danish study (Wennike 1994) found that road markings, which were intended to reduce speed led to the average speed being reduced by 3 km/h. The proportion driving faster than 80 km/h fell by around 45%. In this study, 1 m-wide kerb lanes through a town were marked at the same time as speed limit signs were upgraded. This reduced the width of the carriageway.

Two-way left turn lanes on a two-lane road, which replace a previous four-lane road, have a relatively small effect on road capacity and average speed. The reduction of the number of driving lanes seems to be compensated by the reduced waiting times that occur for trough traffic cause by waiting left turning vehicles. Positive effects have been found for pedestrians, crossing traffic and ambulances (Welch 1999).

**Effect on the environment**

Road markings have no effect on noise and air pollution. Both paints and plastics used for road marking normally contain chemicals that are dangerous to health in high concentrations. Exposure to such substances primarily affects road workers who carry out the road marking. Rumble strips may increase noise.

**Costs**

Estimated costs for some specific types of road markings in Norway in 2005 are summarised in Table 3.13.7. These are averages for all roads, both where road markings are renewed and on roads where this is not done. Project costs and taxes of about 35% of the costs that are shown in Table 3.13.7 have to be taken into account additionally.

Costs for road markings depend on the materials used, traffic volumes, and on the amount of markings that are installed or renewed within one project or one contract (Cottrell and Hanson 2001). Costs for installing rumble strips in USA (maintenance not included) are between \$0.38 and \$3.63 $m^{-1}$, depending on how many kilometres are installed (Perrillo 1998). Maintenance intervals are between 2 and 6 years, depending,

*Table 3.13.7: Costs for road markings in Norway*

| Road marking | Costs (NOK) |
|---|---|
| Average costs of road markings per km per year (Elvik 1996) | 3,500–37,000 |
| Edge or centre line, 10 cm line width, per meter line | 11 |
| Dividing line, 20–30 cm line width, 2+2 m interval, per meter line | 25–35 |
| Rumble strips (marking), per meter line | 15–40 |
| Milled rumble strips, per meter | 40 |
| Chevrons, per piece | 300–1,000 |

among other things, on the type of pavement and on traffic volumes. Maintenance costs are about 50% of the installation costs (Mason 1999).

### Cost–benefit analysis

A cost–benefit analysis for rumble strips has been conducted by Perrillo (1998). According to this analysis, the benefits are 182 times the costs.

A numerical example has been calculated for shoulder rumble strips in Norway. The assumptions in the example are a traffic volume of 2,000 vehicles per day, 0.1 road departure accidents per million vehicle kilometres, and a reduction of road departure accidents by 30%, which lasts for 5 years. The assumed societal costs per kilometre of road are NOK 85,000. The present value of the accident cost savings are NOK 247,000. This is about three times the costs.

## 3.14 Traffic control for pedestrians

### Problem and objective

According to official Norwegian accident statistics, pedestrians run about four times the risk of being killed or injured per kilometre in traffic than car drivers (Bjørnskau 2008). If the risk is calculated on the basis of accident figures that have been corrected for incomplete reporting in official accident statistics, pedestrians run six times the risk of being injured as car drivers.

Traffic control for pedestrians is intended to

- separate pedestrian traffic in time and/or space from vehicular traffic,
- direct pedestrian and cycle traffic to safe crossing locations and
- increase mobility for pedestrians.

### Description of the measure

Traffic control for pedestrians and cyclists includes the following measures:

- Sidewalks/Pavement/Footpath
- Marked crosswalk
- Raised crosswalk

- Refuge in crosswalk
- Lighting at crosswalks
- Grade-separated pedestrian crossing
- Pedestrian guard rails
- School crossing patrols.

Other measures, that may improve safety for pedestrians are dealt with in separate chapters: tracks for walking and cycling (Section 1.1), area-wide traffic calming (Section 3.1), traffic signal control at junctions (Section 3.9), signalised pedestrian crossings (Section 3.10) and one-way streets (Section 3.16).

**Effect on accidents**

The effects of the different measures on accidents are summarised in Table 3.14.1. The results are based on the following studies:

Mackie and Older (1965) (Great Britain)
Jacobs (1966) (Great Britain)
Jacobs and Wilson (1967) (Great Britain)
Wilson and Older (1970) (Great Britain)
Jørgensen and Rabani (1971) (Denmark)
Herms (1972) (USA)
Pegrum Lloyd and Willett (1972) (Australia)
Lalani (1977) (Great Britain)
Cameron and Milne (1978) (Australia)
Polus and Katz (1978) (Israel)
Inwood and Grayson (1979) (Great Britain)
Pfefer, Sorton, Fegan and Rosenbaum (1982) (Japan)
Bagley (1985) (Great Britain)
Vodahl and Giæver (1986b) (Norway)
Yagar (1986) (Canada)
Yagar, Ropret and Kaufman (1987) (Canada)
Boxall (1988) (Great Britain)
Ekman (1988) (Sweden)
Frøysadal (1988) (Norway)
Stewart (1988) (Great Britain)
Blakstad and Giæver (1989) (Norway)
Hunt and Griffiths (1989) (Great Britain)
Dijkstra (1990) (Netherlands)

*Table 3.14.1: Effects of traffic control measures for pedestrians on accidents*

| | Percentage change in the number of accidents | | |
|---|---|---|---|
| Accident severity | Types of accident affected | Best estimate | 95% confidence interval |
| ***Sidewalk/pavement/footpath*** | | | |
| Injury accidents | Pedestrian accidents | −4 | (−7; −1) |
| Injury accidents | Bicycle accidents | −3 | (−28; +31) |
| Injury accidents | Vehicle accidents | +17 | (+6; +30) |
| Injury accidents | All accidents | 0 | (−17; +19) |
| ***Marked crosswalks*** | | | |
| Injury accidents | Pedestrian accidents on two-lane roads | −8 | (−43; +51) |
| Injury accidents | Pedestrian accidents on multi-lane roads | +88 | (−32; +424) |
| Injury accidents | Pedestrian accidents on all roads | +44 | (−6; +121) |
| Injury accidents | Vehicle accidents | +9 | (−25; +59) |
| ***Raised crosswalk vs. no crosswalk*** | | | |
| Injury accidents | All accidents | −65 | (−83; −27) |
| ***Raised crosswalk vs. ordinary marked crosswalk*** | | | |
| Injury accidents | Pedestrian accidents | −42 | (−70; +11) |
| ***Refuge in marked crosswalk (previously no crosswalk)*** | | | |
| Injury accidents | All accidents | 0 | (−26; +36) |
| ***Refuge in marked crosswalk vs. ordinary marked crosswalk*** | | | |
| Injury accidents | Pedestrian accidents | −43 | (−71; +12) |
| Injury accidents | Vehicle accidents | +19 | (−7; +52) |
| Injury accidents | All accidents | −25 | (−55; +24) |
| ***Lighting at crosswalks*** | | | |
| Unspecified | All accidents | −63 | (−79; −36) |
| ***Grade-separated pedestrian crossing*** | | | |
| Unspecified | Pedestrian accidents | −82 | (−90; −68) |
| Unspecified | Vehicle accidents | −14 | (−57; +74) |
| ***Pedestrian guardrails at pedestrian crossing*** | | | |
| Injury accidents | Pedestrian accidents | −29 | (−52; −5) |
| Injury accidents | Vehicle accidents | −8 | (−33; +27) |
| Injury accidents | All accidents | −24 | (−44; −2) |
| ***Pedestrian guardrails with sight gaps at pedestrian crossing*** | | | |
| Injury accidents | All accidents | −48 | (−64; −27) |
| ***School crossing patrols*** | | | |
| Injury accidents | Pedestrian accidents | −35 | (−69; +36) |

Daly, McGrath and VanEmst (1991) (Great Britain)
Blakstad (1993) (Norway)
Borger and Frøysadal (1993) (Norway)
Downing, Sayer and Zaheer-Ul-Islam (1993) (Pakistan)
Jones and Farmer (1993) (Great Britain)
Matsumara, Seo, Umezawa and Okutani (1993) (Japan)
Borger and Frøysadal (1994) (Norway)
Bowman and Vecellio (1994) (USA)
Wachtel and Lewiston (1994) (USA)
Ward et al. (1994) (Great Britain)
Summersgill and Layfield (1996) (Great Britain)
Jones and Tomcheck (2000) (USA)
Koepsell et al. (2002) (USA)
Gårder (2004) (USA)
Zegeer et al. (2005) (USA)

***Sidewalks (pavements, footpaths)*** are usually raised 10–20 cm in relation to the traffic lane and separated from motorised traffic by means of kerbstones. Sidewalks carry pedestrian traffic and sometimes bicycle traffic in both directions. Sidewalks have usually an asphalt surface or concrete or stone paving slabs. The results in Table 3.14.1 indicate that accident rates are lower on roads with sidewalks than on other roads for pedestrians and for cyclists, and higher for motor vehicles. All results refer to accident rates. However, it is not taken into account that accident rates for pedestrians are lower at higher pedestrian volumes. It is likely that pedestrian volumes are higher on roads with sidewalks than on other roads. The reductions that were found for pedestrian and cyclist accidents may therefore be overestimated. Moreover, none of the studies has applied a comparison group.

***Marked crosswalks*** were studied in a large number of studies. However, only few studies have controlled for both pedestrian and vehicle volumes. The results in Table 3.14.1 that refer to pedestrian accidents are based on studies that have controlled for pedestrian and vehicle volumes, either by calculating accident rates as the number of accidents divided by the product of pedestrian and vehicle volume, or by applying multivariate models in which both volumes are included as predictor variables. While no significant difference between marked and unmarked crosswalks was found on two-lane roads, accidents appear to increase on multi-lane roads. The latter result is not statistically significant. When all types of road are regarded together, an increase is found as well. These results refer to accidents occurring either in crosswalks or nearby. The results from these studies are not likely to be affected by regression to the mean or by publication bias. The results from the study by Zegeer et al. (2005) show that pedestrian accident rates in marked crosswalks increase most on multi-lane roads with an AADT of 12,000 or more, while the difference in pedestrian accident risk is not significant in marked vs. unmarked crosswalks on multi-lane roads with an AADT below 12,000.

Studies that have not controlled for pedestrian or vehicle volumes, found that the number of pedestrian accidents at crosswalks is 18% higher than at other locations (95% CI [−14; +61]). Studies that have controlled for either pedestrian or vehicle volumes (but not for both) found a non-significant increase of accident rates as well (+17%, 95% CI [−13; +58]). None of these studies has specified the number of lanes or traffic volumes. Most results refer to crosswalks at junctions, only few refer to accidents at mid-block crosswalks.

It is often assumed that higher accident numbers (total numbers or per pedestrian crossing) are due to more careless behaviour of pedestrians at marked crosswalks. Studies that have investigated pedestrian behaviour found no indication of pedestrians becoming less vigilant or more reckless when crossing marked crosswalks (Knoblauch, Nitzburg and Seifert 2001, Mitman, Ragland and Zegeer 2008, Nitzburg and Knoblauch 2001). However, pedestrian accident rates were found to be greater in a zone of up to 50 m from a marked crosswalk, compared to the accident rate in the crosswalk (Mackie and Older 1965, Jørgensen and Rabani 1971, Vodahl and Giæver 1986a, 1986b, Ekman 1988).

***Raised crosswalks*** are crosswalks in the form of speed humps with a plateau that has about the same height as the sidewalk. The aim is to reduce vehicle speeds. When raised crosswalks are installed at locations where there previously was no crosswalk, the numbers of both pedestrian and vehicle accidents were found to decrease. The results refer to both junctions and mid-block crosswalks. Not all of the crosswalks are marked, and at some locations several raised crosswalks were installed on one stretch of road. None of the studies has controlled for pedestrian or vehicle volumes. Vehicle volumes and vehicle speed are likely to have decreased.

When raised crosswalks are installed as an improvement of previously existing marked crosswalks, pedestrian accidents were found to decrease significantly. This result is based on only one study that has controlled for vehicle volumes, but not for pedestrian volumes (Bowman and Vecellio 1994). A study that has not controlled for any volumes found non-significant increases of both pedestrian and vehicle accidents by ca. 19% (Blakstad 1993).

A ***refuge in marked crosswalk*** is a raised (kerbed) median that separates the two directions of vehicle traffic flow, which may be used by pedestrians to cross in two stages. A refuge also shortens the distance that has to be crossed by pedestrians in each crossing stage, and vehicle traffic has to be observed from only one direction.

The installation of marked crosswalks with refuge at locations where there previously was no marked crosswalk was not found to change the number of accidents. This result is based on only two studies that have not controlled for vehicle or pedestrian volumes. When refuges are installed in existing marked crosswalks, pedestrian accident rates were found to decrease, while vehicle accident rates were found to increase. Both results refer to accident rates and both vehicle and pedestrian volumes are taken into account. None of the results is statistically significant.

***Lighting at pedestrian crossings.*** A large and significant reduction of the number of pedestrian accidents in darkness was found. The result is based on two studies, both of which have applied a control group. However, both compare accident numbers without taking into account possible differences in exposure. Other potential confounding factors or regression to the mean are not controlled for either.

***Grade-separated pedestrian crossings*** were found to reduce pedestrian accidents significantly. The results refer to accident numbers before and after the construction of pedestrian bridges. Exposure or any confounding factors are not controlled for.

***Pedestrian guard rails*** between the pavement and the road leads to a reduction in the number of accidents for both pedestrians and vehicles. The results refer to accident numbers at pedestrian crossings before and after the installation of guardrails and possible changes in exposure are not taken into account.

Pedestrian guardrails can obstruct sight conditions between vehicles and pedestrians walking behind the guardrails who are about to walk out onto the carriageway in order to cross the road (Stewart 1988). This problem can be avoided by using so-called sight guardrails, where individual posts are removed to make the railings more transparent. This type of guardrails appears to have a somewhat greater effect on accidents than ordinary pedestrian guardrails.

***Introducing school crossing patrols*** can lead to fewer accidents involving pedestrians who cross the road, but the reduction is not statistically significant. The reduction in the number of accidents following the introduction of school crossing patrols may be due to the reduction in car speeds. A Danish study concludes that school crossing patrols reduce car speeds by 3 km/h compared with areas where school crossing patrols do not operate (Kjærgaard and Lahrmann 1981).

**Effect on mobility**

Marking crosswalks increases the number of pedestrians crossing at the crosswalk (compared to the number of pedestrians crossing at other locations) and reduces the average waiting time for pedestrians (Hunt 1990, Zegeer et al. 2005). Average waiting times for pedestrians are also shorter compared to signalised pedestrian crossings (Hunt 1990). Mobility for pedestrians, indicated by average waiting times or the proportion of motorists yielding for pedestrians, is further improved by installing raised crosswalks or refuges in marked crosswalks (Blakstad 1993, Huang and Cynecki 2001, Jones and Farmer 1993)

**Effect on the environment**

The measures included in this chapter probably have little or no effect on noise or pollution. Stopping and starting at pedestrian crossings can lead to increased noise and increased exhaust emissions. Raised crosswalks may have the same effects as speed humps, e.g. increased noise and emissions due to braking and accelerating.

**Costs**

The Norwegian cost figures given in Table 3.14.2 apply to the measures included in this chapter.

**Cost–benefit analysis**

For marked crosswalks, no cost–benefit analysis has been conducted. On multi-lane roads, pedestrian accident rates were found to increase in marked crosswalks. On two-lane roads, no significant effect on accident rates was found. The effects on mobility depend on vehicle and pedestrian volumes. The higher the volumes, the greater will be

*Table 3.14.2: Costs of traffic control measures in Norway for pedestrians*

| Measure | Cost in NOK (1995) |
|---|---|
| Marking a pedestrian crosswalk | 5,000 (±3,000) |
| Constructing refuge on pedestrian crosswalk | 10,000 (±3,000) |
| Constructing raised pedestrian crossings | 50,000 (±10,000) |
| Erecting traffic guardrails, per metre | 500 (±100) |

the time benefits to pedestrians and the time losses to motor vehicles. Time benefits and losses will also depend on the proportion of motor vehicles yielding for pedestrians, which varies strongly between crosswalks.

A numerical example has been calculated for constructing a refuge in an existing marked crosswalk. It is assumed that the total number of accidents at the crosswalk is reduced by 25%. No time benefits or delays are assumed for vehicles and pedestrians. The average investment costs are ca. NOK 15,000 at an AADT below 5,000, and NOK 30,000 at an AADT of 5,000. The cost–benefit ratio is 0.84 at an AADT of 1,000, 1.79 at an AADT of 2,000 and 4.5 at an AADT of 5,000. The benefit–cost ratio will also depend on pedestrian volumes and the proportion of motorists yielding for pedestrians.

A numerical example has also been made for the construction of a pedestrian bridge or tunnel at a location with a large pedestrian volume, where vehicles otherwise would have to yield for pedestrians. The example is made under the following assumptions: The total number of accidents is reduced by 14%. The costs and time benefits depend on the traffic volume. The average investment costs are ca. NOK 5.8 million at an AADT of 8,000, NOK 10.6 million at an AADT of 12,000 and ca. NOK 22 million at an AADT of 36,000. Time benefits per vehicle are 1.6, 3.2 and 7 s per vehicle, respectively. For pedestrians, no time benefits are assumed. Even if pedestrians do not have to wait for a gap in vehicle traffic, the crossing of bridges and tunnels takes usually more time than taking the shortest way across the street. The cost–benefit ratio is 0.56 at an AADT of 8,000, 1.10 at an AADT of 12,000 and 2.35 at an AADT of 35,000.

## 3.15 Stopping and parking control

### Problem and objective

Growth in the use of private cars in towns and cities has led to increased demand for parking places. In many places, the existing road and street networks were not designed for current traffic volumes, but nonetheless are used for parking when other parking places are not available. On-street parking obstructs vision, leads to lower capacity and can lead to dangerous situations where cars manoeuvre in and out of parking places along the kerb.

Parking-related accidents comprised 2.4% of all injury accidents reported to the police in Norway, during 1991–95. The most common parking-related accidents are hitting parked vehicles (30%), hitting pedestrians who are crossing the road behind the parked vehicles (25%), colliding when overtaking parked vehicles (15%) and accidents when starting off from a parked position (8%). In addition to injury accidents, a large number of property-damage-only accidents are related to parking.

Stopping and parking controls may have a number of objectives. Improving residential environments, reducing traffic and improving traffic flow and strengthening public transport are important objectives for parking policies in Norway (Hanssen and Stenstadvold 1993). Improving traffic safety is not always the prime objective. Stopping and parking controls are designed to remove or reduce on-street parking, transfer parking to marked parking places or parking lots away from the streets and to prevent vehicles from stopping and parking at places where this severely obstructs vision or hinders movement for other road users, including pedestrians.

**Description of the measure**

Stopping and parking controls include several measures, which can be used in combination and can be used for the same road and street areas at different times. The effects on accidents have been investigated for different types of parking restrictions (ban on on-street parking, one-sided parking restrictions and time-limited parking restrictions), different parking layouts (parallel vs. diagonal) and for marking parking places.

No studies of the effects on accidents have been found for a ban on all stopping, zonal regulation of parking and parking charges in order to reduce short-term parking.

**Effect on accidents**

The results presented here are based on the following studies that have evaluated the effects of different types of parking controls on accidents:

DeRose (1966) (USA): time-limited parking restrictions
LaPlante (1967) (USA): time-limited parking restrictions
Madelin and Ford (1968) (Great Britain): ban on on-street parking
Crossette and Allen (1969) (USA): ban on on-street parking
Good and Joubert (1973) (Australia): ban on on-street parking
Cleveland, Huber and Rosenbaum (1982) (USA): several measures
Main (1984) (Canada): ban on on-street parking
Westman (1986) (Sweden): ban on on-street parking
Blakstad and Giæver (1989) (Norway): ban on on-street parking
Dijkstra (1990) (The Netherlands): several measures

*Table 3.15.1: Effects of different parking control measures on accidents*

| | | Percentage change in the number of accidents | |
|---|---|---|---|
| Accident severity | Types of accident affected | Best estimate | 95% confidence interval |
| ***Introducing parking restrictions (ban on on-street parking)*** | | | |
| Injury accidents | All accidents | −20 | (−26; −14) |
| Property-damage-only accidents | All accidents | −27 | (−30; −25) |
| ***Transition from unrestricted to restricted parking*** | | | |
| Injury accidents | All accidents | −6 | (−14; +3) |
| Property-damage-only accidents | All accidents | +19 | (+13; +24) |
| ***Time-limited parking restrictions*** | | | |
| Unspecified severity | All accidents | −11 | (−17; −4) |
| Unspecified severity | Parking accidents | −79 | (−87; −66) |
| ***One-sided parking ban (on one side of the road)*** | | | |
| Injury accidents | All accidents | +49 | (−15; +159) |
| ***Transition from diagonal parking to parallel parking*** | | | |
| Unspecified severity | All accidents | −35 | (−42; −27) |
| Unspecified severity | Parking accidents | −63 | (−70; −54) |
| ***Marking parking places*** | | | |
| Unspecified severity | All accidents | +51 | (+30; +75) |
| Unspecified severity | Parking accidents | +128 | (+77; +194) |

McCoy, Ramanujam, Moussavi and Ballard (1990) (USA): parking layout and marking parking places
McCoy, McCoy, Haden and Singh (1991) (USA): parking directions
Bonneson and McCoy (1997) (USA): parking ban

Table 3.15.1 shows the effects of stopping and parking controls on accidents on the basis of these studies.

Many of the studies are methodologically weak. They are simple before-and-after studies, which do not control for regression to the mean or long-term trends in the number of accidents. In many cases, the parking control measures have been combined with other measures, so that the effect of the parking regulations by themselves alone cannot be determined. Several studies do not distinguish between injury accidents and property-damage-only accidents.

***Introducing parking restrictions***. Bans on on-street parking are introduced using ‘No parking’ signs. Short-term stops for loading and delivering and for dropping off and picking up are usually permitted. Thus, parking bans do not prevent deliveries of goods. Parking restrictions appear to reduce the number of accidents. However, the studies only show how parking restrictions have affected the street(s) where they are introduced. To the extent that parking may simply be transferred to other streets, it cannot be ruled out that the number of accidents may increase in the streets where parking demand increases.

***The transition from unrestricted to restricted parking***, that is say, parking in marked places or according to certain regulations, appears to have a minor effect on the number of injury accidents. Property-damage-only accidents tend to increase.

***Time-limited parking restrictions*** appear to reduce the number of accidents, especially parking-related accidents. The same applies to changes in parking layout from diagonal parking to parallel parking. One-sided parking bans and marking parking places appear to increase the number of accidents. The explanation for this is not known.

***One-sided parking ban (on one side of the road)*** has been found to increase accident numbers, the effect is however non-significant.

***Transition from diagonal parking to parallel parking.*** In streets where parking is permitted, vehicles can park parallel with the kerb or diagonally to the kerb. Different parking layouts can be indicated using road markings. Parallel parking has been found to reduce accidents, compared to diagonal parking.

***Marking parking places*** has been found to increase accident numbers.

### Effect on mobility

In inner city centres, on-street parking is common. This may prevent access for service vehicles (public transport, emergency vehicles), maintenance and snow clearance. Bans on on-street parking can increase access for such forms of transport. American studies indicate that bans on on-street parking may lead to higher speeds (Crossette and Allen 1969). Increases from 30–45 km/h before the ban to 40–60 km/h after the ban have been found.

### Effect on the environment

In general, a good supply of parking space will lead to increased car usage within an area. This may lead to increased noise and pollution. It is also possible that traffic looking for parking places will increase when parking is controlled. This can be countered by a system showing where parking is available. Studies carried out a short time after parking charges were introduced for the 15,000 or so central parking places in Copenhagen in 1990, found that the amount of parking was reduced by around 25%. This led to a 10% reduction of car traffic in central areas (Hanssen 1996).

## Costs

Parking controls in Norway involve costs for road signs, enforcement, maintenance and operation. Operating expenses include wages, uniforms, traffic wardens' vehicles and parking installations (Solberg 1986b). The costs of one traffic sign are between NOK 1,500 and NOK 3,000. The total costs of introducing parking bans on a 0.5 km-long road may be between NOK 25,000 and NOK 50,000. Figures from 1984–85 show that around half of the municipalities that by then had introduced parking charges, incurred costs of less than NOK 1 million per year (Solberg 1986b). The data included 45 of the 47 municipalities where the measure had been implemented. More than one-third of the municipalities have annual costs of between NOK 1 and 3 million. On average, the municipality's expenses comprise NOK 3,400 per parking place with parking charges. The municipality's total operating costs were around NOK 125 million and the revenue was around NOK 205 million. The larger cities in particular had large revenues from parking. In smaller cities, the annual operating surplus may be between NOK 0.5 and 2 million (Hanssen and Stenstadvold 1993).

Building multi-storey parking facilities costs around NOK 100,000–300,000 per parking place. Annual operating costs for a multi-storey parking facility are around NOK 8,000–20,000 per parking place (Hanssen 1997).

## Cost–benefit analysis

Crossette and Allen (1969) presented a cost–benefit analysis of parking restrictions in two main streets in Yuma, Arizona, USA. The benefit in the form of reduced accident costs was estimated to be $46,000, and the costs of implementing the measure were $3,920. Possible effects on mobility and the environment were not included in this cost–benefit analysis.

An example can be given, in which it is assumed that parking is banned on a street with an AADT of 3,000 vehicles, of which 300 are parking-related. It is assumed that the street has an accident rate of 0.7 injury accidents per million vehicle kilometres. Half the parking-related traffic disappears, and half finds parking places elsewhere. For the latter half, driving distances increases by 500 m. The effect is assumed to last for 10 years.

The effects of parking bans are calculated at around NOK 2.6 million in saved accident costs, around NOK 720,000 in additional costs for parking-related traffic transferred to other streets and around NOK 440,000 in loss of benefit for displaced traffic. The total benefit is estimated to around NOK 1.45 million. The cost of the measure is estimated at NOK 60,000. The benefit is clearly greater than the costs.

## 3.16 One-way streets

### Problem and objective

City streets are often narrow or may have vehicles parked on the kerb. Where there is traffic in both directions, speeds must be kept down, and vehicles may have to brake often to avoid other traffic where conflict and yield points are numerous. This particularly affects the flow of traffic. For pedestrians, the situation becomes difficult when traffic comes from several different directions, especially at intersections where pedestrians normally choose to cross the road. Cyclists may also find crossing roads difficult.

By creating one-way streets, theoretically the number of conflict points at intersections can be considerably reduced. Two-lane roads with traffic in both directions create 32 conflict points for drivers at crossroads. By using two-lane, one-way flow, the number of conflict points is reduced to 16. Furthermore, it becomes easier for pedestrians to cross the road and the capacity of the road increases. On the other hand, one-way streets may lead to longer driving distances.

### Description of the measure

One-way streets are introduced by erecting 'One-way' signs, where the one-way road begins. The sign shows an arrow indicating the direction. At the other end, a 'No Entry' sign is used. One-way streets will often be included in street reclassification plans or in area-wide traffic calming measures (see Section 3.1), where several roads or streets are considered as a whole.

*Table 3.16.1: Effects of one-way streets on the number of accidents*

| | Percentage change in the number of accidents | | |
|---|---|---|---|
| Accident severity | Types of accident affected | Best estimate | 95% confidence interval |
| Injury accidents | All accidents | −1 | (−6; +4) |
| Injury accidents | Pedestrian accidents | +1 | (−11; +14) |
| Property-damage-only accidents | All accidents | −8 | (−12; −5) |

## Effect on accidents

A number of studies evaluating the effects of one-way streets on accidents have been carried out. The results presented in Table 3.16.1 are taken from the following studies:

Bruce (1967) (USA)
Riemersma and Sijmonsma (1979) (The Netherlands)
Parsonson, Nehmad and Rosenbaum (1982) (USA)
Blakstad (1990a) (Norway)
Hocherman, Hakkert and Bar-Ziv (1990) (Israel)
Summersgill and Layfield (1996) (Great Britain)

One-way streets do not appear to be associated with significant changes in the number of injury accidents. There is a small reduction in the number of property-damage-only accidents. A possible explanation for the small reduction in accidents is that one-way streets can lead to increased speeds and increased traffic volume. On average, traffic increased by 22.3% in the before-and-after studies that include data on traffic volume before and after one-way streets were introduced.

## Effect on mobility

One-way streets may lead to longer driving distances for cars. One-way streets increase the capacity of the road. Before-and-after studies in the USA (Parsonson, Nehmad and Rosenbaum 1982) indicate that an increase in traffic of 10–30% in major streets in cities is not unusual. One-way streets can also lead to an increase in speed. Before-and-after studies in Great Britain and the USA (Bruce 1967, Parsonson, Nehmad and Rosenbaum 1982) have found reductions in journey times of between 20% and 60%, depending on how bad the traffic congestion was before one-way streets were introduced.

### Effect on the environment

No studies have been found that show how one-way streets affect the environment conditions. Increased traffic volume and increased speed may lead to increased noise levels and more pollution. On the other hand, better traffic flow can reduce the noise level and lead to less pollution. The actual effects are not known.

### Costs

The direct costs of implementing one-way streets are small. They include planning costs and costs of traffic signs and road markings. The costs can vary from place to place. A minimum outlay would involve setting up one 'One-way' street sign and two 'No Entry' signs. The costs per sign are around NOK 1,500–2,500. Respect for one-way streets is better than for many other traffic control measures (Daas 1980). Nonetheless, a certain amount of enforcement is probably necessary.

### Cost–benefit analysis

A numerical example may indicate the costs and benefits of one-way streets. It is assumed that a pair of collector roads in a city is converted to one-way streets. Each is assumed to have an AADT of 1,500 vehicles and an accident rate of 0.6 injury accidents per million vehicle kilometres. The number of kilometres driven on these two streets is assumed to increase by 20%, while the risk per kilometre driven is assumed to decrease by 20%. It is assumed that speed increases from 30 to 35 km/h. Each street is assumed to be 1 km in length. The lifetime of the measure is set at 10 years.

Under these assumptions, savings in accident costs are calculated at around NOK 450,000. Saved costs of travel time are estimated to around NOK 2.2 million. Increased vehicle operating costs are estimated to be around NOK 690,000. The total benefit is estimated to be around NOK 1.96 million. The cost of the measure is assumed to be around NOK 60,000. This amounts to setting up around 25 traffic signs (12.5 per kilometre of road). The benefit is clearly greater than the cost.

## 3.17 Reversible traffic lanes

### Problem and objective

The hourly volume of traffic on the main road network and on motorways in and around large cities varies considerably over a 24-h period. Traffic is often heavy towards the city during the morning, while there is little traffic out of the city. In the afternoon, the reverse applies. Uneven directional distribution of rush hour traffic creates capacity problems on the main road and motorway network. Some drivers may choose to use the local road network and congestion may tempt some drivers to undertake dangerous overtaking manoeuvres or lane changes.

It is not always possible to expand the capacity of the road system to accommodate the maximum peaks of traffic without delays. An alternative to building more traffic lanes is to make one or more traffic lanes reversible. A reversible traffic lane is designed to serve traffic in both directions, depending on which direction the amount of traffic is greatest. At all times, the traffic lane is only open to traffic in one direction, e.g. towards the city in the morning and out of the city in the afternoon.

**Description of the measure**

Reversible lanes are mostly installed on existing roads where increased traffic has lead to capacity problems in peak hours. Reversible lanes may also be installed at special occasions, such as larger sporting events, concerts or in the case of evacuation. When the usual number of driving lanes is reduced because of road works, reversible lanes may be used as well. A review from the USA showed that 35% of reversible lanes had been installed in order to reduce congestion problems in peak hours, 23% were used at special occasions, 21% were installed for evacuation purposes and 13% have been used in connection with road works (Wolshon and Lambert 2004, 2006a, 2006b).

Reversible lanes are used most frequently on motorways where traffic volumes are largest and where there are no junctions. Reversible lanes are also used in other main roads, and on bridges or in tunnels where an increase of the number of lanes is both difficult and expensive. There are a number of criteria for the installation of reversible lanes by different authorities in the USA (Wolshon and Lambert 2004), such as the requirement of predictable congestion problems, a directional distribution of traffic flows of at minimum 2:1, ideally at least 3:1, a reduction of the average speed in peak hours by at least 25% and no alternative measures. Additionally, the transitions between ordinary driving lanes and reversible lanes must have sufficient capacity and not cause new congestion or other problems. The time intervals in which the driving direction is reversed have to be long enough in order to avoid head-on collisions. Usually, reversible lanes may be used on roads with three or more driving lanes. It is recommended that at least two lanes remain open in both directions at all times in order to avoid delays in the direction with least traffic.

The permitted driving direction in a reversible lane is shown with traffic signs alongside the road and with signs suspended above the road (a green light shows the permitted direction and red light shows the direction of oncoming traffic). Moveable barriers may also be used. In road work zones, moveable devices are used. Reversible lanes should additionally be announced by fixed signs.

Reversible lanes have been used more than 75 years in the USA (Wolshon and Lambert 2004). In England, reversible lanes are used as well (McKenna and King 1987). Reversible lanes are little used in Norway, but have been used in some cities (Kirste 1989, Ragnøy and Eikanger 1983).

Opinions differ on how reversible lanes affect safety. Negative safety effects may be expected for several reasons (Blakstad 1990b, Bretherton and Elhaj 1996, California Department of Transportation 1989, Markovets, Royer and Dorroh 1995, Ragnøy and Eikanger 1983, Wolshon and Lambert 2006b):

- Drivers who are not familiar with reversible lanes may choose the wrong driving lane.
- Increased capacity may lead to increased traffic volumes.
- Reduced congestion may lead to increased speed.
- When reversible lanes are installed on motorways with a median barrier, head-on collisions may increase.
- Lane changes and turning movements at at-grade junctions may get more complex.

On the other hand, there are several factors that can be expected to contribute to positive safety effects, or at least to abate possible negative safety effects (Blakstad 1990b, Bretherton and Elhaj 1996, Markovets, Royer and Dorroh 1995, Ragnøy and Eikanger 1983, Wolshon and Lambert 2006b):

- Reversible lanes may remove traffic from the local road network to the safer network of main roads and motorways.
- Most drivers on the main road network in urban areas in congestion times are using the same routes daily and will soon get familiar with reversible lanes. When there is much traffic, drivers tend to follow vehicle ahead, which reduces the risk of choosing the wrong lane.

A possible increase of accidents immediately after the installation of reversible lanes may therefore not be long-lasting and may even be followed by a decrease in the number of accidents.

**Effect on accidents**

Despite the widespread use of reversible lanes over a long period of time only few empirical studies have been conducted of the effects on accidents, traffic flows, travel times and environment (Wolshon and Lambert 2004). Effects of reversible lanes on accidents have been studied by

Kirste (1989) (Norway)
DeRose (1966) (USA)
Upchurch (1975) (USA)
Agent and Clark (1982) (USA)
Bretherton and Elhaj (1996) (USA)

Based on these studies the effects of reversible lanes on accidents have been estimated as shown in Table 3.17.1.

The summary effects seem to indicate non-significant increases in the numbers of accidents, especially in rush hours. However, all results are non-significant and the results from the individual studies are highly heterogeneous. This indicates that the summary effects may be misleading because the study results are affected by factors that are not accounted for in the analyses. Moreover, none of the studies are well-controlled.

The Norwegian results refer to the installation of reversible lanes on three-lane roads. Some of the roads had previously only two lanes and were extended to three-lane roads, other roads had three lanes, but none of the lanes was reversible. The US studies have investigated the effects of installing reversible lanes on roads with five or six lanes.

Reversible lanes may affect accidents on roads that, previous to the installation of the reversible lanes, had increased traffic volumes due to drivers who wanted to avoid congestion. On such roads, traffic volumes may decrease when reversible lanes are installed on main roads. All available studies have investigated reversible lanes that

*Table 3.17.1: Effects of reversible lanes on accidents*

| | Percentage change in the number of accidents | | |
|---|---|---|---|
| Accident severity | Types of accidents affected | Best estimate | 95% confidence interval |
| Injury accidents | All accidents | +18 | (−16; +66) |
| Unspecified | Accidents in rush hours | +15 | (−3; +37) |
| Unspecified | All accidents | +4 | (−5; +13) |

have been installed with the aim of solving congestion problems in peak hours. None of the studies have investigated reversible lanes that were used for special occasions, evacuation or road works.

**Effect on mobility**

Reversible lanes are primarily a measure that aims at increasing the capacity of roads. The studies referred to in the previous section have found

- improved traffic flows in the direction in which the number of available lanes is increased,
- no change in the total traffic volumes,
- an increase of traffic volumes in peak hours by about 3–7% and
- increased speed and reductions of travel times by about 16–40%.

Travel times may increase in the direction in which the number of available lanes decreases, in this direction, the total amount of traffic is however smaller.

The capacity increase that is achieved by reversible lanes is often not as large as might be expected, because the reversible lane is used by fewer drivers than other lanes, possibly because of safety concerns (Cather and Salazar 1996, Wolshon and Lambert 2004).

A possible measure for increasing the safety in reversible lanes is to close a driving lane between the reversible lane and the outermost lane in the direction that is opposite to the current direction of the reversible lane. This is however only applicable on wide roads. On a six-lane roads, this might, for example, mean opening four lanes in one direction and only one lane in the other direction, and leaving the lane in between unused. The total capacity of the road is obviously reduced and congestion problems may arise in the direction with fewer open lanes. A possible alternative solution that, sometimes, is used is therefore setting up moveable barriers (California Department of Transportation 1989).

**Effect on the environment**

Based on knowledge of the relationship between the quality of traffic flow and exhaust emissions, it has been estimated (Agent and Clark 1982) that air pollution is reduced significantly when reversible traffic lanes are introduced. No changes have been found for noise levels.

## Costs

The costs of setting up reversible traffic lanes depend, among other things, on the length of the lane and whether the road already has sufficient traffic lanes, or whether a new lane must be constructed. If it is assumed that the costs are similar to those incurred in rebuilding roads to current design standards, the cost will be around NOK 3–5 million per kilometre of road. To this must be added annual operating and maintenance costs.

## Cost–benefit analysis

An American cost–benefit analysis of reversible traffic lanes (Agent and Clark 1982) concluded that the benefit–cost ratio was around 7. The analysis concluded that the annual time gain was valued at $329,000, the annual increase in accident costs at $9,350 and the annual capital and operating costs at $43,250.

In order to indicate possible effects of the measure in Norwegian conditions, a numerical example has been worked out. It is assumed that a reversible traffic lane is constructed on a main road with an AADT of 40,000, and an accident rate of 0.108 injury accidents per million vehicle kilometres. The lane is assumed to be 1 km long and costs NOK 3 million to construct and NOK 30,000 per year in operating cost. It is assumed that the lane only serves rush hour traffic. Such traffic is assumed to comprise 25% of the total traffic. The average speed of rush hour traffic is assumed to increase from 30 to 50 km/h or from 40 to 60 km/h. The improved traffic flow is assumed to reduce vehicle operating costs by NOK 0.30 per vehicle kilometre and environmental costs by NOK 0.10 per vehicle kilometre. The number of accidents in rush traffic is assumed to increase by 0%, 5% or 15%. The life time is assumed to be 15 years. The results are summarised in Table 3.17.2. The benefits exceed the costs. The cost–benefit

*Table 3.17.2: Cost–benefit analysis of reversible lanes (million NOK; 2005 prices)*

| Traffic volume (AADT) | Costs per km road (investment and maintenance) | Change in accident numbers (%) | Accident cost savings | Speed increase (km/h) | Time cost savings | Vehicle operation cost savings | Environ-mental cost savings | Cost–benefit ratio |
|---|---|---|---|---|---|---|---|---|
| 40,000 | 9.96 | 0 | 0.0 | 30 to 50 | 81.0 | 11.8 | 3.9 | 9.71 |
| 40,000 | 9.96 | +5 | −0.6 | 30 to 50 | 81.0 | 11.8 | 3.9 | 9.66 |
| 40,000 | 9.96 | +15 | −1.7 | 30 to 50 | 81.0 | 11.8 | 3.9 | 9.54 |
| 40,000 | 9.96 | 0 | 0.0 | 40 to 60 | 50.6 | 11.8 | 3.9 | 6.66 |
| 40,000 | 9.96 | +5 | −0.6 | 40 to 60 | 50.6 | 11.8 | 3.9 | 6.60 |
| 40,000 | 9.96 | +15 | −1.7 | 40 to 60 | 50.6 | 11.8 | 3.9 | 6.49 |

ratios are most strongly affected by the time savings and almost independent of the assumed increases in accident numbers. The time, vehicle operating and environmental cost savings exceed by far the increase in accident costs.

## 3.18 Bus lanes and bus stop design

### Problem and objective

Buses and trams are more often involved in accidents than other vehicles where other road users are injured. Based on Norwegian accident data, the number of injuries per million vehicle kilometres to others is 0.23 for private cars, 0.87 for buses and 11.57 for trams. In other words, buses run four times the risk of injuring other road users as private cars. Trams have a very high risk of injuring others, almost 50 times higher than private cars. Buses and trams travel in much denser and more complicated city traffic than private cars. Buses and trams are also heavy vehicles, and braking and manoeuvring are much more difficult than for private cars.

Constructing up bus lanes and protecting bus stops are intended to separate buses and trams from other traffic, and thus reduce the number of accidents. Another objective with these measures is to increase mobility for public transport and thus shorten journey times.

### Description of the measure

Constructing bus lanes includes rush hour lanes for buses and private cars with several passengers or for buses alone, permanent lanes for buses and taxis or trams and permanent streets for buses and taxis or trams.

Bus stop design includes bus bays and the conversion from refuge stops to kerbside stops.

No studies have been found that show how locating bus stops in accordance with official guidelines (Statens vegvesen, Handbook 017 1993) affects accidents.

### Effect on accidents

Studies of the effects of bus lanes and different types of bus stops on the number of accidents include (Table 3.18.1):

LaPlante (1967) (USA): bus lane for buses in the rush hour
Hvoslef (1973) (Norway): tram stop design

*Table 3.18.1: Effects of bus lanes and different types of bus stops for buses and trams on the number of accidents*

| | Percentage change in the number of accidents | | |
|---|---|---|---|
| Accident severity | Types of accident affected | Best estimate | 95% confidence interval |
| ***Rush hour lanes for buses and private cars with several passengers*** | | | |
| Unspecified degree of injury | All accidents | +61 | (+51; +71) |
| ***Rush hour lanes for buses alone*** | | | |
| Injury accidents | All accidents | +12 | (+4; +21) |
| Property-damage-only accidents | All accidents | +15 | (+3; +28) |
| ***Permanent bus lane for buses and taxis*** | | | |
| Injury accidents | All accidents | +27 | (+8; +49) |
| Unspecified severity | All accidents | −4 | (−8; 0) |
| ***Permanent lane for trams*** | | | |
| Unspecified severity | Accidents involving trams | +16 | (0; +35) |
| ***Permanent public transport street for buses and taxis*** | | | |
| Injury accidents | All accidents | +11 | (+2; +20) |
| Property-damage-only accidents | All accidents | −46 | (−54; −37) |
| ***Permanent public transport street for trams*** | | | |
| Unspecified severity | Accidents involving trams | +16 | (−1; +35) |
| ***Creating bus bays*** | | | |
| Injury accidents | All accidents | −74 | (−90; −34) |
| Property-damage-only accidents | All accidents | +120 | (+9; +348) |
| ***Conversion from refuge stops to kerbside stops*** | | | |
| Injury accidents | All accidents | −55 | (−65; −41) |
| Injury accidents | Pedestrian accidents | −76 | (−82; −67) |

Edminster and Koffman (1979) (USA): public transport street for buses
Skölving (1979) (Sweden): bus lanes
Christiansen et al. (1982) (USA): various measures
Kollektivtrafikberedningen (1982) (Sweden): public transport street for buses
Amundsen (1986) (Norway): bus lane for buses and taxis
Devenport (1987) (Great Britain): various measures
LaPlante and Harrington (1984), cited in Nygaard (1989) (USA): bus lanes
Golob, Recker and Levine (1989) (USA): bus lanes and high-occupancy vehicle lanes
Nygaard (1989) (Norway): bus lane for buses and taxis

Sullivan and Devadoss (1993) (USA): bus lane in rush hour for buses and share-a-ride schemes
Sagberg and Sætermo (1997) (Norway): various measures

The majority of American studies refer to time-limited bus lanes (rush hour lanes), where share-a-ride schemes using private cars are permitted.

Bus lanes appear to lead to an increased number of accidents, at least for injury accidents. The increase is greatest for American-style bus lanes, where share-a-ride schemes with private cars are also allowed. There may be several reasons why this type of bus lane leads to more accidents. Such bus lanes are often constructed in the central reservation or in the left lane of motorways, i.e. where the traffic is fastest. In order to move in or out of such bus lanes, several lane changes may be necessary (large motorways in the USA often have three, four or five traffic lanes in the same direction). There may be major differences in speed between a bus lane and the other traffic lanes. Furthermore, buses and light cars both use the bus lane.

The type of bus lane found in Norway also appears to increase the number of accidents. In Norway, bicycles, mopeds and motorcycles are also permitted in the bus lane. This means that the heaviest and the lightest vehicles use the same traffic lane. When turning right at an intersection, it may be necessary to cross the bus lane. In dense traffic, the differences in speed between a bus lane and the other traffic lanes may be relatively large.

Tram stops in the form of a bay outside the traffic lane are not feasible. Two types of tram stops are found: kerbside tram stops and tram stops at a refuge in the middle of the carriageway. Two studies in Oslo, Norway (Hvoslef 1973, Sagberg and Sætermo 1997), suggest that kerbside tram stops are safer than refuge tram stops. In particular, the risk of pedestrian accidents is lower for kerbside trams stops than for refuge tram stops. A Swedish study (Skölving 1979) indicates that creating bus bays reduces the number of injury accidents but increases the number of property-damage-only accidents. However, the results are very uncertain.

**Effect on mobility**

Organisation for Economic Co-operation and Development (OECD 1977) gives examples of how bus lanes in major cities in America and Western Europe have affected journey times by bus. In the majority of cases, reductions of between 20% and 50% in the journey time have been achieved. In bus lanes, travel speed during rush hours is normally 15–20 km/h. An American study (LaPlante and Harrington 1984) confirms these results. In Chicago, four bus lanes in the city centre reduced the average journey time for bus passengers from 10.25 to 8.00 min (22% reduction). For car drivers, journey times increased immediately after the bus lanes opened, because the bus lanes reduced the number of traffic lanes for car traffic. More stringent traffic control in the following year greatly reduced delays for cars.

Bus lanes in Bangkok, Thailand (Tanaboriboon and Toonim 1983), led to shorter journey times for bus passengers without prolonging the journey time for other traffic. In four out of seven cases, it was actually shortened.

Bus bays can affect travel time for bus passengers and other road users. Swedish model simulations (Skölving 1979) suggest a total time gain of 25–50 s for affected vehicles per stopped vehicle on roads, where the hourly traffic is 500 cars. Affected cars are cars that, if there were no bus bays, would have to stop behind a bus in a traffic lane. In the model calculation, it was assumed that the bus stops for 30 s at the bus stop.

For buses that are required to yield when moving out into the traffic from a bus bay, the average delay was calculated in the same study (Skölving 1979) at between 4 and 11 s per bus, depending on how small a gap the bus driver will accept, with an hourly traffic of 500 cars. These delays can be reduced by removing the yield requirement when a bus moves out onto the road from the bus bay. In Norway, this is done on roads where the speed limit is 60 km/h or lower.

**Effect on the environment**

Few studies have been found concerning the effects of measures improving mobility for public transport on the environment. However, information is available on how driving patterns and average speeds affect conditions, such as air pollution and noise. Information is also available on emissions from buses compared to private cars. On the basis of this, it is possible to estimate the effects on the environment of bus lanes.

A comprehensive Danish study investigated the relationship between driving speeds for buses and emission rates for a number of environmentally harmful substances. The substances covered by the study are CO, HC, NOx and particles. For all the substances mentioned, the study found a marked decrease in emissions with increased driving speeds, especially at speeds of between 10 and 20 km/h, which are often the norm in central areas (Eriksen 1996).

### Costs

A compilation of information on 908 projects (Elvik 1996) shows that creating bus bays costs, on average, NOK 140,000 (1995 prices). No cost figures are available for bus lanes. The costs can be assumed to vary according to how the bus lane is constructed: either in addition to the existing traffic lanes or by road markings within the existing road area. In the first case, the costs may be around NOK 3–5 million per kilometre of road. In the latter case, the costs will be around NOK 50,000–100,000 per kilometre of road.

### Cost–benefit analysis

No Norwegian cost–benefit analyses of bus lanes and bus stop designs for public transport have been reported. A numerical example has been prepared, which may indicate the possible effects of a bus lane and bus bay.

For the bus lane, it is assumed that the AADT of the road is 10,000 vehicles, of which 200 are buses. It is assumed that the road has 0.5 injury accidents per million vehicle kilometres. When constructing bus lanes, it is assumed that the number of injury accidents increases by 25%. The bus's average speed (24 h) is assumed to increase from 20 to 25 km/h. The speed level for other traffic is assumed not to change. It is assumed that the bus lane is created within the existing road area using road markings at a cost of NOK 50,000 per kilometre of road. It is assumed that the road markings will be renewed after 5 years.

The effects of a bus lane of 1 km are estimated at NOK 2.99 million in increased accident costs, NOK 7 million in saved costs of travel time and NOK 0.06 million in saved vehicle operating costs. The total benefit is negative, NOK –1.66 million. The savings in the costs of travel time are not enough to offset the increase in the accident costs.

For the bus bay, the same amount of traffic is assumed as for the bus lane. The risk per bus stop is set at 0.01 injury accidents per bus stop per year. Injury accidents are assumed to reduce by 75% and property-damage-only accidents are assumed to increase by 120%. It is further assumed that each car saves, on average, 1 s when a bus bay is constructed.

The effects of the bus bays are estimated at NOK 48,000 in saved accident costs and NOK 1.18 million in saved costs of travel time, in total NOK 1.23 million. The costs of the measure are calculated at NOK 0.25 million. The benefit is greater than the costs, but the uncertain assumption regarding time savings is decisive for the result.

## 3.19 Dynamic route guidance

### Problem and objective

In large towns and cities, traffic congestion in rush hours is a problem. Queues cause delays and irritation and may tempt some drivers to choose what they assume to be short cuts through residential areas. Drivers do not always know which route would be the most advantageous, taking into account journey time, vehicle operating costs, environmental effects on the surroundings and the accident rate. It is not always the case that the driver's choice of road ensures that the social costs of traffic are the lowest possible. The result may be that the drivers do not find their destination at once and then have to look for it. This will increase the total amount of traffic, and consequently the number of accidents.

An American study (King and Mast 1987) has estimated that around 6% of kilometres driven in America is 'unnecessary driving'. In the study, unnecessary driving is defined as the extra number of kilometres driven because drivers did not always choose the shortest (time-related) route between two points. Driving for pleasure, which has no specific travel purpose, was not classified as unnecessary driving.

The main objective of dynamic route guidance is to utilise the capacity of the road system better by preventing inappropriate choices of route. Thus, unnecessary driving can be prevented. In principle, such a system could also supply information about traffic accidents, direct traffic away from an accident location and give information about the accident rate on different streets, so that drivers can select the safest streets.

### Description of the measure

Dynamic route guidance aims at improving traffic flows, mainly in urban areas. The systems are based on recordings of the amount of traffic and traffic flow (e.g. with the help of electronic loops in the carriageway or video cameras at selected points). There are two different types of dynamic route guidance systems:

1. Information is sent to receiver units in the vehicles.
2. Information is displayed on VMS.

The first type of system assumes that vehicles are equipped with a receiver unit. Based on the traffic flow registrations, the journey time between specific places along specific roads is calculated, continuously updated and sent to the receiver units in vehicles. Based on the estimated travel times, drivers may choose the preferred route. Usually vehicles will also be equipped with Global Positioning System (GPS) that may guide the drivers on the recommended or chosen route.

The second type of dynamic route guidance is based on VMS that display information about events on the road or in the road network, and recommend an alternative route. VMS are usually installed at strategic points on the road network. They may provide information and recommendations in the case of capacity problems, road closures, accidents or other events.

**Effect on accidents**

The primary objective of route guidance VMS is to improve traffic operation, and not safety. They may however affect safety in several ways. Re-routing traffic may reduce accidents on those parts of a road network where traffic volume is reduced. However, on other parts of the network, traffic volume, and thereby the number of accidents, may increase (Annino 1998). The information that is provided to drivers may distract, and thereby increase accident risk (Rothengatter, Carbonell-Vaya, de Ward and Brookhuis 1997, Vaa, Gelau, Penttinen and Spyroupolou 2006). Recommendations on alternative routes may also increase the number of potential conflicts when drivers brake, change lane or search for possible exits (Erke and Gottlieb 1980, Erke, Sagberg and Hagman 2007).

The effects of dynamic route guidance with information sent to receiver units in vehicles have been evaluated in two simulation studies. One is a simulation study for London (Stoneman 1992). The calculation found that dynamic route guidance would hardly affect the number of accidents. Assuming 100% usage, the decrease in accident costs was estimated to be 1.5%. Assuming 10%, 20% and 30% use of dynamic road guidance, the changes in accident costs were even smaller. The other study (Maher, Hughes, Smith and Ghali 1993) calculated the effects of a dynamic route guidance system on journey times and accidents for a simulated road network in a city. The simulations show that the traffic distribution yielding the shortest journey time was associated with the most accidents, and vice versa. The explanation for this is that total journey time is minimised when traffic is spread evenly across the whole road network, so that no part of the road network is more congested than others. However, this type of traffic distribution creates many conflict situations at intersections and therefore contributes to an increase in the number of accidents.

**Effect on mobility**

Research on VMS has shown that information about events (e.g. accidents, congestion, road works) and recommended alternative routes may lead to a re-routing of traffic (e.g. Wendelboe 2003, McKenna 2001, Richards 2000). However, the proportion of drivers actually changing route choice varies considerably, and is seldom more than 40% (Erke, Sagberg and Hagman 2007). In a Swedish study (Davidsson and Taylor 2003), between 6% and 41% of the drivers followed a recommendation on an alternative route in order to avoid congestion. Ramsy and Luk (1997) found that the proportion of diverting vehicles increased by 30% when a road blocking was announced. In the study of Lindkvist (1995), between 5% and 25% of the drivers chose an alternative route, and Cummings (1994) found that only 4–7% of all drivers diverted. In the study of Chatterjee, Hounsell, Firmin and Bonsall (2002), only one-third of all drivers noticed messages about network problems, and few of these drivers diverted. A Norwegian study (Erke, Sagberg and Hagman 2007) found that most drivers avoided a closed road section, either by following a recommendation on VMS or by choosing a different alternative route. While the aim of congestion information is an optimization of traffic flows where 100% compliance with the suggestions would not be desirable, the messages on the variable signs in these studies (closed road section) require almost 100% to achieve maximum effectiveness.

A Japanese model calculation (Kawashima 1991) shows that vehicles using dynamic route guidance can save up to 11% of the journey time. A model calculation for London (Stoneman 1992) found a 6–7% reduction in journey time for vehicles with dynamic route guidance. If 100% of vehicles were equipped, the journey time reduction is estimated to be 6%.

### Effect on the environment

No studies have been found that show the effects of dynamic route guidance on the environment or have attempted to estimate these by means of model calculations.

### Costs

No cost figures are available for dynamic route guidance.

### Cost–benefit analysis

There is no basis for carrying out cost–benefit analyses of dynamic route guidance at present.

## 3.20 VARIABLE MESSAGE SIGNS

### Problem and objective

By using traffic signs, the authorities can control behaviour in traffic and give information to road users. This helps to prevent dangerous behaviour and warns of traffic hazards. However, ordinary traffic signs have two basic limitations in their role as aids in affecting road users' alertness and behaviour.

First, traffic signs are not self-enforcing. In many cases, road users may violate traffic signs for long periods without undesirable consequences from the road user's point of view. On the contrary, behaviour that violates traffic signs, for example, driving faster than the speed limit and parking where parking is forbidden, may often have positive consequences for the road user, in that the destination is reached more quickly and the vehicle can be parked much closer. The police cannot enforce all traffic signs at all times.

Second, the majority of traffic signs are permanent and give the same message the whole time. Traditional traffic signs give few opportunities to vary the content of the message according to the conditions at that place at any time. For example, some places may be especially slippery in certain weather and temperature conditions. It is desirable to warn road users about this problem when it occurs, but only then. A sign that warns of icy roads all year round will not be taken seriously, since it is obvious that the message on the sign cannot be correct at all times.

These limitations can be overcome on some roads by using VMS. VMS are traffic signs on which a message can be displayed or altered as required. For example, there could be a lower speed limit outside a school during school hours than for the rest of the day. VMS can also be used to warn road users of queues, accidents, icy conditions or fog. Detectors and inductive loops in the road surface make it possible to record driver behaviour and to provide immediate feedback on it.

The objective of VMS is to reduce dangerous behaviour by warning road users of conditions that occur seldom, by warning of dangers as they occur, and by giving road users feedback on their behaviour.

### Description of the measure

VMS may use different kinds of technology to display signs or messages (e.g. flip dot, lamp matrix, rotating prisms, fibre optics, light emitting diode [LED]), depending on the type of VMS. Signs that may be displayed as variable signs are, for example, speed limits, different kinds of warning signs and feedback signs.

Variable feedback signs are signs that are activated by traffic, in that they are wired up to recording devices that record the behaviour activating the sign. These signs give feedback either collectively (e.g. percentage who kept the speed limit during a certain period), or individually (e.g. actual speed). Most feedback signs refer to compliance with speed limits. Some signs give feedback on too short headways.

**Effect on accidents**

The effect on accidents or behaviour of VMS has been studied by

Duff (1971) (UK): accident warning signs etc.
Erke and Gottlieb (1980) (Germany): queue warning signs on motorways
Van Houten and Nau (1981) (Canada): collective feedback signs speed)
Janoff, Davit and Rosenbaum (1982) (USA): fog warning signs
Helliar-Symons, Wheeler and Scott (1984) (UK): individual feedback signs speed
Van Houten and Malenfant Rolider (1985) (Canada and Israel): collective feedback signs speed
Helliar-Symons and Ray (1986) (UK): individual feedback signs gaps between vehicles
Amundsen (1988) (Norway): variable speed limits at schools, effect on speed only
Malenfant and Van Houten (1989) (Canada): collective feedback signs pedestrian crossings
Cooper, Sawyer and Rutley (1992) (UK): queue warning signs on motorways
Persaud, Mucsi and Ugge (1995) (Canada): queue warning signs on motorways
Hogema, van der Horst and van Nifterick (1996) (The Netherlands): fog warnings
Rämä and Schirokoff (2003) (Finland): weather-controlled variable speed limits

Table 3.20.1 shows best estimates of changes in the number of accidents associated with the introduction of VMS.

Table 3.20.1 shows that large reductions in the number of accidents are associated with accident warning signs, fog warning signs or collective feedback signs. However, to some extent, the signs studied have been used at accident black spots. Many of the studies are simple before-and-after studies, which do not control for regression to the mean. It is therefore highly likely that the studies overstate the true effect of the signs on the number of accidents.

*Table 3.20.1: Effects of variable message signs on the number of accidents*

| | Percentage change in the number of accidents | | |
|---|---|---|---|
| Accident severity | Types of accident affected | Best estimate | 95% confidence interval |
| ***Accident warning signs*** | | | |
| Injury accidents | Accidents on motorways | −44 | (−59; −22) |
| ***Fog warning signs*** | | | |
| Unspecified severity | Accidents in fog | −84 | (−93; −63) |
| ***Weather-controlled speed limits*** | | | |
| Injury accidents | Accidents in winter | −13 | (ns) |
| Injury accidents | Accidents in summer | −2 | (ns) |
| ***Queue warnings on motorways*** | | | |
| Injury accidents | Rear-end collisions | −16 | (−26; −4) |
| Property-damage-only accidents | Rear-end collisions | +16 | (+1; +34) |
| ***Collective feedback signs for speed*** | | | |
| Unspecified severity | All accidents | −46 | (−62; −24) |
| ***Collective feedback signs for obligation to give way at pedestrian crossings*** | | | |
| Injury accidents | Pedestrian accidents | −65 | (−96; +199) |
| ***Individual feedback signs for speed*** | | | |
| Injury accidents | All accidents | −41 | (−78; +59) |
| ***Individual feedback signs for close following*** | | | |
| Unspecified severity | Rear-end collisions | −6 | (−56; +104) |

Studies of variable speed limits that are combined with variable warning signs for slippery roads in Finland (Rämä and Schirokoff 2003) were found to reduce accidents in winter. The effect is however not statistically significant.

Queue warning signs appear to reduce the number of injury accidents but result in more property-damage-only accidents. Erke and Gottlieb (1980) showed that these signs lead to more frequent lane changes on motorways and to drivers starting to look for exits. This may increase the chances of conflict between vehicles and thus lead to more property-damage-only accidents.

In Norway, variable speed limit signs outside schools have been tested (Amundsen 1988). Studies at nine schools found that the mean speed reduced from around 57 km/h to around 51 km/h, all schools taken together. There was a decrease in speed at all schools, but the size of the decrease varied from around 2 km/h to around 11 km/h. A decrease in speed from 57 to 51 km/h can be expected to reduce the number of injury accidents by around 20% (see Section 3.11, speed limits).

On sections where individual feedback signs for speed have been erected, the number of accidents has reduced by around 41%. The reduction is based on only a few accidents and is not statistically significant. Individual feedback signs for headways appear to produce a small reduction in the number of accidents. The decrease is not statistically significant. Variable feedback signs have only been tested to a limited extent. A number of the studies of the effects of variable feedback signs probably contain uncontrolled regression-to-the-mean effects.

### Effect on mobility

Signs leading to lower average speed reduce mobility, e.g. variable speed limits and fog warning signs. It has been shown that these types of sign reduce the average speed of traffic and thus increase the time needed for travel and transport. The effects of other types of variable signs on mobility are not known. Signs warning of queues were found to reduce congestion on the roads where such signs have been used, because some of the traffic chooses alternative routes (Erke and Gottlieb 1980). If the alternative routes are less congested, this will improve mobility overall.

### Effect on the environment

No studies have been found that indicate the effects of VMS on the environment. Lower speeds can lead to reduced noise and reduced emission of some types of pollutants from vehicles. The actual effects have not been studied.

### Costs

VMS are more expensive than ordinary traffic signs. According to cost estimates published by the US Research and Innovative Technology Administration (RITA), variable speed display signs cost between ca. US$ 3,200 and 4,400, while dynamic message signs cost between ca. US$ 44,000 and 111,000 (2007 prices).

In Norway, a speed sign board with the text ‘Your speed is XX kilometres per hour’ (Vaa, Christensen and Ragnøy 1994) costs NOK 85,000. The price includes the board with the text, the display with light diodes to show speeds, a radar on the top of the board and the trailer upon which the board is mounted.

### Cost–benefit analysis

No cost–benefit analyses of the types of signs described in this chapter have been found nor is it possible to make extensive cost–benefit analyses on the basis of the information available today. Nonetheless, it is possible to make certain assumptions regarding critical values for the effects that make the signs cost-effective or not. Assume, for example, that a collective feedback sign for speed reduces the average speed on a road from 82.5 to 80 km/h for a 1 km long section. The AADT in the direction of the sign is assumed to be 5,000 vehicles and the accident rate is assumed to be 0.25 injury accident per million vehicle kilometres. It is assumed that six property-damage-only accidents occur per injury accident. The number of accidents is assumed to reduce by 10%. In the course of 1 year, the sign will lead to a reduction of around NOK 10,000 in accident costs on this stretch of road. The costs of travel time will increase by around NOK 70,000. The net benefit will therefore be negative. If the gains in time are obtained by driving above the speed limit, however, it is not correct to include the loss of time incurred by forcing people to maintain a legal speed as a loss of benefit in a cost–benefit analysis.

## 3.21 Protecting railway–highway level crossings

### Problem and objective

Collisions between trains and road users often lead to serious injuries. This is because the train's mass is very large in comparison with other vehicles. Protecting railway–highway level crossings is intended to reduce the probability of collisions between trains and road users. This can be done by removing level crossings or equipping them with warning signals and barriers.

### Description of the measure

All level crossings on public roads in Norway are indicated using hazard warning signs no. 134 or no. 135, 'Level Crossing'. At the crossing itself, sign no. 138, 'Railway Line (St. Andrew's cross)' is erected. The level crossing itself can be protected by means of automatic or manned barriers, traffic signals and sound signals or with a manned or unmanned gate. At the end of 2007, the safety installations given in Table 3.21.1 were in use.

*Table 3.21.1: Safety measures at level crossings in Norway, 1996*

| Type of safety installation | Public roads | Private roads |
|---|---|---|
| Automatic full barriers | 85 | 20 |
| Automatic half barriers | 186 | 59 |
| Automatic flashing signals and sound | 10 | 13 |
| Warning signals | 2 | 85 |
| Unmanned gate or no safety measure | 42 | 3,259 |
| Total number of level crossings | 325 | 3,426 |

### Effect on accidents

***Removing level crossings.*** The best way to avoid level crossing accidents is to get rid of the level crossing. When a level crossing is removed, either the crossing traffic disappears completely or the user must be given a new crossing point. This can be done in the form of an interchange or by connection to a multi-use crossing.

***Protecting level crossings.*** The effect of protecting level crossings using signs, light and sound signals and barriers on accidents has been evaluated in several studies. The results presented here are based on the following studies:

Collins (1965) (USA)
California Public Utilities Commission (1965) (USA)
Thomas (1965) (USA)
Schoppert and Hoyt (1968) (USA)
Berg and Oppenlander (1969) (USA)
Schultz, Berg and Oppenlander (1969) (USA)
Planovergangsutvalget (1970) (Norway)
Van Belle, Meeter and Farr (1975) (USA)
Coleman and Stewart (1976) (USA)
Herbert and Smith (1976) (Australia)
Schulte (1976) (USA)
Ricker et al. (1977) (USA)
Zalinger, Rogers and Johri (1977) (Canada)
Amundsen (1980) (Norway)
Ekblom, Kolsrud and Möller (1981) (Sweden)
Eck and Halkias (1985) (USA)
Halkias and Eck (1985) (USA)

*Table 3.21.2: Effects of protecting level crossings between roads and railways on accidents (unspecified severity)*

| | Percentage change in the number of accidents | | |
|---|---|---|---|
| Measure | Types of accident affected | Best estimate | 95% confidence interval |
| Approaching train warning by means of whistle blow | Level crossing accidents | −26 | (−53; +16) |
| Warning of level crossing by means of hazard warning sign | Level crossing accidents | −23 | (−33; −12) |
| Stop sign at level crossing | Level crossing accidents | −65 | (−86; −12) |
| Flashing lights and sound signals at level crossings that previously only had warning signs | Level crossing accidents | −51 | (−64; −33) |
| Barriers at level crossings that previously had flashing lights and sound signals | Level crossing accidents | −45 | (−56; −32) |
| Barriers at level crossings that previously only had warning signs | Level crossing accidents | −68 | (−76; −57) |
| Improving sight conditions at level crossings | Level crossing accidents | −44 | (−68; −5) |

Eck and Shanmugam (1987) (USA)
Hauer and Persaud (1987) (USA)
Abrahamsson, Ohlsson and Sjölinder (1991) (Sweden)
Wigglesworth and Uber (1991) (Australia)
Gitelman and Hakkert (1997) (Israel)
Austin and Carson (2002) (USA)
Park and Saccomanno (2005) (Canada)
Saccomanno and Lai (2005) (Canada)
Saccomanno, Park and Fu (2007) (Canada)
Millegan, Yan, Richards and Han (2009) (USA)

On the basis of these studies, the best estimates of the effect of different safety measures at level crossings on accidents are shown in Table 3.21.2.

Most studies are simple before-and-after studies that do not control for any confounding factors. The results presented above are based only on studies that have controlled for regression to the mean and a potential endogeneity bias in multivariate accident prediction models.

Sound and light signals and automatic barriers greatly reduce the number of accidents on level crossings. Signs warning of level crossings also reduce the number of accidents, but not as much as sound and light signals and barriers. Improving sight conditions at level crossings reduces the number of accidents.

***Measures to increase respect for safety measures.*** A Canadian study (Wilde, Cake and McCarthy 1976) found that respect for the safety equipment (signal and barrier) is related to the length of and variations in the warning time before the train passes the level crossing. The longer the barrier is lowered before the train comes and the more the waiting time varies from train to train, the lower the respect for the installation.

It is possible to equip light and sound signals and barriers with fixed activation times, i.e. a system that adapts warning and lowering times for the barrier to the speed of the train, so that the barrier always goes down at a given time, for example, 30 s before the train passes. American studies (Halkias and Eck 1985, Bowman 1987) indicate that light and sound signals and barriers with fixed activation times result in around 20% fewer accidents than similar installation with variable activation times. The results are based on only a few accidents and are not statistically significant, but nonetheless they indicate that such equipment can improve the safety on level crossings.

### Effect on mobility

Barriers result in longer waiting times for road users at level crossings than are actually strictly necessary for crossing the level crossing. Since the number of trains per day at the vast majority of places is significantly lower than the number of road users per day, only a minority of road users incur such delays. Planovergangsutvalget (1970) estimated the average waiting time per vehicle at a level crossing with an AADT of 10,000 vehicles on the road, 15 trains at night and 15 trains during the day as 0.8 s (all vehicles taken together). It was assumed that the barrier was lowered for 40 s per train and that the number of vehicles arriving per time unit was randomly distributed.

### Effect on the environment

The effects of safety measures on level crossings for environment conditions have not been studied. Sound signals can disturb residential areas, especially at night. Exhaust emission from vehicles may increase as a result of stopping, waiting and starting again. The actual effects have not been quantified.

## Costs

The costs of protecting level crossings vary according to the terrain conditions at the site and the scope of the measures. The following approximate average costs of different measures in Norway can be given:

| Measure | Average cost (NOK) |
|---|---|
| Warning signs | 5,000–10,000 |
| Flashing lights and sound signals | 400,000–600,000 |
| Automatic barriers | 600,000–1,000,000 |
| Annual operating costs for barriers | 5,000–10,000 |

## Cost–benefit analysis

The mean number of accidents per level crossing per year on public roads in Norway is around 0.007 accidents (mean 2003–07). The mean number of accidents at private level crossings per year is 0.00096 accidents (mean 2003–07). These mean values are very low. The majority of accidents at level crossings on public roads occur at level crossings already protected by means of sound or light signals or barriers. The majority of accidents at private level crossings are on unprotected level crossings, i.e. on level crossings where there is only a gate opened and closed by the user.

The number of accidents on level crossings per year is too low for it to be possible to identify any accident black spots at level crossings on the basis of the accident records. It is extremely rare for more than one accident to occur at a level crossing during 1 year. The recorded number of accidents per level crossing per year is largely the result of chance and is a very unreliable measure of the level of safety at level crossings in the long term.

For private level crossings, safety measures in the form of light and sound signals and barriers are not cost-effective in the majority of cases. An investment cost of, e.g. NOK 1 million corresponds to the present value calculated for 25 years (4.5% annual discount rate) of preventing 0.067 injury accidents. This is far more than the current mean number of accidents per level crossing per year, for both public and private level crossings.

This does not mean that the safety measures previously implemented were not worthwhile. An evaluation in an earlier edition of this book (Elvik, Vaa and Østvik 1989, 215) shows that during the period from 1972 to 1979, when safety installations at public level crossings were greatly expanded, investments were around NOK 100,000 per injury accident that was prevented. This is a small investment, considering the fact that the value of preventing a police reported injury accident in Norway is at present NOK 3.56 million.

## 3.22 Environmental zones

### Problem and objective

Local environmental problems associated with road traffic are greatest in cental parts of cities. Many such areas have had a large traffic growth. Neither the road infrastructure nor the buildings and surroundings are however prepared for handling the problems increasing traffic is bringing about. Environmental zones can be installed in order to cope with the local environmental problems of increasing traffic. Such zones aim at improving the environment for residents, pedestrians and cyclists, and the cityscape as a whole. Traffic safety may be improved as well.

In most countries, environmental zones are not (yet) a well established concept. There are numerous different definitions of environmental zones. In Sweden, a preliminary concept has been developed that refers to environmental requirements for heavy traffic within zones in urban areas. In Norway, environmental zones have been defined as follows (Amundsen, Kolbenstvedt and Lerstang 2003): 'A clearly geographically defined area in urban or built up areas, which is vulnerable and traffic burdened, and where special measures are required in order to prevent or reduce several types of environmental impacts, especially from road traffic. Different measures are to be regarded in relationship to each other'.

The specific requirements and measures within an environmental zone can be selected on a local basis, depending on environmental problems, desired quality of the environment, local climatic and topographical conditions. Some measures require authorised decisions. Available resources, implementation costs, and practical aspects of the implementation may limit the possibilities. The choice of measures may have to be adjusted to the time frame within which environmental effects are to be achieved. While some areas may require measures with immediate effects, more long-term measures may be more meaningful in other areas.

### Description of the measure

In Norway, the only city with an environmental zone is Drammen. The measures in this zone are, among others, parking restrictions, city bikes and bicycle parking

(Amundsen, Kolbenstvedt and Lerstang 2003). In Groruddalen, an environmental zone is in preparation with several measures for reducing car traffic and improving cycling and walking conditions (Administrativ samarbeidsgruppe for Groruddalen 2003). Several measures may be used in environmental zones in Norway. Requirements may vary between different areas, depending on existing environmental problems, and on expected developments with and without implementation of environmental zones.

In Sweden, environmental zones have been implemented in the four cities Stockholm, Göteborg, Malmö and Lund. In these cities, particle filters for heavy vehicles are required. In England, a trial is made with 'Clear zones'. Measures in these zones are traffic calming, establishing new cycle routes, park and ride and several improvements of public transport (Amundsen, Kolbenstvedt and Lerstang 2003).

***Where are environmental zones applicable?*** Environmental zones are mainly applicable in parts of cities and built-up areas with high levels of noise and pollution from road traffic. In Sweden, environmental zones are implemented in areas with residential housings, many pedestrians and cyclists, buildings that are vulnerable to traffic, and parks or green spaces that are suffering from emissions from road traffic (Markung 1997). The geographical limits of environmental zones are defined based on the environmental problems and vulnerability of areas. In environmental zones, there may be more restrictive requirements to traffic than in neighbouring areas. The zones should therefore be clearly defined and marked and sufficient information should be provided to road users. Environmental zones should also be enforced in order to make sure that the intended effects are not averted by violations of the restrictions (Kolbenstvedt, Solheim and Amundsen 2000).

***Possbile measures in environmental zones.*** Measures that can be used in environmental zones are measures that aim at reducing traffic volumes or speed or that improve the conditions for pedestrians and cyclists. Restrictions to motorised traffic may be a ban on through traffic or restrictions for specific types of vehicles, either permanently or during certain times. Such restrictions may limit the access e.g. of heavy vehicles, or of vehicles that do not satisfy environmental criteria (Skedsmo and Hagman 2006). Through traffic may also be reduced by one-way traffic in residential streets and by improving main roads or by constructing bypasses (see also Part III, Section 1.3). Parking regulations may also be introduced, e.g. parking restrictions, increased prices or reserved parking space for residents. Speed-reducing measures may be reduced speed limits or physical measures, such as speed humps or narrowings. Reduced traffic volumes and speed may also contribute to making the area more attractive for pedestrians and cyclists. Through traffic may additionally be reduced.

### Effect on accidents

Effects on accidents are dependent on which types of measures are implemented in environmental zones and on the degree to which these measures reduce traffic volumes and speed. When traffic volumes are reduced, accidents in other areas, where traffic volumes might increase, should be taken into account. No evaluations have been found of the safety effects of environmental zones.

### Effect on mobility

Environmental zones may reduce mobility for motorised traffic, especially for heavy traffic, within the respective zones. When the implementation of environmental zones includes the improvement of main roads outside the zones or the construction of bypasses, mobility for through traffic may be improved. Within environmental zones, mobility may be improved for pedestrians and cyclists, depending on the type of measures that are implemented.

### Effect on the environment

Environmental effects depend on the types of measures that are implemented. Most measures aim at improving the environment. In three Swedish cities (Amundsen, Kolbenstvedt and Lerstang 2003), the effects of environmental zones with restrictions for heavy traffic on emissions of particles, HC and NOx, have been evaluated by Trivector (1997). The reductions of emissions in 1997, compared to 1996, were between 15% and 21% for particles, between 5% and 9% for HC and between 1% and 8% for NOx. The restrictions were sharpened in 1999. In Stockholm, emission reductions have also been evaluated in 2001 by Burman and Johansson (2001). It was found that NOx emissions were reduced by 10% and that particle emissions were reduced by about 40% in 2001. Around 90% of all heavy vehicles were found to comply with the demands of the regulations in 2000.

In Norway, Skedsmo and Hagman (2006) have estimated scenarios of introducing charges for trucks for driving in or through geographically defined areas (cities) in order to speed up the replacing of old trucks with newer trucks that conform to European Union (EU) regulations for emissions of new vehicles. The scenarios are however fictitious, and no low emission zones have actually been introduced. Evaluation results are therefore not available (see also cost–benefit analysis).

**Costs**

The costs of environmental zones depend on the types of measures that are implemented. Costs may include costs for the implementation of specific measures, administrative and enforcement costs, and costs to road users such as increased travel times. In the evaluation of low emission zones in Norway (Skedsmo and Hagman 2006), costs are assumed to arise for truck owners (charges and replacing vehicles), and for public authorities (administration and enforcement).

**Cost–benefit analysis**

The benefits of environmental zones are related to environmental, health and safety effects. The annual societal costs of traffic noise are estimated at about NOK 2.5 millions (Norwegian Pollution Control Authority and Directorate for Nature Management 1996). The Norwegian Pollution Control Authority has estimated the total environmental and health costs of $NO_2$ and particle emissions at NOK 3.5 and 5.5 million, respectively.

Trivector (1997) has estimated the societal costs and benefits of low emission zones in Swedish cities. In the city of Göteborg, the costs for truck owners for replacing or improving vehicles have been estimated at about SEK 128 million. The benefits in terms of reduced emissions have been estimated at about SEK 101 million. This is lower than the costs. The environmental benefits have, however, been estimated based on average values for the whole country. Environmental problems of emissions are larger in cities, and the benefits are therefore likely to be somewhat larger than estimated.

Skedsmo and Hagman (2006) have calculated cost–benefit analyses of a low emission zone in Oslo, in which charges are introduced for trucks driving in or through Oslo that have emissions above a defined level. Two scenarios have been estimated. In one scenario, the charges are assumed to reduce emissions by 80% after about 4–5 years. In the second scenario, charges are higher so as to reduce emissions by 80% immediately after introducing the low emission zone. The baseline for both scenarios is the introduction of no extra charges (no low emission zone), which is assumed to lead to a reduction of emissions by 80% in 2020. For both scenarios, the costs exceed the benefits of introducing the low emission zone.

## References

Abel, H. & U. Matthes (2001). *Auswirkungen einer flächendeckenden Einführung von Tempo 30 innerorts auf die Unfallzahlen in der Schweitz*. Prognos AG, Basel.

Abrahamsson, A., K. Ohlsson & K. Sjölinder. (1991). *Litteratursökning gällande olyckspred iktionsmodeller och riskindex för plankorsningar mellan väg och järnväg*. VTI-notat T 105. Väg- och TrafikInstitutet (VTI), Linköping.

Administrativ samarbeidsgruppe for Groruddalen (2003). *Bede miljø i Groruddalen. Planer og hovedstrategier. Miljøsone med 4 innsatsområder*. April 2003.

Agent, K. R. & J. D. Clark. (1982). Evaluation of reversible lanes. *Traffic Engineering and Control*, **23**, 551–555.

Agustsson, L. (2001). *Danish experiences with speed zones/variable speed limits*. Paper presented at the Conference traffic safety on three continents, Moscow, September 19–21, 2001 (available on CD-Rom).

Al-Masaeid, H. R. (1997). Performance of Safety Evaluation Methods. *Journal of Transportation Engineering*, **123**, 364–369.

Amundsen, F. H. (1973a). *Om vikeplikt og forkjørsrett del I. Trafikktekniske undersøkelser ved innføring av forkjørsveger*. TØI-rapport. Transportøkonomisk institutt, Oslo.

Amundsen, F. H. (1973b). *Om vikeplikt og forkjørsrett del II. Trafikkulykkesundersøkelser ved innføring av forkjørsveger*. TØI-rapport. Transportøkonomisk institutt, Oslo.

Amundsen, F. H. (1979). *Trafikkulykker og avkjørsler. En studie av sammenhenger mellom trafikkulykker og avkjørsler langs en del riksveger*. TØI-rapport. Transportøkonomisk institutt, Oslo.

Amundsen, F. H. (1980). Sikkerhetsforholdene ved offentlige planoverganger. *Samferdsel* **8**, 24–25.

Amundsen, F. H. (1981). *Effektmåling av fartsgrense. 60 km/t langs Ev18 i Vestfold. Tredje ettermåling*. TØI-notat 585, revidert utgave 11.11.1981. Transportøkonomisk institutt, Oslo.

Amundsen, F. H. (1983). Effektmåling av fartsgrense 60 km/t langs E18 i Vestfold (4de ettermåling). TØI-notat 620 av 20.10.1982 revidert 19.04.83. Oslo: Institute of Transport Economics.

Amundsen, F. H. (1984). *Vintervedlikehold av gatetun*. TØI-notat 639. Transportøkonomisk institutt, Oslo.

Amundsen, F. H. (1986). *Bruk av fartsdempende tiltak på veger med busstrafikk*. TØI-notat 779. Transportøkonomisk institutt, Oslo.

Amundsen, F. H. (1988). *Variable fartsgrenser og kjørefart. Forsøk ved skoler i Akershus, Østfold og Telemark*. TØI-notat 0871. Transportøkonomisk institutt, Oslo.

Amundsen, F. H. & P. Christensen. (1986). *Sammenheng mellom kjørefart og utforming av boligveger*. TØI-rapport. Transportøkonomisk institutt, Oslo.

Amundsen, F. H., Daas, H.R., Hvoslef, H., Magnussen, P.H. & Sakshaug, K. (1976). *Gangfelt. Utredninger for gangfeltutvalget i 1975*. TØI-rapport. Utgitt i samarbeid med Forskningsgruppen, Institutt for samferdselsteknikk, Norges Tekniske Høgskole. Transportøkonomisk institutt, Oslo.

Amundsen, A. H. Kolbenstvedt, M. & Lerstang, T. (2003). *Miljøsoner – bedre miljø i byer og tettsteder. Muligheter og utfordringer*. Oslo, Transportøkonomisk institutt. TØI rapport 630/2003.

Amundsen, F. H., P. O. Roald, A. Engebretsen (2004). *Kjørefart og personskadeulykker på motorveger med fartsgrense 100 km/t. En evaluering av forsøk på E6 og E18 i Akershus, Buskerud og Vestfold*. Rapport fra Veg- og trafikkavdelingen, TS-seksjonen, 7/2004. Statens vegvesen, Vegdirektoratet, Oslo.

Andersson, B. M. & Nilsson, G. (1974). *Hastighetsbegränsningars effekt på trafikolyckor. Jämförelse mellan hastighetsgränserna 130 och 110 km/h på motorvägar samt hastighetsgränserna 90 och 100 km/h på tvåfältsvägar*. VTI-rapport 59. Statens väg- och trafikinstitut (VTI), Stockholm.

Andersson, G. (2000). *Sänkta hastighetsgränser vintern 1999–2000*. VTI notat 58-2000. Väg- och transportforskningsinstitutet, Linköping.

Andersson, K. (1982). *EMMA-rapport 4. Trafiksäkerhetseffekten av stopplikt*. VTI-rapport 236. Statens väg- och trafikinstitut (VTI), Linköping.

Andreassen, D. C. (1970). Another look at traffic signals and accidents. In: *ARRB Proceedings*, Volume 5, Part 3, 304–316, 1970. Australian Road Research Board, Vermont South, Victoria.

Angenendt, W. (1991). *Sicherheitsverbesserungen in Geschäftsstrassen mit Durchgangsverkehr*. Forschungsberichte der Bundesanstalt für Strassenwesen, 244. Bundeanstalt für Strassenwesen, Bergisch-Gladbach.

Annino, J. M. (1998). *The effects of ITS technology on accident rates*. Toronto, Ontario: Institute of Transportation Engineers, Annual meeting papers.

Annino, J. M. (2003). *Rumble strips in Connecticut. A before/after analysis of safety benefits*. Connecticut Department of Transportation, report CT-902-F-04-3.

Antov, D. & T. Roivas (1999). *Speed experiment in Estonia-impacts on road safety and road user behaviour*. Proceedings of the conference Traffic Safety on two Continents, Malmö, Sweden, September 20–22, 1999. Swedish National Road and Transport Research Institute, Linköping.

Appleyard, D. & M. Lintell (1972). The environmental quality of city streets. The residents viewpoint. *Journal of the American Institute of Planners*, **38**, 84–101.

Arndt, C. G. (1978). Experience with Australias First Pelican Crossings. *Proceedings from Joint ARRB/DOT Pedestrian Conference*.

Askildsen, R. K., Leite, M. E. & Muskaug, R. (1996). *Utvalgsundersøkelser 1995–96. En oppfølging av veileder 8 for NVVP 1998–2007*. Rapport TTS 8/1996. Vegdirektoratet, Transport- og trafikksikkerhetsavdelingen, Transportanalysekontoret, Oslo.

Austin, R. D. & J. L. Carson (2002). An alternative accident prediction model for highway-rail interfaces. Accident Analysis and Prevention, 34, 31–42.

Bach, O. & E. Jørgensen. (1986). *Signaler og ulykker - effekt af ombygninger*. Vejdirektoratet, Sekretariatet for Sikkerhedsfremmende Vejforanstaltninger (SSV), Næstved.

Bagley, J. (1985). An Assessment of the Safety Performance of Pelican Crossings in Relation to Criterion Value. *Proceedings of Seminar M held at PTRC Summer Annual Meeting 1985*, 203–216. PTRC Education and Research Services Ltd.

Baguley, C. (1982). Evaluation of safety of speed control humps. In: *Proceedings (246–250) of Seminar on Short-Term and Area-Wide Evaluation of Safety Measures*, Amsterdam, April 19–21, 1982. Published by SWOV Institute for Road Safety Research on behalf of OECD, Amsterdam.

Baier, R. (1992). Flankierende Massnahmen zur Einrichtung von Tempo 30-Zonen. *Strassenverkehrstechnik*, **Heft 1**, 31–36.

Baier, H. & K. Schlabbach. (1981). Linksabbiegeunfälle an Lichtsignalanlagen in Darmstadt. Vorher-/Nachher-Untersuchung. *Strassenverkehrstechnik*. **Heft 3**, 71–78.

Baier, R., Kiepe, F., Krause, J. et al. (1992). *Forschungsvorhaben Flächenhafte Verkehrsberuhigung. Folgerungen für die Praxis*. Bundesministerium für Raumordnung, Bauwesen und Städtebau, Bundesministerium für Verkehr, Bundesministerium für Umwelt, Naturschutz und Reaktorsicherheit, Bundesministerium für Landeskunde und Raumordnung, Bundesanstalt für Strassenwesen, Umweltbundesamt, Bonn.

Bali, S. Potts, R., Fee, J. A. et al. (1978). *Cost-Effectiveness and Safety of Alternative Roadway Delineation Treatments for Rural Two-Lane Highways*. Report FHWA-RD-78-54. US Department of Transportation, Washington DC.

Barbaresso, J. C. (1987). Relative Accident Impacts of Traffic Control Strategies During Low-Volume Nighttime Periods. *ITE-Journal*, **August**, 41–46.

Basile, A. J. (1962). Effect of Pavement Edge Markings on Traffic Accidents in Kansas. *Highway Research Board Bulletin*, **308**, 80–86.

Bastable, A. J. (1980). The economic and social impact of dynamic signal coordination in Sydney. *ARRB Proceedings*, **Volume 10**, Part 4, 245–251, 1980. Australian Road Research Board, Vermont South, Victoria.

Behrendt, J., Ernst, R.. Hartkopf, G. et al. (1989). *Erfarungsbericht über Zonen-Geschwindigkeitsbeschränkungen*. Unfall- und Sicherheitsforschung Strassenverkehr, Heft 73. Bundesanstalt für Strassenwesen (BASt), Bergisch Gladbach.

Bellis, W. R. (1969). Development of an effective rumble strip pattern. *Traffic Engineering*, **April**, 22–25.

Berg, W. D. & J. C. Oppenlander. (1969). Accident analysis at railroad-highway grade crossings in urban areas. *Accident Analysis and Prevention*, 1, 129–141.

Bhesania, R. P. (1991). Impact of Mast-Mounted Signal Heads on Accident Reduction. *ITE-Journal*, **October**, 25–29.

Bjørnskau, T. (1994). *Spillteori, trafikk og ulykker. En teori om interaksjon i trafikken.* TØI-rapport 287. Transportøkonomisk institutt, Oslo.

Bjørnskau, T. (2008). *Risiko i trafikken 2005–2007*. Report 986/2008. Oslo: Institute of Transport Economics.

Blakstad, F. (1988). *Trafikkteknikk*. Tredje utgave. Tapir forlag, Trondheim.

Blakstad, F. (1990a). *Ulykkesfrekvenser på hovedveger i byområder*. Rapport STF63 A90005. SINTEF Samferdselsteknikk, Trondheim.

Blakstad, F. (1990b). Trefeltsveger med reversible felt: Bedre enn sitt rykte. *Våre Veger*, **17**, 3, 24–27.

Blakstad, F. (1993). *Alternativer til signalregulerte gangfelt*. Rapport STF63 A93002. SINTEF Samferdselsteknikk, Trondheim.

Blakstad, F. & T. Giæver. (1989). *Ulykkesfrekvenser på vegstrekninger i tett og middels tett bebyggelse*. Rapport STF63 A89005. SINTEF Samferdselsteknikk, Trondheim.

Boëthius, P., Ekelöf, L. J., Grunewald, R. et al. (1971). *Trafiksanering-försöksverksamhet. Västerås-Gideonsberg*. Meddelande 34. Chalmers Tekniska Högskola, Institutionen för stadsbyggnad, Göteborg.

Bonneson, J. A. & P. T. McCoy. (1997). *Effect of Median Treatment on Urban Arterial Safety: An Accident Prediction Model.* Paper 970101. 76th Annual Meeting, Transportation Research Board, January 12–16, Washington DC.

Borger, A. & Frøysadal, E. (1993). *Sykkelundersøkelsen 1992*. TØI-rapport 217. Transportøkonomisk institutt, Oslo.

Borger, A. & Frøysadal, E. (1994). *Sykkelbyprosjektet. Intervjuundersøkelser i sykkelbyene Sandnes og Tønsberg/Nøtterøy i 1992*. TØI-rapport 234. Transportøkonomisk institutt, Oslo.

Borges, P., S. Hansen & K. Meulengracht-Madsen. (1985). *Trafiksanering af STORE bygader - nogle eksempler*. Vejdirektoratet, Sekretariatet for Sikkerhedsfremmende Vejforanstaltninger (SSV), Næstved.

Bowman, B. L. (1987). The Effectiveness of Railroad Constant Warning Time Systems. *Transportation Research Record*, **1114**, 111–122.

Bowman, B. L. & R. L. Vecellio. (1994). Effect of Urban and Suburban Median Types on Both Vehicular and Pedestrian Safety. *Transportation Research Record*, **1445**, 169–179.

Boxall, J. A. (1988). School crossing patrols: how effective are they? *Traffic Engineering and Control*, **29**, 586.

Bretherton Jr., W. M. & Elhaj, M. (1996). Is a Reversible Lane System Safe? *Compendium of Technical Papers for the 66TH ITE Annual Meeting*, pp. 277–281, Minneapolis.

Brilon, W. & H. Blanke. (1990). Area-Wide Traffic Calming Measures and Their Effects on Traffic Safety in Residential Areas. *Paper presented at the conference Road safety and Traffic Environment in Europe*, September 26–28, Gothenburg, Sweden.

Brilon, W. & H. Blanke (1992). Flächenhafte Verkehrsberuhigung: Ergebnisse der Unfallanalysen in 6 Modellstädten. *Zeitschrift für Verkehrssicherheit*, **38**, 102–110.

Brilon, W., Kahrmann, B., Senk, W., Thiel, R. & Werner, H. (1985). *Flächenhafte Verkehrsberuhigung. Unfallanalyse Berlin-Charlottenburg*. Bericht zum Forschungsprojekt 8019/9 der Bundesanstalt für Strassenwesen. Bundesanstalt für Strassenwesen, Bergisch-Gladbach.

Brodersen, F., N. O. Jørgensen & H. V. Lund. (1975). *Erfaringer med hastighedsbegrænsninger 1974/75*. RfT-notat 118. Rådet for Trafiksikkerhedsforskning, København,

Brodin, A. & L. Ringhagen. (1975). *Effekt på olyckor och hastigheter av hastighetsgränsen 30 km/h i bostadsområden*. (Rapport Nr 78). Statens väg- och trafikinstitut (VTI), Linköping.

Brown, D. B., S. Maghsoodloo & M. E. McArdle (1990). The Safety Impact of the 65 mph Speed Limit: A Case Study Using Alabama Accident Records. *Journal of Safety Research*, **21**, 125–139.

Brown, H. & Tarko, A. (1999). Effects of access control on safety of urban arterial streets. *Transportation Research Record* 1665, 68–74.

Brownfield, D. J. (1980). Environmental areas-Interim report on a before-and-after accident study. *Traffic Engineering and Control*, **21**, 278–282.

Bruce, J. A. (1967). One-Way Major Arterial Streets. In: *Highway Research Board, Special Report 93*, Improved Street Utilization through Traffic Engineering, 24–35. Highway Research Board, Washington DC.

Brüde, U. & J. Larsson. (1985). *Korsningsåtgärder vidtagna inom vägförvaltningarnas trafiksäkerhetsarbete. Regressions- och åtgärdseffekter*. VTI-rapport 292. Statens väg- och trafikinstitut (VTI), Linköping.

Brüde, U. & J. Larsson. (1988). *Trafiksäkerhetseffekt av LHOVRA-signaler. Analysmetoder och resultat*. VTI-meddelande 575. Väg- och TrafikInstitutet, Linköping.

Brüde, U. & J. Larsson. (1990). *Ändring från stopplikt til väjningsplikt i korsningar på statliga huvudvägnätet. Uppföljning av trafiksäkerhetseffekten*. VTI-meddelande 640. Väg- och TrafikInstitutet, Linköping.

Brüde, U. & J. Larsson. (1992a). *Ändring från stopp- till väjningsplikt. Effekt på antal personskadeolyckor*. VTI-meddelande 695. Väg- och TrafikInstitutet, Linköping.

Brüde, U. & J. Larsson. (1992b). *Trafiksäkerhet i tätortskorsningar*. VTI-meddelande 685. Väg- och TrafikInstitutet, Linköping.

Buran, M., T. Heieraas & S. Hovin. (1995). *Forkjørsregulering av Singsakerringen i Trondheim*. Prosjektoppgave ved Institutt for samferdselsteknikk NTH, Trondheim.

Burman, L. & Johansson, C. (2001). *Stockholms miljözon*. Effekter på luftkvaliteten 2000. Stockholm, Miljøførvaltningen, Stockholms Luft- och Bulleranalys. Rapport nummer 4:01

Burns, A., N. Johnstone & N. Macdonald (2001). *20mph speed reduction initiative*. Development department research programme findings no 104. Scottish Executive, Edinburgh.

Burritt, B. E., Moghrabi, A. & Matthias, J. S. (1976). Analysis of the Relation of Accidents and the 88-km/h (55-mph) Speed Limit on Arizona Highways. *Transportation Research Record*, **609,** 34–35.

Bærum Reguleringsvesen. (1980). *Trafikksanering. Eiksmarka-Østerås-Voll. Erfaringsrapport*. Bærum kommune, Sandvika.

California Public Utilities Commission. (1965). *Accident Reduction at Crossings Protected Under Crossing Protection Fund*. California Public Utilities Commission, San Francisco, 1965.

Cameron, M. H & P. W. Milne. (1978). Pedestrian Exposure and Risk in New South Wales. *Proceedings of Joint ARRB/DoT Pedestrian Conference*, 1978. Department of Transport, Sydney, Australia.

Cather, R.T. & Salazar, R. (1996). *Compendium of Technical Papers for the 66$^{TH}$ ITE Annual Meeting*, pp. 282–288, Minneapolis.

Cedersund, H-Å. (1983). *Olyckor i tätortskorsningar*. VTI-meddelande 362. Statens väg- och trafikinstitut (VTI), Linköping.

Charnock, D. B. & B. A. C. Chessell. (1978). Carrigeway edgelining and the effects on road safety. *Traffic Engineering and Control*, **19**, 4–7, 13.

Chatterjee, K., Hounsell, N.B., Firmin, N.B. & Bonsall, P.W. (2002). Driver response to variable message sign information in London. *Transportation Research Part C: Emerging Technologies*, 10(2), 149–169.

Cheng, E. Y.-C., Gonzalez, E. & Christensen, M.O. (2000). *Application and evaluation of rumble strips on highways*. FHWA Safety Documents.

Chick, C. (1994). An integrated approach to traffic calming, road safety and environmental improvements in the London borough of Hounslow. *Proceedings of Seminar J*. Paper presented at PTRC Summer Annual Meeting September 12–16, 1994, Warwick.

Christensen, J. (1981). *The effects of general speed limits on driving speeds and accidents in Denmark*. Lyngby, Danish Council of Road Safety Research, 1981 (paper presented at the International Symposium on «Traffic Effects of Speed Limits on Traffic Accidents and Transportation Energy Use», Oct. 6–8, Dublin, Ireland.

Christensen, P. (1988). *Utbedringer av ulykkespunkter på riksveger og kommunale veger i perioden 1976–1983. Erfaringsrapport*. TØI-rapport 0009. Transportøkonomisk institutt, Oslo.

Christiansen, D. L. et al. (1982). *Priority for high-occupancy vehicles (HOV). Chapter 8 of Synthesis of safety research related to traffic control and roadway elements. Volume 1*. Report FHWA-TS-82–232. US Department of Transportation, Federal Highway Administration, Washington DC.

Chua C. S. & A. J. Fisher. (1991). Performance Measurements of Local Area Traffic Management: A Case Study. *Australian Road Research*, **21**, 2, 16–34.

Cleveland, D. E., M. J. Huber & M. J. Rosenbaum. (1982). On Street Parking. *Chapter 9 of Synthesis of Safety Research Related to Traffic Control and Roadway Elements. Volume 1*. Report FHWA-TS-82–232. US Department of Transportation, Federal Highway Administration, Washington DC.

Coleman, J. & G. R. Stewart. (1976). Investigation of Accident Data for Railroad-Highway Grade Crossings. *Transportation Research Record*, **611**, 60–67.

Collins, R. O. (1965). *Effectiveness of Automatic Crossing Gates in Northern California, 1954 through 1964*. California Public Utilities Commission, 1965 San Francisco. (sitert etter Brodin og Pettersson 1978).

Cooper, B. R., H. E. Sawyer & K. S. Rutley. (1992). *Analysis of accidents before and after implementation of improved motorway signalling*. Research Report 342. Transport and Road Research Laboratory, Crowthorne, Berkshire.

Corben, B. F. Deery, H.A., Newstead, S.V. et al. (1997). Evaluation of the general effectiveness of countermeasures designed for crashes into fixed roadside objects. Paper submitted to *Accident Analysis and Prevention*.

Cottrell, B. H. (1988). Evaluation of Wide Edgelines on Two-Lane Rural Roads. *Transportation Reseach Record*, **1160**, 35–44.

Cottrell, B.H. & Hanson, R.A. (2001). *Determining the effectiveness of pavement marking materials*. Virginia Transport Research Council: Report VTCR 01-R9.

Craven, R. E. (1986). An analysis of traffic signal safety improvements. In: Effectiveness of highway safety improvements, 73–79. (Carney, J. F. III ed.) American Society of Civil Engineers, New York, NY.

Creasey, F. T., G. L. Ullman & C. L. Dudek. (1989). Delineation of Urban Freeway Gore Area Crash Cushions in Texas. *Transportation Research Record*, 1233, 28–33.

Cribbins, P. D. & C. M. Walton. (1970). Traffic Signals and Overhead Flashers at Rural Intersections: Their Effectiveness in Reducing Accidents. *Highway Research Record* **325**, 1–14.

Crook, A. D. J. (1970). Effect on accidents of area wide traffic control in West London. *Traffic Engineering and Control*, 11, 30–31.

Crossette, J. G. & G. L. Allen. (1969). Traffic Control Measures Improve Safety. *Traffic Engineering*, **39**, 18–21.

Cummings, M. (1994). *Electronic signs strategies and their benefits*. Proceedings of the Seventh International Conference on Road Traffic Monitoring and Control, 141–144. London, UK, 26–28 April 1994.

Daas, H. R. (1978). *Kantstolper. Effektundersøkelse av kantstolper på veger av høy standard og mye trafikk*. TØI-notat 408. Transportøkonomisk institutt, Oslo.

Daas, H. R. (1980). Skilter som virkemiddel i trafikksikkerhetsarbeidet. I *Trafikksanering-aktuelle tiltak, 3–18*. (Muskaug, R. ed) NVF-rapport 1980:11. Nordisk vegteknisk forbund, Oslo.

Dagestad, K. (1989). *Erfaringer med signalregulerte kryss. Ulykkessituasjon i Akerhus*. Statens vegvesen Akershus, Trafikkseksjonen, Oslo.

Dahlen og Toftenes (rådg ingeniører). (1979). *Lyssignalanlegg i Bærum. Trafikksikkerhet*. Utarbeidet for Vegkontoret i Akershus. Haslum.

Dahlen og Toftenes (rådg ingeniører). (1984). *Trafikksikkerhet i signalregulerte kryss*. Utarbeidet for Vegdirektoratet. Haslum.

Dalby, E. (1979). *Area-wide measures in urban road safety. A background to current research*. TRRL Supplementary Report 517. Transport and Road Research Laboratory, Crowthorne, Berkshire.

Dalby, E. & H. Ward. (1981). Application of low-cost road accident countermeasures according to an area-wide strategy. *Traffic Engineering and Control*, **22**, 567–574.

Daltrey, R. A. & D. Healy. (1980). Change in Victorian accident frequency with the introduction of the 100 km/h absolute speed limit in 1974. *ARRB Proceedings Volume 10*, **Part 4**, 158–170.

Daltrey, R. A., D. J. Howie & J. Randall. (1978). Effect of metcon (metropolitan traffic control) on intersection accidents. *ARRB Proceedings, Volume 9*, **Part 5**, 169–173, 1978. Australian Road Research Board, Vermont South, Victoria.

Daly, P. N., F. McGrath & A. B. VanEmst. (1991). *Accidents at pedestrian crossing facilities*. Contractor Report 254. Transport and Road Research Laboratory, Crowthorne, Berkshire.

Datta, T. K. & U. Dutta. (1990). Traffic Signal Installation and Accident Experience. *ITE-Journal*, **September**, 39–42.

Davidse, R., van Driel, C. & Goldenbeld, C. (2004). *The effect of altered road markings on speed and lateral position*. Leidschendam: SWOV-report R-2003-31.

Davidsson, F. & Taylor, N. (2003). ITS modelling in Sweden using CONTRAM. *TRL report 2003/04.*

DeWerd, P. A. M. (1982). Study on the effect of eliminating intermittent signal from traffic light programmes in Eindhoven. In: *Proceedings (148–151) of Seminar on Short-term and Area-wide Evaluation of Safety Measures*, Amsterdam, The Netherlands, April 19–21, 1982. Institute for Road Safety Research SWOV, Leidschendam.

DeRose, F. (1966). Reversible Center-Lane Traffic System-Directional and Left-Turn Usage. *Highway Research Record*, **151**, 1–17.

Devenport, J. (1987). *An evaluation of bus lane safety*. Report ATWP 80. London Accident Analysis Unit, London Research Centre, County Hall. London.

Dietrich, K., Lindenmann, H.P., Hehlen, P. & Thoma, J. (1988). *Auswirkungen von Tempo 80/120 auf die Verkehrssicherheit*. Schweizerische Beratungsstelle für Unfallverhütung bfu/Eidgenössische Technische Hochschule (ETH) Zürich, 1988 (Schlussbericht, April 1988), Zürich.

Dijkstra, A. (1990). *Problemsituaties op verkeersaders in de bebouwde kom: Tweede fase: Selectie van problemsituaties*. SWOV Rapport R-90-13. Stichting Wetenschappelijk Onderzoek Verkeersveiligheid SWOV, Leidschendam.

Dimmen, H. P. & T. Giæver. (1990). *Forkjørsregulering Singsakerringen*. Notat 683/90. SINTEF Samferdselsteknikk, Trondheim.

Downing A., I. Sayer & M. Zaheer-Ul-Islam. (1993). Pedestrian Safety in The Developing World. *Proceedings of Conference on Asian Road Safety 1993 (CARS '93)* Chapter 7, 10–25. Published by OECD and others, Kuala Lumpur.

Drakopoulos, A. & Vergou, G. (2003). *Evaluation of the converging chevron marking pattern at one location in Wisconsin*. Washington: AAA Foundation for Traffic Safety.

Drammen Byplankontor. (1980). *Gatebruksplan Åssiden. Etterprøving av gjennomkjøringsforbudet i Betzy Kjelsbergs vei*. Drammen kommune, Drammen.

Duff, J. T. (1971). Accomplishments in freeway operations outside the United States. *Highway Research Record*, **368**, 9–25.

Eck, R. W. & J. A. Halkias. (1985). Further Investigation of the Effectiveness of Warning Devices at Rail-Highway Grade Crossings. *Transportation Research Record*, **1010**, 94–101.

Eck, R.W., Shanmugam, R. (1987). Physical and operational characteristics of rail-highway grade crossings on low-volume roads. *Transportation Research Record*, **1106**, 246–255.

Edminster, R. & Koffman, D. (1979). *Streets for pedestrians and transit: an evaluation of three transit malls in the United States*. Report UMTA-MA-06-0049-79-1. US Department of Transportation, Urban Mass Transportation Administration, Washington DC.

Ekblom, S., T. Kolsrud & C. Möller. (1981). *Olyckor i plankorsningar mellan väg och järnväg*. TFB S 1981:4. Transportforskningsberedningen, Stockholm.

Ekman, L. (1988). *Fotgängeres risker på markerat overgångsställe jämfört med andre korsningspunkter*. Bulletin 76. Tekniska Högskolan i Lund, Institutionen för trafikteknik, Lund.

Elvestad, B., Freiesleben, O., Poutanen, O-P., Thormar, G. & Helmers, G. (1991). *Forkjørsregulering i bytrafikk*. Rapport STF63 A91007. SINTEF Samferdselsteknikk, Trondheim.

Elvik, R. (1996). *Enhetskostnader for veg- og trafikktekniske tiltak*. Arbeidsdokument TST/0722/96. Transportøkonomisk institutt, Oslo.

Elvik, R. (2002). Optimal speed limits: the limits of optimality models. *Transportation Research Record*, **1818**, 32–38.

Elvik, R. & Muskaug, R. (1994). *Konsekvensanalyser og trafikksikkerhet. Metode for beregning av konsekvenser for trafikksikkerheten av tiltak på vegnettet*. Rapport 281. Transportøkonomisk institutt, Oslo.

Elvik, R., T. Vaa & E. Østvik. (1989). *Trafikksikkerhetshåndbok*. Revidert utgave. Transportøkonomisk institutt, Oslo.

Elvik, R., P. Christensen, A. H. Amundsen (2004). *Speed and road accidents. An evaluation of the Power Model*. Report 740/2004. Institute of Transport Economics, Oslo.

Emerson, J. W. & L. B. West. (1986). *Shoulder rumble strips at narrow bridges*. In: Effectiveness of Highway Safety Improvements, 207–217. (Carney, J. F. III ed). American Society of Civil Engineers, New York, NY.

Engel, U. & T. Andersen. (1994). Sikring af børns skoleveje i Odense kommune. *Dansk Vejtidsskrift*, **4**, 11–13.

Engel, U. & Krogsgård Thomsen, L. (1983). *Trafiksanering på Østerbro. Del 1 - Ulykkesanalyse*. RfT-notat 1/1983. Rådet for Trafiksikkerhedsforskning, København.

Engel, U. & Krogsgård Thomsen, L. (1987) Ny hastighetdsgrænse sparer liv. *Dansk Vejtidsskrift*, **6**, 142–145.

Engel, U. & Krogsgård Thomsen, L. (1988). *Hastigheder, hastighedsgrænser og ulykker. Sammenfatning*. RfT-rapport 27. Rådet for Trafiksikkerhedsforskning, København.

Engel, U. & Krogsgård Thomsen, L. (1989). § 40 gaders sikkerhed. *Dansk Vejtidsskrift*, **8**, 188–190,

Engel, U. & Krogsgård Thomsen, L. (1990). *Effekter af Færdselslovens § 40*. RfT-rapport 29. Rådet for Trafiksikkerhedsforskning, København.

Englund, A. (1978). *TRKs haverikommission. Redogörelse för en försöksverksamhet*. Rapport 1. Försäkringsbranchens Trafiksäkerhetskommitté, Stockholm.

Eriksen, T. (1996). *Framkommelighet-kollektivtrafikk.* I: miljøhåndboken, Del I, 155–163. (Kolbenstvedt, M., H. Silborn and T. Solheim ed). Transportøkonomisk institutt, Oslo.

Eriksson, A. & L. Agustsson (1999). *Hastighedsplanlægning i Mørkhøjkvarteret.* Rapport 182. Vejdirektoratet, København.

Erke, A. & Elvik, R. (2006). Effektkatalog for trafikksikkerhetstiltak (Road safety measures: A catalogue of estimated effects). TØI-Report 851/2006. Oslo: Institute of Transport Economics.

Erke, A., Sagberg, F. & Hagman, R. (2007). Effects of route guidance variable message signs (VMS) on driver behaviour. *Transportation Research Part F*, **10**, 447–457.

Erke, H. & Gottlieb, W. (1980). *Psychologische Untersuchung der Wirksamkeit von Wechselverkehrszeichenanlagen. Verfahren für die zentrale Dokumentation der wegweisenden Beschilderung an Autobahnen.* Heft 289. Forschung Strassenbau und Strassenverkehrstechnik. Bundesminister für Verkehr, Abteilung Strassenbau, Bonn-Bad Godesberg.

European Transport Safety Council. (1996). *Low-cost road and traffic engineering measures for casualty reduction.* Report. European Transport Safety Council, Brussels.

Ewing, R. (1999). *Traffic calming. State of the practice.* Report FHWA-RD-99-135. US Department of Transportation, Federal Highway Administration, Washington DC.

Fahlman, T., H. Norberg & P. Bylund. (1980). *Olycksförändring vid trafiksanering.* Examensarbete 1980:1. Tekniska Högskolan i Stockholm, Institutionen för trafikplanering, Stockholm.

Fairlie, R. B. & Taylor, M. A. P. (1990). Evaluating the safety benefits of local area traffic management. *Proceedings 15th ARRB Conference*, Part 7, 141–166. Australian Road Research Board, Vermont South, Australia.

Farmer, C. M., R. A. Retting & A. K. Lund (1999). Changes in motor vehicle occupant fatalities after repeal of the national maximum speed limit. *Accident Analysis and Prevention*, **31**, 537–543.

Faure, A. & A. de Neuville, A. (1992). Safety in urban areas: the French program «Safer city, accident-free districts». *Accident Analysis and Prevention*, **24**, 39–44.

Fisher, A. J., D. F. Van den Dool, & L. K. Ho. (1989). LATM Operational Successful and Financially Affordable: But are the Users Satisfied? *Proceddings of 1989 National Transport Conference* (62–70), Melbourne, 23–25 May 1989, Preprint of Papers. The Institution of Engineers, Melbourne, Australia.

Fitzpatrick, K. & Balke, K. (1995). An evaluation of flush medians and two-way, left-turn lanes on four-lane rural Highways. Paper 950447, *The 74th Annual Meeting of The Transportation Research Board*, January 22–28, Washington DC.

Ford, S.H. & Calvert, E.C. (2003). Evaluation of a low-cost program of road system traffic safety reviews for county highways. *Transportation Research Record*, **1819**, 231–236.

Forschungsgesellschaft für Strassen- und Verkehrswesen. (1989). *Wirkung von Tempo 30-Zonen*. FGSV-Arbeitspapier Nr 22. Forschungsgesellschaft für Strassen- und Verkehrswesen, Köln.

Forskargruppen Scaft. (1972). *Principer för trafiksanering med hensyn till trafiksäkerhet*. Meddelande 55. Chalmers Tekniska Högskola, Institutionen för stadsbyggnad, Göteborg.

Freiholtz, B. (1991). *Sveriges första miljöprioriterade genomfart*. Åstorp. Publikation 1991:28. Vägverket, Borlänge.

Frith, W. J. & N. M. Derby. (1987). Intersection control by stop and give way signs-the conclusions of Polus. *Accident Analysis and Prevention*, **19**, 237–241.

Frith, W. J. & D. S. Harte. (1986). The safety implications of some control changes at urban intersections. *Accident Analysis and Prevention*, **18**, 183–192.

Frith, W. J. & J. B. Toomath. (1982). The New Zealand open road speed limit. *Accident Analysis and Prevention*, **14**, 209–218.

Frøysadal, E. (1988). *Syklistenes transportarbeid og risiko*. TØI-notat 883. Transportøkonomisk institutt, Oslo.

Frøysadal, E., Granquist, T.E., Helle, K.M. et al. (1979). *Virkninger av trafikkløsninger. Korttidsvirkninger av gågateregulering i Odda sentrum*. TØI-rapport. Transportøkonomisk institutt, Oslo.

Gallaher, M. M., M. Sewell, S. Flint, J. L. Herndon, H. Graff, J. Fenner & H. F. Hull (1989). Effects of the 65-mph speed limit on rural interstate fatalities in New Mexico. *Journal of the American Medical Association*, **262**, 2243–2245

Gitelman, V. & A. S. Hakkert. (1997). The evaluation of road-rail crossing safety with limited accident statistics. *Accident Analysis and Prevention*, **29**, 171–179.

Giæver, T. (1987). *Signalregulerte gangfelt. Vurdering av behov for nye anlegg*. Rapport STF63 A87011. SINTEF Samferdselsteknikk, Trondheim.

Giæver, T. & S. Meland. (1990). *Før-/etterundersøkelse av fysiske fartsdempende tiltak*. Rapport STF63 A90004. SINTEF Samferdselsteknikk, Trondheim.

Giæver, T., Sakshaug, K., Jenssen, G. & Berge, T. (1999). *Effekter av profilert vegmerking*. SINTEF rapport STF22 A99553.

Glad, A., J, Rein & S. Fosser. (1990). *Bilføreres fartsvalg. En undersøkelse av faktorer som påvirker førernes beslutninger*. TØI-rapport 50. Transportøkonomisk institutt, Oslo.

Glennon, J. C. (1986). Accident Effects of Centerline Markings on Low-Volume rural Roads. *Transportation Research Record*, **1027**, 7–13.

Golob, T. F., W. W. Recker & D. W. Levine. (1989). Safety of High-Occupancy Vehicle Lanes Without Physical Separation. *Journal of Transportation Engineering*, **115**, 591–607.

Good, M. C. & P. N. Joubert. (1973). *A review of roadside objects in relation to road safety*. Report No NR/12. Departement of Transport, Australia.

Godwin, S. R. (1992). Effect of the 65 mph speed limit on highway safety in the USA (with comments and reply to comments). *Transport Reviews*, **12**, 1–14.

Greiwe, R. R. (1986). Intersection Management Techniques for the Left-Turning Vehicle: The Indianapolis Experience. *ITE-Journal*, **June**, 23–28.

Griffin, L. I. (1990). *Using The Before-and-After Design with yoked Comparisons to Estimate The Effectiveness of Accident Countermeasures Implemented at Multiple Treatment Locations*. Unpublished manuscript. College Station, TX, Texas Transportation Institute, The Texas A&M University System, Texas.

Griffith, M.S. (2000). *Safety evaluation of rolled-in continuous shoulder rumble strips installed on freeways*. FHWA-RD-00-032.

Grimsgaard, P. (1976). *Trafikkulykker - avkjørsler*. Hovedoppgave i samferdselsteknikk. Norges Tekniske Høgskole, Institutt for samferdselsteknikk, Trondheim.

Grimsgaard, P. (1979). *Spredt bosetting og trafikksikkerhet. En undersøkelse av forholdene i et spredtbygd område med en del av Vindafjord kommune som eksempel*. Notat 1/1979. Rogalandsforskning, Stavanger.

Grue, B., J. L. Langeland & O. I. Larsen. (1997). *Boligpriser. Effekter av veitrafikkbelastning og lokalisering*. TØI-rapport 351. Transportøkonomisk institutt, Oslo.

Grønnerød, E. (1976). *Gulblink på signalanlegg. Bruk av gulblink på signalanlegg i perioder med lite trafikk*. Rapport. Transportøkonomisk institutt, Oslo.

Gunnarsson, S. O. & A. Hagson. (1992). *Visby Innerstad. Bakgrund och effekter av bilbegränsning 1988–91*. TFB-rapport 1992:30. Transportforskningsberedningen, Stockholm.

Gunnarsson, S. O. & L. Olsson. (1974a). *Trafikolyckor i tätort 1. Analys av trafikolyckor i korsningar, Göteborg 1971*. Meddelande 66. Chalmers Tekniska Högskola, Institutionen för stadsbyggnad, Göteborg.

Gunnarsson, S. O. & L. Olsson. (1974b). *Trafikolyckor i tätort 2. Analys av trafikolyckor före respektive efter signalreglering av korsningar*. Meddelande 67. Chalmers Tekniska Högskola, Institutionen för stadsbyggnad, Göteborg.

Gårder, P. (2004). The impact of speed and other variables on pedestrian safety in Maine. *Accident Analysis and Prevention*, **36**, 533–542.

Haakenaasen, B. (1981). *Virkninger av trafikkløsninger. Trafikksaneringen i Rosenborg/Møllenberg-området i Trondheim*. TØI-rapport. Transportøkonomisk institutt, Oslo.

Haakenaasen, B. (1982). *Trafikksanering i Sandefjord sentrum. Tiltak og virkninger*. TØI-notat 634. Transportøkonomisk institutt, Oslo.

Haddeland, J. O. & G. Nielsen. (1991). *Stedet og vegen. Et idehefte om miljøprioritert gjennomkjøring med erfaringer fra gjennomførte prosjekter*. Statens vegvesen, Vegdirektoratet, Miljø- og trafikksikkerhetsavdelingen, Oslo.

Hakkert, A. S. & F. Mahalel. (1978). The effect of traffic signals on road accidents - with special reference to the introduction of a blinking green phase. *Traffic Engineering and Control*, **19**, 212–215.

Halkias, J. A. & R. W. Eck. (1985). Effectiveness of Constant Warning-Time Versus Fixed-Distance Warning Systems at Rail-Highway Grade Crossings. *Transportation Research Record*, **1010**, 101–116.

Hall, J. W. (1987). Evaluation of Wide Egdelines. *Transportation Research Record*, **1114**, 21–30.

Hall, P., R. Hearne & J. O'Flynn, J. (1970). *The 60mph General Speed Limit in Ireland.* An Foras Forbartha, The National Institute for Physical Planning and Construction Research, Dublin.

Hallion, J. V. & R. Michael. (1978). A priority roads study. *ARRB Proceedings, Volume 9*, **Part 5**, 109–119, 1978. Australian Road Research Board, Vermont South, Victoria.

Hanbali, R. M. & C. J. Fornal. (1997). *Methodology for evaluating the effectiveness of traffic responsive systems on intersection congestion and traffic safety*. Paper 970065. 76th Annual Meeting, Transportation Research Board, January 12–16, Washington DC.

Hanssen, J. U. (1996). Parkeringsregulering. I: *Miljøhåndboken, Del I*, 145–154. (Kolbenstvedt, M., H. Silborn and T. Solheim ed). Transportøkonomisk institutt, Oslo.

Hanssen, J. U. (1997). *Parkering. Et virkemiddel i samordnet areal- og transportplanlegging*. TØI-rapport 349. Transportøkonomisk institutt, Oslo.

Hanssen, J. U. & M. Stenstadvold. (1993). *Parkeringspolitikk i teori og praksis.* Rapport 172. Transportøkonomisk institutt, Oslo.

Harper, R. S. (1985). Pelican Crossings. Design and Siting for Safety. *PTRC Summer Annual Meeting, Proceedings of Seminar M*, 217–226.

Hart, M. (1982). Effects on accidents, eliminating throughtraffic of cars in city areas. In *Proceedings (127–134) of Seminar on Short-term and Area-wide Evaluation of Safety Measures*, Amsterdam, The Netherlands, April 19–21, 1982. Institute for Road Safety Research SWOV, Leidschendam.

Harwood, D. W. (1993). *Use of Rumble Strips to Enhance Safety.* National Cooperative Highway Research Program, Synthesis of Highway Practice 191. Transportation Research Board, Washington DC.

Harwood, D. W. & A. D. St John. (1985). *Passing lanes and other operational improvements on two-lane highways.* Report FHWA/RD-85/028. US Department of Transportation, Federal Highway Administration, Washington DC.

Hauer, E. (1991). Should Stop Yield? Matters of Method in Safety Research. *ITE-Journal*, **September**, 25–31.

Hauer, E. & B. N. Persaud. (1987). How to Estimate the Safety of Rail-Highway Grade Crossings and the Safety Effects of Warning Devices. *Transportation Research Record*, **1114**, 131–140.

Haynes, J., Copley, G., Farmer, S. & Helliar-Symons, R.D. (1993). Yellow bar markings on motorway slip-roads. Crowthorne, Berkshire: Transport Research Laboratory (TRL), Project Report 49.

Helberg, N., Hemdorff, S., Højgaard, H. et al. (1996). *Effekt af stoptavler. Effektvurdering af forsøgsopstilling i 4-benede kryds i åpent land.* RfT Arbejdsrapport 8/1996. Rådet for Trafiksikkerhedsforskning, Gentofte.

Helliar-Symons, R. D. (1981). *Yellow bar experimental carriageway markings-accident study.* TRRL Laboratory Report 1010. Transport and Road Research Laboratory, Crowthorne, Berkshire.

Helliar-Symons, R. D. & S. D. Ray. (1986). *Automatic close-following warning sign-further trials.* Research Report 63. Transport and Road Research Laboratory, Crowthorne, Berkshire.

Helliar-Symons, R., P. Webster & A. Skinner. (1995). The M1 Chevron Trial. *Traffic Engineering and Control*, **36**, 563–567.

Helliar-Symons, R.D., Wheeler, A.H. & Scott, P.P. (1984). *Automatic Speed Warning Sign Hampshire Trials.* TRL Laboratory Report 1118. Transport Research Laboratory, Crowthorne, UK.

Helmers, G. & L. Åberg. (1978). *Förarbeteende i gatukorsningar i relation till företrädesregler och vägutformning. En explorativ studie.* VTI-rapport 167. Statens väg- och trafikinstitut (VTI), Linköping.

Henriksson, P. (1992). *Uppskattning av fördröjning och avgasutsläpp i fyrvägskorsningar med olika regleringsformer, speciellt fyrvägsstopp.* VTI-meddelande 700. Väg- och TrafikInstitutet (VTI), Linköping.

Herbert, A. J. & N. M. H. Smith. (1976). Analysing Railway Crossing Accident Data. *Australian Road Research*, **6**, 3, 24–32.

Herms, B. F. (1972). Pedestrian Crosswalk Study: Accidents in Painted and Unpainted Crosswalks. *Highway Research Record*, **406**, 1–13.

Herrstedt, L., Kjemtrup, K., Borges, P. & Andersen, P. S. (1993). *An improved Traffic Environment. A Catalogue of Ideas.* Report 106. Road Data Laboratory, Road Standards Division, Herlev.

Hickey, J. J. (1997). Soulder Rumble Strip Effectiveness: Drift-Off-Road Accident Reductions on the Pennsylvania Turnpike. *Paper 970624. 76th Annual Meeting, Transportation Research Board*, January 12–16, Washington DC.

Hocherman, I., A. S. Hakkert & J. Bar-Ziv. (1990). Safety of One Way Urban Streets. *Transportation Research Record*, **1270**, 22–27.

Hodge, G. A., K. F: Daley & T. N. Nguyen. (1986). Signal co-ordination in regional areas of Melbourne - a road safety evaluation. *ARRB Proceedings, Volume 13*, **Part 9**, 178–190, 1986., Australian Road Research Board, Vermont South, Victoria.

Hoff og Overgaard. (1976). *Den sikkerhedsmæssige effekt af signalregulering i landevejskryds*. Vejdirektoratet, Sekretariatet for Sikkerhedsfremmende Vejforanstaltninger (SSV), Næstved.

Hoffman, M. R. (1974) Two-Way, Left-Turn Lanes Work. *Traffic Engineering*, **August**, 24–27.

Hogema, J. H., R. van der Horst & W. van Nifterick. (1996). Evaluation of an automativ fog-warning system. *Traffic Engineering and Control*, **37**, 629–632.

Hovd, A. (1979). En *undersøkelse omkring trafikkulykker og avkjørsler*. Avhandling til dr ing graden. Meddelelse 22. Norges Tekniske Høgskole, Institutt for veg- og jernbanebygging, Trondheim.

Hovd, A. (1981). *Trafikkulykker i avkjørsler. Sammenhenger mellom ulykkesnivå og avkjørselsavstand, avkjørselstetthet, avkjørsels- og riksvegtrafikk*. Rapport STF61 A81011. SINTEF Vegteknikk, Trondheim.

Hoyt, D. W. (1968) In Further Support of Rumble Strips. *Traffic Engineering*, **November**, 38–41.

Huang, H.F. & Cynecki, M.J. (2001). *The effects of traffic calming measures on pedestrian and motorist behavior*. Report FHWA-RD-00-104.

Huang, H.F. & Zegeer, C.V. (2001). *An evaluation of illuminated pedestrian push buttons in Windsor, Ontario*. Report FHWA-RD-00-102.

Hunt, J. G. (1990). Pedestrian safety and delay at crossing facilities in the United Kingdom. *Proceedings of Road safety and Traffic Environment in Europe in Gothenburg, Sweden*, September 26–28, 1990. VTI-rapport 363A, 17–34. Statens väg- och trafikinstitut, Linköping.

Hunt, J. G. & Griffiths, J.D. (1989). *Accident rates at pedestrian crossings in Hertfordshire*. Contractor Report 154. Transport and Road Research Laboratory, Crowthorne, Berkshire.

Hvoslef, H. (1973). *Trafikksikkerheten i forbindelse med buss og trikk i* Oslo. Notat. Oslo Veivesen, Oslo.

Hvoslef, H. (1974). *Trafikksikkerhet i Oslo. Problemstilling, analyse og løsninger*. Oslo veivesen, Oslo.

Hvoslef, H. (1977). *Trafikkulykker og trafikksikkerhet i Borre*. Arbeidsdokument av 31.8.1977, prosjekt 4559, veiplan for Borre. Transportøkonomisk institutt, Oslo.

Hvoslef, H. (1979) *Risikoforhold i bytrafikk-eksempel fra Haugesund*. Foredrag ved NIF-kurs trafikksikkerhet, vegutforming, trafikkregulering og gatebruk, 8.-10. januar 1979, NTH, Trondheim.

Hvoslef, H. (1980). *Sikker kryssing av hovedgater-kransgater. I: Trafikksanering - aktuelle tiltak, 38–61.* (Muskaug, R ed): NVF-rapport 11:1980. Nordisk Vegteknisk Forbund (NVF), Utvalg 52 Trafikksikkerhet, Oslo.

Høj, J. (1990). *Rumlefelter og støj.* Rapport 89. Vejdatalaboratoriet, Herlev.

Illinois Division of Highways. (1970). Rumble Strips Used as a Traffic Control Device: An Engineering Analysis. *Accident Study Report* **102**, 1970. (sitert etter Harwood, 1993).

Inwood, J & G. B. Grayson. (1979). *The Comparative Safety of Pedestrian Crossings.* TRRL Laboratory Report 895. Transport and Road Research Laboratory, Crowthorne, Berkshire.

Jacobs, G. D. (1966). Pedestrian behaviour on a length of road containing guard rails. *Traffic Engineering and Control*, **8**, 556–561, 565.

Jacobs, G. D. & D. G. Wilson. (1967). *A Study of Pedestrian Risk in Crossing Busy Roads in Four Towns.* RRL Report LR 106. Road Research Laboratory, Crowthorne, Berkshire.

Janoff, M. S., P. S. Davit & M. J. Rosenbaum. (1982). Adverse environmental operations. *Chapter 11 of Synthesis of safety research related to traffic control and roadway elements.* Report FHWA-TS-82-232. US Department of Transportation, Federal Highway Administration, Washington DC.

Janssen, S. T. M. C. & P. J. G. Verhoef. (1989). *Demonstratieproject herindeling en herinrichting van stedelijke gebieden (in de gemeenten Rijswijk en Eindhoven): Eindrapport van het ongevallen onderzoek. Een evaluatie van de maatregelen na een periode van vijf jaar.* R-89-27. Stichting Wetenschappelijk Onderzoek Verkeersveiligheid SWOV, Leidschendam.

Jensen, R. (1968). *Veien og omgivelsene. Oppdragsrapport med studier av randbebyggelse langs E-18 gjennom Vestfold.* Norsk institutt for by- og regionforskning (NIBR), Oslo.

Jernigan, J. D. & C. W. Lynn. (1991). Impact of 65-mph Speed Limit on Virginia's Rural Interstate Highways Through 1989. *Transportation Research Record,* **1318**, 14–21.

Johannessen, S. (1984). *Kjøreatferd i uregulerte T-kryss. Høyreregel eller vikepliktregulering?* Rapport STF63 A84009. SINTEF Samferdselsteknikk, Trondheim.

Johannessen, S. (1985). *Forkjørsregulering i Sandefjord. Studier av trafikkavvikling og sikkerhet på to strekninger i 1983 og 1984.* Rapport STF63 A85003. SINTEF Samferdselsteknikk, Trondheim.

Johannessen, S. & J. Heir. (1974). *Trafikksikkerhet i vegkryss. En analyse av ulykkesforholdene i 187 vegkryss i perioden 1968–72.* Oppdragsrapport 4. Norges Tekniske Høgskole, Forskningsgruppen, Institutt for samferdselsteknikk, Trondheim.

Johansson, R. (1982). *Förhållandet mellan upplevd och verklig olycksrisk*. TFD-rapport 1982:9. Transportforskningsdelegationen, Stockholm.

Johansson, Ö. (1986). *Trafikksäkerhetseffekten av kantstolpar på smala vägar*. Publikation 1986:84. Statens Vägverk, Utvecklingssektionen, Borlänge.

Johns, R. C. & J. S. Matthias. (1977). Relationship of the Color of the Highway Centerline Stripe to the Accident Rate in Arizona. *Transportation Research Record*, **643**, 32–36.

Jones, S. M. & S. A. Farmer. (1993). Pedestrian ramps in Central Milton Keynes: A case-study. *Traffic Engineering and Control*, **34**, 122–128.

Jones, T.L. & Tomcheck, P. (2000). Pedestrian accidents in marked and unmarked crosswalks: A quantitative study. *ITE Journal*, **Sep 2000**, 42–46.

Jurisich, I., Segedin, T., Dunn, R. & Smith, M. (2003). *Experience of using flush medians in Auckland city*. 26th Australian Transport Research Forum, Wellington, New Zealand, 1–3 October 2003.

Jørgensen, N.O., Muskaug, R., Nilsson, G. et al. (1985). *Fartsgrenser-i trafikksikkerhetens tjeneste?* NVF-rapport 1985:6. Nordisk Vegteknisk Forbund, Utvalg 52, Trafikksikkerhet, Oslo.

Jørgensen, N. O. & Z. Rabani. (1971). *Fotgængeres sikkerhed i og ved fodgængerovergange*. RfT-rapport 7. Rådet for trafikksikkerhedsforskning (RfT), København.

Jönrup, H. & Å. Svensson. (1971). *Effekten av hastighetsbegränsningar utanför tätbebyggelse*. Meddelande 10. Statens Trafiksäkerhetsråd, Stockholm.

Kahrmann, B. (1988). Area-wide traffic restraint measures: analysis of accidents in Berlin-Charlottenburg. In: *User Behaviour: Theory and Research*, 424–434. (Rothengatter, J. A. & R. DeBruin. eds): Van Gorcum, Road Assen/Maastricht.

Kallberg, V-P. (1993). Reflector Posts - Signs of Danger? *Transportation Research Record*, **1403**, 57–66.

Kawashima, H. (1991). *Present status of Japanese research programmes on vehicle information and intelligent vehicle systems*. Invited paper presented at DRIVE-conference, February 4–6, Brussels.

Kemper, W. J. & S. R. Byington (1977). Safety aspects of the national 55 MPH speed limit. Public Roads, 41, 58–67.

Kermit, M. L. (1968) Rumble Strips Revisited. *Traffic Engineering*, **February**, 26–30.

Kermit, M. L. & T. C. Hein. (1962). Effect of Rumble Strips on Traffic Control and Driver Behavior. *Highway Research Board Proceedings*, **41**, 469–482.

Kildebogaard, J. & C. Wass. (1982). *EMMA-rapport 3. Signalregulering af fotgængerfelter. Sikkerhetsmæssig effekt*. Rapport nr 29. Udarbejdet for Nordisk Ministerråd. Vejdirektoratet, Vejdatalaboratoriet, Næstved.

King, G. F. & R. B. Goldblatt. (1975). Relationship of accident patterns to type of intersection control. *Transportation Research Record*, **540**, 1–12.

King, G. F. & T. M. Mast. (1987). Excess Travel: Causes, Extent, and Consequences. *Transportation Research Record*, **1111**, 126–134.

Kirste, B. R. (1989). *Trafikksikkerhet på veger med reversible felt*. Hovedoppgave i samferdselsteknikk. Norges Tekniske Høgskole, Institutt for samferdselsteknikk, Trondheim.

Kjærgaard, E. & H. Lahrmann. (1981). *Skolepatruljeblink - en undersøkelse af skolepatruljeblinks effekt på bilernes hastighed*. Særtrykk fra Dansk Vejtidsskrift nr 4, 1981. Vejdirektoratet, Næstved.

Knoblauch, R.L., Nitzburg, M. & Seifert, R.L. (2001). *Pedestrian crosswalk case studies: Richmond, Virginia; Buffalo, New York; Stillwater, Minnesota*. Center for Applied Research, for Federal Highway Administration.

Koepsell, T., McCloskey, L., Wolf, M. et al. (2002). Crosswalk markings and the risk of pedestrian motor vehicle collisions in oder pedestrians. *Journal of the American Medical Association*, **288**, 2136–2143.

Kolbenstvedt, M. Solheim, T. & Amundsen, A. H. (2000). *Miljøhåndboken*. Trafikk og miljøtiltak i byer og tettsteder. Oslo, Transportøkonomisk institutt. ISBN 82-480-0147-4.

Kollektivtrafikberedningen. (1982). *Förbättrad busstrafik i befintliga områden*. Delrapport: bussgators trafiksäkerhet mm. Rapport 1982:1. Kollektivtrafikberedningen (KTB), Solna.

Koshi, M. & S. Kashima. (1981). Effects of speed limit alterations on road safety. IATSS 107 Project Team, *IATSS research* **5**, 6–15.

Kølster Pedersen, S., Kulmala, R, Elvestad, B., Ivarsson, D. & Thuresson, L. (1992). *Trafiksäkerhetsåtgärder i Väg- och Gatumiljö. Exempel hämtade från de nordiska länderna under 1980-talet*. Nordiske Seminar- og Arbejdsrapporter 1992:607. Nordisk Ministerråd, København.

Kraay, J. H., M. P. Mathijssen & F. C. M. Wegman. (1984). *Towards safer residential areas*. Institute for Road Safety Research SWOV, Leidschendam.

Krammes, R.A. & Tyer, K.D. (1991). Post-Mounted Delineators and Raised Pavement Markers: Their Effect on Vehicle Operations at Horizontal Curves on Two-Lane Rural Highways. *Transportation Research Record* **1324**, 59–71.

Kulmala, R. (1995). *Safety at rural three- and four-arm junctions. Development and application of accident prediction models*. VTT Publications 233. Technical Research Centre of Finland, Espoo.

Lahrmann, H. & P. Mathiasen. (1992). Bumpudformning. *Dansk Vejtidsskrift*, **9**, 16–22.

Lalani, N. (1977). Road Safety at Pedestrian Refuges. *Traffic Engineering and Control*, **18**, 429–431.

Lalani, N. (1991). Comprehensive Safety Program Produces Dramatic Results. *ITE-Journal*, October, 31–34.

LaPlante, J. N. (1967). Exclusive Bus Lanes. In: *Highway Research Board, Special Report 93*, Improved Street Utilization through Traffic Engineering, 75–83. Highway Research Board, Washington DC.

LaPlante, J. N. & T. Harrington. (1984). Contraflow Bus Lanes in Chicago: Safety and Traffic Impacts. *Transportation Research Record*, **957**, 80–90

Lie, T. & O. Bettum. (1996). *Miljøgate. Sammendragsrapport fra miljøgateprosjektet.* Statens vegvesen, Vegdirektoratet, Oslo.

Ligon, C.M., Carter, E.C., Joost, D.B. & Wolman, W.W. (1985). *Effects of shoulder textured treatments on safety.* Report FHWA/RD-85/027. Federal Highway Administration, Turner-Fairbank Highway Research Center, Georgetown Pike, VA.

Lillienberg, S. (1971). *Studier av gånggators genomförande. 3. Prästgatan i Östersund. Huvudrapport.* Meddelande 35. Chalmers Tekniska Högskola, Institutionen för stadsbyggnad, Göteborg.

Lillienberg, S., L. Birgersson & L. Husberg. (1971). *Studier av gånggators genomförande. 2. Stora Brogatan i Borås.* Meddelande 32. Chalmers Tekniska Högskola, Institutionen för stadsbyggnad, Göteborg.

Lindenmann, H. P., H. Riedel & J. Thoma. (1987). Fussgänger-Lichtsignalanlagen. Schweitzerische Beratungsstelle für Unfallverhütung, BFU, Bern.

Lindkvist, A. (1995). *A basis for evaluation –capacity, time consumption, and delay.* Deliverable 23 of the TOSCA II project. Swedish National Roads Administration, Gothenburg, Sweden.

Lovell, J. & E. Hauer. (1986). The Safety Effect of Conversion To All-Way Stop Control. *Transportation Research Record*, **1068**, 103–107.

Lum, H. S. & W. E. Hughes. (1990). Edgeline Widths and Traffic Accidents. *Public Roads*, **54,** 1, 153–159.

Lyles, R.W. & Taylor, W.C. (2006). NCHRP Report 559: Communicating changes in horizontal alignment. Transportation Research Board, National Research Council, Washington, DC.

Mackie, A. M., A. R. Hodge & D. C. Webster. (1993). Traffic Calming - Design and Effectiveness of 20 mph Zones. *Proceedings of Seminar C (395–405) of PTRC 21st Summer Annual Meeting*, 13–17 September 1993, University of Manchester Institute of Science and Technology, England.

Mackie, A. M & S. J. Older. (1965). Study of pedestrian risk in crossing busy roads in London inner suburbs. *Traffic Engineering and Control*, **7**, 376–380.

Mackie, A. M & D. Webster (1995). Monitoring of 20mph Zones. *Proceedings of Seminar G (39–50) of the 23rd European Transport Forum (PTRC Summer Annual Meeting)*, 11–15 September 1995, University of Warwick, England.

Madelin, K. B & J. A. Ford. (1968). Gateshead Traffic Management Scheme (2) Implementation, (3) Before and After Studies and Results. *Traffic Engineering and Control*, **10**, 137–139, 181–184.

Mahalel, D & D. M. Zaidel. (1985). Safety evaluation of a flashing-green light in a traffic signal. *Traffic Engineering and Control*, **26**, 79–81.

Maher, M.J., Hughes, P.C., Smith, M.J. & Ghali, M.O. (1993). Accident- and travel time-minimising routeing patterns in congested networks. *Traffic Engineering and Control*, **34**, 414–419.

Mailand, B., E. Obst & H. Strack. (1987). Tempo 30-Versuche in Bonn. *Strassenverkehrstechnik*, **Heft 2**, 44–48.

Main, R. F. (1984). *For Underutilized Collision Reduction Measures*. In: Transport Risk Assessment, 89–120 (Yagar, S. ed). University of Waterloo Press.

Malenfant, L. & R. Van Houten. (1989). Increasing the percentage of drivers yielding to pedestrians in three Canadian cities with a multifaceted safety program. *Health Education Research*, **5**, 275–279.

Malo, A. F. (1967). Signal Modernization. In: *Highway Research Board, Special Report 93*, Improved Street Utilization Through Traffic Engineering, 96–113. Highway Research Board, Washington DC.

Markovets, S., Royer, D. & Dorroh, R. F. (1995). Leetsdale Drive Reversible lane design Study; Denver Colorado. *Compendium of Technical Papers for the 65TH ITE Annual Meeting*, pp. 142–146, Denver.

Markung, B. (1997). Miljözoner i Sverige. Notater til seminar om miljøsoner i Oslo 4/12-1997. Arrangert av Oslo kommunes samferdselsetat, Statens vegvesen Oslo og Statens vegvesen Vegdirektoratet.

Marvin, R.R. & Clark, D.J. (2003). *An evaluation of shoulder rumble strips in Montana*. Report FHWA/MT-03-008/8157.

Mason, D.F. (1999). *An examination of the use and effectiveness of intersection rumble strips in New Brunswick*. New Brunswick: 1999 Annual Conference and Exhibition of the Transportation Association of Canada.

Matsumara, T., Seo, T., Umezawa, M. & Okutani, T. (1993). *Road structure and traffic safety facilities in Japan*. In Proceedings of Conference on Asian Road Safety 1993 (CARS '93), Chapter 8, 13–32. Kuala Lumpur, published by OECD and others.

McBean, P. A. (1982). *The influence of road geometry at a sample of accident sites*. TRRL Laboratory Report 1053. Transport and Road Research Laboratory, Crowthorne, Berkshire.

McCoy, P. T., Ramanujam, M., Moussavi, M. & Ballard, J. L. (1990). Safety Comparison of Types of Parking on Urban Streets in Nebraska. *Transportation Research Record*, **1270**, 28–41.

McCoy, T.A., McCoy, P. T., Haden, R. J. & Singh, V.A. (1991). Safety Evaluation of Converting On-Street Parking from Parallel to Angle. *Transportation Research Record*, **1327**, 36–41.

McFadden, J. & Chandhok, P. (2003). *Evaluating the effectiveness of low cost safety improvements: Effects of shoulder rumble strips on ROR crashes on multi-lane highways*. Institute of Transportation Engineers 2003 Annual Meeting and Exhibit, Seattle, Washington.

McGee, H. W. (1977). Accident Experience With Right Turn on Red. *Transportation Research Record*, **644**, 66–75.

McGee, H. W. & M. R. Blankenship. (1989). *Guidelines for converting stop to yield control at intersections*. National Cooperative Highway Research Program Report 320. Transportation Research Board, Washington DC.

McGee, H. W. & D. L. Warren. (1976). Right Turn on Red. *Public Roads*, **40**, 1, 19–31.

McKenna, M. N. & King, T. A. (1987). Review of Tidal Flow Systems, Traffic Engineering and Control, no. 10, vol. 28, pp. 544–547.

McKenna, R. Q. (2001). *High technology, smart solutions*. High technology international, 119–20.

Millegan, H., X. Yan, S. Richards & L. Han (2009). Evaluation of effectiveness of stop-sign treatment at highway-railroad grade crossings. TRB 2009 Annual Meeting CD Rom. Transportation Research Board, Washington D. C.

Mitman, M.F., Ragland, D.R. & Zegeer, C.V. (2008). *The marked crosswalk dilemma: uncovering some missing links in a 35-year debate*. TRB 2008 Annual Meeting CD-ROM.

Moore, A. F. (1987). *Evaluation of experimental rumble strips*. Report HWA/LA-86/186. Louisiana Department of Transportation and Development, Baton Rouge, LA.

Mullowney, W. L. (1982). Effect of Raised Pavement Markers on Traffic Performance. *Transportation Research Record*, **881**, 20–29.

Musick, J. V. (1960). Effect of Pavement Edge Marking on Two-Lane Rural State Highways in Ohio. *Highway Research Board Bulletin*, **266**, 1–7.

Muskaug, R. (1976a). *Gatebruksplanen i Oslo. Erfaringer fra Ruseløkka/Skillebekk (forsøk 1)*. Oslo kommune, Byplankontoret, Gatebruksplangruppa, Oslo.

Muskaug, R. (1976b). *Gatebruksplanen i Oslo. Erfaringer fra Grünerløkka*. Oslo kommune, Byplankontoret, Gatebruksplangruppa, Oslo.

Muskaug, R. (1983a). *Virkninger av gatetun i Oslo og Sandefjord*. TØI-rapport. Transportøkonomisk institutt, Oslo.

Muskaug, R. (1983b). *Gatetun på Sofienberg. Analyse av før- og etterundersøkelsene i gatetunene på Sofienberg i Oslo*. Arbeidsdokument av 12.7.1983, prosjekt O-693. Transportøkonomisk institutt, Oslo.

Muskaug, R. (1985). *Risiko på norske riksveger. En analyse av risikoen for trafikkulykker med personskade på riks- og europaveger utenfor Oslo, avhengig av vegbredde, fartsgrense, trafikkmengde og avkjørselstetthet.* TØI-rapport. Transportøkonomisk institutt, Oslo.

Muskaug, R., Daas, H. R., Domburg, J. et al. (1979). *Hvordan endringene i trafikkreglene 1978 virket på trafikantenes kunnskap og atferd.* Prosjektrapport. Transportøkonomisk institutt, Oslo.

Nielsen, M. Aa. & L. Herrstedt. (1993). *Effekt af miljøprioriteret gennemfart. Trafiksikkerhed. Vinderup, Skærbæk, Ugerløse.* Vejdatalaboratoriet, Notat 2, Herlev.

Nilsson, G. (1976). *Sammanställning av försök med differentierade hastighetsgränser åren 1968–1972.* VTI-rapprt 88. Statens väg- och trafikinstitut (VTI), Linköping.

Nilsson, G. (1980). *Sänkning av högsta tillåten hastighet från 110 till 90 km/h under sommaren 1979. Effekt på personskadeolyckor.* VTI-meddelande 197. Statens väg- och trafikinstitut, Linköping.

Nilsson, G. (1990). *Sänkning av hastighetsgränsen 110 km/h til 90 km/h sommaren 1989. Effekter på personskadeolyckor, trafikskadade och hastigheter.* VTI rapport nr 358. Väg- och Trafikinstitutet, Linköping.

Nilsson, G. & P-O. Roosmark. (1976). *Förslag till målsättning och kriterier för val av hastighetsbegränsningssystem.* VTI-rapport 76. Statens väg- och trafikinstitut, Linköping.

Nitzburg, M. & Knoblauch, R.L. (2001). *An evaluation of high-visibility crosswalk treatment – Clearrwater, Florida.* FHWA-RD-00-105.

Norwegian Pollution Control Authority & Directorate for Nature Management (1996). Miljøtilstanden i Norge (The state of the environment in Norway). Oslo-Trondheim. ISBN 82-7655- 355-9.

Noyce, D. A. & Elango, V. V. (2004). *Safety evaluation of centerline rumble strips: A crash and driver behavior analysis.* Transportation Research Board: Paper Nr. 04-3932.

Nygaard, H. C. (1989). *Trafikksikkerhet på veger med kollektive felt.* Hovedoppgave i samferdselsteknikk 1989. Norges Tekniske Høgskole, Institutt for samferdselsteknikk, Trondheim.

OECD Road Research Group. (1977). *Bus lanes and busway systems.* OECD, Paris.

OECD Road Research Group. (1979). *Traffic Safety in Residential Areas.* OECD, Paris.

Oslo Byplankontor. (1978). *Trafikksaneringen i Skøyen/Oppsal området. En vurdering av trafikksituasjonen før/etter trafikkomleggingen og de endringer som har skjedd.* Rapport 2/1978. Oslo kommune, Byplankontoret, Oslo.

Outcalt, W. (2001). *Centerline rumble strips.* Colorado Department of Transportation Research Branch: Report CDOT-DTD-R-2001-8.

Owens, R. D. (1967). Effect of Rumble Strips at Rural Stop Locations on Traffic Operation. *Highway Research Record*, **170**, 35–55.

Park, Y-J., F. F. Saccomanno (2005). Evaluating factors affecting safety at highway-railway grade crossings. TRB 2005 Annual Meeting CD Rom. Transportation Research Board, Washington D. C.

Parker, M. R. (1997). Effects of raising and lowering speed limits on selected roadway sections. FHWA.-RD-92-084. US Department of Transportation, Federal Highway Administration, Washington DC.

Parsonson, P. S., I. R. Nehmad & M. J. Rosenbaum. (1982). One Way Streets and Reversible Lanes. *Chapter 7 of Synthesis of Safety Research Related to Traffic Control and Roadway Elements.* Volume 1. Report FHWA-TS-82-232. US Department of Transportation, Federal Highway Administration, Washington DC.

Pegrum, B. V., E. R. Lloyd & P. Willett. (1972). Experience with priority roads in the Perth metropolitan area. *ARRB Proceedings*, Volume 6, Part 2, 363–383, 1972. Australian Road Research Board, Vermont South, Victoria.

Peltola, H. (2000). Seasonally changing speed limits. Effects on speeds and accidents. Transportation Research Record, 1734, 46–51.

Perfater, M. A. (1983). Motorists' Reaction to Exclusive/Permissive Left-Turn Signal Phasing. *Transportation Research Record*, **926**, 7–12.

Perrillo, K. (1998). The effectiveness and use of continuous shoulder rumble strips. FHWA Safety Documents. http://safety.fhwa.dot.gov/roadway_dept/docs/continuousrumble.pdf

Persaud, B., Hauer, E., Retting, R. et al. (1997). Crash reductions related to traffic signal removal in Philadelphia. *Accident Analysis and Prevention*, **29**, 803–810.

Persaud, B. N., K. Mucsi & A. Ugge, A. (1995) *Development and Application of Microscopic Accident Potential Models to Evaluate the Safety Impact of Freeway Traffic Management Systems.* Paper presented at conference Strategic Highway Research Program and Traffic Safety, September 20–22, 1995. Preprint for sessions 21/9, Prague, The Czech Republic.

Persaud, B., Bahar, G., Mollett, C.J. & Lyon, C. (2004). Safety evaluation of permanent raised snow-plowable pavement markers. *Transportation Research Record*, 1897, 148–155.

Persaud, B., Retting, R.A. & Lyon, C. (2004). Crash reduction following installation of centerline rumble strips on rural two-lane roads. *Accident Analysis and Prevention*, 36, 1073–1079.

Pfefer, R.C., Sorton, A., Fegan, J. C. & Rosenbaum, M. J. (1982). *Bicycle Ways. Chapter 15 of Synthesis of Safety Research Related to Traffic Control and Roadway Elements.* Report FHWA-TS-82-233. Washington DC, US Department of

Transportation, Federal Highway Administration, Offices of Research, Development and Technology.

Planovergangsutvalget. (1970). *Innstilling fra utvalg til vurdering av sikkerhetsforholdene ved planoverganger*. Samferdselsdepartementet, Oslo.

Polus, A. (1985). Driver behaviour and accident records at unsignalized urban intersections. *Accident Analysis and Prevention*, **17**, 25–32.

Polus, A. & Katz, A. (1978). An analysis of nighttime pedestrian accidents at specially illuminated crosswalks. *Accident Analysis and Prevention*, **10**, 223–228.

Preusser, D. F., Leaf, W.A., DeBartolo, K.B. et al. (1982). The Effect of Right-Turn-on-Red on Pedestrian and Bicyclist Accidents. *Journal of Safety Research*, **13**, 45–55.

Public Roads Administration, Norwegian Pollution Control Authority and Directorate for Nature Management. (1992). *Sikrere - roligere - renere. Oversettelse av et tysk informasjonshefte om hvordan miljøprioritert gjennomkjøring bør planlegges for mindre støy og luftforurensing i boligveger og hovedgater*. Vegdirektoratet, Statens forurensningstilsyn og Miljøverndepartementet, Oslo.

Ragnøy, A. (1994). Modell *for beregning av kjøretøyers drivstoff-forbruk*. Arbeidsdokument TST/0591/94. Transportøkonomisk institutt, Oslo.

Ragnøy, A. (2004). Endring av fartsgrenser. Effekt på kjørefart og ulykker. Rapport 729. Transportøkonomisk institutt, Oslo.

Ragnøy, A. & M. Eikanger. (1983). *Reversible kjørefelt. En litteraturstudie*. TØI-notat 652. Transportøkonomisk institutt, Oslo.

Ragnøy, A., T. Vaa & R. H. Nilsen. (1990). *Skilting i Norge. Resultater fra registrering og evaluering av 8 vegstrekninger i Østlandsområdet*. TØI-notat 945. Transportøkonomisk institutt, Oslo.

Ramsy, E. & Luk, J. (1997). *Route choice under two Australian travel information systems*. ARRB Research Report ARR 312.

Rasmussen, H. (1990). *Barrierevirkninger av vegtrafikk. Litteraturgjennomgang og resultater fra en undersøkelse i Vålerenga/Gamlebyen i Oslo*. TØI-notat 933. Transportøkonomisk institutt, Oslo.

Rauhala, V. (1980). *Vegstengninger - tungtransportforbud*. In: Trafikksanering - aktuelle tiltak, 62–73. NVF-rapport 11:1980 (Muskaug, R ed). Nordisk Vegteknisk Forbund (NVF), Utvalg 52 Trafikksikkerhet, Oslo.

Rayner, D. S. (1975). Some safety considerations in the conversion of Zebra crossings to Pelican crossings. *Traffic Engineering and Control*, **16**, 123–124.

Richards, A. (2000). *VMS in Southampton: A case study*. Proceedings of the 7th World Congress on Intelligent Transport Systems, Italy: Turin, 6–9 Nov.

Richter, E. D., P. Barach, L. Friedman, S. Krikler & A. Israeli (2004). Raised speed limits, speed spillover, case-fatality rates, and road deaths in Israel: a 5-year follow-up. American *Journal of Public Health*, **94**, 568–574.

Ricker, E.R., Banks, J.F., Brenner, R. et al. (1977). *Evaluation of Highway Safety Program Standards Within the Purview of the Federal Highway Administration - Final report*. Report DOT-FH-11-9129. US Department of Transportation, Federal Highway Administration, Washington DC.

Riemersma, J. B. J. & R. M. M. Sijmonsma. (1979). *Effecten van het instellen van eenrichtingverkeer op de verkeersveiligheid in woonwijken*. Rapport no IZF 1978-C19u. Studiecentrum Verkeerstechniek, Haag.

Rijkswaterstaat dienst verkeerskunde. (1989). *Evaluatie snelheidslimieten. 1 jaar na invoering van nieuw limietenstelsel op autosnelwegen*. ministerie van verkeer en waterstaat, Rotterdam.

Rock, S. M. (1995). Impact of the 65 mph speed limit on accidents, deaths, and injuries in Illinois. *Accident Analysis and Prevention*, **27**, 207–214.

Rosbach, O. (1984). Kantlinjer forbedrer både bilisters og cyklisters sikkerhed. Særtryk fra *Dansk Vejtidsskrift*, **10**.

Rosenbaum, M. J. (1983). A Review of Research Related to the Safety of STOP Versus YIELD Sign Traffic Control. *Public Roads*, **47**, 3, 77–83.

Roszbach, B. (1990). *Safety on motorways*. Third European Workshop on Recent Developments in Road Safety Research April 26–27, 1990. VTI rapport nr 366A. Väg- och Trafikinstitutet, Linköping.

Roth, W. J. (1970). Interchange Ramp Color Delineation and Marking Study. *Highway Research Record*, **325**, 36–50.

Rothengatter, T., Carbonell-Vaya, E., de Ward, D., & Brookhuis, K.A. (1997). On the measurement of driver mental workload. In J.A. Rothengatter & E. Carbonell Vaya (Eds.), *Traffic and Transport Psychology. Theory and application* (161–171). Oxford: Pergamon.

Rumar, K. (1985). *The role of perceptual and cognitive filters in observed behaviour*. In: Human behavior and traffic safety. (Evans, L. and R. C. Schwing eds.) Plenum Press, New York, NY.

Russel, E.R. & Rys, M.J. (2005). *Centerline rumble strips – A synthesis of highway practice*. Washington: NCHRP Synthesis 339.

Rutherford, G. S., R. L. McLaughlin & E. VonBorstel. (1985). Traffic Circles for Residential Intersection Control: A Comparison with Yield Signs Based on Seattle's Experience. *Transportation Research Record* 1010, 65–68.

Rämä, P. & Schirokoff, A. (2003). *Effects of weather controlled variable speed limits on injury accidents*. Paper presented at the ITS in Europe, 24–26 May2004, Budapest.

Saccomanno, F. F., X. Lai (2005). Model for evaluating countermeasures at highway-railway grade crossings. *TRB 2005 Annual Meeting CD Rom*. Transportation Research Board, Washington D. C.

Saccomanno, F. F., P. Y-J. Park & L. Fu (2007). Estimating countermeasure effects for reducing collisions at highway-railway grade crossings. *Accident Analysis and Prevention*, **39**, 406–416.

Sagberg, F. & I-A. Sætermo. (1997). *Trafikksikkerhet for sporvogn i Oslo*. TØI-rapport 367. Transportøkonomisk institutt, Oslo.

Sakshaug, K. (1986). *Fartsgrenseundersøkelsen 1985. Detaljerte resultater fra fartsdelen og ulykkesdelen*. Notat 535/86 og 536/86. SINTEF Samferdselsteknikk, Trondheim.

Salusjärvi, M. (1981). *The speed limit experiments on Public Roads in Finland*. Publications 7/1981. The Technical Research Centre of Finland, Espoo.

Salusjärvi, M. (1982) *Hvordan fartsgrenseendringene har innvirket på fart og ulykker*. SINTEF avd.63 Samferdselsteknikk, 1982 (Oppdragsrapport 74 november 1982) Trondheim.

Samferdselsdepartementet. (1978). *Stortingsmelding 72, 1977–78. Om fart og fartsgrenser*. Samferdselsdepartementet, Oslo.

Sammer, G. (1994). *General 30 kph speed limit in the city. The results of a model project in the city of Graz*. Proceedings of the third international conference on safety and the environment in the 21st century, November 7–10, Tel-Aviv, Israel.

Sawhill, R. B. & D. R. Neuzil. (1963). Accidents and Operational Characteristics on Arterial Streets with Two-Way Median Left-Turn Lanes. *Highway Research Record*, **31**, 20–56.

Schioldborg, P. (1979). *Fotgjenger og bilfører - to forskjellige verdener*? Universitetet i Oslo, Psykologisk institutt, Oslo.

Schlabbach, K., Scharffetter, J., Lauer, P. & Guttenberger, W. (1984). Vorher-/Nachheruntersuchung verkehrsabhängig betriebener Knotenpunkte in Darmstadt. *Strassenverkehrstechnik*, **Heft 2**, 49–56.

Schmutz, J-P. (1977). Der Einfluss von Lichtsignalanlagen bei einzelnstehenden Fussgängerstreifen auf das Unfallgeschehen. *Zeitschrift für Verkehrssicherheit* **23** (2), 72.

Schnüll, R., W. Haller & H. Von Lübke. (1992). *Sicherheitsanliegen bei der umgestaltung von knotenpunkten in Städten*. Forschungsbericht 253. Bundesanstalt für Strassenwesen (BASt), Bergisch Gladbach.

Schnüll, R. & J. Lange. (1992). Speed reduction on through roads in Nordrhein-Westfalen. *Accident Analysis and Prevention*, **24**, 67–74.

Schoppert, D. W. & D. W. Hoyt. (1968). *Factors influencing safety at highway-rail grade crossings*. National Cooperative Highway Research Program Report 50. Highway Research Board, Washington DC.

Schumann, J. (2003). Post-mounted delineators and perception cues for long-ranged guidance during night driving. *Accident Reconstruction Journal*, 14, 44.48.

Schulte, W. R. (1976). Effectiveness of Automatic Warning Devices in Reducing Accidents at-grade Crossings. *Transportation Research Record*, **611**, 49–57.

Schultz, T. G., W. D. Berg & J. C. Oppenlander. (1969). Evaluation of Rail-Highway Grade Crossing Protection in Rural Areas. *Highway Research Record*, **325**, 14–23,

Scott, P. P. & A. J. Barton. (1976). *The effects on road accident rates of the fuel shortage of November 1973 and consequent legislation*. TRRL Supplementary Report 236. Transport and Road Research Laboratory, Crowthorne, Berkshire.

Seim, R. (1994). *Analyse av kryssulykker i Akershus fylke 1990–93*. Hovedoppgave i samferdselsteknikk, høsten 1994. Norges Tekniske Høgskole, Institutt for samferdselsteknikk, Trondheim.

Senneset, G. & E. Skjetne. (1982). *Samkjørte signalanlegg*. Oppdragsrapport 66. Norges Tekniske Høgskole, Forskningsgruppen, Institutt for samferdselsteknikk, Trondheim.

Shebeeb, O. (1995) Safety and Efficiency for Exclusive Left-Turn Lanes at Signalized Intersections. *ITE-Journal*, **July**, 52–59.

Short, M. S., G. A. Woelfl and C-J. Chang. (1982). Effects of traffic signal installation on accidents. *Accident Analysis and Prevention*, **14**, 135–145.

Sidhu, C. S. (1990). Preliminary Assessment of the Increased Speed Limit on Rural Interstate Highways in Illinois. *Transportation Research Record*, 1281, 78–83.

Skedsmo, A. & Hagman, R. (2006). *Miljøavgifter i lavutslippssone (Emission charges in a low emission zones)*. TØI report 848/2006. Oslo: Transportøkonomisk institutt.

Skölving, H. (1979). *Busshållplatser på landsbygd och vid högklassiga trafikleder. Motiv till utforming och placering*. Kunskapsläge 1979–04. Meddelande TU 1979:3. Statens Vägverk, Utvecklingssektionen, Borlänge.

Sliogeris, J. (1992). *110 Kilometre Per Hour Speed Limit-Evaluation of Road Safety Effects*. Report No: GR 92 – 8. VIC ROADS, Road and Environment Safety, Raod Safety Divison, Carlton/Australia.

Smith, R. N. (1990). *Accidents before and after the 65 MPH speed limit in California*. California Department of Transportation Business, Transportation and Housing Agency/Division of Traffic Operations, Sacramento.

Solberg, P. (1986a). *Miljøprioritert veg i Rosendal*. TØI-rapport. Transportøkonomisk institutt, Oslo.

Solberg, P. (1986b). *Parkeringsforhold i norske kommuner-en oversikt-forprosjekt om parkering*. TØI-notat nr 795. Transportøkonomisk institutt, Oslo.

Spolander, K. (1983). *Bilförares olyckrisker - en modell testad på män och kvinnor*. VTI-rapport 260. Statens väg- och trafikinstitut, Linköping.

Stamatiadis, N. & K. R. Agent. (1997). Guidelines for left-turn phasing at signalized intersections. *Paper presented at the Conference Traffic Safety on Two Continents*, Lisbon, Portugal, September 22–24, Lisbon, Portugal.

Statens vegvesen. (1985). *Veiledning. Fartsdempende tiltak i boligområder*. Håndbok 072. Statens vegvesen, Oslo.

Statens vegvesen. (1993). Håndbok-017. *Normaler. Veg- og gateutforming*. Statens vegvesen, Oslo.

Statens vegvesen (2003). Fra riksveg til gate. Evaluering av 16 miljøgateprosjekter. Oslo, Statens vegvesen Vegdirektoratet, 2003. MISA 02/2003.

Statens vegvesen (2005). Handbook 115. *Analyse av ulykkessteder*. Statens vegvesen, Oslo.

Statens Vägverk. (1981). *Olycksreducerande åtgärder i tätort. En føre/efter studie*. PP-meddelande 19. Statens vägverk, Sektionen för planeringsunderlag, Borlänge.

Stewart, D. (1988). Pedestrian guardrails and accidents. *Traffic Engineering and Control*, **29**, 450–455.

Stigre, S. A. (1991). *Forkjørsregulering av overordnet vegnett i Hamar. Effektundersøkelse*. Utarbeidet for Statens vegvesen Hedmark. Rykkinn.

Stigre, S. A. (1993). *Forkjørsregulering av overordnet vegnett i Bærum. Effektundersøkelse*. Utarbeidet for statens vegvesen Akershus. Rykkinn.

Stimpson, W. A., H. W. McGee & W. K. Kittelson. (1977). *Field Evaluation of Selected Delineation Treatments on Two-Lane Rural Highways. Final Report*. US Department of Transportation, Federal Highway Administration, Offices of Research and Development, Washington DC.

Stoneman, B. (1992). *The effects of dynamic route guidance in London. Research* Report 348. Transport Research Laboratory, Crowthorne, Berkshire.

Stølan, A. (1988). *Erfaringer med trafikksaneringer og sammenhengende gang- og sykkelveger*. Oslo, Asplan Samferdsel, 1988. Utgitt av Samferdselsdepartementet, Miljøverndepartementet, Kommunal- og arbeidsdepartementet og Vegdirektoratet. Oslo, Asplan Samferdsel, Oslo.

Sullivan, E. C. & N. Devadoss. (1993). High-Occupancy Vehicle Facility Safety in California. *Transportation Research Record*, **1394**, 49–58.

Summala, H., Karola, J., Radun, I. & Couyoumdjian, A. (2003). *Kohtaamisonnettomuudet päätieverkolla – kehitys ja syyt (Møteulykker på hovedveger)*. Helsinki: Tiehallinnon Selvityksiä 43/2003.

Summersgill, I. & R. E. Layfield. (1996). *Non-junction accidents on urban single-carriageway roads*. TRL Report 183. Transport Research Laboratory, Crowthorne, Berkshire.

Sumner, R. & C. Baguley. (1979a). *Speed control humps in Kensington and Glasgow*. TRRL Supplementary Report 456. Transport and Road Research Laboratory, Crowthorne, Berkshire.

Sumner, R. & C. Baguley. (1979b). *Speed control humps on residential roads*. TRRL Laboratory Report 878. Transport and Road Research Laboratory, Crowthorne, Berkshire.

Sumner, R. & J. Shippey. (1977). *The use of rumble areas to alert drivers*. TRRL Laboratory Report 800. Transport and Road Research Laboratory, Crowthorne, Berkshire.

Tamburri, T. N., Hammer, C, J., Glennon, J. C. & Lew, A. (1968). Elevation of Minor Improvements. *Highway Research Record*, **257**, 34–139.

Tanaboriboon, Y. & S. Toonim. (1983). Impact Study of Bus Lanes in Bangkok. *Journal of Transportation Engineering*, **109**, 247–256.

Taylor, W. C. & T. J. Foody. (1966) Ohio's Curve Delineation Program - An Analysis. *Traffic Engineering*, **June**, 41–45.

Thakkar, J. S. (1984). Study of the Effect of Two-Way Left-Turn Lanes on Traffic Accidents. *Transportation Research Record*, **960**, 27–33.

The California Department of Transportation (1989). Reversible Lanes on Freeways. The Senate Transportation Committee, California.

Thomas, I. L. (1958). Pavement Edge Lines on Twenty-Four Foot Surfaces in Louisiana. *Highway Research Board Bulletin*, **178**, 12–20.

Thomas, R. B. (1965). *Results Accomplished by the Use of the Grade Crossing Protection Fund Established by the Illinois Legislature Beginning September 1, 1955, and Administered by the Illinois Commerce Commission*. Chicago, Illinois Commerce Commission, 1965 (sitert etter Schoppert og Hoyt 1968). Chicago.

Trafiksäkerhetsverket. (1988). *Två- och fyrvägsstopp. Del 2. Fortsatta försök i Malmö*. Trafiksäkerhetsverket, Trafikbyrån, PM 1988:2. Borlänge.

Trivector, A.B. (1997). Utvärdering av miljözon i Stockholm, Göteborg och Malmö. På uppdrag av Stockholms stad, Gatu- och Fastighetskontoret, Trafikkontoret Göteborgs stad och Gatukontoret Malmö.

Ullman, G. L. & C. L. Dudek (1987). Effects of reduced speed limits in rapidly developing urban fringe areas. *Transportation Research Record*, **1114**, 45–53.

Upchurch, J. E. (1975). Reversible Flow on a Six Lane Urban Arterial. *Traffic Engineering* (now ITE-Journal), December, 11–14.

Upchurch, J. (1989). Arizona's Experience with the 65-mph Speed Limit. *Transportation Research Record*, **1244**, 1–6.

US Department of Transportation, National Highway Traffic Safety Administration. (1989). *The Effect of the 65 mph Speed Limit during 1987. A Report to Congress*. US Department of Transportation, National Highway Traffic Safety Administration, Washington DC.

Van Belle, G., D. Meeter & W. Farr. (1975). Influencing factors for railroad-highway grade crossing accidents in Florida. *Accident Analysis and Prevention*, **7**, 103–112.

Van Houten, R., L. Malenfant & A. Rolider. (1985). Increasing driver yielding and pedestrian signaling with prompting, feedback and enforcement. *Journal of Applied Behavior Analysis*, **18**, 103–110.

Van Houten, R. & P. Nau. (1981). A comparison of the effects of posted feedback and increased police surveillance on highway speeding. *Journal of Applied Behavior Analysis*, **14**, 261–271.

Varhelyi, A. (1998). Drivers speed behaviour at zebra crossings: A case study. *Accident Analysis and Prevention*, **30**, 731–743.

Vejdirektoratet. (1996). *Miljøprioriterede gennemfarter. Effekter i 13 byer*. Foreløbig rapport. Vejdirektoratet, København.

Vernon, D. D., L. J. Cook, K. J. Peterson & J. M. Dean (2004). Effect of repeal of the national maximum speed limit law on occurrence of crashes, injury crashes, and fatal crashes on Utah highways. *Accident Analysis and Prevention*, **36**, 223–229.

Virginia Department of Highways and Transportation. (1991). *An Evaluation of the Effectiveness of Rumble Strips*. Traffic and Safety Division Evaluation No 81–5, 1991. (sitert etter Harwood, 1993).

Vodahl, S.B. & Giæver, T. (1986a). *Risiko i vegkryss. Dokumentasjonsrapport*. Rapport STF63 A86011. SINTEF Samferdselsteknikk, Trondheim.

Vodahl, S.B. & Giæver, T. (1986b). *Risiko ved fotgjengerkryssinger*. STF63 A86025. SINTEF Samferdselsteknikk, Trondheim.

Vodahl, S. B. & S. Johannessen. (1977). *Ulykkesfrekvenser i kryss*. Arbeidsnotat nr 7. Resultater av før/etterundersøkelsen. Oppdragsrapport 178. Norges Tekniske Høgskole, Forskningsgruppen, Institutt for samferdselsteknikk, Trondheim.

Vreugdenhil, J. J. (1976). Traffic management schemes for existing residential street layouts on the grid system. *ARRB Proceedings*, **Volume 8**, Session 6B, 1–19. Australian Road Research Board. Vermont South.

Værø, H. (1992). *Effekt af sortpletbekæmpelse i Hillerød*. Vejdirektoratet, Trafiksikkerhedsafdelingen, København.

Vägverket. (1997). *Nollvisionen, fördjupning*. Vägverket, Borlänge. Text located at http://www.vv.se/ts/nollvisn.htm.

Vaa, T., P. Christensen & A. Ragnøy, A. (1994). *Fartsvisningstavle i Vestfold: Virkning på fart*. Rapport 284. Transportøkonomisk institutt, Oslo.

Vaa, T. & S. Johannessen. (1978). *Ulykkesfrekvenser i kryss. En landsomfattende undersøkelse av ulykkesforholdene i 803 kryss i perioden januar 1970 - juni 1976*. Oppdragsrapport 22. Norges Tekniske Høgskole, Forskningsgruppen, Institutt for samferdselsteknikk, Trondheim.

Vaa, T., Gelau, C., Penttinen, M. & Spyroupolou, I. (2006). *ITS and effects on road traffic accidents – State of the art*. Paper presented at the 13th World Congress on ITS, London, 9th oct. 2006.

Wachtel, A. & Lewiston, D. Risk Factors for Bicycle-Motor Vehicle Collisions at Intersections. *ITE-Journal*, **September** 1994, 30–35.

Wahlgren, O. (1972). Effect of temporary speed limits on road accidents. *Traffic Engineering and Control*, **13**, 384–387.

Walker, R. T., G. Gardner & M. McFetridge. (1989). *Urban safety project: The Nelson scheme*. Contractor Report 191. Transport and Road Research Laboratory, Crowthorne, Berkshire.

Walker, R. T. & M. McFetridge. (1989). *Urban safety project: The Bradford scheme*. Contractor Report 190. Transport and Road Research Laboratory, Crowthorne, Berkshire.

Ward, H., Norrie, J.D., Allsop, R.E. & Sang, A.P. (1989a). *Urban safety project: The Sheffield scheme*. Contractor report 134. Transport and Road Research Laboratory, Crowthorne, Berkshire.

Ward, H., Norrie, J.D., Allsop, R.E. & Sang, A.P. (1989b). *Urban safety project: The Reading scheme*. Contractor report 138. Transport and Road Research Laboratory, Crowthorne, Berkshire.

Ward, H., Norrie, J.D., Allsop, R.E. & Sang, A.P. (1989c). *Urban safety project: The Bristol scheme*. Contractor report 192. Transport and Road Research Laboratory, Crowthorne, Berkshire.

Ward, H., Cave, J., Morrison, A. et al. (1994). *Pedestrian Activity and Accident Risk*. The AA Foundation for Road Safety Research, Basingstoke, Hampshire.

Watts, G. R. (1973). *Road humps for the control of vehicle speeds*. TRRL Laboratory Report 597. Transport and Road Research Laboratory, Crowthorne, Berkshire.

Webster, D. C. (1993). *Road humps for controlling vehicle speeds*. TRL Project Report 18. Transport Research Laboratory, Crowthorne, Berkshire.

Webster, D. C & R. E. Layfield. (1993). *An assessment of rumble strips and rumble areas*. TRL Project Report 33. Transport Research Laboratory, Crowthorne, Berkshire.

Webster, D. C. & A. M. Mackie. (1996). *Review of traffic calming schemes in 20 mph zones*. TRL Report 215. Crowthorne, Berkshire, Transport Research Laboratory,

Welch, T.M. (1999). *The conversion of four lane undivided urban roadways to three lane facilities*. Dallas, Texas: TRB/ITE Urban Street Symposium.

Wendelboe, J.T. (2003). *Traffic management applications on the Køge Bugt motorway, Denmark*. Report VIKING MIP2002.

Wennike, F. (1994). Fartdæmpning ved hjælp af afmærkning. *Dansk Vejtidsskrift*, **6/7**, 36.

Westman, K. (1986). *Parkering i innerstaden och olyckskostnader*. VTI-Meddelande nr 460. Statens väg- och trafikinstitut, Linköping.

Wheeler, A. & M. Taylor. (1995). Reducing speeds in villages: the VISP study. *Traffic Engineering and Control*, **36**, 213–219.

Wigglesworth, E. C. and C. B. Uber. (1991). An Evaluation of the Railway Level Crossing Boom Barrier Program in Victoria, Australia. *Journal of Safety Research*, **22**, 133–140.

Wilde, G. J. S., L. J. Cake & M. B. McCarthy. (1976). *An Observational Study of Driver Behaviour at Signalized Railroad Crossings.* Report CIGGT 75-16. Queen's University, Canadian Institute of Guided Ground Transport, Kingston, Ontario.

Willett, P. (1977). Perth's Experience with Pelican Crossings. *Australian Road Research*, **7**,(4), 36–38.

Willis, P. A., P. P. Scott & J. W. Barnes. (1984). *Road edgelining and accidents: an experiment in South-West England.* TRRL Laboratory Report 1117. Transport and Road Research Laboratory, Crowthorne, Berkshire.

Williston, R. M. (1960). Effect of Pavement Edge Markings on Operator Behavior. *Highway Research Board Bulletin*, **266**, 8–27.

Wilson, D. G. & S. J. Older. (1970). *The effects of installing new zebra-crossings in Rugby and Chelmsford.* RRL Report LR 358. Road Reserach Laboratory, Crowthorne, Berkshire.

Wolshon, B. & Lambert L. (2004). *Convertible Roadways and Lanes – A Sythesis of Highway Practice.* NCHRP Sythesis 340, Transportation Research Board, Washington, D.C.

Wolshon, B. & Lambert L. (2006a). Planning and Operational Practices for Reversible Roadways. *ITE Journal*, **8**, 38–44.

Wolshon, B. & Lambert L. (2006b). Reversible Lane Systems: Synthesis of Practice. *Journal of Transportation Engineering*, **12**, 933–944.

Wretling, P. (2000). *Effekt på antalet skadade och dödade personer av sänkt hastighetsgräns i Region Norr vintrarna 94/95–99/00.* VTI notat 74-2000. Väg- och transportforskningsinstitutet, Linköping.

Wu, C.-S., Lee, C.E., Machemehl, R.B. & Williams, J. (1982). Effects of Multiple-Point Detectors on Delay and Accidents. *Transportation Research Record*, **881**, 1–9.

Yagar, S. (1986). *Safety Impacts of Installing Pedestrian Crosswalks.* In: Effectiveness of Highway Safety Improvements, Proceedings of the conference, 137–146 (Carney, J. F. ed). American Society of Civil Engineers, New York, NY.

Yagar, S., M. Ropret & D. Kaufman. (1987). Migration of accidents and injuries at pedestrian crossovers in Toronto. *Proceedings of seminar D (P291) at PTRC 15th Summer Annual Meeting*, 1987, 179–192.

Yee, W. C. K. O. & M. G. H. Bell. (1986). The impact on accidents and driver behaviour of concentric lane-markings in small roundabouts. *Traffic Engineering and Control*, **27**, 255–262.

Young, T. E. (1967). New Traffic Signals. Their Effect on Street Utilization. *In Highway Research Board, Special Report 93, Improved Street Utilization Through Traffic Engineering, 84–95*. Highway Research Board, Washington DC.

Zador, P., J. Moshman & L. Marcus. (1982). Adoption of right turn on red: effects on crashes at signalized intersections. *Accident Analysis and Prevention*, **14**, 219–234.

Zaidel, D.M. & I. Hocherman. (1987). Safety of Pedestrian Crossings at Signalized Intersections. *Transportation Research Record*, 1141, 1–6.

Zalinger, D. A., B. A. Rogers & H. P. Johri. (1977). Calculation of hazard indices for highway-railway crossings in Canada. *Accident Analysis and Prevention*, **9**, 257–273.

Zegeer, C.V., Opiela, K.S. & Cynecki, M.J. (1982). Effect of Pedestrian Signals and Signal Timing on Pedestrian Accidents. *Transportation Research Record*, **847**, 62–72.

Zegeer, C.V., Stewart, J.R., Huang, H.H., Lagerwey, P.A., Feaganes, J. & Campbell, B.J. (2005). *Safety effects of marked versus unmarked crosswalks at uncontrolled locations: Final report and recommended guidelines*. Report FHWA-HRT-04-100.

Øvstedal, L. (1996). *Trafikksanering i utbygde områder*. In: Miljøhåndboken, Del I, 219-232 (Kolbenstvedt, M., H. Silborn and T. Solheim, eds) Transportøkonomisk institutt, Oslo.

Åkerlund, O. & Ö. Johansson. (1980a). *Trafikksäkerhetseffekten av kantstolpar*. Meddelande TU 1980:7. Statens Vägverk, Utvecklingssektionen, Borlänge.

Åkerlund, O. & Ö. Johansson. (1980b). *Trafiksäkerhetseffekten av reflektorer på snöstör*. Meddelande TU 1980:8. Statens Vägverk, Utvecklingssektionen, Borlänge

# 4.

# VEHICLE DESIGN AND PROTECTIVE DEVICES

## 4.0 INTRODUCTION AND OVERVIEW OF 29 MEASURES

This chapter describes 29 measures involving vehicle design and personal safety equipment. The 29 measures are as follows:

4.1 Tyre tread depth
4.2 Studded tyres
4.3 Antilock braking systems (ABS) and disc brakes
4.4 High-mounted stop lamps
4.5 Daytime running lights for cars
4.6 Daytime running lights for mopeds and motorcycles
4.7 Improving vehicle headlights
4.8 Reflective materials and protective clothing
4.9 Steering, suspension and vehicle stability
4.10 Bicycle helmets
4.11 Motorcycle helmets
4.12 Seat belts in cars
4.13 Child restraints
4.14 Airbags in cars
4.15 Seat belts in buses and trucks
4.16 Vehicle crashworthiness
4.17 Driving controls and instruments
4.18 Intelligent cruise control (ICC)
4.19 Regulating vehicle mass (weight)

**The Handbook of Road Safety Measures**

**ISBN: 978-1-84855-250-0**

4.20 Regulating automobile engine capacity (motor power) and top speed
4.21 Regulating engine capacity (motor power) of mopeds and motorcycles
4.22 Under-run guards on heavy vehicles
4.23 Safety equipment on heavy vehicles
4.24 Moped and motorcycle equipment
4.25 Bicycle safety equipment
4.26 Safety standards for trailers and caravans
4.27 Fire safety standards
4.28 Hazardous goods regulations
4.29 Electronic stability control (ESC)

This introductory chapter gives an overview of current knowledge about the effects of these measures on accidents and injuries, effects on mobility and the environment, costs and cost–benefit analysis.

**Amount and quality of research**

Very comprehensive research has been carried out to evaluate the effects on accidents and injuries of most vehicle safety features and forms of personal safety equipment. Table 4.0.1 shows the number of studies, the number of results and the size of the database (sum of statistical weights) for studies of the effects of vehicle design and personal safety equipment on the number of accidents and injuries.

The largest number of studies concerns seat belts, vehicle crashworthiness, daytime running lights on cars and motorcycle helmets. Many studies of vehicle design and personal safety equipment are based on a large accident sample. Meta-analyses have been used to summarise the results for the majority of measures. For some of the measures, however, the available studies do not provide a satisfactory basis for meta-analysis.

The quality of the studies, which have evaluated the effects of vehicle design and personal safety equipment, varies considerably. Experiments have been carried out on antilock braking system (ABS), high-mounted stop lamps, daytime running lights on cars and reflective materials and protective clothing. Good, non-experimental studies are available on seat belts in cars, vehicle crashworthiness and regulating motor power of mopeds and motorcycles. The methodological quality of the studies that have evaluated the other measures is variable.

*Table 4.0.1: The amount of research evaluating the effects on accidents of vehicle design and protective devices*

| Measure | Number of studies | Number of results | Sum of statistical weights | Results last updated |
|---|---|---|---|---|
| 4.1 Tyre tread depth | 4 | 47 | 1,467 | 1997 |
| 4.2 Studded tyres – effect for each car | 12 | 86 | 73,496 | 2001 |
| 4.2 Studded tyres – effect of legislation | 8 | 26 | 145,398 | 2001 |
| 4.3 Antilock braking systems (ABS) and disc brakes | 7 | 172 | 102,005 | 1997 |
| 4.4 High mounted stop lamps | 6 | 19 | 58,742 | 1997 |
| 4.5 Daytime running lights for cars | 25 | 111 | 75,690 | 2003 |
| 4.6 Daytime running lights for mopeds and motorcycles | 16 | 47 | 8,133 | 2003 |
| 4.7 Improving vehicle headlights | 13 | 237 | 81,500 | 1997 |
| 4.8 Reflective materials and protective clothing | 9 | 25 | 3,044 | 1997 |
| 4.9 Steering, suspension and vehicle stability | – | – | – | 1997 |
| 4.10 Bicycle helmets – effect when worn | 17 | 21 | 364 | 2004 |
| 4.10 Bicycle helmets – effect of legislation | 5 | 11 | 18,104 | 2004 |
| 4.11 Motorcycle helmets – effect when worn | 26 | 60 | 1,858 | 1997 |
| 4.11 Motorcycle helmets – effect of legislation | 8 | 73 | 20,778 | 1997 |
| 4.12 Seat belts in cars – effect when worn | 30 | 418 | 358,533 | 1997 |
| 4.12 Seat belts in cars – effect of legislation | 25 | 136 | 1,383,905 | 1997 |
| 4.13 Child restraints – choice of seat in car | 8 | 42 | 2,178 | 2006 |
| 4.13 Child restraints – effect when worn | 19 | 110 | 4,551 | 2006 |
| 4.13 Child restraints – effect of legislation | 7 | 12 | 25,792 | 2006 |
| 4.14 Airbags in cars – frontal airbags | 14 | 190 | 56,039 | 2007 |
| 4.14 Airbags in cars – side airbags | 2 | 53 | 7,708 | 2007 |
| 4.15 Seat belts in buses and trucks | – | – | – | 1997 |
| 4.16 Vehicle crashworthiness | 40 | 230 | 74,524 | 2009 |
| 4.17 Driving control stalks and instruments | 3 | 8 | 515 | 1997 |
| 4.18 Intelligent cruise control (ICC) | – | – | – | 2009 |
| 4.19 Regulating vehicle mass (weight) | 11 | 725 | 121,790 | 1997 |
| 4.20 Regulating motor power | 5 | 5 | - | 2009 |
| 4.20 Intelligent Speed Adaptation (ISA) | 1 | 1 | - | 2009 |
| 4.21 Regulating motor power of mopeds and motorcycles | 14 | 347 | 193,779 | 1997 |
| 4.22 Under-run guard rails on heavy vehicles | 2 | 2 | – | 1997 |
| 4.23 Safety equipment on heavy vehicles | 6 | 60 | 23,569 | 1997 |
| 4.24 Moped and motorcycle equipment | 3 | 6 | 465 | 1997 |
| 4.25 Bicycle safety equipment | 11 | 20 | 695 | 1997 |

*Table 4.0.1: (Continued)*

| Measure | Number of studies | Number of results | Sum of statistical weights | Results last updated |
|---|---|---|---|---|
| 4.26 Safety standards for trailers and caravans | 13 | 121 | 20,387 | 1997 |
| 4.27 Fire safety standards | 3 | 3 | – | 1997 |
| 4.28 Hazardous goods regulations | 9 | 9 | – | 1997 |
| 4.29 Electronic stability control (ESC) | 8 | 38 | 19,386 | 2006 |

## Main elements of the effects on accidents

Vehicle design and personal safety equipment cover two distinct types of measures. These are active safety measures, which are intended to reduce the number of accidents (at a given exposure), and passive safety measures, which are intended to reduce the severity of injuries in the event of accidents.

A distinction can be made between the effects at two levels for both types of measures. One level – the individual level – is the effect on the individual vehicle or the individual user of a specific type of safety equipment. The other level – the aggregate level – is the effect on the total number of accidents or injuries in a society that results from changed use of a measure, e.g. increased use of daytime running lights or seat belts.

The largest reductions of the numbers of injuries have been found for seat belts, motorcycle helmets, increased tyre tread depth, daytime running lights, reflective materials for pedestrians, child restraints and side airbags. These measures were found to reduce the number of injuries in all types of accidents by 15% or more. Large injury reductions in specific types of accidents have also been found for improved vehicle crashworthiness and electronic stability control (ESC). Several types of safety equipment on bicycles and trucks also were found to reduce injuries. Among those measures that may have less effect on the number of accidents and injuries are studded tyres and, with the exception of heavy vehicles and ABS. There is no clear pattern of differences in the effects of active and passive safety measures.

There is no simple relationship between the effects of a measure at individual levels and the effects of the same measure at aggregate levels. Evaluations of laws making seat belt wearing mandatory are a case in point. The probability of driver injury is reduced by around 40–50% when seat belts are worn. Increased use of seat belts will therefore, in otherwise identical conditions, reduce the number of driver fatalities. However, it is not the case that a 10% increase in seat belt use reduces the number of driver fatalities by 5%, or that a 50% increase in seat belt use reduces the number of driver fatalities by

25%, etc. In general, a smaller decrease in the number of fatalities has been found for a given increase in the use of seat belts than might be predicted on the basis of the effect of seat belts on each motorist's risk of a fatal injury. Occasionally, there are examples where the number of driver fatalities has increased after mandatory seat belt use is introduced.

There are many reasons why there is no clear relationship between the effect of using seat belts for the individual motorist and the effect on the total number of fatalities when more motorists start using seat belts. Firstly, the number of fatalities is influenced by several factors other than the use of seat belts. Secondly, the number of fatalities is subject to random fluctuations. Last, but not least, it is not certain that those who start using seat belts when this becomes mandatory are a representative sample of all drivers. If the first drivers to use seat belts are those with the lowest accident involvement rate, the decrease in the total number of fatalities will be smaller than the percentage increase in seat belt use would imply.

There are many other examples of cases where the total effects of a measure are smaller than the sum of the individual effects would imply. Nonetheless, it is clear that many measures involving vehicle design and personal safety equipment have contributed significantly to reducing the number of fatalities and injuries in traffic.

For three of the measures, the effect on accidents has not been extensively evaluated, but some studies have evaluated the effect on intermediate variables, e.g. detection distances or stopping distances. This applies to improvements to car headlights, intelligent cruise control (ICC) and bicycle safety equipment. The effects on detection distances or stopping distances are interpreted here as indications of the potential effect on accidents of these measures.

**Main elements in effects on mobility**

The majority of measures described in this chapter are not intended to improve mobility, with some exceptions. Studded tyres improve mobility in winter driving conditions and ESC improves mobility on wet, snowy or icy roads. Other measures may have more or less unintentional effects on mobility, including traffic volume. An example is mandatory wearing of bicycle helmets, which has led to 20–40% reduction in the amount of cycling. It is not known whether this has led to increased use of other transport modes, or whether cycle trips have simply been cancelled. Speed governors in vehicles, which are activated by the speed limit, may also reduce mobility. Maximum speed governors have been introduced on specific types of heavy vehicles in the EU, but not, as yet, on other vehicles. ICC is mainly intended to improve driving comfort.

It was found to improve traffic flows and to reduce travel times (if a sufficient number of vehicles is equipped with ICC).

There has been much discussion as to whether mandatory use of seat belts or helmets indirectly affects mobility, in that road users, for example, increase their speed when the use of such equipment is made mandatory. Such an effect of the use of seat belts has not been found.

**Main elements in effects on the environment**

Environmental standards have become stricter during recent years, with more stringent standards for pollution emission, fuel consumption and noise levels. On the whole, the measures included in this chapter have little effect on the environment. Measures that have been found to affect the environment are the following:

- The use of studded tyres increases fuel consumption by up to 2% compared to non-studded winter tyres. Studded tyres cause environmental problems because the asphalt is torn up and spread in the form of a fine dust. Some of this dust is inhaled and can lead to health problems.
- Using daytime running lights increases fuel consumption and exhaust emissions by 1–2%.
- Speed governors and intelligent speed adaptation can lead to lower and less variable driving speeds, which will reduce fuel consumption. This can also reduce the noise from road traffic.
- Increasing the weight of the vehicle by 10% increases fuel consumption by around 3%. Among measures contributing to increased weight are under-run guardrails, side rails on heavy vehicles, airbags and ESC.

**Main elements in costs**

The costs of measures involving vehicle design and personal safety equipment vary considerably. Table 4.0.2 gives an overview of available information regarding the costs of the different measures. The costs are, for the most part, one-time costs incurred when buying a vehicle or a piece of equipment. However, some costs are annual running costs.

The available cost estimates are for the most part uncertain and cost estimates are not available for all measures. Cost estimates are not available for steering, suspension and

*Table 4.0.2: Costs of measures involving vehicle design and personal safety equipment calculated per vehicle or per road user in Norway*

| Measure | Cost per car per person (NOK) | Costs from year |
|---|---|---|
| 4.1 Tyre tread depth: change in the requirement from 1.6 to 3 mm | 130 | 1995 |
| 4.2 Studded tyres: set of studded tyres (including wheel rims) | 4,000 | 2007 |
| 4.3 ABS and disc brakes: additional costs | 5,000 | 1997 |
| 4.4 High mounted stop lamps: installation | 250 | 1997 |
| 4.5 Daytime running lights for cars: average annual cost per light vehicle | 140 | 2003 |
| 4.6 Daytime running lights for mopeds and motorcycles: average annual cost per moped/motorcycle | 80 | 2003 |
| 4.8 Pedestrian reflectors: per pair | 20 | 2007 |
| 4.8 Protective clothing for motorcyclists | 7,500 | 1997 |
| 4.10 Bicycle helmets: Per piece, adults | 600 | 2007 |
| 4.11 Motorcycle helmets | 1,500–5,000 | 2008 |
| 4.12 Seat belts in cars: additional cost per car | 2,600 | 1997 |
| 4.13 Child restraints: per piece of equipment | 400–4,000 | 2007 |
| 4.15 Seat belts in buses and trucks: installation of hip belts in school bus, per bus | 16,500 | 1995 |
| 4.16 Vehicle crashworthiness | – | 2009 |
| 4.18 Intelligent cruise control (ICC): additional costs per car | 10,000 | 2009 |
| 4.18 Intelligent speed adaptation (ISA): additional costs per car | 10,000 | 2009 |
| 4.22 Under-run guardrails and side rails on trucks: installation | 13,500 | 1995 |
| 4.23 Side marker lamps on heavy vehicles | 80 | 1995 |
| 4.24 Moped and motorcycle equipment: installation/additional costs | 2,000 | 1995 |
| 4.25 Bicycle safety equipment | 1,200 | 1995 |
| 4.29 Electronic stability control (ESC): additional costs per car | 2,000 | 2006 |

vehicle stability, airbags, regulating vehicle mass, motor power and top speed of cars and motorcycles, safety standards and hazardous goods regulations.

Firstly, the costs of many measures are difficult to identify as part of the total production costs of a vehicle. Car manufacturers make cars and know what they cost. They know less about the additional costs, for example, of increasing a vehicle's weight by 50 kg. Secondly, sales prices for different types of equipment may be affected by special taxes and thus do not reflect the actual costs of production. The cost figures given in Table 4.0.2 are intended to show the social opportunity costs of the measures. The social opportunity costs can deviate from the private costs a car buyer must pay for the different types of equipment, as a result of the special taxes on cars.

### Main elements in cost–benefit analyses

Cost–benefit analyses have not been reported for all the measures involving vehicle design and personal safety equipment. Where the effects and costs of the measures are sufficiently known, numerical examples have been worked out to indicate the costs and benefits. The examples are intended to show costs and benefits for a vehicle or for a road user with an average annual mileage and average accident rate for the type of vehicle. Table 4.0.3 shows the results of the numerical examples for the different measures.

It is possible to estimate costs and benefits for the majority of measures. Amongst the measures for which benefits are clearly greater than costs are seat belts, vehicle crashworthiness, motorcycle helmets and other protective equipment, ESC and most of the measures improving visibility. Less cost-effective measures include more stringent standards for tread depth of car tyres, regulating car motor power, requiring seat belts in buses and possibly speed governors for motor vehicles.

## 4.1 Tyre tread depth

### Problem and objective

During the period 1990–93, 22% of all police-reported injury accidents in Norway occurred on wet, bare roads (Vaa 1995). A number of studies (Satterthwaite 1976, Ivey et al. 1981, Brodsky and Hakkert 1988, Ragnøy 1989) show that the accident rate is higher on wet roads than on dry roads. If the risk on dry, bare roads is set to 1.0, the accident rate on wet, bare roads in Norway is estimated to be around 1.2 in daytime and 1.4 at nighttime (Ragnøy 1989).

A number of factors contribute to explaining why the accident rate is higher on wet roads than on dry roads. Splash and spray contribute to reduced visibility. Worn-out windscreen wipers can increase this problem. Water on the road reduces friction, especially at high speeds. An important factor for friction on wet roads is the tyre tread depth. The gaps in the tread on a car tyre are designed to drain water, which collects between the car tyre and the road when driving, so that friction is maintained. When the tread wears down, the gaps become smaller and the tyre drains less water. This can increase the risk of aquaplaning, i.e. where a film of water forms between the car tyre and the road surface, so that the contact between tyre and road disappears altogether. Tyre tread depth standards are intended to ensure that car tyres give good friction for all road surface conditions.

*Table 4.0.3: Results of numerical examples to indicate the benefit–cost ratio of measures involving vehicle design and personal safety equipment*

| Measure | Benefit–cost ratio |
|---|---|
| 4.1 Tyre tread depth: change in the requirement from 1.6 to 3 mm | 0.3 |
| 4.2 Ban on studded tyres in the four largest cities in Norway | 2.6 |
| 4.3 ABS on cars | 0.7 |
| 4.4 High mounted stop lamps (installation) | 4.1 |
| 4.5 Daytime running lights for cars (mandatory) | 2.5 |
| 4.6 Daytime running lights on motorcycles (mandatory) | 3.8–7.5 |
| 4.7 Improving vehicle headlights – halogen lamps | 9.3 |
| 4.7 Improving vehicle headlights – headlamp washer | 1.0 |
| 4.8 Protective equipment for motorcyclists | 5.3 |
| 4.9 Steering, suspension and vehicle stability | – |
| 4.10 Bicycle helmets for children (7–14 years) | 2.5 |
| 4.10 Bicycle helmets for adults (at least 1.5 km cycle trips per day) | >1 |
| 4.11 Motorcycle helmets | 17.2 |
| 4.12 Seat belts in cars – drivers | 31.7 |
| 4.12 Seat belts in cars – front seat passengers | 13.3 |
| 4.12 Seat belts in cars – rear seat passengers | 1.3 |
| 4.13 Child restraints | 1.13 |
| 4.14 Airbags in cars (frontal/side airbags) | – |
| 4.15 Seat belts in trucks/buses (all seats in buses) | 0.0 |
| 4.16 Vehicle crashworthiness in cars – collapsible steering columns | 16.7 |
| 4.16 Vehicle crashworthiness in cars – laminated front windshield | 30.0 |
| 4.16 Vehicle crashworthiness in cars – head rests | 1.4 |
| 4.16 Vehicle crashworthiness in cars – door protection | 0.9 |
| 4.17 Driving control stalks and instruments – convex mirrors | 0.0 |
| 4.18 Intelligent cruise control (ICC) | 0.6 |
| 4.19 Regulating vehicle mass (weight) | – |
| 4.20 Regulating motor power and top speed of cars | 0.3 |
| 4.20 Intelligent Speed Adaptation (ISA) | 3.7–16.7 |
| 4.21 Regulating motor power of mopeds and motorcycles | – |
| 4.22 Under-run guard rails and side rails on heavy vehicles (trucks) | 3.9 |
| 4.23 Safety equipment for heavy vehicles | – |
| 4.23 Side marker lamps on heavy vehicles | 0.5 |
| 4.24 Moped and motorcycle equipment | – |
| 4.25 Bicycle safety equipment – distance device (side flag) | 2.2 |
| 4.25 Bicycle safety equipment – bicycle lights | 0.1 |
| 4.26 Safety standards for trailers and caravans | – |
| 4.27 Fire safety standards | – |
| 4.28 Hazardous goods regulations | – |
| 4.29 Electronic stability control (ESC): installation in all new vehicles | 4.8 |

**Description of measure**

The minimum permissible tyre tread depth is part of vehicle safety standards. Currently, the following minimum requirements apply in Norway: 1.6 mm for cars and trailers with a total weight of up to 3.5 t; 1.0 mm for cars with a permitted total weight of more than 3.5 t and 3 mm for winter tyres in motorcycles.

Studies of cars in traffic show that the majority observe these standards in Norway (Fosser 1979a, Fosser and Teigen 1981, Statens vegvesen Vegdirektoratet 1982, 1983, Glad 1988). The results of the different studies indicate that less than 5% of cars on the road in Norway have an illegal tyre tread depth on one or more tyres.

**Effect on accidents**

Relatively few studies have evaluated the effect on accidents of tyre tread depth. The following studies have been found which attempt to quantify this effect:

Hankins, Morgan, Ashkar and Tutt (1971) (USA)
Highway Safety Foundation (1971) (discussed in Dijks 1976) (USA)
Glad (1988) (Norway)
Fosser and Ingebrigtsen (1991a) (Norway)

Only two of these studies (Hankins, Morgan, Ashkar and Tutt 1971 and Glad 1988) give details on the number of accidents, which are the basis for the estimating its effect, so that the results can be included in meta-analyses. Based on these two studies, best estimates of the effect of increasing tyre tread depths on accidents are given in Table 4.1.1.

*Table 4.1.1: Effect on accidents of increasing tyre tread depth for car tyres*

| | Percentage change in the number of accidents | | |
|---|---|---|---|
| Accident severity | Type of accident affected | Best estimate | 95% confidence interval |
| ***Increasing tread depth from less than 2 to around 2–3 mm*** | | | |
| Unspecified (all accidents) | All (especially wet roads) | −19 | (−30; −5) |
| ***Increasing tread depth from 2–3 mm to 3–5 mm*** | | | |
| Unspecified (all accidents) | All (especially wet roads) | −9 | (−19; +3) |
| ***Increasing tread depth from 3–5 mm to more than 5 mm*** | | | |
| Unspecified (all accidents) | All (especially wet roads) | +6 | (−1; +12) |

In summary, the results indicate that increasing tyre tread depth is related to decreasing accident numbers up to a treat depth of ca. 5 mm. Increasing tyre tread depth to more than 5 mm has no statistically significant effect on accident rate. These studies have not controlled for confounding factors, but show the simple bivariate relationship between tyre tread depth and accident rate. The results therefore show statistical tendencies only and not the effect of tyre tread depth alone. The results discussed by Dijks (1976) show the same tendencies as the above results. However, this study has not controlled for confounding factors influencing the accident rate. The results are therefore uncertain.

In a Norwegian study, the relationship between the standard of tyres and the accident rate in winter was studied (Ingebrigtsen and Fosser 1991). Tyre tread depth was measured on a scale of 0 to10. The results are therefore not directly comparable with other studies. The study found that when tyre tread depth increases by around 2 mm (calculated from the scale), the accident rate is reduced by around 16% in snow or ice conditions, around 10% on wet, bare roads and around 20% on dry, bare roads. The study controlled for a number of confounding factors affecting the accident rate in winter, in addition to tyre tread depth.

**Effect on mobility**

No studies are available that show how changes in tyre tread depth affects mobility. Drivers who know that their car has poor tyres may drive more carefully than drivers who know that their car has good tyres (Fosser and Ingebrigtsen 1991b, Ingebrigtsen and Fosser 1991, Fosser and Sætermo 1995). This type of behavioural adaptation can take many forms and does not necessarily mean that drivers of cars with poor tyres reduce their speed.

**Effect on the environment**

Tyres with a coarse tread (and thus greater tread depth) generate slightly more noise than tyres with finer treads (Johansen 1975). The differences are small. The most important feature of a car tyre with regard to traffic noise and other environmental effects is whether the tyre is studded or not.

**Costs**

A set of new summer tyres for a car in Norway costs between NOK 2,000 and NOK 3,000. New tyres have a tyre tread depth of around 8 mm. This is worn down to 1 mm in the course of driving 30,000–60,000 km (depending on the road surface and the tyres' strength). On average, wear and tear on tyres cost Norwegian motorists around NOK 0.06 per kilometre (1995 prices) (Statens vegvesen, Handbook 140, 1995). Many drivers in Norway change their tyres before the tread has worn down to 1.6 mm.

### Cost–benefit analysis

Few cars in Norway today have tyres, which have an illegal tyre tread depth. The additional costs that motorists would incur as a result of stricter standards for tyre tread depth are therefore probably small.

If the minimum requirement for tyre tread depth were raised to 3 mm, it is estimated that up to 5% of car tyres in use in Norway today would be illegal. These tyres would have to be changed immediately. In addition, it is likely that many drivers would choose to change their tyres earlier than at present, in order to be sure of being on the safe side.

Changing 5% of the tyres on Norwegian cars and goods vehicles after introducing legislation requiring 3 mm tyre tread depth would cost around NOK 240 million (one-time expense). Assuming that the cars with new tyres are involved in 10% fewer accidents than otherwise, this will prevent some 40 injury accidents during the first year after the measure is implemented. The reduction of accident costs will amount to around NOK 80 million. This is less than the cost of the measure.

## 4.2 Studded tyres

### Problem and objective

During winter, road surface friction is often greatly reduced compared to summer. Snow or ice on the road increase stopping distances and make it more difficult to maintain control of the vehicle. A study of the use of tyres on cars in Norway in the winter of 1993–94 found that the accident rate on snow or ice-covered roads was about twice as high as on bare road surfaces (Fosser 1994). On average, for the years 1990–93, 21% of injury accidents reported to the police in Norway occurred on roads which were completely or partially covered with snow or ice (Vaa 1995).

Studded tyres increase friction and shorten stopping distances on snow or ice-covered roads compared to non-studded tyres, particularly on ice-covered roads. A majority of drivers in Norway therefore choose to use studded tyres in winter. In the winter

1993–94, 81.5% of all vehicle kilometres with passenger cars were driven with studded tyres, 8.2% with winter tyres and 10.3% with summer tyres (Fosser 1994).

The use of studded tyres on bare road surfaces causes the spread of very fine dust formed from particles torn off the road surface. Some of the smallest of these particles can be inhaled and are believed to cause respiratory diseases. In recent years, a policy has therefore been pursued in Norway to reduce the use of studded tyres in major cities. This policy has been successful in bringing down the use of studded tyres in the five largest towns in Norway to less than 50% in winter 1999–2000 (Fridstrøm 2000).

Studded tyres are designed to reduce the number of accidents in winter, especially on snow or ice-covered roads. Another objective is to ensure accessibility by giving sufficient friction to be able to drive on icy roads.

## Description of the measure

Studded tyres are allowed in Norway during the winter months. Some countries have banned the use of studded tyres, while other countries only allow the use of studded tyres during winter or demand extra taxes for their use. Legislation may also govern the number of studs and the type of studs used.

## Effect on accidents

A number of studies have evaluated the effects of studded tyres on the number of accidents in winter. The studies are of two types. One type of study compares the accident rate for cars with studded tyres and cars without studded tyres. The other type of study concerns the effects of a ban on the use of studded tyres.

***Effects of the use of studded tyres on accidents.*** Studies of the effects of studded tyres for the accident rate of each car include the following:

Normand (1971) (Canada)
Steen and Bolstad (1972) (Norway)
Ernst and Hippchen (1974) (Germany)
Roosmark, Andersson and Ahlqvist (1976) (Sweden)
Perchonok (1978) (USA)
Ingebrigtsen and Fosser (1991) (Norway)
Junghard (1992) (Sweden)
Konagai, Asano and Horita (1993) (Japan)

Fosser (1994) (Norway)
Fosser and Sætermo (1995) (Norway)
Roine (1996) (Finland)
Vaa (1997) (Norway)

The results of these studies vary considerably, depending primarily on how well the different studies have controlled for confounding factors affecting the accident rate. The best controlled studies are those of Ingebrigtsen and Fosser (1991), Fosser and Sætermo (1995) and Roine (1996). A meta-analysis of studies that have evaluated the safety effects of studded tyres has been reported by Elvik (1999). On the basis of the three best controlled studies, Table 4.2.1 shows the effect on accident rates in winter when using studded tyres compared with non-studded winter tyres. Cars that use studded tyres seem to have a slightly lower accident rate in winter than cars with non-studded winter tyres. However, the difference is not statistically significant.

***Effects of prohibiting studded tyres on accidents.*** The use of studded tyres is banned in a number of places around the world. The following studies have evaluated the effects on accidents of such bans or related measures designed to discourage the use of studded tyres:

Preus (1973) (Minnesota, USA)
Smith (1973) (Ontario, Canada)
Pucher (1977) (West Germany)
Perchonok (1978) (Minnesota, USA)
Takagi and Horita (1993) (Sapporo, Japan)
Takagi, Shimojo and Onuma (1996) (Hokkaido, Japan)
Hvoslef (1997), see Takagi (1997) (Hokkaido, Japan)
Fridstrøm (2000) (large towns in Norway)

All these studies, except for Fridstrøm's study, are before- and after-studies. They show results varying between an unchanged number of accidents and an increase of around

*Table 4.2.1: Effect on accident rate for cars in winter when using studded tyres compared with non-studded tyres*

| | Percentage difference in accident rate | | |
|---|---|---|---|
| Accident severity | Road surface conditions | Best estimate | 95% confidence interval |
| Unspecified | Snow or ice covered road | −5 | (−20; +12) |
| Unspecified | Bare road (wet or dry) | −2 | (−18; +16) |
| Unspecified | All driving conditions | −4 | (−15; +9) |

10% in the number of accidents. The most recent figures come from Japan. At Hokkaido, in Japan, the number of accidents increased in winter following a ban on studded tyres by around 3% (+2%; +5%) controlling for trends applying to accidents in summer during the same time period (Elvik 1999). The use of studded tyres was reduced from around 90% to around 10%.

Fridstrøm's study (2000) employed multivariate techniques to estimate the effects of changes in the percentage of cars using studded tyres in four major owns in Norway. The study estimated that halving the use of studded tyres, for example from about 80% to about 40%, would lead to an increase of 3% in the number of injury accidents in winter in four major towns in Norway. The estimated increase of the number of accidents was not statistically significant, but is consistent with the findings of other studies.

**Effect on mobility**

Studies of the choice of driving speed with and without studded tyres have given inconsistent results. Carlsson and Öberg (1976) found no difference in speed between cars with studded tyres and cars without studded tyres when driving on bare roads. When driving on snow or ice-covered roads, cars with studded tyres used approximately 2 s less per kilometre than cars without studded tyres. At a speed of 60 km/h, this corresponds to a difference of 2 km/h. More recent studies have given different results. Öberg (1989) found no systematic differences in speed between cars with and without studded tyres in different driving conditions. Fosser and Ingebrigtsen (1991b) found no systematic differences in speed between cars with different types of tyres. Fridstrøm's study (2000) indirectly shows that road users adapt their behaviour to the type of tyres on the car. The study indicated, albeit by means of aggregate data only, that those who have studded tyres tend to slow down less on ice- or snow-covered road surfaces than those who do not have studded tyres.

Observations of behaviour and answers to questionnaires (Fosser and Ingebrigtsen 1991b, Fosser and Sætermo 1995) indicate that drivers adapt their behaviour according to the type of tyres on their car and the standard of the tyres. The answers given in these questionnaires indicate that drivers without studded tyres, and possibly worn-out or poor tyres, drive more carefully than drivers who know their car has good tyres. Behavioural adaptations do not necessarily affect driving speeds alone, but also how often journeys are cancelled because of weather conditions and a feeling of insecurity while driving.

**Effect on the environment**

The used of studded tyres increases asphalt wear and particle pollution and increases noise. The asphalt surface consists of about 90% stone/minerals, about 5% fine particles, and about 5% bitumen (adhesive agent). Studded tyres wear away the stone components of the asphalt, which together with the fine particles is then spread in the form of soot and carbon particles. The carbon consists of large particles, which lie on the road, stick to cars or are spread over the immediate surroundings of the road (Ragnøy, Karlsen and Larsen 2000). Road dust in winter is mainly cause by studded tyres. The amount of road dust depends, amongst other things, on the type of the spikes used, the resistance of the asphalt, vehicle speeds, the proportion of heavy vehicles, and on how much water, snow and ice covers the road surface.

On the basis of research evaluating the effects on human health of inhaling particles, Rosendahl (1996) calculated that in Norway some 90 deaths occur each year as a result of acute pollution, i.e. short periods with abnormally high particle concentration in the air. About 60% of the $PM_{10}$ concentration in the air in Oslo is attributable to road traffic, according to Rosendahl (1996), of which a little under 50% is attributable to the use of studded tyres. Rosendahl has estimated the costs to society of the health-related effects of local air pollution in Oslo in 1992 to NOK 1.728 million. Of this, about NOK 480 million can be attributed to the use of studded tyres.

Studded tyres make more noise than summer tyres (Bang 1996). Norwegian data show that traffic noise level during winter increases by around 2–3 dBA when driving on normal asphalt roads with an even surface, at speeds between 70–90 km/h and around 15–25% heavy vehicles. For pure tyre noise from car tyres, the increase in noise levels can be between 3 and 10 dBA, depending on speed, type of tyres and the quality of the rubber.

Non-studded winter tyres have been found to reduce noise by about 2.3 dB(A) at 50 km/h compared to tyres with spikes of steel, and by about 1.5 dB(A) compared to tyres with environment-friendly spikes. A possible indirect effect of increased use of non-studded tyres is the increased use of low-noise asphalt on heavily trafficked roads.

**Costs**

There are two types of costs involved in the use of studded tyres: direct costs and indirect costs. The direct costs are the costs involved in studding the tyres. The indirect costs are the costs of all the unintentional effects of the use of studded tyres, such as increased wear and tear on the road, pollution and noise. The costs of studding tyres are estimated to NOK 50 per car (four tyres per car) and NOK 58 per tyre for heavy vehicles (Gabestad and Ragnøy 1986). The prices were for Norway in 1985. Converted to 2000 prices, these come to around NOK 80 and around NOK 95, respectively. The indirect costs are discussed in the section on cost–benefit analyses. The introduction of charges on the use of studded tyres is associated with administrative costs that may be covered by the charges.

Reduced use of studded tyres may increase the costs for winter maintenance. On local roads, it has been estimated that winter maintenance costs will increase by about 50–100%, when the proportion of vehicles with studded tyres is reduced from 80% to 20%. On main roads, no increase of winter maintenance costs is assumed (Ragnøy, Karlsen and Larsen 2000).

**Cost–benefit analysis**

A number of cost–benefit analyses have been conducted of the use of studded tyres. Only the most recent of these analyses will be quoted, as the earlier analyses relied on assumptions that may no longer be correct. A numerical example has been calculated, which is based on the most recent information on the use and effects of studded tyres. The example is based on the following assumptions: Halving the use of studded tyres in Oslo increases the number of injury accidents by 8–9% (Fridstrøm 2000). The associated costs are about NOK 20 million per year. The number of vehicle kilometres driven in Oslo in winter is about 1,200 million vehicle kilometres and the average speed is 40 km/h. The number of vehicle hours is then 1,200/40 = 30 million. Halving the use of studded tyres increases travel times by 1% because drivers without studded tyres drive more slowly (Fridstrøm 2000), which corresponds to 0.3 million hours per year. With a time cost of NOK 110 per hour, the increase in travel times corresponds to a societal cost of NOK 33 million per year.

Rosendahl (2000) has estimated the health effects of particle pollution, which is caused by studded tyres in Oslo, at between NOK 2,500 and NOK 7,000 per vehicle and year. A reduction of the use of studded tyres from 80% to 20% would reduce health costs by between NOK 235 and 658 million per year. The cost savings that are related to the health effects of studded tyres are larger than the costs that are associated with an increase of accidents, which would follow a reduction of the use of studded tyres. They are also larger than the effects of studded tyres on travel times. This indicates that the societal benefit of reducing the use of studded tyres in Norwegian cities is greater than the societal costs.

## 4.3 Antilock braking systems and disc brakes

### Problem and objective

Many accidents occur when the driver loses control of the vehicle while braking. An important cause of loss of control is the locking one or more of the wheels when braking. When the wheels lock, the vehicle immediately loses both directional stability and steering control. Official British accident statistics show that the wheels were locked in around 14% of injury accidents involving cars (Grime 1987). Locking wheels in curves means that the vehicle is only steered by centrifugal forces, which results in driving off the road accidents or collisions.

Few drivers are able to use their brakes optimally in emergency situations. When the brake pedal is pressed to the floor, this normally leads to the wheels locking. An ABS is designed to prevent the problems occurring when wheels lock. The objective of ABS is to remove the difficult task of optimising brake pressure, and to prevent the wheels from locking, so that directional stability and steering control can be maintained in a critical situation. On some road surfaces, ABS will also give shorter stopping distances than normal brakes. For heavy vehicles and articulated lorries, it is particularly important to avoid jack-knife accidents and other accidents which result from wheel locking or unstable brakes.

### Description of measure

***Antilock braking system.*** ABS is a so-called closed regulating system. In its simplest form, the system is designed to regulate one wheel and consists of a sensor, which senses the wheel's rotational state (speed, acceleration, deceleration); a control unit, which receives and processes information from the sensor and gives signals for control; and a control valve in the braking circuit wire, which reacts to the control signals from the control unit, so that brake pressure is controlled to avoid brake locking and at the same time give the best possible braking effect, with acceptable leeway for being able to steer (Karlsen 1989).

ABS is available in versions, which work only on front wheels, only on the rear wheels or on all four wheels (Robinson and Duffin 1993, Kahane 1993). On American cars in particular, ABS is used only on the rear wheels on lighter lorries (less than around 4,800 kg), pick-ups, multi-purpose vehicles and 'vans'.

ABS is mandatory within the EU for specific groups of large vehicles (Ross 1993). These have been introduced to improve stability while braking for articulated lorries and truck/trailer combinations, which are assumed to have the greatest problems with stability.

***Disc brakes*** improve a car's handling capability during braking. They enhance resistance to braking losses due to fade or water exposure compared to drum brakes.

### Effect on accidents

The results presented below in Table 4.3.1 are based on the following studies:

Aschenbrenner, Biehl and Wurm (1987) (Germany): cars
Kahane (1993) (USA): smaller lorries and multi-purpose vehicles
Kahane (1994a) (USA): cars
Hertz, Hilton and Johnson (1995a) (USA): cars
Hertz, Hilton and Johnson (1995b) (USA): smaller lorries and multi-purpose vehicles
Highway Loss Data Institute (1995) (USA): cars
Evans and Gerrish (1996) (USA): cars

A distinction is made between effects on cars and effects on other light vehicles (pick-ups, smaller lorries and multi-purpose vehicles).

A relatively small, but statistically significant reduction in the total number of accidents was found for cars equipped with ABS. Statistically significant increases were found for fatal accidents, rollover, single-vehicle accidents and collisions with fixed objects. Statistically significant decreases were found for collisions with pedestrians/cyclists/animals and collisions involving turning vehicles. ABS does not appear to have any effect on rear-end collisions. A study, which examined this type of accident more in detail (Evans and Gerrish 1996), shows that ABS reduces the risk of driving into a vehicle in front by 32%, but increases the risk of being hit from behind by another vehicle by 30%. The net effect for accidents where vehicles are hit from behind is therefore close to zero.

The results from most of the studies summarised in Table 4.3.1 refer to accident rates of cars with ABS vs. cars without ABS. Other differences between cars with and without ABS or between drivers of different types of cars are not controlled for. Only one of the studies (Cummings and Grossman 2007) has controlled for a number of other factors, such as vehicle weight and registration year and prior accidents. This study has investigated the effects on injury accidents with passenger cars. Without controlling for any confounding factors, there were 19% fewer injury accidents per car equipped with ABS (95% CI [−25; −13]). When controlling for confounding variables,

*Table 4.3.1: Effects of ABS on the number of accidents*

| | Percentage change in the number of accidents | | |
|---|---|---|---|
| Accident severity | Type of accident affected | Best estimate | 95% confidence interval |
| ***ABS on cars*** | | | |
| Unspecified | All accidents with cars | −4 | (−5; −3) |
| Injury accidents | All accidents with cars | −1 | (−5; +4) |
| Fatal accidents | All accidents with cars | +6 | (+1; +12) |
| Unspecified | Rollover | +22 | (+11; +34) |
| Unspecified | Single-vehicle accidents (no rollover) | +15 | (+9; +22) |
| Unspecified | Intersection accidents | −2 | (−5; +1) |
| Unspecified | Rear-end collisions | −1 | (−5; +3) |
| Unspecified | Collisions with fixed objects | +14 | (+11; +18) |
| Unspecified | Collisions with turning vehicles | −8 | (−14; −1) |
| Unspecified | Pedestrians/cyclists/animals | −27 | (−40; −12) |
| ***ABS on pick-ups/multi-purpose vehicles/vans*** | | | |
| Unspecified | All accidents with other light vehicles | −7 | (−8; −6) |
| Fatal accidents | All accidents with other light vehicles | +14 | (+11; +18) |
| Fatal accidents | All accidents with pick-up trucks | +10 | (+5; +15) |
| Fatal accidents | Accidents with multi-purpose vehicles | +11 | (−1; +23) |
| Fatal accidents | Accidents with vans | +12 | (0; +26) |
| Unspecified | Rollover | −21 | (−25; −16) |
| Unspecified | Intersection accidents | +3 | (−1; +8) |
| Unspecified | Head-on collisions | +7 | (−3; +18) |
| Unspecified | Rear-end collisions | +16 | (+12; +21) |
| Unspecified | Collisions with fixed objects | −6 | (−8; −3) |
| Unspecified | Collisions with vehicles which are turning | +9 | (+2; +17) |
| Unspecified | Pedestrians/cyclists/animals | −12 | (−15; −8) |

there were 6% more injury accidents with cars equipped with ABS, compared to cars without ABS (95% CI [−5; +17]).

For other light vehicles, a statistically significant decrease in the total number of accidents was found. The increase in fatal accidents is most marked for pick-up vehicles, but is close to statistical significance for vans and multi-purpose vehicles as well. Collisions involving pedestrians/cyclists/animals were found to decrease. The other statistically significant changes in the number of accidents for the pick-up groups, however, go in the opposite direction to the results for cars. There is a decrease in rollovers and in collisions with fixed objects, while collisions involving turning vehicles appear to increase. Rear-end collisions also show a relatively large increase while for cars there was hardly any change at all.

How can these apparently conflicting effects be explained? One possible explanation is the lack of control for confounding factors in most studies.

Another possible explanation is provided by the study by Aschenbrenner, Biehl and Wurm (1987), which indicates that ABS may lead to changes in behaviour in the form of higher speeds and more aggressive driving. The study was made in a taxi company in Munich with two groups of taxis, where the only difference between the groups is whether they were equipped with ABS or not. The taxi drivers were randomly distributed between the groups and told which type of braking system the car had. Their behaviour in traffic was recorded by observers posing as passengers. They drove the same route – a total of 113 trips – distributed equally between taxis with and taxis without ABS. Statistically significant differences in a total of 4 out of 18 types of behaviour were observed. Among the drivers of cars with ABS, it was found that they were less likely to remain within their traffic lane, 'cut corners' to a large extent, were less able to predict changes in traffic, and were more often involved in conflict situations.

One should not rule out the possibility that the results presented here may be partly due to a lack of knowledge or incorrect assumptions among car drivers about how ABS actually function. It is a serious misconception if drivers believe that the main objective of ABS brakes is to reduce stopping distances (Kahane 1994a). ABS only gives a significant reduction in stopping distances under certain road and driving conditions, while stopping distances increase under other conditions. The main purpose of ABS is not to reduce the stopping distance, but to prevent skidding, where loss of steering and control result from locked wheels when braking hard.

***Effect of disc brakes.*** An American study (Kahane 1983a) concluded that cars with disc brakes were involved in 0.17% fewer accidents (−0.10%; −0.24%) than cars without disc brakes. The basis for this figure are changes in the number of accidents, which were caused by brake failure before and after disc brakes were made mandatory in new cars in the United States.

**Effect on mobility**

ABS has no documented effects on mobility.

**Effect on the environment**

ABS has no documented effects on the environment.

### Costs

Few cost figures are available for ABS. A Norwegian report on car policy from 1984 (NOU 1984, 6) raises the question of tax rebates for safety equipment in cars. A tax rebate of NOK 2,500 (1978 prices) for ABS brakes on cars was proposed. Converted to 1995 prices, this corresponds to NOK 6,780. The technology has developed since 1978 and ABS brakes have become more common, so that the costs will probably be much lower. A reasonable estimate of the additional cost of equipping a car with ABS is NOK 5,000. Based on American figures (Kahane 1983a), the cost of disc brakes can be estimated to around NOK 300 per car.

### Cost–benefit analysis

No cost–benefit analyses of ABS have been found. Therefore, a numerical example has been worked out for cars to indicate costs and benefits. For a car with an average annual mileage, the number of injury accidents reported to the police where a car is involved is estimated to around 0.0058 per car per year. It is assumed that ABS reduces this figure by 5%, i.e. 0.00029 accidents prevented per year. This corresponds to around NOK 340 in reduced accident costs per year. In addition, it is assumed that ABS reduces the number of property-damage-only accidents by around 3%. This corresponds to around NOK 30 in reduced compensation payments per car per year. The cost of ABS given as an annuity over a 15-year lifetime for the car is NOK 550. The benefit is around NOK 370. This gives a benefit–cost ratio of around 0.7.

If cars with disc brakes are involved in 0.17% fewer accidents than cars without them, this corresponds to 0.00001 avoided accidents prevented per car per year. The reduced accident costs are around NOK 12 per car per year, which gives a present value of NOK 110 for a 15-year lifetime for a car. The cost of the measure is around NOK 300 per car. The benefit is clearly smaller than the costs.

## 4.4 High-mounted stop lamps

### Problem and objective

The number of accidents involving rear-end collisions increased strongly in the latter half of the 1980s in Norway, but has later stabilised. Such accidents now comprise around 13% of all injury accidents reported to the police. A factor contributing to such accidents may be, in addition to increased traffic density, that the car in front is not noticed quickly enough when the driver brakes. A normal stop lamp (brake lamp) is usually only visible to the car immediately behind that car in a queue. When driving in queues, this means that the driver's delayed reaction spreads backwards through the queue, so that the available reaction time becomes shorter and shorter for each car, the further back it is in the queue. It may be therefore be difficult to avoid rear-end collisions. Use of daytime running lights may also make stop lamps more difficult to notice. On some cars, taillights and stop lamps are located in the same place, but shine with different intensities.

Installing high-mounted stop lamps can counteract these problems. The objective of high-mounted stop lamps is reduce the number of accidents involving rear-end collisions by making it easier to see when the car in front brakes.

**Description of measure**

The most common form of extra, high-mounted stop lamps is a single, extra, centrally located lamp, which is installed either at the top or the bottom of the rear windscreen. High-mounted stop lamps are standard equipment on certain models of cars, but are not mandatory in Norway. In the United States, high-mounted stop lamps have been required on all new cars from 1986.

**Effect on accidents**

The results presented here are based on the following studies:

Malone, Kirkpatrick, Kohl and Baker (1978) (USA)
Reilly, Kurke and Buckenmaier (1980) (USA)
Rausch, Wong and Kirkpatrick (1982) (USA)
Marburger (1983) (Germany)
Kahane (1989a) (USA)
Farmer (1996) (USA)

The first three studies were experiments with taxis in city traffic. They found that high-mounted stop lamps reduced the number of rear-end collisions by around 50%. Subsequent studies show much smaller effects. The best estimate of the effect of one high-mounted stop lamp is currently a 14% decrease in rear-end collisions (−15%; −13%). The best estimate for the effect of two high-mounted stop lamps is a 9% decrease in rear-end collisions (−13%; −4%). The figures for the decrease in accidents refer to cars with high-mounted stop lamps compared with cars without these. They refer to injury accidents and property-damage-only accidents, taken together.

## Effect on mobility

No effects on mobility of high-mounted stop lamps have been documented.

## Effect on the environment

No effects on the environment of high-mounted stop lamps have been documented.

## Costs

Installation of high-mounted stop lamps costs around NOK 200–300 per car.

## Cost–benefit analysis

A number of cost–benefit analyses of high-mounted stop lamps have been reported. A Danish cost–benefit analysis (Somers and Hansen 1984) estimated the cost of equipping all cars in Denmark with high-mounted stop lamps at DKK 201.5 million. The annual additional costs of equipping new cars only with high-mounted stop lamps were estimated to be DKK 12 million, the present value of which for 17 years (the time it takes to change the whole car stock) with 6% annual interest is around DKK125 million. The present value of the benefit of fewer accidents calculated over 17 years with 6% annual interest was estimated to be DKK 133.2 million, if all cars were equipped with high-mounted stop lamps and DKK 72.0 million if new cars only were equipped with high-mounted stop lamps. These results assume a 15% decrease in accidents. The benefit of fewer accidents is, according to this calculation, smaller than the cost of the measure.

A Finnish cost–benefit analysis (Salusjärvi and Potinkara 1987) concluded that one high-mounted stop lamp on new cars only is cost-effective if the decrease in rear-end collisions exceeds 15% in Denmark, 11% in Finland, 7% in Norway and 13% in Sweden. One high-mounted stop lamp is cost-effective on all cars if the decrease in rear-end collisions exceeds 17% in Denmark, 11% in Finland, 8% in Norway and 15% in Sweden.

An American cost–benefit analysis (Kahane 1989a) concluded that the annual costs of compulsory high-mounted stop lamps were $105 million and the annual benefits were $ 910 million. This gives a benefit–cost ratio of around 8.7.

In Norway, around 36% of cars are equipped with high-mounted stop lamps. It would cost around NOK 265 million to equip the remaining 64% of cars with high-mounted stop lamps (one-time cost). Assuming a 14% effect on accidents, this can reduce the number of accidents reported to the police involving rear-end collisions by around 100 per year. The present value of reduced costs of these accidents, calculated over 7.5 years (it is assumed that retrospective fitting of high-mounted stop lamps on cars initially affects older cars, with a shorter remaining lifetime than new cars) at 7% interest per year is around NOK 625 million. To this should be added the reduced costs of property-damage-only accidents, which can be estimated at around NOK 470 million. The total benefit is NOK 1,095 million. This gives a benefit–cost ratio of around 4.1.

## 4.5 Daytime running lights for cars

### Problem and objective

Many traffic accidents occur because road users do not notice each other in time or do not notice each other at all. This is true both for traffic accidents in darkness and traffic accidents in daylight. Vehicle visibility is therefore one of the factors affecting the number of accidents (Attwood 1981, Helmers 1988, Rumar 1980). The eye reacts to contrasts and changes in contrast in the field of vision. When light conditions are particularly difficult, such as at dusk, in rain or in fog, it becomes difficult to see all traffic elements. Driving into the sun when it is low above the horizon also makes it difficult to distinguish different traffic elements from the surroundings. Such sight conditions are more common in countries at Nordic degrees of latitude than in other countries (Koornstra 1993, Nordisk Trafikksikkerhetsråd 1976).

Use of daytime running lights for cars in all light conditions is intended to reduce the number of multi-vehicle accidents by increasing the cars' visibility and making them easier notice in good time.

### Description of the measure

That Norwegian rules of the road §15 contain the following: 'When driving motor vehicles, dipped beam headlights, full beam headlights or approved daytime running lights must always be used.' Vehicles include cars, mopeds and motorcycles. The effects of daytime running lights on mopeds and motorcycles are dealt with in Section 4.6. For new cars, mandatory daytime running lights were introduced in Norway from 1 January 1985 in the form of mandatory use of automatic daytime running lights. Mandatory use of running lights on all cars was introduced on 1 April 1988. The use of daytime running light increased to about 90–95% in 1989–90, compared to 60–65% in 1984–85 and 30–35% in 1980–81 (Elvik 1993, Vaaje 1986).

**Effect on accidents**

A number of studies have evaluated the effects on accidents of daytime running lights on cars. The results presented here are based on the following studies:

Allen and Clark (1964) (USA)
Cantilli (1965) (USA)
Cantilli (1970) (USA)
Andersson, Nilsson and Salusjärvi (1976) (Finland)
Andersson and Nilsson (1981) (Sweden)
Attwood (1981) (Canada and USA)
Stein (1985) (USA)
Vaaje (1986) (Norway)
Sparks, Neudorf and Smith (1989) (Canada)
Schützenhöfer et al. (1990) (Austria)
Hocherman and Hakkert (1991) (Israel)
Elvik (1993) (Norway)
Hansen (1993) (Denmark)
Kuratorium für Verkehrssicherheit (1993) (Austria)
Sparks et al. (1993) (Canada)
Arora et al. (1994) (Canada)
Hansen (1995) (Denmark)
Hollo (1995) (Hungary)
Tofflemire and Whitehead (1997) (Canada)
Hollo (1998) (Hungary)
National Highway Traffic Safety Administration (2000) (USA)
Bergkvist (2001) (USA)
Farmer and Williams (2002) (USA)
Lassarre (2002) (France)
Thompson (2003) (USA)

There are two types of studies. One type tries to determine at the effect on the accident rate for each car of using daytime running lights. The other type of study investigates the effect on the total number of accidents in a country where the use of running lights in daylight is mandatory. Countries presently requiring the use of daytime running lights are Canada (new cars only), Denmark, Finland, Norway, Sweden and Hungary.

*Table 4.5.1: Effects on accidents of using or requiring the use of daytime running lights*

| | Percentage change in the number of accidents | | |
|---|---|---|---|
| Accident severity | Types of accidents affected | Best estimate | 95% confidence interval |
| ***Mandatory daytime running light*** | | | |
| Injury accidents | Pedestrian hit by car | −6 | (−18, +7) |
| Injury accidents | Cyclist hit by car | −10 | (−23, +4) |
| Injury accidents | Front or side collision | −8 | (−12, −5) |
| Injury accidents | Rear-end collisions | +7 | (−1, +14) |
| Injury accidents | Motorcycle hit by car | +3 | (−11, +19) |
| Injury accidents | Multi-vehicle accidents in daylight | −5 | (−9, −1) |
| ***Using daytime running light*** | | | |
| Injury accidents | Pedestrian hit by car | −24 | (−37, −10) |
| Injury accidents | Front or side collision | −10 | (−18, −1) |
| Injury accidents | Rear-end collisions | −14 | (−26, 0) |
| Injury accidents | Multi-vehicle accidents in daylight | −6 | (−9, −3) |

On the basis of the studies mentioned above, the best estimates of the effects on accidents of using or requiring the use of running lights during the day are given in Table 4.5.1.

Use of daytime running lights reduces the number of multi-vehicle accidents by around 6%. The effect is the same for property-damage-only accidents as for injury accidents. Introducing mandatory use of running lights reduces the number of multi-vehicle accidents in daylight by around 5%. The effect varies between different types of accidents. The number of accidents where pedestrians and cyclists are involved is reduced. The same applies to the number of head-on collisions or side impacts between cars.

The figures given above for the effect of mandatory use of daytime running lights refer to an increase in the use of daytime running lights from around 35–40% to around 85–90%. This is representative of the increasing use of daytime running lights found in the Nordic countries following the introduction of mandatory use of running lights.

### Effect on mobility

No effect on mobility of the daytime running lights for cars has been found.

### Effect on the environment

The use of running lights leads to an increase in fuel consumption of around 1–2% (Glad, Assum and Bjørgum 1985). This can lead to increased exhaust emission. Measurements taken at the Technological Institute in Norway (Ørjasæter and Bang 1993) found that the emission of CO (carbon monoxide), HC (hydrocarbons) and $CO_2$ (carbon dioxide) in grams per car with daytime running lights was 0–2% higher than the emission in grams per car without running lights. For $NO_x$ (nitrogen oxide), three out of four measurements found increases in emissions varying between 12% and 29%, while the fourth measurement found a decrease of 7%. On average, the increase was around 14%. None of these changes in exhaust emissions was statistically significant, but the results indicate that the use of running lights may increase the emission of $NO_x$.

### Costs

The direct costs of using running lights in daytime are relatively small. European Transport Safety Council has estimated the costs as follows (ETSC 2003, Table 4.5.2). These estimates are based on the assumption that the regular front lights are used as daytime running lights. Fuel costs are estimated as societal costs, i.e. without taxes.

### Cost–benefit analysis

Assuming 95% of cars in Norway regularly use headlights in daytime and that the average cost per car for this is NOK 145, the total costs of mandatory use of running lights in 2003 was around NOK 305 million. It can further be assumed that around 50% of injury accidents reported to the police, i.e. around 4,300 accidents a year, are multi-vehicle accidents in daylight. A 95% use of running lights can be assumed to lead a 10% lower number of multi-vehicle accidents in daylight than the figure would

*Table 4.5.2: Costs of using daytime running lights (ETSC 2003)*

| Cost component | Average annual cost per vehicle (NOK) |
|---|---|
| Increased fuel consumption (1.6% per light vehicle) | 90 |
| Increased fuel consumption (0.7% per heavy vehicle) | 280 |
| Increased main headlight bulb usage | 50 |
| Total annual costs per light vehicle | 140 |
| Total annual costs per heavy vehicle | 330 |
| Average annual costs per vehicle | 145 |

*Table 4.5.3: Costs and benefits of using daytime running lights*

| Cost and benefit components | Cost per year (million NOK; 2003 prices) |
|---|---|
| Injury accidents prevented | 740 |
| Property damage only accidents prevented | 170 |
| Sum accidents prevented | 910 |
| Costs of increased emissions | 120 |
| Total benefits | 790 |
| Costs of using daytime running lights | 305 |

otherwise be. If no cars in Norway used daytime running lights, there would have been around 215 more multi-vehicle accidents in daylight than there is today. The cost of these accidents can be estimated to around NOK 740 million per year. To this must be added the benefit of preventing property-damage-only accidents, estimated to NOK 170 million per year. It is additionally assumed that the increase of emissions due to the use of daytime running lights is proportional to the increase of fuel consumption. Based on Eriksen, Markussen and Pütz (1999), the annual costs of increased emissions are estimated at NOK 120 million. This gives the following costs and benefits of mandatory use of daytime running lights (Table 4.5.3). The benefit of the measure is estimated to be around 2.5 times as great as the cost.

## 4.6 Daytime running lights for mopeds and motorcycles

### Problem and objectives

Mopeds and motorcycles are more difficult to see in traffic than cars, partly because they are smaller. A number of studies (Dahlstedt 1986, Janoff, Cassel, Fertner and Smierciak 1970, Olson 1989, Thomson 1980, Williams and Hoffman 1979, Wulf, Hancock and Rahimi 1989) indicate that poor visibility is a contributing factor to many accidents involving mopeds or motorcycles. Moped and motorcycle visibility can be increased in a number of ways. One of these is the use of daytime running lights. The objective of mandatory use of daytime running lights for motorcycles is to reduce the number of accidents by making it easier to see motorcycles in traffic.

### Description of the measure

The mandatory use of daytime running lights was introduced for mopeds and motorcycles in Norway on 1 October 1978. Similar laws have been introduced in a number of other places, including the Nordic and other European countries, many American states and in Malaysia. Roadside surveys carried out before the introduction of mandatory use of daytime running lights on mopeds and motorcycles in Norway in 1978 found that 29% of mopeds and motorcycles used daytime running lights (Muskaug et al. 1979). Immediately after mandatory use was introduced, this increased to 75%. In the period between February and June 1979, use of daytime running lights was on average 57%. More recent figures are not available. It is likely that the current use of daytime running lights on mopeds and motorcycles is between 90% and 100%.

**Effect on accidents**

A number of studies have evaluated the effect on accidents of using daytime running lights on mopeds and motorcycles. The results presented here are based on the following studies:

Janoff, Cassel, Fertner and Smierciak (1970) (USA)
Robertson (1976) (USA)
Vaughan, Pettigrew and Lukin (1977) (Australia)
Lalani and Holden (1978) (Great Britain)
Hurt, Ouellet and Thom (1981) (USA)
Waller and Griffin (1981) (USA)
Muller (1982) (USA)
Muller (1983) (USA)
Muller (1984) (USA)
Muller (1985) (USA)
Zador (1985) (USA)
Radin Umar, Mackay and Hills (1995) (Malaysia)
Radin Umar, Mackay and Hills (1996) (Malaysia)
Haworth, Smith, Brumen and Pronk (1997) (Australia)
Bijleveld (1997) (Austria and Denmark)
Yuan (2000) (Singapore)

There are two types of studies. One type tries to determine at the effect on the accident rate for each motorcycle of using daytime running lights (individual effect). Only few and methodologically weak studies have investigated this effect. Based on the best of these studies, the individual effect is estimated at a reduction of multi-vehicle accidents with mopeds or motorcycles at daylight by about 32%. This estimate is statistically not significant (95% CI [−64%; +28%]).

The other type of study investigates the effect on the total number of accidents in a country where the use of running lights in daylight is mandatory for motorcycles. The majority of studies concern the effects of mandatory use of daytime running lights in some states in the USA. Only few of these studies report the proportion of mopeds and motorcycles using daytime running lights or the change in the proportion of mopeds and motorcycles using daytime running lights. The average effect of making the use of running lights on mopeds and motorcycles mandatory is a reduction of around 7% (±2%) in the number of multi-vehicle accidents in daylight.

**Effect on mobility**

No effects on mobility of using daytime running lights on mopeds and motorcycles have been documented.

**Effect on the environment**

No effects on the environment of using daytime running lights on mopeds and motorcycles have been documented.

**Costs**

The European Transport Safety Council has estimated the costs as follows (ETSC 2003) has estimated the annual costs of using daytime running lights for mopeds and motorcycles at about NOK 80 per moped or motorcycle.

**Cost–benefit analysis**

The annual expected number of injury accidents for a moped rider in Norway with an average annual mileage (3,200 km; Rideng 1995) is around 0.005. The corresponding figure for a motorcyclist with an average annual mileage is around 0.01. These figures represent the risk level in a traffic system where the great majority uses daytime running lights. On the basis of the results presented above, it is assumed that the expected number of accidents per moped rider or per motorcyclist if running lights were not used would have been 3% higher than it is today. This equals an increase of 0.00015 injuries per moped rider per year and 0.0003 injuries per motorcyclist per year. The costs of these injuries are respectively NOK 300 and NOK 600 per year. The annual additional costs of using daytime running lights are lower than the benefits in terms of reduced injuries.

## 4.7 Improving vehicle headlights

### Problem and objective

When driving in the dark on roads without street lighting, drivers can only see that part of the road, which is lit by the headlights. At the same time, the eye's ability to discern contrasts is poorer than in daylight. One of the greatest problems of traffic in the dark is the short detection and sight distances between vehicles, and between vehicles and other road users. In such situations, increasing headlight strength helps little, since the oncoming driver will be subject to proportionally more glare.

The accident rate in the dark, according to Swedish studies, is between 1.5 and 2 times higher than in daytime (Brüde, Larsson and Thulin 1980). For pedestrians, the accident rate in the dark increases even more (Ward et al. 1994). There is reason to believe that similar conditions apply in Norway (Bjørnskau 1993). Around 30% of the injury accidents reported to the police occur in the dark. American studies indicate that most driving in the dark is done with dipped headlights (Hisdal 1974a). When driving with dipped headlights, the sight distance is around 30–50 m depending on whether the headlights are correctly adjusted or not. At a speed of 50 km/h, this means that the driver has less than 4 s to stop the car if an unexpected obstacle appears in the road. At higher speeds, the time available is even shorter.

Improving car headlights is intended to give the driver sufficient view of the road ahead without causing glare to other road users, and to make cars easier to see during difficult sight conditions.

### Description of the measure

Improving vehicle headlights includes a number of measures, which can make cars and other road users easy to see, and measures that improve the function of the car headlights.

***Self-levelling headlights*** are equipped with automatic light fitting mechanisms, which ensure that the headlights are correctly adjusted, no matter how the car is loaded (Yerrell 1971, Hisdal 1975). A common error of manually adjusted headlights is that the lights are wrongly aimed, i.e. the light shines up or down too much. Upward-angled lights dazzle other road users, while downward-angled lights reduce the driver's view.

***Headlight washers*** have a spray system and wipers, which clean the headlight glass while driving. Headlight washers are particularly useful when driving on a salted, wet road in winter, when studded tyres are used.

***Halogen lamps*** were introduced in 1959. They have a considerably longer lifetime than other lamps, produce 100% more light and maintain constant light levels throughout the lifetime of the bulb. Traditional filament lamps lose their brightness due to dirt on the inside of the headlight glass. Today, halogen lamps are standard on all cars.

***Dipped headlights***. There are two types of dipped headlights systems, the European system and the American system. The European dipped headlight has a sharp contrast between the lit area and the unlit area. The right-hand light is angled upwards by about 15° to illuminate the edge of the road further ahead than the left-hand light. This is done to make it easier to detect obstacles along the right-hand roadside. The sharp contrast between the lit and unlit areas characterising European dipped headlight systems makes it important that the headlights are correctly aimed. Incorrectly aimed lights can dazzle or may reduce sight distances. American dipped headlights (sealed beam headlights) have a less marked contrast between the lit and the unlit areas, but give stronger light than European dipped headlights. American dipped headlights are less sensitive to incorrect installation than European ones. The differences between the two systems have become smaller over time (Hisdal 1974a). Dipped headlights illuminate the road for 30–50 m in front of the car, while full beam headlights illuminate 100–500 m of road. By increasing the strength of the light, sight distances can be increased, but with an increased chance of dazzling other road users. The net effect depends on whether the advantage of increased sight is greater than the disadvantage of increased dazzle.

***Polarised light*** is filtered light that increases sight. The light is transmitted to a so-called polarisator. One problem with polarised light is the increased dazzle effect for pedestrians, cyclists and other vehicles, which are not equipped with polarisation filters. To avoid being dazzled, special glasses must be worn.

***Curve-fog lamps*** are special lights, which are designed to increase visibility in dense fog. Water droplets in the fog spread the light from standard headlights so that it becomes weaker (Hisdal 1974b). When fog is dense, the effects of standard headlights will be considerably weaker. Special lights, which are mounted low on the vehicle and have a large lateral dispersion, will throw more light on to the carriageway and the roadside near the car. Due to their wide light dispersion, these lights can also help when driving in the dark on sharp curves. This is why they are called curve-fog lamps.

***Emergency signal lights*** use all the direction indicator lights on the car simultaneously to warn of an emergency situation, for example, an emergency stop on the carriageway. Emergency signal lights are mandatory in all cars.

***Vehicle encounter lights.*** When facing oncoming cars in the dark, it is usual to change from full beam to dipped beam in good time before the full beam starts to dazzle the oncoming vehicle (Bjørnskau 1989, 1994a). This can lead to unnecessarily poor visibility conditions. As a result, special vehicle encounter lights have been developed, as well as mechanisms, which delay dipping headlights to give drivers better sight conditions.

Attempts to solve the problem of dipped headlights in oncoming traffic have been made by developing a ***polyellipsoidal light***. This is a light where the transition between lit and unlit areas is even more distinct than with standard European dipped lights (Helmers, Fernlund and Ytterbom 1990). The light intensity in the lit area is stronger than with standard dipped lights.

***Ultraviolet light (UV light)*** is light transmitted by means of shorter wavelengths than the wavelength area, which can be discerned by the human eye. In other words, ultraviolet light is a form of 'invisible light'. This light can reflect from fluorescent (self-lighting) material or material that has some of these characteristics. For example, by using road markings, delineator posts and other objects, which are marked with fluorescent materials or which naturally contain these, they become visible to the car driver long before they are lit by standard dipped headlights.

## Effect on accidents

***Detection distances as an indirect measurement of safety.*** The effects on accidents of the great majority of the measures described above have not been studied. The normal experimental set-up for studying the effects of detection distances is shown in Figure 4.7.1.

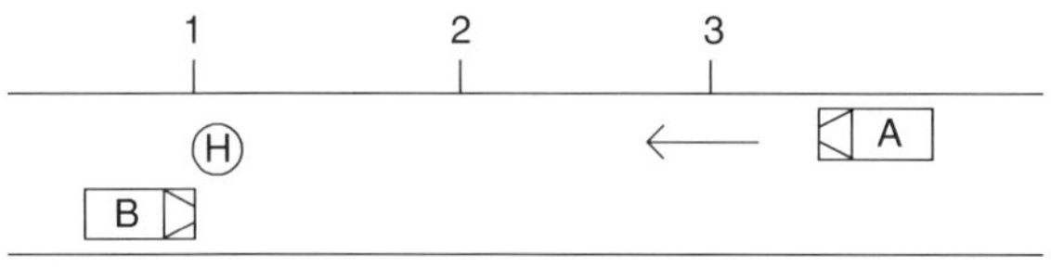


*Figure 4.7.1: Experimental set-up for studying detection distances to obstacles on the carriageway in the dark.*

It is usual to experimentally manipulate two different situations. The most common situation is the '*obstacle in traffic lane*'. Two cars participate in this situation, cars A and car B. Car B is parked while car A drives at a given speed towards car B. At different points in car A's traffic lane, e.g. at point 1, 2 or 3 an obstacle H is placed, for example in the form of a doll lying in the road. The distances 1, 2 or 3 between car B and the obstacle vary between the tests. It is common to place the obstacles either in line with car B, i.e. at point 1 or somewhere in front of car B, e.g. at point 2. The tests measure detection distances between car A and obstacle H under different experimental conditions. The detection distance between car A and obstacle H is the distance between the two when the driver of car A first notices the obstacle. Reference points 1, 2 and 3 are used to measure this distance. The other situation, which has been studied, is '*visibility with full beam headlights*'. Car B does not participate in the test. Car A drives with full beam headlights towards the obstacle H and the detection distance is measured in the same way as for the oncoming obstacle.

Two conditions have been varied experimentally. One is the location of obstacle H in relation to the oncoming car B. The other is lighting equipment on cars A and B. For the latter, four experimental conditions can be distinguished: (1) both cars A and car B are equipped with standard headlights, (2) only car A is equipped with improved headlights, (3) only car B is equipped with improved headlights, (4) both cars are equipped with improved headlights. Here, situation 1 can be regarded as descriptive of the traffic situation before the improved headlights are brought into use. Situations 2 and 3 can be regarded as typical for a traffic situation where 50% of the cars have improved headlamps, and situation 4 can be regarded as typical of a traffic situation where all cars have improved headlamps.

A number of studies have been carried out, especially in Sweden, where the effect of different types of improved lighting equipment on cars on detection distances to obstacles is studied using the method described above. The detection distance to an obstacle can be interpreted as an indication of the safety margin while driving. In this case, the inverse value of the detection distance can be interpreted as an indicator of the potential accident risk:

$$\text{Potential accident risk} = \frac{1}{\text{Detection distance}}$$

If a specific type of lighting equipment increases the detection distance from, e.g. 70 to 90 m, the potential accident risk is reduced from $1/70 = 0.0143$ to $1/90 = 0.0111$, i.e. around 22% ($0.0111/0.0143 = 0.778$). The next section shows the effects of different types of headlights on potential accident risk measured in this way.

One should be aware that this indicator of the potential effect of the measure has great limitations and does not necessarily show the effect the equipment would have on accidents if it were adopted in real traffic. The most important limitation is that the effect only has been studied in a handful of simple and artificial traffic situations. These do not reflect the endless variety of real traffic situations. In real traffic situations, visual pollution and distractions will often occur, which are not found in well-controlled experimental situations. Furthermore, drivers are often unprepared for the situation, in contrast to the tests, where the drivers were prepared for an obstacle to appear. In the tests, the drivers were instructed to maintain a constant speed. In real traffic, it is possible that improved headlights may cause drivers to increase their speed or reduce their alertness. Thus, the safety margin may be reduced.

For these reasons, the effects on potential accident risk, as it is defined above, should be regarded as maximum estimates of the effects of different improvements to headlights on the actual accident rate if the equipment were introduced into normal traffic.

***Effect of improved headlights on detection distances (potential accident risk).*** The effect of different types of improved headlights on detection distances (potential accident risk) have been studied by:

Rumar and Johansson (1964) (Sweden): lamp adjustment
Rumar (1968) (Sweden): halogen lamps
Johansson, Rumar, Forsgren and Snöborgs (1969a) (Sweden): light intensity and polarised light
Johansson, Rumar, Forsgren and Snöborgs (1969b) (Sweden): light intensity and polarised light
Rumar, Helmers and Thorell (1973) (Sweden): American dipped headlights
Helmers and Rumar (1974) (Sweden): light intensity
Hisdal (1974b) (Norway): curve/fog lamps
Knoblauch and Tobey (1980) (USA): emergency signal lights
Helmers and Ytterbom (1984) (Sweden): delayed dipping of full beam headlights
Helmers, Fernlund and Ytterbom (1990) (Sweden): light intensity and polyellipsoidal light
Helmers, Ytterbom and Lundkvist (1993) (Sweden): UV light
Fast (1994) (Sweden): UV light

In addition Cox (1968) and Rumar (1973) have studied the effects of dirt on headlight glass, and thus the potential for improving the situation using headlight washers. Yerrell (1971) has carried out technical tests of the way two mechanisms for

*Table 4.7.1: Effect on potential accident risk rate of improving car headlights*

| | Percentage change in potential accident risk | |
|---|---|---|
| Type of headlight improvement | Best estimate | 95% confidence interval |
| Self-levelling headlights | −15 | (−22; −8) |
| Halogen lamps | −7 | (−9; −5) |
| American dipped headlights (sealed beam) | −23 | (−33; −13) |
| Double light intensity – headlight washers | −5 | (−8; −2) |
| Polarised lights | −29 | (−55; −3) |
| Curve/fog lamps | +6 | (−2; +15) |
| Emergency signal lights | −4 | (−11; +3) |
| Fading full beam | +2 | (−2; +6) |
| Poly-ellipsoidal light | −9 | (−12; −6) |
| Ultraviolet light (UV light) | −24 | (−34; −14) |

self-levelling headlights work. On the basis of these studies, the effect on the potential accident risk of a 100% implementation of the different types of improvement can be estimated as the figures shown in Table 4.7.1 (percentage change in the potential accident risk when driving in the dark).

The effect of ***self-levelling lights*** was estimated on the basis of a study of how the upward or downward angling of headlights affects detection distances. Angle deviations from around 2° downwards to 5° upwards have been studied (Rumar and Johansson 1964). An early study in the Oslo area (Hisdal 1974a) found that the lights on around half the cars had an angle deviation exceeding 0.25°. Downward angling was more common than upward angling. For small installation errors (less than 1°) the effect of self-levelling lights on the detection distance when driving in the dark is smaller than that given above.

***Halogen lamps*** give somewhat greater detection distances than filament lamps. The difference is around 5–10%. American sealed beam dipped headlights increase detection distances by around 20%. It is emphasised that that increased dazzle of pedestrians and cyclists using these lights has not been studied.

Dirt on of headlight glass when driving on roads with large amounts of spray can reduce light intensity by up to 90% (Cox 1968, Rumar 1973). Around 40% of traffic on roads, which are salted in winter in Norway, is on wet, bare roads (Vaa 1995). On unsalted roads, the proportion is around 14%. Under these conditions, headlight glass quickly becomes dirty. The effects of ***headlight washers*** can, according to the studies of the effect of increased light intensity, be estimated to give up to 5% longer detection distances when the light intensity is doubled, ***Polarised light*** lengthens the detection distances by around 30%, but the estimate is very uncertain. In addition, increased dazzle for pedestrians, cyclists, moped riders and motorcyclists has not been taken into account.

***Curve-fog lamps*** do not appear to lengthen detection distances. Observations in fog indicate that the fog needs to be very dense before it becomes more advantageous to use curve/fog lamps than dipped headlights (Hisdal 1974b). If the meteorological sight distance is more 100 m, use of curve/fog lamps will shorten the sight distance.

The effect of ***emergency signal lights*** has been measured using the time to collision as a measure of the safety margin. The time to collision depends on how soon a car is noticed and on how the driver alters his speed after he has noticed a car using emergency signal lights. Cars with emergency signal lights are passed at lower speeds than cars, which are not using these, but the difference is very small.

***Fading full beam*** does not have a favourable effect on detection distances. The increased dazzle caused by these lights more than offsets the advantages of increased sight distances. In Sweden, a special vehicle encounter light has been tested (Morén and Olausson 1986). Essentially, this is an extra full beam headlight, which only lights up on the right side of the road and is not directed towards oncoming traffic. Some 100 professional drivers were asked to evaluate the light after having tested it in normal traffic. More than half thought the light improved sight distances towards oncoming traffic. Interviews were also carried out with some 100 drivers of oncoming vehicles. Thirty percent of these said that the additional light was dazzling. ***Polyellipsoidal lights*** lengthen detection distances by just 10%. Because of the sharp transition between lit and unit areas, however, such lights are very sensitive to adjustments.

***Ultraviolet light*** lengthens detection distances, especially to reflective materials. Light grey and dark materials are detected no earlier with UV light than with ordinary lights.

### Effect on mobility

The effects on mobility of the measures described in this chapter are not known. Measures, which make driving in the dark more comfortable, may lead to more traffic in the dark (changing journey times) and higher speeds.

**Effect on the environment**

No effects on the environment of the measures described in this chapter have been found. For some of the measures, increased dazzle for light traffic (pedestrians, cyclists, moped users and motorcyclists) may be a problem. Additional light equipment on a car leads to increased power consumption and thus greater fuel consumption. This can lead to increased exhaust emission.

**Costs**

The costs of required lights are included in the price of the car and can be difficult to identify. A halogen light bulb for a main headlamp for a car in Norway costs around NOK 50. Where halogen lamps were supplied with the vehicle, the additional cost per set of lights is estimated at around NOK 100–150. Nowadays, it is standard for new cars to be fitted with halogen lamps. Factory-mounted headlamp washers cost around NOK 200–300.

**Cost–benefit analysis**

It is difficult to conduct precise cost–benefit analyses when both the effect on accidents and the costs of the measures are as little known as they are today.

Every year, some 2,800 injury accidents occurring at night are reported to the police in Norway. Assuming that this figure would have been around 5% higher if no cars used halogen lamps would have meant 140 more accidents each year. The annual cost of these accidents is around NOK 280 million. The additional cost per car of halogen lamps is unknown, but from the figures given above, it can be estimated at around NOK 15 per car per year, calculated as an annuity. With 2 million cars, this represents an annual, additional cost of NOK 30 million. This indicates that the benefit of halogen lamps is greater than the costs (280/30 = around 9).

Around 20% of injury accidents reported to the police occur on bare, wet roads. In winter, this corresponds to 600 accidents per year. Assuming that the universal use of headlamp washers can prevent 5% of these accidents, this would prevent 30 accidents per year. The annual cost per car for headlamp washers can be estimated to be NOK 30 (annuity). The total cost is around NOK 60 million. This calculation suggests that the use of headlight washers in Norway can be a cost-effective measure (60/60 = 1.0).

## 4.8 Reflective materials and protective clothing

### Problem and objective

When driving in the dark on roads without street lighting, drivers can only see the part of the road, which is lit by the headlights. At the same time, the eye's ability to discern contrasts is poorer than in daylight. It is particularly difficult to see pedestrians and cyclists in the dark.

Pedestrians, cyclists and people riding mopeds or motorcycles are much more vulnerable to injury in the event of accident than people in cars (see Part I). Around 30% of the injury accidents reported to the police in Norway occur in the dark. The proportion of pedestrian accidents occurring in the dark is close to 40% (Elvik and Muskaug 1994). A Canadian study (Jonah and Engel 1983) shows that pedestrians run more than twice the risk of being injured in the dark compared to daylight. A British study (Ward et al. 1994) shows that pedestrians have a five times higher risk of being injured in the dark than in daylight.

The objective of equipping road users and vehicles with reflective materials is to reduce the probability of accidents by increasing visibility and detection distances. The objective of protective clothing for motorcyclists, cyclists and others in the traffic is to reduce the severity of injuries in the event of accidents.

### Description of the measure

The measures discussed in this chapter include pedestrian reflectors, retro-reflective material on bicycles, retro-reflective number plates and reflectors on the back of cars and protective clothing for motorcyclists.

All types of reflectors designed for use in traffic are made of retro-reflective materials, which reflect light back to the light source. Other materials split the light and reflect only a fraction of it back to the light source (Nordisk trafikksikkerhetsråd 1980). Different types of clothing have different reflective properties. Colour is an important factor determining reflectivity. A dark coat reflects only 5% of the light to which it is exposed, while a light coat reflects around 80% (Trygg Trafikk, emneblokk no. 304, undated). Protective clothing for motorcyclists can lead to increased visibility if textile reflectors are attached. The use of jackets or vests with fluorescent materials increases motorcyclists' visibility in the daylight as well (Fulton, Kirkby and Stroud 1980).

## Effect on accidents

***Pedestrian reflectors.*** Pedestrian reflectors include free-hanging reflectors, permanent textile reflectors and special reflective clothing. Only one study of the effect on pedestrian accidents of pedestrian reflectors has been found. This is a Norwegian study (Elvik 1996a) that has compared pedestrians in traffic and pedestrians in accidents according to the use of reflectors. The study indicates that pedestrian reflectors reduce the risk of pedestrians being run over in the dark by around 85% (−95%; −75%). This large reduction in the accident rate corresponds to the increase in detection distances to pedestrians in the dark by the use of reflectors.

Pedestrians with reflectors can be seen by car drivers at considerably greater distances than pedestrians without reflectors (Nordisk trafikksikkerhetsråd 1975, Blomberg, Hale and Preusser 1984). When using dipped headlights, the detection distance on unlit roads increases from 25–40 m to 130–140 m. When full beam headlights are used, the detection distance increases to more than 400 m.

***Retro-reflective materials on bicycles.*** No studies have been found that quantify how the use of retro-reflective materials on bicycles affects the number of bicycle accidents in darkness. However, some studies have investigated effects on detection distances. Blomberg, Hale and Preusser 1984) showed that spoke reflectors do not lead to increased detection or identification distances for bicycles in the dark, but that an ankle light (white light at the front and a red light at the back) increases the detection distance by 5–35%. Reflectors on cyclists' clothing increased detection distances by 5–10%. Burg and Beers (1978) showed that the detection distance is greater for bicicles with spoke reflectors than for bicycles with reflective tyres, but that the proportion who could correctly identify the bicycle, however, was highest when a bicycle had reflective tyres. A British study (Watts 1984a) showed that the passing distance of cars in the dark in relation to cyclists who wore reflective jackets was around 7% greater (1.13 m as opposed to 1.06 m) than the passing distance to cyclists who wore ordinary, dark-coloured jackets.

***Retro-reflective number plates and reflectors on the back of cars*** are intended to increase visibility in order to reduce the probability of a rear-end collision in darkness. Two studies have been found of the effect on accidents of retro-reflective number plates (Campbell and Rouse 1968, Stoke 1975). The estimated summary effect on the total number of accidents (unspecified severity) is a non-significant reduction by 3% (95% CI [−11; +6]). A Dutch study (Tromp and Noordzij 1991) evaluated the effect of mandatory use of reflectors on lorries in the Netherlands from 1980. The estimated summary effect on the total number of accidents (unspecified severity) is a non-significant increase by 3% (95% CI [−2; +8]). In summary, accident numbers do not seem to be significantly affected.

*Table 4.8.1: Effects of protective clothing for motorcyclists on the number of injuries*

| | Percentage change in the number of injuries | | |
|---|---|---|---|
| Type of accident affected | Type of equipment and injury affected | Best estimate | 95% confidence interval |
| Motorcycle accidents | *Gloves:* hand injuries | −50 | (−63; −33) |
| Motorcycle accidents | *Boots:* foot injuries | −33 | (−45; −17) |
| Motorcycle accidents | *Leather jackets or trousers:* arm/leg injuries | −33 | (−50; −10) |

***Protective clothing for motorcyclists*** includes primarily overalls, gloves and boots. Four studies have been found that quantify the effect on the severity of injury in accidents of protective clothing for motorcyclists. The results of these studies are summarised in Table 4.8.1.

Aldman et al. (1981) (Sweden)
Hurt, Ouellet and Thom (1981) (USA)
Danner, Langwieder, Polauke and Sporner (1984) (Germany)
Aldman et al. (1985) (Sweden)

The use of protective clothing reduces the probability of injury in an accident by 33–50%. This applies to the use of gloves, boots and clothing. The effect is greatest for gloves.

### Effect on mobility

No effects on mobility have been found of the measures discussed in this chapter.

### Effect on the environment

The extent to which retro-reflective materials can have a dazzling effect has been discussed. Normal pedestrian reflectors and reflectors on bicycles do not have a dazzling effect. Nor has it been found that retro-reflective number plates have a dazzling effect (Hisdal 1976). Other effects on the environment have not been found.

### Costs

For the most part, reflectors are handed out free in Norway, for example as part of a marketing campaign. The production costs are around NOK 2–3 per reflector.

Reflectors for use on bicycle spokes cost around NOK 30. Bicycles made in Norway are often supplied with spoke reflectors as standard equipment (Nordisk trafikksikkerhetsråd 1980). 'Jogging vests' in fluorescent colours and with reflectors attached come in various forms and cost between NOK 90 and 105. Protective clothing for motorcycles cost ca. NOK 4,000–9,000 per protective suit, NOK 300–1,000 for gloves and NOK 1,300–2,500 for boots (August 1995).

### Cost–benefit analyses

Some numerical examples have been worked out to indicate the costs and benefits of pedestrian reflectors and protective clothing for motorcyclists.

In 1995, 373 pedestrians were injured in injury accidents in darkness in Norway reported to the police (Statistisk sentralbyrå 1996). Information on the use of reflectors is available for 239 accidents, of which 217 were without reflectors and 22 were with reflectors. Assuming that pedestrians whose use of reflectors was not stated are distributed in the same way as those that are known, the number of injured pedestrians not using reflectors is estimated to be around 340. The cost of these accidents is around NOK 870 million per year. A campaign costing, for example NOK 25 million, will be cost-effective if 10 pedestrian accidents in darkness are prevented. This corresponds to the effect of an increase in the use of reflectors of around 5–10%. Motorcyclists have an accident rate, calculated on the basis of official Norwegian accident statistics, of around 1.5 injured persons per million person kilometres for light motorcycles, and around 1.8 injured persons per million person kilometres for heavy motorcycles. The annual average mileage is around 6,800 km for light motorcycles and around 6,000 km for heavy motorcycles. The annual probability of being injured for a motorcyclist with an annual average mileage is therefore around 0.01. This applies to both light and heavy motorcycles. It is not known how many motorcyclists currently use protective clothing. The probability of injury is assumed to be representative for a motorcyclist who does not use protective clothing.

It is assumed that full protective clothing (gloves, boots and leather clothing) can reduce the annual probability of injury by 40%. This corresponds to around 0.004 injuries prevented per motorcyclist per year. The benefit of this is around NOK 5,700 per motorcyclist per year. Buying full protective clothing costs NOK 7,500. Allowing for 10 years depreciation on protective clothing, the present value of injuries prevented is around NOK 40,000 per motorcyclist. This clearly exceeds the costs of buying the equipment (benefit–cost ratio around 5.3).

## 4.9 Steering, suspension and vehicle stability

### Problem and objective

In a critical situation where quick reactions are needed to avoid an accident, a driver has only the steering wheel and the brakes at his disposal. The driver may totally lack experience regarding what must be done to avoid an accident (Allen 1988). In particular, reflex reactions such as panic braking in curves may lead to loss of steering control, resulting in an accident. When manoeuvring in critical situations, the vehicle may behave very differently than in an ideal driving condition. The combination of steering and braking in difficult conditions may lead to the driver losing control of the vehicle.

Official Norwegian accident statistics do not indicate which manoeuvre was being carried out immediately before the accident. The number of rollover accidents is not registered. However, rollover accidents are registered in the USA. The percentage of rollover accidents in the USA is 2.2% for property-damage-only accidents, 3.8% for injury accidents and 11% for fatal accidents (US Department of Transportation, National Highway Traffic Safety Administration 1995). This shows that rolling over increases the severity of an accident. Rollover increases the probability of being thrown out of the car or of being injured through contact with the interior, such as when the roof is compressed. In the USA, faults were found in the steering mechanism in 21% of articulated lorries involved in accidents. The risk of being involved in an accident is twice as high for articulated lorries with steering defects as for articulated lorries without such defects (Jones and Stein 1989).

Steering, suspension and vehicle stability together should be designed so as to make it possible to carry out all normal manoeuvres – and all imaginable crisis manoeuvres – without losing control of the vehicle. Steering, suspension and vehicle stability must be designed so that the probability of accidents resulting from construction faults, wear and tear, poor design and/or the driver's behaviour, is as low as possible.

### Description of the measure

In this chapter, the effect on accidents of the following characteristics of vehicle steering, suspension and stability are described:

- Steering: loss of motion (play) and slack in steering, four-wheel steering
- Suspension: slack in suspension
- Stability: ratio between a vehicle's track width and the centre of gravity (stability index), baffle plates in tankers.

**Effect on accidents**

No numerical estimates of the effect on accidents of the characteristics of vehicles discussed in this chapter are available. The relative risk is partially known. Factors that affect accident rates are also relatively well known.

***Steering***. A car's steering depends on the design, gauge, centre of gravity and the degree of stability, suspension, load and weight distribution. An important factor in the vehicle's steering is the stability ratio, that is to say the relationship between the gauge (width) and the centre of gravity (height). A narrow gauge combined with a high centre of gravity make the vehicle unstable and thus difficult to steer, especially in a critical situation (Allen 1988, Robertson and Kelley 1989, Harwin and Brewer 1991, Whitfield and Jones 1995).

Certain driving conditions may lead to the car losing its road holding so that steering and stability are reduced. In particular, driving on slippery roads when turning can lead to sideways skidding. This is particularly dangerous if the back part skids more than the front, i.e. when the car starts to rotate. It is important that the road holding on the rear wheels is better than on the front wheels at all speeds (Strandberg 1989). Thus, it can be particularly dangerous to drive with tyres where the tyre tread depth is greater on the front wheels than on the rear wheels, for example on ice-covered roads, or in a situation where there is a likelihood of aquaplaning.

Tests made on special test tracks have shown that the risk of losing control of cars is not affected by defects such as loss of motion in the steering wheel and slack in suspension. The ability to steer past unexpected obstacles in the carriageway was about the same as when there was no loss of motion or slack. Drivers of cars with steering wheel play largely compensate for this type of defect (Arnberg and Odsell 1978). It must be emphasised that the loss of motion studied was no greater than can be expected as the result of normal wear and tear. A very large loss of motion in the steering wheel can be dangerous.

An American study found that heavy vehicles with defective steering mechanisms run twice the risk of being involved in accidents as vehicles without defects (odds ratio 2.0, confidence interval 1.2–3.4) (Jones and Stein 1989). For vehicles where the defects in the steering mechanism were so great that they should have been taken out of use, the accident rate was 1.9 times as high as for the vehicles where the steering was in order.

When a car drives through a curve, the rear wheels follow a flatter path than the front wheels. Thus, the car needs extra space. The increased requirement for space increases with increasing axle distance. The space required can be reduced by reducing the axle distance and increasing the overhang. The space requirements for semi-trailers can be reduced by making the rear axle steerable. Steering on rear axles reduce stability. Uneven carriageways affect the vehicle's steering, which is particularly noticeable in curves (Magnusson and Arnberg 1977). On extremely uneven carriageways, a vehicle's steering may be lost completely. The vehicle's characteristics, especially the state of shock absorbers, will be particularly significant in such conditions.

A German evaluation of the possible effects on safety of four-wheel steering (Gies 1991) maintains that four-wheel steering will give better stability when the traffic situation makes sharp turning manoeuvres necessary. However, there is also a danger that such a system may lead to offsetting behavioural adaptation among drivers.

***Suspension***. Tests introducing slack in the suspension system in cars found that this did not reduce driver performance (Arnberg and Odsell 1978). In the study, the amount of slack did not exceed that which could be expected from normal wear and tear. A vehicle's braking ability, as well as its ability to absorb side forces, depends on the friction between tyres and the road. From the point of view of traffic safety, it is therefore important that maximum friction is maintained on uneven roads (Bunis, Mäkiaho and Odsell 1978). A simulation study of trailers' suspension and shock-absorbing characteristics found that these elements cannot be judged separately. It is the combination of suspension and shock absorbers, which determine the road holding of a trailer. A relatively soft suspension gives better road holding when passing over uneven road surfaces than a relatively hard suspension.

In the USA in 1980, there was an extensive discussion of the relative risk of rollover for the Jeep CJ model. The Jeep CJ's relative rollover rate was around 10–20 times higher than for the total car fleet (Robertson 1989). In spite of this, the manufacturers continued to produce models with high centres of gravity in relation to the gauge. The development of better suspension systems has been suggested as a possible explanation of why there is no perfect relationship between the centre of gravity and gauge, and rollover stability.

***Stability***. Accident statistics show that certain types of car are more often involved in rollover accidents than others (Robertson and Kelley 1989, Whitfield and Jones 1995). Rollover stability is particularly important for heavy vehicles, since the consequences of a rollover can be more serious than when a car overturns. Full-scale English tests have shown that a loaded semi-trailer with a centre of gravity 2.5 m above the ground can overturn at a speed of just 24 km/h on a curve with a radius of 20 m (Kemp, Chinn and Brock 1978). A semi-trailer's rollover stability can be increased, e.g. by

- securing unstable loads,
- lowering the centre of gravity in loaded trailers,

- reducing slack/increasing rigidity through a new type of trailer coupling,
- reinforcing suspension on trailers,
- using a system which warns of overturning danger.

Articulated lorries and semi-trailers usually have a higher centre of gravity than cars, which reduces the overturning stability. Furthermore, the centre of gravity can shift in the wrong direction as a result of the wrong placement of goods, or passengers, if the vehicle is designed for passenger transport. Such changes in the centre of gravity can make these vehicles unstable and liable to overturn.

Moving the centre of gravity forwards in articulated lorries will increase stability. The load on each axle should be lower towards the back, but fully loaded trucks should not pull empty trailers and vice versa. Furthermore, more stringent stability requirements are required for trailers than for trucks. The reason is that a trailer's movements are more powerful than those of a truck, for example, in an avoidance manoeuvre (Strandberg 1978). It is not possible for the driver to manoeuvre the whole articulated lorry according to avoid with the load in question.

As far as road tankers are concerned, rollover stability depends first and foremost on the design of the tanker, how full it is, the baffle plates and the control frequency. When the tanker is 100% full, there is little difference in rollover stability between tankers with circular, elliptical or super-elliptical shape (Strandberg 1978). Model studies show that when the tanker is 50% or 70% full, the elliptical tank form with three vertical baffle plates is the most stable against rollover. With vertical, longitudinal baffle plates the fluid movement resonance is shifted to higher frequencies that than those presumably occur in normal traffic (Lindström 1977). High resonance frequencies are obtained with more baffle plates.

Another group of vehicles particularly susceptible to rollover comprises certain models of jeeps, jeep-type multi-purpose vehicles and small pick-up vans. These cars often have a high centre of gravity in relation to their gauge (Whitfield and Jones 1995). A comparison of the risk of rollover between cars in general and specific types of cars such as the Ford Bronco (1974–87) found that the relative risk of rollover was around 6–11 times higher for the Ford Bronco models (Robertson 1989). Jeeps of the Jeep CJ-5 type (1963–87) and Jeep CJ-7 (1976–86) had a rollover rate, which was 20 and 12 times higher, respectively.

Studies of the rollover rate for a number of models of cars have shown that there is a strong relationship between the rollover rate and the ratio between the gauge and the centre of gravity. Wide, low cars have a low risk of rollover, while narrow, high cars have a high risk of rollover (Robertson 1989, Robertson and Kelly 1989, Harwin and

Brewer 1991, Whitfield and Jones 1995). The exact shape of this relationship is affected by a number of variables, including the suspension system, the wheelbase (car length), car mass (weight) and the ratio between the passenger mass and the car mass. Nonetheless, the relationship is robust, and according to one researcher (Robertson 1989), there is a basis for setting formal stability standards for vehicles. There is a strong relationship between axle distance and the risk of rollover (Harwin and Brewer 1990 and 1991). A measure of stability, which is often used, is the ratio between half the vehicle's gauge and the height of the centre of gravity above the ground. Regression analyses show a clear relationship between this figure and the number of single-vehicle rollover accidents (Harwin and Brewer 1990). A stability index figure close to 1 is associated with the highest number of rollover accidents, while the proportion of accidents tends towards zero when the stability index figure tends towards 1.5–1.6. Even though all the studies were carried out in the USA, it is likely that similar relationships will also apply to European and Japanese models.

### Effect on mobility

Heavy vehicles with poor suspension can damage the road surface (Magnusson, Carlsson and Ohlsson 1984). It has been found that pneumatic suspension is gentler to the body of the car and to passengers than more traditional suspensions systems such as leaf spring suspension, but this does not necessarily mean than pneumatic suspension systems are gentle on the road itself (Transport Research Commission 1984). It is the suspensions' damping characteristics and not the type of suspension, which affect the forces transmitted to the road itself. Damage to the road surface increases the need for maintenance, which can affect traffic.

### Effect on the environment

A potential effect on the environment of better stability is a reduction in potential tanker accidents where leakage, which can harm both people and the environment, can occur. This can include leakage of petrol, chlorine and other chemicals, which may be flammable, explosive or otherwise pollute the environment.

### Costs

No data has been found that indicates the costs of improving steering, suspension and vehicle stability.

### Cost–benefit analysis

Using regression analyses, it has been suggested in the USA that improving the static stability by one-tenth could reduce the number of fatal rollover accidents by around 9 per 100,000 registered vehicles (Robertson 1989). However, the costs of such improvements to static stability are not known. The benefit–cost ratio cannot therefore be calculated.

## 4.10 Bicycle helmets

### Problem and objective

Cyclists run a higher risk of being injured in traffic than any other group of road users (Bjørnskau 2000). Based on the national household travel survey 1997–98, the following estimates for the risk of injury, stated in terms of the number of injured people per million person kilometres of travel in Norway, have been developed on the basis of official accident statistics and the injury register at the National Institute for Public Health (SIFF; Table 4.10.1).

The risk of injury to cyclists is about seven times higher than for car drivers, according to official accident statistics. If hospital records are used as a basis, the risk to cyclists is about 50 times as high as for car drivers. This huge difference is due primarily to the fact that single-vehicle accidents, i.e. accidents where no other vehicles or road users are involved other than the cyclist, are hardly reported at all in official accident statistics. Records at a Norwegian hospital (Schrøder Hansen, Hansen, Walløe and Fjeldsgård 1995) showed that around 44% of injured cyclists, who went to hospital for treatment, had head or facial injuries. A bicycle gives no protection in the event of an accident and the probability of sustaining head injuries if one falls off a bicycle is high. By using bicycle helmets, cyclists can protect themselves from head injuries in the event

*Table 4.10.1: Injured drivers/cyclists per million person kilometres in Norway (different sources)*

| | Injured drivers/cyclists per million person kilometres | |
|---|---|---|
| Form of transport | Official accident statistics | SIFF's register (hospital records) |
| Bicycle | 1.24 | 14.98 |
| Moped/motorcycle | 1.30 | 2.13 |
| Car (driver) | 0.18 | 0.30 |

of an accident. The objective of bicycle helmets is to prevent and reduce the severity of injuries amongst cyclists who are involved in accidents.

## Description of the measure

The most common type of bicycle helmets is helmets with a hard shell, i.e. a helmet which consists of an inner, porous layer covered by a hard shell. Soft helmets without a hard shell, i.e. helmets which consist of a porous, protective layer, are less common. Mandatory wearing of bicycle helmets is intended to ensure that a high proportion of cyclist wear helmets.

## Effect on accidents

***Individual effect of wearing a bicycle helmet***. A number of studies have evaluated the effects of bicycle helmets on the probability of sustaining head injuries in bicycle accidents. The results presented here come from the following studies:

Dorsch, Woodward and Somers (1987) (Australia)
Wasserman et al. (1988) (USA)
Thompson, Rivara and Thompson (1989) (USA)
Thompson, Thompson, Rivara and Wolf (1990) (USA)
Wasserman and Buccini (1990) (USA)
Spaite et al. (1991) (USA)
McDermott, Lane, Brazenor and Debney (1993) (Australia)
Thomas et al. (1994) (Australia)
Maimaris, Summer, Browning and Palmer (1994) (Great Britain)
Schrøder Hansen, Hansen, Walløe and Fjeldsgård (1995) (Norway)
Thompson, Rivara and Thompson (1996) (USA)
Thompson, Nunn, Rivara and Thompson (1996) (USA)
Finvers, Strother and Mohtadi (1996) (Canada)
Jacobson, Blizzard and Dwyer (1998) (Australia)
Shafi et al. (1998) (USA)
Linn, Smith and Sheps (1998) (Canada)
Schrøder Hansen, Engesæter and Viste (2003) (Norway)

On the basis of these studies, best estimates of the effect of bicycle helmets on the probability of being injured in a bicycle accident are given in Table 4.10.2. The results refer to effects on both adults and children.

*Table 4.10.2: Effects on injuries of wearing bicycle helmets*

| | Percentage change in the number of injuries | | |
|---|---|---|---|
| Injury severity | Types of injuries affected | Best estimate | 95% confidence interval |
| ***Bicycle helmet (hard)*** | | | |
| Unspecified | Head injuries | −64 | (−73; −51) |
| Unspecified | Facial injuries | −34 | (−52; −9) |
| Unspecified | Neck injuries | +36 | (0; +86) |
| Unspecified | Other than head injuries | +5 | (−14; +28) |
| ***Soft bicycle helmet*** | | | |
| Unspecified | Head injuries | −41 | (−63: −5) |
| Unspecified | Facial injuries | +14 | (−29; +45) |

Hard bicycle helmets were found to reduce the probability of head injuries and, to a lesser degree, of facial injuries. However, these results seem to be affected by publication bias and methodological weaknesses, and they are likely to be affected by time trends that are not controlled for in most studies (Robinson 2001). The results are therefore highly uncertain and the effects are likely to be overestimated.

Bicycle helmets do not prevent injuries on other parts of the body. Neck injuries have been found to increase by 36%. Soft bicycle helmets have a much smaller protective effect, and the effect on facial injuries is not statistically significant. Effects of bicycle helmets are also likely to be different among children and among adults.

***Potential effects of mandatory wearing of bicycle helmets.*** The effect on the number of injuries amongst cyclists of mandatory wearing of bicycle helmets is determined by three different partial effects, or mechanisms, which can pull in different directions. The three partial effects are the helmet effect, the behavioural effect and the exposure effect. The effect of mandatory wearing of bicycle helmets on the number of cyclists injured can be modelled as the product of the three partial effects.

The helmet effect is the protective effect of bicycle helmets, i.e. less severe injuries in the case of accidents. The size of this effect depends mainly on two factors: (1) What type of cyclists are using a helmet and (2) to what degree the use of bicycle helmet increases.

The behavioural effect is the effect of wearing a helmet on the cyclist's risk of being involved in accidents. A cyclist who uses a helmet is more protected against injury than a cyclist who does not use a helmet. It has been suggested that this can lead to cyclists with helmets cycling less carefully (faster, paying less attention, in more difficult conditions, children being allowed to cycle on their own more than before, etc.) than cyclists without helmets (Bjørnskau 1994b). If mandatory use of helmets leads to less careful behaviour amongst cyclists, this may lead to cyclists being involved in more accidents per kilometre cycled than before (the behavioural effect). Such an effect can totally or partially offset the protective effect of more cyclists using helmets.

The exposure effect is the effect of mandatory wearing of helmets on the amount of cycling. Mandatory use of bicycle helmets has been found to make cycling less attractive, so that the amount of cycling is reduced. Reduced cycling may reduce the total number of injured cyclists, but is likely to increase the accident and injury rate among cyclists (Erke and Elvik 2007).

The effects on the number of injured cyclists of mandatory wearing of bicycle helmets, and of campaigns for the use of helmets, have been evaluated by:

Wood and Milne (1988) (Australia)
Vulcan, Cameron and Watson (1992) (Australia)
Cameron, Vulcan, Finch and Newstead (1994) (Australia)
Scuffham and Langley (1997) (New Zealand)
Robinson (1996) (Australia)

On the basis of the studies, best estimates of the effect of mandatory wearing of bicycle helmets on the number of cyclists injured are given in Table 4.10.3.

In total, mandatory wearing of bicycle helmets seems to have reduced the number of head injuries among cyclists by around 22%. The results are likely to be affected by publication bias, time trends, and methodological weaknesses that have not been controlled for. Another problem with the results is that no clear relationship can be found between the degree to which the use of bicycle helmets increased and the effect on injuries that has been found. If mandatory wearing of bicycle helmets had caused the reductions of injuries that have been found in the studies, one would expect larger increases of helmet wearing to result in larger injury reductions. Since no such

*Table 4.10.3: Effects on injuries of mandatory wearing of bicycle helmets*

| | Percentage change in the number of injuries | | |
|---|---|---|---|
| Injury severity | Types of injuries affected | Best estimate | 95% confidence interval |
| Increased use of helmets | Head injuries | −25 | (−30; −19) |
| Increased risk per km cycled | All injuries | +14 | (+10; +17) |
| Less cycling | All injuries | −29 | (−30; −28) |
| Net effect | All injuries | −22 | (−23; −21) |

relationship has been found, it is doubtful if the injury reductions actually have been due to mandatory wearing of bicycle helmets.

Four studies have discussed the effects of the introduction of mandatory wearing of bicycle helmets in New Zealand (Povey, Frith and Graham 1999, Robinson 2001, Scuffham and Langley 1997, Scuffham et al. 2000). The analyses show the importance of controlling for long-term time trends in the number of injured cyclists. Robinson (2001) concludes that the injury reductions that have been found in many studies are a result of time trends, and not effects of the bicycle helmet law.

### Effects on mobility

If cyclists with helmets cycle faster than other cyclists, this can be interpreted as an increase in mobility. A reduction in the number of cycle trips, which has been found in several studies on the other hand, implies that the cyclists must use other forms of transport, or take exercise in other ways (instead of cycling for exercise).

### Effect on the environment

No effects on the environment of the use of bicycle helmets, or the mandatory wearing of helmets, have been documented.

### Costs

A child's bicycle helmet in Norway costs around NOK 100–400 in 2005. An adult bicycle helmet costs around NOK 400–1,000 in 2005.

### Cost–benefit analysis

A numerical example is calculated for the costs and benefits of using a bicycle helmet for an average adult cyclist. In the example, the cyclist is over 13 years old and has an injury rate of 15 injuries per million cycle kilometres, which is the expected rate according to Bjørnskau (2000). Forty percent of these injuries are expected to be head or facial injuries, resulting in 6.6 expected head or face injuries if no helmet is worn. Most injuries are slight injuries (Schrøder Hansen, Hansen, Walløe and Fjeldsgård 1995). The average cost of cyclist injuries are estimated at NOK 510,000 (Veisten et al. 2007). A bicycle helmet is assumed to cost NOK 600 and to last for 3 or 4 years

*Table 4.10.4: Effects on injuries of mandatory wearing of bicycle helmets*

| Cycle kilometre per day | Expected number of head/face/neck injuries per year | Reduction of head/face/neck injuries per year (%) | Life time of bicycle helmet (years) | Cost–benefit ratio |
|---|---|---|---|---|
| 1 | 0.002 | −10 | 4 | 0.66 |
| 2 | 0.004 | −10 | 4 | 1.31 |
| 5 | 0.011 | −10 | 4 | 3.28 |
| 10 | 0.022 | −10 | 4 | 6.56 |
| 20 | 0.044 | −10 | 3 | 10.05 |
| 30 | 0.066 | −10 | 3 | 15.08 |

depending on the amount of cycling. Bicycle helmets are recommended to be replaced after some years, otherwise they will lose much of their potential protective effect. Table 4.10.4 shows the results from the cost–benefit analysis under the assumption that injuries are reduced by 10%. Based on the current assumptions, using a bicycle helmet on all cycle trips is associated with greater benefits than costs if the average number of cycle kilometres is more than ca. 1.5 km per day. In this numerical example, it is not taken into account that the injury rate may be different depending on the annual number of cycling kilometres or in different age groups.

A numerical example is also calculated for a child between 7 and 14 years. On average, a child in this age group has an annual expected number of injuries of around 0.009. Forty percent of these injuries are assumed to be preventable by a bicycle helmet. The proportion of injuries actually prevented is assumed to be 10%. A bicycle helmet is assumed to cost NOK 400 and to hold for 3 years. Under these assumptions, the cost–benefit ratio of always using a bicycle helmet is 2.5. The effect on injuries is, however, most likely larger and the cost–benefit ratio can therefore be regarded as a lower limit.

## 4.11 Motorcycle helmets

### Problem and objective

Riders of mopeds and motorcycles have a high risk of being injured in traffic. Estimates made on the basis of official Norwegian accident statistics (Bjørnskau 1993) suggest that the risk of injury to moped riders and motorcyclists is 8–10 times higher per million person kilometres than for car drivers. However, not all injuries are reported to the police. If injuries recorded by hospitals are used to estimate risk, the injury rate for moped riders and motorcyclists in traffic is 12–15 times as high as for car drivers.

Mopeds and motorcycles provide minimal protection to riders in the event of an accident. The probability of the accident leading to injuries is therefore high, especially for head injuries. As long as the use of motorcycle helmets is voluntary, experience shows that not all moped riders and motorcyclists choose to wear helmets. In 1976, when the use of helmets was voluntary in Norway, 55% of moped riders and motorcyclists wore helmets (Fosser 1995). Similar experiences have been reported in a number of American states.

Motorcycle helmets are intended to protect against head injuries in the event of accidents and to reduce the severity of such injuries. Mandatory wearing of helmets for moped riders and motorcyclists is intended to reduce the number of injuries for this road user group by ensuring that all moped riders and motorcyclists use helmets.

## Description of the measure

Mandatory wearing of approved helmets when riding mopeds or motorcycles was introduced in Norway on 1 April 1977. Before 1977, the proportion of motorcyclists using a helmet was between 50% and 60%. From 1980 on, the proportion is near 100% (Fosser 1995). The most recent survey found that 98% used helmets in urban areas and 100% in rural areas.

## Effect on accidents

***Individual effect.*** The effect of helmets for moped riders and motorcyclists on the severity of injury in accidents has been evaluated in the following studies:

Cairns and Holbourn (1943) (Great Britain)
Chandler and Thompson (1957) (Great Britain)
Jamieson and D'Arcy (1973) (Australia)
Richardson (1974) (United States)
Kraus, Riggins and Franti (1975a, 1975b) (United States)
Hoffman (1977) (Belgium)
Dare, Owens and Krane (1978) (United States)
McSwain and Lummis (1980) (United States)
National Highway Traffic Safety Administration (1980) (United States)
Andrews (1981) (United States)
Carr, Brandt and Swanson (1981) (United States)
Hurt, Ouellet and Thom (1981) (United States)
Luna, Copass, Oreskovich and Carrico (1981) (United States)

Bachulis, Sangster, Gorrell and Long (1988) (United States)
Evans and Frick (1988) (United States)
May and Morabito (1989) (United States)
Wilson (1989) (United States)
Kelly, Sanson, Strange and Orsay (1991) (United States)
Murdock and Waxman (1991) (United States)
Romano and McLoughlin (1991) (United States)
Offner, Rivara and Maier (1992) (United States)
Shankar et al. (1992) (United States)
Weiss (1992) (United States)
Rutledge and Stutts (1993) (United States)
Gabella et al. (1995) (United States)
Kraus, Peek, Shen and Williams (1995) (United States)

The majority of these studies have been carried out at hospitals or other health institutions where injured moped riders or motorcyclists have come for treatment. A limitation of studies carried out at health institutions is that uninjured motorcyclists, i.e. those who were not injured because they used helmets, are not included. In addition, many of the studies have not controlled for confounding factors affecting injury severity. The results are therefore uncertain. The best estimates of the effect of wearing helmets on the severity of injury are given in Table 4.11.1.

Helmets reduce the number of head injuries among moped riders and motorcyclists by around 44%. The effect is largest for the most serious injuries. There is a tendency for those who use helmets also to incur fewer non-head injuries but this tendency is

*Table 4.11.1: Effects of helmets for moped riders and motorcyclists on the probability of incurring injury: individual effects*

| | Percentage change in number of injuries | | |
|---|---|---|---|
| Injury severity | Type of injury affected | Best estimate | 95% confidence interval |
| Fatal injury (3%) | Head injury | −44 | (−55; −32) |
| Serious injury (17%) | Head injury | −49 | (−58; −39) |
| Slight injury (80%) | Head injury | −33 | (−41; −25) |
| All injuries (100%) | Head injury | −44 | (−22; −41) |
| All levels of severity | Injuries other than head injuries | −8 | (−22; +8) |
| All levels of severity | All types of injury | −25 | (−30; −20) |

not statistically significant. Taking all injuries together, helmets reduce the number of injuries by around 25%.

***Effect of mandatory wearing of helmets.*** There are a number of studies of the effect on the number of injured moped riders and motorcyclists of introducing the mandatory wearing of helmets. The majority of studies are from the United States, where the majority of states introduced mandatory wearing of helmets between 1967 and 1970. Between 1976 and 1978, over half of the 50 states repealed the mandatory wearing of helmets. Since 1990, a number of states have reintroduced compulsory helmet use. The results presented here are based on the following studies:

Koehler (1978) (USA)
Dare, Owens and Krane (1979) (USA)
Asogwa (1980) (Nigeria)
Watson, Zador and Wilks (1980) (USA)
McSwain and Lummis (1980) (USA)
McSwain and Petrucelli (1984) (USA)
Chenier and Evans (1987) (USA)
Kraus, Peek, McArthur and Williams (1994) (USA)

On the basis of the above studies, the best estimates of the effects of introducing or repealing mandatory wearing of helmets for moped riders and motorcyclists are given in Table 4.11.2.

Introducing mandatory wearing of helmets reduces the number of injured moped riders and motorcyclists by around 25%. Repealing helmet wearing laws has been found to significant increases of fatal and other injuries.

*Table 4.11.2: Effects on the number of injured motorcyclists of introducing or repealing mandatory wearing of helmets*

| | Percentage change in the number of injuries | | |
|---|---|---|---|
| Injury severity | Type of injury affected | Best estimate | 95% confidence interval |
| ***Introducing mandatory wearing of helmets*** | | | |
| Fatal injuries | All injuries | −26 | (−33; −19) |
| All personal injuries | All injuries | −27 | (−28; −25) |
| ***Repealing mandatory wearing of helmets*** | | | |
| Fatal injuries | All injuries | +30 | (+25; +35) |
| All personal injuries | All injuries | +8 | (+6; +10) |

### Effect on mobility

No effects on mobility of motorcycle helmets or their mandatory wearing have been documented.

### Effect on the environment

No effects on the environment of motorcycle helmets or their mandatory wearing have been documented.

### Costs

In Norway, a motorcycle helmet cost around NOK 400–1,500 in 1995.

### Cost–benefit analysis

A moped rider or a motorcyclist who drives an average mileage (ca. 3,000 km per year for moped riders and ca 6,000–7,000 km per year for motorcyclists) has an annual expected injury rate of around 0.01 in Norway. This is representative for a situation where almost 100% of moped riders and motorcyclists use helmets. If helmets were not used, it can be assumed that the frequency of injuries would have been $1/0.75 =$ around 33% higher (corresponding to a 25% injury reduction). Helmets are thus assumed to prevent, on average, 0.003 injuries per moped rider or motorcyclist each year. Assuming an average cost per injury of around NOK 1,430,000, this means a saving of around NOK 4,300 per moped rider or motorcyclist per year. The cost of purchasing a helmet in Norway is around NOK 1,000. Calculated as an annuity over a 5-year lifetime, the cost is around NOK 250 per year. This is clearly less than the value of the benefit of injuries prevented. The figures indicate that the use of helmets for moped riders and motorcyclists has a benefit–cost ratio of around 17 ($\pm$ 6). This result is confirmed by American cost–benefit analyses (Muller 1980, Hartunian, Smart, Willemain and Zador 1983).

## 4.12 Seat belts in cars

### Problem and objective

In 1995, a total of 8,727 car occupants were killed or injured in accidents reported to the police (Statistisk sentralbyrå 1996). Of these, 5,623 (64.4%) were killed or injured as the result of impact with the interior of the vehicle, 123 (1.4%) were ejected from the vehicle, 3 (0.03%) were injured by fire, and 17 (0.2%) drowned. Impact with the interior of the vehicle and being ejected are therefore the most common mechanisms of injury in car accidents.

In the event of an accident, a car occupant without a seat belt will continue to move at the same speed at which the car was moving before the accident, and thus will either hit the interior of the car or be thrown out of the vehicle. Ejection drastically increases the probability of sustaining serious injury (Partyka 1979, Grime 1987, Harms 1992).

Seat belts protect people in cars from colliding with the interior of the car and keep them in their seats in the event of an accident. The mechanical energy to which the body is exposed will be greatly reduced. This reduces the probability of personal injuries and can make the injuries less serious. The mandatory use of seat belts is intended to ensure a high usage of seat belts so that the number of persons injured in car accidents is reduced.

## Description of the measure

Since 1971, it has been compulsory to install seat belts in the front seats of cars and vans in Norway. Since 1985, it has been compulsory to install seat belts in the rear seats of private cars. Seat belts must be used, where they are installed, no matter which seat is being used or the age of the person. This regulation was introduced in 1988. New cars and vans must be equipped with three-point seat belts of an approved type for all seats. Two-point belts (lap belts) can only be used in the centre rear seat and for seats where it would otherwise be impossible to install three-point belts. The seat belt must be an automatic retractable belt, that is to say a belt that automatically fits the user and thus is always correctly adjusted (Fosser, Vaa and Torp 1992).

In Norway, the introduction of mandatory use of seat belts in the front seats of light vehicles in 1975 and the introduction of fines were associated with large increases in wearing rates, which had been about 17% in towns and 47% in rural areas before 1975. In 1995, around 70% of drivers of light vehicles used seat belts in towns and cities. In rural areas, the wearing rate was 84%.

## Effect on accidents

***How the effect of seat belts is measured.*** The use of seat belts does not in itself affect the number of accidents, only the probability of being injured when an accident occurs.

The effect of seat belts is therefore measured in terms of how people in cars involved in accidents are distributed according to injury severity. There are four levels of injury severity: fatal injury, serious injuries, slight injuries and no injury. For example, if the use of seat belts reduces the probability of being killed under otherwise identical conditions, relatively fewer of those who wear seat belts will be killed in an accident compared to those who do not use seat belts.

Use of seat belts is not the only factor affecting injury severity in car accidents. Speed, the weight of the vehicle, the type of car, the type of accident and the number of people in the car are examples of other factors that influence the probability of sustaining personal injuries and their severity. In summarising the results of the studies on the effects of seat belts, greatest emphasis is placed on studies that have controlled for both these and other confounding factors affecting injury severity.

***The effect of seat belts on personal injuries in accidents.*** The effect of seat belts on personal injuries in accidents has been subject to much research. The results presented here are based on the following reports:

Bohlin (1967) (Sweden)
Bäckström, Andersson, Forsman and Nilsson (1974) (Sweden)
Kahane (1974) (USA)
Reinfurt, Silva and Seila (1976) (USA)
Dalgaard (1977) (Denmark)
Central Bureau of Statistics (1977) (Denmark)
Hartemann et al. (1977) (France)
Huelke, Lawson, Scott and Marsh (1977) (USA)
Sabey, Grant, Hobbs (1977) (Great Britain)
Toomath (1977) (New Zealand)
Hobbs (1978) (Great Britain)
Perchonok et al. (1978) (USA)
Partyka (1979) (USA)
Cameron (1980) (Australia)
Norin, Nilsson-Ehle, Saretok and Tingvall (1980) (Sweden)
Thomas et al. (1980) (France)
Hobbs (1981) (Great Britain)
Hobbs and Mills (1984) (Great Britain)
Evans (1986) (USA)
Evans (1988) (USA)
Partyka (1988a) (USA)
Tunbridge, Everest, Wild and Johnstone (1988) (Great Britain)

Maghsoodloo, Brown and Shieh (1989) (USA)
Krafft, Nygren, Tingvall (1990) (Sweden)
Conn et al. (1993) (USA)
Dean, Reading and Nechodom (1995) (USA)
Elvik (1995a) (Norway)
Huelke and Compton (1995) (USA)
Evans (1996) (USA)

Based on these reports, the best estimate for the effect of seat belts in accidents is given in Table 4.12.1. The use of seat belts reduces the probability of being killed by 40–50% for drivers and passengers in the front seat and by about 25% for passengers in the rear seats. The effect on serious injuries is almost as great, while the effect on slight injuries is somewhat smaller, around 20–30%. These figures are average figures for all accident types. More detailed analyses indicate that seat belts are most effective in frontal impacts and in running-off-the-road accidents where the probability of being ejected is high if seat belts are not used (Evans 1990b).

*Table 4.12.1: Effect of seat belts on the probability of personal injury in accidents: individual effects*

| | Percentage change in number of injuries | | |
|---|---|---|---|
| Injury severity | Types of accident affected | Best estimate | 95% confidence interval |
| ***Drivers of light vehicles (private cars and vans)*** | | | |
| Fatal | All accidents | −50 | (−55; −45) |
| Serious injuries | All accidents | −45 | (−50; −40) |
| Minor injuries | All accidents | −25 | (−30; −20) |
| All injuries | All accidents | −28 | (−33; −23) |
| ***Front seat passengers in light vehicles (private cars and vans)*** | | | |
| Fatal | All accidents | −45 | (−55; −35) |
| Serious injuries | All accidents | −45 | (−60; −30) |
| Minor injuries | All accidents | −20 | (−25; −15) |
| All injuries | All accidents | −23 | (−29; −17) |
| ***Back seat passengers in light vehicles (private cars)*** | | | |
| Fatal | All accidents | −25 | (−35; −15) |
| Serious injuries | All accidents | −25 | (−40; −10) |
| Minor injuries | All accidents | −20 | (−35; −5) |
| All injuries | All accidents | −21 | (−36; −6) |

***Possible negative effects of seat belts.*** A seat belt holds the body in place on the seat, but it cannot prevent the head from being thrown backward or forward in the event of an accident. It has been claimed that seat belts increase the probability of whiplash injuries when the car is hit from behind, because they contribute to strengthening the movement of the head in relation to the rest of the body. A number of studies have found that a higher proportion of seat belt users have suffered whiplash than non-users (Huelke, Lawson, Scott and Marsh 1977, Sabey, Grant, Hobbs 1977, Cameron 1980, Nygren 1984, Krafft, Nygren and Tingvall 1990). In the majority of these studies, however, the non-injured are not included. An increase in the percentage of those injured, who have a certain type of injury does not necessarily mean that seat belts increase the incidence of this type of injury. If seat belts reduce the incidence of some types of injury more than others, the type of injury, which is least reduced, will make up a greater *percentage* of all *injuries* among seat belt users (Christensen and Borger 1992). This can be shown by means of a numerical example (Table 4.12.2).

The example shows that the percentage of those injured who had sustained neck injuries was around 42% of seat belt users, as opposed to 33% of non-users, in spite of the fact that the number of persons with neck injuries was reduced by 10%. The increase in the percentage with neck injuries amongst seat belt users is nonetheless so large in many studies that this is unlikely to be explained by the fact that the survey is limited to injured persons. At any rate it is clear that seat belts do not reduce the incidence of whiplash injuries to the same extent as other forms of injury and can make such injuries worse when a car is struck from behind.

A contact between the body and the seat belt can also lead to minor injuries such as bruising or in the worst case, broken ribs in accidents where belts are used. However, if an accident is so serious that the seat belt causes such injuries, it is highly probable that the injuries would have been much more serious if the seat belts had not been used.

*Table 4.12.2: Hypothetical effects of seat belts on neck injuries and other types of injury*

| | Persons not using seat belts | | | Persons using seat belts | | | |
|---|---|---|---|---|---|---|---|
| Type of injury | Number of injuries | Percentage of injuries | Percentage of total | Number of injuries | Percentage of injuries | Percentage of total | Change in number of injuries (%) |
| Neck | 250 | 33.3 | 3.6 | 225 | 41.7 | 3.2 | −10 |
| Other | 500 | 66.7 | 7.1 | 315 | 58.3 | 4.6 | −37 |
| All injuries | 750 | 100.0 | 10.7 | 540 | 100.0 | 7.8 | −28 |
| Uninjured | 6250 | | 89.3 | 6460 | | 92.2 | |
| Total | 7000 | | 100.0 | 7000 | | 100.0 | |

***Effects of automatic seat belts.*** An American survey (Nash 1989) shows that automatic seat belts in Toyota Cressidas in the USA have reduced the number of fatalities in such cars by 40% (±8%). Automatic seat belts are attached to the door and fold round the driver when the door is closed. The effect is about as large as for manual seat belts.

***Effects of mandatory use of seat belts.*** The effects of mandatory use of seat belts in light vehicles have been studied in a number of countries. The results presented here are based on the following studies:

Foldvary and Lane (1974) (Victoria, Australia)
Vaughan, Wood and Croft (1974) (New South Wales, Australia)
Crinion, Foldvary and Lane (1975) (South Australia, Australia)
Andreasson and Roos (1977) (Sweden)
Hvidberg Jørgensen (1977) (Denmark)
Jørgensen and Lund (1977) (Denmark)
Møller (1977) (Denmark)
Nielsen, Eriksen, Nordentoft and Weeth (1977) (Denmark)
Toomath (1977) (New Zealand)
Conybeare (1980) (Australia)
Hakkert, Zaidel and Sarelle (1981) (Israel)
Jonah and Lawson (1984) (Quebec, Ontario, Saskatchewan, British Columbia, Canada)
Mackay (1985) (Great Britain)
UK Department of Transport (1985) (Great Britain)
Harvey and Durbin (1986) (Great Britain)
Campbell and Campbell (1988) (States in the USA)
Salmi, Thomas, Fabry and Girard (1989) (France)
Tunbridge (1989) (Great Britain)
Reinfurt, Campbell, Stewart and Stutts (1990) (North Carolina, USA)
States et al. (1990) (New York, USA)
Asch, Levy, Shea and Bodenhorn (1991) (New Jersey, USA)
Evans and Graham (1991) (States in the USA)
Rock (1993) (Illinois, USA)
Elvik (1995a) (Norway)
Koushki, Ali and Al-Saleh (1996) (Kuwait)

The results of these studies vary. Figure 4.12.1 shows the relationship between the percentage increase in the use of seat belts and the percentage change in the number of motorists killed following the introduction of mandatory use of seat belts in light vehicles. Fig. 4.12.1 shows that there is a tendency for the percentage decrease in the

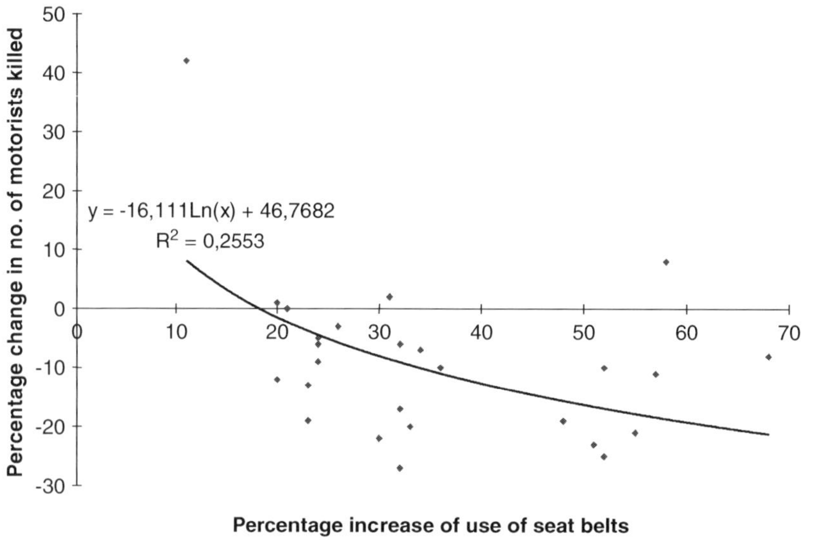


*Figure 4.12.1: Relationship between the increase in the use of seat belts following the introduction of seat belt legislation and changes in the number of motorists killed.*

number of motorists killed to be greater when the relative increase in the use of seat belts, following the introduction of mandatory use, is large than when it is small.

Figure 4.12.2 shows corresponding results for injured motorists. There is a smaller percentage decrease in the number of injured motorists than the number of motorists who are killed.

In Figs. 4.12.1 and 4.12.2 the individual data points have not been weighted by the number of accidents they are based on. When the results are weighted and grouped, the best estimate of the effect of mandatory seat belt use is shown in Table 4.12.3.

The mandatory use of seat belts has, on average, led to a decrease of around 10–15% in the number of car occupants killed or seriously injured. The total number of car occupants injured is reduced by about 10%. The more seat belts are used, the greater the decrease in the number of injured persons in light vehicles. The greatest decrease observed is around 15–20%.

There are examples that show that even a relatively large increase in the wearing rate of seat belts (e.g. over 30%) has only led to a small decrease (less than 10%) in the number of persons injured in light vehicles. This may be due to the fact that the safest

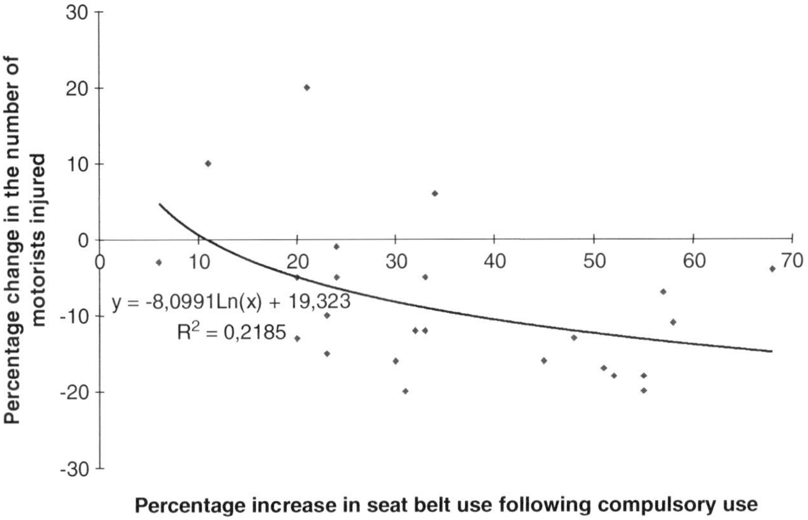


*Figure 4.12.2: Relationship between increase in use of seat belts following legislation and changes in the number of motorists injured.*

*Table 4.12.3: Effects of compulsory use of seat belts on the number of persons injured*

| | Percentage change in number of injured persons | | |
|---|---|---|---|
| Injury severity | Group of road user | Best estimate | 95% confidence interval |
| ***Legislation which has led to an increase of less than 25% in the use of seat belts*** | | | |
| Fatal | People in light vehicles | −7 | (−9; −5) |
| All injuries | People in light vehicles | +0.7 | (+0.4; +1) |
| ***Legislation which has led to an increase of 25–49% in the use of seat belts*** | | | |
| Fatal | People in light vehicles | −8 | (−9; −7) |
| All injuries | People in light vehicles | −14 | (−15; −13) |
| ***Legislation which has led to an increase more than 50% in the use of seat belts*** | | | |
| Fatal | People in light vehicles | −21 | (−22; −20) |
| All injuries | People in light vehicles | −16 | (−16; −15) |
| ***Average effect of all legislation making use of seat belts mandatory*** | | | |
| Fatal | People in light vehicles | −11 | (−12; −10) |
| Serious injuries | People in light vehicles | −18 | (−19; −18) |
| Slight injuries | People in light vehicles | −8 | (−8; −7) |
| All injuries | People in light vehicles | −12 | (−15; −10) |
| ***Effects of compulsory seat belt use for traffic groups not covered by the legislation*** | | | |
| Fatal | All other groups | +7 | (+5; +8) |
| All injuries | All other groups | +7 | (+6; +8) |

drivers are those who first start using seat belts and are most inclined to comply with the legislation on mandatory seat belt use. Danish (Jørgensen and Lund 1977), Norwegian (Nordisk Trafikksikkerhetsråd 1984) and American (Evans 1987) surveys indicate that drivers who use seat belts have a lower accident rate per kilometre driven than drivers who do not use seat belts.

It has been claimed (Adams 1985, 1994) that the mandatory use of seat belts encourages car drivers to drive with less care because they feel protected by the seat belt. Less careful driving has been assumed to lead to more pedestrian and cyclist injuries. Following the introduction of the mandatory use of seat belts, the number of injured pedestrians, cyclists and motorcyclists has increased slightly. A simple explanation for this may be an increase in traffic volume. The assumption that use of seat belts leads to less careful driving has received little support in the research that is available. A detailed study of drivers' behaviour before and after the introduction of mandatory seat belt use in Newfoundland in Canada and in Great Britain (O'Neill, Lund, Zador and Ashton 1985) found no indications of less careful driving behaviour. A Dutch survey (Janssen 1994) on the other hand, found a weak tendency towards increasing speed among drivers who normally did not use seat belts and who took part in a trial where they were forced to use seat belts.

**Effect on mobility**

The use of seat belts has no documented effect on mobility.

**Effect on the environment**

The use of seat belts has no documented effect on the environment.

**Costs**

Today seat belts are standard equipment in all cars and vans. Exact costs are therefore difficult to find. Based on previous editions of this book, the costs per seat for installing seat belts are estimated as NOK 530–640 for a three-point seat belt in driver seats and other seats.

**Cost–benefit analysis**

A number of cost–benefit analyses have been reported (Hakkert 1969, Bolstad 1972, US Department of Transportation 1976, National Transportation Safety Board 1979,

Transport Canada 1986). All the analyses show that the benefit of seat belts clearly outweighs the costs. The benefit–cost ratio is estimated to be between 3 and 8.

In order to illustrate the costs and benefits of using seat belts in Norway today, a numerical example has been worked out. It is assumed that a private car covers 200,000 km in the course of its lifetime (15 years). The risk of personal injury can be estimated (Bjørnskau 1993) to about 0.32 injuries per million kilometres driven for drivers and about 0.27 injuries per million person kilometres for passengers. These figures apply to a situation involving 60–80% use of seat belts. It is therefore assumed that the risk of injury if seat belts are not used is 0.40 per million kilometres driven for drivers and 0.35 per million person kilometres for passengers. The expected number of persons injured in the course of a vehicle's lifetime can then be estimated to be 0.08 for drivers, 0.04 for front seat passengers and 0.02 for rear seat passengers.

The benefits of using seat belts throughout a vehicle's lifetime are estimated to NOK 19,000 for drivers (present value 15 years, 7% interest). The installation cost for seat belts for drivers seats is ca. NOK 600. The corresponding benefit for front seat passengers is calculated to be NOK 8,000 and the cost NOK 600. For rear seat passengers, the benefit is calculated at ca. NOK 2,000 and the cost at NOK 1,500.

The calculations show that the benefit of using seat belts exceeds the installation costs for seat belts for all the seats in a car. The time involved in putting on and taking off seat belts is not included. The time involved is estimated at 8 s per journey per person (Blomquist 1977, 1979). A private car is used on average a little under 1,000 times a year (Rideng 1994). This corresponds to around 1,800 person journeys per car per year (the number of persons is on average 1.82 per trip). If seat belts are used by everyone on every trip, the time involved in putting on and taking off seat belts amounts to 4 h per car per year. The costs per hour amount to NOK 340 per year for all seats in the car, or a present value of NOK 3,115 for the whole lifetime of the vehicle. By way of comparison, the benefit of using seat belts is calculated at ca. NOK 29,000 for all seats in the vehicle taken together. The cost is small and means little in the cost–benefit value of using seat belts.

## 4.13 Child restraints

### Problem and objective

Children in cars, who are not restrained by seat belts or in some other way, have a great risk of being injured by striking the interior of the car or being thrown out through a door or window in the event of rollover, collision or sudden braking. A child who uses a child seat/seat belt or other forms of child restraints will be kept in place on the seat if an accident occurs and will reduce speed at the same rate as the vehicle so that the force that affects the body is spread over a longer period and a longer distance than if child restraints were not used.

A passenger in the rear seat who is not restrained can also be a danger to people in the front seats in head-on collisions. People in the front seat have suffered serious injuries from non-restrained rear seat passengers (Roberts 1983, Nordisk trafikksikkerhetsråd 1984). A number of studies have indicated that children have a smaller risk than adults of being injured in traffic accidents (Norin, Saretok, Jonasson and Samuelsson 1978). Based on data from Norin, Nilsson-Ehle, Saretok and Tingvall (1980), it has been calculated that children between the ages of 1 and 14 years have a 22% lower risk of being injured in car accidents than adults aged between 15 and 56 (Nordisk trafikksikkerhetsråd 1984). Nonetheless, many children are injured in cars.

Child restraints in cars are intended to keep the child in its place on the seat so that in the event of sudden braking or collision, the child is not thrown against the interior or out of the car. The equipment must be able to absorb kinetic energy without itself injuring the child and must be easy to use. As long as the use of child restraints is not mandatory, not all parents will secure their children sufficiently. The mandatory wearing of child restraints is intended to reduce the number of injured children by ensuring that a high proportion of them are restrained in cars.

## Description of the measure

Child restraints include the following measures:

- Choice of seat in the car for a child (front seat or rear seat)
- Restraining small children using carrycots or child car seats
- Restraining larger children using seat belts, possibly in conjunction with a cushion

For children of different sizes (weights), the following methods of restraint are recommended:

***Group 0: 0–9 kg (0–9 months).*** Children up to the age of 10 months must lie/sit in approved child restraints, which restrain both the child and the seat. The seat should be rearward facing.

***Group 1: 9–18 kg (10 months to 3–4 years).*** The child should sit in a child car seat, which has its own seat belt to restrain the child and a three-point seat belt to secure the child seat. It is recommended that the car seat be rearward facing.

***Group 2: 15–25 kg (3–4 years to 6–7 years).*** An ordinary three-point seat belt can be combined with a cushion or seat, which raises the child up so that the seat belt fits the child closely over the shoulder and the hips.

***Group 3: 22–36 kg (6–7 years to 10–12 years).*** A three-point seat belt can be used in combination with a cushion, which raises the child up so that the seat belt goes across the shoulder and the hips.

Not all child seats perform equally well in crash tests (Carlsson and Hattrem 1995). For a good performance, it is also important that the child restraint is correctly installed and used. The proportion of small children that are restrained is around 90–95% in countries such as Norway, Sweden, USA, Great Britain and Australia (Amundsen and Elvik 2006, Anund et al. 2003, US Department of Transportation 2004). Restraints are, however, often not used correctly. Proportions of incorrect use of child restraints range from 15% up to 80% (Amundsen and Elvik 2006, Anund et al. 2003, Arbogast et al. 2004, Decina and Lococo 2005, Decina and Knoebel 1997). Usual mistakes among others are that a belt is not properly fastened, not installing a child seat correctly on the car seat or that a belt us lying around a child's neck or under the arms. When child restraints are not installed properly, they may be less effective in reducing injuries, but serious injuries are for the most part reduced all the same (Arbogast et al. 2004). When children are placed in a child seat, especially in a rear-facing child seat, on the front seat, and when a front airbag is installed and not deactivated, the child will most likely sustain severe or fatal injuries when the airbag inflates in a collision (NHTSA 2001).

**Effect on accidents**

***Choice of seat in car.*** A number of studies have compared injury rates in different seating positions in the car. The following studies have examined how the choice of seats in a car affects injury rates among children:

Nielsen (1974) (Denmark)
Williams and Zador (1977) (USA)
Norin, Saretok, Jonasson and Samuelsson (1978) (Sweden)
Dalmotas et al. (1984) (Canada)
Kahane (1986) (USA)
Tingvall (1987) (Sweden)

Agran, Castillo and Winn (1992) (USA)
Durbin et al. (2006) (USA)

On the basis of these studies, it is estimated that placing non-restrained children on the rear seat rather than the front reduces injuries with 26% (95% CI [−29; −22]). For restrained children it is estimated that injuries are reduced by 14% (95% CI [−23; −4]).

***Child car seats and seat belts.*** A number of studies have evaluated the effect of child restraints in cars on the risk of injury in accidents:

Williams and Zador (1977) (USA)
Melvin, Stalnaker and Mohan (1978) (USA)
Norin and Andersson (1978) (Sweden)
Norin, Saretok, Jonasson and Samuelsson (1978) (Sweden)
Scherz (1979) (USA tates)
Norin, Nilsson-Ehle, Saretok and Tingvall (1980) (Sweden)
Dalmotas et al. (1984) (Canada)
Wagenaar (1985) (USA)
Kahane (1986) (USA)
Aldman, Gustafsson, Nygren and Tingvall (1987) (Sweden)
Carlsson, Holmgren and Norin (1987) (Sweden)
Tingvall (1987) (Sweden)
Partyka (1988b) (USA)
Langwieder and Hummel (1989) (Germany)
Agran, Castillo and Winn (1992) (USA)
Arbogast et al. (2004) (USA)
Jakobsson, Isaksson-Hellman and Lundell (2005) (Sweden)
Durbin et al. (2006) (USA)
Elliot, Kallan, Durbin and Winston (2006) (USA)

On the basis of these studies, best estimates of the effect of different child restraints for use in cars are given in Table 4.13.1.

***For babies, carrycots fastened with car seat belts*** reduce the probability of the baby being injured by around 25%. This result is not statistically significant and based on only one study.

***Child car seat, combined with a seat belt,*** has been found to be associated with large and significant injury reductions among children between the ages of 0 and 9. For children under the age of 5, rear-facing seats are more effective than front-facing seats.

*Table 4.13.1: Effects of child restraints in cars on the child's risk of injury as a car passenger*

| | | Percentage change in the number of injuries | |
|---|---|---|---|
| Injury severity | Types of accidents affected | Best estimate | 95% confidence interval |
| ***Restraining babies using carry cots*** | | | |
| All injuries | All accidents | −25 | (−75; +120) |
| ***Restraining children with child seats and seat belts*** | | | |
| All injuries (0–4 year old children) | All accidents (forward facing seat) | −55 | (−76; −39) |
| All injuries (0–4 year old children) | All accidents (rear-facing seat) | −71 | (−83; −51) |
| Severe injuries/fatalities (0–4 year old children) | All accidents (rear-facing seat) | −90 | (−96; −77) |
| All injuries (5–9 year old children) | All accidents | −57 | (−64; −50) |
| ***Restraining children using child car seat instead of seat belt only*** | | | |
| Severe injuries (1–7 year old children) | All accidents | −71 | (−79; −59) |
| ***Restraining children using seat belts only*** | | | |
| All injuries (0–4 year old children) | All accidents | −32 | (−35; −29) |
| All injuries (5–9 year old children) | All accidents | −24 | (−34; −14) |
| All injuries (10–14 year old children) | All accidents | −46 | (−52; −39) |
| Severe injuries (10–14 year old children) | All accidents | −71 | (−79; −59) |

No studies are available for older children, which distinguish between forward- and rear-facing child car seats. Children who are older than 10 years can, in most cases, use the car's standard seat belts.

For children between the ages of 1 and 7, the probability of being injured is reduced by about 70% when an ***adequate child seat is used instead of a seat belt only***. The effect of using a child seat as compared to a seat belt only is largest for more serious injuries.

***Use of seat belts alone*** for children also has been found to be associated with large and significant injury reductions, although the effects are somewhat smaller than the effects of child seats combined with seat belts.

***Effects of mandatory wearing of child restraints in cars.*** The effect of mandatory wearing of child restraints in cars has been studied in Norway and the USA. The results presented here are based on the following studies:

Lawless and Siani (1984) (USA)
Guerin and MacKinnon (1985) (USA)

Wagenaar (1985) (USA)
Wagenaar, Webster and Maybee (1987) (USA)
Evans and Graham (1990) (USA)
Elvik (1995b) (Norge)
Rock (1996) (USA)

On the basis of these studies, the best estimate of the effect of mandatory wearing of child restraints in cars is a decrease of 15% ($\pm$1%) in the number of children injured in cars in the age groups covered by this legislation.

### Effect on mobility

No effects on mobility of using child restraints in cars, or the mandatory use of these, have been documented.

### Effect on the environment

No effects on the environment of using child restraints in cars, or the mandatory wearing of these, have been documented.

### Costs

Prices for different types of child restraints in Norway as of 2005 are given in Table 4.13.2. Prices for seat belts are not given, since these are standard equipment. The Norwegian Roads Administration advises against the purchase of used equipment because worn-out equipment may not offer sufficient protection.

*Table 4.13.2: Effects of child restraints in cars on the child's risk of injury as a car passenger*

| Type of equipment | Prices (NOK) |
|---|---|
| Steel frame with safety net | 1,000–1,500 |
| Baby seat | 1,300–3,000 |
| Child seat (groups 1 and 2) | 1,000–4,000 |
| Child seat (groups 2 and 3) | 1,000–3,000 |
| Cushions without back – simple | 350–700 |
| Cushions with back/neck supports | 1,000–2,500 |
| Child-safer (seat belt device) | 400 |

### Cost–benefit analysis

Based on Norwegian official accident statistics from the years 2000–05, about 6 children are killed in car accidents each years, 4 are very seriously injured, 20 are seriously injured and 370 are slightly injured each year. In total, there are over 400 children younger than 15 years who are killed or injured in car accidents each year. In total, there are about 860,000 children in Norway who belong to families owning a car. About 90% of them are restrained while travelling in a car.

A numerical example is calculated based on the assumption than the risk of being fatally injured is reduced by 60%, that the risk of being very severely or severely injured is reduced by 50% and that the risk of being slightly injured is reduced by 40% when an appropriate child restraint is used. When 90% of all children are restrained properly, the annual number of prevented fatalities is 8.1, the number of prevented serious injuries is 21.6 and the number of prevented slight injuries is 222. The societal benefit of the prevented fatalities and injuries is about NOK 565 million per year. Under the assumption that 250,000 child restrains at a unit cost of NOK 2,000 are purchased each year, the total annual cost of child restraints is about NOK 500 million. This is less than the benefit. The cost–benefit ratio of using child restraints under the present assumptions is 1.13 and indicates that using child restraints is profitable.

## 4.14 Airbags in cars

### Problem and objective

The use of seat belts reduces injuries in traffic accidents, but cannot protect against all types of injury. For example, a seat belt does not keep the head in place in accidents and cannot prevent the head from hitting parts of the vehicles interior. It has been found that seat belts do not prevent whiplash injuries to the same extent as other injuries (see Section 4.12). Airbags, when used together with seat belts, are designed to give drivers and front seat passengers in cars better protection against injuries, which result from collisions with the car's interior in the event of accidents.

### Description of the measure

An airbag is a compressed balloon, which inflates in the event of a collision. There are several types of airbags that provide protection in different types of accidents and for different body regions.

***Frontal airbags.*** The most common type of airbags is frontal airbags, which are installed in the steering wheel or in the dashboard in front of the passenger seat in the front of the car. They aim at preventing injuries to the head, neck and upper body in frontal collisions. Frontal airbags are activated when the longitudinal deceleration of the vehicle exceeds a defined limit. They vary in size and in how powerfully they inflate. Ideally, front airbags deploy so fast that the drivers or passengers head does not reach the steering wheel or front panel, respectively, before it hits the deploying airbag, without inflicting injuries that would not have occurred without the airbag. Airbags may however cause injuries, such as burns, abrasions or eye injuries, and they may cause fatal injuries, mostly injuries to the thorax or dislocations of the vertebtrae. Injuries caused by airbags are most frequent and most serious among small and fragile persons, such as children, older people or small women, and they are most often observed in collisions at low speeds, in which injuries otherwise would not have been equally serious. How many and how serious injuries are caused by airbags depends on how powerfully the airbags deploy. In the USA, the criteria for testing airbags have therefore been revised in 1997. Previously, airbags had to be tested in crash tests with high impact speed. From 1997, testing in sled tests with lower impact speeds were allowed, which made it possible to reduce speed and power with which airbags inflate. Additionally, on–off buttons could be installed, which make it possible to deactivate the airbag, e.g. for small people. Airbags are for the most part reliable, but it may happen that airbags do not inflate when they should do so or vice versa. About two-thirds of all recalls of airbags are due to erroneous inflation (Klanner, Ambos and Paulus 2004).

In USA, front airbags are mandatory equipment in all new cars. In Europe, airbags are not mandatory, but most new vehicles are equipped with frontal airbags. Driver airbags are standard equipment in 96% of all new cars and passenger airbags are standard equipment in 93% of all new cars (Klanner, Ambos and Paulus 2004).

***Side airbags*** aim at protecting the head and thorax of car drivers and passengers, especially in side collisions. Injury rates in side collisions are larger than in frontal collisions because the vehicle's sides cannot absorb energy to the same degree as the vehicle's front side (McCartt and Kyrychenko 2006). Side airbags are installed in the seat, door or roof, and they are designed to protect the torso, the head or both torso and head. Some side airbags are connected to an overturning detector and they may prevent car occupants from being ejected from the car (Kahane 2007). Side airbags were first introduced in the mid-1990s, but installed in larger numbers of cars first after 2000. In 2003 about 20% of all new cars in the USA were equipped with side airbags (Kahane 2006) and in 2006 over 90% of all new cars in the USA were equipped with side airbags (McCartt and Kyrychenko 2006). In Germany about 75% of all new cars in 2004 had side airbags (torso bags) as standard equipment, but only 7% had head bags as standard equipment (Klanner, Ambos and Paulus 2004).

***Other types of airbags,*** which are under development and not standard equipment in cars, are foot and knee airbags; airbags for motorcyclists, which are integrated in protective clothes; and airbags for the protection of pedestrians, which are installed in vehicle's bonnet.

### Effect on accidents

***Effects of frontal airbags on killed or injured drivers and adult front seat passengers.*** Most studies of frontal airbags have investigated the effects on driver fatalities, and most studies have been conducted in the USA.

Zador and Ciccone (1993) (USA)
Edwards (1995) (USA)
Ferguson, Lund and Greene (1995) (USA)
Joksch (1995) (USA)
Kahane (1996) (USA)
Malliaris, DeBlois and Digges (1996) (USA)
Lenard, Frampton and Thomas (1998) (Great Britain)
Segui-Gomez (2000) (USA)
Cuerden, Hill, Kirk and Mackay (2001) (Great Britain)
Cummings, McKnight, Rivara and Grossman (2002) (USA)
Braver, Kyrychenko and Ferguson (2005) (USA)
Meyer and Finney (2005) (USA)
Kahane (2006) (USA)
Olson et al. (2006) (USA)

The results from these studies are summarised in Table 4.14.1. Results are reported for belted and unbelted drivers and from studies that have statistically controlled for belt use. No results are reported when seat belt use is unspecified. These results are likely to be confounded by seat belt use, which is higher in airbag-equipped vehicles (Meyer and Finney 2005).

Reductions of fatal injuries and serious injuries by about 15% have been found among belted drivers and passengers in airbag-equipped cars. The largest effect has been found in frontal collisions. In other types of collisions, the effects are smaller and not significant. The effect that has been found for serious injuries is about equally large as the effect for fatal injuries. Unbelted drivers do not benefit from airbags, and they have increased risk of fatal injuries in accidents that are not collisions (mostly single-vehicle accidents) when a front airbag is installed in the car.

*Table 4.14.1: Effects of frontal airbags on killed or injured car occupants*

| | Percentage change in the number of injuries | | |
|---|---|---|---|
| Injury severity | Types of accidents | Best estimate | 95% confidence interval |
| ***Belted drivers*** | | | |
| Fatal | All accidents | −15 | (−24; −5) |
| Fatal | Frontal collisions | −22 | (−28; −16) |
| Fatal | Frontal collisions, 12 o'clock* | −21 | (−26; −15) |
| Fatal | Non-frontal collisions* | −2 | (−8; +5) |
| Fatal | Non-collisions | −14 | (−31; +7) |
| Seriously injured | Frontal collisions | −20 | (−25; −14) |
| ***Drivers, belt use statistically controlled*** | | | |
| Fatal | All accidents | −5 | (−14; +5) |
| Fatal | Frontal collisions | −25 | (−47; +5) |
| Fatal | Non-frontal collisions | +3 | (−4; +11) |
| ***Unbelted drivers*** | | | |
| Fatal | All accidents | −1 | (−11; +9) |
| Fatal | Frontal collisions | −13 | (−18; −7) |
| Fatal | Non-frontal collisions | −2 | (−21; +22) |
| Fatal | Non-collisions | +21 | (+8; +36) |
| ***Belted passengers*** | | | |
| Seriously injured | Frontal collisions | −28 | (−43; −10) |

*Combined effect for belted drivers and statistical control for seat belt use.

When belt use is statistically controlled for, the effects are non-significant, and the effect for all accidents is smaller when belt use is statistically controlled for than when only belted drivers are included in the analysis. Additionally, sensitivity analyses indicate that the results are likely to be affected by other factors than belt use and accident types that are not controlled for in the studies. When other factors such as impact speed are statistically controlled for, both the sign and direction of the effects on fatalities may change (Farmer 2006, Meyer 2006). Even if most results are statistically significant, the results must therefore be regarded as highly uncertain.

***Effects of frontal airbags with reduced energy.*** The effectiveness of revising the test criteria for airbags in the USA 1997 has been investigated by comparing the effectiveness of airbag models from before and after 1997. The results are shown in the upper part of Table 4.14.2. These results are based on the same studies as have been summarised in Table 4.14.1. Studies that have not been conducted in the USA have been excluded. Airbags in car models from before 1997 can be assumed to be tested according to the old criteria. Airbags in car models from after 1997 are assumed to be for the most part tested according to the revised criteria, which allow the design of less powerfully inflating airbags. The latter group consists, however, not exclusively of airbag models post-1997, and not enough information is available to identify only airbags models from after 1997. The effectiveness of airbags from after 1997 in preventing fatalities seems to be greater than the effectiveness of pre-1997 airbags both in frontal collisions and in all accidents.

Some studies have directly compared airbags that have been tested according to the revised criteria (sled-tested airbags) and airbags that have been tested according to the previous criteria (Kahane 2006, Braver, Kyrychenko and Ferguson 2005). The results from these studies are summarised in the lower part of Table 4.14.2.

When sled-tested airbags are compared to airbags that are tested according to the criteria from before 1997, significant reductions of fatalities have been found among belted drivers in frontal collisions and among children. Among belted drivers in

*Table 4.14.2: Effects of front airbags on the number of killed or injured car occupants*

| | Percentage change in the number of injuries | | |
|---|---|---|---|
| Injury severity | Types of accidents/occupants affected | Best estimate | 95% confidence interval |
| ***US airbags pre-1997 vs. no airbag, belted drivers*** | | | |
| Fatal | All accidents | −13 | (−23; 0) |
| Fatal | Frontal collisions | −21 | (−27; −14) |
| ***US airbags post-1997 vs. no airbag, belted drivers*** | | | |
| Fatal | All accidents | −21 | (−39; +3) |
| Fatal | Frontal collisions | −30 | (−42; −16) |
| ***Sled tested airbag (post-1997) vs. full power airbag; belted drivers*** | | | |
| Fatal | Frontal collisions | −5 | (−6; −4) |
| Fatal | Non-frontal collisions | +2 | (−5; +9) |
| ***Sled tested airbag (post-1997) vs. full power airbag; unbelted drivers*** | | | |
| Fatal | Frontal collisions | −1 | (−8; +7) |
| Fatal | Non-frontal collisions | +8 | (+2; +15) |
| ***Sled tested airbag (post-1997) vs. full power airbag; passengers*** | | | |
| Fatal | Frontal collisions, belted | −5 | (−17; +9) |
| Fatal | Frontal collisions, unbelted | −7 | (−19; +7) |
| ***Sled tested airbag (post-1997) vs. full power airbag; children, unspecified use of child restraints*** | | | |
| Fatal | Frontal collisions | −60 | (−81; −17) |

non-frontal collisions and among unbelted drivers in front collisions, the fatality rate remains about unchanged. Among drivers who are not belted, the fatality rate in non-frontal collisions is increasing. These resuls refer to all types of passenger cars. These results indicate that the revision of the test criteria for airbags in the USA in 1997 has improved the effectiveness of airbags in reducing fatalities. No results are, however, available for all types of accidents, and no overall effect for all types of accidents can be estimated for the effectiveness of sledtesting airbags.

***Factors that affect the effectiveness of frontal airbags in reducing fatalities*** have been investigated in a number of studies. The results can be summarised as follows:

- Airbags have no effect on injuries when the seat belt is not used.
- Seat belt force limiters may increase the effectiveness of airbags.
- Airbags seem to be more effective in larger or heavier vehicles than in smaller or lighter vehicles, although the difference is not large or significant (Ferguson, Lund and Greene 1995, Joksch 1995).
- The groups of people who are most vulnerable to airbag injuries are older people, short people and women (Yoganandan et al. 2007a, Segui-Gomez 2000).
- Airbags are more likely to prevent serious injuries in more severe accidents. At lower speeds (below 30 km/h), airbags are not likely to reduce injuries and may even increase injuries and fatalities (Frampton et al. 2000, Joksch 1995, Meyer and Finney 2005, Huere, Foret-Bruno, Faverjon and Le Coz 2001).
- Effects on behavioural adaptation (e.g. less careful driving in airbag-equipped cars) have not been found (Sagberg and Sætermo 1996).
- Vehicles that are equipped with airbags are often more expensive, and socio-economic status is assumed to be a moderator variable for choice of car and driver behaviour (McCartt and Kyrychenko 2006, Farmer 2006).

Finally, methodological aspects of studies of airbag effectiveness seem to affect the results. Relevant methodological aspects are, among other things, the type of control group used, control for accident severity, the type of database used in the analysis and control for confounding variables.

***Effects of frontal airbags on head injuries.*** Reduced risk of head injuries, cranial fracture, neck injuries and maxillofacial fractures have been found in several studies (Barnes, Morris, Fildes and Newstead 2002, Lenard, Frampton and Thomas 1998, Morris, Barnes and Fildes 2001a, Morris et al. 2001b, Mouzakes et al. 2001). Analyses of accident data from Germany and Great Britain have found fewer serious injuries to the head and face (AIS 2+) among belted drivers who have sustained severe injuries (MAIS 2+) in airbag-equipped vehicles compared to vehicles without airbag. Airbags have been found to increase the risk of eye injuries among occupants who are wearing glasses. The risk of eye injuries is smaller in airbags with reduced energy (Duma et al. 2005). Results for facial injuries are inconclusive. Frampton et al. (2000) found reduced risk of facial injuries in airbag-equipped cars, whereas other studies (Barnes, Morris, Fildes and Newstead 2002, Dalmotas, Hurley, German and Digges 1996) found reduced risk.

***Effects of frontal airbags on arm injuries.*** The most frequent airbag-caused injuries are injuries to arms, wrists and hands (Frampton et al. 2000). Increased risk of arm injuries has been found in a number of studies (Atkinson et al. 2002, Barnes, Morris, Fildes and Newstead 2002, Frampton et al. 2000, Jernigan and Duma 2003, Johnston, Desantis-Klinich, Rhule and Saul 1997, Lenard, Frampton and Thomas 1998, Morris, Barnes and Fildes 2001a, Morris et al. 2001b). Most airbag-caused arm injuries are dislocations or fractures (Jernigan, Rath and Duma 2005). The risk of airbag-caused arm injuries depends on how the driver is holding the steering wheel (Atkinson et al. 2002).

***Effects of frontal airbags on thorax injuries.*** The most frequent airbag-caused fatal injuries are thorax injuries (e.g. aortic dissection) and dislocations of neck vertebrae (Cunningham, Brown, Gradwell and Nee 2000). Matthes et al. (2006) found 30% greater risk for thorax injuries in airbag-equipped cars than in cars without airbags.

***Effects of frontal airbags on child fatalities in the passenger front seat.*** The effects of frontal airbags on fatalities among children seated in the passenger front seat have been investigated by Kahane (2006), Glass, Segui-Gomez and Graham (2000) and Graham et al. (1998). Significant results from these studies are summarised in Table 4.14.3. The results show that children below 5 years are most at risk, independent of the use of restraints. Older children have increased fatality rates only when unrestrained. Injury rates among children can be reduced by seating children in the back seat, or by deactivating the airbag if a child is seated in the front passenger seat (Kahane 1996).

*Table 4.14.3: Effects of front airbags on the number of killed or injured car occupants*

| | Percentage change in the number of fatalities | | | |
|---|---|---|---|---|
| Age (years) | Types of accidents affected | Restraint | Best estimate | 95% confidence interval |
| Under 1 | Frontal collisions | Unspecified | +310 | (+68; +898) |
| 1–5 | Frontal collisions | Restrained | +92 | (+5; +251) |
| 1–5 | Frontal collisions | Unrestrained | +177 | (+53; +403) |
| 1–5 | All accidents | Unrestrained | +155 | (+6; +512) |
| 6–10 | Frontal collisions | Unrestrained | +94 | (+6; +256) |

***Injuries caused by airbags***. Deploying airbags may cause injuries to the face, head, neck, arms, wrists and hands and to the thorax (see above). The noise and gasses from deploying airbags may cause hearing damages and injuries to the air passages. In a study of fatally injured car drivers of airbag-equipped vehicles, Cammisa, Reed, Ferguson and Lund (2000) found that 15% had died from injuries that had been inflicted by the airbag. The risk of airbag-caused injuries increases when car occupants sit close to the airbag. The recommended minimum distance is 25–30 cm. Injury rates increase also when occupants are sitting out of position, i.e. in non-standard sitting positions. This is a possible explanation for the finding of Langwieder, Hummelt and Mueller (1997), according to which airbag-caused injuries more often occur among passengers than among drivers.

***Effects of side airbags.*** The effects of side airbags on fatalities and injuries have been studied in USA by McCartt and Kyrychenko (2006) and Kahane (2007). The results are summarised in Table 4.14.4.

Side airbags seem to reduce fatalities in most types of accidents. Since larger effects have been found when belt use is statistically controlled for than when belt use is unspecified and not statistically controlled for, the overall effect on all accidents may be somewhat smaller than shown in Table 4.14.4. The effectiveness in preventing fatalities has been found to be greater when torso- and head airbags are combined, than when torso-airbags are the only types of side airbags. Significant reductions of head injuries have also been found in crash tests (Kahane and Tarbet 2006).

Results from in-depth accident studies in Germany and USA do not indicate that side airbags cause injuries that would not have occurred otherwise (Gehre, Kramer and

*Table 4.14.4: Effects of frontal airbags on the number of killed or injured car occupants*

| | | Percentage change in the number of injuries | |
|---|---|---|---|
| Injury severity | Types of accidents | Best estimate | 95% confidence interval |
| ***Drivers, unspecified seat belt use*** | | | |
| Fatal | All accidents | −32 | (−42; −20) |
| Fatal | Collisions | −34 | (−54; −6) |
| Fatal | Single-vehicle accidents | −12 | (−26; +5) |
| ***Drivers and passengers, belt use statistically controlled for*** | | | |
| Fatal | Head-on collisions | −11 | (−22; +2) |
| Fatal | Side impact on driver/passenger nearside | −22 | (−28; −15) |
| Fatal | Side impact on driver/passenger farside | −20 | (−34; −4) |
| Ejected fatalities | Side impact | −11 | (−31; +15) |

Schindler 2003, Yoganandan Pintar, Zhang and Gennarelli 2007b). Crash tests have also shown that side airbags are less dangerous to children than frontal airbags. Depending on the type of airbag however, injuries to the neck and spine may occur all the same.

***Other types of airbags.*** Foot and knee airbags have up to now only been tested in crash tests. For foot airbags, reductions of injuries to the feet in serious head-on collisions of up to 80% have been found (Kippelt, Buss, Feldhoff and Thelen 1998). A study of knee airbags found a protective effect and no injuries inflicted to knees by the airbags (Schroeder and Bosch 2005).

### Effect on mobility

Airbags have no documented effects on mobility.

### Effect on the environment

Airbags are filled with nitrogen gas. On inflation, natrium hydroxide is released, which reacts with the air to create a powder. This power is not dangerous. There is no evidence showing that inflation of airbags has resulted in damage to hearing (Fosser, Vaa and Torp 1992).

### Costs

No recent cost estimates are available for the installation of airbags in new vehicles. In Norway, the costs for frontal airbags in new vehicles have been estimated at about NOK 5,000 (1995 prices). In the USA, the costs have been estimated to be about US$ 300 (NHTSA 2001).

The costs for replacing deployed frontal airbags have been estimated at about US$ 1,000 for passenger airbags and about US$ 1,200 for driver airbags (Evans 2004). These estimates take into account that the windscreen often has to be replaced as well.

### Cost–benefit analysis

Numerical examples are calculated for installing frontal and side airbags in all new cars. Since no cost estimates are available, it is estimated at which costs the benefits will exceed the costs, assuming different effects on driver and front seat passenger fatalities. For serious injuries, the same effect as for fatalities is assumed. No effects of airbags on slight injuries are assumed in the numerical example. Under the assumption that driver and passenger fatalities and serious injuries are reduced by 15%, the benefits of installing frontal airbags in all new vehicles exceed the costs, when the costs do not exceed NOK 4,680. Under the assumption of a reduction of fatalities and serious injuries by 5%, the respective figure is NOK 2,400. For side airbags, the equipment of all new vehicles has larger benefits than costs if the costs do not exceed NOK 10,700 under the assumption that driver and passenger fatalities and serious injuries are reduced by 20%. When the fatality and serious injury reduction is 5%, the respective figure is NOK 5,350. In these numerical examples, it is assumed that about 90% of all drivers and passengers are using seat belts. For unbelted drivers and passengers no effects on fatalities or injuries of frontal airbags are assumed.

Vehicles that are equipped with side airbags are for the most part also equipped with frontal airbags. No empirical results are, however, available about the combined effects of frontal and side airbags.

## 4.15 Seat belts in buses and trucks

### Problem and objective

The dimensions of the vehicle itself provide occupants of heavy vehicles with greater protection against injury in accidents than occupants of smaller vehicles. In Norway, according to official accident statistics (1990–93), the proportion of uninjured drivers in injury accidents was 90% among bus drivers and 78% among truck drivers. In passenger cars, only 53% of all drivers involved in injury accidents were injured themselves. In buses, not only the driver but also the passengers are exposed to the risk of injury. This risk is not just caused by traffic accidents in which the bus is involved, but also by sudden braking and turning manoeuvres, which can lead to passengers hitting the interior of the bus, hitting each other or falling out of their seats. Standing passengers in buses can easily fall over when the bus makes sudden movements. In Norway (1985–86), it has been estimated that the true numbers of injured persons in buses was 241 in traffic accidents (127 according to official accident statistics) and 156 in other types of bus accidents (none in official accident statistics) (Vaa 1993). These injury figures refer to all people on board in buses.

Seat belts in heavy vehicles (lorries and buses) are intended to reduce the probability and the severity of injuries to drivers and passengers in heavy vehicles.

**Description of the measure**

Seat belts in heavy vehicles must be installed in a different way from seat belts in passenger cars and vans. This is partly due to the fact that the driver's seat in heavy vehicles, as a rule, is spring-mounted, which means that the seat belt must be able to adapt to the movements of the seat. The back of seats in passenger seats in buses, especially city buses, are often too low for the shoulder strap in a three-point seat belt to be secured effectively (Khasnabis, Dusseau and Dombrowski 1991). However, technical solutions have been developed for both lorries and buses, which have proved to function satisfactorily in crash tests using dummies.

**Effect on accidents**

No studies have been found that quantify the effect on the number of injuries and the severity of injuries of the use of seat belts in heavy vehicles. An American evaluation of the potential of seat belts in reducing the number of injuries in buses (Khasnabis, Dusseau and Dombrowski 1991) concludes that it is difficult to predict the effect. A three-point seat belt will hold the body in place, but not the head, which can be thrown into the seat in front in the event of a head-on collision. Since the seat backs are often low, whiplash injuries can occur in the event of rear-end collisions. A person who is held in his/her bus seat in the event of accident can put so much extra loading on the seat that the seat mounting snaps. In city buses, with frequent stops and many people getting on and off, seat belts must also be simple to put on and off, and be vandal-proof.

In another American evaluation of costs and benefits of making seat belts compulsory in school buses in Florida, it was assumed that seat belts (both lap belts and three-point belts) could reduce the probability of injury by 0–20% (Baltes 1995). The estimate is very uncertain and based in part on poorly documented assumptions (Transportation Research Board 1989).

**Effect on mobility**

No studies have been found that indicate how seat belts in heavy vehicles affect mobility. If the use of seat belts in city buses becomes widespread, more time may be needed at each bus stop to give passengers time to take seat belts on and off.

## Effect on the environment

No studies have been found that show how seat belts in heavy vehicles can affect the environment. Seat belts will increase the weight of the vehicle very slightly. This can lead to a very small increase in fuel consumption.

## Costs

An American study (Baltes 1995) shows the installation costs for seat belts in school buses to be US$ 1,500 (January 1995) for lap belts, US$ 3,800 per bus for three-point seat belts and US$ 4,644 per bus for four-point seat belts. The annual maintenance costs are respectively US$ 35, 40 and 40. Converted to Norwegian kroner according to the dollar exchange rate in January 1995 (6.70) and purchasing power parity for private consumption between the USA in Norway in 1991 (1.64) (Elvik 1995a), this results in the following figures in Norwegian kroner per bus:

| Type of seat belt | Installation costs (NOK) | Annual maintenance costs (NOK) |
|---|---|---|
| Lap belts | 16,500 | 385 |
| Three-point belts | 41,700 | 440 |
| Four-point belts | 51,000 | 440 |

## Cost–benefit analysis

An American cost–benefit analysis (Baltes 1995) concludes that far too few injuries occur in school buses, and that the effect of seat belts is far too uncertain, for it to be cost-effective to equip these vehicles with seat belt. However, no benefit–cost ratio is given.

Assuming that around 400 people in buses are injured each year in Norway, of whom it can be roughly estimated that 300 could have used seat belts (the others are assumed to be standing passengers), the number of injured persons per bus per year is around 0.01. Assuming further that seat belts reduce the number of injuries by 10%, 100% use of seat belts in all seats on a bus would reduce the number of injured persons per bus per year by 0.001. The benefit of this can be estimated at around NOK 400 per bus per year. It costs a minimum of NOK 16,500 to equip a bus with seat belts. This is far more than the benefit of injuries prevented. Even if seat belts could eliminate all injuries to bus passengers, the measure would not be cost-effective.

## 4.16 Vehicle crashworthiness

### Problem and objective

Cars are involved in the majority of traffic accidents. Car occupants (drivers and passengers) comprised around 65% of all those who were injured or killed and around 59% of all those who were killed in injury accidents reported to the police in Norway in the years 2001–06. In the last 40 years, vehicle crashworthiness has considerably improved. In Norway, the percentage of fatalities in police-reported injury accidents decreased from 4.8% in 1970 to 2.8% in 2000 and to 2.5% in the years 2001–06. In Sweden, it decreased from 5.6% in 1970 to 2.6% in 2000, although both vehicles masses and speed have increased over this period. Information from insurance statistics indicates that an increasing number of traffic accidents lead to property damage only.

Crashworthiness refers to all aspects of the vehicle's construction, which influences the severity of injuries for occupants and, according to some definitions, also properties of the vehicle, which affect injury severity among pedestrians in collisions with the vehicle.

### Description of the measure

Vehicle crashworthiness depends on a number of properties of vehicles that affect the probability of occupants sustaining severe or fatal injuries in a collision. Occupants may sustain injuries from colliding with the vehicles interior. Characteristics of the vehicles interior, such as the steering wheel, instrument panel, front windscreen and doorframe, affect the probability and severity of such injuries (Harms 1992, NHTSA 1995, Thomas and Bradford 1995). The construction of a vehicle's body affects the degree to which the vehicle absorbs collision forces and reduces G forces on the occupants. It also affects the degree to which a survival space remains for the occupants in (serious) collisions. Ideally, deformation of parts of the vehicle absorb a maximum of collision forces, while at the same time, a part of the vehicle remains stable so as to protect occupants from being crushed. In side impacts, occupant protection is more difficult to achieve because less vehicle mass is available to absorb collision forces without reducing survival space for the occupants. The probability to survive frontal collisions at high speeds is limited both by the complete crushing of the vehicle and by inertial forces on the occupants (Wood, Veyrat, Simms and Glynn 2007).

In this chapter, the effects on the risk of severe or fatal injuries are described for cars with different test results in standardized crash tests, general improvements of vehicles crashworthiness and some individual properties of cars, which are assumed to be related to crashworthiness.

***Crash test results.*** When testing the crashworthiness of vehicles in crash tests, the forces on the occupants in standardized collisions are measured with instrumented dummies. In the USA, all new vehicles have to be assessed by a New Car Assessment Programme (NCAP). In Europe, cars also have to fulfil certain safety standards. Additionally, cars may be tested by EuroNCAP (European NCAP), which is voluntary for car manufacturers. EuroNCAP exists since 1997. It evaluates new cars by testing four aspects of crashworthiness:

- Adult occupant protection: frontal, the side and pole impact tests, whiplash test
- Pedestrian protection: collision tests with adult and child pedestrians
- Child occupant protection: frontal and side impact tests with 18-month-old and 3-year-old sized dummies, clarity of instructions and seat installation in the vehicle to ensure that the child seat can be fitted safely and securely (since 2003)
- Safety assist: presence and design of ESC, seat belt reminder and speed limitation devices (since 2009)

Each of these aspects is rated on a scale from 1 to 5 stars (pedestrian protection on a scale of 1 to 4 stars). Since 2009, an overall rating is provided, ranging from 1 to 5 stars, based on the ratings of all four ratings.

In the USA, crash tests are performed according to guidelines issued by the NHTSA (USNCAP) and by the IIHS. Both crash tests are performed as frontal impact tests with airbag-equipped vehicles. In Australia (ANCAP), crash tests are also performed as frontal impact tests.

***General improvements of vehicle crashworthiness.*** During the last decades, vehicle crashworthiness has generally improved and more recent vehicle models are therefore often assumed to be safer than older models.

***Individual characteristics of vehicles.*** Improvements to the vehicle crashworthiness are often introduced simultaneously and it is therefore difficult to evaluate the effects of isolated aspects of vehicle crashworthiness. Vehicle characteristics that are assumed to affects injury severity and that have been investigated empirically are as follows:

- *Collapsible steering columns* have been standard equipment in American cars since the end of the 1960s and are now required in all cars. A collapsible steering column may be equipped with a cut-off joint, which snaps when exposed to pressure, or with a telescopic construction, so that it does not intrude into the compartment.
- *Laminated front windscreens* are constructed with several thin layers of glass glued together. This strengthens the front windscreen, which prevents the head from going through the front windscreen in an accident.

- Improved *front windscreen fastening* is intended to prevent the windscreen coming loose in an accident. If the front windscreen comes loose, this greatly increases the risk of the driver and front seat passenger being thrown out of the car.
- *Padding and changing the location of the instrument panel* means that the steering wheel and dashboard are filled with foam rubber or some other relatively soft material, while at the same time the instrument panel and the individual instruments are located in such a way that the probability of drivers or passengers hitting them in an accident is reduced, or so that the contact points lead to the minimum amount of damage possible.
- *Headrests* are either adjustable cushions or extended (prolonged) seat backs. Headrests are intended to reduce the uncontrolled movements of the head rearwards and forwards when a car is struck from behind and thus reduce the probability of neck injuries.
- *Safer door locks* involve changes to the design of door locks, which are intended to prevent the doors from swinging open in an accident. If the doors are opened, the probability of being thrown out of the car increases, resulting in more serious injuries.
- *Reinforcement bars* in doors are intended to protect against injuries in side impacts. These bars increase the doors' resistance against deformation, so that the compression of the compartment is reduced.
- *Crush-resistant roof* is intended to prevent the roof being compressed when a vehicle overturns and lands on its roof.

**Effect on accidents**

***Validity of crash test results.*** The relationship between crash test ratings and the risk for serious or fatal injuries to the occupants in real accidents has been investigated in a number of studies. The results vary considerably and can partly be explained with methodological aspects of the studies. An overall effect has therefore not been calculated. In general, there are two groups of studies. The first group of studies compared crash test ratings with injury/fatality risk in accidents under more or less identical conditions as the crash tests (e.g. impact point, speed, vehicle mass). In most of these studies, reduced risk of serious of fatal injuries was found in cars with better crash test ratings (Zador, Jones and Ginsburg 1984, Jones and Whitfield 1988). According to Kahane (1994b), drivers of cars with a good crash test rating have ca. 20–25% lower fatality risk than drivers of cars with a poor crash test rating in head-on collisions between two similar vehicles, one of which has a good rating and one of which has a poor rating. Only one study (Nirula, Mock, Nathens and Grossman 2004) found no difference in injury severity between drivers of cars with different ratings in the USNCAP.

The second group of studies investigated relationships between crash test ratings and injury/fatality risk in accidents in more general circumstances. These studies are for the most part based on large numbers of accidents. Three studies found no relationship (Campbell 1982, Grush, Marsh IV and 67 South 1983, Stewart and Rodgman 1985). According to four more recent studies, better crash test results are associated with lower injury severity, although the relationships were not always strong or consistent (Australia: Newstead and Cameron 1997, 1999, USA: Newstead, Narayam, Cameron and Farmer 2003, Farmer 2005). In general, stronger relationships were found between crash test ratings and injuries or fatalities in frontal impacts than between crash test ratings and injuries/fatalities in all accidents. The strongest relationships were found in Australian studies. Injury severity in vehicles with intermediate ratings was not always significantly different from injury severity in vehicles with good or poor ratings, and not even always in between these. Relationships were not always consistent between different groups of vehicles. Newstead, Narayam, Cameron and Farmer (2003) found relationships between crash test ratings and injury severity only when ratings from USNCAP and IIHS were combined, but not for ratings from one test only.

There are several possible explanations for the weak and inconsistent relationships that were found in these studies. Newstead, Narayam, Cameron and Farmer (2003) argue that information on injury severity is hardly comparable between police-reported accidents and crash test ratings, and that this may have contributed to the weak relationships. Although the studies controlled for driver age and gender, driver behaviour may not have been adequately controlled for.

Harless and Hoffer (2007) compared fatality risks of drivers in cars with different USNCAP ratings. In order to control for differences between drivers of different types of cars, comparisons were made only within vehicle lines for which several crash test results were available. The results show the following fatality rates compared to vehicles with a 5-star rating:

- 4 stars: 1.07 (1.00; 1.15)
- 3 stars: 1.14 (1.04; 1.24)
- 2 stars: 1.36 (1.11; 1.66)
- 1 star: 1.18 (1.00; 1.49)

When the same analyses were conducted without restriction to comparisons within vehicle lines, the relationship between crash test rating and fatality rates is weaker and inconsistent. This indicates that weak relationships found in other studies may be partly due to confounding effects of driver characteristics.

***General improvements in vehicle crashworthiness.*** When investigating the effects of general improvements of vehicle crashworthiness, it is important to take into account other changes over time and differences between drivers of different (old vs. new) vehicles. Three studies were found that investigated the effects of vehicle registration year on injury rates. Two of them concluded that newer vehicles are safer (Martin and Lenguerrand 2008, Broughton 2003), while one concluded that older vehicles are safer (Fosser, Christensen and Fridstrøm 2000). The explanations for the findings are improvements of crashworthiness over time and behaviour adaptation among drivers (drivers of older cars assumed to drive more cautiously), respectively.

Table 4.16.1 shows the relative fatality/injury accident rates for vehicles in different age groups. The rates in the oldest age group are set equal to one. Fosser, Christensen and Fridstrøm (2000) studied the relationship between the age of vehicles and injury accident rates. In contrast to the other two studies, it was found that accident rates increase continuously at later registration years, when controlling for annual mileage, car owner's gender, age and province of residence. Broughton (2003) estimated the numbers of fatalities and serious injuries in accidents in 1990 and 1998 if vehicle safety had remained at the same level as in 1980. Compared with the estimated fatality numbers, the actual numbers decreased for cars with later registration years. Martin and Lenguerrand (2008) investigated the relationship between the age of vehicles and the probability of a driver being fatally injured in a head-on collision. The results show that driver fatality rates decrease continuously with later registration years when controlling for a number of other factors, such as vehicle mass and power of both vehicles in the collisions, age and gender of the drivers of both vehicles, impact zone and road category.

*Table 4.16.1: Relative fatality/injury accident rates for vehicles in different age groups*

| | Fosser, Christensen and Fridstrøm (2000) | | Broughton (2003) | | Martin and Lenguerrand (2008) | |
|---|---|---|---|---|---|---|
| | Registration year | Injury accidents | Registration year | Fatal/serious injury accidents | Registration year | Fatalities in head-on collisions |
| Oldest | 1962–70 | *1.00* | 1980 | *1.00* | Before 1991 | *1.00* |
| More recent | 1971–75 | 1.36 | 1990 | 0.91 | 1991–93 | 0.95 |
| ... | 1976–81 | 1.47 | 1998 | 0.80 | 1994–96 | 0.86 |
| ... | 1982–85 | 1.80 | | | 1997–99 | 0.79 |
| ... | 1986–92 | 1.95 | | | 2000–02 | 0.62 |
| Most recent | | | | | 2003–05 | 0.57 |

***Individual characteristics of vehicles.*** The effects on injuries and fatalities of a number of individual properties of vehicles have been investigated in the following studies:

Lundstrom and Cichowski (1969) (USA): collapsible steering columns
Mackay, Siegel and Hight (1970) (Great Britain): laminated front windscreens
Nahum, Siegel and Brooks (1970) (USA): collapsible steering columns
Levine and Campbell (1971) (USA): collapsible steering columns
O'Day and Creswell (1971) (USA): collapsible steering columns
O'Neill, Haddon, Kelley and Sorenson (1972) (USA): headrests
States et al (1972) (USA): headrests
New York State Department of Motor Vehicles (1973) (USA): collapsible steering columns
McLean (1974) (USA): collapsible steering columns, headrests, bars in car doors
Huelke, Lawson and Marsh (1977) (USA): crush-resistant roofs
Cameron and Wessels (1979) (Australia): headrests
Kahane (1981) (USA): collapsible steering columns
Kahane (1982a) (USA): headrests
Kahane (1982b) (USA): bars in doors
Kahane (1984) (USA): various measures
Nygren (1984) (Sweden): headrests
Kahane (1985) (USA): laminated front windscreens, improved fastening of front windscreens
Nygren, Gustafsson and Tingvall (1985) (Sweden): headrests
Kahane (1988) (USA): instrument panel
Kahane (1989b) (USA): door locks and crush-resistant roofs
Friedel, Glaeser and Krupp (1992) (Germany): headrests
Kahane (1994c) (USA): crash test performance criteria
Moffatt and Padmanaban (1995) (USA): crush-resistant roofs

On the basis of these studies, the effect on the severity of injury in accidents of the different measures can be estimated as stated in Table 4.16.2.

Front windscreens with improved fastenings reduce the probability of ejection considerably. Injuries, which are due to contact with the front windscreen, however, are not reduced as much. Padding and relocation of the instrument panel reduce the probability of injuries in head-on collisions by around 20%. Headrests appear to be associated with an increase in the number of fatalities in rear-end collisions. It is not known why this is the case, but many adjustable headrests are adjusted too low. They then act as neck breakers in accidents, rather than as an aid to preventing neck injuries. Adjustable headrests reduce neck injuries in rear-end collisions by around 15%, while

*Table 4.16.2: Effects of crashworthiness on the number of injured persons in accidents*

| | | Percentage change in the number of injuries | |
|---|---|---|---|
| Type of accident affected | Injury severity | Best estimate | 95% confidence interval |
| ***Collapsible steering columns compared with rigid*** | | | |
| Head-on collision | Fatal injury | −12 | (−15; −8) |
| | All injuries | −24 | (−29; −19) |
| ***Laminated front windscreen compared with toughened front windscreen*** | | | |
| Head-on collision | Fatal injury | −20 | (−24; −17) |
| | Serious injury | −30 | (−32; −29) |
| | Slight injury | −9 | (−10; −8) |
| ***Front windscreens with improved fastening to the car*** | | | |
| Thrown out of the car | Fatal injury | −15 | (−19; −12) |
| | All injuries | −55 | (−63; −46) |
| Contact with front windscreen | All injuries | −4 | (−6; −2) |
| ***Padding and changed design of the instrument panel*** | | | |
| Head-on collision | All injuries (cars) | −22 | (−35; −6) |
| | All injuries (other vehicles) | −18 | (−40; +14) |
| ***Head rests (compared with cars without these)*** | | | |
| Rear-end accident | Fatal injury (all types of injury) | +12 | (+1; +24) |
| | Neck injuries (adjustable) | −14 | (−17; −11) |
| | Neck injuries (fixed) | −25 | (−34; −17) |
| ***Safer door locks*** | | | |
| Rollover accidents (ejection) | Fatal injury | −13 | (−18; −8) |
| ***Reinforcement bars in doors*** | | | |
| Side impacts | Fatal injury | −1 | (−4; +2) |
| | All injuries | −16 | (−18; −13) |
| Single-vehicle accidents | Fatal injury | −19 | (−22; −17) |
| | All injuries | −21 | (−26; −16) |
| ***Crush resistant roofs*** | | | |
| Rollover accidents | Fatal injury | −75 | (−79; −72) |
| | All injuries | −35 | (−36; −32) |
| ***Results (good/poor) in crash tests with specific performance requirements*** | | | |
| Tested accident types | Fatal injury | −20 | (−29; −10) |

fixed head supports reduce such injuries by around 25%. The effect of safer door locks is only known for fatal injuries in rollover accidents. Locks satisfying Federal Motor Vehicle Safety Standard 206 are associated with a 13% lower risk of fatal injury in rollover accidents than locks that do not satisfy this standard. Reinforcement bars in the doors reduce the probability of injuries in side impacts and in single-vehicle accidents where the first point of contact is on the driver's side of the vehicle. The decrease in the probability of being injured is around 15–20%. More rigid roofs give a lower probability of injury in a rollover than a roof, which is compressed. The results apply to the difference between a roof, which is crushed less than 12 cm in an accident, and a roof, which is crushed more than this.

### Effect on mobility

No effects on mobility of crashworthiness as described in this chapter have been documented.

### Effect on the environment

Some measures improving crashworthiness increase the weight of the car. These include reinforcement bars in doors and headrests. Increasing the weight of the car increases fuel consumption and the emission of polluting gases, which are directly related to fuel consumption.

### Costs

Few cost figures are available for the measures described in this chapter. Kahane (1981) states the cost of collapsible steering wheel columns to be US$ 8.41 (1978 figures) per car, plus an increase in weight of 0.5 kg. Laminated front windscreens cost US$ 6 per car in 1982. In the same report, Kahane states that the price of improved windscreen fastenings gave a cost saving of around US$ 15 dollars per car. Kahane (1982a) states the cost of headrests in 1981 in US dollars at US$ 24.33, plus a weight increase of 4.7 kg per car for adjustable headrests, and US$ 6.65 plus a weight increase of 1.7 kg per car for permanent headrests. Kahane (1982b) states that costs of reinforcement bars in doors are US$ 28.29 (1982 prices) plus a weight increase of 11.8 kg per car.

### Cost–benefit analysis

Collapsible steering columns are effective in head-on collisions. The average number of head-on collisions with injuries per vehicle per year, according to official Norwegian accident statistics, is around 0.0006. This is representative for a situation where the majority of cars have collapsible steering wheel columns. Without these, the number of head-on collisions involving injuries per car per year would be around 0.00075. In other words, flexible steering wheel columns prevent 0.00015 injury accidents per car per year. The present value of saved accident costs, calculated over 15 years, is around NOK 3,000. The costs of collapsible steering wheel columns are around NOK 180, of which NOK 170 is construction costs and NOK 10 is for increased petrol consumption. This gives a benefit–cost ratio of around 16.7.

Laminated front windscreens reduce injuries in the event of head-on collisions. Relying on the same assumptions as given above, this measure can be estimated to prevent around 0.00015 injury accidents per vehicle per year. This gives the same saved accident costs as above, NOK 3,000 per vehicle. The cost per vehicle is around NOK 100, which gives a benefit–cost ratio of around 30.

Headrests prevent injuries in rear-end collisions. The expected number of rear-end collisions involving injuries per car per year is around 0.00055. This figure applies to a situation where the majority of cars have headrests. Headrests can be estimated to prevent around 0.0001 injury accidents per car per year. The present value of saved accident costs, calculated over 15 years, is around NOK 720. The cost of the measure is around NOK 520 per car, of which NOK 430 is the cost of installing head supports and NOK 90, the cost of increased fuel consumption. The benefit–cost ratio is around 1.4.

Reinforcement bars in doors prevent injuries in side impacts. The expected number of such collisions per car per year is around 0.0005. It is assumed that this figure can be reduced by 15% with the use of reinforcement bars, i.e. 0.000075 injury accidents prevented per car per year. The present value of saved accident costs, calculated over 15 years, is around NOK 680 per car. The cost of the measure can be estimated to be NOK 720 per car. Of this, NOK 500 is the cost of installing the bars, and NOK 220 is the additional cost of fuel. The benefit–cost ratio is thus around 0.95.

## 4.17 Driving controls and instruments

### Problem and objective

Different types of human error are often regarded as the most important contributory factor to traffic accidents. Examples of common human errors are omission errors (a task is not carried out), carrying out a task incorrectly, in the wrong order, or with inadequate timing, attention errors (e.g. overlooking something) or carrying out a task to a too great or little extent (Swain and Guttman 1980, Kantowitz and Sorkin 1983). Driving errors probably occur relatively often, but a driving error does not necessarily have serious consequences. The probability of committing driving errors can increase dramatically in critical situations, which require faster reactions from the driver (Swain and Guttman 1980). The chance of carrying out a wrong action also increases when the amount of information and thus the workload are large, for example when driving through a complicated intersection with numerous information signs and several traffic elements. The probability of errors while driving is also related to the design of driving controls and instruments.

The objective is to design a car's driving controls and instruments in such a way that the number of errors is reduced so that the probability of accidents becomes as small as possible.

### Description of the measure

The design of the driver environment comprises among other things the design of the steering wheel, gear stick, pedals and hand brake, instrument panel, indicators, driving controls on the dashboard, control functions for headlights, direction indicators, windscreen wipers, windscreen washers, front headlight washers, defroster equipment, heating and air-conditioning equipment, instrument and compartment lighting, lights and horn, seat belt locks and warning lights, radio, cassette/CD player and possibly a mobile telephone.

The design of these controls and instruments can affect the probability of driver errors, and thereby influence safety. The design of the driver environment can be adapted to the human form, senses, perception and information processing, e.g. by adjusting the visibility, location and adjustability.

Mirrors are part of the driving environment. A problem with mirrors is often that they do not cover all the fields behind the car. Blind zones may hide another vehicle, a cyclist or pedestrian. Mirrors, which are designed so as to minimize blind zones, are often designed in a way that may lead to misjudgements of e.g. distances. It has been claimed that convex mirrors may lead to misjudgement of speed and distance (Mortimer and Jorgeson 1974, Luoma, Sivak and Flannagan 1995). Convex mirrors were found to reduce the visibility of cars behind and to lead to an underestimation of the speed of passing cars. Drivers were found to prefer flat mirrors and to use those more often than convex mirrors (Mortimer and Jorgeson 1974).

### Effect on accidents

Four studies have been found, which have evaluated the effects on accidents of different types of wing mirrors: Smith, Mulholland and Burger (1985), Cross (1991),

Behrensdorff and Hansen (1994) and Luoma, Sivak and Flannagan (1995). Flat mirrors produce blind zones in the rearward field of vision. As a result, several types of convex mirrors have been tested, which are designed to cover these blind zones. The results from the studies of the effects on accidents are somewhat inconsistent and do, in summary, not indicate that there are significant effects on accidents.

In an American field experiment, Smith, Mulholland and Burger (1985) investigated the effects of a convex mirror on the passenger side. A non-significant reduction in accidents of 18% in mirror-related accidents was found.

In the study by Cross (1991), three groups with a total of 5,200 vans in a transport company were compared, which had different combinations of mirrors. The results showed that trucks with flat wing mirror on the left side and a convex mirror on the right side had 17.6% fewer accidents where 'blind zones could have contributed to the accident' (Cross 1991) than trucks with only flat wing mirrors on both sides.

Behrensdorff and Hansen (1994) investigated the effects of convex mirrors (wide-angle mirrors and close-up mirrors) on the passenger's side. It was assumed that these mirrors could reduce the number of accidents when turning right, but increase the number of accidents with traffic from the right, because the mirror is so large that it can reduce the view to the right. The results show that injury accidents increase (not significant) and that fatal accidents are reduced (significant).

In the Finnish study (Luoma, Sivak and Flannagan 1995), two types of mirror were installed on the driver's side: a multi-radius mirror and a convex mirror. Flat mirrors were used as a control group. A multi-radius mirror is a mirror having a convex central element while the adjoining peripheral part has a progressively reduced curve radius towards the outer edge of the mirror. In the Finnish study, the effect on accidents related to lane changes was studied. The results from these studies are summarised in Table 4.17.1. Multi-radius mirrors and convex mirrors appear to reduce the number of accidents when changing lanes, but the reduction is not statistically significant.

**Effect on mobility**

No effects on mobility have been documented. There may be indirect effects when a design affects the predictability of driver behaviour. For example, a design, which encourages the use of direction indicators, may increase mobility by making driver signals to other road users more reliable and behaviour more predictable.

*Table 4.17.1: Effects of different types of mirrors on the number of accidents*

| | Percentage change in the number of accidents | | |
|---|---|---|---|
| Accident severity | Types of accident affected | Best estimate | 95% confidence interval |
| ***Right-hand mirror on lorries/goods vehicles: convex only*** | | | |
| Not specified | 'Mirror-related' accidents | −18 | (−36; +6) |
| ***Right-hand mirror on lorries: 1 flat+1 convex*** | | | |
| All accidents | 'Mirror related' accidents | +5 | (−10; +23) |
| Injury accidents | Right turn accidents | +18 | (−6; +48) |
| Fatal accidents | Right turn accidents | −44 | (−66; −6) |
| Injury accidents | Counter-part from the right | +9 | (−6; +26) |
| Fatal accidents | Counter-part from the right | −7 | (−32; +10) |
| ***Mirror on driver's side on passenger car*** | | | |
| All accidents (multi-radius mirror) | *Changing lane* | −21 | (−43; +10) |
| All accidents (convex mirror) | Changing lane | −23 | (−46; +9) |

## Effect on the environment

No effects on the environment of improving driving controls and instruments have been documented.

## Costs

Improvements and standardisation of driving controls and instruments will probably not result in increased costs for anyone. With the mass production of components such as switches, indicator lights etc, standardisation will actually produce an economic benefit.

## Cost–benefit analysis

The lack of information about costs of the measures makes it difficult to carry out cost–benefit analyses. Replacing a mirror on a car, for example replacing a flat mirror with a convex mirror, will cost between NOK 500 and NOK 1,500. This can reduce accidents when changing lanes by around 20%. Such accidents comprise around 0.5% of injury accidents reported to the police. This means that the expected number of injury accidents when changing lanes per car per year is around 0.00002. The expected number of injury accidents prevented per car per year with convex mirrors is therefore 0.000004. This gives a saving in accident costs of around NOK 4 per car per year. This is undoubtedly less than the cost of the measure.

## 4.18 Intelligent cruise control

### Problem and objective

According to official Norwegian accident statistics, there was an increase in the number and proportion of rear-end collisions. In 1993–84, this type of accident made up ca. 10% of all accidents involving injuries. From 1990 to 2006, the proportion was around 20% in most years. In 1991 the USA's National Safety Council reported 11.3 million accidents involving vehicles. Of these, 2.7 million, or around 24%, were rear-end collisions. This includes property-damage-only accidents (National Safety Council 1992).

Many rear-end accidents are associated with a lack of driver attention. An American study found that 63% of all rear-end collisions were caused by lack of driver attention alone, 15% were related to the consumption of alcohol, 14% were a combination of lack of attention and driving too close to the car in front, 2% were a combination of high speed and lack of attention, 2% were due to poor judgement and 3% were due to sight and visibility conditions (McGehee, Mollenhauer and Dingus 1994). The driver's perceptual abilities with regard to judging the relative speed of a car directly ahead is relatively poorly developed (Hofmann 1966). According to American studies of rear-end collisions, collisions with stationary vehicles are the most common. In 1990, these comprised around 70% of rear-end collisions in the USA (McGehee, Mollenhauer and Dingus 1994).

Lack of attention may have its roots in lack of information about driver behaviour in cars that are ahead in a queue of cars. For example, a driver will seldom see the brake lights on cars, which are two cars or more ahead in the queue. Car manufacturers in Europe, Japan and the USA have invested in a very comprehensive research activity to develop solutions, which are effective in reducing rear-end collisions (Becker et al. 1995a, 1995b, Butsuen, Doi and Sasaki (1995), Farber and Bailey 1993, Farber and Paley 1993, Kemeny and Piroird 1991, Nelson, Farber, Burgett and Sheridan 1994, Satoh and Tanigushi 1994, Schwertberger 1994).

ICC is intended to prevent the car behind from driving into the car in front. ICC is also intended to increase driving comfort.

### Description of the measure

ICC can be seen as an expansion of the so-called 'Cruise Control' (Chira-Chavala and Yoo 1994). With cruise control, the car can be set at a fixed, constant speed that the car maintains until the driver turns it off. ICC means that the car is set at automatic regulation of speed also with regard to distance to the car in front. As a result, acceleration/deceleration is also affected through regulation of the accelerator and/or brake. ICC is also referred to as adaptive cruise control or following distance warning systems.

Different systems for ICC have been studied in field studies and in simulator studies. Field studies were conducted by Becker et al. (1995a, 1995b), Butsuen, Doi and Sasaki (1995), Fancher and Ervin (1994), Satoh and Tanigushi (1994). Simulator studies were conducted by Rothengatter and Heino (1994), Nilsson (1995), Nilsson, Alm and Janssen (1992) and Janssen and Nilsson (1992). The systems that were studied vary with respect to how speed is regulated, what kinds of warnings are given to the driver and which possibilities the drivers have to take over control from the system. Some systems use both autonomous braking and the accelerator pedal, while others only apply reduced engine power or gear brakes. Warnings can be given to driver in the form of visual or auditory information or as increased counter-pressure of the accelerator pedal. In most systems, the driver can take over control from the system.

Some studies have conducted evaluations of idealised systems where, under given assumptions, the effects on accidents and mobility are simulated (Marburger, Klöckner and Stöcker 1989, Farber and Bailey 1993, Farber and Paley 1993, Malaterre and Fontaine 1993, Chira-Chavala and Yoo 1994).

**Effect on accidents**

No studies of the effects on accidents of ICC have been found. ICC has consistently been found to reduce the time drivers spend driving at short-time headways (Regan et al. 2006). A number of studies have estimated potential changes in the number of accidents when driving with ICC (Marburger, Klöckner and Stöcker 1989, Malaterre and Fontaine 1993, Farber and Bailey 1993, Farber and Paley 1993, Chira-Chavala and Yoo 1994). The different estimates of potential effects are summarised in Table 4.18.1. There is a remarkable consistency with regard to possible effects on rear-end collisions. All estimates are close to a 50% decrease. As regards the effect on the total number of accidents, there is a greater spread in the effect estimates. This may be due to the fact that the proportion of rear-end collisions varies from country to country and depends on whether property-damage-only accidents are included or not.

Regan et al. (2006) estimated that ICC in combination with Intelligent Speed Adaptation (ISA) would reduce fatal accidents by up to 9% and serious injury accidents by up to 7%.

*Table 4.18.1: Potential effects on the number of accidents of ICC*

| | Percentage change in the number of accidents | |
|---|---|---|
| Study | Rear-end collisions | All accidents |
| Marburger, Klöckner and Stöcker (1989) (proposal 1) | – | −3.0 |
| Marburger, Klöckner and Stöcker (1989) (proposal 2) | – | −2.3 |
| Malaterre and Fontaine (1993) | −45 | −5.0 |
| Farber and Paley (1993) | −50 | −11.9 |
| Chira-Chavala and Yoo (1994) | −52 | −7.5 |
| Average – all calculations | −49 | −5.9 |

It should be noted that the results of the above mentioned studies are not based on accidents. Behavioural adaptation effects are not taken into account. Such effects may occur, as was shown by Rudin-Brown and Parker (2004). Subjects driving with ICC had in this study longer response times for hazard detection and lane position variability increased significantly. At the same time, driver workload was reduced.

**Effect on mobility**

ICC may affect mobility in that it regulates headways and speed. Broqua, Lerner, Mauro and Morello (1991) have estimated that when driving in queues is harmonised with a headway of 1 s – and that 20% and 40% of cars, respectively, are equipped with ICC – then the volume of traffic may *increase* by respectively 6% and 13%. When the headways are harmonised to 2 s, the volume of traffic will be *reduced* by respectively 6% and 13%, with the same proportions of vehicles having the system as given above (Broqua 1991, referred to in Chira-Chavala and Yoo 1994). According to Kesting, Treiber, Schönhof and Helbing (2008), congestion can be considerably reduced when at least 25% of all vehicles are equipped with ICC and travel times can be reduced already at lower equipment rates.

**Effect on the environment**

ICC may lead to reduced emission of pollution because speeds are harmonised and the frequency of queues at a standstill can be reduced. The actual effect is not known.

**Costs**

ICC as optional equipment in new cars costs ca. €1,300 (2009 prices).

### Cost–benefit analysis

No cost–benefit analyses of autonomous/or automated distance regulators are available. In order to indicate possible benefit effects and costs, a numerical example has been worked out. It is assumed that the measure costs NOK 6,200 per vehicle (a one-off cost). It is further assumed that the number of rear-end collisions can be reduced by 45%. This applies to both injury accidents and property-damage-only accidents. The number of police-reported injury accidents prevented per car per year for cars with an average annual mileage and an average accident rate can be estimated to 0.00025 accidents per car per year. In addition, it can be estimated that 0.00375 property-damage-only accidents are avoided per car per year. The present value of reduced accident costs accumulated over 15 years can be estimated at around NOK 2,500 for injury accidents and around NOK 1,000 for property-damage-only accidents. In total, this is around NOK 3,500. This is less than the cost of the measure. Possible effects on mobility and the environment are, however, not included in this analysis.

## 4.19 Regulating vehicle mass (weight)

### Problem and objective

Unprotected road users, i.e. pedestrians and cyclists, are termed unprotected because they must absorb all the kinetic energy, which is released in an accident from their own body. They have no surrounding mass, which can absorb this energy. People in cars have much greater protection against energy absorption because much of the energy conversion occurs in the car's bodywork, not only in the human bodies, which are in the car. As a result, injury severity is reduced for people in cars. This is clearly shown in official Norwegian accident statistics, which show how the proportion of injured drivers of all drivers involved in injury accidents varies between vehicles with different mass. The figures refer to injury accidents reported to police in Norway in the period 1990–93 (Table 4.19.1). Table 4.19.1 clearly shows that the proportion of uninjured drivers increases with the mass of the vehicle.

Mass, therefore, is central in explaining differences in injury risks between road user groups with different mass. According to Harms (1992), the relative speed change in a head-on collision (often called delta $V$, symbolised by $\Delta V$) is proportional to the mass ratio between the vehicles. When two cars, one weighing 20 t and one weighing 2 t, both with a speed of 80 km/h, collide head-on, the change in speed is 14.5 km/h for the heavy vehicle and 145.5 km/h for the light vehicle. The sum of the speed changes is equal to the relative collision speed (80+80 km/h = 160 km/h). The probability of being injured in an accident depends strongly on the relative speed change in an accident. As a result,

*Table 4.19.1: Relationship between vehicle mass and the proportion of all drivers involved in injury accidents in Norway who were injured*

| Vehicle group | Typical mass (kg) | Drivers distributed by percentage | | Number involved |
|---|---|---|---|---|
| | | Injured drivers | Uninjured drivers | |
| Lorry | 20,000 | 21.8 | 78.2 | 2,723 |
| Bus | 12,000 | 9.9 | 90.1 | 1,157 |
| Van or pickup | 2,000 | 37.6 | 62.4 | 2,985 |
| Combined car | 1,500 | 32.1 | 67.9 | 1,273 |
| Taxi | 1,500 | 28.4 | 71.6 | 659 |
| Car | 1,200 | 46.8 | 53.2 | 38,666 |
| Heavy motorcycle | 400 | 91.0 | 9.0 | 1,547 |
| Light motorcycle | 200 | 88.0 | 12.0 | 251 |
| Moped | 100 | 90.0 | 10.0 | 2,977 |
| Bicycle | 25 | 95.3 | 4.7 | 4,150 |
| Pedestrian | | 99.3 | 0.7 | 4,545 |

vehicle mass is important both for the distribution of injuries between different groups of vehicles and road users, and for the total number of injuries. Evans (1990b) illustrates this with some examples. A road user who swaps his car for a motorcycle would increase his own risk, but make it safer for all others. If a road user changes to a bigger and heavier car, he or she will be safer, but all others will incur increased injury risk. One assumption made in these examples is that the accident involvement rate is independent of the size of the car, which is hardly the case. In the USA, it has been shown that large cars have a higher risk of being involved in accidents than small cars (Evans 1985a, 1985b).

Several researchers have established relationships between the size of a car and the probability of injury, which can be considered almost as laws of nature in traffic accidents where vehicles are involved, when all other factors are identical (Campbell and Reinfurt 1973, Negri and Riley 1974, Grime and Hutchinson 1979a, 1979b, Evans 1990b):

- The lighter the vehicle, the smaller the risk of injury for other road users
- The heavier the vehicle, the smaller the risk of injury for the people in the car.

These rules apply to a wide spectrum of vehicles, from mopeds, motorcycles, small cars and larger cars to smaller and larger lorries (Evans and Frick 1993). Variations in injury risk attributable to car mass are first and foremost a question of the distribution of risk between vehicle and road user groups. It is less clear what significance the mass of the vehicle has for the total number of injuries in traffic and whether it is possible to reduce this by setting specific standards for vehicle mass. In order to be able to say that a difference in the injury risk between small and large cars is due to the mass of the car, other explanations for this difference must be ruled out. This is seldom possible.

The objective of a possible regulation of car mass, as a traffic safety measure, is to influence the distribution of the car fleet according to mass, so that the total number of injured persons in traffic is as low as possible with a given number of cars and a given accident rate per kilometre driven.

## Description of the measure

Measures, which could be used to regulate car mass, include a ban on the use of cars under a given weight, a ban on the use of cars above a given weight and tax regulations with a view to optimise the weight distribution in a fleet of cars.

## Effect on accidents

***Method for describing the effects of car mass on the number of injuries***. In order to indicate the effect of mass on the number of injuries, a distinction must be made between three types of accidents: (1) collisions between cars, (2) single-vehicle accidents with cars and (3) collisions between cars and lighter road users. The best basis for indicating the effects of vehicle mass are collisions between vehicles (Broughton 1996a, 1996b, 1996c).

***The significance of mass on the number of injuries.*** The results presented here are based on the following studies:

Perchonok et al. (1978) (USA)
Grime and Hutchinson (1979a, 1979b) (Great Britain)
Evans (1984) (USA)
Evans (1985b) (USA)
Bryden and Fortuniewicz (1986) (USA)
Evans and Wasielewski (1987) (USA)
Partyka (1990) (USA)
Björketun (1992) (Sverige)
Evans and Frick (1992) (USA)
Tapio, Pirtala and Ernvall (1995) (Finland)
Broughton (1996c) (Great Britain)

The majority of these studies do not state the total effects on the number of injuries of changes in car mass. As a whole, they deal only with internal risk, i.e. how increases in mass affect the risk of injury to those who occupy the car whose mass is increased. These figures only tell half the story, because they do not say anything about the risks to others caused by an increasing car mass.

The most comprehensive data refer to effects on the driver's own risk of increasing the mass of a car. The results of these studies are summarised in Table 4.19.2, which shows the relative fatality rates for drivers of cars with different mass in crashes with cars with a different mass (Evans and Frick 1992).

The table shows the fatality rate for drivers of car 1 in collision with car 2. The figures on the diagonal, printed in bold italics, show the effect on fatality rate of a universal increase in car mass, i.e. going over to a fleet of cars where all cars have equal mass, but a mass, which is greater than the mass that the smallest cars have today. This shows the effect of *increased mass per se*. It is only when mass increases to more than around 1,400 kg that fatality rate is reduced.

Only four of the above studies (Evans and Wasielewski 1987, Björketun 1992, Tapio, Pirtala and Ernvall 1995, Broughton 1996c) have tried to measure the effects of car mass on both the risk of injury to people in the car and the risk of injury to the counterpart in multi-vehicle accidents The results of these four studies are summarised in Figure 4.19.1.

*Table 4.19.2: Relative fatality rate for drivers of car 1 in collision with car 2 (fatality rate in crashes between the lightest cars is set at equal to 1.00)*

| | Car 2 | | | | | | | | |
|---|---|---|---|---|---|---|---|---|---|
| Car 1 | 830 | 960 | 1080 | 1180 | 1290 | 1400 | 1460 | 1560 | 1640 |
| 830 | *1.00* | 1.51 | 2.15 | 1.99 | 2.32 | 2.48 | 2.19 | 2.31 | 2.28 |
| 960 | 1.01 | *1.45* | 1.71 | 1.63 | 1.97 | 2.10 | 2.17 | 1.88 | 1.94 |
| 1080 | 0.85 | 1.06 | *1.63* | 1.56 | 1.63 | 1.58 | 1.69 | 1.59 | 1.58 |
| 1180 | 0.61 | 0.77 | 0.99 | *1.40* | 1.31 | 1.31 | 1.56 | 1.31 | 1.66 |
| 1290 | 0.43 | 0.72 | 0.87 | 1.00 | *1.07* | 1.10 | 1.04 | 1.14 | 1.40 |
| 1400 | 0.46 | 0.61 | 0.71 | 0.83 | 0.93 | *0.90* | 1.00 | 0.98 | 1.11 |
| 1460 | 0.32 | 0.43 | 0.69 | 0.70 | 0.73 | 0.83 | *0.86* | 0.99 | 0.96 |
| 1560 | 0.28 | 0.33 | 0.48 | 0.50 | 0.62 | 0.62 | 0.80 | *0.85* | 0.96 |
| 1640 | 0.19 | 0.20 | 0.33 | 0.44 | 0.50 | 0.57 | 0.59 | 0.65 | *0.72* |

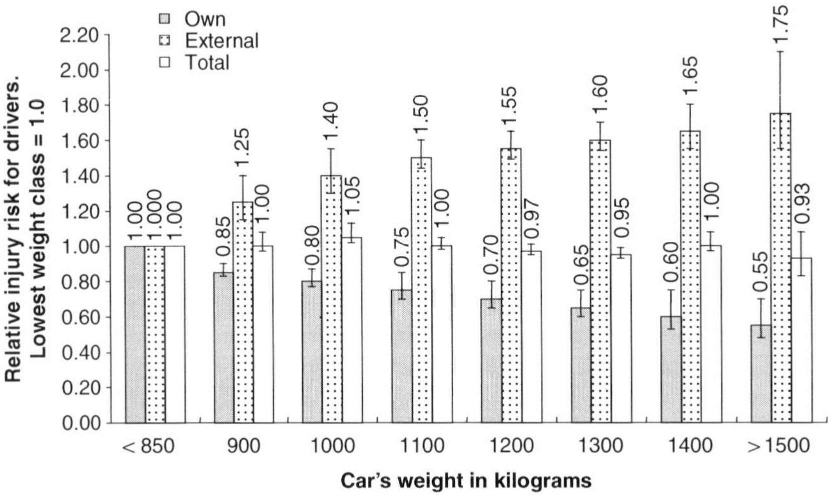


*Figure 4.19.1: The relationship between the car's specific weight in kilograms and the relative risk of injury in collisions where cars are involved.*

The relative risk of injury for the light cars is set equal to 1.00. The numbers at the top of the columns show the relative risk of injury for heavier vehicles. The lines above the columns show the uncertainty in the relative risk. Figure 4.19.1 shows that the risk of injury for people sitting in a car decreases when the weight of the car increases and is around 50% lower in cars of more than 1,500 kg than for cars weighing less than 850 kg. On the other hand, the risk of cars injuring others increases the heavier they are. The external risk of the heaviest cars is around 75% higher than the external risk of the lightest cars. The total number of injured persons in frontal impacts, where cars are of different weights are involved, is almost independent of car mass. This implies that the increase in the external risk with increasing weight offsets the gain in internal risk.

A number of estimates have been made of the possible effects on the total number of injuries of changing the average weight of a whole car fleet. Klein, Hertz and Borener (1991) calculated the effect of reducing the average weight of vehicles from around 1,680 to 1,225 kg in the states of Texas and Maryland in the USA. For Texas, it was calculated that the number of injured persons would increase by 11%, while for Maryland, the calculated increase was 4%. The increase was statistically significant only in Texas. Broughton (1995) calculated the effect of a 5% reduction in weight of all cars in Great Britain to a 3.8% decrease in the number of seriously injured people in cars in urban areas and a 2.9% decrease in the number of seriously injured people in cars in rural areas. In the USA, small lorries and multi-purpose vehicles (sports utility vehicles [SUV]) weighing around 1,750–2,000 kg have become more common in recent years, while at the same time, passenger cars are becoming lighter (Kahane 1997). As result, there is an increasing difference in weight between passenger cars and multi-purpose vehicles. Kahane estimated the effect of a weight reduction of around 50 kg for multi-purpose vehicles to a decrease of around 1% in the number of injured persons in multi-vehicle accidents where these cars were involved. For passenger cars, a similar weight reduction was estimated to produce an increase of around 2% in the number of injured persons in multi-vehicle accidents in which cars are involved.

These calculations are hypothetical and only take the weight or mass of the car into account. If drivers thought that their cars would protect them less well than they do today, for example, by cars being lighter and smaller, it is possible that this would lead to more careful driving behaviour, which would have just as great an effect on the number of injury accidents as changes in mass itself.

In recent years, vehicle safety has improved considerably. Swedish accident statistics show that the difference in fatality rates between large and small cars has decreased (Folksam 2009, Figure 4.19.2).

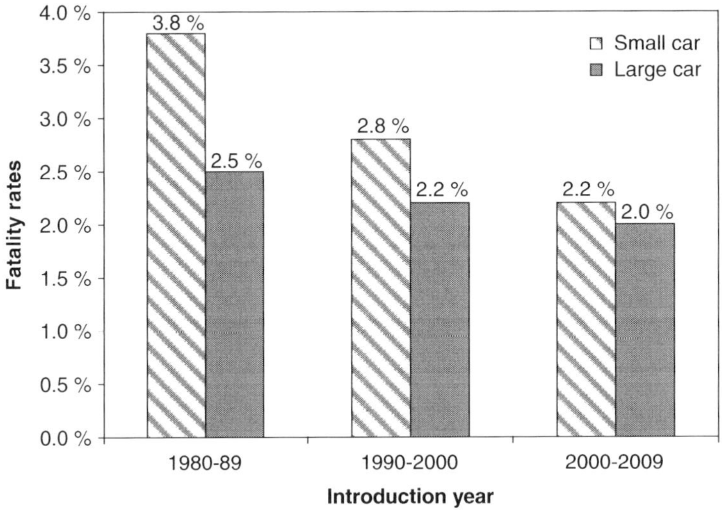


*Figure 4.19.2: Change of fatality rates in small and large cars over time (Folksam 2009).*

### Effect on mobility

Measures intended to change weight distribution in a given fleet of vehicles may have direct or indirect effects on mobility. Measures that remove a group of light and/or heavy vehicles or intended to produce a more even distribution of weight in the car fleet can lead to more homogenous behaviour in traffic, for example in the form of less variations in speed. This can lead to better mobility in traffic and reduce the need for overtaking. The actual effects have not been studied.

### Effect on the environment

Changes in the mass of a car can affect the environment as a result of the relationship between car mass and fuel consumption. On the basis of information from 48 car models (Opplysningsrådet for veitrafikken 1993), Figure 4.19.3 shows the relationship between weight and fuel consumption, calculated in litres per Norwegian mile (10 km) at 90 km/h.

Figure 4.19.3 shows that large cars use more fuel than light cars. This can also lead to increased emission and pollution.

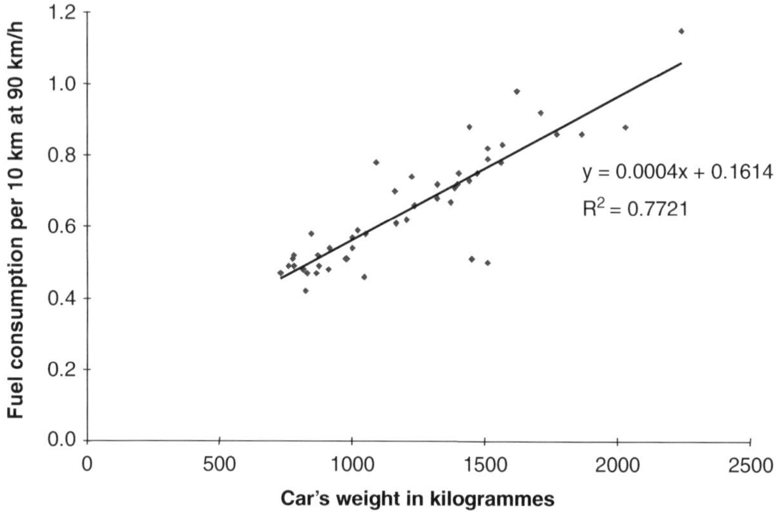


*Figure 4.19.3: Relationship between car mass and fuel consumption (Opplysningsrådet for veitrafikken).*

### Costs

No cost figures are available for the potential measures, which are described here.

### Cost–benefit analyses

The costs and benefits of the measures that are designed to regulate car mass cannot be calculated, as no cost figures are available for such measures.

## 4.20 Regulating automobile engine capacity (motor power) and top speed

### Problem and objective

Vehicle speed is one of the main contributing factors to (serious) accidents, and the risk of fatal injuries increases in the fourth power with increasing speed (Elvik, Christensen and Amundsen and Elvik 2006). Both engine capacity and top speeds of vehicles have increased and road standards improved in most countries. Speed limits and speed enforcement are not always sufficient to limit actual driving speed to the legal maximum speed, or to the speed that is appropriate for given driving conditions. There is currently no regulation of the development of increasing engine powers and top speeds. Regulating automobile engine capacity and limiting the top speed are intended to prevent the benefits of increased crashworthiness in vehicles and road design from being offset as a result of increased speeds or other forms of careless driving.

### Description of the measure

There is an EU directive that prescribes speed limiters in goods vehicles above 3.5 t and in all vehicles used for the carriage of passengers and which have more than eight passenger seats. These groups of vehicles must now have maximum speed governors for 90 and 100 km/h, respectively.

While a maximum speed governor sets a general limit for the maximum driving speed, which cannot be exceeded, Intelligent Speed Adaptation (ISA) regulates the maximum driving speed depending on the actual speed limit. Speed may be regulated either throughout the whole road system or only in specific areas, such as cities or particular stretches of road. The maximum tolerable speed may be defined as the current speed limit, or other conditions may be taken into account as well, such as construction zones, pedestrian crossings, traffic, road and weather conditions. ISA can influence driving speed by simply displaying the actual speed limit, by making the gas pedal exert a counter force at speeds above the current limit (or advisable speed) and by additionally reducing motor power or applying the brakes either with or without permitting the driver to over steer the system. The whole system may or may not allow the driver to switch it on or off (Várhelyi, Hjälmdahl, Hydén and Drasköczy 2004, Carsten and Tate 2005).

### Effect on accidents

***Engine capacity***. A number of studies have evaluated the relationship between engine capacity and the accident rate. A synthesis of the results of these studies using meta-analysis is not possible.

A Norwegian study compiled injury statistics from the Gjensidige insurance company (Elvik and Skaansar 1989). It compared the number of accidents reported to the insurance company for six makes of car, each with the standard model and the GTI model. The GTI models have considerably more powerful engines than the standard models. For all six makes, the GTI models had a higher accident rate than the standard models. If the accident rate for the standard model is set equal to 1.00, the GTI models had accident rates of 1.22–2.42, with an average of 1.75. However, the differences in the accident rate are not necessarily due to the car's characteristics alone. Different drivers choose different models of cars and the results do not control for driver characteristics.

A German study (Bock et al. 1989) investigated the relationship between weight per unit of engine capacity and the number accidents per 100 registered cars involved in accidents was studied. A vehicle weighing 1,000 kg, which weighs less than 10 kilos per kilowatt engine performance, has an engine producing more than 100 kilowatts. A car of equal weight, which weighs more than 35 kilos per kilowatt engine power, has an engine providing a maximum of 28 kilowatts. Cars with the most powerful engines (less than 10 kg/kW engine performance) had around 65% more accidents per 100 cars than cars with the least powerful engines (35 or more kg/kW engine performance). However, annual mileage, driver characteristics and the passive safety of the cars were not controlled for. The observed relationship may therefore in part be due to these factors, not to engine capacity alone.

The British Department of Transport (UK Department of Transport 1993) compared accident involvement of cars of different sizes and with different engine capacity. In total, cars with high engine performance ('high engine performance' is not defined) have around 14% more accidents per 10,000 cars than cars with standard engine performance. For the smallest cars, accident rate increases by 40–50% when engine performance increases. For larger cars, there is no difference in accident rate between cars with normal engine performance and cars with high engine performance. Driver characteristics and annual mileage were not controlled for. A supplement to the report shows that cars with an engine capacity greater than 1,500 $cm^3$ have an annual mileage of 15,100–19,600 km, as opposed to 9,500–13,200 km for cars with an engine size below 1,500 $cm^3$ (UK Department of Transport 1993). The differences in mileage account completely for the differences in accident rate per 10,000 cars.

A French study (Fontaine and Gourlet 1994) investigated the car's accident rate per kilometre driven for cars with different weight and engine performance per ton weight (kilowatt per ton). The effect of increased engine performance on the risk level varies substantially with the weight of the car. Taking all weight classes together, cars with an engine, which produces more than 50 kW/t, have a 25% higher risk than cars with an engine, which produces less than 50 kW/t. However, a consistent relationship between engine performance and accident rate has only been found for vehicles in the 800–1,000 kg weight class. More in-depth analyses show that a relationship between car engine performance and accident rate has only been found for young drivers (Fontaine and Gourlet 1994). For drivers aged between 30 and 64 years, no such relationship was found.

Figure 4.20.1 shows the results of a German study (Schepers and Schmid 1996), where the risk of being involved in injury accidents per million kilometres driven is compared for cars with different engine performance in kilowatts. The age of the car was controlled for. A distinction is made between four age groups for cars. The figure shows that cars with a high engine capacity do not have higher accident rates than cars with smaller engine capacity. Rather, there is a tendency that the accident rate decreases with increasing engine performance. Driver characteristics are not controlled for in this figure.

In summary, the results of the studies vary. The best controlled studies are the British, the French and the German studies. These studies indicate that the relationship between engine performance and accident rate weakens the more confounding factors a study controls for. This pattern corresponds with the findings in similar studies of the relationship between engine performance and the accident rate of motorcycles (see Section 4.21).

It is therefore difficult to draw any general conclusions from these studies. The results do not show the effects of engine performance alone, but rather engine performance combined with a number of other factors, which also influence accident rate. If, despite these weaknesses, one interprets the results of these studies as showing true effects, the French and British studies indicate that cars with particularly high engine performance

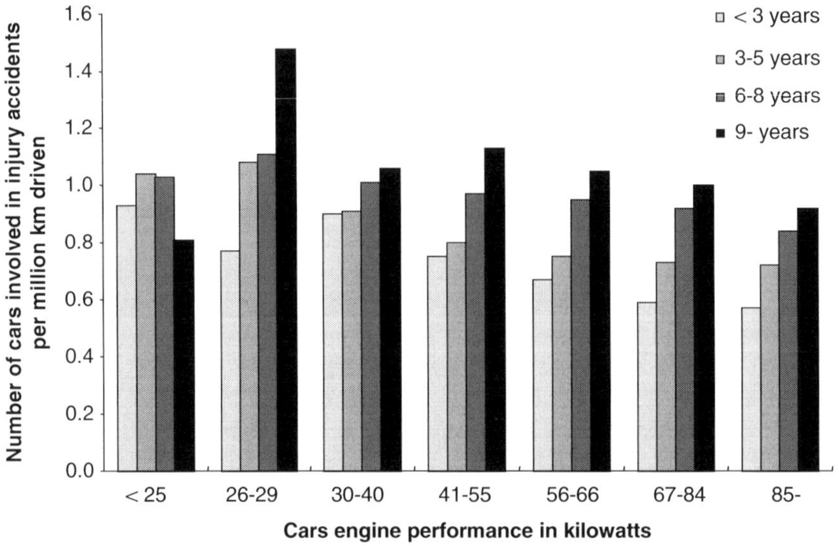


*Figure 4.20.1: Risk of being involved in injury accidents for cars with different engine performance: German results (Schepers and Schmid 1996).*

have, at most, a 15–25% higher risk than cars with standard engine performance, given the weight of the car. On the other hand, the German study does not indicate that accident rate increases with increasing engine performance.

***Intelligent speed adaptation (ISA).*** Field trials in which ISA was installed in private cars have been conducted in several countries:

Almqvist and Nygård (1997) (Sweden)
Duynstee, Katteler and Martens (2001) (Netherlands)
Madsen (2001) (Denmark)
Hjälmdahl and Várhelyi (2004) (Sweden)
Várhelyi, Hjälmdahl, Hydén and Draskóczy (2004) (Sweden)
Carsten and Tate (2005) (UK)
Regan et al. (2006) (Australia)
Driscoll, Page, Lassare and Ehrlich (2007) (France)
Vlassenroot et al. (2007) (Belgium)
Adell, Várhelyi and Hjälmdahl (2008) (Sweden)
Adell and Várhelyi (2008) (Sweden)
Wallén-Warner and Åberg (2008) (Sweden)

All studies were conducted in urban areas, except for the Danish and French studies, which included both urban and rural areas. In most studies, an active accelerator pedal was used, i.e. the gas pedal exerts a counter force at speeds above the current limit. Reduced driving speeds with ISA were found almost consistently. Greater speed reductions were found

- among drivers with a positive attitude towards ISA and among drivers who do not enjoy speeding,
- among the top speeds,
- during the first time after installation of ISA, effects decreased during the first 6 months; however, average speeds remained below the speed level before installation of ISA,
- when ISA applied an active accelerator pedal than when only visual/acoustic warnings are given to the drivers.

Speed changes were often found to be different at different speed limits. Results are however inconsistent. Many drivers are reluctant to drive much slower than the surrounding traffic. The average speed of the surrounding traffic and traffic volume are therefore likely to affect speed reductions with ISA. Speed changes were not studied with respect to these factors. Increased average speed was in some studies found among drivers who had driven well below the speed limit before the installation of ISA. Those drivers often increased their speed and drove at a constant speed closer to the speed limit with ISA. Speed variance was also found to be reduced with ISA, i.e. drivers drove at more constant speeds and accelerated and decelerated less.

Several studies investigated effects on certain types of driver behaviour, e.g. giving way to pedestrians at pedestrian crossings and speed changes in approaches to intersections or in other situations were speed has to be adjusted. Behaviour at pedestrian crossings was found to be improved in some studies, but on the whole driver behaviour seemed to be mostly unchanged with ISA. The number of violations (other than speeding) was found to increase among drivers with ISA in the study by Hjälmdahl and Várhelyi (2004).

Effects of ISA on accidents were only investigated in one study. Várhelyi, Hjälmdahl, Hydén and Draskóczy (2004) found no difference in the number of police-reported accidents among drivers with and without ISA. ISA drivers had twice as many self-reported accidents than other drivers.

Based on observed changes of speed and speed variance Carsten and Tate (2005) estimated that injury accidents would be reduced by between 10% and 36% and that fatal accidents would be reduced by between 18% and 59% if all cars were equipped with ISA. Results from the French ISA trial (Driscoll, Page, Lassare and Ehrlich 2007) indicate that fatalitites may be reduced by between 4% and 16% and that serious injuries may be reduced by between 0% and 11%, depending on the type of system. Regan et al. (2006) estimated that ISA may reduce fatal accidents by up to 8% and serious injury accidents by up to 6%, based on observed speed changes.

**Effect on mobility**

Top performance speeds for modern cars are well over the maximum speed limit in Norway (100 km/h). Internationally, speed limits of around 110–130 km/h are not uncommon on motorways. There is no top speed limit on most of the motorway network in Germany. The most probable effects of the introduction of maximum speed governors will therefore be an increase in travel time costs, mostly for drivers who drive faster than the speed limit. A calculation for Norway suggests an increase in time consumption in traffic of around 7% if all vehicles were equipped with a top speed governor connected to the speed limit (Elvik 1996b).

Most studies of ISA found that travel times in vehicles equipped with ISA increased because of reduced average travel speeds. However, if all vehicles in an urban area were equipped with ISA, traffic flow is likely to improve, which is likely to be associated with reduced average travel times and congestion (Davidsson 1995, Várhelyi, Hjälmdahl, Hydén and Draskóczy 2004).

**Effect on the environment**

Cars with high-performance speeds use more fuel than cars with low-performance speeds and thus cause more exhaust emission if the high-speed potential is used. ISA is likely to reduce emissions, especially on roads with high speeds (Vaa and Christensen 1992, Vaa, Christensen and Ragnøy 1993, Vaa Christensen and Ragnøy 1995). Emission reductions are affected both by reduction of high speeds and by improved traffic flows (Várhelyi, Hjälmdahl, Hydén and Draskóczy 2004, Almqvist and Nygård 1997).

**Costs**

No cost figures for regulating cars' engine capacity are available. There will be direct and indirect costs. Direct costs are the costs of drafting regulations covering engine capacity and information regarding these regulations and necessary checks and enforcement of such regulations. The indirect costs are the losses to car buyers who have their freedom of choice in buying a car curtailed, and may not be able to buy the model they really want any longer. In principle, these costs can be quantified in the form of compensation, which must be given to those who, as the result of this legislation, would no longer be able to buy the car they want in order to cover the loss of benefit these people would suffer as a result of this limitation in their freedom of choice. It is currently not possible to quantify any of these types of costs.

The costs of ISA consist of costs for the installation and maintenance of infrastructure (digital maps and sensors), in-vehicle equipment costs and costs for updating of maps. The infrastructure costs are dependent on the type of system, i.e. on the type of information that is used for calculating top speed (posted speed limit, specific situations, traffic and weather conditions).

**Cost–benefit analysis**

A number of cost–benefit analyses have been reported for Intelligent Speed Adaptation (ISA).

Elvik (2003) performed an analysis of introducing ISA in Sweden. Requiring new cars to have ISA starting in 2011 was found to have a benefit–cost ratio of 1.37. The cost of installing ISA per vehicle was estimated at SEK 10,000 (about €1,000) and annual costs of running and updating the system was set to SEK 500 (€50) per car per year.

Carsten and Tate (2005) investigated costs and benefits of several scenarios for the introduction of ISA in Great Britain. Costs of installing an intervening ISA were estimated to be £2,361 (€2,640) per car in the year 2000 and £372 (€417) per car in the year 2010. Annual operating costs were set to £5 per car in the year 2000 and £1 per car in the year 2010. Benefit–cost ratio was estimated to between 3.7 and 16.7, depending on the type of ISA used and the assumptions made regarding future growth in traffic. Benefits exceeded costs by a wide margin in all scenarios.

COWI (2006) performed a cost–benefit analysis of ISA applying to the European Union. Two scenarios were compared: the ‘do nothing’ scenario and the ‘do-something’ scenario. In the first scenario, it was assumed that 20% of cars would have ISA by 2025; in the latter scenario, all cars would have ISA by 2025. The benefit–cost ratio was estimated at 3.3 for the do-something scenario.

Elvik (2007) performed a cost–benefit analysis of requiring new cars in Norway to have ISA, starting in 2007. Benefit–cost ratio was estimated at 1.95.

All these analyses indicate that the benefits of ISA are greater than the costs. All analyses adopted a societal perspective, in which the benefits of violating speed limits are disregarded and not treated as a societal benefit in cost–benefit analyses. The analyses of Carsten and Tate (2005) and COWI (2006) did not include any costs of additional travel time at all. The analyses of Elvik (2003, 2007) included costs of additional travel time below the speed limit. The rationale for doing this was that ISA systems were assumed not to be perfect, so that in a traffic stream in which all vehicles are equipped with ISA, mean speed will be slightly below the speed limit.

It should be noted that ISA most probably is a road safety measure that represents a so-called social dilemma. This term refers to a situation in which a cost–benefit analysis made according to a societal perspective can give very different results from a cost–benefit analysis adopting a road user perspective. It is, for example, likely to road users will treat all additional costs of travel time as a loss, not just the additional travel time below the speed limit. Moreover, part of the accident costs is external; hence, road users are not likely to include the full accident savings in their private assessments of the costs and benefits of ISA.

## 4.21 Regulating engine capacity (motor power) of mopeds and motorcycles

### Problem and objective

Riders and passengers on mopeds and motorcycles have a higher risk of injury than any other group of road users who use motor vehicles.

Mopeds and motorcycles give users minimal protection against injury in the event of accidents. The speed at the time of an accident very strongly influences the severity of injuries. In the majority of motorised countries, attempts have been made to regulate speed and engine performance on mopeds and motorcycles, in order to reduce the accident rate for these vehicles and the severity of injuries in accidents (Mayhew and Simpson 1989). The most common form of regulation is the division of mopeds and motorcycles into different classes on the basis of engine performance, combined with licensing regulations for riders of different types of mopeds and motorcycles. A commonly found rule is that only persons who have experience of riding mopeds or smaller motorcycles are given driving licences for the largest motorcycles. It is also common to set limits for engine capacity for different types of mopeds and motorcycles, combined with the ban on engine tuning, which increases engine output beyond the legal limits.

Regulating engine capacity of mopeds and motorcycles, together with driving licensing riders of regulations for mopeds and motorcycles, is intended to reduce the risk of injury for mopeds and motorcycles.

## Description of the measure

In Norway, mopeds and motorcycles are divided into the following classes, based on engine performance (Forlaget Last og Buss A/S 1997):

| Class | Greatest engine size ($cm^3$) | Greatest effect (kW) | Maximum top speed (km/h) |
|---|---|---|---|
| Moped | 50 | 4.00 | 45 |
| Light motorcycle | 100 | 5.15 | 80 |
| Medium-weight motorcycle | None | 25.00 | $>80$ |
| Heavy motorcycle | None | None | $>80$ |

Medium-weight and heavy motorcycles have an engine capacity above $100\,cm^3$. Regulations of engine capacity for different types of motorcycle are combined with the following driving licence regulations (Grøndahl Dreyer 1995):

| Class | Age limit (years) | Training requirements, etc. |
|---|---|---|
| Moped | 16 | Compulsory training and moped driving licence |
| Light motorcycle | 16 | Compulsory training and driving licence |
| Heavy motorcycle | 18 | Compulsory training and driving licence |

Furthermore, there is a ban on tuning of mopeds. A Norwegian study (Fosser and Christensen 1992) showed that tuning of mopeds is relatively common. Of 922 mopeds studied, 36% had been tuned-up at the time they were studied; 14% had previously been tuned-up but had now been tuned down again.

## Effect on accidents

***Ban on engine tuning of mopeds.*** Despite the ban on engine tuning of mopeds, tuning them up is nonetheless widespread among groups of young people who use mopeds regularly (Fosser and Christensen 1992). A Norwegian study found the following relative accident rates for tuned-up mopeds compared to non-tuned mopeds 1.48 (95%

CI [1.10; 2.01]) for injury accidents, and 1.18 (95% CI [1.03; 1.37]) for property-damage-only accidents.

Tuning up mopeds increases the accident rate. Based on the relative accident rates given above, it can be estimated that if no mopeds were tuned up, the number of injury accidents could be reduced by around 14% (−21%; −4%) and the number of property-damage-only accidents by around 7% (−11%; −1%).

A German study (Löffelholz and Nicklisch 1977) confirms these results. The study showed that mopeds, which were tuned up so that the cylinder volume was above 50 $cm^3$, had an accident rate, which was around 2.8 times as high (for injury accidents) as that of non-tuned mopeds.

***Ban on driving heavy motorcycles for young drivers.*** A ban on young riders riding heavy motorcycles has been introduced in Australia and Great Britain. In Victoria, Australia, learner riders and riders with new driving licences (the first year after passing the driving test) were banned from riding motorcycles with an engine capacity above 260 $cm^3$ (Troup, Torpey and Wood 1984). A before-and-after study found that the number of injuries per licence holder went down by around 33% among riders covered by the ban (−38%; −27%). Among riders who were not covered by the ban, the number of injuries per licence holder increased by 8% (−3%; +21%). This change was not statistically significant.

In Great Britain, riders with new driving licences (learner permits) were banned from riding motorcycles above 125 $cm^3$ in 1982 (Broughton 1987). Earlier, the limit was 250 $cm^3$. A before-and-after study found the changes in the number of injury accidents for different groups of riders and motorcycles, which are shown in Table 4.21.1.

*Table 4.21.1: Effects of a ban on riding heavy motorcycles for young drivers on the number of accidents*

| | Percentage change in the number of accidents | | |
|---|---|---|---|
| Group | Size of motorcycle | Best estimate | 95% confidence interval |
| Test group (new riders) | Less than 125 $cm^3$ | +24 | (+21; +29) |
| | More than 125 $cm^3$ | −79 | (−80; −77) |
| | All sizes | +2 | (−1; +5) |
| Control group (experienced) | Less than 125 $cm^3$ | +7 | (+2; +12) |
| | More than 125 $cm^3$ | −16 | (−18; −14) |
| | All sizes | −10 | (−13; −8) |

The number of accidents decreased markedly in the age group covered by the ban and for the type of motorcycle to which the ban applied. However, this decrease was more than offset by an increase in the number of accidents involving light motorcycles. In total, therefore, the number of accidents did not reduce for new riders. For experienced riders in the same period, there was a decrease of around 10% in the number of injury accidents. On the basis of this, the measure cannot be said to have improved the safety for new riders.

***Regulating engine capacity for heavy motorcycles.*** A number of studies evaluated the relationship between engine capacity on mopeds and motorcycles and the accident rate of these vehicles. These studies include:

Kraus, Riggins and Franti (1975a, 1975b) (United States)
Nordisk Trafikksikkerhetsråd (1975) (Sweden)
Hurt, Ouellet and Thom (1981) (United States)
Lekander (1983) (Sweden)
Kallberg (1986) (Finland)
Carstensen (1987) (Denmark)
Koch (1987) (Germany)
Broughton (1988) (Great Britain)
Ingebrigtsen (1989) (Norway)
Mayhew and Simpson (1989) (Canada)
Ingebrigtsen (1990) (Norway)
Taylor and Lockwood (1990) (Great Britain)
Rogerson, Lambert and Allen (1992) (Australia)

The results of these studies vary substantially. There is a tendency for well-controlled studies to find a weaker relationship between engine capacity and accident rate than poorly controlled studies. Well-controlled studies control for as many confounding variables as possible. The best controlled study is by Ingebrigtsen (1990). The study controlled for gender, age, experience, make of motorbike, year and model, annual mileage and a variable intended to measure willingness to take risks. Having controlled for these factors, the relationship between engine capacity for heavy motorcycles and the relative accident rate was as given in Table 4.21.2.

On the basis of these figures, it can be concluded that there is scarcely any gain in safety to be obtained by banning heavy motorcycles or regulating these more stringently than is the case today.

*Table 4.21.2: Effect of engine capacity on heavy motorcycles on the relative accident rate*

| | | Relative accident rate | |
|---|---|---|---|
| Motorcycle capacity | Type of accident affected | Best estimate | 95% confidence interval |
| 101–425 $cm^3$ | All | 1.00 | (0.85; 1.18) |
| 426–625 $cm^3$ | All | 1.03 | (0.83; 1.28) |
| 626–825 $cm^3$ | All | 1.04 | (0.86; 1.25) |
| 826 and more $cm^3$ | All | 1.05 | (0.88; 1.26) |

### Effect on mobility

No effects on mobility of measures for regulating engine capacity of mopeds and motorcycles have been documented. Measures, which limit top speed, may reduce mobility. Measures, which forbid the use of a certain type of motorcycle for a given group of riders, reduce riders' choices with regard to the type of motorcycle.

### Effect on the environment

No effects on the environment of measures to regulate engine capacity of mopeds and motorcycles are known.

### Costs

The direct costs of regulating engine capacity for a moped and motorcycle are not known. These costs consist of: (1) administrative costs of drafting legislation, (2) costs for information connected with legislation and (3) control and enforcement costs.

Regulating the engine capacity of mopeds and motorcycles also involves indirect costs, in that riders' opportunities to choose the motorcycles they would prefer to ride will be curtailed. In principle, this cost can be quantified in the form of suitable compensation to motorcyclists for the loss of benefit associated with the lack of opportunity to buy and ride their first choice of motorcycle. The amount of any such compensation is currently unknown.

### Cost–benefit analyses

If there were no tuned-up mopeds, the number of moped accidents involving injuries could be reduced by around 14%. Estimated on the basis of the official Norwegian accident record for 1995, this would comprise around 75 injured persons prevented per year. This represents a saving of around NOK 110 million. If it were possible to remove all tuned-up mopeds from traffic for a cost, which is less than this, this will be a cost-effective measure. Regarding the engine capacity of heavy motorcycles, the best studies indicate that there is no gain in safety to be obtained by regulating this more stringently than at present.

## 4.22 Under-run guards on heavy vehicles

### Problem and objective

In frontal impacts between lorries and other road users, it is usually the other road users who are injured. Accidents in which road users fall or are pulled under a truck or trailer are known as under-run accidents. In the majority of cases, these lead to much more serious injuries than if under-run had been avoided (Fosser 1979b). Motorcyclists, cyclists and pedestrians are particularly vulnerable to serious injuries if they end up under a lorry. Car passengers often become seroiusly injured even at low impact speeds, and other occupant protection systems often become ineffective.

A Swedish study found that 35% of fatal accidents involving lorries in frontal impacts with two-wheeled vehicles and pedestrians led to these being run over by the lorry (Högström, Svenson and Thörnquist 1973). An American study suggested that a car crashing into a truck from the rear would run under it in more than 90% of the cases (Minahan and O'Day 1977). Under-runs from the side occurred in 75% of frontal impacts between passenger cars and lorries.

Under-run guardrails on lorries and large trailers are designed to prevent cars and other vehicles from driving or being pulled under the overhang of large vehicles.

### Description of the measure

Under-run guards are rails or grates on the back of a lorry or trailer. Side under-run protection can also be rails or grates on the side of the vehicle between the wheel axles. The rail can be made of steel or light metal and either be a rigid construction or a flexible, energy-absorbing structure. Under-run guards on the back of heavy vehicles are obligatory in EU countries since 2007.

### Effect on accidents

Swedish laboratory tests have shown that under-run guardrails significantly reduce the risk of injury, especially combined with the use of seat belts in passenger cars (Högström, Svenson and Thörnquist 1974). However, it is not possible, on the basis of these tests, to state any exact figures for the effect on the severity of injury of equipping all heavy vehicles with under-run guardrails and side under-run protection.

A study of the distribution of points of impacts in 581 collisions found that in 44% of accidents, other road users (cars, two-wheeled vehicles and pedestrians) hit the vehicle between the wheels on the side or from the back (Fosser 1979b). A Swedish analysis of 187 fatal accidents between cars and lorries in the period 1970–72 found that 28% were frontal impacts from the side or from the back (Högström, Svenson and Thörnquist 1974).

A British analysis of 111 fatal accidents (Robinson and Riley 1991) where cars drove under lorries concluded that under-run guardrails at the front of the lorry could certainly have prevented 11 deaths, probably have prevented 32 deaths and possibly have prevented 59 deaths. The authors estimate 32 fatalities prevented out of 111 (29%) as the best estimate of the effects of under-run guardrails.

### Effect on mobility

Under-run guardrails and side under-run protection have no documented effect on mobility.

### Effect on the environment

Under-run guardrails and side under-run protection increase the weight of a vehicle. At a given permitted weight, this may lead to a small reduction in the maximum payload. Increasing the vehicle's weight can also increase fuel consumption. No studies have been found, which quantify these possible effects.

### Costs

Car manufacturers have given the following estimates for costs (excluding taxes) of under-run guardrails and side under-run protection respectively in Norway (February 1996):

| Car's weight (tons) | Under-run guardrails (NOK) | Side under-run protection (NOK) |
|---|---|---|
| 3.5–13 | 3,200 | 4,500 |
| >13 | 3,200 | 7,800 |

### Cost–benefit analysis

A Norwegian cost–benefit analysis using costs figures from 1976 shows that under-ride guardrails are cost-effective (the benefit in kroner is greater than the cost) if all injuries associated with driving under a lorry can be eliminated. If the under-ride guardrails only prevent 50% of injuries at the actual point of contact, they are not cost-effective (Sæther 1980). The same analysis concluded that side under-run protection is cost-effective for an annual mileage of around 10,000–20,000 km and above (Sæther 1980).

These analyses were based on figures, which are more than 30 years old. It cannot therefore be assumed that they are valid today. The cost of under-run guardrails and side under-run protection is NOK 10,000 for a lorry under 13 t and NOK 13,500 for a lorry over 13 t. The expected number of injury accidents per lorry per year is around 0.014. The expected annual cost of injury accidents per car is around NOK 39,000. The costs of under-run guardrails and side under-run protection are around NOK 13,500 per vehicle.

Assuming, somewhat conservatively, that under-run guardrails at the rear and side under-run protection along both sides of a lorry reduce injury costs by 15% per year, this then comprises around NOK 53,000 expressed at present value for 15 years. This is around 3.9 times more than the cost of the measure.

## 4.23 Safety equipment on heavy vehicles

### Problem and objective

Heavy vehicles, with their large mass, represent a hazard to other road users. In accidents involving heavy vehicles, it is normally the other part in the accident, which suffers the most serious injuries. An overview produced on the basis of injuries

*Table 4.23.1: Distribution of injuries among users of a vehicle and injuries to other road users in accidents where the vehicle or road user is involved*

| Type of vehicle | Injuries to users of the vehicle | Injuries to other road users | Ratio between other/own injuries |
|---|---|---|---|
| Lorry | 132 | 795 | 6.02 |
| Bus | 221 | 378 | 1.71 |
| Van or pickup | 301 | 616 | 2.05 |
| Car | 15,622 | 5,128 | 0.33 |
| Motorcycle | 1,233 | 270 | 0.22 |
| Moped | 2,316 | 144 | 0.06 |
| Cycle | 12,801 | 413 | 0.03 |
| Pedestrians | 3,248 | 49 | 0.02 |
| Other groups | 589 | 910 | 1.54 |
| All groups | 36,463 | 8,703 | 0.24 |

recorded in the injury surveillance system of the National Institute of Public Health in Norway (Hagen 1993, Elvik 1994) shows the following distribution of injuries to persons in the vehicle and other road users for different types of vehicle (Table 4.23.1). Lorries cause six times as many injuries to other road users as the number of injured persons in the lorry itself. The table shows that there is a strong relationship between the dimensions of the vehicle and the distribution of injuries between occupant injuries and injuries to other road users.

The number of vehicles involved in injury accidents per million vehicle kilometre has been estimated to be 0.45 for cars and trucks and 0.89 for buses. Accidents where heavy vehicles are involved more often lead to fatalities or serious injuries than accidents where only light vehicles are involved. However, the number of vehicle kilometres travelled by trucks in Norway is not very well known (Borger 1991, Sætermo 1995). As a result, estimates of risk are uncertain.

Protective equipment in heavy vehicles is intended to reduce the number of accidents where heavy vehicles are involved and reduce the severity of injuries in such accidents.

**Description of the measure**

Protective equipment in heavy vehicles includes the following types of equipment and regulations, which are intended to reduce the number of accidents and the severity of injuries in accidents involving heavy vehicles (Fosser 1984): total weight limits and length limits for heavy vehicles, ABS, side marker lamps, extra mirrors and wide-angle mirrors, under-run guardrails and side under-run protection, seat belts, fire extinguishers and first aid equipment. Seat belts are described in Section 4.15, mirrors in Section 4.17 and under-run guardrails and side under-run protection in Section 4.22.

## Effect on accidents

The effect of the measures listed above on accidents has not been extensively evaluated. Estimates of the effect on accidents are only available for total weight, length, ABS, extra mirrors and side marker lamps. In addition, studies have evaluated the relationship between technical defects and the accident rate. The following studies, the results of which are summarised in Table 4.23.2, are available:

Kommunikationsdepartementet (1977) (Sweden): articulated lorry length
Vallette, McGee, Sanders and Enger (1981) (USA): weight and length
Kahane (1983b) (USA): side marker lamps
Jones and Stein (1989) (USA): technical defects
Statistiska Centralbyrån (1994) (Sweden): weight
Hertz, Hilton and Johnson (1995b) (USA): ABS

*Table 4.23.2: Effect of protective equipment on heavy vehicles on the number of accidents*

| | | Percentage change in the number of accidents | |
|---|---|---|---|
| Accident severity | Type of accident affected | Best estimate | 95% confidence interval |
| ***Increasing the total weight by ca. 3–5 t*** | | | |
| Injury accidents | All accidents with heavy vehicles | +22 | (+11; +33) |
| ***Increasing the length of articulated lorries by around 1 m*** | | | |
| Unspecified (all accidents) | All accidents with articulated lorries | +2 | (−7; +12) |
| ***ABS*** | | | |
| Fatal accidents | Head-on collisions and side impacts | +21 | (+13; +30) |
| Unspecified (all accidents) | Head-on collisions and side impacts | −12 | (−13; −11) |
| ***Side marker lamps*** | | | |
| Injury accidents | Side impacts in darkness | −8 | (−10; −6) |
| Property damage only accidents | Side impacts in darkness | −7 | (−8; −6) |
| ***Articulated lorries with technical defects compared to non-defective vehicles (relative risk)*** | | | |
| Unspecified (all accidents) | All accidents with articulated lorries | +72 | (+35; +118) |

***Increasing the total weight*** of a lorry or articulated lorry by 3–5 t increases the risk of injury accidents by about 22%. This is partly due to the fact that increased weight increases braking distances. However, it does not necessarily follow from this that stricter weight limitations on heavy vehicles will reduce the number of accidents. More stringent weight limits require a larger number of vehicles to transport a given amount to goods. This will increase the number of kilometres driven, which will contribute to more accidents. The difference in mass between heavy and light vehicles, even after a considerable total weight reduction (e.g. from 50 to 25 t), will still be large enough for heavy vehicles to cause injuries to other road users (Harms 1992).

***Increasing the length*** of articulated lorries by around 1 m in the region of around 10–25 m appears to have little effect on the number of accidents. Long-articulated lorries require more room and take longer time to pass than shorter lorries. Seen in isolation, these factors probably contribute to increasing the accident rate. On the other hand, a long-articulated lorry can carry a larger load than a short one. More stringent regulation will therefore probably increase the number of lorries and articulated lorries on the roads.

***Antilock braking systems*** on smaller lorries reduce the total number of head-on and side impacts, as well as driving off the road and overturning. The number of fatal accidents appears to increase. The explanation for this apparent difference in effect between fatal accidents and less serious accidents is not known. A possible explanation may be that the increased manoeuvrability provided by ABS in emergency situations makes it easier to avoid accidents, while, at the same time, accidents, which do occur, occur at greater speeds than they did before.

***Side marker lamps*** are small lights fitted on the side of a car to indicate its size. They appear white at the front and red at the back. These lights are mandatory in the USA (Kahane 1983b). Side marker lamps reduce the number of side impacts in darkness by around 7–8%.

***Articulated lorries with one or more technical defects*** have an accident rate, which is around 70% higher than for articulated lorries with no technical defects (Jones and Stein 1989). This indicates that improving technical condition, e.g. as a result of vehicle inspections, can reduce the number of accidents involving articulated lorries.

### Effect on mobility

Increasing weight and heavy vehicles are likely to reduce the speed of these vehicles, and increasing length makes overtaking more difficult for other vehicles. No effects on mobility are documented for other measures discussed in this chapter.

### Effect on the environment

Heavy vehicles create more noise per vehicle than light vehicles. The emission of exhaust gases is also greater, but it has a different chemical composition than that of light vehicles, since heavy vehicles are usually diesel-driven. Except for large changes in total weight limits, the measures discussed in this chapter will have little measurable effect on the environment.

### Costs

No figures are available that show the direct costs of changes in the rules for weight and length of heavy vehicles. The greatest costs of such changes will probably be indirect costs in the form of increased transport costs for industry. The following average transport prices per ton kilometre for transport by lorry in Norway have been estimated for 1993 (Hagen 1995):

| Pay load in tons | Price in NOK per ton kilometre |
|---|---|
| 3.5–4.9 | 4.50 |
| 5.0–7.9 | 3.20 |
| 8.0–9.9 | 2.63 |
| 10.0–11.9 | 1.68 |
| 12.0 and more | 0.98 |

The price per ton kilometre decreases strongly with increasing payload per vehicle. More stringent weight limitations on heavy vehicles mean that more vehicles will be required to transport the same amount of goods. The number of ton kilometres will be the same, but society will pay, for example, three times as much for transport (NOK 3.20 per ton kilometre with a load of 5–8 t, as opposed to NOK 0.98 per ton kilometre with a load more than 12 t) and the transport companies will drive twice as many vehicle kilometres than they do today.

No cost figures for ABS have been found. For side marker lamps, the costs can be estimated, on the basis of an American study (Kahane 1983b), to be around NOK 250–275 per car.

### Cost–benefit analysis

In Section 4.7, the benefit–cost ratio of side marker lamps was estimated to be 1.3. The result stems from an American study. It is difficult to calculate the costs and benefits of, for example, more stringent weight limitations on heavy vehicles. A numerical example has been made for a possible transport system where the heaviest vehicles drive 100 million kilometres per year and carry 1,500 million ton kilometres of goods (15 t per kilometre driven). The number of injury accidents where these vehicles are involved is assumed to be 75 per year (0.75 per million vehicle kilometres).

With a weight limitation of 7.5 t, the number of kilometres driven will approximately be doubled to 200. The number of accidents per million vehicle kilometres is assumed to go down to 0.45. The number of injury accidents will then be 90 (200 × 0.45), that is to say, 15 more than before the weight limitation was introduced. In addition, transport costs per ton kilometre will be approximately tripled.

Of the 2,800 injury accidents in darkness, around 560 are side impacts at intersections. If all cars had side marker lamps, about 7% of these accidents could be prevented, i.e. around 40 accidents per year. The total cost of these accidents is around NOK 80 million per year. Based on the American cost figures, the annual cost per car of side marker lamps is estimated to be NOK 80. This amounts to NOK 160 million for the total fleet of cars in Norway. This indicates that it is not very likely that side marker lamps are cost-effective in Norway (80/160 = 0.5). An American cost–benefit analysis of side marker lamps on cars (Kahane 1983b) concluded that best estimates of the best estimate of the benefit–cost ratio is around 1.3 with an area of uncertainty from around 0.8 to around 1.9.

## 4.24 Moped and motorcycle equipment

### Problem and objective

Riders and passengers on mopeds and motorcycles have a high risk of injury in traffic and minimal protection against injury in the event of an accident. They are much less protected against injuries in accidents than car occupants. The probability for people on mopeds or motorcycles being injured when they are involved in a traffic accident is around 70%.

A particular problem for mopeds and motorcycles is that they are more difficult to notice in traffic than cars, partly because they are smaller. A number of studies (Janoff, Cassel, Fertner and Smierciak 1970, Williams and Hoffman 1979, Thomson 1980, Dahlstedt 1986, Olson 1989, Wulf, Hancock and Rahimi 1989) indicate that poor visibility is a contributory factor in many accidents involving mopeds or motorcycles.

Safety equipment on mopeds and motorcycles is intended to reduce the number accidents in which these vehicles are involved and the severity of the accidents, partly by making them more visible, partly by making them easier to steer and by building mopeds and motorcycles in such a way that they protect drivers and passengers against injury in the event of an accident.

**Description of the measure**

The following measures for making mopeds and motorcycles safer are discussed in this chapter: extended front wheel forks, raised foot rests, lowered seats, front windscreens on motorcycles, coating to protect knees and legs and two-stroke engines.

Daytime running lights are described in Section 4.6. Otherwise, see Section 4.8 for discussion of protective clothing for motorcyclists, Section 4.11 for a description of helmets for moped users and motorcyclists and Section 4.21 for a description of regulating engine performance of motorcycles and mopeds

**Effect on accidents**

The following studies have evaluated the effect on accidents of different types of equipment described above:

Kraus, Riggins and Franti (1975a, 1975b) (USA)
Hurt, Ouellet and Thom (1981) (USA)
Rogerson (1991) (Australia)

On the basis of these studies, best estimates of the effect on the number of injury accidents of the different types of equipment are shown in Table 4.24.1. It should be emphasised that these results are very uncertain. The studies are simple case–control studies that did not control for confounding factors.

***Lengthening the front wheel fork*** by up to 25 cm has no effect on the accident rate for mopeds and motorcycles.

***Raising footrests.*** Low footrests can be a problem when driving in curves. If the footrest comes into contact with the road, there is a great danger of the motorcyclist losing control of the machine. Raising the footrests is associated with a tendency to reduce the number of accidents, but the change is not statistically significant.

*Table 4.24.1: Effects of different types of equipment on mopeds and motorcycles on the number of accidents*

| | Percentage change in the number of accidents | | |
|---|---|---|---|
| Type of equipment | Type of accident affected | Best estimate | 95% confidence interval |
| Extended front wheel fork | All accidents | −2 | (−27; +32) |
| Raised foot rests | Accidents in curves | −27 | (−51; +8) |
| Lowered seat | All accidents | −21 | (−45; +12) |
| Front windscreen | All accidents | −44 | (−54; −31) |
| Coating for knees/legs | All accidents | −32 | (−46; −14) |
| Two-stroke engines | All accidents | +62 | (+41; +86) |

***Lowering the seat*** lowers the motorcycle's centre of gravity and thus may make it more stable. Lowering the seat is associated with a tendency to reduce the number of accidents, but again the changes are not statistically significant.

***A 'front windscreen'*** on motorcycles made of plastic can have two advantages. The first is that it makes the motorcycle is easier to see, and the second that draughts in the face of the motorcycle rider can be reduced. Motorcycles with front windscreens have fewer accidents than motorcycles without these.

By installing a coat of ***light metal on the front*** of the motorcycle, the machine becomes easier to see and the coat protects knees and legs in the event an accident, at least when speeds are low. Motorcycles with this type of coat have fewer accidents than motorcycles without them.

***A two-stroke engine*** produces a lower effect at a given cylinder volume than a four-stroke engine. It has therefore been assumed that two-stroke engines have a lower accident rate than four-stroke engines. However, an Australian study (Rogerson 1991) found no support for this assumption. On the contrary, two-stroke bikes had higher accident rates than four-strokes. Driver characteristics were not controlled for.

## Effect on mobility

No effect on mobility of the measures to increase safety for mopeds and motorcycles described in this chapter has been documented.

### Effect on the environment

No effects on the environment have been documented.

### Costs

No cost figures are available.

### Cost–benefit analysis

No cost–benefit analyses of the safety measures for mopeds and motorcycles covered by this chapter are available.

## 4.25 Bicycle safety equipment

### Problem and objective

It is estimated that almost half of single-vehicle accidents on bicycles are related to road design and maintenance. Two Norwegian studies show that 10–15% of self-reported accidents amongst adults are connected with bicycle-related conditions. The corresponding proportion for children is estimated to be 2–8%. For example, this refers to a lack of or failure of lights, brakes and gear systems or defective parts on a bicycle (Borger and Frøysadal 1993, 1994).

Safety equipment on bicycles is designed to prevent bicycle accidents by making bicycles more visible, easier to manoeuvre and easier to stop.

### Description of the measure

The following types of bicycle equipment have been studied: lamps and reflectors, brakes, handlebars (height and design), drop handlebars and gears, wheel diameter and wheel distance, distance markers and spoke protectors. No studies of the effects on accidents have been found for bicycle bells and for child seats and child wagons.

### Effect on accidents

Effects of different types of safety equipment on bicycles on the number of accidents have not been studied to any great extent. The majority of studies, which have been carried out, are only concerned about the effects on different risk factors related to the number of accidents, for example stopping distance, detection distance or passing distance. The effects on such factors should be interpreted as potential safety effects. The following studies have evaluated the potential effects of different types of safety equipment on bicycles:

Rice and Roland (1970) (the effects of brakes on stopping distances)
Arnberg, Tydén and Norén (1975) (wheel diameter and height of handlebars; effect on frequency of errors when manoeuvring while cycling on roads)
Oranen (1975) (distance marker effect on passing distances)
Watts (1980) (brake blocks and the effect of rim construction on stopping distances)
Blomberg, Hale and Preusser (1984) (spoke reflectors and other types of reflectors on bicycles; effect on detection distances)
Watts (1984a) (effects of different types of reflectors on jackets on passing distances)
Watts (1984b) (distance marker effect on passing distances)
Watts (1984c) (pedal reflectors and rear lights; effect on detection distances)
Fosser (1986) (brake type effect on braking times)
Angenendt and Hausen (1989) (distance marker effect on passing distances)
Borger (1995)

On the basis of these studies, the figures in Table 4.25.1 can be given for the effect on potential accident risk of different types of equipment.

***Reflectors and lamps*** increase detection distance to bicycles in the dark and, all other things being equal, thus reduce the risk of accidents. No favourable effect of spoke reflectors has been found, but other forms of reflectors, including reflectors on cyclists clothing, appear to improve the chances of being detected when cycling in the dark.

***Brakes.*** A brake, which works on the front wheel, gives a shorter stopping distance than one that only operates on the rear wheel (Rice and Roland 1970). Stopping lengths are shortest with brakes operating on both wheels. Rim brakes give slightly shorter stopping distances than hub brakes. Hand brakes give shorter stopping distances than pedal brakes. Synthetic brake blocks work better than brake blocks made of rubber. Leather brake blocks work best during wet weather, while rubber brake blocks work least well.

*Table 4.25.1: Effects on potential accident rates of different types of equipment on bicycles*

| | | Percentage change in potential risk | |
|---|---|---|---|
| Type of equipment | Types of accidents affected | Best estimate | 95% confidence interval |
| ***Reflectors and lamps*** | | | |
| Pedal reflectors | Multi-vehicle accidents in darkness | −75 | (−85; −60) |
| Spoke reflectors | Multi-vehicle accidents in darkness | +9 | (+1; +18) |
| Cyclist's ankle light | Multi-vehicle accidents in darkness | −22 | (−35; −9) |
| Reflectors on cyclist's jacket | Multi-vehicle accidents in darkness | −10 | (−15; −5) |
| Taillight (lit) | Rear-end collisions in darkness | −80 | (−67; −90) |
| ***Brakes*** | | | |
| Brakes on front wheel vs. back wheel | All bicycle accidents | −28 | (−30; −26) |
| Brakes on both wheels vs. back wheel | All bicycle accidents | −48 | (−51; −46) |
| Rim brakes vs. hub brakes | All bicycle accidents | −5 | (−7; −3) |
| Hand brake vs. pedal brakes | All bicycle accidents | −22 | (−25; −20) |
| Synthetic brake blocks vs. rubber | Bicycle accidents in dry weather | −20 | (−25; −10) |
| | Bicycle accidents in wet weather | −40 | (−50; −30) |
| Rubber brake blocks vs. leather | Bicycle accidents in dry weather | −5 | (−25; +5) |
| | Bicycle accidents in wet weather | +190 | (+30; +250) |
| ***Drop handlebars and gears*** | | | |
| Drop handlebars compared to standard handlebars | All bicycle accidents | +78 | (+38; +129) |
| Bicycles with two to five gears compared with bicycles without gears | All bicycle accidents | −17 | (−32; +1) |
| Bicycles with more than five gears compared with bicycles without gears | All bicycle accidents | +62 | (+25; +109) |
| ***Other*** | | | |
| High handlebars vs. standard handlebars | Overturning accidents with bicycles | +55 | (+40; +80) |
| Small wheels vs. standard wheels | Overturning accidents with bicycles | +30 | (+5; +55) |
| Distance markers | Multi-vehicle accidents involving bicycles | −7 | (−10; −4) |
| Spoke protectors | All bicycle accidents | −37 | (−74; +55) |

***Handlebars.*** Bicycles with high handlebars are more difficult to steer than bicycles with normal handlebars. This leads to more mistakes in manoeuvring on the road. High handlebars are also a potential risk factor, which can injure the cyclist if he has to extricate himself in the event of a collision or overturning.

***Drop handlebars and gears.*** Drop handlebars are associated with an accident rate almost 80% higher than standard handlebars (controlling for number of gears). Bicycles with up to five gears have a slightly lower accident rate than bicycles without gears. More than five gears are associated with an increase of the accident rate of around 60%. It is emphasised that these results are based on one study only and rely on self-reported accidents. The majority of self-reported accidents led to injuries, which were so minor that medical treatment was not necessary.

***Wheel diameter and wheel distance.*** At a given rotation speed, wheels with a large diameter will have a stabilising effect and will contribute to keeping the bicycle in an upright position (Rice and Roland 1970). Small wheels reduce stability. Any increase in the wheel distance will, under otherwise similar conditions, increase stability. Large wheel distances are good for cycling on straight stretches, but have a negative effect in sharp turning and avoidance manoeuvres (Rice and Roland 1970). On the other hand, the danger of overturning is smaller with increasing wheel distance.

***Distance markers*** in a horizontal position increase passing distances between bicycles and other vehicles by around 5–10%.

***Spoke protection.*** Spoke protectors are largely measures to protect children who sit on the back of a bicycle without a child seat, from injuries, which may occur if the legs get caught in the spokes. The probability of incurring an injury, which requires medical treatment, is reduced by around 37% when spoke protectors are used.

**Effect on mobility**

Bicycle safety equipment has no documented effects on mobility. Use of certain dynamo lamps can make it heavier to pedal. The same may occur when carrying children by bicycle.

Bicycle gears must be considered primarily as a tool for increasing mobility, and not safety. On cycles without gears, the speed is determined by how quickly the cyclist pushes the pedals round. Today, bicycles are built with up to, or more than, 20 gears. This makes it possible to regulate the exchange of energy between the pedals and the chain, so that it becomes easier to keep an even speed on the pedals, independent of the terrain.

**Effect on the environment**

Bicycle safety equipment has no documented effects on the environment.

## Costs

The table below shows the costs of different types of safety equipment from a Norwegian manufacturer (Øglænd DBS 1995):

| Type of equipment | Price per unit (NOK, 1995 price) |
|---|---|
| Lamps | 100–1,000 |
| Bicycle bells | 35–85 |
| Distance markers | 35 |
| Spoke protectors | 100 |
| Child seat | 400–750 |
| Child cycle wagons | 3,500–6,000 |

In an estimate for the years 1976 and 1977 (Næss 1980), the following elements of a bicycle were regarded as safety equipment: taillight with an electric circuit, reflectors on the back mud guard, pedals and forks, distance markers, dynamo lamps, 50% of the braking system and spoke protectors. It was estimated that these elements comprised on average around 27% of the price of a new bicycle. A new bicycle without gears costs around NOK 3,000–4,000 in 1995. A new bicycle with gears costs between NOK 4,000 and 8,000.

## Cost–benefit analysis

It is difficult to evaluate the costs and benefits of bicycle safety equipment, since the effects on accidents are largely unknown. Nonetheless, simple numerical examples can be given. According to the figures presented above, it can be assumed that two lamps, which work as they should, reduce multi-vehicle accidents in darkness by 20%. The total cost is NOK 1,000 per bicycle. Each year, around 180 bicycle accidents, which occur in the dark, are reported in official accident statistics. The extent of under-reporting is high. Self-reported lamp use among cyclists is around 80%, while surveys carried in traffic indicate that the use of lamps is around 50%. Assuming that 60% of bicycles, which are used in the dark, are equipped with lamps and that there are 2,650,000 bicycles in Norway (Borger and Frøysadal 1993), the cost of equipping the remaining 40% of bicycles with lamps is estimated at NOK 1,060 million. The number of accidents prevented (police reported) can be estimated at around 15. This gives an annual saving of around NOK 30 million. Assuming a 5-year lifetime for the lamps, the cost calculated as an annuity will be around NOK 260 million. The benefit of accidents prevented in this case is smaller than the cost of the measure (30/260).

## 4.26 Safety standards for trailers and caravans

### Problem and objective

Driving with a trailer is more difficult than driving without a trailer. Stability, road holding, acceleration and braking all change when driving with trailers. Reversing with a trailer can cause special problems for many drivers.

Various Norwegian studies have estimated the accident rate while driving with trailers, compared to driving without trailers (Gabestad 1979, Hvoslef 1990, Borger 1991, Sætermo 1995). On the basis of these studies, the accident rate while driving with trailers can be estimated as follows when the accident rate while driving without trailers is set equal to 1.00 (Table 4.26.1).

Driving with caravans or trailers does not appear to be associated with an increased accident rate. However, semi-trailers appear to have around 30% higher risk than driving articulated lorries alone. It is emphasised that these figures are uncertain and other possible differences between driving with and without trailers, which may affect the accident rate, have not been controlled for. Safety standards for vehicle trailers are intended to make driving with trailers as safe as possible and ideally as safe as driving without trailers.

### Description of the measure

Possible measures for reducing the number of accidents and the accident rate when driving with trailers include

- a ban on driving with trailers, on whole or part of the road network,
- regulating the types of trailers that can be used,
- special speed limits for certain car and trailer combinations,

*Table 4.26.1: Relative accident rate when driving with trailers in Norway (risk when driving without trailers = 1.00)*

| | | Relative accident rate when driving with a trailer | | |
|---|---|---|---|---|
| Type of vehicle | Type of trailer | Lower limit | Best estimate | Upper limit |
| Car | Camping | 0.29 | 0.49 | 0.81 |
| Lorry | Trailer | 0.97 | 1.01 | 1.06 |
| Lorry | Semi-trailer | 1.21 | 1.30 | 1.40 |

- total weight limits for trailers,
- improved brakes for trailers,
- better suspension and shock absorption for trailers,
- better stability, control and tracking for trailers.

## Effect on accidents

The effect of the measures included in this chapter on accidents is largely unknown. A number of factors, which influence the level of risk, are known and are discussed.

***Ban on driving with trailers.*** Driving with trailers usually means that the load capacity increases. If there were a ban on driving with trailers, they would have to be replaced with cars with a similar payload. Any ban on driving with trailers will therefore, as a minimum, lead to an increase in the total number of vehicle kilometres corresponding to the number of kilometres driven with trailers. A number of studies have compared the accident rate when driving with trailers with the accident rate when driving without trailers. These include the following studies:

Hutchinson and Seyre (1977) (USA)
Gabestad (1979) (Norway)
McGee, Abbott and Rosenbaum (1982) (USA)
Muskaug (1984) (Nordic countries)
Transportation Research Board (1986) (USA)
Carsten (1987) (USA)
Stein and Jones (1988) (USA)
Jovanis, Chang and Zabaneh (1989) (USA)
Hvoslef (1990) (Norway)
Borger, (1991) (Norway)
Lyles, Campbell, Blower and Stamadiadis (1991) (USA)
Mingo, Esterlitz and Mingo (1991) (USA)
Blower, Campbell and Green (1993) (USA)
Sætermo (1995) (Norway)

A number of these studies concern driving with two trailers, i.e. a semi-trailer with a tow-trailer behind the semi-trailer. American studies indicate that semi-trailers with trailers have a higher accident rate than semi-trailers without trailers. When driving a passenger car with a trailer, American studies indicate that the risk is around 2.4 times as high as driving without trailers. For heavy vehicles, the risk increases by around 30% when driving with trailers. Thus, for heavy vehicles, a ban on driving with trailers will hardly reduce the number of accidents, since on average, trailers probably increase the vehicle's payload by more than 30%.

***Regulating the types of trailers which can be used.*** Norwegian risk estimates, based on the studies listed above, indicate that articulated lorries have an accident rate which is 25% lower than that for semi-trailers (−30%; −15%). Assuming that an articulated lorry can replace a semi-trailer, this means that replacing semi-trailers by articulated lorries can reduce the number of accidents correspondingly.

***Special speed limits when driving with trailers.*** No studies have been found that show the effects of special speed limits while driving with trailers on the number of accidents. An American study (Garber and Gadiraju 1992) of the effects of keeping the speed limit at 55 miles/h (88 km/h) for heavy vehicles when this was increased to 65 miles/h (105 km/h) for passenger cars concluded that this vehicle-differentiated speed limit did not improve safety. The same conclusion was reached in a Swedish study (Carlsson, Nilsson and Wretling 1992), where the effects of a maximum speed governor of 80 km/h for heavy vehicles were evaluated.

One problem with vehicle-related speed limits is that increased speed differences between vehicles lead to more catching up and overtaking situations. This counteracts the gain in safety produced by a reduction in speed, so that the net effect on the number of accidents is almost zero.

***Total weight limits for trailers.*** It is not known to what extent overloading of car trailers occurs. Increased trailer weight, under otherwise identical conditions, leads to longer braking distances.

***Improved trailer brakes.*** Trailers have different types of brakes. Push load brakes are breaking systems for trailers where the brakes are activated by the trailer's pushing forces to the vehicle pulling the trailer. Co-ordinated (non-independent) brakes are brakes for articulated lorries, where the whole articulated lorry's braking can be controlled by the driver (Forlaget Last og Buss A/S 1997). When braking with push load brakes, a transfer of weight from trailer to the ball-bearing occurs in the trailer connection fitting. If the pressure on the ball-bearing (ball-bearing pressure) is high, the pressure on the front axle is reduced. This can lead to premature locking of the car's front wheels when braking (Odsell 1978). The weight transfer can be reduced by prolonging the stretches on the trailer and by having the lowest possible centre of gravity on this. This pressure can be affected by changing the air pressure in the trailer's tyres and by more even distribution of the load in the trailer. For the majority of trailers, the optimal ball-bearing pressure probably lies in the area of 50–75 kg, evaluated with driving characteristics and braking functions in mind (Odsell 1978).

***Improved suspension and shock absorbers on trailers.*** A Swedish model study using data simulation evaluated the suspension and shock-absorbing features, which are needed on single-axle trailers from the point of view of traffic safety (Bunis, Mäkiaho and Odsell 1978). The result showed that it is a combination of suspension/shock absorbers, which determines the vehicle's road holding. Suspension and shock absorbers cannot be evaluated separately. Soft suspension increases the road holding when driving on uneven parts of the carriageway, but may also lead to the trailer tilting in curves. This can be counteracted by installing anti-roll stabilisers. In the Swedish study, the results from model calculations were compared with result from field studies. It was concluded that the model was satisfactory for studying actual driving with trailers.

***Improved stability for trailers.*** The stability of vehicles and trailers can be increased by keeping the centre of gravity of the trailer as low above the ground as possible. An even distribution of the load, so that trailer is neither too heavy at the front nor at the back, increases steering stability. An evaluation of the static rollover stability of articulated lorries 18, 19 or 22 m in length, by means of data simulation, concluded that the factors that have the greatest effect on static rollover stability are the height of the centre of gravity, the gauge, tilting rigidity of the suspension and the height of the centre of the suspension (Karlsen 1991). Dynamic rollover risks in avoidance manoeuvres are affected most by the speed of the control manoeuvres (how quickly the driver turns the steering wheel) (Karlsen 1991).

### Effect on mobility

A vehicle with a trailer will reduce mobility for other vehicles on some roads. This is particularly true of roads with a relatively large number of gradients. Mobility can be increased by means of passing lanes on roads with steep and/or long gradients.

### Effect on the environment

A vehicle with a trailer has higher fuel consumption than a vehicle without a trailer. Thus, the amount of exhaust gas will also increase. Driving with trailers, however, comprises such a small proportion of the total number of kilometres driven that this must be seen as a problem of minor significance. Nonetheless, the number of kilometres driven will probably increase if trailers are forbidden and have to be replaced by more cars without trailers.

### Costs

No detailed cost figures are available. Nor is it possible to calculate the costs of new legislation for use of trailers on the basis of the information available.

### Cost–benefit analysis

Cost–benefit analyses of different regulations of the use of trailers and requirements governing trailers are not possible as long as information about costs and effect on accidents of different measures is as inadequate as it is today. A possible ban on driving with trailers for lorries in Norway would increase transport costs for industry, since the cost per ton kilometre falls with increasing vehicle dimensions (Hagen 1995). The cost of using, for example, two lorries, each with a load of 8 t, is greater than the cost of an articulated lorry with a load of 16 t.

## 4.27 Fire safety standards

### Problem and objective

Although fire is not common in accidents, there are every year a number of accidents were fire breaks out. The risk of fire increases with vehicle age (Parsons 1995). Fire may be caused by dangerous goods, but they may also break out in the engines of vehicles or when fuel leaks. Injuries sustained in fire are often fatal. For the period 1985–94, the frequency of injuries in fires, which occurred in accidents, is shown in Table 4.27.1.

Burns are difficult to treat and can result in serious impairment. For this reason, it is important to prevent this type of injury. The objective of fire safety standards is to reduce the probability of fires in vehicles.

*Table 4.27.1: Injuries caused by fire in injury accidents reported to the police in Norway 1985–94*

| Injury severity | Injured by fire | Injuries in total | Burns per 10,000 injuries |
|---|---|---|---|
| Killed | 29 | 2,182 | 133 |
| Very seriously injured | 3 | 1,325 | 23 |
| Seriously injured | 6 | 7,970 | 8 |
| Slightly injured | 31 | 69,384 | 4 |

**Description of the measure**

In this chapter, the effects of the following measures designed to reduce fires in vehicles are discussed:

- Safety requirements for fuel tank installations in the USA
- The location of the fuel tank in the vehicle
- Design of fuel pipes and fuel caps

In addition to these, fire-extinguishing equipment either in the vehicle or at other accessible places can contribute to reducing the extent of fires.

**Effect on accidents**

An American study has investigated the effects of safety standards for fuel system installations, which aim at reducing the chances of fuel-fed fires caused by fuel system breaching in vehicle crashes. The standards cover fuel tank fixings, resistance to mechanical stress (cracks, rust, deformation in accidents etc), choice of materials (flammability of materials) insulation against the exhaust system and the design of fuel pipes and caps (Parsons 1995). They apply to passenger cars, light trucks and school buses. The study found no change in the number of fires in fatal accidents, a significant decrease 12% in the number of fires in injury accidents and a significant decrease by 20% in the number of fires in all accidents taken together. These results refer to fires in car accidents. No effects were found in accidents with light trucks or school buses.

A Danish study has investigated how the location of the engine affects the risk of fires (Fredriksen 1971). The study showed that the number of fires per 1,000 registered cars is lowest when the engine is at the front and the fuel tank at the rear (0.19 fires per 1,000 cars). The number of fires is somewhat higher when the engine is at the back and the fuel tank at the front of the car (0.25 fires). The largest number of fires was found when both engine and fuel tank are at the back of the car (0.70 fires). These figures show fires per registered vehicle, not fires per accident in which the vehicles are involved. The differences in fire rate between different locations of engines and petrol tanks may therefore be due to the fact that different cars have different risks of being involved in accidents. Nonetheless, it appears that locating the engine and the petrol tank close to each other is not a good idea. The figure for cars with both the engine and petrol tank at the back concerns the NSU Prinz model, which was the only car that had such a construction and which is no longer manufactured.

A similar Swedish study (Rångtell 1973) of 79 fuel fires, which occurred in traffic accidents, found that 68% of these occurred in cars with a fuel tank at the rear, and 32% in cars with a fuel tank at the front. The cars' share of the total car fleet was respectively 80% and 20%. This indicates that the risk of petrol fires is around 1.9 times higher when the fuel tank is placed at the front than when it is placed at the rear.

The same study (Rångtell 1973) studied changes in petrol fires in Volkswagen cars after the 1968 model was equipped with the new filling pipe to the petrol tank and a new petrol cap. The number of petrol fires per year went down from 17 in 1967 to 5–11 each year between 1968 and 1971.

### Effect on mobility

Measures against fires in cars have no known effect on mobility.

### Effect on the environment

Measures against fires in cars have no known effect on the environment.

### Costs

No information is available about the costs of fire safety standards.

### Cost–benefit analysis

Since the cost of measures to prevent car fires is unknown, it is not possible to make cost–benefit analyses. Moreover, fire is a very seldom event and estimates of the expected number of fatalities in fire are therefore highly incertain.

## 4.28 Hazardous goods regulations

### Problem and objective

Hazardous goods is a generic term for materials which, by their very nature, represent particular risks to life, health, the environment and material goods. Hazardous goods are formally defined as those materials that are regarded as hazardous goods in accordance with the ADR Convention (see below). ADR divides hazardous materials and objects into hazard classes on the basis of their characteristics. The hazard classes in ADR are as defined as follows:

Class 1 Explosive materials and objects
Class 2 Gases, compressed, liquid, or soluble under pressure
Class 3 Flammable liquids
Class 4.1 Flammable solids
Class 4.2 Self-igniting solids
Class 4.3 Materials, which produce flammable gases on contact with water
Class 5.1 Oxidising materials
Class 5.2 Organic peroxides
Class 6.1 Poisonous materials
Class 6.2 Infectious materials
Class 7 Radioactive materials
Class 8 Corrosive materials
Class 9 Other hazardous materials and objects

The objectives of regulating the transport of hazardous goods

- directing the transport of goods to vehicles and transport routes where the probability of accidents and the expected amount of damage in an accident are as low as possible,
- ensuring that goods are loaded, packaged and marked in a responsible manner,
- ensuring that the goods are handled in such a way that the additional risk attributable to hazardous goods is as small as possible,
- enabling those who transport hazardous goods to limit the extent of injury in an accident by informing them about the nature of the goods and measures to reduce injury and damage caused by the goods,
- organising quick help-and-rescue measures in the event of an accident.

**Description of the measure**

Safety measures for the transport of hazardous goods are given by Acts of Parliament, regulations and other legislation.

***The ADR agreement***. The ADR (Agreement on Dangerous Goods by Road) Convention is the European Agreement Concerning the International Carriage of Dangerous Goods by Road (1957), which has been introduced into the directives 94/55/EC of the European Union from 1994. It applies to the majority of countries in

Europe and concerns road transport of hazardous goods, which cross the borders of member countries. The rules, which state how this transport should be carried out, are found in appendices A and B to the agreement, as well as in attachments to these appendices. The regulations are virtually the same as international regulations governing the transport of hazardous goods by rail (RID).

***Norwegian regulations.*** Road transport of hazardous goods in Norway is regulated by the Regulations on Road Transport of Hazardous Goods. The main rule contained in these regulations is that road transport of hazardous goods must be done in accordance with the legislation in the ADR agreement. For drivers in Norway, a specific proof of competence is required for transporting hazardous goods (all hazard classes) in tankers, in containers with a total transport volume per transport unit of more than 3,000 L, or where the vehicle's total permitted weight is more than 3.5 t, and when transporting class 1 hazardous goods (explosive materials). When driving within Norway, proof of competence is only required when the vehicle's permitted weight is over 3.5 t.

***Vehicle and equipment standards.*** Vehicles that transport hazardous goods must be in first-class condition. The following special equipment is required: fire extinguishers, special warning lights with an orange light and a tool kit. The requirements for personal safety equipment depend on the nature of the load. Tankers and vehicles with a permitted total weight above 3.5 t for the transport of explosive materials must have special permits. Vehicles carrying hazardous goods must have orange warning signs on the front and the rear. Tankers and tank containers must have orange signs with numbers stating the type of load and the nature of the hazardous material. As a rule, each tanker or tank compartment should have its own sign. Tankers and vehicles, which carry explosive or radioactive goods, must also be marked on both sides and on the back with danger signs.

## Effect on accidents

Few studies have been found, which indicate the effects of regulating transport of hazardous goods. The following types of evidence are discussed here:

- Accident rates when transporting hazardous goods vs. other goods
- Expected number of accidents when transporting specific types of hazardous goods
- Effects of a ban on transport on specific roads and recommended transport routes
- Potential effect of different measures accidents during transport of hazardous goods.

***Accident rates when transporting hazardous goods compared to other goods.*** Estimates of the risk of injury accidents for the transport of flammable goods compared to other goods transport are available for Norway for the period 1980–85 (Elvik 1988) and 1990–94 (Borger 1996) and for Sweden for the period 1988–90 (Nilsson 1994). The studies showed that the risk of injury accidents for the transport of flammable goods on roads is around 75% lower than the risk of injury for transport of other goods.

***Choice of mode of transport when carrying hazardous goods.*** A number of studies have compared the expected number of accidents for different modes of transport for the transport of a given type of hazardous goods between a given pair of destinations (Jenssen 1977, Elvik 1985, Purdy 1993, Fredén 1994). In Table 4.28.1, the results of these studies are compared. For each destination, the most dangerous mode of transport is assigned a risk of 1. The risk for other modes of transport is expressed as the risk relative to the most dangerous. The results are inconsistent as regards the safest and the most dangerous mode of transport. However, all studies show that there can be great differences in risk between different modes of transport.

***Experiences with transport bans and recommended transport routes.*** Transporters of hazardous goods may be required to use specific routes. In an experiment carried out in Windsor, England, no effect on accidents of banning heavy transport from specific city streets was found (Barton 1980). Information regarding compliance with the ban is not available. A similar ban on heavy transport in the town of Lymm (Christie and Prudhoe 1980) led to a reduction of 65% in heavy traffic through the town. The number of accidents involving heavy vehicles went down from three in the 4-year period before the ban to zero in the first 10 years after the ban. These figures are too small to be able to draw statistically meaningful conclusions about changes in the number of accidents.

***Evaluations of possible measures against possible accidents during the transport of hazardous goods.*** Russell (1993) described 11 possible types of accidents when

*Table 4.28.1: Results of risk analyses for the transport of hazardous goods*

| | | Relative expected accident rates (most hazardous = 1.00) | | | | |
|---|---|---|---|---|---|---|
| Destinations | Type of hazardous goods | Ship | Road | Train | Road and rail | Ship and train |
| Herøya-Hurum | Chlorine | 0.37 | 1.00 | | 0.64 | |
| Rjukan-Herøya | Ammonia | | 0.92 | | 1.00 | 0.42 |
| Unspecified | Chlorine | | 0.18 | 1.00 | | |
| 15 km planned road | Petrol | | 1.00 | 0.23 | | |
| 15 km planned road | Ammonia | | 1.00 | 0.01 | | |

transporting hazardous goods to a group of experts and asked them to evaluate the effects of different possible measures to reduce the probability and consequences of the different possible accidents. The study was based on a so-called Delphi technique, where the aim was to achieve consensus among the experts about the effects of different measures. One type of accident was driving off the road with subsequent leakage of hazardous materials in the vicinity of a densely populated area. In order to prevent this type of accident, an emergency exit ramp for heavy vehicles was regarded as potentially the most effective measure, with an anticipated effect of a 70% reduction in accidents. Heavy guardrails were assumed to reduce such accidents by 30% (Russell 1993).

### Effect on mobility

Safety measures for hazardous goods have no documented effect on mobility.

### Effect on the environment

Safety measures for hazardous goods may reduce the extent of discharge of hazardous materials in accidents. This may limit damage to the environment. Quantified effects are not available.

### Costs

In 1991, training for instructors and drivers for the ADR certificate cost around NOK 3.2 million (Hagen 1993). Other direct cost figures for safety measures for hazardous goods are not available.

### Cost–benefit analysis

No studies are available of the costs and benefits of current safety measures for hazardous goods. A cost–benefit analysis of improved road links between Esso's refinery at Slagentangen and the E18 highway found that social benefits correspond to investments of around NOK 80–110 million (Nicolaysen 1995). Possible effects of the investments on accidents and the environment were not included in this analysis. Only savings in direct transport costs were evaluated.

## 4.29 Electronic stability control

### Problem and objective

Loss of control is a contributing factor to many severe accidents, especially to road departure, turnover, and head-on collisions. Control loss may occur at too high speed in curves, i.e. collision avoidance manoeuvres, under low friction conditions or combinations of these (Sferco, Page, Le Coz and Fay 2001). A number of studies have estimated the proportions of accidents that involve skidding or loss of control, mostly based on in-depth studies of injury or fatal accidents (Campbell, Smith and Najm 2003, Insurance Institute for Highway Safety 2005, Langwieder, Gwehenberger, Hummel and Bende 2003, Sferco, Page, Le Coz and Fay 2001, Unselt, Breuer, Eckstein and Frank 2004, Zobel, Friedrich and Becker 2000). These studies yield quite consistent results. In summary, loss of control or skidding has been a contributing factor in between about 40% and 50% of all single-vehicle accidents, in about 10% of all multi-vehicle accidents (mostly head-on collisions), and in between about 20–40% of all accidents (Erke 2008). Larger proportions of fatal accidents have been found to involve skidding or loss of control than other injury accidents.

For most drivers, it is difficult to predict at what point over- or understeering will occur, or to react adequately. Driver reactions may even worsen the situation (e.g. exaggerated countersteering). Additionally, drivers have no possibility to counteract over- or understeering by braking individual tyres.

### Description of the measure

ESC aims at preventing skidding and loss of control in cases of oversteering or understeering. A central processing unit compares continuously a number of driving parameters, such as speed, side slip, yaw characteristics and steering wheel position. When these parameters indicate the beginning of over- or understeering, adequate counteractions are initiated, such as braking individual wheels and reducing engine power, among other things, and other control systems may be activated (ABS, electronic brake power distribution, traction control and engine drag torque control), thereby skidding and the probability of control loss are reduced. ESC does usually not overrun the driver inputs (speed and steering wheel movements) but it may do so if this is necessary to regain stability.

ESC has been introduced as optional equipment in luxury class cars from ca. 1995, and from 1997 the proportion of cars that are equipped with ESC as standard equipment has been steadily increasing. In 2004 the proportion of new vehicles that had ESC as standard equipment was 36% in the EU, 67% in Germany and 70% in Sweden (Deutscher Verkehrssicherheitsrat 2006; Folksam). The proportion of all vehicles in the EU has been estimated to be about 9% in 2005 and is predicted to reach 50% by 2025, if no legal requirements are introduced (European Commission 2005).

**Effect on accidents**

The effects of ESC on accidents have been estimated in the following studies:

Aga and Okada (2003) (Japan)
Dang (2004) (USA)
Lie, Tingvall, Krafft and Kullgren (2004) (Sweden)
Bahouth (2005) (USA)
Farmer (2006) (USA)
Page and Cuny (2006) (France)
Kreiss, Schüler and Langwieder (2006) (Germany)
Thomas (2006) (Great Britain)

The results from these studies are summarised in Table 4.29.1.

Large and significant accident reductions have been found for all types of accidents that are assumed to be affected by ESC. These are single-vehicle accidents, accidents

*Table 4.29.1: Effects on accidents of ESC*

| | Percentage change in the number of accidents | | |
|---|---|---|---|
| Accident severity | Types of accidents affected | Best estimate | 95% confidence interval |
| Unspecified | Single-vehicle accidents | −49 | (−55; −42) |
| Unspecified | Loss of control | −41 | (−62; −7) |
| Injury | Rollover | −69 | (−82; −45) |
| Unspecified | Head-on collisions | −13 | (−17; −8) |
| Unspecified | Side impact | −7 | (−14; 0) |
| Unspecified | Multi-vehicle accidents | +3 | (+1; +5) |
| Injury | Single-vehicle accidents | −46 | (−64; −18) |
| Fatal | Single-vehicle accidents | −49 | (−62; −33) |
| Injury | Head-on collisions | −10 | (−15; −5) |
| Fatal | Head-on collisions | −79 | (−97; +61) |
| Injury | Multi-vehicle accidents | +2 | (+1; +3) |
| Fatal | Multi-vehicle accidents | −32 | (−43; −20) |

involving loss of control, rollover accidents and head-on collisions. The size of the effects is about equal to the proportions of the respective types of accidents that are assumed to involve skidding or loss of control (see above, Problem and objective). Larger effects have been found on fatal accidents than on injury accidents, except for single-vehicle accidents. No effect estimate could be computed for all accidents. Effects of ESC have been found to be larger on icy or snowy roads and the smallest effects on dry roads (Farmer 2006, Kreiss, Schüler and Langwieder 2006, Lie, Tingvall, Krafft and Kullgren 2006).

A sensitivity analysis indicates that the estimated effects on single-vehicle accidents may be somewhat overestimated, most likely because of methodological weaknesses. For the effect on head-on collisions, there are no such indications (Erke 2008).

**Effect on mobility**

An ESC-equipped vehicle is easier to drive on snowy or icy roads and less likely to require snow chains or studded tyres than a vehicle without ESC. Mobility under difficult driving conditions is therefore improved.

**Effect on the environment**

ESC has no documented effects on the environment. Tyre wear may be somewhat reduced, and the need for studded tyres may be reduced as well. The additional weight and power consumption are most likely neglectable for fuel consumption.

**Costs**

The additional costs for equipping a new passenger car with ESC have been estimated at about NOK 2.000 (€250, European Commission 2005). The costs are, however, dependent on what other safety devices (e.g. ABS and traction control) are installed in a vehicle. The installation of ESC in used cars is most likely more expensive than selling the car and buying a new one. The costs for ESC may be reduced when less expensive yaw sensors become available, which are currently under development. ESC is more expensive for SUV and heavy vehicles than for passenger cars.

**Cost–benefit analysis**

A cost–benefit analysis has been calculated for installing ESC as standard equipment in all new vehicles from 2007. It is assumed that 10% of all vehicle kilometres were driven with ESC in 2006 that this proportion increases to 100% by 2023, and that ESC costs NOK 3,000 per vehicle. A discount rate of 4.5% is used in the analysis. It is further assumed that fatalities are reduced by 25%, that critical and serious injuries are reduced by 15% and that slight injuries are reduced by 5%. Based on these assumptions, the cost–benefit ratio of installing ESC in all new vehicles is 4.8.

## References

Adams, J. G. U. (1985). Smeed's Law, seat belts and the Emperor's new clothes. In: *Human Behavior and Traffic Safety*, 193–257. (Evans, L. & R. C. Schwing eds.). Plenum Press, New York, NY.

Adams, J. G. U. (1994). Seat belt legislation: the evidence revisited. *Safety Science*, **18**, 135–152.

Adell, E. & Várhelyi, A. (2008). Driver comprehension and acceptance of the active accelerator pedal after long-term use. *Transportation Research Part F*, **11**, 37–51.

Adell, E., Várhelyi, A. & Hjälmdahl, M. (2008). Auditory and haptic systems for in-car speed management – A comparative real life study. *Transportation Research Part F*, **11**, 445–458.

Aga, M. & Okada, A. (2003). Analysis of vehicle stability control\s effectiveness from accident data. ESV paper 541.*18th ESV Conference*. Nagoya.

Agran, P. F., D. N. Castillo & D. G. Winn. (1992). Comparison of motor vehicle occupant injuries in restrained and unrestrained 4- to 14-years-olds. *Accident Analysis and Prevention*, **24**, 349–355.

Aldman, B., Cacciola, I., Gustafsson, H. et al. (1981). The Protective Effect Of Different Kinds Of Protective Clothing Worn By Motorcyclists. *Journal of Traffic Medicine*, **9**, 57–58.

Aldman, B., Kajzer, J., Gustafsson, H. et al. (1985). The Protective Effect of a Specially Designed Suit for Motorcyclists. *Proceedings (1095–1100) of the Tenth International Technical Conference on Experimental Safety Vehicles, held at Oxford, England, July 1–4, 1985*. US Department of Transportation, National Highway Traffic Safety Administration, Washington DC.

Aldman, B., Gustafsson, H., Nygren, Å. & Tingvall, C. (1987) Child restraints. A prospective study of children as car passengers in road traffic accidents with respect to restraint effectiveness. *Acta Paediatrica Scandinavica*, **Supplement 339**, 1987, paper II (reprinted in Tingvall, 1987).

Allen, M. J. & J. R. Clark. (1964). Automobile running lights - a research report. *American Journal of Optometry and Archives of American Academy of Optometry*, **41**, 293–315.

Allen, R. W. (1988). Crash avoidance models and driver/vehicle handling. In: *Proceedings (8–16) of Roads and Traffic Safety on Two Continents*, Gothenburg, Sweden, 9–11 September 1987. VTI-rapport 331 A. Väg- och TrafikInstitutet, Linköping.

Almqvist, S. & Nygård, M. (1997). *Dynamic speed adaptation: A field trial with automatic speed adaptation in an urban area*. Bulletin 154, Department of Traffic Planning and Engineering, University of Lund, Sweden.

Amundsen, A. & Elvik, R. (2006). *Revisjon av Trafikksikkerhetshåndboken: kapittel 4.13 sikring av barn i bil (Revision of the Handbook of Road Safety Measures, Chapter 4.13 Child restraints)*. Working document No. SM/1825/2006. Oslo: Institute of Transport Economics.

Andersson, K. & G. Nilsson. (1981). *The effects on accidents of compulsory use of running lights during daylight in Sweden*. VTI-report 208A. National Road and Traffic Research Institute, Linköping.

Andersson, K., G. Nilsson & M. Salusjärvi. (1976). *Effekt på trafikolyckor av rekommenderad och påkallad användning av varselljus i Finland*. VTI-rapport 102. Statens väg- och trafikinstitut, Linköping.

Andreasson, R. & K. Roos. (1977). Effects of Sweden's Seat Belt Law. In: *Proceedings of the Sixth International Conference of the International Association for Accident and Traffic Medicine* (45–55), January 31–February 4, Melbourne, Australia.

Andrews, J. C. (1981). Motorcycle helmets - last chance for life. *Journal of Traffic Medicine*, **9**, 22–25.

Angenendt, W. & Hausen, C. (1989). *Zur Sicherheitswirkung von Fahrradkellen*. Forschungsberichte der Bundesanstalt für Strassenwesen 197. Bundesanstalt für Strassenwesen (BASt), Bergisch Gladbach.

Anund, A., Falkmer, T., Forsman, Å. et al. (2003). *Child safety in cars – Literature Review*. VTI Report 489A, Swedish National Road and Transport Research Institute (VTI), Linköping.

Arnberg, P. R. & O. Odsell. (1978). *Degradation of steering and suspension components affecting driver-vehicle performance during emergency situations*. VTI-rapport 109A. Statens väg- och trafikinstitut, Linköping.

Arnberg, P.W., T. Tydén & B. Norén. (1975). *Manövrerings- och balansegenskaper hos olike cykeltyper. En litteraturgenomgång och en experimentell studie*. VTI-rapport 45. Statens väg- och trafikinstitut, Stockholm.

Arbogast, K.B., Durbin, D.R., Cornejo, R.A. et al. (2004). An evaluation of the effectivness of forward facing child restraint systems. *Accident Analysis and Prevention*, **36**, 585–589.

Arora, H., Collard, D., Robbins, G. et al. (1994). *Effectiveness of Daytime Running Lights in Canada*. Report TP 12298 (E). Transport Canada, Ottawa.

Asch, P., Levy, D.T., Shea, D. & Bodenhorn, H. (1991). Risk compensation and the effectiveness of safety belt use laws: a case study of New Jersey. *Policy Sciences*, **24**, 181–197.

Aschenbrenner, K.M., B. Biehl & G. W. Wurm. (1987). *Einfluss Der Risikokompensation auf die Wirkung von Verkehrsicherheitsmassnahmen am Beispiel ABS*. Schriftenreihe Unfall- und Sicherheitsforschung Strassenverkehr, Heft 63, 65–70. Bundesanstalt für Strassenwesen (BASt), Bergisch Gladbach.

Asogwa, S. E. (1980). The crash helmet legislation in Nigeria: a before-and-after study. *Accident Analysis and Prevention*, **12**, 213–216.

Atkinson, P. Hariharan, P., Mari-Godwa, S., Telehowski, P., Martin, S., Van-Hoof, J. & Atkinson, T. (2002). *An under-hand steering wheel grasp procedures significant injury risk to the upper extremity during airbag deployment*. Association for the Advancement of Automotive Medicine, Barrington, IL, USA.

Attwood, D. A. (1981). *The Potential of Daytime Running Lights as a Vehicle Collision Countermeasure*. SAE Technical Paper 810190. Society of Automotive Engineers, Warrendale, PA.

Bachulis, B.L. Sangster, W., Gorrell, G.W. & Long, W.B. (1988). Patterns of injury in helmeted and nonhelmeted motorcyclists. *The American Journal of Surgery*, **155**, 708–711.

Bahouth, G. (2005). Real world crash evaluation of vehicle stability control (VSC) technology. *49th Annual Proceedings Association for the Advancement of Automotive Medicine*, September 12–14, 2005.

Baltes, M. R. (1995). To Belt or Not To Belt: Should Florida Mandate Installation of Safety Restraints in Large School Buses? *Transportation Research Record*, **1485**, 97–104.

Bang, J. R. (1996). Vinterdekk uten pigger eller med miljøpigger. I: Kolbenstvedt, M.; Silborn, H.; Solheim, T. (Red): *Miljøhåndboken*, **Del 1**, 339–345. Transportøkonomisk institutt, Oslo.

Barnes, J.S., Morris, A.P., Fildes, B.N. & Newstead, S.V. (2002). Airbag effectiveness in real world crashes. *Proceedings Vehicle Safety 2002 - IMechE*, 28–30 May, London, England.

Barton, A. J. (1980). *The effects on accident frequencies of lorry controls in the Windsor area*. TRRL Supplementary Report 631. Transport and Road Research Laboratory, Crowthorne, Berkshire.

Becker S., Bork, M., Dorissen, H.T. et al. (1995a). Summary of experience with autonomous intelligent cruise control (AICC). Part 1: Study objectives and methods. *Proceedings of the First World Congress on Applications of Transport Telematics and Intelligent Vehicle-Highway Systems*, Paris 30 November–3 December 1994, 4, 1828–1835. Paris.

Becker S., Bork, M., Dorissen, H.T. et al. (1995b). Summary of experience with autonomous intelligent cruise control (AICC). Part 2: Results and conclusions. *Proceedings of the First World Congress on Applications of Transport Telematics and Intelligent Vehicle-Highway Systems,* Paris 30 November–3 December 1994, 4, 1836–1843. Paris.

Behrensdorff, I. & L. K. Hansen. (1994). *Sidespejle på lastbiler-brug og effekt af nærzone- og vidvinkelspejle.* RfT-rapport 1/1994. Rådet for Trafiksikkerhedsforskning, København.

Bergkvist, P. (2001). Daytime running lights (DRLs) – a North American success story. Paper 395. *Proceedings of 17th Enhanced Safety Vehicle Conference.* Washington DC, U.S. Department of Transportation.

Bijleveld, F. D. (1997). *Effectiveness of daytime motorcycle headlights in the European Union.* Report R-97-9. Leidschendam, SWOV Institute for Road Safety Research.

Björketun, U. (1992). *Fordonsfaktorer.* Upublisert rapportmanuskript datert 1992-04-02. Väg- og trafikinstitutet (VTI), Linköping.

Bjørnskau, T. (1989). Rasjonalitetsmodeller og virkeligheten. Kan laboratorieeksperimenter med gjentatte Fangens Dilemma-spill ha empirisk relevans? *Norsk Statsvitenskapelig Tidsskrift*, **5**, 237–249.

Bjørnskau, T. (1993). *Risiko i veitrafikken 1991/92.* TØI-rapport 216. Transportøkonomisk institutt, Oslo.

Bjørnskau, T. (1994a). *Spillteori, trafikk og ulykker: En teori om interaksjon i trafikken.* TØI-rapport 287. Transportøkonomisk institutt, Oslo.

Bjørnskau, T. (1994b). *Hypoteser om atferdstilpasning (risikokompensasjon).* Arbeidsdokument TST/0512/94. Transportøkonomisk institutt, Oslo.

Bjørnskau T. (2000). *Risiko i veitrafikken 1997/98.* Oslo, Transportøkonomisk institutt, TØI rapport 483/2000.

Blomberg, R. D., A. Hale & D. F. Preusser. (1984). *Conspicuity for pedestrians and bicyclists: definition of the problem, development and test of countermeasures.* Report DOT HS-806 563. US Department of Transportation, National Highway Traffic Safety Administration, Washington DC.

Blomquist, G. C. (1977). Economics of Safety and Seat Belt Use. *Journal of Safety Research*, **9**, 179–189.

Blomquist, G. C. (1979). Value of Life Saving: Implications of Consumption Activity. *Journal of Political Economy*, **87**, 540–558.

Blower, D., K. L. Campbell & P. E. Green. (1993). Accident rates for heavy truck-tractors in Michigan. *Accident Analysis and Prevention*, **25**, 307–321.

Bock, O., Brühning, E., Dilling, J. et al. (1989). *Aufbereitung und Auswertung von Fahrzeug- und Unfalldaten.* Heft Unfall- und Sicherheitsforschung Strassenverkehr, 71. Bundesanstalt für Strassenwesen (BASt), Bergisch Gladbach.

Bohlin, N. I. (1967). *A Statistical Analysis of 28,000 Accident Cases with Emphasis on Occupant Restraint Value*. SAE Technical Paper 670925. Society of Automotive Engineers, 1967 (reprinted 1968). New York, NY.

Bolstad, A. (1972). *Nyttekostnadsanalyser av bilbelter*. TØI-rapport. Transportøkonomisk institutt, Oslo.

Borger, A. (1991). *Eksponering tunge kjøretøy*. Arbeidsdokument TST/0308/91. Transportøkonomisk institutt, Oslo.

Borger, A. (1995). Sammenligning av syklisters risiko for ulike sykkeltyper og ved ulik bruk av sikkerhetsutstyr på grunnlag av sykkelundersøkelsene. Arbeidsdokument TST/0651/95. Transportøkonomisk institutt, Oslo.

Borger, A. (1996). *Risikoberegning for transport av farlig gods på veg 1990–94*. Arbeidsdokument TST/0721/96. Transportøkonomisk institutt, Oslo.

Borger, A. & E. Frøysadal. (1993). *Sykkelundersøkelsen 1992*. TØI-rapport 217. Transportøkonomisk institutt, Oslo.

Borger, A. & E. Frøysadal. (1994). *Sykkelbyprosjektet. Intervjuundersøkelser i sykkelbyene Sandnes og Tønsberg/Nøtterøy i 1992*. Rapport 234. Transportøkonomisk institutt, Oslo.

Braver, E.R., Kyrychenko, S.Y. & Ferguson, S.A. (2005). Driver mortality in frontal crashes: Comparison of newer and older airbag designs. *Traffic Injury Prevention,* **30**, 24–30.

Brodsky, H. & A. S. Hakkert. (1988). Risk of a road accident in rainy weather. *Accident Analysis and Prevention*, **20**, 161–176.

Broqua, F., Lerner, G., Mauro, V. & Morello, E. (1991). Cooperative driving: Basic concepts and a first assessment of intelligent cruise control strategies. *Proceedings DRIVE Conference, Advanced telematics in road transport, Brüssel*, February 1991, 908–929.

Broughton, J. (1987). *The effect on motorcycling of the 1981 Transport Act*. TRRL Research Report 106. Transport and Road Research Laboratory, Crowthorne, Berkshire.

Broughton, J. (1988). *The* relation *between motorcycle size and accident risk*. TRRL Research Report 169. Transport and Road Research Laboratory, Crowthorne, Berkshire.

Broughton, J. (1995). *The likely effects of downsizing on driver casualties in two-car accidents*. TRL Report 171. Transport Research Laboratory, Crowthorne, Berkshire.

Broughton, J. (1996a). The theoretical basis for comparing the accident record of car models. *Accident Analysis and Prevention*, **28**, 89–99.

Broughton, J. (1996b). The British index for comparing the accident record of car models. *Accident Analysis and Prevention*, **28**, 101–109.

Broughton, J. (1996c). Further aspects of the British index of secondary car safety. *Accident Analysis and Prevention*, **28**, 791–798.

Broughton, J. (2003). The benefits of improved car secondary safety. *Accident Analysis and Prevention*, **35**, 527–535.

Brüde, U., J. Larsson & H. Thulin. (1980). *Trafikolyckors samband med linjeföring - för olika belagd bredd, hastighetsgräns, årstid, ljusförhållanden och region*. VTI-meddelande 235. Statens väg- och trafikinstitut (VTI), Linköping.

Bryden, J. E. & J. S. Fortuniewicz. (1986). Traffic barrier performance related to vehicle size and type. *Transportation Research Record*, **1065**, 69–78.

Bunis, G., I. Mäkiaho & O. Odsell. (1978). *Fjädrings- och dämpningsegenskaper hos enaxliga släpvagnar*. VTI-rapport 165. Statens väg- och trafikinstitut, Linköping.

Burg, A. & J. Beers. (1978). Reflectorization for Nighttime Conspicuity of Bicycles and Motorcycles. *Journal of Safety Research*, **10**, 69–77.

Butsuen, T., A. Doi & H. Sasaki. (1995). Development of a collision avoidance system with automatic brake control. *Proceedings of the First World Congress on Applications of Transport Telematics and Intelligent Vehicle-Highway Systems,* Paris 30 November–3 December 1994, 4, 2078–2086. Paris.

Bäckström, C.-G., Andersson, C.-E., Forsman, E. & Nilsson, L.-E. (1974). Road Accidents with SAAB 99. *Journal of Traffic Medicine*, **2, 1**, 1–5.

Cairns, H. & H. Holbourn. (1943). Head injuries in motor-cyclists with special reference to crash helmets. *British Medical Journal*, **May 15, 1943**, 591–598.

Cameron, M. H. (1980). The effect of seat belts on minor and severe injuries measured on the Abbreviated Injury Scale. *Proceedings of the Eighth International Conference of the International Association for Accident and Traffic Medicine* (72–98), University of Aarhus, June 10–13, Aarhus, Denmark.

Cameron, M. H. & J. P. Wessels. (1979). *The effectiveness of Australian* design rule 22 *for head restraints*. Report CR 5. Road Safety and Traffic Authority, Victoria, Melbourne.

Cameron, M.H., Vulcan, A.P., Finch. C.F. & Newstead, S.V. (1994). Mandatory bicycle helmet use following a decade of helmet promotion in Victoria, Australia - an evaluation. *Accident Analysis and Prevention*, **26**, 325–337.

Cammisa, M.X., Reed, R.T., Ferguson, S.A. & Lund, A.K. (2000). *Driver fatalities in frontal crashes of airbag-equipped vehicles: A review of 1989–96 NASS cases*. SAE Technical Papers 2000-01-1003.

Campbell, B.J. (1982). *A comparison of NHTSA car safety ratings with injuries in highway crashes*. Highway Safe. Highlights 15, 1–3.

Campbell, B, J. & F. A. Campbell. (1988). Injury reduction and seat belt use associated with occupant restraint laws. In: *Preventing Automobile Injury. New Findings from Evaluation Research*, 24–50. (Graham, J. D. ed). Auburn House Publishing Company, Dover, MASS.

Campbell, B. J. & D. W. Reinfurt. (1973). *Relationship between driver crash injury and passenger car weight*. Highway Safety Research Center, University of North Carolina, Chapel Hill, NC.

Campbell, B. J. & W. S. Rouse. (1968). Reflectorized License Plates and Rear End Collisions at Night. *Traffic Safety Research Review*, **12**, 2, 40–45.

Campbell, B.N., Smith, J.D. & Najm, W.G. (2003). *Examining of crash contributing factors using national crash databases*. NHTSA report DOT-VNTSC-NHTSA-02-07.

Cantilli, E. J. (1965). Daylight "Lights-On" Plan By Port of New York Authority. *Traffic Engineeering*, **36**, 17, December.

Cantilli, E. J. (1970). Accident Experience with Parking Lights as Running Lights. *Highway Research Record*, **332**, 1–13.

Carlsson, A., G. Nilsson & P. Wretling. (1992). *Hastighetsgräns 80 km/h för tunga lastbilar. Konsekvensanalys av träfik- och trafiksäkerhetseffekter*. VTI-meddelande 683. Väg- och Trafikinstitutet, Linköping.

Carlsson, G., J. Holmgren & H. Norin. (1987). The child in the Volvo car. *Proceedings (VTI-report 332A, 214–236) of Roads and Traffic Safety on Two Continents*, 9–11 September, Gothenburg, Sweden.

Carlsson, G. & G. Öberg. (1976). *Dubbdäcks effekt på fordons restider*. VTI-rapport 70. Statens väg- och trafikinstitut, Linköping.

Carlsson, T. & H. Hattrem. (1995). Spedbarna dårligst sikret. *Motor*, **nr 9**, 6–9.

Carr, W. P., D. Brandt & K. Swanson. (1981). Injury patterns and helmet effectiveness among hospitalized motorcyclists. *Minnesota Medicine*, **64**, 521–527.

Carsten, O. (1987). Safety Implications of Truck Configuration. *Transportation Research Record*, **1111**, 17–26.

Carsten, O.M.J. & Tate, F.N. (2005). Intelligent speed adaptation: accident sacings and cost-benefit analysis. *Accident Analysis and Prevention*, **37**, 407–416.

Carstensen, G. (1987). *Motorcykelstørrelse og uheldsrisiko - analyse af tre uheldsmaterialer*. RfT-notat 1/1987. Rådet for Trafiksikkerhedsforskning, København.

Central Bureau of Statistics (1977). *Færdselsuheld 1976. Kap 4, Analyse af sikkerhedsselens skadeforebyggende virkning*. Danmarks Statistik, København.

Chandler, K. N. & J. K. L. Thompson. (1957). The effectiveness of present-day crash helmets for motorcyclists. *Operations Research Society Quarterly*, **8**, 63–71.

Chenier, T. C. & L. Evans. (1987). Motorcyclist fatalities and the repeal of mandatory helmet wearing laws. *Accident Analysis and Prevention*, **19**, 133–139.

Chira-Chavala, T. & S. M. Yoo. (1994). Potential safety benefits of intelligent control systems. *Accident Analysis and Prevention*, **26**, 135–146.

Christensen, P. & A. Borger, A. (1992). *Betydningen av bruk av bilbelter og hodestøtter for nakkeslengskader*. Arbeidsdokument TST/0382/92. Transportøkonomisk institutt, Oslo.

Christie, A. W. & J. Prudhoe. (1980). *Effects of lorry control at Lymm, Cheshire*. TRRL Supplementary Report 566. Transport and Road Research Laboratory, Crowthorne, Berkshire.

Conn, J.M., Chorba, T.L., Peterson, T.D. et al. (1993). Effectiveness of Safety-Belt Use: A Study Using Hospital-Based Data for Nonfatal Motor-Vehicle Crashes. *Journal of Safety Research*, **24**, 223–232.

Conybeare, J. A. C. (1980). Evaluation of Automobile Safety Regulations: The Case of Compulsory Seat Belt Legislation in Australia. *Policy Sciences*, **12**, 27–39.

COWI. (2006). *Cost-benefit assessment and prioritization of vehicle safety technologies*. Final report. The European Commission, Brussels.

Cox, N. T. (1968). *The effect of dirt on vehicle headlamp performance*. RRL Report LR 240. Road Research Laboratory, Crowthorne, Berkshire.

Crinion, J. D., L. A. Foldvary & J. C. Lane. (1975). The effect on casualties of a compulsory seat belt wearing law in South Australia. *Accident Analysis and Prevention*, **7**, 81–89.

Cross, R. (1991). Blind luck = Bad luck. The need for custom mirrors. *Commercial Carrier Journal*, **September**, 56–58.

Cuerden, R., Hill, J., Kirk, A. & Mackay, M. (2001). The potential effectiveness of adaptive restraints. *International IRCOBI Conference on the Biomechanics of Impact*, Isle of Man, UK, 10–12 October.

Cummings, P. & Grossman, D.C. (2007). Antilock brakes and the risk of driver injury in a crash – A case control study. *Accident Analysis and Prevention*, **39**, 995–1000.

Cummings, P., McKnight, B., Rivara, F.P. & Grossman, D.C. (2002). Association of driver airbags with driver fatality: A matched cohort study. *British Medical Journal*, **324**, 1119–1122.

Cunningham, K., Brown, T.D., Gradwell, E. & Nee, P.A. (2000). Airbag associated fatal head injury: case report and review of the literature on airbag injuries. *Journal of Accident Emergency Medicine*, **17**, 139–142.

Dahlstedt, S. (1986). *A comparison of some daylight motorcycle visibility treatments*. VTI-report 302A. Swedish Road and Traffic Research Institute, Linköping.

Dalgaard, J. B. (1977). *Dræbt i bil. Ulykkesårsager og selevirkning. En trafikmedicinsk undersøgelse*. Retsmedicinsk institut, Århus.

Dalmotas, D.J., Dance, D.M., Gardner, W.T. et al. (1984). *Current Activities in Canada Relating to the Protection of Children in Automobile Accidents*. SAE Paper 840529. SAE Report P-141, Advances in Belt Restraint Systems: design, performance and usage. Society of Automotive Engineers, Warrendale, Pa.

Dalmotas, D.J., Hurley, J., German, A. & Digges, K. (1996). Airbag deployment crashes in Canada. *Proceedings of the 15*th *International Technical Conference on the Enhanced Safety of Vehicles*, Melbourne, Australia, 13–16 May, **Vol 1**, 155–168.

Dang, J.N. (2004). *Preliminary results analysing the effectiveness of electronic stability control systems*. NHTSA, DOT HS 809 790.

Danner, M., Langwieder, K., Polauke, J. & Sporner, A. (1984). *Schutzkleidung für motorisierte Zweiradfahrer*. Bericht zum Forschungsprojekt 7806/7. Bundesanstalt für Strassenwesen (BASt), Bergisch-Gladbach.

Dare, C.E., Owens, J.C. & Krane, S.W. (1978). *Impact of motorcycle helmet usage in Colorado*. Report DOT HS-803 680. US Department of Transportation, National Highway Traffic Safety Administration, Washington DC.

Dare, C.E., Owens, J.C. & Krane, S.W. (1979). Effects of motorcycle safety helmet use on injury location and severity: before-and-after helmet law repeal in Colorado. *ITE Journal*, **October**, 9–15.

Davidsson, F. (1995). Dynamisk hastighetsanpassning – scenario 2020 (Dynamic speed adaptaion – scenario 2020). TFK, PM, Stockholm, Sweden.

Dean, J. M., J. C. Reading & P. J. Nechodom. (1995). Overreporting and Measured Effectiveness of Seat Belts in Motor Vehicle Crashes in Utah. *Transportation Research Record*, **1485**, 186–191.

Decina, L.E. & Knoebel, K.Y. (1997). Child safety seat misuse patterns in four states. *Accident Analysis and Prevention*, **29**, 125–132.

Decina, L.E. & Lococo, K.H. (2005). Child restraint system use and misuse in six states. *Accident Analysis and Prevention*, **37**, 583–590.

Dijks, A. (1976). Influence of tread depth on wet skid resistance of tires. *Highway Research Record*, **621**, 136–147.

Dorsch, M. M., A. J. Woodward & R. L. Somers. (1987). Do bicycle safety helmets reduce severity of head injury in real crashes? *Accident Analysis and Prevention*, **19**, 183–190.

Driscoll, R. Page, Y. Lassare, S. & Ehrlich, J. (2007). LAVIA : an evaluation of the potential safety benefits of the French intelligent speed adaptation project. In: *Proceedings of the 51 st Annual Conference of the Association for the Advancement of Automotive Medicine AAAM*, Melbourne, Australia, 484–505.

Duma, S.M., Rath, A.L., Jernigan, M.V., Stitzel, J.D. & Herring, I.P. (2005). The effects of depowered airbags on eye injuries in frontal automobile crashes. *American Journal of Emergency Medicine*, **23**, 13–19.

Durbin, D.R., Chen, I., Smith, R. et al. (2006). Effects of seating position and appropriate restraint use on risk of injury to children in motor vehicle crashes. *Pediatrics*, **115**, 305–309.

Duynstee, L., Katteler, H. & Martens, G. (2001). Intelligent speed adaptation: selected results of the Dutch practical trial. *Proceedings of the 8th World Congress of Intelligent ransprot Systems*, Sydney, Australia.

Edwards, W.R. (1995). An effectiveness analysis of Chrysler driver airbags after five years exposure. *Proceedings of the Fourteenth International Technical Conference on Enhanced Safety of Vehicles*, May 23–26, 1994, Munich, 556–561.

Elliot, M.R., Kallan, M.J., Durbin, D.R. & Winston, F.K. (2006). Effectiveness of child safety seat vs seat belt in reducing risk for death in children in passenger vehicle crashes. *Archives of Pediatrics & Adolescent Medicine*, **160**, 617–621.

Elvik, R. (1985). *Risikoanalyse av fire alternativer for transport av ammoniakk og ammoniumnitrat fra Rjukan fabrikker til Porsgrunn fabrikker*. Arbeidsdokument av 14.10.1985 (prosjekt O-1182). Transportøkonomisk institutt, Oslo.

Elvik, R. (1988). *Risiko ved transport av farlig gods på veg-foredrag presentert på NIF-kurs i april 1988*. Arbeidsdokument TS/0018/88. Transportøkonomisk institutt, Oslo.

Elvik, R. (1993). The effects on accidents of compulsory use of daytime running lights for cars in Norway. *Accident Analysis and Prevention*, **25**, 383–398.

Elvik, R. (1994). The external costs of traffic injury: definition, estimation and possibilities for internalization. *Accident Analysis and Prevention*, **26**, 719–732.

Elvik, R. (1995a). *Virkninger av bilbelter i Norge*. Arbeidsdokument TST/0667/95. Transportøkonomisk institutt, Oslo.

Elvik, R. (1995b). *Virkninger av påbud om sikring av barn i bil i Norge*. Arbeidsdokument TST/0684/95. Transportøkonomisk institutt, Oslo.

Elvik, R. (1996a). *Virkninger av fotgjengerrefleks på antall fotgjengerulykker i mørke*. Arbeidsdokument TST/0704/1996. Transportøkonomisk institutt, Oslo.

Elvik, R. (1996b). *Potensielle virkninger på ulykker og tidsbruk i trafikken av en toppfartssperre på motorkjøretøy*. Arbeidsdokument TST/0748/96. Transportøkonomisk institutt, Oslo.

Elvik, R. (1999). The effects on accidents of studded tires and laws banning their use: a meta-analysis of evaluation studies. *Accident Analysis and Prevention*, **31**, 125–134.

Elvik, R. (2003). How would setting policy priorities according to cost-benefit analyses affect the provision of road safety? *Accident Analysis and Prevention*, **35**, 557–570.

Elvik, R. (2007). *Prospects for improving road safety in Norway*. Report 8897. Institute of Transport Economics, Oslo.

Elvik, R., Christensen, P. & Amundsen, A.H. (2004). *Speed and road accidents: an evaluation of the power model*. TØI report 740/2004. Oslo: Institute of Transport Economics.

Elvik, R. & R. Muskaug. (1994). *Konsekvensanalyser og trafikksikkerhet*. TØI-rapport 281. Transportøkonomisk institutt, Oslo.

Elvik, R. & E. Skaansar. (1989). *Utviklingen av bilenes fartsressurser etter ca 1960*. Arbeidsdokument TST/0158/89. Transportøkonomisk institutt, Oslo.

Eriksen, K. S., Markussen, T. & Pütz, K. (1999). *Marginale kostnader ved transportvirksomhet*. TØI rapport 464. Oslo, Transportøkonomisk institutt.

Erke, A. (2008). Effects of electronic stability control (ESC) on accidents: A review of empirical evidence. *Accident Analysis and Prevention*, **40**, 167–173.

Erke, A. & Elvik, R. (2007). Making vision zero real: Preventing pedestrian accidents and making them less severe. Report 889. Oslo: Institute of Transport Economics.

Ernst, R. & L. Hippchen. (1974). *Zur Auswirkung der Spikesreifenverwendung auf den Verkehrsablauf. Strassenbau und Strassenverkehrstechnik*, Heft 170. Bundesminister für Verkehr, Abteilung Strassenbau, Bonn.

European Commission (2005). *Cost-benefit assessment and priorisation of vehicle safety technologies*. European Commission Directorate General Energy and Transport: Interim Report.

European Transport Safety Council (ETSC). (2003). *Cost effective EU transport safety measures*. Draft report. Brussels, ETSC.

Evans, L. (1984). Driver fatalities versus car mass using a new exposure approach. *Accident Analysis and Prevention*, **16**, 19–36.

Evans, L. (1985a). Driver behavior revealed in relations involving car mass. In: *Human behavior and traffic safety*, 337–353. (Evans, L. & R. C. Schwing eds). Plenum Press, New York, NY.

Evans, L. (1985b). Driver age, car mass and accident exposure – a synthesis of available data. *Accident Analysis and Prevention*, **17**, 155–170.

Evans, L. (1986). The effectiveness of safety belts in preventing fatalities. *Accident Analysis and Prevention*, **18**, 229–241.

Evans, L. (1987). Belted and unbelted driver accident involvement rates compared. *Journal of Safety Research*, **18**, 57–64.

Evans, L. (1988). Rear seat restraint system effectiveness in preventing fatalities. *Accident Analysis and Prevention*, **20**, 129–136.

Evans, L. (1990a). Restraint effectiveness, occupant ejection from cars, and fatality reductions. *Accident Analysis and Prevention*, **22**, 167–176.

Evans, L. (1990b). Discussion of "The problem of compatibility in car-to-car collisions" by Thomas et al. *34th Annual Proceedings of Association for the Advancement of Automotive Medicine,* 269–273, October 1–3, 1990, Scottsdale, Arizona.

Evans, L. (1996). Safety-belt effectiveness: the influence of crash severity and selective recruitment. *Accident Analysis and Prevention*, **28**, 423–433.

Evans, L. (2004). Airbag benefits, airbag costs. Science Serving Society, SAE International.

Evans, L. & M. C. Frick. (1988). Helmet effectiveness in preventing motorcycle driver and passenger fatalities. *Accident Analysis and Prevention*, **20**, 447–458.

Evans, L. & M. C. Frick. (1992). *Driver fatality risk in two-car crashes - dependence on masses of driven and striking car*. Paper 920480. 71st Annual Meeting of the Transportation Research Board, Washington DC.

Evans, L. & M. C. Frick. (1993). Mass ratio and relative driver fatality risk in two-vehicle crashes. *Accident Analysis and Prevention*, **25**, 213–224.

Evans, L. & P. H. Gerrish. (1996) Antilock brakes and risk of front and rear impact in two-vehicle crashes. *Accident Analysis and Prevention*, **28**, 315–323.

Evans, L. & P. Wasielewski. (1987). Serious or fatal driver injury rate versus car mass in head-on crashes between cars of similar mass. *Accident Analysis and Prevention*, **19**, 119–131.

Evans, W. N. & J. D. Graham. (1990). An estimate of the lifesaving benefit of child restraint use legislation. *Journal of Health Economics*, **9**, 121–142.

Evans, W. N. & J. D. Graham. (1991). Risk Reduction or Risk Compensation? The Case of Mandatory Safety-Belt Use Laws. *Journal of Risk and Uncertainty*, **4**, 61–73.

Fancher, P. & Ervin, R. (1994). Implications of intelligent cruise control (ICC) systems for the driver's supervisory role. *Proceedings of the First World Congress on Applications of Transport Telematics and Intelligent Vehicle-Highway Systems,* Paris 30 November–3 December 1994, 4, 2071–2078. Paris.

Farber, E. & D. Bailey, D. (1993). Using the REAMACS model to compare the effectiveness of alternative rear end collision-warning systems. Paper presented at *the conference Strategic Highway Research Program (SHRP) and Traffic Safety on Two Continents,* Hague, The Netherlands.

Farber, E. & M. Paley. (1993). Using freeway traffic data to estimate the effectiveness of rear-end collision countermeasures. Paper presented at *the conference Strategic Highway Research Program (SHRP) and Traffic Safety on Two Continents.* Hague, The Netherlands.

Farmer, C. M. (1996). Effectiveness estimates for center high mounted stop lamps: a six-year study. *Accident Analysis and Prevention*, **28**, 201–208.

Farmer, C.M. (2005). Relationships of frontal offset crash test results to real world driver fatality rates. *Traffic Injury Prevention*, **6**, 31–37.

Farmer, C.M. (2006). Effects of electronic stability control: An update. *Traffic Injury Prevention*, **7**, 319–324.

Farmer, C. M. & Williams, A. F. (2002). Effects of daytime running lights on multiple-vehicle daylight crashes in the United States. *Accident Analysis and Prevention*, **34**, 197–203.

Fast, P. T. (1994). Field test of UV-headlamps at a 100 km test site. In: *Towards an Intelligent Transport System, Proceedings of the First World Congress on Applications of Transport Telematics and Intelligent Vehicle-Highway Systems*, 2172–2179, Paris.

Ferguson, S. A., A. K. Lund & M. A. Greene. (1995). *Driver Fatalities in 1985–1994 Airbag Cars.* Insurance Institute for Highway Safety, Arlington VA.

Finvers, K.A., Strother, R.T. & Mohtadi, N. (1996). The Effect of Bicycling Helmets in Preventing Significant Bicycle-Related Injuries in Children. *Clinical Journal of Sport Medicine*, **6**, 102–107.

Foldvary, L. A. & J. C. Lane. (1974). The effectiveness of compulsory wearing of seat-belts in casualty reduction. *Accident Analysis and Prevention*, **6**, 59–81.

Folksam (2009). *Statistics published by Folksam*, http://folksam.se/testergodarad/bilen/krocktest/statistik (accessed 14.04.2009).

Fontaine, H. & Y. Gourlet. (1994). *Sécurité des véhicules et de leurs conducteurs.* Rapport INRETS 175. Institut National de Recherche sur les Transports et leur Sécurité, Paris.

Forlaget Last og Buss AS. (1997). *Kjøretøyforskriften nr 1, 1997. Ajour pr 1. april 1997.* Forlaget Last og Buss AS, Oslo.

Fosser, S. (1979a). *Dekkutrustning på vogntog og lastebiler om vinteren*. TØI-notat 503. Transportøkonomisk institutt, Oslo.

Fosser, S. (1979b). *Underkjøringshinder på godsbiler. En analyse av mulighetene for å redusere skadeomfanget mellom godsbiler og andre trafikanter*. Rapport. Transportøkonomisk institutt, Oslo.

Fosser, S. (1984). *Sikkerhetsutstyr på lastebiler og vogntog*. Arbeidsdokument revidert 21.12.1984 (prosjekt O-582 tunge kjøretøy). Transportøkonomisk institutt, Oslo.

Fosser, S. (1986). *Bremseforsøk med barnesykler*. TØI-notat 767. Transportøkonomisk institutt, Oslo.

Fosser, S. (1994). *Dekktyper på personbiler hver vinter fra 1991/92 til 1993/94*. Rapport 277. Transportøkonomisk institutt, Oslo.

Fosser, S. (1995). *Bilbelte- og hjelmbruk fra 1973 til 1993*. TØI-notat 996. Transportøkonomisk institutt, Oslo.

Fosser, S. & P. Christensen. (1992). *Mopedtrimming og trafikksikkerhet*. TØI-rapport 131. Transportøkonomisk institutt, Oslo.

Fosser, S., Christensen, P. & Fridstrøm, L. (2000). Older cars are safer. In *10th International Conference on Traffic Safety on Two Continents*, 243–251.

Fosser, S. & Ingebrigtsen, S. (1991a). *Dekkstandardens betydning for trafikkulykker om vinteren*. Rapport 75. Transportøkonomisk institutt, Oslo.

Fosser, S. & Ingebrigtsen, S. (1991b). *Dekkstandardens betydning for person- og varebilføreres fartsvalg på glatt føre*. TØI-notat 947. Transportøkonomisk institutt, Oslo.

Fosser, S. & I-A. Sætermo. (1995). *Vinterdekk med eller uten pigger - betydning for trafikksikkerheten*. Rapport 310. Transportøkonomisk institutt, Oslo.

Fosser, S. & H. Teigen. (1981). *Mønsterdybde i dekk på person- og varebiler i trafikken vinteren 1981*. TØI-notat 558. Transportøkonomisk institutt, Oslo.

Fosser, S., T. Vaa & A. K. Torp. (1992). *Sikring av barn og voksne i bil. Et informasjonshefte om bilbelter, barnesikring og luftputer - lovgivning, sikkerhetseffekt, bruk og feilbruk*. Rapport 111. Transportøkonomisk institutt og Gjensidige forsikring, Oslo.

Frampton, R., Sferco, R., Welsh, R., Kirk, A. & Fay, P. (2000). Effectiveness of airbag restraints in frontal crashes: What European field studies tell us. *Proceedings of the 2000 Internationall IRCOBI Conference on the Biomechanics of Impact*, September 20–22, Montpellier, Frankrike, s. 425–438.

Fredén, S. (1994). *Användning av analysmetoden - Ett fiktivt beräkningsexempel*. VTI-rapport 387:6. Väg- och transportforskningsinstitutet, Linköping.

Fredriksen, P. (1971). *Bilbrande opstået i forbindelse med færdselsuheld*. RfT-rapport 10. Rådet for Trafiksikkerhedsforskning, København.

Fridstrøm, L. (2000). *Piggfrie dekk i de største byene*. TØI rapport 493. Transportøkonomisk institutt, Oslo.

Friedel, B., K-P. Glaeser & R. Krupp. (1992). Kopfstützen in Personenkraftwagen. *Zeitschrift für Verkehrssicherheit*, **38**, 4–9.

Fulton, E. J., C. Kirkby & P. G. Stroud. (1980). *Daytime motorcycle conspicuity*. TRRL Supplementary Report 625. Transport and Road Research Laboratory, Crowthorne.

Gabella, B., Reiner, K.L., Hoffman, R.E. et al. (1995). Relationship of helmet use and head injuries among motorcycle crash victims in El Paso county, Colorado, 1989–1990. *Accident Analysis and Prevention*, **27**, 363–369.

Gabestad, K. O. (1979). *Eie og bruk av campingtilhenger*. TØI-rapport. Transportøkonomisk institutt, Oslo.

Gabestad, K. O. & A. Ragnøy. (1986). *Samfunnsøkonomiske vurderinger av piggdekkforbud*. TØI-notat 798. Transportøkonomisk institutt, Oslo.

Garber, N. J. & R. Gadiraju. (1992). Impact of Differential Speed Limits on the Speed of Traffic and the Rate of Accidents. *Transportation Research Record*, **1375**, 44–52.

Gehre, C., Kramer, S., Schindler, V. (2003). *Seitenairbag und Kinderrueckhaltesystem*. Technische Universitaet Berlin, Institut fuer Strassen- und Schienenverkeht (ILS). Abschlussbericht zum Forschungsprojekt 82.176/2000 (ITRD-Nummer D707307) der Bundesanstalt fuer Strassenwesen.

Gies, S. (1991). *Die Sicherheitsrelevanz neuer Fahrhilfen in Kraftfahrzeugen*. Forschungsbericht 238. Bundesanstalt für Strassenwesen (BASt), Bergisch Gladbach.

Glad, A. (1988). *Piggdekkstandard og ulykkesrisiko. Forslag til gjennomføring av en undersøkelse og resultater fra en forundersøkelse*. Arbeidsdokument TS/0049/88. Transportøkonomisk institutt, Oslo.

Glad, A., T. Assum & E. Bjørgum. (1985). *Kjøremåte, bilvedlikehold og drivstofforbruk. Grunnlagsmateriale for en kampanje for drivstoffsparing blant vanlige bilister*. Rapport NORD. Nordisk Ministerråds Sekretariat, Oslo.

Glass, R.J., Segui-Gomez, M. & Graham, J.D. (2000). Child passenger safety: Decisions about seating location, airbag exposure, and restraint use. *Risk Analysis*, **20**, 521–527.

Graham, J.D., Goldie, S.J., Segui-Gomez, M., Thompson, K.M., Nelson, T., Glass, R., Simpson, A. & Woerner, L. (1998). Reducing risks to children in vehicles with passenger airbags. *Pediatrics*, **102**, 1–7.

Grime, G. (1987). *Handbook of road safety research*. Butterworth, London.

Grime, G & Hutchinson, T.P. (1979a). Vehicle mass and driver injury. *Ergonomics* **22**, 93–104.

Grime, G & Hutchinson, T.P. (1979b). *Some implications of vehicle-weight for the risk of injury to drivers*. Research Report. Transport Studies Group, University College London.

Grush, E.S., Marsh IV, J.C. 67 South, N.E. (1983). Comparison of high-speed crash test results with fatality rates. In: *Proceedings of the 27th Annual Conference of the American Association for Automotive Medicine*, Arlington Heights, IL, 189–209.

Grøndahl Dreyer. (1995). *Vegtrafikklovgivningen. Ajourført pr 1. februar 1995.* Grøndahl Dreyer, Oslo.

Guerin, D. & D. P. MacKinnon. (1985). An Assessment of California Child Passenger Restraint Requirement. *American Journal of Public Health*, **75**, 142–144.

Hagen, K-E. (1993). *Samfunnsøkonomisk regnskapssystem for trafikkulykker og trafikksikkerhetstiltak.* TØI-rapport 182. Transportøkonomisk institutt, Oslo.

Hagen, K-E. (1995). *Analyse av kostnadsutviklingen i innenlandske godstransporter. Sammenlikning med nordiske land.* TØI-rapport 297. Transportøkonomisk institutt, Oslo.

Hakkert, A. S. (1969). The economic savings from wearing seat belts. *Accident Analysis and Prevention*, **1**, 153–158.

Hakkert, A. S., D. M. Zaidel & E. Sarelle. (1981). Patterns of safety belt usage following introduction of a safety belt wearing law. *Accident Analysis and Prevention*, **13**, 65–82.

Harless, D.W. & Hoffer, G.E. (2007). Do laboratory frontal crash test programs predict driver fatality risk? Evidence from within vehicle line variation in test ratings. *Accident Analysis and Prevention*, **39**, 902–913.

Hankins, K.D., Morgan, R.B., Ashkar, B. & Tutt, P.R. (1971). Influence of Vehicle and Pavement Factors on Wet-Pavement Accidents. *Highway Research Record*, **376**, 66–84.

Hansen, L. K. (1993). *Kørelys i Danmark. Effektvurdering af påbudt kørelys i dagtimerne.* Notat 2/1993. Rådet for Trafiksikkerhedsforskning, København.

Hansen, L. K. (1995). *Kørelys. Effektvurdering baseret på uheldstal efter knap 3 års erfaring med kørelys.* Arbejdsrapport 1/1995. Rådet for Trafiksikkerhedsforskning, København.

Harms, P. L. (1992). *Crash injury investigation and injury mechanisms in road traffic accidents. State-of-the-art review.* HMSO (on behalf of the Transport Research Laboratory). London.

Hartemann, F., Thomas, C., Henry, C. et al. (1977). Belted or Not-Belted: The Only Difference Between Two Matched Samples of 200 Car Occupants. Paper 770917. *Proceedings of Twenty-First Stapp Car Crash Conference*, 97–150.

Hartunian, N.S., Smart, C.N., Willemain, T.R. & Zador, P.L. (1983). The Economics of Safety deregulation: Lives and Dollars Lost due to Repeal of Motorcycle Helmet Laws. *Journal of Health Politics, Policy and Law*. **8**, 76–98.

Harvey, A. C. & J. Durbin. (1986). The Effects of Seat Belt Legislation on British Road Casualties: A Case Study in Structural Time Series Modelling. *Journal of the Royal Statistical Society, Series A*, **149**, 187–227.

Harwin, E.A. & H. K. Brewer. (1990). Analysis of the relationship between vehicle rollover stability and rollover risk using the NHTSA CARDfile accident database. *Journal of Traffic Medicine*, **18**, 109–122.

Harwin, E. A. & Brewer, H. K. (1991). Vehicle rollover stability and rollover risk. *Accident Reconstruction Journal*, **18**, 22–23, 33.

Haworth, N., Smith, R., Brumen, I. & Pronk, N. (1997). *Case-control study of motorcycle crashes*. Report CR 174. Clayton, VIC, Monash University Accident Research Centre.

Helmers, G. (1988). *Daytime running lights-a potent traffic safety measure?* VTI-report 333 A. Swedish Road and Traffic Research Institute, Linköping.

Helmers, G., M. Fernlund & U. Ytterbom. (1990). *Optimisation of the low beam pattern of illumination. Some experimental results related to the illumination above the cut-off*. VTI-report 353A. Swedish Road and Traffic Research institute, Linköping.

Helmers, G. & K. Rumar. (1974). *High beam intensity and obstacle visibility*. Report 150. Department of psychology, University of Uppsala.

Helmers, G. & U. Ytterbom. (1984). *Visibility Effects of a Rapidly Fading High Beam as an Option to the Ordinary Low Beam*. VTI-report 275A. Swedish Road and Traffic Research Institute, Linköping.

Helmers, G., U. Ytterbom & S-O. Lundkvist. (1993). *Upptäcktsavstånd till hinder på vägen i UV-ljus. Mätning i en simulerad fullskalig trafiksituation*. TFB & VTI forskning/research 9, 1993. Transportforskningsberedningen og Statens väg- och trafikinstitut, Stockholm og Linköping.

Hertz, E., J. Hilton & D. M. Johnson. (1995a). *An analysis of the crash experience of light trucks equipped with antilock braking systems*. Report DOT HS 808 278. US Department of Transportation, National Highway traffic Safety Administration, Washington DC.

Hertz, E., J. Hilton & D. M. Johnson. (1995b). *An analysis of the crash experience of Passenger Cars Equipped with Antilock Braking Systems*. Report DOT HS 808 279. US Department of Transportation, National Highway traffic Safety Administration, Washington DC.

Highway Loss Data Institute (HLDI). (1995). *Three Years On-the-Road Experience with Antilock Brakes*. HLDI Special Report A-47. Highway Loss Data Institute, Arlington, Va.

Highway Safety Foundation. (1971). *A study of relationships between tire tread depth and the likelihood of accident involvement*. The Highway Safety Foundation, (sitert etter Dijks 1976). Mansfield, Ohio.

Hisdal, B. (1974a). *Kjøretøyers lysbruk og trafikksikkerhet: nærlys og lyktinnstilling*. SI-rapport. Sentralinstituttet for industriell forskning, Oslo.

Hisdal, B. (1974b). *Kjøretøyers lysbruk og trafikksikkerhet: kurve-tåkelys*. SI-rapport. Sentralinstituttet for industriell forskning, Oslo.

Hisdal, B. (1975). *Kjøretøyers lysbruk og trafikksikkerhet: justering av nærlys*. SI-rapport. Sentralinstituttet for industriell forskning, Oslo.

Hisdal, B. (1976). Kjøretøyers lysbruk og trafikksikkerhet. Retroreflekterende kjennemerker. Sentralinstitutt for industriell forskning, Oslo.

Hjälmdahl, M. & Várhelyi, A. (2004). Speed regulation by in-car active accelerator pedal – effects on driver behaviour. *Transportation research part F*, **7**, 77–94.

Hobbs, C. A. (1978). *The effectiveness of seat belts in reducing injuries to car occupants*. TRRL Laboratory Report 811. Transport and Road Research Laboratory, Crowthorne, Berkshire.

Hobbs, C. A. (1981). *Car occupant injury patterns and mechanisms*. TRRL Supplementary Report 648. Transport and Road Research Laboratory, Crowthorne, Berkshire.

Hobbs, C. A & P. J. Mills. (1984). *Injury probability for car occupants in frontal and side impacts*. TRRL Laboratory Report 1124. Transport and Road Research Laboratory, Crowthorne, Berkshire.

Hocherman, I. & A. S. Hakkert. (1991). The use of daytime running lights during the winter months in Israel-evaluation of a campaign. *Proceedings of the third workshop of ICTCT in Cracow, Poland*, November 1990, 123–131. Bulletin 94, Lund Institute of Technology, Department of Traffic Planning and Engineering, University of Lund.

Hoffman, G. R. (1977). The effectiveness of the helmet for the motorcyclist (machine under 50 cc) and the importance of alcoholemia in traffic accidents. *Journal of Traffic Medicine*, **5**, 36–37.

Hofmann, E. R. (1966). Note on detection of vehicle velocity changes. *Human Factors*, **8**, 139–141.

Hollo, P. (1995). Changes of the DRL-regulations and their effect on traffic safety in Hungary. *Paper presented at the conference Strategic Highway Safety Program and Traffic Safety, Prague, The Czech Republic*, September 20–22, 1995. Preprint for sessions on September 21.

Hollo, P. (1998). Changes in the legislation on the use of daytime running lights by motor vehicles and their effect on road safety in Hungary. *Accident Analysis and Prevention*, **30**, 183–199.

Huelke, D. F. & C. P. Compton. (1995). The effects of seat belts on injury severity of front and rear seat occupants in the same frontal crash. *Accident Analysis and Prevention*, **27**, 835–838.

Huelke, D.F., Lawson, T.E.; Scott, R. & Marsh, J.C. (1977). The Effectiveness of Belt Systems in Frontal and Rollover Crashes. *Journal of Traffic Medicine*, **5, 1**, 8–21.

Huelke, D. F., T. E. Lawson & C. J. Marsh. (1977). Injuries, restraints and vehicle factors in rollover car crashes. *Accident Analysis and Prevention*, **9**, 93–107.

Huere, J.F., Foret-Bruno, J.Y., Faverjon, G. & Le Coz, J.Y. (2001). Airbag efficiency in frontal real world accidents. *Proceedings of the 17*th *International Technical Conference on the Enhanced Safety of Vehicles*, Amsterdam, 4–7 June 2001, paper 2001-S1-O-193.

Hurt, H. H., J. V. Ouellet & D. R. Thom. (1981). *Motorcycle Accident Cause Factors and Identification of Countermeasures. Final Report*, Volume 1, Technical Report. Report DOT-HS-805 862. US Department of Transportation, National Highway Traffic Safety Administration, Washington DC.

Hutchinson, J. W. & R. V. Seyre. (1977). *Recreational vehicle accident investigation study*. Report DOT HS-802 631. US Department of Transportation, National Highway Traffic Safety Administration, Washington DC.

Hvidberg Jørgensen, E. (1977). Undersøgelse af sikkerhedsselelovens virkning ved analyse af data fra 15 danske hospitaler. I: *Virkningen af lov om påbudt brug af sikkerhedssele*, 35–58. RfT-rapport 21, Rådet for Trafiksikkerhedsforskning, København.

Hvoslef, H. (1990). *Yrkesrisiko i transport*. Notat fra Trafikksikkerhetskontoret i Vegdirektoratet, 27.4.1990. Statens vegvesen Vegdirektoratet, Oslo.

Hvoslef, H. (1997). *Kommentarer fra Japan om trafikk- og ulykkessituasjonen på Hokkaido*. Notat av 21.1.1997. Vegdirektoratet, Stabskontor for kvalitetssikring innenfor trafikksikkerhet og miljø, Oslo.

Högström, K., Svenson, L. & Thörnquist, B. (1973). *Olycksfallsundersökning. Tung lastvagn/oskydad trafikant*. Rapport 1. AB Volvo Lastvagnar Trafiksäkerhetsavdelingen, Göteborg.

Högström, K., L. Svenson & B. Thörnquist. (1974). *Olycksfalls undersökning. Dödsolyckor tung lastvagn/personvagn*. Rapport 2. AB Volvo Lastvagnar Trafiksäkerhetsavdelingen, Göteborg.

Ingebrigtsen, S. (1989). *Motorsykler, mopeder og ulykker*. TØI-rapport 30. Transportøkonomisk institutt, Oslo.

Ingebrigtsen, S. (1990). *Risikofaktorer ved ferdsel med moped og motorsykkel*. TØI-rapport 66. Transportøkonomisk institutt, Oslo.

Ingebrigtsen, S. & S. Fosser. (1991). *Dekkstandardens betydning for trafikkulykker om vinteren*. TØI-rapport 75. Transportøkonomisk insituttt, Oslo.

Insurance Institute for Highway Safety (2005). Electronic Stability Control. Status Report, 4(1), 2–4.

Ivey, D.L., Griffin III, L.I., Newton, T.M. et al. (1981). Predicting wet weather accidents. *Accident Analysis and Prevention*, **13**, 83–99.

Jacobson, G.A., Blizzard, L. & Dwyer, T. (1998). Bicycle injuries: road trauma is not the only concern. *Australian and New Zealand Journal of Public Health*, **22 (4)**, 451/455.

Jakobsson, L., Isaksson-Hellman, I., Lundell, B. (2005). Safety for the growing child – experience form Swedish accident data. *Childhood Injury Prevention Symposium*, Paper no 05-0330.

Jamieson, K. G. & K. D'Arcy. (1973). Crash helmets reduce head injuries. *The Medical Journal of Australia*, **2**, 806–809.

Janoff, M.S., Cassel, A., Fertner, K.S., Smierciak, E.S. (1970). Daytime *Motorcycle Headlight and Taillight Operation.* Report DOT HS-800 321. US Department of Transportation, National Highway Safety Bureau, Washington DC.

Janssen, W.H. (1994). Seat-belt wearing and driving behavior: an instrumented-vehicle study. *Accident Analysis and Prevention*, **26**, 249–261.

Janssen, W.H. & L. Nilsson. (1992). *An experimental evaluation of in-vehicle collision avoidance systems.* VTI särtryck nr 181/1992 Väg- och Trafikinstitutet, Linköping.

Jenssen, T. K. (1977). *Risiko ved klortransport.* TØI-rapport. Transportøkonomisk institutt, Oslo.

Jernigan, M.V. & Duma, S.M. (2003). The effects of airbag deployment on severe upper extremity injuries in frontal automobile crashes. *American Journal of Emergency Medicine*, **21**, 100–105.

Jernigan, M.V., Rath, A.L. & Duma, S.M. (2005). Severe upper extremity injuries in frontal automobile crashes: The effects of depowered airbags. *American Journal of Emergency Medicine*, **23**, 99–105.

Johansen, J. (1975). *Dekkstøy-en del av trafikkstøyen. En undersøkelse av dekkstøy på fire vegdekketyper.* Internrapport 617. Statens vegvesen, Veglaboratoriet, Oslo.

Johansson, G., Rumar, K., Forsgren, J.-B. & Snöborgs, M. (1969a). *Experimentella studier av polariserat mötesljus II. Siktsträcka som funktion av strålkastarintensitet under olika atmosfärförhållanden.* Rapport S38. Psykologiska institutionen, Uppsala Universitet.

Johansson, G., Rumar, K., Forsgren, J.-B. & Snöborgs, M. (1969b). *Experimentella studier av polariserat mötesljus IV. Siktsträcka vid möten mellan koventionellt halvljus och polariserat mötesljus.* Rapport S40. Psykologiska institutionen, Uppsala Universitet.

Johnston, K.L., Desantis-Klinich, K., Rhule, D.A. & Saul, R.A. (1997). *Assessing arm injury potential from deploying airbags.* SAE Technical paper 970400, 259–273.

Joksch, H.C. (1995). *Update of airbag fatalities approximation for passenger car fleet.* University of Michigan, Transportation Research Institute, Report UMTRI-05-33.

Jonah, B. A. & G. R. Engel. (1983). Measuring the relative risk of pedestrian accidents. *Accident Analysis and Prevention*, **15**, 193–206.

Jonah, B. A. & J. J. Lawson. (1984). The effectiveness of the Canadian mandatory seat belt use laws. *Accident Analysis and Prevention*, **16**, 433–450.

Jones, I. S. & H. S. Stein. (1989). Defective equipment and tractor-trailer crash involvement. *Accident Analysis and Prevention*, **21**, 469–481.

Jones, I.S. & Whitfield, R.A. (1988). Predicting injury risk with New Car Assessment Program crashworthiness ratings. *Accident Analysis and Prevention*, **20**, 411–419.

Jovanis, P. P., H-L. Chang & I. Zabaneh. (1989). Comparison of Accident Rates for Two Truck Configurations. *Transportation Research Record*, **1249**, 18–29.

Junghard, O. (1992). Estimating the traffic safety effect of studded tires. *Accident Analysis and Prevention*, **24**, 357–361.

Jørgensen, N. O. & H. V. Lund. (1977). Undersøgelse af virkningen af sikkerhedsseleloven ved anvendelse af uheldsdata fra Danmarks Statistik. I: RfT-rapport 21, *Virkningen af lov om påbudt brug af sikkerhedssele,* 13–34. Rådet for Trafiksikkerhedsforskning, København.

Kahane, C. J. (1974). *Usage and Effectiveness of Seat and Shoulder Belts in Rural Pennsylvania Accidents*. NHTSA Technical Note DOT HS-801 398. US Department of Transportation, National Highway Traffic Safety Administration, Washington DC.

Kahane, C. J. (1981). *An evaluation of federal motor vehicle safety standards for passenger car steering assemblies. Standard 203 - impact protection for the driver. Standard 204 - rearward column displacement.* Report DOT HS 805 705. US Department of Transportation, National Highway Traffic Safety Administration, Washington DC.

Kahane, C. J. (1982a). *An evaluation of head restraints. Federal Motor Vehicle Safety Standard 202.* Report DOT HS 806 108. US Department of Transportation, National Highway Traffic Safety Administration, Washington DC.

Kahane, C. J. (1982b). *An evaluation of side structure improvements in response to Federal Motor Vehicle Safety Standard 214.* Report DOT HS 806 314. US Department of Transportation, National Highway Traffic Safety Administration, Washington DC.

Kahane, C. J. (1983a). *A Preliminary Evaluation of Two Braking Improvements for Passenger Cars. Dual Master Cylinders and Front Disc Brakes.* Report DOT HS-806 359. US Department of Transportation, National Highway Traffic Safety Administration, Washington DC.

Kahane, C. J. (1983b). *An Evaluation of Side Marker Lamps for Cars, Trucks and Buses.* Report DOT HS-806-430. US Department of Transportation, National Highway Traffic Safety Administration, Washington DC.

Kahane, C. J. (1984). *The National Highway Traffic Safety Administration's evaluations of Federal Motor Vehicle Safety Standards.* SAE Technical Paper 840902. Society of Automotive Engineers, Warrendale, Pa.

Kahane, C. J. (1985). *An evaluation of windshield glazing and installation methods for passenger cars.* Report DOT HS 806 693. US Department of Transportation, National Highway Traffic Safety Administration, Washington DC.

Kahane, C. J. (1986). *An Evaluation of Child Passenger Safety. The Effectiveness and Benefits of Safety Seats.* Report DOT HS 806 890. US Department of Transportation, National Highway Traffic Safety Administration, Washington DC.

Kahane, C. J. (1988). *An evaluation of occupant protection in frontal interior impact for unrestrained front seat occupants of cars and light trucks.* Report DOT HS 807 203. US Department of Transportation, National Highway Traffic Safety Administration, Washington DC.

Kahane, C. J. (1989a). *An Evaluation of Center High Mounted Stop Lamps Based on 1987 Data*. Report DOT HS 807 442. US Department of Transportation, National Highway Traffic Safety Administration, Washington DC.

Kahane, C. J. (1989b). *An evaluation of door locks and roof crush resistance of passenger cars-Federal Motor Vehicle Safety Standards 206 and 216*. Report DOT HS 807 489. US Department of Transportation, National Highway Traffic Safety Administration, Washington DC.

Kahane, C. J. (1993). *Preliminary Evaluation of the Effectiveness of Rear-Wheel Antilock Brake Systems for Light Trucks*. Draft Report December 1993. US Department of Transportation, National Highway Traffic Safety Administration, Washington DC.

Kahane, C. J. (1994a). *Preliminary Evaluation of the Effectiveness of Antilock Brake Systems for Passenger Cars*. Report DOT HS 808 206. US Department of Transportation, National Highway Traffic Safety Administration, Washington DC.

Kahane, C. J. (1994b). *Correlation of NCAP performance with fatality risk in actual head-on collisions*. Report DOT HS 808 061. US Department of Transportation, National Highway Traffic Safety Administration, Washington DC.

Kahane, C. J. (1994c). *Fatality Reduction by Automatic Occupant Protection in the United States*. Paper 94-S5-O-08. US Department of Transportation, National Highway Traffic Safety Administration, Washington DC.

Kahane, C. J. (1996). *Fatality Reduction by Airbags. Analyses of Accident Data through Early 1996*. Report DOT HS 808 470. US Department of Transportation, National Highway Traffic Safety Administration, Washington DC.

Kahane, C. J. (1997). *Relationships between Vehicle Size and Fatality Risk in Model Year 1985–93 Passenger Cars and Light Trucks*. Report DOT HS 808 570. US Department of Transportation, National Highway Traffic Safety Administration, Washington DC.

Kahane, C.J. (2006). An evaluation of the 1998–1999 redesign of frontal airbags. NHTSA Technical Report DOT-HS-810-685.

Kahane, C.J. (2007). An evaluation of side impact protection: FMVSS 214 TTI(d) improvements and side airbags. NHTSA Report DOT HS 810 748.

Kahane, C.J. & Tarbet, M.J. (2006). HIC test results before and after the 1999–2003 head impact upgrade of FMVSS 201. NHTSA Technical Report Nr. DOT HS 810 739.

Kallberg, V-P. (1986). *Motorcykelolyckor i Finland*. VTT-rapport 423. Statens tekniska forskningscentral, Esbo.

Kantowitz, B. H & R. D. Sorkin. (1983). *Human Factors: Understanding People-System Relationships*. John Wiley & Sons, New York.

Karlsen, P. G. (1989). *Vurdering av forskjellige blokkeringsfrie bremsesystemer (ABS) under nordiske veg- og vinterforhold*. Rapport 40/1989. Teknologisk institutt, Avdeling for kjøretøyteknikk, Oslo.

Karlsen, P. G. (1991). *Vurdering av kjøreegenskaper og stabilitet til vogntog*. Rapport 52/1991. Teknologisk institutt, Oslo.

Kelly, P., Sanson, T., Strange, G. & Orsay, E. (1991). A prospective study of the impact of helmet usage on motorcycle trauma. *Annals of Emergency Medicine*, **20**, 852–855.

Kemeny, A. & Piroird, J.M. (1991). A simulator for cooperative driving. *Proceedings of the DRIVE Conference*, Brussels, February 1991, pp. 930–942.

Kemp, R. N., B. P. Chinn & G. Brock. (1978). *Articulated vehicle roll stability: methods of assessment and effects of vehicle characteristics*. TRRL Laboratory Report 788. Transport and Road Research Laboratory, Crowthorne, Berkshire.

Kesting, A., Treiber, M., Schönhof, M. & Helbing, D. (2008). Adaptive cruise control design for active congestion avoidance. *Transportation Research Part C*, **16**, 668–683.

Khasnabis, S., R. A. Dusseau & T. J. Dombrowski. (1991). Safety Implications of Seat Belts on Transit Buses. *Transportation Research Record*, **1322**, 9–16.

Kippelt, U., Buss, W., Feldhoff, U. & Thelen, M. (1998) Protectino devices and development tools for reducing foot and leg injuries in frontal crashes. *Proceedings of the International IRCOBI Conference on the Biomechanics of Impact*, September 16–18, Goeteborg, Sweden, 161–172.

Klanner, W., Ambos, R. & Paulus, H. (2004). Unfallverletzungen in Fahrzeugen mit Airbag (Accident injuries in vehicles with airbags). Berichte der Bundesanstalt für Straßenwesen, *Fahrzeugtechnik*, **Heft F 53**.

Klein, T. M., E. Hertz & S. Borener. (1991). *A collection of recent analyses of vehicle weight and safety*. Report DOT HS 807 677. US Department of Transportation, National Highway Traffic Safety Administration, Washington DC.

Knoblauch, R. L. & H. N. Tobey. (1980). *Safety Aspects of Using Vehicle Hazard Warning Lights*. Volume 1. Executive Summary. Report DOT FHWA/RD-80/101. US Department of Transportation, Federal Highway Administration, Washington DC.

Koch, H. (1987). *The correlation between and the influence of age, riding experience and engine performance on the involvement of motorcycle beginners in accidents. Results of multivariate evaluations of a survey*. Institute for Two-Wheeled Safety, Bochum.

Koehler, M. (1978). *Evaluation of Motorcycle Safety Helmet Usage Law. Final Report*. College Station, TX, Texas A&M University, Texas.

Kommunikationsdepartementet. (1977). *Långa fordon och fordonskombinationer. Betänkande avgivet av trafiksäkerhetsutredningen*. Ds K 1977:1. Kommunikationsdepartementet, Stockholm.

Konagai, N., M. Asano & N. Horita. (1993). Influence of Regulation of Studded Tire Use in Hokkaido, Japan. *Transportation Research Record*, **1387**, 165–169.

Koornstra, M. J. (1993). *Daytime running lights: Its safety revisited*. SWOV Report D-93-25. SWOV Institute for Road Safety Research, Leidschendam.

Koushki, P. A., Y Ali & O. I. Al-Saleh. (1996). Safety-Belt Law in Kuwait: Observed and Reported Compliance and Impacts on Road Safety. *Transportation Research Record*, **1560**, 13–17.

Krafft, M., C. Nygren & C. Tingvall. (1990). Rear seat occupant protection. A study of children and adults in the rear seat of cars in relation to restraint use and characteristics. *Journal of Traffic Medicine*, **18, 2**, 51–60.

Kraus, J.F., Peek, C., McArthur, D.L. & Williams, A. (1994). The effect of the 1992 California motorcycle helmet use law on motorcycle crash fatalities and injuries. *Journal of the American Medical Association*, **272**, 1506–1511.

Kraus, J.F., Peek, C., Shen, H. & Williams, A. (1995). Motorcycle crashes: injuries, rider, crash and vehicle characteristics associated with helmet use. *Journal of Traffic Medicine*, **23**, 29–35.

Kraus, J. F., R. S. Riggins & C. E. Franti. (1975a). Some epidemiologic features of motorcycle collision injuries. I. Introduction, methods and factors associated with incidence. *American Journal of Epidemiology*, **102**, 74–98.

Kraus, J. F., R. S. Riggins & C. E. Franti. (1975b). Some epidemiologic features of motorcycle collision injuries. II. Factors associated with severity of injuries. *American Journal of Epidemiology*, **102**, 99–109.

Kreiss, J.-P., Schüler, L. & Langwieder, K. (2006). The effectiveness of primary safety features in passenger cars in Germany. ESV-paper No. 05-0145. *19th-ESV-Conference*, Washington DC (USA).

Kuratorium für Verkehrssicherheit; Institut für Verkehrstechnik und Unfallstatistik. (1993). *Fahren mit Licht - auch am Tag. Analyse der verkehrsunfälle beim Kraftwagendienst der Österreichischen Bundesbahnen und bei der Österreichischen Post- und Telegraphenverwaltung nach Einführung der Verwendung des Abblendlichtes auch am Tag*. Wien.

Lalani, N. & E. J. Holden (1978). The Greater London "Ride Bright" campaign-its effect on motorcyclist conspicuity and casualties. *Traffic Engineering and Control*, **19**, 404–407.

Langwieder, K., Gwehenberger, J., Hummel, T., Bende, J. (2003). Benefit potential of ESP in real accident situations involving cars and trucks. *16 th International Technical Conference on the Enhanced Safety of Vehicles*, Nagoya (Japan).

Langwieder, K. & T. Hummel. (1989). Children in Cars – Their Injury Risks and the Influence of Child Protection. *Proceedings, Volume 1 (39–49), of Twelfth International Technical Conference on Experimental Safety Vehicles*, May 29–June 1, Gothenburg, Sweden.

Langwieder, K., Hummelt, T. & Mueller, C. (1997). *Der Airbag im Realunfall: Leistung und Schwaechen, Erkenntnisse aus der Unfallforschung*. VDI-Bericht 1354, 55–102.

Lassarre, S. (2002). *Évaluation de l'expérimentation des feux de croisement de jour dans Les Landes*. Rapport 244, Décembre 2002. Paris, INRETS.

Lawless, E. W. & T. A. Siani. (1984). *Child Passenger Safety Legislation: Implementation and Enforcement*. SAE Paper 840521. SAE Report P-141, Advances in Belt Restraint Systems: design, performance and usage. Warrendale, Pa, Society of Automotive Engineers, Warrendale.

Lekander, T. (1983). Motorcykelstatistik. I: *Motorcykelsäkerhet-Ett seminarium, 4–8*. (Lövsund, P. ed), VTI-rapport 253. Statens väg- och trafikinstitut, Linköping.

Lenard, J., Frampton, R. & Thomas, P. (1998). The influence of European airbags on crash injury outcome. *16th International Conference on the Enhanced Safety of Vehicles*, Windsor, Canada. Paper number 98-S5-O-01.

Levine, D. N. & B. J. Campbell. (1971). *Effectiveness of Lap Seat Belts and Energy Absorbing Steering System in the Reduction of Injuries*. Report DOT HS 011 537. Chapel Hill, NC, University of North Carolina, Chapel Hill.

Lie, A., Tingvall, C., Krafft, M. & Kullgren, A. (2004). The effectiveness of ESP in Reducing real life accidents. *Traffic Injury Prevention*, **5**, 37–41.

Lie, A., Tingvall, C., Krafft, M. & Kullgren, A. (2006). The effectiveness of electronic stability control (ESC) in reducing real life crashes and injuries. *Traffic Injury Prevention*, **7**, 38–43.

Lindström, M. (1977). *Vältningsstabilitet för tankfordon-med och utan langsgående skvalpskott*. VTI-rapport 115. Statens väg- och trafikinstitut, Linköping.

Linn, S., Smith, D. & Sheps, S. (1998). Epidemiology of bicycle injury, head injury, and helmet use among children in British Columbia: a five year descriptive study, *Injury Prevention*, **4**, 122–125.

Löffelholz, H. & F. Nicklisch. (1977). Stellungsnahme zu einer Änderung der Nationalen Vorschriften für Kleinkrafträder und Fahrräder mit Hilfsmotor. In: *Unfall- und Sicherheitsforschung Strassenverkehr*, **Heft 9**, 101–143, 1977. Bundesanstalt für Strassenwesen (BASt), Bergisch Gladbach.

Luna, G.K., Copass, M.K., Oreskovich, M.R. & Carrico, C.J. (1981). The role of helmets in reducing head injuries from motorcycle accidents: a political or medical issue? *The Western Journal of Medicine*, **135**, 89–92.

Lundstrom, L. C. & W. G. Cichowski. (1969). *Field Experience with the Energy Absorbing Steering Column*. SAE Technical Paper 690183. Warrendale, PA, Society of Automotive Engineers, Warrendale.

Luoma, J., M. Sivak & M. J. Flannagan. (1995). Effects of driver-side mirror type on lane-change accidents. *Ergonomics*, **38**, 1973–1978.

Lyles, R.W., Campbell, K.L., Blower, D.F. & Stamadiadis, P. (1991). Differential Truck Accident Rates for Michigan. *Transportation Research Record*, **1322**, 62–69.

Mackay, G. M., A. W. Siegel & P. V. Hight. (1970). Tempered versus HPR Laminated Windshields: A Comparative Study of United Kingdom and United States Collisions. Report DOT HS 008 627, *Proceedings of the Fourteenth Stapp Car Crash Conference*. Society of Automotive Engineers, New York, NY.

Mackay, M. (1985). Seat belt use under voluntary and mandatory conditions and its effect on casualties. In: *Human Behavior and Traffic Safety*, 259–283. (Evans, L & R. C. Schwing. eds) Plenum Press, New York, NY.

Madsen, J.R. (2001). *INFATI – brugertest adfærdsændringer (ISA – user test of behaviour changes)*. Trafikforskningsgruppen Aalborg Univseritet.

Maghsoodloo, S., D. B. Brown & Y-I. Shieh. (1989). A Quantification of the Impact of Restraining Systems on Passenger Safety. *Journal of Safety Research*, **20**, 115–128.

Magnusson, G. & P. W. Arnberg. (1977). *Vägjämnhetens inverkan på bilars broms- och styrbarhet. En litteraturstudie*. VTI-rapport 134. Statens väg- och trafikinstitut, Linköping.

Magnusson, G., H-E. Carlsson & E. Ohlsson. (1984). *Inverkan av tunga fordons fjädringsegenskaper och däcksutrustning på vägens nedbrytning*. VTI-rapport 270. Statens väg- och trafikinstitut, Linköping.

Maimaris, C., Summer, C.L., Browning, C. & Palmer, C.R. (1994). Injury patterns in cyclists attending an accident and emergency department: a comparison of helmet wearers and non-wearers. *British Medical Journal*, **308**, 1537–1540.

Malaterre, G. & H. Fontaine. (1993). The potential safety impacts of driving aids. *Recherche transports sécurité* English issue no **9**, December 1993. Paris/Arcueil, INRETS.

Malliaris, A.C., DeBlois, J.H. & Digges, K.H. (1996). Airbag field performance and injury patterns. *SAE transactions* **15(6)**, 751–774.

Malone, T.B., Kirkpatrick, M., Kohl, K.S. & Baker, C. (1978). *Field Test Evaluation of Rear Lighting Systems*. Report DOT-HS 803 467. US Department of Transportation, National Highway Traffic Safety Administration, Washington DC.

Marburger, E.A. (1983). *Zum Einfluss zusätzlicher Hochgesetzter Bremsleuchten auf das Unfallgeschehen*. Bundesanstalt für Strassenwesen (BASt), Bergisch Gladbach.

Marburger, E. A., J-H. Klöckner & U. Stöcker. *Assessment of the potential accident reduction by selected Prometheus functions*. Federal Highway Research Institute (BASt), September 1989 (Pro-General/Reports of the launcing phase). Bergisch Gladbach.

Martin, J.L. & Lenguerrand, E. (2008). A population based estimation of the driver protection provided by passenger cars: France 1996–2005. *Accident Analysis and Prevention*, **40**, 1811–1821.

Matthes, G., Schmucker, U., Lignitz, E., Huth, M., Ekkernkamp, A. & Seifert, J. (2006). Does the frontal airbag avoid thoracic injury? *Archives of Orthopaedic and Trauma Surgery*, **126**, 541–544.

May, C & D. Morabito. (1989). Motorcycle helmet use, incidence of head injury, and cost of hospitalization. *Journal of Emergency Nursing*, **15**, 389–392.

Mayhew, D. R. & H. M. Simpson. (1989). *Motorcycle engine size and traffic safety*. Traffic Injury Research Foundation of Canada, Ottawa, Ontario.

McCartt, A.T. & Kyrychenko, S.Y. (2006). *Efficacy of side airbags in reducing driver deaths in driver-side car and SUV collisions*, IIHS, Arlington, VA.
McDermott, F.T., Lane, J.C., Brazenor, G.A. & Debney, E.A. (1993). The effectiveness of bicyclist helmets: A study of 1710 casualties. *The Journal of Trauma*, **34**, 834–845.
McGee, H. W., P. F. Abbott & M. J. Rosenbaum. (1982). *Commercial Vehicles. Chapter 14 of Synthesis of Safety Research Related to Traffic Control and Roadway Elements*. Report FHWA-TS-82-233. US Department of Transportation, Federal Highway Administration, Washington DC.
McGehee, D., Mollenhauer, M.A & Dingus, T.A. (1994). The decomposition of driver human factors in front-to-rear end automobile crashes. *Proceedings of the First World Congress on Applications of Transport Telematics and Intelligent Vehicle-Highway Systems,* Paris 30 Nov-3 Dec 1994, 4, 1726–1733. Paris.
McLean, A. J. (1974). Collection and Analysis of Collision Data for Determining the Effectiveness of Some Vehicle Systems. Mich, Motor Vehicle Manufacturers Association, Detroit.
McSwain, N. E. & M. Lummis. (1980). Impact of repeal of motorcycle helmet law. *Surgery, Gynecology and Obstetrics*, **151**, 215–224.
McSwain, N. E. & E. Petrucelli. (1984). Medical consequences of motorcycle helmet nonusage. *The Journal of Trauma*, **24**, 233–236.
Melvin, J. W., R. L. Stalnaker & D. Mohan. (1978). Protection of Child Occupants in Automobile Crashes. SAE Technical Paper 780904. *Printed in Proceedings of Twenty-Second Stapp Car Crash Conference*, October 24–26, Ann Arbor, Michigan.
Meyer, M. (2006). Commentary on "Another look at Meyer and Finney's 'Who wants airbags?'". *Chance,* **19**, 23–24.
Meyer, M. & Finney, T. (2005). Who wants Airbags? *Chance*, **18(29)**, 3–16.
Minahan, D.J. & J. O'Day. (1977). Fatal car-into-truck/trailer underride collisions. *The HSRI Research Review*, **8**, 1–15.
Mingo, R. D., J. R. Esterlitz & B. L. Mingo. (1991). Accident Rates of Multiunit Combination Vehicles Derived from Large-Scale Data Bases. *Transportation Research Record*, **1322**, 50–61.
Moffatt, E. A. & J. Padmanaban. (1995). The relationship between vehicle roof strength and occupant injury in rollover crash data. *39th Annual Proceedings, Association for the Advancement of Automotive Medicine,* 245–267, October 16–18, Chicago, IL.
Morén, B. & M. Olausson. (1986). *REMARK MÖTESLJUS-Utvärdering av enkätstudie och fältförsök*. VTI-meddelande 502. Statens väg- och trafikinstitut, Linköping.
Morris, A., Barnes, J. & Fildes, B. (2001a). Some effects of Australian Design Rule (ADR) 69 on frontal crashes. *International Journal of Crashworthiness*, **6**, 499–509.

Morris, A., Barnes, J., Fildes, B., Bentivegna, F. & Seyer, K. (2001b). *Effectiveness of ADR69: A Case control study of crashed vehicles equipped with airbags*. Monash University Accident Research Center, Report Nr. CR 199.

Mortimer, R. G & C. M. Jorgeson. (1974). Driver's Vision and Performance with Convex Exterior Rearview Mirrors. Paper presented at *Automobile Engineering Meeting, Society of Automotive Engineers,* Toronto, Canada October 21–25, 1974. Ann Arbor, Highway Safety Research Institute, Toronto, Canada.

Mouzakes, J., Koltai, P.J., Kuhar, S., Bernstein, D.S., Wing, P. & Salsberg, E. (2001). The impact of airbags and seat belts on the incidence and severity of maxillofacial injuries in automobile accidents in New York state. *Archives of Otolaryngology – Head & Neck Surgery*, **127**, 1189–1193.

Muller, A. (1980). Evaluation of the costs and benefits of motorcycle helmet laws. *American Journal of Public Health*, **70**, 586–592.

Muller, A. (1982). An Evaluation of the Effectiveness of Motorcycle Daytime Headlight Laws. *American Journal of Public Health*, **72**, 1136–1141.

Muller, A. (1983). How Effective Are Daytime Motorcycle Headlight Laws? A Response to Zador's Criticism. *American Journal of Public Health*, **73**, 809–810.

Muller, A. (1984). Daytime headlight operation and motorcyclist fatalities. *Accident Analysis and Prevention*, **16**, 1–18.

Muller, A. (1985). Motorcycle Headlight-Use Laws: A Contrasting View. *American Journal of Public Health*, **75**, 547–549.

Murdock, M. A. & K. Waxman. (1991). Helmet use improves outcomes after motorcycle accidents. *The Western Journal of Medicine*, **155**, 370–372.

Muskaug, R. (1984). *Tunge kjøretøy og sikkerhet på veg. Forprosjekt*. TØI-notat 692. Transportøkonomisk institutt, Oslo.

Muskaug, R., Daas, H. R., Domburg, J. et al. (1979). *Hvordan endringene i trafikkreglene 1978 virket på trafikantenes kunnskap og atferd*. 2. opptrykk. Rapport. Transportøkonomisk institutt, Oslo.

Møller, L. (1977). *Bilistuheld i Århus før og efter sikkerhedsseleloven*. I RfT-rapport 21, Virkningen af lov om påbudt brug af sikkerhedssele, 89–131. Rådet for Trafiksikkerhedsforskning, København.

Nahum, A. M., A. W. Siegel & S. Brooks. (1970). The Reduction of Collision Injuries: Past, Present and Future. Report DOT HS 008 627, *Proceedings of the Fourteenth Stapp Car Crash Conference*. Society of Automotive Engineers, New York, NY.

Nash, C. E. (1989). The effectiveness of automatic belts in reducing fatality rates in Toyota Cressidas. *Accident Analysis and Prevention*, **21**, 517–527.

National Highway Traffic Safety Administration. (1980). *A report to the Congress on the effect of motorcycle helmet use law repeal-a case for helmet use*. US Department of Transportation, National Highway Traffic Safety Administration, Washington DC.

National Highway Traffic Safety Administration. (1995). *National Accident Sampling System Crashworthiness Data System 1991–1993*. Report DOT HS 808 298. US Department of Transportation, National Highway Traffic Safety Administration, Washington DC.

National Highway Traffic Safety Administration (NHTSA). (2000). *A preliminary assessment of the crash-reducing effectiveness of passenger car daytime running lamps (DRLs)*. Report DOT HS 808 645. Washington DC, U.S. Department of Transportation.

National Safety Council. (1992). *Accident facts*. National Safety Council, Chicago.

National Transportation Safety Board. (1979). *Safety effectiveness evaluation of the National Highway Traffic Safety Administration's Rulemaking process. Volume 2: Case history of Federal Motor Vehicle Safety Standard 208: Occupant Crash Protection*. Report NTSB-SEE-79-5. US Department of Transportation. National Transportation Safety Board, Washington DC.

Negri, D. B. & R. K. Riley. (1974). *Two car collision study II*. Report DOT-HS-245-2-478-4. State of New York Department of Motor Vehicles, Albany, NY.

Nelson, D. C., Farber, G., Burgett, A. & Sheridan, T. (1994). Collision avoidance systems: Issues and opportunities-a summary of workshop results. *Proceedings of the First World Congress on Applications of Transport Telematics and Intelligent Vehicle-Highway Systems*, Paris 30 November–3 December 1994, 4, 2102–2109.

New York State Department of Motor Vehicles. (1973). *VSDSS Research Studies*. Report DOT HS 800 780. Springfield, Va, National Technical Information Service, Springfield.

Newstead, S.V. & Cameron, M.H. (1997). *Correlation of results from the New Car Assessment Program with real crash data*. Report No 115, Monash University Accident Research Centre.

Newstead, S.V. & Cameron, M.H. (1999). *Updated correlation of results from the Australian New Car Assessment Program with real crash data from 1987 to 1996*. Report No 152, Monash University Accident Research Centre.

Newstead, S.V., Narayam, S. Cameron, M.H. & Farmer, C.M. (2003). US consumer crash test results and injury risk in police-reported crashes. *Traffic Injury Prevention*, **4**, 113–122.

NHTSA (2001). *Fifth/sixth report to congress effectiveness of occupant protection systems and their use*. NHTSA Report Nr. DOT HS 809 442.

Nicolaysen, B. (1995). *Samfunnsøkonomiske gevinster av bedre veiforbindelse mellom Slagentangen og E-18*. TØI-notat 1002. Transportøkonomisk institutt, Oslo.

Nielsen, H.V., Eriksen, E., Nordentoft, E.L. & Weeth, R. (1977). Virkningen af sikkerhedsselelovgivningen i Danmark. I RfT-rapport 21, *Virkningen af lov om påbudt brug af sikkerhedssele*, 59–79. Rådet for Trafiksikkerhedsforskning, København.

Nielsen, K. R. (1974). *Børn i biler. En undersøkelse udført ved Retsmedicinsk Institut Århus Universitet.* RFT-notat 128. Rådet for Trafiksikkerhedsforskning, København.

Nilsson, G. (1994). *Vägtransporter med farligt gods-Farligt gods i vägtrafikolyckor.* VTI-rapport 387:3., Väg- och transportforskningsinstitutet, Linköping.

Nilsson, L. (1995). *Driving with autonomous intelligent cruise control in critical traffic situations: Effects on driver behaviour, workload and attitudes.* Sv RTI '91-'94. DALTM/AICC safety study. Swedish Road and Transport Research Institute (VTI). Linköping.

Nilsson, L., H. Alm & W. Janssen. (1992). *Collision avoidance systems-effects of different levels of task allocation on driver behaviour.* VTI särtryck nr 181/1992. Väg- och Trafikinstitutet, Linköping.

Nirula, R., Mock, C.N., Nathens, A.B. & Grossman, D.C. (2004). The new car assessment program: Dies it predict the relative safety of vehicles in actual crashes? *Trauma Injury Infect. Crit. Care*, **57**, 779–786.

Nordisk Trafikksikkerhetsråd. (1975). *Motorcyklar och mopeder-trafiksäkerhet och konstruktion.* NTR-rapport 13. Nordisk Trafikksikkerhetsråd, Stockholm.

Nordisk Trafikksikkerhetsråd. (1976). *Varselljus-bilbelysning under dagtid.* NTR-rapport 17. Nordisk Trafikksikkerhetsråd, Stockholm.

Nordisk Trafikksikkerhetsråd. (1980). *Bättre synbarhet - cyklar, cyklister, mopedister, motorcyklister.* NTR-rapport 29. Nordisk Trafikksikkerhetsråd, Stockholm.

Nordisk Trafikksikkerhetsråd. (1984). *Sikring av voksne og barn i personbilers bakseter. En beregning av virkningen av alternative bestemmelser.* NTR-rapport 37. Nordisk Ministerråd, Oslo.

Norges Offentlige Utredninger (NOU) (1984). *NOU 1984:6 Personbilpolitikk-personbilen i norsk samferdsel.* Universitetsforlaget, Oslo.

Norin, H. & B. Andersson. (1978). *Kan barn använda bilbälte?* Göteborg, AB Volvo Personvagnar, Trafikolycksforskningen, Göteborg.

Norin, H., Saretok, E., Jonasson, K. & Samuelsson, S. (1978) *Barnet i Volvobilen. Om Volvos forskning för ökad barnsäkerhet.* Göteborg, AB Volvo Personvagnar, Göteborg.

Norin, H., Nilsson-Ehle, A., Saretok, E. & Tingvall, C. (1980). *Injury-reducing effect of seat belts on rear seat passengers.* Volvo Car Corporation and The Swedish Road Safety Office, Göteborg and Borlänge.

Normand, J. (1971). Influence of studded tires on winter driving safety in Quebec. *Highway Research Record*, **352**, 50–61.

Nygren, Å. (1984). Injuries to car occupants-some aspects of the interior safety of cars. *Acta Oto-Laryngologica Scandinavica*, **Supplement 395**, 1–164.

Nygren, Å., H. Gustafsson and C. Tingvall. (1985). Effects of Different Types of Headrest in Rear-End Collisions. *Proceedings of Tenth Experimental Safety Vehicle Conference*, 85–90.

Næss, K. (1980). *Sikkerhetsutstyr for trafikant og kjøretøy.* Arbeidsdokument av 5.2.1980, prosjekt 4650 (økonomiske analyser av trafikksikkerhet). Transportøkonomisk institutt, Oslo.

O'Day, J. & J. S. Creswell. (1971). *Can the Effect of Changes in Vehicle Design be seen in Mass Accident Data?* HIT Lab Reports, Mich, University of Michigan, Ann Arbor.

O'Neill, B., Haddon, W., Kelley, A.B. & Sorenson, W.W. (1972). Automobile Head Restraints - Frequency of Neck Injury Claims in Relation to the Presence of Head Restraints. *American Journal of Public Health*, **62**, 399–406.

O'Neill, B., Lund, A.K., Zador, P. & Ashton, S. (1985). Mandatory belt use and driver risk taking: an empirical evaluation of the risk-compensation hypothesis. In: *Human Behavior and Traffic Safety*, 93–118. (Evans, L. & R. C. Schwing eds.) Plenum Press, New York, NY.

Odsell, O. (1978). *Påskjutsbromsars funktion och driftsäkerhet.* VTI-rapport 160. Statens väg- och trafikinstitut, Linköping.

Offner, P. J., F. P. Rivara & R. V. Maier. (1992). The impact of motorcycle helmet use. *The Journal of Trauma*, **32**, 636–642.

Olson, C.M., Cummings, P., Rivara, F.P. (2006). Association of first- and secondgeneration airbags with front occupant death in car crashes: a matched cohort study. *American Journal of Epidemology*, **164**, 161–169.

Olson, P. L. (1989). Motorcycle Conspicuity Revisited. *Human Factors*, **31**, 141–146.

Opplysningsrådet for veitrafikken. (1993). *Tekniske data. Personbiler.* Juni 1993. Opplysningsrådet for veitrafikken, Oslo.

Oranen, L. (1975). *Investigations into light traffic I.* Reports from Liikenneturva 16. Liikenneturva, Central Organization for Traffic Safety, Helsinki.

Page, Y. & Cuny, S. (2006). Is electronic stability control effective on French roads? *Accident Analysis and Prevention*, **38**, 357–364.

Parsons, G. (1995). Motor Vehicle fires in Traffic Crashes and the effects of the fuel system integrity standard. *Accident Investigation Quarterly*, **6**, 20–40.

Partyka, S. C. (1979). Fatal accidents in the first fifteen months of the National Crash Severity Study. *Proceedings of Twenty-Third Conference of the American Association for Automotive Medicine* (77–89), Louisville, KY, October 3–6, Louisville.

Partyka, S. C. (1988a). *Papers on Adult Seat Belts-Effectiveness and Use.* Report DOT HS 807 285. US Department of Transportation, National Highway Traffic Safety Administration, Washington DC.

Partyka, S. C. (1988b). *Lives Saved by Child Restraints from 1982 through 1987.* Report DOT HS 807 371. US Department of Transportation, National Highway Traffic Safety Administration, Washington DC.

Partyka, S. C. (1990). Differences in reported car weight between fatality and registration data files. *Accident Analysis and Prevention*, **22**, 161–166.

Perchonok, K. (1978). *Studded Tires and Highway Safety. An Accident Analysis.* National Cooperative Highway Research Program Report 183. TRB, National research Council, Washington DC.

Perchonok, K., Ranney, T.A., Baum S. et al. (1978). *Hazardous Effects of Highway Features and Roadside Objects. Volume 2: Findings.* Report FHWA-RD-78-202. US Department of Transportation, Federal Highway Administration, Washington DC.

Povey, L.J., Frith, W.J. & Graham, P.G. (1999). Cycle helmet effectiveness in New Zealand. *Accident Analysis and Prevention*, **31**, 763–770.

Preus, C. K. (1973). After studs in Minnesota. *Highway Research Record*, **477**, 11–15.

Pucher Ingenieurbüro (1977). *Überprüfung der Auswirkung des Verbotes der Spikes-Reifen.* FP 7541/3. Bundesanstalt für Strassenwesen (BASt), Bergisch Gladbach.

Purdy, G. (1993). Risk analysis of the transportation of dangerous goods by road and rail. *Journal of Hazardous Materials*, **33**, 229–259.

Radin Umar, R. S., G. M. Mackay & B. L. Hills. (1995). Preliminary Analysis of Motorcycle Accidents: Short-Term Ompacts of the Running Headlights Campaign and Regulation in Malaysia. *Journal of Traffic Medicine*, **23**, 17–28.

Radin Umar, R. S., Mackay, G. M. & Hills, B. L. (1996). Modelling of conspicuity-related motorcycle accidents in Seremban and Shah Alam, Malaysia. *Accident Analysis and Prevention*, **28**, 325–332.

Ragnøy, A. (1989). *Trafikksikkerhet og drensasfalt.* Arbeidsdokument TST/0143/89. Transportøkonomisk institutt, Oslo.

Ragnøy, A., Karlsen, P. G. & Larsen, S. (2000). Vinterdekk uten pigger. I: Kolbenstvedt, M.; Solheim, T.; Amundsen, A. H. *Miljøhåndboken. Trafikk og miljøtiltak i byer og tettsteder*, 413–420. Oslo, Transportøkonomisk institutt.

Rausch, A., J. Wong & M. Kirkpatrick. (1982). A field test of two single, center, high mounted brake light systems. *Accident Analysis and Prevention*, **14**, 287–291.

Regan, M.A., Triggs, T.J., Young, K.L. et al. (2006). *On-road evaluation of intelligent speed adaptation, following distance warning and seat-belt reminder systems: Final results of the TAC SafeCar project.* Report No. 253. MUARC.

Reilly, R. E., D. S. Kurke & C. C: Buckenmaier. (1980). *Validation of the reduction of rearend collisions by a high mounted auxiliary stoplamp.* Report DOT-HS 805 360. US Department of Transportation, National Highway Traffic Safety Administration, Washington DC.

Reinfurt, D.W., Campbell, B.J., Stewart, J.R. & Stutts, J.C. (1990). Evaluating the North Carolina safety belt wearing law. *Accident Analysis and Prevention*, **22**, 197–210.

Reinfurt, D. W., C. Z. Silva & A. F. Seila. (1976). *A Statistical Analysis of Seat Belt Effectiveness in 1973–75 Model Cars Involved in Towaway Crashes.* Report DOT-HS-5-01255. US Department of Transportation, National Highway Traffic Safety Administration, 1976 (sitert etter Berard-Andersen 1978). Washington DC.

Rice, R. S. & R. D. Roland. (1970). *An Evaluation of the Performance and Handling Qualities of Bicycles*. Technical report CAL No VJ-2888-K. Cornell Aeronautical Laboratory, Cornell University, Buffalo, NY.

Richardson, H. A. (1974). *A motorcycle safety helmet study*. NHTSA Staff Report PB-231 318. US Department of Transportation, National Highway Traffic Safety Administation, Washington DC.

Rideng, A. (1994). *Transportytelser i Norge 1946-1993*. Rapport 256. Transportøkonomisk institutt, Oslo.

Rideng, A. (1995). *Transportytelser i Norge 1946-1994*. TØI-rapport 303. Transportøkonomisk institutt, Oslo.

Roberts, A. K. (1983). *The effect of rear seat passengers on front seat occupants in frontal impacts*. TRRL Laboratory Report 1079. Transport and Road Research Laboratory, Crowthorne, Berkshire.

Robertson, L. S. (1976). An instance of effective legal regulation: motorcyclist helmet and daytime headlamp laws. *Law and Society*, **Spring**, 467–477.

Robertson, L. S. (1989). Risk of fatal rollover in utility vehicles relative to static stability. *American Journal of Public Health*, **79**, 300–303.

Robertson, L. S. & A. B. Kelley. (1989). Static stability as a predictor of overturn in fatal motor vehicle crashes. *The Journal of Trauma*, **29**, 313–319.

Robinson, B. J. & A. R. Duffin. (1993). The performance and reliability of antilock braking systems. Braking of Road Vehicles. *Proceedings (115–126) of the Institution of Mechanical Engineers*, 23–24 March 1993, Institution of Mechanical Engineers (IMechE), Birdcage Walk, London. Published by Mechanical Engineers Publications Limited, London.

Robinson, B. J. & B. S. Riley. (1991). Improving HGV Safety-Front Underrun Guards and Antilock Braking Systems. *Proceedings of 13th International Technical Conference on Experimental Safety Vehicles,* 1275–1284, November 4–7, 1991, Paris, France.

Robinson, D. L. (1996). Head injuries and bicycle helmet laws. *Accident Analysis and Prevention*, **28**, 463–475.

Robinson, D.L. (2001). Changes in head injury with the New Zealand bicycle helmet law. *Accident Analysis and Prevention*, **33**, 687–691.

Rock, S. M. (1993). Risk compensation and the Illinois seat belt use law. *Accident Analysis and Prevention*, **25**, 537–544.

Rock, S. M. (1996). Impact of the Illinois child passenger protection act: a retrospective look. *Accident Analysis and Prevention*, **28**, 487–492.

Rogerson, P. (1991). *Accident involvement and exposure by type of motorcycle*. Vic Roads Report GR 91-5. VicRoads, Hawthorn, Victoria.

Rogerson, P., J. Lambert & P. Allen. (1992). *Motorcycle accident involvement by power to weight ratio for novice and experienced drivers*. Report GR 92-11. Vic Roads, Kew, Victoria, Australia.

Roine, M. (1996). Estimation of the effects of studded tyres using disaggregated accident models. In: *KFB&VTI forskning/research* **18**, **del 1**, 143–157. Komminukationsforskningsberedningen og Statens Väg- och Transportforskningsinstitut, Stockholm og Linköping.

Romano, P. S. & E. McLoughlin. (1991). Helmet use and fatal motorcycle injuries in California, 1987–1988. *Journal of Head Trauma Rehabilitation*, **6**, 21–37.

Roosmark, P-O., K. Andersson & G. Ahlqvist. (1976). *Dubbdäcks effekt på trafikolyckor*. VTI-rapport 72. Statens väg- och trafikinstitut, Linköping.

Rosendahl, K. E. (1996). *Helseeffekter av luftforurensning og virkninger på økonomisk aktivitet. Generelle relasjoner med anvendelse på Oslo*. Rapport 96/8. Statistisk sentralbyrå, Oslo.

Rosendahl, K. E. (2000). *Helseeffekter og samfunnsøkonomiske kostnader av luftforurensning*. SFT rapport 1718. Oslo, Statens forurensningstilsyn.

Ross, C. F. (1993). Trailer ABS for the future. *Proceedings (203–214) of the Institution of Mechanical Engineers,* 23–24 March 1993, Institution of Mechanical Engineers (IMechE), Birdcage Walk, London. Published by Mechanical Engineers Publications Limited, London.

Rothengatter, J. A. & Heino, A. (1994). Safety evaluation of collision avoidance systems. *Proceedings of the First World Congress on Applications of Transport Telematics and Intelligent Vehicle-Highway Systems*, Paris 30 November–3 December 1994, 4, 2047–2054. Paris.

Rudin-Brown, C.M. & Parker, H.A. (2004). Behavioural adaptation to adaptive cruise control (ACC): implications for preventive strategies. *Transportation Research Part F: Traffic Psychology and Behaviour*, **7**, 59–76.

Rumar, K. (1968). *Halogenstrålkastare och konventionella strålkastare. En jämförelse av siktsträckor*. Rapport S33. Psykologiska institutionen, Uppsala Universitet, Uppsala.

Rumar, K. (1973). *Dirty headlights - frequency and visibility effects*. Report 136. Department of psychology, University of Uppsala.

Rumar, K. (1980). Running lights - conspicuity, glare and accident reduction. *Accident Analysis and Prevention*, **12**, 151–157.

Rumar, K., G. Helmers & M. Thorell. (1973). *Obstacle visibility with European halogen H4 and American sealed beam headlights*. Report 133. Department of psychology, University of Uppsala.

Rumar, K. & G. Johansson. (1964). *Siktsträckor under morkertrafik vid möte med felinställt halvljus*. Rapport 13. Psykologiska institutionen, Uppsala Universitet, Uppsala.

Russell, E. R. (1993). Rating Countermeasures for Mitigation of Hazardous Materials Incidents. *Journal of Transportation Engineering*, **119**, 211–225.

Rutledge, R. & J. Stutts. (1993). The association of helmet use with the outcome of motorcycle crash injury when controlling for crash/injury severity. *Accident Analysis and Prevention*, **25**, 347–353.

Rångtell, H. (1973). *Trafikolykor med bensinbränder i bilar 1969-71*. VTI-rapport 23. Statens väg- och trafikinstitut, Stockholm.

Sabey, B. E., B. E. Grant & C. A. Hobbs. (1977). *Alleviation of injuries by use of seat belts*. TRRL Supplementary Report 289. Transport and Road Research Laboratory, Crowthorne, Berkshire.

Sagberg, F. & Sætermo, I.A. (1996). *Atferdstilpasning til kollisjonsputer og blokkeringsfrie bremser*. TØI-rapport 335/1996. Oslo: Transportøkonomisk institutt.

Salmi, L.R., Thomas, H., Fabry, J. & Girard, R. (1989). The effect of the 1979 French seat-belt law on the nature and severity of injuries to front-seat occupants. *Accident Analysis and Prevention*, **21**, 589–594.

Salusjärvi, M. & T. Potinkara. (1987). *Kostnadsnyttaanalys av tilläggsbromsljus*. VTT-meddelande 658. Statens Tekniska Forskningscentral (VTT), Esbo.

Satoh H. & I. Tanigushi. (1994). A new control method of adaptive cruise control. *Proceedings of the First World Congress on Applications of Transport Telematics and Intelligent Vehicle-Highway Systems,* Paris 30 November–3 December 1994, 4, 2094–2101. Paris.

Satterthwaite, S. P. (1976). An assessment of seasonal and weather effects on the frequency of road accidents in California. *Accident Analysis and Prevention*, **8**, 87–96.

Schepers, A. & M. Schmid. (1996). *Unfallrisiko von Pkw unterschiedlicher Fahrzeugtypen*. Mensch und Sicherheit Heft M 62. Bundesanstalt für Strassenwesen (BASt), Bergisch Gladbach.

Scherz, R. G. (1979). Epidemiology of Childhood Motor Vehicle Related Accidents. SAE Technical Paper 791013. Printed in *Proceedings (291–305) of Twenty-Third Stapp Car Crash Conference,* October 17–19, 1979, Warrendale, PA, Society of Automotive Engineers, San Diego, California.

Schroeder, G. & Bosch, U. (2005). Is the kneebag safe in out of position situations? Berichte der Bundesanstalt fuer Strassenwesen, *Fahrzeugtechnik*, **55**, 189–191.

Schrøder Hansen, K., Hansen, T.E., Walløe, A. & Fjeldgård, K. (1995). *Sykkelulykker og sykkelskader. En epidemiologisk registrering i Bergen.* Haukeland sykehus, Bergen.

Schrøder Hansen, K., Engesæter, L.B. & Viste, A. (2003). Protective Effect of Different Types of Biycle Helmets. *Traffic Injury Prevention*, **4**, 285–290.

Schützenhöfer, A., Koch, U. & Henökl, H. (1990). *Effektivitätsuntersuchung des Modellversuches Fahren mit Licht am Tag der Grazer Verkehrsbetriebe (Evaluation of the DRL-experiment on the fleet of the Graz Authority)*. Kuratorium für Verkehrssicherheit, Landesstelle Steiermark, Graz.

Schwertberger, W. (1994). Autonomous intelligent cruise control in commercial vehicles. *Proceedings of the First World Congress on Applications of Transport Telematics and Intelligent Vehicle-Highway Systems*, Paris 30 November–3 December 1994, 4, 1886–1891.

Scuffham, P. & J. Langley. (1997). *Trends in cycle injury in New Zealand under voluntary helmet use*. Unpublished manuscript, November 1994. Injury Prevention Research Unit, University of Otago, Dunedin, New Zealand.

Scuffham, P., Alsop, J., Cryer, C. et al. (2000). Head injuries to bicyclists and the New Zealand bicycle helmet law. *Accident Analysis and Prevention*, **32**, 565–573.

Segui-Gomez, M. (2000). Driver airbag effectiveness by severity of the crash. *American Journal of Public Health*, **90**, 1575–1581.

Sferco, R., Page, Y., Le Coz, J.Y. & Fay, P.A. (2001). Potential effectiveness of electronic stability programs (ESP) – what European field studies tell us. *Proceedings of the 17th international technical conference on the enhanced safety of vehicles*, Amsterdam.

Shafi, S., Gilbert, J.S., Loghmanee, F., Allen, J.E. Caty, M.G., Glick, P.L., Garden, C.S. & Azizkhan, R.G. (1998). Impact of Bicycle Helmet Safety Legislation on Children Admitted to a Regional Pediatric Trauma Center. *Journal of Pediatric Surgery*, **33**, **2**, 317–321.

Shankar, B.S., Ramzy, A.I., Soderstrom, C.A. et al. (1992). Helmet use, patterns of injury, medical outcome, and costs among motorcycle drivers in Maryland. *Accident Analysis and Prevention*, **24**, 385–396.

Smith, P. (1973). Winter accident experience in Ontario with and without studded tires. *Highway Research Record*, **477**, 16–26.

Smith, R.L., M. U. Mulholland & W. J. Burger. (1985). *Field test evaluation of rearview mirror systems for commercial vehicles*. Report No DOT HS 806 948 US Department of Transportation, Washington DC.

Somers, R. L. & A. Hansen. (1984). The cost of rear-end collisions in Denmark and the potential savings from a high center-mounted auxiliary brake light. *Accident Analysis and Prevention*, **16**, 423–432.

Spaite, D.W., Murphy, M., Criss, E.A. et al. (1991). Prospective Analysis of Injury Severity Among Helmeted and Nonhelmeted Bicyclists Involved in Collisions with Motor Vehicles. *The Journal of Trauma*, **31**, 1510–1516.

Sparks, G. A., R. D. Neudorf & A. E. Smith. (1989). *An analysis of the use of daytime running lights in the CVA fleet in Saskatchewan*. Traffic Safety Services Department, SaskAuto, Saskatoon, Saskatchewan.

Sparks, G.A., Neudorf, R.D., Smith, A.E. et al. (1993). The effect of daytime running lights on crashes between two vehicles in Saskatchewan: a study of a government fleet. *Accident Analysis and Prevention*, **25**, 619–625.

Statens vegvesen Vegdirektoratet. (1982). Registrering av lysbruk, $CO_2$-utslipp (avgass) og dekkutrustning av personbiler sommeren/høsten 1981. Statens vegvesen Vegdirektoratet, Oslo.

Statens vegvesen Vegdirektoratet. (1983). *Undersøkelse av mønsterdybde i dekk på personbiler sommeren/høsten 1983*. Vegdirektoratet, Vegtrafikkavdelingen, Oslo.

Statens vegvesen. (1995). *Håndbok 140. Konsekvensanalyser. Del I. Prinsipper og metodegrunnlag.* Statens vegvesen, Oslo.

States, J.D., Balcerak, J.C., Williams, J.S. et al. (1972). Injury Frequency and Head Restraint Effectiveness in Rear-End Impact Accidents. *Proceedings of Sixteenth Stapp Car Crash Conference* 228–245.

States, J.D., Annechiarico, R.P., Good, R.G. et al. (1990). A time comparison stidy of the New York state safety belt use law utilizing hospital admission and police accident report information. *Accident Analysis and Prevention*, **22**, 509–521.

Statistisk sentralbyrå (1996). *Veitrafikkulykker 1995.* NOS C 332. Oslo-Kongsvinger.

Statistiska Centralbyrån (1994). *Trafikskador 93.* Sveriges officiella statistik. Statistiska Centralbyrån, Stockholm.

Steen, L. E. & A. Bolstad. *Piggdekk-bruk og sikkerhet. En analyse av vegtrafikkulykkene vinteren 1971/72.* TØI-rapport. Transportøkonomisk institutt, Oslo. (1972).

Stein, H. (1985). *Fleet Experience with Daytime Running Lights in the United States.* SAE Technical Paper 851239. Warrendale, PA, Society of Automotive Engineers, Warrendale.

Stein, H. S. & I. S. Jones. (1988). Crash Involvement of Large Trucks by Configuration: A Case-Control Study. *American Journal of Public Health*, **78**, 491–498.

Stewart, J.R. & Rodgman, E.A. (1985). Comparison of NCAP test results with driver injury rates in highway crashes. In *Proceedings of the 29th Annual Conference of the American Association for Automotive Medicine*, Arlington Heights, IL, 181–197.

Stoke, C. B. (1975). *Reflectorized license plates: Do they reduce night rear-end collisions?* Reprint number 93. Charlottesville, VA, University of Virginia and Virginia Highway and Transportation Research Council, Charlottesville.

Strandberg, L. (1978). *Tankfordons sidstabilitet.* VTI-rapport 147. Statens väg- och trafikinstitut, Linköping.

Strandberg, L. (1989). Skidding accidents and their avoidance with different cars. *Twelfth International Technical Conference on Experimental Safety Vehicles, Göteborg, May 29–June 1, 1989*, Proceedings **Vol 2**, pp 825–828. US Department of Transportation, Washington DC.

Swain, A. D. & H. E. Guttman. (1980). *Handbook of human reliability analysis with emphasis on nuclear power plant applications. Draft report for interim use and comment.* Technical Report NU-REG/CR-1278. US Nuclear Regulatory Commission, Washington DC.

Sætermo, I-A. (1995). *Risiko for tunge kjøretøy.* Arbeidsdokument TST/0637/95. Transportøkonomisk institutt, Oslo.

Sæther, J. P. (1980). *Økonomisk vurdering av underkjøringshinder på lastebiler.* Arbeidsdokument av 29.4.80 (prosjekt 4650 økonomiske analyser av trafikksikkerhet). Transportøkonomisk institutt, Oslo.

Takagi, H. (1997). *Letter to Mr H. Hvoslef*, dated January 16, 1997. Hokkaido Development Bureau, Sapporo.

Takagi, H. & N. Horita. (1993). Influences and problems of studded-tire regulation in Hokkaido. *Monthly report of Civil Engineering Research Institute*, **483**, 1–29, Hokkaido Development Bureau,Sapporo.

Takagi, H.A. Shimojo & H Onuma (1996). Effects of road environments and traffic conditions under studded tires regulation in Hokkaido. Preprint F-1. Prepared for *4th international Symposium on Snow Removal and Ice Control Technology*. Hokkaido Development Bureau, Civil Engineering Research Institute, Sapporo.

Tapio, J., P. Pirtala & T. Ernvall. (1995). *The accident involvement and injury risk rates of car models*. Report 30. Publications of Road and Transport Laboratory, University of Oulu.

Taylor, M. C. & C. R. Lockwood. (1990). *Factors affecting the accident liability of motorcyclists – a multivariate analysis of survey data*. TRRL Research Report 270. Transport and Road Research Laboratory, Crowthorne, Berkshire.

Thomas, C., Faverjon, G., Henry, C. et al. (1980). Comparative study of 1624 belted and 3242 non-belted occupants: results on the effectiveness of seat belts. *Proceedings of the Twenty-Fourth Conference of the American Association for Automotive Medicine (*422–436), October 7–9.

Thomas, P. & M. Bradford. (1995). The nature and source of the head injuries sustained by restrained front-seat car occupants in frontal collisions. *Accident Analysis and Prevention*, **27**, 561–570.

Thomas, S., Acton, C., Nixon, J. et al. (1994). Effectiveness of bicycle helmets in preventing head injury in children: case-control study. *British Medical Journal*, **308**, 173–176.

Thomas, P. (2006). Crash involvement risks of cars with electronic stability control systems in Great Britain. *International Journal of Vehicle Safety*, **1**, 267–281.

Thompson, D.C., Thompson, R.S., Rivara, F.P. & Wolf, M. E. (1990). A Case-Control Study of the Effectiveness of Bicycle Safety Helmets in Preventing Facial Injury. *American Journal of Public Health*, **80**, 1471–1474.

Thompson, D.C., Rivara, F.P. & Thompson, R.S. (1996). Effectiveness of Bicycle Safety Helmets in Preventing Head Injuries. A Case-Control Study. *Journal of the American Medical Association*, **276**, 1968–1973.

Thompson, D.C., Nunn, M.E., Rivara, F.P. & Thompson, R.S. (1996). Effectiveness of Bicycle Safety Helmets in Preventing Serious Facial Injuries. A Case-Control Study. *Journal of the American Medical Association*, **276**, 1974–1974.

Thompson, P. A. (2003). *Daytime running lamps (DRLs) for pedestrian protection.* SAE technical paper series 2003-01-2072. Warrendale, PA, Society of Automotive Engineers.

Thompson, R. S., F. P. Rivara & D. C. Thompson. (1989). A case-control study of the effectiveness of bicycle safety helmets. *The New England Journal of Medicine*, **320**, 1361–1367.

Thomson, G. A. (1980). The role frontal motorcycle conspicuity has in road accidents. *Accident Analysis and Prevention*, **12**, 165–178.

Tingvall, C. (1987). Children in cars. Some aspects of the safety of children as car passengers in road traffic accidents. *Acta Paediatrica Scandinavica,* **Supplement 339**. Almqvist og Wiksell, Stockholm and Göteborg.

Tofflemire, T. S. & Whitehead, P. C. (1997). An evaluation of the impact of daytime running lights on traffic safety in Canada. *Journal of Safety Research*, **28**, 257–272.

Toomath, J. B. (1977). Compulsory seat belt legislation in New Zealand. *Proceedings of the Sixth International Conference of the International Association for Accident and Traffic Medicine* (21–39), January 31–February 4, Melbourne, Australia.

Transport Canada. (1986). *Background paper on motor vehicle occupant protection in Canada.* Report 8078E. Transport Canada, Road Safety, Ottawa.

Transportation Research Board. (1986). *Twin Trailer Trucks.* Special Report 211. National Research Council, Washington DC.

Transportation Research Board. (1989). *Improving School Bus Safety*. Special Report 222. National Research Council, Washington DC.

Transport Research Commission (1984). *Konsekvenser av höjd axeltryck för bussar.* TFK-rapport 1984:5. Transportforskningskommissionen, Stockholm.

Tromp, J. P. M. & P. C. Noordzij. (1991). *Het effect van markeringen aan de achterzijde van vrachtwagens. Ongevallen met geparkeerde vrachtwagens en achterannrijdingen tegen rijdende vrachtwagens.* SWOV Rapport R-91-25. Stichting Wetenschappelijk Onderzoek Verkeersveiligheid SWOV, Leidschendam.

Troup, G. A., S. E. Torpey & H. T. Wood. (1984). Engine capacity restrictions for novice motorcyclists-the Victorian experience. *ARRB Proceedings*, **Volume 12**, Part 7, 1–12.

Trygg Trafikk. (undated). *Vi reflekterer på refleks.* Emneblokk nr 304 fra Trygg Trafikk. Trygg Trafikk, Oslo.

Tunbridge, R. J. (1989). *The long term effect of seat belt legislation on road user injury patterns.* Research Report 239. Transport and Road Research Laboratory, Crowthorne, Berkshire.

Tunbridge, R.J., Everest, J.T., Wild, B.R. & Johnstone, R.A. (1988). *An in-depth study of road accident casualties and their injury patterns.* Research Report 136. Transport and Road Research Laboratory, Crowthorne, Berkshire.

UK Department of Transport (1985). *Compulsory Seat Belt Wearing.* Report by the Department of Transport. Her Majesty's Stationary Office, London, Great Britain.

UK Department of Transport (1993). *Cars: Make and Model: Injury accident and Casualty Rates*. Great Britain: 1991. Transport Statistics Report. UK Department of Transport, London.

Unselt, T., Breuer, J., Eckstein, L. & Frank, P. (2004). Avoidance of loss of control accidents through the benefits of ESP. *FISITA Conference* paper no. F2004V295, Barcelona.

US Department of Transportation. (1976). *The Secretary's Decision concerning Motor Vehicle Occupant Crash Protection*. US Department of Transportation, Washington DC.

US Department of Transportation (2004). Misuse of child restraints. Report DOT HS 809 671.

Vallette, G.R., McGee, H., Sanders, J.H. & Enger, D.J. (1981). *The effect of truck size and weight on accident experience and traffic operations. Volume III: Accident experience of large trucks*. Report FHWA/RD-80/137. US Department of Transportation, Federal Highway Administration, Washington DC.

Várhelyi, A., Hjälmdahl, M., Hydén, C. & Draskóczy, M. (2004). Effects of an active accelerator pedal on driver behaviour and traffic safety after lon-term use in urban areas. *Accident Analysis and Prevention*, **36**, 729–737.

Vaughan, R. G., K. Pettigrew & J. Lukin. (1977). *Motorcycle crashes: A two level study*. Sydney, NSW, Traffic Accident Research Unit, Department of Motor Transport, Sydney.

Vaughan, R. G., R. Wood & P. G. Croft. (1974). Some aspects of compulsory seat belt wearing. *ARRB Proceedings*, **Volume 7, part 5**, 103–127.

Veisten, K., Sælensminde, K., Alvær, K. et al. (2007). Total costs of bicycle injuries in Norway: Correcting injury figures and indicating data needs. *Accident Analysis and Prevention*, **39**, 1162–1169.

Vlassenroot, S., Broekx, S., DeMol, J. et al. (2007). Driving with intelligent speed adaptation: final results of the Belgian ISA-trial. *Transportation Research Part A*, **41**, 267–279.

Vulcan, A. P., M. H. Cameron, & W. L. Watson. (1992). Mandatory Bicycle Helmet Use: Experience in Victoria, Australia. *World Journal of Surgery*, **16**, 389–397.

Vaa, T. (1993). *Personskader og risiko ved bussreiser. Reviderte beregninger*. Rapport 160. Transportøkonomisk institutt, Oslo.

Vaa, T. (1995). *Salting og trafikksikkerhet. Del 2: Sammenligning av ulykkesfrekvens på saltet og usaltet vegnett. Saltingens effekt på kjørefart*. Rapport STF63 A95004. SINTEF Samferdselsteknikk, Trondheim.

Vaa, T. (1997). *Piggfrie dekk i Trondheim? Erfaringer fra kjøring med ulike typer vinterdekk sesongen 1996/97*. Report STF A97612. Trondheim, SINTEF Bygg og miljø, avdeling samferdsel.

Vaa, T. & P. Christensen. (1992). *Økt politikontroll. Virkning på fart og subjektiv oppdagelsesrisiko*. TØI-rapport 142. Transportøkonomisk institutt, Oslo.

Vaa, T., P. Christensen & A. Ragnøy. (1993). *Evaluering av aksjon for redusert fart på E6-Akershus*. Arbeidsdokument TST/0422/93. Transportøkonomisk institutt, Oslo.

Vaa, T., P. Christensen & A. Ragnøy. (1995). *Politiets fartskontroller: Virkning på fart og subjektiv oppdagelsesrisiko ved ulike overvåkingsnivåer*. TØI-rapport 301. Transportøkonomisk institutt, Oslo.

Vaaje, T. (1986). *Kjørelys om dagen reduserer ulykkestallene*. Arbeidsdokument av 15.8.1986, Q-38 CRASH. Transportøkonomisk institutt, Oslo, Norway.

Wagenaar, A. C. (1985). Mandatory Child Restraint Laws: Impact on Childhood Injuries Due to Traffic Crashes. *Journal of Safety Research*, **16**, 9–21.

Wagenaar, A. C., D. W. Webster & R. G. Maybee. (1987). Effects of Child Restraint Laws on Traffic Fatalities in Eleven States. *The Journal of Trauma*, **27**, 726–732.

Waller, P. F.; Griffin, L. I. (1981). *The impact of a motorcycle lights-on law: an update*. Report HSRC A71. Chapel Hill, NC, University of North Carolina, Highway Safety Research Center.

Wallén-Warner, H., Åberg, L. (2008). The long-term effects of an ISA speed-warning device on drivers speeding behaviour. *Transportation Research Part F*, **11**, 96–107.

Ward, H., Cave, J., Morrison, A. et al. (1994). *Pedestrian Activity and Accident Risk*. Report published jointly by AA Foundation for Road Safety Research, University of London Centre for Transport Studies and Steer Davies Gleave, London.

Wasserman, R. C. & R. V. Buccini. (1990). Helmet protection from head injuries among recreational bicyclists. *The American Journal of Sports Medicine*, **18**, 96–97.

Wasserman, R.C., Waller, J.A.; Monty, M.J. et al. (1988). Bicyclists, Helmets and Head Injuries: A Rider-Based Study of Helmet Use and Effectiveness. *American Journal of Public Health*, **78**, 1220–1221.

Watson, G. S., P. L. Zador & A. Wilks. (1980). The repeal of helmet use laws and increased motorcyclist mortality in the United States, 1975–1978. *American Journal of Public Health*, **70**, 579–585.

Watts, G. R. (1980). *Pedal cycling braking performance – effects of brake block and rim design*. TRRL Supplementary Report 619. Transport and Road Research Laboratory, Crowthorne, Berkshire.

Watts, G. R. (1984a). *Evaluation of conspicuity aids for pedal cyclists*. TRRL Laboratory Report 1103. Transport and Road Research Laboratory, Crowthorne, Berkshire.

Watts, G. R. (1984b). *Evaluation of pedal cycle spacers*. TRRL Supplementary Report 820. Transport and Road Research Laboratory, Crowthorne, Berkshire.

Watts, G, R. (1984c). *Pedal cycle lamps and reflectors – some visibility tests and surveys*. TRRL Laboratory Report 1108. Transport and Road Research Laboratory, Crowthorne, Berkshire.

Weiss, A. A. (1992). The effects of helmet use on the severity of head injuries in motorcycle accidents. *Journal of the American Statistical Association*, **87**, 48–56.

Whitfield, R. A.; & I. A. Jones. (1995). The Effect of Passenger Load on Unstable Vehicles in Fatal, Untripped Rollover crashes. *American Journal of Public Health*, **85**, 1268–1271.

Williams, A. F. & P. Zador. (1977). Injuries to children in automobiles in relation to seating location and restraint use. *Accident Analysis and Prevention*, **9**, 69–76.

Williams, M. J. & E. R. Hoffman. (1979). Motorcycle conspicuity and traffic accidents. *Accident Analysis and Prevention*, **11**, 209–224.

Wilson, D. (1989). *The Effectiveness of Motorcycle Helmets in Preventing Fatalities*. Report DOT HS 807 416. US Department of Transportation, National Highway Traffic Safety Administration, Washington DC.

Wood, D.P., Veyrat, N., Simms, C. & Glynn, C. (2007). Limits for survivability in frontal collisions: Theory and real-life data combined. *Accident Analysis and Prevention*, **39**, 679–687.

Wood, T. & P. Milne. (1988). Head injuries to pedal cyclists and the promotion of helmet use in Victoria, Australia. *Accident Analysis and Prevention*, **20**, 177–185.

Wulf, G., P. A. Hancock & M. Rahimi. (1989). Motorcycle Conspicuity: An Evaluation and Synthesis of Influential Factors. *Journal of Safety Research*, **20**, 153–176.

Yerrell, J. S. (1971). *The performance of two self-levelling headlamp systems*. RRL Report LR 378. Road Research Laboratory, Crowthorne, Berkshire.

Yoganandan, N., Pintar, F., Stemper, B.D., Gennarelli, T.A. & Weigelt, J.A. (2007a). Biomechanics of side impact. Injury criteria, aging occupants, and airbag technology. *Journal of Biomechanics,* **40**, 227–243.

Yoganandan, N., Pintar, F., Zhang, J. & Gennarelli, T.A. (2007b). Lateral impact injuries with side airbag deployment – A descriptive study. *Accident Analysis and Prevention*, **39**, 22–27.

Yuan, W. (2000). The effectiveness of the "ride-bright" legislation for motorcycles in Singapore. *Accident Analysis and Prevention*, **32**, 559–563.

Zador, P. L. (1985). Motorcycle Headlight-Use Laws and Fatal Motorcycle Crashes in the US, 1975–83. *American Journal of Public Health*, **75**, 543–546.

Zador, P. L. & M. A. Ciccone. (1993). Automobile Driver Fatalities in Frontal Impacts: Airbags Compared with Manual Belts. *American Journal of Public Health*, **83**, 661–666.

Zador, P.L., Jones, I.S. & Ginsburg, M. (1984). Fatal front-to-front collisions and the results of 35 MPH frontal barrier impacts. In: *Proceedings of the 28th Annual Conference of the American Association for Automotive Medicine*, Arlington Heights, IL.

Zobel, R., Friedrich, H. & Becker, H. (2000). Accident research with regard to crashworthiness and crash avoidance. *Conference Vehicle Safety*, 7–9 June 2000, London, UK.

Öberg, G. (1989). *Dubbade och odubbade personbilers reshastighet.* VTI-notat T 59. Statens väg- och trafikinstitut, Linköping.

Øglænd DBS A/S. (1995). *Den store norske sykkelboken 1995.* Øglænd DBS A/S, Sandnes.

Ørjasæter, J. & J. R. Bang. (1993). *Utslipp med og uten kjørelys.* Rapport. Teknologisk institutt, Avdeling for kjøretøyteknikk, Oslo.

# 5.

# Vehicle and Garage Inspection

## 5.0 Introduction and overview of four measures

This chapter describes following four measures concerning motor vehicle inspection and garage regulation and inspection:

5.1 Vehicle safety standards
5.2 Periodic motor vehicle inspections
5.3 Roadside vehicle inspections
5.4 Garage regulation and inspections

It is obvious that the technical condition of a vehicle may affect road safety. This applies to both new and used vehicles. As far as new vehicles are concerned, the authorities can influence traffic safety by setting more stringent safety standards for new vehicles. With respect to used vehicles, technical inspections are the most realistic measure. Different forms of technical inspections of motor vehicles are found in the majority of motorised countries. Periodic inspection of motor vehicles has been introduced in the EU countries, the majority of American states and in New Zealand. Roadside inspection of vehicles is less common, but is found in some places in the United States. As far as we know, a separate law setting standards for garages is only found in Norway. The systems for approval and inspection for new vehicles (compliance control) in the form of vehicle regulations, and an associated system for model approval of motor vehicles, are almost similar in all motorised countries.

**The Handbook of Road Safety Measures**

**ISBN: 978-1-84855-250-0**

This introductory chapter gives an overview of current knowledge about these measures and their effects on accidents, mobility and the environment, as well as costs and cost–benefit analysis.

**Amount and quality of research**

Different indicators of the amount of research into vehicle inspection and garage regulation and inspection are shown in Table 5.0.1. The largest number of studies, and the most comprehensive studies, have evaluated safety standards for new vehicles and periodic inspections of vehicles. Roadside vehicle inspection has been less studied. Only one study has evaluated garage regulation and inspection. Meta-analyses have been used to summarise the results of the studies for all measures except garage regulation and inspection.

A number of studies have been carried out, especially in the United States, evaluating the effects of new safety standards for vehicles on the number of fatalities. Some of these studies are based on very large accident samples. Most of the studies are multivariate analyses, i.e. statistical studies of how a number of factors, including new safety standards for vehicles, affect traffic safety. Generally, the studies are methodologically sound.

A number of studies have also evaluated periodic motor vehicle inspections, carried out in Norway, Sweden, the United States and New Zealand. By far, the best study of this measure is a Norwegian study carried out in the period 1986–91 (Fosser 1991, 1992). This study was designed as an experiment and based on 205,000 passenger cars and vans. The effect of periodic inspections of heavy vehicles (lorries and buses) has not been studied to any great extent, and our knowledge about this is highly uncertain.

There are few studies of the effect on accidents of roadside inspections of vehicles. These studies are all subject to weaknesses in study methodology. The effects stated for roadside inspections of vehicles on accidents are therefore very uncertain.

*Table 5.0.1: The amount of research evaluating the effects on accidents of vehicle and garage inspections*

| Measure | Number of studies | Number of results | Sum of statistical weights | Results last updated |
|---|---|---|---|---|
| 5.1 Vehicle safety standards | 12 | 33 | 52,602,777 | 1997 |
| 5.2 Periodic vehicle inspections | 17 | 107 | 1,306,011 | 1997 |
| 5.3 Roadside vehicle inspections | 6 | 6 | 571,957 | 2002 |
| 5.4 Garage regulation and inspections | 1 | 1 | 0 | 1997 |

The effect on accidents of regulation and inspection of garages is unknown and has only been investigated indirectly in one Norwegian study of how well garages fulfill the standards set by law.

**Main elements of effects on accidents**

Safety standards for new vehicles have developed considerably, for example, in the form of standards for safety belts, airbags, laminated front windscreens, head rests, collapsible steering wheel columns, dual master braking systems, high mounted stop lamps, etc. Studies in the United States indicate that more stringent safety standards for vehicles have reduced the number of people killed in traffic by around 30%. The effect on injuries and property damage is less known.

Periodic vehicle inspection has no effect on the number of accidents for passenger cars and vans, which are up to 12 years old. A possible explanation for this result is that the drivers adapt their driving behaviour according to the technical condition of the vehicle, and drive more carefully when they know that the vehicle has technical defects. Such behavioural adaptations are not very well known, but a number of studies indicate that they do occur. Another possible explanation is that the some of the technical defects identified by periodic inspections are too trivial to affect safety.

The effect of periodic inspections of heavy vehicles is poorly known. However, it is known that technical defects in heavy vehicles increase the accident rate for these vehicles. This means that technical inspections, in principle, can reduce the accident rate for heavy vehicles.

The results of US studies indicate that roadside inspections of vehicles can reduce the numbers of accidents. Quantifying the effect is difficult. Roadside inspections allow insp-ectors to pick out the vehicles in the poorest technical condition for inspection. Technical roadside inspection of motor vehicles can, in principle, be combined with other kinds of enforcement, for example, concerning the use of seat belts and daytime running lights.

The effect on accidents of garage regulation and inspection is unknown.

**Main elements of effects on mobility**

This chapter describes the measures that are not primarily intended to affect mobility, but may do so indirectly. It has been suggested that drivers may adapt their driving behaviour to the technical condition of the vehicle and vehicle characteristics (e.g. increase speed); however, this assertion has little support. The vast majority of studies that have evaluated the effects of new safety standards for vehicles conclude that these standards have reduced the number of people killed in traffic. It is therefore not correct that drivers adapt their behaviour to such an extent that the new safety standards for cars do not have any effect on the number of accidents. Behavioural adaptations of a more moderate degree may occur. Traffic speed has increased over a long period, and it is reasonable to assume that developments in the form of more powerful engines, greater acceleration and higher top speeds in new cars are some, but certainly not all, factors that explain this growth. Less is known about how awareness of technical defects in a vehicle affects behaviour. Some studies indicate that drivers of small vehicles try to compensate for technical defects in their vehicles through more careful behaviour. Taken as a whole, the available studies provide no basis for quantifying the effects on mobility of the measures included in the chapter.

**Main elements of effects on the environment**

In parallel with the development of new safety standards for vehicles over the last 20–30 years, environmental standards have also become more stringent. This applies to standards for emissions, fuel consumption and noise levels. US studies indicate that this has led to less pollution from vehicle traffic. In the United States, the decrease in emissions from each vehicle has been so large that the total level of pollution has been reduced, despite an increase in traffic volume. Older vehicles often pollute more than new vehicles. Technical inspections can reduce emissions from older vehicles, but experiences to date are limited and give little basis for quantifying the effect.

**Main elements of costs**

The Norwegian Public Roads Administration's costs for vehicle and garage inspections are shown in Table 5.0.2. The annual costs per vehicle are estimated based on the total annual costs for the Public Roads Administration and for car owners and 2 million registered vehicles (cars, vans, buses, trucks and combined vehicles).

The costs of compliance control for vehicle safety standards and garage regulation and inspection for car owners are not known. US estimates of the costs of more stringent safety standards for cars indicate that these costs are of the order of magnitude of NOK 13,000–22,000 per vehicle.

**Main elements in cost–benefit analyses**

The US cost–benefit analysis indicates that more stringent safety standards for vehicles have a benefit–cost ratio between 1.9 and 7.2.

*Table 5.0.2: Costs for vehicle and garage inspections in Norway*

| | Total annual costs (million NOK) | | Annual costs per vehicle (NOK) | | |
|---|---|---|---|---|---|
| Measure | Roads administration | Car owners | Roads administration | Car owners | Results last updated |
| 5.1 Compliance control for vehicle safety standards | 5 | | 2.5 | | 1995 |
| 5.2 Periodic vehicle inspections | 77 | 72 | 38.5 | 36 | 1995 |
| 5.3 Roadside vehicle inspections | 22 | 7 | 11 | 3.5 | 1995 |
| 5.4 Garage regulation and inspections | 2 | | 1 | | 1995 |

Periodic inspection of light vehicles, as carried out in Norway at present, has a benefit–cost ratio of around 0.2, assuming that the inspections lead to a reduction in the pollution emissions from inspected cars by around 10%. If this effect on emissions is not realised, the benefit–cost ratio of periodic inspection of light vehicles is zero, since the measure does not affect the number of accidents. Assuming a decrease in the number of accidents for heavy vehicles of around 5% per inspected vehicle for the first year following inspection (see Section 5.2), periodic inspection of heavy vehicles has a benefit–cost ratio of around 2.6.

The effects on the number of accidents of roadside inspections are very uncertain and any cost–benefit assessment should be treated as a numerical example only. In the example, it is assumed that there is a decrease in the number of accidents, associated with a 50% increase in inspections, of 0.7% for light vehicles and 1.7% for heavy vehicles. The benefit is then substantially greater than the cost. The example shows that roadside inspections of vehicles can be cost-effective, even with a very small effect on the number of accidents.

The cost–benefit value of regulation and inspection of garages is not known.

## 5.1 Vehicle safety standards

### Problem and objective

Safety standards for vehicles have developed considerably. The United States has led the way in this development, but other motorised countries have adopted the standards set by US authorities for vehicles, partly to be able to sell cars to the United States. New safety standards for vehicles are largely set as the result of international co-operation. Great emphasis is placed on the international harmonising of regulations in this area, primarily to avoid trade problems and secure competitive conditions.

The general standards for vehicles in Norway are contained in the Vehicle Regulations (Forlaget Last og Buss A/S 1995). To ensure that these regulations are being adhered to, a system has been introduced for model approval (compliance control) of vehicles. Model approval is a general regulation of a specific model type or a type of vehicle on the basis of an inspection of one example of this vehicle. The system of model approval only applies to series-produced vehicles. Vehicles that are not covered by the model approval system must be inspected individually (individual regulation).

Model approval and individual regulation are intended to ensure that all vehicles (brand-new, converted and second-hand imported vehicles) meet the technical standards that the vehicle legislation sets for new vehicles, and do not have defects. Another objective is to simplify vehicle regulation for new vehicles.

Random checks are carried out on model-approved vehicles to ensure that the system of model approval is respected. Compliance control of older vehicles is intended to ensure that vehicles are not being sold with technical defects.

## Description of the measure

The measures described in this chapter include mainly safety standards for new vehicles (discussed later in the chapter). No studies have been found on the effects on accidents of model approval of new vehicles, random checks of model-approved vehicles and technical inspection on change of ownership.

## Effect on accidents

The effects on accidents of model approval, inspection of approved vehicles, individual regulation and inspections on change of ownership are not known. The effect is indirect and depends on how the new standards set for vehicles have affected safety. If the new safety standards for vehicles have improved safety, the inspection of these standards may contribute to increase safety.

The safety standards that the American authorities have introduced for new vehicles from the middle of the 1960s include (Crandall, Gruenspecht, Keeler and Lave 1986) standards for dual-master braking systems, head rests, laminated front windscreens, collapsible steering wheel columns and seat belts and/or airbags in cars. Many of the standards were introduced around 1970. In the United States, a number of studies have evaluated how the introduction of these safety standards has affected traffic safety, primarily the number of traffic fatalities. The first study was carried out by Peltzman (1975), and concluded that safety standards for vehicles had improved safety for drivers and passengers, but reduced safety for other road users, particularly pedestrians and cyclists. He interpreted this to be a result of behavioural adaptation on the part of car users. The idea was that the safety standards for vehicles protected those inside in the vehicle better from injury in the event of accidents, but that less careful driving, induced by this increased protection, reduced safety for other road users.

Peltzman's results and his interpretation of them have been very controversial in the United States and have provided the impetus for a number of studies to verify his findings. Studies that have evaluated the effects of Federal motor vehicle safety standards in the United States include

Peltzman (1975)
Joksch (1976)
Robertson (1977a)
Robertson (1977b)
Robertson (1981)
Crandall and Graham (1984)
Graham (1984)
Graham and Garber (1984)
Orr (1984)
Robertson (1984)
Garbacz (1985)
Crandall, Gruenspecht, Keeler and Lave (1986)

These studies were carried out at different times after the safety standards were introduced. By around 1980, the vehicle fleet in the United States had been renewed to such an extent that the safety standards covered the majority of vehicles. On the basis of the studies, the following estimates (Table 5.1.1) of the effects of the safety standards for vehicles in the United States can be made (percentage change in the number of people killed, with the lower and upper limits for 95% confidence interval in parentheses).

Peltzman's study and the other earlier studies referred to the effects of the safety standards set before 1972, at which time not all standards had been implemented and much of the vehicle fleet had not yet benefited from standards that had been introduced. The only study that has evaluated the effect of all the standards in the list

*Table 5.1.1: Effects of more stringent safety standards for vehicles on the numbers killed in the USA*

| | | Percentage change in the numbers killed | |
|---|---|---|---|
| Safety standards for vehicles | Injuries affected | Best estimates | 95% confidence interval |
| Few standards, ca. 1972 | Car occupants killed | −15 | (−16, −14) |
| Several standards, ca. 1976 | Car occupants killed | −25 | (−26, −24) |
| All standards, ca. 1980 | Car occupants killed | −40 | (−41, −39) |
| All standards, ca. 1980 | Killed outside vehicles | +7 | (+6, +8) |
| All standards, ca. 1980 | All road users | −30 | (−31, −29) |

above is Crandall, Gruenspecht, Keeler and Lave (1986). This study found that the total number of fatalities in traffic accidents in the United States in 1981 was around 30% lower than it would otherwise have been as a result of the more stringent safety standards for vehicles. There was a decrease of around 40% in the number of motorists killed and an increase of around 7% in the number of road users in other groups killed (pedestrians, cyclists and motorcyclists).

### Effect on mobility

The effects of more stringent safety standards for vehicles on mobility have not been documented. Traffic speed has increased in the last 20–30 years, but this may be partly due to improvements in the road network, not just due to technical improvements of vehicles.

### Effect on the environment

In parallel with the more stringent safety standards for vehicles in the last 25–30 years, environmental standards have also been tightened up considerably. This particularly affects standards with regard to emissions, but also standards regarding fuel consumption and noise levels. Between 1970 and 1983, the total emission of hydrocarbons (HC) from passenger cars in the United States, according to Crandall, Gruenspecht, Keeler and Lave (1986), went down by 55%. The same study found a 46% decrease in the emission of carbon monoxide (CO) and a 12% decrease in the emission of nitrogen oxide (NO) in the same period. The number of kilometres driven by passenger cars increased in the United States by 36% from 1970 to 1983. Petrol consumption per kilometre for an average 1984 model passenger car in the United

States was about half that of a 1968 model (Crandall, Gruenspecht, Keeler and Lave 1986).

As far as the effect of safety standards on the environment is concerned, the results are more mixed. A number of these standards including standards for dual master braking systems, collapsible steering wheel columns, reinforcement bars in doors and laminated front windscreens increase the weight of the vehicle, and thus the fuel consumption. However, the weight increase is very slight, less than 50 kg for all types of safety equipment taken together.

### Costs

The costs of more stringent safety standards for vehicles, and the system of model approval and individual regulation for implementing these standards, are of two types. One is the administrative costs of carrying out the regulations. The other is the vehicle owners' additional costs, to the extent that new vehicle safety standards have made vehicles more expensive.

The Norwegian Public Roads Administration's costs for model approval and registration of vehicles in Norway in 1992 were NOK 50.6 million (Hagen 1994). These also include the costs of the vehicle registrations, which form most of the activity in this area. The cost of model approval and individual vehicle approval can be estimated at about NOK 5 million per year.

Vehicle owners' costs resulting from more stringent safety standards for cars are not well known. An early Norwegian study (Berthelsen and Sager 1976) estimated the cost of safety components for vehicles at around 7% of the price of the new vehicle. Crandall, Gruenspecht, Keeler and Lave (1986) have tried to estimate the costs of more stringent safety standards for vehicles in the United States in the period 1966–84. The cost per vehicle of the safety standards, calculated in 1984 dollars, was estimated at around US$ 610–1,040 per vehicle.

### Cost–benefit analysis

Crandall, Gruenspecht, Keeler and Lave (1986) have estimated the benefit–cost ratio of more stringent safety standards for cars in the United States to be between 0.56 and 2.15, if the prevention of one fatality is valued at US$ 300,000 (1981 values). If the prevention of a fatality is valued at $1 million, the benefit–cost ratio is estimated to be between 1.89 and 7.16.

On average, a light vehicle in Norway is involved in around 0.004 injury accidents reported to the police per car per year. The expected annual cost per passenger car in injury accidents can be estimated to around NOK 7,000. In addition, the costs of property damage only accidents comprise around NOK 2,000 per vehicle per year.

If the cost of safety standards for vehicles is set at NOK 18,000 per vehicle, it corresponds to an annual added cost of NOK 2,000 per vehicle per year (annuity). This means that the benefits of the safety standards are greater than the costs if they reduce the expected number of injury accidents per vehicle per year by around 30%. From 1977 to 1994, the number of injury accidents reported to the police per vehicle per year went down from around 0.009 to around 0.006, that is, about 33%. This reduction is not due exclusively to more stringent safety standards for cars, but may partly be due to such standards. The use of seat belts, child restraints and daytime running lights increased significantly in this period.

## 5.2 Periodic motor vehicle inspections

### Problem and objective

As a result of normal use, many parts of a motor vehicle are exposed to wear and tear, which may eventually develop into serious technical defects. The majority of drivers are not able to detect anything other than serious and obvious defects in the vehicle. In many ways, modern vehicles are much more difficult for owners to inspect and repair than vehicles were 30–40 years ago.

Roadside surveys of vehicles show that the older vehicles have more technical defects than newer vehicles. A Norwegian study of the technical condition of passenger cars (Fosser and Ragnøy 1991) shows that older vehicles have more technical defects than newer vehicles. The number of technical defects increases almost linearly with the vehicle's age. It increases from 0.89 for 4-year-old vehicles to 5.57 for ≥13-year-old vehicles. Twenty nine per cent of cars that were used in 1990 had no defects. A study of articulated lorries in Vestfold, Norway (Fosser 1987), found that there were defects in 39% of the lorries and 61% of the trailers.

Rather little is known about how technical defects affect accident rate. An American study (Jones and Stein 1989) found that articulated lorries with technical defects had around 1.7 times as high an accident involvement rate as articulated lorries with no technical defects. On the basis of the study, it can be estimated that if no articulated lorries had technical defects, the number of accidents involving articulated lorries would go down by 37%.

A literature study carried out for the EU Commission (Rompe and Seul 1985) contains the results of 28 studies, including official accident statistics, where attempts have been made to classify accidents according to the factors that were judged to have caused the accident. In the official accident statistics, the proportion of accidents attributed to technical failure of the vehicle varies between 1.3% and 11.4% (on average, around 4%). According to in-depth studies of accidents, the proportion of accidents attributed to technical failure of the vehicle varies between 1.5% and 24.4% (on average, around 8.5%).

These figures should be taken with a grain of salt. As a rule, more than one factor contributes to an accident; designating one of them as the most important can be somewhat arbitrary. Different in-depth studies have used different criteria to identify contributory factors. Technical failure of a vehicle will normally be listed as a contributory factor to an accident only if it occurred suddenly, for example, if a tyre blew out or if the brakes suddenly failed. The figures say little about the potential for preventing accidents through improving technical defects in vehicles.

Periodic motor vehicle inspection is intended to prevent accidents that are due to technical defects in vehicles, by detecting such defects and ensuring that they are repaired, or possibly banning the use of vehicles with serious defects.

**Description of the measure**

Periodic inspection of motor vehicles is the regular inspection of vehicles carried out in inspection halls. In Norway, such inspections can be carried out either at the state-owned inspection stations or by approved garages.

**Effect on accidents**

A number of studies have evaluated the effects of periodic vehicle inspection on accidents. The results presented here are based on an analysis of the following studies:

Mayer and Hoult (1963) (USA)
Buxbaum and Colton (1966) (USA)
Fuchs and Leveson (1967) (USA)
Foldvary (1971) (USA)
Little (1971) (USA)
Colton and Buxbaum (1977) (USA)
Schroer and Peyton (1979) (USA)

Crain (1980) (USA)
VanMatre and Overstreet (1981) (USA)
Berg, Danielsson and Junghard (1984) (Sweden)
Loeb and Gilad (1984) (USA)
Loeb (1985) (USA)
White (1986) (New Zealand)
Loeb (1987) (USA)
Robinson (1989) (USA)
Fosser (1991) (Norway)
Moses and Savage (1992) (USA)

The majority of studies have been carried out in the United States and are more than 20 years old. All of these studies have significant methodological flaws (Vaaje 1985, Fosser 1991, 1992). The methodologically best study in this area is the Norwegian study (Fosser 1991). The study covered 204,000 passenger cars. These were randomly assigned to three groups. One group was inspected annually through a 3-year period. The second group was inspected once in the course of 3 years. The third group was not inspected in the course of the period of the study. On the basis of this study, the effect of periodic inspection of passenger cars is estimated to be:

- Effect on injury accidents: −2% (95% CI [−10%; +7%])
- Effect on property damage only accidents: +1% (95% CI [−1%; +3%])

There were no statistically significant changes in the number of accidents per insured vehicle day or per kilometre driven. The results refer to passenger cars that are less than 12 years old.

Only one study has been found that indicates the effects of periodic inspection of heavy vehicles on the number of accidents (Moses and Savage 1992). The study concerns general inspections of haulage companies, where the vehicle's technical condition is inspected together with compliance with driving and rest-hour regulations and administrative conditions for the running of the company. In the study, a distinction was made between three groups of companies: (1) companies that keep to the rules satisfactorily (satisfactory), (2) companies that can be given conditional approval (conditional) (i.e. to say, they are approved providing that certain deficiencies are corrected) and (3) companies that operate in conflict with the rules (not approved). The accident rate was calculated for each group of companies. Table 5.2.1 shows the results of the calculations. Companies given conditional approval had the lowest accident rate, both for injury accidents and for all accidents.

*Table 5.2.1: Accident rate in different groups of haulage companies in the USA (Moses and Savage 1992)*

| | Groups of companies | | |
|---|---|---|---|
| Accidents per million vehicle kilometres | Satisfactory | Conditional | Not approved |
| Injury accidents | 0.319 | 0.294 | 0.422 |
| All accidents | 5.284 | 3.128 | 5.632 |

*Table 5.2.2: Theoretically attainable effect on accidents of periodic inspection of heavy vehicles (calculated on the basis of the risk figures in Table 5.2.1*

| | Implicit effect of inspections (%) | |
|---|---|---|
| Groups compared | Injury accidents | All accidents |
| Conditional approval vs. not approved | −30 | −44 |
| Satisfactory vs. not approved | −24 | −6 |
| Satisfactory vs. conditional approval | +9 | +69 |
| Satisfactory and conditional approval together vs. not approved | −26 | −16 |
| Satisfactory vs. conditional approval and not approved together | −2 | +40 |

A number of comparisons can be made between the three groups (Table 5.2.2). The two comparisons where two groups are compared with the third (the two bottom rows in Table 5.2.2) may give an indication of the possible effects on accidents. For injury accidents, the results indicate a reduction, but for all accidents, the results are conflicting. The effects of inspections may depend on how accurate the inspection authority is in selecting vehicles for inspection. If only the most defective vehicles are targeted for inspection and if inspection leads to a complete repair of these vehicles, a relatively large decrease in the number of injury accidents can be achieved. A less selective choice of vehicles will have a smaller effect on accidents.

## Effect on mobility

No studies have been found that show if and how periodic motor vehicle inspection affects mobility. If periodic inspection reduces the probability of vehicles stopping in traffic in case of emergency resulting from technical defects, such a measure may contribute to improving mobility.

It is possible that the driver's knowledge of the vehicle's technical condition affects driving behaviour. A US study found that drivers of older vehicles kept a greater distance to the vehicle driving in front than drivers of new vehicles (Evans and Wasielewski 1983). A Norwegian study (Ingebrigtsen and Fosser 1991) found that drivers adapt their driving behaviour in the winter to how good they think their car tyres are. This adaptation affects the accident rate.

### Effects on the environment

Vehicle ignition systems, carburettors and exhaust systems wear out can be wrongly adjusted or may leak if they are used for a long period without being checked. This can increase fuel consumption and the emission of pollution. Leaks in the exhaust system can increase the level of noise.

A literature study carried out for the EU Commission (Rompe and Seul 1985) concludes that correcting wrongly adjusted ignition and carburettor systems, as a result of periodic inspections, can reduce the emissions of CO from each vehicle by 20%. For HC, it was concluded that a 10% reduction in emission could be achieved. For NOx, no effect of periodic inspection was estimated.

The effect of emission control carried out in connection with periodic vehicle inspection depends on the type of inspection carried out and the type of exhaust gas purification system the vehicle has (Torp 1996). A distinction can be made between two types of inspections: (1) idling inspections, where the quantities of CO and HC in exhaust gases from a vehicle are measured and (2) driving cycle inspections, where emissions are measured in greater detail in a laboratory, by running the engine in different gears and with different revolutions per minute. The type of inspection currently carried out by the Norwegian Public Roads Administration is of the first type (idling inspection).

### Costs

In 1995, the Norwegian Public Roads Administration used around 140 man-years on periodic motor vehicle inspection, including calling in vehicles for inspection. The total costs can be estimated to around NOK 77 million (assuming NOK 550,000 per working year). This does not include the costs incurred by road users for vehicle inspection (time and vehicle costs).

## Cost–benefit analyses

A number of cost–benefit analyses of periodic motor vehicle inspections have been carried out. Loeb and Gilad (1984) calculated the costs and benefits of periodic vehicle inspection in the state of New Jersey in the United States as follows:

| Cost and benefit components | Value in million dollars |
|---|---|
| Saved accident costs | 103.5 |
| Total benefit | 103.5 |
| Direct inspection costs | 15.1 |
| Cost of road users time | 50.9 |
| Operating costs for vehicles associated with inspection | 17.6 |
| Total costs | 83.6 |
| Benefit–cost ratio | 1.24 |

It was assumed that there was a decrease in accidents of around 20%. In a subsequent analysis, based on information from all the states in the United States, Loeb (1985) estimated the benefit–cost ratio of periodic vehicle inspection as around 1.03. In this analysis, the benefit consisted only of fewer accidents. The cost items included were the same as shown above.

An evaluation produced for the EU Commission (Rompe and Seul 1985) estimated the benefit–cost ratio of compulsory, periodic vehicle inspection in all member countries of the EU in 1985 as 1.62. It was assumed that there was a 5% decrease in the number of accidents and a 3% saving in fuel consumption. The costs included direct inspection costs, costs of time spent and operating costs of vehicles involved in driving to and from the inspection hall. The benefit–cost ratio varied according to this analysis between different EEC countries, from 1.02 (Italy) to 3.86 (Luxembourg).

A cost–benefit analysis of periodic vehicle inspection in Sweden (Riksrevisionsverket 1989) assumed that there was a 2–10% decrease in accidents, a 12–20% decrease in the emission of CO and particles and a 1.5–3% reduction in fuel consumption. The estimated cost–benefit ratios range between 1.15 and 5.97.

A more recent Swedish cost–benefit analysis (Hjalte 1991) examined critically some of the values in the analysis reported above. The results of this analysis are given below.

According to this analysis, the benefit–cost ratio of periodic vehicle inspection in Sweden is between 0.17 and 0.36.

| | Amount in million Swedish kroner | |
|---|---|---|
| Cost and benefit components | Minimum value | Maximum value |
| Saved accident costs | 365 | 365 |
| Saved environmental costs | 115 | 190 |
| Saved fuel costs | 26 | 53 |
| Benefit of extended vehicle lifetime | 0 | 0 |
| Total benefits | 506 | 608 |
| Direct inspection costs | 550 | 550 |
| Road users' time costs | 230 | 360 |
| Loss of income for the transport business | 195 | 195 |
| Vehicles operating costs at inspection | 115 | 200 |
| Additional costs of repairs | 580 | 1,740 |
| Total costs | 1,680 | 3,055 |

Moses and Savage (1997) have carried out a cost–benefit analysis of inspections of heavy vehicles in the United States. A distinction was made between two types of inspection: company visits, where vehicles were inspected and a number of other elements of the company's operations were considered, and roadside inspections carried out at weighing stations. For company inspections, the benefit–cost ratio was estimated as 4.14, and for roadside inspections 0.87. The inspections were assumed to reduce the accident rate in the road haulage industry as a whole by around 5% per year. Of this, 4% was assumed to be a direct result of the inspections and 1% was as a result of a deterrent effect.

For Norwegian conditions, a provisional cost–benefit analysis can be made on the basis of the following assumptions:

| Factor | Assumption |
|---|---|
| Effect on accidents per year for light vehicles | 0% |
| Effect on accidents per year with heavy vehicles | −5% |
| Road users' time consumption per inspection of light vehicles | 1 h |
| Rod users' time consumption per inspection of heavy vehicles | 2 h |
| Driving distance per vehicle to and from periodic inspections | 30 km |
| Effect on emissions of CO, HC and NOx (inspected vehicles only) | −10% |
| Number of inspected light vehicles | 165,000 |
| Number of inspected heavy vehicles | 65,000 |

*Table 5.2.3: Costs and benefits of periodic vehicle inspections as carried out in Norway today*

| | Amount in million NOK (1995) | |
|---|---|---|
| Cost and benefit components | Light vehicles | Heavy vehicles |
| Reduced accident costs | 0 | 92 |
| Reduced environmental costs | 31 | 70 |
| Total benefits | 31 | 162 |
| Direct inspection costs | 43 | 36 |
| Opportunity cost of public expenditures | 9 | 7 |
| Road users time costs | 17 | 44 |
| Vehicle operating costs | 5 | 6 |
| Total costs | 74 | 93 |
| Benefit–cost ratio | 0.17 | 2.60 |

It has been assumed that idling inspections of exhaust gases are carried out in conjunction with periodic inspections. Costs and benefits calculated on the basis of inspections carried out in 1995, including EEA inspections, are given in Table 5.2.3:

The way in which periodic inspection is carried out in Norway today is probably not cost-effective for light vehicles. The measure can be cost-effective for heavy vehicles, assuming that both a reduction in accidents and an environmental gain are achieved. Each of these benefit components on its own is not enough to offset the cost of the measure.

## 5.3 Roadside vehicle inspections

### Problem and objective

As a result of normal use, a number of vehicle elements are exposed to wear and tear. Without regular inspection and maintenance, dangerous defects may occur. Older vehicles are generally in poorer technical condition than new cars. A Norwegian roadside survey of the technical condition of passenger cars (Fosser and Ragnøy 1991) in 1990 found that vehicles that were less than 4 years old had, on average, 0.89 technical defects per vehicle. Vehicles that were 13 years older or more had, on average, 5.57 technical defects per vehicle. As far as heavy vehicles are concerned, less is known regarding the relationship between age and technical condition. It is known, however, that many heavy vehicles are technically defective (Ragnøy and Sagberg 1999). A US study (Jones and Stein 1989) found that articulated lorries with technical defects had an accident rate 1.7 times higher than articulated lorries without technical defects.

An advantage of roadside inspections of vehicles is that only vehicles that are actually used will be inspected. Trained inspectors are good at identifying those vehicles that tend to be in the poorest technical condition. On the contrary, testing requiring advanced equipment cannot be done at the roadside. Roadside inspection of vehicles is intended to identify technical defects in vehicles in use and reduce the number of accidents by ensuring that defects are repaired or that the vehicles are removed from traffic.

**Description of the measure**

Roadside inspection of vehicles in Norway comprises inspections carried out by the Norwegian Public Roads Administration and by the police, partly together and partly independently. The number of light vehicles (under 3.5 t) inspected tripled between 1985 and 1990–91. More recently, the number of light vehicles inspected has gone down again. The frequency of inspections (the number of inspections per light vehicle per year) increased from 0.07 in 1985 to 0.17 in 1990, but has later reduced to 0.08. The number of inspected heavy vehicles almost quintupled from 1985 to 1992, but later went down. The frequency of inspection increased from 0.43 in 1985 to 1.88 in 1992 and went down again to 0.47 in 1996.

**Effect on accidents**

The following few studies have evaluated the effects of roadside inspections of vehicles on accidents:

Crain (1980) (USA)
VanMatre and Overstreet (1981) (USA)
Fridstrøm and Bjørnskau (1989) (Norway), see also Fridstrøm and Ingebrigtsen (1991)
Jones and Stein (1989) (USA)
Moses and Savage (1992) (USA)
Gou et al. (1999) (Canada)
Elvik (2002) (Norway)

These studies are very different and difficult to summarise. Studies by Crain (1980) and VanMatre and Overstreet (1981) compare the level of traffic risk between states that have or do not have roadside inspections in the United States. Both studies found that the states that have roadside inspections have a fatality rate that is around 15% lower (± 1%) than states that do not conduct roadside inspections. For injury accidents, the risk in states with roadside inspections was 14% lower (±0.2%) than in states without roadside inspections. The studies do not describe the scope or quality of roadside inspections. Both studies have controlled for a number of confounding factors (around 8–10), which might explain differences in the level of risk between the states.

Studies by Jones and Stein (1989) and Moses and Savage (1992) compare the accident rates for heavy vehicles with and without technical defects. These studies only indicate the *theoretical or maximum conceivable* effect on the accident rate of removing technical defects in heavy vehicles. Another study by Jones and Stein (1989) shows a maximum possible effect on accident rates (injury and property damage only) by removing technical defects in heavy vehicles of 37% (95% CI [−50; −20]). The other study (Moses and Savage 1992) shows a maximum possible effect on accident rates from removing technical defects in heavy vehicles of 26% (95% CI [35; −16]) for injury accidents and 16% (95% CI [−18; −13]) for property damage only accidents. In practice, it would be difficult to carry out inspections that are so comprehensive that all heavy vehicles could be guaranteed to be free of technical defects at all times. The effect on accidents that can be achieved in practice is therefore smaller than the theoretical maximum effect.

A Canadian study (Gou et al. 1999) estimated that technical defects had contributed to 15% of accidents involving heavy vehicles. Again, this estimate should be interpreted as showing the maximum effect on accident rate that can be attained by removing all technical defects from heavy vehicles.

A Norwegian study (Fridstrøm and Bjørnskau 1989, Fridstrøm and Ingebrigtsen 1991) examined the factors responsible for the variation in the number of accidents per county and per month in Norway in the period 1974–86. The study found that roadside inspections, measured on the basis of the average frequency of inspections per county and per month, was estimated to reduce the number of injury accidents by around 0.4% (95% CI [−2.3; +1.4]). The effect was not statistically significant. A more detailed analysis found that roadside inspections, as they were carried out in the period 1974–86, contributed to a 5% reduction in the number of injured vehicle users per county and per month, but a 5% increase in the number of pedestrians and cyclists injured per county and per month. For injuries in total, there was a decrease of 1.5% per county and per month. This result was not statistically significant at the 5% level.

In another Norwegian study (Elvik 2002), the relationship between the frequency $f$ of inspections of heavy vehicles and their accident rate was evaluated. The study controlled for changes in the business cycle, the recruitment of new drivers and long-term trend. It was found that doubling the frequency of inspections (e.g. from 0.5 to 1.0 per car per year) was associated with a 6.7% (95% CI [−18.4; +5.1]) reduction of accident rate.

Taken as a whole, these studies do not provide a very firm basis for quantifying the effect of roadside inspections of vehicles on the number of accidents. All results indicate that the existence of roadside inspections, or an increase in the frequency of inspections, contributes to reducing the number of accidents. Furthermore, there seems to be a reason to conclude that the effect on accidents is greater for heavy vehicles than for light vehicles. Nonetheless, quantifying the effect is difficult.

We have decided to place greatest emphasis on the Norwegian results. The results of Fridstrøm and Bjørnskau's (1989) study, with the number of injured persons as a dependent variable, is assumed largely to represent the effect of roadside inspections of light vehicles, since the majority of injured persons are inside such vehicles or are injured by them. The calculated effects of a 50% increase in the frequency of inspections on the number of injury accidents are

- −0.7% (95% CI [−1.7; +0.3]) for light vehicles
- −3.4% (95% CI [−9.2; +2.5]) for heavy vehicles.

Both these effects apply to all accidents with light vehicles and heavy vehicles, respectively, not just accidents where inspected vehicles are involved.

### Effect on mobility

No studies have been found that show how roadside inspection of vehicles affects mobility. The inspections are normally carried out at outdoor inspection stations, parking places or lay-bys where they do not obstruct other traffic. Traffic passing an inspection point can therefore flow more or less normally. Inspecting a passenger car would, on the average, take about 15 min, whereas a heavy vehicle takes about 30 min.

### Effect on the environment

No studies have been found that show how roadside inspections of vehicles affect the environment. In roadside inspections, it is possible to carry out idling inspections of exhaust emission (see Section 5.2, periodic inspection, for further discussion). Visual inspection can show to some extent where emissions are abnormally high. Leakage from the exhaust system can, at least in serious cases, be detected from noise levels. To the extent that roadside inspections also include exhaust emission and leakage in the exhaust system, and ensure that defects are repaired, they can reduce environmental problems related to exhaust gases and noise. The actual effects have not been documented.

### Costs

In Norway, about 50 man-years were spent on roadside inspections of vehicles in the year 2000. An increase in the manpower devoted to such inspections to about 80 man-years has been planned. The cost of this increase will amount to about 21 million NOK per year.

### Cost–benefits analysis

No cost–benefit analyses have been found for roadside inspections of vehicles. In order to indicate the possible effects of increasing the number of such inspections, a numerical example has been worked out.

An increase in the number of inspections as planned by the Norwegian government will cost about 21 million NOK. It can be assumed that the number of accidents involving heavy vehicles is reduced by 5%, whereas there is no effect on accidents involving light vehicles. Assuming that only heavy vehicles are inspected, one may estimate the savings in accident costs to 161 million NOK per year. Stopping for inspections will impose delays worth about 4 million NOK on operators of heavy vehicles. Hence, benefits come to 157 million NOK and costs (including the opportunity cost of taxes) come to 25 million NOK. Benefits are clearly greater than costs.

## 5.4 Garage regulation and inspections

### Problem and objective

In order for a vehicle to be technically in order at all times, it must be maintained. Such maintenance often requires the vehicle being repaired, since parts and equipment are exposed to wear and tear. Following accidents and other damage, vehicles must often be repaired. Repairs to vehicles can be done privately to some extent, but are usually done at a garage. However, it has been documented that garages do not always carry out satisfactory work. To ensure that garage work maintains a certain standard, a special act governing the inspection and regulation of garages has been issued. The reasoning behind the Garages Act is to set standards for garages to ensure that garage work is of a high quality, which in turn will result in lower accident rates for the vehicles.

Garage regulation and inspection is intended to ensure a high quality of repairs and to protect garage customers from unskilled repair work.

## Description of the measure

The main rule in Norway according to legislation regulating vehicle repair garages is that a commercial garage must be approved (authorised) by the Norwegian Public Roads Administration. In order to be approved, a garage must fulfill detailed standards regarding personnel, premises, equipment and machinery, storage areas for vehicles and repair data. Some of maintenance and repair work to vehicles is exempt from authorisation standards. Examples of such works are charging and changing batteries, changing tyres, repairs to vehicle instruments and replacing window glass. The Garage Regulation and Inspection Act does not cover work vehicle owners carry out on their own vehicles.

## Effect on accidents

The effect on accidents of garage regulation and inspection has not been documented. The effect is indirect and difficult to study. The causal chain from the Garages Act to accidents is as follows:

Regulation of garages → Garage standards → Repair standards
→ Technical condition → Accidents

By setting standards for garages, the aim is to achieve a better standard of garages. It is then assumed that this leads to a better standard of repairs carried out at the garages, so that vehicles have fewer technical defects. Fewer technical defects in vehicles are assumed to reduce the number of accidents.

No studies have been found where all the links in this causal chain have been studied. A study of how the Garages Act is implemented (Elvik 1983) found that garages frequently inspected by the Vehicle Inspection Authority (Biltilsynet) (Norwegian Public Roads Administration, traffic stations) more often meet the standards in the Act than garages that are seldom inspected. Among 72 garages inspected every other year, 68% satisfied the standards of the Act regarding garages. Among 88 garages inspected every eighth year, 42% satisfied the legal standards for garages.

In the same study, the quality of repairs of technical defects detected during inspections was studied in a follow-up inspection of 682 vehicles. Of these, 247 had been repaired privately and 435 had been repaired at a garage. The proportion of technical defects satisfactorily repaired was 86.5% for the garages and 84.8% for private repair work. For garages satisfying the law's standards for garages, the proportion of satisfactory repairs was 90.3%. For garages not satisfying the law's standards, the proportion of satisfactory repairs was 81.7% (Elvik 1983). These differences are small, but indicate that garages that meet the standards laid down by law do better work than garages that do not meet the legal standards.

However, it should be borne in mind that many of the technical defects studied were trivial defects, which the majority of vehicle owners can deal with themselves. These include, for example, incorrect air pressure in tyres, worn-out tyres, dead light bulbs or worn-out windscreen wipers. If more complicated work is needed, professional qualifications and access to correct tools and equipment are important for the quality of the work. The study does not show what the quality of the garages' work would have been without the standards laid down by law.

### Effect on mobility

The Garages Act has no documented effects on mobility.

### Effect on the environment

The Garages Act has no documented effects on the environment.

### Costs

In Norway, the Norwegian Public Roads Administration's costs of regulation and inspection of garages is of the order of NOK 2 million per year.

### Cost–benefit analysis

The effects of the Garages Act are not known. As a result, there is no basis for making a cost–benefit analysis of the Act.

## References

Berg, G., S. Danielsson, S. & O. Junghard. (1984). *Trafiksäkerhet och periodisk fordonskontroll.* VTI-rapport 281. Väg- och TrafikInstitutet (VTI), Linköping.

Berthelsen, J. & T. Sager. (1976). *Oversikt over utgiftene til trafikksikkerhet i Norge.* TØI-rapport. Transportøkonomisk institutt, Oslo.

Buxbaum, R. C. & T. Colton. (1966). Relationship of Motor Vehicle Inspection to Accident Mortality. *Journal of the American Medical Association*, **197**, 31–36.

Colton, T. & R. C. Buxbaum. (1977). Motor vehicle inspection and accident mortality. In: *Statistics and Public Policy*, 131–142. (Fairley, W. B. & F. Mosteller, eds). Addison-Wesley, Reading, MA.

Crain, W. M. (1980). *Vehicle Safety Inspection Systems. How Effective?* AEI studies 258. American Entreprise Institute for Public Policy Research, Washington DC.

Crandall, R. W. & J. D. Graham. (1984). Automobile Safety Regulation and Offsetting Behavior: Some New Empirical Estimates. *American Economic Review, AEA Papers and Proceedings*, **74**, 328–331.

Crandall, R. D., Gruenspecht, H. K., Keeler, T. E. & Lave, L. B. (1986). *Regulating the Automobile*. The Brookings Institution, Washington DC.

Elvik, R. (1983). *Bilverkstedloven. En undersøkelse av reparasjonsstandard, verkstedstandard og hvordan verkstedene vurderer loven*. TØI-rapport. Transportøkonomisk institutt, Oslo.

Elvik, R. (2002). The effect on accidents of technical inspections of heavy vehicles in Norway. *Accident Analysis and Prevention*, **34**, 753–762.

Evans, L. & P. Wasielewski. (1983). Risky driving related to driver and vehicle characteristics. *Accident Analysis and Prevention*, **15**, 121–136.

Foldvary, L. A. (1971). *A Review of Vehicle Inspection in relation to road safety*. Report NR/9. Australian Department of Transport, Canberra.

Forlaget Last og Buss A/S. (1995). *Kjøretøyforskriften*. Ajourført pr 1. november 1994. Forlaget Last og Buss A/S, Oslo.

Fosser, S. (1987). *Feil og mangler ved vogntog kontrollert på Solum utekontrollstasjon ved E-18 i Vestfold*. TØI-notat 825. Transportøkonomisk institutt, Oslo.

Fosser, S. (1991). *Effekt av periodisk bilkontroll på ulykkesrisiko. Resultater fra et 4-årig eksperiment med 205.000 person- og varebiler i Norge*. TØI-rapport 70. Transportøkonomisk institutt, Oslo.

Fosser, S. (1992). An experimental evaluation of the effects of periodic motor vehicle inspection on accident rates. *Accident Analysis and Prevention*, **24**, 599–612.

Fosser, S. & A. Ragnøy. (1991). *Teknisk stand på personbiler i trafikken 1990*. TØI-rapport 80. Transportøkonomisk institutt, Oslo.

Fridstrøm, L. & T. Bjørnskau. (1989). *Trafikkulykkenes drivkrefter. En analyse av ulykkestallenes variasjon i tid og rom*. TØI-rapport 39. Transportøkonomisk institutt, Oslo.

Fridstrøm, L. & S. Ingebrigtsen. (1991). An aggregate accident model based on pooled, regional time-series data. *Accident Analysis and Prevention*, **23**, 363–378.

Fuchs, V. R. & I. Leveson. (1967). Motor Accident Mortality and Compulsory Inspection of Vehicles. *Journal of the American Medical Association*, **201**, 657–661.

Garbacz, C. (1985). A note on Peltzman's theory of offsetting consumer behavior. *Economics Letters*, **19**, 183–187.

Gou, M.; Clément, B.; Birikundavyi, S.; Bellavigna-Ladoux, O.; Abraham, E. (1999). Effect of heavy-vehicle mechanical condition on road safety in Quebec. Paper presented at *the 1999 Annual meeting of the Transportation Research Board*, Washington DC (Available on CD-ROM).

Graham, J. D. (1984). Technology, Behavior, and Safety: An Empirical Study of Automobile Occupant-Protection Regulation. *Policy Sciences*, **17**, 141–151.

Graham, J. D. & S. Garber. (1984). Evaluating the Effects of Automobile Safety Regulation. *Journal of Policy Analysis and Management*, **3**, 206–224.

Hagen, K-E. (1994). *Rullering av samfunnsøkonomisk regnskapssystem for trafikkulykker og trafikksikkerhetstiltak (SRT) for 1992*. Arbeidsdokument TST/0570/94. Transportøkonomisk institutt, Oslo.

Hjalte, K. (1991). *Bilprovningsåtgärder-ett räkneexempel*. Bilaga till Bilaga 7, Beräkningar, till Samhällsekonomisk prioritering av trafiksäkerhetsåtgärder. TFB & VTI forskning/research 7:7, 1991. Transportforskningsberedningen och Väg- och Trafikinstitutet, Stockholm och Linköping.

Ingebrigtsen, S. & S. Fosser. (1991). *Dekkstandardens betydning for trafikkulykker om vinteren*. TØI-rapport 75. Transportøkonomisk institutt, Oslo.

Joksch, H. C. (1976). Critique of Sam Peltzman's study the effects of automobile safety regulation. *Accident Analysis and Prevention*, **8**, 129–137.

Jones, I. S. & H. S. Stein. (1989). Defective equipment and tractor-trailer crash involvement. *Accident Analysis and Prevention*, **21**, 469–481.

Little, J. W. (1971). Uncertainties in evaluating periodic motor vehicle inspection by death rates. *Accident Analysis and Prevention*, **3**, 301–313.

Loeb, P. D. (1985). The Efficacy and Cost-Effectiveness of Motor Vehicle Inspection Using Cross-Sectional Data-An Econometric Analysis. *Southern Economic Journal*, **52**, 500–509.

Loeb, P. D. (1987). The determinants of automobile fatalities. With special consideration to policy variables. *Journal of Transport Economics and Policy*, **21**, 279–287.

Loeb, P. D. & B. Gilad. (1984). The efficacy and cost-effectiveness of vehicle inspection. *Journal of Transport Economics and Policy*, **18**, 145–164.

Mayer, A. J. & T. F. Hoult. (1963). *Motor Vehicle Inspection. A Report on Current Information, Measurement, and Research*. Institute for Regional and Urban Studies, Wayne State University.

Moses, L. N. & I. Savage. (1992). The effectiveness of motor carrier safety audits. *Accident Analysis and Prevention*, **24**, 479–496.

Moses, L. N. & I. A Savage. (1997). Cost-Benefit Analysis of US Motor Carrier Safety Programmes. *Journal of Transport Economics and Policy*, **31**, 51–67.

Orr, L. D. (1984). The Effectiveness of Atomobile Safety Regulation: Evidence from the FARS Data. *American Journal of Public Health*, **74**, 1384–1389.

Peltzman, S. (1975). The Effects of Automobile Safety Regulation. *Journal of Political Economy*, **83**, 677–725.

Ragnøy, A. & F. Sagberg. (1999). *Vogntog, kjøreatferd og kjøretøytilstand. Betydningen av sjåførenes arbeidssituasjon og rammebetingelser i næringen.* TØI rapport 468. Transportøkonomisk institutt, Oslo.

Riksrevisionsverket. (1989). *Den statliga fordonskontrollen. Revisionsrapport.* Dnr 1987:1479. Riksrevisionsverket, Stockholm.

Robertson, L. S. (1977a). A Critical Analysis of Peltzman's «The Effects of Automobile Safety Regulation. *Journal of Economic Issues*, **11**, 587–600.

Robertson, L. S. (1977b). State and federal new-car safety regulation: effects on fatality rates. *Accident Analysis and Prevention*, **9**, 151–156.

Robertson, L. S. (1981). Automobile Safety Regulations and Death Reductions in the United States. *American Journal of Public Health*, **71**, 818–822.

Robertson, L. S. (1984). Automobile Safety Regulation: Rebuttal and New Data. *American Journal of Public Health*, **74**, 1390–1394.

Robinson, R. C. (1989). *Compulsory motor vehicle inspection: implications for driver behavior and motor accident mortality.* Unpublished PhD dissertation. The State University of New York at Buffalo, Buffalo, NY.

Rompe, K. & E. Seul. (1985). *Advantages and disadvantages of conducting periodic roadworthiness tests to monitor the mechanical condition of private cars, the impact of such tests on road safety, environmental protection and the renewal of the vehicle fleet, and the scope for introducing roadworthiness testing throughout the European Community.* Report VII/133/85-EN. Commission of the European Communities, Directorate-General for Transport, Brussels.

Schroer, B. J. & W. F. Peyton. (1979). The effects of automobile inspections on accident rates. *Accident Analysis and Prevention*, **11**, 61–68.

Torp, C. (1996). Kontroll av kjøretøyer. I: *Miljøhåndboken*, Del I, 346–352. (Kolbenstvedt, M., H. Silborn & T. Solheim, eds.) Transportøkonomisk institutt, Oslo.

Vaaje, T. (1985). *Periodisk kjøretøykontroll og trafikksikkerhet. En litteraturstudie.* TØI-notat 749. Transportøkonomisk institutt, Oslo.

VanMatre, J. G. & G. A. Overstreet. (1981). Motor Vehicle Inspection and Accident Mortality: A Reexamination. *Journal of Risk and Insurance*, **48**, 423–435.

White, W. T. (1986). Does periodic vehicle inspection prevent accidents? *Accident Analysis and Prevention*, **18**, 51–62.

# 6.

# Driver Training and Regulation of Professional Drivers

## 6.0 Introduction and overview of 12 measures

This chapter describes 12 measures that cover requirements for drivers, basic driver training, and professional driver training, including driving emergency service vehicles and transporting school children. The 12 measures are as follows:

6.1 Driving licence age limits
6.2 Health requirements for drivers
6.3 Driver performance standards
6.4 Basic driver training
6.5 The driving test
6.6 Training and testing moped and motorcycle riders
6.7 Training and testing professional drivers
6.8 Graduated driving licences (GDLs)
6.9 Motivation and incentive systems in the workplace
6.10 Regulation of driving and rest hours
6.11 Safety standards for emergency driving
6.12 Safety standards for school transport

This introduction describes the amount and quality of research evaluating the effects of these measures on road safety. The main elements in current knowledge of the effects of the measures on mobility and the environment as well as costs and cost–benefit assessment are also described.

**The Handbook of Road Safety Measures**

**ISBN: 978-1-84855-250-0**

## Amount and quality of research

Comprehensive research has been carried out to evaluate the effects on accidents of requirements for drivers, basic driver training and professional driver training. Table 6.0.1 gives an overview of this research for the different measures. The largest number of studies refers to health requirements for drivers, treatment of problem drivers, graduated licensing and basic driver training. Meta-analyses have been used to summarise research results for all measures in this chapter, apart from safety standards for emergency driving and safety standards for transporting school children.

The quality of research varies. Good experimental studies have been reported for basic driver training and the treatment of problem drivers. These experiments are among the methodologically best studies to be found for any road safety measure. For other measures, the quality of research is not as good. Few studies have evaluated the effects of motivation and incentive systems in the workplace, safety standards for emergency driving and safety standards for transporting school children. Many studies have evaluated health requirements for drivers, but the quality of the methods is sometimes poor.

## Main elements of effects on accidents

A number of driver training measures and regulations for professional drivers have been found to reduce the number of accidents. Studies indicate that increasing the

*Table 6.0.1: Amount of research evaluating the effects on accidents of driver training and regulation of professional drivers*

| Measure | Number of studies | Number of results | Statistical weights | Results last updated |
|---|---|---|---|---|
| 6.1 Driving licence age limits | 10 | 70 | 22,026 | 2004 |
| 6.2 Health requirements for drivers | 50 | 298 | >100,000 | 2002 |
| 6.3 Driver performance standards | 17 | 58 | 16,498 | 1997 |
| 6.4 Basic driver training | 25 | 107 | 29,400 | 1997 |
| 6.5 The driving test | 8 | 22 | 247,701 | 1997 |
| 6.6 Training and testing moped and motorcycle riders | 18 | 65 | 4,298 | 1997 |
| 6.7 Training and testing professional drivers | 11 | 25 | 47,096 | 1997 |
| 6.8 Graduated driving licences (GDL) | 29 | 96 | 120,698 | 2006 |
| 6.9 Motivation and incentive systems in the workplace | 3 | 7 | 244 | 1997 |
| 6.10 Regulation of driving and rest hours | 10 | 344 | 7,198 | 1997 |
| 6.11 Safety standards for emergency driving | 7 | 7 | 0 | 1997 |
| 6.12 Safety standards for school transport | 4 | 4 | 0 | 1997 |

licensing age by 1 year in the 16–21 age group reduces the accident rate in the first year of driving by around 5–10%. GDLs with restrictions on, e.g. driving at night have been found to reduce accidents during the learner period by between 5% and 10%. The largest effects have been found for the GDL programmes with most restrictions, especially restrictions on nighttime driving and on the maximum number of violations. The studies have, however, several methodological weaknesses that may have contributed to the results. Formal training for professional drivers, in particular training in defensive driving taught at the workplace, combined with motivation and incentive systems, can reduce the accident rate by around 20%. Bright yellow fire engines have been found to be involved in fewer accidents than red fire engines.

Health requirements may reduce the number of accidents. A large number of studies have found increased accident rates among drivers with several types of medical conditions. Regulation of driving and rest periods may also have an effect on accidents. If driving and rest period rules in Norway were adhered to 100%, the number of injury accidents involving the vehicles that are subject to these rules would probably be around 2–7% lower than it is today.

Measures that have not been found to reduce accidents are knowledge tests, formal driver training offered by traffic schools, formal training and testing of moped and motorcycle riders, with the possible exception of driving tests, and the use of blue lights on the roof of emergency vehicles.

Special driver trainings may increase the number of accidents. Skid trainings have been found to increase accidents among young male car drivers, professional drivers and drivers of emergency vehicles.

The effect on accidents of safety standards for transporting school children has not been evaluated.

**Main elements of effects on mobility**

The measures in this area are not primarily intended to affect mobility. Nonetheless, the following measures may have indirect effects on mobility:

- Driving licence age limits and health requirements for drivers can contribute to limiting the number of drivers and thus the amount of driving. The effect on the amount of driving of current age limits and health requirements cannot be quantified.
- Night driving curfews and other restrictions on new drivers limit the mobility of these drivers.

- Regulations for driving and rest hours affect the transport time for goods. It has been estimated that 100% adherence to the current rules will increase the time taken for goods transport by least 2.6%.
- A number of measures including sirens, choice of colour and permission to deviate from the traffic regulations are intended to increase mobility for emergency service vehicles. It is probable that these measures contribute to increasing mobility for emergency service vehicles.
- The provision of transport to and from school for children influences their choice of mode of travel to and from school and the time spent on these journeys.

No effects on mobility have been documented for the other measures in this area.

**Main elements of effects on the environment**

The majority of measures in this area have no known effect on the environment. Noise from emergency service vehicles can be a local environmental problem in the areas where there is a considerable amount of emergency service vehicle activity (close to accident and emergency departments, fire stations and police stations).

**Main elements of costs**

The costs of the measures in Norway described in this chapter are shown in Table 6.0.2. For driving licence age limits, driver performance standards, and regulation of driving and rest hours, the costs consist mainly of administrative and enforcement costs. No cost estimates are available related to individual drivers.

**Main elements of cost–benefit analysis**

Cost–benefit analyses are available to varying degrees for the measures described in this chapter. The benefits in terms of prevented accidents have not been found to be larger than the costs for any of the measures. This is especially true for the measures that have not been found to reduce accidents, i.e. driver training and testing, blue lights on the roof of emergency vehicles and special driver trainings. Health requirements for drivers are also unlikely to be beneficial from a societal point of view.

Basic driver training, training and testing of moped and motorcycle riders, training and testing of professional drivers and safety requirements for driving emergency service vehicles improve mobility and accessibility. At present, this benefit is, however, too

*Table 6.0.2: Average costs of measures concerning requirements for drivers, driver training and professional driver training in Norway*

| Measure | Average cost per driver/ vehicle (NOK) | Cost estimates from year |
|---|---|---|
| 6.1 Driving licence age limits | – | 2004 |
| 6.2 Health requirements for drivers: cost of health check | 300 | 1995 |
| 6.3 Driver performance standards | – | |
| 6.4 Basic driver training, per person | 20,240 | 1995 |
| 6.5 The driving test | 710 | 1995 |
| 6.6 Training and testing of moped and motorcycle riders | – | |
| 6.7 Training and testing professional drivers | 15,000–20,000 | 1995 |
| 6.8 Graduated driving licences (GDL) | – | |
| 6.9 Motivation and incentive systems in the workplace: costs per 10,000 driving kilometre | 500–2,500 | 1995 |
| 6.10 Regulation of driving and rest hours | – | |
| 6.11 Safety standards for emergency driving: ambulance | 30,000 | 1995 |
| 6.11 Safety standards for emergency driving: fire engine | 10,000 | 1995 |
| 6.11 Safety standards for emergency driving: police car | 17,500 | 1995 |
| 6.11 Safety standards for emergency driving: driver training, 80 lessons | 14,000 | 1995 |
| 6.12 Safety standards for school transport | 135–21,000 | 1995 |

little known for meaningful cost–benefit analyses to be made. Gains in mobility while driving emergency service vehicles improve paramedical care and have additionally been found to reduce fatal and critical injuries.

## 6.1 Driving licence age limits

### Problem and objective

The risk for drivers of being involved in injury accidents varies considerably by age. On the basis of a number of studies from different countries, the risk of an injury accident for drivers in different age groups has been estimated as shown in Figure 6.1.1. These results are based on the following studies:

Broughton (1988) (Great Britain)
Fontaine (1988) (France)
Mercer (1989) (Canada)
Massie, Campbell and Williams (1995) (USA)

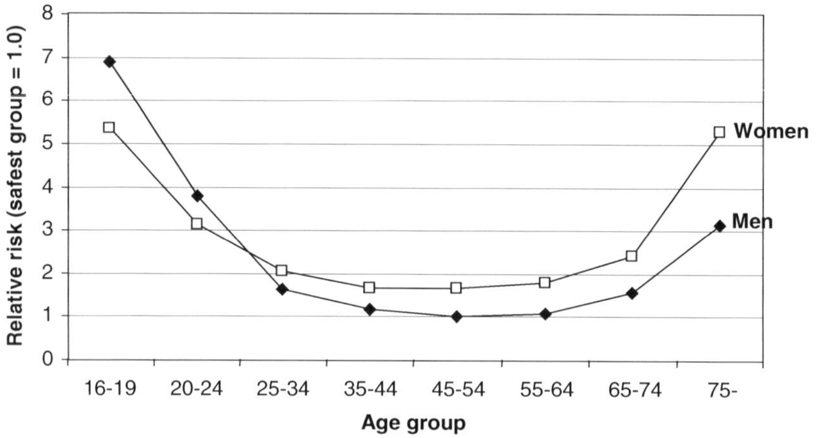


*Figure 6.1.1: Drivers' risk of injury accidents, based on nine studies (Elvik 2002).*

Diamantopoulou, Skalova, Dyte and Cameron (1996) (Victoria, Australia)
Hautzinger, Tassaux-Becker and Hamacher (1996) (Germany)
Bjørnskau (2000) (Norway)
Bernhoft (2001) (Denmark)
Nilsson (2002) (Sweden)

The accident risk in the group with the lowest risk is set equal to one. The relative risk in the other groups is estimated as an average of all nine studies. The results from all studies are highly consistent. All studies have found the highest accident risk in the youngest age group and the lowest accident risk in the middle age groups. Young men have a higher risk than young women. From the age of 30, women have a higher risk than men. For drivers over the age of 65, the risk of injury increases somewhat, but is not high, as it is for the youngest drivers. The high risk for young and inexperienced drivers, according to Evans (1991, 41), has been found so often that 'it could almost be called a law of nature'.

There are several explanations for the higher accident risk of women. First, women drive less than men, and accident risk has been found to decrease with increasing annual driving distances. Second, women often drive smaller cars than men, and smaller cars provide less protection in accidents than larger cars. Third, women drive more in urban areas where accident risk is higher than in rural areas or on motorways. Fourth, driver behaviour has been found to be different among men and women in some respects, e.g. women stop more often at traffic signals changing from green to yellow than men, which increases the risk of rear-end collisions. On acceleration lanes, women often drive more slowly than men in order to wait for a gap, instead of accelerating and than merging into the traffic on the main lane (Bjørnskau 1994).

The relationship between age and risk of injury is best known for car drivers. However, among moped and motorcycle riders, young riders also have the highest risk (Ingebrigtsen 1989, 1990). The objective of driving licence age limits is to limit the number of accidents involving drivers who, because of their age, are not fit to drive motor vehicles.

**Description of the measure**

At present, the following limits for driving licences or provisional driving licences apply in Norway with respect to:

- the age at which one can start practising learning to drive
- the earliest age at which one can acquire an ordinary driving licence for the first time
- the latest age at which one can acquire a driving licence for the first time.

An overview is provided in Table 6.1.1 (Cappelen Akademisk Forlag 2003).

New regulations for practice driving have come into effect in March 2004. Mainly, practice driving is allowed for 2 years before the minimum age for obtaining an ordinary driving licence for car, moped, motorcycle, tractor and snow scooter, but in some cases, not before the age of 15 years.

Ordinary driving licences A, B, BE, S and T are valid until the licence holder reaches 100 years of age. After the age of 70, drivers must always keep a medical certificate with their driving licence. There is no upper age limit for driving licences in Norway, apart from acquiring a driving licence for the first time. Driving licences C, CE, D and DE are valid for 10 years. The upper age limits for licence C, CE, D, DE, D1 and DE1 do not apply to drivers who had licence in one of these classes earlier. Driving licences in these classes have a shorter period of validity if the holder is 60 years old or above. On expiry of the period of validity, a new driving test is not normally required. The licence is renewed when the licence holder appears at the public roads administration and pays the fee for the issuing of a new licence. In 1991, 87.5% of all B licences were issued to persons between 18 and 24 years.

In the majority of European countries, the age limit for driving licences for cars is 18 years. In Great Britain, it is 17 years. In the majority of American states, the licensing

*Table 6.1.1: Age limits for practice driving and issuing of driving licences (regulation valid from 1 March 2004)*

| Driving licence class | Practice driving permitted from | Driving licence first issued at age | Driving licence last issued at age |
|---|---|---|---|
| M Moped | 15 years | 16 years/18 years (moped over 150 kg) | No limit |
| A Motorcycle (all) | 17 years/20 years (heavy MC) | 21 years/18 years (heavy MC if less than 2 years experience) | No limit |
| A1 Light motorcycle | 15 years | 16 years | No limit |
| S Snow scooter | | 16 years | No limit |
| T Tractor | 15 years | 16 years | No limit |
| B/BE Passenger car, van | 16 years | 18 years | No limit |
| E Trailer for B, C, C1, D, D1 | Same as class BE, C1E, CE, D1E and DE, respectively | | |
| C/CE Truck | 18 years[1] | 21 years[2] | 60 years |
| C1/C1E Light truck | 18 years[1] | 18 years | 65 years |
| D/DE Bus | 20 years/19 years (if part of vocational training) | 21 years | 60 years |
| D1/D1 E Minibus | 20 years/19 years(if part of vocational training) | 21 years | 65 years |

[1]Practice driving in classes C, CE, C1, C1E, D, DE, D1 and D1E requires driving licence B (not relevant if part of vocational training).
[2]18 years if licence class B available and if licence is part of vocational training.

age is 16 years. In some areas, it is 15 years and in a few places, it is 17 years. In New Zealand, the licensing age for cars is 15 years, but the driving licence is graduated, which means that new drivers do not have full driving privileges from the first day.

## Effect on accidents

In the course of the first 5–7 years of driving, the accident rate drops dramatically. In a Norwegian study, it was found that the number of accidents in a group of drivers who had the driving licence for 8–10 months was reduced by 50% compared with drivers who had the driving licence for only 1–2 months (Sagberg 1997). The accident risk during the first months after obtaining the driving licence depends on the length of the period with practice driving and the amount of practice driving. A Swedish study has investigated the effects of reducing the age limit for practice driving from 18 to 16 years. A reduction of the number of accidents by 35% was found during the first year after obtaining the unrestricted driving licence among the drivers who actually had started practice driving at the age of 16 (Gregersen 1997). A similar study has been conducted in Norway after the reduction of the age limit for practice driving to the age of 16. In this study, no difference was found between the accident numbers of drivers who had started practice driving at the age of 16 and drivers who had started practice driving at the age of 17 (Sagberg 2002). The difference between the Norwegian and the Swedish study results may be explained with a far larger amount of practice driving in Sweden compared with Norway.

***Effects of the age of new drivers on accidents.*** The decrease in risk in the first years of driving is due to a combination of age, experience and other factors. Young drivers are usually also inexperienced. It is therefore difficult to separate the effect of age as such from the effect of experience and annual driving distances. A number of studies have investigated the partial effect of (increasing) age. These studies have controlled for the effects on accidents of other variables such as experience and annual driving distance.

Ferdun, Peck and Coppin (1967) (USA): car drivers
Shaoul (1975) (Great Britain): car drivers
Spolander (1983) (Sweden): car drivers
Drummond (1986) (Australia): car drivers
Glad (1988) (Norway): car drivers
Engel and Krogsgård Thomsen (1989) (Denmark): moped drivers
Ingebrigtsen (1990) (Norway): motorcycle drivers
Maycock, Lockwood and Lester (1991) (Great Britain): car drivers
Forsyth, Maycock and Sexton (1995) (Great Britain): car drivers
Rutter and Quine (1996) (Great Britain): motorcycle drivers

The best of these studies are the two most recent British studies of car drivers. On the basis of these two studies, the effect on accidents of the drivers' age at the time of obtaining the driving licence has been estimated as shown in Table 6.1.2.

*Table 6.1.2: Effects on accidents of increasing the drivers age at the time of obtaining the driving licence with 1 year during the first year after obtaining the driving licence*

| | Percentage change in the number of accidents | | |
|---|---|---|---|
| Increase of drivers age at the time of obtaining the driving licence | Type of accidents affected | Best estimate | 95% Confidence interval |
| From 16 to 17 years | All accidents | −10 | (−20; +5) |
| From 17 to 18 years | All accidents | −7 | (−15; +1) |
| From 18 to 19 years | All accidents | −6 | (−17; +4) |
| From 19 to 20 years | All accidents | −6 | (−22; +13) |
| From 20 to 21 years | All accidents | −5 | (−29; +27) |

The accident risk seems to be reduced with increasing age. The largest decreases have been found in the youngest age groups. None of the effects is statistically significant. The results are all the same likely to be realistic. All results point in the same direction and the results are consistent in all of the studies cited above. A similar studies of drivers of heavy motorcycles (Ingebrigtsen 1990) also found that an increase of the beginner age from 18 to 19 years led to a reduction of accident risk by about 10% (95% CI [−16%; −4%]).

On the basis of the results shown in Table 6.1.1, it can be calculated that the accident risk of drivers aged 21 is 16% smaller than that of the drivers aged 18. This difference is far smaller than the difference in accident risk between these two ages that has been found in other studies (between 50% and 60%). This is due to the fact that the results in Table 6.1.1 show the isolated effects of increasing age, whereas the total decrease of the accident risk with increasing age is a combined effect of increasing age, experience and other factors that affect a drivers' accident risk.

These results do not say much about the potential effects of changing the age limits for obtaining a driving licence of a certain class. Changing the age limit may not only affect accidents with vehicles in the respective category but also accidents with other vehicles or modes of transport. For example, reducing the minimum age for obtaining a driver licence for cars may make mopeds less attractive, and reversely, increasing the minimum age for driving a car may increase the amount of moped driving.

The studies by Maycock, Lockwood and Lester (1991) and Forsyth, Maycock and Sexton (1995) have estimated the annual contributions of increasing age and increasing experience on the accident risk of young drivers. Figure 6.1.2 shows the results from

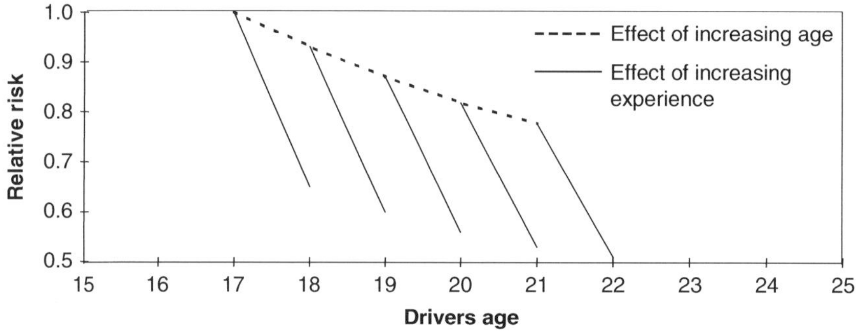


*Figure 6.1.2: Annual contributions of increasing age and increasing experience on the accident risk of young drivers.*

these studies. The dotted line indicates the decrease of accident risk that can be attributed to increasing age. The solid lines indicate the effect on accident risk of 1-year driving experience. These lines drop much steeper than the dotted line that indicates the effect of increasing age, i.e. the effect of 1-year experience is greater than the effect of increasing age by 1 year. The last solid line for experience that starts at the age of 21 ends at the risk that has been found for 22-year-old drivers compared with 17-year-old new drivers, which is about 50 lower than the risk of the 17-year-old new drivers (value 0.5 in Figure 6.1.2).

***Effects of changes in age limit for driving licences.*** Only two studies have been found of the effects of changing the age limit for driving licences. In Quebec, Canada, the age limit for driving licence for car was reduced from 18 to 16 years in 1962. It has been estimated that this led to an increase in the number of accidents (all levels of injury severity and all road user groups) of 12%, an increase in the number of injury accidents of 4% and an increase in the number of fatalities of 20% (Gaudry 1987). In Denmark, the age limit for moped riding was raised from 15 to 16 years in 1980. The number of injury accidents with moped riders aged 15 years or less went down by 80% (−82%, −78%), when drivers aged 20 years or more were used as comparison group (Engel and Krogsgård Thomsen 1989). The study does not show whether the number of accidents with 15-year-old drivers increased in other road user groups.

***Older drivers' risk levels – upper age limits.*** Older drivers have an injury rate that is somewhat higher than that of middle-aged drivers. If the risk of injury for all drivers is set equal to 1.0, the corresponding rate for older drivers has been estimated to the numbers given in Table 6.1.3 in a number of studies.

The studies from Norway and Sweden found inconsistent results for drivers in the age group 65–74 years. These drivers may possibly have a slightly higher injury accident risk than the average for all drivers, but the difference is small. Drivers who are older

*Table 6.1.3: Older drivers' risk of injury accident in Norway and Sweden according to a number of studies (average risk = 1.0)*

| | | Average = 1.00 | |
|---|---|---|---|
| Study | Country and year | 65–74 years | 75 years and older |
| Bjørnskau (1988) | Norway 1984–85 | 0.83 | 3.30 |
| Bjørnskau (1993) | Norway 1991–92 | 1.54 | 1.65 |
| Bjørnskau (2000) | Norway 1997–98 | 0.94 | 1.94 |
| Thulin (1987) | Sweden 1984–85 | 1.20 | 5.00 |
| Thulin and Nilsson (1994) | Sweden 1992 | 0.69 | 2.19 |

than 75 years clearly have a higher risk of injury accidents than the average driver. In both Norway and Sweden, it appears that the increase in risk for the older drivers has reduced over time. A possible explanation for this tendency is that older drivers are now more experienced and, to a large extent, are more used to a heavily motorised society than they were a few years ago.

In spite of the high risk, the absolute number of injury accidents among older drivers is considerably lower than among the youngest drivers. Many older drivers drive less often and only in simple traffic conditions, that is to say during daylight, on roads they know and at times when traffic is light. No country has introduced an upper age limit for driving licences.

In Norway, a medical certificate is required for drivers above the age of 70. This is intended to ensure that the older drivers who are not fit to drive a car for health reasons are prevented from driving. However, it is known that this system is interpreted liberally (Brækhus 1996), so it must be assumed that a number of older drivers with health impairments that increase the accident rate are still driving. A selection of drivers based only on age would result in many 'false positives', i.e. many drivers who actually are fit to drive would lose their driving licence. More valid criteria would therefore be required to identify drivers with increased accident risk (see Section 6.2).

A Norwegian study has evaluated the validity of several tests of vision and cognitive functions that were assumed to be relevant for driving skills (Ulleberg and Sagberg 2003). Driving abilities were assessed by experienced driving instructors and tests. Even if the driving skills of drivers above 75 years were rated somewhat lower than those of drivers between 69 and 74 years, the results do not indicate that age alone is a significant predictor of driving skills. Four tests of vision and cognitive functions were more valid indicators of driving skills.

### Effect on mobility

Driving licence age limits may have two effects on mobility. One possible effect concerns travel opportunities. The more stringent the age limit, the fewer the number of drivers. Those who cannot drive must cater to their needs for transport in other ways or refrain from travelling. The other possible effect concerns the quality of the traffic flow. It is possible that by removing all drivers who drive more slowly than others from traffic, traffic flow could improve in certain situations (Bjørnskau 1994). Neither of the two possible effects mentioned here have been documented.

### Effect on the environment

No effect on the environment of driving licence age limits has been documented. If age limits decrease the total amount of driving, the environmental effects of driving will be reduced as well.

### Costs

The direct costs of administering the system of age limits for driving licences are small. Additional costs may arise for those who have not reached or who have exceeded the age limit and who have to use other modes of travel. The system of medical certificates for older drivers entails some costs, which are described in Section 6.2.

### Cost–benefit analysis

The direct costs of driving licence age limits are small. Any indirect costs are too little known for it to be possible to make a meaningful cost–benefit evaluation.

## 6.2 Health requirements for drivers

### Problem and objective

In road traffic, situations often occur that require quick decisions and reactions from drivers of motor vehicles. According to the law, no one should drive motor vehicles if they are not fit enough to drive safely. The health of the driver is one of the factors determining how fit he or she is to drive.

A Norwegian study of the results of autopsies of 230 killed car drivers found that 27 drivers (12%) had died of natural causes, and not of injuries sustained in the accidents (Alvestad and Haugen 1999). The main causes for these deaths were acute cardiovascular diseases. These accidents are often road departures and occur often at low speeds. This indicates that the drivers had had some advance warnings and had managed to reduce the severity of the accidents.

The objective of regulating driver health is to ensure that all drivers satisfy certain minimum health conditions in order to drive, and to limit the number of drivers who, for health reasons, are not fit to drive.

**Description of the measure**

The health requirements for drivers are laid down in the European driving licence regulations. For driving licence A, B, BE and T, the following requirements for health and fitness apply:

- Visual acuity must be at least 6/12 when both eyes are tested simultaneously, including when a driver uses spectacles or contact lenses. The field of vision must be normal in at least one eye.
- Epileptic seizures or other types of seizures with cramps or loss of consciousness must not have occurred during the last 2 years.
- Locomotion must be adequate for safe and satisfactory manoeuvring of the vehicle.
- With respect to other illnesses, the decision as to whether a driving licence can be issued lies with the Norwegian Public Roads Administration, on the basis of information obtained from the doctor.

For driving licence C, CE, D, DE, D2 and D2E (buses and lorries), the requirements are the same, but there are stricter requirements for visual acuity and the non-occurrence of epilepsy or other attacks involving cramps or loss of consciousness and heart attack or other coronary heart disease.

As a rule, when applying for a driving licence A, B, BE or T in Norway, no medical certificate is required. The applicant gives a statement of health on the application form for the driving licence (Steen and Gjerstad 1993). For applicants who use spectacles or contact lenses while driving, a statement from an authorised optician is normally adequate. Applicants who have had epileptic fits, heart attacks or serious disturbances to the heart rhythm, as well as insulin-dependent diabetics must produce a statement from a specialist. If health problems occur after a driving licence has been issued, the main rule is that the driver must consult his doctor and that the doctor then decides whether the driver is still fit enough to have a driving licence. People who suffer epileptic fits or other type of fits involving cramps or loss of consciousness cannot drive a motor vehicle until 2 years have elapsed since the last attack.

Drivers who hold a licence A, B, BE or T and who are above 70 years need a valid medical certificate. There are, however, no formal requirements for such certificates, and certificates are issued based on subjective judgements of the doctors (Brækhus 1996).

When applying for a driving licence C1(E), C(E), D1(E) and D(E), a medical certificate is required about the occurrence of, e.g. epilepsy, mental disorders, alcohol or drug abuse, diabetes and coronary diseases.

The following section describes the relationship between a number of health impairments and accidents, the relevance of health problems for the total number of accidents in Norway and the effects on accidents of medical checkups for drivers.

## Effect on accidents

***The relationship between health impairments and accidents.*** Estimates of the relative risk of drivers with diseases are summarised in Table 6.2.1. The results are based on a meta-analysis (Vaa 2003) of the effects on traffic safety of diseases that are described in the EU directive about driver licensing (CD 91/439/EEC; The Council of the European Communities 1991). The results are based o the following studies:

- *Visual impairments:* Hofstetter (1976), Hills and Burg (1977), Janke (1983), Decina and Staplin (1993), Gresset and Meyer (1994), Marottoli et al. (1994), McCloskey, Koepsell, Wolf and Buchner (1994), Lewandowski (1995), Johansson (1997), Maag, Vanasse, Dionne and Laberge-Nadeau (1997), Owsley, McGwin and Ball (1998), McGwin, Sims, Pulley and Roseman (2000), Owsley et al. (2002)
- *Hearing impairments:* Coppin and Peck (1965), Ysander (1966), McCloskey, Koepsell, Wolf and Buchner (1994)
- *Arthritis/motoric disorders:* Mäki and Linnoila (1976), MacPherson, Perl, Starmer and Homel (1984), Koepsell et al. (1994), McGwin, Sims, Pulley and Roseman (2000), Vernon et al. (2002)
- *Coronary diseases:* Waller (1965; see Larsen 1976), Waller (1967), Crancer and Quiring (1968; see Larsen 1976), Crancer and O'Neall (1969; see Larsen 1976), MacPherson, Perl, Starmer and Homel (1984), Koepsell et al. (1994), Johansson (1997), McGwin, Sims, Pulley and Roseman (2000), Vernon et al. (2002)
- *Diabetes:* Waller (1965), Crancer and Quiring (1968), Ysander (1970), MacPherson, Perl, Starmer and Homel (1984), Hansotia and Broste (1991), Koepsell et al. (1994), McGwin, Sims, Pulley and Roseman (2000), Vernon et al. (2002)
- *Neurological disorders:* Waller (1965), Hansotia and Broste (1991), Janke (1993), Koepsell et al. (1994), Adler, Rottunda, Bauer and Kuskowski (2000), McGwin, Sims, Pulley and Roseman (2000), Lings (2001), Schultheis, Marheis, Nead and DeLuca (2002), Vernon et al. (2002)
- *Mental disorders:* Waller (1967), Mäki and Linnoila (1976), MacPherson, Perl, Starmer and Homel (1984), Friedland et al. (1988), Ball and Owsley (1991), Drachman and Swearer (1993), Cooper, Tallman, Tuokko and Beattie (1993), Janke (1993), Leveille et al. (1994), Marottoli et al. (1994), Koepsell et al. (1994), Fitten et al. (1995), Trobe et al. (1996), Johansson (1997), Nada-Raja et al. (1997), Bédard, Molloy and Lever (1998), Withaar and Brouwer (1999), McGwin, Sims, Pulley and Roseman (2000), Vernon et al. (2002)

*Table 6.2.1: Relative risk of accidents for drivers with diseases; relative risk of drivers without disease = 1 (Vaa 2003)*

| Diseases | Relative risk | Confidence interval |
|---|---|---|
| ***Visual impairments (all types)*** | 1.09 | (1.04; 1.15) |
| Field of vision | 0.90 | (0.69; 1.17) |
| Progressive eye diseases | 0.86 | (0.50; 1.49) |
| Reduced visual acuity | 1.13 | (1.05; 1.22) |
| Reduced visual acuity (<80%) | 1.19 | (1.07; 1.33) |
| Reduced visual acuity (<50%) | 1.14 | (1.00; 1.29) |
| Reduced visual acuity (<25%) | 1.24 | (1.04; 1.47) |
| ***Hearing impairments*** | 1.19 | (1.02; 1.40) |
| ***Arthritis/motor disorders*** | 1.17 | (1.004; 1.36) |
| ***Coronary diseases (all types)*** | 1.23 | (1.09; 1.38) |
| Cardiac arrhythmia | 1.27 | (1.09. 1.47) |
| Abnormal arterial blood pressure | 1.03 | (0.86; 1.22) |
| Angina pectoris | 1.52 | (1.10; 2.09) |
| Heart attack | 1.09 | (0.62; 1.92) |
| ***Diabetes mellitus*** | 1.56 | (1.31; 1.86) |
| Neurological disorders | 1.75 | (1.61; 1.89) |
| Disease or surgery that affects the central or peripheral nervous system (including stroke, traumatic brain damage, etc.) | 1.35 | (1.08; 1.67) |
| Epilepsy/other seizures | 1.84 | (1.68; 2.02) |
| ***Mental disorders*** | 1.72 | (1.48; 1.99) |
| Serious mental disorders | 2.01 | (1.60; 2.52) |
| Serious disorders related to ageing, e.g. Alzheimer, dementia | 1.45 | (1.14; 1.84) |
| Alcoholism | 2.00 | (1.89; 2.12) |
| ***Pharmaceuticals and psychoactive substances*** | 1.58 | (1.45; 1.73) |
| Misuse of pharmaceuticals/drugs | 1.96 | (1.70; 2.25) |
| Prescribed use of pharmaceuticals/drugs | 1.49 | (1.35; 1.64) |
| Psychoactive substances (including alcohol) | 1.96 | (1.74; 2.20) |
| Cyclic antidepressants | 1.42 | (1.33; 1.52) |
| Analgetics (opiates) | 1.21 | (1.08; 1.36) |
| Antihistamines | 1.10 | (0.91; 1.32) |
| Benzodiazepine (including diazepam) | 1.54 | (1.24; 1.90) |
| ***Renal diseases: serious kidney failure*** | 0.87 | (0.54; 1.34) |

- *Alcoholism:* Janke (1993), Vernon et al. (2002)
- *Pharmaceuticals and psychoactive substances:* Bø et al. (1975; see Larsen 1976), Mäki and Linnoila (1976), Smart and Fejer (1976), Honkanen et al. (1980), Hingson et al. (1982), MacPherson, Perl, Starmer and Homel (1984), Benzodiazepine/Driving Collaborative Group (1993), Beylich et al. (1994), Leveille et al. (1994), Koepsell et al. (1994), Marottoli et al. (1994), Hemmelgarn et al. (1997), Neutel (1998), McGwin, Sims, Pulley and Roseman (2000), Longo et al. (2000), Longo, Lokan and White (2001), Mathijssen, Koornstra and Commandeur (2002), Vernon et al. (2002)
- *Renal diseases:* Ysander (1966), McGwin, Sims, Pulley and Roseman (2000)

The results in Table 6.2.1 are based on studies that vary considerably in size and quality. Many studies have not sufficiently controlled for confounding factors, i.e. for factors that are related to the diseases and that affect accident risk. Many studies include only small numbers of subjects. Not all studies provide information about the average annual driving distance of the drivers in the study and control groups. Information about the severity of the accidents is not always available, but it is likely that most studies include injury and property damage only accidents. All main groups of diseases, except renal diseases, have been found to increase accident risk significantly.

The largest increase has been found for alcoholism, which increases accident risk by about 100%. Alcoholism refers only to the diagnosis of the disease, and not to drink-driving that has a far larger effect on accident risk. Other diseases with large effects on accidents are neurological diseases, mental diseases and use or misuse of pharmaceuticals or drugs. The increase of accident risk in these groups of diseases is between about 60% and 100%. The highest relative risk was found for sleeping diseases (including narcolepsy and sleep apnoe). The relative risk for these diseases has been found to be 3.71 (Vaa 2003). These diseases are, however, not included in the list of diseases in the Appendix of the EU directive.

Diseases with relatively small effects on accidents are visual impairments, hearing impairments, motoric disorders and cardiovascular diseases. These diseases increase accident risk by about 10–20%. Reduced visual acuity means the ability to perceive details that are not in movement.

The accident risk of physically disabled drivers with specially designed cars has been studied in Norway (Sagberg, Amundsen, Glad and Midtland 2003). The number of accidents per million kilometre was 10.3 for this group of drivers and 10.1 for all drivers. This is practically the same risk. Injury and property damage only accidents reported to insurance companies were included in this analysis.

***Relevance of illness and health problems for the total number of accidents in Norway.*** The significance of these health impairments for the total number of accidents depends on the prevalence in the population. A disease that increases accident risk is of greater importance for the total number of accidents if 20% of all drivers have this disease than when 5% of all drivers have the disease. For several types of health impairments, the prevalence among drivers has been estimated as shown in Table 6.2.1. These figures are adjusted for the fact that the proportions of licence holders are smaller in the older age groups, in which the impairments have a higher prevalence than in younger age groups. On the basis of the relative risk of drivers with health impairments and the estimated prevalence of these impairments among drivers, Elvik (2000) has estimated the proportions of accidents that might be avoided if drivers with health impairments would be eliminated from traffic. These proportions are also shown in Table 6.2.2. They are based on the assumption that drivers with diseases drive as much as other drivers. If drivers with diseases drive less, the proportions of accidents that might be avoided by eliminating these drivers from traffic are over-estimated.

***Effects on accidents of medical checkups for drivers.*** Only one study has been found that tried to evaluate the effects on accidents of medical checkups for drivers (Popkin and Stewart 1992). The study is from North Carolina in the United States and compared the number of accidents per driver per year before and after drivers underwent medical checkups. The results of the study are compiled in Table 6.2.2. Drivers who underwent medical checkups are compared with normal drivers, that is to say drivers of the same gender, age and ethnic background. The table shows that drivers who had undergone medical checkups had significantly more accidents than normal drivers. This is a result of the way in which drivers are referred for medical checkups. Such referrals are made in North Carolina when a driver, on the basis of the official accident record (which contains data of the accident history for the individual driver), appears to have an abnormally high number of accidents, and it is suspected that this may be due to health problems. The most common reason for referral is suspicion of alcoholism. Drivers in this group are not shown in Table 6.2.3.

*Table 6.2.2: Estimates of the prevalence of health impairments among drivers*

| Health impairment | Source | Prevalence among drivers (%) | Accidents avoided if drivers with impairments were eliminated from traffic (%) |
|---|---|---|---|
| Visual impairments | Stensholt, Bergsaker and Skog (1992) | 3 | 0.39 |
| Hearing impairments | SSB (1996) | 2 | 0.38 |
| Motoric disorders | SSB (1996) | 10 | 1.67 |
| Coronary diseases | SSB (1996) | 10 | 2.25 |
| Mental disorders | SSB (1996) | 5 | 3.47 |

*Table 6.2.3: Changes in the number of accidents per driver per year before and after medical checkups of drivers in North Carolina, USA, specified for different illnesses*

| | | Accidents per driver per year | | |
|---|---|---|---|---|
| Group of illness | Number of drivers | Before medical checkups | After medical checkups | Normal drivers |
| Heart diseases | 1,274 | 0.069 | 0.048 | 0.044 |
| Strokes, fainting, fits, etc. | 1,035 | 0.218 | 0.088 | 0.058 |
| Somatic illnesses | 289 | 0.166 | 0.074 | 0.054 |
| Failing eyesight | 263 | 0.090 | 0.038 | 0.052 |
| Deteriorating mental condition | 265 | 0.119 | 0.072 | 0.062 |

The type of illness a driver has is identified at a medical checkup. Necessary medication and treatment will be prescribed. Furthermore, the doctor gives advice on how the driver should adapt his driving to his illness. In some cases, restrictions on the driving licence are also imposed. Table 6.2.3 shows that number of accidents per driver per year went down in all groups following medical checkups. However, due to the way drivers are selected, this reduction may be due to regression to the mean. Popkin and Stewart (1992) did not control for regression to the mean.

Experience shows that regression to the mean in driver accident data can be very large (Weber 1972, Hauer and Persaud 1983). On the basis of information given by Hauer and Persaud (1983), the regression effect has been calculated. The expected number of accidents without medical checkups is calculated for the different groups and compared with number of accidents following medical checkups. The expected number of accidents per driver per year without a medical checkup was estimated to 0.060 for heart disease (actual number 0.048), 0.082 for strokes, fainting, etc. (actual 0.088), 0.074 for somatic illnesses (actual 0.074), 0.063 for sight problems (actual 0.038) and 0.067 for mental impairment (actual 0.072). In the majority of groups, the decrease in the number of accidents following medical checkups is no greater than could be expected from regression to the mean. Taking all groups of illnesses together, the annual number of accidents per driver went down by 6% after medical checkups (from an expected total of 434 accidents over the course of 2 years to 407).

**Effect on mobility**

Driver health requirements may have two types of effect on mobility. One effect is to limit mobility, that is to say, to reduce travel opportunities for drivers who, as a result of poor health, are excluded from driving cars. These people must meet their needs for travel without driving.

The other possible effect concerns the quality of the traffic flow. One possible effect is particularly connected with older drivers. Senile dementia can reduce the ability to find the way. An American study (Kaszniak, Keyl and Albert 1991) found that 81% of drivers with senile dementia had got lost at one time or another. Drivers with dementia can also make serious mistakes such as driving on to motorways in the wrong direction. This type of behaviour creates dangerous situations and can affect traffic flow. The actual effects have not been quantified.

**Effect on the environment**

No effects on the environment of health requirements for drivers have been documented.

**Costs**

The direct costs of health requirements for drivers are related to the medical checkups which must be carried out to ensure that drivers satisfy the health requirements. Medical certificates are mandatory for applications for driving licences C, CE, D and DE (buses and lorries), and for drivers above 70 years of age for all driving licence classes.

In 1995, some 7,000 new driving licences C, CE, D and DE were issued in Norway. It is assumed that a similar number of medical checkups were carried out. Further, it can be assumed that annually there are some 20,000 driving licence holders who reach 70 years of age and therefore require a medical certificate (this figure can be expected to increase over time). After the age of 75, the medical certificate must be renewed annually. It is assumed that there are around 5,000 renewals of this type each year. The cost of each medical checkup is set at NOK 300. Thus, the costs will be NOK 2.1 million for applicants for driving licences for buses and lorries and NOK 7.5 million for licence holders over the age of 70 years.

**Cost–benefit analysis**

The direct costs of the current system of medical checkups for drivers correspond to the costs of some five injury accidents reported to the police each year. It is not known how many drivers are refused driving licences each year, or who have their licences suspended because they do not fulfil the health requirements for drivers. It is possible the figure may be large enough to prevent five injury accidents per year.

It has been documented that a number of drivers who ought to wear spectacles or contact lenses while driving do not do so, and thus see less well than they could do with optimal correction of vision (Stensholt, Bergsaker and Skog 1992). Nonetheless, only around 3% of drivers do not meet the sight requirements for drivers. With optimal correction, this proportion can be reduced to 0%. All that is normally required is that the driver visits the optician or eye specialist and obtains spectacles or contact lenses.

If the cost of glasses or contact lenses is set at NOK 2,000 per driver (a relatively low figure, since advanced sight correction in the form of progressive spectacles normally costs more), the total cost will be around NOK 160 million (one-off expense). The number of injury accidents prevented can be estimated at around 40. Reduced accident costs are around NOK 80 million. This indicates that the gain in the form of fewer accidents of improving the vision of those drivers who have poor vision is not large enough to offset the cost of this. However, improved vision will also increase driving comfort, and most people who are wearing glasses or contact lenses do so also while not driving.

The mean annual number of accidents (including property damage) per driver per year in Norway is around 0.09. A reduction in this number of 6% as a result of medical checkups (see Table 6.2.3) corresponds to 0.0054 accidents prevented per driver per year, of which 0.0003 are injury accidents and around 0.0051 are property damage accidents. The savings from this are around NOK 675 per year. Annual medical checkups costing less than this per driver per year can therefore be cost-effective. In practice, a 6% decrease in the expected number of accidents cannot be expected for all drivers because the majority of drivers probably do not have health problems affecting their accident rate.

Cost–benefit analyses of health requirements for drivers have been conducted in the EU project IMMORTAL. It is estimated that the benefits of denying or withdrawing a driving licence is beneficial only if the accident risk is at least six times as high as the accident risk of an average driver. None of the health problems studied has been found to increase accident risk by a factor of 6 or greater. The analyses do not indicate that health requirements for drivers may be beneficial from a societal point of view.

## 6.3 Driver performance standards

**Problem and objective**

A certain level of knowledge and skill is needed to be able to drive motor vehicles safely. The ability to learn to drive motor vehicles safely varies among the population.

If there were no minimum standards for driver performance to obtain driving licences, actual knowledge and skill would vary considerably among drivers. Minimum standards for driver performance are intended to prevent people who, due to ignorance or a lack of skill, are unsuitable to drive motor vehicles from obtaining driving licences. They are designed to prevent new drivers from being involved in accidents as a result of a lack of elementary driving proficiency. Another objective with these standards is to promote mobility by setting minimum standards for adapting to other traffic.

## Description of the measure

In Norway, the driver performance standards for cars cover (Statens vegvesen, Vegdirektoratet 1994) the following aspects: Drivers must be aware of the limitations of different road user groups and they should know how fatigue, age, the use of alcohol and illnesses affect driver behaviour and performance. Drivers must also have some knowledge about how the vehicle functions, and be able to decide whether brakes, tyres and wheels, steering, headlights and safety equipment are in good condition. Knowledge of the road and the traffic environment includes knowledge of traffic regulations, and all traffic signs. Requirements for basic driving skills are described in great detail. They include, among many other things, hill starts, correct behaviour in junctions, choice of driving lanes, judging speed and distance, overtaking and correct use of headlights at night. In addition, the driver must know about the risks involved in driving, and the number and causes of traffic accidents. Requirements for knowledge of behaviour in traffic also include traffic regulations and other rules for behaviour in traffic. With regard to driver responsibility, the driver must know the rules regarding responsibilities in the event of traffic accidents and motor vehicle insurance requirements.

Effects on accidents have been investigated for certain knowledge requirements for drivers and for specific skill trainings. Specific trainings include skid training, night driving courses and courses for older drivers. It has also been investigated how drivers' accident risk is affected by being active in motor sports.

## Effect on accidents

Effects on accidents have been investigated for certain knowledge requirements and for trainings of specific skills.

***Knowledge requirements.*** The relationship between drivers' theoretical knowledge and their accident rate has been evaluated in a number of studies, including

Waller and Goo (1969) (USA)
Wallace and Crancer (1971) (USA)
Hoinville, Berthoud and Mackie (1972) (Great Britain)
Pedersen and Christensen (1973) (Norway)
Raymond and Tatum (1977) (Great Britain)
Dreyer and Janke (1979) (USA)
Stoke (1980) (USA)
Strang, Deutsch, James and Manders (1982) (Australia)

The main finding in the studies is that there is no clear statistical relationship between different indicators of knowledge and driver accident rates.

An early British study investigated the relationship between knowledge and accident rate among motorcyclists (Raymond and Tatum 1977). The study found that among riders who had undergone formal training, there was no association between knowledge and accident rates. However, among riders who had *not* had formal training, but who had only learnt informally (through relatives, friends, etc.), there was a positive correlation between knowledge and accident rates. The better the rider's knowledge, the higher the accident rate.

Drivers with specific learning disabilities may have a higher accident rate than other drivers. An American study (Waller and Hall 1980) found that drivers who chose to undergo an oral theory test for the driving test had 20% more accidents per driver than drivers who took the standard, written theory test.

Taken together, the studies that have evaluated the relationship between drivers' knowledge and accident rate do not provide a basis for clear conclusions. Most of the studies are old and methodologically relatively poor. It is not always clear what knowledge has been studied.

***Training of specific skills.*** A number of studies have evaluated how training in special driving skills affects driver accident rates. A number of different types of skills and trainings have been studied. Table 6.3.1 shows best estimates of the effects on accidents per driver on the basis of the following studies.

The effects on accidents of *skid training* have been studied by

Eriksson (1983) (Sweden): ambulance drivers
Hess and Born (1987) (Switzerland): volunteers among car drivers
Glad (1988) (Norway): new car drivers

*Table 6.3.1: Effects of skill and training of skill for drivers on the number of accidents per driver*

| | Percentage change in the number of accidents | | |
|---|---|---|---|
| Accident severity | Type of accident affected | Best estimate | 95% Confidence interval |
| ***Skid training*** | | | |
| Unspecified | Accidents in icy conditions, passenger cars | +12 | (+7; +18) |
| Unspecified | Accidents in icy conditions, ambulance drivers | +45 | (−35; +220) |
| Unspecified | Accidents in icy conditions, drivers of heavy vehicles | +22 | (+9; +36) |
| ***Night driving course for passenger cars*** | | | |
| Unspecified | Accidents in darkness | +11 | (+4; +20) |
| ***Courses for older drivers*** | | | |
| Unspecified | Accidents with older drivers | −1 | (−5; +1) |
| ***Drivers who take part in motor sports compared with normal drivers*** | | | |
| Injury accidents | All types of accident | −48 | (−69; +48) |
| Property damage only accidents | All types of accident | −37 | (−49; −23) |

Siegrist and Ramseier (1992) (Switzerland): volunteers among car drivers
Keskinen, Hatakka, Katila and Laapotti (1992) (Finland): new car drivers
Christensen and Glad (1996) (Norway): new heavy vehicle drivers

The effects on accidents of *night driving* have been studied by

Glad (1988) (Norway): new car drivers
Keskinen, Hatakka, Katila and Laapotti (1992) (Finland): new car drivers

The effects on accidents of *courses for older drivers* have been studied by

McKnight, Simone and Weidman (1982) (USA)
Janke (1994) (USA)
Berube (1995) (USA)
Ulleberg (2006) (Norway)

Comparisons of *drivers taking part in motor sports* and normal drivers have been made by

Williams and O'Neill (1974) (USA)
Moe (1992) (Norway)

Skid training and night driving courses are intended to make drivers particularly aware of the hazards of slippery roads and darkness. The majority of the courses in skid training and night driving, which have been studied, are also intended to teach skills in avoiding accidents in critical situations, for example practising evasive manoeuvres and the control of skidding in curves.

***Skid training*** appears to increase the number of accidents for drivers who have received the training. The increase is smallest for passenger car drivers and greatest for ambulance drivers. The explanation for these results is not known. However, it is possible that training that places emphasis on mastering slippery roads may give some drivers an unrealistic belief in their own ability to drive on icy roads. This may result in less careful behaviour in icy conditions.

Courses for ***night driving*** do not in general appear to reduce the number of accidents.

***Improvement courses for older drivers.*** Courses for older drivers are mostly voluntary and aim at improving driving skills. These courses are based on the assumption that driving skills decrease from an age of 65. Courses for older drivers do not appear to affect the number of accidents per driver to any great extent. The explanation for this is not known. A possible reason is that older drivers continue to drive to a higher age when they have taken a course than they would otherwise have done.

***Drivers who are active in motor sports.*** In the United States and Norway, studies have been carried out where the accident involvement in normal traffic for drivers who are active in motor sports has been compared with the accident rate for normal drivers. These studies indirectly indicate the effects of driving skills, since drivers who are actively involved in motor sport must be assumed to have better driving skills than other drivers.

Without taking into account difference in annual driving distance, drivers who are active in motor sports have on average 23% more accidents per driver in normal traffic than other drivers. Annual driving distance was not stated in the US study. In the Norwegian study, this information was included. It found that motor sport drivers had a 48% (−69%, +48%) lower risk of being involved in injury accidents per kilometre driven than normal drivers. The motor sport drivers' risk of being involved in property damage only accidents was 37% (−49%, −23%) lower than for normal drivers. Motor sport drivers drove much longer distances each year than normal drivers. This can probably explain some of the difference in the accident rate. The accident rate per kilometre declines the further one drives per year (Forsyth, Maycock and Sexton 1995).

Most of the results presented show that training in special skills does not reduce the accident rate. There is a tendency in the opposite direction. It cannot be concluded from this that the good driving skills per se are detrimental to traffic safety. The explanation for the results given above is probably related to the way in which a driver chooses to apply his skills in traffic. A driver who knows that he or she has good skills may be tempted to adopt less careful driving behaviour than a driver who is less sure of his own abilities.

**Effect on mobility**

The effects, if any, of driver performance standards on mobility have not been documented. One of the requirements for drivers is that they must be able to drive in a way that does not unnecessarily obstruct other traffic.

**Effect on the environment**

No effects on the environment of driver performance standards have been documented.

**Costs**

The direct costs of setting driver performance standards are small. The standards may indirectly lead to costs in that training is necessary to meet them. The costs of training are described in other chapters.

Costs of setting driver performance standards in Norway include the costs of inspecting driving schools and of those who train driving instructors. The annual costs incurred by the Norwegian Public Roads Administration in Norway for inspecting driving schools can be estimated at NOK 8 million (Statens vegvesen, Vegdirektoratet 1993, 1995). The cost of running the state driver instructor school is around NOK 10 million per year (Borger 1992).

**Cost–benefit analysis**

No cost–benefit analyses of the driver performance standards have been found. It is not possible to analyse costs and benefits of these standards without including the costs of the training, which is required to satisfy the standards. Costs and benefits of training are dealt with in Sections 6.5–6.8.

A cost–benefit analysis of courses for older drivers has been computed by Ulleberg (2006). According to this analysis, the benefits of the course that has been evaluated in Norway are about three times the cost, when accidents are reduced by 20%.

Gebers and Peck (2003) have estimated the accident reduction that must be obtained in order for a course to be cost-effective. Measures that cost $5 per driver are cost-effective when accidents are reduced by 1%, measures that cost $25 would be cost-effective when accidents are reduced by 4% and measures that cost $100 per drivers would be cost-effective when accidents are reduced by 7%. This analysis refers to different measures. It is based on the assumption that all drivers for whom the probability of getting involved in an accident during the following 3 years are participating.

## 6.4 Basic driver training

### Problem and objective

Safe driving requires good knowledge, good skills and a good understanding of risk. These skills can be acquired by means of continuous and varied exposure to traffic, that is by means of driving. Drivers who are experienced have acquired high skills and are, partly for that reason, much safer than drivers with little experience. Young and inexperienced drivers have a considerably higher accident rate than other drivers.

Around 1980, drivers in Norway aged 18 and 19 years had an injury rate around six to seven times higher than the average for all drivers. In the middle of the 1980s and in 1991–92, the risk for drivers aged between 18 and 19 years was around three to four times higher than the average (Bjørnskau 1988, 1993). Drivers aged between 20 and 24 had an injury rate that was around 1.5 times higher than the average. A similar pattern is found in all motorised countries. Figure 6.4.1 shows young drivers' relative risk of injury in 10 motorised countries when the average risk for drivers is set equal to 1.00. The risk estimates are taken from different sources and apply to slightly different years, but show a striking consistency (Norway: Bjørnskau 1993, Sweden: Thulin and Nilsson 1994, Denmark: Danmarks statistik 1982, The Netherlands: Poppe 1993, Germany: Hautzinger and Tassaux 1989, France: Fontaine 1988, Great Britain: Broughton 1988, United States: Massie, Campbell and Williams 1995, Canada: Stewart and Sanderson 1984, New Zealand: Toomath and White 1982).

In all countries represented in Figure 6.4.1, the youngest drivers had an injury rate that is three to five times higher than average. Accidents with young and inexperienced drivers are therefore a great problem in many countries. Comprehensive research has

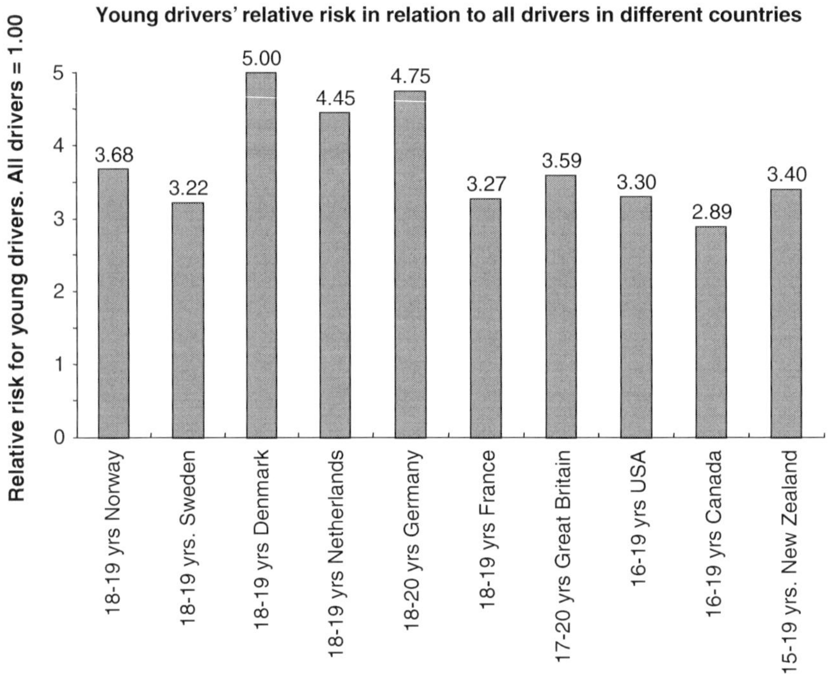


*Figure 6.4.1: Young drivers' relative risk of injury in different countries. Average for all drivers in each country = 1.00.*

been carried out to find solutions to this problem (Marek and Sten 1977, Summala 1985, Jonah 1986, Michon 1988, Gregersen 1995).

The question posed by many is: how can the safety benefits of increased driving experience be transferred to new drivers in such a way that the high accident rate can be reduced? Driver training is intended to give new drivers a lower accident rate than they would otherwise have had, and speed up the decrease in the accident rate that occurs as drivers become more experienced.

## Description of the measure

Basic driver training is here taken to mean formal training of new drivers, i.e. drivers who have not previously driven vehicles. Formal training is formally organised training, given according to an educational programme at private or state driving schools. Purely informal training is self-training and training given by family members or friends. As a rule, this type of training does not follow any formal plan. Integrated driver training is a mixture of formal and informal training. Integrated training is an organised combination of driving lessons at driving schools and private training with parents or others acting as mentors. The mentor and the pupil are given a form of 'homework' from the driving school in the form of a number of driving lessons (or possibly a number of kilometres driven) to be completed within a certain time.

### Effect on accidents

***Formal training compared with informal training.*** A number of studies have compared formal driver training with informal training. The results presented here are based on the following studies:

Ferdun, Peck and Coppin (1967) (USA)
Skelly (1968) (Great Britain)
McGuire (1971) (USA)
Harrington (1972) (USA)
Shaoul (1975) (Great Britain)
Schuster (1978) (USA)
Dreyer and Janke (1979) (USA)
McKnight and Edwards (1982) (USA)
Strang, Deutsch, James and Manders (1982) (Australia)
Stock et al. (1983) (USA)
Wynne-Jones and Hurst (1984) (New Zealand)
Lund, Williams and Zador (1986) (USA)
Glad (1988) (Norway)
Keskinen, Hatakka, Katila and Laapotti (1992) (Finland)
Gregersen (1993) (Sweden)
Hatakka, Keskinen, Katila and Laapotti (1996) (Finland)

For the most part, these results refer to the number of accidents per driver or per kilometre driven during the first 1–2 years after the driving test has been passed. The results do not indicate that formal driver training reduces accidents among novice drivers in this period.

The results vary greatly, depending on study design. The best studies were designed as experiments, where drivers were randomly distributed between formal and informal training. This type of study design controls for all confounding factors. Experiments with formal training show that drivers who have undergone formal training have exactly the same mean number of accidents per driver ($0 \pm 4\%$) as drivers who have not undergone formal training. However, the number of accidents per kilometre has been found to be 11% higher (95% CI [+8; +15]) among drivers with formal training than those who have not undergone formal training.

When all studies are combined (experiments and poorer study designs), they show that drivers who have undertaken formal training have 2% fewer accidents (95% CI [−4; 0]) per driver than those who have not. The number of accidents per kilometre driven, all studies taken together, is 4% lower for drivers with formal training than for drivers without such training (95% CI [−6; −2]).

***Elements in formal training that can affect the effect of formal training.*** The results given above refer to all types of formal training. However, there are a number of elements in formal training that can influence the effect of such training such as amount of training and the training method. Trainings of specific skills are described in Sections 6.3 and 6.4.

***Amount.*** A number of the studies listed above state the number of driving lessons pupils have had in formal training. Figure 6.4.2 shows the relationship between the number of driving lessons and the effect of formal training on driver accident rates. The figure shows that an increasing number of driving lessons is related to an *increasing* accident rate. Normally, it is assumed that an increase in the amount of training reduces accident rate. The results in Figure 6.4.2 come for the most part from experimental studies, in which the pupils themselves did not choose the number of driving lessons but were randomly allocated in a training programme. The unexpected result cannot therefore be explained by the assumption that pupils with poorer learning abilities have to take more driving lessons.

***Method.*** The most common form of driving instruction is driving in normal traffic. However, the other methods have also been tested. An early US study (Jones 1973) found that there was no difference in accident rate between drivers who were trained in driving simulators and drivers who were trained in regular traffic. The driving simulators used were, however, relatively simple, and only a few driving lessons (less than 10) were given.

Two studies (Dreyer and Janke 1979, Strang, Deutsch, James and Manders 1982) have compared trainings given in driving ranges and in normal traffic. A driving range is an area of roadway closed to normal traffic and where a simple road system has been constructed. Pupils drive alone in groups and can be directed by the instructor via radio. One study (Dreyer and Janke 1979) found that drivers who were trained in driving ranges had around 33% (−52%; −5%) fewer accidents per driver than drivers

*Figure 6.4.2: Relationship between the number of driving lessons and the effect of formal training on the driver's accident rate.*

who were trained in regular traffic. The other study (Strang, Deutsch, James and Manders 1982) found that drivers who were trained in driving ranges had 12% (−33%; +17%) fewer accidents per kilometre driven than drivers who underwent informal training. A group of drivers who underwent part of the formal training in driving ranges and the rest in regular traffic had 15% fewer accidents (−11%; +48%) per kilometre driven than drivers who only had informal training. None of these differences was statistically significant.

In Sweden, the effects of integrated driver training on accidents have been studied (Gregersen 1993, 1994). The integrated driver training was based on an increased amount of training for new drivers through systematic co-operation between the driving schools and pupils' mentors. No effect on accidents of this type of training was found.

In France, a system of mentor-supported training connected with car insurance has been expanded in recent years (Heggdal, Pedersen and Conradi 1990). A study of the effects of mentor-supported training in France on accidents (Belloc and Ivaldi 1991) concluded that the measure reduced the participants' annual accident rate per kilometre driven by around 24%. The study did not control for potential self-selection bias, i.e. the fact that the measures largely appealed to the safest drivers. Such bias may well have affected the results.

***Changes in basic automobile training in the Nordic countries.*** In 1986, driver training in Denmark was revised. The changes made included (Carstensen 1994): (1) more emphasis was placed on defensive driving, (2) the first 3–4 h of practical training were carried out in driving ranges, (3) exercises in practical training were re-organised, starting with the simplest and going on to more difficult exercises, (4) emergency situation training on ranges was introduced from 1990 and (5) a new theory test was introduced. A study of how these changes affected the number of accidents concluded that the number of accidents involving drivers aged 18 and 19 went down by 7–21%, depending on the method of estimation (Carstensen 1996). This estimate is based on aggregate accident statistics and does not control for changes in annual driving distance per driver.

In 1989, a 'traffic safety package' in driver training was introduced in Norway. This comprised 10 lessons in compulsory country road driving and 8 lessons in theory. Studies (Sikveland and Hagen 1991, Sikveland 1993, 1994, Opdal 1994) of how the traffic safety package affected accidents claim that the total number of accidents among drivers aged 18 and 19 went down by around 25% (95% CI [−30; −25]) in the period after the traffic safety package was introduced. However, the studies contain no information about the number of drivers and their driving distances, and therefore, do not show the effects of the traffic safety package on driver accident rates.

In Finland, driver training in two phases was introduced in 1990 (Keskinen, Hatakka, Katila and Laapotti 1992). Among other measures, compulsory skid training and night driving courses were introduced. The driving licence issued after phase one of the training is provisional. Ordinary driving licences are issued when phase two of the training has been completed. A study of how the new driver training system in Finland has affected traffic safety found no difference in the number of accidents per kilometre driven between drivers who had undergone the old training and drivers who had undergone the new training.

In Sweden, the age limit for starting to learn driving in passenger cars was reduced from 17.5 years to 16 years from 1 September 1993. A study of the effect of the 16-year age limit for learner driving in Sweden (Gregersen 1997) found that drivers who started learning to drive at the age of 16 had on average driven 118 h before their driving test, as opposed to an average of 47 h for those who took their driving test before the age limit was reduced. Drivers who started learning to drive at 16 had, on average, a 35% (95% CI [−45; −24]) lower risk of injury per kilometre driven than drivers who started learning to drive at 17.5. For property damage only accidents, the decrease in the accident rate was 25% (95% CI [−39; −7]). Possible self-selection bias in the study has not been controlled for.

***Discussion and summary.*** The main impression from the studies presented above is that formal training of new drivers has not been found to reduce the number of accidents. The methodological quality of research evaluating driver training is in general somewhat better than the quality of research evaluating other road safety measures (Elvik 1991, 1992). A number of well-controlled experiments have been carried out. There is a clear tendency that the methodologically better the study, the less favourable the effects of training on accidents. Only in the methodologically poorest studies, effects of formal driver training on accidents been found.

There are several possible explanations for the lack of effects on accidents. First, it is sometimes assumed that the training schemes evaluated are not good enough. This argument is discussed by Johansson (1991), who concludes that it is very implausible. This conclusion is supported here. It is far more probable that the best training programmes have been evaluated rather than the poorest. By 'best' training programmes is meant the most thoroughly thought-out and planned programmes.

Second, accidents may be too insensitive a measure of the effect of training. Accidents are rare and very often random events, influenced by many factors other than the knowledge and skills of the individual driver. This argument is somewhat plausible. Christensen (1992) has found that several of the studies referred to above were based on so small samples that only major changes in accident rates, for example more than 30%, could be detected statistically. However, this objection carries less weight when the results of many studies are combined in a meta-analysis, as is done here. When all studies are combined, they show that drivers with formal training have 1.9% fewer accidents per driver than drivers without formal training. A 95% confidence interval for this estimate is from 3.8% fewer accidents to an unchanged number of accidents. This means that a difference of 2% in the number of accidents per driver – rather than 1.9% – would have been statistically significant at the 5% level. In other words, the results have a combined power to detect differences in the accident rates as small as 2%. It is not correct to refer to results with this level of statistical power as 'insensitive'.

Third, pupils may adapt their behaviour according to their perceived ability as drivers. Several studies show that special skills training leads to more accidents. The explanation for this is unlikely to be that good skills per se are negative for traffic safety. The explanation is more likely related to the way a driver chooses to use his skill in traffic. A driver who knows that he or she is skilled may be tempted to drive less carefully than a driver who is more uncertain of his own skills and who therefore chooses a more careful way of driving. In an experiment with skid training, Gregersen (1996) found support for this hypothesis. Drivers who were taught to control their cars in icy conditions evaluated their own skills in such conditions as better than drivers who were taught to understand that they could not control the vehicle in icy conditions.

### Effect on mobility

No studies are available that show how formal driver training affects mobility.

### Effect on the environment

No studies are available that show how formal driver training affects the environment.

### Costs

The costs of basic driver training in Norway comprise the following components (Borger 1992, Christensen 1992, 1995, 1997):

- costs of running the National Driving Instructors College
- the Norwegian Public Roads Administration's costs for inspecting traffic schools and for driving tests and issuing driving licences
- the pupils' costs for formal training, textbooks, private practice driving and driving test
- the Norwegian Public Roads Administration's costs.

Of these costs, running the National Driving Instructors College and inspection of driving schools are treated as costs of driver performance standards (see Section 6.3). Cost to candidates and the Norwegian Public Roads Administration for driving tests are counted as a part of the costs of this measure, not as costs of training as such.

A Norwegian calculation for 1991 (Borger 1992), updated to 1995 (Christensen 1995), found the costs of the different elements of driver training, which are reported in Table 6.4.1. The total costs are calculated by assuming an annual number of pupils of around 57,000. The average cost per pupil is around NOK 14,200 and the total cost is around NOK 812 million.

### Cost–benefit analysis

No cost–benefit analysis of basic automobile driver training is available. The results presented above do not indicate that formal training of new drivers reduces the number

*Table 6.4.1: Costs of basic driver training in Norway (NOK, 1995 prices)*

| Training element | Cost per pupil (NOK) | Total costs (million NOK) |
|---|---|---|
| Theory course at driving school | 850 | 48.5 |
| Compulsory driving lessons (9.5 h) | 2,375 | 135.4 |
| Other driving lessons at driving schools | 6,490 | 369.9 |
| Total paid lessons at driving school | 9,715 | 553.8 |
| Pupils' time costs for driving lessons | 890 | 50.7 |
| Purchase of text books | 200 | 11.4 |
| Costs of private practice driving | 1,300 | 74.1 |
| Travel costs to and from driving lessons | 1,135 | 64.7 |
| Time costs for reading text books | 1,000 | 57.2 |
| Total costs of basic driver training | 14,240 | 811.9 |

of accidents. However, the most important reason why people want to learn to drive is not a desire to prevent accidents. Having a driving licence increases individual travel opportunities considerably. The value of this benefit and of the possible effects of driver training on mobility and the environment are too little known for meaningful cost–benefit analyses to be possible.

## 6.5 The driving test

### Problem and objective

Basic driver training is ideally intended to give new drivers the knowledge and skills they need to drive safely. However, not all new drivers are equally highly motivated for all elements of driver training. Without some form of control of how training works in practice, there is a risk that some new drivers undergo training without really learning very much. In order to prevent people who lack elementary skills from starting to drive, most countries require that new drivers pass a test – the driving test – before they are granted a driving licence. The driving test is intended to ensure that new drivers fulfil certain minimum driver performance standard to motivate drivers to acquire knowledge and skills and to identify drivers who are unfit to drive.

### Description of the measure

The driving test in Norway consists of a theoretical part and a practical part. The theory test is a written test. The practical test (the driving test) consists of driving in normal traffic with an examiner in the car.

## Effect on accidents

There are a number of methodological problems in measuring the effect of the driving test on accidents. In Norway, almost everyone who takes the driving test ultimately gets a driving licence, even though 20–30% fail at the first attempt. Those who do not pass the driving test, even after many attempts, are not allowed to drive cars and thus cannot be exposed to the risk of accidents as car drivers. It is therefore not possible to compare the accident rate for drivers who have passed the driving test with drivers who have not passed this test, in order to determine whether drivers who fail the driving test have a higher accident rate than drivers who pass it. The possibilities for studying the effects of the driving test on accidents are associated with the following situations:

- When a new or a stricter driving test is introduced, the number of accidents before and after the changes can be compared.
- Upon abolishing driving tests. Earlier, driving licences had to be renewed by means of a renewal test in Norway. This was abolished in 1975. Other countries have also abolished renewal tests. This gives opportunities to study changes in the number of accidents from before to after this change.
- For drivers taking the driving test, the relationship between the number of attempts to pass the test and the accident rate can be investigated.
- The relationship between the total points attained in the driving test and the accident rate can be investigated.

All these methods have weaknesses. Methods 1 and 2 primarily measure the effects of the existence of a driving test, not the potential of the test to discriminate between safe and less safe drivers. As for methods 3 and 4, all drivers studied have passed the driving test, even though some drivers were probably close to failing. Because of these methodological problems, the validity of the results presented below cannot be taken for granted.

Studies that have attempted to measure effects of the driving test on the number of accidents include:

Hoinville, Berthoud and Mackie (1972) (Great Britain): optional advanced driving test
Christensen, Glad and Pedersen (1974) (Norway): renewal test
Stoke (1980) (USA): theory tests
McKnight and Edwards (1982) (USA): textbooks and theory tests
Kelsey and Janke (1983) (USA): repeal of renewal test
Stock et al. (1983) (USA): written examination before the driving test
Kelsey, Janke, Peck and Ratz (1985) (USA): repeal of renewal tests
Janke (1990) (USA): repeal of renewal theory tests

Lyles, Narupiti, Johar (1995) (USA): optional professional driving test for heavy vehicles
Hagge and Romanowicz (1996) (USA): more stringent driving tests for heavy vehicles

All studies of ***theory tests*** were designed as experiments. On the basis of the studies, the effect of a theory test on driver accident rates is estimated to be exactly zero (95% CI [−1; +1]), i.e. drivers who take a theory test have exactly the same accident rate as drivers who do not take a theory test.

Studies of ***practical tests*** are more diverse. Hoinville, Berthoud and Mackie (1972) studied accident rates among drivers who took an optional, advanced driving test, which was the entrance test for membership of the Institute of Advanced Motorists. Drivers who passed the tests at the first or second attempt (58% of drivers) had a 25% lower accident rate than drivers who failed the test (42% of the drivers). Drivers who had failed the official driving test at least once before they passed (25% of drivers) had no more accidents than drivers who had passed the official driving test on their first attempt (Hoinville, Berthoud and Mackie 1972).

On the basis of the studies by Hoinville, Berthoud and Mackie (1972) and Stock et al. (1983), the relationship between the percentage not passing the driving test and the difference in accident rate between drivers who have passed the test and drivers who have failed the test can be investigated. The higher the failure rate for the driving test, the greater is the difference in the accident rate between drivers who pass the test and drivers who fail the test. This can be interpreted as evidence that a difficult driving test discriminates more effectively between safe and less safe drivers than an easier driving test. This interpretation is supported by a British study (Fazakerley and Downing 1980) that showed that the longer the driving test was, the more candidates began to make serious errors (errors that leads to a candidate failing). The study showed that 18% of candidates had committed a serious error after 30 min. After 90 min, the proportion had increased to 41%.

An American study (Stock et al. 1983) found that drivers who passed the final pre-test in their formal training had a 7% lower accident rate than drivers who failed this test; 30% of drivers failed the pre-test.

Another American study (Hagge and Romanowicz 1996) reviewed the effects of more stringent driving tests (both theory tests and practical tests) for drivers of heavy vehicles in California. The number of injury accidents increased by around 5% (95% CI [+4; +6]) after the more stringent driving test was introduced. Reasons for this increase are not known.

***Effects of abolishing renewal tests in Norway.*** On the basis of a comprehensive literature survey (Christensen, Glad and Pedersen 1974), the renewal driving test was abolished in Norway in 1975. The last year in which renewal tests were carried out was 1974, when some 158,000 renewal tests were taken. The rule was that the driving licence had to be renewed every 10th year, and more often for older drivers. In order to study possible effects on traffic safety of abolishing the renewal test, accident statistics for drivers for 1974 and 1976 have been compared (Table 6.5.1). If renewal tests had an effect on safety, changes in the number of accidents for drivers with driving licences that were 10 years old or older should have been expected, shown in italics in Table 6.5.1. However, the changes observed between 1974 and 1976 for this group of drivers do not differ significantly from the changes found for other groups of drivers. No effect on road safety of abolishing renewal test in Norway in 1975 is found. This corresponds with expectations based on the literature survey made in advance (Christensen, Glad and Pedersen 1974).

## Effect on mobility

In order to pass the driving test, the candidate must not drive in such a way as to unnecessarily obstruct other traffic. To the extent that candidates who do not meet this requirement fail the driving test, this can increase mobility.

## Effect on the environment

No effects on the environment of the driving test have been documented.

*Table 6.5.1: Number of drivers involved in injury accidents in Norway in 1974 and 1976 according to drivers' age and the age of the driving licence*

| | Number of drivers involved in injury accidents reported to the police | | | |
|---|---|---|---|---|
| Age | Age of driving licence | Before (1974) | After (1976) | Change (%) |
| 18–26 years | Up to 10 years | 2,673 | 2,774 | +3.8 |
| | Age not stated | 1,000 | 981 | −1.9 |
| 27 years and more | Up to 10 years | 1,494 | 1,507 | +0.9 |
| | 10 years and more | 1,427 | 1,476 | +3.4 |
| | Age not stated | 2,927 | 3,124 | +6.7 |
| Not stated | All | 476 | 404 | −15.1 |
| Total | | 9,997 | 10,266 | +2.7 |

*Table 6.5.2: Costs of driving tests in Norway (NOK, 1995 prices)*

| Driving licence class | Cost unit | Cost per candidate (NOK) | Total costs (million NOK) |
|---|---|---|---|
| B (car) | Candidate costs | 1,970 | 148.7 |
| | Norwegian Public Roads Administration costs | 710 | 53.5 |
| C, D (bus, truck) | Total candidate costs | 2,060 | 5.3 |
| | Total Norwegian Public Roads Administration costs | 710 | 1.8 |
| CE (articulated) | Total candidate costs | 2,180 | 9.9 |
| | Total Norwegian Public Roads Administration costs | 760 | 3.5 |

### Costs

The costs of driving tests in Norway are of two types. These are costs to candidates of renting a car for the driving test, paying fees and time costs and costs to the Public Roads Administration's costs for developing driving tests and issuing driving licences. In principle, the fees are intended to cover the Norwegian Public Roads Administration's costs. Nonetheless, in order to give an overview, all costs are shown in Table 6.5.2 (Borger 1992, Christensen 1995, 1997).

### Cost–benefit analysis

No cost–benefit analyses of the driving test, as it is implemented in Norway, are available. The percentage failing in class B in 1995 was around 28%. The vast majority of those who fail take a new test and pass. It is not known how many of those who take the driving test never obtain a driving licence. The results of the studies presented above indicate that those who fail the driving test have an accident rate about 5% higher than those who pass. Since the vast majority of these still obtain driving licences in Norway, because they take the tests several times, the gain in traffic safety that could be realised by denying the failed candidates a licence is not realised at present. Therefore, it is not possible to quantify the possible benefits from driving tests in Norway.

## 6.6 Training and testing of moped and motorcycle riders

### Problem and objective

Moped and motorcycle riders have an extremely high rate of injury. Moped riders and motorcyclists have an 8–10 times higher risk of injury than car occupants (Bjørnskau 1993). Although the number of uninjured riders and passengers per million person kilometres was 0.17 for cars, it was 1.45 for mopeds, 1.96 for light motorcycles and 1.68

for heavy motorcycles. Estimates of risk for different age groups of moped riders and motorcyclists are uncertain. Figure 6.6.1 is based on two Norwegian studies (Ingebrigtsen 1989, 1990). It shows the relative risk of accidents for the youngest riders of mopeds and motorcycles. The average accident rate for all riders is set equal to 1.00. The youngest riders have a higher accident rate than the average rider of mopeds, light motorcycles and different groups of heavy motorcycles. The difference in risk between the youngest riders and the average rider is smallest for mopeds. This is due to the fact that mopeds are ridden almost exclusively by 16-year-old drivers, who therefore also contribute significantly to the average accident rate. For heavy and light motorcycles, the youngest riders have an accident rate that is 30–60% than the average for all riders. This pattern corresponds to the findings for passenger cars.

Formal training and testing of moped riders and motorcyclists is intended to reduce the rider accident rates by giving them knowledge about and skills in safe driving.

**Description of the measure**

Formal training is mandatory for moped riders and motorcyclists in Norway. It comprises theoretical and practical training. Basic moped rider training covers subjects

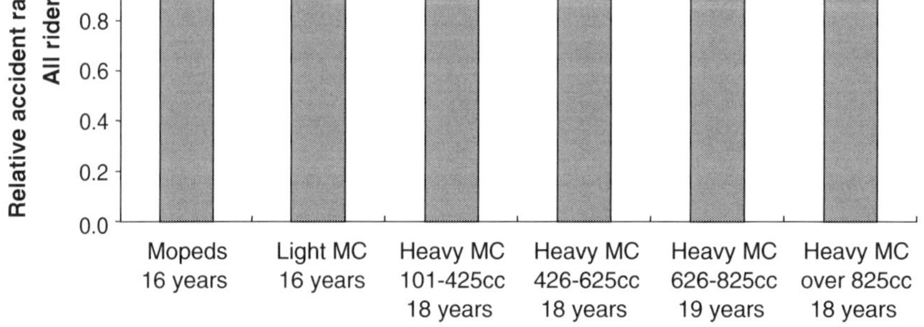


*Figure 6.6.1: Relative accident rate for the youngest riders of mopeds and motorcycles, compared with the average accident rate for all riders in Norway. Average accident rate for all riders of each type of moped or motorcycle = 1.00.*

such as the risks involved in moped riding, factors that affect the level of risk, use of personal safety equipment, moped construction and how it works. Practical exercises are made in a driving range and in real traffic. All candidates must pass a theoretical and a practical test.

### Effect on accidents

Studies that have evaluated the effects on accidents of various types of training for moped and motorcycle riders include

Kraus, Riggins and Franti (1975) (USA): optional training
Raymond and Tatum (1977) (Great Britain): optional training
Russam (1979) (Japan): optional training
Satten (1980) (USA): optional training
Hurt, Ouellet and Thom (1981) (USA): optional training
Jonah, Dawson and Bragg (1981) (Canada): driving tests
Jonah, Dawson and Bragg (1982) (Canada): optional training
Mortimer 1984 (USA): optional training
Troup, Torpey and Wood (1984) (Australia): ban on heavy motorcycles for new riders
Adams, Collingwood and Job (1985) (Australia): optional training
Daltrey and Thompson (1987) (Australia): driving tests
Broughton (1987) (Great Britain): ban on heavy motorcycles for new riders
Mortimer (1988) (USA): optional training
Steffens, Gawatz and Willmes (1988) (Germany): optional training
Engel and Krogsgård Thomsen (1989) (Denmark): compulsory training
McDavid, Lohrmann and Lohrmann (1989) (Canada): optional training
Ingebrigtsen (1990) (Norway): compulsory training
Koch (1991) (Germany): GDLs
Waller (1992) (USA): optional training
Lloyd et al. (1994) (USA): optional training

On the basis of these studies, best estimates of the effect of training are given in Table 6.6.1.

Optional training does not reduce the number of accidents among moped and motorcycle riders. Riders who have undertaken formal training in fact have more accidents than those who have not undertaken such training. The explanation for this result is not known. Many of the studies of formal training of moped and motorcycle riders give little information about the form of training and how it was carried out.

*Table 6.6.1: Effects of formal training and testing of moped riders and motorcyclists on number of accidents*

| | Percentage change in the number of accidents | | |
|---|---|---|---|
| Accident severity | Accident types affected | Best estimate | 95% Confidence interval |
| ***Optional formal training*** | | | |
| Unspecified | All accident types (per rider) | +18 | (+1; +37) |
| Unspecified | All accident types (per km driven) | +44 | (+33; +56) |
| ***Compulsory formal training*** | | | |
| Unspecified | All accident types (per rider) | −3 | (−8; +1) |
| ***Driving tests for moped and motorcycle riders*** | | | |
| Unspecified | All accident types (per rider) | −13 | (−14; −1) |
| ***GDL for the first two years for moped and motorcycle*** | | | |
| Unspecified | All accident types (per rider) | −0 | (−7; +6) |
| ***Ban on new riders riding heavy motorcycles (accidents in total)*** | | | |
| Unspecified | Accidents with heavy motorcycles | −74 | (−77; −71) |
| Unspecified | Accidents with lighter motorcycles | +17 | (+8; +26) |
| Unspecified | All motorcycle accidents | +14 | (+8; +20) |

A number of studies (Raymond and Tatum 1977, Satten 1980) show that motorcyclists who have had formal training drive less than motorcyclists without formal training. Riders, who ride little, have a higher accident rate per kilometre driven than riders who ride a great deal. Part of the explanation of the difference in the accident rate per kilometre driven between riders with formal training and riders without this may therefore be that riders with formal training ride less than riders without this.

The introduction of compulsory moped rider training in Denmark (Engel and Krogsgård Thomsen 1989) and Norway (Ingebrigtsen 1990) has not led to fewer accidents per rider. There is a tendency towards a small decrease, but it is not statistically significant.

Only two studies have evaluated driving tests. A Canadian study (Jonah, Dawson and Bragg 1981) found that those who took an optional driving test had rather more accidents than those who did not take this test. An Australian study (Daltrey and Thompson 1987), on the contrary, found that introducing compulsory driving tests, combined with training, led to fewer accidents per rider. The Australian study contributes most to the summary result given above.

A German study (Koch 1991) found that GDL for new riders, i.e. driving licences, which do not permit new riders to ride the heaviest motorcycles, did not lead to fewer accidents. This finding is consistent with the results of a British study (Broughton 1987) of the ban on new riders riding heavy motorcycles. The study found that the transition to lighter motorcycles among new riders was so great that it more than offset the gain of fewer riders riding heavy motorcycles. An Australian study (Troup, Torpey and Wood 1984) showed that bans on new riders driving heavy motorcycles reduced the number of accidents involving heavy motorcycles. However, in the study, a possible increase in accidents for light motorcycles resulting from such a ban was not studied. As a result, one should not put as much emphasis on the result of this study as on the British study.

### Effect on mobility

No effects on mobility of the measures described in this chapter have been found.

### Effect on the environment

No effects on the environment of the measures described in this chapter have been documented.

### Costs

No cost figures are available for moped and motorcycle training. On the basis of cost figures for car driver training in Norway (Christensen 1995), the costs of compulsory moped and motorcycle training can be roughly estimated to be around NOK 8,000 per rider for moped rider training and around NOK 10,000 per rider for motorcycle training.

### Cost–benefit analysis

The results presented above do not indicate that formal training of moped and motorcycle riders reduces their accident rates. Accordingly, it cannot be assumed that this type of training produces any benefit in the form of fewer accidents.

With regard to driving tests, the results are inconsistent, but tend to indicate that those who take a test have around 13% fewer accidents than those who do not pass or do not take the test. No statistics are available that show how many of those who fail the moped certificate test, or the driving test for motorcycles, give up their attempts to obtain a driving licence. Most of those who fail the driving test take a new test and eventually get a driving licence. There is therefore no basis for cost–benefit analysis of driving tests for moped and motorcycle riders.

## 6.7 Training and testing of professional drivers

### Problem and objective

Professional drivers drive far more than any other group of the population. No doubt this gives them considerable and varied experience, which may be useful for safe driving. On the contrary, professional drivers are more exposed to risk in traffic than most people. Furthermore, many professional drivers drive large, heavy vehicles that expose other road users to risk. For these reasons, it may be appropriate to set more stringent standards for professional drivers than for other road users.

The injury accident rate for professional drivers is no higher than the corresponding rate for other groups of drivers. The statistics in Table 6.7.1 shows the number of drivers involved in injury accidents per million kilometres driven in Norway in the period 1988–93. Taxis, vans, lorries and tankers carrying flammable goods all have an accident rate that is close to, or lower than, the rate for passenger cars. Buses and trams

*Table 6.7.1: Risk of being involved in injury accidents for drivers of different types of vehicles in Norway*

| Vehicle group | Vehicles involved in injury accidents | Million kilometres | Involved per million vehicle kilometres |
|---|---|---|---|
| Tanker for flammable goods | 30 | 251 | 0.12 |
| Combined car | 1,764 | 5,950 | 0.30 |
| Taxi | 997 | 3,193 | 0.31 |
| Van | 4,557 | 14,166 | 0.32 |
| Passenger car | 57,743 | 130,114 | 0.44 |
| Lorry | 4,317 | 9,636 | 0.45 |
| Bicycle | 5,707 | 7,108 | 0.80 |
| Pedestrians | 7,370 | 8,818 | 0.84 |
| Bus | 1,694 | 1,974 | 0.86 |
| Moped | 4,592 | 2,627 | 1.75 |
| Light motorcycle | 459 | 206 | 2.23 |
| Heavy motorcycle | 2,362 | 1,012 | 2.33 |
| Tram | 207 | 18 | 11.40 |

Based on official Norwegian accident statistics 1988–93.

have a higher risk of being involved in injury accidents than other vehicles. This is probably partly attributable to the fact that these vehicles are driven in complex city traffic to a greater extent than other vehicles.

Professional drivers are more experienced than other drivers. This ought to imply a lower accident rate than for other drivers. Inexperienced professional drivers are more often involved in accidents than experienced professional drivers. A Norwegian study (Nygård and Tellnes 1994) showed that the proportion of drivers who had been involved in one or more traffic accidents in 1993 was ca. 41% among drivers with less than 5 years experience, and declined to ca. 18% among drivers with 15 or more experience. A corresponding pattern has been found for car drivers and moped and motorcycle riders.

Formal training and testing of professional drivers is intended to prevent clearly unsuitable drivers from becoming professional drivers and to give professional drivers a lower accident rate than they would have had without formal training and testing. Furthermore, it is desirable to aim for a lower accident rate for professional drivers than for other groups of road users.

### Description of the measure

The measures described in this chapter include training and testing of professional drivers and special training for drivers who carry dangerous goods.

### Effect on accidents

***Training and testing of professional drivers.*** A number of studies have evaluated the effects of formal training of professional drivers, including people who drive a great deal as part of their work (for example, craftsmen). The results presented here are based on the following studies:

Payne and Barmack (1963) (USA): training with emphasis on anticipatory driving
O'Day (1970) (USA): courses in defensive driving
Eriksson (1983) (Sweden): skid training for ambulance drivers
Manders and Rennie (1984) (Australia): courses in defensive driving
Downing (1988) (Pakistan): training for bus drivers with emphasis on defensive driving
Beilock, Capelle and Page (1989) (USA): general training of lorry drivers
Gray (1990) (Great Britain): courses in defensive driving
Gregersen and Morén (1990) (Sweden): courses including driving with commentary

Lähdeniemi (1995) (Finland): courses in defensive driving for bus drivers
Christensen and Glad (1996) (Norway): compulsory skid training for heavy vehicles
Hagge and Romanowicz (1996) (USA): more stringent driving tests for heavy vehicles
King (1996) (USA): courses in defensive driving
Valset (1996) (Norway): courses for bus drivers

The training measures that have been covered by the studies can be roughly divided into three groups: (1) courses in defensive driving, (2) skid training and (3) more stringent driving tests. The methodological quality of the studies varies. A number of studies, for example Gray (1990), are simple before-and-after studies, where uncontrolled regression to the mean may have influenced the results. Other studies, for example Gregersen and Morén (1990), are experiments with full control of all confounding factors. The greatest emphasis is placed on the results of the methodologically best studies. Best estimates of the effect on accidents of the different measures are given in Table 6.7.2 (percentage change in the total number of accidents, or number of accidents per driver, or per kilometre driven).

Training professional drivers in more defensive driving reduces the accident rate by around 20%. In larger companies, such measures are often combined with bonus schemes or other reward systems for accident-free driving. Skid training appears to be associated with more accidents, both among ambulance drivers and drivers of lorries and articulated lorries. More stringent driving tests do not lead to fewer accidents. There is a weak tendency towards an increase in the accident rate, explanation for which is not known. Hagge and Romanowicz (1996) indicate that methodological problems may be one possible explanation for the result of the study.

*Table 6.7.2: Effects of training and testing professional drivers on the number of accidents*

| | Percentage change in the number of accidents | | |
|---|---|---|---|
| Accident severity | Type of accident affected | Best estimate | 95% Confidence interval |
| ***Course in defensive driving for experienced drivers*** | | | |
| Unspecified | All types of accidents (per km driven) | −20 | (−33; −5) |
| ***Skid training for ambulance drivers*** | | | |
| Unspecified | Accidents in icy conditions (per driver) | +45 | (−35; +220) |
| ***Skid training for drivers of heavy vehicles*** | | | |
| Unspecified | Accidents in icy conditions (per km driven) | +22 | (+9; +36) |
| ***More stringent driving tests for drivers of heavy vehicles*** | | | |
| Injury accidents | All types of injury (total accidents) | +5 | (+4; +6) |

***Training testing of drivers of tankers carrying dangerous goods.*** Tankers carrying flammable goods have a 73% lower accident rates than other lorries (see above; Muskaug 1984, Elvik 1988, Borger 1996, Christensen and Glad 1996). One cannot claim that all the difference in risk is attributable to different driver requirements, but more stringent training of drivers of tankers for flammable goods may be one of the factors that contribute to the difference in risk. Other factors may be stricter standards for vehicles, differences in the road and traffic environment in which tankers carrying flammable goods and other lorries travel and the selection and training of personnel in companies.

### Effect on mobility

No effects on mobility of the training measures for professional drivers described in this chapter have been documented.

### Effect on the environment

It is not known how the training measures described in this chapter affect the environment.

### Costs

The total costs of training and testing of professional drivers in Norway are not known precisely. Table 6.7.3 gives cost figures for training professional drivers on the basis of information obtained from a sample of larger driving schools.

### Cost–benefit analysis

No cost–benefit analyses of formal training of professional drivers are available. The only measure described in this chapter that clearly appears to reduce the number of accidents is training in defensive driving. This measure reduces the number of accidents by around 20%.

The expected number of injury accidents per heavy vehicle per year in Norway is around 0.01. A 20% reduction of this figure corresponds to around 0.002 accidents prevented per vehicle per year. This represents a reduction of accident costs of around NOK 2,200 per vehicle per year. All the training measures described earlier cost considerably more than this. It is therefore highly unlikely that the current formal

*Table 6.7.3: Costs of training professional drivers in Norway (1995 prices)*

| | Driving licence class | | | |
|---|---|---|---|---|
| Course element | C | CE | D | ADR |
| Theory course | 2,750 | 2,000 | 2,750 | 2,250 |
| Driving lesson | 470 | 510 | 470 | |
| Skid training | 2,500 | 5,000 | 2,500 | |
| Rental of car for driving test | 950 | 1,000 | 950 | |
| Fee for theory test | 150 | 200 | 100 | |
| Fee for practical test | 300 | 400 | 300 | 150 |
| Fee for issue of driving licence | 120 | 120 | 120 | 120[1] |
| Average cost per pupil based on the prices given above[2] | 15,400 | 20,930 | 15,820 | 2,520 |
| Package price from driving schools | 15,540 | 21,190 | 15,490 | |

[1]Fee for ADR certificate of competence.
[2]This cost includes compulsory ADR training.

training of professional drivers in Norway results in gains in traffic safety that are greater than the cost of this training.

## 6.8 Graduated driving licences (GDLs)

### Problem and objective

Young and inexperienced drivers have a higher accident rate than any other group of drivers. Current driver training does not appear to be adequate to eliminate this high risk. However, in the first few months after the acquisition of a driving licence, the accident rate decreases strongly for novice drivers (Glad 1996, Sagberg 1996). The accident rate reduces as both age and experience increase, i.e. the accident rate that new drivers have on passing their driving test is lower than the increasing age of those who pass the test (Maycock, Lockwood and Lester 1991).

A number of studies have investigated the factors that contribute to the high risk of young and inexperienced drivers. Young drivers are more prone to have single-vehicle accidents in which high speed or risky driving are contributing factors (Lam 2003, Masten 2004, Kirk and Stamatidis 2001). Head-on collisions and accidents in darkness or on icy roads, which are also often caused by speeding and risky driving, are over-represented among young drivers as well (Sten, Hole, Borch and Thingelstad 1977, Williams 1985, Massie, Campbell and Williams 1995). Contrary to older drivers, younger drivers are more likely to be involved in accidents when they are driving with passengers (Lam 2003, Masten 2004). The risk for these types of accidents decreases more than the risk for other types of accidents within the first 6 months after obtaining the drivers licence (Lam 2003, Masten 2004).

A possible explanation for the high accident rate of novice drivers in demanding driving conditions is cognitive overload (Gregersen 1995). Among inexperienced drivers, not all elements of vehicle driving have become automated to the same extent as among more experienced drivers. Inexperienced drivers therefore need to use more mental capacity for the actual driving than experienced drivers. Under demanding driving conditions, this can lead to overload. Additionally, young drivers tend to over-estimate their own abilities and to under-estimate dangerous situations (Johansson 1982, Spolander 1983, Rumar 1985). Therefore, their driving is more risky and less according to their abilities compared to more experienced drivers (Masten 2004).

GDLs are intended to reduce the degree of difficulty in novice drivers' acquisition of driving skills when they drive on their own. As drivers become more experienced, the restrictions are lifted and drivers are given full driving privileges.

**Description of the measure**

GDL has been widely introduced in United States and in Canada from about 1995. Other countries that have introduced GDL programmes are, among others, New Zealand, Australia, and Sweden. In Germany, a pilot project is conducted with a GDL system. GDL consists mostly of three phases:

- the learner phase, in which accompanied driving is permitted,
- the intermediate phase with several restrictions on unaccompanied driving, such as lower BAC limits, restrictions on driving at night, on motorways or with passengers, and often with a limit for the number of violations that may be committed and
- the last phase without restrictions.

Some of the programmes are combined with education or tests. Some programmes provide incentives by shortening the learner or intermediate phase when a course or test is taken. A detailed description of all GDLs programmed in the United States is provided by Shope and Molnar (2003) and Williams and Mayhew (2004). The GDL programmed in the United States were classified by the Insurance Institute for Highway Safety (Morrisey, Grabowski, Dee and Campbell 2006) as good, fair or marginal programmes, depending on the length of the learner phase and the type and amount of restrictions.

Probationary driving licence was introduced in Germany in 1992 and in Austria in 1992. The probationary period lasts for 2 years. Drivers who are arrested for different traffic violations during this period must take a special course in Germany. In Austria, the probationary period is extended by 1 year and a psychological course must be taken.

### Effect on accidents

The following studies have investigated the effects of *GDL* on accidents, mostly in United States and in Canada:

McKnight, Hyle and Albrecht (1983) (Maryland, USA)
Hagge and Marsh (1986) (California, USA)
Jones (1994) (Oregon, USA)
Langley, Wagenaar and Begg (1996) (New Zealand)
Boase and Tasca (1998) (Ontario, Canada)
Driver Education (1998) (Ontario, Canada)
Ulmer, Preusser, Ferguson and Williams (1999) (Louisiana, USA)
Bouchard et al. (2000) (Quebec, Canada)
Gregersen, Nyberg and Berg (2003) (Sweden)
Ulmer et al. (2000) (Florida, USA)
Agent et al. (2001) (Kentucky, USA)
Foss, Feaganes and Rodgman (2001) (North Carolina, USA)
Mayhew and Simpson (2001) (Ontario, Canada)
Mayhew, Simpson, Des Groseilliers and Willia (2001) (Nova Scotia, Canada)
Shope, Molnar, Elliott and Waller (2001) (Michigan, USA)
Ulmer, Ferguson, Williams and Preusser (2001) (Connecticut, USA)
Simard et al. (2002) (Quebec, Canada)
Cooper, Gillen and Atkins (2004) (California, USA)
Rice, Peek-Asa and Kraus (2004) (California, USA)
Shope and Molnar (2004) (Michigan, USA)
Wiggins (2004) (British Columbia, Canada)
Dow, Wilson and Hildebrand (2005) (New Brunswick, Canada)
Morrisey, Grabowski, Dee and Campbell (2006) (USA): comparison of GDL programmes classified as good, fair or marginal

Two studies have investigated the effects of *probationary driving licences*:

Meewes and Weissbrodt (1992) (Germany)
Bartl (2004) (Austria)

The effects of *night restrictions*, which are not part of GDL programmes, have been studied in the United States by:

McKnight, Hyle and Albrecht (1983) (Maryland)
Preusser, Williams, Lund and Zador (1990) (Detroit, Cleveland, Columbus)
Preusser, Zador and Williams (1993) (47 towns)
Preusser, Williams, Zador and Blomberg (1984) (12 states)

Table 6.8.1 summarizes the results from these studies.

***Night restrictions.*** According to the results shown in Table 6.8.1, night restrictions lead to a significant reduction of nighttime accidents. The effect is, however, smaller than that should be expected if there were full compliance with the nighttime restrictions. No significant effect is found when all accidents are regarded together.

***Probationary driving licence.*** For probationary driving licence, a small but significant reduction of accidents has been found.

***GDL.*** The results for GDL seem to be affected by publication bias. Table 6.8.1 shows therefore both the original effect estimates and the effect estimates that have been controlled for publication bias with the trim and fill method. The reduction of injury accidents is not significant when publication bias is controlled for; the reduction of accidents with unspecified severity, which includes both injury and property damage only accidents, remains significant when publication bias is controlled for. For fatal accidents a larger, but non-significant reduction has been found. This result is based on too few effect estimates for controlling for publication bias.

The largest effect of GDL has been found on night accidents and single-vehicle accidents. The effect on accidents involving illegal BAC is not significant. None of these results is controlled for publication bias because there are too few effect estimates for each of the results, although they may be affected by publication bias as well.

The type and amount of restriction in GDL programmes affects the effect on accidents according to the study by Morrisey, Grabowski, Dee and Campbell (2006). A large and significant reduction of all accidents was only found for programmes classified as 'good'. A significant reduction of nighttime accidents was only found for the

*Table 6.8.1: Effects on accidents of driving restrictions and GDL*

| | Percentage change in the number of accidents | | |
|---|---|---|---|
| Accident severity | Types of accidents affected | Best estimate | 95% Confidence interval |
| ***GDL*** | | | |
| Unspecified | All accidents | | |
| | Controlled for publication bias: | −11 | (−18; −3) |
| | Not controlled for publication bias: | −18 | (−23; −13) |
| Injury accidents | All accidents | | |
| | Controlled for publication bias: | −6 | (−12; 0) |
| | Not controlled for publication bias: | −14 | (−19; −9) |
| Fatal accidents | All accidents | −28 | (−50; +5) |
| Unspecified | Night time accidents | −31 | (−46; −12) |
| Unspecified | Single vehicle accidents | −21 | (−29; −13) |
| Unspecified | Accidents involving illegal BAC | −23 | (−56; +35) |
| ***GDL USA, 'good' programmes***[1] | | | |
| Fatal accidents | All accidents | −19 | (−33; −6) |
| Fatal accidents | Daytime accidents | −29 | (−49; −9) |
| Fatal accidents | Nighttime accidents | −10 | (−30; +10) |
| ***GDL USA, 'fair' programmes***[1] | | | |
| Fatal accidents | All accidents | −5 | (−13; +4) |
| Fatal accidents | Daytime accidents | +2 | (−9; +12) |
| Fatal accidents | Nighttime accidents | −13 | (−24; −1) |
| ***GDL USA, 'marginal' programmes***[1] | | | |
| Fatal accidents | All accidents | −1 | (−12; +10) |
| Fatal accidents | Daytime accidents | +1 | (−15; +17) |
| Fatal accidents | Nighttime accidents | +2 | (−15; +18) |
| ***GDL for motor cyclists*** | | | |
| Injury accidents | All accidents | −25 | (−36; −12) |
| ***Probationary driving licence*** | | | |
| Injury accidents | All accidents | −3 | (−4; −1) |
| ***Night restrictions*** | | | |
| Injury accidents | All accidents | −7 | (−17; +5) |
| Injury accidents | Nighttime accidents | −36 | (−43; −28) |

[1]GDL programmes divided into 'good', 'fair' and 'poor' according to the study by Morrisey, Grabowski, Dee and Campbell (2006).

programmes classified as 'fair'. No information is available on the proportions of programmes in each of the three groups that include nighttime restriction. The effect of the restrictions is due to both reduced exposure and increased age of unrestricted licence holders (Shope and Molnar 2003, McKnight and Peck 2002).

Only few studies have investigated the effects of GDL on men and women. Jones (1994) who have studies GDL in Oregon found an effect of GDL only among men (reduction of accidents by 16%), but not among women. In Sweden, equal effects have been found among men and women (Gregersen, Nyberg and Berg 2003).

In addition to publication bias, the results for GDL are likely to be affected by several other methodological weaknesses that may have contributed to over-estimated accident reductions. First, most studies have not controlled for general trends in accident numbers. The studies that have controlled for trend found reduced or no overall effect of GDL on accidents, as compared with the effect without control for trend (Langley, Wagenaar and Begg 1996, Masten and Hagge 2004, Mayhew and Simpson 2001). Second, the introduction of a GDL programme usually leads to an increase of new licence holders immediately before the programme is introduced, and to a reduction of new licence holder afterwards (Simard et al. 2002). When comparing accidents before and after introduction and GDL are compared without taking into account the change in the number of licence holders, an accident reduction will be found, even if accidents per licence holders remained the same as before. All the same, many studies have only estimated effects on accidents per population. When controlling for the change in the number of licence holders, the decrease of the accidents numbers is consequently smaller than otherwise (Gregersen, Nyberg and Berg 2003, Masten and Hagge 2004).

***GDL, effect of practice driving.*** The aim of GDL programmes is to provide learner drives with driving possibilities under conditions with relatively low risk, and most learners also utilise this possibility (Mayhew 2003). The effect of driving in the learner phase has been evaluated in Sweden, where the GDL programme has fewer restrictions than in most US programmes. In Sweden, the minimum age for the learner phase was reduced from 17.5 to 16 years, whereas the minimum age for unrestricted driving remained at 18 years. Among the young drivers who started driving at 16 years, accident risk after having obtained the unrestricted licence was reduced by 46%, whereas accident risk among young drivers who had started at 17.5 years did not change (Gregersen, Nyberg and Berg 2003). A further result from the study by Gregersen is that the accident risk after having obtained the unrestricted licence is about 30 times as large as during the learner phase.

***GDL, effect of driving school lessons and tests.*** Only some GDL programmes include obligatory theoretical or practical driving lessons with tests, some programmes provide voluntary driving lessons, and other include not training at all. A number of studies have investigated the effects of obligatory or voluntary driving lessons, and found no effects on accidents, violations or risky driving (Christie 2001, Masten 2004, Mayhew 2003, McKenna, Yost, Munzenrider and Young 2000, Page, Ouimet and Cuny 2004). A reduction of the demands on training in Norway, Sweden, Denmark and Finland, however, has been found to increase accidents (Christie 2001). A Danish study has found positive effects of driving lessons only on accident involving low speed, easy driving manoeuvres or other vehicles. These effects lasted only for the first year after obtaining a licence, and no effects were found on single-vehicle accidents (Carstensen 2002). Studies of the effects of driving tests have not found any effects on accidents either (Mayhew 2003).

Two studies from Canada (Boase and Tasca 1998, Wiggins 2004) and one study that has been conducted in 47 states of the United States before the introduction of GDL (Levy 1990) found larger effects of the amount of driving than that of driving lessons. Driving lessons have been found to increase accidents by almost 30% when the learner period can be shortened as an incentive for taking driving lessons (Wiggins 2004).

***Effect of restrictions in GDL programmes.*** Most GDL programmes (except the one in Sweden) involved an increase of the restrictions during the learner phase. In most cases, a learner phase had existed already before the introduction of GDL, but only with few restrictions. All results refer to accidents before an unrestricted licence has been obtained. Effects of GDL after an unrestricted licence has been obtained have been studied by

Agent et al. (2001) (Kentucky, USA)
Mayhew, Simpson, Desmond and Williams (2003) (Nova Scotia, Canada)
Ulmer et al. (2000) and Ulmer, Ferguson, Williams and Preusser (2001) (Florida and Connecticut, USA)

All studies found accident reductions before the unrestricted licence has been obtained, but no effects afterwards.

Effects of GDL programmes with and without restrictions on driving at night, lower BAC limit for learners and a reduced maximum number of violations are compared in Table 6.8.2.

*Nighttime restrictions.* The results indicate that night restrictions reduce nighttime accidents. Larger effects on accidents when GDL involves night restrictions have also

*Table 6.8.2: Effects on accidents (unspecified severity) of restrictions in GDL programmes*

| | Percentage change in the number of accidents | | |
|---|---|---|---|
| Restrictions | Types of accidents affected | Best estimate | 95% Confidence interval |
| Night restrictions | All accidents | −18 | (−23; −12) |
| No night restrictions | All accidents | −19 | (−29; −9) |
| Night restrictions | Nighttime accidents | −46 | (−54; −36) |
| No night restrictions | Nighttime accidents | −10 | (−15; −5) |
| Lower BAC limit | All accidents | −17 | (−24; −9) |
| No lower BAC limit | All accidents | −20 | (−28; −12) |
| Violation restrictions | All accidents | −21 | (−28; −14) |
| No violation restrictions | All accidents | −15 | (−19; −11) |

been found in the studies by Shope and Molnar (2003), Masten (2004), Lin and Fearn (2003) and Boase and Tasca (1998). Doherty and Andrey (1997) have estimated that nighttime restrictions reduce all accidents by 10% and fatal accidents by 24% whereas the amount of driving only was reduced by 4%. The study by Cooper, Gillen and Atkins (2004), on the contrary, found no effect of nighttime restrictions on driving at night or on accidents.

*Lower BAC limit.* No overall effect on accidents was found of lower BAC limits. The comparison refers to all types of accidents, not specifically to accidents involving alcohol. Results from studies that have investigated the effects of lowered BAC limits are inconsistent. Masten (2004) found reduced accident numbers when controlling for trends. Studies that have not controlled for trend found accident reductions, but these may be due to trends (Masten 2004, Boase and Tasca 1998). Shope, Molnar, Elliott and Waller (2001) found a reduction of accidents involving alcohol, but the reduction was smaller than would have been expected based on the general trend in accident numbers.

*Violation restrictions.* The results in Table 6.8.2 show that accident reductions are larger in GDL programmes with violation restrictions than those without violation restrictions. The same result has been obtained in the study by Masten (2004).

*Passenger restrictions.* Young drivers have increased accident risk when driving with passengers (Lin and Fearn 2003). Restrictions on driving with passengers has been found to reduce accidents during the first 6 months (Masten and Hagge 2004).

*Restrictions on driving on motorways.* Some GDL programmes include restrictions on driving on motorways or on roads with high speed limits. Results of accident studies of the effects of such restrictions are contradictory. Doherty and Andrey (1997) found more accidents; Boase and Tasco found fewer accidents when GDL programmes included restrictions for driving on high-speed roads.

Restrictions in GDL programmes may reduce accidents by reducing exposure, if there is compliance to the restrictions. Accordingly, increased enforcement may be expected to improve the effectiveness of restrictions (Masten and Hagge 2004). Restrictions may also lead to more careful driving, even if there is a lack of compliance. Although there mostly is high support for restrictions (Mayhew 2003), there is not always compliance (Goodwin and Foss 2004, Masten and Hagge 2003, Rice, Peek-Asa and Kraus 2004). Most young drivers have reported that they drive more carefully in order to avoid being caught (Goodwin and Foss 2004).

**Effect on mobility**

Graduated licences with restrictions reduce mobility for drivers who are subject to them. For other age groups, mobility may possibly be improved since the measure may lead to less traffic and fewer accidents. On the contrary, this applies mostly to late evening and at night, when problems of traffic congestion are smaller than they are in daytime.

**Effect on the environment**

GDL may have an indirect effect on the environment to the extent that these measures contribute to reducing traffic volume.

**Costs**

The direct costs of imposing driving restrictions for young drivers are probably small. A certain amount of enforcement is necessary to ensure compliance with, for example, a nighttime curfew. A GDL programme may involve higher costs, e.g. administrative costs for issuing licences several times for each new driver and costs for pursuing violations that are often associated with more severe penalties. This may require a new sanction system, for example a penalty point system.

In addition to the direct costs, driving restrictions for young drivers have indirect costs in the form of the loss of benefit on the grounds of reduced driving. This loss of benefit may be important since many young drivers enjoy driving and, to some extent, also drive for pleasure.

### Cost–benefit analysis

The costs and benefits of GDL are related to the type and amount of restrictions, and on the type of licensing system GDL is compared with. A numerical example is calculated under the assumption that a GDL system reduces the number of accidents for young drivers by 5–10% for the first 2 years when they drive alone. Assuming that this measure is limited to drivers aged 18 or 19, this corresponds to the prevention of some 25–50 injury accidents per year in Norway. This corresponds to a gain of NOK 50–100 million per year. If it is assumed that graduated licences apply for the first 2 years of driving for drivers who are 18 when they pass the driving test, and for the first year for drivers who are 19 when they pass the driving test, the measure will cover some 150,000–180,000 drivers at any one time. The gain from the measure thus works out at NOK 280–670 per driver per year. If the sum of the direct and indirect costs of GDL is less than this, calculated per driver, such a measure would be cost-effective.

## 6.9 Motivation and incentive systems in the work place

### Problem and objective

Professional drivers have a fatality rate per 100 million person hours that is about three times higher than the average for all other professions in Norway (Fosser and Elvik 1996). Being a professional driver is a dangerous occupation compared to other lines of work.

Human behaviour can be influenced by means of rewarding desirable behaviour (Chaplin and Krawiec 1970). The driver's motivation to drive safely is an important factor influencing his accident rate. Knowledge, skills, road design, road markings and information do not help if the driver's motivation for safe driving is overshadowed by other motives such as mobility, enjoyment of speed and the need for strong stimuli (Sagberg 1994).

Motivation or incentive systems in the workplace are intended to influence employees' driving behaviour – or other aspects of working environment – in such a way that the number of accidents goes down.

### Description of the measure

It may be worth distinguishing between two strategies that can potentially affect both the number of accidents or the severity of injuries among professional drivers. First, there are measures that are generally directed towards the company's operating conditions and working environment – i.e. background conditions under which professional drivers work and which can affect the number of accidents – in the form of time pressure, the company's knowledge of safety in general and motivational conditions as functions of external conditions and working environments. The second strategy includes measures targeted at types of behaviour that are assumed to contribute to accidents, or measures that will reduce injury severity in the event of accidents, such as the use of seat belts.

## Effect on accidents

Three studies have evaluated the effects of different types of incentive and motivation measures on accidents. The effects of the following measures on accidents have been investigated in three studies. Misumi (1982, Japan) investigated the effects of group discussions among drivers at the workplace. Gregersen and Morén (1990, Sweden) and Gregersen, Brehmer and Morén (1996) studied the effects of driver training, group discussions, bonuses for accident-free driving and campaigns. Sagberg (1994, Norway) studied the effects of a combination of driver training, group discussions, bonuses for accident-free driving and campaigns. The first study is a simple before-and-after study, whereas the last two are before-and-after studies with comparison groups.

When all results are combined, the summary effect on accidents is zero (95% CI [−12; +13]). However, the results are highly inconsistent between the studies. The result of the Japanese study (Misumi 1982) is very uncertain and probably contains uncontrolled regression to the mean effects. In the Norwegian study, there were organizational changes during the study period that resulted in increased time, pressure and stress. This may at least partly explain the finding that accidents increased by about 300%. When these results are excluded, the best estimate of the effect of the measure is a reduction in the number of accidents of 18% (95% CI [−28; −6]). The largest effect, a reduction by almost 50%, was achieved in the group that used group discussions to influence behaviour. In the groups that used driver training, bonuses for accident-free driving and the multiple measures that were used in the Norwegian study, reductions in accidents of 32%, 16% and 20%, respectively, were achieved. However, in the last group, where campaigns were used, there was an increase of 36%.

## Effect on mobility

Motivation and incentive systems have no documented effects on mobility.

*Table 6.9.1: Overview of costs and cost reductions associated with the use of motivation and incentive programmes in the Swedish telecommunications industry*

| Measure/group | Cost of measure per 10,000 km | Change in accident costs per 10,000 km 1987 | Change in accident costs per 10,000 km 1988 | Time (years) before costs are paid back |
|---|---|---|---|---|
| Bonus | 454 | −102 | −279 | 1.6 |
| Driver training | 2,575 | −160 | −368 | 7 |
| Group discussions | 649 | −90 | −555 | 1.2 |
| Campaign | 938 | −26 | −342 | 2.7 |
| Control | 0 | −117 | −103 | – |

SEK in thousands (from Gregersen and Morén 1990).

### Effect on the environment

Motivation and incentive systems have no documented effects on the environment.

### Costs

In Gregersen and Morén's study, the costs of the measure, together with changes in the accident costs, were calculated (Table 6.9.1). None of the applied strategies resulted in savings that balanced the costs during the period in which the measures were implemented (Gregersen and Morén 1990). In a group where campaign measures were used, the number of accidents increased by 36%. No explanation is given of how this finding is compatible with a saving in accident costs.

### Cost–benefit analysis

In the Swedish study, it has been estimated how long it will take to recover the costs of the measures, assuming that the reduction of accidents was maintained at the level that was observed in 1988 (Gregersen and Morén 1990). Table 6.9.1 shows that group discussions would recover costs most rapidly, in 1.2 years. The bonus system was almost equally effective, whereas driver training was the most expensive measure, taking 7 years for the costs to be recovered.

## 6.10 Regulation of driving and rest hours

### Problem and objective

Driving requires paying continual attention to the road, other road users and the vehicle itself. Long periods of driving without a break can reduce alertness and lengthen reaction times (Lisper, Dureman, Ericsson and Karlsson 1971, Lisper 1977). This can increase the probability of accidents.

In all countries with a high level of motorisation, regulations have been introduced regarding how long drivers of heavy vehicles can drive without breaks and the length of the rest periods they must take per 24-h period and per week.

In professional driving, in particular the transport of goods over long distances, there can be a conflict of interest between traffic safety and the desire to get the goods to their destination as fast as possible (Waller 1986). In order to reduce the risk of accidents, regulations have been introduced regarding driving and rest periods in professional driving. Regulating driving and rest periods is intended to reduce accidents when driving professionally, by preventing drivers from driving too long without breaks and rest.

**Description of the measure**

Driving and rest hours in Norway are regulated for buses (with the exception of mini buses) and trucks (goods transport vehicles with a total permitted weight of 3.5 t or more). The main contents of these rules are as follows:

- Daily driving time must not exceed 9 h. Twice a week this may be extended to 10 h per day.
- Weekly driving times: After a maximum of six daily driving periods, the driver must take a weekly break. The total driving time during 14 days must not exceed 90 h.
- Longest driving time without a break: Drivers must not drive for more than 4.5 h without a break of at least 45 min. For inland transport, the authorities may decide that the length of a break can be reduced to 30 min. The driver must not carry out any other type of work during these breaks. Breaks in driving cannot be counted as part of the daily rest period.
- Rest periods: In each 24-h period, the driver must take a rest of at least 11 continuous hours. The daily rest can be shortened to 9 h for a maximum of three times in the course of 1 week.
- Weekly break: Each week, the rest period must be extended to a weekly rest of at least 45 continuous hours. The weekly rest can be reduced to 36 h if it is taken at the driver's home, or at the place where the vehicle belongs, or to 24 h if these rest is taken elsewhere.

In order to enforce these regulations, all vehicles that are covered by the driving and rest hour rules must have a tachnograph registering driving hours and stationary periods. If several drivers use the same vehicle, separate graphs must be available for each driver.

**Effect on accidents**

No studies are available that show the effect on accidents of all parts of the driving and rest hour regulations. A number of studies were found that deal with individual aspects of driving and rest hours.

***Longest continuous driving period without a break.*** The following studies have evaluated the relationship between the length of driving periods without a break and accident rate:

Harris and Mackie (1972) (USA)
Hackman, Larson and Shinder (1978) (USA)
Mackie and Miller (1978) (USA)
Hamelin (1987) (France)
Jones and Stein (1987) (USA)
Stein and Jones (1988) (USA)
Lin, Jovanis and Yang (1993) (USA)
Frith (1994) (New Zealand)

Figure 6.10.1 shows the relationship between the longest continuous driving period without a break and the accident rate for lorries according to these studies. The accident rate in the first hour of driving is set equal to 1.00. The accident rate in the subsequent hours (2, 3, etc.) is stated as the ratio of the accident rate in that hour to the risk for the first hour. Numbers above 1.00 mean that the accident rate is higher than that in the first hour.

The largest accident sample refers to accidents of unspecified severity. For these accidents, there are no statistically significant differences in the accident rate for the first 5 h. The accident rate increases from the sixth hour. It is highest in the tenth hour, with a relative risk of 1.63 (i.e. 63% higher than the first hour; 95% CI [1.34; 1.97]). For injury accidents, no statistically significant differences in the accident rate have been found for the first 8 h. For the ninth hour, the relative risk is 1.31 (95% CI [1.02; 1.69]). For the tenth hour, it is 3.10 (95% CI [2.23; 4.31]). For property damage only accidents, the accident rate shows a tendency to decrease when the number of hours driven increases. However, this tendency is not statistically significant for the first 6 h.

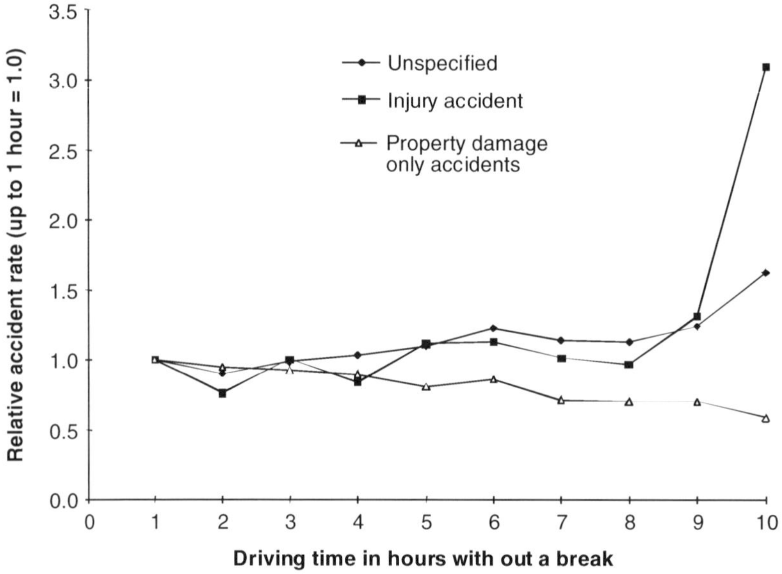


*Figure 6.10.1: Accident rate per hour driven for different numbers of hours driven without a break for lorry drivers.*

The risk is lowest in the tenth hour, with a relative risk of 0.59 (95% CI [0.32; 1.06]), which is not statistically significant.

The result for property damage only accidents is atypical. Studies where changes in accident rate has not been studied hour by hour, but where a number of hours are considered together (Jones and Stein 1987, Stein and Jones 1988), also show that the accident rate (for accidents of unspecified severity) increases with increasing driving periods without breaks:

| Driving time without a break (h) | Relative risk (95% CI) |
|---|---|
| 0–2 | 1.00 |
| 2–5 | 1.23 (1.05; 1.45) |
| 5–8 | 1.29 (1.08; 1.53) |
| >8 | 1.80 (1.20; 2.70) |

These results can be applied to estimate the increase in accident rate attributable to violating the regulations governing: (1) longest driving period without a break (4.5 h)

*Table 6.10.1: Effect on accident rate of breaking the driving and rest regulations for lorry drivers*

| Compliance with regulations | Accident severity | Relative risk (95% CI) |
|---|---|---|
| Driving up to 4.5 h without a break | Unspecified | 1.00 |
| Driving more than 4.5 h without a break | Unspecified | 1.22 (1.09; 1.36) |
| Driving up to 4.5 h without a break | Injury | 1.00 |
| Driving more than 4.5 h without a break | Injury | 1.32 (1.10; 1.59) |
| Driving up to 9 h per day | Unspecified | 1.00 |
| Driving more than 9 h per day | Unspecified | 1.49 (1.19; 1.87) |
| Driving up to 9 h per day | Injury | 1.00 |
| Driving more than 9 h per day | Injury | 3.12 (2.10; 4.64) |

and (2) longest daily driving times (9 h), compared to driving in compliance with these regulations. The results concerning property damage only accidents are not used. The results of these estimates with regard to lorry drivers are shown in Table 6.10.1.

Driving that violates the rules regarding breaks in driving after 4.5 h and the longest daily driving time of 9 h leads to an increased accident rate. The increase is greater for injury accidents than for accidents of unspecified severity. Furthermore, driving that violates the regulations concerning longest daily driving times leads to a greater increase in accident rate than driving that violates the regulations concerning breaks when driving.

Figures 6.10.2 shows how the accident rate for bus drivers varies with the length of driving without a break. The results refer to accidents of unspecified severity and are taken from one study only (Harris and Mackie 1972). There is no increase in accident rate up to and including the eighth hour. In the ninth hour, the relative risk is 1.37 (0.98; 1.94), and in the tenth hour, the relative risk is 1.58 (0.92; 2.69). On the basis of these values, it can be calculated that driving buses in conflict with the rules on breaks when driving after 4.5 h leads to a relative risk of 1.03 (0.87; 1.21), i.e. an increase of 3% in relation to legal driving. The increase is not statistically significant. Violating the regulations governing the longest period of driving of 9 h per day has a relative risk of 1.75 (0.97; 3.16) in relation to legal driving. This increase is very close to statistical significance at the 5% level.

***Length of breaks when driving.*** After 4.5 h driving, a break of 45 min must be taken, which can be shortened to 30 min. The significance of the length of breaks in driving for bus drivers has been studied by Pokorny, Blom, Van Leeuwen and Van Nooten (1987). The study was carried out in the Netherlands and concerned drivers of scheduled city buses. Drivers of such buses normally have two types of break in driving during the

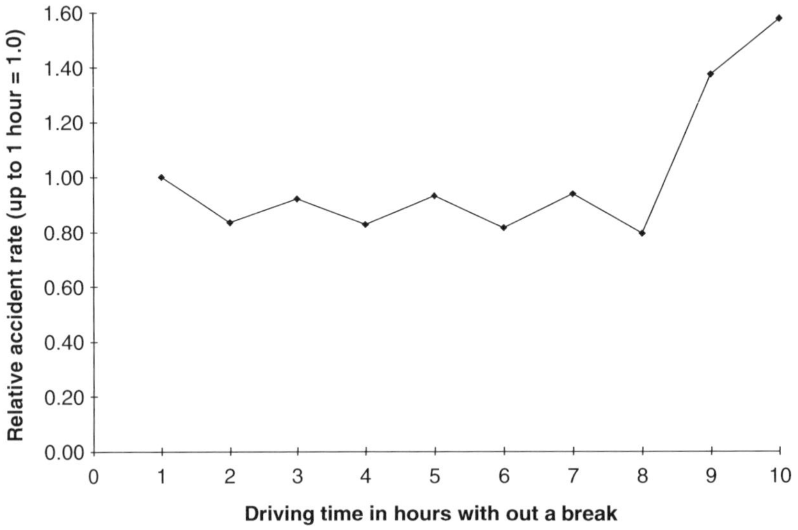


*Figure 6.10.2: Accident rate per hour driven for different numbers of hours driven without a break for bus drivers.*

working day. One type of break is the so-called regulating time of a bus route. The regulating time is the time between the bus arriving at its destination in one direction until it must start back in the opposite direction. The regulating time is usually 5–15 min. If the bus is delayed, the regulating time will be shorter or may disappear entirely.

The other type of break for bus drivers are scheduled rest breaks, such as meal breaks or breaks in connection with shift changes (changing drivers). The scheduled rest breaks are usually between 30 and 60 min. Pokorny et al. studied the relationship between the length of the break and accident rate, for breaks that varied between 0 and more than 100 min. The majority of breaks were between 10 and 50 min.

Drivers who had breaks of up to 69 min had an accident rate that is around 4% lower than drivers who did not have breaks at all (95% CI [−24; +21]). The difference was not statistically significant. A number of such comparisons between shorter and longer breaks have been carried out. The results are summarised in Table 6.10.2.

In the majority of cases, longer breaks led to slightly lower accident rates. This applied whatever the length of the break at the outset. None of the results are statistically significant. Taking all lengths of breaks together, longer breaks (on average, they were

*Table 6.10.2: Effects of length of breaks in driving on bus drivers' accident rate*

| Length of break before (minutes) | Length of break after (minutes) | Change in accident rate (%) (95% CI) |
|---|---|---|
| 0 | 1–69(average 20) | −4 (−24; +21) |
| 10–14 | 15–89 (average 30) | −14 (−50; +48) |
| 15–19 | 20–99 (average 45) | −14 (−51; +51) |
| 25–29 | 30 to >100 (average 65) | −17 (−60; +72) |
| 30–39 | 40 to >100 (average 65) | −5 (−44; +60) |
| 40–49 | 50 to >100 (average 75) | +89 (−18; +334) |
| 50–59 | 60 to >100 (average 85) | −22 (−67; +83) |
| All driven | All lengths | −4 (−19; +14) |

lengthened to around 60 min) led to a decrease in the accident rate of 4% (95% CI [−19; +14]). The length of breaks in driving, in other words, is of relatively little importance for the accident rate, but may possibly reduce it a little.

On the basis of these results, the risk attributable to violations of the regulations on the length of breaks can be estimated. The accident rate when the driver takes a legal break of 45 min or more is set equal to 1.00. The accident rate when the driver takes a break of 30–45 min is then 1.15 (95% CI [0.58; 2.28]). The accident rate when the driver takes a break of less than 30 min is 0.94 (95% CI [0.69; 1.59]).

***Length of the daily break for lorry drivers.*** Lin, Jovanis and Yang (1994) have studied the effect of the length of the daily rest for lorry drivers on accident rate. The risk with a daily rest of up to 10.5 h was set equal to 1.00. The relative risk when taking a daily rest of 10.5–13.75 h was estimated to 0.88. When taking daily rest of 13.75–25.75 h, the relative risk was 0.87 and with a daily rest of more than 25.5 h, the relative risk was 0.81. The uncertainty in the result is not stated, but none of them were statistically significant.

The minimum legal daily rest is 11 h. On the basis of the results stated above, the relative accident rate when the driver takes an illegal daily rest (less than 11 h) compared with a legal daily rest is around 1.17 (approximate uncertainty from 0.95 to 1.40, estimated on the basis of *T*-values given in Lin, Jovanis and Yang).

***The significance of continuous daily rest periods.*** In the United States, long-distance transport drivers may take their daily rest in the vehicle. The driver cabin on articulated lorries in the United States is often equipped with a small sleeping area behind the driver's seat (sleeper berth). A study of the significance that an interrupted daily rest in the vehicle (for example, 2 × 4 h breaks from driving) has for the risk of fatal accidents

(Hertz 1988) concluded that drivers who have an interrupted daily rest had 3.05 times (95% CI [2.36; 3.94]) as high a risk of being involved in a fatal accident as drivers who had an unbroken daily rest.

***Length of weekly working hours for bus drivers.*** A Norwegian study (Nygård and Tellnes 1994) has studied the effects of different aspects of working hours for bus drivers on accident rate. The sample consisted of around 1,500 drivers, of whom 87% were bus drivers. The accidents are self-reported accidents. Figure 6.10.3 shows the most important results of the study.

Figure 6.10.3 shows the effects on the accident rate of (1) the length of the normal weekly working period in hours, (2) the amount of overtime in the previous month and (3) whether the driver has fixed working hours during the day or does shift work. The accident rate is expressed as the number of accidents per driver. Since drivers who do a lot of overtime, for example, also drive more kilometres, it is not clear that the number of accidents per kilometre driven would show the same tendencies as the number of accidents per driver. Figure 6.10.3 shows that when the risk is set equal to 1.00 for drivers who work up to 30 h per week, the risk is 1.57 (95% CI [1.19; 2.07]) for drivers

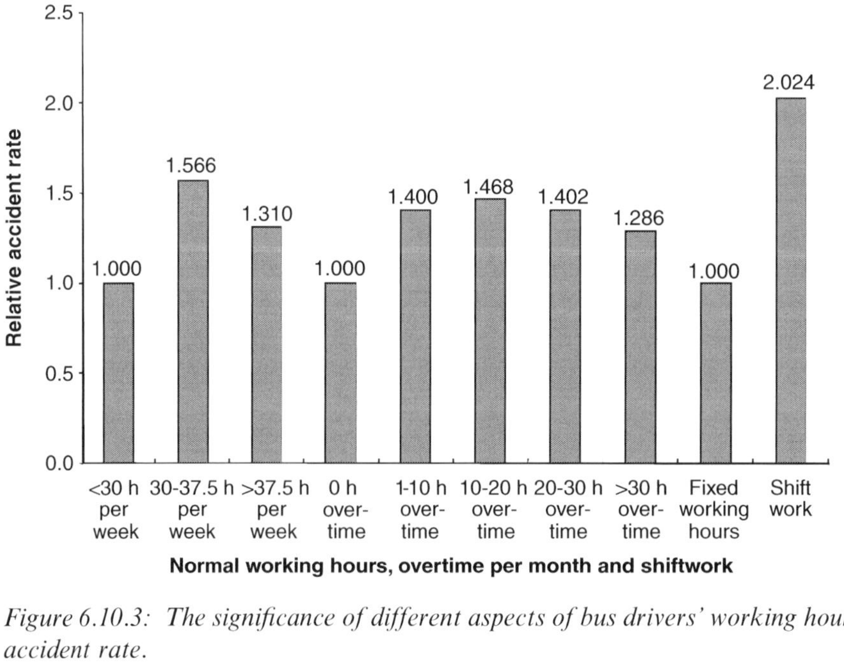


*Figure 6.10.3: The significance of different aspects of bus drivers' working hours for their accident rate.*

who work 30–37.5 h per week and 1.31 (95% CI [0.97; 1.76]) for drivers who work more than 37.5 h per week. Thus, there is a tendency towards an increasing accident risk rate with longer weekly working hours.

***The amount of overtime per month for bus drivers.*** Figure 6.10.3 shows that when the risk for drivers who do not work overtime is set equal to 1.00, it is 1.40 (95% CI [1.03; 1.90]) for drivers who work up to 10 h overtime per month; 1.47 (95% CI [1.07; 2.0]) for drivers who work 10–28 h overtime per month; 1.40 (95% CI [0.95; 2.08]) for drivers who work 20–30 h overtime per month and 1.29 (95% CI [0.91; 1.83]) for drivers who work more than 30 h overtime per month. In other words, overtime work, whatever its extent, contributes to increasing the accident rate for bus drivers.

***Fixed working hours compared with shift work for bus drivers.*** According to Figure 6.10.3, bus drivers who work in shifts have a relative risk of 2.02 (1.61; 2.54) when the accident rate for drivers who work fixed hours during the day is set equal to 1.00.

***The significance of the economic operating conditions on the accident rate for the transport industry.*** The significance of the economic operating conditions for the transport industry for the accident rate of lorries is not well known. The question is discussed in an OECD report (OECD Scientific Expert group 1996) that concludes that very little information is to be found in this area. One hypothesis that has been discussed is that the strong competition pushes down profit margins and that the companies adapt to this by cutting down on maintenance, which can lead to increased accident rates. The OECD report refers to the results of a US study where the relationship between different indicators of the transport companies' financial results and their accident rates are studied. Table 6.10.3 shows one of the results of this study. There is a tendency for the accident rate to be highest in companies with poor financial results, i.e. where operating costs exceed the operating income (the company operates with a loss). However, this tendency is not found for the most profitable companies, although the reasons for this are not known.

*Table 6.10.3: Relationship between operating results and accident rates for lorry transport companies in the USA (OECD 1996)*

| Operating costs divided by operating income ( × 100) | Accidents per million vehicle kilometre |
|---|---|
| More than 100 | 1.38 |
| 98–100 | 1.23 |
| 96–98 | 0.97 |
| 94–96 | 0.87 |
| Below 94 | 1.26 |

### Effect on mobility

An important reason for violating the driving and rest hour regulations is that it is possible to save time in this way. To this extent, driving and rest hour regulations may be said to reduce mobility (extended transport time). However, it is impossible to say how much current driving times would need to be extended to correspond with the driving and rest regulations. For Norway, it can be estimated that the time used for transport has to be increased by 2.6%, if the regulations regarding rest breaks when driving and longest daily driving times were to be respected 100%. The effects for the use of time of violations of the rest period regulations cannot be calculated on the basis of the information available.

### Effect on the environment

No studies have been found that show how the regulations on driving and rest periods affect the incidence of different working environment problems among professional drivers, or how these regulations effect traffic noise or air pollution.

### Costs

The costs of driving and rest regulations fall into two categories. One type is direct costs of enforcement. In 1995, these costs in Norway were estimated at around NOK 5 million. The other type of cost involved in driving and rest hour regulations is the extra time costs incurred in adhering to these regulations. These extra costs are difficult to estimate satisfactorily since it is not known how much time would be used for transport without current driving and rest hour regulations. A minimum estimate for the time costs that the driving and rest regulations entail for lorry drivers can be based on the increase in the time used for transport which would entail 100% respect for these regulations. This increase is calculated to be 2.6%. This comprises around 1 million hours per year. The cost of this increase in transport time is estimated to around NOK 260 million per year.

### Cost–benefit analysis

No cost–benefit analyses of driving and rest hour regulations are available. In order to indicate possible effect of these regulations, a numerical example has been worked out. With 100% compliance with the current regulations, the number of accidents for the groups of vehicles covered by the rules would be around 4.3% lower than it is today.

This represents around 40–45 fewer accidents involving heavy vehicles per year, which corresponds to around NOK 112 million in saved accident costs. The increase in time costs of adhering to the driving and rest regulations is not included as a loss of benefit for transport companies since a benefit obtained by breaking the law should not count as a societal benefit in a cost–benefit analysis (Elvik 1997). It is not known how much driving and rest hour checks would need to be increased in order to achieve 100% respect, but even an increase of 10 times the current levels will cost less than the benefit which 100% respect for the driving and rest hour regulations would give in the form of fewer accidents.

## 6.11 Safety standards for emergency driving

### Problem and objective

In order to be able to fulfil their function, emergency service vehicles need to be able to get through traffic quickly. At the same time, safety standards must be maintained when driving. These requirements are not always easy to reconcile. In order to give emergency service vehicles the best chance of fulfilling their function, the drivers of these vehicles are allowed to ignore certain laws, i.e. regulations regarding traffic behaviour, traffic signs, speed regulations, parking and traffic control. (The Road Traffic Act § 11). Other road users are required to give way to emergency service vehicles when the driver uses flashing blue lights.

Emergency service driving includes driving with blue lights and/or sirens in ambulances/doctors cars, police cars, police motorcycles or fire engines. Emergency service vehicles do not necessarily need to be marked; for example, unmarked police cars can also use blue lights and sirens. Sirens cannot be used alone. Doctors are not allowed to carry out emergency call-out driving unless the vehicle is registered as an emergency service vehicle.

In two Norwegian studies, the accident rate in emergency service vehicle driving has been estimated for ambulances, fire engines and police cars (Frøyland 1983, Fosser 1986). The results of these studies with respect to the risk of injury accidents are shown in Table 6.11.1.

All emergency service vehicles have accident rates that are higher than the average for all road traffic. The risk increases during emergency call-out driving. In emergency call-out driving, the accident rate for ambulances, fire engines and police cars was, respectively, around 10, 20 and 60 times higher than the average for all road traffic. During normal driving, ambulances do not have a higher accident rate than other

*Table 6.11.1: Accident rate for injury accidents in emergency call-out driving in Norway*

| | Injury accidents per million kilometre driven | | |
|---|---|---|---|
| Type of emergency service vehicle | Emergency call-out driving | Normal driving | All driving |
| All road traffic | – | – | 0.41 |
| Ambulances | 3.9 | 0.49 | 1.16 |
| Fire engines | 10.4 | – | 1.90 |
| Police cars | 23.5 | 1.04 | 1.73 |

traffic, but the accident rate for police cars is around 2.5 times as high. The accident rate for fire engines in normal traffic is unknown.

Injury accidents occurring during emergency call-out driving result in more severe injuries than injury accidents otherwise (Frøyland 1983, Fosser 1986). This may be attributable to the fact that the accidents occur at a higher speed than normal traffic. Around 75% of all accidents with emergency service vehicles are collisions with other vehicles. Accidents at junctions are the most frequent. Pedestrians, cyclists and motorcycles are very seldom involved in accidents with emergency service vehicles. People in ambulances may be particularly vulnerable to injuries in the event of collisions. This particularly concerns patients, and nurses or others who are in the ambulance with the patient (Turbell 1980).

Safety standards for emergency driving are designed to reduce the risk associated with such driving and, ideally, to make such driving as safe as road traffic in general.

### Description of the measure

As stated previously, during emergency call-out driving, drivers of emergency service vehicles are allowed to ignore some traffic regulations. This is conditional on warnings being given, using blue lights and/or sirens. If this is done, other road users are required to give way to emergency service vehicles. Safety standards for emergency call-out driving cover safety standards for vehicles and drivers.

***Safety standards for vehicles.*** Emergency service vehicles must be equipped with special warning lights. For ambulances, fire engines and police cars, rotating, blue warning lights on the roof are the most common. Blue warning lights can also be placed on the car's radiator, which is often done on unmarked police cars and ambulances. However, blue is not the 'the best choice' with regard to light intensity and range. The highest intensity is achieved with white light. For coloured light, yellow gives the highest intensity of all colours (Rubin and Howett 1981). The use of red colour on fire engines is probably largely due to historical reasons. No research-based support for the use of red for visual, safety or psychological reasons has been found (Solomon and King 1995). An eye with normal night vision is colour-blind to red in the dark (Southall 1961). Golden yellow is the most visible colour for everybody, even for those who have reduced vision and/or are colour-blind (Lahr and Heinsen 1959). Certain colour combinations have wrongly been considered as advantageous with regard to visibility. In fact, some colours and combinations of colours can break up contours and contrasts, so that vehicles become more difficult to detect. Combinations of red and white are the least visible, whereas those of black and yellow are the most visible (Nathan 1969).

Emergency service vehicles must have sirens that warn other road users in good time. The sirens must be easy to hear, difficult to mistake for other noises, easy to determine their direction and should not cause too much discomfort for other road users and for the drivers of the emergency service vehicles (Dahlstedt 1980a). Direction detection can be difficult since sound can often be reflected. There are several types of sirens for emergency service vehicles. Electronic sirens have one or more loudspeakers operated by electrical impulses from an electronic signal generator. Purely mechanical or electro-mechanical sirens are not used to any great extent any more (Rubin and Howett 1981). There are three main types of sirens (Rubin and Howett 1981): 'wail' (a continuous cyclical (rough) sound that rises or falls evenly), 'yelp' (a 'wail' sound with faster changes between high and low tones) and 'hilo' (a sound with two fixed notes at different pitches, with an even interchange between the high and low tones). The most common are probably the electronic two-tone signals ('high-low' or 'Hilo'). Some experts think these are best because they can be heard inside a car to a greater extent than other electronic sound patterns (Dahlstedt 1980a). Others do not agree with this judgement (Potter et al. 1977).

***Safety standards for drivers.*** Driving emergency service vehicles in an emergency is demanding. Emergency call-out driving requires a high degree of attention and quick reactions. People who drive the emergency service vehicles in emergencies or ambulance with patient(s) in Norway must comply with the medical requirements for professional drivers, must be at least 20 years old and not more than 70, must have a driving licence for the specific group of vehicles, together with a certificate of competence, or must have passed a driving test. The certificates of competence can also be acquired after passing a course.

## Effect on accidents

***Safety standards for vehicles.*** In an experiment in the United States, the warning light was removed from the roof of half of the new standard police cars, which were supplied in 1982 (Raub 1985). These cars had warning lights placed on the front grill and in the rear window. The groups of patrol cars were otherwise identical with regard to stripes, symbols and the text 'State Police'. Vehicles with and without warning lights on the roof were randomly allocated among police officers. Sixty five percent fewer accidents per kilometre driven were registered among drivers who drove cars without warning lights on the roof. Moreover, fuel consumption was reduced by 7% and productivity in patrol duties (speed checks) increased by 25%. All changes were statistically significant. Drivers of cars without warning lights stated that they were aware that the vehicles might be less visible, which had made them more conscious of safety.

Analyses of accidents where emergency service vehicles have crashed with other vehicles show that the driver of the other vehicle had not always noticed the light, sirens or markings on the vehicle (Transportforskningsdelegationen 1979). The results are highly similar for the different vehicle groups. In 40–50% of accidents, the other drivers stated that they had not noticed the warning lights. The proportion is practically the same for sirens. The only group that stands out is fire engines, which were detected more easily than police cars and ambulances. This may be due to the fact that fire engines are normally larger than other vehicles, and several may often appear in quick succession in an emergency call-out.

An American experiment found that sirens may have a relatively low degree of detection (Potter et al. 1977). The study found that the sirens did not give satisfactory warning in any of these cases. A driver sitting in a vehicle with the windows closed, driving at 80 km/h with the radio on will not hear a penetrating siren until the distance between the vehicles is 100 m. If the radio is on loudly, there is a danger that a siren will not be heard at all (Moe 1983). Several studies have concluded that the noise level of sirens must be increased significantly if they are to be heard by other road users in all situations. The noise levels that will be necessary to ensure this will not be acceptable for the drivers of emergency service vehicles, other road users and people living along stretches of road near emergency service vehicle stations (Potter et al. 1977, Dahlstedt 1980a, 1980b, Dahlstedt 1991). Drivers of emergency service vehicles must be aware of this in order to avoid unrealistic notions of the extent to which these sirens are actually heard by other road users.

In a US study, the effect of the colour of fire engines on accidents was studied by comparing a group of red and red/white fire tenders with lemon yellow/white vehicles in the fire service in Dallas, Texas (Solomon and King 1995). Warning lights and sirens were used in all call-outs to the fire but not on the return journey. In 80% of all accidents, and 93% of accidents at intersections, warning lights and sirens were being used. Twenty accidents were recorded that were judged to be related to visibility. Of these, red and red/white vehicles were involved in 16 accidents (7 involving injuries) and lemon yellow/white vehicles in 4 accidents (1 involving injury). The results from the study show that red and red/white fire tenders were involved ca. twice as often in accidents as the lemon yellow/white vehicles. Compared with the accident rate for all vehicles in Dallas, Texas, the red and the red/white and lemon yellow/white vehicles have respectively 20 and 10 times higher accident rates.

***Safety standards for drivers.*** Training of emergency service vehicle drivers has not been standardised. It is therefore difficult to draw any general conclusions about the effects of training for emergency service vehicle drivers. Some emergency service vehicle drivers are given special skid training. The effect of this type of training has been studied in Sweden (Eriksson 1983). Training was carried out on an ice driving circuit. It covered exercises in correct braking, avoidance manoeuvres and the control of skids. The training lasted 4 h. The study found that male drivers who had received skid training were more often involved in accidents for a 6-month period after they had undergone this training than drivers who had not had such training. For women and men with longer periods of employment, no statistically significant changes in accident rate were found, although there was a tendency towards a decrease for women. For all drivers taken together, the accident rate increased by around 45%.

***Other measures.*** In an experiment carried out in Northampton, 14 intersections were equipped with receivers to receive signals from fire engines on call-out so that these would be given priority with a green traffic signal when they arrived at an intersection. An evaluation showed that the probability of being given a green sign increased to around 90%, which in turn reduced the journey time from the fire station to the scene of the fire by around 10% (Griffin and Johnson 1980). In an earlier experiment in giving fire engines on call-out a 'green light', the journey time on call-out was reduced by up to 50% (Honey 1972). German experiments show a reduction in the number of traffic regulation violations on call-out as well as reduction in the journey time (Bosserhoff and Swiderski 1984). It was found that the number of call-outs using the opposite carriageway was reduced from 43% to 12%, running a red light was reduced by 63% to 0, the number of vehicles crossing the emergency vehicles' pathway reduced from 13% to 1% and critical situations were reduced from 10% to 0. Effects on accidents were not studied in these three studies.

### Effect on mobility

Warning other road users with sirens and/or blue lights on vehicles is intended to improve accessibility for emergency service vehicles. Tests in actual traffic in Oslo have shown that sirens give increased mobility when they are used in combination with blue lights (Dahlstedt 1980c). Average time savings were around 15 s/km driven. Using sirens alone has a larger effect on mobility than blue lights alone. In certain traffic situations, there also appear to be differences between the types of sirens with respect to effect on mobility.

In tests where fire engines were given a 'green light', the journey time on call-out is reduced by 10–50% (Honey 1972, Griffin and Johnson 1980). The effects of other measures such as the colour of emergency service vehicle and driving training, on accessibility, have not been documented.

### Effect on the environment

Sirens on emergency service vehicles produce considerable amounts of noise, both within the vehicle and in the surroundings. The median values from measuring 73 sirens were around 94 dB(A) measured in the driver's seat, 104 dB(A) 7 m in front of the vehicle and 105 dB(A) 21 m in front (Dahlstedt 1980a).

Noise within the vehicle is dangerous to health with long-term exposure. Drivers of emergency service vehicles should not be exposed more than 30–60 min per day to avoid long-term hearing damage (Dahlstedt 1980a).

Increasing the noise level of sirens to warn other road users better is not a realistic measure because noise would then reach the pain threshold. However, better sound insulation is possible, as is protecting drivers in other ways against siren noise, which is dangerous to health. However, other road users are not protected, especially pedestrians and cyclists who cannot protect themselves against the noise of sirens other than by blocking their ears. A very high noise level can produce long-term damage to hearing even with short exposure.

### Costs

Early in the 1980s, cost figures were compiled in Norway for safety equipment on emergency service vehicles (Elvik 1985). The cost figures include blue lights, sirens, painting using specific colours, ABS brakes and extra front headlights. Converted to 1995 prices, the costs of these types of equipment are estimated to be around NOK 30,000 per ambulance, around NOK 10,000 per fire engine and around NOK 17,500 per police car.

Cost figures for driving training were also collected in the early 1980s. Training of ambulance personnel was reckoned to cost around NOK 77,000 per pupil. However, this also included medical training, not just driver training. The cost of skid training course lasting 4 h is estimated to be NOK 800–1,000 per pupil. A course in emergency service vehicle driving costs around NOK 14,000 for 80 lessons.

### Cost–benefit analysis

The studies referred to above do not indicate that the measures implemented at present reduce the accident rate for emergency service vehicles. In fact, the results presented above rather tend to indicate the opposite. Removing the light from the roof reduces the accident rate. The same applies to painting fire engines in different colours to those used at present. Skid training increases the accident rate. In a cost–benefit analysis of standards for emergency service vehicle driving, effects on travel time and the chance of saving lives and limiting material damage must also be included. The benefits of safety standards for emergency service vehicle driving are at present too little known for cost–benefit analyses to be made.

## 6.12 Safety standards for school transport

### Problem and objective

According to the official Norwegian accident record, 98 children under the age of 15 were killed or injured on roads on their way to or from school in 1994 and 97 children were killed or injured in 1995. However, the purpose of the journey in accident statistics is only given for drivers. This means that injuries that occurred on journeys to and from school while a passenger in a car or on a bus are not included in the values given above. A study of accidents among schoolchildren in Østfold, Norway, found that 75% of accidents on journeys to or from school occurred on bicycles. This is primarily due to a high number of single-vehicle accidents involving bicycles. Slightly more than 10% of accidents occurred when the child was a passenger in a car or on public transport (Kolbenstvedt 1986).

In Sweden, children's accident rates in traffic have been estimated right down to the age of 1 year. Figure 6.12.1 shows the estimated injury rate, expressed as the number of injured persons per million person kilometre for different modes of travel among children in Sweden (Thulin and Nilsson 1994). Children's injury rates are highest as pedestrians and cyclists. As pedestrians, children have a higher risk than in other modes of travel and a higher risk than adult pedestrians. The youngest children have

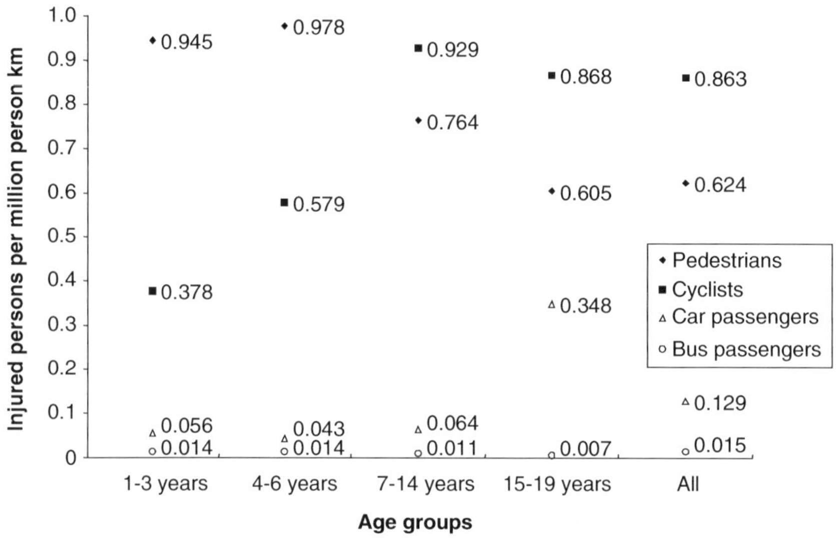


*Figure 6.12.1: Children's risk of injury in traffic in Sweden. Number of injured children per million person kilometre in 1994.*

the highest risk as pedestrians, especially in the age group 4–6 years. Next highest is the risk to young children when they cycle. However, the risk estimates are based on official accident statistics for Sweden, where, as in Norway, there is significant under-reporting of cycle injuries among children, especially for single-vehicle accidents with bicycles. According to Figure 6.12.1, the safest way for children to travel is as passengers in cars or buses. The injury risk rate is particularly low for buses.

School transport is intended to give children safer journeys to school than alternative methods of travel from door to door.

## Description of the measure

Pupils in Norway are entitled to school transport if the distance between home and school is 4 km at elementary school level and 6 km at secondary school level. However, some municipalities offer school transport independent of the distance between home and school, in order to give children safer transport to and from school (Norges offentlige utredninger 1995).

Safety standards for school transport are here taken to mean all measures to make school journeys as safe as possible. This covers the transport itself as well as measures to make such transport as safe as possible. Measures described here are

- school transport with buses at different distances to school
- special safety standards for school buses
- improving bus stops
- training bus drivers
- training pupils.

Some of these measures are also discussed in other chapters, but are included here in order to give as full as possible an overview of possible measures.

## Effect on accidents

***School transport with buses at different distances to school.*** A Norwegian study has evaluated the amount of transport and costs of alternative boundaries for school transport for pupils in different classes in elementary schools (Engebretsen and Hagen 1996). The effects of different transport boundaries on the number of accidents were not calculated. These effects depend on which alternative transport modes would have been chosen instead of school bus transport, which cannot be known with certainty. Table 6.12.1 shows the number of person kilometre per year that would be transferred to or from school bus transport according to the alternative school transport boundaries given.

The average injury rate for bus passengers, estimated on the basis of the Norwegian official accident register, is around 0.05 injured persons per million person kilometre. It is assumed that children's injury risk as bus passengers is the same as the average injury risk for a bus passenger. The average injury risk for car passengers is around 0.15 injured persons per million person kilometre, calculated on the basis of the official

*Table 6.12.1: Number of person kilometre transferred to or from buses for different transport boundaries for school transport in Norway*

| | Changing transport boundary | | | |
|---|---|---|---|---|
| Age level (years) | From km | To km | Transferred person km | To or from |
| 6 | 4 | 2 | 8,387,000 | To bus |
| 7–9 | 4 | 2 | 23,403,000 | To bus |
| 13–15 | 4 | 5 | 10,526,000 | From bus |

accident record. Assuming that the variation in risk by age is the same in Norway as in Sweden, the injury risk for children in cars can be estimated to 0.05 injured persons per million person kilometre for 6-year-old children, and around 0.075 injured persons per million person kilometre for children aged 7–14 years. The injury risk for children aged between 7–14 years who cycle, estimated on the basis of the official Norwegian accident record and the 1992 survey of cycling (Borger and Frøysadal 1993), is 0.63 injured persons per million person kilometre. The same accident rate is assumed for 6-year-olds. Children's injury risk as pedestrians has not been documented in Norway. Assuming the same variation by age as in Sweden, the risk of injury can be roughly estimated to be around 1.00 injured persons per million person kilometre for 6-year olds and 0.95 injured persons per million person kilometre for 7- to 14-year-olds.

On the basis of these assumptions about the risk of injury, the possible effects on the number of injured children of changes in transport boundaries given in Table 6.12.1 can be calculated. The expected number of injuries with buses for 6-year-old is $0.05 \times 8.387 = 0.4$ per year. A good alternative to buses are cars, which give the same expected annual number of injuries as buses. The worst alternative to buses is that 6-year-olds walk, which gives an expected number of injuries of 8.4 per year. Cycling to and from school is regarded as unrealistic for this age group. Changing the transport boundary from 4 to 2 km for 6-year-olds could therefore prevent between 0 and 8 injuries per year, with 2–4 as the most probable figure. A similar calculation for 7- to 9-year-olds shows that changing the transport boundary limit from 4 to 2 km could prevent between 0.5 and 21 injuries per year, with 5–8 as the most probable. Extending the transport boundary from 4 to 5 km for 13- to 15-year-olds may lead to 0.25–9.5 more accidents per year, with 3–5 as the most probable. These results are very uncertain, but indicate the order of magnitude of changes likely to be observed for injury accidents.

***Special safety standards for school buses.*** In a US study (Transportation Research Board 1989), a number of possible measures for buses were evaluated. The effects of the measures are not documented, but approximate estimates have been produced. The possible effects are estimated to be:

| Measure | Approximate decrease in accidents (%) |
|---|---|
| Seat belts | 0–20 |
| Higher seat backs | 0–20 |
| Warning indicators at crossings | 5–25 |
| Sensors for obstacles in front of the wheels | 10–50 |
| Stop signal arm | 0–30 |
| Exterior loudspeaker system | 0–20 |

Warning indicators and stopping signal arms are installed on the bus to make other road users aware of children crossing the road. The sensors detect obstacles in front of the wheels of a bus, so that pupils are not run over.

***Improvements to bus stops, etc.*** Bus stops should be located such that the walking distance is as short as possible and so that, as far as possible, pedestrians can use footpaths or other areas which are separate from vehicle traffic. Guidelines for the design of bus stops in Norway are given in the road design standards (Statens vegvesen, handbook 017, 1993). Bus stops designed as bus bays offer better safety than bus stops on the road (see Section 3.18, *bus lanes and improvements to bus stops*). Guide rails in bus bays can also increase safety. Erecting pedestrian barriers between the pavements of footpaths and the road leads to a reduction in the number of accidents for both pedestrians and vehicles. Using school patrols to protect crossing points for children also reduces the number of accidents, but the results are uncertain (see Section 3.14, *traffic control for pedestrians and cyclists*). Lighting in bus bays can be assumed to reduce the number of accidents (see Section 1.18, *road lighting*).

***Training school bus drivers.*** In several states in the United States, drivers who drive school buses must undergo special training in school transport (Transportation Research Board 1989). The effect of such training on accidents is not known. However, it has been found that training bus drivers in defensive driving can reduce the accident rate per driver by around 20% (see Section 6.7, *training professional drivers*).

***Training children.*** It has been found that teaching children aged between 5 and 12 the right way to cross a road can reduce the number of accidents involving children who cross the road by 10–20% (see Section 7.2, *training schoolchildren*).

## Effect on mobility

As a rule, school bus transport provides children with faster school journeys than other modes of travel.

## Effect on the environment

No effects of school transport on noise and pollution have been documented. The feeling of security can be improved with school transport.

*Table 6.12.2: Costs of safety measures in school buses*

| Measure | Type of cost | Cost per bus NOK |
|---|---|---|
| Seat belts | Installation cost | 15,000 |
| | Annual maintenance | 440 |
| High seat backs | Installation cost | 2,000 |
| Warning indicator | Installation cost | 2,650 |
| | Annual maintenance | 265 |
| Obstacle sensors | Installation cost | 21,000 |
| | Annual maintenance | 1,060 |
| Stop signal alarm | Installation cost | 2,650 |
| | Maintenance cost | 135 |
| External loudspeaker system | Installation cost | 2,650 |
| | Annual maintenance | 135 |

Based on the Transportation Research Board (1989).

## Costs

In a US report, the cost of a number of safety requirements for buses have been calculated (Transportation Research Board 1989). Converted to 1995 Norwegian kroner, the costs of the different measures are given in Table 6.12.2. It can be seen that the cost of installing all types of safety equipment on a bus can be considerable.

## Cost–benefit analyses

The additional cost of providing school transport for all 6-year-old children in Norway living 2 km or more from school, compared with 4 km from school, is NOK 28.3 million. The number of injuries prevented per year is 2–4 that corresponds to a monetary benefit of NOK 3–6 million. The corresponding additional cost of reducing the school transport boundary from 4 to 2 km for 7- to 9-year-old children is NOK 79.6 million. The number of injuries avoided is 5–8 per year, which corresponds to reduced accident costs of NOK 7.5–12 million per year. This is less than the cost of the measure. Increasing the transport boundary from 4 to 5 km gives a saving of NOK 35.8 million kroner per year. The number of injured children will increase by 3–5 that represents an additional cost of NOK 4.5–7.5 million per year.

Even using the most optimistic assumptions as a basis regarding the effects of school bus transport on the number of accidents among children, expanding the current transport system does not appear to be a cost-effective measure based on the effect on the injury figures alone. If gains in mobility and in the feeling of safety for both parents and children are included, the result may be different. These possible beneficial effects are, however, too little known to be included in a cost–benefit analysis.

## References


Adams, A., V. Collingwood & R. F. S. Job. (1985). *Evaluation of the 1982 Australia Post motorcycle training scheme.* Research Note RN 3/85. Sydney, Traffic Authority of New South Wales, Traffic Accident Research Unit, Sydney.

Adler, G., Rottunda, S., Bauer, M. & Kuskowski, M. (2000). The older driver with Parkinson's disease. *Journal of Gerontological Social Work*, **34(2)**, pp 39–49.

Agent, K.R., Steenbergen, L., Pigman, J.G., Kidd, P.S., McCoy, C. & Pollack, S.H. (2001) Impact of partial graduated driver's license on teen motor vehicle crashes in Kentucky. *Transportation Research Record*, **1779**, 54–61.

Alvestad, M., Haugen, O.A. (1999). Death behind the wheel. *Tidsskrift For Den Norske Laegeforening [The Journal of the Norwegian Medical Association]*, **119(7)**, 966–968.

Ball, K. & Owsley, C. (1991). Identifying Correlates of Accident Involvement for the Older Driver. *Human Factors*, **33**, 583–595.

Bartl, G. (2004). *Ansätze für mehr Verkehrssicherheit von Fahranfängern in Österreich.* Berichte der Bundesanstalt für Straßenwesen. Unterreihe Mensch und Sicherheit, 161.

Bédard, M., Molloy, D. W., & Lever, J. A. (1998). Factors associated with motor vehicle crashes in cognitively impaired older adults. *Alzheimer Disease and Associated Disorders* **12(3)**, 135–139.

Beilock, R., R. B. Capelle & E. B. Page. (1989). Speed and Training Factors Associated with Heavy Truck Accidents. *Transportation Quarterly*, **43**, 571–589.

Belloc, B. & M. Ivaldi. (1991). *Evaluation de l'Apprentissage anticipe de la Conduite.* Rapport 9101. Université des Sciences Sociales de Toulouse, Faculté des Sciences Économiques, Groupe de Recherche en Économie Mathematique et Quantitative, Toulouse.

Benzodiazepine/Driving Collaborative Group (1993). Are benzodiazepines a risk factor for road accidents? *Drug and Alcohol Dependence*, **33 (1993)**, 19–22.

Bernhoft, I. M. (2001). *Risiko i trafikken 1997–1999.* Notat 9 2001. Danmarks Transportforskning, Lyngby.

Berube, E. (1995). *Evaluation of Mature Driver Improvement Program Home-Study Courses.* Report RSS-95-157. California Department of Motor Vehicles.

Beylich, K-M., Bjørneboe, A., Chritophersen, A. S., Fosser, S., Glad, A. & Mørland, J. (1994). *Frequency of alcohol and other intoxicants in blood samples from drivers involved in accidents.* TØI-rapport 248. Institute of Transport Economics, Oslo.

Bjørnskau, T. (1988). *Risiko i persontransport på veg*. TØI-rapport 0002. Transportøkonomisk institutt, Oslo.

Bjørnskau, T. (1993). *Risiko i veitrafikken 1991/92*. TØI-rapport 216. Transportøkonomisk institutt, Oslo.

Bjørnskau, T. (1994). *Spillteori, trafikk og ulykker. En teori om interaksjon i trafikken*. TØI-rapport 287. Transportøkonomisk institutt, Oslo.

Bjørnskau, T. (2000). *Risiko i veitrafikken 1997/98*. TØI rapport 483/2000. Oslo: Transportøkonomisk institutt.

Boase, P. & Tasca, L. (1998). *Graduated Licensing System Evaluation*. Ministry of Transportation of Ontario, Safety Policy Branch: Interim Report '98, 410, SPB-98-101.

Borger, A. (1992). *Samfunnsøkonomiske kostnader ved føreropplæringen*. Arbeidsdokument TST/0352/92. Transportøkonomisk institutt, Oslo.

Borger, A. (1996). *Risikoberegning for transport av farlig gods på veg 1990–94*. Arbeidsdokument TST/0721/96. Transportøkonomisk institutt, Oslo.

Borger, A. & E. Frøysadal. (1993). *Sykkelundersøkelsen 1992*. TØI-rapport 217. Transportøkonomisk institutt, Oslo.

Bosserhoff, D. & D Swiderski. (1984). Priority for emergency vehicles by intervention in signal-setting programs. *Traffic Engineering and Control*, **25**, 314–316, 326.

Bouchard, J., Dussaud, C., Simard, R., Gendreau, M. & Lemire, A.M. (2000). *The Quebec graduated licensing system for novice drivers: A two-year evaluation of the 1997 reform*. Conference on alcohol, drugs, and traffic safety, Stockholm.

Broughton, J. (1987). *The effect on motorcycling of the 1981 Transport Act*. TRRL Research Report 106. Transport and Road Research Laboratory, Crowthorne, Berkshire.

Broughton, J. (1988). *The variation of car drivers' accident risk with age*. Research report 135. Transport and Road Research Laboratory, Crowthorne, Berkshire.

Brækhus, A. (1996). *Demens og bilkjøring. Dagens situasjon og praksis vedrørende helseattest for førerkort*. Upublisert rapportmanuskript. Ullevål sykehus, hukommelsesklinikken, Oslo.

Cappelen Akademisk Forlag (2003). *Vegtrafikklovgivningen 2003. Vegtrafikkloven med trafikkregler og forskrifter*. Ajourført pr 27.februar 2003. Oslo, Cappelen Akademisk Forlag.

Carstensen, G. (1994). Evaluation of a New Driver Education in Denmark. In: *Proceedings of the Conference Strategic Highway Research Program (SHRP) and Traffic Safety on Two Continents*, Part 2, 287–298. September 22–24, Hague, Netherlands.

Carstensen, G. (1996). *Køreuddannelsen til personbil - effekt på uheldsudviklingen*. Rapport 2/1996. Rådet for Trafiksikkerhedsforskning, København.

Carstensen, G. (2002). The effect of accident risk of a change in driver education in Denmark. *Accident Analysis and Prevention,* **34**, 111–121.

Chaplin, J. P. & T. S. Krawiec. (1970). *Systems and Theories of Psychology*. Second Edition. Holt, Rinehart and Winston, London.

Christensen, P. (1992). *Kostnader ved alternativer for føreropplæring*. Arbeidsdokument TST/0381/92. Transportøkonomisk institutt, Oslo.

Christensen, P. (1995). *Beregning av kostnader forbundet med føreropplæring*. Arbeidsdokument TST/0652/95. Transportøkonomisk institutt, Oslo.

Christensen, P. (1997). *Beregning av føreropplæringskostnader*. TØI-notat 1056. Transportøkonomisk institutt, Oslo.

Christensen, P. & A. Glad. (1996). *Obligatorisk glattkjøringskurs for førere av tunge biler. Effekt på ulykkesrisikoen*. TØI-rapport 334. Transportøkonomisk institutt, Oslo.

Christensen, P., A. Glad & T. O. Pedersen. (1974). *Fornyet førerprøve som virkemiddel i trafikksikkerhetsarbeidet*. TØI-rapport 197. Transportøkonomisk institutt, Oslo.

Christie, R. (2001). *The effectiveness of driver training as a road safety measure: A review of the literature*. Royal Automobile Club of Victoria: Report 01/03.

Cooper, D., Gillen, D. & Atkins, F. (2004). *Impacts of California's graduated licensing law of 1998*. Institute of Transportation Studies, University of California, Berkley: Research Report UCB-ITS-RR-2004-1.

Cooper, P. J., Tallman, K., Tuokko, H. & Beattie, B.L. (1993). Vehicle Crash Involvement and Cognitive Deficit in Older Drivers. *Journal of Safety Research*, **24**, 9–17.

Coppin, R.S. & Peck, R.C. (1965). *The totally deaf driver in California – Part II*. Sacramento, California, Department of Motor Vehicles.

Dahlstedt, S. (1980a). *Akustiska utryckningssignaler I: Ljudnivåer inuti, och utanför, utryckningsfordon*. TØI-notat 544. Transportøkonomisk institutt, Oslo.

Dahlstedt, S. (1980b). *Akustiska utryckningssignaler II: Hörbarhet hos signaler med olika karaktär*. TØI-notat 545. Transportøkonomisk institutt, Oslo.

Dahlstedt, S. (1980c). *Akustiska utryckningssignaler III: Utryckningsfordons framkomlighet med olika signaler*. TØI-notat 546. Transportøkonomisk institutt, Oslo.

Dahlstedt, S. (1991). *Larmanordningar för utryckningsfordon. En litteraturstudie*. VTI-rapport 327. Väg- och Trafikinstitutet (VTI), Linköping.

Daltrey, R. & B. Thompson. (1987). *Evaluation of motorcycle rider training and licensing schemes: Time series analysis*. Research Note RN/87/8. Melbourne, Research and Investigations Branch, Road Traffic Authority – Victoria.

Danmarks statistik. (1982). *Færdselsuheld 1981. Kapittel 4 Personskader i forhold til transportmængde*. Statistiske meddelelser 1982:8. Danmarks statistik, København.

Decina, L.E. & Staplin, L. (1993) Retrospective evaluation of alternative vision screening criteria for older and younger drivers. *Accident Analysis and Prevention*. **Vol 25**, 267–275.

Diamantopoulou, K., Skalova, M., Dyte, D., & Cameron, M. (1996). *Crash risks of road user groups in Victoria (88)*. Melbourne, Australia: Monash University Accident Research Centre.

Doherty, S.T. & Andrey, J.C. (1997). Young drivers and graduated licensing: The Ontario case. *Transportation,* **24**, 227–251.

Dow, T., Wilson, F. & Hildebrand, E. (2005). *Effects of the graduated licensing program on young drivers in New Brunswick*. University of New Brunswick, Transportation Group. Fredericton, NB: Canadian Multidisciplinary Road Safety Conference XV.

Downing, A. (1988). The effectiveness of a retraining programme for bus drivers in Pakistan. In: *Road User Behaviour. Theory and Research*, 682–689. (Rothengatter, J. A. & R DeBruin eds.) Van Gorcum, Assen.

Drachman, D. A. & Swearer, J. M. (1993). Driving and Alzheimer's disease: The risk of crashes. *Neurology*, **43**, 2448–2456.

Dreyer, D. & M. Janke. (1979). The effects of range versus nonrange driver training on the accident and conviction frequencies of young drivers. *Accident Analysis and Prevention*, **11**, 179–198.

Driver Education (1998). *Teen crash rates drop under GDL*. Driver Education, 1998.

Drummond, A. E. (1986). *Driver Licensing Age and Accident Involvement Rates of Young Drivers*. Report GR/86/15. Hawthorn, Victoria, Road traffic Authority, Hawthorn.

Elvik, R. (1985). *Kostnader til trafikksikkerhetstiltak i 1982. Sammenlikning med kostnader til tiltak i 1973 og 1978 og ulykkeskostnader de samme år*. TØI-notat 756. Transportøkonomisk institutt, Oslo.

Elvik, R. (1988). *Risiko ved transport av farlig gods på veg - foredrag presentert på NIF-kurs i april 1988*. Arbeidsdokument TS/0018/88. Transportøkonomisk institutt, Oslo.

Elvik, R. (1991). *Effektmåling av føreropplæring. Et eksempel på Effektmålingenes Jernlov?* Arbeidsdokument TST/0300/91. Transportøkonomisk institutt, Oslo.

Elvik, R. (1992). *Kan vi stole på resultatene av forskning om virkninger av føreropplæring?* Arbeidsdokument TST/0347/92. Transportøkonomisk institutt, Oslo.

Elvik, R. (1997). *Vegtrafikklovgivning, kontroll og sanksjoner. Potensialet for å bedre trafikksikkerheten og nytte-kostnadsvurdering av ulike tiltak*. TØI-notat 1073. Transportøkonomisk institutt, Oslo.

Elvik, R. (2000). *Improving Road Safety in Sweden. An Analysis of the Potential for improving Safety, the Cost-Effectiveness and Cost-Benefit Ratios of Road Safety Measures. Main Report*. TØI rapport 490/2000. Oslo: Transportøkonomisk institutt.

Elvik, R. (2002). *A framework for cost-benefit analysis of policy options designed to control impaired driving*. Draft report of Deliverable P1 to project IMMORTAL. Oslo, Institute of Transport Economics, Norway.

Engebretsen, Ø. & K-E. Hagen. (1996). *Omfanget av skoleskyss og kostnader ved alternative skyssgrenser i barne- og ungdomsskolen.* TØI-rapport 333. Transportøkonomisk institutt, Oslo.

Engel, U. & L. Krogsgård Thomsen. (1989). Færdselsundervisning og propaganda-en færdselssikkerhedsfremmende foranstaltning? *Dansk Vejtidsskrift*, **12**, 295–297.

Eriksson, R. (1983). *Utvärdering av utbildning vid trafikövningsplatser.* Examensarbete. Pedagogiska institutionen, Uppsala Universitet, Uppsala.

Evans, L. (1991). *Traffic Safety and The Driver.* Van Nostrand Reinhold, New York, NY.

Fazakerley, J. A. & A. J. Downing. (1980). *A comparison of two methods of driver testing.* TRRL Laboratory report 931. Transport and Road Research Laboratory, Crowthorne, Berkshire.

Ferdun, G. S., R. C. Peck & R. S. Coppin. (1967). The Teen-Aged Driver. An Evaluation of Age, Experience, Driving Exposure and Driver Training as They relate to Driving Record. *Highway Research Record*, **163**, 31–53.

Fitten, L.J., Perryman, K.M., Wilkinson, C.J., Little, R.J., Burns, M.M., Pachana, N., Mervis, J.R., Malmgren, R., Siembieda, D.W. & Ganzell, S. (1995). Alzheimer and vascular dementias and driving. *Journal of the American Medical Association*, **273**, 1360–1364.

Fontaine, H. (1988). Usage de l'automobile et risque d'accident. *Recherche Transports Sécurité*, **20**, 5–12.

Forsyth, E.; Maycock, G.; Sexton, B. (1995). *Cohort study of learner and novice drivers: Part 3, accidents, offences and driving experience in the first three years of driving.* Project Report 111. Transport Research Laboratory, Crowthorne, Berkshire.

Foss, R.D., Feagernes, J.R. & Rodgman, E.A. (2001). Initial effects of graduated driver licensing on 16-year old driver crashes in North Carolina. *Journal of the American Medical Association,* **286**, 1588–1592.

Fosser, S. (1986). *Ulykkesrisiko ved politiets utrykningskjøring.* TØI-rapport. Transportøkonomisk institutt, Oslo.

Fosser, S. & R. Elvik. (1996). *Dødsrisiko i vegtrafikken og andre aktiviteter.* TØI-notat 1038 Transportøkonomisk institutt, Oslo.

Friedland, R.P., Koss, E., Kumar, A., et al. (1988). Motor Vehicle Crashes in Dementia of the Alzheimer Type. *Annals of Neurology*, **24**, 782–786.

Frith, W. J. (1994). A case-control study of heavy vehicle drivers' working time and safety. *Proceedings 17th ARRB Conference, Part 5*, 17–30, 1994. Australian Road Research Board, Vermont South.

Frøyland, P. (1983). *Risiko ved utrykningskjøring. En analyse av ulykker og risiko i utrykningsetatene i Norge, og en analyse av ambulansetjenesten basert på en undersøkelse i fire fylker.* TØI-rapport. Transportøkonomisk institutt, Oslo.

Gaudry, M. (1987). *Responsibility for accidents: Relevant results selected from the DRAG model.* Publication # 544. Centre for transport research, University of Montreal.

Glad, A. (1988). *Fase 2 i føreropplæringen. Effekt på ulykkesrisikoen.* TØI-rapport 15. Transportøkonomisk institutt, Oslo.

Glad, A. (1996). *Effekt på trafikksikkerheten av økt kjøretrening i føreropplæringen.* Arbeidsdokument TST/0749/96. Transportøkonomisk institutt, Oslo.

Goodwin, A.H. & Foss, R.D. (2004). Graduated driver licensing restrictions: Awareness, compliance, and enforcement in North Carolina. *Journal of Safety Research*, **35**, 367–374.

Gebers, M.A. & Peck, R.C. (2003). Using traffic conviction correlates to identify high accident-risk drivers. *Accident Analysis and Prevention*, **35**, 903–912.

Gray, I. (1990). An attempt to reduce accidents in a company car fleet by driver training and encouragement of low risk driving habits. *Journal of Traffic Medicine*, **18**, 139–141.

Gregersen, N. P. (1993). *Integrerad förarutbildning. Ett försök med strukturerat samarbete mellan trafikskola och privatlärare.* VTI-rapport 376. Väg- och Trafikinstitutet (VTI), Linköping.

Gregersen, N. P. (1994). Systematic cooperation between driving schools and parents in driver education, an experiment. *Accident Analysis and Prevention*, **26**, 453–461.

Gregersen, N. P. (1995). *Prevention of road accidents among young novice car drivers.* Linköping University Medical Dissertations No 444. Department of Community Medicine, Faculty of Health and Swedish Road and Transport Research Institute, Linköping.

Gregersen, N. P. (1996). Young drivers' overestimation of their own skill – an experiment on the relation between training strategy and skill. *Accident Analysis and Prevention*, **28**, 243–250.

Gregersen, N. P. (1997). *Utvärdering av 16-årsgräns för övingskörning.* VTI-rapport 418. Väg- och Transportforskningsinstitutet, Linköping.

Gregersen, N. P., B. Brehmer & B. Morén. (1996). Road safety improvement in large companies. An experimental comparison of different measures. *Accident Analysis and Prevention*, **28**, 297–306.

Gregersen, N. P. & B. Morén. (1990). *Trafiksäkerhetsåtgärder i Televerket: Ett jamförande försök att minska skador och kostnader under körträning, gruppsamtal, bonus och kampanj.* VTI-rapport nr 348. Linköping, Väg- och Trafikinstitutet.

Gregersen, N.P., Nyberg, A. & Berg, H.Y. (2003). Accident involvement among learner drivers – an analysis of the consequences of supervised practice. *Accident Analysis and Prevention*, **35**, 725–730.

Gresset, J.A. & Meyer, F.M. (1994). Risk of accidents among elderly car drivers with visual acuity equal to 6/12 or 6/15 and lack of binocular vision. *Ophthal Physiol Opt*, **14, January**, 33–37.

Griffin, R. M. & D. Johnson, D. (1980). Northampton fire priority demonstration scheme – a report on the first part of the "before" study and EVADE. *Traffic Engineering and Control*, **21**, 182–185.

Hackman, K. S., E. E. Larson & A. E. Shinder. (1978). *Analysis of accident data and hours of service of interstate commercial motor vehicle drivers.* Report PB 286 718. US Department of Transportation, Federal Highway Administration, Washington DC.

Hagge, R. A. & W. C. Marsh. (1986). *An evaluation of the traffic safety impact of provisional licensing.* Interim report. Sacramento, CA, Department of Motor Vehicles, Sacramento.

Hagge, R. A. & P. A. Romanowicz. (1996). Evaluation of California's commercial driver license program. *Accident Analysis and Prevention*, **28**, 547–559.

Hamelin, P. (1987). *Lorry drivers' time habits in work and their involvement in traffic accidents.* Institut national de recherche sur les transports et leur sécrurité (INRETS), Paris.

Hansotia, P., & Broste, S.K. (1991). The effect of epilepsy or diabetes mellitus on the risk of automobile accidents. *New England Journal of Medicine*, **324(1)**, 22–26.

Harrington, D. M. (1972). The young driver follow-up study: an evaluation of the role of human factors in the first four years of driving. *Accident Analysis and Prevention*, **4**, 191–240.

Harris, W. & R. R. Mackie. (1972). *A study of the relationships among fatigue, hours of service, and the safety of operations of truck and bus drivers.* Report BMCS-RD-71-2. US Department of Transportation, Federal Highway Administration, Washington DC.

Hatakka, M., Keskinen, E., Katila, A. & Laapotti, S. (1996). Professional and private driver training in Finland – evaluation of results. In: *Proceedings of International Conference on Traffic and Transport Psychology*, Valencia, Spain, May 22–25, 245–249.

Hauer, E. & B. N. Persaud. (1983). A Common Bias in Before-and-After Accident Comparisons and Its Elimination. *Transportation Research Record*, **905**, 164–174.

Hautzinger, H. & B. Tassaux. (1989). *Verkehrsmobilität und Unfallrisiko in der Bundesrepublik Deutschland. Ergebnisbericht.* Forschungsbericht 195. Bundesanstalt für Strassenwesen, Bergisch Gladbach.

Hautzinger, H., Tassaux-Becker, B., Hamacher, R. (1996). *Verkehrsunfallrisiko in Deutschland (Road accidents in Germany).* Berichte der Bundesanstalt für Straßenwesen, Heft M 58.

Heggdal, M. Aa., K. Pedersen & T. Conradi. (1990). *La Conduite Accompagnée. Fransk føreropplæring går nye veier. Inntrykk fra en studietur til Frankrike 11–15. januar 1990.* Vegdirektoratet, Opplæringskontoret, Oslo.

Hemmelgarn, B., Suissa, S., Huang, Abolvin, J-F. & Pinard, G. (1997). Benzodiazepine use and the risk of motor vehicle crash in the elderly. *The Journal of the American Medical Association*, **278(1)**, 27–31.

Hertz, R. P. (1988). Tractor-trailer driver fatality: the role of nonconsecutive rest in a sleeper berth. *Accident Analysis and Prevention*, **20**, 431–439.

Hess, E. & P. Born. (1987). *Erfolgskontrolle von Antischleuderkursen*. Bfu-Report 10. Schweitzerische Beratungsstelle für Unfallverhütung (BFU), Bern.

Hills, B. L. & Burg, A. (1977). *A reanalysis of California driver vision data: general findings*. TRRL Laboratory Report 768. Transport and Road Research Laboratory, Crowthorne, Berkshire.

Hingson, R; Heeren, T; Mangione, T; Morelock, S; and Mucatel, M. (1982). Teenage Driving after Using Marijuana or Drinking And Traffic Accident Involvement. *Journal of Safety Research*, **13**, 33–37.

Hofstetter, H. W. (1976). Visual acuity and highway accidents. *Journal of the American Optometric Association*, **47**, 887–893.

Hoinville, G., R. Berthoud & A. M. Mackie. (1972). *A study of accident rates amongst drivers who passed or failed an advanced driving test*. Report LR 499. Transport and Road Research Laboratory, Crowthorne, Berkshire.

Honey, D. W. (1972). Priority routes for fire appliances. *Traffic Engineering and Control*, **13**, 166–167.

Honkanen, R., Ertama, L., Linnoila, M., Alha, A, Lukkari, I., Karlsson, M., Kiviluoto, O. & Puro, M. (1980). Role of drugs in traffic accidents. *British Medical Journal*, **281**, 1309–1312.

Hurt, H. H., J. V. Ouellet & D. R. Thom. (1981). *Motorcycle Accident Cause Factors and Identification of Countermeasures*. Final Report, Volume 1, Technical Report. Report DOT-HS-805 862. US Department of Transportation, National Highway Traffic Safety Administration, Washington DC.

Ingebrigtsen, S. (1989). *Motorsykler, mopeder og ulykker*. TØI-rapport 30. Transportøkonomisk institutt, Oslo.

Ingebrigtsen, S. (1990). *Risikofaktorer ved ferdsel med moped og motorsykkel*. TØI-rapport 66. Transportøkonomisk institutt, Oslo.

Janke, M. K. (1983). Accident Rates of Drivers with Bioptic Telescopic Lenses. *Journal of Safety Research*, **14**, 159–165.

Janke, M. K. (1990). Safety effects of relaxing California's clean-record requirement for driver license renewal by mail. *Accident Analysis and Prevention*, **22**, 335–349.

Janke, M.K. (1993). Reportable medical conditions and driver risk. *Alcohol, Drugs and Driving*, **9(3-4)**, 167–183.

Janke, M. K. (1994). The Mature Driver Improvement Program in California. *Transportation Research Record*, **1438**, 77–83.

Johansson, K. (1997). *Older Automobile Drivers: Medical Aspects*. Doctor's Dissertation. Department of Clinical Neuroscience and Family Medicine, Division of Geriatric Medicine, Traffic Medicine Center, Karloinska Institute, Stockholm, Sweden.

Johansson, R. (1982). *Förhållandet mellan upplevd och verklig olycksrisk*. TFD-rapport 1982:9. Transportforskningsdelegationen, Stockholm.

Johansson, R. (1991). *Funderingar kring varför trafiksäkerhetsutbildning ofta har så begränsade trafiksäkerhetseffekter.* VTI-notat TF 54-11 (1991-02-26). Väg- och Trafikinstitutet (VTI), Linköping.

Jonah, B. A. (1986). Accident risk and driver risk-taking behaviour among young drivers. *Accident Analysis and Prevention*, **18**, 255–271.

Jonah, B. A., N. E. Dawson & B. W. E. Bragg. (1981). Predicting accident involvement with the motorcycle operator skill test. *Accident Analysis and Prevention*, **13**, 307–318.

Jonah, B. A., N. E. Dawson & B. W. E. Bragg. (1982). Are formally trained motorcyclists safer? *Accident Analysis and Prevention*, **14**, 247–255.

Jones, B. (1994). The effectiveness of provisional licensing in Oregon: An analysis of traffic safety benefits. *Journal of Safety Research*, **25**, 33–46.

Jones, I. S. & H. S. Stein. (1987). *Effect of driver hours of service on tractor-trailer crash involvement.* Arlington, Va, Insurance Institute for Highway Safety, Arlington.

Jones, M. H. (1973). *California driver training evaluation study.* Final report. California Department of Motor Vehicles, Sacramento.

Kaszniak, A. W., P. M. Keyl & M. S. Albert. (1991). Dementia and the Older Driver. *Human Factors*, **33**, 527–537.

Kelsey, S. L. & M. K. Janke. (1983). Driver License Renewal By Mail in California. *Journal of Safety Research*, **14**, 65–82.

Kelsey, S. L., Janke, M., Peck, R.C. & Ratz, M. (1985). License Extensions for Clean-Record Drivers: A 4-Year Follow-Up. *Journal of Safety Research*, **16**, 149–167.

Keskinen, E., Hatakka, M., Katila, A. & Laapotti, S. (1992). *Onnistuiko kuljettajapetuksen uudistus? Seurantaprojektin loppuraportti.* Psykologian Tutkimuksia 94. Turun Yliopisto, Turku.

King, R. D. (1996). *Bus Occupant Safety.* Synthesis of Transit Practice 18. Transportation Research Board, National Academy Press, Washington DC.

Kirk, A. & Stamatidis, N. (2001). Crash rates and traffic manoeuvres of young drivers. *Transportation Research Record*, **1779**, 68–74.

Koch, H. (1991). Der Einfluss des Stufenführerscheins auf das Unfallgeschehen 18- und 19jähriger Motorradfahranfänger. *Zeitschrift für Verkehrssicherheit*, **37**, 66–70.

Koepsell, T.D., Wolf, M.E., McCloskey, L., Buchner, D.M., Louie, D., Wagner, E.H. & Thompson, R.S. (1994). Medical Conditions and Motor Vehicle Collision Injuries in Older Adults. *Journal of the American Geriatrics Society*, **42**, 695–700.

Kolbenstvedt, M. (1986). *Trafikkulykker og reisevaner blant skolebarn i Østfold 1985. Resultater fra en spørreundersøkelse blant 10.500 grunnskoleelever.* TØI-rapport. Transportøkonomisk institutt, Oslo.

Kraus, J. F., R. S. Riggins & C. E. Franti. (1975). Some epidemiologic features of motorcycle collision injuries. I. Introduction, methods and factors associated with incidence. *American Journal of Epidemiology*, **102**, 74–98.

Lahr, L. E. & A. C. Heinsen. (1959). Visibility of colors: A field study of the relative visibility of various colors. *California Fish and Game Quarterly*, **45**, 208–209.

Lam, L.T. (2003). Factors associated with young drivers' car crash injury: Comparisons among learner, provisional, and full licenses. *Accident Analysis and Prevention,* **11**, 913–920.

Langley, J. D., A. C. Wagenaar & D. J. Begg. (1996). An evaluation of the New Zealand graduated driver licensing system. *Accident Analysis and Prevention*, **28**, 139–146.

Larsen, H.O.E. (1976). Road user behaviour and medical handicap – A critical review of literature. Working document. Oslo: Institute of Transport Economics.

Leveille, S.G., Buchner, D.M., Koepsell, T.D., McCloskey, L.W., Wolf, M.E. & Wagner, E.H. (1994). Psychoactive medications and injurious motor vehicle collisions involving older drivers. *Epidemiology,* **5**, 591–598.

Levy, D.T. (1990). Youth and traffic safety: The effects of driving age, experience, and education. *Accident Analysis and Prevention,* **22**, 327–334.

Lewandowski, I. (1995). *Syn hos trafikanter*. Inger Lewandowski Consult, Mjøndalen.

Lin, M.L. & Fearn, K.T. (2003). The provisional license: Night time and passenger restrictions, a literature review. *Journal of Safety Research,* **34**, 51–61.

Lin, T-D., P. P. Jovanis & C-Z. Yang. (1993). Modeling the Safety of Truck Driver Service Hours Using Time-Dependent Logistic Regression. *Transportation Research Record*, **1407**, 1–10.

Lin, T-D., P. P. Jovanis & C-Z. Yang. (1994). Time of Day Models of Motor Carrier Accident Risk. *Transportation Research Record*, **1467**, 1–8.

Lings, S. (2001). Increased driving accident frequency in Danish patients with epilepsy. *Neurology*, **57**, 435–439.

Lisper, H-O. (1977). *Trötthet i trafiken: En empirisk och teoretisk översikt*. Bilag 1 (229–276) i SOU 1977:2, Bilarbetstid. Kommukiationsdepartementet, Stockholm.

Lisper, H-O., Dureman, I., Ericsson, S. & Karlsson, N.G. (1971). Effects of sleep deprivation and prolonged driving upon subsidiary reaction time. *Accident Analysis and Prevention*, **2**, 335–341.

Lloyd, L. E. et al. (1994). Evaluation of the Texas motorcycle operator training course. Paper submitted to *Accident Analysis and Prevention* (unpublished).

Longo, M.C., Hunter, C.E., Lokan, R.J., White, J.M. & White, M.A. (2000). The prevalence of alcohol, cannabinoids, benzodiazepines and stimulants amongst injured drivers and their role in driver culpability. Part I: The prevalence of drug use in drivers, and characteristics of the drug-positive group. *Accident Analysis and Prevention*, **32** (2000) 613–622.

Longo, M.C., Lokan, R. J. & White, J.M. (2001). The relationship between blood benzodiazepines concentration and vehicle crash culpability. *Journal of Traffic Medicine*, **29(1–2)**. 36–43, 2001.

Lund, A. K., A. F. Williams & P. L. Zador. (1986). High school driver education: Further evaluation of the DeKalb County study. *Accident Analysis and Prevention*, **18**, 349–357.

Lyles, R. W., S. Narupiti & S. Johar. (1995). *Relationship between CDL Test scores and driver safety*. Paper 950074. 74th Annual Meeting, Transportation Research Board, January 22–28, Washington DC.

Lähdeniemi, E. (1995). *Effects of defensive driving training in a bus company*. Research Reports 41/1995. The Central Organization for Traffic Safety in Finland (Liikenneturva), Helsinki.

Maag, U., Vanasse, C., Dionne, G. & Laberge-Nadeau, C. (1997). Taxi drivers' accidents: how binocular vision problems are related to their rate and severity in terms of the number of victims. *Accident Analysis and Prevention*, **29**, 217–224.

Mackie, R. R. & J. C. Miller. (1978). *Effects of hours of service, regularity of schedules, and cargo loading on truck and bus driver fatigue*. Report PB 290 957. US Department of Transportation, National Highway Traffic Safety Administration, Washington DC.

MacPherson, R.D., Perl, J., Starmer, G.A., Homel, R. (1984). Self-reported drug-usage and crash-incidence in breathalyzed drivers. *Accident Analysis and Prevention*, **16**, 139–148.

Manders, S. M. & G. C. Rennie. (1984). *An Evaluation of an Advanced Driver Training Course Involving Company Drivers*. Report 1/84 (GR). Road Traffic Authority, Road Safety and Traffic Bureau, Melbourne.

Marek, J. & T. Sten. (1977). *Traffic environment and the driver. Driver behavior and training in international perspective*. Charles C. Thomas Publisher, Springfield, IL.

Marottoli, R.A., Cooney, L.M., Wagner, D.R., Doucette, J., & Tinetti, M.E. (1994). Predictors of Automobile Crashes and Moving Violations Among Elderly Drivers. *Annals of Internal Medicine*, **121**, 842–846.

Massie, D. L., K. L. Campbell & A. F. Williams. (1995). Traffic accident involvement rates by driver age and gender. *Accident Analysis and Prevention*, **27**, 73–87.

Masten, S.V. (2004). *Teenage driver risks and interventions*. California Department of Motor Vehicles: Report RSS-04-207.

Masten, S.V. & Hagge, R.A. (2003). *Evaluation of California's graduated driver licensing program*. California Department of Motor Vehicles.

Masten, S.V. & Hagge, R.A. (2004). Evaluation of California's graduated driver licensing program. *Journal of Safety Research*, **35**, 523–535.

Mathijssen, M.P.M., Koornstra, M.J. & Commandeur, J.J.F. (2002). *Het effect van alcohol-, drugs- en geneesmiddelengebruik op het letselrisico van automobilisten*. Leidschendam, Stichting Wetenschappelijk Onderzoek Verkeersveiligheid (SWOV), SWOV-report nr R-2002-14.

Maycock, G., C. R. Lockwood & J. F. Lester. (1991). *The accident liability of car drivers*. Research Report 315. Transport and Road Research Laboratory, Crowthorne, Berkshire.

Mayhew, D.R. (2003). The learner's permit. *Journal of Safety Research, 34*, 35–43.

Mayhew, D.R. & Simpson, H.M. (2001). *Graduated licensing for motorcyclists*. Ottawa, Ontario: Traffic Injury Research Foundation.

Mayhew, D.R., Simpson, H.M., Des Groseilliers, M. & Williams, A.F. (2001). Impact of the graduated driver licensing program in Nova Scotia. *Journal of Crash Prevention and Injury Control,* **2**, 179–192.

Mayhew, D.R., Simpson, H.M., Desmond, K, & Williams, A.F. (2003). Specific and long-term effects of Nova Scotia's graduated licensing program. *Traffic Injury Prevention,* **4**, 91–97.

McCloskey, L.W., Koepsell, T.D., Wolf, M. E. & Buchner, D.M. (1994). Motor vehicle collision injuries and sensory impairments of older drivers. *Age and Ageing*, **23**, 267–273.

McDavid, J. C., B. A. Lohrmann & G. Lohrmann. (1989). Does Motorcycle Training Reduce Accidents? Evidence from a Longitudinal Quasi-Experimental Study. *Journal of Safety Research*, **20**, 61–72.

McGuire, F. L. (1971). Psychological and educational methods of influencing driver behavior. In: *Volume 2 of Proceedings of international Symposium on psychological aspects of driver behaviour,* held at Noordwijkerhout, The Netherlands.

McGwin, G., Sims, R.V., Pulley, L. & Roseman, J.M. (2000). Relations among chronic medical conditions, medications, and automobile crashes in the elderly: A population-based case-control study. *American Journal of Epidemiology*, **152**, 424–431.

McKenna, C.K., Yost, B., Munzenrider, R.F. & Young, M.L. (2000). *An evaluation of driver education on Pennsylvania*. Pennsylvania Transportation Institute: Report PA-2000-025+97-04(59).

McKnight, A. J. & R. Edwards. (1982). An experimental evaluation of driver license manuals and written tests. *Accident Analysis and Prevention*, **14**, 187–192.

McKnight, A. J., P. Hyle & L. Albrecht. (1983). *Youth license control demonstration project*. Report DOT HS 806 616. US Department of Transportation, National Highway Traffic Safety Administration, Washington DC.

McKnight, A.J. & Peck, R.C. (2002). Graduated driver licensing: What works? *Injury Prevention,* **8**, 32–38.

McKnight, A. J., G. A. Simone & J. R. Weidman. (1982). *Elderly Driver Retraining. Final Report*. Report DOT-HS-806 336. Washington DC, US Department of Transportation, National Highway Traffic Safety Administration,

Meewes, V. & G. Weissbrodt. (1992). *Führerschein auf Probe. Auswirkungen auf die Verkehrssicherheit*. Heft 87, Reihe Unfall- und Scherheitsforschung Strassenverkehr. Bundesanstalt für Strassenwesen (BASt), Bergisch-Gladbach.

Mercer, G. W. (1989). Traffic accidents and convictions: group totals versus rate per kilometer driven. *Risk Analysis*, **9**, 71–77.

Michon, J. A. (1988). Should drivers think? In: *Road User Behaviour. Theory and Research*, 508-517 (Rothengatter, J. A. & R. DeBruin. Eds.). Van Gorcum, Assen.

Misumi, J. (1982). Action Research on Group Decision Making and Organizational Development. In: *Social Psychology, Selected Revised Papers, XXIInd International Congress of Psychology, Leipzig, GDR*, July 6-12, 1980, 94–98 (Hiebsch, H. ed.) North-Holland Publishing Company, Amsterdam.

Moe, D. (1992). *Motorbaner og trafikksikkerhet.* Rapport STF63 A92010. SINTEF Samferdselsteknikk, Trondheim.

Moe, J. (1983). *Akuttmedisin og transport av syke og skadede.* Teknologisk Forlag, Oslo.

Morrisey, M.A., Grabowski, D.C., Dee, T.S. & Campbell, C. (2006). The strength of graduated drivers license programs and fatalities among teen drivers and passengers. *Accident Analysis and Prevention,* **38**, 135–141.

Mortimer, R. G. (1984). Evaluation of the motorcycle rider course. *Accident Analysis and Prevention*, **16**, 63–71.

Mortimer, R. G. (1988). A Further Evaluation of the Motorcycle Rider Course. *Journal of Safety Research*, **19**, 187–196.

Muskaug, R. (1984). *Tunge kjøretøy og sikkerhet på veg. Forprosjekt.* TØI-notat 692. Transportøkonomisk institutt, Oslo.

Mäki, M. & Linnoila, M. (1976). Traffic accident rates among Finnish out-patients. *Accident Analysis and Prevention*, **8**, 39–44.

Nada-Raja S., Langley, J.D., McGee, R., Williams, S.M., Begg, D.J. & Reeder, A.I. (1997). Inattentive and behavioural and driving offences in adolescence. *Journal of the American Academy of Child and Adolescence Psychiatry*, **36**, 515–522.

Nathan, R. A. (1969). What's the safest color for a motor vehicle? *Traffic Safety,* **69**, 13, September.

Neutel, I. (1998). Benzodiazepine-related traffic accidents in young and elderly drivers. In Hindmarch, I & Riedel, W.J (eds). *Drugs & Driving, Human Psychopharmacology Clinical and Experimental*, **November 1998**, S115–S123

Nilsson, G. (2002). *The three dimensions of exposure, risk and consequence.* Unpublished manuscript. Swedish national road and transport research institute, Linköping.

Norges offentlige utredninger. (1995). NOU 1995:18. *Ny lovgivning om opplæring*. Oslo.

Nygård, J. F. & G. Tellnes. (1994). *Arbeidsmiljø, helse og trafikksikkerhet blant yrkessjåfører. Delrapport 1: Basisregistrering. Gruppe for trygdemedisin*, Universitetet i Oslo.

O'Day, J. (1970). A before and after analysis of accidents involving students of the defensive driving course. *Accident Analysis and Prevention*, **2**, 175–188.

OECD Scientific Expert group. (1996). *Training truck drivers.* OECD, Paris.

Opdal, L. (1994). *Evaluering av TS-pakkens virkning på trafikkulykker*. Hovedoppgave i pedagogikk, våren 1994. Universitetet i Oslo, Det samfunnsvitenskapelige fakultet, Pedagogisk Forskningsinstitutt, Oslo.

Owsley, C., McGwin, G., & Ball, K. (1998). Vision Impairment, Eye Disease, and Injurious Motor Vehicle Crashes in the Elderly. *Ophthalmic Epidemiology*, **5(2)**, 101–113.

Owsley, C., McGwin Jr., G., Sloane, M. E., Wells, J., Stalvey, B. T. & Gauthreaux, S. (2002). Impact of cataract surgery on motor vehicle crash involvement by older adults. *The Journal of the American Medical Association*, **288(7)**, 841–849.

Page, Y., Ouimet, M.C. & Cuny, S. (2004). An evaluation of the effectiveness of the supervised driver training system in France. *Association for the Advancement of Automotive Medicine 48th Annual Conference*. Biscane, FL.

Payne, D. E. & J. E. Barmack. (1963). An experimental field test of the Smith-Cummings-Sherman driver training system. *Traffic Safety Research Review*, **7**, 10–14.

Pedersen, T. O. & P. Christensen. (1973). *En kartlegging av bilføreres forståelse av vikepliktregler og skilt*. TØI-rapport 139. Transportøkonomisk institutt, Oslo.

Pokorny, M.L.I., Blom, D.H.J., van Leeuwen, P. et al. (1987). Shift Sequences, Duration of Rest Periods, and Accident Risk of Bus Drivers. *Human Factors*, **29**, 73–81.

Popkin, C. L. & J. R. Stewart. (1992). Can the crash risk for medically impaired drivers be reduced? *Journal of Traffic Medicine*, **20**, 49–57.

Poppe, F. (1993). *Verkeersrisico's in Nederland. 1. De cijfers*. SWOV rapport R-93-57. 2. Verantwoording. SWOV rapport R-93-58. Stichting Wetenschappelijk Onderzoek Verkeersveiligheid, Leidschendam,

Potter, B. C. et al. (1977). *Effectiveness of audible warning devices on emergency vehicles*. Report DOT-TSC-OST-77-38. US Department of Transportation, Washington DC.

Preusser, D.F., Williams, A.F., Lund, A.K. & Zador, P.L. (1990). City curfew ordinances and teenage motor vehicle injury. *Accident Analysis and Prevention*, **22**, 391–397.

Preusser, D.F., Williams, A.F., Zador, P.L. & Blomberg, R.D. (1984). The effect of curfew laws on motor vehicle crashes. *Law and Policy*, **6**, 115–128.

Preusser, D. F., Zador, P.L. & Williams, A.F. (1993). The effect of city curfew ordinances on teenage motor vehicle fatalities. *Accident Analysis and Prevention*, **25**, 641–645.

Raub, R. A. (1985). Removal of roof-mounted emergency lighting from police patrol vehicles: An evaluation. *Transportation Research Record*, **1047**, 83–88.

Raymond, S. & Tatum, S. (1977). *An evaluation of the effectiveness of the RAC/ACU motor cycle training scheme – final report*. University of Salford, Department of Civil Engineering, Road Safety Research Unit, Salford.

Rice, T.M., Peek-Asa, C. & Kraus, J.F. (2004). Effects of the California graduated driver licensing program. *Journal of Safety Research,* **35**, 375–381.

Rubin, A. I. & G. L. Howett. (1981). *Emergency vehicle warning systems*. NBS Special publication 480-37. National Bureau of Standards, Washington.

Rumar, K. (1985). The role of perceptual and cognitive filters in observed behaviour. In: *Human behavior and traffic safety*, 151–170. (Evans, L. & R. C. Schwing. eds) Plenum Press, New York, NY.

Russam, K. (1979). *Motorcycle training and licensing in Japan*. TRRL Laboratory Report 916. Transport and Road Research Laboratory, Crowthorne, Berkshire.

Rutter, D. R. & Quine, L. (1996). Age and experience in motorcycling safety. *Accident Analysis and Prevention*, **28**, 15–21.

Sagberg, F. (1994). *Motivasjon og trafikksikkerhet blant yrkessjåfører: Utprøving av skadeforebyggende tiltak ved Oslo posterminal*. TØI-rapport 263. Transportøkonomisk institutt, Oslo.

Sagberg, F. (1996). *Evaluering av ny ordning for førerkort klasse B. Foreløpige resultater vedrørende ulykkesrisiko*. Arbeidsdokument nr TST/0766/96 Transportøkonomisk institutt, Oslo.

Sagberg, F. (1997). *Unge føreres risikoutvikling: Evaluering av endrede regler for føreropplæring og førerprøve i klasse B*. TØI rapport 371/1997. Oslo: Transportøkonomisk institutt.

Sagberg, F. (2002). *Mengdetrening, kjøreerfaring og ulykkesrisiko*. TØI rapport 566/2002. Oslo: Transportøkonomisk institutt.

Sagberg, F., Amundsen, A.H., Glad, A. & Midtland, K. (2003). *Trafikksikkerhet for spesialtilpassede biler for førere med fysisk funksjonshemning*. TØI rapport 626/2003. Oslo: Transportøkonomisk institutt.

Satten, R. S. (1980). Analysis and Evaluation of the Motorcycle Rider Course in Thirteen Northern Illinois Counties. *Proceedings of International Motorcycle Safety Conference,* **Volume 1**, 145–163. Linthicum, Md, Motorcycle Safety Foundation, Linthicum.

Schultheis, M.T., Marheis, R.J., Nead, R. & DeLuca, J. (2002). Driving behaviors following brain injury: Self-report and motor vehicle records. *J Head Trauma Rehabil.*, **17(1)**, 38–47.

Schuster, D. H. (1978). Cognitive Accident-Avoidance Training for Beginning Drivers. *Journal of Applied Psychology*, **63**, 377–379.

Shaoul, J. (1975). *The use of accidents and traffic offences as criteria for evaluating courses in driver education*. The University of Salford, Department of Civil Engineering, Road Safety Research Unit, Salford.

Shope, J.T. & Molnar, L.J. (2003). Graduated driver licensing in the United States: Evaluation results from the early programs. *Journal of Safety Research,* **34**, 63–69.

Shope, J.T. & Molnar, L.J. (2004). Michigan's graduated driver licensing program: Evaluation of the first four years. *Journal of Safety Research,* **35**, 337–344.

Shope, J.T., Molnar, L.J., Elliott, M.R. & Waller, P.F. (2001). Graduated driver licensing in Michigan. *Journal of the American Medical Association,* **286**, 1593–1598.

Siegrist, S. & E. Ramseier. (1992). *Erfolgskontrolle von Fortbildungskursen für Autofahrer*. Bfu-Report 18. Schweitzerische Beratungsstelle für Unfallverhütung (BFU), Bern.

Sikveland, R. (1993). *18-19-årige bilførere innblandet i politiregistrerte personskadeulykker i Vestfold 1988, 1990-91-92*. Statens vegvesen Vestfold, Trafikant- og kjøretøyavdelingen, Tønsberg.

Sikveland, R. (1994). *Rapport om 18-19-årige bilførere innblandet i politiregistrerte personskadeulykker i Vestfold 1988, 1992, 1993*. Statens vegvesen Vestfold, Trafikant- og kjøretøyavdelingen, Tønsberg.

Sikveland, R. & R. M. Hagen. (1991). *Antall 18-19 årige bilførere innblandet i politiregistrerte personskadeulykker i Vestfold 1986, 1988, 1990*. Statens vegvesen Vestfold, Biltilsynsavdelingen, Tønsberg.

Simard, R., Gendreau, M., Bouchard, J., Lemire, A.M. & Dussault, C. (2002). The new graduated licensing system in Quebec: Impact on new drivers and on nighttime single crashes. *The Quebec graduated licensing system for novice drivers: A two-year evaluation of the 1997 reform*. Conference on alcohol, drugs, and traffic safety, Stockholm.

Skelly, G. B. (1968). *Aspects of driving experience in the first year as a qualified driver*. Report LR 149. Transport and Road Research Laboratory, Crowthorne, Berkshire.

Smart, R. G. & Fejer, D. (1976). Drug use and driving risk among high school students. *Accident Analysis and Prevention*, **8**, 33–38.

Solomon, S. S. & J. G. King. (1995). Influence of color on fire vehicle accidents. *Journal of Safety Research*, **26**, 41–48.

Southall, J. P. (1961). *Introduction to physiological optics*. Dover Publications, New York.

Spolander, K. (1983). *Bilförares olycksrisker. En modell testad på män och kvinnor*. VTI-rapport 268. Statens Väg- och Trafikinstitut, Linköping.

SSB (1996). Statistics Norway, http://www.ssb.no

Statens vegvesen Vegdirektoratet. (1993). *Normalplan for føreropplæring. Obligatorisk opplæring i glattkjøring for fører av buss, lastebil og vogntog*. Vegdirektoratet, Oslo.

Statens vegvesen Vegdirektoratet. (1994). *Normalplan for føreropplæring. Førerkort klasse B*. November 1994. Vegdirektoratet, Oslo.

Statens vegvesen Vegdirektoratet. (1995). *Veileder 9. Norsk veg- og vegtrafikkplan 1998-2007. Virkninger av tiltak-trafikksikkerhet*. Vegdirektoratet, plan- og budsjettstaben, Trafikkavdelingen, Oslo.

Statens vegvesen. (1993). *Veg- og gateutforming*. Håndbok 017. Vegdirektoratet, Oslo.

Steen, T. & L. Gjerstad. (1993). Førerkortmedisin. Oversikt over saksgang og praksis. *Tidsskrift for den Norske Lægeforening*, **113**, 2277–2280.

Steffens, U., R. Gawatz & G. Willmes. (1988). *Wirksamkeit von Mofakursen*. Unfall- und Sicherheitsforschung Strassenverkehr, Heft 67. Bundesanstalt für Strassenwesen (BASt), Bergisch Gladbach.

Stein, H. S. & I. S. Jones. (1988). Crash Involvement of Large Trucks by Configuration: A Case-Control Study. *American Journal of Public Health*, **78**, 491–498.

Sten, T., Hole, G., Borch, K. & Thingelstad, H. (1977). *Bilføreropplæring i to faser. Innstilling fra arbeidsgruppen for planlegging av bilføreropplæring i to faser*. Statens vegvesen, Vegdirektoratet, Oslo,

Stensholt, E., T. Bergsaker O-J. Skog. (1992). *Synsproblemer i trafikken. Rapport fra en optometrisk undersøkelse av unge og eldre bilførere*. Rapport 1/1992. Norsk optometrisk forskningsinstitutt, Kongsberg.

Stewart, D. E. & R. W. Sanderson. (1984). The Measurement of Risk on Canada's Roads and Highways. In: *Transport Risk Assessment*, 1–21(Yagar, S. ed). University of Waterloo Press, Waterloo, Ontario.

Stock, J. R., Weaver, J.K. & Ray, H.W. et al. (1983). *Evaluation of Safe Performance Secondary School Driver Education Curriculum Demonstration Project*. Report DOT-HS-806 568. US Department of Transportation, National Highway Traffic Safety Administration, Washington DC.

Stoke, C. B. (1980). Effectiveness of written test of drivers' knowledge of rules of the road. *Transportation Research Record*, **782**, 1–8.

Strang, P.M., Deutsch, K.B., James, R.S. & Manders, S.M. (1982). *A comparison of on-road and off-road driver training*. Report 1/1982. Road Safety and Traffic Authority, Canberra, Australia.

Summala, H. (1985). Modeling Driver Behavior: A Pessimistic Prediction? In: *Human Behavior and Traffic Safety*, 43–65. (Schwing, R. C. & L. Evans. Eds.) Plenum Press, New York, NY.

The Council of the European Communities (1991). *Council Directive of 29. July 1991 on driving licenses (91/439/EEC)*. Official Journal L 237, 24/08/1991, p. 0001–0024.

Thulin, H. (1987). *Olika åldersgruppers risker och exponering i trafiken*. VTImeddelande 536. Väg- och transportforskningsinstitutet, Linköping.

Thulin, H. & G. Nilsson. (1994). *Vägtrafik. Exponering, skaderisker och skadekonsekvenser för olika färdsätt och åldersgrupper*. VTI-rapport 390. Väg- og transportforskningsinstitutet, Linköping.

Toomath, J. B. & W. T. White. (1982). New Zealand survey of driver exposure to risk of accidents. *Accident Analysis and Prevention*, **14**, 407–411,

Transportation Research Board. (1989). *Improving School Bus Safety. Special* Report 222. National Research Council, Washington DC.

Transportforskningsdelegationen (TFD). (1979). *Olyckor vid utryckningskörning*. TFD-rapport 1979:10. Transportforskningdelegationen, Stockholm.

Trobe, J.D., Waller, P.F., Cook-Flannagan, C.A., Teshima,S.M. & Bieliauskas, K.A. (1996). Crashes and violations among drivers with Alzheimer disease. *Archives of Neurology*, **53**, 411–416.

Troup, G. A., S. E. Torpey & H. T. Wood. (1984). Engine capacity restrictions for novice motorcyclists-the Victorian experience. *ARRB Proceedings,* **Volume 12**, **Part 7**, 1–12.

Turbell, T. (1980). *Barriärkollision med ambulans.* VTI-meddelande 206. Statens Väg- och Trafikinstitut (VTI), Linköping.

Ulleberg, P. (2006). *Blir man bedre billist etter oppfriskningskurs? Evaluering av kurset "Bilfører 65+" (Evaluation of the "Driver 65+" refresher course for elderly drivers).* TØI Report 841/2006. Oslo: Institute of Transport Economics.

Ulleberg, P. & Sagberg, F. (2003). *Syn og kognitiv funksjon blant bilførere over 70 år.* Betydning for kjøreferdighet. TØI rapport 668/2003. Oslo: Transportøkonomisk institutt.

Ulmer, R.G., Preusser, D.F., Ferguson, S.A., Williams, A.F. (1999). Teenage crash reduction associated with delayed licensure in Louisiana. *Journal of Safety Research*, **30**, 31–38.

Ulmer, R.G., Preusser, D.F., Williams, A.F., Ferguson, S.A., Farmer, C.M. (2000). Effect of Florida's graduated driver licensing programon the crash rate of teenage drivers. *Accident Analysis and Prevention*, **32**, 527–532.

Ulmer, R.G., Ferguson, S.A., Williams, A.F., Preusser, D.F. (2001). Teenage crash reduction associated with delayed licensure in Connecticut. *Journal of Safety Research*, **32**, 31–41.

Valset, P. (1996). Undersøkelse viser: Bedre trafikksikkerhet blant yrkessjåfører. I: *Sikker yrkestransport, temabilag til Transportforum,* **11**, 17–19. Transportbedriftenes Landsforening, Oslo.

Vernon, D.D., Diller, E.M., Cook, L.J., Reading, J.C., Suruda, A.J. & Dean., J.M. (2002). Evaluating the crash and citation rates of Utah drivers licenced with medical conditions, 1992-1996. *Accident Analysis and Prevention*, **34**, 237–246.

Vaa, T. (2003). *Impairment, diseases, age and their relative risks of accident involvement: Results from meta-analysis.* Deliverable R1.1 from EU-project IMMORTAL. TØI report 690. Oslo, Institute of Transport Economics.

Wallace, J. E. & A. Crancer. (1971). Licensing examinations and their relation to subsequent driving record. *Behavior Research in Highway Safety*, 53–65.

Waller, F. L. (1992). *An analysis of the impact of the Texas Department of Public Safety motorcycle operator training program upon motorcycle related traffic accidents.* An applied research project submitted to the Department of Political Science, Southwest Texas State University, in partial fulfillment for the requirements for the degree of Master of Public Administration, Spring.

Waller, J. A. (1967). Cardiovascular disease, aging, and traffic accidents. *Journal of Chronical Diseases*, **20**, 615–520.

Waller, J. A. & J. T. Goo. (1969). Highway crash and citation patterns and chronic-medical conditions. *Journal of Safety Research*, **1**, 13–27.

Waller, P. F. (1986). The highway transportation system as a commons: implications for risk policy. *Accident Analysis and Prevention*, **18**, 417–424.

Waller, P. F. & R. G. Hall. (1980). Literacy-A Human Factor in Driving Performance. SAE Paper 800385, In: *Accident Causation*, 15–25. (Evans, L. ed.) Report SP-461. Warrendale, PA, Society of Automotive Engineers, Warrendale.

Weber, D. C. (1972). An analysis of the California driver record study in the context of a classical accident model. *Accident Analysis and Prevention*, **4**, 109–116.

Wiggins, S. (2004). *Graduated licensing program: Interim evaluation report – year 3*. Victoria, British Columbia: Insurance Corporation of British Columbia.

Williams, A. F. (1985). Nighttime driving and fatal crash involvement of teenagers. *Accident Analysis and Prevention*, **17**, 1–5.

Williams, A.F. & Mayhew, D.R. (2004). *Graduated licensing: A blueprint for North America*. Insurance Institute of Highway Safety (http://www.iihs.org/laws/state_-laws/grad_license.html).

Williams, A. F. & B. O'Neill. (1974). On-the-road driving record of licensed race drivers. *Accident Analysis and Prevention*, **6**, 263–270.

Withaar, F.K. & Brouwer, W.H. (1999). Measuring driving performance in older subjects with cognitive impairment. In *Proceedings of a workshop on the methodology for performance scoring during driving assessment*. Held at the Mobility Advice and Vehicle Information Service, Monday 28 July 1999, Crowthorne.

Wynne-Jones, J. D. & P. M. Hurst. (1984). *The AA Driver Training Evaluation*. Traffic Research Report 33. Ministry of Transport, Road Transport Division, Wellington, New Zealand.

Ysander, L. (1966). The safety of drivers with chronic disease. *British Journal of Industrial Medicine*, **23**, 28–36.

Ysander, L. (1970). Sick and handicapped drivers. *Acta Chirurgica Scandinavia, Supplementum*, **409**.

# 7.

# Public Education and Information

## 7.0 Introduction and overview of three measures

This chapter deals with the effects of three measures in the field of road safety education and information. The three measures are given below:

7.1 Education of pre-school children
7.2 Education in schools
7.3 Road user information and campaigns

Road safety education for children is defined as special educational measures for children and young people who are not old enough to acquire a driving licence for motor vehicles.

The main elements in current knowledge of the effects of these measures on accidents, mobility and the environment, together with costs and cost–benefit evaluations, are described in this introductory chapter.

### Amount and quality of research

Table 7.0.1 gives an overview of the amount of research that has evaluated measures within the area of public education and information. Meta-analyses have been carried to summarise the findings of studies for all measures.

The Handbook of Road Safety Measures

ISBN: 978-1-84855-250-0

*Table 7.0.1: Number of studies, number of results and sum of statistical weights for studies in the field of road safety education and information*

| Measure | Number of studies | Number of results | Sum of statistical weights | Results last updated |
|---|---|---|---|---|
| 7.1 Education of pre-school children | 3 | 15 | 2,077 | 1997 |
| 7.2 Education in schools | 4 | 9 | 388 | 1997 |
| 7.3 Road user information and campaigns | 38 | 123 | >10,000 | 2009 |

The largest number of studies – and the most comprehensive studies – are on road safety education and campaigns. There are relatively few studies of the effects of education for pre-school children (up to 6 years old). The effects on accidents of education in schools have been studied slightly more.

A number of studies have evaluated the effects of road user education and information on knowledge and attitudes. Fewer studies have considered the effects on behaviour in traffic, and fewer still have investigated effects on accidents. This chapter mainly emphasises on presenting results of studies that have quantified effects on accidents. There are two main reasons for this. First, the relationship between knowledge, attitudes and behaviour on the one hand, and accidents on the other hand, is relatively poorly understood. Second, reductions in the number of accidents and injuries is the ultimate objective of all measures that try to influence knowledge, attitudes and behaviour in traffic.

The quality of the studies varies. All studies concerning education of pre-school children and education in schools are non-experimental. Both experimental and non-experimental studies of information and campaigns have been reported.

## Main elements in effect on accidents

Two types of educational measures for pre-school children, namely, Childrens Traffic Club and organised training in the correct way to cross the road, have been studied in Norway. It has been found there that children who belong to the Childrens Traffic Club have fewer traffic accidents than children who are not members; in Sweden, the opposite has been found. Unfortunately, it is not possible to give a satisfactory explanation for these conflicting results. Training children in the correct way to cross a road in areas they use regularly has been found to reduce the number of accidents involving children aged between 5 and 9 by around 10% in the United States and Great Britain.

Educational measures in schools that have been evaluated include training in the correct way to cross the road in areas that children use regularly and cycling proficiency training (balance, manoeuvring, indicating and braking). A decrease in the number of accidents as a result of training in crossing roads has been found but not as a result of cycling training.

Road user information and campaigns were found to reduce accidents only when combined with enforcement. Without accompanying enforcement, no effects on accidents were found.

**Main elements in effects on mobility**

Most of the measures in this area have no known effects on mobility.

**Main elements in effects on the environment**

Road user education and information have no known effects on the environment apart from those that possibly result from changes in driving speeds. Lower and less variable driving speeds in the region 60–100 km/h can reduce exhaust emissions.

**Main elements in costs**

The costs of road user education and information are not well known. With regard to education for pre-school children, the only documented costs in Norway are the costs to the Norwegian Council for Road Safety for running the Childrens Traffic Club. In 1995, these amounted to NOK 4.2 million. The costs to the Norwegian Council for Road Safety for producing teaching material for road safety education in schools was NOK 1.4 million in 1995. Other costs of road safety education in school are not known, since the scope is too little known. The total costs of road user information and campaigns are estimated to be between NOK 15 and 20 million per year.

**Main elements in the cost–benefit values of the measures**

The information available about traffic safety education for pre-school children is insufficient to make a cost–benefit analysis of the measure.

Road user information and campaigns are relatively cheap measures. However, campaigns alone (without accompanying enforcement) were not found to reduce accidents and are therefore most likely not cost-effective. When combined with enforcement, the cost-effectiveness depends for the most part on costs of enforcement and the effects of the enforcement on accidents.

## 7.1 Education of pre-school children (0–6 years)

### Problem and objective

In 1995, 292 children in Norway up to the age of 6 were killed or injured in traffic accidents according to the official accident statistics (Statistisk sentralbyrå 1996). The actual number of traffic injuries among children is considerably higher. On the basis of a Norwegian study in 1991 (Borger 1991), the number of injured persons registered at the National Institute for Public Health was compared with the number of injured persons registered in official accident statistics in 1990. When all road user groups are taken together, the level of injury reporting for children aged between 0 and 6 was 15%. For road users in other age groups, the level of reporting was 40%. Under-reporting of bicycle accidents is particularly high among children. Accidents where one or more motor vehicles are involved have a high level of reporting. However, even in such accidents, there is a tendency for injuries to children to be reported less often than injuries to adults.

Children do not have the same ability to master safe behaviour in traffic as adults do (Bérard-Andersen 1985). Children below school age do not understand traffic signs, rules and road markings. They do not have the same ability as adults and older children to judge speed and distance. Sight and hearing are not fully developed among children. For example, they cannot switch their gaze from far to near (and vice versa) as quickly as adults and have more difficulty in judging where sound is coming from. They are small and therefore cannot get the same overview of traffic as adults. The ability to do several things simultaneously is not fully developed among the youngest children. Nor do children have the same ability to generalise learning from one situation to another as adults do. For example, this means they cannot simply transfer the rules for crossing the road correctly from the place where they learned the rules to another place. Children like to play, and they often act impulsively. Children who are 6 years old or younger do not have the ability to adopt another person's perspective and therefore cannot imagine how a traffic situation appears from a driver's point of view, for example. A number of studies show that there is a significant difference between 6-year and 7-year-olds with regard to their ability to be safe on their own in traffic and their ability to learn safe behaviour (Midtland 1995).

Educational measures for pre-school children are intended to

- influence behaviour of children;
- give parents knowledge of the ability of children to move safely in traffic; and
- motivate parents to improve children's safety.

**Description of the measure**

Children learn how to behave in traffic in several ways: (1) by copying the behaviour of others, (2) through their own experiences in traffic and (3) through organised educational measures. Educating pre-school children refers to the last type of education.

**Effect on accidents**

In a comprehensive literature survey, OECD (1983) concludes that the majority of studies of effects of road safety education for pre-school children are inadequate. A few of the studies have attempted to measure the effect of education on the number of accidents.

The effect on accidents of the Childrens Traffic Club has been studied in Norway and Sweden. The Norwegian study (Schioldborg 1974) found that children who were members of the Childrens Traffic Club had, on average, a 30% lower risk in traffic than children who were not (95% CI [−50; −3]). The study was controversial (Knudsen 1975a, 1975b, Schioldborg 1975a, 1975b). Membership is voluntary and it cannot be ruled out that the observed differences in risk may be due to the fact that parents of children who are members may be more motivated to teach their children safer behaviour in traffic than the parents of non-members. This type of bias has been found in many studies of voluntary educational measures (OECD 1983).

The Swedish study (Gregersen and Nolén 1994) found that children who were members of the Childrens Traffic Club had on average a 67% higher risk of being injured in traffic per 100 hours spent in traffic (95% CI [+39; +100]) than children who were not members.

These two studies show highly conflicting results; both studies are non-experimental. It is possible that both results may be due to weaknesses in study methods. The Norwegian study found that children who were members of the Childrens Traffic Club had better knowledge and safer behaviour than non-members. These differences may, however, be due to self-selection. The Swedish study is more recent than the Norwegian study. It also used other types of accidents than traffic accidents as a comparison, but does not contain information about knowledge and behaviour. It is impossible to say with certainty why the results are so different.

In the cities of Los Angeles (California), Columbus (Ohio) and Milwaukee (Wisconsin) in the United States, an information film about the correct way to cross a road was shown on children television at the same time as information material was distributed in pre-schools and schools (Blomberg, Preusser, Hale and Leaf 1983a, 1983b). A before and after study found that the measure reduced dart-out accidents among school-children aged between 5 and 9 by around 10% (95% Ci [−15; −7]). Dart-out accidents are accidents that occur when a child runs out into the road in front of a car. The measure was specifically directed at this type of accident.

### Effect on mobility

Educational measures for pre-school children have no documented effects on traffic mobility.

### Effect on the environment

Education can reduce feelings of insecurity or anxiety. To the extent a person may feel safer without actually being so, this must be regarded as an unwanted effect. There is no benefit in creating a false sense of security for children in traffic. No effects on physical environmental factors have been documented of educational measures for pre-school children.

### Costs

Trygg Trafikk's costs for the Childrens Traffic Club in 1995 were ca. NOK 4.2 million, which were largely covered by membership fees (Trygg Trafikk 1996).

### Cost–benefit analysis

A cost–benefit analysis of the campaign to reduce dart-out accidents in Los Angeles, Columbus and Milwaukee concludes that the measure was highly cost-effective

(OECD 1986). The effect of the Childrens Traffic Club on accidents among children is too uncertain to form the basis for carrying out a cost–benefit analysis of the measure.

## 7.2 Education in schools (6–18 years old)

### Problem and objective

According to official statistics, among the total number of people killed or injured in traffic accidents in Norway, 727 were children aged between 7 and 14 and 1,488 were young people aged between 15 and 18 (Statistisk sentralbyrå 1996). The actual number of injured children is considerably higher. On the basis of a study made in 1991 (Borger 1991), the number of injured persons registered by the National Institute for Public Health was compared with the number of injured persons register in official accident statistics in 1990. It has been estimated that the level of reporting of traffic injuries to children in Norway aged between 7 and 14 was 17%. For road users above the age of 15, the level of reporting is 40%. For bicycle accidents and moped and motorcycle accidents in particular, there is a tendency for injuries to children to be reported less often than injuries to adults.

Organised road safety education in schools is designed to give children lower accident rates than they would otherwise have, by practising knowledge and skills so that children can travel as safely as possible.

### Description of the measure

Road safety education in Norwegian primary schools is not a separate subject, but is offered as an integrated part of other subjects. Traffic-related subjects are dealt within several of the compulsory subjects, as well as being taught in cross-disciplinary lessons and in practical, social and cultural studies. Since road safety education is not a compulsory subject, there are no recommendations regarding the number of lessons. There is a reason to believe that the amount of road safety education varies considerably from place to place and from teacher to teacher.

Questionnaires among pupils aged between 13 and 15 in 1987 showed that the proportion pupils who had not had any road safety education was 73% among grade 7 pupils, 64% among grade 8 pupils and 52% among grade 9 pupils. The proportion of pupils who chose road safety as an optional subject was 3% in grade 7, 6% in grade 8 and 24% in grade 9 (Moe and Tyldum 1987).

On the basis of a questionnaire in 1994, Sagberg (1994) also showed that there was little or no road safety education in school. In grades 1–4, there were approximately one to two lessons in how to walk in areas with road traffic, in the use of reflectors and on general road safety education.

## Effect on accidents

A number of studies have evaluated the effects of road safety education for children on the number of accidents involving children as active road users. Broadly speaking, a distinction can be made between training in the right way to cross a road and cycle proficiency training. The following studies have been found evaluating the effects on accidents of these measures:

Sargent and Sheppard (1974) (Great Britain): crossing the road
Downing and Spendlove (1981) (Great Britain): crossing the road
Fortenberry and Brown (1982) (USA): crossing the road
Blomberg, Preusser, Hale and Leaf (1983a, 1983b) (USA): crossing the road
Preusser and Lund (1988) (USA): crossing the road
Preston (1980) (Great Britain): cycling proficiency training

Table 7.2.1 shows the effect on accidents of different measures estimated on the basis of these studies.

Training children in the right way to cross a road appears to lead to fewer accidents when crossing the road, particularly among children aged between 9 and 12. The results shown above are largely based an educational programme shown on children's television in the United States. Training in the right way to cross a road is based on teaching children simple rules to follow at specific places where they walk regularly.

*Table 7.2.1: Effects on accidents of road safety education for schoolchildren*

| | Percentage change in the number of accidents | | |
|---|---|---|---|
| Accident severity | Types of accidents affected | Best estimate | 95% Confidence interval |
| ***Education in the right way to cross a road*** | | | |
| Injury accidents with children 5–9 years | Crossing the road | −11 | (−15; −7) |
| Injury accidents with children 9–12 years | Crossing the road | −20 | (−32; −7) |
| ***Cycling proficiency training*** | | | |
| Injury accidents with children 6–16 years | Cycling accidents | −6 | (−17; +7) |

Cycle proficiency training does not appear to lead to statistically significant changes in the number of accidents. Cycling proficiency training teaches more general skills, some of which may be difficult to apply in everyday cycling. This may be one reason why training in the right way to cross the road appears to be more effective than cycling proficiency training.

### Effect on mobility

No effects on mobility of road safety education in school are known.

### Effect on the environment

No effects of road safety education in schools on the environment have been documented.

### Costs

The costs of road safety education in Norwegian schools are not known precisely because the actual scope of educational activities is not known. The educational material used is to a large extent produced by Trygg Trafikk. The organisation's expenses for educational material in 1995 were around NOK 1.4 million (Trygg Trafikk 1996).

### Cost–benefit analysis

No cost–benefit analyses of road safety education in schools are available. Since both the scope and the content of current education are very incompletely known, it is not possible to perform a meaningful cost–benefit analysis.

## 7.3 Road user information and campaigns

### Problem and objective

Some types of behaviour strongly increase the risk of accident and injury. These include exceeding the speed limit (Munden 1967, Wasielewski 1984, Elvik, Christensen and Amundsen 2004), the use of alcohol (Glad 1985, Assum and Glad 1990), crossing red lights (Sakshaug and Sten 1979, Gårder 1982, Garber et al. 2007) and non-use of seat belts (Nordisk Trafikksikkerhetsråd 1984, Evans 1987). It has been estimated that if road users respected road traffic legislation perfectly (100%), the number of injured road users could be reduced by 27% (±18%) and the number road accident fatalities could be reduced by 48% (±30%) (Elvik 1997). The current amount of police enforcement is not sufficient to ensure 100% respect for road traffic legislation.

Reasons why drivers (and other road users) do not obey traffic rules or behave in ways that are unfavourable for safety may be, among other things, unfavourable attitudes and a lack of knowledge about traffic rules and possible consequences of not obeying traffic rules (accident risk, risk of being caught by the police). It is often assumed that improving knowledge and attitudes will eventually lead to a (favourable) change in behaviour. However, the relationship between knowledge/attitudes and behaviour is only weak; even if one succeeds in changing these, a corresponding change in behaviour will not necessarily occur. There are many other determinants of road user behaviour besides knowledge and attitudes, for example, a desire to reach the destination as fast as possible (speeding), forgetfulness (non-use of seat belts), sleepiness or monotony (road departure accidents).

Road user information and campaigns are intended to reduce accidents by promoting safer behaviour in traffic, by giving road users improved knowledge and more favourable attitudes towards such behaviour. Another objective is to inform about enforcement.

### Description of the measure

Road user information and campaigns includes information though different types of media, such as newspapers, journals, the Internet, TV, radio, cinemas, letters and brochures that are sent directly to specific target groups, famous people as promoters, posters and advertisement hoardings and signs along the roadside. The information may be directed towards specific target groups (e.g., by sending letters or using target-group-specific types of print or online media) or towards the general public (e.g., signs along the roadside).

Information and campaigns are often directed towards specific types of behaviour. The largest part of (evaluated) campaigns is directed towards speeding or drink-driving. Some campaigns aim at influencing attitudes only, whereas others are combined with police enforcement. In the latter case, the campaigns inform about the ongoing enforcement, while the enforcement strengthens the message by the campaign.

Information and campaigns in Norway are mostly produced by governmental bodies and by organisations supported by government, such as the Norwegian Council for Road Safety. Insurance organisations, motoring organisations and other voluntary organisations also implement information measures.

**Effect on accidents**

The following studies have evaluated the effects of information campaigns on the number of accidents:

Anderson (1978) (USA)
Maisey and Saunders (1981) (Australia)
Haynes, Pine and Fitch (1982) (USA)
Blomberg, Preusser, Hale and Leaf (1983a, 1983b) (USA)
Lane, Milne and Wood (1983) (Australia)
Sali (1983) (USA)
Wolfe (1983) (USA)
Fosser (1984), see Elvik (1995) (Norway)
Harte and Hurst (1984) (New Zealand)
Armour, Monk, South and Chomiac (1985) (Australia)
Dowling (1986) (USA)
Glad (1986), see Elvik (1995) (Norway)
Blomberg, Preusser and Ulmer (1987) (USA)
Moe, Sakshaug and Stene (1987) (Norway)
Spoerer (1989) (Germany)
Smith, Maisey and McLaughlin (1990) (Australia)
Stene (1987), see Elvik (1995) (Norway)
Moe and Stene (1990), see Elvik (1995) (Norway)
Schlabbach (1990) (Germany)
Studsholt (1990) (Denmark)
Behrensdorff and Johansen (1991) (Denmark)
Nagatsuka (1991) (Japan)
Drummond, Sullivan and Cavallo (1992) (Australia)
Fosser, Christensen and Ragnøy (1992), see Elvik (1995) (Norway)
Oei and Polak (1992) (Netherlands)
Wells, Preusser and Williams (1992) (USA)
Cameron et al. (1993) (Australia)
Machemer et al. (1994) (Germany)
Britt and Bergman (1995) (USA)

Stuster (1995) (USA)
Taylor and Ahmed (1995) (USA)
Törnros (1995) (Sweden)
Oei and Goldenbeld (1996) (the Netherlands)
Sävenhed et al. (1996) (Sweden)
Cameron et al. (1997) (Australia)
Voas, Holder and Gruenewald (1997) (USA)
Amundsen, Elvik and Fridstrøm (1999) (Norway)
Delhomme et al. (1999) (several countries)

The results are summarised in Table 7.3.1. All results, with the exception of pedestrian, driving-off-the-road and keep-your-distance campaigns, are based on a random effects model of meta-analysis and controlled for publication bias. A more detailed description of the analyses is given in Vaa, Assum, Ulleberg and Veisten (2004).

The results show that significant reductions of accident numbers were found for drink-driving campaigns. For most other types of campaigns, reductions were found as well; however, these are non-significant. The results refer mainly to changes of accident

*Table 7.3.1: Effects on accidents of road user information and campaigns*

| | Percentage change in number of injuries | | |
|---|---|---|---|
| | Types of accident affected | Best estimate | 95% confidence interval |
| ***Theme of campaign*** | | | |
| All campaigns | All accidents | −9 | (−13; −5) |
| Drink-driving campaigns | All accidents | −14 | (−21; −8) |
| Australian drink-driving campaigns | All accidents | −13 | (−22; −4) |
| Speeding campaigns | All accidents | −8 | (−20; +3) |
| Other single-theme campaigns | All accidents | −10 | (−19; −1) |
| Pedestrian campaigns (reflector use) | Pedestrian accidents | +3 | (−2; +8) |
| Driving off the road campaigns | Road departure accidents | −3 | (−16; +11) |
| Keep your distance campaigns | Rear-end collisions | −9 | (−17; +1) |
| Multi-theme campaigns | All accidents | +1 | (−7; +9) |
| ***Combination with enforcement*** | | | |
| Campaign only (no enforcement) | All accidents | +1 | (−9; +12) |
| Campaign and enforcement | All accidents | −13 | (−19; −6) |
| Campaign and enforcement and education | All accidents | −14 | (−22; −5) |
| Local individualised campaigns | All accidents | −39 | (−56; −17) |

numbers in the campaign period. Some studies also include a period after the campaign period. The results are based on all types of campaigns, regardless of whether these are combined with enforcement. Some campaigns are combined with enforcement, e.g. the Australian drink-driving campaigns are an accompanying measure for a high-intensity enforcement campaign with DUI checkpoints (see also Section 8.7). Other campaigns are isolated information campaigns without accompanying enforcement, e.g. the pedestrian campaigns that aim at increasing reflector use among pedestrians (which is not mandatory).

When campaigns are divided into groups according to whether or not they are combined with enforcement, only those campaigns that are combined with enforcement were found to reduce accidents. Campaigns alone do not seem to have any effect at all. Only local individualized campaigns were found to reduce accidents significantly, also without targeted enforcement.

***Effects of information campaigns on behaviour.*** In an Australian meta-analysis (Elliott 1993), the results of a large number of studies on how road user information and campaigns affect behaviour are summarised. Table 7.3.2 presents a number of results from this study. The majority of studies (Maisey and Saunders 1981) concerned campaigns for the use of seat belts. The greatest increases in seat belt use occurred after the campaign, whereas its initial use was low. Among the campaigns against drink-driving, only some studies have used roadside surveys in order to evaluate the effects on drink-driving, whereas other studies have used self-reported drink-driving, which must be assumed to be a non-optimal measure that is likely to lead to biased results in favour of the campaigns. Among the campaigns against speeding, some of the campaigns were combined with enforcement, while others were not.

Taken together, these results indicate, despite some methodological weaknesses (e.g., self-reported behaviour, effects from campaigns not separated from effects from enforcement), that it is possible to change road user behaviour by means of information and campaigns.

*Table 7.3.2: Effects of road user information and campaigns on behaviour (Elliott 1993)*

| Type of behaviour | Measure of effect | Before the campaign | After the campaign | Percentage change |
|---|---|---|---|---|
| Use of seat belts | Number of users (%) | 61.6 | 73.7 | +20 |
| Drink-driving | Percentage of drink-driving (%) | 29.8 | 24.2 | –19 |
| Speeding | Number of violations (%) | 50.5 | 40.1 | –21 |
| Use of bicycle helmets | Number of users (%) | 12.4 | 19.8 | +60 |

On the basis of his meta-analysis, Elliott (1993) concludes the following regarding the conditions for succeeding with an information campaign for safer behaviour in traffic:

- Greater changes in behaviour are achieved when the initial proportion of road users exhibiting the desired behaviour was low than when a high proportion of road users had the desired behaviour at the start.
- Greater changes in behaviour are achieved when information campaigns are combined with increased police enforcement than when they are not.
- Campaigns clearly stating which type of behavioural change is desired, and why it is important to change behaviour, lead to greater behavioural changes than campaigns that simply encourage people to be careful in general terms.
- The use of television as a medium in the campaign appears to lead to greater changes in behaviour than other media. This may possibly be due to the fact that television is a medium that reaches a wider public than any other media.

**Effect on mobility**

Changes in behaviour as a result of information campaigns may affect mobility. For example, lower speeds lead to increased journey times. Results are, however, inconsistent as to whether campaigns affect speed. A campaign in Darmstadt, Germany to maintain the 30 km/h speed limit found that mean speed was reduced from 39.1 to 34.8 km/h, and the proportion of the drivers who drove at speeds of 30 km/h or less increased from 13% to 32%. Similar changes in other areas (control areas) were not studied (Schlabbach 1990). A campaign for lower speeds and greater headways between vehicles on motorways in England and Wales in order to reduce the number of accidents on motorways indicates that there was little, if any, effect on speed or headways (Christie 1990). In a nationwide campaign in Sweden, together with local campaigns in Mjølby, Sala and Sandviken, where the objectives included reducing speed, an effect on speed could only be detected in Sala. In that city, mean speed went down by 0.9 km/h (Nolén and Johansson 1993). A campaign warning of hazards associated with blind curves in the Netherlands led to lower speeds in curves where specific information about the hazard was given. The test persons in the study signed up for this voluntarily, and it is uncertain to what extent the same result could be achieved through a standard information campaign (Hendrickx and Vlek 1991).

**Effect on the environment**

Road user information campaigns have no documented effect on the environment.

**Costs**

The costs of road user information and campaigns vary according to the content, scope and method of the activity. Exact estimates of costs cannot be given because information is a routine activity in many organisations. Costs were estimated for a number of different campaigns in Sweden. The annual costs vary between SEK 2 and 19 million. The estimates refer to the total costs of the campaigns, i.e. to the costs for all components of the campaigns including enforcement or other measures (the largest cost estimate refers to a campaign that involves Intelligent Speed Adaptation [ISA], see Section 4.20).

**Cost–benefit analyses**

Cost–benefit analyses have not been calculated. Campaigns were not found to have any effect on accidents when not combined with enforcement. When combined with enforcement, accident reductions were found. Studies of the effects of enforcement (see Section 8.7) do not indicate that accompanying campaigns increase the effectiveness of enforcement significantly. On a general basis, it is therefore most likely that campaigns are not cost-effective.

## References

Amundsen, A.H., Elvik, R. & Fridstrøm, L. (1999). *Evaluering av "Sei i frå" kampanjen i Sogn og Fjordane*. TØI rapport 425/1999, Transportøkonomisk institutt, Oslo.

Anderson, J. W. (1978). The effectiveness of traffic safety material in influencing the driving performance of the general driving population. *Accident Analysis and Prevention*, **10**, 81–94.

Armour, M., Monk, K., South. D. & Chomiac, G. (1985). *Evaluation of the 1983 Melbourne random breath testing campaign: casualty accident analysis*. Road Traffic Authority report (8/85). 18p.

Assum, T. & Glad, A. (1990). *Alkohol og trafikk i Norge: En situasjonsrapport*. Arbeidsdokument nr TST/0189/90. Institute of Transport Economics, Oslo.

Behrensdorff, I. & Johansen, H. J. (1991). Kampagnen "Stop spritkørsel – osse de andres". Spørgeskemaundersøgelse blant unge på vej til "Grøn koncert". Gentofte, Rådet for Trafiksikkerhedsforskning. Arbeidsnotat, 1.

Bérard-Andersen, K. (1985). *Om barn, trafikk og oss voksne*. Revidert utgave. Temahefte nr 9 i temaserien Samferdsel. Transportøkonomisk institutt, Oslo.

Blomberg, R.D., Preusser, D.F., Hale, A. & Leaf, W.A. (1983a). *Experimental Field Test of Proposed Pedestrian Safety Messages-Volume II.* Report DOT HS-806-522. US Department of Transportation, National Highway Traffic Safety Administration, Washington, DC.

Blomberg, R.D., Preusser, D.F., Hale, A. & Leaf, W.A. (1983b). *Experimental Field test of Proposed Pedestrian Safety Messages. Volume III.* Report DOT HS-806-523. US Department of Transportation, National Highway Traffic Safety Administration, Washington, DC.

Blomberg, R.D., Preusser, D.F., Ulmer R.G. (1987). *Deterrent effects of mandatory license suspension for DWI conviction. Final report.* U.S. Department of Transportation, National Highway Traffic Safety Administration (Report DOT HS 807 138).

Borger, A. (1991). *Underrapportering av trafikkulykker.* TØI-notat 975. Transportøkonomisk institutt, Oslo.

Britt, J. W. & A. B. Bergman. (1995). *Law Enforcement, Pedestrian Safety and Driver Compliance with Crosswalk Laws: Evaluation of a Four-Year Seattle Campaign.* Paper 950261. 74th Annual Meeting of the Transportation Research Board, Washington, DC.

Cameron, M., Diamantoupoulou, K., Mullan, N., Dyte, D. & Gantzer, S. (1997). *Evaluation of the country random breath testing and publicity program in Victoria 1993–1994.* Monash University Accident Research Centre (report N°126). 60p.

Cameron, M., Haworth, N., Oxley, J., Newstead, S. & Le, T. (1993). *Evaluation of Transport Accident Commission Road Safety Television Advertising.* Monash University Accident Research Centre (report N°52).

Christie, N. (1990). The Effectiveness of the 1988 Police National Motorway Safety Campaign. *Proceedings (35–49) of Road Safety and Traffic Environment in Europe,* Gothenburg, Sweden, September 26–28, 1990. VTI-rapport 365 A. Statens väg- och trafikinstitut (VTI), Linköping.

Delhomme, P., Vaa, T., Meyer, T. et al. (1999). *Evaluated Road Safety Media Campaigns: An Overview of 265 Evaluated Campaigns and Some Meta-Analysis on Accidents.* INRETS. Project funded by EC and partners under EU 4th Framework Programme. Paris March 1999.

Dowling, A. M. (1986). *Stop-DWI: The First Four Years – an Evaluation Update.* Conducted for the New York state department of motor vehicles by the Institute for Traffic Safety Management and research.

Downing, C. S. & J. Spendlove. (1981). *Effectiveness of a campaign to reduce accidents involving children crossing roads near parked cars.* TRRL Laboratory Report 986. Transport and Road Research Laboratory, Crowthorne, Berkshire.

Drummond, A. E., Sullivan, G., Cavallo A. (1992). *An evaluation of the random breath testing initiative in Victoria 1989–1990: quasi-experimental time series approach.* Monash University Accident Research Centre (report N°37). 105p.

Elliott, B. (1993). *Road Safety Mass Media Campaigns: A Meta Analysis*. Report CR 118. Department of Transport and Communications, Federal Office of Road Safety, Canberra, Australia.

Elvik, R. (1995). *Virkninger av informasjonskampanjer i Norge på antall trafikkulykker*. Arbeidsdokument TST/0689/95. Transportøkonomisk institutt, Oslo.

Elvik, R. (1997). *Vegtrafikklovgivning, kontroll og sanksjoner. Potensialet for å bedre trafikksikkerheten og nytte-kostnadsvurdering av ulike tiltak*. TØI-notat 1073. Transportøkonomisk institutt, Oslo.

Elvik, R., P. Christensen, A. H. Amundsen (2004). *Speed and road accidents. An evaluation of the Power Model*. TØI Report 740/2004. Institute of Transport Economics, Oslo.

Evans, L. (1987). Belted and unbelted driver accident involvement rates compared. *Journal of Safety Research*, **18**, 57–64.

Fortenberry, J. C. & D. B. Brown. (1982). Problem identification, implementation and evaluation of a pedestrian safety program. *Accident Analysis and Prevention*, **14**, 315–322.

Fosser, S. (1984). *Effektmåling av forsikringsbransjens refleksaksjon i 1983*. Arbeidsdokument av 4.1.1984, prosjekt O-717. Resultater fra førmåling i 1982 og ettermåling i 1983. Transportøkonomisk institutt, Oslo.

Fosser, S., P. Christensen & A. Ragnøy. (1992). *Effekten av kampanjen: "Hold avstand-92"*. TØI-rapport 139. Transportøkonomisk institutt, Oslo.

Garber, N.J., Miller, J.S., Abel, R.E., Eslambolchi, S. & Korukonda, S.K. (2007). *The impact of red light cameras (photo-red enforcement) in Virginia*. Final report VTRC 07-R2. Virginia Transportation Research Council. Charlottesville, Virginia.

Glad, A. (1985). *Omfanget av og variasjonen i promillekjøringen. Reviderte resultater fra en landsomfattende promilleundersøkelse i 1981–82*. TØI-notat 740. Transportøkonomisk institutt, Oslo.

Glad, A. (1986). *Aksjonen "Bedre bilist-85". Resultater av en evaluering av aksjonen*. TØI-rapport. Transportøkonomisk institutt, Oslo.

Gregersen, N. P. & S. Nolén. (1994). Children's road safety and the strategy of voluntary traffic safety clubs. *Accident Analysis and Prevention*, **26**, 463–470.

Gårder, P. (1982). *Gåendes säkerhet i trafiksignaler*. Bulletin 43. Tekniska Högskolan i Lund, Institutionen för trafikteknik, Lund.

Harte, D.S. & Hurst, P.M. (1984). Evaluation of operation checkpoint-Accident data. *Road traffic safety seminar 15–17 august 1984*. Road traffic safety research council, Wellington, New Zealand. *Seminar papers*, **Vol 2**, pp.153–167.

Haynes, R.S., Pine, R.C., Fitch, H.G. (1982). Reducing accidents with organizational behaviour modification. *Academy of Management Journal*, **25(2)**, 407–416.

Hendrickx, L. & C. Vlek. (1991). Effects of Risk Information on Speed Choice in Blind Curves. In: *Behavioural Research in Road Safety*. Proceedings (139–147) of a Seminar held at Nottingham University, 26–27 September 1990. (Grayson, G. B. & J. F. Lester. eds). Publication PA2038/91. Transport and Road Research Laboratory, Crowthorne, Berkshire.

Knudsen, K. (1975a). Virkninger av Barnas Trafikklubb. En kritisk kommentar. *Tidsskrift for samfunnsforskning*, **16**, 250–253.

Knudsen, K. (1975b). Replikk. *Tidsskrift for samfunnsforskning*, **16**, 259–261.

Lane, J., P. Milne & T. Wood. (1983). *Evaluation of the 1981/82 Rear Seat Belt Campaign*. Australia, Road Traffic Authority, Hawthorn, Victoria.

Machemer, E., Runde, B., Wolf, U., Büttner, D., Tucke, M., Kley, H., Pieper, M., Schopuis, R., Timmer, H., Trecksel, H. & Wundram, A. (1994). *Delegierte belohnung und intensivierte Verkehrs-überwachung im Vergleich*. BAST (Berichte der Bundesanstalt für Strassenwesen), Mensch und Sicherheit (Heft M 48).

Maisey, G.E. & Saunders, C.M. (1981). *An evaluation of the 1980/81 Christmas/New Year traffic enforcement blitz*. Road Traffic Authority, Research and statistics division, Western Australia (report N°16).

Midtland, K. (1995). *Seksåringers forutsetninger for å ferdes trygt i trafikken*. TØI-notat 999/1995. Transportøkonomisk institutt, Oslo.

Moe, D., K. Sakshaug & T. M. Stene. (1987). *Evaluering av utforkjøringskampanjen 1986*. Rapport STF63 A87006. SINTEF Samferdselsteknikk, Trondheim.

Moe, D. & T. M. Stene. (1990). *Evaluering av utforkjøringskampanjen 1989*. Rapport STF63 A90003. SINTEF Samferdselsteknikk, Trondheim.

Moe, D. & T. Tyldum. (1987). *Forestillinger om bil og MC-kjøring blant ungdom. Spørreskjemaundersøkelse*. Rapport STF63 A87004. SINTEF Samferdselsteknikk, Trondheim.

Munden, J. M. (1967). *The* relation *between a driver's speed and his accident rate*. RRL Report LR 88. Road Research Laboratory, Crowthorne.

Nagatsuka, Y. (1991). Effectiveness of model driving with a safety campaign sticker on the rear outside of the body of buses, trucks and taxis: an action research. Transportation research institute, Haifa. *Proceedings of the Second International Conference on New Ways for Improved Road Safety and Quality of Life (Tel Aviv, Israel, October 7–10)*, pp. 9–10.

Nolén, S. & R. Johansson. (1993). *Utvärdering av lokal hastighetskampanj i Mjölby, Sala och Sandviken*. VTI-meddelande 707. Statens väg- och trafikinstitut (VTI), Linköping.

Nordisk Trafikksikkerhetsråd. (1984). *Sikring av voksne og barn i personbilers bakseter. En beregning av virkningen av alternative bestemmelser*. NTR-rapport 37. Nordisk Ministerråd, Oslo.

OECD Scientific expert group. (1983). *Traffic Safety of Children*. OECD, Paris.

OECD Scientific expert group. (1986). *Effectiveness of road safety education programmes*. OECD, Paris.

Oei, H.L., Goldenbeld, C. (1996). *Snelheidscampagne 1995 in Eindhoven. Leidschendam: Stichting Wetenschap- pelijk Onderzoek Verkeersveiligheid*. SWOV (Rapport N° R-96-31).

Oei, H.L. & Polak, P.H. (1992). *Effect van automatische waarschuwing en toezicht op snelheid en ongevallen. Resultaten van een evaluatie-onderzoek in vier provincies*. SWOV, Leidschendam (Rapport N° 92–23).

Preston, B. (1980). Child cyclist accidents and cycling proficiency training. *Accident Analysis and Prevention*, **12**, 31–40.

Preusser, D. F. & A. K. Lund. (1988). And keep on looking: a film to reduce pedestrian crashes among 9 to 12 year olds. *Journal of Safety Research*, **19**, 177–185.

Sagberg, F. (1994). *En spørreundersøkelse om trafikksikkerhetstiltak for barn og ungdom*. Arbeidsdokument TST/0546/94. Transportøkonomisk institutt, Oslo.

Sakshaug, K. & T. Sten. (1979). *Fotgjengere i signalregulerte kryss*. Oppdragsrapport 39. Forskningsgruppen, Institutt for Samferdselsteknikk, Norways Tekniske Høgskole, Trondheim.

Sali, G.J. (1983). Evaluation of Boise traffic enforcement project. Washington, DC, *Transportation Research Record*, **910**, 68–93.

Sargent, K. J. & D. Sheppard. (1974). *The development of the Green Cross Code*. TRRL Laboratory Report 605. Transport and Road Research Laboratory, Crowthorne, Berkshire.

Schioldborg, P. (1974). *Barn, trafikk og trafikkopplæring. En analyse av Barnas Trafikklubb*. Universitet i Oslo, Psykologisk institutt, Oslo.

Schioldborg, P. (1975a). Virkninger av Barnas Trafikklubb. En kommentar til Knud Knudsen. *Tidsskrift for samfunnsforskning*, **16**, 254–258.

Schioldborg, P. (1975b). Svarreplikk. *Tidsskrift for samfunnsforskning*, **16**, 263–264.

Schlabbach, K. (1990). Improvement of Traffic Safety by Local Public Relations Campaigns. *Proceedings (51–64) of Road Safety and Traffic Environment in Europe*, Gothenburg, Sweden, September 26–28, 1990. VTI-rapport 365 A. Statens väg- och trafikinstitut (VTI), Linköping.

Smith, D.I., Maisey, G.E. & McLaughlin, K.L. (1990). Evaluation of the first year of random breathtesting in Western Australia. 15th *arrb conference, Darwin, northern territory (26–31 august, Victoria)*. Australian Road Research Board Proceedings, 15(7), pp. 93–106.

Spoerer, E. (1989). *Einflus von Informationen zur Verkehrssicherheit auf unfallbeteiligte Kraftfahrer*. BAST (Berichte der Bundesanstalt für Strassenwesen), Bergisch Gladbach.

Statistisk sentralbyrå. (1996). *Vegtrafikkulykker 1995*. NOS Publikasjon C 332, Oslo-Kongsvinger.

Stene, T. M. (1987). *Evaluering av fotgjengerkampanjen 1987*. Rapport STF63 A88006. SINTEF Samferdselsteknikk, Trondheim.

Studsholt, P. (1990). Campaigns against drunken driving among young drivers. *Proceedings of road safety and traffic in Europe (Conference, Gothenburg, Sweden september 26–28)*. In National Swedish Road & Traffic Research Institute, Linköping, Sweden (report N°HS-041 279, VTI-365 A), pp. 26–33.

Stuster, J.W. (1995). *Experimental evaluation of municipal enforcement programs*. Washington, DC, National Highway Traffic Safety Administration (Report No DOT HS 808 325).

Sävenhed, H., Brüde, U., Nygaard, B., Petterson, H-E. & Thulin, H. (1996). *Heja Halland: An evaluation of a traffic campaign*. Statens vaeg- och transportforskningsinstitut, Linkoeping, Sweden (VTI Meddelande, 779).

Taylor, W.C. & Ahmed, A.R. (1995). *Evaluation of the "Share-the-road "campaign*. Final Report. Michigan State University, USA (Report GLCTTR 71-95/01). 75p.

Trygg Trafikk. (1996). *Årsberetning 1995*. Trygg Trafikk, Oslo.

Törnros, J. (1995). *Intensified random breath testing in southern Sweden*. Statens vaeg- och transportforskningsinstiut, Linkoeping, Sweden (VTI Meddelande, 746).

Voas, R.B., Holder, H.D., Gruenewald, P.J. (1997). The effect of drinking and driving interventions on alcohol-involved traffic crashes within a comprehensive community trial. *Addiction*, **92** (**Supplement 2**), S221–S236.

Vaa, T., Assum, T., Ulleberg, P. & Veisten, K. (2004). *Effekter av informasjonskampanjer på atferd og trafikkulykker (Effects of information campaigns on behaviour and accidents)*. TØI Report 727/2004. Institute of Transport Economics, Oslo.

Wasielewski, P. (1984). Speed as a measure of driver risk: observed speeds versus driver and vehicle characteristics. *Accident Analysis and Prevention*, **16**, 89–103.

Wells, J.K., Preusser, D.F. & Williams, A.F. (1992). Enforcing alcohol-impaired driving and seat belt use laws, Binghamton, NY. *Journal of Safety Research*, **23**, 63–71.

Wolfe, A. C. (1983). *Interim (two-year) evaluation report on the Oakland county alcohol enforcement/education project*. University of Michigan Transport Research Institute, USA (report N°83–12).

# 8.

# Police Enforcement and Sanctions

## 8.0 Introduction and overview of 13 measures

This chapter describes 13 measures in the area of enforcement and sanctions. Some measures are directed towards specific law violations: speeding, non-wearing of seat belts, red-light running and driving under the influence of alcohol (DUI). Sanctions are largely issued in the form of punishment, but also to some extent in the form of reward and motivational measures (motor vehicle insurance). Some laws are also described, which are a relevant background to police enforcement and sanctions. The 13 measures are as follows:

8.1 Stationary and manual speed enforcement
8.2 Automatic speed enforcement
8.3 Seat belt enforcement
8.4 Patrolling
8.5 Red-light cameras
8.6 Demerit point systems and licence suspension
8.7 Fixed penalties
8.8 DUI laws
8.9 DUI enforcement
8.10 Restrictions for DUI-convicted drivers
8.11 Treatment of DUI-convicted drivers
8.12 Penalties and imprisonment
8.13 Motor vehicle insurance

**The Handbook of Road Safety Measures**

**ISBN: 978-1-84855-250-0**

## Amount and quality of research

Table 8.0.1 gives an overview of the amount of research that has evaluated measures within the area of enforcement and sanctions. There are a relatively large number of studies reporting on the effects of the measures on accidents. The majority of studies deal with measures against DUI, speeding and red-light running. Some studies are based on very large accident samples, in particular the sections on DUI laws, DUI enforcement and motor vehicle insurance. Meta-analyses have been used to summarise research results for all measures, except fixed penalties, where no studies were found to be suitable for meta-analysis.

The quality of the research varies, but the majority of the studies have used experimental or quasi-experimental designs or multivariate methods. For a number of measures, systematic differences in the results have been found depending on study quality. These measures are seat belt enforcement, red-light cameras, DUI enforcement and DUI laws. For these measures, only results from the best studies are presented.

Changes in enforcement, sanctions and laws are seldom introduced as individual measures. Usually more than one measure is introduced (or changed) in order to achieve a reduction in the prevalence of a specific traffic law violation. This is a methodological challenge, because it is difficult or impossible to separate the effects from different measures. On some areas, a number of multivariate studies have been found, which have investigated the effects of different types of measures based on large accident numbers from different legislations and over many years. These are especially studies of DUI laws (Section 8.8), and laws about penalties and imprisonment (Section 8.12). For treatment of DUI-convicted drivers (Section 8.11). In contrast, there are hardly any well-controlled studies available. This type of measure is often used in combination with sanctions and there are for the most part systematic differences between drivers who do and who do not receive a treatment. The results are therefore not always attributable to the treatments studied.

The United States has contributed the most by way of studies. Especially DUI laws have been studied on a large scale in the USA. Australia has contributed to a large part of the studies of DUI enforcement. The United Kingdom, Norway and Australia have contributed many studies of automatic speed and red-light running enforcement.

## Main elements in effects on accidents

***Stationary and manual speed enforcement*** was found to reduce accidents. When combined with patrolling, no effects on accidents were found. ***Automatic speed***

*Table 8.0.1: The amount of research evaluating the effects on accidents of police enforcement and sanctions*

| Measure | Number of studies | Number of results | Statistical weights | Results last updated |
|---|---|---|---|---|
| 8.1 Stationary and manual speed enforcement | 12 | 52 | 5,415 | 2009 |
| 8.2 Automatic speed enforcement | 16 | 68 | 13,332 | 2009 |
| 8.3 Seat belt enforcement | 17 | 66 | 103,388 | 2009 |
| 8.4 Patrolling | 18 | 74 | 29,065 | 2008 |
| 8.5 Red-light cameras | 23 | 116 | 27,569 | 2007 |
| 8.6 Demerit point systems and licence suspension | 17 | 51 | 10,940 | 2008 |
| 8.7 Fixed penalties* | 5 | 5 | – | 2008 |
| 8.8 DUI laws | 45 | 222 | 376,128 | 2008 |
| 8.9 DUI enforcement | 40 | 98 | 43,852 | 2008 |
| 8.10 Restrictions for DUI convicted drivers | 6 | 14 | 3,499 | 2008 |
| 8.11 Treatment of DUI convicted drivers | 11 | 21 | 2,689 | 2008 |
| 8.12 Penalties and imprisonment | 13 | 38 | 38,447 | 2008 |
| 8.13 Motor vehicle insurance | 9 | 31 | 85,114 | 2008 |

*The results refer to effects on violations; no summary effects have been calculated.

***enforcement*** is associated with a significant reduction in the number of injury accidents of 16%. The effect is greater for fatal accidents than for other accidents.

***Seat belt enforcement*** has been found to increase seat belt use by ca. 20%. However, these effects are difficult to generalise since the size of the increase in wearing rate depends on the initial level.

No effects on accidents have been found of most types of ***police patrols***. When an unmarked car is used for patrolling with a special focus on speeding, a small but significant increase in accident numbers was found.

***Red-light enforcement*** was found to lead to an increase in the total number of accidents at junctions. Side collisions, which are the target accidents of red-light enforcement, were found to be reduced. However, this effect is more than offset by an increase in rear-end collisions.

***Demerit point systems*** were not found to reduce accidents. However, components of such systems may reduce accidents. Warning letters and courses for drivers with critical numbers of penalty points may reduce the accident involvement of the respective drivers. ***Licence suspension*** was found to be effective only among drivers whose licence has been suspended, and only while the licence actually was suspended. No effects were found on drivers in general or on drivers whose licence was reinstated. It was also found that many drivers with a suspended licence continue driving illegally.

***Fixed penalties*** for non-use of seat belts were found to increase the use of seat belts. No effects on speeding were found because of increased fixed penalties for speeding.

***DUI laws:*** The two laws that have the greatest and best documented effect on accidents are an increase of the minimum legal drinking age from 18 to 21 and a blood alcohol concentration (BAC) level of 0.02 for young drivers. Per se BAC laws and administrative licence suspension laws have found to lead to small but significant reductions of the number of fatal accidents in states that adopt such laws. The effects of reducing (existing) BAC levels are uncertain. Two American laws that have been found to be effective in reducing fatal accidents are dram shop laws and open container laws. Dram shop laws impose civil liability on liquor stores and other commercial establishments that sell alcoholic beverages to minors or obviously intoxicated persons. Open container laws prohibit consuming alcohol in a car while driving. The effects on accidents are, however, not large and may be not be generalised to other countries than the USA.

Laws that were not found to have any effect on accidents are reduced BAC limits for DUI-convicted drivers, anti-plea bargaining laws, social host liability and laws that allow random breath testing. High alcohol prices, prohibition of advertising for alcohol and reduced availability of alcohol do not seem to reduce alcohol accidents either. Reduced availability of alcohol (local prohibition, reduced density of licensed premises, shorter opening hours) was found to lead to increased numbers and lengths of trips related to purchase and consumption of alcohol, and may therefore have a negative impact on safety.

***DUI enforcement*** was found to reduce accident numbers, especially during the first months after the implementation of a new enforcement programme or an increase in the amount of enforcement. The enforcement methods that are used in Australia, in the form of highly visible checkpoints where many drivers are tested, have been found to be most effective.

***Restrictions for DUI-convicted drivers*** include licence suspension, vehicle impoundment and alcolock. Licence suspension was found to be effective in reducing accidents while the licence is suspended, but not after the licence has been reinstated. Vehicle impoundment was found to have greater and more long-lasting effects than licence suspension, both among drivers who actually have a vehicle impounded and among drivers who are in danger of vehicle impoundment (e.g. because the licence is suspended). No studies of the effects of alcolock on accidents were found. Drink driving is likely to be reduced, but no effects were found after alcolock is removed from the vehicles.

***Treatment of DUI-convicted drivers*** includes educational measures with a focus on behaviour changes, and therapeutic measures with a focus on alcohol problems. Results from evaluation studies are inconsistent. Differences in accident involvement that have been found between treated and untreated drivers are often likely to be due to other factors than the treatment, such as the number of previous DUI convictions. Educational measures may be effective in reducing recidivism among drivers without alcohol problems. Among alcoholics, education has no effect. Treatment seems to be most effective in combination with sanctions. Some studies found increased accident involvement among drivers who had chosen treatment as an alternative to licence suspension.

Penalties and imprisonment do not seem to have any effect on accident numbers. This refers to both the total number of accidents (in jurisdictions with severe sanctions) and convicted drivers. However, combined programmes, which include sanctions, treatment and monitoring, have been found to reduce recidivism. Such programmes, often administered by DUI courts, include for the most part a requirement of total abstinence from alcohol and are quite comprehensive and restrictive.

Different elements of ***insurance schemes*** have different effects on accidents. More stringent laws requiring liability insurance appear to have led to increases in accident numbers. Introducing no-fault insurance and lower compensation limits also appear to lead to more accidents. Policyholders who have collision insurance have the same claims frequency as policyholders who do not have this kind of insurance, while paying accrued bonuses in cash (reverse bonus system) has been found to be associated with a reduction of 22% in accidents.

**Main elements in effects on mobility**

The measures in this area are not primarily intended to affect mobility, but there are some exceptions. Speed enforcement reduces speed. Licence suspension and restrictions for DUI-convicted drivers may affect individual mobility. However, compliance is not high as long as driving is not made physically impossible. Red-light cameras may have a negative effect on traffic flow and on junction capacity because more drivers stop at a yellow traffic signal, instead of driving through the intersection.

## Main elements in effects on the environment

To the extent that these measures reduce speed, they will also contribute to some extent to reducing noise and exhaust gas emissions from vehicles. Red-light cameras will probably have some effect on the environment in that more drivers may stop on a yellow traffic signal, with the result that their vehicles stands idling throughout one signal light phase, instead of driving through the intersection without stopping. This increases exhaust gas emissions.

## Main elements in costs

Table 8.0.2 shows the estimated costs for Norway of the measures in the area of enforcement and sanctions.

## Main elements in cost–benefit analyses

Cost–benefit analyses have only been carried out to a limited extent with respect to enforcement and sanctions. For a number of measures, numerical examples have been worked out to indicate costs and benefits.

An issue relevant to the cost–benefit analysis of enforcement is whether the benefit to those who commit traffic violations, e.g. in the form of time saved through speeding,

*Table 8.0.2: Costs of enforcement and sanctions in Norway*

| Measure | Costs (million NOK) | Results last updated |
|---|---|---|
| 8.1 Stationary and manual speed enforcement | 130 | 2009 |
| 8.2 Automatic speed enforcement | –* | |
| 8.3 Seat belt enforcement | 37 | 1994 |
| 8.4 Patrolling | 130 | 2008 |
| 8.5 Red-light cameras | 0 | 2007 |
| 8.6 Demerit point systems and licence suspension | – | 2008 |
| 8.7 Fixed penalties | – | 2008 |
| 8.8 DUI laws | 1 | 2008 |
| 8.9 DUI enforcement | 40 | 1995 |
| 8.9 DUI enforcement, prosecution, imprisonment, licence suspension | 164 | 1995 |
| 8.11 Treatment of DUI convicted drivers | – | 2008 |
| 8.12 Penalties and imprisonment | 112 | 2008 |
| 8.13 Motor vehicle insurance | 11.5 | 2008 |

*No cost estimates available.

*Table 8.0.3: Benefit–cost ratios of enforcement and sanctions in Norway*

| Measure | Benefit–cost ratio |
|---|---|
| 8.1 Tripling stationary speed enforcement | 1.5 |
| 8.2 Automatic speed enforcement | 2–27 |
| 8.3 Increased seat-belt enforcement at a cost of NOK 100 million annually | 1.0 |
| 8.4 Patrolling | –[1] |
| 8.5 Red-light cameras | –[1] |
| 8.6 Demerit point systems | –[1] |
| 8.7 Fixed penalties | –[2] |
| 8.8 Zero BAC limit for drivers under the age of 21 | 11 |
| 8.9 Tripling drink driving enforcement | 1.2 |
| 8.10 Alcolock in heavy vehicles | $<1$ |
| 8.10 Driving licence suspension for drink driving (current practice) | 9.2 |
| 8.11 Treatment of DUI-convicted drivers | –[2] |
| 8.12 Imprisonment | –[1] |
| 8.13 Motor vehicle insurance | –[2] |

[1]No accident reductions were found for these measures.
[2]No results available.

should be counted as a social benefit in a cost–benefit analysis of measures intended to curb violations. This issue is discussed in greater detail in a working report (Elvik 1997a). It is concluded that benefits achieved by violating the law cannot be regarded as a social benefit to be included in a cost–benefit analysis. Road user benefits from violating the law are therefore disregarded in cost–benefit analyses. This means, for example, that increased costs of travel time for road users who have to reduce their speed because of speed enforcement are not included. The benefit–cost ratio for a number of measures has been estimated as shown in Table 8.0.3.

The analyses show that an increase in enforcement is probably cost-effective with regard to speed, drink driving and the use of seat belts. Speed cameras, driving licence suspension and a zero BAC limit for young drivers are very cost-effective measures, as used at present. For several measures, no cost–benefit ratios have been calculated since no accident reductions have been found.

## 8.1 Stationary and manual speed enforcement

### Problem and objective

Exceeding the speed limit is probably the most common form of traffic violation. Many drivers would drive faster than the speed limit – a few considerably faster – if they knew for sure that the police were not enforcing speed on a particular road. Even though the actual risk of apprehension may be very low, the mere possibility that speeds may be checked by the police influences behaviour. An analysis of the effect of the police strike in Finland in 1976 found that average speed changed little, while the number of major violations of the speed limit increased by 50–100% (Summala, Näätänen and Roine 1980). Stationary speed enforcement is intended to ensure compliance with the speed limit, thus reducing the number and severity of accidents.

**Description of the measure**

A distinction should be made between speed enforcement using stationary methods and speed enforcement using 'mobile' methods or police patrols. The distinction is relevant because halo effects have been found in time and space for stationary enforcement, but not for mobile patrols (Shinar and McKnight 1985, Vaa 1993). 'Halo effects' in time and space means that an effect can be found during a given period of time and/or at a certain distance from the spot where the speed enforcement is carried out. The mechanism, which establishes the halo effects, is through the visibility of enforcement symbols as marked cars and uniformed police officers. The analyses distinguish between two types of stationary speed enforcement: One, often found in the Nordic countries, is with an unobtrusive/hidden observation site, which measures driving speeds, and a clearly visible apprehension site some distance downstream. The other, predominantly found in the USA and hence labelled 'American type', is when the same car measures driving speeds, pursuits and apprehends the offender in case of speed violations. In addition, it should be pinpointed that these types of speed enforcement are done manually.

The categorisation of the stationary methods should be regarded with some precaution as many of the studies lack a thorough description of the methods that have been applied. The following techniques of stationary speed enforcement are used:

- Stationary speed enforcement using radar/laser or instruments that measure mean speed between two fixed observation points, and stopping sites staffed by uniformed police officers and marked cars.
- As above, but labelled 'American type' as when one Highway Patrol unit, sometimes one officer alone in a car, both measures, pursuits and apprehends a speed violator.
- Composite speed enforcement including at least one stationary, visible speed enforcement element. This term is used when more than one enforcement method is applied. In its simplest form, it comprises both a stationary and a patrolling/mobile element; in a complex form, it may cover several enforcement methods as defined by McCartt and Rood (1989), which comprised several methods, among them aeroplanes as observation posts and visible stopping sites with marked cars.

**Effect on accidents**

The effects of speed enforcement on accidents have been evaluated in the following studies:

Novak and Shumate (1961) (USA)
Ekström, Kritz and Strömgren (1966) (Sweden)
Munden (1966) (UK)
Mason (1970a, 1970b) (USA)
Saunders (1977) (Australia)
Brackett and Beecher (1980) (USA)
Leggett (1988) (Australia)
Salusjärvi and Mäkinen (1988) (Finland)
McCartt and Rood (1989) (USA)
Andersson (1991) (Sweden)
Statens vegvesen Buskerud/UP (1996) (Norway)
Pez (2002) (Germany)

For all types of enforcement, the relationship between the following factors and the size of the effect on accidents have been investigated: the country in which the study (and the enforcement) was conducted, the visibility of the enforcement (visible vs. hidden), whether or not the enforcement was conducted at randomly chosen times and places and the type of publicity that accompanied the enforcement (no publicity, local publicity, e.g. in local media, or a more comprehensive publicity campaign). Other aspects studied include whether the effects on accidents vary according to injury severity and whether study quality affected the results.

Table 8.1.1 shows the effect on accidents of stationary speed enforcement.

For ***stationary visible enforcement with radar/laser***, a significant decrease of the number of accidents was found. Most results refer to injury accidents. There is no significant difference between the effects on injury accidents and accidents with unspecified severity (mostly property damage only). All studies are from countries other than the United States (Australia, Sweden, Finland) and all studies have applied some kind of comparison group.

***Stationary visible enforcement with radar/laser 'American type'*** was not found to reduce accidents. There is no variation in effects with respect to accident severity.

*Table 8.1.1: Effects on accidents of stationary speed enforcement*

| | | Percentage change in the number of accidents | |
|---|---|---|---|
| Characteristics of enforcement | Accident severity | Best estimate | 95% confidence interval |
| ***Stationary visible enforcement with radar/laser*** | | | |
| All | Unspecified | −17 | (−31; −2) |
| ***Stationary visible enforcement with radar/laser 'American type'*** | | | |
| All | Unspecified | −1 | (−5; +4) |
| ***Composite speed enforcement*** | | | |
| All | ***Unspecified*** | | |
| | Without control for publication bias: | −7 | (−15; +1) |
| | With control for publication bias: | −1 | (−11; +9) |

***Composite speed enforcement*** shows a tendency of reducing the number of accidents, but it is not significant, and the results seem to be affected by publication bias. When publication bias is controlled for, the effect on accidents diminishes almost to zero. The effect on accidents does not seem to be consistently affected by any of the factors investigated.

## Effect on mobility

A number of Norwegian studies have shown that speed goes down where speed enforcement increases. The average reduction in speed is around 2 km/h. A time-halo effect of between 2 days and 10 weeks after the period of intensified speed enforcement has been found (Vaa, Christensen and Ragnøy 1995). The distance-halo effects vary from around 1 to 22 km (Vaa 1993).

## Effect on the environment

A lower speed level reduces both noise and exhaust emissions from vehicles.

## Costs

In a recent policy analysis (Elvik 2007), the current annual costs of speed enforcement in Norway were estimated to be roughly NOK 130 million. The level of speed enforcement in Norway remained stable during the year from 1995 to 2003 (Elvik and Christensen 2004).

### Cost–benefit analysis

In an English study where the number of accidents was reduced by 25% as the result of increasing enforcement by a factor of 6–8, the benefit–cost ratio was estimated to be between 0.3 and 1.8 (Munden 1966). In an American study where enforcement was increased in six counties in Texas, the benefit–cost ratio was estimated to be around 3.3–5.7 (Roop and Brackett 1980). For speed enforcement by means of observing and measuring speed from the air, which has been tested in Australia, the benefit–cost ratio was 12.1 (Kearns 1988).

Leggett (1988) estimated the benefit–cost ratio of a long-term, low-intensity stationary speed enforcement to be 4.

In a road safety policy analysis for Norway, Elvik (2007) estimated costs and benefits of different increases in speed enforcement. Doubling the level of speed enforcement was estimated to have a benefit–cost ratio of 2, tripling the level of enforcement was estimated to have a benefit–cost ratio of 1.5 and quintupling the level of enforcement was estimated to have a benefit–cost ratio of 1.0.

## 8.2 Automatic speed enforcement: Speed cameras

### Problem and objectives

Exceeding the speed limit is probably the most common traffic law violation among drivers. Only a very small proportion of all traffic violations are detected. The ***objective*** risk of being apprehended is very low. For example, a Swedish estimate indicates that only around 3 out of every 10,000 incidences of speeding are detected by the police (Nilsson and Engdahl 1986). A Norwegian estimate from 1976 indicated that the risk of being apprehended for speeding was less than 1 in 1,000, even for road sections that had the highest levels of enforcement (Endresen 1978).

Speed cameras (automatic speed enforcement) are intended to provide an enhanced capacity for enforcement by applying technical solutions that do not require the presence of police officers at the scene of an offence.

### Description of the measure

Systems for automatic enforcement, including speed cameras, are designed to detect traffic violations and identify the vehicle/driver automatically, i.e. without police officers being physically present at the scene. Identification is based on photographs of the vehicle and driver, usually from the front, but sometimes from the rear.

## Effect on accidents

The effects of speed cameras on accidents have been evaluated in the following studies:

Bourne and Cooke (1993) (Australia)
Cameron, Newstead, Diamantopoulou and Oxley (2003) (Australia)
Elvik (1997) (Norway)
Fuller (2006) (Ireland)
Gains, Heydecker, Shrewsbury and Robertson (2004) (UK)
Goldenbeld and van Schagen (2005) (The Netherlands)
Hook, Kirkwood and Evans (1995) (UK)
Jones, Sauerzapf and Haynes (2008) (UK)
Kang (2002) (Korea)
Lamm and Kloeckner (1988) (Germany)
London Accident Analysis Unit (1997) (UK)
Newstead and Cameron (2003) (Australia)
Nuyts (2006) (Belgium)
Oei and Polak (1992) (The Netherlands)
Stefan (2006) (Ireland)
Tay (2000) (New Zealand)

For all types of speed cameras, the relationship between the following factors affects and the size of the effect on accidents has been investigated: the country in which the study (and the enforcement) was conducted, the visibility of the enforcement (visible vs. hidden), whether or not the enforcement was conducted at randomly chosen times and places and the type of publicity that accompanied the enforcement (no publicity, local publicity e.g. in local media, or a more comprehensive publicity campaign). Other aspects studied include whether the effects on accidents differ according to injury severity and whether study quality affects the results. Table 8.2.1 shows the effect on accidents of speed cameras.

***Fixed (visible) speed cameras***: The results in Table 8.2.1 indicate that fixed speed cameras reduce accidents of all severities by 24%. However, when publication bias is controlled for, the effect is reduced to −16%. Most of the results refer to injury accidents. For fatal accidents, a larger effect was found.

*Table 8.2.1: Effects on accidents of speed cameras*

| | Percentage change in the number of accidents | | |
|---|---|---|---|
| Characteristics of enforcement | Accident severity | Best estimate | 95% confidence interval |
| ***Fixed (visible) speed cameras*** | | | |
| All | Unspecified | | |
| | *Without control for publication bias:* | −24 | (−29; −19) |
| | *With control for publication bias:* | −16 | (−23; −8) |
| All | Fatal accidents | −39 | (−60; −7) |
| Less than doubled enforcement | Unspecified severity | −17 | (−28; −5) |
| More than doubled enforcement | Unspecified severity | −35 | (−51; −15) |
| New type of enforcement | Unspecified severity | −24 | (−29; −19) |
| ***Mobile (hidden) speed cameras*** | | | |
| All | Injury accidents | −10 | (−22; +4) |
| All | Fatal accidents | −16 | (−33; +5) |
| ***Section control*** | | | |
| All | Injury accidents | −30 | (−61; +25) |

Larger effects were found when the number of speed cameras was more than doubled than when it was less than doubled or when speed cameras were introduced as a new type of enforcement. These results are not controlled for publication bias and the effects may therefore be somewhat overestimated. Almost all speed cameras are signposted and well visible for drivers, the effects of signposting and visibility could therefore not be investigated. Speed camera programmes were sometimes, but not always, accompanied by different types of publicity, either as local publicity, or a part of wider, more comprehensive publicity campaign. The effects on accidents are practically identical, irrespective of the type of publicity (not shown in Table 8.2.1).

All results for fixed speed cameras are based only on studies that have applied some kind of comparison group. Studies that have not applied a comparison group found systematically larger effects, probably due to a lack of control for confounding factors, and where therefore omitted from the analyses.

***Mobile (hidden) speed cameras*** were found to reduce injury accidents by 10% and fatal accidents by 16%. Neither result is statistically significant. The enforcement was invisible to drivers in all cases. In about half of the programmes, the speed cameras were accompanied by a publicity campaign. All studies have applied some kind of comparison group.

For both fixed and mobile speed cameras, the effects on injury accidents are slightly larger when the enforcement is accompanied by a publicity campaign than when no there is no accompanying publicity. The differences in the effects are, however, only small and not significant (not shown in Table 8.2.1).

***Section control*** was found to reduce injury accidents by 30%. This result is based on only one study (Stefan 2006), which does not include many accidents. It is therefore not statistically significant.

### Effect on mobility

Speed cameras may affect mobility in that the average speed is reduced.

### Effect on the environment

A measure reducing high speed will reduce exhaust emissions and traffic noise.

### Costs

According to information provided by the Norwegian Public Roads Administration, costs were estimated as follows:

- Installing a camera box: NOK 87,000
- Installing a wet film camera: NOK 156,000
- Installing a digital camera: NOK 320,000
- Annual operating costs per camera: NOK 100,000.

### Cost–benefit analysis

A study by Mäkinen and Oei (1992) estimated the costs of speed cameras in the Netherlands to Dfl 360,000 and the benefit in terms of a reduction in accidents to Dfl 924,000 (Dfl = Dutch guilders). This gives a benefit–cost ratio of 2.6.

A Norwegian study by Brekke (1993) estimated accident savings at NOK 80 million. The total cost of setting up and operating the system was around NOK 3 million. This gives a benefit–cost ratio of 26.7.

The total costs of a Dutch 5-year program with mobile (hidden) cameras were €5 million. If saving two fatalities, at an estimated €15.4 million, the B/C ratio would be 3 (Goldenbeld and van Schagen 2005).

A study made for the European Union (ICF Consulting 2003) concluded that by adopting best practice in the use of speed cameras in all EU-countries, a benefit–cost ratio of 5.9 could be attained. Best practice was defined as installing the same number of speed cameras per kilometre of road as in Great Britain, which at the time of the study had the highest density of speed cameras.

According to a road safety policy analysis for Norway (Elvik 2007), extending the use of speed cameras according to a plan prepared by the Public Roads Administration has a benefit–cost ratio of 2.1. Converting existing speed cameras to a system of section control was estimated to have a benefit–cost ratio of 2.3.

## 8.3 Seat belt enforcement

### Problem and objective

Many studies have shown that the risk of being killed or injured in a road accident is reduced considerably by wearing seat belts. According to Section 4.12, analyses of the effect of seat belts show that the risk of being seriously injured or killed is reduced by 45–50% if seat belts are worn.

In Norway, the use of seat belts has increase from under 40% in 1973 (35% in rural areas and 13% in urban areas) to ca. 90% in 2007 (93% in rural areas and 90% in urban areas). This is partly due to the introduction of fines, and more or less regular increases of these, and partly to an increase of enforcement. In other countries, even higher usage rates have been achieved. In Germany, the proportion of drivers using seat belts is 96%, 97% and 99% in urban areas, rural areas and on motorways, respectively (Heinrich 1991). In England, the usage rates are 92% in rural areas and 95% in urban areas (Broughton 1991). In the USA, seat belt use was estimated to be 75% in 2002 (Shults et al. 2004). In states with primary seat belt laws, the usage rate is ca. 80% on average, while it is on average 69% in states with secondary seat belt laws.

The objective of seat belt enforcement is to increase seat belt usage among drivers and passengers in vehicles in order to reduce the severity of injuries in accidents.

## Description of the measure

Seat belt enforcement is often conducted at checkpoints by the police (in Norway also by the Public Roads Administration). Mobile police patrols can also enforce the use of seat belts. With a primary seat belt law the police are allowed to stop drivers solely for being unbelted. With a secondary law, police can issue tickets for the non-use of seat belts only if a driver is stopped for another reason (e.g. speeding). Primary laws were found to increase seat belt usage rates in states that previously only had secondary laws (Shults et al. 2004).

Seat belt enforcement is often conducted in combination with other types of enforcement (e.g. speed enforcement) and is often accompanied by information in media or by publicity campaigns. An example is the STEP program (Selective Traffic Enforcement Program) from USA and Canada. STEP includes the enforcement of several traffic law violations and public information (Vaa 1996). Another example is the campaign 'Click it or ticket', which has a strong focus on police enforcement and which led to an increase of the proportion of drivers using seat belts by 17% (from 81% to 95%) in Washington (Salzberg and Moffat 2004).

## Effect on accidents

Seat belt enforcement aims at reducing the usage of seat belts, and thereby to reduce the number of seriously of fatally injured persons in road accidents. Most studies have investigated the effect on seat belt use, only few studies have investigated the effects on the numbers of fatalities or injuries.

***Effects on seat belt use of seat belt enforcement*** were investigated in the following studies:

Gundy (1988) (Netherlands)
Gras and Noordzij (1987) (Netherlands)
Lund, Stuster and Fleming (1989) (Netherlands)
Vissers (1989) (Netherlands)
Dosselaar, van Winterink and Benjamins (1988) (Netherlands)
Beke and Wilbers (1990) (Netherlands)
Reinfurt, Campbell, Stewart and Stutts (1990) (USA)
Hagenzieker (1991) (Australia)
Mathijssen (1992) (Netherlands)
Streff, Molnar and Christoff (1992) (USA)

Wells, Preusser and Williams (1992) (USA)
Kaye, Sapolsky and Montgomery (1995) (USA)
Salzberg and Moffat (2004) (USA)
Geary, Ledingham and Maloney (2005) (USA)
Nuyts and Vesentini (2006) (Belgium)

The results are summarised in Table 8.3.1. Effects are reported both during the enforcement period and for a period after the enforcement period.

The results show that seat belt enforcement increases seat belt use by 21% during the enforcement period, and by 15% afterwards. Even if the increases are smaller in the after period for all subgroups of results, all results are statistically significant. The results do not seem to be affected by publication bias. There are several factors that affect the effectiveness of seat belt enforcement.

Larger increases of seat belt use have been found in studies that have applied a comparison group than in studies that have not done so. This indicates that the results in the other subgroups may be overestimated. However, the differences between the

*Table 8.3.1: Effects on seat belt use of seat belt enforcement*

| | Before–during | | Before–after | |
|---|---|---|---|---|
| | Best estimate | 95% confidence interval | Best estimate | 95% confidence interval |
| All results | +21 | (+16; +27) | +15 | (+10; +20) |
| Studies without comparison | +38 | (+10; +73) | +11 | (+1; +23) |
| Studies with comparison | +20 | (+14; +26) | +17 | (+11; +22) |
| Nighttime | +40 | (+31; +50) | +12 | (0; +26) |
| Day-time | +11 | (+3; +19) | +10 | (+4; +17) |
| Increase of enforcement | +30 | (+18; +44) | +19 | (+11; +28) |
| Changed form of enforcement | +18 | (+12; +25) | +12 | (+7; +16) |
| Publicity campaign | +24 | (+17; +31) | +20 | (+13; +28) |
| Local publicity | +21 | (+12; +31) | +17 | (+7; +28) |
| Comprehensive program | +17 | (+10; +25) | +9 | (+6; +12) |
| No publicity | | | −13 | (−19; −8) |
| Announced checkpoints | +21 | (+14; +27) | +19 | (+13; +25) |
| Checkpoints not announced | +11 | (+2; +21) | +9 | (+1; +17) |

other subgroups of results do not change when only studies that have applied a comparison group are regarded.

The results indicate that the effects of seat belt enforcement on seat belt use are larger at night than during daytime, possibly because seat belt use is often lower at night than at daytime. The results indicate further that the effects are greater when the intensity of enforcement increases than when a new form of enforcement is introduced. This finding may be related to the finding that seat belt enforcement that is accompanied by publicity has greater effects on seat belt use than comprehensive programs, which aim at reducing a number of different traffic violations.

When seat belt checkpoints are not announced with road signs, greater effects have been found than when checkpoints are not announced. The announcement of checkpoints with road signs was intended as an indicator of how well visible the checkpoints are to drivers. It is assumed that more visible enforcement has greater effects (Zaal 1994). However, when seat belt enforcement is announced, some drivers may think that they will be able to fasten the seat belt whenever they see a checkpoint (Erke and Vaa 2008).

The changes in usage rates are on average greater when the initial usage rate was lower (Shults et al. 2004). The relationship between usage rate in the before period and the change in the usage rate is shown in Figure 8.3.1 based on the studies that are summarised above. The change in the usage rate is shown as odds ratio, i.e. 1 indicates no change, and valued above 1 indicate an increase of seat belt use.

***Effects on seat belt use of campaigns and incentive programmes.*** The effects of campaigns and incentives on seat belt use have been investigated in a meta-analysis by Hagenzieker, Bijleveld and Davidse (1997). The results show an increase in seat belt use by ca. 10%. However, the results may be affected by publication bias (larger estimates of effect were found in larger studies).

***Effects on accidents and fatalities of seat belt enforcement***. Effects on accidents have been investigated in two studies (Wells, Preusser and Williams 1992, Williams, Reinfurt and Wells 1996). The results show a decrease by 4%, 6% and 8% for all accidents, fatal accidents and injury accidents, respectively. None of the results is statistically significant. Salzberg and Moffat (2004) studied the effects on fatalities. The results show that the number of fatalities was reduced by 13% after the introduction of the campaign ‘Click it or ticket’ (seat belt use increased by 17%). However, the study has not controlled for other factors and the results may therefore be affected by time trends, regression effects and other safety measures.

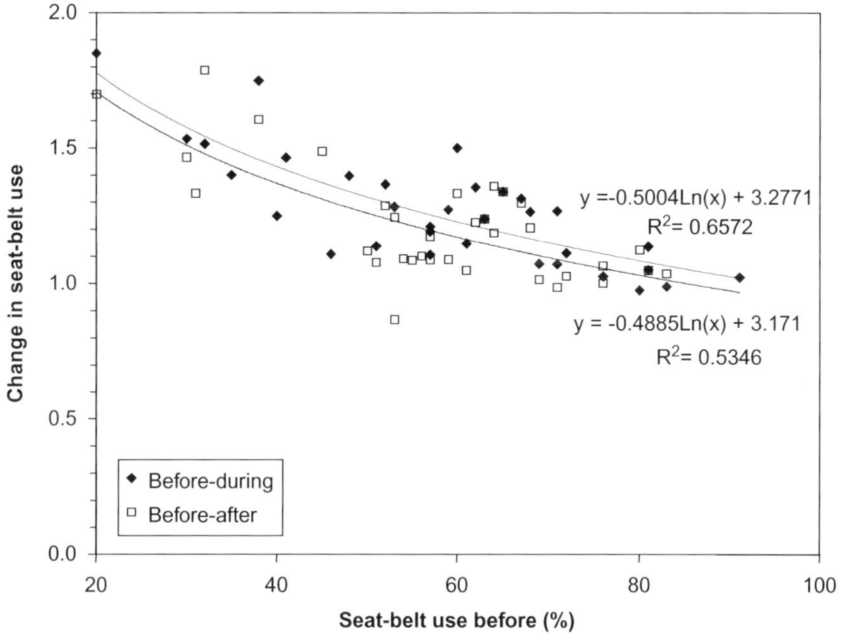


*Figure 8.3.1: Relationship between seat belt usage rates before enforcement and change in the usage rate during and after the enforcement period.*

***Possible reduction of the numbers of fatalities and injuries.*** Based on the effects on fatalities and injuries that have been found of seat belt use, it can be estimated to what degree seat belt enforcement may decrease the number of fatalities and serious injuries in road accidents. In 2004–06, the proportion of drivers using seat belts in Norway was ca. 87% in urban areas and ca. 94% in urban areas. On motorways, it was ca. 89%. Based on Norwegian accident data, it is estimated that the number of fatally injured drivers and car passengers could be reduced by about 9% in rural areas and by about 5% in urban areas if all drivers and passengers were using seat belts. The numbers of seriously injured could be reduced by 4% in urban and by 2% in rural areas. This applies if seat belts reduce the risk of fatal or very serious injuries by 40% and the risk of serious injuries by 20%.

However, a usage rate of 100% is unrealistic. It must also be taken into account that non-users of seat belts, who continue driving unbuckled after increased enforcement, are likely to be different from drivers who start using seat belts when enforcement is increased. Among drivers who are not using seat belts, there are more young men, more drunk drivers, more who drive at high speed, more who commit other traffic offences and accident risk is higher among drivers who do not use seat belts (Preusser, Lund, Williams and Blomberg 1988a, Vaa 1996, Evans 1987a, 1987b, Kim, Nitz, Richardson and Li 1995). Accident risk is 35% higher and the number of traffic convictions is 69% higher among drivers not using seat belts than among drivers using seat belts according to Hunter, Stewart, Stutts and Rodgman (1990). When assuming that increased enforcement increases the usage rate for seat belts from 87% to 90% in urban areas, and from 94% to 96% in rural areas, the proportion of prevented fatalities and very serious injuries is ca. 2% in urban and rural areas and ca. 1% in rural areas. It is assumed that accident risk among drivers who start using seat belts is 10% higher than among drivers who were using seat belts before enforcement increased, and that drivers who continue not using seat belts have a 40% higher accident risk.

***Effects on the use of child restraints of an enforcement and education programme*** have been studied by Decina, Temple and Dorer (1994). The results show an increase by 13%, which is not statistically significant (95% CI [−7; +38]).

### Effect on mobility

The measure has no documented effect on mobility.

### Effect on the environment

The measure has no documented effect on the environment.

### Costs

The costs of police enforcement of the use of seat belts in Norway have been estimated at NOK 37.4 million (Hagen 1994). In 1996, the police registered 56,813 violations of the seat belt law (Utrykningspolitiet, årsberetning 1997).

### Cost–benefit analysis

Based on Norwegian accident statistics and the estimated effects of increased seat belt use on the numbers of killed or injured road users, it has been estimated at what maximum costs increased seat belt enforcement would be beneficial from a societal point of view. It is assumed that increased enforcement would increase the usage rates for seat belts from 87% to 90% in urban areas and from 94% to 96% in rural areas. The estimated numbers of prevented fatalities and injuries and the corresponding

*Table 8.3.2: Estimated effects of increased seat belt use on numbers of fatalities, injuries and prevented accident costs*

| | Seat belt use | | | | |
|---|---|---|---|---|---|
| | Annual numbers (currently) | | Annual numbers prevented (increased enforcement) | | |
| Injury severity | 87% (urban) | 94% (rural) | 90% (urban) | 96% (rural) | Saved annual accident costs (million NOK) |
| Fatal | 10 | 128 | 0.2 (2.1%) | 2.2 (1.7%) | 62.9 |
| Very serious | 4 | 52 | 0.1 (2.1%) | 0.9 (1.7%) | 17.4 |
| Serious | 31 | 465 | 0.3 (0.9%) | 3.1 (0.7%) | 20.0 |
| Minor | 888 | 5,278 | 0 (0%) | 0 (0%) | 0 |
| All severities | 932 | 5,923 | 0.5 | 6.1 | 100.3 |

accident costs are summarised in Table 8.3.2. The following assumptions are made: Seat belt use reduces the risk of being killed or very severely injured by 40% and the risk of being severely injured by 20%. Accident rates are assumed to be 10% higher among drivers who currently are not using seat belts, but who will start to do so. Accident risk among drivers who will continue driving unbuckles is assumed to be 40% higher than among drivers who are currently using seat belts. Effects on seat belt use are assumed only among drivers of cars and vans, not among drivers of trucks and buses. The results in Table 8.3.2 show that increased seat belt use might save accident costs of about NOK 100 million annually. Under the current assumptions, increased seat belt enforcement would be beneficial from a societal point of view if the assumed increases in seat belt use were achieved and if the costs do not exceed NOK 100 million annually.

## 8.4 Patrolling

### Problem and objective

Police resources for enforcement are limited. The police cannot be everywhere all the time. The effect of stationary enforcement is limited both in time and space (Hauer, Ahlin and Bowser 1982, Armour 1984, Vaa and Christensen 1992, Vaa 1993, Vaa, Christensen and Ragnøy 1995). The police therefore also use enforcement techniques that cover larger geographic areas than those covered by stationary enforcement. Mobile enforcement using patrols are intended to extend the coverage of enforcement in time and space. The objective of police patrols is to ensure compliance with road traffic legislation.

## Description of the measure

A distinction is made between stationary methods and mobile methods of enforcement. The distinction is relevant because halo effects have been found in time and space for stationary enforcement but not for patrols (Shinar and McKnight 1985, Vaa 1993). On the other hand, patrols can be used in a more general way than stationary enforcement, since the latter is usually confined to enforcing speed, drink driving or the use of seat belts. Patrols are carried out using both marked patrol cars and civilian vehicles.

## Effect on accidents

A distinction is made between studies of patrolling directed towards different kinds of violations. Most studies have evaluated the effect of increasing the amount or intensity of patrolling. Some studies have evaluated the effects of a changed form of patrolling.

Four studies have evaluated the effects of patrolling on accidents where there is ***no specific focus on a certain kind of violation***:

Shoup (1973) (USA): patrols using motorcycles in city streets in Los Angeles
Williams and Robertson (1975) (USA): patrols at weekends on highways in rural areas in Michigan
Lund and Jørgensen (1974) (Denmark): patrols during 1 year on the main A1 road in Sjælland

Several studies have investigated the effects of patrolling with a ***special focus on driving under the influence (DUI)***. In most studies, the amount of patrolling was increased at the same time as publicity campaigns aimed at reducing DUI were conducted. In some studies, there were additional improvements of administrative procedures and police officers were trained to detect DUI. Special police units enforcing only DUI were investigated by Stuster and Blowers (1995) and Wiliszowski and Jones (2003). Studies of DUI patrolling are:

Toomath (1974) (New Zealand)
Zador (1976) (USA)
Ross (1977) (UK)
Hurst and Wright (1981) (New Zealand)
Amick and Marshall (1983) (USA)
Sali (1983) (USA)
Wolfe (1985) (USA)
Voas and Hause (1987) (USA)

Stuster and Blowers (1995) (USA)
Wiliszowski and Jones (2003) (USA)

Patrolling with a ***special focus on speeding*** has been investigated in the following studies:

Diamantopoulou, Cameron and Shtifelman (1998, 1999) (Australia)
Diamantopoulou and Cameron (2002) (Australia)
Novak and Shumate (1961) (USA)

Table 8.4.1 shows the effect of patrolling on accidents.

No significant effects of patrolling, with no special focus on a specific kind of violations and with a special focus on DUI, were found. Patrolling with a special focus on speeding and a marked car was not found to reduce the number of accidents either. When an unmarked car was used, patrolling with a special focus on speeding was found to significantly increase the number of injury accidents.

On the whole, the results do not indicate that patrolling has a significant effect on accidents. Moreover, in most studies, a new form of or increased patrolling was not the only measure implemented.

*Table 8.4.1: Effects on accidents of patrolling*

| | Percentage change in the number of accidents | | |
|---|---|---|---|
| Accident severity | Types of accident affected | Best estimate | 95% confidence interval |
| ***Patrolling with no focus on a specific kind of violations*** | | | |
| Injury accidents | All accidents | 0 | (−9; +11) |
| Unspecified | All accidents | +10 | (−4; +27) |
| ***Patrolling with a special focus on DUI*** | | | |
| Fatal accidents | All accidents | −3 | (−9; +4) |
| Injury accidents | All accidents | −2 | (−6; +1) |
| ***Patrolling with a special focus on speeding – marked car*** | | | |
| Injury accidents | All accidents | −2 | (−8; +4) |
| ***Patrolling with a special focus on speeding – unmarked car*** | | | |
| Injury accidents | All accidents | +6 | (+1; +13) |

### Effect on mobility

A mobile, marked, police patrol unit may create a more even traffic flow and speed for vehicles in the immediate vicinity, both in front and behind. Time-halo effects were not reported for mobile patrols, which indicates that patrolling gives 'instantaneous effects' to a greater extent than stationary forms of speed enforcement.

### Effect on the environment

Lower speed levels reduce both noise and exhaust emissions from vehicles. Increased patrolling may reduce crime (Albuquerque Police Department 2001).

### Costs

On the basis of Norwegian figures for 1992 (Hagen 1994), the costs of patrolling for 1995 can be estimated at around NOK 130 million. However, in addition to patrols, the cost estimate includes other types of enforcement, such as enforcement of driving and rest hour regulations, overtaking/road markings, distance to the vehicle in front and compliance with yield signs. It is not possible to isolate the costs attributable to mobile patrols.

### Cost–benefit analysis

No significant effects of patrolling on accidents have been found. A cost–benefit analysis is therefore not conducted.

## 8.5 Red-light cameras

### Problem and objective

Red-light running in junctions contributes to about one-third of injury accidents and to a still larger proportion of fatal accidents in signalised junctions. Accidents involving red-light running are typically side impacts, which are more severe than for example rear-end collisions (Garber et al. 2007). Red-light running occurs for the most part within the first few seconds after the lights turn to red. Red-light cameras are intended to reduce accidents at junctions, caused by disrespect for traffic signals.

## Description of the measure

Red-light cameras are installed in signalised junctions. A photograph is taken of a vehicle running against a red traffic signal, often from the front to allow identification of the drivers. Vehicles are detected by sensors under the road surface, which compare information about vehicle speed at the stop line and the signal phase. Usually two photographs are taken of vehicles crossing the stopping line at red, one as the vehicle crosses the line and another as the vehicle continues through the intersection. Red-light cameras are often signposted, either to increase their deterrent effect or because of data privacy.

Several other measures aim to reduce red-light running and accidents associated with red-light running. Such measures are re-timing of signal phasing, variable warning signs in the approaches to signalised junctions and detection systems for automatic regulation of green phases.

## Effect on accidents

***Red-light cameras.*** The effects of red-light cameras on accidents have been elaborated in 23 studies, most of them from USA:

South, Harrison, Portans and King (1988) (USA)
Hillier, Ronczka and Schnerring (1993) (Australia)
Mann, Brown and Coxon (1994) (Australia)
Andreassen (1995) (Australia)
MVA Consultancy (1995) (Great Britain)
Fox (1996) (Great Britain)
Hooke, Knox and Portas (1996) (Great Britain)
Ng, Wong and Lum (1997) (USA)
Giæver and Tveit (1998) (Norway)
Vinzant and Tatro (1999) (USA)
City of Charlotte (2001) (USA)
California State Authority (2002) (USA)
Golob, Cho, Curry and Golob (2002) (USA)
Retting and Kyrychenko (2002) (USA)
Chin and Quddus (2003) (Singapore)
Burkey and Obeng (2004) (USA)
Yaungyai (2004) (USA)
Council et al. (2005a) (USA)

Garber et al. (2005) (USA)
Garber et al. (2007) (USA)
Shin and Washington (2007) (USA)
Helai, Chor and Haque (2008) (Singapore)

The studies used different methods and most results are likely to be affected by methodological weaknesses of the studies (Shin and Washington 2007, Retting, Ferguson and Farmer 2008). One such weakness is a lack of control for regression to the mean, which occurs when red-light cameras are installed in junctions with exceptionally high numbers of accidents. The control for spillover effects also may affect study results. Spillover effects may occur when junctions in the vicinity of camera junctions are used as a control group, and when red-light running in these junctions are reduced as well after the installation of red-light cameras. The lack of control for characteristics of the junctions, such as traffic volume, also may affect study results.

The estimated effects of red-light cameras on accidents are summarised in Table 8.5.1. The results are based only on studies that have controlled for regression to the mean, spillover effects and a number of other factors (Burkey and Obeng 2004, Council et al. 2005b, Garber et al. 2007, Retting and Kyrychenko 2002, Shin and Washington 2007).

The total number of accidents seems to increase after the installation of red-light cameras. The effect is, however, not significant. For rear-end collisions, a significant increase has been found. Rear-end collisions may occur when vehicles are braking abruptly and unexpectedly for the following vehicles. A Norwegian study showed that an increasing number of vehicles stopped at yellow after red-light cameras were installed (Giæver and Tveit 1998). Following this evaluation, red-light cameras were dismounted and rear-end collisions dropped to the level before their installation (Statens vegvesen Vestfold 1996).

*Table 8.5.1: Effects on accidents at signalised junctions of red-light cameras*

| | Percentage change in the number of accidents | | |
|---|---|---|---|
| Accident severity | Types of accidents affected | Best estimate | 95% confidence interval |
| Unspecified | All accidents | +15 | (−3; +38) |
| Injury accidents | All accidents | +13 | (−10; +43) |
| Unspecified | Rear-end collisions | +43 | (+20; +70) |
| Unspecified | Side impacts | −10 | (−31; +19) |

Most accidents in which red-light running is a contributing factor are side impacts. For these accidents, a non-significant decrease has been found. Since side impact collisions often are more severe than rear-end collisions, it is often assumed that the overall effect of red-light cameras on injury severity is a reduction, even if rear-end collisions increase (City of Charlotte 2001). However, such an effect is not observable in Table 8.5.1. The effects on injury accidents and on accidents with unspecified severity (which include property damage only accidents) are almost identical.

Some studies indicate that red-light cameras affect accidents in neighbouring signalised junctions without cameras (McGee and Eccles 2003, Shin and Washington 2007). The results are however not unambiguous. When comparing results from studies that have and studies that have not controlled for changes of accident numbers in neighbouring junctions, the results are not consistent either.

In the study by Washington and Shin (2005), the largest reductions of side impact collisions were found in junctions with long signal phases, large traffic volumes and high speed. When red-light cameras were announced with signs, the reduction of side impact collisions and the increase of rear-end collisions was larger than when cameras were not announced.

A number of studies found reduced red-light running in camera junctions of between 20% and 80% (Arup 1992, Chin 1989, Giæver and Tveit 1998, Retting, Williams, Farmer and Feldman 1999a, 1999b). An Australian study found larger effects on red-light running among passenger cars than among heavy vehicles and an increase of the effect during the first 7 weeks after installation of red-light cameras (Lau 1986). Several studies found reductions of red-light running in junctions where no cameras were installed (Andreassen 1995, Fleck and Smith 1999, McGee and Eccles 2003).

***Extended yellow phased and all red phase.*** Reduced red-light running has been found in several studies that have evaluated the effects of an extended yellow phase and of an all red phase. Retting, Ferguson and Farmer (2008) also found reduced accident numbers in junctions where signal phases were changed in accordance with the recommendations of the Institute of Transportation Engineers. The greatest reduction was found for pedestrian and bicycle accidents, which were reduced by 37%. All injury accidents were reduced by 12%. Re-timing of signal phases with an increased yellow phase and an all red phase led to a reduction of side impacts and left turn accidents and to reduced red-light running (Datta, Schattler and Datta 2000). A reduction of red-light running when the yellow phases were extended was found by Retting, Ferguson and Farmer (2008). Both red-light running and accidents were reduced when clearance intervals were lengthened in signalised junctions in the study by Schattler, Hill and Datta (2002). Criteria for signal phasing are different between different countries and may vary between different junctions. Results from studies of signal phasing can therefore not easily be transferred to other junctions or countries (Eccles and McGee 2001).

***Variable signs before signalised junctions.*** Three studies studied warning signs with flashers, which give advance warnings to drivers approaching a signalised intersection and who will arrive at the intersection at red signal (Farraher, Weinholzer and Kowski 1999, Schultz, Peterson and Eggett 2007, Schultz-Grant, Peterson, Giles and Eggett 2006). Such signs are mostly installed on roads with high speed and large traffic volumes. All three studies found short-term reductions of red-light running, but no long-term effects. One year after installation, both red-light running and speed had returned to their respective previous levels. Schulz et al. even found increased speed and red-light running 8 months after the installation of the advance warning signs. A possible explanation is that drivers became familiar with the phasing of signals and advance warning sings and used the information from the advance warning signs to increase speed when this makes it possible to arrive at the signalised intersection before the signals turn red. The effects on heavy vehicles were more favourable and more long-lasting than the effects on passenger cars in the study by Farraher et al. Among heavy vehicles, red-light running was reduced by about 60% and speed was reduced by about 20%.

***Detection system for automatic regulation of green phases.*** Bonneson et al. (2002) evaluated a system that detects vehicles approaching signalised junctions on rural high-speed roads, and which controls the signal phased accordingly. After the installation of the system, accidents were significantly reduced by 39%, delays were reduced by 14%, the proportion of vehicles arriving at red signal was reduced by 9% and red-light running was reduced by 58%.

### Effect on mobility

Red-light cameras may affect mobility, because some drivers will stop at a yellow traffic signal instead of driving through the intersection. In some cases, this may reduce the flow of traffic.

### Effect on the environment

It is possible that red-light cameras may have some effect on the environment in that more drivers choose to stop at the yellow traffic signal, so the vehicle stands idling though a whole phase instead of driving though the intersection without stopping.

### Costs

On the basis of information given by Hagen (1992) and Krohn (1996), Elvik (1997b) calculated the costs of red-light cameras at a typical signal controlled junction to around NOK 160,000 per intersection per year. It is assumed that each intersection is equipped with four boxes and one camera. Investment costs were converted to annual capital costs by assuming 10 years depreciation time and 7% discount rate.

In a British study (Hooke, Knox and Portas 1996), the average fixed costs for red-light cameras are estimated at about £9,200 and the average recurrent costs at about £5,600 per camera site, with an average of 7 cameras per site. These costs include costs for material, installation, signposting and planning.

A USA study (Kriz, Moran and Regan 2006) estimated the costs per camera at about $55,000 and additional $25,000 for system equipment, setup and implementation. Maintenance costs are estimated at about $60,000 per camera over a 5-year period (4% discount rate).

### Cost–benefit analysis

Since no reduction of the total number of accidents has been found, no cost–benefit analysis of red-light cameras is conducted. Red-light cameras increase revenues from fines. From a societal perspective, this is a redistribution of resources and does not count as either benefit (for the state) or cost (for drivers).

## 8.6 Demerit point systems and licence suspension

### Problem and objective

The number of traffic law violations is one of the best single predictors of future involvement in accidents. Previous accident involvement is a still better predictor (Chen, Cooper and Pinili 1995). Violations that are associated with accident involvement include speeding, disregard of right-of-way and red-light running (Masten and Peck 2004). Demerit point systems may affect violations and accidents in several ways. Drivers may become generally more cautions in order to avoid getting demerit points. Drivers who have gathered a certain amount of demerit points may drive more cautiously in order to avoid licence suspension. Drivers who get their licence suspended because the number of demerit points has exceeded a critical limit should not be driving at all. More cautions driving and reduced exposure are assumed to reduce the number of violations and accidents.

## Description of the measure

With a demerit point system, traffic convictions are recorded for all drivers, usually in the form of demerit points, and sanctions are imposed when a driver has obtained a critical number of demerit points. Sanctions may be warning letters, mandatory driver improvement courses or licence suspension, depending on the number of demerit points. Demerit points are recorded only for violations that are considered serious or related to accidents, but that are not by themselves sufficient for licence suspension or more severe sanctions. Violations for which licence suspension is frequently used as a sanction are severe speed limit violations and DUI.

Studies have been made to assess the extent to which demerit point systems are reliable in identifying those drivers who are more often involved in accidents than other drivers (Brown and Thiebaux 1970, Chipman 1982, Smiley, Persaud, Hauer and Duncan 1989, Schade 1992, Chen, Cooper and Pinili 1995). Systems in which the number of demerit points is assigned on the basis of the assumed severity of an offence are particularly unreliable (Smiley, Persaud, Hauer and Duncan 1989, Chen, Cooper and Pinili 1995).

## Effect on accidents

***Demerit point systems.*** Only two studies were found that have evaluated demerit point systems as a whole. The demerit point system that was introduced in Norway in 2004 has been evaluated by Stene, Sakshaug and Moe (2008). No effect was found on the total number of fatalities or severely injured road users. Speed in general did not change. The only effect that was found is an increase in self-reported cautious driving among drivers who had accumulated enough demerit points to get a warning letter, the last step before licence suspension.

A habitual offenders program from USA (which in practice resembles a demerit point system) was evaluated by Li and Waller (1976). No difference in violations or accident involvement was found between drivers who had or had not been informed about having reached the status of a habitual offender.

Components of demerit point systems and licence suspension have been investigated in a number of studies. These components are driver improvement and similar courses, warning letters, licence suspension and a special driving test.

***Courses and letters.*** The effects on accidents of *driver improvement courses* for drivers who have accumulated a certain number of demerit points have been evaluated by the following studies:

Schuster (1969) (USA)
Helander (1984) (USA)
Drummond and Torpey (1985) (Victoria, Australia)
Utzelmann and Haas (1985) (Germany)
Kadell (1987) (California, USA)
Bloch (1997) (USA)
Stephen (2004) (USA)

*Defensive driving and similar courses* for specific groups of drivers, which are not directly related to a penalty point system have been studied by the following:

Harano and Peck (1972) (USA): driver improvement course for young drivers
Kaestner and Speight (1975) (USA): defensive driving course for problem drivers
O'Day (1970) (USA): defensive driving course for professional drivers
Peck, Kelsey, Ratz and Sherman (1980) (USA): driver improvement course for problem drivers
Planek, Schupack and Fowler (1974) (USA): voluntary defensive driving course
Prothero and Seals (1978) (USA): defensive driving course for problem drivers
Utzelmann (1983) (Germany): theory courses and driving lessons for young drivers

Effects of *group discussions* between problem drivers under the guidance of a government representative have been studied by the following:

Kaestner and Syring (1967) (USA): interviews with drivers and psychological tests
Marsh, Coppin and Peck (1967) (USA): group discussions
Kaestner and Syring (1968) (USA): interviews with drivers and psychological tests
Fuchs (1980) (USA): interviews with drivers
Kadell (1987) (USA): group discussions and self-study courses
Prothero and Seals (1978) (USA): group discussions
Struckman-Johnson, Lund, Williams and Osborne (1989) (USA): several courses

The effects on accidents of *warning letters* sent to drivers who have accumulated a certain amount of demerit points have been evaluated by the following:

Epperson and Harano (1975) (California, USA)
Helander (1984) (USA)
Jones (1987) (Connecticut, USA)

Jones (1997) (Oregon, USA)
Kaestner, Warmoth and Syring (1967) (Oregon, USA)
Lynn, Jernigan, Norris and Froning (1993) (USA)
McBride and Peck (1970) (California, USA)

Table 8.6.1 shows the effects on accidents. All results refer to accidents involving drivers having either visited a course or received a warning letter.

Courses and warning letters were found to reduce accidents by around 10%. Group discussions do not seem to have any effect on accidents. The effect of warning letters is statistically significant, also when controlling for publication bias. It is not known how long-lasting the effects on accidents are. The effects of warning letters may be different depending on the contents of the letters and characteristics of the drivers receiving them (Kaestner, Warmoth and Syring 1967, McBride and Peck 1970, Epperson and Harano 1975, Jones 1997). The results are not consistent.

Driver improvement courses are often voluntary and drivers are rewarded with the deletion of a certain amount of demerit points. Therefore, drivers visiting a course are hardly comparable to drivers not visiting a course, which makes it difficult to assess the effect of the courses. Those drivers participating in a course may have had fewer accidents than drivers not participating even if none of them had participated in a course.

*Table 8.6.1: Effects on accidents of courses and warning letters*

| | Percentage change in the number of accidents | | |
|---|---|---|---|
| Accident severity | Types of accidents affected | Best estimate | 95% confidence interval |
| ***Driver improvement courses*** | | | |
| Unspecified | All accidents | −11 | (−22; +1) |
| ***Defensive driving and other courses (not directly related to penalty point system)*** | | | |
| Unspecified | Accidents with problem drivers | −9 | (−19; +2) |
| Unspecified | Accidents with young drivers | −13 | (−20; −4) |
| Unspecified | Accidents with professional drivers | +15 | (+6; +24) |
| Unspecified | Accidents with voluntary participants | −33 | (−52; −6) |
| ***Group discussions*** | | | |
| Unspecified | All accidents | −1 | (−3; +1) |
| ***Warning letters*** | | | |
| Unspecified | All accidents | | |
| | *Not controlled for publication bias:* | −13 | (−17; −10) |
| | *Controlled for publication bias:* | −10 | (−14; −6) |

Masten and Peck (2004) conducted a meta-analysis of several measures on accidents and violations. Their results show that driver improvement and similar courses reduce accidents with young drivers. Among professional drivers, accidents were found to increase. No significant effects were found on problem drivers.

***Licence suspension***. Studies of the effects of licence suspension are highly heterogeneous with respect to the groups of drivers and the time periods included in the studies. Summary effects have therefore not been calculated. An overview of the studies is shown in Table 8.6.2. The effects of licence suspension as a sanction for DUI are described in Section 8.10.

*Table 8.6.2: Effects on accidents of licence suspension: overview of studies*

| | | | | Percentage change | |
|---|---|---|---|---|---|
| | Drivers | Control group | Effect variable | Best estimate | 95% confidence interval |
| Campbell and Ross (1968) | All drivers, 1 year after introduction of new law | All drivers before introduction of new law | Accidents | −4 | (non-significant) |
| Kaestner and Speight (1975) | Drivers with suspended licence (1 year, incl. 1 month while licence suspended) | Drivers without suspended licence (no sanctions) | Accidents or penalties | −2 | (−29; +35) |
| | Drivers with probationary driving licence (1 year, incl. 1 month while probationary licence) | Drivers without suspended licence (no sanctions) | Accidents or penalties | −22 | (−44; +8) |
| Jones (1987) | Drivers with suspended licence | Drivers having received warning letter | Accidents | −37 | (−67; +21) |
| McKnight and Edwards (1987) | Young drivers threatened by a two-week licence suspension | Young drivers threatened by mandatory personal interview | Accidents | −7 | (−13; 0) |
| | Young drivers two years after two-week licence suspension | Young drivers two years after personal interview | Accidents | −9 | (−18; 0) |
| Stephen (2004) | Drivers with suspended licence | Drivers visiting course instead of licence suspension | Accidents | −57 | (−62; −50) |
| | | Drivers with no sanctions | Accidents | −82 | (−84; −80) |
| Strathman, Kimpel, and Leistner (2007) | Drivers 1.5 years after licence suspension | Same group of drivers before suspension of licence | Accidents | −11 | |

Licence suspension has been found to be an effective sanction for those drivers who actually get their licence suspended, although many studies have found that many drivers with a suspended licence continue driving. Reduced accident involvement may be due to reduced exposure or to more cautious driving in order to avoid detection (Masten and Peck 2004).

Campbell and Ross (1968) evaluated the effects of licence suspension as a sanction for drivers convicted of speeding. The result refers to all drivers, not only those with a suspended licence. The result may be affected by increased speed enforcement and regression to the mean.

The remainder of the results refers only to drivers who were threatened by licence suspension or who actually had their licence suspended. Most studies have applied methodologically strong study designs. Kaestner and Speight (1975) and McKnight and Edwards (1987) conducted experimental studies; in the study by Jones (1987), drivers were matched with respect to earlier violations and accidents. Strathman, Kimpel and Leistner (2007) compared accident involvement of drivers before and after licence suspension and controlled for regression to the mean.

In the study by Stephen (2004), there were likely systematic differences between drivers who had their licence suspended and other drivers. Drivers who participated in a course did so voluntarily in order to avoid licence suspension, and drivers with no sanctions had committed fewer violations.

***Special driving test***. Effects of a special driving test for drivers with a critical number of penalty points were studied by Staplin 1993 (USA). Drivers who had taken the test had 17% fewer accidents in the following year than other drivers (95% CI [−27; −4]). However, there may have been other differences between drivers who had and who had not taken the test.

### Effect on mobility

Drivers with a suspended licence will have reduced mobility. Otherwise there are no documented effects of demerit point systems or licence suspension.

### Effect on the environment

There are no documented effects on the environment.

### Costs

No information is available about the costs of a demerit point system. Costs include the costs of a central conviction register and costs of sanctions imposed on drivers with a critical number of demerit points. A large part of there costs will be administrative costs.

### Cost–benefit analysis

For demerit point systems as a whole, no cost estimates are available and no effects on accidents have been documented. A cost–benefit analysis has therefore not been conducted. Individual components of demerit point systems may be cost-effective. Warning letters may be especially cost-effective since the costs are quite low (Jones 1997, Marsh 1992, Marsh and Healy 1995, Strathman, Kimpel and Leistner 2007). Licence suspension may be cost-effective as well. According to McKnight and Edwards (1987) the suspension of one driving licence costs ca. US$ 3, while a personal interview costs ca. US$ 70 per participant. Since drivers with a suspended licence have been found to have fewer accidents, licence suspension must be cost-effective when compared to personal interviews.

## 8.7 Fixed penalties

### Problem and objective

Many of the most common traffic violations are committed thousands of times each year. This is particularly true of illegal parking, speeding and the non-use of seat belts. It is normally assumed that violations have to be punished in order to deter people from committing them. This assumption is supported by the experience gained in Norway in the period 1975–79, when the non-wearing of seat belts was not punished, although a seat belt law had been passed. Figure 8.7.1 shows the usage rate for seat belts before and after the introduction of fines on 1 October 1979. At that time, the fine for non-use was NOK 200 (Elvik and Christensen 2004).

If the sanctions against the most common violations of traffic regulations were to be administered by the courts, with standard appeal procedures, the legal service would be overloaded with cases, many of which are trivial. It would take a long time from the violation was committed until the sanction was imposed. This is ineffective, if the objective is to change road user behaviour. It is more effective to impose sanctions immediately after the violation (Chaplin and Krawiec 1970). In order to impose fast, effective sanctions for the most common traffic violations, fixed penalties have been

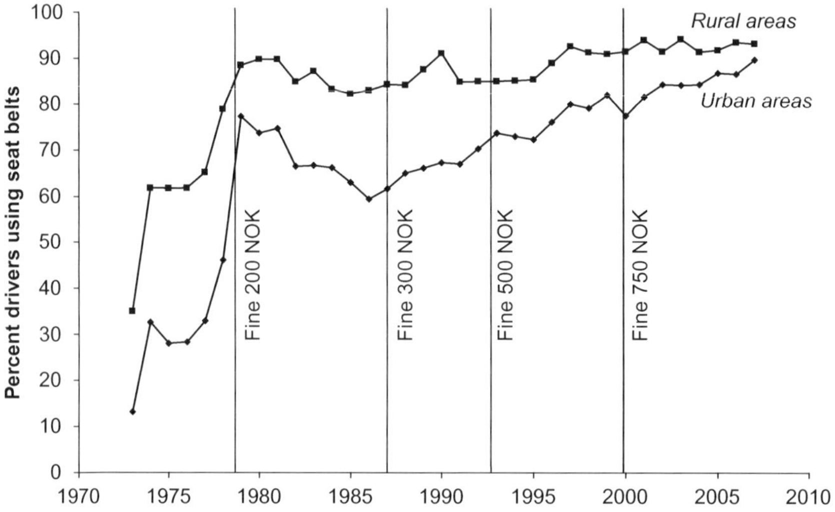


*Figure 8.7.1: Changes in seat belt usage rate among drivers in Norway 1973–95 inside and outside towns.*

introduced. The objective of fixed penalties is to simplify the use of sanctions, so that the most common violations can be dealt with quickly and the costs of administering the sanctions can be reduced.

**Description of the measure**

There are a number of sanctions against traffic violations in Norway (Østvik 1987). Some of these are regarded as punishments in the legal sense of that term. Other sanctions are not regarded as punishments and can be imposed without registering the violator as an offender. Fixed penalties and fines are used for the most usual violations. They can be administered on scene, without involving a court. A number of traffic violations can be sanctioned using fixed penalties, e.g. for speeding, disregarding certain road signs and red-light running.

**Effect on accidents**

The effect of fines and fixed penalties on accidents has so far not been quantified. Some studies have investigated the relationship between changes in fines and fixed penalties and changes in traffic violations. The results cannot be summarised by means of meta-analysis.

Nilsson and Åberg (1986) studied the effects on speeding of a doubling of fixed penalties for speeding in Sweden 1982. No significant changes in speed or other violations were found.

Andersson (1989) studied the effects of increased fixed penalties for speeding on speeding and found it to be between 33% and 50% in Sweden in 1987. The proportion of drivers driving above the speed limit was nearly unchanged at six measuring points (49.5% before and 50.1% after the increase of the fixed penalties).

Fridstrøm (1999) investigated the effects of fines on seat belt use for non-use of seat belts by means of econometric models. The results show that a 10% increase in fines (fixed prices) corresponded to an increase of seat belts from 70% to ca. 72.5% in urban areas. In rural areas, the estimated effect was smaller.

Elvik and Christensen (2004, 2007) investigated the effects of fines for non-use of seat belts and of fixed penalties for speeding in Norway. An increase of fines for non-use of seat belt by NOK 100 was estimated to increase seat belt use by 8.2% in urban areas and by 2.7% in rural areas. However, in the years 1995–2004, the amount of seat belt enforcement increased in Norway. It is therefore not known to what extent the increase in seat belt use was attributable to increased fines or increased enforcement. Increased fixed penalties for speeding were not found to be associated with reduced speeding.

Cedersund (2008) investigated the effects on the number of drivers driving above the speed limit of a doubling of the fixed penalties for speeding in Sweden in 2006. A significant decrease of the proportion of speeding drivers from 40.6% to 32.2% was found. Contrary to the expectation, the largest effects were not found at speed cameras, but on roads without speed cameras.

The results from these studies are somewhat inconsistent. Only two studies have investigated effects on seat belt use. The results indicate an increase in seat belt use when fines are increased. The effects may, however, partly be due to increased enforcement. Four studies have investigated effects on speeding. Three of them have not found significant effects of increased fixed penalties and one study found a reduction of speeding.

On the whole, the results do not support any clear conclusions. Increased fines and fixed penalties may reduce violations, but they do not always seem to do so.

**Effect on mobility**

No effects of fixed penalties on mobility have been documented.

### Effect on the environment

No effects of fixed penalties on the environment have been documented.

### Costs

It is very difficult to estimate the costs of fixed penalties to society in a meaningful way. According to economic theory, fixed penalties cannot be regarded as a cost as such, but only as a transfer of money from road users to the state (see for example Sager 1974). Tickets and simple fines are sanctions for violations of the law, not payment for the use of resources that have alternative uses.

Nonetheless, there are costs to society of having a system of fixed penalties. Firstly, a certain level of enforcement must be maintained in order for sanctions to have a deterrent effect. Secondly, forms used to impose fixed penalties must be printed and distributed. Thirdly, there must be an apparatus for dealing with any objections to imposed penalties. In other words, the system of fixed penalties is not without costs, even though the penalties are not in themselves a cost.

### Cost–benefit analysis

No cost–benefit analysis has been carried out for fixed penalties, since there is not sufficient information about the costs and since effects on accidents are not known. However, the existence of fines or fixed penalties seems to be associated with fewer violations. There is higher compliance with laws when violations are punished than when they are not. Since the total costs of a system of fixed penalties are assumed to be smaller than for many other sanctions, it is likely that these sanctions are cost-effective.

## 8.8 DUI LEGISLATION

### Problem and objective

Driving under the influence of alcohol (DUI) probably increases the risk of road accidents more than any other traffic law violation (Assum and Glad 1990). Alcohol impairs perception, information processing and judgements, increases reaction times and may reduce inhibitions (Glad and Vaas 1993). A number of laws aim at reducing the occurrence of drink driving by providing the legal background for police enforcement and sanctions, or by restricting the availability or consumption of alcohol.

***Accidents involving alcohol.*** The relative accident rates for drivers with different BACs were estimated on the basis of the roadside survey in Norway in 1981–82 and the official road traffic accident statistics (Glad 1985a, 1985b, Assum and Glad 1990, Glad and Vaas 1993). The results are summarised in Figure 8.8.1. Results from more recent risk studies are similar. For example, Assum et al. (2005) found the following relative risk of involvement in injury accidents at different BAC levels: 2.1 (0.2–0.5 BAC), 8.3 (0.5–0.8 BAC), 17.6 (0.8–1.3 BAC) and 87.2 (above 1.3 BAC).

The proportion of fatal accidents involving alcohol has been estimated at ca. 12% in Norway (Haldorsen 2007) and at 41% in USA (NHTSA 2002). In Norway, drivers with BAC over 1.5 account for about 20% of driving under the influence of alcohol, more than 50% of drivers with illegal BAC levels are involved in injury accidents and almost 80% of drivers with illegal BAC levels are killed in accidents (Glad 1985c, Assum and Ingebrigtsen 1990).

Accidents involving alcohol are overrepresented among nighttime accidents, mostly at weekend nights, and among single-vehicle accidents, and they are often more severe

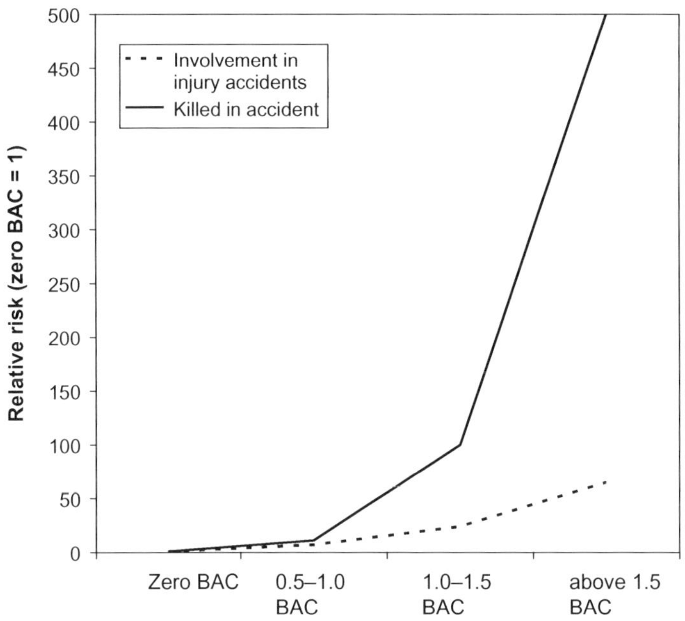


*Figure 8.8.1: Risk with different blood alcohol concentrations in relation to sober drivers in Norway (Glad and Vaas 1993).*

than other accidents. Among drivers involved in alcohol accidents, young drivers and men are overrepresented (Assum and Glad 1990, Glad 1985b, Peck, Gebers, Voas and Romano 2008).

***DUI-convicted drivers*** have in many studies been found to be different from other drivers (Hubicka, Laurell and Bergman 2008). For example, DUI-convicted drivers are often young men, have a low socioeconomic status, have alcohol problems, commit more other traffic violations, drive more often without a valid licence, have more convictions for non-traffic related crime, use more drugs and have more psychiatric problems than other drivers (Assum and Glad 1990, Christophersen 1990, Ferguson, Sheehan, Davey and Watson 1999, Glad and Vaas 1993, Lapham, Kapitula, de Baca and McMillan 2006, McMillen et al. 1992, Ruud and Glad 1990, Wheeler and Hissong 1988).

The proportion of relapse among DUI-convicted drivers is large (Baca, Miller and Lapham 2001). According to a Norwegian study, about 40% of DUI-convicted drivers received one or more new convictions during a 6-year period following the first conviction (Gjerde and Mørland 1991). Studies conducted in the USA have estimated that about 28% of all drivers with one DUI conviction will receive more DUI convictions in the future, and that a DUI-convicted driver has on average driven between 60 and 90 times above the legal BAC limit without being caught (Jones and Lacey 2000, Lapham, Kapitula, de Baca and McMillan 2006, Quaye and Boase 2004).

***Multiple DUI offenders.*** Drivers with a particularly high risk of future accidents and DUI convictions are drivers with more than one previous DUI conviction, alcoholics, drivers convicted for high BAC levels and young drivers (Harrison, Newman, Baldock and McLean 2003, Hubicka, Laurell and Bergman 2008, Marowitz 1998, Breckendridge, Winfree, Maupin and Clason 2000). Multiple DUI offenders have on average higher risk of accidents involving alcohol and are often caught with higher BAC levels than drivers with only one DUI conviction. They seem to be quite resistant to most sanctions (Lapham, Kapitula, de Baca and McMillan 2006, Nochajski and Stasiewicz 2006) and less responsive to DUI enforcement measures, such as checkpoints (Harrison, Newman, Baldock and McLean 2003) and to psychological treatment (Breckendridge, Winfree, Maupin and Clason 2000) than other drivers. Reasons may be alcohol addiction and a social background that does not encourage any change of drinking or driving habits (Ferguson, Sheehan, Davey and Watson 1999). Jones and Lacey (2000) found that drivers with more than one previous DUI conviction have a lower risk of accidents not involving alcohol. Possible explanations are reduced exposure or more cautions driving (while sober) while the licence is suspended.

### Description of the measure

DUI laws described in this chapter include laws that provide a legal background for police enforcement and sanctions, and laws that restrict the availability or consumption of alcohol. More detailed descriptions of these laws are given in the following sections, which summarize the effects on accidents. Private interest groups that may affect DUI or DUI laws are also treated in this chapter. Laws about the use of penalties and jail as DUI sanctions are described in Section 8.12.

### Effect on accidents

Effects of DUI laws on accidents have been investigated in a large number of studies of highly varying quality. A problem in many studies is that the effects of laws cannot be isolated from the effects of other measures. For example, the introduction of new DUI laws is often accompanied by increased enforcement, and in many cases, several DUI laws are changed or introduced at the same time. Other methodological problems include the choice of comparison groups and the control for time trends, among many other things. The results that are presented in the present chapter are based, as far as possible, only on studies that have at a minimum controlled for time trends and for other laws or measures aiming at reducing DUI. Most of these studies have investigated the relationship between accidents and DUI laws in several legislations over several years, and also controlled for background factors, such as demographics, alcohol sales and economic indicators. Such studies might, in principle, have investigated interaction effects between different laws (e.g. the effects of per se BAC laws with and without administrative licence suspension laws). However, interaction effects are only rarely reported.

***Per se laws: BAC 0.10 and 0.08 (USA).*** Most states in the USA have per se BAC laws according to which it is illegal to drive with BAC over 0.08 or 0.10, independent of driving behaviour or accident involvement. Per se BAC laws also imply that primary enforcement of DUI is legal. In 2001, per se laws were introduced in 19 states and in 2003 in all states except Massachusetts, which had per se laws (Bernat, Dunsmuir and Wagenaar 2004). The following studies have evaluated the introduction of per se laws:

Evans, Neville and Graham (1991)
Bernat, Dunsmuir and Wagenaar (2004)
Voas, Tippetts and Fell (2000)
Tippetts, Voas, Fell and Nichols (2005)
Kaplan and Prato (2007)
Dee (2001)

Eisenberg (2001)
Voas, Tippetts and Fell (2003)

Based on these studies, the effect on fatal accidents of introducing per se BAC laws is a significant reduction by 6% (95% CI [−7; −5]). This implies that the number of fatal accidents was reduced by 6% when a BAC 0.10 law was introduced or when a BAC 0.10 law was replaced by a BAC 0.08 law. Time trends and effects of other DUI laws are controlled for in all studies. The results are consistent between the studies and do not seem to be affected by confounding variables or publication bias. The results may to a certain degree be affected by endogeneity and therefore to a certain degree underestimated. The introduction of BAC 0.08 laws was more likely in states with initially higher proportions of fatal accidents involving alcohol than in other states.

Large variation in the effectiveness of per se laws has been found between different states (Bernat, Dunsmuir and Wagenaar 2004, Wagenaar et al. 2007a). Results indicate that per se laws are not effective in states where no DUI checkpoints are conducted (Tippetts, Voas, Fell and Nichols 2005), and it is likely that per se laws are more effective in states with an administrative licence suspension law (Apsler, Char, Harding and Klein 1999).

The results are not consistent as regards differential effects on drivers with different BAC levels. Wagenaar et al. (2007a) found no difference in the effectiveness of per se laws depending on the BAC level of drivers involved in fatal accidents, while the results of the study by Hingson, Heeren and Winter (1996) indicate that per se laws are more effective in preventing fatal accidents at higher BAC levels than fatal accidents at lower BAC levels and Dee (2001) found larger effects during weekends than on working days.

***Reduced BAC limit: From 0.08 to 0.05.*** The illegal BAC level has been reduced from 0.8 to 0.5 in New South Wales and in Queensland (Australia) in 1980 and in 1982, respectively. The effects on accidents have been studied by

Henstridge, Homel and Mackay (1997) (New South Wales and Queensland, Australia)
Homel (1994) (New South Wales, Australia)
Smith (1988) (Queensland, Australia)
Bernhoft and Behrensdorff (2000) (Denmark)

In summary, it has been found that fatal accidents in which alcohol is involved or assumed to be overrepresented are reduced by 2% (95% CI [−17; +6]) and that injury accidents in which alcohol is assumed to be overrepresented are reduced by 13% (95% CI [−16; −9]). No significant effect has been found on injury accidents at daytime

(−6%, 95% CI [−17; +8]). A study that has been conducted in the Australian city of Adelaide did not find any change in the proportion of drivers involved in accidents in which BAC levels were at or above 0.08.

Bartl and Esberger (2000) found that the number of injury accidents involving alcohol decreased by about 10% (95% CI [−14; −6]) after the illegal BAC level was reduced from 0.08 to 0.05 in Austria in 1998. However, more severe sanctions were introduced at the same time and the number of BAC tests conducted by the police increased. It is therefore not clear to what extent the change in the number of alcohol accidents is due to the changed BAC limit, other measures against DUI or other factors that have not been controlled for in this study.

***Reduced BAC limit: From 0.05 to 0.02 (Sweden).*** In Sweden, the illegal BAC limit was reduced from 0.05 to 0.02 in 1990. At the same time, the limit for aggravated drink driving was reduced from 0.15 to 0.10 and the sanctions for aggravated drink driving were increased. These changes were evaluated in two studies (Borschos 2000, Norström and Laurell 1997). Both studies found reductions of the numbers of fatal and injury accidents by about 10%. However, it is not unlikely that the results are affected by confounding variables, such as time trends, other DUI laws and a doubling of the number of random breath tests in the same time period (Glad and Vaa 1997).

***Reduced BAC limit for DUI-convicted drivers.*** In Maine (USA), a law was introduced in 1988, which defined the illegal BAC limit for DUI-convicted drivers at 0.05. In 1995, this limit was reduced to BAC 0.00. No effects of these changes in law have been found on accidents or recidivism (Jones and Rodriguez-Iglesias 2004).

***Reduced BAC limit for young drivers.*** Young drivers have a higher accident risk than other drivers and alcohol increases accident rate more for young drivers than for other drivers (Peck, Gebers, Voas and Romano 2008). Laws making it illegal for young drivers (under age 21, which also is the minimum legal drinking age) to drive at any BAC above 0.01 or 0.02 have therefore been introduced in the USA and in Australia. The effects of these laws have been evaluated by

Maisey (1984) (Australia)
Haque, Strang and Crabb (1986) (Australia)
Haque and Cameron (1989) (Australia)
Hingson, Heeren and Winter (1994) (USA)
Bartl and Esberger (2000) (Austria)
Eisenberg (2001) (USA)

*Table 8.8.1: Effects on accidents of reduced BAC limits for young drivers*

| | Percentage change in the number of accidents | | |
|---|---|---|---|
| Accident severity | Types of accidents affected | Best estimate | 95% confidence interval |
| Fatal accidents | Accidents involving alcohol (young drivers) | −18 | (−20; −15) |
| Fatal accidents | All accidents (young drivers) | +3 | (−3; +9) |
| Injury accidents | Accidents involving alcohol (young drivers) | −3 | (−7; +0) |

Whetten-Goldstein, Sloan, Stout and Liang (2000) (USA)
Voas, Tippetts and Fell (2003) (USA)

The results are summarised in Table 8.8.1. In most studies, graduated driving licence (GDL) programs existed when the BAC laws were introduced. Studies of the introduction of GDL are not included in the analysis.

The number of fatal accidents involving alcohol with young drivers decreased significantly after the introduction of reduced BAC limits for young drivers. No effects have been found on other fatal accidents or on injury accidents. The results are not likely to be very much affected by methodological weaknesses.

***Licence suspension***. Administrative licence suspension laws allow the police to suspend the licence of drivers who do not pass a BAC test without involving a court. Laws about licence suspension in court define licence suspension as a standard sanction for drivers convicted of DUI in court. *Administrative licence suspension laws* have been evaluated in the following studies, most of which have been conducted in the USA; only the study by Sen (2001) was conducted in Canada.

Evans, Neville and Graham (1991)
Ruhm (1996)
Voas, Tippetts and Fell (2000)
Whetten-Goldstein, Sloan, Stout and Liang (2000)
Young Likens (2000)
Dee (2001)
Eisenberg (2001)
Sen (2001)
Voas, Tippetts and Fell (2003)
Bernat, Dunsmuir and Wagenaar (2004)
Kaplan and Prato (2007)
Wagenaar et al. (2007a)

*Table 8.8.2: Effects on accidents of licence suspension laws*

| | Percentage change in the number of accidents | | |
|---|---|---|---|
| Accident severity | Types of accidents affected | Best estimate | 95% confidence interval |
| ***Administrative licence suspension laws*** | | | |
| Fatal accidents | All accidents | −4 | (−5; −3) |
| Fatal accidents | Accidents involving alcohol | −8 | (−11; −5) |
| Fatal accidents | Accidents involving alcohol (proxy) | −5 | (−7; −3) |
| ***Laws about licence suspension in court*** | | | |
| Fatal accidents | All accidents | −2 | (−7; +4) |
| Fatal accidents | Accidents involving alcohol | −4 | (−8; +0) |

Laws about *licence suspension in court* have been evaluated in the following studies, all of which have been conducted in the USA:

Wagenaar et al. (2007b)
Young and Likens (2000)
Whetten-Goldstein, Sloan, Stout and Liang (2000)

The results are summarised in Table 8.8.2. All results refer to the general effects of the laws, i.e. effects on all drivers independent of any DUI convictions. The effects of licence suspension on drivers who actually get their licence suspended are described in Section 8.10 (restrictions for DUI-convicted drivers).

Administrative licence suspension laws have been found to reduce the number of fatal accidents. The largest effect has been found on fatal accidents involving alcohol. The result that refers to accidents involving alcohol (proxy) is based on types of accidents in which alcohol is overrepresented, but not all of which are known to involve alcohol (e.g. weekend night accidents). Laws about licence suspension in court seem to be less effective than administrative licence suspension laws and none of the results is statistically significant. All results are relatively consistent between the studies and do not seem to be affected by publication bias or confounding factors.

***Anti-plea bargaining laws*** have been evaluated by Evans, Neville and Graham (1991). No relationship was found between the introduction of anti-plea bargaining laws and fatal accidents. The estimated percentage change of the number of fatal accidents is 0% (95% confidence interval (−5; +7). A recidivism study (Surla and Koons 1988) indicates that anti-plea bargaining laws reduced the proportion of drivers with multiple DUI convictions.

***Reduced minimum legal drinking age (USA).*** The minimum legal drinking age was increased from 18 to 21 in several states of the USA. Three studies have evaluated these changes (Brown and Maghsoodloo 1981, Ferreira and Sicherman 1976, Naor and Nashold 1975) and found a significant increase of the number of accidents involving drivers in the relevant age group by 22% (95% CI [+6; +40]).

***Increased minimum legal drinking age (USA).*** From 1984 in the USA, sanctions were imposed on all states that have a minimum legal drinking age below 21, and by 1989, all states had introduced a minimum legal drinking age of 21. The increase of the minimum legal drinking age in states of the USA has been evaluated in the following studies:

Naor and Nashold (1975)
Ferreira and Sicherman (1976)
Brown and Maghsoodloo (1981)
Wagenaar (1982)
Hingson et al. (1983)
Cook and Tauchen (1984)
Males (1986)
Dyke and Womble (1988)
Eisenberg (2001)
Voas, Tippetts and Fell (2003)

These studies have found a significant decrease of the total number of accidents involving drivers in the relevant age groups by 16% (95% CI [−24; −7]). No significant differences were found in the effects of involving or not involving alcohol on accidents. Most studies have controlled for accidents involving drivers not directly affected by the legal changes.

***Dram shop laws*** impose civil liability on liquor stores and other commercial establishments that sell alcoholic beverages to minors or obviously intoxicated persons who subsequently cause death or injury to third parties, e.g. in an accident. The effects of dram shop laws on accidents have been investigated in the following studies, all of which have been conducted in the USA:

Ruhm (1996)
Whetten-Goldstein, Sloan, Stout and Liang (2000)
Young and Likens (2000)
Dee (2001)
Eisenberg (2001)

In summary, dram shop laws were found to reduce the number of fatal accidents by 14% (95% CI [−21; −5]) and the number of fatal accidents involving alcohol by 17% (95% CI [−24; −9]). The results are significant, but there is significant heterogeneity in the results and the effects are not significantly different for fatal accidents involving alcohol and other fatal accidents. This indicates that other factors than dram shop laws may have contributed to the results.

***Social host liability laws*** impose civil liability on private persons who serve alcohol to minors or obviously intoxicated persons who subsequently cause death or injury to third parties, e.g. in an accident. The effect of social host liability on accidents has been investigated by Whetten-Goldstein, Sloan, Stout and Liang (2000). No significant effect on the number of fatal accidents was found.

***Availability of alcohol.*** A number of laws aim at restricting the availability of alcohol in order to reduce the negative social and health effects of alcohol consumption. Among these are accidents, but a reduced number of road accidents is not always the main focus. Laws that restrict alcohol availability are total or local prohibitions against the sale of all alcohol or types of alcoholic beverages, laws that regulate the density of establishments selling or serving alcohol and laws that affect alcohol prices, usually by imposing taxes. In summary, studies that have investigated the effects of such laws on road accidents did not find reduced accident numbers, although several studies found that alcohol consumption in a geographical area is related to the number of accidents involving alcohol (Gruenewald and Ponicki 1995, Kaplan and Prato 2007, Voas, Tippetts and Fell 2003).

During the ***prohibition*** that was introduced in the USA in 1920, both liver cirrhosis and the number of drivers arrested for drink driving was strongly reduced. After the end of the prohibition in 1933, liver cirrhosis and the number of drivers arrested for drink driving increased strongly. The changes in the occurrence of liver cirrhosis indicate that the changes in the number of arrested drunken drivers was not only due to changes in police enforcement (Dills, Jacobson and Miron 2005).

***Local alcohol prohibition*** still exists in a number of counties in states of the USA. Effects on accidents have been studied by

Colón (1983)
Colón (1991)
Joksch (1991)
Giacopassi and Winn (1995)
Brown, Jewell and Richer (1996)

Ruhm (1996)
Young and Likens (2000)
Baughman, Conlin, Dickert-Conlin and Pepper (2001)
Schulte Gary, Aultman-Hall, McCourt and Stamatiadis (2003)
Webster, Pimentel and Clark (2008)

The results are too heterogeneous for calculating a summary effect. The results seem, at the first sight, unexpected. Most studies found more accidents or fatalities in counties with local alcohol prohibition (dry counties), compared to counties without local alcohol prohibition (wet counties) and some studies found non-significant or inconsistent effects. In summary, the results indicate that dry counties may have more accidents than wet counties for several reasons, but that local alcohol prohibition is not necessarily one of the causes and may even reduce the number of accidents. Dry counties may have more accidents than wet counties because people drive more in order to buy or consume alcohol, because of geographical (less urban, longer driving distances) or social (more men with alcohol and drug problems and criminal records arrested for DUI) differences, or because local alcohol prohibitions are more likely to be introduced in counties with many (alcohol related) accidents. When controlling for the number of alcohol-related fatal accidents before the introduction of local alcohol prohibition, Baughman, Conlin, Dickert-Conlin and Pepper (2001) and Brown, Jewell and Richer (1996) found that dry counties have fewer – not more – accidents than wet counties.

***Alcohol outlet density***. The relationship between alcohol outlet density and accidents involving alcohol has been investigated by

Colón and Cutter (1983)
Giacopassi and Winn (1995)
Gruenewald and Ponicki (1995)
Jewell and Brown (1995)
Stevenson, Brewer and Lee (1998)
Whetten-Goldstein, Sloan, Stout and Liang (2000)
McCarthy (2003)
Meliker et al. (2004)
Treno, Johnson, Remer and Gruenewald (2007)

The studies are too heterogeneous for calculating a summary effect. The results resemble the results from studies of local alcohol prohibition. Some studies found more accidents in areas with a high outlet density, while others found no relationship. A possible explanation for the inconsistent results is that low outlet density can lead to reduced alcohol availability (longer distances, higher prices), which may reduce alcohol-related accidents, and to more driving related to the purchase and consumption of alcohol, which may increase accidents. Moreover, areas with a high outlet density are generally more densely inhabited areas, which also may affect the number of alcohol-related accidents (McCarthy 2003).

***Alcohol prices.*** The relationship between alcohol taxes or indicators of alcohol prices and accidents has been studied by

Saffer and Grossman (1987)
Walsh (1987)
Saffer and Chaloupka (1989)
Evans, Neville and Graham (1991)
Sloan, Reilly and Schenzler (1994)
Gruenewald and Ponicki (1995)
Ruhm (1996)
Dee (1999)
Whetten-Goldstein, Sloan, Stout and Liang (2000)
Young and Likens (2000)
Sen (2001)
McCarthy (2003)
Voas, Tippetts and Fell (2003)
Kaplan and Prato (2007)

No summary effect can be computed since all studies have used different indicators of alcohol prices or alcohol taxes. The results are inconsistent and it seems most likely that alcohol prices do not directly affect the number of accidents. Some studies have found that higher alcohol prices are related to fewer road fatalities. However, this has been found for both alcohol-related and non-alcohol-related accidents, and the results may be affected by other factors than alcohol prices. Moreover, several studies have not found any relationship between alcohol prices and accidents. An Irish study found a relationship between alcohol consumption and accidents (Walsh 1987). However, the results of this study indicate that alcohol consumption is more strongly affected by incomes and unemployment than by alcohol prices.

***Open container laws*** prohibit consumption of alcohol while driving. The effects on accidents have been investigated by Evans, Neville and Graham (1991), Eisenberg (2001) and Whetten-Goldstein, Sloan, Stout and Liang (2000). In summary, it was found that fatal accidents involving alcohol are significantly reduced by 9% (95% CI [−13; −5]). No significant effect was found on the total number of fatal accidents (−4%; 95% CI [−9; +0]).

***Anti-consumption laws,*** which prohibit the consumption of alcohol for all car occupants, have been studied by Whetten-Goldstein, Sloan, Stout and Liang (2000). No significant effects have been found, neither on fatal accidents involving alcohol (−3%; 95% CI [−11; +5]), nor on the total number of fatal accidents (−6%; 95% CI [−15; +3]).

***Random breath testing laws*** allow the police to breath test drivers without suspicion. Effects on accidents have been studied by

Evans, Neville and Graham (1991)
Eisenberg (2001)
Ruhm (1996)
Whetten-Goldstein, Sloan, Stout and Liang (2000)
Saffer and Chaloupka (1989)

Random breath testing laws do not seem to have any direct effect on accidents. The summary effect on fatal accidents is a non-significant reduction by 1% (95% CI [−4; +2]). No difference has been found between the effects on fatal accidents involving alcohol and on the total number of fatal accidents.

***Private interest groups*** may affect the introduction of new laws, publicity accompanying new laws and publicity against drink driving in general. One such interest group is Mothers Against Drink Driving (MADD) in the USA. The effects of MADD activities on the number of fatal accidents has been investigated in three well-controlled studies (Eisenberg 2001, Rogers and Schoenig 1994). All studies found that MADD activity is related to reductions of the numbers of fatal accidents, both with and without alcohol involved. Rogers and Schoenig (1994) have estimated that MADD reduces fatal accidents by between 9% and 11%, while the introduction of several DUI laws (per se laws, increased penalties, administrative laws) reduced fatal accidents by between 2% and 8%.

No studies have been found of the effects of interest groups that are interested in selling alcohol on law changes or on accidents. A literature review (Nelson 2001) found no relationship between advertising for alcohol and alcohol consumption, and no effect of prohibiting advertising for alcohol on alcohol consumption.

## Effect on mobility

No effects on mobility in general have been documented. Drivers with a suspended licence will have reduced mobility. Laws that restrict the availability of alcohol have been found to increase driving distances on trips related to purchase or consumption of alcohol.

### Effect on the environment

No effects on the environment of any of these measures have been documented. Laws that reduce the availability of alcohol (local prohibition, outlet density, alcohol taxes) may have positive or negative social and health effects, if they reduce alcohol consumption or stimulate illegal activities in order to produce or purchase alcohol.

### Costs

The direct costs of DUI laws are mainly administrative costs, i.e. the costs incurred in developing, introducing and administering these laws. Additional costs are related to the enforcement of the laws. Costs for courts may change as well. For example, administrative laws reduce court costs. Laws that reduce the availability of alcohol may have more general economic consequences, such as taxes on alcohol sales.

### Cost–benefit analysis

Costs and benefits of the reduced BAC limits for young drivers have been evaluated in an American cost–benefit analysis (Miller, Lestina and Spicer 1998). The analysis referred to the possible introduction of a 0.00 BAC limit for drivers under the age of 21 years (16 is the most common age for driving licences for cars in the USA). The benefit was estimated to around US$ 0.042 per kilometre driven for drivers aged between 16 and 21 years. The costs were estimated to around US$ 0.0038 dollars per kilometre driven for the same drivers. The costs consisted of a loss of benefit, attributable to the fact that previously legal driving became illegal, and additional costs of sanctions (withdrawal of driving licences and possible prosecution). According to this analysis, the benefit was around 11 times greater than the costs. The same study found that the accident costs of driving with BAC above 0.8 were greater than the driver's benefit from these trips.

No cost–benefit analyses have been calculated for other DUI laws. It is difficult to specify the costs, and the effects of laws depend on accompanying measures, such as police enforcement. Moreover, many laws aim not only at reducing road accidents, and cost–benefit analyses should therefore also include social and health effects.

## 8.9 DUI ENFORCEMENT

### Problem and objectives

Police enforcement is conducted in order to detect and punish those drivers who are driving with illegal BAC levels, preferably before they get involved in accidents. Another purpose of police enforcement is to deter drivers from driving at illegal BAC levels. It is assumed that a high subjective risk of detection (in combination with the expected sanctions) deters from drink driving (Homel 1988). According to deterrence theory, the effect of police enforcement will be greater the higher the intensity and the more unpredictable enforcement is.

### Description of the measure

The types of police enforcement that are described in this section are DUI checkpoints, i.e. stationary police enforcement, where drivers are stopped in order to investigate whether they are driving at illegal BAC levels. DUI checkpoints vary with respect to amongst other things

- whether all drivers are stopped, drivers are stopped at random or only when they arouse suspicion, and whether all drivers who are stopped are tested or only those drivers whose behaviour indicates alcohol;
- how BAC is tested, e.g. by behavioural indicators, breath tests or passive detectors; blood tests are normally taken only when there is an indication of drink driving, e.g. a positive result from a breath test;
- how large and visible checkpoints are; checkpoints may be conducted by unmarked or marked police cars, in Australia and New Zealand special buses are used, so-called booze buses, which are highly visible and equipped for testing a large number of drivers;
- whether checkpoints are conducted at random times or places or more targeted at times and places where a high proportion of drivers with illegal BAC is suspected.

Moreover, checkpoints may be more or less publicised in media or campaigns. Some checkpoint programmes are conducted as 'Blitzes' with short periods of high-intensity enforcement, followed by periods with no or little enforcement.

In order to conduct DUI checkpoints, random stopping of drivers has to be permitted, i.e. stopping drivers without suspicion and, preferably, also to randomly breath test drivers independent of behaviour or accident involvement. Such laws have been implemented in most motorised countries. In order to conduct checkpoints effectively, it is an advantage if breath test results (instead of blood samples) are permitted as evidence in court.

Types of enforcement that are not described in this section are police patrols that specialised on DUI enforcement (see Section 8.4) and BAC tests that the police conduct as a part of regular police work (e.g. in combination with speed enforcement or after accidents).

**Effect on accidents**

The following 40 studies have been found the effects of DUI checkpoints on accidents:

Cameron, Strang and Vulcan (1981) (Australia)
Cameron and Strang (1982) (Australia)
Ross (1982) (UK)
Kearns and Goldsmith (1984) (Australia)
McLean et al. (1984) (Australia)
Thomson and Mavrolefterou (1984) (Australia)
Armour (1984) (Australia)
Hardes et al. (1985) (Australia)
L'Hoste, Duval and Lassarre (1985) (France)
Mercer (1985) (Canada)
Voas, Rhodenizer and Lynn (1985) (USA)
Frank (1986) (Australia)
Åberg, Engdahl and Nilsson (1986) (Sweden)
Derby and Hurst (1987) (New Zealand)
Barnes (1988) (Australia)
Homel (1988) (Australia)
King (1988) (Australia)
Evans, Neville and Graham (1991) (USA)
Smith, Maisey and McLaughlin (1990) (Australia)
Cameron, Cavallo and Sullivan (1992) (Australia)
Wells, Preusser and Williams (1992) (USA)
Bailey (1995) (New Zealand)
Jones et al. (1995) (USA)
Stuster and Blowers (1995) (USA)
Törnros (1995) (Sweden)
Mara, Davies and Frith (1996) (New Zealand)
Mercer, Cooper and Kristiansen (1996) (Canada)

Cameron et al. (1997) (Australia)
Henstridge, Homel and Mackay (1997) (Australia)
Holder, Voas and Gruenwald (1997) (USA)
Lacey, Jones and Fell (1997) (USA)
Ryan, Hendrie and Allotey (1997) (Australia)
Diamantopoulou and Cameron (1998) (Australia)
Newstead, Cameron and Narayan (1998) (Australia)
Lacey and Jones (2000) (USA)
Agent, Green and Langley (2002) (USA)
Mathijssen and de Craen (2004) (The Netherlands)
Miller, Blewden and Zhang (2004) (New Zealand)
Fell, Langston and Tippetts (2005) (USA)
Tay (2005) (Australia)

The most important results are summarised in Table 8.9.1.

All results in Table 8.9.1 refer to the effects of DUI checkpoints on the total numbers of accidents in those areas where the checkpoints are conducted. No distinction is made between different types of accidents (with or without alcohol involved) or between different accident severities. Some studies have investigated the effects of introducing DUI checkpoints as a new type of enforcement, while others have investigated the effects of increasing the amount or intensity of DUI enforcement. No differences have been found in the results of these two types of studies.

*Table 8.9.1: Effects on accidents of DUI checkpoints*

| | Percentage change in the number of accidents | |
|---|---|---|
| Studies included | Best estimate | 95% confidence interval |
| ***All studies*** | | |
| Without control for publication bias: | −17 | (−20; −14) |
| With control for publication bias: | −14 | (−18; −11) |
| ***Studies with a comparison group*** | | |
| Without control for publication bias: | −13 | (−15; −10) |
| With control for publication bias: | −9 | (−12; −7) |
| ***Australian studies*** | | |
| Without control for publication bias: | −22 | (−26; −17) |
| With control for publication bias: | −17 | (−22; −11) |
| *Australia, studies with a comparison group* | −13 | (−14; −12) |

The results in Table 8.9.1 show that the results are affected by methodological aspects of the studies. The overall effect that has been found is a reduction of the number of accidents by 17%. When controlling for publication bias, this reduces to a reduction by 14%. Greater effects have been found in studies without a comparison group than in studies with a comparison group.

Significantly greater effects have been found in Australia than in other countries. Studies from Australia that have applied a comparison group have found an accident reduction of 13%. This result does not seem to be affected by publication bias. A 13% reduction can therefore be regarded as the upper limit of what may be expected from DUI checkpoints, since the effects in Australia have been found to be greater than in other countries, and the result is based on the methodologically best studies.

There are a number of differences between DUI checkpoints in Australia and in other countries that may have contributed to the favourable results for Australian DUI checkpoints:

- The amount of drink driving was initially greater in Australia than in most other countries, and alcohol was involved in more fatal accidents than in other countries.
- The number of BAC tests per driver is high in Australia compared to other countries. In Victoria and New South Wales, the proportion of licence holders who were BAC-tested per year was 51% in 1994 and 37% in 1998. In Sweden, this proportion is ca. 17%, which is the second highest in Europe (the proportion is still higher in Finland, but Finland is not represented among the studies included in the meta-analysis).
- DUI checkpoints in Australia are often conducted with booze buses, the checkpoints are highly visible and easily recognizable as DUI enforcement.

A number of other factors that may affect the effectiveness of DUI checkpoints have been investigated. The results are summarised as follows:

- The greatest effects have been found during the first 6 months of checkpoints programs.
- The effects are likely to be greater when all drivers who are stopped at a checkpoints are BAC-tested than when drivers are tested on suspicion only. It was not possible to investigate the effects of stopping all drivers vs. stopping drivers randomly or selectively.
- No differences in effects have been found with respect to accident severity. Most studies have investigated effects on injury accidents or fatal accidents.
- The effects do not seem to depend on whether or not accidents involve alcohol. A possible explanation for this finding is that information on actual involvement of

alcohol was not available in most studies. Many studies have therefore used a proxy measure for alcohol accidents (e.g. accidents at weekend nights). Even if alcohol is overrepresented in these accidents, there will be some overlap between accidents involving and not involving alcohol.
- Media campaigns were not found to affect the effectiveness of the checkpoints.

### Effect on mobility

DUI enforcement has no general effect on mobility. Testing of drivers at checkpoints will cause delays for all drivers who are tested.

### Effect on the environment

DUI enforcement has no general effects on the environment.

### Costs

The cost of current DUI enforcement in Norway has been estimated to be about NOK 40 million (1995 prices) annually (Elvik 1997a). In addition to the enforcement costs come costs for prosecution and imprisonment of drunk drivers (NOK 93 million), costs for licence suspension (NOK 17 million) and costs for new driving tests and replacement of driving licences (NOK 14 million). The sum of these costs is NOK 164 million NOK.

### Cost–benefit analysis

In a Norwegian cost–benefit analysis (Elvik 2006), it was assumed that tripling random breath testing could lead to a 3% decrease in the number of fatal accidents, a 1% decrease in the number of other injury accidents and a 1% decrease in the number of property-damage-only accidents. This gives a total benefit of NOK 340 million per year, consisting of NOK 312 million in reduced accident costs and NOK 2 million in reduced environmental costs. The cost of increasing enforcement was estimated to NOK 266 million. The benefit is therefore greater than the costs (314/266 = 1.2).

## 8.10 Restrictions for DUI-convicted drivers

### Problem and objective

Drivers who are driving at illegal BAC levels are a danger to themselves and others. DUI offenders, and especially multi-DUI offenders, were found to be quite resistant to both punishment and treatment. Among the reasons are attitudes, lifestyle and alcohol addiction. All these factors are difficult to change with non-voluntary measures. Removing such drivers from traffic is therefore an option to reduce accidents.

### Description of the measure

The measures described in this chapter are licence suspension, vehicle suspension and alcolock. Jail terms and surveillance are described in Sections 8.11 and 8.12.

The most common measure is ***licence suspension***. Many countries have introduced administrative laws that allow the police to suspend the licence of drivers with an illegal BAC level, without involving the court. The risk of detection for drivers without a valid licence is small, as long as they are not involved in accidents. A number of studies found that up to 75% of drivers with a suspended licence continue driving illegally (Peck and Voas 2002). The effects of laws about licence suspension are described in Section 8.8 DUI laws.

An electronic driving licence, which permits starting a vehicle engine only while valid, might increase the compliance of drivers with a suspended licence. However, no studies have been found.

Several countries (some states in the USA, New Zealand, Canada) have introduced laws that allow the ***impoundment or confiscation of the vehicles*** of drivers with a suspended licence or with illegal BAC levels (Voas and DeYoung 2002). Many laws are administrative, i.e. the vehicle can be impounded immediately by the police whenever a driver has an illegal BAC level or no valid licence. Impounded vehicles can be returned to the owner after the impoundment period (usually as long as the licence is suspended) against the payment of a fee. Vehicles can also be impounded if the driver is not the owner of the vehicle. In such cases, the reinstatement of the vehicle to the owner is possible under certain conditions. As alternatives to vehicle impoundment, also the licence plate may be seized, a sticker may be attached to the licence plate or the vehicle registration may be withdrawn. Vehicle confiscation (vehicles are not returned to the owner, but sold on an auction) is more rarely used, mainly because of expensive administrative procedures and low value of confiscated vehicles.

It has been found that drivers whose vehicle is impounded have fewer opportunities to drive illegally than drivers from whom only the licence is suspended. Especially drivers who got a borrowed vehicle impounded may have reduced opportunities to borrow a vehicle in the future (Voas and DeYoung 2002).

***Alcolock*** aims at preventing driving only while drunk, not driving in general. Alcolock is a device that is installed in vehicles and that requires the driver to provide a breath test in order to start the engine. When the breath sample contains alcohol above a defined limit, the engine will not start (Assum and Hagman 2006). DUI-convicted drivers may be required to install alcolock in their vehicles, e.g. as a part of a treatment program or probation conditions, or as an alternative to licence suspension. Alcolock may also be installed in specific types of vehicles where the risk associated with DUI is especially high, such as buses, taxis or snow scooters.

**Effect on accidents**

***Licence suspension***. Three studies have been found that have evaluated the specific effects of licence suspension, i.e. the effect on drivers whose licence has been suspended after a DUI offence. The studies differ with respect to the time periods studied and the proportions of the study periods in which the licences actually have been suspended. Summary effects are therefore not calculated, but the results of all three studies are summarised in Table 8.10.1.

Hagen (1978) and Preusser, Blomberg and Ulmer (1988b) studied accident involvement of drivers during a longer time period, with only small proportions of this period in which the licence actually has been suspended. Significant accident reductions were found during the whole period. Siskind (1996) studied the accident involvement of drivers during the period in which the licence was suspended, compared to the accident involvement of the same drivers after the reinstatement of the licences. The results indicate that the accident reductions are larger while the licence is suspended than after reinstatement of the licences. The effect is smaller among drivers with more than two DUI offences than among drivers with 'only' one or two DUI offences. The numbers of DUI offences and of total traffic offences was also reduced during the licence suspension period.

A number of studies have shown that between 32% (Williams, Hagen and McConnell 1984) and 75% (Peck and Voas 2002) of drivers whose licence is suspended continue driving illegally. Traffic offences were recorded for 61% of drivers with a suspended licence (Williams, Hagen and McConnell 1984). Parker (2003) found that a driver without a valid licence is involved in 20% of all accidents. A Danish study showed that

*Table 8.10.1: Effects on accidents of licence suspension. Summary of studies*

| | | | Percentage change in the number of accidents | | |
|---|---|---|---|---|---|
| | Drivers | Study period | Accidents affected | Best estimate | 95% confidence interval |
| Hagen (1978), California, USA | Multiple DUI offenders | 6 years, including a period with suspended licence | Injury accidents | −35 | (−47; −21) |
| | | | Alcohol related accidents | −25 | (−37; −9) |
| Preusser, Blomberg, and Ulmer (1988b), Wisconsin, USA | First-time DUI offenders | 1 year; including a period of 3–6 months with suspended licence | All accidents | −21 | (−28; −24) |
| | | | Injury accidents | −16 | (−28; −3) |
| Siskind (1996) | All DUI offenders | Licence suspended | All accidents | −65 | (−70; −60) |
| | Multiple DUI offenders (more than two DUI offences) | Licence suspended | All accidents | −56 | (−71; −36) |

ca. 50% of all drivers who were involved in injury accidents and who had an illegal BAC level (above 0.5), had no valid driving licence. It is unlikely that licence suspension has any effect on drivers who do not have a valid licence (Bernhoft and Behrensdorff 2000).

***Vehicle impoundment***. Seven studies have been found that have evaluated the effects of vehicle impoundment or similar measures. The studies differ with respect to the type of measure studied, the groups of drivers and the time periods studied. One study (Beirness, Simpson, Mayhew and Jonah 1997) has investigated the simultaneous introduction of two laws and it is not known to what degree the results are due to the law on vehicle impoundment. Summary effects are therefore not calculated, but the results of six studies are summarised in Table 8.10.2. General effects refer to effects on all drivers, independent of whether or not a vehicle was impounded. Specific effects refer to the effects on those drivers whose vehicle was impounded.

All studies are well controlled and found that vehicle impoundment and similar measures reduce drink driving, other traffic offences and accidents. Positive effects were found for all drivers (general effect) and for drivers who got their vehicle impounded (specific effect) during the impoundment period and afterwards. The results indicate that vehicle impoundment has greater and more long-lasting effects than licence suspension. The effects may in part be due to deterrence, either because drivers want to avoid further penalties, or problems with persons from whom they borrow vehicles. The effects may also be due to reduced availability of vehicles and less driving. Drivers may have more problems borrowing vehicles and not all impounded vehicles are retrieved by the owner.

***Alcolock***. Several studies found that an alcolock reduces DUI offences while it is installed in vehicles of DUI-convicted drivers (Beck, Rauch, Baker and Williams 1999, Bjerre 2005, Bjerre and Laurell 2000, Bjerre and Thorsson 2008, Coben and Larkin 1999, Nochajski and Stasiewicz 2006, Voas, Marques, Tippetts and Bierness 1999). In most studies, participation in an alcolock program was voluntary, often in exchange for reduced sanctions. However, not all drivers participate in an alcolock program, even if sanctions are reduced (DeYoung 2002, Voas and Marques 2004, Voas, Blackman, Tippetts and Marques 2002). It is therefore likely that there are differences between participants and non-participants. Moreover, participation in an alcolock program is often associated with treatment and total abstinence from alcohol. Therefore, differences between drivers participating and not participating in alcolock programs are likely to be due to other factors than (only) alcolock.

Effects on recidivism were not found in all studies, and some studies found that licence suspension is more effective in reducing recidivism (in the suspension period) than

*Table 8.10.2: Effects on accidents of vehicle impoundment: summary of studies*

| | | | | Effect on accidents | |
|---|---|---|---|---|---|
| | Drivers | Control group | Accidents/ violations | Best estimate | 95% confidence interval |
| ***Vehicle impoundment (law): General effect*** | | | | | |
| Sen (2001) | States with a law about vehicle impoundment | States without a law about vehicle impoundment | Accidents | −19% | (−18; +54) |
| ***Vehicle impoundment as a sanction for driving without a licence: Specific effect*** | | | | | |
| DeYoung (1999, 2000) | Drivers 1 year after vehicle has been impounded | Drivers with suspended licence (before introduction of vehicle impoundment law) | Accidents | −29% | (−41; −15) |
| | Drivers with suspended licence (after introduction of vehicle impoundment law) | Drivers with a valid licence | Accidents | No sign. difference | |
| ***Vehicle impoundment as a sanction for DUI convicted drivers: Specific effect*** | | | | | |
| Voas, Tippetts and Fell (2000), Voas, Tippetts and Lange (1997) | Drivers with an impounded vehicle | DUI convicted drivers without impounded vehicle (admin. mistake) | DUI and other traffic violations | ca. −50% to 60% | |
| | Drivers 1 year after impoundment of vehicle | DUI convicted drivers without impounded vehicle (admin. mistake) | DUI and other traffic violations | ca. −25% to 30% | |
| ***Confiscation of vehicles from DUI convicted drivers: Specific effect*** | | | | | |
| Crosby (1996) | Drivers whose vehicle has been confiscated | | Traffic violations | ca. −50% | |
| ***Sticker on registration plate of vehicles of drivers with a suspended licence: Specific effect*** | | | | | |
| Voas, Tippetts and Lange (1997) | Drivers with a suspended licence, no sticker on registration plate | Drivers with a suspended licence before introduction of law | Accidents | −7 | (−21; +10) |
| | Drivers with a suspended licence, and a sticker on registration plate | Drivers with a suspended licence before introduction of law | Accidents | −13% | (−17; −9) |
| ***Impoundment of registration plate of DUI-convicted drivers: Specific effect*** | | | | | |
| Rogers (1994) | Drivers with impounded licence plate, 2 years | | DUI | ca. −50% | |

alcolock (DeYoung 2002). After removing alcolock from the vehicles of DUI offenders, the difference between drivers participating and not participating in alcolock programs disappeared (Bax et al. 2001, Beck, Rauch, Baker and Williams 1999, DeYoung 2002, Nochajski and Stasiewicz 2006, Voas, Marques, Tippetts and Bierness 1999).

Trials with alcolock in commercial vehicles were made in Sweden (Bjerre and Kostela 2008, Bjerre 2005) and in Norway (Assum and Hagman 2006). In these studies, alcolock was installed in all vehicles of the companies participating in the studies. The proportion of all engine starts that was prevented by alcolock was 0.34% in the first trial in Sweden (Bjerre 2005) and 0.19% in the second trial in Sweden (Bjerre and Kostela 2008) at a limit of BAC 0.02. In a study of alcolock for DUI offenders, the respective proportion was 0.57% at a limit of BAC 0.04 (Marques, Tippetts, Voas and Beirness 2001). The drivers know that a breath test has to be provided in order to start the engine. The results are therefore unlikely to be representative of the proportion of times an engine would have been started at BAC level above the limit if alcolock had not been installed in the vehicles. Moreover, it is not known how reliable the breath tests of alcolock are.

No studies have been found on the effects of alcolock on accidents that are based on a sufficient number of accidents to allow meaningful conclusions.

### Effect on mobility

Mobility is reduced for drivers whose licence is suspended or whose vehicle is impounded. Many drivers with a suspended licence have been found to continue driving illegally. Vehicle impoundment may also affect the mobility of other persons, e.g. family members. Alcolock only reduces mobility for drivers with illegal BAC levels.

### Effect on the environment

Licence suspension and vehicle impoundment are likely to reduce the total number of vehicle kilometres driven. This effect is likely to be marginal and without significant impact on the environment. Social consequences of vehicle impoundment and alcolock that have been discussed are the costs that these measures imply for the convicted drivers. Drivers without sufficient economic resources may not be able, e.g. to retain or replace an impounded vehicle or to participate in an alcolock program.

### Costs

No recent cost estimates are available for licence suspension and vehicle impoundment. The costs are for the most part only administrative costs. Drivers whose vehicles have been impounded usually have to pay all costs related to transport and storage of the vehicles, as well as administrative costs. Impounded vehicles that are not reclaimed by the owner and confiscated vehicles are sold on auctions. However, these vehicles have for the most part no large value.

The costs of alcolock have been estimated at ca. EUR 1,700 for installation and EUR 225 annually in maintenance costs.

### Cost–benefit analysis

A Norwegian cost–benefit analysis found that the benefit of suspending the licences of DUI-convicted drivers is approximately nine times as large as the costs (Elvik 1997a). The benefits consist of NOK 281 million in prevented accident costs and NOK 2 million in prevented environmental costs. The costs are estimated at NOK 14 million administrative costs and NOK 17 million for issuing new licences. It is assumed that the number of accidents among drivers who had their driving licences withdrawn is reduced by 18% during the period of suspension.

Vehicle impoundment has been found to reduce accidents. If the costs are borne by the vehicle owners, and if these costs are not taken into account in an analysis from a societal point of view, vehicle impoundment is likely to be a cost-effective measure.

No cost–benefit analysis has been calculated for alcolock, since no estimate of the effects on accidents is available. In Norway, it has been estimated that the installation of alcolock in all heavy vehicles (above 7.5 t) would be cost-effective if ca. 30% of all fatal and serious injury accidents involving heavy vehicles would be prevented. This is highly unlikely since the proportion of vehicle kilometre driven under the influence of alcohol is below 1% according to a number of studies. Installing alcolock in all heavy vehicles is therefore unlikely to be a cost-effective measure.

## 8.11 Treatment of DUI-convicted drivers

### Problem and objective

Many DUI offenders, especially multiple offenders and drivers convicted of driving at high BAC levels, have alcohol problems or are addicted to alcohol. Sanctions such as licence suspension, penalties or imprisonment have not been found to be effective in reducing alcohol problems or DUI offences among alcohol-addicted drivers (Fowler and Alcorn 2002).

Treatments with educational or therapeutic measures aim at changing drinking or drink driving behaviour and may be used as supplements or alternatives to classical sanctions. However, there is some discussion about the question of whether drink driving should be regarded as a health problem or as a criminal act (Ferguson, Sheehan, Davey and Watson 1999). Both points of view have some legitimacy (McKnight 1995): Addicted drivers are unlikely to impose less risk on other road used as long as their addiction is not treated, and as long as drink driving is regarded as criminal the individual driver, not society, will have to bear the costs.

**Description of the measure**

Many countries use treatment of DUI offenders in combination with sanctions as a measure for reducing drink driving. Some general aspects of DUI treatment are as follows.

***Focus on problems.*** Therapeutic measures have a main focus on alcohol problems and are used mainly for drivers with the most serious alcohol problems. A problem with therapy is that the effectiveness may be limited if participation is compulsory (Ferguson, Sheehan, Davey and Watson 1999). For the treatment of non-alcoholics, measures with an educational focus are more relevant. Some programs have a moral focus (e.g. victim impact panels). When drivers without alcohol problems are the target group, the total number of drivers and the potential for changing behaviour are greater, but drivers with alcohol problems (or a criminal background) have the highest risk per driver ('prevention paradox', Woodall et al. 2004). Drivers with a criminal background are often excluded from treatment offers.

***Voluntaries.*** DUI-convicted drivers may be obliged to undergo a treatment, but participation in a treatment program is mostly (at least partly) voluntary. Incentives for participation may be reduced sanctions, or treatment may be a precondition for reinstatement of the driving licence.

***Follow-up and monitoring.*** Some treatment programs merely require attendance at a certain number of courses or meetings. Other programs include extensive requirements of the drivers, such as abstinence from alcohol, and measures to monitor compliance. For example, drivers may be required to show up for regular interviews and blood tests, and in some cases electronic monitoring is used to monitor compliance with house arrest (alternative to jail) or driving prohibitions.

**Effect on accidents**

The effects of treatment of DUI-convicted drivers have been evaluated in a large number of studies. However, in most cases, treatment was not the only measure and there were systematic differences between treated and untreated drivers. Another problem is that most studies only have evaluated effects in the treatment period. However, behaviour changes during treatment can often, at least partly, be explained in terms of a desire to avoid sanctions if probation conditions are violated.

***Effects of education on recidivism.*** Bartl et al. (2002) reviewed six studies that found recidivism reductions of about 50% among DUI-convicted drivers without alcohol problems who had participated in an education programme. Study periods were between 1 and 6 years following the course. According to Bartl. et al. (2002), all studies are relatively well controlled. All of the evaluated courses lasted 3–8 weeks, had a maximum of 10 participants and had a focus on self-reflection rather than on education. Rider et al. (2007) conducted an experimental study and found that a program that focuses on driving instead of drinking was more effective in reducing recidivism among first-time DUI offenders than a program with a main focus on drinking behaviour. The study covered 2 years after the education program had been finished.

***Effects of education on accidents.*** Evaluation studies of a course for drivers convicted of alcohol-related reckless driving by the California Department of Motor Vehicles (2002, 2003, 2004, 2005, 2006, 2007, 2008) found that accidents 1 year after completion of the course were reduced by on average 5%, which is not statistically significant (95% CI [−13; +4]). The result refers to drivers who had participated in the course. A study of an education program for young drivers (Lacey, Wiliszowski and Jones 2003) found no effect on the total number of accidents involving young drivers. The program was directed at all young drivers, independent of DUI convictions. Education has not been found to be effective among drivers who are alcoholics (McKnight 1995).

***Effects of treatment on recidivism.*** Three studies have been found the effects of treatment on recidivism. All are relatively well controlled. Two studies (Langworthy and Latessa (1993; 1996) indicate that recidivism is reduced immediately after treatment, but not when a period of 3.5 years after treatment is considered. Peck, Arstein-Kerslake and Helander (1994) did not find any long-lasting effects either.

***Effects of treatment on accidents.*** In a meta-analysis of 105 studies Wells-Parker et al. (1995) found that education and treatment programs reduced accidents and recidivism by about 7–9%. However, the summary effects are not significant and there is large variation in the results between studies. Moreover, the results may be affected by publication bias (the largest effects have been found in the smallest studies) and methodologically weaker studies found larger effects than stronger studies. This indicates that other factors than the treatment are likely to have contributed to the results. Green, French and Haberman (1991) found that drivers who completed a treatment program had fewer accidents than drop-outs. This may, however, be due to differences between the drivers. Nochajski, Miller, Wieczorek and Whitney (1993) found that treatment is less effective among drivers with criminal records.

***Effects of treatment and licence suspension on recidivism.*** Several studies found that licence suspension has greater effects on recidivism than treatment. It has also been found that treatment has greater effects in combination with sanctions than without additional sanctions (DeYoung 1995, 1999, Watson 1998, Wells-Parker et al. 1995, Nochajski and Stasiewicz 2006). DeYoung (1995, 1999) found that treatment in combination with licence suspension reduced recidivism, but not treatment alone. These findings refer to the treatment period.

***Effects of treatment as an alternative to licence suspension on accidents.*** Three studies have investigated accident involvement of drivers who could choose either licence suspension or treatment. The results show that drivers who had chosen treatment had significantly more non-alcohol accidents that drivers who had chosen treatment (+27%; 95% CI [+29; +34]), and equal numbers of alcohol-related accidents (Preusser, Ulmer and Adams 1976, Hagen, Williams and McConell 1979, Sadler, Perrine and Peck 1991). The results refer to a period of 4 years after conviction. The studies have not controlled for differences between the drivers other than age. A study of a penalty point system (Stephen 2004) also found that participation in a course instead of licence suspension increased accident involvement.

***Effects of imprisonment and treatment on accidents.*** Woodall et al. (2004) found that combining a jail sentence with obligatory treatment in prison has no effect on accident involvement during a period of between 1 and 7 years following imprisonment. Drivers who received treatment in prison and a 6-month follow-up period were compared with comparable drivers who were sentenced to prison only. The effect that was found on the number of accidents was a non-significant reduction of 6% (95% CI [−20; +9]).

### Effect on mobility

Treatment and education have no general effects on mobility, except when combined with licence suspension or imprisonment.

### Effect on the environment

There are no documented effects on the environment.

### Costs

The costs of treatment and education depend on the type of programme.

### Cost–benefit analysis

There is large variation in both costs and effects of treatment and education programs. Therefore no cost–benefit analysis has been conducted.

## 8.12 Fines and imprisonment

### Problem and objective

Road traffic legislation contains a threat of punishment for those who violate it. Punishment is intended to create both a general and a specific deterrent effect. General deterrence is intended to prevent violations from being committed. Specific deterrence is intended to prevent violators from repeating the violation.

### Description of the measure

***Traffic tickets and imprisonment*** are the most stringent forms of sanction for traffic violations. In contrast to sanctions such as fixed penalties, licence suspension or vehicle impoundment, tickets and jail cannot be administered by the police, but only by courts. Tickets and jail sentences as standard sentences are often differentiated according to the severity of the DUI offence and previous DUI offences. Imprisonment may be unconditional or in probation.

***Alternative sanctions and probation conditions.*** Mandatory monitoring and treatment programmes are sometimes used as alternatives to imprisonment, or monitoring and treatment programmes may be parts of probation conditions. The aims of such measures are both cost savings (compared to imprisonment) and reducing recidivism (Jones, Wiliszowski and Lacey 1996, Jones and Lacey 1999). Recidivism has often been found to be lower following such alternative programmes than following imprisonment.

***DUI courts.*** In many states of the USA, courts have been established, which specialize in severe DUI offences. These courts combine classical sanctions (penalties, jail) with comprehensive and restrictive programmes, including, for example, demands for alcohol abstinence, treatment and monitoring. Measures that may be used in such programmes include regular interviews and alcohol tests, electronic monitoring, antabuse, alcolock and community work.

## Effect on accidents

***Effects of laws about minimum penalties or jail sentences on fatal accidents (general effects).*** The effect of laws that define minimum penalties or minimum jail sentences for DUI-convicted drivers have been evaluated in a number of studies from the USA that are based on state-level data on fatal accidents over several years. The minimum jail sentence is in most cases one or two days, and never above 10 days. The results refer to the general effects of the laws, i.e. the effect on all drivers.

Evans, Neville and Graham (1991)
Ruhm (1996)
Young and Likens (2000)
Whetten-Goldstein, Sloan, Stout and Liang (2000)
Dee (2001)
Eisenberg (2001)
Sen (2001)
Wagenaar et al. (2007b)

No effects of penalties or jail sentence on fatal accidents were found. The summary effect is a reduction of 1% (95% CI [−9; +7]), independent of whether or not accidents involve alcohol.

***Effects of imprisonment on accidents and recidivism (general effects).*** Several studies have investigated the effects of imprisonment as a standard sanction for DUI-convicted drivers in single states of the USA on the total number of accidents in the respective states.

Ross, McCleary and LaFree (1990)
Epperlein (1987)
Robertson, Rich and Ross (1973)
Jones, Joksch, Lacey and Schmidt (1988)

None of these studies have found any effects on accidents or recidivism.

***Effects of increased penalties on accidents (general effects).*** Several studies have investigated the effects of increasing penalties for DUI or speeding on drink driving, speeding and the total number of accidents. The studies are too heterogeneous for calculating meaningful summary effects.

One well-controlled study found a significant relationship between penalties for drink driving and the number of alcohol-related driver fatalities (Young and Likens 2000). Neustrom and Norton (1993) found a significant reduction of nighttime injury accidents during 3 years following the introduction of more severe penalties (−9%; 95% CI [−11; −8]) but this change may be due to other factors.

None of the other studies found large or significant effects of increased penalties on accidents. Briscoe (2004) found no effect on the number of fatal accidents and an increase of the number of likely alcohol-related injury accidents after the penalties for drink driving were doubled in New South Wales (Australia) in 1998. Hingson et al. (1987) found a possible short-term effect of the introduction of more severe penalties for drink driving, but no long-term effect on single-vehicle nighttime fatal accidents. No effect was found on self-reported drink driving and only few drivers believed that it was likely that drunken drivers would be stopped by the police.

***Effects of increased penalties on driver behaviour (general effects).*** McCartt and Northrup (2003) have evaluated the introduction of increased penalties for drivers with high BAC levels in several states of the USA (BAC above 0.15 or 0.20). Only small reductions were found of the number of drivers with BAC above the critical levels. In Sweden, the penalties for speeding were doubled in 1982. Åberg, Nilsson and Engdahl (1989) found no effects on speed. Only one-third of all drivers knew the penalties.

***Effects of penalties and imprisonment on accidents (specific effects).*** Mann et al. (1991) have evaluated the effects of several sanctions on accident involvement of DUI-convicted drivers. They found reduced accident involvement among drivers convicted of licence suspension, but no effects on penalties or jail sentences.

***Effects of increased penalties on recidivism (specific effects).*** Recidivism was unchanged among drivers who were sentenced to prison compared to drivers sentenced to other penalties (Martin, Annan and Forst 1993). DeYoung (1995) found increased recidivism among drivers sentenced to prison compared to drivers sentenced to licence suspension or treatment. In the latter study, a number of other differences between drivers, which may have contributed to the findings, are statistically controlled for.

***Effects of monetary penalties instead of imprisonment on accidents (general effects).*** A change of the standard sanctions for DUI offences from jail to a differentiated use of monetary penalties, conditional and unconditional jail sentences in Norway and Sweden has been evaluated by Ross and Klette (1995) and Vaas and Elvik (1992). No significant change was found in the total number of injury accidents (−3%, 95% CI [−8; +2]) and a significant reduction of the number of fatal accidents by 18% (95% CI [−25; −10]). The only factor controlled for in these studies is trend. Several other changes in the study period have not been taken into account, e.g. an increase of police enforcement and the reduction of the illegal BAC limit from 0.05 to 0.02 in Sweden. Therefore, it cannot be concluded that monetary penalties instead of jail reduce fatal accidents, only that mandatory jail sentences are not under all conditions more effective than monetary penalties.

***Effects of alternative sanctions and DUI courts on recidivism (specific effects).*** The effects of alternative sanctions and DUI courts on recidivism have been evaluated in a number of well controlled studies that have been conducted over several years (Breckendridge, Winfree, Maupin and Clason 2000, Carey et al. 2008, Crancer 2003, Eibner, Morral, Pacula and MacDonald 2006, Jones, Wiliszowski and Lacey 1996, Jones and Lacey 1999, Lapham, Kapitula, de Baca and McMillan 2006). The results of these studies show that recidivism is reduced among drivers who are sentenced to treatment and monitoring in addition to imprisonment, when compared to drivers who were only sentenced to prison. Greater effects have been found of more restrictive programmes and among drivers with less criminal background.

### Effect on mobility

The measures presented in this chapter do not have any general effect on mobility. Imprisonment and restrictions imposed by DUI courts reduce mobility, as is the aim of these measures.

### Effect on the environment

The measure has no documented effect on the environment.

### Costs

No recent cost estimates are available for the sanctions described in this chapter. Imprisonment has high costs as compared to penalties. Alternative sanctions have lower costs than imprisonment, but may be costly for the convicted DUI offenders.

### Cost–benefit analysis

In an early Norwegian cost–benefit analysis (Sager 1974), fines are compared to imprisonment as punishments for drink driving. The analysis included three types of savings gained by imposing fines instead of prison sentences: reduced prison costs, reduced production losses and increased freedom in the use of time. The value of these savings, if all those prosecuted for drink driving were fined instead of imprisoned, was estimated to be NOK 17.3 million for 1970. It was assumed that the incidence of drink driving and the number of traffic accidents would not be affected by the measure. An alternative using low fines was also analysed, in which it was assumed that there was some increase in traffic accidents. According to this analysis, fines are a more cost-effective form of punishment than imprisonment.

The results of the studies summarised above do not indicate that imprisonment reduces accident involvement compared to fines. The results also indicate that alternative sanctions for serious DUI offences reduce recidivism in comparison to imprisonment only. Since both fines and alternative sanctions are less expensive than imprisonment, both types of sanctions will be more cost-effective than imprisonment.

## 8.13 Motor vehicle insurance

### Problem and objective

The costs of a road accident may run into millions. This applies, for example, to accidents where someone suffers permanent injuries and is no longer able to work. Very few people have the resources to pay these costs themselves. Insurance distributes the costs of road accidents among all the policyholders, so that the individual is protected against personal financial ruin if he or she is involved in an accident in which he, she or others are injured.

The protection that insurance offers against serious financial consequences of road accidents may imply that road accidents are perceived to be less serious than they otherwise would have been, so that road users become less careful. Therefore, it has been claimed that the existence of motor vehicle insurance in itself adversely affects road safety (Wilde 1991). In order to counteract possible negative effects, the insurance companies calculate premiums on the basis of the customer's accident rate and provide other incentives for safer driving, the purchase of safer vehicles and the use of safety equipment for vehicles.

## Description of the measure

Knowledge of the relationship between insurance schemes and road safety is poor. Aspects of insurance systems that have been studied are described in the following.

***Liability insurance*** covers all injuries and property damage to others. In a collision between two vehicles, the liability insurance covers all personal injuries (for both parties), as well as the property damage sustained by the innocent part in the collision. Damage to the responsible part's own vehicle is not covered by liability insurance. Liability insurance is compulsory in all motorised countries. However, the extent to which this is implemented and the type of liability insurance vary. In American compensation law, a so-called fault system (tort liability) is standard. This means that in order to obtain compensation, it must be proved that the person who caused the accident acted negligently (was at fault).

***No-fault insurance.*** A number of states in the United States have introduced a so-called no-fault system, which functions in practice as a legal principle for sharing responsibility. Under a no-fault system, compensation can be claimed even if the person who caused the damage was not negligent or guilty in the accident. The insurance system in Norway follows the same principle under the name objective responsibility. In calculating compensation, costs are allocated based on the distribution of guilt. It is normal practice to combine this type of system with lower limits for what can be compensated, e.g. as a rule, medical expenses less than NOK 10,000 will not be compensated.

***Bonus system.*** The bonus system means that the insurance premium is reduced by a given percentage for each year in which no claims are filed, but that it is increased if a claim is made for which the insurance company must make a payment. Not all countries have, or have ever, had a bonus system in vehicle insurance. The bonus systems currently found are not equally rigorous in all countries. Rigour in a bonus system denotes the size of the difference, measured in monetary terms, between the highest and lowest bonuses, and how rigorously the system punishes claims in the form of loss of bonus (Lemaire 1995).

***Paying accrued bonus in cash.*** Another way of implementing a bonus system is to let the policyholder pay the whole basic premium for a specified number of years and then pay back the accrued bonus at the end of the period in the form of cash. This makes the bonus system more visible than the present system and thus may increase the effect of the bonus system.

***Collision insurance*** covers damage to one's own vehicle in accidents for which the driver is held responsible. Collision insurance is optional. It is possible that those who take out this type of insurance are less careful than others, since they know that damage to their own car will be covered, even though they may be the guilty party in an accident. It is therefore of interest to evaluate whether policyholders with collision insurance have a higher or lower accident rate than policyholders without this type of insurance.

**Effect on accidents**

Studies that have quantified the effect of different aspects of insurance systems on accidents include the following:

Landes (1982) (USA): no-fault insurance and lower compensation limits
Zador and Lund (1986) (USA): no-fault insurance and lower compensation limits
Gaudry (1987) (Canada): tightening up liability insurance; no-fault insurance
Ingebrigtsen and Fosser (1991) (Norway): collision insurance
Vaaje (1991) (Norway): paying bonuses in cash
Vaaje (1992) (Norway): paying bonuses in cash
Bjørnskau (1994) (Norway): collision insurance
Lemaire (1995) (Several countries): rigour of bonus systems
Negrin (1995) (Several countries): introducing a bonus system
Cohen and Dehejia (2004) (USA): tort liability, no-fault insurance

On the basis of these studies, Table 8.13.1 shows best estimates of the effect on accidents of the different elements in insurance schemes.

The effects of ***compulsory liability insurance*** have been studied in Quebec, Canada, by Gaudry (1987) and by Cohen and Dehejia (2004) in the USA. The proportion of vehicles with liability insurance increased from 70% to 85% in Canada and from 87% to ca. 90% in USA. The results indicate that compulsory liability insurance increases the number of accidents. However, only the effect on property-damage-only accidents is significant. Cohen and Dehejia estimated that the number of fatal accidents increases by 2% for every percentage increase in the proportion of vehicles with liability insurance.

*Table 8.13.1: Effect on accidents of different elements in insurance arrangements*

| Accident severity | Percentage change in the number of accidents | | |
|---|---|---|---|
| | Types of accidents affected | Best estimate | 95% confidence interval |
| ***Compulsory liability insurance*** | | | |
| Fatal accidents | All types of accidents | +17 | (−23; +78) |
| Injury accidents | All types of accidents | +15 | (−3; +36) |
| Property damage only accidents | All types of accidents | +30 | (+25; +36) |
| ***No-fault insurance and lower compensation limits*** | | | |
| Fatal accidents | All types of accidents | +2 | (−0; +3) |
| Injury accidents | All types of accidents | +26 | (+19; +33) |
| Property damage only accidents | All types of accidents | +10 | (+7; +13) |
| ***Introduction of a bonus system*** | | | |
| Fatal accidents | All types of accidents | +1 | (−3; +6) |
| Injury accidents | All types of accidents | −3 | (−4; −2) |
| ***Paying accrued bonus in cash*** | | | |
| Unspecified | Accidents involving young drivers | −22 | (−24; −20) |
| ***Collision insurance (policy holders with this vs. policy holders without)*** | | | |
| Unspecified | All accidents | +23 | (−20; +88) |

Introducing ***no-fault insurance*** has been found to increase the numbers of accidents. Cohen and Dehejia (2004) compared drivers with no-fault insurance and drivers with tort liability insurance. Their results indicate that no-fault insurance is related to less risky driving.

***Bonus systems*** were introduced in Switzerland in 1963; Germany in 1968; Belgium, France and Austria in 1971; Italy in 1976 and the Netherlands in 1982 (Negrin 1995). Negrin (1995) claims, on the basis of an overview of the frequency of claims the year before the bonus system was introduced and the frequency of claims in the same country in 1993, that this has led to fewer accidents in the countries listed above. However, it is very doubtful whether the data Negrin uses supports the conclusion he has drawn. Firstly, a bonus system may affect the reporting of accidents to the insurance companies. The chance of losing bonus may be a motive for not reporting minor damage to the companies. Secondly, the length of the periods that Negrin compares varies considerably from country to country. Thirdly, it has not been taken into account that the claims frequency may have been affected by a number of conditions other than the bonus system.

Negrin's information about when the bonus systems were introduced in different countries has been used as the basis for a simple study carried out specially for this book on the basis of the IRTAD database. The study was designed thus:

- For each country that has introduced a bonus system, one or more other countries were chosen to form comparison groups. Countries forming the comparison groups were chosen on the basis of having similar long-term trends in the number of accidents.
- Countries in the comparison group had unchanged bonus systems for the whole period covered by the study.
- The study was based on information on the numbers killed and injured in traffic 1 year before, and 1 year after, the introduction of the bonus system. The year in which the bonus system was introduced was omitted from the study.

With these limitations, it was possible to evaluate the effects of introducing a bonus system in Belgium (with The Netherlands as a comparison group), in Austria (with Switzerland as a control group) and The Netherlands (with the Nordic countries as the comparison group). The study indicates that the number of injured persons in the first year with the bonus system went down by around 3%. There was no statistically significant change in the number of fatalities.

Bonus systems in different countries are not all equally rigorous. Lemaire (1995) has developed an index for the rigour of bonus systems. If a rigorous bonus system encourages safer behaviour on the road than does a lenient bonus system, then countries having the most rigorous bonus systems ought also to have the lowest risk in traffic. Figure 8.13.1 shows the relationship between the rigour of the bonus system and the fatality rate in traffic in 15 motorised countries, based on data published by IRTAD in 1994. The countries are ordered from 1 to 15 according to the rigour of the bonus system. The country ranked as number 1 has the most rigorous bonus system. The countries listed in Figure 8.13.1 are also rank-ordered according to the fatality rate, where 1 is the lowest rate and 15 is the highest. The fatality rate is measured by the number of fatalities per 100 million vehicle kilometres. The figure shows that the more rigorous the bonus system, the lower the fatality rate. Since a number of potentially confounding factors have not been controlled for, this figure must be interpreted with care. It only shows a statistical relationship, not a causal relationship.

***Paying accrued bonus in cash.*** The Gjensidige insurance company has introduced a new bonus system for policyholders aged between 18 and 22. Instead of normal premium or rebates, policyholders are awarded a cash bonus for each year they drive without accidents from the age of 18 to 22. If no claims are made in the course of this 5-year

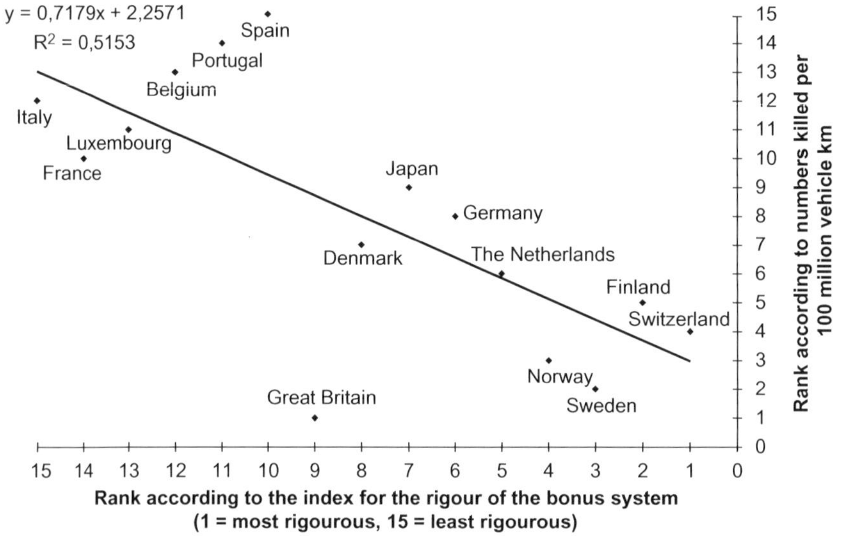


*Figure 8.13.1: Relationship between the rigour of bonus systems and fatality rate in traffic (15 countries, rank-ordered).*

period, NOK 6,000 in accrued bonuses is paid out. Studies (Vaaje 1991 1992) indicate that this has reduced the accident frequency in this age group by about 20%.

***Collision insurance.*** Norwegian studies (Ingebrigtsen and Fosser 1991, Bjørnskau 1994) do not indicate that policyholders with collision insurance have a higher or lower accident frequency than policyholders without this type of insurance. In both studies, a large number of confounding factors were controlled for.

### Effect on mobility

No studies have been found which show how insurance schemes affect mobility.

### Effect on the environment

No studies have been found that show how insurance systems affect the environment.

### Costs

In 2007 a total of NOK 11,500 million was paid in insurance premiums in motor vehicle insurance in Norway. This includes all coverage in this type of insurance, i.e. theft and vandalism insurance, not just vehicle insurance. The compensation payments from motor vehicle insurance in 2007 were NOK 4,300 million. On average, the insurance premium per registered vehicle is around NOK 5,000 per year.

The insurance industry in Norway estimates that around 0.5% of premiums is used for activities, which the insurance companies regard as damage prevention (Pihl and Hamre 1989). In 1995, this comprised around NOK 37 million.

### Cost–benefit analysis

No cost–benefit analyses have been found for different elements of insurance schemes for motor vehicles. For the individual, insurance represents a loss, since the policyholder pays a premium, which in the long term costs more than any damage for which it provides cover. The premium also covers the company's administrative costs and services. Nonetheless, many people think insurance is a good thing, since it replaces large, unpredictable expenses with a more even flow of predictable expenses. The main reason for making liability insurance compulsory is to protect the injured party from major financial loss, and also not to affect the number of injuries or damage.

Compulsory no-fault insurance was found to increase the number of accidents. Legal and administrative costs on the other hand are reduced compared to tort liability (Cohen and Dehejia 2004). Which of these two effects is greater is not known.

## References

Agent, K.R., Green, E.R. & Langley, R.E. (2002). *Evaluation of Kentucky's "You drink and drive. You loose" campaign.* Report KTC-02-28/KSP1-02-2F. Lexington, Kentucky: University of Kentucky, Kentucky Transportation Center.

Albuquerque Police Department (2001). *Safe streets program.* Report DOT HS 809 278. National Highway Traffic Safety Administration.

Amick, D.R & Marshall, P.B. (1983). Evaluation of the Bonneville, Idaho, DUI Accident Prevention Program. *Transportation Research Record*, **910**, 81–92.

Andersson, G. (1989). *Hastigheter som funktion av toleransgräns, övervakningsintensitet och påföljd.* VTI-Report 337. Linköping: Statens Väg- och Trafikinstitut.

Andersson, G. (1991). *Effekter på hastigheter av intensifierad övervakning med radar.* Forskning/Research nr 6. Stockholm og Linköping: Transportforskningsberedningen (TFB) and Statens väg- och trafikinstitut (VTI).

Andreassen, D. (1995). *A long term study of red light cameras and accidents.* Research report ARR 261. Victoria, Australia: Australian Road Research Board.

Apsler, R., Char, A.R., Harding, W.M. & Klein, T.M. (1999). *The effects of 0.08 BAC laws.* Report DOT HS 808 892. US Department of Transportation, National Highway Traffic Safety Administration.

Armour, M. (1984). *A review of the literature on police traffic law enforcement.* In: Proceedings of the 14th Australian Road Research Board Conference, 14, 17–24.

Arup (1992). *Red light camera evaluation study—implementation in Brisbane.* Report No. 6221, Arup Transportation Planning for Queensland Transport, Melbourne, Australia.

Assum, T. & Glad, A. (1990). *Alkohol og trafikk i Norge: En situasjonsrapport.* Arbeidsdokument nr TST/0189/90. Oslo: Institute of Transport Economics.

Assum, T. & Hagman, R. (2006). *Alkolås i buss.* TØI rapport 842/2006. Oslo: Transportøkonomisk institutt.

Assum, T. & Ingebrigtsen, S. (1990). *Ulykker med alkoholpåvirkede førere 1987.* TØI-notat 0915. Oslo: Institute of Transport Economics.

Assum, T. Mathijsen, M.P.M., Houwing, S., Buttress, S.C., Sexton, B., Tunbridge, R.J. & Oliver, J. (2005). *The prevalence of drug driving and relative risk estimations – a study conducted in the Netherlands, Norway and United Kingdom.* Deliverable D-R4.2. Project IMMORTAL, funded by the European Commission under the Transport RTD Programme of the 5th Framework Programme.

Baca, J.C., Miller, W.R. & Lapham, S. (2001). A multiple risk factor aproach for predicting DWI recidivism. *Journal of Substance Abuse Treatment,* **21**, 207–215.

Bailey, J.P.M. (1995). An evaluation of compulsory breath testing in New Zealand. I: Alcohol, Drugs and Traffic Safety T'95: *Proceedings of the 13th Internastional Conference on Alcohol, Drugs and Traffic Safety*, **Volume 1** (Kloeden, C. N and A. J. McLean. eds.) Adelaide.

Barnes, J.W. (1988). *The effect of the introduction of random breath testing in New South Wales on accident patterns.* In: Seminar Papers, Volume 2: Road Traffic Safety Seminar 14–16 September 1988, Road Traffic Safety Research Council, Wellington, NZ, pp. 125–155.

Bartl, G., Assailly, J.-P. Chatenet, F., Hatakka, M. , Keskinen, E. & Willmes-Lenz, G. (2002). *EU-Project "Andrea" Analysis of Driver Rehabilitation Programmes.* Wien: Kuratorium fuer Verkehrssicherheit.

Bartl, G. & Esberger, R. (2000). Effects of lowering the legal BAC limit in Austria. *Proceedings of the 15th Conference on Alcohol, Drugs and Traffic Safety*, Stockholm, Sweden.

Baughman, R., Conlin, M., Dickert-Conlin, S. & Pepper, J. (2001). Slippery when wet: the effects of local alcohol access laws on highway safety. *Journal of Health Economics*, **20**, 1089–1096.

Bax, C., Kärki, O., Evers, C., Bernhoft, I.M. & Mathijssen, R. (2001). *Alcohol Interlock Implementation in the European Union; Feasibility study*. Leidschendam, The Netherlands: SWOV Institute for Road Safety Research.

Beck, K., Rauch, W., Baker, E., & Williams, A. (1999). Effects of ignition interlock licence restrictions on drivers with multiple alcohol offenses: A random trial in Maryland. *American Journal of Public Health*, **89**, 1696– 1700.

Beirness, D.J., Simpson, H.M., Mayhew, D.R. & Jonah, B.J. (1997). The impact of administrative license suspension and vehicle impoundment for DWI in Manitoba. In: Mercier-Guyon, C. (Ed.), *14th International Conference on Alcohol, Drugs and Traffic Safety*. Annecy, France, pp. 919–925.

Beke, B.M.W.A. & Wilbers, P.T. (1990). *Autogordelcampagne Zeeland : een bedrijfsgerichte benadering versus een publieksgerichte benadering*. Arnhem: Advies- en Onderzoeksgroep Beke.

Bernat, D.H., Dunsmuir, W.T.M. & Wagenaar, A.C. (2004). Effects of lowering the legal BAC to 0.08 on single-vehicle nighttime fatal traffic crashes in 19 jurisdictions. *Accident Analysis and Prevention*, **36**, 1089–1097.

Bernhoft, I.-M. & Behrensdorff, I. (2000). *Alkohol og bilkørsel – effekt af ændret promillegrænse (Alcohol and driving – effects of the changed illegal BAC level)*. Rapport 1. København: Danmarks Transportforskning.

Bjerre, B. (2005). Primary and secondary prevention of drink driving by the use of alcolock device and program: Swedish experiences. *Accident Analysis and Prevention*, **37**, 1145–1152.

Bjerre, B., & Kostela, J. (2008). Primary prevention of drink driving by the large-scale use of alcolocks in commercial vehicles. *Accident Analysis and Prevention*, **40**, 1294–1299.

Bjerre, B., & Laurell, H. (2000). The Swedish alcohol ignition interlock programme. In H. Laurell, & F. Schlyter (Eds.), *Alcohol, drugs and traffic safety-T2000*. Stockholm7 Ekonomi-Print.

Bjerre, B. & Thorsson, U. (2008). Is an alcohol ignition interlock programme a useful tool for changing the alcohol and driving habits of drink-drivers? *Accident Analysis and Prevention*, **40**, 267–273.

Bjørnskau, T. (1994). *Spillteori, trafikk og ulykker. En teori om interaksjon i trafikken (Game theory and accidents. A theory of interaction in road traffic)*. TØI-Report 287. Oslo: Institute of Transport Economics.

Bloch, S.A. (1997). *The effectiveness of Traffic Violator Schools: An examination of their effects on driver knowledge, attitudes, and performance.* Los Angeles, CA: Automobile Club of Southern California.

Bonneson, J.A.D, Middleton, D., Zimmerman, K., Charan, H. & Abbas, M. (2002). *Intelligent detection control system for rural signalized intersections.* Report FHWA/TX-02/4022-2.

Borschos, B. (2000). An evaluation of the Swedish drink driving legislation implemented on February 1, 1994. In: H. Laurell & F. Schlyter (Eds.), *International Conference on Alcohol, Drugs and Traffic Safety*, Stockholm.

Bourne, M.G. & Cooke, R.G. (1993). Victoria's speed camera program. In: R.V. Clarke (ed.), *Crime Prevention Studies,* Vol. 1, Monsey, NY: CriminalJustice Press, pp. 177–192.

Brackett, R. Q., & Beecher, G. P. (1980). *Longitudinal evaluation of speed control strategies.* College Station, Human Factors Division, Texas Transportation Institute/Texas A&M University (Final Report – Vol 1).

Breckendridge, J.F., Winfree, L.T., Maupin, J.R. & Clason, D.L. (2000). Drunk drivers, DWO "drug court" treatment, and recidivism: Who fails? *Justice Research and Policy*, **2**, 87–106.

Brekke, G. (1993). Automatisk trafikkontroll: Har spart Bergen for 40 personskadeulykker. Bergen, Statens Vegvesen/Hordaland vegkontor, "Veg i vest", Nr 3, pp. 6–7.

Briscoe, S. (2004). Raising the bar: Can increased statutory penalties deter drinks-drivers? *Accident Analysis and Prevention*, **36**, 919–929.

Broughton, J. (1991). Restraint use by car occupants: Great Britain, 1982–91. I: *Strategies to increase the use of restraint systems.* Report no R-91-60-sidene 34–38. (Hagenzieker, M. P. ed.) SWOV Institute for Road Safety Research, Leidschendam.

Brown, D.B. & Maghsoodloo, S. (1981). A study of alcohol involvement in young driver accidents with the lowering of the legal age of drinking in Alabama. *Accident Analysis and Prevention*, **13**, 319–322.

Brown, M.G. & Thiebaux, H.J. (1970). The predictive power of driver demerit points: A case study of male drivers in Nova Scotia. *Accident Analysis and Prevention*, **10**, 297–312.

Brown, R.W., Jewell, R.T. & Richer, J. (1996). Endogenous alcohol prohibition and drunk driving. *Southern Economic Journal*, **62**, 1043–1053.

Burkey, M.L. & Obeng, K. (2004). *A detailed investigation of crash risk reduction resulting from red light cameras in small urban areas. Updated Final Report.* Greensboro: Urban Transit Institute, North Carolina Agricultural/Technical State University.

California Department of Motor Vehicles (2002, 2003. 2004, 2005, 2006, 2007, 2008). *Annual report of the California DUI Management Information System.* Sacramento, California.

California State Authority (2002). *Red light camera programs*. Report 2001–125. Sacramento, CA.

Cameron, M., Cavallo, A. & Sullivan, G. (1992). *Evaluation of the random breath testing initiative in Victoria 1989–1991*. Report No 38. Monash University Accident Research Centre Australia.

Cameron, M., Diamantopoulou, K., Mullan, N., Dyle, D., Gantzer, S. (1997). *Evaluation of the country random breath testing and publicity program in Victoria, 1993–1994*. Report 126. Melbourne: Monash University Accident Research Centre.

Cameron, M.H., Newstead, S.V., Diamantopoulou, K., & Oxley, P. (2003). *The interaction between speed camera enforcement and speed-related mass media publicity in Victoria, Australia*. In: Annual Proceedings of the Association for Advanced Automotive Medicine, 47, 267–82.

Cameron, M.H. & Strang, H.J. (1982). Effect of intensified random breath testing in Melbourne during 1978 and 1979. *ARRB Proceedings*, **11**, 1–12.

Cameron, M.H, Strang, P.M. & Vulcan, A.P. (1981). Evaluation of random breath testing in Victoria, Australia. In: *Alcohol, Drugs and Traffic Safety*, **Vol III**, 1364–1381. (Goldberg, L. ed.) Almqvist & Wiksell International, Stockholm.

Campbell, D.T. & Ross, H. L. (1968). The Connecticut crackdown on speeding. Time-series data in quasi-experimental research. *Law and Society Review*, **3**, 32–53.

Carey, S.M., Fuller, B.E., Kissick, K., Taylor, E. & Zold-Kilbourn, P. (2008). *Michigan DUI courts outcome evaluation*. Portland, OR: NPC Research; Lansing, MI: Michigan Supreme Court, State Court Administrative Office.

Cedersund, H-Å. (2008). *Hur påverkades hastigheterna av höjda böter*? VTI-notat 19-2008. Linköping, Väg- och transportforskningsinstitutet.

Chaplin, J.P. & Krawiec, T.S. (1970). *Systems and Theories of Psychology*. Second Edition. Holt, Rinehart and Winston Inc., London.

Chen, W, Cooper, P. & Pinili, M. (1995). Driver accident risk in relation to the penalty point system in British Columbia. *Journal of Safety Research*, **26**, 9–18.

Chin, H. C. (1989). Effect of automatic red-light cameras on red-running. *Traffic Engineering and Control*, **30**, 175–179.

Chin, H.C. & Quddus, M.A. (2003). Applying the random effect negative binomial model to examine traffic accident occurrence at signalized intersections. *Accident Analysis and Prevention*, **35**, 253–259.

Chipman, M.L. (1982). The role of exposure, experience and demerit point levels in the risk of collision. *Accident Analysis and Prevention*, **14**, 475–483.

Christophersen, A. (1990). Kombinasjonsrus-et alvorlig trafikkproblem. *Samferdsel*, **29(3)**, 34–35.

City of Charlotte. (2001). *SafeLight crash analysis 2001*. http://www.charmeck.org/Departments/Transportation/Special + Programs/SafeLight + Crash + Analysis + 2001.htm (accessed 17. sept. 2007).

Coben, J.H. & Larkin, G.L. (1999). Effectiveness of ignition interlock devices in reducing drunk driving recidivism. *American Journal of Preventive Medicine*, **16**, 81–87.
Cohen, A., Dehejia, R.H. (2004). The effect of automobile insurance and accident liability laws on traffic fatalities. *The Journal of Law and Economics*, **47**, 357–393.
Colón, I. (1983). County level prohibition and alcohol-related fatal motor vehicle accidents. *Journal of Safety Research*, **14**, 101–104.
Colón, I. (1991). Letters to the editor, response: Does county-level prohibition increase fatal motor vehicle accidents? *Journal of Safety Research*, **22**, 49–51.
Colón, I. & Cutter, H.S. (1983). The Relationship of Beer Consumption and State Alcohol And Motor Vehicle Policies To Fatal Accidents. *Journal of Safety Research*, **14**, 83–89.
Cook, P.J. & Tauchen, G. (1984). The effect of minimum drinking age legislation on youthful auto fatalities 1970–1977. *The Journal of Legal Studies*, **XIII (1)**, 169–190.
Council, F.M., Persaud, B., C., Eccles, Lyon, K. & Griffith (2005a). *Safety evaluation of red-light cameras*. Report FHWA-HRT-05-048.
Council, F.M., Persaud, B., Lyon, C., Eccles, K., Griffith, M, Zaloshnja, E. & Miller, T. (2005b). Implementing red light camera programs. *Transportation Research Record*, **1922**, 38–43.
Crancer, A. (2003). *An analysis of Idaho's Kootenai County DUI court*. http://www.ndci.org/pdf/Kootenai_County_DUI_Evaluation.pdf (accessed 3. nov. 2008).
Crosby, I. (1996). *Portland's asset forfeiture program: The effectiveness of vehicle seizure in reducing rearrest among "problem" drunk drivers. Policing in central an eastern Europe*. College of Police and Security Studes, Slovenia.
Datta, T.K., Schattler, K. & Datta, S. (2000). Red light violations and crashes at urban intersections. *Transportation Research Record*, **1734**, 52–58.
Decina, L.E., Temple, M.G. & Dorer, H.S. (1994). Increasing child safety-seat use and proper use among toddlers. *Accident Analysis and Prevention*, **26**, 667–673.
Dee, T.S. (1999). State alcohol policies, teen drinking and traffic fatalities. *Journal of Public Economics*, **72**, 289–315.
Dee, T.S. (2001). Does setting limites save lives? The case of 0.08 BAC laws. *Journal of Policy Analysis and Management*, **20**, 111–128.
Derby, N.M & Hurst, P.M. (1987).The effects of random stopping in New Zealand. In: *Alcohol, Drugs and Traffic Safety-T86*, 421–427. (Nordzij, P. C & R. Roszbach. eds) Excerpta Medica, Amsterdam.
DeYoung, D.J. (1999). An evaluation of the specific deterrent effects of vehicle impoundment on suspended, revoked, and unlicensed drivers in California. *Accident Analysis and Prevention*, **31**, 45–53.

DeYoung, D.J. (2000). An Evaluation of the General Deterrent Effect of Vehicle Impoundment on Suspended and Revoked Drivers in California. *Journal of Safety Research*, **31**, 51–59.

DeYoung, D.J. (2002). An evaluation of the implementation of ignition interlock in California. *Journal of Safety Research*, **33**, 473– 482.

DeYoung, D.J. (1995). *An evaluation of the effectiveness of California drinking driver programs*. Report CAL-DMV-RSS-95-146. Sacramento, Cal., California Department of Motor vehicles.

Diamantopoulou, K. & Cameron, M. (1998). *Localised effects on crashes of the country random breath testing and publicity program in Victoria*. In: Proceedings of the 19th ARRB Conference, Sydney, Australia, p. 50–65.

Diamantopoulou, K., Cameron, M. (2002). *An evaluation of the effectiveness of overt and covert speed enforcement achieved through mobile radar operations*. Report No. 187. Monash University Accident Research Centre MUARC, Clayton, Victoria.

Diamantopoulou, K., Cameron, M. & Shtifelman, M. (1998). *Evaluation of Moving Mode Radar for Speed Enforcement in Victoria, 1995–1997*. Report No.141. Monash University Accident Research Centre.

Dills, A.K., Jacobson, M. & Miron, J.A. (2005). The effect of alcohol prohibition on alcohol consumption: evidenve from drunkenness arrests. *Economic Letters*, **86**, 279–284.

Dosselaar, M., van Winterink, J.M.G., & Benjamins, H. (1988). *Actie autogordel Utrecht 1988: evaluatieverslag*. Utrecht: Werkgroep Actie Autogordel Utrecht.

Drummond, A.E. & Torpey, S.E. (1985). *Driver improvement program evaluation*. Report No 11/85. Victoria, Road Traffic Authority, Victoria.

Dyke, J.V. & Womble, K. (1988). *The impact of minimum drinking age laws on fatal crash involvements an update of the NHTSA analyses*. DOT HS 807 349 NHTSA Technical Report. National Highway Traffic Safety Administration/U.S: Department of Transportation, Washington, DC.

Eccles, K.A. & McGee, H.W. (2001). *A history of the yellow and all-red intervals for traffic signals*. Report IR-113. Washington, DC, Institute of Transportation Engineers.

Eibner, C., Morral, A.R., Pacula, R.L. & MacDonald, J. (2006). Is the drug court modell exportable? The cost-effectiveness of a driving-under-the-influence court. *Journal of Substance Abuse Treatment*, **31**, 75–85.

Eisenberg, D. (2001). *Evaluating the effectiveness of a 0.08% BAC limit and other policies related to drunk driving*. Standord, CA: Stanford Institute for Economic Policy Research, Stanford University.

Ekström B., Kritz, L-B. & Strömgren, L. (1966). *Försök med förstärkt trafikövervakning på europavägarna 3 och 18 sommaren 1965*. Statens Trafiksäkerhetsråd, Stockholm.

Elvik, R. (1997a). *Vegtrafikklovgivning, kontroll og sanksjoner. Potensialet for å bedre trafikksikkerheten og nytte-kostnadsvurdering av ulike tiltak*. TØI-notat 1073/97. Oslo: Institute of Transport Economics.

Elvik R. (1997b). Effects of accidents of automatic speed enforcement in Norway. *Transportation Research Record*, **1597**, 1–19.

Elvik, R. (2006). Are individual preferences always a legitimate basis for evaluating the costs and benefits of public policy?: The case of road traffic law enforcement. *Transport Policy*, **13**, 379–385.

Elvik, R. (2007). *Prospects for improving road safety in Norway*. Report 897. Oslo: Institute of Transport Economics.

Elvik, R. & Christensen, P. (2004). *Virkninger av økte satser for gebyr og forenklet forelegg på lovlydighet i trafikken*. TØI rapport 725/2004. Oslo- Transportøkonomisk institutt.

Elvik, R., Christensen, P. (2007). The deterrent effect of increasing fixed penalties for traffic offences: The Norwegian experience. *Journal of Safety Research*, **38**, 689–695.

Endresen, C. (1978). *Politiets farstovervåking og bilførernes oppfatninger av den*. TØI Report. Oslo: Institute of Transport Economics.

Epperlein, T. (1987). Initial deterrent effects of the crackdown on drinking drivers in the state of Arizona. *Accident Analysis and Prevention*, **19**, 285–303.

Epperson, W.V. & Harano, R.M. (1975). An evaluation of some additional factors influencing the effectiveness of warning letters. *Accident Analysis and Prevention*, **7**, 239–247.

Erke, A. & Vaa, T. (2008). *Evaluering av bruk av skilt ved bilbeltekontroller*. TØI-rapport 951/2008. Oslo: Transportøkonomisk institutt.

Evans, L. (1987a). Belted and Unbelted driver Accident Involvement Rates Compared. *Journal of Safety Research*, **18**, 57–64.

Evans, L. (1987b). Estimating Fatality Reductions from Increased Safety Belt Use. *Risk Analysis*, **7**, 49–57.

Evans, W.D., Neville, D. & Graham, J. (1991). General deterrence of drunk driving: Evaluation of recent American policies. *Risk Analysis*, **11**, 279–289.

Farraher, B.A.B., Weinholzer, R. & Kowski, M.P. (1999). *The effect of advanced warning flashers on red light running*. Report CD-006. Washington DC: Institute of Transportation Engineers.

Fell J.C., Langston E.A. & Tippetts A.S. (2005). *Evaluation of four state impaired driving enforcement demonstration programs: Georgia, Tennessee, Pennsylvania and Louisiana*. In: 49th Annual Proceedings Association for the Advancement Automotive Medicine, September 12–14, Boston, Massachusetts, pp. 311–326.

Ferguson, M., Sheehan, M., Davey, J. & Watson, B. (1999). *Drink driving rehabilitation: the present context*. Road Safety Research Report CR 184.

Queensland, Australia: Centre for Accident Research and Technology, Queensland University of Technology.

Ferreira, J. & Sicherman, A. (1976). The impact of Massachusetts' reduced drinking age on auto accidents. *Accident Analysis and Prevention*, **8**, 229–239.

Fleck, J.L. & Smith, B.B. (1999). *Can we make red light runners stop? Red light photo enforcement in San Francisco, California*. San Francisco Department of Parking and Traffic. http://www.ci.sf.ca.us/dpt/press.htm.

Fowler, W.E. & Alcorn, J. (2002). The use of legal motivators in the treatment of drunken driers: Questioning the assumptions. *The Chronicle*, **50**, 10–12.

Fox, H. (1996). *Accidents at signal controlled junctions and pelican crossings in Glasgow*. Scottish Office Central Research Unit, Glasgow.

Frank, L. (1986). *The effect of the 1983 RBT 'blitz' on the frequency of casualty accidents in Melbourne residential streets*. Report No. GR/86/16. Road Traffic Authority of Victoria.

Fuchs, C. (1980). Wisconsin driver improvement program: A treatment-control evaluation. *Journal of Safety Research*, **12**, 107–114.

Fuller, R. (2006). Mission impossible? A retrospective of the effectiveness of a high-intensity enforcement campaign. In: *Behavioural research in road safety: Eleventh seminar proceedings*. Twelfth Seminar. London: Department for Transport.

Gains, A., Heydecker, B., Shrewsbury, J., & Robertson, S. (2004). *The national safety camera programme. Three-year evaluation report*. London: PA Consulting Group.

Garber, N.J., Miller, J.S., Abel, R.E., Eslambolchi, S. & Korukonda, S.K. (2007). *The impact of red light cameras (photo-red enforcement) in Virginia*. Final report VTRC 07-R2. Virginia Transportation Research Council. Charlottesville, Virginia.

Garber, N.J., Miller, J.S., Eslambolchi, S., Khandelwal, R., Mattingly, K.M., Sprinkle, K.M. & Wachendorf, P.L. (2005). *An evaluation of red light camera (photo-red) enforcement programs in Virginia*. Final Report VTRC 05-R21. Virginia Transportation Research Council. Charlottesville, Virginia.

Gaudry, M. (1987). *Responsibility for accidents: relevant results selected from the DRAG model*. Publication # 544, Centre de recherche sur les transports, Université de Montréal.

Geary, L.L., Ledingham, K.A. & Maloney S.C. (2005). Connecticut statewide sTEP wave evaluation. *Journal of Safety Research*, **36**, 333–340.

Giacopassi, D. & Winn, R. (1995). Alcohol availability and alcohol-related crashes: Does distance make a difference? *The American Journal of Drug and Alcohol Abuse*, **21**, 407–416.

Giæver, T. & Tveit, Ø. (1998). *Erfaringer med automatisk rødlyskontroll – vurdering av videre drift*. SINTEF rapport STF22 A97067.

Gjerde, H. & Mørland, J. (1991). Høy recidivisme blant promillekjørere. *Samferdsel*, **20(8)**, 30.

Glad, A. (1985a). *Omfanget av og variasjonen i promillekjøringen.* TØI-notat av 28.5.1985. Oslo: Institute of Transport Economics.

Glad, A. (1985b). *Omfanget av og variasjonen i promillekjøringen. Reviderte resultater fra en landsomfattende promilleundersøkelse i 1981–82.* TØI-notat nr 740. Oslo: Institute of Transport Economics.

Glad, A. (1985c). *Research on drinking and driving i Norway. A survey of recent research on drinking and driving and on drinking drivers.* TØI-notat. Oslo: Institute of Transport Economics.

Glad, A. & Vaa, T. (1997). Lavere promillegrense krever mer kontroll. *Samferdsel*, **4**, 9–10.

Glad, A. & Vaas, K. (1993). *Ruspåvirket kjøring og ruspåvirkete førere. Et informasjonshefte om situasjonen i Norge.* Transportøkonomisk institutt/Rusmiddeldirektoratet, Oslo.

Goldenbeld, C. & van Schagen, I. (2005). The effects of speed enforcement with mobile radar on speed and accidents. An evaluation study on rural roads in the Dutch province Friesland. *Accident Analysis and Prevention*, **37**, 1135–1144.

Golob, J.M., Cho, S., Curry, J.P./Golob, T.F. (2002). *Impacts of the San Diego photo red light enforcement system on traffic safety.* Report UCI-ITS-WP-02-11. Irvine, California: Institute of Transportation Studies.

Gras, J.A. & Noordzij, P.C. (1987). *Actie autogordels Gelderland: een evaluatie.* Leiden: Rijksuniversiteit Leiden, Werkgroep Veiligheid.

Green, R.E., French, J.F., Haberman, P.W. (1991). The effects of combining sanctions and rehabilitation for driving under the influence: an evaluation of the New Jersey Alcohol Countermeasures Program. *Accident Analysis and Prevention*, **23**, 543–555.

Gruenewald, P.J. & Ponicki, W.R. (1995). The relationship of the retail availability of alcohol and alcohol sales to alcohol-related traffic crashes. *Accident Analysis and Prevention*, **27**, 249–259.

Gundy, C.M. (1988). The effectiveness of combination of police enforcement and public information for improving seat-belt use. I: *Road User Behaviour - Theory and Research*, (Rothengatter, J. A & R. A. de Bruin, eds) Van Gorcum, Assen/Maastricht.

Hagen, K-E. (1992). *Kostnads- og inntektsanalyse av politiets trafikkontroller.* (TØI-Report nr 116/1992. Oslo: Institute of Transport Economics.

Hagen, K-E. (1994). *Rullering av samfunnsøkonomisk regnskapssystem for trafikkulykker og trafikksikkerhetstiltak (SRT) for 1992.* Arbeidsdokument TST/0570/94. Oslo: Institute of Transport Economics.

Hagen, R.E. (1978). The efficacy of licensing controls as a countermeasure for multiple DUI offenders. *Journal of Safety Research*, **10**, 115–122.

Hagen, R. E., Williams, R. L. & McConell, E. J. (1979). The traffic safety impact of alcohol abuse treatment as an alternative to mandated licensing controls. *Accident Analysis and Prevention*, **11**, 275–291.

Hagenzieker, M. (1991). The effects of enforcement and rewards on safety-belt use: A field study in the Netherlands. I: *Proceedings of the internastional road safety symposium* in Copenhagen, Denmark, September 19–21, 1990, 65–68. (Koornstra, M. J. & J. Christensen eds). SWOV Institute for Road Safety Research, Leidschendam.

Hagenzieker, M., Bijleveld, F.D. & Davidse, R. (1997). Effects of incentive programs to stimulate safety belt use: A meta-analysis. *Accident Analysis and Prevention*, **29**, 759–777.

Haldorsen, I. (2007). *Dybdeanalyser av dødsulykker i vegtrafikken – Nasjonal årsrapport for ulykkesanalysegruppenes arbeid i 2006*. Rapport 09/2007, Statens vegvesen.

Haque, M.O. & Cameron, M. (1989). Effect of the Victorian zero BAC legislation on serious casualty accidents: July 1984-December 1985. *Journal of Safety Research*, **20**, 129–137.

Haque, O., Strang, P. & Crabb, M. (1986). *Evaluation of the Victorian BAC legislation.* Interim Report RN/86/5. Evaluation and Statistical Sevices Section/Road Traffic Authority – Victoria.

Harano, R. M. & Peck, R.C. (1972). The effectiveness of a uniform traffic school curriculum for negligent drivers. *Accident Analysis and Prevention*, **4**, 13–45.

Hardes, G., Gibberd, R.W., Lam, P. et al. (1985). Effects of random breath testing on hospital admissions of traffic accident casualties in the Hunter Health Region. *Medical Journal Aus*, **142**, 625–626.

Harrison, W., Newman, S., Baldock, M. & McLean, J. (2003). *Drink-driving enforcement — Issues in developing best practice*. Austroads Publication No. AP–R220/03. Sydney NSW, Australia: Austroads Incorporated.

Hauer E., Ahlin, F.J. & Bowser, J.S. (1982). Speed enforcement and speed choice. *Accident Analysis and Prevention*, **14**, 267–278.

Heinrich, H.C. (1991). Strategies to increase the use of restraint systems: Report about Germany. I: *Strategies to increase the use of restraint systems*. (Hagenzieker, M.P ed). (Report no R-91-60-sidene 29-33). SWOV Institute for Road Safety Research, Leidschendam.

Helai, H., Chor, C.H. & Haque, M.M. (2008). Severity of driver injury and vehicle damage in traffic crashes at intersections: A Bayesian hierarchical analysis. *Accident Analysis and Prevention*, **40(1)**, 45–54.

Helander, C. J. (1984). Intervention Strategies for Accident-Involved Drivers: An Experimental Evaluation of Current California Policy and Alternatives. *Journal of Safety Research*, **15**, 23–40.

Henstridge, J., Homel, R., Mackay, P., 1997. *The long-term effects of random breath testing in four Australian states: A time series analysis*. No. CR 162 Canberra, Australia: Federal Office of Road Safety.

Hillier, W., Ronczka, J. & Schnerring, F. (1993). *An evaluation of red-light cameras in Sydney*. Research Note 1/93 - February 1993. Roads and Traffic Authority, New South Wales, Road Safety Bureau, New South Wales.

Hingson, R., Heeren, T., Kovenock, D., Mangione, T., Meyers, A.M.; Lederman, R. & Scotch, N.A. (1987). Effects of Maine's 1981 and Massachusett's 1982 Driving-Under-the-Influence legislation. *American Journal of Public Health*, **77**, 593–597.

Hingson, R. Heeren, T. & Winter, M. (1994). Lower legal blood alcohol limits for young drivers. *Public Health Rep.*, **109**, 738–744.

Hingson, R. Heeren, T. & Winter, M. (1996). Lowering state legal blood alcohol limits to 0.08%: the effect on fatal motor vehicle crashes. *American Journal of Public Health*, **86**, 1297–1299.

Hingson, R.W., Scotch, N., Mangione, T., Meyers, A., Glantz, L., Heeren, T., Lin, N., Mucatel, M. & Pierce, G. (1983). Impact of legislation raising the legal drinking age in Massachusetts from 18 to 20. *American Journal of Public Health*, **73**, 163–170.

Holder, H.D., Voas, R.B. & Gruenwald, P.J. (1997). *A comprehensive community program to prevent alcohol-involved crashes: Early results from a trial in the U.S.* In: Proceedings of the 14th International Conference of Alcohol, Drugs and Traffic T'97, Annecy, France.

Homel, R. (1988). *Policing and punishing the drinking driver. A study of general and specific deterrence.* Springer Verlag, New York/Berlin.

Homel, R. (1994). Drink-driving law enforcement and the legal blood alcohol limit in New South Wales. *Accident Analysis and Prevention*, **26(2)**, 147–155.

Hook, D., Kirkwood, A., & Evans, D. (1995). Speed cameras in Oxfordshire. *Highways and Transportation*, **42**, 11–13.

Hooke, A., Knox, J. & Portas, D. (1996). *Cost benefit analysis of traffic light & speed cameras.* Police Research Series Paper 20. London: Police Research Group.

Hubicka, B., Laurell, H. & Bergman, H. (2008). Criminal and alcohol problems among Swedish drunk drivers – predictors of DUI relapse. *International Journal of Law and Psychiatry*, **31**, 471–478.

Hunter, W.W., Stewart, R., Stutts, J.C. & Rodgman, E.A. (1990). Observed and self-reported seat belt wearing as related to prior traffic accidents and convictions. *Accident Analysis and Prevention*, **22**, 297–300.

Hurst, P.M & P.G. Wright. (1981). Deterrence at last. The Ministry of Transport's Alcohol Blitzes. In: *Alcohol, Drugs and Traffic Safety*, **VOL III**, 1283–1297. (Goldberg, L. ed) Almqvist & Wiksell International, Stockholm.

ICF Consulting. (2003). *Cost-benefit analysis of road safety improvements.* Final Report. London: ICF Consulting Ltd.

Ingebrigtsen, S. & Fosser, S. (1991). *Dekkstandardens betydning for trafikkulykker om vinteren.* TØI-Report 75. Oslo: Institute of Transport Economics.

Jewell, R.T. & Brown, R.W. (1995). Alcohol availability and alcohol-related motor vehicle accidents. *Applied Economics*, **27**, 759–765.

Joksch, H.C. (1991). Letters to the editor: Does county-level prohibition increase fatal motor vehicle accidents? *Journal of Safety Research*, **22**, 49–51.

Jones, A.P., Sauerzapf, V., & Haynes, R. (2008). The effects of mobile speed camera introduction on road traffic crashes and casualties in a rural county of England. *Journal of Safety Research*, **39**, 101–110.

Jones, B. (1987). Oregon's habitual traffic offender program: An evaluation of the effectiveness of license revocation. *Journal of Safety Research*, **18**, 19–26.

Jones, B. (1997). Age, gender and the effectiveness of high-threat letters: An analysis of Oregon's driver improvement advisory letters. *Accident Analysis and Prevention*, **29**, 225–234.

Jones, R.K., Joksch, H.C., Lacey, J.H. & Schmidt, H.J. (1988). *Field Evaluation of Jail Sanctions for DWI*. Report DOT HS 807 325. Washington DC: National Highway Traffic Safety Administration.

Jones, R.K., Joksch, H.C., Lacey, J.H. et al. (1995). *Site report: Wichita, Kansas, field test of combined speed, alcohol and safety belt enforcement strategies*. Report DOT HS 808 244.

Jones, RK & Lacey, JH. (1999). *Evaluation of a day reporting center for repeat DWI offenders*. DOT HS 808 989. Washington, DC: National Highway Traffic Safety Administration.

Jones, R.K. & Lacey, J.H. (2000). *State of Knowledge of Alcohol-Impaired Driving: Research on Repeat DWI Offenders*. Washington DC: National Highway Traffic Safety Administration.

Jones, R.K. & Rodriguez-Iglesias, C. (2004). *Evaluation of lower BAC limits for convicted OUI offenders in Maine*. Report DOT HS 809 827. Washington DC: National Higway Traffic Safety Administration.

Jones, R.K., Wiliszowski, C.H. & Lacey, J.H. (1996). *Evaluation of alternative programs for repeat DWI offenders*. Report DOT HS 808 493. Washington DC: National Highway Traffic Safety Administration.

Kadell, D. (1987). Traffic safety impacts of the Home Instruction/Point Reduction Incentive (HI/PRI) program. *Journal of Safety Research*, **18**, 149–178.

Kaestner, N.; Speight, L. (1975). Successful alternatives to license suspension: The defensive driving course and the probationary license. *Journal of Safety Research*, **7**, 56–66.

Kaestner, N. & Syring, E. M. (1967). Accident and violation reduction through brief driver improvement interviews. *Traffic Safety Research Review*, December, **11**, 99–105.

Kaestner, N. & Syring, E. M. (1968). Follow-up of brief driver improvement interviews in Oregon. *Traffic Safety Research Review*, December, **12**, 111–117.

Kaestner, N., Warmoth, E.J. & Syring, E.M. (1967). Orgeon study of advisory letters: The effectiveness of warning letters in driver improvement. *Traffic Safety Research Review*, **11**, 67–72.

Kang, J.G. (2002). Changes of speed and safety by automated speed enforcement systems. *IATSS Research*, **26**, 38–44.
Kaplan, S. & Prato, C.G. (2007). Impact of BAC limit reduction on different population segments: A Poisson fixed effect analysis. *Accident Analysis and Prevention*, **39**, 1146–1154.
Kaye, B. K., Sapolsky, B.S. & Montgomery, D.J. (1995). Increasing seat belt use through PI&E and enforcement: The Thumbs Up Campaign. *Journal of Safety Research*, **26**, 235–245.
Kearns, I.B. (1988). *The effect of aerial speed enforcement on traffic crashes*. Research note RN 4/88. Traffic Authority of New South Wales.
Kearns, I.B. & Goldsmith, H.J. (1984). *The impact on traffic crashes of the introduction of random breath testing in New South Wales*. In: Proceedings of the 12th Australian Road Research Board Conference, pp. 81–95.
Kim, K., Nitz, L., Richardson, J. & Li, L. (1995). Personal and behavioral predictors of automobile crash and injury severity. *Accident Analysis and Prevention*, **27**, 469–481.
King, M. (1988). *Random breath testing operation and effectiveness in 1987*. Australian Department of Transport, Road Safety Division, (Report Series 7/88), Australia.
Kriz, K., Moran, C. & Regan, M. (2006). *An analysis of a red-light camera program in the city of Milwaukee*. University of Wisconsin-Madison.
Krohn, F. (1996). *Automatisk trafikkontroll-oppsummering av effekter*. Rapport nr TTS 7/1996. Statens vegvesen/Vegdirektoratet, Transport og trafikksikkerhetsavdelingen-Transportanalysekontoret/Via Nova, Oslo.
Lacey, J.H. & Jones, R.K. (2000). *Evaluation of New Mexico's anti-DWI efforts*. Report DOT HS 809 024. Washington DC, National Highway Traffic Safety Administration.
Lacey, J.H., Jones, R.K. & Fell, J.C. (1997). *The effectiveness of the 'Checkpoint Tennessee' program"*. In: Mercier-Guyon, C. (Eds.), Alcohol, Drugs, and Traffic Safety, CERMT, Annecy, Vol. 2, pp. 969–975.
Lacey, J.H., Wiliszowski, C.H. & Jones, R.K. (2003). *An impact evaluation of underage drinking prevention projects*. Report DOT HS 809 670. Washington DC: National Highway Traffic Safety Administration.
Lamm, R. & Kloeckner, J.H. (1988). Increase of Traffic Safety by Surveillance of Speed Limits with Automatic Radar Devices on a Dangerous Section of a German Autobahn: A Long-Term Investigation. *Transportation Research Record*, 974, 8–16.
Landes, E.M. (1982). Insurance, liability, and accidents: A theoretical and empirical investigation of the effects of no-faults accidents. *Journal of Law and Economics*, **25**, 49–65.
Langworthy, R. & Latessa, E.J. (1993). Treatment of chronic drunk drivers: the turning point project. *Journal of Criminal Justice*, **21**, 265–276.

Langworthy, R. & Latessa, E.J. (1996). Treatment of chronic drunk drivers: A four-year follow-up of the turning point project. *Journal of Criminal Justice*, **24**, 273–281.

Lapham, S.C., Kapitula, L.R., de Baca, J. & McMillan, G.P. (2006). Impaired-driving recidivism among repeat offenders following an intensive court-based intervention. *Accident Analysis and Prevention*, **38**, 162–169.

Lau, H. (1986). *Evaluation of a red light camera at a pedestrian operated signal crossing*. Road Traffic Authority, Victoria/Australia.

Leggett, L. M. W. (1988). *The effect on accident occurrence of long-term, low-intensity police enforcement*. Proceedings of the 14th ARRB Conference, Part 4, 92–104, 1988.

Lemaire, J. (1995). *Bonus-Malus Systems in Automobile Insurance*. Kluwer Academic Publishers, Boston.

L'Hoste, J., Duval, H. & Lassarre, S. (1985). Experimental study of the effective-ness of random alcohol testing in France. In: *Alcohol, Drugs and Traffic Safety, Proceedings of the Ninth International Conference on Alcohol, Drugs and Traffic Safety* - San Juan, Puerto Rico, 1983, 831–839. (Kaye, S. & G. W. Meier. eds) US Department of Transportation, Washington DC.

Li, L.K. & Waller, P.F. (1976). *Evaluation of the North-Carolina habitual offender law*. Chapel Hill, NC: University of North Carolina, Highway SAfety Research Center.

London Accident Analysis Unit. (1997). *West London Speed Camera Demonstration Project Analysis of accident and casualty data 36 months 'after' implementation and comparison with the 36 months 'before' data*. London Research Centre (United Kingdom). London Accident Analysis Unit.

Lund, A., Stuster, J. & Fleming, J.A. (1989). Special publicity and enforcement of California's belt use law: Making a "secondary" law work. *Journal of Criminal Justice*, **17**, 329–341.

Lund, H.V. & Jørgensen, N.O. (1974). *Et forsøg med skærpet politiovervågning på hovedvej A1*. (Rapport 16), Rådet for trafiksikkerhedsforskning, København.

Lynn, C.W., Jernigan, J.D., Norris, A. & Froning, P. (1993). Investigation of the effectiveness of the Virginia Habitual Offender Act. *Transportation Research Record*, **1401**, 90–99.

Maisey, G.E. (1984). *The effect of lowering the statutory alcohol limit for first year drivers from 0.08 to 0.02 gm/100 ml*. Research Report 84/2. Research & Statistics Section/Police Department/Traffic Licensing and Services Centre, Perth.

Males, M.A. (1986). The minimum purchase age for alcohol and young-driver fatal crashes: A long-term view. *The Journal of Legal Studies*, **XV**, 181–212.

Mann, R.E. Vingilis, E.R., Gavin, D., Adlaf, E. & Anglin, L. (1991). Sentence severity and the drinking driver: Relationships with traffic safety outcome. *Accident Analysis and Prevention*, **23**, 483–491.

Mara M.K., Davies, R.B. & Frith, W.J. (1996). *Evaluation of the effects of compulsory breath testing and speed cameras in New Zealand*. In: Proceedings of the 18th ARRB

Transport Research Conference and Transit New Zealand Land Transport Symposium, Christchurch, New Zealand, Part 5, pp. 269–282.

Marowitz, L.A. (1998). Predicting DUI recidivism: blood alcohol concentration and driver record factors. *Accident Analysis and Prevention*, **30**,545–554.

Marques, P.R., Tippetts, A.S., Voas, R.B. & Beirness, D.J. (2001). Predicting repeat DUI offenses with the alcohol interlock recorder. *Accident Analysis and Prevention*, **33**, 609–619.

Marsh, W.C., Coppin, R. S. & Peck, R. C. (1967). A Reevaluation of Group Driver Improvement Meetings. *Highway Research Record*, **163**, 120–131.

Marsh, W.C. (1992). *Negligent-operator treatment evaluation system: Program effectiveness*. Report No 6, CAL-DMV-RSS-92-137. Research and Development Section, Department of Motor Vehicles, Sacramento, California.

Marsh, W.C.& Healy, E.J. (1995). *Negligent-operator treatment evaluation system: Program effectiveness*. Report No 7, CAL-DMV-RSS-95-153. Research and Development Office, Department of Motor Vehicles, Sacramento, California.

Mann, T.S., Brown, S.L. & Coxon, C.G.M. (1994). *Evaluation of the effects of installing red light cameras at selected Adelaide intersections*. South Australian Department of Transport Office of Road Safety, September 1994, Walkerville.

Martin, S.E, Annan, S. & Forst, B. (1993). The special deterrent effects of a jail sanction on first-time drunk drivers: A quasi-experimental study. *Accident Analysis and Prevention*, **25**, 561–568.

Mason, B. (1970a): *Operation 500*: Final Report # IV A-1 U.S. 101 Accidents. State of California, Department of California Highway Patrol, Operational Planning and Analysis Section. March 1970.

Mason, B. (1970b): *Operation 500*: Final Report # IV A2 I-80 Accidents. State of California, Department of California Highway Patrol, Operational Planning and Analysis Section. June 1970.

Masten, S.V. & Peck, R.C. (2004). Problem driver remediation: A meta-analysis of the driver improvement literature. *Journal of Safety Research*, **35**, 403–425.

Mathijssen, M.P.M. (1992). *Integraal verkeerstoezicht in de subregio Leiden: effecten op het gebruik van autogordels*. Leidschendam, Stichting: Wetenschappelijk Onderzoek Verkeersveiligheid SWOV.

Mathijssen, M.P.M. & de Craen, S. (2004). *Evaluatie van de regionale verkeershandhavingsplannen (Evaluation of the regional traffic management plan)*. SWOV Report R-2004-4.

McBride, R.S. & Peck, R. C. (1970). Modifying negligent driving behaviour through warning letters. *Accident Analysis and Prevention*, **2**, 147–174.

McCarthy, P. (2003). Alcohol-related crashes and alcohol availability in grass-roots communities. *Applied Economics*, **35**, 1331–1338.

McCartt, A.T. & Northrup, V.S. (2003). *Enhanced sanctions for higher BACs: Evaluation of Minnesotas high-BAC law*. Report DOT HS 809 677. Washington DC: National Highway Traffic Safety Association.

McCartt A.T. & Rood, D.H. (1989). *Evaluation of the New York State Police 55 MPH Speed Enforcement Project*. (Final Report DOT HS 807 618). US Department of Transportation, National Highway Traffic safety Administration, Washington DC.

McGee, H.W. & Eccles, K.A. (2003). *Impact of red light camera enforcement on crash experience*. NCHRP Synthesis 310. Washington, DC.

McKnight, A.J. (1995). Meta-analysis of remedial interventions with drink/drive offenders: A useful clarification of what is and is not known. *Addiction*, **90**, 1591–1592.

McKnight, A.J. & Edwards, M.L. (1987). A taste of suspension: The preventive and deterrent value of limited license suspension. *31st Annual Conference of the American Association for Automotive Medicine*.

McLean, A.J., Clark, M.S., Dorsch, M., Holubowycz, O.T. & McCaul, K.A. (1984). *Random breath testing in South Australia: effects on drink-driving, accidents and casualties*. NHMRC Road Accident Research Unit, University of Adelaide, Adelaide.

McMillen, D.L., Adams, M.S., Wells-Parker, E., Pang, M.G. & Anderson, B.J. (1992). Personality traits and behaviour of alcohol-impaired drivers: A comparison of first and multiple offenders. *Addictive Behaviors* **17**, 407–414.

Meliker, J.R., Maio, R.F:, Zimmerman, M.A., Kim, H.M., Smith, S.C. & Wilson, M.L. (2004). Spatial analysis of alcohol-related motor vehicle crash injuries in southeastern Michigan. *Accident Analysis and Prevention*, **36**, 1129–1135.

Mercer, G.W. (1985). The relationships among driving while impaired charges, police drinking-driving roadcheck activity, media coverage and alcohol-related casualty traffic accidents. *Accident Analysis and Prevention*, **17**, pp. 467–474.

Mercer, G.W., Cooper, P.J. & Kristiansen, L. (1996). *A cost/benefit analysis of a 5-month intensive alcohol-impaired driving road check campaign*. In: Proceedings of the 40th Annual Conference of the Association for the Advancement of Automotive Medicine, Vancouver, British Columbia, Canada, 1996, pp. 283–292.

Miller T., Blewden M. & Zhang J.F. (2004). Cost savings from a sustained compulsory breath testing and media campaign in New Zealand. *Accident Analysis and Prevention*, **36**, 783–94.

Miller, T.R., Lestina, D.C. & Spicer, R.S. (1998). Highway crash costs in the United States by driver age, blood alcohol level, victim age, and restraint use. *Accident Analysis and Prevention*, **30**, 137–150.

Munden, J.M. (1966). An *experiment in enforcing the 30 mile/h speed limit*. RRL Report No 24. Road Research Laboratory, Harmondsworth.

MVA Consultancy (1995). *Running the red: an evaluation of Strathclyde Police's red light camera initiative.* http://www.scottishexecutive.gov.uk/Publications/1999/01/47e3bf41-bf11-470a-83bf-7f57095d0f0f (accessed 17.9.07).
Naor, E.M. & Nashold, R.D. (1975). Teenage driver fatalities following reduction in the legal drinking age. *Journal of Safety Research*, **7**, 74–79.
Negrin, D. (1995). Bonus/malus ou non? L'assurance automobile et la prevention des accidents. Paper presented at *OECD workshop on Automobile Insurance and Traffic Safety*, 10–12 May 1995, Tallinn, Estonia.
Nelson, J.P. (2001). Alcohol advertising and advertising bans: a xurvey of reseach methods, results and policy implications. *Advertising and Differentiated Products*, **10**, 239–295.
Neustrom, M.W. & Norton, W.M. (1993). The impact of drunk driving legslation in Louisiana. *Journal of safety research*, **24**, 107–121.
Newstead, S.V., & Cameron, M.H. (2003). *Evaluation of crash effects of the Queensland speed camera program.* Report No. 204. Victoria, Australia: Monash University, Accident Research Center.
Newstead, S., Cameron, M. & Narayan, S. (1998). *Further modelling of some major factors influencing road trauma trends Victoria: 1990–1996.* Report No. 129. Monash University Accident Research Centre, Australia.
Ng, C.H., Wong, Y.D. & Lum, K.M. (1997). The impact of red-light surveillance cameras on road safety in Singapore. *Road & Transport Research*, **6**, 72–81.
NHTSA (2002). *Traffic safety facts 2001.* Report DOT HS 809 484. US Department of Transportation, National Highway Traffic Safety Adminstration.
Nilsson, E. & Åberg, L. (1986). *Övervakning och påföljd.* TFD-forskning 1976–1983. TFB-rapport 1986:11. Transportforskningsberedningen, Stockholm.
Nilsson, R. & Engdahl, S. (1986). *Riktlinjer för trafikövervakningens utforming.* TFB-rapport 1986: 15. Stockholm: Transportforskningsberedningen.
Nochajski, T.H., Miller, B.A., Wieczorek, W.F. & Whitney, R. (1993). The effects of a dringing-driver treatment program. Does criminal history make a difference? *Criminal Justice and Behavior*, **20**, 174–189.
Nochajski, T.H. & Stasiewicz, P.R. (2006). Relapse to driving under the influence (DUI): A review. *Clinical Psychology Review*, **26**, 179–195.
Norström, T. & Laurell, H. (1997). Effects of lowering the legal BAC limit in Sweden. In: C. Mercier-Guyon (Ed.). *Proceedings of the 14th Internatinoal Conference on Alcohol, Drugs and Traffic Safety*, Annecy, France.
Novak, J.W. & Shumate, R.P. (1961). The use of "control groups" in highway accident research: A field study. *Traffic safety Research Review*, 20–24.
Nuyts, E. (2006). *Effectiviteit van onbemande camera's.* Report RA-2006-90. Limburg: Provinciale Hogeschool.

Nuyts, E. & Vesentini, L. (2006). *Effect van een gordelcampagne in Antwerpen*. Steunpunt Verkeersveiligheid, RA-2006-76, Diepenbeek.

O'Day, J. A. (1970). Before and after analysis of accidents involving students of the defensive driving course. *Accident Analysis and Prevention*, **2**, 175–188.

Oei, H.L. & Polak, P.H. (1992). *Effect van automatische waarschuwing en toezicht op snelheid en ongevallen. Resultaten van een evaluatie-onderzoek in vier provincies*. Rapport 92–23. SWOV, Leidschendam.

Parker, J.G. (2003). Enforcing suspended licenses: Tough laws, technology yield results. *Traffic Safety*, **103**, 8–9.

Peck, R., Voas, R.B. (2002). Forfeiture programs in California: Why so few? *Journal of Safety Research*, **33**, 245–258.

Peck, R.C. Arstein-Kerslake, G.W. & Helander, W.J. (1994). Psychometric and biographical correlates of drunk-driving recidivism and treatment program compliance. *Journal of Studies on Alcohol*, **55**, 667–678.

Peck, R.C., Gebers, M.A., Voas, R.B. & Romano, E. (2008). The relationship between blood alcohol concentration (BAC), age, and crash risk. *Journal of Safety Research*, **39**, 311–319.

Peck, R. C., Kelsey, S. L., Ratz, R. & Sherman, B. R. (1980). The effectiveness of accredited traffic violator schools in reducing accidents and violations. *Journal of Safety Research*, **12**, 68–77.

Pez, P. (2002). Weniger Unfälle durch Öffentlichkeitsarbeit und Verkehrsüberwachung. *Zeitschrift für Verkehrssicherheit*, **48**, 58–64.

Pihl, A. & Hamre, B. (1989). *Forsikringsnæringens skadeforebyggende arbeid*. Rapport. Norges forsikringsforbund, Oslo.

Planek, T.W., Schupack, S.A. & Fowler, R.C. (1974). An evaluation of the National Safety Council's defensive driving course in various states. *Accident Analysis and Prevention*, **6**, 271–297.

Preusser, D.F., Lund, A.K., Williams, A.F. & Blomberg, R.D. (1988a). Belt use by high-risk drivers before and after New York's seat belt use law. *Accident Analysis and Prevention*, **20(4)**, 245–250.

Preusser, D.F., Blomberg, R.D. & Ulmer, R.G. (1988b). Evaluation of the 1982 Wisconsin drinking and driving law. *Journal of Safety Research*, **19(1)**, 29–40.

Preusser, D.F, Ulmer, R.G. & Adams, J.R. (1976). Driver record evaluation of a drinking driver rehabilitation program. *Journal of Safety Research*, **8(3)**, 98–105.

Prothero, J. C. & Seals, T. A. (1978). Evaluation of Educational Treatment for Rehabili-tation of Problem Drivers. *Transportation Research Record*, **672**, 58–63.

Quaye, K. & Boase, P. (2004). First time drinking and driving offenders – unraveling the myth with ignition interlock and short-term suspension data. *17th Meeting of the International Council on Alcohol, Drugs and Traffic Safety*. Glasgow, Scotland: August 8–13, 2004.

Reinfurt, D.W., Campbell, B.J., Stewart, J.R. & Stutts, J.C. (1990). Evaluating the North Carolina safety belt wearing law. *Accident Analysis and Prevention*, **22**, 197–210.

Retting, R.A., Williams, A.F., Farmer, C.M. & Feldman, A.F. (1999a). Evaluation of red light camera enforcement in Fairfax Virginia. *ITE Journal* **69**, 30–34.

Retting, R.A., Williams,A.F., Farmer, C.M. & Feldman,A.F. (1999b). Evaluation of red light camera enforcement in Oxnard California. *Accident Analysis and Prevention* **31**, 169–174.

Retting, R.A., Ferguson, S.A. & Farmer, C.M. (2008). Reducing red light running through longer yellow signal timing and red light camera enforcement: Results of a field investigation. *Accident Analysis and Prevention*, **40(1)**, 327–333.

Retting, R.A. & Kyrychenko, S.Y. (2002). Reductions in injury crashes associated with red light camera enforcement in Oxnard, California. *American Journal of Public Health*, **92**, 1822–1825.

Rider, R., Voas, R.B., Kelley-Baker, T., Grosz, M. & Murphy, B. (2007). Preventing alcohol-related convictions: The effect of a novel curriculum for first-time offenders on DUI recidivism. *Traffic Injury Prevention*, **8**, 147–152.

Robertson, L.S., Rich, R.F. & Ross, H.L. (1973). Jail sentences for driving while intoxicated in Chicago: A judicial policy that failed. *Law & Society Review*, **8(1)**, 55–67.

Rogers, A. (1994). Effect of Minnesota's license plate impoundment law on recidivism of multiple DWI violators. *Alcohol, Drugs and Driving*, **10**, 127–134.

Rogers, P.N., Schoenig, S.E. (1994). A time series evaluation of California's 1982 driving-under-the-influence legislative reforms. *Accident Analysis and Prevention*, **26**, 63–78.

Roop, S.S. & Brackett, R.Q. (1980). *Evaluation of project increased traffic law enforcement*. Final report (80)05-09-C1-AA. College Station, TX: Texas A&M University.

Ross, H.L. (1977). Deterrence regained: The Cheshire constabulary's "Breathalyzer Blitz". *The Journal of Legal Studies*, **VI(1)**, 241–249.

Ross, H.L. (1982). *Deterring the Drinking Driver. Legal policy and Social Control.* Lexington Books, D.C. Heath and Company, Lexington; Massachusetts.

Ross, H.L. & Klette, H. (1995). Abandonment of mandatory jail for impaired drivers in Norway and Sweden. *Accident Analysis and Prevention*, **27**, 2, 151–157.

Ross, H.L., McCleary, R. & LaFree, G. (1990). Can mandatory jail laws deter drunk driving? The Arizona case. *The Journal of Criminal Law & Criminology*. **81(1)**, 156–170.

Ruhm, C.J. (1996). Alcohol policies and highway vehicle fatalities. *Journal of Health Economics*, **15**, 435–454.

Ruud, J. & Glad, A. (1990). *De promilledømte. En undersøkelse av innsatte ved Ilseng arbeidskoloni.* (TØI-Report nr 0056/1990). Oslo: Institute of Transport Economics.

Ryan, G.A., Hendrie, D. & Allotey, P. (1997). *Random breath testing in Western Australia.* In: Proceedings of the 41st Annual Conference of the Association for the Advancement of Automotive Medicine, Orlando, Florida, pp. 11–30.

Sadler, D.D., Perrine, M.W. & Peck, R.C. (1991). The long-term traffic safety impact of a pilot alcohol abuse treatment as an alternative to license suspensions. *Accident Analysis and Prevention*, **23(4)**, 203–224.

Saffer, H. & Chaloupka, F. (1989). Breath testing and highway fatality rates. *Applied Economics*, **21**, 901–912.

Saffer, H. & Grossman, M. (1987). Beer taxes, the legal drinking age, and youth motor vehicle fatalities. *Journal of Legal Studies*, **16**, 351–374.

Sager, T. (1974). *Økonomisk vurdering av bot eller fengsel som promilledom*. TØI-notat nr 161. Oslo: Institute of Transport Economics.

Sali, G.J. (1983). Evaluation of Boise Selective Traffic Enforcement Project, *Tranportation Research Record*, **910**, 68–93.

Salusjärvi, M. & Mäkinen T. (1988). *Experiment med hastighetsövervakning i Vanda*. Nordisk Kommitté för Transportforskning, 1988 (ISBN 87-88453-07 3).

Salzberg, P.M. & Moffat, J.M. (2004). Ninety five percent: An evaluation of law, policy, and programs to promote seat belt use in Washington state. *Journal of Safety Research*, **35**, 215–222.

Saunders, C.M. (1977). *A study on increased intensity of traffic law enforcement as a means of reducing accidents*. Report no 8. Reseach and Statistics Division, Road Traffic Authority, Perth, Australia.

Schade, F.-D. (1992). Rückfallsrisiko bei Geschwindigkeitsdelikten-trotz Ahndung unverändert? *Zeitschrift für Verkehrsicherheit*, **38**, 114–120.

Schattler, K.L., Hill, C. & Datta, T.K. (2002). Clearance interval design and red light violations. *ITE Conference Todays Transport Challenge: Meeting Our Customers Expectations*. Palm Harbor, Florida.

Schulte Gary, Aultman-Hall, L., McCourt & Stamatiadis, N. (2003). Consideration of driver home county prohibition and alcohol-related vehicle crashes. *Accident Analysis and Prevention*, **35**, 641–648.

Schultz-Grant, G., Peterson, R., Giles, B. & Egget, D.L. (2006). *Evaluation of advance warning signal installation*. Report UT-06.11. Provo, Utah: Brigham Young University, Department of Civil and Environmental Engineering.

Schultz, G.G., Peterson, R. & Eggett, D.L. (2007). *Evaluating the long term effectiveness of blank-out overhead dynamic warning signals*. TRB Paper No. 07-0783. Washington: Transportation Research Board 86 th Annual Meeting.

Schuster, D. H. (1969). Follow-up evaluation of the performance of driver imprivement classes for problem drivers. *Journal of Safety Research*, **1**, 80–87.

Sen, A. (2001). Do stricter penalties deter drinking and driving? An empirical investigation of Canadian impaired driving laws. *Canadian Journal of Economics*, **34**, 149–164.

Shin, K. & Washington, S. (2007). The impact of red light cameras on safety in Arizona. *Accident Analysis and Prevention*, **39(6)**, 1212–1221.

Shinar D. & McKnight, A.J. (1985). The effects of enforcement and public information on compliance. In: *Human Behaviour and Traffic safety* (Schwing R. C. & Evans L. eds). Plenum Press, New York.

Shoup, D.C. (1973). Cost effectiveness of urban traffic law enforcement. *Journal of Transport Economics and Policy*. **January**, **7**, 32–57.

Shults, R.A., Elder, R.W., Aleet, D.A., Thompson, R.S. & Nichols, J.L. (2004). Primary enforcement seat belt laws are effective even in the face of rising belt use rates. *Accident Analysis and Prevention*, **36**, 491–493.

Siskind, V. (1996). Does license disqualification reduce reoffence rates? *Accident Analysis and Prevention*, **28**, 519–524.

Sloan, F.A., Reilly, B.A., & Schenzler, C. (1994). Effects of prices, civil and criminal sanctions, and law enforcement on alcohol-related mortality. *Journal of Studies on Alcohol*, **55(4)**, 454–465.

Smiley, A., Persaud, B., Hauer, E. & Duncan, D. (1989). Accidents, convictions and demerit points: An Ontario driver records study. *Transportation Research Record*, **1238**, 53–64.

Smith, D.I. (1988). Effect on traffic safety of introducing a 0.05% blood alcohol level in Queensland, Australia. Medicine, *Science and the Law*, **28**, 165–170.

Smith, D.I., Maisey, G. E. & McLaughlin, K. (1990). Evaluation of the first year of random breath testing in Western Australia. *Proceedings of the 15th ARRB Conference*, 93–106. Australian Road Research Board, Vermont South, Victoria, Australia.

South, D., Harrison, W., Portans, I. & King, M. (1988). *Evaluation of the red light camera program and the owner onus legislation*. Report No SR/88/1. Road Traffic Authority, Hawthorne/Australia.

Staplin, L. (1993). Cost-effective driver improvement treatment in Pennsylvania. *Transportation Research Record*, **1401**, 26–36.

Statens vegvesen (1996). *Automatisk Trafikkontroll: Forslag til revisjon av retningslinjer (av 30.august 1993) for valg av strekninger for ATK-fart og ATK-rødlys*. Oslo, Statens vegvesen Vegdirektoratet, Kontor for drift og trafikkteknikk, oktober 1996.

Statens vegvesen Vestfold (1996). *Evaluering av ATK = Rødlys*. Brev av 1996-03-06 fra Statens vegvesen Vestfold til Vegdirektoratet v/Transportanalysekontoret (referanser hhv 96/0019 and 96/39 TAN). Oslo, Statens vegvesen Vegdirektoratet, Kontor for drift & trafikkteknikk, oktober 1996.

Stefan, C. (2006). *Section control – Automatic speed enforcement in the Kaisermühlen tunnel (Vienna, A22 motorway)*. Wien: Kuratorium für Verkehrssicherheit.

Stene, T.M., Sakshaug, K. & Moe, D. (2008). *Evaluering av prikkbelastning av førerkort*. Rapport SINTEF A4448. Trondheim: SINTEF Teknologi og Samfunn.

Stephen, M. (2004). *What is the effect of drier education programs on traffic crash and violation rates?* Report FHWA.AZ.04-546. Phoenix, Arizona, Arizona Department of Transportation.

Stevenson, M., Brewer, R.D. & Lee, V. (1998). The spatial relationship between licenced alcohol outlets and alcohol-related motor vehicle crashes in Gwinnett County, Georgia. *Journal of Safety Research*, **29**, 197–203.

Strathman, J.G., Kimpel, T.J. & Leistner, P. (2007). *Evaluation of the Oregon DMV driver improvement program.* Report FHWA-OR-RD-07-08. Washington DC, Federal Highway Administration and Salem, OR, Oregon Department of Transport.

Streff, F.M., Molnar, L.J. & Christoff, C. (1992). Increasing safety belt use in a secondary enforcement state: Evaluation of a three-county sepcial enforcement program. *Accident Analysis and Prevention*, **24**, 369–383.

Struckman-Johnson, D.L., Lund, A.K., Williams, A.F. & Osborne, D.W. (1989). Comparative effects of driver improvement programs on crashes and violations. *Accident Analysis and Prevention*, **21(3)**, 203–215.

Stuster, J.W. & Blowers, P.A. (1995). *Experimental evaluation of sobriety checkpoint programs.* Report DOT HS 808 287. Washington DC, National Highway Traffic Safety Association.

Summala, H., Näätänen, R., & Roine, M. (1980). Exceptional conditions of police enforcement: Driving speeds during the police strike. *Accident Analysis & Prevention*, **12**, 179–184.

Surla, L.T. & Koons, S.M. (1988). *Evaluation of the elimination of plea bargaining for DWI (Driving While Intoxicated) offenders – Final report.* Report MMI-935-86. US Department of Commerce, National Technical Information Center.

Tay, R. (2000). Do speed cameras improve road safety? In: *Traffic and transportation studies: international conference on traffic and transportation studies.* Beijing, China, July 2000: 44–57.

Tay R. (2005). The effectiveness of enforcement and publicity campaigns on serious crashes involving young male drivers: Are drink driving and speeding similar? *Accident Analysis and Prevention*, **37**, pp.922–929.

Thomson, J. & Mavrolefterou, K. (1984). Assessing the effectiveness of random breath testing. *ARRB Proceedings*, **12**, **Part 7**, 72–80.

Tippetts, A.S., Voas, R.B., Fell, J.C. & Nichols, J.L. (2005). A meta-analysis of .08 BAC laws in 19 jurisdictions in the United States. *Accident Analysis and Prevention*, **37**, 149–161.

Toomath, J.D. (1974). *Short-term traffic 'Blitzes'.* Traffic Research Report No. 11. Traffic Research Section, Road Transport Division, Ministry of Transport, N.Z.

Treno, A.J., Johnson, F.W., Remer, L.G. & Gruenewald, P.J. (2007). The impact of outlet densities on alcohol-related crashes: A spatial panel approach. *Accident Analysis and Prevention*, **39**, 892–901.

Törnros, J. (1995). *Intensifierad övervakning med utandningsprov. Försök i södra Sverige.* VTI meddelande nr 746. Väg- och transportforskningsinstitutet, 1995 Linköping.

Utzelmann, H. D. (1983). Nachschulung für auffällige junge Fahranfänger. *Zeitschrift für Verkehrssicherheit*, **29**, 74–76.

Utrykningspolitiet (1997). *Årsberetning 1996*. Utrykningspolitiet, Oslo.

Utzelmann, H.D. & Haas. R. (1985). Evaluation der Kurse für mehrfach auffällige Kraftfahrer. *Shriftenreihe Unfall- und Sicherheitsforschung-Strabenverkehr*, **Heft 53**, 1985. Bundesanstalt für Strabenwesen, Bergisch-Gladbach.

Vinzant, J.C. & Tatro, B.J. (1999). *Evaluation of the Effects of Photo Radar Speed and Red Light Camera Technologies on Motor Vehicle Crash Rates*. Prepared forth City of Mesa Police Department, Arizona State University, and B.J. Tatro Consulting.

Vissers, J.A.M.M. (1989). *Autogordelactie Regionaal Orgaan voor de Verkeersveiligheid ROV-Brabant 1988: een evaluatie*. In opdracht van het Regionaal Orgaan voor de Verkeersveiligheid ROV-Brabant. Veenendaal, Traffic Test, 43, p. 21.

Voas, R. B., Blackman, K. O., Tippetts, A. S., & Marques, P. R. (2002). Evaluation of a program to motivate impaired driving offenders to install ignition interlocks. *Accident Analysis and Prevention*, **34**, 449– 551.

Voas, R.B. & DeYoung, D.J. (2002). Vehicle action: Effective policy for controlling drunk and other high-risk drivers? *Accident Analysis and Prevention*, **34**, 263–270.

Voas R. B & Hause, J. M. (1987). Deterring the drinking driver: The Stockton experience. *Accident Analysis and Prevention*, **19**, 81–90.

Voas, R. B., & Marques, P. R. (2004). Emerging technological approaches for controlling the hard core DUI offender in the U.S. *Traffic Injury Prevention*, **5**, 309–316.

Voas, R. B., Marques, P. R., Tippetts, A. S., & Bierness, D. J. (1999). The Alberta interlock program: The evaluation of a province-wide program on DUI recidivism. *Addiction*, **94**, 1857–1867.

Voas, R.B., Rhodenizer & E. C. Lynn (1985). *Evaluation of Charlottesville Checkpoint Operations*. Report HS-806-989. National Highway Traffic Safety Administration (NHTSA), U.S. Department of Transportation, Washington DC.

Voas, R. B., Tippetts, A.S. & Fell, J. (2000). The relationship of alcohol safety laws to drinking drivers in fatal crashes. *Accident Analysis and Prevention*, **32**, 483–492.

Voas, R.B., Tippetts, A.S. & Fell, J.C. (2003). Assessing the effectiveness of minimum legal drinking age and zero tolerance laws in the United States. *Accident Analysis and Prevention*, **35**, 579–587.

Voas, R.B., Tippetts, A.S. & Lange, J.E. (1997). Evaluation of a method for reducing unlicensed driving: The Washington and Oregon license plate sticker laws. *Accident Analysis and Prevention*, **29**, 627–634.

Vaa, T. (1993). *Politiets trafikkontroller: Virkning på atferd og ulykker. En litteraturstudie*. TØI-Report nr 204/1993. Oslo: Institute of Transport Economics.

Vaa, T. (1996). *Bruk av bilbelter, strategier for økt bruk, virkning av økt bruk på drepte og skadde, omfang av politets kontrollvirksomhet, kjennetegn ved ikke-brukere*. TØI-arbeidsdokument nr TST/0751/1996. Oslo: Institute of Transport Economics.

Vaa, T. & Christensen. P. (1992). *Økt politikontroll. Virkning på fart og subjektiv oppdagelsesrisiko*. TØI-Report nr 142/1992. Oslo: Institute of Transport Economics.

Vaa, T., Christensen, P. & Ragnøy, A. (1995). *Politiets fartskontroller: Virkning på fart og subjektiv oppdagelsesrisiko ved ulike overvåkingsnivåer*. TØI-Report nr 301/1995. Oslo, Transportøkonomisk institutt.

Vaaje, T. (1991). Rewarding in insurance: return of part of premium after a claim-free period. In: *Enforcement and Rewarding: Strategies and Effects, Proceedings of the International Road safety Sym-posium* in Copenhagen, Denmark, September 19–21, 1990, 154–156(Koornstra, M. J. & J. Christensen. eds). SWOV Institute for Road Safety Research, Leid-schendam.

Vaaje, T. (1992). Rewarding youth drivers after claim-free period by return of part of premium. Paper presented at *International Conference on Automobile In-surance and Road Accident Prevention*, Amsterdam, April 6–8, 1992, hosted by OECD. Amsterdam.

Vaas, K. & Elvik, R. (1992). *Føreres kunnskap om og holdning til promillelovgivningen*. TØI-Report nr 104/1992. Oslo: Institute of Transport Economics.

Wagenaar, A.C. (1982). Preventing highway crashes by raising the legal minimum age for drinking: An empirical confirmation. *Journal of safety research*, **12**, 57–71.

Wagenaar, A.C., Maldonado-Molina, M.M., Ma, L., Tobler, A.L. & Komro, K.A. (2007a). Effects of legal BAC limits on fatal crash involvement: Analyses of 28 states from 1976 through 2002. *Journal of Safety Research*, **38**, 493–499.

Wagenaar, A.C., Maldonado-Molina, M.M., Erickson, D.J., Ma, L., Tobler, A.L. & Komro, D.J. (2007b). General deterrence effects of US statutory DUI fine and jail penalties. *Accident Analysis and Prevention*, **39**, 982–994.

Walsh, B. (1987). Do excise taxes save lives? the Irish experience with alcohol taxation. *Accident Analysis and Prevention*, **19**, 433–448.

Washington, S. & Shin, K. (2005). *The impact of red light cameras (automated enforcement) on safety in Arizona*. Report FHWA-AZ-05-550.

Watson, B.C. (1998). The effectiveness of drink driving license actions, remedial programs and vehicle-based sanctions. *18th ARRB Reseach Conference*, 66–87.

Webster, J.M., Pimentel, J.H. & Clark, D.B. (2008). Characteristics of DUI offenders convivted in wet, dry, and moist counties. *Accident Analysis and Prevention*, **40**, 976–982.

Wells, J.-A.K., Preusser, D.F. & Williams, A.F. (1992). Enforcing Alcohol-Impaired Driving and Seat Belt Use Laws, Binghamton, NY. *Journal of Safety Research*, **23**, 63–71.

Wells-Parker, E.N., Bangert-Drowns, R. Allegrezza, J. McMillen, R. & Williams, M. (1995). Final Results From a Meta-Analysis of Remedial Interventions with DUI Offenders. *Addiction*, **90**, 907–926.

Wheeler, G.R. & Hissong, R.V. (1988). Effects of criminal sanctions on drunk drivers: Beyond incarceration. *Crime & Delinquency*, **34**, 29–42.

Whetten-Goldstein, K., Sloan, F.A., Stout, E., Liang, L., 2000. Civil liability, criminal law, and other policies and alcohol-related motor vehicle fatalities in the United States: 1984–1995. *Accident Analysis and Prevention*, **32 (November (6))**, 723–733.

Wilde, G.J.S. (1991). Economics and accidents: a commentary. *Journal of Applied Behavior Analysis*, **24**, 81–84.

Wiliszowski, C.W. & Jones, R.K. (2003). *Enforcement of the Austin Police Department DWI enforcement unit*. Mid-America Research Institute, Incorporated ; National Highway Traffic Safety Administration.

Williams, A.F, Reinfurt, D. & Wells, J.K. (1996). Increasing seat belt use in North Carolina. *Journal of Safety Research*, **27(1)**, 33–41.

Williams, A.F & Robertson, L.S. (1975). The fatal crash reduction program: A reevaluation. *Accident Analysis and Prevention*, **7**, 27–44.

Williams, , R.L., Hagen, R.E. & McConnell, E.J. (1984). A driving record analysis of suspension and revocation effects on the drinking offender. *Accident Analysis and Prevention*, **16**, 333–338.

Wolfe, A.C. (1985). Evaluation of the special alcohol enforcement/education project in Oakland County, Michigan. In: Kaye, S. & Meier, G. W. (Eds): *Alcohol, Drugs and Traffic Safety. Proceedings of the Ninth International Conference on Alcohol, Drugs and Traffic Safety* - San Juan, Puerto Rico, 1983, 1575–1595. US Department of Transportation, Washington DC.

Woodall, W.G., Kunitz, S.J., Hongwei, Z., Wheeler, D.R., Westerberg, V. & Davis, K. (2004). The prevention paradox, traffic safety, and driving-while-intoxicated treatment. *American Journal of Preventive Medicine*, **27**, 106–111.

Yaungyai, N. (2004). *Evaluation update of red light camera program in Fairfax county, Virginia*. Masters Thesis. Virginia Tech, April 30, 2004.

Young, D.J. & Likens, T.W. (2000). Alcohol regulation and auto fatalities. *International Review of Law and Economics*, **20**, 107–126.

Zaal, D. (1994). *Traffic law enforcement: A review of the literature*. Monash University Accident Research Center, Report No. 53.

Zador, P. (1976). Statistical evaluation of the effectiveness of "alcohol safety action projects". *Accident Analysis and Prevention*, **8**, 51–66.

Zador, P. & Lund, A. (1986). Re-Analyses of the Effects of No-Fault Auto Insurance on Fatal Crashes. *Journal of Risk and Insurance*, **2**, 226–241.

Østvik, E. (1987). *Sanksjoner i vegtrafikken. Straff og andre reaksjoner vi kan og bør nytte*. TØI-Report. Oslo: Institute of Transport Economics.

Åberg, L., Engdahl, S. & Nilsson, E. (1986). *Intensifierad övervakning med utandningsprov (Intensified control with breath tests)*. Transportforskningsberedningen, 1986:12. Liber distribution, Stockholm.

Åberg, L, Nilsson, E. & Engdahl, S. (1989). *Höjda hastighetsböter. Effekter på förares kunskaper ombötesbelopp och val av hastighet*. TFB-meddelande nr 100. Transportforsknings-beredningen, Stockholm.

# 9.

# Post-Accident Care

## 9.0 Introduction and overview of three measures

This chapter describes three measures in the area of post-accident care:

9.1 Emergency medical services
9.2 Rescue helicopters
9.3 Automatic crash notification

All three measures aim at reducing the severity of injuries sustained in accidents, not at reducing the number of accidents. This introduction describes the amount and quality of research evaluating the effects of these measures on injury severity. Main elements in current knowledge of the effects of the measures on mobility and the environment, together with their costs and benefits, are also described.

### Amount and quality of research

Table 9.0.1 gives an overview of the amount of research that has evaluated measures within the area of post-accident care.

Meta-analysis has been used to summarize the effects of emergency medical services (EMS) and rescue helicopters. For automatic crash notification (ACN), no studies are available that have empirically investigated the effects on accident severity. Potential effects on fatality rates were investigated in three studies based on accident data and in-depth accident analyses.

The Handbook of Road Safety Measures

ISBN: 978-1-84855-250-0

*Table 9.0.1: The amount of research evaluating the effects on accident severity of post-accident care*

| Measure | Number of studies | Number of results | Statistical weights | Results last updated |
|---|---|---|---|---|
| 9.1 Emergency medical services | 8 | 13 | 305 | 2009 |
| 9.2 Rescue helicopters | 18 | 48 | 923 | 2009 |
| 9.3 Automatic crash notification | 3 | 3 | – | 2006 |

## Main elements in effects on accident severity

Post-accident care aims at reducing the severity of injury outcomes of accidents. In the case of serious injuries, a major factor that determines the outcome, i.e. the chances to survive, is the time to definitive care. The time between accident occurrence and definitive care can be shortened by shortening the notification time, the time it takes an ambulance to reach the accident scene, the on-scene time of the EMS and the transport time to the hospital. ACN aims at reducing notification times.

Most evidence indicates that advanced medical treatment at the accident scene may decrease survival chances, compared with a 'scoop and run' approach, when the treatment delays transport to definitive care. There are, however, differences between different types of injuries. Decision criteria about how to treat which patients may therefore also influence the injury outcomes.

When the distance from an accident scene to the nearest hospital is long (more than ca. 100 km), transport may be speeded up by helicopter. However, study results indicate for the most part that helicopter transport does not improve survival changes, except possibly for some patients with initially intermediate survival chances.

## Main elements in effects on mobility

The measures in this area are not primarily intended to affect mobility. There may be effects on mobility when accident scenes are cleared more quickly and thereby congestion is reduced.

## Main elements in effects on environment

The measures in this area do not have direct impact on the environment.

### Main elements in costs

Table 9.0.2 shows the estimated costs for Norway of the measures in the area of post-accident care.

### Main elements in cost–benefit analyses

Cost–benefit analyses have only been carried out to a limited extent. For EMS, no cost–benefit analyses are available (Table 9.0.3).

*Table 9.0.2: Costs of post-accident care*

| Measure | Costs (NOK) | Costs from year |
|---|---|---|
| 9.1 Emergency medical services | – | – |
| 9.2 Rescue helicopters (per mission) | 180,000 | 1997 |
| 9.3 Automatic crash notification – investment infrastructure, per unit | 240,000–400,000 | 2006 |
| 9.3 Automatic crash notification – training of personnel, per person | 2,400–4,000 | 2006 |
| 9.3 Automatic crash notification – vehicle equipment, per vehicle | 1,200–2,400 | 2006 |

*Table 9.0.3: Benefit–cost ratios of post-accident care*

| Measure | Benefit–cost ratio |
|---|---|
| 9.1 Provision of medical services | – |
| 9.2 Rescue helicopters: Ambulance missions | 5.9 |
| 9.3 Automatic crash notification (ACN) | 0.23–1.65 |

## 9.1 Emergency medical services

### Problem and objective

One of the factors that affect the injury outcome of traffic accidents is the provision of EMS. The faster and the more effectively an injured person is treated medically, the greater are the chances of surviving and making a full recovery.

Serious injuries that are sustained in traffic accidents are often time-critical. Trauma, which are unspecific, extensive and life-threatening injuries, should be treated within 10 min, and more extensive medical care should be provided within 1 h, preferably at a specially equipped trauma centre (Champion 2005). When not treated timely and adequately, trauma may lead to incapacitating injuries or death. Less-serious injuries and injuries that lead to immediate death are to a lesser degree dependent on immediate treatment. The proportion of traffic fatalities who are killed within the first minutes after an accident is between ca. 37% and 50% (Akella et al. 2003, Bachmann and Prezotti 2001, Clark and Cushing 2002, Henriksson, Öström and Eriksson 2001). In such cases, the sustained injuries are most likely not survivable under any circumstances, even with immediate and optimal medical help (NOU 1998).

The proportion of people who were fatally injured in road accidents involving personal injury has decreased in most countries during the past ca. 30 years. For example, in Great Britain, this percentage was 2.1 in 1970, and was reduced to 1.1 in 2000. In Norway, the percentage decreased from 4.8 in 1970 to 2.8 in 2000, and in Sweden, it decreased from 5.6 in 1970 to 2.6 in 2000. It has been hypothesised that the reduction in the proportion killed of all those who are involved in injury accidents is, at least in part, attributable to an improved provision of EMS. In a study from the USA that is based on annual fatality data from 50 states over 14 years (Noland 2003), it was found that improved medical services has been one of the most important factors in reducing the total number of fatalities.

The objective of the provision of EMS is to ensure fast and adequate medical treatment and transport to a hospital in the event of traffic accidents in order to maximise the probability of survival and full recovery.

### Description of the measure

Those aspects of EMS that are described in this chapter are pre-hospital times, treatment strategies at the accident scene and telemedicine. First aid by lay persons is described as well. Other aspects of EMS and treatment at hospital are outside the scope of this book.

***Pre-hospital times.*** The total pre-hospital time consists of the time from the occurrence of an accident or injury (although many studies start counting when the EMS is notified) until the arrival of the patient at hospital. The response time of the EMS is usually defined as the time from the emergency call until the ambulance reaches the accident scene. Response times depend among other things on the distance to the nearest hospital, the availability of ambulances and ambulance personnel, road and traffic conditions and the accurateness of the descriptions of the accident location. The on-scene time is the time spent by the EMS at the accident scene and depends to a large degree on the medical treatments that are provided. The transport time to the hospital depends on the distance to the hospital and on transport mode and conditions.

Delays between the accident and medical treatment were found to be larger on roads with low traffic volumes in rural areas (Brodsky 1993, Virtanen 2005), where there are often long distances to the nearest hospital. Accidents that are likely to be associated with delayed medical treatment are single-vehicle accidents, which are over-represented on rural roads and at night. These accidents are often severe and there are often no other people who may call an ambulance (Mäkelä and Kärki 2004, Tiehallinto 2005).

The total pre-hospital time depends additionally on the notification time, i.e. the time between the accident and the emergency call. Notification times and their effect on injury outcomes are described in Section 9.3. Delays in transport, e.g. due to long distance to the hospital or traffic conditions, contribute to the total time it takes until injured persons are provided medical treatment. Rescue helicopters can be used for faster transport. Their effects are described in Section 9.2.

***First aid by lay persons.*** When obtaining a driving licence, it is in many countries mandatory to take a first aid course, and, e.g. in Germany, all drivers are obliged to provide first aid when arriving at an accident scene.

***Treatment strategies at the accident scene.*** A general distinction can be made between two strategies: advanced life support (*ALS*) means that seriously injured people are provided professional medical treatment, including invasive treatments and medication, at the accident scene by specially trained paramedics or by doctors. Because of the prolonged on-scene times, this is often at the cost of a delay of definitive care at hospital. The other strategy, basic life support (*BLS*, also called ‘Load and go’ or ‘Scoop and run’), aims at transporting patients as fast as possible to a (specialised) hospital. Medical treatment involves only non-invasive techniques and is provided only to the degree that is necessary to keep the patient alive during transport.

ALS is generally more common in more developed countries (Sethi et al. 2009). However, the decision of which patients receive ALS, and possibly treatment by a doctor, remains an issue. There are differences between different types of injuries, e.g. patients with a cardiac arrest are most likely to profit from a scoop and run approach (BLS), blunt trauma patients may profit more from ALS than penetrating trauma patients (Liberman, Mulder and Sampalis 2000, Oppe and De Charro 2001). There are also differences between different types of ALS treatment (e.g. intubation is less likely to have detrimental effects than fluid resuscitation, Regel, Stalp, Lehmann and Seekamp 1997). A study from the United States showed that BLS ambulance crews can not always safely determine which patients may require ALS (Cone and Wydro 2001), and that the use of specified criteria reduced the proportion of ALS responses to emergency calls where ALS was not necessary (Culley et al. 1994).

***Treatment at hospitals.*** Injury outcomes are also affected by the treatment of injured persons at hospital. The treatment of trauma is more effective in a trauma centre than in other hospitals (Sampalis et al. 1993, Morrisey, Ohsfeldt, Johnson and Treat 1996). The most specialised hospitals are usually centralised, and better treatment is therefore often related to longer transport. The treatment of less-serious injuries at a trauma centre may have overall negative effects because it binds resources without improving the outcome of the treatment substantially. The quality of the treatment at hospital is also essential for the probability of surviving serious injuries. Many studies of the causes of death among trauma patients found that quite large proportions died during treatment, and that inadequate treatment in many cases contributed to the fatal outcome (Henriksson, Öström and Eriksson 2001, Morrisey, Ohsfeldt, Johnson and Treat 1996). Treatment strategies at hospital and measures to improve treatment at hospitals are beyond the scope of this book.

***Telemedicine*** is the use of telecommunications technology for medical diagnosis and patient care. Applications for the most part are related to direct patient care or to the transfer of radiological or computer tomography images (Benger 2000, Currell, Urquhart, Wainwright and Lewis 2009). Possible applications in the context of EMS are teleconsultation of EMS personnel with hospitals or the use of portable devices with audio and video equipment for the communication of lay persons with emergency physicians while providing first aid (Auerbach, Schreyøgg and Busse 2006).

## Effect on accidents

***Pre-hospital times.*** A number of studies have investigated the relationship between response times and the chances of surviving traffic accidents. The studies differ and are not suitable for synthesis in the form of meta-analysis. Response times are defined somewhat differently in different studies (e.g. total time from accident to hospital or time from notification to arrival of the EMS at the accident scene). Almost all studies found that longer response times are associated with higher fatality rates. However, many studies have not controlled for other factors that may affect the injury outcomes of accidents and the results may therefore not reflect the effects of response times alone. Such factors are, for example, accident severity and the type of treatment (e.g. ALS vs. BLS, see below) that may be related to the response times. For example in rural areas, where response times on the average are longer than in urban areas, accidents are often more severe.

Several studies have compared injury outcomes of accidents between geographical areas with different average response times, and controlled for a number of other factors that are likely to be relevant for the injury outcomes. All studies found that fatality rates are lower in areas with shorter response times or with better access to EMS.

The study that has controlled for most factors is the study by Sampalis et al. (1993). When controlling for type and severity of injury, age, the type of pre-hospital treatment and in-hospital care, patients with pre-hospital times of more than 1 h were 3.01 times more likely not to survive the first 6 days at hospital (95% CI [1.27; 5.06]). A number of other studies also found that longer pre-hospital times are associated with increased fatality rates when controlling for other factors. Brodsky and Hakkert (1983) found that fatality rates are highest in areas with long response times and lowest in areas with short response times. When controlling for other factors such as the speed at the time of the accident and the person's age, the fatality rates are ca. 38% higher than in other areas. Maio et al. (1992) found that fatality rates are almost twice as high in rural areas, compared with urban areas (relative risk in rural areas = 1.96). When controlling for accident characteristics, age and sex of the driver, the relative risk was reduced to 1.51. This means that a large part of the difference in fatality rates can be explained by accident and driver characteristics. A possible explanation for the remaining difference in fatality rates between rural and urban areas is better access to medical services in urban areas. In a similar study, Muelleman et al. (2007) found that the fatality rates in the most rural counties in Nebraska is about twice as high as in other areas in Nebraska (relative risk = 1.98; 95% CI [1.18–3.31]) when controlling for speed limit, age, alcohol involvement and injury severity. Feero, Hedges, Simmons and Irwin (1995) compared response times (the total time until the arrival at the hospital) between 'unexpected survivors' of accidents in urban areas in which major injuries (trauma) were sustained and 'unexpected deaths'. The unexpected survivors had on average shorter out-of-hospital times than the unexpected deaths (20.8 vs. 29.3 min). The EMS on-scene times and transport times were also shorter among the unexpected survivors. The results are statistically significant, although they are based on very small case numbers (13 unexpected survivors and 20 unexpected deaths).

***First aid by lay persons.*** No studies were found of the effect of first aid provided by lay persons on the injury outcomes of road accidents. In the case of cardiac arrest, significant improvement of survival chances was documented in some studies (Engdahl, Bång, Lindkvist and Herlitz 2001). Skills acquired in first aid trainings are not always adequate, are not retained to a large degree even over 6 months and re-training is not always successful (Chamberlain et al. 2002). Ertl and Christ (2007) studied the performance of lay persons in two emergency situations: unconscious trauma victim with severe bleeding and cardiopulmonary resuscitation. Those lay helpers who acted only based on their current knowledge performed quite poorly on most criteria (e.g. only ca. 10% checked the patients airways). Those lay helpers who were provided assistance by a handheld 'Personal Digital Assistant' performed significantly better. The Personal Digital Assistant provided standardized instructions with images, text and verbal instructions. However, in the absence of evidence for the effectiveness of improved lay assistance on injury outcomes (Auerbach, Schreyøgg and Busse 2006), it is not possible to estimate the possible effects of improving first aid trainings or providing assistance to lay persons in emergency situations.

***Treatment strategies at the accident scene.*** The following studies compared fatality rates between trauma patients who received different kinds of treatments at the accident scene:

Murphy, Cayten, Stahl and Glasser (1993) (USA)
Sampalis et al. (1993) (Canada)
Rainer et al. (1997) (Great Britain)
Nicholl et al. (1998) (Great Britain)
DiBartolomeo et al. (2001) (Italy)
Oppe and De Charro (2001) (the Netherlands)
Liberman et al. (2003) (Canada)
Iirola, Laaksonen, Vahlberg and Pälve (2006) (Finland)
Roudsari et al. (2007) (different countries)
Shepherd, Trethewy, Kennedy and Davis (2008) (Australia)

On the basis of these studies, summary effects were calculated for treating trauma patients with more advanced medical treatments compared with less advanced medical treatments. Most studies compared ALS versus BLS. All studies investigated the effects on fatality outcomes. Studies that investigated only effects among penetrating trauma patients or among cardiac arrest patients are not included in the analysis.

Only one of the studies has controlled for injury severity, response times and treatment at hospital (Sampalis et al. 1993). No significant effect on fatality rates was found of ALS, compared with BLS. ALS increased the fatality rate by 8% (95% CI [−36; +82]).

On the basis of all the studies that have controlled for injury severity, more advanced treatment has no significant effect on the fatality rate (+1%; 95% CI [−25; +38]). One of these studies has compared ALS treatment by doctors with ALS treatment by paramedics who are not doctors (Roudsari et al. 2007). This study found that doctors decreased fatality rates significantly by 30% (95% CI [−46; −7]). When this study is excluded from the analysis, ALS increases fatality rates non-significantly by 18% (95% CI [−5; +47]), compared with BLS.

It is important to take into account that more advanced medical treatment (ALS, doctors on ambulances) is usually provided to more seriously injured patients. When injury severity is not controlled for, it is therefore likely that those patients who are treated with more advanced methods will have a higher fatality rate than other patients, even if the treatment improves the survival chances ('Simpsons paradox', Oppe and De Charro 2001). When results are summarised from those studies that have not controlled for injury severity, fatality rates are on average 152% higher (95% CI [+37; +362]) among patients receiving ALS compared with patients receiving BLS. This corresponds to the results of the meta-analysis by Liberman, Mulder and Sampalis (2000). In this study, it was found that patients treated with ALS had on average 159% higher fatality risk than patients treated with BLS. Many of the studies included in the meta-analysis have not controlled for injury severity. There may be other differences between patients who are provided different treatments that are related to the injury outcomes, such as type of injuries and transport times.

ALS was found to be related to longer on-scene times in a number of studies. On average, the on-scene time was 18.5 min for ALS versus 13.5 min for BLS (Liberman, Mulder and Sampalis 2000). The longer on-scene times are related to the (time-consuming) treatments provided with ALS and should therefore be treated as a characteristic of ALS, rather than as a confounding variable. Longer on-scene times may contribute to lower survival chances.

Another methodological problem is that it is rarely possible to investigate the effects of different types of treatment on fatality rates before arrival at the hospital. Ambulance crews with no doctor on board have only limited possibilities to declare death. Pre-hospital fatality rates may therefore not be comparable between different ambulance crews. At hospital, fatalities during the first hours after arrival are most likely to be affected by the pre-hospital treatment, while later fatality rates depend on many other factors (e.g. type and quality of treatment at the hospital).

***Telemedicine***. Studies of the application of telemedicine on the injury outcomes of accidents were not found. A possible benefit of the use of teleconsultation is that the proportion of patients who are retrieved by ambulance, and especially by helicopter, is reduced. This was found in a study by Mathews, Elcock and Furyk (2008). Schmidt et al. (1992) studied mortality rates among trauma patients who were retrieved by helicopter. Mortality was higher among those trauma patients who were treated by a trauma surgeon who was a member of the flight crew, compared with those who were treated by a nurse/paramedic team with remote medical control. The patients were comparable as regards type and severity of injury.

### Effect on mobility

Better provision of medical services has no documented effects on mobility in traffic. If an accident scene is cleaned up more quickly, the hindrance to other traffic caused by an accident may be reduced.

### Effect on the environment

Better provision of medical services has no documented effects on the environment in traffic.

### Costs

No cost figures are available for EMS for those injured in traffic accidents.

### Cost–benefit analysis

No cost–benefit analyses of improved provision of medical services for those injured in traffic accidents have been found.

## 9.2 Rescue helicopters

### Problem and objective

When seriously injured or ill persons are at a long distance from the nearest hospital, it may take a long time until an ambulance reaches them and they can be brought to a hospital for definitive care. Serious injuries are often time dependent, i.e. the time it takes until the first medical care is provided and the time until treatment at hospital are often critical for survival (see Section 9.1).

Ambulance helicopters aim at providing medical care as fast as possible to patients who are out of the reach of ground ambulances or who would not be reached in time otherwise, and to transport these patients to a hospital where the most adequate definitive care can be provided. For injured patients, treatment at a trauma centre is often most adequate, which may be at a still longer distance than the nearest general hospital.

**Description of the measure**

Rescue helicopters can be used both for search and rescue missions and for ambulance transport. When used for ambulance transport, the aim is mainly to ensure fast transport of injured persons to a hospital, especially over long distances, when transport by ground ambulance would take long time. For transport over short distance, car is usually a faster mode. An Australian study found that helicopters under normal circumstances were faster than ground ambulances at distances over 100 km (Shepherd, Trethewy, Kennedy and Davis 2008). Rescue helicopters on ambulance missions are often accompanied by a doctor.

Helicopters have longer response times than ground ambulances (Nicholl, Brazier and Beeby 1994). On-scene times were found to be longer as well by Nicholl, Brazier and Snooks (1995). No significant differences in on-scene times were found in other studies (Schwartz, Jacobs and Juda 1990, Oppe and De Charro 2001). In a Norwegian study, it was found that ambulance helicopters had a mean response time of 26 min; 98% of all patients were reached within 1 h. Since there are large regional differences in the distances to the nearest hospital, helicopters may have a compensating effect in reducing the regional differences in the accessibility of EMS (Heggestad and Børsheim 2002).

Ambulance helicopters are intended to be used for those patients who are in most need of a fast provision of medical care. However, a large proportion (60–70%) of trauma patients who are transported by helicopter has non-life threatening injuries, especially in urban areas. This was found in a meta-analysis of 22 peer-reviewed studies by Bledsoe et al. (2006). In the study by Norton et al. (1996), over 60% of all requests for helicopter ambulance were considered inappropriate.

**Effect on accidents**

A number of studies have evaluated the effect of ambulance helicopter transport on the probability of surviving an accident or an acute illness. The results presented here are based on the following studies:

Baum (1980) (Germany)
Larsen et al. (1981) (Norway)

Baxt and Moody (1983) (USA)
Søreide, Sandstad, Buxrud and Holme (1985) (Norway)
Harboe et al. (1985) (Norway)
Baxt et al. (1985) (USA)
Baxt and Moody (1987) (USA)
Schiller et al. (1988) (USA)
Boyd, Corse and Campbell (1989) (USA)
Schwartz, Jacobs and Juda (1990) (USA)
Karper, Indrebø and Hjort (1991) (Norway)
Magnus and Kristiansen (1992) (Norway)
Heggestad (1993) (Norway)
Nicholl, Brazier and Beeby (1994) (Great Britain)
Nicholl, Brazier and Snooks (1995) (Great Britain)
Hotvedt et al. (1996) (Norway)
Cunningham, Rutledge, Baker and Clancy (1997) (USA)
Brathwaite et al. (1998) (USA)
DiBartolomeo et al. (2001) (Italy)

The results of the studies are summarised in Table 9.2.1.

The results indicate a non-significant decrease of the number of fatalities among patients who are seriously ill. Among trauma patients, no overall effect on fatality rates was found. Among those seriously injured (ISS > 16 or initial survival probability

*Table 9.2.1: Effects on fatality risk of ambulance helicopters*

| | Percentage change in number of fatalities | | |
|---|---|---|---|
| Injury severity | Types of patients affected | Best estimate | 95% confidence interval |
| ***All studies*** | | | |
| All | Unspecified/illness | −6 | (−15; +3) |
| All | Trauma | +2 | (−17; +25) |
| Less serious | Trauma | +4 | (−50; +118) |
| Serious | Trauma | −17 | (−24; −9) |
| ***Studies from before 1990*** | | | |
| Serious | Trauma | −20 | (−35; −2) |
| ***Studies from 1990 or later*** | | | |
| All | Trauma | −6 | (−17; +6) |
| Serious | Trauma | −4 | (−17; +11) |

below 0.75), a significant decrease of fatalities was found. Most studies have either stratified the results according to injury severity or compared patients with similar levels of injury severity. Fatality rates are therefore for the most part compared between groups of patients with similar injury severity. However, there is a tendency in most studies for patients transported by helicopter to be more seriously injured, even if the difference in injury severity between helicopter and ground-transported patients is not statistically significant. Most studies have not statistically controlled for injury severity or initial survival probabilities. It is therefore not clear to what degree the results are attributable to helicopter transport alone.

The effectiveness of ambulance helicopters is likely to have changed over time. In earlier studies, helicopters could often offer more advanced medical care than ground transport. However, pre-hospital medical care has improved considerably and the greatest advantage of helicopters is now mainly increased speed when patients are picked up in remote areas where ground ambulances take a long time, or where patients are difficult to reach, except by air (Bledsoe 2003). In accordance with this assumption, greater fatality reductions were found in earlier studies than in more recent studies. In studies from 1990 or later, a non-significant decrease of fatality rates was found for both serious injuries and all injuries. The result that refers to all injuries is based on two studies that have controlled for injury severity: Nicholl, Brazier and Snooks (1995) and Brathwaite et al. (1998). The latter study conducted a supplementary analysis with interaction effects between helicopter transport and injury severity as additional predictor variables. The results show that helicopter transport does not improve survival chances for those patients who are either slightly injured (ISS $< 16$) or very severely injured (ISS $> 60$; an ISS value of 75 indicates a fatality). For those patients with an injury severity between ISS $= 16$ and 60, helicopter transport improved survival chances.

In summary, the results indicate that helicopter transport does not seem to improve survival chances, especially in more recent years. Only for some seriously injured patients whose survival chances are not extremely low, there may be a slight benefit.

The proportion of missions of ambulance helicopters that has been classified as life-saving is 3.7% (95% CI [3.4; 4.1]). This result is based on all studies listed earlier; no distinction is made between trauma patients and patients suffering from acute illness.

**Effect on mobility**

No effects on mobility have been documented.

### Effect on the environment

No effects on the environment have been documented.

### Costs

Transport by ambulance helicopters is known to be expensive. In Norway, NOK 129.9 million were spent on rescue missions with helicopters per year in 1997, which corresponds to ca. NOK 180,000 per mission. Ambulance missions are somewhat less expensive.

### Cost–benefit analysis

A cost–benefit analysis has been conducted of the National Air Ambulance Helicopter Service in Norway by Elvik (1996). It was based on an estimated percentage of lifesaving missions of 6% and 20% of missions that improve the quality of life. It was concluded that the current service in Norway carried out by these helicopters had a benefit–cost ratio of around 5.4. Rescue helicopters carry out both search and rescue missions and ambulance transport. For the search and rescue missions, the benefit–cost ratio of current services is around 4.9. For ambulance services, the benefit–cost ratio was calculated to be around 5.9.

## 9.3 Automatic crash notification

### Problem and objective

The time from an accident until the arrival of an ambulance at the accident scene is in many cases critical for the outcome of injuries. Many severe injuries are time-critical and may become incapacitating or fatal if medical treatment is not provided within short time. The total time until the arrival of the ambulance consists of the notification time, i.e. the time from the accident until the EMS is notified, and the response time of the ambulance, i.e. the time taken by the ambulance from the emergency call until the arrival at the accident scene. The relationship between response times and injury outcomes is described in more detail in Section 9.1.

In a Swedish study (Henriksson, Öström and Eriksson 2001), it has been estimated that 27% of all persons killed in road accidents died because they were found too late or because of delays in medical treatment. In such cases, shorter notification times might have reduced the probability of the injuries becoming fatal. The proportion of traffic fatalities who are killed within the first minutes after an accident is between ca. 37% and 50% (Akella et al. 2003, Bachmann and Prezotti 2001, Clark and Cushing 2002, Henriksson, Öström and Eriksson 2001). In such cases, the sustained injuries are most likely not survivable under any circumstances, even with immediate and optimal medical help (NOU 1998).

The notification time depends on a number of factors. It increases when injured car occupants do not have mobile phones or are not able to use them and when no other road users, who might notify the EMS, pass the accident scene. Notification times are longest in rural areas, at night and after accidents that involve game or loss of control (Virtanen 2005).

ACN aims at reducing response times by shortening the notification time and by improving the information about the accident location.

**Description of the measure**

ACN systems use information from the car in order to detect (serious) accidents. For example, airbag sensors may be used, or more advanced systems may be developed. The information that is sent to the emergency service central includes a minimum information about the fact that an accident has occurred, about the location of the accident and vehicle information. More advanced systems may additionally send information about, e.g. the type of accident or the number of people involved.

There are a number of different ACN systems, with different technical properties. The usefulness of ACN depends on the reliability of the system, i.e. the degree to which (serious) accidents are correctly detected and reported and the degree to which less severe accidents (property damage only or minor injury) are not reported. Another issue on which the usefulness depends is the compatibility of ACN systems between different countries (Bachmann and Prezotti 2001). A system that is being developed in Europe, based on the emergency number 112, is eCall (eSafety Forum 2004). The system aims at improving communication along the whole service chain, that is accident location → emergency service central → ambulance → hospital, and thereby reducing delays that are due to late notification or imprecise information on the accident location.

**Effect on accidents**

ACN aims at reducing notification times and thereby the probability of serious injuries to become incapacitating or fatal.

No empirical studies of the effects of injury outcomes have been found, but some studies have estimated likely effects on fatalities and serious injuries. An overview of the results from these studies is given in Table 9.3.1. The results are shown as intervals of the estimated likely upper and lower limits of the possible reductions of fatalities and severe injuries. Only studies that provide a comprehensible description of the methods are included in the overview, other studies are not included.

Clark and Cushing (2002) and Evanco (1999) have estimated potential fatality reductions with statistical models that are based on large numbers of fatalities and serious injuries, for which information about notification times was available. Virtanen (2005) has conducted an in-depth analysis of fatal accidents in Finland, based on reports from the police, hospitals and EMS.

There are several factors that can be assumed to affect the effectiveness of ACN. The effectiveness in preventing fatalities is assumed to be greatest after serious accidents with long notification times, such as accidents rural areas, nighttime accidents, game accidents and single-vehicle accidents (Bachmann and Prezotti 2001, Clark and Cushing 2002, Garrison, Gough, Swanson and Cunningham 2002, Virtanen 2005). The effects can also be assumed to be related to the response times and the adequacy of the medical treatment provided. When response times are long, shorter notification times may be of limited value since the most serious injuries require treatment within 1 h at a maximum. When no adequate treatment is provided (e.g. inadequate decisions as regards advanced vs. basic life support or choice of hospital, see Section 9.1), shorter notification times may also be of limited value. Measures that reduce the type of serious accidents in which ACN is most beneficial are likely to reduce the effectiveness of ACN in terms of the total numbers of lives saved. Such measures are, for example, electronic stability control and shoulder rumple strips.

*Table 9.3.1: Effects on numbers of fatalities and serious injuries of automatic crash notification*

| Studies | Types of accidents affected | Number of fatalities/injuries in the study | Percentage change in the number of fatalities |
|---|---|---|---|
| Clark and Cushing (2002) (USA) | All accidents | 30,875 | (−1.5; −6) |
| Evanco (1999) (USA) | Accidents in rural areas | 25,761 | (−7; −12) |
| Virtanen (2005) (Finland) | All accidents | 919 | (−3;−8) |

### Effect on mobility

ACN may improve traffic flows if shorter notification times reduce the time it takes to clear accident scenes. The effects of ACN on notification times are, however, most likely only small when traffic volumes are high because there are many other road users that may notify the EMS. On roads where no other road users may notify the EMS, there is no great danger of congestion.

### Effect on the environment

No effects on the environment have been documented. If congestion is reduced, this would have positive environmental effects.

### Costs

The implementation of ACN requires (at a minimum) the installation of in-vehicle systems, which detect serious accidents and send information to the emergency service central. The infrastructure of the emergency service central has to be adjusted to the requirements of ACN, and the personnel of the emergency service central has to be trained in the use of ACN. Cost estimates vary widely between different studies. High and low estimates of the costs for ACN are estimated as follows. In-vehicle systems cost between €150 and €200 (Virtanen 2005). This refers to the installation in new vehicles. Costs for the installation in used vehicles may be much higher, depending on the equipment of the car (e.g. airbag sensors, GPS) and on the compatibility of the equipment with the required ACN equipment. Infrastructure costs may be between €30,000 and €50,000 per emergency service central. In Norway, there is one emergency service central per about 100,000 inhabitants (Abele, Kerlen and Krueger 2005). The training of the personnel costs between €300 and €500 per employee per year. It is assumed that four employees per emergency service central have to be trained each year. Additional costs may occur when communication infrastructure is additionally installed for the communication between emergency service central, hospital and ambulance. This would require both technical equipment and training of personnel. More advanced detection systems that provide, for example, information on the type of accident and the occupants of the involved vehicles would also be associated with additional costs.

### Cost–benefit analysis

A numerical example is calculated for implementing ACN in Norway. The costs are assumed to be as described in the previous section. The effect on the number of

*Table 9.3.2: Cost–benefit ratios of automatic crash notification under different cost and benefit assumptions*

| | High benefit (−8% fatalities) | Medium benefit (−4% fatalities) | Low benefit (−1.5% fatalities) |
|---|---|---|---|
| High costs | 1.22 | 0.61 | 0.23 |
| Low costs | 1.65 | 0.82 | 0.31 |

fatalities is assumed to be high (−8%), medium (−4%) or low (−1.5%). Infrastructure is assumed to hold for 20 years; the project time is 18 years. During this time, a penetration rate of 100% can be achieved among all cars that meet the requirements for the installation of ACN. No installation of vehicle equipment in used cars is assumed. The discount rate in the numerical example is 4.5%. Cost–benefit ratios are calculated under the assumption of high costs (€200 per car, €50,000 per emergency service central and €500 training per employee) or low costs (€150 per car, €10,000 per emergency service central and €300 training per employee) and low, medium or high benefits (−1.5%, −4% or −8% fatalities, respectively). The cost–benefit ratios are shown in Table 9.3.2. The benefits are larger than the costs only under the assumption of high benefits (8% fatality reduction). Under the assumption of medium or low benefits, the costs exceed the benefits, independent of the costs. These figures are similar to the results from Virtanen (2005), according to which the cost–benefit ratio is 0.55 under the assumption of small benefits and high costs, and 2.32 under the assumption of large benefits and low costs.

The numerical example is based on the assumption of a 100% reliable system, i.e. on the assumption that notifications are sent to the EMS in all cases of accidents in which someone sustained life-threatening injuries, and that no notifications are sent after accidents in which no life-threatening injuries occur. When no notification is sent in the case of an accident with a seriously injured person, the benefits would be reduced. When a notification is sent in the case of an accident with no life-threatening injury (e.g. property damage only, minor injuries or immediately fatal injuries), the costs would increase, and negative effects may occur because the EMS would be on duty unnecessarily.

## References

Abele, J., Kerlen, C. & Krueger, S. (2005). Exploratory study on the potential socio-economic impact of the introduction of intelligent safety systems in road vehicles (SEiSS). Teltow: VDI/VDE.

Akella, M., Bang, C., Beutner, R., Delmelle, E. Batta, R., Blatt, A. Rogerson, P. & Wilson, G. (2003). Evaluating the reliability of automated collision notification systems. Accident Analysis and Prevention, **35**, 349–360.

Auerbach, H., Schreyøgg, J. & Busse, R. (2006). Cost-effectiveness of telemedical devices for preclinical traffic accident emergency rescue in Germany. Technol Health Care, **14**, 189–197.

Bachmann, L.R. & Prezotti, G.R. (2001). Automated collision notification (ACN). Field operational test evaluation report. DOT HS 809 304.

Baum, H. (1980). Kosten-Nutzen-Analyse des Hubschrauber-Luftrettungssystems. Algemeine Deutsche Automobil Club, Deutschland.

Baxt, W. G. & P. Moody. (1983). The impact of a rotorcraft aeromedical emergency care service on trauma mortality. The Journal of the American Medical Association, **249**, 3047–3051.

Baxt, W. G. & P. Moody. (1987). The impact of advanced prehospital emergency care on the mortality of severely brain-injured patients. The Journal of Trauma, **27**, 365–369.

Baxt, W.G., Moody, G., Cleveland, H.C. et al. (1985). Hospital-based rotorcraft aeromedical emergency care services and trauma mortality: a multicenter study. Annals of Emergency Medicine **14**:9, 859–864.

Benger, J. (2000). A review of telemedicine in accident and emergency: the story so far. J Accid Emerg Med, **17**, 157–64.

Bledsoe, B.E. (2003). EMS myth 6: Air medical helicopters save lives and are cost-effective. Emergency Medical Services, **32**, 88–90.

Bledsoe, B.E., Wesley, A.K., Eckstein, M., Dunn, T.M., O'Keefe, M.F. (2006). Helicopter scene transport of trauma patients with non-life-threatening injuries: a meta-analysis. Journal of Trauma, **60**, 1265–1266.

Boyd, C. R., Corse, K. M. & R. C. Campbell. (1989). Emergency interhospital transport of the major trauma patient: Air versus ground. The Journal of Trauma, **29**, 789–793.

Brathwaite, C.E.M., Rosko, M., McDowell, R. et al. (1998). A critical analysis of on-scene helicopter transport on survival in a statewide trauma system. Journal of Trauma, **45**, 140–144.

Brodsky, H. (1993). The call for help after injury road accidents. Accident Analysis and Prevention, **25**, 123–130.

Brodsky, H. & A. S. Hakkert. (1983). Highway fatal accidents and accessibility of emergency medical services. Social Science and Medicine, **17**, 731–740.

Chamberlain D., Smith A., Woollard M., et al. (2002). Trials of teaching methods in basic life support (3): comparison of simulated CPR performance after first training and at 6 months, with a note on the value of re-training. Resuscitation, **53**, 179–187.

Champion, H. R. (2005). New tools to reduce deaths and disabilities by improving emergency care. Paper Number 05-0191.

Clark, D. E. & Cushing, B.M. (2002). Predicted effect of automatic crash notification on traffic mortality. Accident Analysis and Prevention **34**, 507–513.

Cone, D.C. & Wydro, G.C. (2001). Can basic life support personnel safely determine that advanced life support is not needed? Prehospital Emergency Care, **5**, 360–365.

Culley, L.L., Henwood, D.K., Clark, J.J. et al. (1994). Increasing the efficiency of emergency medical services by using criteria based dispatch. *Annals of Emergency Medicine*, **24**, 847–872.

Cunningham, P., Rutledge, R., Baker, C.C. & Clancy, T.V. (1997). A comparison of the association of helicopter and ground ambulance transport with the outcome of injury in trauma patients transported from the scene. The Journal of Trauma: Injury, Infection, and Critical Care, **43**, 940–946.

Currell, R., Urquhart, C., Wainwright, P. & Lewis, R. (2009). Telemedicine versus face to face patient care: effects on professional practise and health care outcomes (Review). The Cochrane collaboration. John Wiley & Sons Ltd.

DiBartolomeo S., Sanson G., Nardi G., et al. (2001). Effects of 2 patterns of prehospital care on the outcome of patients with severe head injury. *Archives of Surgery*, **136(11)**,1293–1300.

Elvik, R. (1996). Nytte-kostnadsanalyse av redningshelikoptrene. TØI-notat 1033. Transportøkonomisk institutt, Oslo.

Engdahl, J., Bång, A., Lindkvist, J. & Herlitz, J. (2001). Factors affecting short- and long-term prognosis among 1069 patients with out-of-hospital cardiac arrest and pulseless electrical activity. Resuscitation, **51**, 17–25.

Ertl, L. & Christ, F. (2007). Significant improvement of the quality of bystander first aid using an expert system with a mobile multimedia device. Resuscitation, **74**, 286–295.

eSafety Forum (2004). Memorandum of understanding for realization of interoperable in-vehicle eCall. Retrieved March 16 2006 from http://europa.eu.int/information_society/activities/esafety/doc/esafety_library/mou/invehicle_ecall_mou.pdf.

Evanco, W. M. (1999). The potential impact of rural mayday systems on vehicular crash fatalities. Accident Analysis and Prevention **31**, 455–462.

Feero, S., Hedges, J.R., Simmons, E. & Irwin, L. (1995). Does out-of-hospital EMS time affect trauma survival? American Journal of Emergency Medicine, **13**, 133–135.

Garrison, H.G., Gough, S.B., Swanson, M.S. & Cunningham, P.R.G. (2002). The react project: Rural enhancement on access and care for traumata. National Highway Traffic Safety Administration, U.S. DOT HS 809 521.

Harboe, S., O. V. Eielsen, S. A. Hapnes, E. Søreide & H. Mikkelsen. (1985). Erfaringer med legebemannet helikopter ved Sentralsjukehuset i Rogaland. Tidsskrift for den Norske Lægeforening, **105**, 1863–1866.

Heggestad, T. (1993). Statens luftambulanse-i hvilken retning? Nasjonale virksomhetsdata for 1992, samt utviklingstrekk i 5-årsperioden 1988–1992. Rapport STF81 A93028. SINTEF Norsk institutt for sykehusforskning, Trondheim.

Heggestad, T. & Børsheim, K.Y. (2002). Accessibility and distribution of the Norwegian national air emergency service. *Air Medical Journal*, **21**, 39–45.

Henriksson, E., Öström, M. & Eriksson, A. (2001). Preventability of vehicle-related fatalities. Accident Analysis and Prevention, **33**, 467–475.

Hotvedt, R., Kristiansen, I.S., Førde, O.H. et al. (1996). Which groups of patients benefit from helicopter evacuation? The Lancet, **347**, 1362–1366.

Iirola, T.T., Laaksonen, M.I., Vahlberg, T.J. & Pälve, H.K. (2006). Effect of physician-staffed helicopter emergency medical service on blunt truma patient survival and prehospital care. European Journal of Emergency Medicine, **13**, 335–339.

Karper, S., Indrebø, T. & Hjort, P.F. (1991). Legehelikopter i fjellbygder. Evaluering av ett års drift av Dombåsbasen. Tidsskrift for den Norske Lægeforening, **111**, 221–224.

Larsen, A.V., Blikra, G., Grimeland, J. et al. (1981). Evaluering av legebemannet luftambulansetjeneste. Helsedirektoratet, Oslo.

Liberman, M., Mulder, D., Lavoie et al. (2003). Multicenter Canadian study of prehospital trauma care. Annals of Surgery, **237**, 153–160.

Liberman, M., Mulder, D., Sampalis, J. (2000). Advanced or basic life support for trauma: Meta-analysis and critical review of the literature. Journal of Trauma, **49**, 584–599.

Maio, R.F., Green, P.E., Becker, M.P. et al. (1992). Rural motor vehicle crash mortality: the role of crash severity and medical resources. Accident Analysis and Prevention, **24**, 631–642.

Magnus, A. K. & I. S. Kristiansen. (1992). Legehelikopter og transport av pasienter med akutt hjerteinfarkt. Tidsskrift for den Norske Lægeforening, **112**, 512–514.

Mathews, K.A., Elcock, M.S. & Furyk, J.S. (2008). The use of telemedicine to aid in assessing patients prior to aeromedical retrieval to a tertiary referral centre. *Journal of Telemedicine and Telecare*, **14**, 309–314.

Morrisey, M.A., Ohsfeldt, R.L., Johnson, V. & Treat, R. (1996). Trauma patients: An analysis of rural ambulance trip reports. Journal of Trauma: Injury, Infection and Critical Care, **41**, 741–746.

Muelleman, R.L., Wadman, M.C., Tran, T.P., Ullrich, F., Anderson, J.R. (2007). Rural Motor Vehicle Crash Risk of Death is Higher After Controlling for Injury Severity. The Journal of Trauma, **62**, 221–226.

Murphy, J.G., Cayten, C.G., Stahl, W.M. & Glasser, M. (1993). Dual response run in prehospital trauma care. Journal of Trauma, **35**, 356–362.

Mäkelä, O. & Kärki, J.-L. (2004). Tievalaistuksen vaikutus liikenneturvallisuuteen ja ajonopeuksiin (The effect of road lighting on safety and speed). Tiehallinnon selvityksiä 18/2004.

Nicholl, J. P., Brazier, J. E. & N. R. Beeby. (1994). The costs and effectiveness of the Cornwall and Isles of Scilly ambulance service helicopter unit. Final report to the DoH. Medical Care Research Unit, University of Sheffield, Sheffield.

Nicholl, J.P., Brazier, J.E. & Snooks, H.A. (1995). Effects of London helicopter emergency medical service on survival after trauma. British Medical Journal, **311**, 217–222.

Nicholl, J., Hughes, S., Dixon, S., Turner, J. & Yates, D. (1998). The costs and benefits of paramedic skills in prehospital trauma care. Health Technology Assessment, **2(17)**, 1–72.

Noland, R.B. (2003). Traffic fatalities and injuries: the effect of changes in infrastructure and other trends. Accident Analysis and Prevention, **35**, 599–611.

Norton, R., Wortman, E., Eastes, L. et al. (1996). Appropriate Helicopter Transport of Urban Trauma Patients. Journal of Trauma, **41**, 886–891.

NOU (1998). Hvis det haster.... Norges offentlige utredninger NOU 1998:9.

Oppe, S. & De Charro, F.T. (2001). The effect of medical care by a helicopter trauma team on the probability of survival and the quality of life of hospitalised victims, Accident Analysis and Prevention, **33**, 129–138.

Rainer, T.H., Houlihan, K.P.G., Robertson, C.E. et al. (1997). An evaluation of paramedic activities in prehospital trauma care, Injury, **28**, 623–627.

Regel, G., Stalp, M., Lehmann, U. & Seekamp, A. (1997). Prehospital care, importance of early intervention on outcome. *Acta Anaesthesiologica Scandinavica Supplementum*, **110**, 71–76.

Roudsari, B., Nathens, A B., Cameron, P., Civil, I., Gruen, R.L., Koepsell, T.D., Lecky, F.E., Lefering, R.L., Liberman, M., Mock, C.N., Oestern, H.-J., Schildhauer, T.A., Waydhas, C. & Rivara, F.P. (2007). International comparison of prehospital trauma care systems. Injury, **38**, 993–1000.

Sampalis, J.S., Lavoie, A., Williams, J.I. et al. (1993). Impact of on-site care, prehospital time, and level of in-hospital care on survival in severely injured patients. Journal of Trauma, **34**, 252–261.

Schiller, W.R., Knox, R., Zinnecker, H. et al. (1988). Effect of helicopter transport of trauma victims on survival in an urban trauma center. The Journal of Trauma, **28**, 1127–1131.

Schmidt, U., Frame, S.B., Nerlich, M.L. et al. (1992). On-scene helicopter transport of patients with multiple injuries -. comparison of a German and an American system. The Journal of Trauma, **33**, 553–555.

Schwartz, R. J., Jacobs, L. M. & R. J. Juda. (1990). A comparison of ground paramedics and aeromedical treatment of severe blunt trauma patients. Connecticut Medicine, **54**, 660–662.

Sethi, D.D., Kwan, I., Kelly, A.M., Roberts, I.G. & Bunn, F. (2009). Advanced trauma life support training for ambulance crews (Review). The Cochrane Collaboration.

Shepherd, M.V., Trethewy, C.E., Kennedy, J. & Davis, L. (2008). Helicopter use in rural trauma. Emergency Medicine Australasia, **20**, 494–499.
Søreide, E., Sandstad, O., Buxrud, T. & Holme, J.A. (1985). Kritisk syke og skadde. En deskriptiv studie av pasienter behandlet og transportert av legebemannet ambulansehelikopter. Tidsskrift for den Norske Lægeforening, **105**, 1216–1219.
Tiehallinto (2005). Liikenneonnettomuudet yleisillä teillä 2004. Helsinki: Tiehallinnon tilastoja 3/2005.
Virtanen, N. (2005). Automaattisen hätäviestijärjestelmän vaikutukset onnettomuus-tilanteessa. Helsinki: AINO julkaisut 14/2005.

# 10.

# General-Purpose Policy Instruments

## 10.0 Introduction and overview of 13 measures

This chapter describes 13 general-purpose policy instruments affecting road safety:

10.1 Organisational measures
10.2 Information for decision-makers
10.3 Quantified road safety targets and road safety programmes
10.4 Safe community programmes
10.5 Exposure control
10.6 Land use plans (urban and regional planning)
10.7 Road plans and road construction
10.8 Road safety audits and inspections
10.9 Motor vehicle taxation
10.10 Road pricing
10.11 Changes in the modal split of travel
10.12 Road traffic legislation
10.13 Regulating commercial transport

The term 'general-purpose policy instruments', refers to policy instruments that are applied in many areas of public policy. An important characteristic of such measures is that the objectives are very complex and often conflicting. Improving road safety is often not the only objective, and in many cases, it is not the most important. For example, some of the objectives in controlling land use in society through urban and

**The Handbook of Road Safety Measures**

**ISBN: 978-1-84855-250-0**

regional planning include protecting areas of unspoilt nature and valuable landscape areas, encouraging business development in the municipality, reducing energy consumption and air pollution and improving road safety.

Measures in this area are also often complex and they come in different forms and varieties. This makes it difficult to generalise about their effects. The effects depend on the way in which these measures are designed, implemented and used.

Some of these measures are concerned with the design of the institutional framework for road safety policy. Such measures are intended to affect the objectives that government sets for road safety or the amount of resources allocated to road safety measures and the type of information used to make decisions about road safety measures. It is obvious that the causal relationship between institutional measures and the number of accidents and injuries is extremely complex and consists of many steps. Therefore, it is difficult, and perhaps not always possible or meaningful, to quantify the effects of such measures on accidents and injuries.

**Amount and quality of research**

The amount and quality of research that has evaluated the effects of general-purpose policy instruments on the number of accidents and injuries varies considerably. The most comprehensive research refers to land use plans, road plans and regulating commercial transport. Comprehensive research has also evaluated the relationship between traffic volume and the number of accidents. The relationship between the modal split of transport, and the number of accidents has been less well studied.

Meta-analysis has been used to summarise knowledge of the effects of quantified road safety targets and road safety programmes, safe community programmes, exposure control, land use plans, road plans, changes in the modal split of transport, road traffic legislation and regulating commercial transport. There is no basis for using meta-analysis for the remaining general-purpose policy instruments. Table 10.0.1 shows the amount of research that has evaluated the effects of general-purpose policy instruments on road safety.

All the studies are non-experimental and are not always of a particularly good methodological quality. This means that the knowledge of these effects is uncertain. It may seem somewhat surprising that the effects of general-purpose policy instruments are not better known. These measures are potentially among the most drastic that can be taken to affect the number of accidents. However, as mentioned above, these measures are highly complex and sometimes affect the number of accidents or injuries

*Table 10.0.1: Overview of the number of studies, number of results and statistical weights for studies of the effects of general-purpose policy instruments on traffic safety*

| Measure | Number of studies | Number of results | Statistical weights | Results last updated |
|---|---|---|---|---|
| 10.1 Organisational measures | 7 | 7 | – | 1997 |
| 10.2 Information for decision-makers | 11 | 11 | – | 1997 |
| 10.3 Quantified road safety targets and road safety programmes | 1 | 35 | 71,716 | 2001 |
| 10.4 Safe community programmes | 7 | 20 | 28,119 | 1997 |
| 10.5 Exposure control | 11 | 76 | 700,800 | 2008 |
| 10.6 Urban and regional planning | 12 | 50 | 1,680 | 1997 |
| 10.7 Road plans and road construction | 10 | 16 | – | 1997 |
| 10.8 Road safety audits and inspections | 5 | 5 | – | 2009 |
| 10.9 Motor vehicle taxation | 3 | 24 | – | 1997 |
| 10.10 Road pricing | 14 | 14 | – | 2009 |
| 10.11 Changes in the modal split of travel | 7 | 66 | 85,183 | 1997 |
| 10.12 Road traffic legislation | 1 | 9 | 8,711 | 1997 |
| 10.13 Regulating commercial transport | 6 | 18 | 186,468 | 2008 |

only indirectly. Furthermore, they do not lend themselves very easily to randomised controlled trials. This means that it is more difficult to evaluate the effects of general-purpose policy instruments than it is to evaluate the effects of smaller, simpler measures.

## Main elements in effects on accidents

The effects of ***organisational measures and information for decision-makers*** on accidents are unknown. The relationship between these measures and the number of accidents is too indirect to be meaningfully measured. ***Quantified road safety targets and road safety programmes*** have been found to be associated with a small improvement in road safety. This result is, however, very uncertain.

***Local community safety programmes*** have been found to reduce the number of accidents in some, but not all communities significantly. To succeed, a community needs good local accident statistics, a capability to identify the most important local accident problems and ways of creating a strong motivation for improving safety. These conditions do not always exist.

***Traffic volume*** is the single most important factor affecting the number of accidents. Measures affecting traffic volume are therefore likely to affect the number of accidents as well. However, the relationship between volume and accidents is complex and predictions of the effects of changing volumes on accidents are hardly possible.

***Land use plans and the pattern of land use*** in an area can affect the number of accidents by influencing traffic volume, the modal split of traffic, how traffic is distributed between various roads and the accident rate for each road or mode of transport. Traffic separation in residential areas has been found to reduce the accident rate. Designing access roads so that speed is kept low also contributes to reducing the number of accidents.

***Road plans and road construction*** can also affect the number of accidents by influencing traffic volume, the distribution of traffic on the road network and the accident rate of each road. Increasing road capacity in areas with capacity problems on the road network can generate more traffic. New roads are usually safer than old roads. The net effect of road construction on the number of accidents thus depends on which partial effect is strongest: increased traffic or reduced accident rate per kilometre driven.

***Road safety audits and inspections*** are systematic checks to ensure that road and traffic facilities are designed in such a way that they do not create unnecessary hazards to traffic or contain defects, which can easily be corrected. Experiences with road safety audits in several are very favourable.

***Vehicle taxation*** affects the numbers of vehicles and the use of each vehicle, and thereby both traffic volume and its composition. ***Road pricing*** may affect total traffic volumes and the distribution of volumes during the day. Thereby, also accidents may be affected.

***Changes in the modal split of travel.*** The risk of injury varies considerably between different means of transport. A transition from individual to public transport in large cities may reduce the number of injury accidents. However, there may be an increase in the number of unreported falls among pedestrians, which are not counted as a road traffic accident in official accident statistics. Major changes in the number of accidents are difficult to imagine, because it is difficult to achieve major changes in the modal split of transport.

***Road traffic legislation*** includes a number of acts and regulations. The effects of such legislation on the number of accidents depend on (1) the risk represented by the actions or risk factors subject to legal regulation and (2) the level of compliance with the legislation. It has been estimated that number of injured persons in traffic in Norway could be around 27% (±18%) lower if perfect compliance with current legislation was realised. The number of road accident fatalities in Norway could be 48% (±30%) lower assuming 100% compliance with road traffic legislation.

***Regulating commercial transport.*** Commercial transport has to a large extent been deregulated in the last 15–20 years. Studies from a number of countries do not indicate that the deregulation of commercial transport has significantly affected the number of road accidents.

## Main elements in effects on mobility

Improving accessibility and mobility is an important objective of many of the general-purpose policy instruments, including land use plans, road plans, road pricing and legislation of road traffic. When road capacity increases, or when a new road with a better design than the existing road is built, mobility is improved. Road pricing that leads to less, or more evenly distributed, traffic improves mobility for remaining traffic. An increase in the number of people who use public transport will also improve mobility, at least to the extent that it reduces the amount of car traffic. The existence of speed limits probably means that the speed level is lower than it otherwise would have been. Vehicle taxation and road traffic legislation reduce travel demand, in that they increase road users' generalised travel costs (i.e. the sum of direct expenses of travel and all other sacrifices or disadvantages of travel).

## Main elements in effects on the environment

Measures curbing travel demand contribute to reducing all the environmental impacts of traffic that are proportional to the amount of road traffic. This is true of the bulk of environmental problems attributable to road traffic, including noise, barrier effects, air pollution, fuel consumption and land use. Measures reducing traffic congestion also reduce environmental problems, primarily air pollution. Limiting traffic volume in residential areas is a highly valued environmental benefit, which not only contributes to less noise and pollution, but also to increased safety and a more pleasant environment in a wide sense. The actual environmental effects of the general-purpose policy instruments are not very well documented.

## Main elements in costs

The costs of the general-purpose policy instruments are difficult to estimate. One of the problems is that these measures have complex goals. The costs therefore ought to

*Table 10.0.2: Cost of organisational measures, Norway*

| Measure | Amount in million NOK (1995) | | |
|---|---|---|---|
| | Administrative costs | Implementation costs | Transfers |
| 10.1 Organisational measures[1] | 5 | | |
| 10.2 Information for decision-makers | | 20 | |
| 10.3 Quantified road safety targets and road safety programmes[2] | | 189 | |
| 10.4 Safe community programmes[1] | | 5 | |
| 10.5 Exposure control[3] | | | |
| 10.6 Urban and regional planning[4] | 324 | 3, 316 | |
| 10.7 Road plans and road construction[5] | 330 | 4,256 | |
| 10.8 Road safety audits[1] | 10 | 50 | |
| 10.9 Motor vehicle taxation | 653 | | 29,581 |
| 10.10 Road pricing | 128 | | 1,037 |
| 10.11 Changes in the modal split of transport[6] | | | 4,478 |
| 10.12 Road traffic legislation | | 659 | |
| 10.13 Regulating commercial transport (2009 prices) | 5–10 | | |

[1]Approximate calculation of the order of magnitude of the costs.
[2]The figure refers to costs of special traffic safety measures in the Norwegian road and road traffic plan 1994–97.
[3]The costs are entered under other measures, including land use plans, road plans, vehicle taxation and road pricing.
[4]Implementation costs are the municipalities' spending on transport and communications.
[5]Implementation costs are grants for national highway investments, special road safety measures excepted.
[6]National and county council subsidies for the operation of public transport.

be allocated between the different goals, according to their importance. There is too little information available to make such an allocation possible. In Table 10.0.2 the total costs of the general-purpose policy instruments are shown, to the extent that they are known. The table shows that the costs of these measures are substantial.

A distinction is made between three types of costs of general-purpose policy instruments: (1) administrative costs, including the cost of developing land use plans and road plans and for collecting vehicle taxes; (2) implementation costs, which includes the costs of implementing land use plans, road plans or other measures; and (3) financial transfers, which includes the payment of vehicle taxation and toll fees. The cost figures in Table 10.0.2 are taken from easily accessible sources and are not an adequate estimate of the social opportunity costs of the measures (i.e. the value of the resources consumed).

The costs of legislation include the costs of enforcement and sanctions.

### Main elements in cost–benefit analyses

It is not feasible to carry out meaningful cost–benefit analyses of general-purpose policy instruments on the basis of current knowledge. Firstly, the effects of these measures are quite uncertain. Secondly, the costs are not well known. Thirdly, the effects of the measures on other policy objectives than improving road safety are only partly known. The cost–benefit analyses, which can be made can be summarised as follows.

***Quantified road safety targets and targeted road safety programmes*** have a high benefit–cost ratio, provided the road safety programmes contain long-term measures that are known to reduce the number of accidents. The same applies to local community safety programmes.

The costs and benefits of ***land use plans and road plans*** depend on the content. Road construction is usually most cost-effective when there is a high traffic volume and when there are severe problems connected with traffic (high risks, congestion and environmental problems).

***Road safety audits*** are generally an effective road safety measure. A number of cost–benefit analyses conclude that the benefits exceed the costs by a good margin.

The cost-effectiveness of ***vehicle taxation*** and ***road pricing*** depend on the size of the external effects of road traffic. External effects refer to the disadvantages of road traffic in terms of accidents, congestion and environmental problems. When these external effects are severe, it is cost-effective to curb traffic demand or to distribute traffic more evenly in time to reduce these effects. According to an analysis carried out by Statistics Norway, current Norwegian vehicle taxation is cost-effective, i.e. the benefits of a reduction of accidents and environmental problems, attributable to this taxation, are greater than the loss of benefits from suppressed traffic demand. Introducing road pricing in Oslo, Norway, would also be cost-effective.

Similar points of view apply with regard to ***road traffic legislation***. If having no legislation encourages dangerous behaviour or behaviour that damages the environment, it is cost-effective to try to reduce the incidence of such behaviour by means of legislation. A number of elements of road traffic legislation are cost-effective. The costs and benefits to society of ***regulating commercial transport*** depend not only on how such legislation affects the external effects of transport, but also on how it affects transport prices. In practice, the regulation of commercial transport can easily turn into protection for producers at the expense of consumers. One effect of such regulation may be that prices are higher than they otherwise would have been. Analyses indicate that the deregulation of the transport market, which has taken place in a number of countries in the last 15–20 years, has been cost-effective. ***Subsidising public transport*** is normally cost-effective in city areas where roads are congested and the external effects of transport are large.

## 10.1 Organisational measures

### Problem and objective

The responsibility for developing and implementing road safety measures is usually divided among a number of governmental agencies at the national, regional and local level. An extensive division of responsibility can make it difficult to implement road safety measures in the most cost-effective way.

The objective of organisational measures are to ensure that adequate resources are available for road safety purposes based on the targets and priorities set by the authorities, and to ensure the most effective utilisation of these resources, through an appropriate division of work and responsibility. Organisational measures should also ensure that road safety measures are not unintentionally given low priority due to a lack of clarity in the distribution of tasks between the public agencies, inadequate organisation of the work or poorly defined responsibility for traffic safety.

### Description of the measure

Organisational measures are defined as all measures that (1) affect the power that governmental agencies have to introduce road safety measures, (2) alter systems for the allocation of resources for road safety purposes or (3) alter the division of tasks and responsibilities between governmental agencies. Organisational measures can include setting up or closing down certain agencies (offices, departments, etc.), allocating new tasks to certain agencies, changing the method of planning of measures and changing financial responsibility. The following measures are included:

- Empowering public agencies to introduce road safety measures
- Systems for resource allocation for safety purposes, including incentive systems for local authorities
- Formalising responsibility for introducing road safety measures and detailed planning of measures
- Defining the extent of legal responsibility for the design and maintenance of public roads.

Experience from Norway and from other countries will be included, since a number of significant problems in these areas have much in common with other countries.

## Effect on accidents

***Empowering public agencies.*** Power can be defined as the product of interest in a decision and control of the outcome of the decision (Hernes 1975). Interest refers to the difference in utility of different possible outcomes of a decision. Control refers to the ability to increase the probability that the most desirable outcome will occur (Elvik 1993a, 1993b). Does any single governmental agency have both interest in and control over road accidents?

A problem pointed out by a number of researchers (Trinca et al. 1988, Køltzow 1990, 1993, Elvik 1993c, 1993d), is that the public bodies have only a relatively small direct financial interest in improving road safety. The financial benefit of fewer road accidents accrues primarily to road users, but does not show up in the road budget. However, the road budget contains the largest public expenses for road safety measures. This point of view is developed in Table 10.1.1, which shows the distribution of annual accident costs (injury accidents only) and costs of road safety measures between sectors of society in Norway (Hagen 1994, Elvik 1993e, 1994, 1995, Statistisk sentralbyrå 1993). The cost figures include both direct expenditures and the valuation of loss of quality of life. The loss of quality of life is treated as an internal cost to road users. The figures in the table are rough estimates of the size of the costs and their approximate distribution across the administrative levels and sectors.

*Table 10.1.1: Distribution of accident costs and costs of road safety measures among sectors of society in Norway (amounts in million NOK 1993 prices; injury accidents only)*

| | | Amount in million NOK (1993) | |
|---|---|---|---|
| Administrative level | Sector | Accident costs | Cost of measures |
| State | Health sector | 160 | |
| | Social security | 1,160 | |
| | Road sector | | 2,180 |
| | Justice and police | 170 | 350 |
| | Other sectors | 570 | 30 |
| County councils | Health sector | 330 | |
| | Road sector | | 320 |
| | Other sectors | 210 | 10 |
| Municipality | Health sector | 90 | |
| | Road sector | | 280 |
| | Other sector | 410 | 10 |
| Road users | Road users | 13,400 | 5,520 |
| Total | | 16,500 | 8,700 |

The table shows that the greatest costs to the public sector of road accidents are not incurred by the same agencies as those who pay the costs of the road safety measures. There is, in other words, a weak relationship between the interest in road safety (the prospect of a financial gain) and the control of road safety measures. The accident costs to the public consist of costs for health services, social security payments and loss of income through loss of taxes (as a result of sick leave, etc.). Most of the costs of road safety measures refer to road construction and maintenance. The current system of public budgets in Norway does not encourage the use of cost–benefit analysis or other efficiency assessment tools. The effects of this on the priority given to road safety in public budgets are not known.

***Systems for the allocation of resources in the public sector – incentive systems.*** Are public budgets prepared in a way that ensures that the maximum benefit of measures, funded by these budgets, reaped? In Norway, this question has been discussed in relation to how public funds for national highways investments are allocated between the counties. The pattern of allocation that was laid down in the Norwegian Road Plan in the 1960s has later proved to be highly stable (Bjørnland 1989, Elvik 1993c, 1995a). However, the current allocation is not based on cost–benefit analyses (Killi and Ryntveit 1996). Increasing use of cost–benefit analyses for road planning appears to have had little impact on the distribution of investment funding between counties, or on the priority given to different investment projects in each county. The question is therefore whether the allocation between counties of state funds for national road investments can be explained in another way.

This question has been studied by Elvik (1995a), who compared three models for the distribution of public funds for national road investments between counties: (1) an economic benefit model, where the allocation was assumed to be the result of cost–benefit analyses; (2) a game theoretic model, where it was assumed that the counties formed informal coalitions to ensure an allocation, which was advantageous for the majority of counties; and (3) an engineering standards model, where the investment funds are distributed according to technical criteria, based on the objective of achieving a certain minimum standard of roads in all counties. Analyses of the allocation of national highway funding between counties in the periods 1990–93 and 1994–97, supported both the game theory model and the engineering standards model. The economic benefit model received little support (Elvik 1995a).

One problem experienced by many countries is that local authorities do not always implement mandates from central government regarding road safety measures. In the United States, the federal government has tried to solve this problem by threatening non-compliant states with the withdrawal of road funding if they do not comply with federal guidelines (Campbell 1991). Experiences with such threats are mixed. Around

1970, the federal government succeeded in forcing the states to adopt of motorcycle helmet-wearing laws. However, strong opposition to this measure forced the federal government to abandon this policy in 1976. The result was that about half the states repealed the motorcycle helmet-wearing laws. The national speed limit of 55 mph (88 km/h), which was introduced in the United States in early 1974 to save fuel, met a similar fate. Federal government threatened states that did not enforce the speed limit with the withdrawal of 10% of the road funding. When matters came to a head in 1987, the federal government lost and the speed limit was initially raised to 65 mph. Later, the national speed limit was repealed altogether. In other cases, the federal government in the United States has been successful in bringing pressure to bear on the states (Campbell 1991). For example, the states were forced to raise the minimum drinking age from 18 to 21 years, which all the states (some rather unwillingly) have done. The federal government has also been successful in forcing the states to pass seat belt laws.

In the Netherlands, the central government introduced a reward system for municipalities that succeeded in improving road safety (Wegman, Van Selm and Herweijer 1991). Each municipality, or coalition of municipalities with more than 20,000 inhabitants, could apply for a public subsidy for road safety measures. Municipalities that applied for the subsidy agreed to try to reduce the number of traffic injuries by 5% between 1986 and 1987, 10% between 1986 and 1988 and 15% between 1986 and 1989. If this reduction was achieved, the municipality received a reward of 5,000 guilders per traffic injury prevented. The first year when the system was in use, 98% of municipalities signed up for it. The effects of the system on the number of persons injured in traffic have not been evaluated.

In Austria, the municipalities were encouraged to implement road safety measures with the objective of reducing the number of injury accidents by 10% during the period 1 June 1986 to 31 May 1987, compared with the annual average for 1984 and 1985 (Risser, Michalik and Stratil 1987). No public financial subsidies were offered to the municipalities. Nonetheless, 100% of the municipalities in Austria were willing to participate in ‘Action minus 10%’. A study of accident trends in the first 4 months of the campaign found a decrease of around 5% in the number of injury accidents (Risser, Michalik and Stratil 1987). The total number of injury accidents reported to the police in Austria decreased from an average of 47,211 during 1984–85 to 44,570 during 1986–87. This is a decrease of 5.6%. A similar programme has been implemented in France.

***Responsibility for initiatives for new measures – special road safety agencies.*** In Norway, no single public agency has legal responsibility for proposing or developing new road safety measures. Responsibility for road safety spread across a number of administrative levels and authorities creates problems of co-ordination, which could be solved by setting up a special road safety authority (Køltzow 1990, 1993). A number of motorised countries including the United States, New Zealand and Sweden have or have had such agencies (National Highway Traffic Safety Administration in USA, established in 1966; Trafiksäkerhetsverket in Sweden, established in 1967, abolished in 1993; Land Transport Safety Authority in New Zealand, start date unknown). A comparison of the relative number of road accident fatalities in five countries during the periods 1966–70 and 1986–90 (Elvik 1993d) showed that countries with traffic safety agencies (USA and Sweden) have not accomplished greater reductions in the number of road accident fatalities than countries without traffic safety agencies (Denmark, Finland and Norway).

***Legal responsibility for the design of roads.*** The Norwegian Road Traffic Act places the legal responsibility for preventing accidents primarily on the road user, by stating that everyone is required to travel considerately and carefully, in a way not causing damage or creating a hazard (Road Traffic Act § 3). In many other countries, including the United States, government – primarily the road authorities – is legally responsible for keeping roads in a safe condition. The American rules imply that the road authorities can be held responsible for injuries resulting from poor road design or road maintenance (Baldwin 1980). In Norway, road authorities can only be held legally responsible for injuries to road users when evidence of gross negligence on their part is found and they can be produced in court.

Liability for compensation gives the road authorities a financial incentive to maintain the roads in a safe condition (Baldwin 1980). However, this may also have adverse impacts. In the United States, the legal responsibility of highway agencies has become so extensive that even minor upgrading of a road can be interpreted as an indirect admission that the road was not previously safe for traffic (Baldwin 1980). In turn, this can make highway agencies abstain from improving a road. This can also lead to safety assessment of a road being based on purely formal criteria, for example, whether or not it is in line with the road design standards, and not according to the actual accident rate (Hauer 1993).

## Effect on mobility

Effects on mobility have not been evaluated. Measures that affect traffic volumes or the modal split of transport are likely to also affect mobility.

## Effect on the environment

Measures that affect traffic volumes or the modal split of transport, as well as measures that aim at improving the environment, are likely to have effects on the environment.

### Costs

The direct costs associated with the organisational measures are largely unknown. Introducing a system where highway agencies are held responsible for deficiencies in road design and maintenance will increase their payments for accidents. It is not possible say how much such payments would increase.

### Cost–benefit analysis

It is extremely difficult to judge the costs and benefits of organisational measures. If the measures lead to more effective use of road safety measures, the benefit–cost ratio may be very high. If the measures do not have this effect, they may well entail costs that otherwise would have been avoided. At present, the cost–benefit value of the organisational measures discussed above is not known.

## 10.2 Information for decision-makers

### Problem and objective

Decisions concerning the use of road safety measures need to be based on information about the number of accidents, when and where accidents occur, the road user groups that are involved, the factors that contribute to accidents and the measures that can be taken to reduce the number of accidents or injury severity. The objective of providing information for decision-makers is to give them the best possible knowledge about the number of road accidents, types of accidents and the effects of road safety measures, including the costs of the measures, in order to avoid ineffective priority setting.

### Description of the measure

Information for decision-makers generally means providing available information for government and people working with road safety, including information concerning the following topics:

- The number of accidents and types of accidents
- Road safety measures and their effects, including the results of road safety research
- Technical standards for different measures
- Costs of the measures

- Formal methods for priority setting of measures
- The attitudes of the general public to various measures.

Information for decision-makers concerning road safety is currently found in a number of different sources. This chapter will review some of the most important sources.

## Effect on accidents

There is no simple relationship between the supply of professional information and the number of accidents. Better information makes it possible to make better decisions.

***Access to and quality of accident data.*** The most frequently used source of data on accidents in planning road safety measures is the official accident record. It is a well-known fact that far from all reportable accidents involving injuries are, in fact, reported (Borger, Fosser, Ingebrigtsen and Sætermo 1995). Under-reporting of accidents is in more detail described in Part I of this book.

***Knowledge of road safety and desired priorities among decision-makers.*** A number of studies have evaluated the amount of knowledge that decision-makers at different levels have regarding road safety, and which types of measures these decision-makers want to prioritise. An interview survey among 30 leading decision-makers (Køltzow 1990, 1993) elicited their priorities for road safety measures under two conditions: (1) measures they would use if costs were not to be considered and (2) measures they felt to be the most cost-effective. The measures that were mentioned are the following (the number of times the measures were mentioned is given in brackets; each person interviewed could mention more than one measure):

| Preferred measures if costs were not important | Preferred measures if costs were to be considered |
|---|---|
| Traffic engineering measures (84) | Police enforcement (35) |
| Legislation and police enforcement (49) | Traffic engineering (33) |
| Changes in attitude, training and information (44) | Changes in attitude, training and information (15) |
| Increased public transport (6) | |
| Changes in the organisation of traffic safety agencies (2) | |

***The relationship between knowledge of effects of measures and attitudes to the use of the measures.*** Two American studies have evaluated the relationship between knowledge of the effects of a road safety measure and attitudes to the use of the measure. The measure studied was the mandatory use of seat belts in cars. Slovic, Fischhoff and Lichtenstein (1978) studied how the two methods of presenting risk information influenced attitudes to the mandatory use of seat belts. One group was told that the probability of being killed per trip was 0.000000286 (1 per 3.5 million). In this group, 54% were in favour of the mandatory use of seat belts. A second group was told that the lifetime probability of being killed in traffic accidents is around 0.01 (1 per 100). In this group, 78% were in favour of mandatory use of seat belts. Runyan and Earp (1985) divided a sample of students randomly into one group that was told about the effects of seat belts, and a second group that was not given this information. Both groups were asked about their attitudes to mandatory use of seat belts. Sixty percent were in favour of such legislation in the group that had been told about the effect of seatbelts, as opposed to just 22% in the group that was not given this information. The study shows that the attitude to a particular traffic safety measure depends on the level of knowledge regarding the effects of the measure.

***Decision-maker perception of popular attitudes to different measures.*** A study carried out on behalf of the Norwegian Association of Public Transport Companies and the Oslo Tram Company Stangeby (1994) compared politicians' attitudes to traffic restrictions with the general public's attitudes to the same restrictions, and politicians' perception of the attitude, which they thought the majority of the general public had to such traffic restrictions. With regard to measures designed to reduce traffic congestion in town centres, the proportion in favour of different measures was as follows:

| | Percentage in favour of various measures | | |
|---|---|---|---|
| Measure | Municipal politicians | What the politicians thought people wanted | The general public |
| Parking restrictions | 61 | 31 | 43 |
| Pedestrian streets | 68 | 38 | 53 |
| Limiting the amount of traffic in cities | 72 | 24 | 64 |

The politicians were largely in favour of the restrictive measures, but did not think the general public would be in favour of them. However, a higher proportion of the general public was in favour of such restrictive measures than politicians thought to be the case. To the extent that the politicians have an inaccurate perception of public attitude to different measures, this may prevent them from taking measures that they believe will not be supported by the public, but would in fact be widely supported.

***Decision-makers' use of formal methods for priority setting of measures.*** Cost–benefit analyses are carried out routinely for all major investments on national roads in Norway. A number of studies (Odeck 1991, 1996, Elvik 1993a, 1995a, Fridstrøm and Elvik 1995, Nyborg and Spangen 1996a, 1996b) show that actual priority setting for road investments in Norway is not based on cost–benefit analyses. Possible explanations of why so little weight is placed on the results of cost–benefit analyses may be that many people do not think that the analyses include all the relevant impacts of road investments; scepticism regarding the economic valuation of a number of effects and institutional traditions, which make it difficult to deviate from earlier decisions, even if those were not based on cost–benefit analyses. Interviews with members of the parliamentary committee for transport (in the 1990–93 election term) show that the attitude towards cost–benefit analyses follows a right–left axis. The attitude to such analyses is most favourable among politicians who are to the right (Nyborg and Spangen 1996a, 1996b).

### Effect on mobility

No effects of information for decision-makers on mobility have been documented.

### Effect on the environment

No effects of information on road safety for decision-makers on the environment have been documented.

### Costs

Little information is available regarding the costs of information for decision-makers.

### Cost–benefit analysis

No cost–benefit analyses of information on road safety for decision-makers have been reported. The costs of such information probably correspond to the costs to society of some 10–20 injury accidents each year. It is possible that the sensible use of such information could prevent a corresponding number of accidents each year.

## 10.3 Quantified road safety targets and road safety programmes

### Problem and objective

The current number of road accidents and accident victims is regarded as unacceptably high by the governments of most countries. It has therefore become increasingly common to set quantified targets for improving road safety, in particular, for reducing the number of road accident fatalities. Many countries in Europe, as well as Australia and New Zealand have set quantified road safety targets and developed targeted road safety programmes designed to realise these targets. Previously, most countries had only qualitative target formulations, such as 'to continue to improve road safety', which did not state how much road safety was to be improved and how soon an improvement was to be realised. Quantified road safety targets aim to strengthen the commitment to improve road safety by stating in clear terms the improvement to be aimed for within a certain period. A quantified target will also make it easier to assess the need for introducing road safety measures in order to realise the target.

**Description of the measure**

Road safety targets can be formulated in many ways (Elvik 1993d, OECD 1994). A quantified road safety target usually states the reduction aimed for in the number of road accidents or road accident victims within a certain period. For the most part, the targets refer to road accident fatalities at the national level. Most of the road safety targets are quite ambitious, and aim for a reduction of the number of road accident fatalities of some 40–50% during periods of between 5 and 15 years. In addition to the targets for fatalities, some countries have set targets for reducing the number of injured road users, in particular, those seriously injured. Most countries belonging to the European Union (EU) have set quantified road safety targets.

**Effect on accidents**

The main problem in measuring the effects of quantified road safety targets on road safety is that there are few units of observation (few countries that have set quantified targets), while there are very many factors affecting road safety for each unit of observation. It is therefore difficult to rule of out the effects of confounding factors.

A study has been made in which the effects of 22 quantified targets set by national governments and 13 quantified targets set by regional or local governments on road safety performance were evaluated (Elvik 2001a). The International Road Traffic and Accident Database (IRTAD) was used as a source. The study concluded that it was not possible to evaluate the effects of quantified road safety targets on road safety performance in a sufficiently rigorous manner to conclude anything about their effects. If the tendencies present in the data are taken as showing real effects, the study shows that a quantified road safety target is associated with a slight improvement in road safety performance, amounting to a net reduction of the number of road accident fatalities of about 0.8% per year. The largest improvement in road safety performance is associated with ambitious, long-term targets set by national governments.

One reason why quantified road safety targets apparently do not influence road safety very much may be that effective safety programmes have not been implemented, and that the targets have, in effect, served a symbolic function mainly.

### Effect on mobility

The effects of quantified road safety targets and targeted safety programmes on mobility depend on the safety measures included in such programmes. Reducing speed limits may be one of the measures considered. On the other hand, improving roads is often also part of a road safety programme. The net effect on mobility is difficult to predict.

### Effect on the environment

The impacts of road traffic on the environment are closely related to traffic volume. Only one national road safety plan is known to have included a target for curbing traffic growth. That was the Dutch national road safety plan for the period 1985–2010, which contained a target stating that kilometres of driving in the Netherlands should not increase by more than 35% from 1985 to 2010 (Ministry of Transport, Public Works and Water Management 1996). Traffic has already increased by more than this target value, but so far no drastic measures have been taken in the Netherlands to curb further growth in traffic.

In most cases, targeted road safety programmes take future growth in traffic for granted and do not seek to influence it. To a very large extent, these programmes also take modal split for granted. As a consequence, targeted road safety programmes do not normally contain measures that will have much of an effect on the environment.

### Costs

The costs of a targeted road safety programme depend on the measures it contains. Some examples of the costs estimated for a number of national road safety programmes are given. The annual total cost of all road safety measures (public as well as private) currently used in the Netherlands has been estimated to about US$ 1.7 billion (Ministry of Transport, Public Works and Water Management 1996). A corresponding estimate for Norway puts the cost at about US$ 1 billion per year

(Elvik 1999). For Sweden, the annual total cost of road safety programmes has been estimated to about US$ 2.6 billion (Sund 2000). All these estimates refer to the total cost of all ongoing safety programmes in both the public and private sector.

The marginal cost of additional measures that are introduced as part of a targeted road safety programme is generally substantially less than the total cost of all safety programmes that are operated at any time. As an example, the annual cost of all road safety measures in Norway, whose marginal benefits are greater than the marginal cost, amounts to about US$ 0.5 billion (Elvik 1999). In Denmark, the marginal cost of the road safety plan for the period, 2001–12, is estimated to about US$ 0.13 billion per year (Færdselssikkerhedskommissionen 2000).

### Cost–benefit analysis

The costs and benefits of targeted road safety programmes are likely to vary substantially, making it difficult to provide typical figures. Analyses of road safety policy in Norway (Elvik 1999) and Sweden (Elvik and Amundsen 2000, Elvik 2001b) indicate that it is, in principle, possible to achieve a reduction of the number of road accident fatalities of about 50% by introducing measures whose benefits are greater than the costs. The analyses also show that current road safety policies in Norway and Sweden are not fully realising the potential for reducing traffic fatalities by introducing cost-effective measures. To the extent that setting a quantified road safety target strengthens interest in applying cost-effective measures, it may result in more efficient priority setting for such measures.

## 10.4 Safe community programmes

### Problem and objective

A common problem in accident and injury prevention work is lack of motivation (Hoff 1996). The success of accident prevention is therefore to some extent dependent on showing by means of good examples that this type of work can succeed. Such examples can motivate others. A necessary condition for success in preventing accidents is that people must be aware of how many accidents that actually occur, must know who the accidents affect and the circumstances surrounding the accidents. Existing accident statistics often give an incomplete picture of the accident problem.

In order to demonstrate good examples of accident prevention at the local level, the World Health Organisation has launched the concept of safe communities (Hoff 1996).

In order to be designated as a safe community, a local community must fulfil several requirements regarding accident prevention. Local community safety programmes are designed to create a better basis for local accident prevention by giving examples of how such work can be organised and by reducing the number of injured persons in those societies where the programmes are implemented.

**Description of the measure**

Safe community programmes are accident prevention programmes that have the following characteristics:

- The systematic recording of accidents in a local community over a given period of time. Normally, hospitals or other health institutions are responsible for the records.
- On the basis of accident records, the dominant accident problems in the local community are identified and published.
- A steering group for accident prevention is set up, with participation from all parties that are presumably able to contribute to preventing accidents, usually including the municipality (administration and politicians), schools, the health service, the police, the fire service, representatives of trade and industry and voluntary organisations.
- A quantified target for accident reduction during a given period is set and a set of measures designed to achieve this target is developed.
- Changes in the number of accidents and injuries are monitored and information on new developments is given to all those participating in the programme.
- The effects of the programme on the number of accidents are studied, the results are published and changes may be made in the targets or in the safety programme.

Programmes containing these elements have been introduced in a number of local communities, both in Norway and in other countries. The programmes have been directed both towards traffic accidents and towards other types of accidents.

**Effect on accidents**

The results presented here (Table 10.4.1) are based on the following studies that have evaluated safe community programmes:

Tellnes (1984) (Værøy, Norway)
Schelp (1987) (Falköping, Sweden)
Guyer et al. (1989) (cities in Massachusetts, USA)

*Table 10.4.1: Effects of local community safety programmes on the number of injury accidents*

| | Percentage change in the number of accidents | | |
|---|---|---|---|
| Source of accident data | Types of accidents affected | Best estimate | 95% confidence interval |
| Special records | Traffic accidents | −29 | (−35; −22) |
| Official accident record | Traffic accidents | +8 | (+6; +9) |
| Special records | Non-traffic accidents | −17 | (−22; −12) |

Haugen et al. (1991) (Bø i Telemark, Norway)
Davidson et al. (1994) (Harlem, New York, USA)
Ytterstad and Wasmuth (1995) (Harstad, Norway)
Hingson et al. (1996) (Massachusetts, USA)

Table 10.4.1 shows that a decrease of 29% in the number of traffic accidents has been achieved. This has been estimated on the basis of the special accident records set up in local communities as part of the programmes. The number of other types of accidents has been reduced by 17%. Accidents included in the official accident record increase by around 5–10%. The explanation for this is probably that the level of reporting of traffic accidents in the official record has increased.

**Effect on mobility**

The effects of local community safety programmes on mobility depend on the types of measures included in such programmes. In Harstad, Norway, where a comprehensive programme was introduced in the period, 1985–92, the following measures were included (Ytterstad and Wasmuth 1995): information (brochures, lectures, guidance for parents, etc.), black spot treatment on the road network, a rental system for safety equipment for children in cars, free installation of high mounted brake lights on cars and police enforcement. Most of these measures do not affect mobility.

**Effect on the environment**

No effects of local community safety programmes on the environment have been documented.

### Costs

None of the studies of local community safety programmes referred to in this chapter give any information about the total costs of the programmes. Thus, it is difficult to provide cost figures.

### Cost–benefit analysis

No formal cost–benefit analyses of local community safety programmes are available.

## 10.5 Exposure control

### Problem and objective

The single most important factor influencing the number of road accidents is traffic volume. This applies in both the short term and the long term. The more traffic there is, the more traffic accidents can be expected to occur, all other conditions being equal. Studies in the Nordic countries (Fridstrøm et al. 1993, 1995) indicate that variation in traffic volume, measured on the basis of fuel consumption, explain around 65–75% of the systematic variation in accident counts. Even if the total number of accidents increases with increasing volumes, the accident rates for individual road users usually decrease.

Limiting the amount of traffic can thus affect the number of accidents and accident risk. Congestion and environmental problems that are related to road traffic can be affected as well (Grue, Larsen, Rekdal and Tretvik 1997, Kolbenstvedt, Silborn and Solheim 1996). A basic principle in road safety policy is 'to allow individuals to choose the most adequate means of transport for own purposes, when concerns of mobility, safety and accessibility are reflected in the external conditions' (Samferdsels-departementet, St meld 24, 2003–04). There is therefore no direct regulation of road traffic. However, the amount of traffic may be influenced by a number of other instruments that are not conflicting with the principle of free choice of means of transport. Many road safety measures have also been found to affect traffic volumes. Knowledge of the relationship between volumes and accidents are necessary for predicting the effects of such measures on accident numbers and rates. For example, if a safety measure leads to increasing volume and if the accident rate decreases, the conclusion that the safety measure has led to decreased accident risk may be wrong if the increase in volume has led to the reduced accident risk.

Regulating traffic volume measure is designed to limit or reduce the amount of traffic in order to reduce the number of road traffic accidents.

**Description of the measure**

***Measures of exposure.*** Traffic volumes are often expressed as annual average daily traffic (AADT), which is the average number of vehicles on a section of road per day over a whole year. However, there may be large variations in traffic volume during the day, and corresponding variations in accident numbers and rates. Accident rates can therefore differ between roads with different distributions of volumes over the day, even when the roads have the same AADT. Moreover, AADT does not take into account variations in volume of different types of vehicles, which may have different relationships between volume and accidents.

AADT is therefore not necessarily the most adequate exposure measure when investigating the relationship between volume and accidents. Other exposure measures may be more adequate, i.e. yield more reliable and stronger relationships with accidents. Examples are hourly volumes or volume–capacity ratios. One may also include other predictors in addition to a volume measure, e.g. capacity or rush hour percentage. Moreover, the relationship between volume and accidents depends on the function that is used in accident modelling (e.g. a linear or a logarithmic transformation). If this transformation does not reflect the 'true' relationship with accidents, only weak relationships will be found.

***Measures that affect the amount of traffic.*** The amount of road traffic can be influenced using a number of measures. These measures are described in greater detail in other chapters in this book. Only the main elements are described here. Land use plans establish both the main principles and the details of land use in a specific area, which affects both the total volume of traffic and the modal split of travel (see Section 10.6). Road plans and road construction determine the supply of road capacity in an area and the standard of the roads. Both elements influence traffic volume and the quality of the traffic flow (see Section 10.7). Motor vehicle taxation influences the number of vehicles purchased and the extent to which these are used (see Section 10.9). Road pricing can affect the total volume of traffic, the distribution of traffic over the 24-h period and the modal split of traffic (see Section 10.10). The number of vehicles in the traffic system can be reduced by changing from travelling individually to using public transport (see Section 10.11). In principle, regulating commercial transport makes it possible to regulate the amount of traffic by limiting the numbers of those allowed to operate commercial transport and regulating the areas where such transport can take place (see Section 10.13). A number of traffic control measures can be used to limit the amount of traffic locally. Examples of such measures include traffic calming, parking regulations and dynamic route guidance (see Chapter 3, Traffic control).

### Effect on accidents

The relationship between exposure control and the number of accidents is indirect. In order to quantify the effect of measures affecting traffic volume on the number of accidents, it is important to know both the effect of the measures on traffic volume and the relationship between traffic volume and the number of accidents.

***The relationship between traffic volume and the number of accidents.*** The relationship between traffic volume and the number of accidents has been evaluated in a large number of studies. The results presented here are based on the following studies, all of which have used regression models in which accident numbers are estimated based on volume and a number of other predictor variables, such as road characteristics:

Knuiman, Council and Reinfurt (1993) (USA)
Miaou (1994) (USA)
Hadi, Aruldhas, Chow and Wattleworth (1995) (USA)
Milton and Mannering (1996) (USA)
Gharaibeh, Hicks and Hall (1997) (USA)
Ivan and O'Mara (1997) (USA)
Milton and Mannering (1998) (USA)
Wang, Hughes and Steward (1998) (USA)
Vogt and Bared (1998) (USA)
Anderson, Bauer, Harwood and Fitzpatrick (1999) (USA)
Brown and Tarko (1999) (USA)
Council and Steward (1999) (USA)
Abdel-Aty and Radwan (2000) (USA)
Ivan, Wang and Bernardo (2000) (USA)
Sakshaug (2000) (Norway)
Sawalha and Sayed (2001) (USA)
Strathman, Duecker, Zhang and Williams (2001) (USA)
Greibe (2003) (Denmark)
Bauer, Harwood, Hughes and Richard (2004) (USA)
Hauer, Council and Mohammedshah (2004) (USA)
Shankar et al. (2004) (USA)
Chang (2005) (Taiwan)
Lord, Washington and Ivan (2005) (USA)

Stefan (2006) (Østerrike)
Caliendo, Guida and Parisi (2007) (Italy)
Davies, Cenek and Henderson (2008) (New Zealand)
Haynes et al. (2008) (New Zealand)
Lord, Guikema and Geedipally (2008) (USA).

Almost all studies have used AADT as an exposure measure. From all studies, the estimated percentage increase of the number of accidents has been calculated for an increase in traffic volume by 1%. The results are highly heterogeneous. This indicates that the relationship between volumes and accidents is different under different conditions. The results also indicate that the relationship between volume and the number of accidents is not likely to be linear, i.e. that the number of accidents increases at a lower rate than volume. However, the percentage increase of accident numbers is not necessarily constant, although this is implicitly assumed in many accident models.

Based on the studies listed above, it has been estimated that a volume increase by 1% is related to an increase in the total number of accidents (unspecified severity) by 0.88% (95% CI [0.77; 0.99]). For single vehicle accidents, the estimated increase is smaller (+0.4%; 95% CI [0.29; 0.53]). The latter result indicates that the risk of single vehicle accidents increases at a lower rate than the risk of other accidents.

***Traffic volumes and capacity.*** Traffic volumes that are above the capacity of a road are often associated with decreased accident rates (Fridstrøm and Ingebrigtsen 1991), and congestion may even be favourable for safety (Zhou and Sisiokipu 1997). When traffic volumes exceed a roads capacity, speed is reduced and there are fewer single vehicle accidents. Increasing the capacity of roads on which there is more traffic than the road is designed for, may therefore increase accident rates (Ivan, Wang and Bernardo 2000). However, when the capacity of a road increases more than the traffic volumes, traffic flows, speed and safety are usually improved (Harwood 1995).

***Effects of measures that influence traffic volume.*** The effects of measures that are intended to influence traffic volume are described in greater detail elsewhere in this book. Table 10.5.1 summarises the effects of a number of measures affecting traffic volume and the total number of injury accidents. The effects on volume and accidents have been estimated independently (i.e. not based on an assumed relationship between volume and accidents).

The first three measures in Table 10.5.1 have been found to reduce both volume and accidents. Building new main roads and the abolition of all vehicle taxation were found to increase volume and accidents.

*Table 10.5.1: The effects of a number of measures that influence traffic volume on traffic volume and the number of injury accidents*

| | Percentage change (95% confidence interval) | |
|---|---|---|
| Measure | Traffic volume | Accidents |
| Compacting towns from ca. 600 $m^2$ per inhabitant to ca. 300 $m^2$ per inhabitant | −33 (−45; −15) | −30 (−40; −12) |
| Traffic calming in residential areas (local streets are closed to through traffic) | −30 (−35; −25) | −25 (−33; −20) |
| Introducing toll roads, etc. in Oslo, Bergen, Trondheim and Tromsø | −7 (−10; −3) | −5 (−11; +1) |
| Building new main roads with increased road capacity in cities (Norwegian data) | +13 (+2; +25) | +10 (+2; +20) |
| Abolition of all vehicle taxation (purchase, ownership and use) | +37 (+35; +40) | +33 (+30; +37) |

## Effect on mobility

When traffic volumes are reduced, the traffic flow will, other things being equal, improve (Grue, Larsen, Rekdal and Tretvik 1997). On the other hand, when traffic volumes are reduced, mobility may be reduced for those who otherwise would have used the car.

## Effect on the environment

The environmental problems that are caused by road traffic may be reduced both by a reduction in traffic volumes and when traffic flow is improved.

## Costs

The costs of measures that affect the amount of traffic are of two types: direct costs and indirect costs. The direct costs are the costs of implementing measures influencing traffic volume. The indirect costs are the loss of benefit attributable to a reduced demand for travel. Both the direct and the indirect costs of measures that affect the amount of traffic are little known and difficult to estimate.

## Cost–benefit analysis

The benefits of limiting or reducing road traffic vary considerably, depending on the size of the external effects of traffic. In the largest city areas in Norway, the external costs of car use are so high that road pricing, or other exposure control measures particularly at the busiest times of the day, may be cost-effective.

## 10.6 Land use plans (urban and regional planning)

### Problem and objective

The development of large areas without the direction of a long-term land usage plan can lead to unnecessary traffic or a complicated and dangerous traffic system, which may increase the number of accidents (Fridstrøm et al. 1993, 1995). In urban areas, the risk of injury accidents per kilometre driven is higher than in rural areas (Elvik and Muskaug 1994). An increase in the size of urban areas may therefore increase the accident rate. The objective of land use planning used as a traffic safety measure is to

- locate roads, residential areas, workplaces and other industries in such a way that traffic volume and travel distances are minimised,
- create a road network that separates access roads from roads for through traffic and ensures that traffic volume on access roads is as small as possible,
- design individual roads so that the accident rate on the road is low and
- make the traffic system simple and easily understandable for all road users.

Land use plans may have a number of other objectives including promoting industrial development or housing development, protecting agricultural land, protecting recreational areas, making the flow of traffic more effective or using specific resources more effectively. It is possible that these objectives may conflict with traffic safety objectives. The contents of this chapter are limited to the use of the land use planning for promoting road safety.

### Description of the measure

Land usage in an area can be determined using different types of plans. The most important of these are county plans, municipal plans, precinct plans, local development plans and building plans. These types of plans can be seen as a hierarchy. County plans contain regulations that are used as a basis for municipal plans. Municipal plans give guidelines for the development of precinct plans, local development plans and building plans. Local development plans give guidelines for the development of building plans.

**Effect on accidents**

Land use plans and land usage can influence traffic safety by affecting traffic volume, the distribution of traffic on different types of roads, the modal split of transport, accident rates on each road and the location of industries that generate a lot of traffic in such a way that traffic to and from these industries can use public transport or those parts of the road network that have the lowest accident rate.

***The relationship between land usage, the amount of traffic and the number of accidents.*** Certain land use patterns induce more traffic than others. For example, the construction of large numbers of single family houses with gardens and vehicle access to each house, leads to an increase in the use of private cars and a decrease in the use of public transport (Hall 1975). Nonetheless, it is not obvious exactly which land usage patterns lead to the least amount of traffic (Loder and Bayly 1973, Espedal and Omland 1982, Brindle 1984). It has also proved difficult to quantify the relationship between land usage patterns and traffic volume (Hanssen 1993a). However, a number of studies have shown that increasing development density is related to a reduction of the amount of travel per inhabitant.

An international overview of the relationship between land use and traffic in 32 cities (Newman and Kenworthy 1989) showed that there is a strong negative relationship between development density and traffic volume. Figure 10.6.1 shows the relationship between development density (inhabitants per hectare) and traffic per inhabitant per year (kilometres driven per inhabitant) in the 32 cities, which were included in the study.

In 21 towns in Norway, the urban area per inhabitant increased from 450 to 554 $m^2$ from 1970 to 1990 (Larsen and Saglie 1995). This means that the development density reduced from 22 to 18 inhabitants per hectare. In an international context, Norwegian towns and cities have a very low development density. Another Norwegian study (Næss 1996) also shows that increasing development density is related to a reduction of the amount of traffic per inhabitant.

***Distribution of traffic across the road network.*** A number of studies show that there are large variations in the accident rate between different types of road. Table 10.6.1 summarises the results of the studies in the form of relative accident rates for different types of roads and traffic environments based on the following sources:

Krenk (1985) (Denmark)
UK Department of Transport (1992) (UK)
Elvik and Muskaug (1994) (Norway)

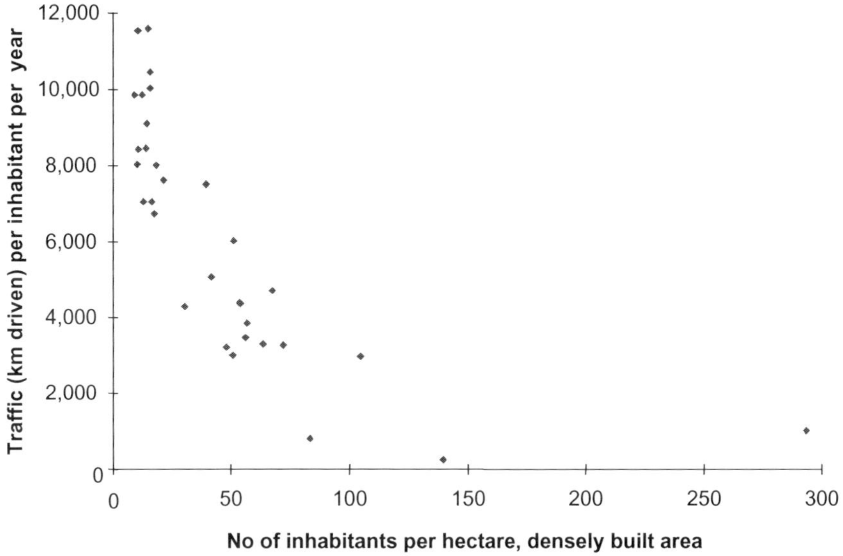


*Figure 10.6.1: Relationship between development density and traffic per inhabitant in 32 cities (Newman and Kenworthy 1989).*

*Table 10.6.1: Relative accident rate on different types of roads in different countries*

| | | Relative accident risk of injury accidents in different countries | | | | | | |
|---|---|---|---|---|---|---|---|---|
| | Type of road | DK | FIN | GB | N | NL | S | USA |
| Rural areas | Motorway | 1.00 | 1.00 | 1.00 | 1.00 | 1.00 | 1.00 | 1.00 |
| | Main road | 3.97 | 2.91 | 2.90 | 2.28 | 2.08 | 1.29 | 2.72 |
| | Collector road | 4.67 | 3.27 | 4.10 | 3.46 | 4.17 | 2.34 | 4.56 |
| | Access road | 5.67 | 6.11 | | 5.53 | | 1.34 | 8.66 |
| Urban areas | Main road | 11.00 | 7.86 | 9.60 | 5.22 | 18.44 | 2.15 | 5.68 |
| | Collector | 9.11 | 6.82 | 9.20 | 6.46 | 8.89 | 3.96 | 5.61 |
| | Access road | 9.98 | 7.35 | | 12.13 | 10.32 | 3.09 | 8.81 |
| All | All | 4.61 | 3.75 | 5.65 | 4.04 | 7.30 | 2.22 | 4.64 |

Injury accidents. Accident rate on motorways = 1.00. Country abbreviations: DK = Denmark, FIN = Finland, GB = Great Britain, N = Norway, NL = The Netherlands, S = Sweden, USA = USA. Source: see the text.

Poppe (1993) (The Netherlands)
Thulin (1991) (Sweden)
Tielaitos (1997) (Finland)
US Department of Transportation (1991) (USA)

Relative accident rates are used because absolute rates are not directly comparable between different countries, due to differences in accident reporting. It is emphasised that the classification of road types in this table is rough and approximate, and is only intended to demonstrate main patterns. It has not been possible to obtain accident rates for all types of roads in all countries included in the table. Thus, some cells do not show any accident rate.

Table 10.6.1 shows that motorways have the lowest rate of injury accidents of all roads. On average, the accident rate on motorways is about 25% of the average for all public roads. Main roads in rural areas also have a lower accident rate than the average for all public roads. All roads in urban areas have a higher rate of injury accidents than the average for public roads. The accident rate on access roads in densely populated areas is on average around 7, when the accident rate on motorways is set equal to 1.00. It follows from this that the more traffic there is on access roads in densely populated areas, the higher the number of accidents will be. Traffic volume on access roads in densely populated areas can be limited by building roads in such a way that through traffic is prevented, by building short access roads and by building access roads in such a way that speeds are kept down.

***Design principles for roads and road systems*** include the degree of separation and differentiation of the road network in residential areas (physically separated facilities for pedestrians and cyclists, and no through traffic), the types of connection between the local road network and the main road network (main road goes into or through an area vs. main road goes around an area) and through traffic on local roads (dead-end streets vs. streets where through traffic is possible). Studies evaluating the effects of these design principles for safety in residential areas include

Hvoslef (1976) (Norway): degree of separation
Bennett and Marland (1978) (UK): through traffic
OECD (1979) (several countries): all design principles
Hvoslef (1980) (Norway): degree of separation

Table 10.6.2 shows the best estimates of the effects of different design principles on the public health risk (injured persons per 1,000 inhabitants per year) attributable to road accidents in residential areas. All three design principles were found to be related to reduced health risk. However, the studies are to some extent based on simple

*Table 10.6.2: Effects of design principles for the road network in residential areas on the public health risk attributable to traffic accidents*

| | Percentage change in health risk | | |
|---|---|---|---|
| Design principle | Groups compared | Best estimate | 95% confidence interval |
| Degree of separation | Totally separated vs. not separated | −64 | (−66; −61) |
| Form of connection | External vs. internal feeding | −33 | (−52; −6) |
| Through traffic | No through traffic vs. through traffic possible | −72 | (−75; −70) |

*Table 10.6.3: Relative accident rates on roads in urban areas depending on the type of activity along the road*

| | | Relative risk | |
|---|---|---|---|
| Building density | Type of building | Norway | Germany |
| Medium | Housing | 1.00 | 1.00 |
| | Mixed | | 0.97 (0.84; 1.12) |
| | Industrial | 0.86 (0.70; 1.05) | 1.24 (1.04; 1.47) |
| Dense | Housing | 1.00 | 1.00 |
| | Mixed | | 1.59 (1.39; 1.82) |
| | Industrial | 1.03 (0.84; 1.27) | 1.42 (1.23; 1.63) |

comparisons, and the results may be affected by confounding factors, e.g. different traffic volumes in different areas may have contributed to the results.

***The effect of the nature of the surroundings and the design of access roads.*** Roads in urban areas have a higher accident rate than roads in rural areas (see Table 10.6.1). However, accident rate is also influenced by the nature of the activity along the road. A Norwegian study (Blakstad 1990) and a German study (Köhler and Schwamb 1993) have compared the accident rate on roads residential areas, industrial areas and areas with mixed land usage. Table 10.6.3 shows the results of these comparisons (injury accidents per million vehicle kilometres). The accident rate on roads in residential areas is set equal to 1.00. In Norway, there does not appear to be a significant difference in accident rate between residential areas and other areas. In Germany, a tendency has been found for the accident rate to be higher in industrial areas and areas with mixed land usage than in residential areas.

The accident rate on access roads in residential areas depends on the design of the road and the number of dwellings it serves. A British study (Bennett and Marland 1978) found that the health risk attributable to accidents on access roads in residential areas

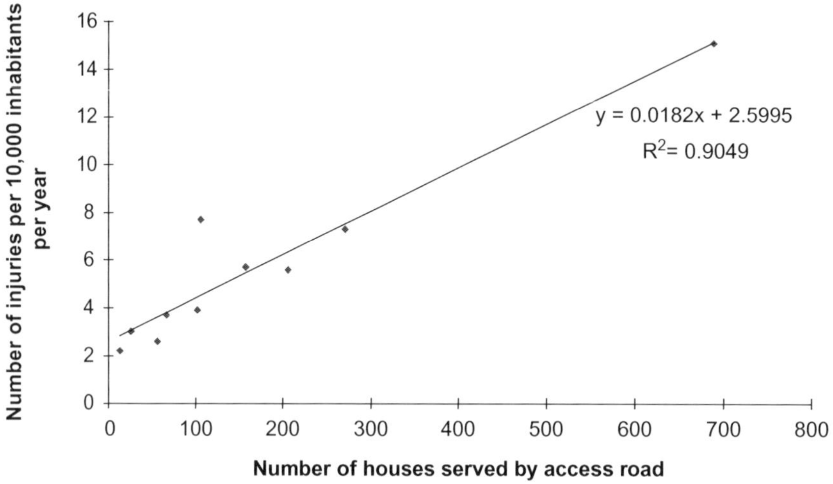


*Figure 10.6.2: Relationship between the public health risk attributable to traffic accidents in residential areas and the number of houses served by access roads (Bennett and Marland 1978).*

increased with an increasing number of dwellings served by the access road. The relationship between the number of houses served by a road and health risk is shown in Figure 10.6.2. The relationship may be explained by differences in traffic volume. Access roads connecting many houses lead to more traffic than access roads serving only a few houses.

A Norwegian study has calculated the accident rates on access roads, depending on speed limit and on speed humps (Blakstad and Giæver 1989). The results of the study are summarised in Table 10.6.4. Accident rates on access roads in residential areas can be reduced by lowering the speed limit level and introducing physical speed reduction measures.

***Relocation of businesses.*** Land use plans are usually regarded as very long-term tools in social planning. The physical structure of society changes slowly. Nonetheless, relocation is common. Even though the actual building mass in an area may change little, the relocation of industries within an area may have major consequences for transport. Studies of the relocation of businesses show that the length of the journey to work may increase and that the modal split of transport may change (Hanssen 1993b, 1995). In summary, the studies indicate that locating workplaces in a city centre contributes to increasing the numbers using public transport and reduces the number of cars used to get to work. Locating a business on the outskirts of a large city will

*Table 10.6.4: Accident rate on access roads with different forms of traffic control (Blakstad and Giæver 1989)*

| | | Injury accidents per million vehicle kilometres | |
|---|---|---|---|
| Speed limit | Physical measure | Medium density | Dense |
| 50 | None | 1.43 (±0.51) | 1.95 (±3.82) |
| 40 | None | 1.43 (±1.98) | 3.17 (±2.07) |
| 30 | None | 0.74 (±0.51) | 1.96 (±0.75) |
| 30 | Speed humps | 0.48 (±0.54) | |

often increase the total amount of transport (number of person kilometres) on journeys to and from work.

When Gjensidige moved from the centre of Oslo to the outskirts of the city (Lysaker), for example, the proportion of those who drove to work increased from 17% to 35%. Studies of the relocation of offices from the city centre in San Francisco found that the employees had roughly the same distance to travel, but the proportion using public transport reduced from 56% to 3%, while the use of cars tripled (Strand 1993). Moving the banking industry out of the centre of Trondheim was associated with a reduction of 69% of the number of those using public transport, and a reduction of 67% of the number of those walking or cycling to work. Car usage increased by 190% (Lervåg 1985). A study of the modal split of transport in a company that moved from a more peripheral location to a more central city location in Oslo found that the proportion of those travelling by public transport and the numbers walking or cycling to work increased. At the same time, the number of car journeys reduced by 35% (Fosli 1995).

**Effect on mobility**

Few studies have attempted to quantify the effect of land use plans and land usage patterns on mobility. In an overview of land usage and transport in 32 major cities in the world (Newman and Kenworthy 1989), information concerning the average speed on the main road network in the cities was also obtained for 30 cities. There was a tendency, albeit with significant spread, for the average speed to increase when the number of kilometres driven per inhabitant per year increases. Assuming that the number of kilometres driven per inhabitant per year is highest in cities with low development density, this implies that the average speed is highest in a dispersed development pattern with low density, and lowest in a dense development pattern with relatively low land usage.

## Effect on the environment

The severity of environmental problems caused by road traffic is strongly related to traffic volume. All other conditions being equal, a land use pattern inducing a lot of traffic will increase environmental problems (noise and pollution). Studies indicate that inhabitants in cities with a low development density use on average 25% more energy for transport than inhabitants in cities with high density (Næss 1996). The construction of large shopping centres near main roads can generate increased traffic (Engebretsen 1991). Speed-reduction measures on access roads in residential areas can have adverse effects on both noise and air pollution (see also Section 3.12, Speed-reducing devices).

## Costs

The costs of land use planning and the development of an area vary considerably depending on local conditions. A development pattern requiring the construction of new roads will normally be more expensive than a development pattern where existing roads can be used to a large extent. Norwegian studies indicate that concentrated development patterns produce somewhat lower total investment and operating costs than dispersed patterns (Næss 1996).

The factors that affect the costs of the development of an area most strongly are the topography (terrain), the type of land, the type of building, building density, the installation of main technical systems, alignment, dimensions and mass balance for technical installations. Roads comprise approximately one-third of building land costs and by establishing building plots on both sides of the road, and/or reducing the width of the plot, the number of road metres per plot can be reduced (Fiskaa and Stabell 1988). Under otherwise identical conditions, narrower roads are cheaper than wide roads (Hoffmann 1982, Kolbenstvedt and Strand 1986).

## Cost–benefit analysis

Examples of formal cost–benefit analyses of land use plans, where costs and benefits of different development principles are quantified, have not been found. It is difficult to do good cost–benefit analyses of land use planning, because the measure has a large number of objectives that cannot always be expressed in a meaningful way. Among the qualities valued by many people in a residential area are the view, pretty countryside, little pollution, little traffic, few accidents, a low crime rate, peace and quiet and low living expenses. In industrial areas, good accessibility is valued highly. At present, no satisfactory monetary valuation of all these qualities is available. The basis for cost–benefit analyses of land use plans is therefore inadequate.

## 10.7 Road plans and road construction

### Problem and objective

In order to ensure a high level of road safety, road planning needs to be based on the best knowledge available of the effects of road design on road safety. Formal road planning affects the degree to which roads and industries are located so that traffic volumes and accident rates are as low as possible and to which traffic is segregated according to different characteristics and needs. They also contribute to identify places that have particular needs for safety measures and to introduce effective measures at such sites.

### Description of the measure

In this chapter, the effects of road designs standards on road safety are described and it also discusses whether new traffic is induced by new roads or by expanding existing roads.

### Effect on accidents

***Elements of design standards.*** Road design standards specify in detail the 'correct' design of different elements of a road. These standards are not based exclusively on the results of research showing which road design is the safest (Hauer 1988, Jenssen 1988). They have been developed gradually as increasing vehicle traffic has made it necessary to plan better roads. The relationships between road characteristics, many of which are described in design standards, and accidents have been investigated in numerous studies. The results are summarised in the sections of Chapter 1 (Road design and road equipment).

***Safety on new and old roads.*** In an American study (Chatfield 1987), the fatality rate on roads opened to traffic in the years 1967–71 was compared with the fatality rate for roads opened to traffic before 1967. Figure 10.7.1 shows the results of the study. The new roads had around 20% (95% CI [−28; −12]) fewer fatal accidents per 100 million vehicle miles than the older roads. On both older and new roads the fatality rate drops dramatically with increasing traffic volume. This may, in part, be due to the fact that speeds drop and that the standard of roads with heavy traffic is often better than that of roads carrying little traffic.

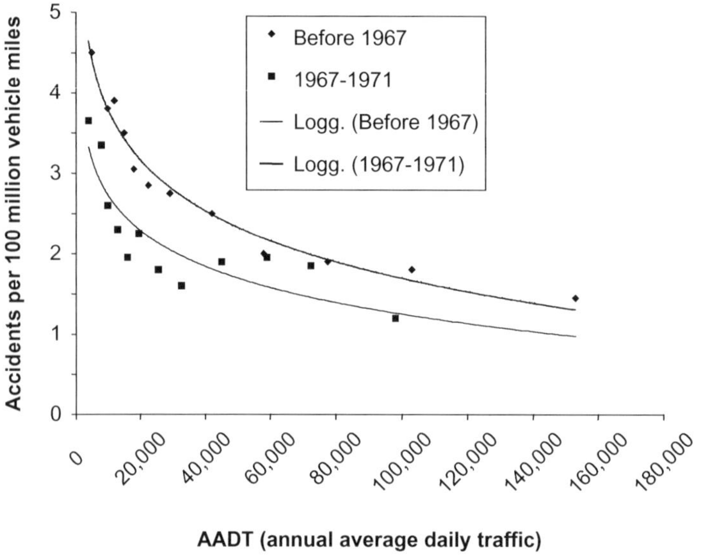


*Figure 10.7.1: Number of fatal accidents per 100 million vehicle miles on roads in the USA opened at different times (Chatfield 1987).*

*Table 10.7.1: Injury accidents per million vehicle kilometres on roads built in different decades and with different road widths in Sweden (Björketun 1991)*

| | Reported injury accidents per million vehicle kilometres | | | |
|---|---|---|---|---|
| Construction decade | Narrow roads | Average width | Wide roads | All roads |
| 1950s | 0.31 | 0.29 | 0.28 | 0.30 |
| 1960s | 0.32 | 0.28 | 0.41 | 0.33 |
| 1970s | 0.28 | 0.26 | 0.26 | 0.27 |
| All decades | 0.29 | 0.27 | 0.31 | 0.29 |

In a Swedish study (Björketun 1991), the accident rate on roads designed and built in the 1950s, the 1960s and the 1970s were compared. Table 10.7.1 shows the results of the study, stated in terms of the number of injury accidents per million vehicle kilometres on roads built in different decades and with different road widths. From the 1950 to the 1960s there was no decrease in the accident rate. Roads built in the 1970s, however, have a lower accident rate than older roads. On these roads, the rate of injury accidents is around 18% lower than on roads built in the 1960s and around 10% lower than on roads built in the 1950s (Björketun 1991).

A number of Norwegian studies provide information about the accident rate on roads built in recent years and make it possible to compare these with roads built earlier (Smeby 1992, Holt 1993). The accident rates do not show any systematic pattern. Some of the new stretches of road have lower accident rates than normal for this type of road, while others have higher rates.

***New traffic induced by new roads.*** One question that has been discussed, particularly in connection with the development of the main road network in large cities where the road network has capacity problems, is whether new roads induce so much new traffic that the benefit of a lower accident rate per kilometre driven is offset by an increase in the number of kilometres driven. The following Norwegian studies indicate how much new traffic results from a road construction:

Haakenaasen (1980): bypass road in Gol
Kolbenstvedt et al. (1989): Vålerenga tunnel in Oslo
Amundsen and Gabestad (1991): The Oslo tunnel in Oslo
Sandelien (1992): a number of road projects in Norway
Holt (1993): motorway between Trondheim and Værnes
Statens vegvesen Sør-Trøndelag (1996): expansion from two to four lanes in Trondheim

Table 10.7.2 shows the estimated percentage of induced traffic based on these studies. The amount of induced traffic depends on a number of conditions (Sandelien 1992), including what road provision the area had previously (if any), the size of the increase in road capacity, whether there were previously road capacity problems or not, how much time can be saved by using a new road, whether the new road is a toll road, etc.

### Effect on mobility

It is important to take account of accessibility and mobility in road planning. A main objective of road construction is to ensure more effective and less time-consuming travel. One question that is often discussed is whether developing roads in large towns and cities improves mobility, or whether the roads soon fill up with increased traffic, so that mobility becomes as bad as before (Downs 1962, Mogridge 1996). A study in California (Hansen and Huang 1997) estimated that the number of vehicle kilometres increased by 0.7–0.9% for each percentage increase in road capacity, measured in lane kilometres. This implies that the growth in traffic almost keeps level with the increase in road capacity and that the flow of traffic does not particularly improve, no matter how large road capacity is provided.

*Table 10.7.2: Percentage of new traffic or new journeys on roads in Norway*

| Type of road | Time period for increase in traffic | Induced traffic (% of journeys) | |
|---|---|---|---|
| | | Best estimate | 95% confidence interval |
| Roads to areas without roads | First year | +220 | (+127; +351) |
| Bridge to relieve ferry | On opening | +69 | (+41; +97) |
| Bridge to relieve ferry | After 10 years | +67 | (+25; +109) |
| Tunnel that reduces distance | On opening | +73 | (+22; +124) |
| New main roads in cities | First 2–3 years | +11 | (−8; +30) |
| Increased road capacity in cities | First 3–8 years | +14 | (+3; +25) |

### Effect on the environment

Many road projects affect the environment. Estimates made on the basis of the Norwegian road and road traffic plan for the period, 1998–2007, show that the number of people exposed to unacceptably high noise along national highways (trunk roads excepted) is expected to reduce from 83,668 in 1998 to 76,602 by the year 2008 if the recommended strategy is adopted. The number of people exposed to particularly high concentration of particles in the air is expected, during the same period to reduce from 20,735 in 1998 to 14,611 in 2008.

### Costs

In 1993, the Norwegian Public Roads Administration spent NOK 332 million on planning national highway constructions in Norway. This represented 5.3% of the construction costs (Statens vegvesen 1994). In 1987, around NOK 24 million was used for county road construction planning, which corresponded to 3.5% of the construction costs.

### Cost–benefit analysis

Cost–benefit analyses are carried out for all investment projects on national highways in Norway. Five alternative investment strategies were developed for the road plan period, 1998–2007:

- A mobility strategy
- An environmental strategy
- A road safety strategy
- A district strategy (only in 15 of 19 counties)
- A recommended strategy.

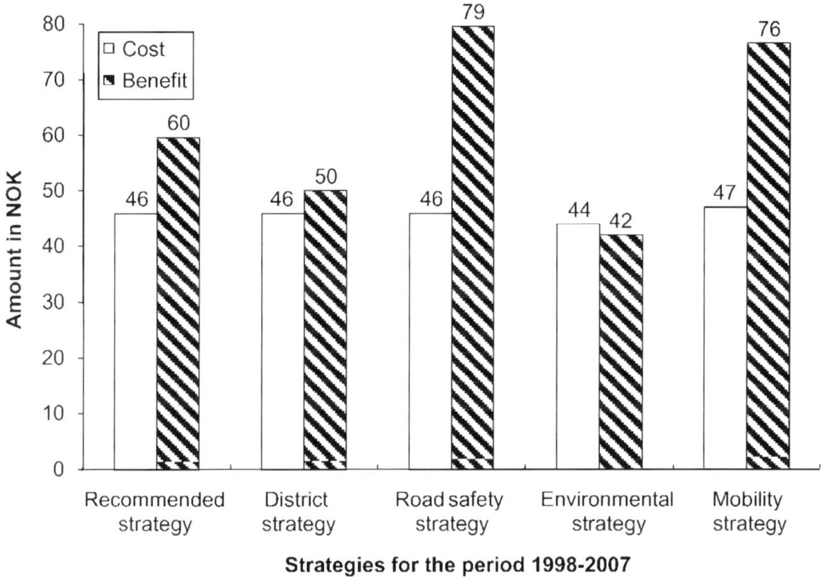


*Figure 10.7.2: Costs and benefits of alternative strategies for the road plan period 1998–2007 in Norway (Samferdselsdepartementet, St meld 37, 1996–97).*

The strategies are named according to the policy objective that is given highest priority in the strategy. The recommended strategy is a mixture of the other four strategies. Figure 10.7.2 shows the estimated total benefit and estimated costs of the alternative strategies for the period, 1988–2007 (Samferdselsdepartementet, St meld 37, 1996–97).

The estimated benefits are the sum of benefits for mobility, road safety and the environment. Figure 10.7.2 shows that the road safety strategy gives the greatest total benefit and has the best benefit–cost ratio. In the recommended strategy, the benefit (present value) is around NOK 20 billion less than in the road safety strategy.

## 10.8 Road safety audits and inspections

### Problem and objective

In most countries, the planning and design of public roads, road maintenance and traffic control is based on comprehensive sets of regulations and guidelines, which normally have been produced by the national roads administrations. One of the several objectives of these detailed technical regulations governing road design, road maintenance and traffic control is to ensure road safety. However, on several occasions completely new projects have been designated as accident black spots after just a few years. There may be many reasons for this:

- The guidelines are not up to date with the newest knowledge about road safety, because they normally not are updated very frequently.
- The guidelines are a compromise between conflicting objectives.
- The guidelines are not followed as intended.
- The project costs, environmental restrictions, and political restraints force the road planner or designer to make compromises, which do not always lead to the safest road design.
- The road environment, traffic volume and road user behaviour change after (re)opening of the road.

Road safety audits and inspections are intended to detect defects in road design or traffic control, which may affect road safety, and to ensure that these are corrected in order to prevent accidents.

**Description of the measure**

Road safety audit was introduced in Great Britain (Brownfield 1996) and Denmark (Jørgensen and Nilsson 1995) in the beginning of the 1990s and has now more or less been adopted in 23 European countries, Australia and several states in the United States (Matena, Löhe and Vaneerdewegh 2005). In addition, various forms of road safety inspections have also been applied in many European countries (Lutschounig, Nadler and Mocsari 2005).

Road safety audit and inspection are proactive road safety management. An audit deals with the design of new or reconstructed roads and inspection deals with existing roads. The purpose is to make new, reconstructed and existing roads as safe as possible before construction is started and/or accidents occur. Both road safety audit and inspection focus solely on road safety without regard for other possibly conflicting objectives.

Throughout the world, several definitions of road safety audit and inspection exist. Based on reviews of the different definitions, Matena et al. (2007) and Cardoso, Stefan, Elvik and Sørensen (2007) have formulated the following general definitions:

- ***Road safety audit***: A formal systematic road safety assessment of a road scheme carried out by an independent, qualified auditor who reports on the project's accident potential for all kinds of road users.

- ***Road safety inspection***: A preventive tool consisting of a regular, systematic, on-site inspection of existing roads, covering the whole road network carried out by trained safety expert teams, resulting in a formal report on detected road hazards and safety issues, requiring a formal response by the relevant road authority.

Road safety audit ought to be carried out in one or more of the following stages in the development of the road projects: the planning stages, the preliminary design stages and detailed design stages, before the road is opened to traffic and shortly after the road has been opened to traffic (Matena et al. 2007). Road safety inspection could be done as a periodic inspection every 2–4 years, as a dedicated inspection every fourth year or as an ad hoc inspection on identified roads with possible safety problems (Cardoso, Stefan, Elvik and Sørensen 2007).

Three different parties are usually involved in the process: the client responsible for the project, the designer of the road schemes and the auditor making the audit or inspection. The process and how to conduct an audit or inspection is normally described in detail in national handbooks for road safety audit and inspection. These handbooks often contain sets of checklists, or items to be investigated in a road safety audit or inspection. The audit or inspection should been done by an authorised auditor. Several countries have standardised training courses and examinations.

### Effect on accidents

Only few studies have been found where attempts were made to quantify the effect of road safety audits on accidents.

In a Danish study of 13 road construction projects with road safety audits, it was concluded that the auditor's comments led to improvements that were estimated to prevent 25–28 accidents per year (Jørgensen and Nilsson 1995). The road safety audit entailed an additional cost around DKR 12 million. The total construction costs were around DKR 1 billion.

In a German study, it was estimated that a road safety audit may prevent up to 70% of all accidents on newly constructed roads (BASt 2002).

The Surrey Country Council in Great Britain undertook a study of 19 audited and 19 non-audited traffic schemes. Comparisons were made between the effects of the projects on injury accidents. For sites with audited schemes, the average number of casualties dropped by 1.25 per year from 2.08 to 0.83, while casualty crashes at the not

*Table 10.8.1: Summary of effects on injury accident to be expected as a result of road safety inspection (Elvik 2006a)*

| Treatment | Accident that are influenced | Expected accident reduction (%) |
|---|---|---|
| Removing sight obstacles | All accidents | 0–5 |
| Flattening side slopes | Road departure accidents | 5–25 |
| Providing clear recovery zones | Road departure accidents | 10–40 |
| Guardrails along embankments | Road departure accidents | 40–50 |
| Guardrail end treatment | Vehicles striking guardrail ends | 0–10 |
| Yielding light poles | Vehicles striking poles | 25–75 |
| Signing of hazardous curves | Road departure accidents in curves | 0–35 |
| Correcting erroneous signs | All accidents | 5–10 |

audited dropped by only 0.26 per year from 2.60 to 2.34 (Surrey Country Council 1994).

An evaluation of road safety inspection for 300 high-crash locations in New York reports a 20–40% reduction in accidents (FHWA 2006). Another US study conducted in South Carolina showed that road safety inspection had an accident reduction of 12.5–23.4% and one site had a reduction of 60% in fatalities (FHWA 2006).

Road safety inspection may lead to the implementation of several different measures. Elvik (2006a) summarised the effects of the most frequently used measures (Table 10.8.1).

### Effect on mobility

No effects of road safety audits on mobility have been found.

### Effect on the environment

No effects of road safety audits on the environment have been found.

### Costs

The costs of road safety audit can vary greatly depending on the size of the project and the stage in which the audit takes place. A distinction can be made between time costs and extra costs for reconstruction.

*Table 10.8.2: Estimated costs of audit and inspection in different countries (Matena, Löhe and Vaneerdewegh 2005, Lutschounig, Nadler and Mocsari 2005, SWOV 2007, FHWA 2006)*

| | Audit costs (€ per stage) | Audit costs (% of construction costs) | Inspection costs |
|---|---|---|---|
| Australia | 600–6,000 | 0.2 (in average) | 10,000 €/km |
| Austria | 700–2,500 (per km road length) | 0.1–0.15 | 1 working day/10 km |
| Belgium | – | – | – |
| Czech Republic | 1,000–3,000 | – | – |
| Denmark | – | <0.5 | – |
| Germany | 800–5,000 | ≪ < < 1.0 | – |
| Norway | – | 0.1–1.0 | <50,000 €/km (construction costs inclusive) |
| Portugal | – | 4–7 (of planning costs) | 3 working day/40 km |
| The Netherlands | 3,200–4,600 | – | – |
| United Kingdom | 700–1,400 | 0.5 | – |
| United States | 2,000–5,000 ($ per stage) | – | – |

The costs of road safety audit related to the time spent to make the audit are summarised in Table 10.8.2 for different countries. The cost of an audit ranges between 600 and 6,000 € per stage or between 700 and 2,500 €/km. This corresponds to about 0.1–1.0% of the construction costs or 4–7% of the planning costs.

In Denmark (Jørgensen and Nilsson 1995), the costs of road safety audits are calculated to be around 150,000 €, if the additional costs for the implementation of the measures proposed by the auditors is included. The additional cost of implementing measures proposed by the auditors comprised 1.15% of the total construction costs of the roads. Estimates of added costs are around 1–2% of the total project costs (SWOV 2007).

Table 10.8.2 also summarises the costs for road safety inspection. The costs are about 10,000 €/km or 0.75–1 working day/10 km. If the construction costs of interventions are included the costs are up to 50,000 €/km.

## Cost–benefit analysis

The main advantages of road safety audits are that accidents can be prevented before any accidents occur and deficits can be treated before the road is built. This gives an effective and inexpensive road safety management. Cost–benefit analyses of road safety audits

*Table 10.8.3: Estimated benefit—costs (B/C) ratio of audit and inspection in different countries (Rosebud 2003, Macaulay and Mcinerney 2002, SWOV 2007)*

| | Audit, B/C ratio | Inspection, B/C ratio |
|---|---|---|
| Australia | 3–242 | 2.4–84 |
| Denmark | 1.46 | – |
| Germany | 4–99 | – |
| Norway | 1.34 | – |

were conducted in Denmark, Germany, Norway and Australia. Table 10.8.3 summarises the results. The benefit–costs ratios vary from about 1.34 in Norway to up to 242 in Australia. In Australia, the benefit–cost ratio was found to be greater than 10 for approximately 75% of all implemented recommendations (Macaulay and Mcinerney 2002).

In Australia, the benefit–cost ratio for road safety inspections has also been estimated. It is between 2.4 and 84. About 47% of all the recommendations had a benefit–cost ratio over 5 (Macaulay and Mcinerney 2002).

## 10.9 Motor vehicle taxation

**Problem and objective**

Using a motor vehicle gives rise to a number of costs for society. These costs include the construction and maintenance of public roads, traffic control, police enforcement, accident costs, environmental costs, time costs and congestion costs. The extent to which motor vehicles are used depends on how much users have to pay to acquire, own and use the vehicle (Fridstrøm and Rand 1993). The amount of traffic, and thus the number of accidents, can therefore be affected by changing the level and form of vehicle taxation.

Many of the costs of owning and using a motor vehicle are paid for by the users in the form of direct out-of-pocket expenses. However, this does not apply to all costs. Some accident costs and a very large part of the environmental costs are external, that is to say, they are not charged to those who bring about these costs. The bulk of congestion costs on roads are also external.

An issue that has often been discussed is whether the users of motor vehicles pay the full costs to society associated with the use of vehicles through taxes on the purchase, ownership and use of motor vehicles. If the external costs are not covered by taxation, this implies that society is subsidising the use of motor vehicles. In principle, it is possible to affect the number of traffic accidents through taxing the purchase, use and ownership of motor vehicles. Possible objectives of systems of vehicle taxation include managing travel demand, limiting the number and use of vehicles with particularly high levels of risk, promoting the safest possible composition of the vehicle fleet with regard to age, size or other characteristics and promoting the increased use of safety equipment. In addition, vehicle taxation has a purely fiscal objective, i.e. it is a source of revenue for the state.

**Description of the measure**

The costs of using motor vehicles can be divided into internal and external costs (Larsen 1991). Internal costs are all costs that the users of motor vehicles cover themselves when they buy and use a vehicle. External costs are all costs that are not covered by the users of motor vehicles themselves, but are inflicted on other members of society, such as people who are affected by noise and pollution from road traffic, or the public sector.

A number of attempts have been made to estimate the external costs of using motor vehicles in Norway (Samferdselsdepartementet 1996, Eriksen and Hovi 1995). The most important results from this study are shown in Table 10.9.1. The external costs of using motor vehicles in Norway in 1993 were estimated at almost NOK 23.3 billion. The Norwegian government's income from special taxes on motor vehicles in 1993 was NOK 20.2 billion (Opplysningsrådet for veitrafikken 1996).

**Effect on accidents**

No studies have been found that show the effect of changes in vehicle taxation on accidents. The effect will be indirect, by affecting travel demand, which in turn affects the number of accidents.

*Table 10.9.1: External costs of the use of motor vehicles in Norway (Eriksen and Hovi 1995)*

| | Amount in million NOK (1993 prices) | |
|---|---|---|
| Cost post | Best estimate | Confidence interval |
| Wear and tear on roads | 1,580 | (1,580; 1,580) |
| Road accidents | 8,022 | (8,022; 8,022) |
| Noise | 2,857 | (2,857; 2,857) |
| Air pollution | 10,733 | (7,708; 15,990) |
| Total | 23,192 | (22,167; 28,449) |

*Table 10.9.2: Expected effects on the amount of travel (number of person km) of different possible changes in vehicle taxes in Norway (Fridstrøm and Rand 1993)*

| | Percentage change in number of person km | | | |
|---|---|---|---|---|
| | Private cars | | Bus | |
| Change in tax | Short term | Long term | Short term | Long term |
| Increasing annual tax by NOK 2,000 | | −8 | | +6 |
| Increasing petrol prices by NOK 5 per litre | −10 | −26 | +6 | +24 |
| Vehicle taxes abolished, no increase in other taxes | | +27 | | −4 |
| Vehicle taxes abolished, income tax increased correspondingly | | +25 | | −4 |
| 50% lower purchase tax, and ca. 50% higher fuel tax | | +2 | | −3 |
| 50% increase in fixed costs of keeping a car | | −17 | | +16 |
| 50% reduction in fixed costs of keeping a car | | +14 | | −6 |
| 50% increase in variable costs of keeping a car | −8 | −20 | −2 | +8 |
| 50% reduction in variable costs of keeping a car | +16 | +26 | +2 | −3 |

***Simulated effects of alternative tax systems.*** On the basis of the national transport model for Norway, Fridstrøm and Rand (1993; see Fridstrøm 1993) have estimated the expected effects of different possible changes in vehicle taxation on the total number of journeys. Table 10.9.2 summarises the results of the calculations.

Short-term effects are immediate adaptations, given the current vehicle fleet. Long-term effects also include adaptations in the form of changes in the vehicle fleet. The estimates show that vehicle taxes influence travel demand. If vehicle taxation were abolished, the number of person kilometres driven by car would increase by 25–30%. The number of vehicle kilometres would increase even more, by 35–40%, because the use of cars would become more individual. If traffic were to increase by this amount, the number of injury accidents would be expected to increase by 25–30%.

The figures presented above indicate that the total taxation on vehicles needs to increase by around 25% in Norway in order for the taxes to cover the external costs of the use of vehicles. This increase in taxation would reduce the amount of traffic by around 10–15%, depending to some extent on how the increase in taxation is implemented. This could reduce the number of injury accidents by 5–10%.

***Increases in tax for high risk vehicles.*** From 1 January 1974 purchase tax for new motorcycles increased considerably in Norway (NOU 1975:42). In 1974, fewer new motorcycles were registered than in previous years. The number of motorcycles registered for the first time before and after 1974 was

| 1969 | 1970 | 1971 | 1972 | 1973 | 1974 | 1975 | 1976 |
|---|---|---|---|---|---|---|---|
| 4,203 | 3,821 | 3,598 | 3,638 | 3,710 | 3,462 | 3,525 | 3,949 |

There was a decrease of 248 in the number of motorcycles registered for the first time between 1973 and 1974. This decrease was no greater than the corresponding decrease in the number of motorcycles registered for the first time between 1969 and 1970. In both 1975 and 1976, the number of motorcycles registered for the first time increased again. Increases in taxation therefore appear to have had only a short-term, limited effect on the number of new motorcycles.

***Use of taxes to affect the composition of the vehicle fleet according to age and size.*** In public discussions on vehicle taxation, it is claimed that older cars are less safe than new cars and that the taxation system should therefore encourage a faster renewal of the car fleet. In 1996, the scrap fee in Norway was temporarily increased from NOK 1,000 to NOK 6,000 for specific groups of older cars. The number of scrapped cars increased significantly in 1996 in relation to previous years.

The relationship between the age of the car and accident rate is not well known. Without further study, it is not possible to say what effect the age of the car has on the risk of injury accidents in Norway today.

The relationship between the weight of the vehicle and its crashworthiness has also been much discussed (see Section 4.19). It is correct that heavy vehicles protect occupants from injury. On the other hand, they represent an increased risk of injury for occupants of lighter cars. The difference in the level of protection against injury between cars of different weights in the current car fleet is entirely due to differences in mass, and not due to mass as such. A British calculation of the effects of changes in mass of the car fleet (Broughton 1995) concluded that if the average mass were reduced by 5%, the number of injured drivers would be reduced by around 1.5%. This calculation indicates that there would be a favourable effect on safety in Norway if everyone had smaller cars than they do today, and if the differences in weight between cars were reduced.

**Effect on mobility**

Vehicle taxation contributes to reducing travel demand. This leads to less traffic on the roads than there would have been if all vehicle taxation were abolished. In and around the larger cities and towns in Norway, the road network is congested during certain times of the day. On these roads, less traffic will have a favourable effect on the flow of traffic for the remaining traffic.

### Effect on the environment

The severity of environmental problems associated with road traffic is closely related to traffic volume (Kolbenstvedt, Silborn and Solheim 1996). Current Norwegian vehicle taxation contributes to curbing travel demand and thus the total extent of environmental problems. General vehicle taxation is not designed with a view to affecting local environmental problems.

In a Norwegian study of the effects of environmental taxation effects on transport (Fridstrøm, Ramjerdi, Svae and Thune-Larsen 1991), the effects of increasing the carbon dioxide ($CO_2$) tax on fuel were estimated. An extrapolation of current developments (the reference alternative) was compared to a policy where the taxes on fossil fuels were increased (taxation alternative). It was estimated that emissions of $CO_2$ in 2000 would be 4% lower in the taxation alternative than in the reference alternative. For 2025, a reduction in emission of 14% was estimated if the taxation alternative were chosen instead of the reference alternative.

### Costs

The social opportunity costs of motor vehicle taxation are not well known. These costs consist of the direct collection costs and the net value of gains or losses in efficiency caused by the taxation. Among the gains in efficiency is the limitation of the external effects of road traffic. These external effects have been estimated to be around NOK 25 billion for Norway in 1995. The costs include the loss of consumer surplus for journeys not made, due to current taxation. This loss is unknown.

In an estimate of the marginal costs of different forms of taxation, Brendemoen and Vennemo (1993) conclude that taxes on petrol, mineral oil and $CO_2$ emissions are clearly the most cost-effective forms of taxation in Norway. The explanation for this is that these forms of taxation contribute to limiting environmental problems. When the environmental costs of different forms of consumption are included, petrol taxation, mineral oil taxation and $CO_2$ taxation have a negative social marginal cost in Norway. This means that the advantages these taxes in terms of less environmental problems are valued more highly than the costs that they entail in terms of a reduction in consumption causing environmental problems (Brendemoen and Vennemo 1993).

On the basis of this study, it is concluded that general vehicle taxation does not lead to any net opportunity costs in Norway.

#### Cost–benefit analysis

If vehicle taxation in Norway were to be abolished, the number of kilometres driven by cars would increase by 35–40%. Calculating, as a very rough approximation, that the external effects of driving would increase correspondingly, this represents an added cost of around NOK 9–10 billion.

According to Brendemoen and Vennemo's study (1993), mentioned above, Norwegian consumers value the benefit of reduced environmental problems more highly than the costs of taxation. The external costs of road traffic are currently very probably greater than vehicle taxes, implying that it would be cost-effective to increase these.

### 10.10 Road pricing

#### Problem and objective

The costs to society of using motor vehicles vary considerably across different types of road and traffic flow conditions. On roads with light traffic that run through undeveloped areas, the external effects of driving motor vehicles in the form of accidents, noise, air pollution emission, undesirable land usage and barriers for local travel are relatively small. In dense rush hour traffic on main roads in large towns and cities, these external effects are considerably greater. Furthermore, traffic congestion inflicts large costs on all road users.

Econ (2003) and Eriksen, Markussen and Pütz (1999) have estimated the external costs of road traffic in Norway for different types of vehicles in urban and rural areas. Costs that were included in the estimates are costs associated with road wear and tear, accidents, noise, emission of $CO_2$, local exhaust gas emissions and local emission of dust and particles. Figure 10.10.1 shows the results of the calculations for different types of vehicles. In addition, taxes that are proportional to the distance driven are also given, per kilometre driven. Figure 10.10.1 shows that the external costs per kilometre driven in Norway are higher in urban than in rural areas for all types of vehicle. Furthermore, the average external costs are higher than the taxation rates for all types of vehicle. In rush hour traffic in the largest cities, the external congestion costs are considerable.

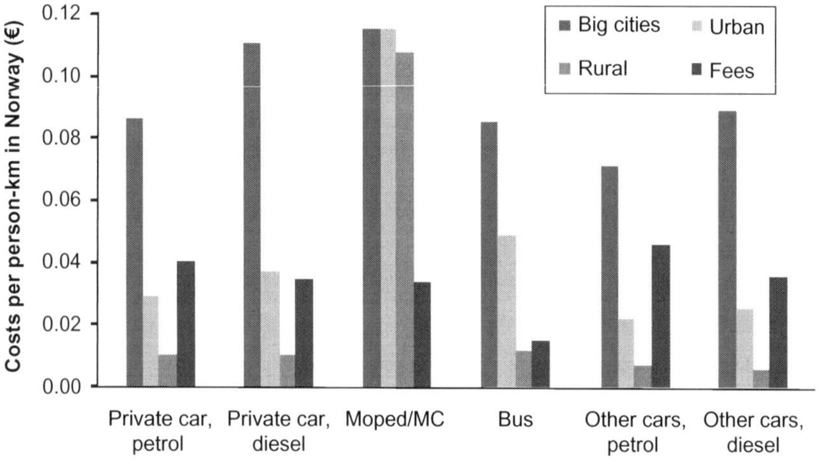


*Figure 10.10.1: Marginal, external costs per person kilometre of travel for different forms of transport in Norway in Euros (Econ 2003).*

Road pricing makes it possible to charge road users for the full costs, which they inflict upon society. The objective is to ensure that road users make their travel behaviour choices based on the best available information of the social costs, which their choice entails.

## Description of the measure

Road pricing is an economic concept that means that motorists directly pay for driving on a particular roadway or in a particular area. The road charges includes fuel taxes, licence fees, parking taxes, tolls, and congestion charges, including those that may vary by time of day, by the specific road, or by the specific vehicle type, size and weight being used.

Road pricing is not primarily intended as a road safety measure. There are three explicit or implicit goals of road pricing (Jensen-Butler et al. 2008): (1) to collect revenue, (2) to reduce traffic and nuisance (externalities as congestion, environmental damage, noise, etc.) and (3) to promote efficiency.

The principle of the first item is to generate funds that normally are dedicated to roadway projects. The rates are set to maximise revenues or recover specific costs. Shifts to other routes and transport modes are not desired.

The strategy of the second and partly the third item is normally described as 'transportation demand management', also called 'mobility management'. The goal is often to reduce peak volumes. Revenue is normally not dedicated to roadway projects. Variable rates may be used during congested periods. Travel shifts to other modes and times are considered desirable. The reason for using road pricing to reduce rush hour traffic or to spread this in time is that it is not considered feasible to expand the road capacity in large cities to such an extent that congestion will disappear (Newbery 1990, Winston 1991, Jones and Hervik 1992, Jansson 1994, Lindberg 1994, Verhoef 1994, Bergan and Wærness 1995, Larsen and Minken 1995, Mayeres, Ochelen and Proost 1996, Meland 1996, Atkins 2006, VTPI 2008, Jensen-Butler et al. 2008).

Road pricing may be divided into different categories with different objectives (VTPI 2008):

- Road toll (fixed rates): A fixed fee for driving on a particular road. The goal is to raise revenues.
- Congestion pricing (time variable): A fee that is higher under congested conditions, intended to shift some vehicle traffic to other routes, times and modes. The goal is to raise revenue and reduce traffic congestion.
- Cordon fees (toll rings): Fees charged for driving in a particular area. The goal is to reduce congestion in major urban centres.
- A high-occupancy vehicle lane that accommodates a limited number of lower-occupant vehicles for a fee. The goal is to favour high-occupancy vehicle lanes compared with a general-purpose lane, and to raise revenues.
- Distance-based fees: A vehicle use fee based on how many kilometre a vehicle drives. The goal is to raise revenues and reduce various traffic problems.
- Pay-as-you-drive insurance: Prorates premiums by kilometre so vehicle insurance becomes a variable cost. The goal is to reduce various traffic problems, particularly accidents.
- Road space rationing: Revenue-neutral credits used to ration peak-period roadway capacity. The goal is to reduce congestion on major roadways or urban centres.

Road pricing can be implemented at various scales: a point in the road network, such as a bridge, a roadway section, a roadway or a corridor, all roads in an area, such as a centre of a city, roadways at regional centres or throughout a region, or certain roads in a county.

A variety of pricing methods can be used to collect fees as pass, toll booths, electronic tolling, optical vehicle recognition or global positioning system (GPS) (VTPI 2008). GPS are not used as road pricing yet, but several pilots have been made, and a nationwide system is under development in the Netherlands planned to start in 2011 for goods traffic and in 2012 for private traffic (Ministerie van Verkeer en Waterstaat 2007). EU also plans a united European GPS road pricing system for lorries.

## Effect on accidents

In principle, toll-funded roads may affect road safety by influencing traffic volume and speed. Congestion pricing may reduce vehicle travel (VTPI 2008). Finally, pay-as-you-drive insurance probably has a favourable effect on road safety.

***Congestion charging in London.*** London has had a congestion charge in the central area since 2003. During the first years, the scheme resulted in a 12% reduction in total vehicle kilometres, a 30% reduction in car traffic, and a 28% reduction in accidents. Moped and motorbike journeys increased 10–15%, while moped and motorbike accidents decreased 4%. Pedestrian injuries declined by 6% (Richards 2006; Jensen-Butler et al. 2008). A later evaluation by TfL (2007) concludes that recent trends in injury accidents in central London continue to reflect traffic changes brought about by charging. The latest findings suggest that reduction in accidents in the charging zone is perhaps slightly greater than might otherwise have been expected. However, there is some evidence of possibly detrimental trends to accidents involving taxis and bicycles.

***Congestion charging in Stockholm.*** Stockholm has a congestion pricing system on a permanent basis since August 2007 after a 7-month trial period. The system is operated with automatic number plate recognition. For the first 7 months it is estimated that the congestion charging has entailed a decline in the number of personal injury accidents of 5–10% within the congestion tax area (City of Stockholm 2006; Jensen-Butler et al. 2008).

***The AKTA road pricing experiment in Copenhagen.*** In 2001–03, an experiment of GPS road pricing was carried out in Copenhagen among 500 car drivers. In this project, the overall reduction in accidents has been 4% corresponding to a 5.4% reduction in car mileage. In the charging zone, the estimated reduction in accidents was 6–8% compared to an 8–10% reduction in traffic (Sulkjær et al. 2005, Jensen-Butler et al. 2008).

***Pay-as-you-speed project in Denmark.*** The project is the first ISA project based on pay-as-you-drive principles. If speeding, the driver gets penalty points, which decrease the driver's chance of a potential 30% discount on the cost of the automobile insurance. The preliminary result is based on 38 participants. The key results are that free flow speed is reduced by 2.4 km/h on 50 km/h roads and 4.8 km/h on rural 80 km/h roads, and the mileage with speeding above 5 km/h has been reduced from 16% to 3% on 50 km/h and from 29% to 2% on rural 80 km/h roads (Agerholm, Tradisauskas, Harms and Lahrmann 2007). According to the power model of speed and road accident (Elvik, Christensen and Amundsen 2004) this speed reduction corresponds to reduction of injury accident by 9% on 50 km/h roads and 11% on 80 km/h rural roads.

***Tolls in Norway with alternative choice of road.*** A study of route choices in the area around Drammen, Norway, in 1977, between destinations where it was possible to use both the toll road and national highways where no tolls were payable, found that around 18% of traffic between these points used the old national road network (Kristiansen and Østmoe 1978). The study estimated that half of the traffic that chose the old national highway network, i.e. around 9% of the total traffic, would have chosen the toll road if no fees were payable on that road. The effect of this displacement of traffic was not quantified on accidents. On the basis of normal accident rates for national highways, it is estimated that the total number of accidents on the two roads would have been around 17% lower with no fees than the actual number. Traffic on the national highway would then have been considerably lower, while traffic on the toll road would have increased about 12.5%.

***Effects of toll ring roads in Bergen, Oslo and Trondheim and of local fuel taxes in Tromsø, Norway.*** The effects of the toll rings on traffic volume in Bergen, Oslo and Trondheim, and the local fuel tax in Tromsø, have been the subject of a number of studies (Bergen: Larsen 1987, 1988; Oslo: Solheim 1992, Ramjerdi 1995; Trondheim: Meland 1994, Polak and Meland 1994). In Bergen, the decrease in vehicle traffic during the first year following the opening of the toll road, during the part of the day when tolls were payable is estimated to be 6–7%. No transfer to public transport was found. In Oslo, the decrease in car traffic is estimated to be 3–10% for the first year after the toll ring was opened. No transition to public transport could be found in Oslo either. In Trondheim, the decrease in vehicle traffic in the period when tolls are payable was estimated at 8% for the year after the ring road was open. In Tromsø, the decrease in vehicle traffic was estimated at 7% during the first year after the local fuel tax was introduced. Table 10.10.1 shows changes in the number of injury accidents per year from before to after the introduction of tolls/taxation systems in the four Norwegian cities (Bergen: 1985–86; Oslo: 1989–90; Trondheim: 1990–92; Tromsø: 1989–91).

In all the cities where toll rings or local fuel taxes have been introduced, the number of injury accidents reduced in the first year after these systems were introduced. On average, the decrease is around 5% (95% CI [−11; +1]), which corresponds well with the reduction of traffic in the cities.

***Road pricing system in Gothenburg.*** In Sweden, possible effects of a fully developed road pricing system in the Gothenburg area have been simulated using a traffic assignment programme as part of the so-called Test-Oriented Scenario Assessment

*Table 10.10.1: Changes in the number of injury accidents in Norwegian cities with toll rings, compared with towns in the rest of Norway*

| | Accidents in the four cities | | Accidents in other towns | | |
|---|---|---|---|---|---|
| City | Before | After | Before | After | Change (%)[1] |
| Bergen | 525 | 458 | 4,189 | 4,375 | −16 |
| Oslo | 1,108 | 1,122 | 3,089 | 3,194 | −2 |
| Trondheim | 274 | 239 | 4,042 | 3,771 | −7 |
| Tromsø | 70 | 62 | 4,127 | 4,170 | −13 |
| All | 1,977 | 1,881 | 15,447 | 15,510 | −5 |

[1]Net change in the four cities, controlled for changes in other towns.

(TOSCA) Project (Delegationen för Transporttelematik 1994). It was assumed that each vehicle was automatically debited (using electronic micro chips) for a sum corresponding to the marginal, external costs of driving. If the system were fully developed, it was calculated that accidents could reduce by 15%.

### Effect on mobility

The effects of road pricing on mobility depend on the design of the system. A toll road will normally have better mobility than the old road network. With a fully developed road pricing system, some of the current rush hour traffic may disappear or travel at different times. This will reduce congestion as shown in, for example London and Stockholm (Jensen-Butler et al. 2008). Estimates for Oslo show that the benefits of differentiating prices (Ramjerdi 1995) in the toll ring according to the amount of traffic would be greater than the costs. In other words, the benefits in the form of increased mobility for the remaining traffic are greater than the costs in the form of loss of benefit for the displaced traffic. Simulations for the Gothenburg area show that a fully developed road pricing system can lead to an increase in the average speed of around 10% (Delegationen för Transporttelematik 1994). Pay-as-you-speed projects will probably reduce the average speed. In a Danish experience, speed was reduced by about 5% among car drivers participating in the project (Agerholm, Tradisauskas, Harms and Lahrmann 2007).

### Effect on the environment

The effects of road pricing on the environment depend on the design of the system and its effects on traffic volumes and flows. An estimate of the effects of increased toll rates in rush hour in the toll ring in Oslo found that fuel consumption in rush hour could be reduced by around 23–28% (Larsen and Rekdal 1996). For the whole of Oslo and Akershus, Norway, taken together, the decrease in fuel consumption over the whole 24-h period is estimated to be 1–4%. All other conditions being equal, reduced fuel consumption will reduce air pollution.

In London and Stockholm, a 16% and 13% reduction in $CO_2$ emission was observed. The effect on NOx and PM10 is estimated to be respectively 8% and 7% in London and 9% and 13% in Stockholm. For Copenhagen, the reduction for $CO_2$ emission and local emission (NOx, PM10 and PM5) is estimated to 1–3% for the whole Copenhagen region (Jensen-Butler et al. 2008).

A simulation of a fully developed road pricing system in the Gothenburg area found that the total emissions from road traffic would be reduced by around 11% (Delegationen för Transporttelematik 1994).

Neither London nor Stockholm can identify significant changes in noise level as a consequence of road charging, although there seems to be a slight overall reduction of 0–3 dB. In Copenhagen study, however, there is an estimated overall 2% reduction in noise exposure measured in terms of a so-called noise annoyance index (Jensen-Butler et al. 2008).

### Costs

The costs of road pricing and toll ring roads are of two types: direct costs and indirect costs. The direct costs are costs of collecting payment. These consist of building and running toll systems, including manning the toll stations and debt collection from those who do not pay. The indirect costs are as follows: (1) delays at toll stations for people who have to pay. With a fully developed road pricing system based on electronic microchips and automatic vehicle identification, such delays can be avoided. (2) Loss of benefit from cancelled journeys due to tolls or road pricing. The total costs are the sum of the direct and indirect costs.

In a fully developed road pricing system these costs are offset in the form of savings in journey time for the remaining traffic. As mentioned above (under *effects on mobility*), in given cases these savings can be greater than the gross costs of a road pricing system.

For the Norwegian toll ring in Bergen, Oslo and Trondheim, Meland (1996) gives costs in NOK million (Table 10.10.2). The cost figures in Table 10.10.2 cannot be added, since they are a mixture of investment costs and annual costs. Ramjerdi (1995) has

*Table 10.10.2: Costs of the Norwegian toll ring in Bergen, Oslo and Trondheim (Meland 1996)*

| | Amount in million NOK (1992–93) | | |
|---|---|---|---|
| Place | Cost of installation | Operating costs per year | Fees paid per year |
| Bergen | 19 | 12.5 | 64.8 |
| Oslo | 255 | 74.0 | 634.7 |
| Trondheim | 57 | 6.0 | 74.0 |

*Table 10.10.3: Costs and benefits of different road pricing systems in Oslo, Norway (Ramjerdi 1995)*

| | Annual amount in million NOK (1993) | | | | | |
|---|---|---|---|---|---|---|
| | Current road network | | | Fully developed main road network | | |
| Costs and benefits | Current system | Optimal toll ring | Optimal road pricing | No tolls | Current system | Optimal toll ring |
| Benefit for remaining traffic | 55.4 | 114.5 | 170.2 | 224.0 | 266.7 | 299.0 |
| Loss of benefit for lost traffic | 33.6 | 19.4 | 19.3 | −3.5 | 28.8 | 13.8 |
| Loss of time when paying tolls | 4.8 | 1.1 | Not known | 0.0 | 5.4 | 0.5 |
| Total benefit | 17.0 | 94.0 | 150.9 | 227.5 | 232.5 | 284.7 |
| Costs of collecting tolls | 96.6 | 70.0 | Not known | 0.0 | 96.6 | 70.0 |
| Net benefit | −79.6 | 24.0 | Not known | 227.5 | 135.9 | 214.7 |

converted the investment costs for the toll ring in Oslo to an annual capital cost. This amounts to NOK 27 million.

The set-up costs for the London congestion charging scheme was about £58 million. The most recent forecast of net revenue is £68 million, based on gross revenue of £164 million and operational costs of £97 million (Jensen-Butler et al. 2008). The electronic truck toll collection system in Germany (MAUT) had an estimated investment cost on €700 million (Rtt 2009). The planned national GPS road pricing system in the Netherlands is estimated to costs €1.3–4.4 billion in investment and €500–1,100 million annually for operation (Ministerie van Verkeer en Waterstaat 2007).

## Cost–benefit analysis

Ramjerdi (1995) has carried out a cost–benefit analysis of alternative road pricing system in Oslo, Norway. The results of the analysis are shown in Table 10.10.3.

Introducing road pricing in Oslo would give greater benefits than the current toll ring. It is cost-effective to introduce road pricing in Oslo, independent of whether or not the main road network is to be financed by an extension of the current toll stations.

## 10.11 Changes in the modal split of travel

### Problem and objective

The risk of personal injury varies considerably between different forms of transport. Estimates of risk for different modes of transport are provided in Chapter 3 of Part I of this book. All forms of individual transport involve a higher risk of personal injury than public transport. The risk of injury is particularly high for pedestrians, cyclists and riders of mopeds or motorcycles. It is therefore reasonable to believe that the number of persons injured in traffic could be reduced if a higher proportion of journeys were made using public transport, and a lower proportion using private means of transport.

Nonetheless, it is important to be aware of the fact that the risk estimates based on official accident statistics, can give misleading results as far as differences in risk between different forms of transport are concerned (Vaa 1993). This is primarily due to the fact that the level of under-reporting of injuries in official statistics varies between different forms of transport. Furthermore, public transport cannot be used from door-to-door to the same extent as private forms of transport. Using public transport normally means that a larger proportion of a specific journey must be done on foot or by means of another personal form of transport than when private transport is used for the whole journey.

Changes in the modal split of travel is intended to contribute to reducing the total number of injuries in traffic by encouraging people to use the modes of travel that have the lowest expected number of injuries for a given travel distance.

### Description of the measure

The term 'changes in the modal split of travel' is used here to denote changes in the distribution of a given number of person kilometres across difference forms of travel. The phrase 'main mode of travel' refers to the mode of travel used for the largest part of the distance on any journey. More than one mode of travel can be used during a single journey. The following measures are discussed:

- Changes in the supply of public transport
- Changing the main mode of transport for journeys of a given length
- The accident rate on roads and streets with and without public transport
- Measures that can affect the demand for public transport.

## Effect on accidents

***Changes in the supply of public transport*** have been investigated in the following studies, the results of which are summarised in Table 10.11.1:

Boot, Wassenberg and Van Zwam (1982) (The Netherlands): public transport strikes
Allsop and Turner (1986) (Great Britain): fare increases
Allsop and Robertson (1994) (Great Britain): increases and decreases in fares

Public transport strikes in The Hague in the Netherlands from 7 to 27 May 1981 led to a very large reduction in the supply of public transport. Only regional buses were running. Compared to the corresponding days in the years 1978, 1979 and 1980, both injury accidents and property-damage-only accidents increased. The increase in injury accidents only affected bicycle accidents and accidents involving mopeds and motorcycles. The increase in property-damage-only accidents was largest for cars, but also included other types of vehicles. Traffic counts showed that cycle traffic increased by 45% during the strike. Car traffic increased by 10% (Boot, Wassenberg and Van Zwam 1982).

*Table 10.11.1: Effect of changes in the availability of public transport on accidents*

| | Percentage change in the number of accidents | | |
|---|---|---|---|
| Accident severity | Type of accident affected | Best estimate | 95% confidence interval |
| ***Pubic transport strike (very limited public transport)*** | | | |
| Injury accidents | All accidents | +18 | (−1; +41) |
| Property damage only accidents | All accidents | +31 | (+25; +38) |
| ***Higher fares (transition from public to private transport)*** | | | |
| Injury accidents | All accidents | +4 | (+3; +6) |
| ***Lower fares (transition from private to public transport)*** | | | |
| Injury accidents | All accidents | +0 | (−1; +1) |

In 1982, fares for London Transport in London (buses and underground) increased by about 90%. In the first year after the increase in prices, the number of injured persons in London was about 4% higher than otherwise expected. The number of injured pedestrians and bus passengers reduced. The number of injured cyclists, moped riders, motorcyclists and car passengers increased. Rush hour traffic using London Transport in and out of central areas of London went down by 14% from 1981 to 1982. Rush hour traffic by individual means of transport in and out of London increased in the same period by 19% (UK Department of Transport 1989).

In 1983, fares on London Transport were reduced by 25%. The total number of injured persons did not change. The number of injured pedestrians and bus passengers increased and the number of persons in other road user groups, who were injured, decreased. Rush hour traffic using London Transport increased from 1982 to 1983 by 11%. Rush hour traffic for other modes went down by 10%.

***Individual risk with different forms of transport – changing form of transport.*** A number of studies have been carried out where the injury risk of different forms of transport to an individual traveller has been estimated. The studies are based on somewhat different assumptions and are therefore not suitable for a synthesis in the form of a meta-analysis.

Forsström (1982) studied the risk of injury on door-to-door journeys in the Gothenburg area. He found that the risk of being injured on average was about 12% higher when a form of public transport was used as the main mode of transport (i.e. for the major part of the journey) than when an individual form of transport was used as the main mode of transport. However, the injuries were less serious when public transport was used. The study found that pedestrians, cyclists and people on mopeds and motorcycles could reduce their risk by using public transport. However, car drivers and car passengers would run a higher risk by changing to public transport. This is due to the fact that the increased walking distance to and from bus stops will lead to more falls, if public transport is used.

Lie and Muskaug (1982) estimated the risk for door-to-door journeys on the basis of risk figures for Haugesund, Norway. They found that buses were the safest form of transport. Jørgensen (1988) found in a study for Greater Copenhagen that the risk was lowest when using suburban trains. The study also found that car users could reduce their total risk of injury by using regional trains or buses.

Vaa (1993) calculated the risk for door-to-door journeys where buses are used as the main mode of transport. The study shows that official accident figures give a very misleading picture of the risk of injury on bus journeys. According to the official statistics, 303 people were registered as injured in traffic accidents in Norway where buses were involved. The actual figure, estimated on the basis of the injury record at the National Institute for Public Health was estimated to 632. There were a further 156 people who were injured in falls on board buses, without the bus being involved in a traffic accident, and 2,389 people injured in falls walking to or from the bus stop. In total, the number of persons injured on bus journeys was estimated to 3,177 per year, of whom only 303 were registered in the official accident statistics.

Hagen and Ingebrigtsen (1993) used Vaa's risk figures to estimate the potential for reducing the number of injured persons by changing from using cars to using the train or bus for journeys to work in Akershus County in Norway. They found that a transition from car to bus did not reduce the expected number of injured persons. However, the transition to train could reduce the number of persons injured, especially if the journey to the railway station was made by car.

Elvik (1997a) estimated possible changes in injury risk in Norway when changing from bicycle, moped, motorcycle or car to either bus or train. The estimates were carried out both on the basis of official injury figures and estimated true injury figures. The calculations were carried out for the whole country and for Oslo. For Oslo, trams were also included. Furthermore, a separate estimate was made for travellers aged between 18 and 24 years of age. The study contains a very large number of results. The study shows that the number of injured persons can be reduced if cyclists and people on mopeds or motorcycles start using buses or trains. This applies whatever the length of the journey and independently of whether estimates rely on official accident statistics or on estimates of the total number of injuries. The study found that for car drivers, the official number of injured persons could probably be reduced by using buses or trains. The unrecorded injuries from falls will, however, increase so much that no overall gain in safety can be expected if car users start using buses or trains. This applies at least for short journeys.

The main results of the studies presented above can be summarised in the following points:

- The number of injured persons can be reduced if cyclists and people using mopeds or motorcycles start using buses or trains.
- The number of injured persons in official accident statistics can probably be reduced if car users start using the bus or the train. However, unrecorded injuries are likely to increase, in particular, involving falls on the way to or from the bus or train.
- Trams are the least safe form of public transport. On short journeys, buses are safest and on long journeys, trains are the safest.

- Falls when walking to or from public transport stops contribute substantially to the total risk of door-to-door journeys using public transport. Short distances between bus stops can reduce walking distances and thus the number of injuries. Better road maintenance, especially during the winter, can also reduce the number of falls.

***Accident rate on roads with and without public transport.*** Two Norwegian studies (Hvoslef 1973, 1974, Blakstad 1990) have compared the accident rate on roads and streets with and without public transport. The results of these studies are shown in Table 10.11.2. There is a tendency for the accident rate to be higher in streets with public transport, particularly in streets with both buses and trams than in streets without public transport. This may be partly due to the fact that public transport generates more pedestrian traffic, and that public transport, in particular, trams, are less able to make evasive manoeuvres in critical situations than private cars and other smaller vehicles.

***Measures that affect the demand for individual and public transport.*** Among the measures that affect the demand for individual and public transport are prices for transport services (including fuel prices and vehicle prices), journey times (including waiting times and walking time) and other aspects of public transport, such as availability of seats.

The effects of these factors with respect to individual choices of transport in Norway have been summarised by Fridstrøm and Rand (1993) and Stangeby and Norheim (1995). Table 10.11.3 is based on these reports. The table shows the effect of different factors in the form of demand elasticity. Demand elasticity shows the percentage by which demand changes when the factor that influences demand is changed by 1%.

*Table 10.11.2: Number of injury accidents reported to the police per million vehicle kilometer on roads and streets with and without public transport, Norway (sources: Hvoslef 1973, 1974, Blakstad 1990)*

| | | Public transport | | |
|---|---|---|---|---|
| Study | Type of road or street | None | Bus alone | Bus and tram |
| Hvoslef (1974) | Two lanes, densely populated | 1.35 | 1.49 | 2.88 |
| Blakstad (1990) | Four lanes, medium density of population | (0.42) | 0.70 | (0.57) |
| | Two lanes, medium density of population | 0.31 | 0.43 | (0.91) |
| | Four lanes, densely populated | 1.18 | 1.24 | 1.00 |
| | Two lanes, densely populated | 0.94 | 0.91 | 1.36 |

Accident rates given in brackets are based on only a few accidents and are very uncertain.

*Table 10.11.3: Demand elasticities for individual and public transport, Norway (Fridstrøm and Rand 1993, Stangeby and Norheim 1995)*

| Factor | Mode of transport | Elasticity of demand in the short and long term: Short term | Long term |
|---|---|---|---|
| Costs of keeping a car (+1%) | Car | | −0.41 |
| | Bus | | 0.26 |
| | Train | | 0.27 |
| | Aeroplane | | 0.24 |
| Car usage costs (+1%) | Car | −0.21 | −0.43 |
| | Bus | −0.05 | 0.12 |
| | Train | −0.01 | 0.18 |
| | Aeroplane | 0.02 | 0.17 |
| Journey time by car (+1%) | Car | | −0.51 |
| | Bus | | −0.04 |
| | Train | | 0.14 |
| | Aeroplane | | 0.23 |
| Public transport ticket price (+1%) | Bus | −0.30 | −0.65 |
| | Train | −0.70 | −1.10 |
| | Underground | −0.20 | −0.40 |
| | Car | 0.16 | 0.16 |
| Journey time by public transport (+1%) | Departure time | −0.24 | −0.24 |
| | Waiting time | −0.37 | −0.37 |
| | Travel time | −0.26 | −0.26 |
| | Car driving | 0.16 | 0.16 |
| Frequency of departures (+1%) | Public transport | 0.15 | 0.15 |
| | Car journeys | −0.04 | −0.04 |

A distinction is made between short-term and long-term elasticity. Short-term elasticity refers to the direct effects on transport demand, occurring within a period of 1–3 years. Long-term elasticity shows more long-term effects, occurring within a period of 8–10 years. Increases in car ownership costs lead to less driving and a somewhat increased demand for public transport. The percentage decrease in car driving is greater than the increase in public transport. The same applies if car usage costs increase. Increased journey time by car reduces the use of cars, but does not in itself lead to significantly more public transport. Increased fares on public transport lead to less use of public transport and more car driving. The same applies if journey times with public transport become longer. Increasing the number of departures increases the use of public transport and can reduce car traffic.

### Effect on mobility

Journey times on most of the road network in Norway are scarcely affected by the modal split of transport. In and around the larger cities, however, mobility can be affected by the model split of travel. Cars take up more road space per person per kilometre than public transport, and therefore consume more road capacity for a given number of person kilometres (Kolbenstvedt, Silborn and Solheim 1996). By switching to public transport, road capacity is utilised more effectively, so that the flow of traffic improves.

### Effect on the environment

Emissions from different forms of transport into the air vary according to traffic flow patterns and the technical condition of the vehicle. Typical emission coefficients are shown in Table 10.11.4 (Solheim, Hammer and Johansen 1994). Public transport vehicles for the majority of pollutants pollute more per kilometre driven than cars. Electrically powered transport does not emit air pollution. Nonetheless, a certain amount of emission for these forms of transport has been stipulated, in order to take account of the fact that producing electricity can pollute, and that electricity used for transport has alternative uses. The emission per person kilometre depends on how well public transport utilises its capacity. The more person kilometres are performed for a given number of public transport kilometres, the lower the amount of emissions per person kilometre. On the basis of the emission figures in Table 10.11.4, Solheim, Hammer and Johansen estimated the expected effects of the following

*Table 10.11.4: Emission coefficients in grams per kilometre driven from vehicles, Norway (Solheim, Hammer and Johansen 1994)*

| | Emission in grams per kilometre driven | | | | |
|---|---|---|---|---|---|
| Type of pollutant | Car | Bus | Train[1] | Underground[1] | Tram[1] |
| NOx | 2.3 | 24.6 | 1.13 | 0.91 | 1.03 |
| $SO_2$ | 0.03 | 1.5 | 1.89 | 1.51 | 1.72 |
| VOC[2] | 0.0 | 2.6 | 0.15 | 0.12 | 0.14 |
| CO | 21.0 | 4.8 | 0.01 | 0.01 | 0.01 |
| Particles | 0.08 | 1.1 | 0.09 | 0.08 | 0.09 |
| $CO_2$ | 310.0 | 1,104.0 | 1,210.09 | 968.07 | 1,102.52 |

[1]The emissions are calculated by assuming that electricity is produced by oil-fired power stations.
[2]VOC = Volatile, organic compounds (largely hydrocarbons).

measures on the total emissions in Oslo and Akershus, Norway, to affect the modal split of travel:

- Increasing fuel prices by 30%
- Reducing bus driving times by 25%
- Reducing fares by 25%
- Increasing the number of kilometres driven by public transport by 25%.

The effects of different combinations of these measures were also estimated. Measures transferring travel to public transport can be expected to reduce pollution. Increasing fuel prices has the greatest effect, because this produces the greatest decrease in car traffic. Increasing the supply of public transport, seen in isolation, has little effect on pollution.

### Costs

The costs of running public transport are considerable. Parliamentary report 32 (1995–96; Samferdselsdepartementet 1996) gives the following figures for state subsidies for public transport in Norway in 1994:

| Type of subsidy | NOK million |
|---|---|
| County council subsidies for local routes | 2,678 |
| Oslo municipality's subsidy for Oslo Sporveier | 519 |
| State operating subsidy for the Norwegian State Railway | 772 |
| State subsidy for domestic flights | 289 |
| State subsidy for Hurtigruten (coastal express) | 220 |
| Total state subsidies for public transport | 4,478 |

In total, public subsidies for running public transport are close to NOK 4.5 billion per year. In addition, in recent years, the state has given around NOK 200 million per year for investments in public transport in the larger cities.

### Cost–benefit analysis

A cost–benefit analysis of subsidies to Oslo Sporveier (Larsen 1993) tried to estimate how large a subsidy should be offered to Sporveien based on an objective of achieving the greatest possible social benefit from the subsidy (maximising the consumer surplus). The social benefit in this case was measured on the basis of consumer surplus (see the Definitions of technical terms, Part III). Generalised travel costs, the sum of direct expenses and time costs, were used as a basis for calculating the consumer surplus. The optimal subsidy for Sporveien was estimated under different assumptions.

The annual subsidy for Oslo Sporveier when the study was carried out (1992) was NOK 481 million. If Sporveien were to be given complete freedom to select an optimal combination of fares and routes, at the same time if road pricing was introduced to ensure that car drivers were charged the social marginal costs of car driving, the optimum subsidy would be NOK 296 million. If road pricing were not introduced, the optimal subsidy would be NOK 514 million, because car traffic in Oslo would then be too. The analysis found that under most of the assumptions made, it is optimal to give Oslo Sporveier a greater subsidy than the company receives today.

## 10.12 Road traffic legislation

**Problem and objective**

Road user behaviour is of great importance for road safety. In order to make behaviour as predictable and as safe as possible, government has issued rules to regulate traffic behaviour. The idea is everyone travels more safely when these rules are adhered to than when they are violated. In order to ensure that the rules are complied with, the police enforce them. Violating the rules can be sanctioned with fines or imprisonment, among other things.

The design of vehicles, roads and traffic control are among the factors influencing road user behaviour. In order to ensure that the rules of the road and other rules directed at road users are complied with, it is important that other parts of the system are adapted to suit this. Road traffic legislation also includes the standards set by government regarding the design of roads, traffic control and vehicles.

Road traffic legislation is intended to reduce the number of traffic accidents by banning particularly dangerous behaviour and regulating behaviour so that it becomes homogeneous and predictable.

**Description of the measure**

Road traffic legislation, in Norway, denotes regulations with the force of law that are part of the Road Traffic Act or are based on this. These regulations are comprehensive and detailed, but a detailed description will not be given here.

## Effect on accidents

***The relationship between drivers' violation rates and their accident rate.*** A number of studies have evaluated the relationship between the number of traffic violations a driver has been convicted for, and the driver's accident rate. These studies include

Peck, McBride and Coppin (1971) (USA)
Harrington (1972) (USA)
Goldstein (1973) (USA)
Chipman (1982) (Canada)
Evans and Wasielewski (1982) (USA)
Evans and Wasielewski (1983) (USA)
Wasielewski (1984) (USA)
Smiley, Persaud, Hauer and Duncan (1989) (Canada)
West, Elander and French (1992) (Great Britain)

All these studies show that drivers who have been convicted for numerous violations have a higher accident rate per driver than drivers who have been convicted for few or no violations. Both the probability of being convicted and the number of accidents per driver are closely related to the driver's annual driving distance. It is therefore important to control for annual driving distance when studying the relationship between the number of traffic convictions and accident rate. Only the studies carried out by Chipman (1982) and West, Elander and French (1992) have controlled for driving distance. Figure 10.12.1 shows the relationship between the number of traffic convictions and accident rate according to Chipman's study. The accident rate increases with an increase in the number of violations, but not dramatically. There were too few women with six or more convictions to estimate their accident rate.

The results presented in Figure 10.12.1 do not refer to any specific type of violations. Research on the relationship between driving under the influence of alcohol (DUI) and accidents found consistently that drivers convicted for DUI, and especially multiple DUI offenders, are far more likely to get involved in accidents than other drivers (see Section 8.6).

***Possible effects of 100% compliance with road traffic legislation on the number of people killed or injured.*** An estimate has been made of the potential for reducing the number of people killed or injured in traffic in Norway if road traffic legislation were complied with 100% (Elvik 1997b). The results of this estimation are given in Table 10.12.1. It seems clear that better respect for road traffic legislation would improve traffic safety.

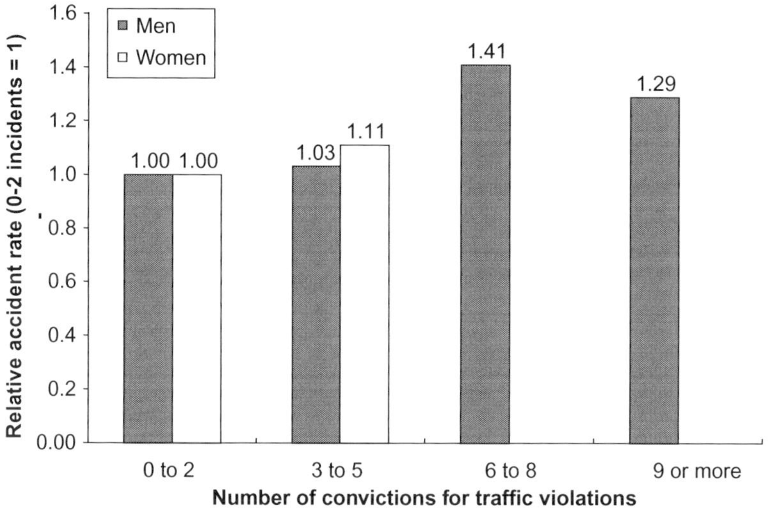


*Figure 10.12.1: The relationship between the number of traffic violations for which a driver has been convicted for and the driver's accident rate, Canada (Chipman 1982).*

*Table 10.12.1: Potential for reducing the numbers killed and injured in traffic in Norway assuming 100% respect for road traffic legislation (Elvik 1997b)*

| | Percentage change in the number of accidents (95% confidence interval) | |
|---|---|---|
| Main group of regulations | Injured | Killed |
| Speed limits | −9 (±5) | −15 (±8) |
| Use of safety equipment | −5 (±3) | −14 (±8) |
| Drink driving regulations | −3 (±2) | −10 (±7) |
| Other behaviour regulations in traffic | −8 (±6) | −7 (±5) |
| Technical requirements for vehicles | −1 (±1) | −1 (±1) |
| Driver requirements | −1 (±1) | −1 (±1) |
| Total potential | −27 (±18) | −48 (±30) |

***Effects of changes in legislation.*** A number of changes have been made to road traffic legislation in Norway. The effect of a number of these changes on the number of accidents has been studied. Table 10.12.2 summarises the results of studies that have evaluated the effects of these measures on the number of injury accidents or the number of people injured in traffic. The figures refer to the effects in the measure's target group, and not the total effects. For example, the target group for the compulsory use of

*Table 10.12.2: Effects of changes in road traffic legislation in Norway on the number of injuries/injury accidents in the target groups of each legislation*

| | Percentage change | |
|---|---|---|
| Changes in the law | Best estimate | 95% confidence interval |
| Repeal of the requirement for renewed driving tests, 1975 (see Section 6.5) | +1 | (−7; +9) |
| Compulsory helmets for mopeds/motorcycles, 1977 (see Section 3.11) | +42 | (+31; +57) |
| Sharpening up yield requirements at pedestrian crossings, 1978 (Hvoslef 1984) | +11 | (−2; +26) |
| Fines for non-use of seat belts, 1979 (Elvik 1995b) | −6 | (−10; −3) |
| Compulsory use of seat belts in the rear seats, 1985 (Elvik 1995c) | −6 | (−10; −2) |
| Automatic daytime running lights on new cars in 1985 (Elvik 1993c) | −2 | (−10; +7) |
| Compulsory daytime running lights on all cars in 1988 (Elvik 1993c) | −5 | (−13; +4) |
| Compulsory use of child restraints in 1988 (Elvik 1995c) | −11 | (−17; −5) |
| Changes in punishment for drink driving in 1988 (Vaas and Elvik 1992; see also Section 8.6) | +3 | (−5; +13) |

helmets on mopeds and motorcycles is drivers and passengers on mopeds and motorcycles. The target group for tightening up the yield requirement on pedestrian crossings is pedestrians who cross roads using pedestrian crossings.

Most of the measures do not appear to have led to statistically significant changes in the number of accidents. The mandatory use of seat belts in cars (front and rear seat) and child restraints appear to have reduced the number of injured persons. On the other hand, mandatory use of helmets for drivers of mopeds and motorcycles does not appear to have reduced the number of injuries. The numbers increased after the helmet-wearing law was introduced. The explanation for this increase is not known. An increased level of reporting of accidents involving mopeds or motorcycles is one possible explanation. Another possibility is changes in behaviour among moped users and motorcyclists after they started to wear helmets.

Effects of changes in drink driving legislation are described in Section 8.6.

**Effect on mobility**

The effects of road traffic legislation on mobility vary, depending on the content of the legislation. Some of the regulations in the road traffic legislation limit mobility in order to promote traffic safety. Speed limits are the best example of this, but drink driving legislation may also be regarded as reducing travel opportunities. Road traffic legislation also contains regulations prohibiting behaviour that unnecessarily hinders traffic, and parking that creates obstacles for traffic. The net effect of the legislation on mobility is not known and is difficult to judge on an informal basis.

### Effect on the environment

The effects of road traffic legislation on the environment have not been documented. The Norwegian regulations also cover noise levels and emission levels for motor vehicles. Since 1989, catalytic converters have been mandatory on all new cars in Norway. It has been documented that this contributes to reducing air pollution (Statens forurensningstilsyn 1993). Mandatory use of daytime running lights contributes to an increase in fuel consumption and an insignificant increase in pollution emissions (Ørjasæter and Bang 1993). Other effects of road traffic legislation on the environment have not been documented.

### Costs

The costs involved in road traffic legislation are of two types: direct costs and indirect costs. The direct costs consist of the costs of drawing up legislation and the cost of enforcement and sanctions. The indirect costs are additional costs that road users incur in the form of more expensive vehicles or increased journey times. One of the characteristics of legislation as a policy instrument is that the direct costs are often small and the indirect costs are often large (Friedman 1987). No estimates of the total costs of road traffic legislation are available. Table 10.12.3 compiles available estimates of costs (Elvik 1993d; Hagen 1994).

*Table 10.12.3: The cost of road traffic legislation in Norway (most important sources: Elvik 1993d, Hagen 1994)*

| | Annual costs in million NOK (1995) | |
|---|---|---|
| What the cost affects | Costs in public budgets | Costs for road users |
| Drawing up legislation, etc. | 10 | |
| Police enforcement | 320 | |
| Roadside vehicle inspections | 186 | 339 |
| Punishments for violations | 143 | |
| Vehicle safety standards, etc. | | 975 |
| Training requirements, etc. | | 778 |
| Total, all legislation | 659 | 2,092 |

*Table 10.12.4: Cost–benefit analysis of selected legislation of road traffic*

| Legislation or measure | Benefit–cost ratio |
|---|---|
| ***Existing regulations*** | |
| Mandatory use of daytime running lights on vehicles | 3.3 (±0.4) |
| Mandatory use of daytime running lights on mopeds/motorcycles | 8.7 (±10.0) |
| Mandatory use of helmets of mopeds/motorcycles | 18.0 (±6.0) |
| Mandatory use of seat belts for drivers | 31.7 (±5.7) |
| Mandatory use of seat belts for front-seat passengers | 13.3 (±3.5) |
| Mandatory use of seat belts for rear-seat passengers | 1.3 (±0.9) |
| Mandatory use of child restraints in cars | 1.3 (±0.6) |
| Mandatory use of under-ride guardrails on lorries | 4.0 (±2.0) |
| ***Possible new regulations*** | |
| Compulsory use of additional high-mounted stop lamps on cars | 3.6 (±0.3) |
| ***Enforcement measures*** | |
| Tripling stationary speed enforcement | 6.5 (±3.9) |
| Tripling drink driving enforcement | 1.2 (±0.4) |
| Tripling seat belt enforcement | 3.6 (±2.2) |
| Current use of speed cameras | 8.9 (±2.9) |
| ***Sanctions*** | |
| Withdrawing driving licences for drink driving | 9.2 (±1.0) |

The estimate shows that the annual costs of road traffic legislation in Norway currently amount to around NOK 2.75 billion. Of this, around NOK 660 million is charged to public budgets, while the rest are costs incurred by road users. Road user costs consist both of direct outlays, for example in the form of payment for mandatory driving lessons, and costs of time incurred as the result of different measures, such as vehicle inspections.

## Cost–benefit analysis

A distinction can be made between cost–benefit analyses of (1) existing regulations, (2) new regulations, (3) enforcement of existing regulations and (4) sanctions of violations of road traffic regulations. Table 10.12.4 shows cost–benefit analyses of selected regulations (Elvik 1997b). The table shows that all items of current legislation that have been analysed are cost-effective. The introduction of additional, high-mounted stop lamps on all vehicles would also be cost-effective. Increasing the amount of enforcement is cost-effective. Any benefit to road users of violating the law is not included in a cost–benefit evaluation of the enforcement measures (Elvik 1997b).

## 10.13 Regulating commercial transport

### Problem and objective

It can be estimated that about 10–15% of vehicle kilometres driven on public roads in Norway is commercial transport (Rideng and Vågane 2008). Commercial transport refers to all kinds of transport of people or goods that are made for hire. Commercial transport is often performed by means of large and heavy vehicles, like buses or trucks. The time spent in transport can influence income. It is important to get people or goods to their destinations within a certain time. The combination of time pressure and large vehicles may represent a particular risk. This is one of the reasons why the Norwegian government has regulated commercial transport since the 1940s. Regulation has taken the form of legislation requiring permission from a public body in order to start a commercial transport business.

Permission to start commercial transport is given when an application is sent to the appropriate public body and the applicant satisfies a number of formal requirements. The current law regulating commercial transport in Norway was passed in 2002. The law comprises commercial transport in the form of taxis, buses and goods haulage.

In principle, the regulatory system adopted in Norway makes it possible to regulate the commercial transport business in detail by determining the number of permissions given and the conditions attached to these.

### Description of the measure

The commercial transport act of 2002 regulates non-scheduled transport of people (taxi), scheduled transport of people (buses run on a time table), transport of people by means of ferry, and transport of goods by means of motor vehicle. The main provision of the act states that in order to engage in any of these forms of commercial transport, permission is needed. Permission is given when an applicant satisfies a set of requirements concerning personal honesty, financial basis and knowledge of the transport sector. Permission to operate buses may be given following a competition among bids.

No permission is needed to transport goods as part of another business (i.e. a business whose purpose is not transport). Organised transport of employees to and from work does not require permission.

Competitive bidding is generally applied when awarding permissions to operate buses. It is also common that so called incentive contracts are used in public transport.

According to such contracts, transport companies are rewarded for increasing ridership, reducing delays and operating cost-effectively. Permissions for commercial transport of people are given on a needs basis, i.e. new permissions will not be given unless there is sufficient demand for travelling. Permissions for transporting goods are not given on the basis of need, and the freight transport industry is characterised by intense competition among transport firms.

At the international level, there has been a strong tendency to liberalise and deregulate commercial transport in the past 30 years. Liberalising means that the conditions for getting permissions are relaxed. Deregulation means that anyone who wants to start a transport firm is free to do so. No formal permission is needed. The transport sector in Norway is not deregulated in this sense, but it is characterised by competition between transport firms. Competition either takes the form of competitive bidding for contracts or by the presence of multiple firms offering transport services in the same area.

Commercial transport is subject to a number of regulations with respect to, for example, driving and resting hours, abstention from the consumption of alcohol in working hours and periodic inspection of vehicles.

**Effect on accidents**

Elvik (2006b) has summarised the results of 25 studies evaluating the effects on safety of liberalisation, introduction of competitive bidding and deregulation of commercial transport. No statistically significant changes in the number of accidents can be detected as a result of deregulation of commercial transport by road. The best estimate was an increase of 2% in the number of accidents (95% CI [−4; +8]).

As far as aviation was concerned, no statistically significant changes in the number of accidents associated with deregulation were found. With respect to railways, an accident reduction of 25% was found following deregulation. This reduction is statistically significant, but it is not clear that it can be attributed to deregulation exclusively.

On the whole, regulating commercial transport appears to have little effect on safety. One possible reason for this is that commercial transport is subject to a number of safety regulations that have remained in force even if the purely economic regulation, i.e. regulating the number of firms permitted to operate, is abolished. These safety regulations comprise technical standards for vehicles, laws requiring abstention from alcohol, standards for driver training and regulation of service hours.

**Effect on mobility**

The effect of regulating commercial transport on mobility is not known. Commercial transport of goods is characterised by large economies of scale (Hagen 1995). This means that the cost per tonne kilometre is lowest when large vehicles that cover long distances per unit of time are used. In a competitive market, transport firms offering low prices will strengthen their position; this may lead to an increased use of large vehicles travelling long distances. This is optimal in terms of transport economics, and may, in principle, favour road safety as well. Concentrating transport to large vehicles implies that a given amount of goods requires fewer vehicles to be transported than would otherwise be the case.

**Effect on the environment**

Large goods vehicles require space, produce noise and have quite high emissions, in particular, when they are fully loaded and drive at the maximum speed permitted by the road and the motor power of the vehicle. Cars with a gross weight of more than 3.5 t should have a speed governor. The maximum speed is 90 km/h for trucks and 100 km/h for buses. Table 10.13.1 shows estimates of the marginal environmental costs per vehicle kilometre of driving for different types of goods vehicles (Samstad, Killi and Hagman 2005). Costs are highest in major cities. The marginal environmental costs are lower for passenger trains than for buses. The effects of regulating commercial transport on the environment are not known.

**Costs**

The direct costs of administering the law regulating commercial transport are small. The law is administered by the counties. The statistics for counties (Statistics Norway, KOSTRA) suggest that costs may be in the order of NOK 5–10 million per year.

The costs for applicants are unknown. Indirect costs in terms of higher costs for transport than would be the case for a deregulated market are also unknown.

**Cost–benefit analysis**

No cost–benefit analyses of regulating commercial transport have been reported for Norway. American studies (Moses and Savage 1989) indicate that deregulation of

*Table 10.13.1: Marginal external costs per vehicle kilometre for different types of motor vehicles: 2005 prices (NOK per vehicle kilometre; 1 NOK = 0.12 Euro)*

| | | NOK per vehicle kilometre | | |
|---|---|---|---|---|
| Type of vehicle | Component | Major cities | Small cities | Rural areas |
| Car, gasoline | Greenhouse gases | 0.103 | 0.103 | 0.103 |
| | Local pollution | 0.064 | 0.041 | 0.016 |
| | Traffic noise | 0.310 | 0.310 | 0.000 |
| | All components | 0.477 | 0.454 | 0.119 |
| Car, diesel | Greenhouse gases | 0.106 | 0.106 | 0.106 |
| | Local pollution | 0.600 | 0.191 | 0.009 |
| | Traffic noise | 0.309 | 0.309 | 0.000 |
| | All components | 1.015 | 0.606 | 0.115 |
| Van, diesel | Greenhouse gases | 0.170 | 0.170 | 0.170 |
| | Local pollution | 0.699 | 0.227 | 0.014 |
| | Traffic noise | 0.310 | 0.310 | 0.000 |
| | All components | 1.179 | 0.707 | 0.184 |
| Bus | Greenhouse gases | 0.538 | 0.538 | 0.538 |
| | Local pollution | 4.575 | 2.038 | 0.178 |
| | Traffic noise | 2.906 | 2.925 | 0.000 |
| | All components | 8.019 | 5.501 | 0.716 |
| Goods vehicle, diesel, 3.5–7.5 t | Greenhouse gases | 0.280 | 0.280 | 0.280 |
| | Local pollution | 1.745 | 0.799 | 0.075 |
| | Traffic noise | 1.967 | 1.942 | 0.000 |
| | All components | 3.992 | 3.021 | 0.355 |
| Goods vehicle, diesel, 23+ t | Greenhouse gases | 0.641 | 0.641 | 0.641 |
| | Local pollution | 4.003 | 1.747 | 0.167 |
| | Traffic noise | 3.226 | 3.214 | 0.000 |
| | All components | 7.870 | 5.602 | 0.808 |
| Passenger train | Greenhouse gases | 0.654 | 0.654 | 0.654 |
| | Local pollution | 2.784 | 0.825 | 0.206 |
| | Traffic noise | 1.856 | 1.650 | 0.000 |
| | All components | 5.294 | 3.129 | 0.860 |
| Freight train | Greenhouse gases | 2.270 | 2.270 | 2.270 |
| | Local pollution | 7.423 | 2.474 | 0.687 |
| | Traffic noise | 4.949 | 5.567 | 0.000 |
| | All components | 14.642 | 10.311 | 2.957 |

aviation and goods haulage in the United States led to lower prices and increased the demand for transport. Safety did not deteriorate.

## References

Abdel-Aty, M. & Radwan, A.E. (2000). Modeling traffic accident occurrence and involvement. *Accident Analysis and Prevention,* **32**, 633–642.

Agerholm, N., Tradisauskas, N., Harms, L. & Lahrmann, H. (2007). *Preliminary results from the Danish ISA project spar paa farten – behaviour*. 14th World Congress On Intelligent Transport Systems-ITS for a Better Life. Beijing.

Allsop, R. E. & S. A. Robertson. (1994). Road Casualties in London in Relation to Public Transport Policy. *Journal of Transpo t Economics and Policy*, **28**, 61–82.

Allsop, R. E. & E. D. Turner. (1986). Road casualties and public transport fares in London. *Accident Analysis and Prevention*, **18**, 147–156.

Amundsen, F. H. & K. O. Gabestad. (1991). *Oslotunnelen. Erfaringer fra planleggingen og det første driftsåret*. Rapport 14, 1991. Vegdirektoratet, Plan- og anleggsavdelingen, Oslo.

Anderson, I.B., Bauer, K.M., Harwood, D.W. & Fitzpatrick, K. (1999). Relationship to safety of geometrical design consistency measures for rural two-lane highways. *Transportation Research Record*, **1658**, 43–51.

Atkins (2006). *World Review of Road Pricing – phase 2, final report*. Commission for Integrated Transport.

Baldwin, D. G. (1980). Uses of road liability law in improving road safety decision-making. *The HSRI Research Review*, **10**, **4**, 2–6, 1980. Highway Safety Research Institute, University of Michigan.

BASt (2002). *Sicherheitsaudit für Strassen (SAS) in Deutschland*. Berichte der BASt; Verkehrstechnik Heft V98.

Bauer, K.M., Harwood, D.W., Hughes, W.E. & Richard, K.R. (2004). Safety effects of using narrow lanes and shoulder-use lanes to increase the capacity of urban freeways. *Transportation Research Record*, **1897**, 71–80.

Bennett, G. T. & J. Marland. (1978). *Road accidents in traditionally designed local authority estates*. TRRL Supplementary Report 394. Transport and Road Research Laboratory, Crowthorne, Berkshire.

Bergan, R. & E. Wærness. (1995). *De norske kjøretøyavgiftene*. ECON-rapport 124/95. Econ Analyse, Oslo.

Björketun, U. (1991). *Linjeföring samt prediktion av olyckor utifrån linjeföringsdata för vägar projekterade/byggda under 1950-, 1960- respektive 1970-talet*. VTI-meddelande 641. Statens Väg- och Trafikinstitut (VTI), Linköping.

Bjørnland, D. (1989). *Vegen og samfunnet. En oversiktlig fremstilling og analyse i anledning Vegdirektoratets 125- årsjubileum 1864–1989*. Vegdirektoratet, Oslo.

Blakstad, F. (1990). *Ulykkesfrekvenser på hovedveger i byområder*. Rapport STF63 A90005. SINTEF Samferdselsteknikk, Trondheim.

Blakstad, F. & T. Giæver. (1989). *Ulykkesfrekvenser på vegstrekninger i tett* og *middels tett bebyggelse*. Rapport STF63 A89005. SINTEF Samferdselsteknikk, Trondheim.

Boot, T. J. P. M., P. W. Wassenberg & H. H. P. van Zwam. (1982). Changes in the road accident pattern as a result of a strike at the municipal public transport undertaking in The Hague. In: *Proceedings (117–124) of Seminar on Short-term and Area-wide Evaluation of Road Safety Measures*, Amsterdam, April 19–21, 1982. SWOV Institute for Road Safety Research, Leidschendam.

Borger, A., S. Fosser, S. Ingebrigtsen & I.-A. Sætermo. (1995). *Underrapportering av trafikkulykker*. TØI-rapport 318. Transportøkonomisk institutt, Oslo.

Brendemoen, A. & H. Vennemo. (1993). Hva koster det å øke skattene? *Økonomiske analyser*, **8**, 22–28.

Brindle, R. E. (1984). *Town planning and road safety. A review of literature and practice*. Office of Road Safety Report CR 33; ARRB Special Report SR 28. Department of Transport, Office of Road Safety, Canberra, Australia.

Broughton, J. (1995). *The likely effect of downsizing on driver casualties in two-car accidents*. TRL Report 171. Transport Research Laboratory, Crowthorne, Berkshire.

Brown, H. & Tarko, A. (1999). Effects of access control on safety of urban arterial streets. *Transportation Research Record*, **1665**, 68–74.

Brownfield, J. (1996). The Application of Safety Audit Principles as a Means of Accident Prevention. *Proceedings*, **Vol 4A**, 11–27, of the *Conference Road Safety in Europe and Strategic Highway Research Program (SHRP)*, Prague, the Czech Republic, September 20–22, 1995. Swedish National Road and Transport Research Institute, Linköping.

Caliendo, C., Guida, M. & Parisi, A. (2007). A crash-prediction model for multilane roads. *Accident Analysis and Prevention*, **39**, 657–670.

Campbell, B. J. (1991). Incentives for corporate and political behavior. In: *Enforcement and Rewarding: Strategies and Effects, Proceedings of the International Road Safety Symposium* in Copenhagen, Denmark, September 19–21, 1990, 123–125 (Koornstra, M. J. & J. Christensen, eds). SWOV Institute for Road Safety Research, Leidschendam.

Cappelen akademisk forlag (2007). *Vegtrafikklovgivningen*. 47. utgave. À jour per 1.3.2007. Cappelen akademisk forlag, Oslo.

Chang, L.Y. (2005). Analysis of freeway accident frequencies:Negative binomial regression versus artificial neural network. *Safety Science*, **43**, 541–557.

Cardoso, J.L., Stefan, C., Elvik, R. & Sørensen, M. (2007). *Road Safety Inspection – Best Practice Guidelines and Implementations*. Steps, report D5, Ripcord-Iserest.

Chatfield, B. V. (1987). *System-Wide Safety Improvements: An Approach to Safety Consistency*. National Cooperative Highway Research Program Report 132. Transportation Research Board, Washington, DC.
Chipman, M. L. (1982). The role of exposure, experience and demerit point levels in the risk of collision. *Accident Analysis and Prevention,* **14**, 475–483.
City of Stockholm (2006). *Facts and results from the Stockholm trials*. City of Stockholm, Congestion Charge Secretariat.
Council, F. & Steward, J. (1999). Safety effects of the conversion of rural two-lane to four-lane roadways based on cross-sectional models. *Transportation Research Record,* **1665**, *35–43.*
Davidson, L. L. et al. (1994). The Impact of the Safe Kids/Healthy Neighborhoods Injury Prevention Program in Harlem, 1988 through 1991. *American Journal of Public Health,* **84**, 580–586.
Davies, R.B., Cenek, P.D. & Henderson, R.J. (2008). The effect of skid resistance and texture on crash risk. *International Safer Roads Conference*, Cheltenham England, 11–14 May 2008.
Delegationen för transporttelematik. (1994). *Vägval för IT i trafiken.* K 1994:08. Norstedts, Stockholm.
Downs, A. (1962). The Law of Peak-Hour Expressway Congestion. *Traffic Quarterly*, **16**, 393–409.
Econ (2003). *Eksterne marginale kostnader ved transport.* Report 2003-054, Econ analyse, Oslo.
Elvik, R. (1993a). *Hvor rasjonell er trafikksikkerhetspolitikken? En analyse av investeringsprogrammet på Norsk veg- og vegtrafikkplan. Rapport 175.* Transportøkonomisk institutt, Oslo.
Elvik, R. (1993b). Om å konstituere interesser gjennom formelle organisasjonsstrukturer. TØI-særtrykk 35. *VTIs* og *TFBs Forskardagar* 1993, del 3, 83–91.
Elvik, R. (1993c). The effects on accidents of compulsory use of daytime running lights for cars in Norway. *Accident Analysis and Prevention*, **25**, 383–398.
Elvik, R. (1993d). Quantified road safety targets: a useful tool for policy making? *Accident Analysis and Prevention*, **25**, 569–583.
Elvik, R. (1993e). *Økonomisk verdsetting av velferdstap ved trafikkulykker. Dokumentasjonsrapport.* TØI-rapport 203. Transportøkonomisk institutt, Oslo.
Elvik, R. (1994). The external costs of traffic injury: definition, estimation and possibilities for internalization. *Accident Analysis and Prevention,* **26**, 719–732.
Elvik, R. (1995a). Explaining the distribution of State funds for national road investments between counties in Norway: Engineering standards or vote trading? *Public Choice*, **85**, 371–388.
Elvik, R. (1995b). *Virkninger av bilbelter i Norge.* Arbeidsdokument TST/0667/95. Transportøkonomisk institutt, Oslo.

Elvik, R. (1995c). *Virkninger av påbud om sikring av barn i bil i Norge*. Arbeidsdokument TST/0684/95. Transportøkonomisk institutt, Oslo.

Elvik, R. (1997a). *En sammenstilling av beregninger av potensielle virkninger på ulykkene av å overføre reiser fra individuell til kollektiv transport*. Arbeidsdokument TST/0860/97. Transportøkonomisk institutt, Oslo.

Elvik, R. (1997b). *Vegtrafikklovgivning, kontroll og sanksjoner. Potensialet for å bedre trafikksikkerheten og nytte-kostnadsvurdering av ulike tiltak*. TØI-notat 1073. Transportøkonomisk institutt, Oslo.

Elvik, R. (1999). *Bedre trafikksikkerhet i* Norge. TØI rapport 446. Transportøkonomisk institutt, Oslo.

Elvik, R. (2001a). *Quantified road safety targets. An assessment of evaluation methodology*. Report 539. Institute of Transport Economics, Oslo.

Elvik, R. (2001b). Improving road safety in Norway and Sweden: analysing the efficiency of policy priorities. *Traffic Engineering and Control*, **42**, 1, 9–16.

Elvik, R. (2006a). *Road safety inspection: safety effects and best practice guidelines*. Report 850/2006, Institute of transport Economics, Oslo.

Elvik, R. (2006b). Economic deregulation and transport safety: A synthesis of evidence from evaluation studies. *Accident Analysis and Prevention*, **38**, 678–686.

Elvik, R. & Amundsen, A. H. (2000). *Improving road safety in Sweden. Main report*. Report 490. Institute of Transport Economics, Oslo.

Elvik, R., Christensen, P. & Amundsen, A. (2004). Speed and road accidents: An evaluation of the Power Model. Report 740. Oslo: Institute of Transport Economics.

Elvik, R. & R. Muskaug. (1994). *Konsekvensanalyser og trafikksikkerhet*. TØI-rapport 281. Transportøkonomisk institutt, Oslo.

Engebretsen, Ø. (1991). *Næringsvirksomheters arealbruk og trafikkskaping. Kunnskapsbehov og datamuligheter*. TØI-notat 0959. Transportøkonomisk institutt, Oslo.

Eriksen, K. S. & I. B. Hovi. (1995). *Transportmidlenes marginale kostnadsansvar*. TØI-notat 1019. Transportøkonomisk institutt, Oslo.

Eriksen, K. S., Markussen, T. E. & Pütz, K. (1999). *Marginale kostnader ved Transportvirksomhet*. Report 464/1999, Institute of Transport Economics, Oslo.

Espedal, T. G. & I. Omland. (1982). *Trafikksikkerhet i arealplaner-en litteraturstudie*. Rapport S-2-1982. Rogalandsforskning, Stavanger.

Evans, L. & P. Wasielewski. (1982). Do accident-involved drivers exhibit riskier everyday driving? *Accident Analysis and Prevention*, **14**, 57–64.

Evans, L. & P. Wasielewski. (1983). Risky driving related to driver and vehicle characteristics. *Accident Analysis and Prevention,* **15**, 121–136.

FHWA (2006). *FHWA Road Safety Audit Guidelines*. FHWA-SA-06-06, Federal Highway Administration, US Department of Transportation.

Fiskaa, H. & N. Stabell. (1988). *Fysisk detaljplanlegging. Reguleringsplan og bebyggelsesplan*. Norsk institutt for by- og regionplanlegging, Trondheim.

Forsström, Å. (1982). *Commuting accidents. A study of commuting accidents and casualties in some Swedish regions during 1971.* Publications edited by the Departments of Geography, University of Gothenburg, Series B no 69. Göteborg.

Fosli, O. (1995). *Transport, arealbruk og miljø. Ein studie av dei transportmessige verknadene av IDG Norges omlokalisering frå Hasle til Galleri Oslo.* Hovedoppgave i samfunnsgeografi. Universitetet i Oslo, Samfunnsvitenskapelig fakultet, Oslo.

Fridstrøm, L. (1993). *Lommeboka, prisen eller reisetiden: Hva får oss til å velge transportmiddel på lengre reiser?* Foredrag ved Transportøkonomisk institutts 35-års-jubileum, 17.11.

Fridstrøm, L. & R. Elvik. (1995). *The barely revealed preference behind road investment priorities.* Working paper TST/685/95. Institute of Transport Economics, Oslo.

Fridstrøm, L. et al. (1993). *Explaining the variation in road accident counts.* Report Nord 1993:35. Nordic Council of Ministers, Copenhagen.

Fridstrøm, L. et al. (1995). Meauring the contribution of randomness, exposure, weather, and daylight to the variation in road accident counts. *Accident Analysis and Prevention*, **27**, 1–20.

Fridstrøm, L. & S. Ingebrigtsen. (1991). An aggregate accident model based on pooled, regional time-series data. *Accident Analysis and Prevention*, **23**, 363–378.

Fridstrøm, L., F. Ramjerdi, P.C. Svae & H. Thune-Larsen. (1991). *Miljøavgifters virkning på samferdselen.* TØI-rapport 77. Transportøkonomisk institutt, Oslo.

Fridstrøm, L. & L. Rand. (1993). *Markedet for lange reiser i Norge.* TØI-rapport 220. Transportøkonomisk institutt, Oslo.

Friedman, D. (1987). Law and economics. In: *The New Palgrave. A Dictionary of Economics,* Volume 3, K to P, 144–148 (Eatwell, J.; Milgate, M.; Newman, P. eds): Macmillan, London.

Færdselssikkerhedskommissionen. (2000). *Hver ulykke er én for meget. Trafiksikkerhed starter med dig. Mod nye mål 2001–2012.* Trafikministeriet, København.

Gharaibeh, N.G., Hicks, J.E., Hall, J.P. (1997). Analysis of accidents, traffic and pavement data. *Conference on Traffic Congestion and Traffic Safety in the 21st Century.* Chicago, Illinois.

Goldstein, L. G. (1973). *Behavioral aspects of highway safety relevant to preparation of the beginning driver: a review of research.* The California Traffic Safety Task Force, California.

Greibe, P. (2003). Accident prediction models for urban roads. *Accident Analysis and Prevention*, **35**, 273–285.

Grue, B., Larsen, O. I. Rekdal, J. & Tretvik, T. (1997). *Køkostnader og køprising i bytrafikk.* TØI-rapport 363. Transportøkonomisk institutt, Oslo.

Guyer, B. et al. (1989). Prevention of Childhood Injuries: Evaluation of the Statewide Childhood Injury Prevention Program (SCIPP). *American Journal of Public Health*, **79**, 1521–1527,

Hadi, M., Aruldhas, J., Chow, L. & Wattleworth, J. (1995). Estimating safety effects of cross-section design for various highway types using negative binomial regression. *Transportation Research Record*, **1500**, 169–177.

Hagen, K-E. (1994). *Rullering av samfunnsøkonomisk regnskapssystem for trafikkulykker og trafikksikkerhetstiltak (SRT) for 1992*. Arbeidsdokument TST/0570/94. Transportøkonomisk institutt, Oslo.

Hagen, K-E. (1995). *Analyse av kostnadsutviklingen i innenlandske godstransporter. Sammenlikning med nordiske land*. TØI-rapport 297. Transportøkonomisk institutt, Oslo.

Hagen, K-E. & S. Ingebrigtsen. (1993). *Samfunnsøkonomiske kostnader og innsparingspotensiale ved fall- og trafikkulykker i Akershus*. TØI-rapport 199. Transportøkonomisk institutt, Oslo.

Hall, P. (1975). *Urban and Regional Planning*. Penguin Books, Harmondsworth, Middlesex.

Hansen, M. & Y. Huang. (1997). Road supply and traffic in California urban areas. *Transportation Research, Series A*, **31**, 205–218.

Hanssen, J. U. (1993a). *Sammenhenger mellom arealbruk og transport på lokalt nivå. Sammenfatning av en litteraturstudie*. TØI-rapport 211. Transportøkonomisk institutt, Oslo.

Hanssen, J. U. (1993b). *Transportmessige virkninger av næringsvirksomheters lokalisering*. TØI-rapport 215. Transportøkonomisk institutt, Oslo.

Hanssen, J. U. (1995). Transportation impacts of office relocation. *Journal of Transport Geography*, **3**, 247–256.

Harrington, D. M. (1972). The young driver follow-up study: an evaluation of the role of human factors in the first four years of driving. *Accident Analysis and Prevention*, **4**, 191–240.

Harwood, D.W. (1995). Relationships between operational and safety considerations in geometric design improvements. *Transportation Research Board*, **1512**, 1–6.

Hauer, E. A. (1988). *Case for Science-Based Road Safety Design and Management*. Paper presented at "Highway-Safety: At the Crossroads", San Antonio, Texas, 1988. Proceedings published by the American Society of Civil Engineers.

Hauer, E. (1993). Introduction. In: *The Traffic Safety Toolbox: A Primer on Traffic Safety*, 3–10. Institute of Transportation Engineers, Washington, DC.

Hauer, E., Council, F.M., Mohammedshah, Y. (2004). Safety models for urban four-lane undivided road segments. *Transportation Reseach Record*, **1897**, 96–105.

Haugen, A-M. et al. (1991). Bø prøvekommune for trafikksikring på lokalplanet. Rapport, Bø, Bø kommune og Statens vegvesen Telemark.

Haynes, R., Lake, I.R., Kingham, S., Sabel, C.E., Pearce, J., Barnett, R. 2008. The influence of road curvature on fatal crashes in New Zealand. *Accident Analysis and Prevention*, **40**, 843–850.

Hernes, G. (1975). *Makt og avmakt*. Universitetsforlaget, Oslo.

Hingson, R. et al. (1996). Reducing Alcohol-Impaired Driving in Massachusetts. The Saving Lives Program. *American Journal of Public Health*, **86**, 791–797.

Hoff, S. A. (1996). Trygge lokalsamfunn som nasjonal strategi. I: *Et tryggere Norge-veien videre*, 19–21. (Lund, J. ed): Skadeforebyggende forums årskonferanse og årsmøte i Oslo, 24. april 1996. Skadeforebyggende forum, Oslo.

Hoffmann, J. U. (1982). *Vegsystemet i boligområder. En vurdering av mulighetene for reduserte byggekostnader og konsekvensene av slike besparelser*. TØI-notat 619. Transportøkonomisk institutt, Oslo.

Holt, A. G. (1993). *Trafikksikkerhetsvurdering E6 øst*. Notat 794/93. SINTEF Samferdselsteknikk, Trondheim.

Hvoslef, H. (1973). *Trafikksikkerheten i forbindelse med buss og trikk*. Notat. Oslo Veivesen, Oslo.

Hvoslef, H. (1974). *Trafikksikkerhet i Oslo. Problemstilling, analyse og løsninger*. Oslo Veivesen, Oslo.

Hvoslef, H. (1976). *Trafikkulykker med barn og eldre i Oslo*. TØI-notat 318. Transportøkonomisk institutt, Oslo.

Hvoslef, H. (1980). *Trafikanters skaderisiko i bytrafikk. En analyse av ulykker og reiseaktivitet i Haugesund*. TØI-rapport. Transportøkonomisk institutt, Oslo.

Hvoslef, H. (1984). *De nye gangfeltreglene ga kortvarig virkning*. Notat. Vegdirektoratet, Trafikksikkerhetskontoret, Oslo.

Haakenaasen, B. (1980). *Korttidsvirkninger av omkjøringsvegen på Gol*. TØI-rapport. Transportøkonomisk institutt, Oslo.

Ivan, J.N., O'Mara, P.J., 1997. Prediction of traffic accident rates using Poisson regression. *Transportation Research Board 76 th Annual Meeting*, Washington, DC.

Ivan, J.N., Wang, C. & Bernardo, N.R. (2000). Explaining two-lane highway crash rates using land use and hourly exposure. *Accident Analysis and Prevention,* **32**, 787–795.

Jansson, J. O. (1994). Accident Externality Charges. *Journal of Transport Economics and Policy*, **28**, 31–43.

Jensen-Butler, C., Sloth, B., Larsen, M.M., Madsen, B. & Nielsen, O.A. (2008). *Road Pricing, the Economy and the Environment*. Springer Verlag, Berlin.

Jenssen, J. A. (1988). *Vegsystem og arealplanlegging*. Foredrag på NIF-kurs om Ny Vegnormal 28. september 1988. Norske Sivilingeniørers Forening, Oslo.

Jones, P. & A. Hervik. (1992). Restraining car traffic in European cities: An emerging role for road pricing. *Transportation Research, Series A*, **26**, 133–145.

Jørgensen, N. O. (1988). *Trafikrisiko i nærtrafik*. Notat 88-4. Institut for veje, trafik og byplan. Danmarks Tekniske Højskole, København.

Jørgensen, N. O. & P. K. Nilsson. (1995). *Trafiksikkerhedsrevisionsprojektet. Evaluering*. Det eksterne panels rapport. Rapport nr 33. Vejdirektoratet, København.

Killi, M. & A. K. Ryntveit. (1996). *Fakta om fordeling av riksvegmidler*. Arbeidsdokument TØ/0933/96. Revidert. Transportøkonomisk institutt, Oslo.

Knuiman, M., Council, F. & Reinfurt, D. (1993). The effects of median width on highway accident rates. *Transportation Research Record,* **1401**, 70–80.

Kolbenstvedt, M. et al. (1989). *Korttidsvirkninger av Vålerenga-tunnelen i noen gatestrekninger i Vålerenga/Gamlebyen.* TØI-notat 0907. Transportøkonomisk institutt, Oslo.

Kolbenstvedt, M., H. Silborn & T. Solheim (ed) (1996). *Miljøhåndboken. Del 1.* Transportøkonomisk institutt, Oslo.

Kolbenstvedt, M. & A. Strand. (1986). *Atkomstveger i boligområder. Bilfrihet eller blandingstrafikk?* Barn og Bomiljø rapport 36. Norsk institutt for by- og regionforskning og Transportøkonomisk institutt, Oslo.

Krenk, F. (1985). *Metoder og resultater i den koordinerede uheldsstatistik* 1978–82. Rapport 27. Vejdatalaboratoriet, Herlev.

Kristiansen, K. S. & K. Østmoe. (1978). *Bompengefinansiering ved alternative vegvalg.* TØI-rapport. Transportøkonomisk institutt, Oslo.

Köhler, U. & R. Schwamb. (1993). *Erweiterung und Verifizierung des Modells zur Abschätzung des Unfallgeschehens und der Unfallkosten auf Innerörtlichen Netzelementen.* Schlussbericht. Forschungsbericht FE-Nr 70186/88. Frankfurt am Main, Ingenieursozietät BGS,

Køltzow, K. (1990). *Beslutningstakere, holdningsendring og trafikkulykkene.* TØI-rapport 53. Transportøkonomisk institutt, Oslo.

Køltzow, K. (1993). Road safety rhetorics versus road safety politics. *Accident Analysis and Prevention,* **25**, 647–657.

Larsen, O. I. (1987). *Bompengeringen i Bergen. Erfaringer og virkninger på trafikken.* TØI-rapport. Transportøkonomisk institutt, Oslo.

Larsen, O. I. (1988). The toll ring in Bergen, Norway – The first year of operation. *Traffic Engineering and Control,* **29**, 216–222.

Larsen, O. I. (1991). *Samfunnsøkonomiske kalkyler for transportstrategier. Veiledningsgruppen for transportplanarbeidet i de 10 største byområdene.* Transportøkonomisk institutt, Oslo.

Larsen, O. I. (1993). *Samfunnsnytte av tilskudd til kollektivtrafikk.* TØI-rapport 208. Transportøkonomisk institutt, Oslo.

Larsen, O. I & H. Minken. (1995). *Kriterier for optimal transportpolitikk i byer.* Arbeidsdokument TRU/0479/95. Transportøkonomisk institutt, Oslo.

Larsen, O. I & J. Rekdal. (1996). *Køprising i et miljøperspektiv. En simulering av tidsdifferensierte bompenger i Oslo.* TØI-rapport 324. Transportøkonomisk institutt, Oslo.

Larsen, S. L. & I. L. Saglie. (1995). *Tettstedsareal i Norge.* NIBR-rapport 1995:3. Norsk institutt for by- og regionforskning, Oslo.

Lervåg, H. (1985). *Arealbruk og transport.* NIBR-notat 1985:14. Norsk institutt for by- og regionplanlegging, Trondheim.

Lie, T. & R. Muskaug. (1982). *Valg av reisemåte påvirker trafikksikkerheten.* TØI-notat 611. Transportøkonomisk institutt, Oslo.

Lindberg, G. (1994). *Traffic Charges. The Swedish experience of getting prices right.* Centre for Research on Transport and Society, Borlänge.

Loder, B. N. & L. J. Bayly (1973). *A review of town planning in* relation to *road safety.* Report Nr 17 by the Expert Group on Road Safety. Australian Government Publishing Service, Canberra, Australia.

Lord, D., Washington, S.P., Ivan, J.N. (2005). Poisson, Poisson-gamma and zero-inflated regression models of motor vehicle crashes: balancing statistical fit and theory. *Accident Analysis and Prevention*, **37**, 35–46.

Lord, D., Guikema, S.D., Geedipally, S.R. (2008). Application of the Conway–Maxwell–Poisson generalized linear model for analyzing motor vehicle crashes. *Accident Analysis and Prevention*, **40**, 1123–1134.

Lutschounig, S., Nadler, H. & Mocsari, T. (2005). *Description of the current practice of RSI.* Report D5.1, Ripcord-Iserest.

Macaulay, J. & Mcinerney, R. (2002). *Evaluation of the proposed action emanating from road safety audits.* Australian Road Research Board, Austroads, Sydney.

Matena, S., Löhe, U. & Vaneerdewegh, P. (2005). *Road Safety Audit – Current Practice.* Report D4.1, Ripcord-Iserest.

Matena, S., Weber, R., Huber, C. et al. (2007). *Road Safety Audit – Best Practice Guidelines, Qualification for Auditors and Programming.* Report D4, Ripcord-Iserest.

Mayeres, I.; Ochelen, S.; Proost, S. (1996). Marginal external costs of urban transport. *Transportation Research, Series D*, **1**, 111–130.

Meland, S. (1994). *RVU Trondheim* 1992. *Evaluering av bomringen i Trondheim.* Rapport STF63 A94006. SINTEF Samferdselsteknikk, Trondheim.

Meland, S. (1996). Bompenger og vegprising. In: *Miljøhåndboken*, Del 1, 116–129. (Kolbenstvedt, M., H. Silborn & T. Solheim eds): Transportøkonomisk institutt, Oslo.

Miaou, S.-P. (1994). The relationship between truck accidents and geometric design of road sections: Poisson versus negative binomial regressions. *Accident Analysis and Prevention,* **26**, 471–482.

Milton, J. & Mannering, F. (1996). *The relationship among highway geometries, traffic-related elements and motor-vehicle accident frequencies.* Report WA-RD 403.1. Washington State Department of Transport.

Milton, J. & Mannering, F. (1998). The relationship among highway geometries, traffic-related elements and motor-vehicle accident frequencies. *Transportation,* **25**, 395–413.

Ministerie van Verkeer en Waterstaat (2007). Making a start on price per kilometre.

Ministry of Transport, Public Works and Water Management. (1996). *Long-range programme for road safety. Putting policy into practice.* Dutch Ministry of Transport, Public Works and Water Management, The Hague.

Mogridge, M. J. H. (1996). *Will increased urban road capacity reduce congestion? A review of theories, disputes and available evidence.* NIBR Working Paper 1996:117. Norwegian Institute for Urban and Regional Reearch, Oslo.

Moses, L. N. & Savage, I. (1989). Introduction. In Moses, L. N.; Savage, I. (Eds): *Transportation Safety in an Age of Deregulation*, 3–7. Oxford University Press, New York.

Newbery, D. (1990). Pricing and congestion: Economic principles relevant to pricing roads. *Oxford Review of Economic Policy*, **6**, 2, 22–38.

Newman, P. W. G. & J. R. Kenworthy. (1989). *Cities and Automobile Dependence: A Sourcebook*. Avebury Technical, Aldershot.

Norges Offentlige Utredninger. (1975). NOU 1975:42. *Motorvognavgiftene*. Universitetsforlaget, Oslo.

Nyborg, K. & I. Spangen. (1996a). *Politiske beslutninger om investeringer i veger. Intervjuer med medlemmer i Stortingets samferdselskomité*. TØI-notat 1026. Transportøkonomisk institutt, Oslo.

Nyborg, K. & I. Spangen. (1996b). Politiske beslutninger om veiinvesteringer. *Økonomiske analyser*, **3**, 1996, 3–9.

Næss, P. (1996). Miljømessig effektiv lokalisering av arbeidsplasser og boliger. In: *Miljøhåndboken*, Del 1, 95–106. (Kolbenstvedt, M., H. Silborn & T. Solheim, T. eds) Transportøkonomisk institutt, Oslo.

Odeck, J. (1991). Om nytte-kostnadsanalysens plass i beslutningsprosessen i vegsektoren. *Sosialøkonomen*, **3**, 1991, 10–15.

Odeck, J. (1996). Ranking of regional road investment in Norway. Does socio-economic analysis matter? *Transportation*, **23**, 123–140.

OECD-Road Research Group. (1979). *Traffic Safety in Residential Areas*. OECD, Paris.

OECD Scientific Expert Group. (1994). *Targeted Road Safety Programmes*. OECD, Paris.

Opplysningsrådet for veitrafikken. (1996). *Bil- og Veistatistikk 1996. Publikasjon 1000–96*. Opplysningsrådet for veitrafikken, Oslo.

Peck, R. C., R. S. McBride & R. S. Coppin S. (1971). The distribution and prediction of driver accident frequencies. *Accident Analysis and Prevention*, **2**, 243–299.

Polak, J. & S. Meland. (1994). An assessment of the effects of the Trondheim toll ring on travel behaviour and the environment. In: *Towards an Intelligent Transport System. Proceedings of the First World Congress on Applications of Transport Telematics and Intelligent Vehicle-Highway Systems*, 994–1001. Edited by ERTICO. Artech House, London.

Poppe, F. (1993). *Verkeersrisico's in Nederland. 1. De cijfers*. SWOV rapport R-93-57. 2. Verantwoording. SWOV rapport R-93-58. Stichting Wetenschappelijk Onderzoek Verkeersveiligheid, Leidschendam.

Ramjerdi, F. (1995). *Road Pricing and Toll Financing with Examples from Oslo and Stockholm*. Doctoral Thesis. Institute of Transport Economics and Royal Institute of Technology, Oslo and Stockholm.

Richards, M.G. (2006). *Congestion Charging in London: The Policy And The Politics*. Palgrave.

Rideng, A. & Vågane, L. (2008). *Transportytelser i Norge 1946–2007*. Rapport 979. Transportøkonomisk institutt, Oslo.

Risser, R., C. Michalik & A. Stratil. (1987). *Aktion "Minus 10 Prozent" in Österreich. Eine dokumentation der Startphase*. Forschungsberichte der Bundesanstalt für Strassenwesen (BASt), Bereich Unfallforshung, 159. Bundesanstalt für Strassenwesen (BASt), Bergisch Gladbach.

Rosebud (2003). *Screening of efficiency assessment experiences – report state of the art*. Report D2, WP1, Rosebud, Road Safety and Environmental Benefit-Cost and Cost-effectiveness Analysis for use in Decision making.

Rtt (2009). LKW-MAUT Electronic Toll Collection System for Heavy Goods Vehicles. Germany, www.roadtraffic-technology.com.

Runyan, C. W. & J. A. Earp. (1985). Epidemiological Evidence and Motor Vehicle Policy Making. *American Journal of Public Health*, **75**, 354–357.

Sakshaug, K. (2000). Sammenheng mellom ulykkesfrekvens, ulykkeskostnad og veggeometri utenfor tettbygd strøk (Relationship between crash frequency, crash cost and road geometry in rural areas). Report STF22 A00555. Trondheim, SINTEF Bygg og miljøteknikk.

Samferdselsdepartementet. (1996). *Stortingsmelding 32, 1995–96*. Om grunnlaget for samferdselspolitikken. Samferdselsdepartementet, Oslo.

Samferdselsdepartementet. (1997). *Stortingsmelding 37, 1996–97. Norsk veg- og vegtrafikkplan 1998–2007*. Samferdselsdepartementet, Oslo.

Samferdselsdepartementet. (2003–2004). Stortingsmelding 24. Nasjonal Transportplan 2006–2015. Oslo: Samferdselsdepartementet (Ministry of Transport).

Samstad, H., Killi, M. & Hagman, R. (2005). *Nyttekostnadsanalyse i transportsektoren: parametre, enhetskostnader og indekser*. Rapport 797. Transportøkonomisk institutt, Oslo.

Sandelien, B. (1992). *Økt vegkapasitet = økt trafikk?* TØI-rapport 119. Transportøkonomisk institutt, Oslo.

Sawalha, Z. & Sayed, T. (2001). Evaluating safety of urban arterial roadways. *Journal of Transportation Engineering*, **127**, 151–158.

Schelp, L. (1987). *Epidemiology as a Basis for Evaluation of a Community Intervention Programme on Accidents*. Academic Thesis. Sundbyberg, Karolinska Institute, Department of Social Medicine, Kronan Health Centre, Sweden.

Shankar, V.N., Chayanan, C., Sittikariya, S. et al. (2004). Marginal impacts of design, traffic, weather, and related interactions on roadside crashes. *Transportation Research Record*, **1897**, 156–163.

Slovic, P., B. Fischhoff & S. Lichtenstein. (1978). Accident probabilities and seat belt usage: a psychological perspective. *Accident Analysis and Prevention*, **10**, 281–285.

Smeby, T. (1992). Erfaringer fra Norge. Ulykkesfrekvenser på 3-felts veger i Akershus. Beregninger basert på politiregistrerte personskadeulykker. *Via Nordica, Dokument*, 255–257. Nordiska Vägtekniska Förbundets XVI kongress, 9–11.6. Tammerfors, Finland.

Smiley, A., Persaud, B., Hauer, E. & Duncan, D. (1989). Accidents, Convictions, and Demerit Points: An Ontario Driver Records Study. *Transportation Research Record*, **1238**, 53–64.

Solheim, T. (1992). *Bompengeringen i Oslo. Effekter på trafikk og folks reisevaner. Sluttrapport fra før-/etterundersøkelsen.* Prosam-rapport 8. Transportøkonomisk institutt, Oslo.

Solheim, T., F. Hammer & K. W. Johansen. (1994). *Kollektivt og forurensende? Miljøeffekter av å forbedre kollektivtilbudet i norske byer.* TØI-rapport 245. Transportøkonomisk institutt, Oslo.

Stangeby, I. (1994). *Holdninger til bil og kollektivtransport. En intervjuundersøkelse blant befolkningen og politikere i Oslo.* TØI-rapport 288. Transportøkonomisk institutt, Oslo.

Stangeby, I. & B. Norheim. (1995). *Fakta om kollektivtransport. Erfaringer og løsninger for byområder.* TØI-rapport 307. Transportøkonomisk institutt, Oslo.

Statens forurensningstilsyn. (1993). *Utslipp fra veitrafikken i Norge. Dokumentasjon av beregningsmetode, data og resultater.* SFT-rapport 93:12. Statens Forurensningstilsyn, Oslo.

Statens vegvesen. (1994). *Vegdata. Driftsregnskap-driftsstatistikk 1993. Håndbok 056. (Norwegian Public Roads Administration handbook 056)* Vegdirektoratet, Oslo.

Statens vegvesen Sør-Trøndelag. (1996). *E6 Omkjøringsvegen. Et prosjekt i Trondheimspakken.* Brosjyre utgitt i 1996. Statens vegvesen Sør-Trøndelag, Trondheim.

Statistisk sentralbyrå. (1993). *Statistisk Årbok 1993.* NOS C 85. Oslo-Kongsvinger.

Stefan, C. (2006). *Predictive model of injury accidents on Austrian motorways.* Wien: KfV, Kuratorium für Verkehrssicherheit,

Strand, A. (1993). *Trafikksikkerhetsmessige hensyn i arealplanleggingen.* Forelesning ved EEU-kurs Trafikksikkerhet 29.10.93. Norges Tekniske Høgskole, Institutt for samferdselsteknikk, Trondheim.

Strathman, J.G., Duecker, K.J., Zhang, J. & Williams, T. (2001). *Analysis of design attributes and crashes on the Oregon highway system.* Oregon: Center for Urban Studies, Portland State University, Report SPER 312.

Sulkjær, P., Bonnevie, N., Nielsen, O. A., Kristensen, J. P. & Meiner, M. L. (2005). *Forsøg med kørselsafgifter I København.* Københavns Kommune, Danmarks tekniske Universitet, Vejdirektoratet and Rambøll, København.

Sund, B. (2000). *Samhällets kostnader för olyckor. Kostnader för det förebyggande arbetet.* Räddningsverket, Karlstad.

Surrey Country Council (1994). *Road safety Audit: An investigation into casualty savings – Discussion report*. Surrey Country Council Highways Management Division.

SWOV (2007). The Road Safety Audit and Road Safety Inspection, SWOV Fact sheet, SWOV, Leidschendam.

Tellnes, G. (1984). Resultater av skadeforebyggende arbeid i lokalsamfunnet. *Tidsskrift for den Norske Lægeforening*, **104**, 1838–1842.

TfL (2007). *Central London Congestion Charging – impacts monitoring*. 5th annual report, Transport for London (TfL), Mayor of London, London.

Thulin, H. (1991). *Trafikantgruppers skadetal, risker och hälsoförluster i olika trafikmiljöer-en tabellsammanställning*. Bilaga 2 till Samhällsekonomisk prioritering av trafiksäkerhetsåtgärder. TFB & VTI forskning/research rapport 7:2 1991. Transportforskningsberedningen och Statens väg- och trafikinstitut, Stockholm och Linköping.

Tielaitos-Finnish National Road Administration. (1997). *Public Roads in Finland 1.1.1997*. Finnra Statistical Reports 1/1997. Finnish National Road Administration, Helsinki.

Trinca, G., Johnston, I.R., Campbell, B.J. et al. (1988). *Reducing Traffic Injury-A Global Challenge*. Royal Australasian College of Surgeons, Melbourne.

UK Department of Transport. (1989). *Transport Statistics Great Britain 1978–1988*. London., Her Majesty's Stationary Office.

UK Department of Transport. (1992). *Transport Statistics Great Britain 1982–1992*. London, Her Majesty's Stationary Office.

US Department of Transportation. (1991). *Fatal and Injury Accident Rates on Public Roads in the United States*. Washington, DC, US Department of Transportation, Federal Highway Administration.

Verhoef, E. (1994). External effects and social costs of road transport. *Transportation Research, Series A*, **28**, 273–287.

Vogt, A. & Bared, J. (1998). Accident models for two-lane rural segments and intersections. *Transportation Research Record*, **1635**, 18–29.

Vaa, T. (1993). *Personskader og risiko ved bussreiser. Reviderte beregninger*. TØI-rapport 160. Transportøkonomisk institutt, Oslo.

Vaas, K. & R. Elvik. (1992). *Føreres kunnskap om og holdning til promillelovgivningen*. TØI-rapport 104. Transportøkonomisk institutt, Oslo.

VTPI (2008). *Road pricing, Congestion Pricing, Value pricing, Toll Roads and HOT Lanes*. Victoria Transport Policy Institute.

Wang, J., Hughes, W.E. & Steward, R. (1998). *Safety effects of cross-section design on rural multi-lane highways*. International Symposium on Highway Geometric Design Practices. Boston, MA.

Wasielewski, P. (1984). Speed as a measure of driver risk: observed speeds versus driver and vehicle characteristics. *Accident Analysis and Prevention*, **16**, 89–103.

Wegman, F. M. C., J. Van Selm & M. Herweijer. (1991). Evaluation of a stimulation plan for municipalities in the Netherlands. *Safety Science*, **14**, 61–73.

West, R., J. Elander & D. French. (1992). *Decision making, personality and driving style as correlates of individual accident risk.* Contractor Report 309. Crowthorne, Berkshire, Transport Research Laboratory,

Winston, C. (1991). Efficient Transportation Infrastructure Policy. *Journal of Economic Perspectives,* **5**, 113–127,

Ytterstad, B. & H. Wasmuth. (1995). The Harstad injury prevention study: Evaluation of hospital-based injury recording and community-based intervention for traffic injury prevention. *Accident Analysis and Prevention,* **27**, 111–123.

Zhou, M. & Sisiokipu, V. (1997). On the relationship between volume to capacity ratios and accident rates. *Transportation Research Record*, **1581**, 47–52.

Ørjasæter, J. & J. R. Bang. (1993). *Utslipp med og uten kjørelys.* Rapport. Teknologisk institutt, Avdeling for kjøretøyteknikk, Oslo.

# PART III

## Vocabulary and Index

# Definitions of Technical Terms

| | |
|---|---|
| Annual average daily traffic | The number of vehicles passing a road during one year, divided by 365 |
| Abbreviated injury scale (AIS) | A scale for injury severity measuring the threat to life posed by injuries. AIS 1 is a minor injury, AIS 6 is a fatal injury |
| Accessibility | The possibility of reaching a destination; the ease of getting to a place; the easier it is to reach a place, the more accessible it is |
| Access control | Regulation of the use of access roads to an arterial road. In full access control, no access roads are permitted. In partial access control, access roads may be permitted on certain conditions. In no access control, access roads can be freely constructed |
| Access road | Road providing access to abutting properties; in general, an access road serves local traffic only and is at the bottom of the road hierarchy |
| Accident | A sudden and unintentional event resulting in damage to property, people or the environment |
| Accident black spot | A location where there is an abnormally high number of accidents; sometimes also referred to as a hazardous road location |
| Accident cost | The value of all resources lost or used as a result of an accident; comprehensive costs also include a monetary valuation of lost quality of life as a result of accidents |
| Accident density | The number of accidents per kilometre of road per year |

| | |
|---|---|
| Accident migration | The tendency for accidents to 'move' to new places as a result of the treatment of a black spot |
| Accident rate | The number of accidents per unit of exposure; most commonly, the number of accidents per million vehicle kilometres of travel |
| Accident reporting | Formal systems established to report road traffic accidents to public authorities. In general, the police are entrusted to report accidents |
| Accident severity | The severity of an accident is generally measured by the change in speed associated with it, often referred to as delta $V$ ($\Delta V$) |
| Accident statistics | Records of reported accidents kept by highway authorities or other governmental bodies |
| Aggregation | The adding of elementary units to form a new unit of observation |
| Acceleration | Increase of speed |
| Acceleration lane | Driving lane reserved for vehicles to increase their speed when entering a motorway (freeway) |
| Antilock brakes | Brakes that prevent lockup of wheels, i.e. keep the wheels rolling throughout deceleration |
| Alignment | The curvature of a road in space (vertical and horizontal) |
| Allergy | Excessive sensitivity to a substance or set of substances |
| Anthropometric | Resembling the human body in terms of physical size, shape and weight; anthropometric dummies are used in crash testing of cars |
| Arterial road | A main road designed to serve a large traffic volume |
| Articulated lorry | A lorry (truck) pulling a trailer |

| | |
|---|---|
| Autocorrelation | Correlation between successive observations in a time-series |
| Automatic enforcement | The enforcement of traffic regulations by means of equipment that records offences routinely without the presence of police officers at the scene |
| Axiom | Statement assumed to be true; self-evident truth |
| Axle load | The weight carried by an axle on a vehicle and transmitted to the road |
| Before-and-after study | A commonly employed study design used to evaluate the effects of road safety measures by comparing the number of accidents before and after the measure was introduced. There are many variants of before-and-after studies, see discussion in Part I of the book |
| Benefit–cost ratio | The benefits of a programme divided by its costs; sometimes referred to as cost–benefit ratio |
| Bias | Systematic errors; a sample is biased if observations made in the sample cannot be generalised to the population of interest |
| Black spot | A road location with an abnormally high number of accidents; sometimes referred to as a hazardous road location |
| Blood alcohol content (BAC) | The amount of alcohol in the blood stream; often expressed as a percentage. BAC can be measured in a number of ways; often milligrams of alcohol per millilitre of blood is used |
| Break-away pole | Lighting pole designed to fold upon impact |
| Bypass road | A road built around a town in order to lead long distance traffic away from it |
| Candela | Unit for luminance; one candela roughly corresponds to the amount of light emitted by a candle |

| | |
|---|---|
| Car | A four-wheeled vehicle powered by an engine and designed for transporting goods or people. Cars are often classified as passenger cars, vans, utility vehicles, trucks (lorries) and buses |
| Capacity (of a road) | The capacity of road is the largest number of vehicles that can pass a point on the road per unit of time |
| Case–control study | Study that compares those who have a certain characteristic (e.g., having been involved in an accident) to a control group not having the characteristic. Case–control studies, of which there are many variants, are frequently used in epidemiology to determine risk factors for accidents or disease |
| Cause | Anything that produces something (an effect); in accident research, the term 'cause' is controversial; if used at all, it usually denotes risk factors that are statistically associated with accidents |
| Centre line | A broken or continuous painted line marking the division between opposing traffic streams |
| Channelisation | Measures taken in junctions in order to separate the various traffic movements through it |
| Chicanes | Obstacles put alternately on the left and right side of the road to keep speed down |
| Collector road | Road that collects traffic from access roads and feeds it onto arterial roads |
| Confidence interval | A measure of the statistical uncertainty of an estimate. A 95% confidence interval will contain the true value of the estimated variable in 95 of 100 cases sampled the same way as the case at hand |
| Confounding | The influence on study results of factors other than those a study seeks to measure |

| | |
|---|---|
| Confounding factors | Any factors that may lead to confounding, e.g. to effects that may erroneously be mixed up with the effects of a road safety measure |
| Conspicuity | The distinctness of an object from its surroundings |
| Construct validity | Also referred to as theoretical validity; construct validity denotes the extent to which a study can measure empirically the theoretical concepts it employs |
| Consumer's surplus | The net benefit to a consumer of consuming a good (see Part I of the book) |
| Control of confounding factors | To control for confounding factors is to try to eliminate their influence on study results. Control of confounding factors can be accomplished through study design or statistical analysis |
| Coordinated traffic signals | A set of traffic signals linked in order to allow traffic to pass through several consecutive junctions without having to stop |
| Correlation | The strength of the statistical association between two variables. A correlation is often measured by a coefficient taking on values between −1 and +1. The value 0 indicates no association |
| Cost | Use of resources that have alternative uses. Costs are generally measured in monetary terms, but the concept of cost includes any use of resources, not just direct out-of-pocket expenses |
| Cost–benefit analysis | A formal analysis of costs and benefits of a programme, in which all relevant impacts are converted to monetary terms |
| Cost–benefit ratio | See benefit–cost ratio above |
| Crashworthiness | The performance of a car in protecting occupants from injury in an accident |

| | |
|---|---|
| Crest curve | The top of a hill; the segment of a road where it changes from going uphill to going downhill |
| Dashboard | Panel on the inside front of a car compartment, to which the steering wheel is mounted, containing an instrument panel, as well as a glove compartment and a compartment for a radio |
| Daytime running lights | The use of vehicle headlights during daytime in order to enhance vehicle conspicuity |
| Dazzling (glare) | Temporary loss of vision due to exposure to an intensive source of light; dazzling is in most cases a discomfort only and does not permanently harm the eyes |
| Deceleration | Reduction of speed |
| Deflection | Change of direction; roundabouts are built so as to force entering vehicles to deflect, thereby reducing speed |
| Deformation pole | Lighting pole that deforms upon impact |
| Demerit point system | A system in which points are entered in a driver's record when the driver is convicted of a traffic offence; when a certain number of points have been accumulated within a certain period, the driver's licence may be suspended |
| Dependent variable | Variable that depends on, or is influenced by, other variables |
| Deregulation | The repeal of restrictions on entry to a trade; measures taken to ensure competitive markets |
| Design speed | The speed at which vehicles are assumed to travel when a road is designed, i.e. when alignment is determined at the planning stage of a road |
| Detection distance | The longest distance at which an object can be seen, although not necessarily identified (see recognition distance) |

| | |
|---|---|
| Deterministic | A phenomenon is deterministic if it occurs with necessity and is not subject to random influences; the opposite of stochastic |
| Differentiation | The separation in time or in space of different types of traffic or categories of road users |
| Discounting | Conversion of future payments to present values by means of a discount rate |
| Discount rate | An interest rate, stated in constant prices, and used to convert future payments to their value today (present value) |
| Divided highway | A road that is used as a median to separate opposing traffic streams |
| Drink-driving | Driving with alcohol in the blood stream |
| Driving and resting hour regulations | Regulations setting limits to the longest hours professional drivers are allowed to drive per day, or per week without taking a rest, the minimum duration of which is generally also specified |
| Driving range | An enclosed circuit used for driver training; a driving range will usually consist of various types of roads and junctions |
| Driving simulator | An instrumented model of a car mounted in a laboratory for testing driver behaviour in controlled conditions |
| Edge line | Broken or continuous white line marking the outer edge of a road |
| Elasticity | The ratio between two relative changes. As an example, an accident elasticity with respect to traffic volume states the percentage of change in the number of accidents if traffic volume changes by 1%. An elasticity can be positive or negative, depending on the direction of the relationship between the variables to which the elasticity applies |

| | |
|---|---|
| Electronic stability control (ESC) | ESC is a vehicle safety system that detects and prevents skidding |
| Emission | To emit something is to send it out; motor vehicles emit noise and air pollution |
| Energy | The capacity for doing work that, however, may be only partly available for use |
| Enforcement | Actions taken to ensure compliance with legislation; traffic enforcement is usually done by the police |
| Environmental street | A street that has been redesigned in order to keep speed down and make the street more pleasant looking |
| Ergonomics | A field of study dealing with the mutual adjustment between human beings, machines and the working environment |
| Expected number of accidents | The mean number of accidents (per unit of time) expected to occur in the long for a given exposure and a given level of risk. Technically, the expected number of accidents is the mean value of a random variable whose sampling space consists of the recorded number of accidents |
| Experiment | Randomised controlled trial, i.e. a study in which subjects are randomly allocated between different experimental conditions, such as receiving or not receiving a treatment. Randomisation ensures control of all confounding factors (see above) |
| Exposure | The amount of activity that is exposed to risk. In road safety studies, exposure usually denotes the amount of travel |
| External costs | Costs attributable to the external effects of economic activity (see below) |
| External effect | An effect on utility (see below) of production or consumption, not taken into account by the economic agent whose production or consumption causes the effect |

| | |
|---|---|
| External validity | The extent to which the results of a study, or set of studies, can be generalised to other settings or populations than those in which the study or studies were made |
| Fatal injury | According to the Vienna convention, a fatal injury is one that results in death within 30 days of the accident. Most highly motorised countries apply this definition of a traffic accident fatality |
| Fixed penalty | A fine imposed according to a fixed rate and normally settled out of court |
| Fluorescent | A material is fluorescent if it becomes luminous when exposed to light |
| Friction | The resistance against sliding of two objects touching each other. Friction is measured by means of a coefficient taking on values between 0 (no friction) and 1 (maximum friction) |
| Game mirrors | Coloured glass prisms intended to deter animals from crossing a road |
| Generalised costs of travel | The sum of all monetary outlays and other costs of travel, such as the use of time |
| Geometric design | The design of a road with respect to horizontal and vertical curves. See alignment |
| Goodness-of-fit | How well a statistical model fits the data; one way of measuring it is in terms of the squared correlation coefficient that measures the degree to which the variance of the dependent variable is reduced when it is regressed on one or more independent variables |
| Hazard | A hazard is anything that may cause damage or injury in the event of an accident (see above) |
| Headlamp adjustment | The light from maladjusted headlamps will aim either too high, thereby dazzling oncoming traffic, or too low, thereby reducing own sight distance |

| | |
|---|---|
| Health risk | The rate of traffic injuries per 100,000 inhabitants per year |
| Hump | A speed-reducing device in the form of an elevation of the road surface, often designed as a circular segment |
| Hydrocarbons | Chemical compounds of hydrogen and carbon; fuel not fully burnt by a combustion engine running on fossil fuels |
| Incidence | The rate of new cases (especially of illness) occurring per unit of time per inhabitant |
| Incomplete accident reporting | Refers to the fact that not all accidents that actually occur are recorded in official accident statistics |
| Indifference | Inability to form a preference; equal in terms of utility |
| Injury accident | An accident that results in injury to one or more persons; such accidents are normally required to be reported in official accident statistics |
| Instrument panel | The part of the dashboard of a car set aside for instruments showing, e.g., speed, engine revolutions per minute, fuel tank filling level |
| Insurance | The spreading of financial risk among a large number of individuals (policyholders), in order to protect individuals from large economic losses in case of an accident |
| Integration of traffic, woonerfs | The deliberate mixing of traffic in a way that keeps speed low, thus permitting the use of motor vehicles in streets where children are allowed to play |
| Interchange | Grade separated intersection, where the intersecting road are connected by means of ramps leading from one level to another |

| | |
|---|---|
| Internal validity | The extent to which one can infer that there is a causal relationship between variables, such as whether a safety measure is the main cause of changes in safety rather than, for example, confounding factors not controlled for by a study |
| Intersection (junction) | A point where two or more roads cross or meet |
| Jackknifing | The folding of an articulated vehicle around the coupling, resulting in loss of control |
| Junction | The same as an intersection (see above) |
| Kinetic energy | The amount of mechanical work produced in moving a body across a surface. Kinetic energy depends on mass and speed |
| Legislation | Acts or provisions that have the force of law, i.e. that give the police the right to enforce and courts of law the right to impose penalties |
| Lane line | Road marking to indicate lanes of traffic, for traffic moving in the same direction |
| Load sensing brake valves | Devices that register the weight of a vehicle and control the application of brake force according to vehicle weight |
| Lorry (truck) | Heavy motor vehicle designed for goods transport |
| Macro-texture | The size and roughness of stones in a road surface |
| Marginal benefit | The additional benefit associated with a small increase in the variable generating benefit |
| Marginal cost | The additional cost associated with a small increase in the variable generating cost |
| Marked pedestrian crossing (crosswalk) | A location marked with road markings to permit pedestrians to cross the road |
| Mass (of a vehicle) | The mass of a body is its weight |

| | |
|---|---|
| Mean speed of traffic | The mean speed of vehicles passing a measurement point on the road |
| Median | Physical separation between opposing traffic streams; on motorways (freeways), the median will often be a wide grass-covered area |
| Methodological | Pertaining to the methods used; a methodological interpretation of a study usually rejects the study because the research methods were not good enough |
| Micro-texture | The roughness of each stone in a road surface |
| Mini roundabout | A small roundabout in which the diameter of the central island is less than about 5 m |
| Mixed traffic | The mixture of unprotected and protected road users on the same road |
| Mobility | Use of the transport system for surmounting distance; mobility is generally described in terms of the amount of travel and the time spent travelling; the less time it takes to cover a given distance, the higher is mobility |
| Modality (statistical) | Statistical distributions can be described as unimodal (having one peak), bimodal (two peaks) or multimodal (several peaks) |
| Modal split | The distribution of travel by mode. Modes include walking, cycling, driving a car, taking the bus, taking the train and so on |
| Modes of travel | The means used for transport; the main modes include walking, cycling, driving or using public transport |
| Moped | A small motorcycle |
| Motorcycle | A two-wheeled vehicle powered by an engine |

| | |
|---|---|
| Motorway (freeway) | Road designed for use by motor vehicles only; built according to high design standards in order to serve high traffic volumes at a high speed. Motorways do not have accesses to adjacent properties |
| Multi-vehicle accident | An accident involving more than one vehicle; bicycles are usually counted as vehicles |
| Narcotics | Substances used legally or illegally to reduce pain, anxiety or otherwise affect mental state |
| Newton | Unit for force. One Newton is the force that gives a mass of 1 kilogram an acceleration of 1 meter per square second; $1\,\text{N} = 1\,\text{kg}\,\text{m/s}^2$ |
| Nitrogen oxides | Chemical compounds of nitrogen and oxygen; exposure to nitrogen oxides may damage health |
| Optical guidance | Guidance on the alignment of a road given by means of signs or markings |
| Optimal speed | The speed that minimises the total costs to society of travel; total costs include cost of accidents, cost of travel time, vehicle operating costs and cost of environmental impacts |
| Outlier | An atypical observation; a highly deviant value |
| Overhang | That part of a motor vehicle that is in front of front wheels or behind the rear wheels |
| Pareto optimality | A state in which it is not possible to increase utility for one person without thereby reducing it for another person |
| Potential Pareto improvement | The usual test for a welfare improvement in cost–benefit analysis; a potential Pareto improvement occurs when those who gain utility from an action can compensate those who lose utility by the action and still retain a net gain in utility. This criterion is usually assumed to be satisfied when the benefits of an action are greater than the costs of it |

| | |
|---|---|
| Poisson distribution | Statistical distribution for rare events named after the French mathematician Simeon Denis Poisson, who first described it. The Poisson distribution is generally used as a model to describe pure random variation in the number of accidents |
| Preference | Rank ordering of objects or outcomes in terms of their desirability |
| Prevalence | The proportion of people in the population who are found to have a disease at a certain point in time |
| Primary traffic signal | The first signal a driver encounters in a signal controlled junction |
| Priority road | A road where traffic has priority, meaning that traffic entering from minor roads must give way |
| Probability | The long-term frequency of occurrence of an event in repeated trials that have the event as one of the possible outcomes; how likely something is to happen |
| Probability sampling | Sampling technique yielding a sample that is representative of the population from which it is drawn, by ensuring that each individual has an identical probability of being sampled; samples obtained this way are often referred to as random samples |
| Radar | Device used to measure the speed of vehicles |
| Random | Not systematic; an event occurs at random if it is not voluntary and cannot be predicted |
| Randomisation | Allocation of experimental subjects at random to different experimental conditions |
| Random variation in the number of accidents | Variation in the recorded number of accidents around a given expected number of accidents |
| Range (of observations) | The difference between the most extreme observations in a sample |

| | |
|---|---|
| Rationality | The use of reason to form opinions or make decisions. An action is rational if it is the best means to realise the objectives set for the action |
| Recidivism | The repetition of offences by previously convicted offenders |
| Refuge | A small traffic island, marked by kerbstone |
| Regression-to-the-mean | The tendency for an abnormally high number of accidents to return to values closer to the long-term mean; conversely, abnormally low numbers of accidents tend to be succeeded by higher numbers |
| Reliability | The reproducibility of observations; the similarity of repeated measures of the same phenomenon under controlled conditions; trustworthiness |
| Residual term | The difference between a value estimated by means of a statistical model and the actual value of an observation; small values for the residuals is generally regarded as desirable |
| Retardation | Slowing down; the same as deceleration (see above) |
| Retro-reflection | Materials are retro-reflective if they reflect light back to the source of light |
| Risk | The possibility of an unwanted event; usually the possibility will be quantified as a probability and the event will be described in terms of its consequences, resulting in this definition of risk: Risk = Probability × Consequence |
| Risk compensation | The tendency of road users to compensate for changes in the road system that are perceived as improving safety by adapting behaviour |
| Risk factor | A factor that affects the probability of accident occurrence or the severity of the consequences of an accident |

| | |
|---|---|
| Roundabout | Junction in which traffic (in countries driving on the right) moves counter-clockwise around a central traffic island; there is usually offside priority, meaning that entering vehicles must give way to circulating traffic |
| Rumble strips | Road markings that produce noise in the car when driven on |
| Sag curve | The bottom of a downhill; the point at which a road turns from going downhill to going uphill |
| Secondary traffic signal | A traffic signal mounted on the far side of a junction, to repeat information given by the primary signal (see above) |
| Self-selection | A voluntary decision made to join a sample or a safety programme; samples obtained by self-selection will often be biased |
| Separation | The physical separation of groups of road users or traffic streams in time or space |
| Significance (statistical) | A result is statistically significant if there is a low probability that it was caused by chance variation alone |
| Single-vehicle accident | An accident involving just one vehicle |
| Skewness (statistical) | A distribution is skew if most of the values observed are either above or below the mean value for the distribution; a skew distribution will typically have a long 'tail' in one direction |
| Speed | The distance covered per unit of time; speed is often measured in kilometres per hour |
| Speeding | Violations of the speed limit |
| Speed cameras | Cameras used to enforce speed limits, by taking pictures of offending vehicles |
| Speed limit | The highest speed permitted by legislation; speed limits are often signposted |

| | |
|---|---|
| Speed variance | The variation of speed in a traffic stream |
| Statistical validity | The extent to which the results of a study are free from statistical errors, random as well as systematic |
| Study quality | The extent to which a study is free of methodological weaknesses |
| Systematic variation in the number of accidents | Variation in the long-term expected number of accidents |
| Test of significance | Statistical test applied in order to decide if a finding is due to chance, at a stated probability |
| Theoretical validity | The extent to which a study successfully tests a theory; sometimes also referred to as construct validity (see above) |
| Time series | A series of observations made at different points in time, but usually at fixed intervals (e.g., monthly) |
| Traffic accident | Accident that occurs in traffic, i.e., involving one or more vehicles in motion |
| Traffic calming | Measures taken to reduce traffic volume and/or speed, in particular in residential areas |
| Traffic congestion | The formation of queues in traffic, sometimes leading to a complete standstill |
| Traffic control | Measures taken to control traffic; includes speed limits, parking regulations, traffic signals and signs |
| Traffic risk | The number of accidents or injured road users per unit of travel; most often per person kilometre of travel |
| Traffic stream | A set of vehicles following each other in the same direction |
| Traffic volume | The number of vehicles that pass a certain point during a certain period; the amount of driving |

| | |
|---|---|
| Transitional curve | The transition between a straight road section and the point at which a curve has minimum radius |
| Travel speed | The mean speed of a vehicle between points A and B |
| Trend | Systematic changes over time in a series of observations |
| Trip generation | The number of trips originating from a certain location |
| Uncertainty | Lack of knowledge; in decision theory, uncertainty refers to a situation in which the probability associated with the various possible outcomes of a decision is unknown |
| Unprotected road user | A road user who is not protected from injury by means of a hard shell surrounding the road user; in general, pedestrians and cyclists are regarded as unprotected; sometimes motorcycle riders are also included |
| Utility | The degree to which preferences are satisfied; the benefits that people derive from consumption |
| Validity | A study is valid if its results closely approximate the truth, which means that there should be no reason to believe that the results are influenced by erroneous observations or poor research methods |
| Valuation, monetary | Determining how valuable something is; in monetary valuation, the value is stated in monetary terms |
| Vehicle kilometres of travel | A frequently used measure of exposure; the product of the number of vehicles used and the distance each vehicle is driven |
| Vertical curve | A crest or sag curve (see above) |
| Visual acuity | The ability to see small details in objects |
| Visual field (field of view) | The size of the area a person can see measured horizontally and vertically |

| | |
|---|---|
| Volume/capacity ratio | The ratio between traffic volume and the capacity of a road |
| Welfare | The quality of life measured in terms of overall levels of individual satisfaction (happiness) |
| Willingness to pay | The amount of money a person is willing to pay to obtain a non-market good, e.g., safer traffic |
| Yield (give way) | The duty to give way to traffic; to enter a road only when this does not obstruct other traffic |

# List of abbreviations

| | |
|---|---|
| AADT | Annual average daily traffic |
| ABS | Anti-lock braking system |
| ACN | Automatic crash notification |
| ADR agreement | Agreement on dangerous goods by road |
| AIS | Abbreviated injury scale |
| ALS | Advanced life support |
| BAC | Blood alcohol concentration |
| BLS | Basic life support |
| CI | Confidence interval |
| DUI | Driving under the influence of alcohol |
| EMS | Emergency medical service |
| ESC | Electronic stability control |
| EuroNCAP | European new car assessment programme |
| FHWA | Federal Highway Administration (USA) |
| GDL | Graduated driving licence |
| ICC | Intelligent cruise control |
| IIHS | Insurance Institute for Highway Safety |
| ISA | Intelligent speed adaptation |
| ISS | Injury severity score |
| km/h | Kilometres per hour |
| MADD | Mothers against drink-driving |
| MAIS | Maximum abbreviated injury scale |
| mph | Miles per hour |
| MUTCD | Manual on Uniform Traffic Control Devices |
| NCAP | New car assessment programme |
| NHTSA | National Highway Traffic Safety Administration (USA) |
| OECD | Organisation for Economic Co-operation and Development |
| TØI | Transportøkonomisk institutt (Institute of transport economics), Norway |
| VMS | Variable message sign |
| WHO | World Health Organisation (a body of the United Nations) |

# Subject Index